THE DELL
CROSSWORD
DICTIONARY

THE DELL CROSSWORD DICTIONARY

COMPILED AND EDITED BY KATHLEEN RAFFERTY

REVISED AND UPDATED BY MARGARET S. DOHERTY

EDITORIAL CONSULTANT, ROSALIND MOORE

A DELL BOOK

Published by
Dell Publishing Co., Inc.
1 Dag Hammarskjold Plaza
New York, New York 10017

Dell © TM 681510, Dell Publishing Co., Inc.

ISBN: 0-440-16309-9

Printed in the United States of America

Two Previous Editions
New Edition
First printing—August 1985

ABOUT THIS BOOK . . .

Looking for an "Assam silkworm"? Can't find a "Brazilian coin"? Don't know a "candlenut tree"? They're easily found —with the aid of this book.

The purpose of this dictionary is to give puzzlers the pleasure of COMPLETING, down to the last two-letter word, every crossword that they begin. It is meant to eliminate the frustration of filling in "all but a few" of those final puzzle squares. Here, in a handy, easy-to-use format, is a complete 432-page reference book, including the exclusive cross-referenced Word-Finder, where puzzle solvers can find all those little-known, but much-used, crossword words.

We believe this book is the most useful book ever published for crossword solvers. It is the outgrowth of many years of exhaustive research and was prepared by Kathleen Rafferty who was, for many years, editor-in-chief of the Dell crossword magazines and books.

ABOUT THIS EDITION

Many of the words and definitions used in crosswords remain the same today as when this dictionary was first compiled. However, new words have come into our language since that time, and today's crosswords utilize these words. Since such words, in the main, are in specialized areas, this edition has been expanded by adding to the Special Section, instead of including additional words and definitions in the general section. This arrangement of the new information will make it easier for you to find the words you need to complete your puzzles!

In this edition, the Special Section now includes such listings as Computer Terminology, Aerospace, and Acronyms and Abbreviations. Though not new to the language, sections on Music and Sports, among others, have also been added. Both the Gazetteer and the First and Last Names sections have been completely revised and updated. You will undoubtedly find the all-new Celebrities' Original Names section entertaining, as well as a handy reference.

These new additions have been compiled from material I have gathered, both as solver and editor, over the past twelve years. The lists are in no way meant to be all-inclusive; they are not intended as exhaustive reference works, but as invaluable puzzle-solving aids.

Margaret S. Doherty

TABLE OF CONTENTS

DEFINITIONS SECTION 5

All the important crossword puzzle words are listed alphabetically by definition.

Look under group headings for these special word listings:

Birds 19
Birthstones 20
Card games 65
Colors 33
Combining forms 34
Constellations 36
English authors 50
Fabrics 53, 54
Fish 57
French words 61–63
Gems 65
German words 66
Greek letters 91
Greek numbers 71
Hebrew letters 91
Hebrew months 102
Insects 81

Italian words 83
Knights of the Round Table 134
Latin words 89–90
Men's names and nicknames 96
Moslem months 102
Musical instruments 81, 105
Planets 118, 119
Prefixes 122
Scottish words 138–40
Spanish words 151–52
Suffixes 158
Trees 168
Wedding anniversaries 179
Women's names and nicknames 183

SPECIAL SECTION
READY REFERENCE WORD LISTS

Acronyms, Initials,
    Abbreviations 250
Aerospace:
  Astronauts and Missions 236
  Rockets, Launch Vehicles 237

Satellites, Capsules,
    Spacecraft 234
Armor, Heraldry—Heraldic
    Terms 194
Biblical References 196
Celebrities' Original Names 210

Chemical Elements and
    Symbols **195**
Coins, Money **190**
Computer Terminology **238**
First and Last Names **202**
Gazetteer or Geographical
    Dictionary **224**
Gods (Deities), Goddesses, and
    Mythology **198**
Indians, Indian Tribes **192**
Measures **188**
Music:
    Composers **244**
    Musical Terms **242**
Names from Shakespeare
216

Pen Names **214**
Sports:
  Kentucky Derby Winners
  246
  Sports figures:
    Baseball **247**
    Basketball **249**
    Football **248**
    Ice Hockey **249**
  Triple Crown Winners **246**
Tribes **191**
U.S. Authors **215**
U.S. Presidents Information
220
U.S. States Information **222**
Weights **189**

WORD-FINDER 256

Every essential two-, three-, and four-letter word in the English language. Cross-referenced to the Definitions section for utmost aid to
solving. You can complete unfinished puzzle words with this section.

ABBREVIATIONS USED IN THIS BOOK

abbr. .... abbreviation
Abyssin. .... Abyssinia(n)
Afgh. .... Afghanistan
Afr. .... Africa(n)
Am. .... American
Arab. .... Arabia(n)
Arch. .... Architecture
A.-S. .... Anglo-Saxon
Austr. .... Austria(n)
Austral. .... Australia(n)
Babyl. .... Babylonian
Bibl. .... Biblical
biol. .... biology
bot. .... botany; botanical
Braz. .... Brazil(ian)
Cent. Am. ... Central America(n)
Chin. .... Chinese
comb. form .... combining form
Dan. .... Danish
Du. .... Dutch
Du. E. Ind. ... Dutch East Indies
E. .... East
Egyp. .... Egypt(ian)
E. Ind. .... East Indies
Eng. .... England; English
Eur., Europ. .... Europe(an)
fort. .... fortification
Fr. .... France; French
geol. ...... geology; geological
geom. .... geometry
Ger. .... German(y)
Goth. .... Gothic
govt. .... government
Gr. .... Greek
Hebr. .... Hebrew
Her. .... heraldry
Himal. .... Himalayan
Holl. .... Holland
Ind. .... India(n)
Indo-Chin. .... Indo-Chinese
Ir. .... Ireland; Irish
Is. .... Island

Ital. .... Italian; Italy
Jap. .... Japan(ese)
Lat. .... Latin
math. .... mathematics
med. .... medical
Medit. .... Mediterranean
Mex. .... Mexican; Mexico
milit. .... military
Min. .... Minor
mus. .... music; musical
myth. .. mythological; mythology
N., No. .... North
naut. .... nautical
N. Hebr. .... New Hebrides
N. T. .... New Testament
N. Z. .... New Zealand
Nor. .... Norway; Norwegian
O. Eng. .... Old English
P. I. .... Philippine Islands
P. R. .... Puerto Rico
Pacif. .... Pacific
Pers. .... Persian
pert. .... pertaining
pharm. .... pharmacy
philos. .... philosophical
poet. .... poetry
Polyn. .... Polynesia(n)
Port. ..... Portugal; Portuguese
Pruss. .... Prussian
R. C. .... Roman Catholic
Rom. .... Roman
Russ. .... Russian
S. .... South
S. Afr. .... South African(n)
Scot. .... Scottish
Sp. .... Spanish
Teut. .... Teutonic
Turk. .... Turkey; Turkish
W. .... West
W. Ind. .... West Indian
WW .... World War
zool. .... zoology

4

DEFINITIONS
SECTION

CROSSWORD DEFINITIONS
AND ANSWERS

HOW TO USE THIS SECTION:

Here are crossword DEFINITIONS, arranged alphabetically.

Look up the DEFINITION of a crossword word, and you will find, in bold-face type, the word you want.

There are two kinds of crossword definitions. One is the almost unvarying definition: "Bitter vetch" or "Vetch" is used to define ERS. If you look in this dictionary under "B" for "bitter vetch" or under "V" for "vetch" you will find it there.

The other kind of definition, far more common, is the more varied definition where the puzzle-maker can choose from among many descriptive words when he defines a puzzle word: "India nurse," "Oriental nurse," "Oriental maid," "Oriental nursemaid" are all used in crossword puzzles as definitions for AMAH. For efficiency's sake, crossword words with varying definitions are listed here under the ESSENTIAL definition word. In the case of AMAH, the listing is under "nurse," "maid," and "nursemaid".

So, if you don't find your wanted word under the first word of the definition given, look for it under the other words of the definition.

The length of a word is important to crossword solvers, and so, when a definition fits two or more words the words are arranged according to length. For example: adage .... SAW, MAXIM, PROVERB.

Remember to use also the efficiently-arranged reference word lists in the SPECIAL SECTION, beginning on page 187.

A

Aaron's brother .... MOSES
Aaron's sister .... MIRIAM
Aaron's miracle worker ... ROD
Aaron's son, oldest .... NADAB
abaca .... LINAGA
abaca, top-quality ..... LUPIS
Abadan's land .... IRAN
abalone shell money
                    ULLO, UHLLO
abandon   MAROON, DISCARD
abandoned .... DERELICT
abate .... EBB, LESSEN
abatement .... LETUP
abbess .... AMMA
abbey: Sp. .... ABADIA
abbot: Lat. .... ABBAS
abbreviations
          PTA, SRO, NATO (1949
                    pact)
abdominal .... VENTRAL
Abel's brother .... CAIN
abhor   HATE, DETEST, LOATHE
Abie's girl .... ROSE
Abijah's son .... ASA
ability ...... POWER, TALENT
abject .... BASE

abode, blissful .... EDEN
abode of dead .. HADES, SHEOL
abode of dead: Egypt.
                    AALU, AARU
abound .... TEEM
abounding .... RIFE
about .. OF, RE, ANENT, CIRCA
about: Lat. .... CIRCITER
above ..... O'ER, OVER, UPON
abrade .... RUB, CHAFE
Abraham's birthplace ..... UR
Abraham's brother
                 HARAN, NAHOR
Abraham's father ...... TERAH
Abraham's nephew .... LOT
Abraham's son
              ISAAC, ISHMAEL
Abraham's wife . SARAH, SARAI
abrasive .... EMERY
abrogate .... ANNUL
abrupt flexure .... GENU
Absalom's cousin ..... AMASA
Absalom's sister ..... TAMAR
abscond ..... ELOPE, LEVANT
absence, license for .... EXEAT
absent ..... OFF, OUT, AWAY,
                    GONE
absolute .... UTTER, PLENARY
absolve sins .... SHRIVE

absorbed .... RAPT
abstruse .... ESOTERIC
abundance, in .... GALORE
abundant ...... RIFE, AMPLE
abuse: India .... GALI, GALEE
abuse ... VIOLATE, MISTREAT
abusive, be .... REVILE
abusive charges .... MUD
abut ...... ADJOIN, BORDER
abyss .... GULF, HOLE, CHASM
Abyssinian .... KAFA, KAFFA
Abyssin. fly .... ZIMB
Abyssin. grain .... TEFF
Abyssin. Hamite . AFAR, AGAO,
                 BEJA, AFARA
Abyssin. language ...... SAHO
Abyssin. mountain wolf
                    KABERU
Abyssin. ruler's title ... NEGUS
Abyssin. ox .. GALLA, SANGA,
                 SANGU
Abyssin. Semitic dialect
              GEEZ, GHESE
Abyssin. tree .... KOSO
Abyssin. tribesman .... SHOA
Abyssin. vizier .... RAS
accent .... TONE
accent, Irish .. BLAS, BROGUE

access .... ENTREE
accommodate .... LEND
"— accompli" .... FAIT
according to . ALA, AUX, ALLA
accost .... HAIL, GREET
account entry ...ITEM, DEBIT,
                    CREDIT
accumulate .... AMASS,
              HOARD, ACCRUE
accumulation .... FUND
accustomed .... USED, WONT,
                 ENURED
acetic acid ester .... ACETATE
acetone derivative ... ACETOL
acetylene .... ETHIN, ETHINE
Achilles' adviser ... NESTOR
Achilles' father ... PELEUS
Achilles' mother .... THETIS
Achilles' slayer ...... PARIS
acid, kind of .. AMINO, BORIC
acid radical ... ACYL, ACETYL
acidity .... ACOR
acknowledge .... OWN
acknowledge frankly .. AVOW
acorns, dried ...... CAMATA
acoustics apparatus ... SIRENE
acquainted .... VERSANT
acquiesce .... ASSENT

6

a acquiesce, fully ..... ACCEDE
acquire .... WIN, GAIN, REAP
acrobat of India .... NAT
Acropolis of Thebes .. CADMEA
across: comb. form
.... TRAN, TRANS
acrostic, Hebrew .... AGLA
act ...... DEED, FEAT, EMOTE
act: Lat. ...... ACTU, ACTUS
action, put into .... ACTUATE
action word .... VERB
active ... SPRY, AGILE, BRISK,
.... LIVELY, NIMBLE
actor .... HISTRIO, HISTRION
actor's group .... TROUPE
actor's hint .... CUE
actor's valet .... DRESSER
actual .... REAL, TRUE
actual being .... ESSE
actuality .... FACT
adage .... SAW, MAXIM,
.... PROVERB
Adam's ale .... WATER
Adam's 1st mate: legend
.... LILITH
Adam's grandson .... ENOS
Adam's son . ABEL, CAIN, SETH
adapt .... FIT
adept .... ACE
b add on .... AFFIX, ANNEX,
.... ATTACH
adder, common .... ASP
additions .... ADDENDA
addition, bill's .... RIDER
adequate .... DUE, FULL,
.... AMPLE, EQUAL
adhere .... CLING, STICK,
.... CLEAVE
adherent .... IST
adhesive .. GUM, GLUE, PASTE
ADJECTIVE ENDING, see SUF-
.... FIX, ADJECTIVE
adjust ..... FIX, SET, ADAPT,
.... ATTUNE, ORIENT
adjutant .... AIDE
adjutant bird .... ARGALA,
.... HURGILA, MARABOU
admonish .... WARN, EXHORT,
.... REPROVE
admonisher .... MONITOR
adolescence .... TEENS,
.... YOUTH, NONAGE
adopted son of Mohammed . ALI
Adriana's servant .... LUCE
adroit ...... READY, HABILE,
.... SKILLFUL
adulterate .. DEBASE, DEFILE,
.... DENATURE
advance guard .... VAN
advantage .... USE, GAIN,
.... PROFIT, BENEFIT

c adventitious lung sound .. RALE
adventure ...... GEST, GESTE
adviser, woman ...... EGERIA
Aeëtes' daughter ..... MEDEA
Aegir's wife .... RAN
Aeneas' wife .... CREUSA
Aeneid author VERGIL, VIRGIL
Aesir ... TIU, TYR, ULL, FREY,
.... LOKE, LOKI, ODIN, THOR,
.... VALE, VALI, DONAR,
.... FREYA, BRAGI, WODEN,
.... BALDER
affectionate ... FOND, WARM,
.... LOVING, TENDER
affirm .. AVER, POSIT, ASSERT
affirmative .... AY, AYE,
.... YEA, YES
affirmative vote .... AY, AYE,
.... YEA, YES
afflict ...... TRY, VEX, PAIN,
.... DISTRESS
affluence ...... EASE, RICHES,
.... WEALTH
affray .... BRAWL, FIGHT,
.... MELEE
Afghan prince .. AMIR, AMEER
Afghan title .... KHAN
afresh .... ANEW
d afraid: obsolete .... REDDE
AFRICAN .... see also SOUTH
.... AFRICAN and AFRICAN in
.... SPECIAL SECTION
AFRICAN ANTELOPE
.... see ANTELOPE
Afr. bass .... IYO
Afr. bustard .... KORI
Afr. cotton garment .... TOBE
Afr. disease .... NENTA
Afr. worm .... LOA
Afr. grass, millet-like .. FUNDI
Afr. hornbill .... TOCK
Afr. plant .... ALOE
Afr. scrub .... BITO
Afr. soldier .... ASKARI
Afr. squirrel .... XERUS
Afr. stockade .... BOMA
Afr. tableland ...... KAROO
Afrikaans ...... TAAL, BOERS
aft .... ABAFT, ASTERN
after awhile .... ANON
aftermath .... ROWEN
afterpart of ship's keel
.... SKAG, SKEG
afterpiece, comic ..... EXODE
aftersong .... EPODE
again .... ENCORE
against .... CON, ANTI,
.... CONTRA, VERSUS
agalloch wood .. AGAR, ALOE,
.... GAROO
Agamemnon's son .... ORESTES

agate stone .... ACHATE
age .... EON, ERA, AERA, RIPEN, PERIOD
aged .... OLD, ANILE, SENILE
agave fiber .... ISTLE
agency, depression-era .. N R A
agency, govt. ..... E C A, F H A
agency, wage, price .... E S A
agency, ration-book .... O P A
agency, World-War II .. O P A
agent ...... DOER, FACTOR, FACIENT
agents acted through .. MEDIA
aggregate . SUM, MASS, TOTAL
agitate .... STIR
agitation ...... STIR, DITHER, TUMULT
agitation, be in state of SEETHE
agnomen .... NAME
agree .... GIBE, JIBE, TALLY, ASSENT, CONCUR
agreeable: old Eng. ... AMENE
agreeableness of letters EUTONY
agreement ...... MISE, PACT, CONCORD, ENTENTE
agriculture goddess .... CERES, VACUNA, DEMETER
Agrippina's son .... NERO
Ahasuerus' minister .. HAMAN
ahead .. ON, BEFORE, FORWARD
Ahiam's father .... SACAR
aid ... ABET, ASSIST, SUCCOR, FURTHER
aim ...... END, GOAL, ASPIRE
aims, with the same .... AKIN
air .. AER, ARIA, MIEN, TUNE
air apparatus ...... AERATOR
air current, ascending THERMAL
air, fill with .... AERATE
air, fresh .... OZONE
air passage ...... FLUE, VENT
air spirit .... SYLPH
air, upper .... ETHER, AETHER
aircraft, motorless .... GLIDER
airplane ...... JET, AERO
airplane: Fr. .... AVION
airport marker ...... PYLON
airport, Paris .... ORLY
airship . AERO, BLIMP, PLANE
airy .... LIGHT, ETHEREAL
ait .... ISLE
Ajax, tale about ...... MYTH
Ajax's father ...... TELAMON
akin .... SIB
alang grass .... LALANG
alarm . SCARE, SIREN, AROUSE
alas! .. ACH, HEU, OCH, OIME
alas: Irish .. OHONE, OCHONE
alas: poetic .... AY
Alaska glacier .... MUIR

ALBANIAN see COINS, TRIBES, GAZETTEER in SPECIAL SECTION
Albanian dialect .. GEG, CHAM, GHEG, TOSK
albatross, sooty ...... NELLY
alchitran .... TAR, PITCH
alcohol radical .... AL
alcohol, solid . STERIN, STEROL
alcoholic drink .... GIN, RUM, RHUM
Alcott heroine ...... JO, AMY, MEG, BETH
alcove ...... BOWER, RECESS
alder tree: Scot .... ARN
ale mug .... TOBY
ale, sour .... ALEGAR
alewife fish .... POMPANO
ALEUTIAN see TRIBES, GAZETTEER in SPECIAL SECTION
Alexandrian theologian . ARIUS
Alexander victory
        ISSUS, ARBELA
alfalfa .... LUCERN, LUCERNE
Alfonso's queen .... ENA
alga .... NORI
alga, one-cell .... DIATOM
algae genus, fan-shaped
        PADINA
algarroba tree ...... CALDEN
Algerian governor .... DEY
ALGERIA—see SPECIAL SECTION
ALGONQUIN .... see Page 192
Ali Baba's word ...... SESAME
Ali, caliph descendants ALIDS
Alien in Hebrew territory . GER
alienate ... WEAN, ESTRANGE
align ... TRUE, ALINE, RANGE
alkali ...... LYE, REH, USAR
alkaline solution .... LYE
alkaloid . CAFFEIN, CAFFEINE
alkaloid, calabar bean
        ESERINE
all: Lat. .... TOTO
all religions, believer in
        OMNIST
all right ...... OKAY, OKEH
allanite .... CERINE
allay ...... CALM, ASSUAGE, RELIEVE
alleged force .... OD
allegory, religious ... PARABLE
Allepo native .... SYRIAN
alleviate .... EASE, ALLAY, LESSEN
alley .... MIB, MIG
alliance ... UNION, LEAGUE
alliance, Western ...... NATO
alligator .... LAGARTO

a

alligator pear ..... AVOCADO
alligator, S.A. ...... CAIMAN, CAYMAN
allot .... METE, GRANT, ASSIGN, PORTION
allotment .... QUOTA, RATION
allow .... LET
allowance TARE, TRET, RATION
alloy ...... MOKUM, OROIDE
alloy, aluminum ...... DURAL
alloy, copper .... BRASS
alloy, copper-tin ... BRONZE
alloy, gold-silver: Egyp. . ASEM
alloy, lead-tin .. CALIN, TERNE
alloy, non-ferrous ...... TULA
alloy, yellow .... AICH
allspice .... PIMENTO
allure .... TICE, TOLE, TEMPT, ENTICE
allusion .... HINT
almond emulsion ..... ORGEAT
almost .... ANEAR
alms box or chest ...... ARCA
aloe .... AGAVE
aloe derivative .... ALOIN
aloes product .... ALOIN
alone, on stage .. SOLA, SOLUS
along .... ON, BESIDE
alp .... PEAK

b

alpaca .... PACO
alphabet letter, old .... RUNE
Alps, Austro-It.
      TIROL, TYROL, TIROLO
Alps, one of .... BLANC
Alps pass .... CENIS
Alps, river rising in .. RHONE
Altar constellation ..... ARA
altar end of church .... APSE
altar screen .... REREDOS
altar shelf . GRADIN, RETABLE
altar side curtain .... RIDDEL
altar top .... MENSA
alternate .... ROTATE
alternative ...... OR, EITHER
alumni .... GRADS
always .. AY, AYE, EER, EVER
amadou .... PUNK
amass ...... HOARD, GATHER
amateur TIRO, TYRO, NOVICE
Amazon cetacean ...... INIA
Amazon tributary .. APA, ICA
ambary .... DA
ambary hemp ...... NALITA
ambassador .. ENVOY, LEGATE
amber fish
        RUNNER, MEDREGAL
Amen-Ra's wife .... MUT
amend ALTER, EMEND, REVISE
amendment, document . RIDER
amends, make .... ATONE
ament .... CHAT

c

Am. artist ..... WEST, HICKS, HOMER, MARIN, PEALE, BENTON, COPLEY, INNESS, CORBINO, ALBRIGHT
AMERICAN INDIAN ...... see INDIANS, Page 192
Am. aloe fiber .... PITA, PITO
Am. author . ADE, POE, AMES, BAUM, HARTE, WYLIE, YERBY, CORWIN, FERBER, HERSEY, KANTOR, MORLEY
Am. author, illustrator ... PYLE
Am. capitalist .... ASTOR
Am. caricaturist ... REA, NAST
Am. dramatist . AKINS, BARRY, ODETS, CROUSE
Am. editor .... BOK
Am. educator .... MANN
Am. explorer . BYRD, FREMONT
Am. general
        LEE, OTIS, GREENE
Am. humorist ...... ADE, NYE, COBB, NASH, ROGERS
Am. jurist .... TANEY
Am. inventor ... IVES, MORSE, TESLA, EDISON
American: Mex. ..... GRINGO
Am. nature writer BEEBE, SETON
Am. nighthawk .... PISK
AM. PAINTER see AM. ARTIST

d

Am. patriot .... HALE, OTIS, ALLEN, REVERE
Am. philanthropist ...... RIIS
Am. philosopher ..... EDMAN
Am. pianist
  ARRAU, DUCHIN, LEVANT
Am. poet . POE, AUDEN, BENET, FROST, GUEST, RILEY, STEIN, MILLAY
Am. poetess ... STEIN, LOWELL
Am. sculptor .... CALDER
AM. SINGER ... see SOPRANO
Am. statesman
      CLAY, BARUCH, DULLES
Am. suffragist .... CATT
Am. surgeon .... PARRAN
AM. WRITER see AM. AUTHOR
AMERIND (means any American Indian) See pages 192, 193
amide, pert. to .... AMIC
a mine: Corn. .... BAL
ammonia compound .. AMIN, AMIDE, AMINE
ammoniac plant .... OSHAC
ammunition . SHOT, SHRAPNEL
ammunition, short for: . AMMO, AMMU
ammunition wagon ... CAISSON
among ...... IN, MID, AMID
amorously, stare .. LEER, OGLE
amount assessed ...... RATAL

Amount

a   amount staked in gambling **MISE**
amuse .... **DIVERT**
ampere................. **WEBER**
amphibian .... **FROG, TOAD, ANURAN**
amphibian, order HYLA, **ANURA**
amphitheater .... **ARENA**
amphitheater, natural ... **CIRQUE**
amplification factor......... **MU**
amulet ..... **CHARM, PERIAPT**
analyze...... **ASSAY, DISSECT**
analyze grammatically ... **PARSE**
ancestor of Irish .. **IR, ITH, MIL, MILED**
ancestor of man, Hindu .. **MANU**
ancestral spirit, P. I. ..... **ANITO**
ancestral .... **AVITAL**
ancestral spirits **LARES, MANES**
anchor **FIX, TIE, MOOR, KEDGE**
anchor part............. **FLUKE**
anchor, small, light ..... **KEDGE**
anchor tackle .... **CAT**
ancient Asiatic........... **MEDE**
ancient Briton............ **CELT**
ancient Chinese.......... **SERES**
anchovy sauce........... **ALEC**
ancient city, Asia Minor . **MYRA, NICAEA**
ancient country .... **GAUL**
Ancient Egyp. kingdom **SENNAR**
ancient flute .... **TIBIA**
ancient Greece division **AETOLIA**
ancient invader, India.... **SAKA, SACAE**

b   ancient people of Gaul.... **REMI**
ancient Persian .... **MEDE**
ancient Persian money... **DARIC**
ancient philosophy ...... **YOGA**
ancient race .... **MEDES**
ancient Slav ..... **VEND, WEND, VENED**
ancient times ...... **ELD, YORE**
ancient tribe of Britons ... **ICENI**
ancient weight .... **MINA**
and .. **TOO, ALSO, PLUS, WITH**
and: Lat.................... **ET**
and not .... **NOR**
and so on: abbr........... **ETC.**
Andes cold higher region . **PUNA**
Andes grass .... **ICHU**
Andes mountain....... **SORATA**
andiron.................. **DOG**
"Andronicus,—"........ **TITUS**
anecdotage or anecdotes . **ANA, TALES**
anent .... **RE, ABOUT, BESIDE**
anent, close— .... **TO**
anesthetic ...... **GAS, ETHER**
Angel of Death........ **AZRAEL**
angel, Pers............... **MAH**

c   anger .... **IRE, RAGE, RILE, CHOLER**
anger, fit of... **PIQUE, TEMPER**
angle, 57 degrees..... **RADIAN**
angle of leaf and axis...... **AXIL**
angle of leafstalk............ **AXIL**
angle of stem, pert. to... **AXILE**
Anglo-Saxon "G" ... **YOK, YOGH**
A.–S. god of peace .... **ING**
A.–S. lord's man **THANE, THEGN**
A.–S. king .... **INE**
A.–S. money (coin) .... **ORA**
A.–S. slave .... **ESNE**
A.–S. warrior... **THANE, THEGN**
Angora goat .... **CHAMAL**
angry .... **HOT, MAD, SORE, IRATE**
animal, Afr..... **CIVET, GENET, POTTO, ZEBRA, GENETTE**
animal, ant-eating .... **ECHIDNA**
animal, aquatic... **SEAL, OTTER, WHALE, DUGONG, WALRUS, MANATEE**
animal, arboreal...... **TARSIER**
animal, Austral....... **ECHIDNA**
animal, badgerlike, Java **TELEDU**
animal body .... **SOMA**
animal, draft........ **OX, OXEN**

d   animal, fabulous........ **DRAGON**
animal, giraffelike .... **OKAPI**
animal, India .... **DHOLE**
animal, Madagascar .... **FOSSA, FOUSSA**
animals of area .... **FAUNA**
animal-plant life .... **BIOTA**
animal, Peru .... **ALPACA**
animal, sea .... **SEAL, CORAL, WHALE, WALRUS, DUGONG, MANATEE**
animal, S. Afr. .... **ZORIL**
animal, S. Am. . **APARA, COATI**
animal trail . **RUN, SLOT, SPUR, SPOOR**
animating principle .... **SOUL**
ankle.. **TALUS, TARSI, TARSUS**
ankle, pert. to......... **TARSAL**
Annamese measure .... **TAO**
Annapolis student **PLEB, PLEBE**
annatto seeds: Sp. .. : **ACHIOTE**
anneal ... **TEMPER, TOUGHEN**
annex........ **ADD, ELL, WING, ATTACH**
annihilate............ **DESTROY, DISCREATE**
ANNIVERSARY .. see WEDDING
announce............. **HERALD**
annoy ... **IRK, TRY, VEX, RILE, PEEVE, TEASE, BOTHER, MOLEST, PESTER, DISTURB**

10

a annual, as winds .... ETESIAN
annuity, form of .... TONTINE
annul .... UNDO, VOID,
CANCEL, REVOKE
annular die .... DOD
annulet: Her. .... VIRE
anoint ... OIL, ANELE, ENELE
another ... NEW, ADDITIONAL
ant .... EMMET, PISMIRE
antarctic bird ...... PENGUIN
antarctic icebreaker ..... ATKA
antecedent . PRIOR, ANCESTOR
antelope, Afr. .... GNU, KOB,
BISA, GUIB, KOBA, KUDU,
ORYX, POKU, PUKU, TORA,
ADDAX, ELAND, ORIBI,
RHEBOK
antelope, Afr., large .. IMPALA
antelope, Afr., small .. DUIKER
antelope, Ind.
SASIN, NILGAI, NILGAU
antelope, Siberian ..... SAIGA
antelope, tawny .... ORIBI
antenna HORN, PALP, AERIAL
FEELER
antenna, with nodose
NODICORN
anthracite, inferior ..... CULM
anti-aircraft shells ..... FLAK
anti-tank gun .... PIAT
b antic ... DIDO, CAPER, PRANK
antique red color .. CHAUDRON
antiseptic ... EUPAD, EUSOL,
IODIN, SALOL, CRESOL,
IODINE
antiseptic, mercury
EGOL, METAPHEN
antitoxin ...... SERA, SERUM
antler point .... SNAG, TINE,
PRONG
antler, unbranched ...... DAG
antlers, stag's .... ATTIRE
"Anthony and Cleopatra" character .... IRAS
anvil .... INCUS, TEEST
anxiety .... CARE
any: dialect .... ONI
any one .... AN
aoudad .... ARUI
apathy ... ENNUI, DOLDRUMS
ape .... ORANG
ape, long-tailed, India ... KRA
appellation ..... NAME, TITLE
APERTURE . see also OPENING
aperture .... GAP, HOLE,
SLOT, VENT, ORIFICE
apex, at the .... APICAL
aphasia, motor ...... ALALIA
aphorism .. SAW, RULE, SUTRA
Aphrodite .... VENUS

c Aphrodite, got apple from
PARIS
Aphrodite, love of ... ADONIS
Aphrodite's mother .... DIONE
Aphrodite's son .... EROS
apocopate .... ELIDE
Apocrypha, book from . ESDRAS
Apollo's instrument ...... BOW,
LUTE, LYRE
Apollo's mother LETO, LATONA
Apollo's sister
DIANA, ARTEMIS
Apollo's son .... ION
Apollo's twin .... ARTEMIS
Apollo's vale, sacred .... TEMPE
apoplexy, plant .... ESCA
Apostle (12) .... JOHN, JUDE
(THADDEUS), JAMES, JUDAS,
PETER (SIMON PETER), SI-
MON, ANDREW, PHILIP,
THOMAS (DIDYMUS), MAT-
THEW (LEVI), MATTHIAS,
BARTHOLOMEW
Apostle, Capernaum MATTHEW
Apostles, teaching of . DIDACHE
apparent ..... OVERT, PLAIN,
EVIDENT
apparition .. SPECTER, SPECTRE
appear .... LOOK, LOOM, SEEM
appearance . AIR, MIEN, GUISE
d appease ...... CALM, ALLAY
PLACATE
appellation ..... NAME, TITLE
append .... ADD, AFFIX,
ATTACH
appendage, caudal ...... TAIL
appetizer . CANAPE, APERITIF
apple ... POME, TREE, FRUIT,
PIPPIN
apple acid .... MALIC
apple seed .... PIP
apple tree .... SORB
apple tree genus ...... MALUS
apple, winter .... ESOPUS
apples, crushed .... POMACE
apple-like fruit .... POME
appoint .. SET, NAME, CHOOSE
apportion DEAL, METE, ALLOT
appraise RATE, VALUE, ASSESS
apprise ...... ADVISE, NOTIFY
approach ...... NEAR, ANEAR,
ACCESS
appropriate, ... APT, FIT, MEET
appropriate, not INAPT, UNFIT
apricot, Jap. .... UME
apricot, Korean . ANSU, ANZU
apricots .... MEBOS
apropos ...... PAT, FITTING
apteryx .... KIWI
aptitude ..... FLAIR, ABILITY

11

Aptitude

a aptitude, natural .... **FLAIR, TALENT**
aquamarine .... **BERYL**
AQUATIC . see SEA or MARINE
Arab .... **GAMIN, SEMITE**
Arab cloak, sleeveless .... **ABA**
Arab drink .... **BOSA, BOZA, BOZAH**
Arab name .... **ALI**
Arab's state of bliss ..... **KEF**
Arabia, people of .... **OMANI**
ARABIAN . see ARAB, ARABIA, SPECIAL SECTION
Arabian chief . **SAYID, SAYYID**
Arabian chieftain **AMIR, EMIR, AMEER, EMEER**
Arabian chieftain's domain **EMIRATE**
Arabian cloth .... **ABA**
Arabian district .... **TEMA**
Arabian garment .... **ABA**
Arabian jasmine .... **BELA**
Arabian judge .... **CADI**
"Arabian Nights" dervish . **AGIB**
Arabian noble . **AMIR, EMIR, AMEER, EMEER**
Arabian nomadic tribesman **SLEB**
Arabian sailboat .. see VESSEL, ARAB
Arabian sleeveless garment **ABA**
b Arabian tambourine **TAAR, DAIRA, DAIRE**
Arabic jinni, evil **AFRIT, AFREET, AFRITE**
Arabic letter . **GAF, KAF, MIM, WAW, ALIF, DHAL**
Arabic script .... **NESKI**
Arabic surname .... **SAAD**
arachnid . **MITE, TICK, SPIDER**
Arawakan language .... **TAINO**
arbitrator ... **UMPIRE, REFEREE**
arboreal .... **DENDRAL**
arc .... **LINE, CURVE**
arch of heaven .... **COPE**
arch, pointed .... **OGIVE**
archaeology, mound ..... **TERP**
archangel .... **URIEL**
archbishop .... **PRIMATE**
archbishop, Canterbury **BECKET**
archer in Eng. ballad **CLIM, CLYM**
archetype ... **MODEL, PATTERN**
archfiend .... **SATAN**
architect's drawing ..... **EPURE**
architecture, school of **BAUHAUS**
architecture, type **DORIC, IONIC**
ARCTIC ..... see GAZETTEER
Arctic . **NORTH, POLAR, FRIGID**

c arctic air force base .... **THULE**
arctic dog .... **SAMOYED**
arctic gull genus ..... **XEMA**
arctic plain .... **TUNDRA**
Arden .... **FOREST**
ardor ... **ELAN, ZEAL, FERVOR**
area measure .. **RADII, RADIUS**
area, small .... **AREOLA**
areca .... **BETEL**
arena .... **FIELD**
Ares' mother .... **ENYO**
Ares' sister .... **ERIS**
ares, 10 .... **DECARE**
Argonaut ... **JASON, ACASTUS**
Argonauts' leader ...... **JASON**
Argonauts' ship .... **ARGO**
argument .... **AGON, DEBATE, HASSLE**
arhat .... **LOHAN**
aria ...... **AIR, SOLO, SONG, TUNE, MELODY**
arias .... **SOLI**
aridity, having .... **XERIC**
arikara .... **REE**
arise ...... **REBEL, ACCRUE, APPEAR**
arista .... **AWN**
Arizona aborigine ...... **HOPI**
ARIZONA INDIAN see page 192
d **ARIZONA** ... see also SPECIAL SECTION
Ark, porter of: Bible ..... **BEN**
Ark's landing place .... **ARARAT**
arm .... **LIMB, TENTACLE**
arm, movable with verniers **ALIDADE**
arm of sea . **BAY, FIRTH, FRITH**
armadillo ..... **APAR, APARA**
armadillo, Braz. . **TATU, TATOU**
armadillo, giant . **TATU, TATOU**
armadillo, large 12-banded **TATOUAY**
armadillo, 6-banded .. **PELUDO**
armadillo, small .. **PEBA, PEVA**
armadillo, 3-banded .... **APAR, APARA, MATACO, MATICO**
armed band .... **POSSE**
armed galley of old Northmen **AESC**
ARMOR .... see also SPECIAL SECTION, page 194
armor bearer .... **ARMIGER**
armor, body .... **CUIRASS**
armor, chain .... **MAIL**
armor, horse .. **BARD, BARDE**
armor, leg ... **JAMB, JAMBE**
armor, leg below knee **GREAVE**
armor, lower body ..... **CULET**

12

a armor part .... **LORICA**
armor part, throat ... **GORGET**
armor, skirt .... **TACE, TASSE, TASSET**
armor, thigh ... **CUISH, TUILE, CUISSE, TUILLE**
armpit .... **ALA**
army .... **HOST, TROOPS**
army group .... **CADRE**
army provisioner ...... **SUTLER**
aroid, an .... **ARAD, ARUM**
aromatic herb
DILL, MINT, SAGE
aromatic herb, carrot genus
CARUM
aromatic herb-plant .... **NARD**
aromatic seed
CUMIN, CUMMIN
aromatic seed, plant ... **ANISE**
aromatic substance ... **BALSAM**
aromatic weed .... **TANSY**
around .... **CIRCA**
arouse .... **FIRE, STIR, PIQUE**
arpeggio .... **ROULADE**
arquebus support ...... **CROC**
arraign ..... **ACCUSE, INDICT**
arrange ...... **FIX, SET, FILE, DISPOSE**
arrangement: comb. form . **TAX, TAXI, TAXO, TAXEO, TAXIS**
b arrangement, pert. to . .**TACTIC**
array .. **DECK, ORDER, ATTIRE**
arrest .... **NAB, HALT**
arrest writ .... **CAPIAS**
arris .... **PIEN**
arrow .... **BOLT, DART**
arrow, body of .... **STELE**
arrow, fit string to ..... **NOCK**
arrow, spinning .... **VIRE**
arrow wood .... **WAHOO**
arrowroot .... **PIA, ARARU**
arroyo .... **HONDO**
art: Lat. .... **ARS**
art style ...... **DADA, GENRE**
Artemis . **UPIS, DELIA, PHOEBE**
Artemis' twin .... **APOLLO**
Artemis' victim ...... **ORION**
artery, largest .... **AORTA**
artery of neck ...... **CAROTID**
artful .... **SLY, WILY**
arthritis aid **ACTH, CORTISONE**
Arthur's foster brother ... **KAY**
Arthurian lady
ENID, ELAIN, ELAINE
article .... **AN, THE, ITEM**
article, Fr. ...... **LA, LE, DES, LES, UNE**
article, Ger. .... **DAS, DER**
article, Sp. . . **EL, LA, LAS, LOS**
articulated joint ...... **HINGE**
artifice ... **RUSE, WILE, TRICK**

c artificial language .... **RO, IDO**
ARTIST .... see also PAINTER
and under Country
of each artist
artist, primitive .... **MOSES**
artless .... **NAIVE**
arum family plant **TARO, CALLA**
arum plant ..... **ARAD, AROID**
Aryan .... **MEDE, SLAV**
as .. **QUA, LIKE, SINCE, WHILE**
as far as .... **TO**
as it stands: mus. .... **STA**
as written: mus. .... **STA**
asafetida .... **HING**
asbestos .... **ABISTON**
ascent .... **UPGO, CLIMB**
ascetic, ancient .... **ESSENE**
asceticism, Hindu .... **YOGA**
ash, fruit, seed ..... **SAMARA**
ash key .... **SAMARA**
ashy pale .... **LIVID**
ASIA .. see also SPECIAL SEC-
TION
Asia Minor district, old **IONIA**
Asia Minor region, pert. to
EOLIC, AEOLIC
Asia native, S.E. .... **SHAN**
Asiatic ancient people .. **SERES**
d Asiatic country .. see page 210
Asiatic cow .... **ZO, ZOH**
Asiatic evergreen ...... **BAGO**
Asiatic fowl .... **SAT**
Asiatic gangster .... **DACOIT**
Asiatic sardine .... **LOUR**
Asiatic shrub .... **TEA, TCHE**
Asiatic tree .... **ACLE, ASAK, ASOK, ASOKA**
"— asinorum" .... **PONS**
askew .... **WRY, AGEE, ALOP, AWRY**
aspect ... **SIDE, FACET, PHASE**
asperse .... **SLANDER**
aspire .... **HOPE**
ass, wild
KULAN, ONAGER, QUAGGA
assail .... **BESET, ATTACK**
ASSAM .... see also SPECIAL
SECTION, Page 191
Assam hill tribe .... **AKA**
Assam mongol .... **NAGA**
Assam silkworm .... **ERI, ERIA**
Assam tribe, Naga Hills
AO, NAGA
assault .... **ONSET, STORM**
assault, prolonged ...... **SIEGE**
assayer .... **TESTER**
assaying cup .... **CUPEL**
assemble .... **MEET, MUSTER, COLLECT**

a assembly .... DIET, SYNOD,
      SESSION, GATHERING
assembly, A.-S. GEMOT, GEMOTE
assembly, China, Hawaii .. HUI
assembly, Dutch .... RAAD
assent, solemn .... AMEN
assert .... AVER, POSIT, STATE
assert formally .... ALLEGATE
assess ...... TAX, LEVY, VALUE
assessment RATE, SCOT, RATAL
asseverate .... AVER
assignor of property ... CEDENT
assimilate .. ABSORB, DIGEST
assistance AID, HELP, SUPPORT
assistant .... AIDE
associate .. ALLY, COLLEAGUE
association, trade GILD, GUILD
assuage .... MITIGATE
ASSYRIAN .. see also SPECIAL
      SECTION, Page 198
Assyrian king .... PUL
Assyrian queen, myth.
      SEMIRAMIS
asterisk .... STAR
astern ..... AFT, BAFT, ABAFT
astringent .... ALUM, STYPTIC
astringent, black ...... KATH
astringent fruit .... SLOE
astrologer of India ... JOSHI

b astronomical ...... URANIC
astron. luminous "cloud"
      NEBULA
Aswan, ancient .... SYENE
asylum ...... HAVEN, REFUGE
at all .... ANY
at any time .... EVER
at odds .... OUT
at the home of: Fr. ..... CHEZ
Atahualpa, king ... ... INCA
atap palm .... NIPA
atelier .... STUDIO
Athamas' wife .... INO
Athena ... PALLAS, MINERVA
Athena, appellation, title . ALEA
Athena, possession of .. EGIS
Athenian .... ATTIC
Athenian bronze coin CHALCUS
Athenian demagogue ... CLEON
Athens, last king of .. CODRUS
athlete, famous ...... THORPE
a-tiptoe .... ATIP
atmospheric pressure, of BARIC
at no time: poet. ...... NEER
atoll's pool .... LAGOON
atom part .... PROTON
atomic machine
      BETATRON, RHEOTRON
atomic physicist .. BOHR, RABI,
      UREY, FERMI, PAULI,
      COMPTON, MEITNER
      MILLIKAN

c atomic submarine .... SKATE,
      SARGO, TRITON, NAUTILUS
atone for .... REDEEM
attach .... ADD, FIX, TIE,
      APPEND
attack .... BESET, ONSET
attack, mock .... FEINT
attar .... OTTO
attempt .... TRY, STAB, ESSAY
attendant, hunter's
      GILLY, GILLIE
attention ... EAR, CARE, HEED
attest ..... VOUCH, CERTIFY
attic .... LOFT, GARRET
Attica resident .... METIC
Attila .... ATLI, ETZEL
attitudinize .... POSE
attribute .. IMPUTE, ASCRIBE
attune .... KEY, ACCORD
auction .... SALE
audience ...... EAR, HEARING
auditory .... OTIC, AURAL
auger .... BORE, BORER
augment .... EKE
augur .... BODE, PORTEND
augury ...... OMEN, PORTENT
auk genus .. ALCA, ALLE, URIA
auk, little ...... ROTCH, ROTCHE
aura, pert. to .... AURIC

d aureola .... HALO
auric acid salt ...... AURATE
auricle .... EAR
auricular ...... OTIC, EARED
aurochs .. TUR, URUS, AURUS
aurora .... EOS, DAWN
auspices .... EGIS, AEGIS
Australasian harrier-hawk
      KAHU
Australasian shrub genus
      HOYA
AUSTRALIA . see also SPECIAL
      SECTION
Australian boomerang .. KILEY
Austral. food .... KAI
Austral. gum tree
      KARI, TUART
Austral. hut .... MIAM, MIMI
Austral. marsupial
      TAIT, KOALA
Austral. scaly-finned fish
      MADO
Austral. tree, timber .. PENDA
Austrian folk dance .. DREHER
Austr. violinist .... MORINI
author .... PARENT
author, boys' .. ALGER, HENTY
author, nature stories .. SETON
authoritative .... MAGISTRAL
author unknown: abbr. .. ANON

14

a
authority, name as	**CITE, QUOTE**
auto, old	**JALOPY, JALOPPY**
automaton	**ROBOT**
automaton: Jew. legend	**GOLEM**
automobile "shoe"	**TIRE, TYRE**
ave	**HAIL**
avena	**OAT**
avenger: Hebr.	**GOEL**
average	**PAR, MEAN, NORM, USUAL, MEDIAL**
averse	**LOTH, LOATH**
Avesta division	**YASNA, GATHAS, YASHTS**
avid	**KEEN, EAGER**
avifauna	**ORNIS**
avocado, Mex.	**COYO**
avoid	**SHUN, ESCHEW**

c
avouch	**AVER, ASSERT**
away	**OFF, GONE, ABSENT**
aweather, opposed to	**ALEE**
aweto	**WERI**
awkward	**INEPT**
awkward fellow	**LOUT**
awn	**ARISTA**
awned	**ARISTATE**
awry	**AGEE, AJEE, AGLEY**
axilla	**ALA**
axilla, pert. to	**ALAR**
axillary	**ALAR**
axis deer	**CHITAL**
Aztec god, sowing	**XIPE**
Aztec "Noah" (hero)	**NATA**
Aztec "Noah's" wife	**NANA**
Aztec spear	**ATLATL**

B

b
babbler: Scot.	**HAVEREL**
Babism, founder	**BAB**
babul tree pods	**GARAD**
baby animal: Fr.	**TOTO**
baby carriage	**PRAM**
BABYLONIAN GODS, DEITY, see also GODS and also SPE-CIAL SECTION on page 198	
Babylonian abode of dead	**ARALU**
Babylonian city	**IS**
Babylonian chief gods	**EA, ANU, BEL, HEA, ENKI**
Babylonian chief goddess	**ISTAR, ISHTAR**
Babylonian chief priest of shrine	**EN**
Babylonian division	**SUMER**
Babylonian hero	**ETANA**
Babylonian lunar cycle	**SAROS**
Babylonian neighbor	**ELAMITE**
Babylonian numeral	**SAROS**
Babylonian priestess	**ENTUM**
Babylonian purgatory	**ARALU**
Bacchanals' cry	**EVOE**
bacchante	**MAENAD**
Bacchus' follower	**SATYR**
Bacchus' son	**COMUS**
back	**AID, AFT, FRO, ABET, HIND, REAR, SPONSOR**
back, call	**REVOKE**
back door	**POSTERN**
back, flow	**EBB, RECEDE**
back, lying on	**SUPINE**
back of neck	**NAPE**
back, pert. to	**DORSAL**

d
back, take	**RETRACT**
back, thrust	**REPEL**
back, toward	**RETRAL**
back: Zool.	**NOTA, NOTUM**
backbone	**CHINE, SPINE**
bacteria-free	**ASEPTIC**
bacteriologist's wire	**OESE**
bacteriostatic subst.	**CITRININ**
badge, Jap.	**MON**
badger	**DAS, BAIT**
badgerlike animal	**PAHMI, RATEL**
badgers, Old World	**MELES**
baffle	**FOIL, POSE, ELUDE**
bag	**SAC**
bag net	**FYKE**
bagatelle	**TRIFLE**
bagpipe, hole in	**LILL**
bagpipe sound	**SKIRL**
bailiff, old Eng.	**REEVE**
baize fabric	**DOMETT**
baker bird	**HORNERO**
baking chamber	**OST, KILN, OAST, OVEN**
baking pit	**IMU**
balance	**REST, POISE, SCALE**
balance, sentence	**PARISON**
Balance, The	**LIBRA**
balancing weight	**BALLAST**
Balder's killer	**LOK, LOKE, LOKI**
Balder's wife	**NANNA**
baldness	**ACOMIA**
Balkan	**SERB**
ball, low	**LINER**
ball, to hit	**LOB, BUNT, SWAT**

Ball

ball, yarn thread .... CLEW
ballad .... LAY, DERRY
ballet jump .... JETE
ballet skirt .... TUTU
ballet turn .... FOUETTE
balloon basket CAR, NACELLE
ball-rope missile

BOLA, BOLAS
balm of Gilead ..... BALSAM
balsalike wood ...... BONGO
balsam .... FIR, TOLU, RESIN
Balt .... ESTH
BALTIC ... see also SPECIAL
SECTION
Baltic Finn .... VOD
Baltimore stove .... LATROBE
Balto-Slav .... LETT
Baluchistan tribe ...... REKI
Baluchistan tribesman .. MARI
"Bambi" author ...... SALTEN
bamboo .... REED
bamboo shoots, pickled ACHAR
Bana's daughter: Hindu USHA
banal .... STALE, TRITE
banana genus .... MUSA
banana, kind of .. PLANTAIN
banana, Polyn. .... FEI
band .... BELT, TAPE,
STRIP, FILLET
band: Arch. .. FACIA, FASCIA
band, muscle, nerve .. TAENIA
band, narrow .. STRIA, STRIAE
bandage ...... STUPE, TAENIA
bandicoot .... RAT
bandmaster, Am. ..... SOUSA
banish ..... EXILE, RELEGATE
bank .... RELY, DEPEND
bank, of a river ... RIPARIAN
bank, river .... RIPA
banker, India .. SARAF, SHROFF
banner .... FLAG,
ENSIGN, BANDEROLE
banter ... CHAFF, PERSIFLAGE
BANTU   see also TRIBES in
SPECIAL SECTION, Page 191
Bantu .... KAFIR, KAFFIR
Bantu, Congo ... RUA, WARUA
Bantu language .... ILA
Bantu nation .... GOGO
Bantu-speaking tribe
RAVI, RORI, PONDO
Bantu tribesman ..... DUALA
baobab, dried .... LALO
baobab leaves, powdered . LALO
baptism font .... LAVER
baptismal basin .... FONT
bar .... RAIL, INGOT,
HINDER, STRIPE
bar legally .... ESTOP
bar, supporting .... FID
barb, feather .... HARL, HERL

Barbados native .... BIM
barbarian .... HUN, GOTH
Barbary ape .... MAGOT
barber ..... SHAVER, TONSOR
bard, Goth. .... RUNER
bare ..... BALD, MERE, NUDE
bargain ...... DEAL, PALTER
bargain: Dutch .... KOOP
barge .... HOY
bark .... BAY, YAP, YIP
bark, bitter .. NIEPA, NIOTA
bark, inner .... CORTEX
bark, lime tree .. BAST, BASTE
bark, medicinal .... COTO
bark, paper mulberry .. TAPA
bark, pert. to ..... CORTICAL
bark remover .... ROSSER
bark, rough exterior .... ROSS
barking .... LATRANT
barn owl genus .... TYTO
barometric line ...... ISOBAR
barony, Jap. .... HAN
barracuda, small SPET, SENNET
barrelmaker .... COOPER
barrel slat .... STAVE
barren land .... USAR
Barrie character ..... ALICE
barrow, Russ. .... KURGAN
base .... LOW, VILE
base, architectural
SOCLE, PLINTH
base, attached by .... SESSILE
baseball position: abbr. .... LF,
RF, SS
Bashan, king of .... OG
bashful .... COY, SHY, TIMID
basilica, Rome ..... LATERAN
basin: Geol. .... TALA
basis of argument .. PREMISE
basket .... KISH, CABAS,
PANIER, PANNIER
basket, coarse .... SKEP
basket, Eng. ...... PED, CAUL
basket, fish .... WEEL, CRAIL,
CREEL, WICKER
basket grass, Mex. ..... OTATE
basket, large .... HAMPER
basket strip .... RAND
basketball player ..... CAGER
basketry rod .... OSIER
Basra native .... IRAQI
bass, Europ. .... BRASSE
basswood .... LINDEN
bast fiber .... RAMIE
bat .... RACKET
batfish .... DIABLO
bathe .... LAVE
bathing-suit .... MAILLOT
baths, Roman ..... THERMAE
Bathsheba's husband
URIA, URIAH

16

a baton .... ROD
batrachian ...... FROG, TOAD
batter .... RAM
battering machine ...... RAM
battery plate .... GRID
battle, Am. Rev. ... CONCORD
battle area .... SECTOR
battle, Arthur's last .. CAMLAN
battle ax ... TWIBIL, TWIBILL
battle, Civil War, Tenn. SHILOH
battle cry, Irish .. ABU, ABOO
battle, Eng.-Fr. CRECY, CRESSY
battle formation .... HERSE
battle, Franco-Pruss. .. SEDAN
battle, 100 Years War
                  CRECY, CRESSY
"Battle Hymn of Republic"
     author .... HOWE
battle, WWI .. MARNE, SOMME,
                YPRES, VERDUN
battlefield .... ARENA
bauble .... BEAD
bay .... COVE, BIGHT, INLET
bay, Orkney, Shetland ... VOE
bay tree .... LAUREL
bay window .... ORIEL
bazaar .... FAIR
be foolishly overfond ... DOAT,
                         DOTE
be silent: music .... TACET
b be still .... SH, HUSH, QUIET
beach .... SHORE, STRAND
beach cabin .... CABANA
beads, prayer .... ROSARY
beak .... NEB, NIB, BILL
beam, supporting
           TEMPLET, TEMPLATE
bean .... SOY, URD, LIMA
bean, E. Ind. .... URD
bean, field .... PINTO
bean, green .... HARICOT
bean, poisonous ... CALABAR
bean, S. Am. .... TONKA
bean tree .... CAROB
bear .. STAND, YIELD, ENDURE
Bear constellation ...... URSA
bear, nymph changed to
                      CALLISTO
bear, Austral. .... KOALA
bear witness .. VOUCH, ATTEST
beard of grain .. AWN, ARISTA
bearded seal .... MAKLUK
bearer, Ind. .... SINDAR
bearing .... MIEN, ORLE
bearing plate .... GIB
bear's-ear .... ARICULA
beast of burden .... ASS,
                  BURRO, LLAMA
beat .... WIN, CANE, DRUB,
           FLAP, POMMEL, PULSE
beat about: naut. ...... BUSK

c beater, mortar .... RAB
beauty, goddess of: Hindu
     SRI, SHRI, SHREE, LAKSHMI
beauty, Greek .... LAIS
beaver .... CASTOR
beaver skin .... PLEW
beche-de-mer ..... TREPANG
beckon .... NOD
bed .... KIP, PALLET
bed of dry stream .... DONGA
bed of press, handle .. ROUNCE
bed: slang .... DOSS
Bedouin headband cord .. AGAL
bee, honey, genus ...... APIS
bee house ..... APIARY, HIVE
bee, male .... DRONE
bee tree .... LINDEN
bees, pert. to .... APIAN
bee's pollen brush ...... SCOPA
beech tree genus ...... FAGUS
beechnuts .... MAST
beefwood: Polyn. ...... TOA,
                 TOOA, BELAH
beehive, straw .... SKEP
Beehive State .. see page 209
beer ..... ALE, BOCK, LAGER
beer ...... Afr. millet ...... POMBE
beer ingredient .. HOPS, MALT
beer mug .... STEIN
beer, P. 1. rice ..... PANGASI
d beet variety .... CHARD
Beethoven's birthplace . BONN
beetle .... DOR, ELATER
beetle, burrowing ...... BORER
beetle, click .... ELATER
beetle, fruit-loving .... BORER
beetle genus, ground .. AMARA
beetle, ground .... CARAB
beetle, sacred Egyp. .. SCARAB
beetle, wood .... SAWYER
befall .... HAP
before .... ERE, PRE,
                    ANTERIOR
before: obs. .... ERER
before: naut. .... AFORE
beget .... EAN, SIRE
"Beggar's Opera" dramatist
                        GAY
beginner .... TIRO, TYRO,
             NOVICE, NEOPHYTE
beginning .... GERM, ONSET,
             ORIGIN, INITIAL
beginning .... NASCENCY
behave toward .... TREAT
behind .... AFT, AREAR,
                   ASTERN
behold ..... LO, ECCE, VOILA
behoove .... DOW
beige .... ECRU
being .... ENS, ENTITY

17

Being

a
being, abstract **ENS, ESSE, ENTIA**
being, essential .... **ENS**
Bela, son of .... **IRI**
beleaguerment .... **SIEGE**
Belem .... **PARA**
belief .... **CREED,
FAITH, TENET**
believe .... **TROW,
CREDO, CREDIT**
believer in god of reason **DEIST**
bell, alarm .... **TOCSIN**
bell, sacring .... **SQUILLA**
bell tower .... **BELFRY,
CAMPANILE**
bell's tongue .... **CLAPPER**
bellbird, N.Z. .... **MAKO**
bellowing .... **AROAR**
below: nautical .... **ALOW**
belt .... **CEST, SASH**
belt, sword .... **BALDRIC,
BAWDRIC, BALDRICK**
ben .... **BENE**
bench ...... **EXEDRA, SETTLE**
bench, judge's .. see JUDGE'S
BENCH
bench in a galley ..... **BANK**
bend .... **SNY, FLEX, GENU,
STOOP, FLEXURE**
benediction .... **BENISON**
benefactor .... **PATRON**
beneficiary: Law .... **USES**

b
benefit .... **BOON, AVAIL**
Bengal native .... **KOL**
Bengal singer .... **BAUL**
Benjamin's first born ... **BELA**
bent .... **PRONATE**
bequeath .... **WILL**
bequest .... **DOWER**
Berber arrowroot .... **RIFF**
Bermuda arrowroot
ARARU, ARARAO
Bermuda grass .. **DOOB, DOUB**
berserk .... **AMOK, AMUCK**
beseech .... **PRAY,
OBTEST, ENTREAT**
beside .... **BY**
besides .. **TOO, YET, ALSO, ELSE**
bestow .... **AWARD,
CONFER, IMPART**
bets, fail to pay
WELCH, WELSH
betel leaf ...... **BUYO, PAUN**
betel nut .... **SERI, SIRI,
BONGA, SIRIH**
betel palm .. **ARECA, PINANG**
betel pepper ..... **IKMO, ITMO**
Bethuel's son .... **LABAN**
betoken .... **DENOTE**
betroth .... **AFFY**
between: prefix .... **INTER**
Bevan's nickname .... **NYE**

c
bevel .... **BEZEL, SLANT**
bevel out .... **REAM**
bevel ship timber ...... **SNAPE**
bevel to join .. **MITER, MITRE**
BEVERAGE ... see also DRINK
beverage .... **ADE, ALE,
TEA, BEER**
beverage, curdled .... **POSSET**
beverage, hot wine .... **NEGUS**
beverage, Polyn.
KAVA, KAWA
beverage, S. Am. .... **MATE**
bewitch .... **HEX, SPELL**
beyond: comb. form .. **ULTRA**
Bhutan pine .... **KAIL**
biased person .... **BIGOT**
BIBLICAL .. see also SPECIAL
SECTION
Biblical city .... **DAN,
BABEL, EKRON**
Biblical character .. **ARA, IRA,
ERI, ARAN, ATER, ONAN**
Biblical country . **EDOM, ENON
SEBA, SHEBA**
Biblical driver .... **JEHU**
Biblical judge .... **ELI,
ELON, GIDEON, SAMSON**
Biblical king **OG, ASA, AGAG,
AHAB, ELAH, OMRI, SAUL,
HEROD, NADAB**

d
Biblical kingdom .... **ELAM,
MOAB, SAMARIA**
Biblical land .... **NOD**
Biblical lion .... **ARI**
BIBLICAL MEASURE ...... see
HEBREW MEASURE
BIBLICAL MOUNT see Page 197
Biblical name .. **ED, ER, IRI,
ONO, REI, TOI, ABIA, ADER,
ANER, ANIM, ASOM, DARA,
ENOS, IRAD, IVAH, REBA,
ABIAM, AHIRA, AMASA,
ASEAS**
Biblical name for part of Arabia
SHEBA
Biblical ornaments ..... **URIM**
Biblical priest, high ...... **ELI,
AARON, ANNAS**
Biblical region .. **ARAM, EDAR**
Biblical ruler .... **IRA**
Biblical sacred objects .. **URIM**
Biblical serpent .. **NEHUSHTAN**
Biblical son .... **HAM**
Biblical spy .... **CALEB**
Biblical tower .... **EDAR**
Biblical town in Samaria **ENON**
BIBLICAL TRIBE .... see
Page 197
Biblical weed .... **TARE**
Biblical well; spring . **AIN, ESEK**
Biblical wild ox .... **REEM**

18

a Biblical witch's home .. ENDOR
Biblical woman RAHAB, LEAH
Biblical word .. SELAH, MENE
Biblical word of reproach RACA
bicarbonate .... SODA
bice blue .... AZURITE
bicker .... CAVIL
bicycle for two ...... TANDEM
biddy .... HEN
"— bien" .... TRES
big casino .... TEN
bile .... GALL
bill .... DUN, NEB, BEAK
bill of fare .... MENU, CARTE
bill, part of .... CERE
billiard shot .. CAROM, MASSE
billow .... SEA, WAVE
bind .... TAPE, SWATH
biography .... LIFE, MEMOIR
biological .. BIOTIC, BIOTICAL
biological reproductive body
                        GAMETE
biotic community .... BIOME
bird .... CLEE, COCK, CROW,
     DOVE, FINK, GLED, HUIA,
     IIWI, JACU, KALA, KIWI,
     KOEL, KORA, KUKU, KYAH,
     LARK, LOON, LORO, LORY,
     LOUN, LOWA, LULU, LUPE,
     MAKO, MAMO, MIRO,
     MOHO, MORO, MYNA,
b   NENE, PAPE, PEHO, PISK,
     RAIL, RAYA, ROOK, RUFF,
     RURU, RYPE, SKUA, SMEE,
     SMEW, SORA, STIB, SWAN,
     TEAL, TERN, TOCK, TOCO,
     TODY,   UTUM,   WAEG,
     WREN,   YENI,   YUTU,
     DRAKE, ROBIN, SERIN, EL-
     ANET, SHRIKE, SISKIN,
bird, Am. .... TOWHEE
bird, Arctic .. BRANT, FULMAR
bird, Austral. ...... EMU, KOEL,
               COOEE, COOEY
bird, black ANI, ROOK, RAVEN
bird, blue .... JAY
bird, C. & S. Am. ...... COIN,
          CONDOR, CONDORES
bird cry .... CAW, COO
bird, diving ...... AUK, LOON,
              LOUN, SMEW
bird, ducklike .... COOT
bird, extinct .... MOA,
              DODO, MAMO
bird, Europ. .... GLEDE, TEREK
bird genus ...... CRAX, RHEA
bird, gull-like .... TERN
BIRD, HAWAIIAN ...... see
          HAWAIIAN BIRD
bird house .... COTE
bird, hunting .... FALCON

c bird, India .... SARUS
              SHAMA, ARGALA
bird, laughing .... LOON
bird life .... ORNIS
bird, long-legged
              AGAMI, STILT
bird, marsh .... RAIL,
              SORA, BITTERN
bird, mythical .... ROC
bird, national .... EAGLE
bird nest collector .. OOLOGIST
bird of prey ...... ERN, ERNE,
          HAWK, KITE, EAGLE,
          CORMORANT
bird, orange .... ORIOLE
bird order ..... PICI, RASORES
bird, oscine .. CHAT, ORIOLE
BIRD, OSTRICHLIKE ...... see
          OSTRICHLIKE BIRD
bird, Persian .... BULBUL
BIRD, SEA .. see SEA BIRD
bird, shore RAIL, SORA, SNIPE,
     WADER, AVOCET, PLOVER
bird, small .... TIT, PIPIT
bird, small brown ...... WREN
BIRD, S. AM. .... see
              S. AMER. BIRD
bird, swimming .. LOON, GREBE
bird, talking .. MYNA, MYNAH
d bird, tropical ...... ANI, ANO,
          TROGON, JACAMAR
bird, U. S.
     COLIN, VEERY, TANAGER
BIRD, WADING .... see
          .. WADING BIRD
bird, wading, Afr.
          UMBER, UMBRETTE
bird, water see WADING BIRD
BIRD, WEB-FOOTED .... see
          WEB-FOOTED BIRD
bird, W. Ind. .... TODY
bird, white-plumed .... EGRET
bird, white-tailed .. ERN, ERNE
birds .... AVES
bird's beak .... NEB, NIB
bird's cry .... CAW, WEET
birds of region ...... ORNIS
birds' route .... FLYWAY
biretta .... CAP
birth, by .... NEE
birth, of one's .... NATAL
birthmark
     MOLE, NEVUS, NAEVUS
birthplace, Apollo, Diana DELOS
birthplace, Constantine's
              NIS, NISH
birthplace, Mohammed's MECCA
birthplace, Muses, Orpheus
              PIERIA

a birthstone .... Jan., **GARNET;**
Feb., **AMETHYST;** March,
**JASPER, AQUAMARINE,
BLOODSTONE;** April, **DIA-
MOND;** May, **AGATE, EM-
ERALD;** June, **PEARL,
MOONSTONE;** July, **ONYX,
RUBY;** Aug., **CARNELIAN,
SARDONYX, PERIDOT;**
Sept., **SAPPHIRE;** Oct.,
OPAL; Nov., **TOPAZ;** Dec.,
TURQUOISE, ZIRCON
birthwort, Europ. .. **CLEMATITE**
bishop .... **PRELATE**
bishop of Rôme .... **POPE**
bishopric .... **SEE**
bishop's attendant ... **VERGER**
bishop's hat
HURA, MITER, MITRE
bishop's office .... **LAWN**
bishop's seat .... **SEE, APSE**
bishop's title, East .... **ABBA**
bite .... **CHAM, MORSEL**
bite upon .... **GNAW**
biting .... **ACERB, ACRID**
bitter .... **ACERB, ACRID**
bitter almonds compound
AMARINE
bitter drug .... **ALOE**
bitter vetch .... **ERS**
b bittern .... **HERON**
bivalve .... **CLAM, MUSSEL**
bivalve genus .... **PINNA**
bizarre .... **OUTRE**
black .... **JET, EBON, INKY,
RAVEN, SABLE, TARRY,
NIGRINE**
black and blue .... **LIVID**
black buck .... **SASIN**
black gum tree genus **NYSSA**
black haw .... **SLOE**
black kelpie .... **BARB**
black nightshade ... **DUSCLE**
Black Sea arm ... **AZOF, AZOV**
blackbird
ANI, MERL, MERLE, RAVEN
blackbird, Europ.
OSSEL, OUSEL, OUZEL
blackbird: variant ...... **ANO**
blacken .... **INK, SOOT**
black-fin snapper ...... **SESI**
blackfish .... **TAUTOG**
Blackmore heroine .... **LORNA**
blacksnake .... **RACER**
blacksmith's block .... **ANVIL**
blackthorn fruit .... **SLOE**
blackwood, India ...... **BITI**
blade .... **OAR**
Blake's symbolic figure .. **ZOA**
Blake's symbolic figures **ZOAS**
blanch .... **ETIOLATE**

c blanket, cloak-like .. **PONCHO**
blanket, coarse wool .. **COTTA**
blanket, horse ...... **MANTA**
blanket, Sp.-Am. ..... **SERAPE**
blast furnace, stone in .. **TYMP**
blaubok, S. Afr. ...... **ETAAC**
blaze star .... **NOVA**
bleach .... **CHLORE**
bleaching vat .... **KEIR, KIER**
bleak .... **RAW**
blesbok .... **NUNNI**
bless .... **SAIN**
bless: Yiddish .... **BENSH**
blessing
BOON, GRACE, BENEFICE
blight .... **NIP**
blight of drought, India **SOKA**
blind, as hawks .... **SEEL**
blind dolphin .... **SUSU**
blind god, Teut. **HOTH, HODER**
blind impulse to ruin ... **ATE**
blindness .... **CECITY**
blister .. **BLEB, BULLA, BULLAE**
block, small arch
DENTEL, DENTIL
block, wood .... **NOG**
blockhead .... **ASS, DOLT**
blood factor .... **RH**
blood, lack of red
ANEMIA, ANAEMIA
d blood of gods .... **ICHOR**
blood, part of .... **SERUM**
blood, pert. to ...... **HEMAL,
HEMIC, HAEMAL, HAEMIC**
blood vessel .... **VEIN**
blood vessel, main .... **AORTA**
blood, watery part of
SERA, SERUM
blood sucker .... **LEECH**
blood-sucking parasite .. **TICK**
blouse, long .... **TUNIC**
blow.... **COUP, CRIG, ONER,
SWAT, WAFT**
blubber, piece of ..... **LIPPER**
blubber, to strip .... **FLENSE**
blue .... **CADET, PERSE,
SMALT, COBALT**
blue-dye yielding herb **WOAD**
blue dyestuff .... **WOAD**
"Blue Eagle" .... **NRA**
blue-footed petrel ...... **TITI**
blue grass (genus) ..... **POA**
blue grape anthocyanin
ENIN, OENIN
blue gray
CHING, MERLE, SLATE
blue, greenish .... **BICE,
SAXE, TEAL, EMAIL**
blue mineral .... **IOLITE**
blue-pencil .... **EDIT**
blue pointer shark ..... **MAKO**

a
blue pine	LIM
Bluebeard's wife	FATIMA
bluebonnet	LUPINE
bluff	CRUSTY
bluish-white metal	ZINC
blunder	ERR
blunt	DULL
blushing	ROSY
boa, ringed	ABOMA
boast	BRAG, VAUNT
boastful air	PARADO

BOAT . see also SHIP, CANOE, GALLEY, VESSEL,

boat	ARK, TUB, PUNT
boat, assault	LST
boat, Ceylon, India	DONI, DHONI
boat, collapsible	FALTBOAT, FOLDBOAT
boat, dispatch	AVISO
boat, E. Ind.	DONI, DHONI
boat, Egypt	BARIS
boat, Eskimo .. BIDAR, CAYAK, KAYAK, UMIAK, OOMIAC, OOMIAK, UMIACK	
boat, fishing	TROW, DOGGER, CORACLE
boat, fishing, North Sea	COBLE
boat, flat-bottomed	SCOW, BARGE

b
boat, freight	LIGHTER
boat front	BOW, PROW
boat, Ind. landing	MASOOLA
boat, landing	LCI, LST
boat, Levantine	BUM
boat, light	WHERRY
boat, mail	PACKET
boat, Malay .... PAHI, PRAH, PRAO, PRAU, PROA, PRAHU, PRAHO	
boat, Manila Harbor ..	BILALO
boat, military	PONTOON
boat, Nile 2-masted	SANDAL
boat, P. I.	BANCA, BANKA
boat, racing ..	SCULL, SHELL
boat, river	BARGE, FERRY, PACKET
boat, river Chin. ...	SAMPAN
boat, small	DORY
boat, 3-oar	RANDAN
boat, used on Tigris	GUFA, KUFA
boat, with decks cut	RASEE, RAZEE
bob bait for fish	DIB
bobbin .. PIRN, REEL, SPOOL	
bobbins, frame for	CREEL
bobwhite	COLIN
Boche	HUN
bodice, India	CHOLI
bodily motion, pert. to	GESTIC

c
body	SOMA, LICHAM
body, heavenly . STAR, COMET	
body of laws	CODE
body of men	FORCE
body of persons	CORPS
body of retainers	RETINUE
body of writing	TEXT
body, part of THORAX, THORACES	
body, pert. to SOMAL, SOMATIC	
body, trunk of .. TORSE, TORSO	
body: zool.	SOMA
Boer general	BOTHA
bog. FEN, MIRE, QUAG, MARSH	
boggy	FENNY
boil	STEW, SEETHE
boil down	DECOCT
boiled rice without salt: P. I.	CANIN
boiler, disk for hole in ..	SPUT
"Bolero" composer	RAVEL
boll weevil	PICUDO
Bolshevik leader	LENIN
bolt	SCREEN
bomb, defective	DUD
bombardment, short, intense	RAFALE
bombast	ELA
bombastic TURGID, OROTUND	
Bombyx	ERI

d
bond	NEXUS
bond-stone	PERPEND
bondman ...... SERF, VASSAL	
bonds, chem. with 2 double	DIENE
bone	OS
bone, ankle TALUS, ASTRAGAL	
bone, arm	ULNA
bone, arm, pert. to ...	ULNAR
bone, breast STERNA, STERNAL, STERNUM	
bone, ear ..... ANVIL, INCUS	
bone: Greek	OSTE
bone, leg .... FEMUR, TIBIA, FIBULA, TIBIAE	
bone, pelvic, hip	ILIUM
bone, pert. to	OSTEAL
bone scraper	XYSTER
bone, skull	VOMER
bones	OSSA
bones, dorsal	ILIA
bones, end of spine ..	SACRA
bones, hip	ILIA
bonnet monkey ZATI, MUNGA	
bonnyclabber	SKYR
bony	OSTEAL
book .... MO, TOME, PRIMER	
book, case for FOREL, FORREL	
book, largest	FOLIO
book, manuscript CODEX, CODICES	

Book

a
book, map .... ATLAS
book, Bible .. see SPECIAL SEC-
          TION, Page 196
book of devotions .... MISSAL
book of feasts, Catholic ORDO
book of hours .. HORA, HORAE
book palm, tree .... TARA
book, The .... BIBLE
books, Bible .... GOSPEL
bookbinding style ...... YAPP
bookkeeping entry
        DEBIT, CREDIT
booklet .... BROCHURE
boor OAF, CLOD, LOUT, CHURL
boot, Eskimo .... KAMIK
booth .... STALL
booth, Oriental market
       SUQ, SOOK, SOUK
bootlace .... LACET
booty ..... LOOT, PELF, SWAG
booty, take .... REAVE
borax, crude .... TINCAL
border ...... HEM, RIM, EDGE,
     RAND, SIDE, MARGE
border on .... ABUT
bore .... TIRE, EAGRE,
    WEARY, CALIBER
borecole .... KAIL, KALE
boredom .... ENNUI
boric acid salts ...... BORATE

b
born .... NEE
born, being .... NASCENT
born: old Eng. .... NATE
Bornean squirrel shrew
           PENTAIL
Borneo native .. DYAK, DAYAK
boron, pert. to ...... BORIC
borough .... BURG
borrowed stock: Irish law DAER
bosh .... ROT, POOH
boss .... STUD
boss on shield ...... UMBO
Bostonian .... HUBBITE
botanical suffix ..... ACEAE
botanist .... MENDEL
botch .... FLUB, MESS
both ears, involving use of
         BINAURAL
bother ... ADO, FUSS, TODO,
    TEASE, MOLEST, PESTER
bo-tree .... PIPAL
bottle, glass water .. CARAFE
bottle, oil, vinegar
      CRUET, FLASK
bottomless pit .... ABADDON
boundary ...... LINE, MERE,
     METE, LIMIT
boundaries, mark off
      DEMARCATE
bounder .... CAD
bounding line .... SIDE

c
bounds .... AMBIT
bouquet .... AROMA
bovine .... OX, COW
bovine, male .... STEER
bow of ship .... PROW
bow, low Oriental
     SALAM, SALAAM
bow-shaped .... ARCATE
bower .... ARBOR
bowfin .... AMIA
bowl: cricket .... YARK
bowling term .... SPARE
bowstring hemp IFE, PANGANE
box .... BIN, BINN, CASE,
    CIST, SPAR, CHEST
box, ecclesiastic ...... ARCA
box canyon: Sp. ...... CAJON
box, metal .... CANISTER
box opener .... PANDORA
box, papyrus rolls, Rom.
          CAPSA
box, sacred, ancient Rom. CIST
box sleigh .... PUNG
boxing glove, Rom. .... CESTUS
boxing term .... KO, TKO
BOY'S NAME .. see MAN'S
    NAME
boy ... BUB, BUD, LAD, TAD
boys in blue .... ELI'S
B.P.O.E. member ...... ELK

d
brace .... PAIR, TRUSS
braced aback: nautical ABOX
bracing .... TONIC
brag .... BOAST, VAUNT
Brahman rule .. SUTRA, SUTTA
Brahmany bull .... ZEBU
braid ... PLAT, PLAIT, QUEUE
braid, kind of .... LACET
brain canal-passage .... ITER
brain, layer in .... OBEX
brain opening .... LURA, PYLA
brain part .... PIA
brain: P. I. .... UTAC
brain ridges .... GYRI
brain tissue .... TELA
brain ventricle opening
         PYLA
branch .... ARM, LIMB, RAMI,
    RAME, RAMUS, SPRIG
branch-like RAMOSE, RAMOUS
branchia .... GILL
branch of learning ...... ART
brass, man of .. TALOS, TALUS
brassart .... BRACER
"Brave Bulls" author .... LEA
brawl ...... MELEE, FRACAS
BRAZIL ..... see also SPECIAL
      SECTION
Brazil drink .... ASSAI
Brazil red .... ROSET
Brazil dance .... SAMBA
Brazil heron .... SOCO

a Brazil Negro .... MINA
Brazil plant ..... YAGE, YAJE
Brazil rubber tree .. ULE, HULE
Brazil tree ...... APA, ANDA
Brazil capital .... RIO
breach .... GAP
bread, hard-baked ...... RUSK
bread crumbs, dish with
PANADA
breadfruit: P. I. .... RIMA
breadfruit: P. R. ... CASTANA
bread-tree seeds ..... DIKA
break .... SNAP
break in .... STAVE
breakers .... SURF
breakwater ...... MOLE, PIER
breastbone, of ..... STERNAL
breastplate .... URIM
breastwork .... PARAPET
breastplate, Gr.
THORAX, THORACES
breath of life .... PRANA
breathed .... SPIRATE
breathing, harsh
RALE, STRIDOR
breech-cloth, Polyn. .. MALO
breeches: Scot. .... TREWS
breed ...... REAR, RAISE
Bremen's river ...... WESER
breviary ... PORTAS, PORTASS
b brewer's ferment .. LOB, LOBB
brewer's vat .... TUN
brewing .... MALTING
brewing, one
GAAL, GAIL, GYLE
bribe .... SOP
brick carrier .... HOD
brick, sun-dried ...... ADOBE
bricklayer .... MASON
bricklayer's helper ...... CAD
bridal wreath .... SPIREA
bridge .... SPAN
bridge, floating ... PONTOON
bridge, maneuver ... FINESSE
bridge, Mississippi ..... EADS
bridge part TRESSEL, TRESTLE
brief .... SHORT, TERSE
brigand .... LATRON
Brigham Young U. site PROVO
bright .... APT, NITID
bright colored fish
BOCE, OPAH, WRASSE
bright: music .... ANIME
brilliance .... ECLAT, ORIENCY
brilliant group .... PLEIAD
bring forth .... EAN
bring on oneself ...... INCUR
bring together ...... COMPILE
bring up ...... REAR, RAISE
brisk: music .... ALLEGRO
bristle .... SETA

c bristles .... SETAE
bristle, pert. to .... SETAL
bristly .... SETOSE
Britain's ancient inhabitant
PICT
BRITISH .. also see ENGLISH
British conservative ..... TORY
British king, legendary .. LUD,
BELI, BRAN, BRUT, LUDD,
NUDD
Britisher, early .... PICT
Brittany; city, ancient ...... IS
broach .... RIMER
broad band: Her. ...... FESS
broadbill, E. Ind. ...... RAYA
broadbill duck ...... SCAUP
broken glass to remelt ... CALX
broken seed coats ..... BRAN
broken spike of grain ... CHOB
broken stone, etc. ... RUBBLE
Bronte heroine .... EYRE
bronze, Rom. money ..... AES
brood ...... SET, NIDE, COVEY
brook, small ..... RUN, RILL
broom of twigs .... BESOM
broom-corn millet
HIRSE, KADIKANE
brother .. FRA, FRIAR, FRATER
brought up .... BRED
brow of hill; Scot. ...... SNAB
d brown ... TAN, SEAR, SEPIA,
UMBER, BISTER, RUSSET,
SIENNA, SORREL
– brown kiwi .... ROA
brown, pale .... ECRU
brown, red-yellow ..... PABLO
brown, yellowish dull ... DRAB
brown-skinned race ... MALAY
brown sugar .... PANELA
browned .... RISSOLE
brownie ..... NIS, NIX, NISSE
Browning poem, girl in PIPPA
browse .... GRAZE
Brünnhilde's mother ... ERDA
brushwood .... TINET, TINNET
brusque ...... BLUNT, TERSE
Brythonic .... CORNISH
Brythonic sea god ...... LER
bubble .... BLEB
buck, 4th year .... SORE
Buddha .... FO
Buddha, Jap. AMIDA, AMITA
Buddha's foe .... MARA
Buddha's mother ...... MAYA
Buddha's tree .... PIPAL
Buddhist angel .... DEVA
Buddhist language ..... PALI
Buddhist church in Jap. .. TERA
Buddhist monastery, Jap. TERA
Buddhist Mongol ...... ELEUT
Buddhist monk .... BO, LAMA

Buddhist

a
Buddhist pillar .... LAT
Buddhist monument .. STUPA
Buddhist novice ...... GOYIN
Buddhist priest .... LAMA
Buddhist relic .... STUPA
Buddhist sacred city .. LASSA
Buddhist sacred dialect PALI
Buddhist sacred mountain OMEI
Buddhist saint LOHAN, ARHAT
Buddhist scripture SUTRA, SUTTA
Buddhist sect, Jap. ..... ZEN
Buddhist shrine TOPE, STUPA,
    DAGABA, DAGOBA, DAG-
    HOBA, DHAGOBA
Buddhist spirit of evil .. MARA
buds, pickled .... CAPERS
buffalo, India
    ARNA, ARNI, ARNEE
buffalo pea .... VETCH
buffalo, water, P. I. CARABAO
buffet ...... SLAP, SMITE, TOSS
buffoon .. FOOL, MIME, ZANY,
    CLOWN, MUMMER, JESTER
bug .... BEETLE
bugaboo: S. Afr. GOGA, GOGO
bugle call
    TATOO, TATTOO, TANTARA
bugle note .... TIRALEE
build .... REAR, ERECT
builder .... ERECTOR

b
builder, jetty-dam ...... EADS
building site .... LOT
building wing .... ELL, ANNEX
bulb, edible .... SEGO
bulb, Indian food
    CAMAS, CAMASS, CAMMAS
bulb-like stem .... CORM
BULGARIAN .. see also SPE-
    CIAL SECTION
Bulgarian czar .... BORIS
bulge, as eyes .... BUG
bulk .... MASS
bull, girl carried off on EUROPA
bull, sacred Egyp. .... APIS
bullet, size of
    CALIBER, CALIBRE
bullet sound ...... ZIP, PHIT,
    PHUT, PIFF
bullfight .... CORRIDA
bullfight cry .... OLE
bullfighter on foot .. TORERO
bullfighter's queue .... COLETA
bullfinch, Eng. .... ALP
bully .... HECTOR
bulrush .... TULE
Bulwer-Lytton heroine .. IONE
bumblebee .... DOR
bumpkin .... LOUT
bunch .... TUFT, WISP
bunch grass .... STIPA
bundle .... BALE, PACK

c
bundle, small .... PACKET
bundle, twig, stick .... FAGOT
bundling machine ...... BALER
bungle .... BOTCH
bunting .. ESTAMIN, ETAMINE,
    ORTOLAN, ESTAMENE
bunting bird .... CIRL
buoy, Eng. .... DAN
buoy, kind of .CAN, NUN, NUT,
    BELL, SPAR, WHISTLING
buoyancy .... FLOTAGE
burbot .... LING
burbot genus .... LOTA, LOTE
Burchell's zebra ...... DAUW
burden ... LADE, LOAD, ONUS
burden bearer .... ATLAS
burglar .... YEGG
burial place, Polyn. ...... AHU
BURMA .. see also SPECIAL
    SECTION
Burma Buddhist (native) MON
Burma chief .... BO, BOH
Burmese capital, ancient AVA
Burmese demon (devil) .. NAT
Burmese gibbon .... LAR
Burmese governor WUN, WOON
Burmese hill-dweller .... LAI
Burmese hills .... NAGA
Burmese knife .. DAH, DHAO
Burmese language .. WA, PEGU
Burmese mongoloid ..... LAI

d
Burmese native (s) WA, LAI, WAS
Burmese premier .... UNU
Burmese 3-string viol .. TURR
Burmese wood sprite .... NAT
burn incense .... CENSE
burn .... ASH, CHAR, SERE
Burnett, Frances, heroine SARA
burning bush .... WAHOO
burning, malicious .... ARSON
burnish .... RUB
burrowing animal MOLE, RATEL
burst asunder .... SPLIT
burst forth .... ERUPT
bury .... INTER, INHUME
bush or bushy clump .... TOD
bushel, fourth of ...... PECK
Bushmen .... SAN, SAAN
bushy .... DUMOSE
business .... TRADE
business cartel .... TRUST
"Bus Stop" author ..... INGE
bustard genus .... OTIS
bustle .... ADO, TODO
bustle about .... FISK
busy, to be .... HUM
but .... YET, ONLY, STILL
butcher's hook ...... GAMBREL
butter, illipe .... MAHUA
butter, India .... GHI, GHEE
butter, liquid ..... GHI, GHEE

24

a
butter tree	SHEA
butter tub	FIRKIN
butterbur	OXWORT
butterfly	IO, SATYR
butterfly, large	IDALIA
butterfly-lily	SEGO
button	STUD
button, part of	SHANK
buyer	VENDEE
buyer: Law	EMPTOR

c
buzzard	BUTEO
buzzing sound	WHIR, WHIZ
by	AT, PER, PAST, ALONG, BESIDE
by birth	NEE
by hand, bred	CADE
by means of	PER
bygone	AGO
Byron poem	LARA
Byzantine capital	NICAEA

C

b
C, mark under	CEDILLA
caama	ASSE
cab, Near East	ARABA
cabal	PLOT
cabbage	COLE, KAIL, KALE, KEAL
cabbage type	SAVOY
cabin, main	SALOON
cabinet, open, bric-a-brac	ETAGERE
cactus fruit, edible	COCHAL
cactus, genus	CEREUS
cactus-like	CACTOID
caddis fly worm	CADEW
Caddoan Indian	REE
cadet	LAD
Cadmus' daughter	INO
Caen's river	ORNE
Caesar's conspirator-slayer	CASCA, BRUTUS, CASSIUS
cafe	CABARET
caffein in tea	THEIN, THEINA, THEINE
caffein-rich nut	COLA, KOLA
cage	MEW
Cain's brother	ABEL
Cain's land	NOD
Cain's son	ENOCH
Cain's wife, Byron poem	ADAH
cake, rich	TORTE, TORTEN
cake, small	BUN, BUNN
calabar bean alkaloid	ESERIN, ESERINE
calamity	WOE, DISASTER
calcium oxide	LIME
calf of leg, pert. to	SURAL
calf's cry	BLAT
caliber	BORE, DIAMETER
calico colors, mix	TEER
calico horse	PINTO, PIEBALD
calico-printing method	LAPIS
California army base	ORD
Calif. fish	RENA, REINA
Calif. fort	ORD

d
Calif. herb	AMOLE
Calif. motto	EUREKA
Calif. shrub, berry	SALAL
Calif. wine valley	NAPA
Caliph	ALI, IMAM
call	CRY, DUB, DIAL, NAME, ROUSE, WAKEN, MUSTER
call for hogs	SOOK
call forth	EVOKE, SUMMON, ELICIT, EVOCATE
call, to attract attention	HEY, PST, HIST, PIST
calling	METIER, VOCATION
Calliope's sister	ERATO
calm	LAY, COOL, LULL, QUIET, STILL, PLACID, SERENE, SMOOTH, SOOTHE
calorie	THERM, THERME
calumniate	MALIGN
calumny	SLANDER
Calvinists, Scotch	BEREANS
calyx leaf	SEPAL
cam	TAPPET
cambric	PERCALE
cambric grass	RAMIE
CAME	see COME
camel: Anglo-Ind.	OONT
camel hair cloth	ABA
camel hair robe	ABA
camel-like animal	LLAMA
Camelot lady	ENID
cameo stone	ONYX
camera platform	DOLLY
Cameroons tribe	ABO
"Camille" author	DUMAS
camlet	PONCHO
camp, fortified	TABOR
camp, pert. to	CASTRAL
camphor, kind of	ALANT
campus, restrict. to Eng.	GATED
Canaanite month	BUL
Canada goose	OUTARDE
canal bank	BERM, BERME
canal betw. N. and Balt. Seas	KIEL

a

canary yellow ...... MELINE
canasta play .... MELD
cancel .. DELE, ANNUL, ERASE
candid ...... OPEN, FRANK
candidates list .. LEET, SLATE
candle ... DIP, TEST, TAPER
candle holder
     SCONCE, GIRANDOLE
candle wick .. SNAST, SNASTE
candlenut tree .... AMA
candlenut tree fiber ...... AEA
cane ... RATTAN, MALACCA
Canio's wife "I Pagliacci"
     NEDDA
canister, tea, alloy for .. CALIN
canna plant .... ACHIRA
cannabis .... HEMP
cannon .... MORTAR
cannon, old
     MOYENNE, ROBINET
CANOE .. see also BOAT
canoe, Afr. .. BONGO, BUNGO
canoe, Hawaii ...... WAAPA
canoe, Malabar ...... TONEE
canoe, Malay (South Seas) out-
     rigger .. PAHI, PRAH,
     PRAO, PRAU, PROA,
     PRAHU
canoe, Maori .... WAKA

b

canoe, P. I. .. BANCA, BANKA
canon .... LAW, RULE
canonical hour .. SEXT (noon),
     LAUDS, NONES, PRIME,
     MATINS, TIERCE
canopy .. COPE, SHADE, TESTER
cant TIP, TILT, SLANG, CAREEN
cant-hook .... PEAVY, PEEVY,
     PEAVEY, PEEVEY
cantankerous command. . SCAT
cantata, pastoral .. SERENATA
canticle, Scripture ...... ODE
"Cantique de Noel" composer
     ADAM
CANTON .. see the country in
     SPECIAL SECTION
canvas .. DUCK, TUKE, SAILS
canvas, piece of .... TARP
canvas shelter .... TENT
canyon mouth .... ABRA
canyon, small ...... CANADA
CAP .. see HEADGEAR
capable .... ABLE
cape ..'...... NES, RAS,
     NASE, NAZE, NESS
cape, early .... COPE
cape, fur ...... PALATINE
Cape Horn native .... ONA
cape, Pope's .. FANON, ORALE
Cape Verde native ..... SERER
Capek creature ...... ROBOT

c

caper .... DIDO, LEAP, ANTIC
CAPITAL .. see SPECIAL SEC-
     TION
caprice WHIM, FANCY, VAGARY
captain, fiction .... AHAB
captain, Nile ...... RAIS, REIS
capture BAG, NAB, NET, SEIZE
car .... SEDAN
car, last CABOOSE, CAMBOOSE
car, old make .... REO
caracal .... LYNX
Caradoc .... BALA
caravan .... CAFILA
caravansary
     CHAN, KHAN, SERAI
caravel, Columbus NINA, PINTA
carbolic acid ...... PHENOL
carbon, powdery ...... SOOT
CARD .. see also GAME, CARD
card ... ACE, PAM, SIX, TEN,
     TWO, FOUR, JACK, KING,
     NINE, TREY, KNAVE,
     POSTAL
card game like bridge .. VINT
card game, 3-handed ... SKAT
card game, old ...... TAROT
card game, Sp. ...... OMBER,
     OMBRE
card holding .... TENACE
card in euchre .... BOWER
card, playing
     TAROC, TAROT, TAROCCO

d

card wool ...... TUM, TEASE
cards, highest ...... HONORS
care for .... RECK, TEND
care, heavy .... CARK
careen ...... TIP, LIST, TILT
caress .... PET
cargo .... LOAD, PORTAGE
cargo, put on .... LADE, LOAD
"Carmen" composer .... BIZET
carnation .... PINK
carnelian .... SARD
carnivore, Afr. ...... RATEL
carol .... NOEL, SING
carol singer .... WAIT
carom .... RICOCHET
carousal ORGY, BINGE, SPREE
carouse .... REVEL
carp .... ID, CAVIL
carp, Jap. .... KOI
carp, red-eyed .... RUD, RUDD
carpet, Afgh...HERAT, HERATI
carpet, Caucasian BAKU, KUBA
carpet, India .... AGRA
carpet, Pers. ... KALI, SENNA
carriage .. GIG, MIEN, POISE,
     CALASH, LANDAU, CARIOLE
carriage: Fr. .... FIACRE
carriage, India .... EKKA
carriage, Java, Oriental SADO

a carried away .... RAPT
carrier, of Orient .... HAMAL
Carroll heroine .... ALICE
carrot-family plant .... ANISE
carrot-like herb genus .. MEUM
carrot ridges .... JUGA
carry ...... LUG, BEAR, TOTE
carry across water .... FERRY
carry on (a war) ...... WAGE
cart, heavy .... DRAY
carte .... MENU
Carthage, of .... PUNIC
Carthage queen .... DIDO
cartograph .... MAP
cartoonist
    ARNO, CAPP, NAST, KIRBY
carve in itaglio ...... INCISE
case, grammatical .... DATIVE
case of explosives .... PETARD
case, toilet, small
                ETUI, ETWEE
casing, bore-hole ...... LINER
cask .. KEG, TUB, TUN, BUTT,
    CADE, TIERCE, PUNCHEON
cassava .. AIPI, JUCA, YUCA
cassia leaves .... SENNA
cast, founded .. FUSIL, FUSILE
cast metal mass .. PIG, INGOT
cast off MOLT, SHED, MOULT
b caste AHIR, BICE, GOLA, JATI
caste, agricultural ...... MEO
caste, gardener .... MALI
caste, low KOLI, KULI, PARIAH
caste, Tamil merchant
                    CHETTY
caster ...... CRUET, ROLLER
casting mold .... DIE
castor-oil bean poison RICIN
castor-oil plant .... KIKI
Castor's killer .... IDAS
Castor's mother .... LEDA
cat .... ANGORA
cat, Afr.
    CIVET, GENET, GENETTE
cat, Am.
    PUMA, COUGAR, OCELET
cat cry .. MEW, MIAU, MIAW,
    MIAOU, MIAOW, MIAUL
cat genus .... FELIS
cat-headed goddess, Egypt BAST
cat, spotted
    PARD, MARGAY, OCELET
cat, tailless .... MANX
catalogue ..... LIST, RECORD
catamaran ...... BOAT, RAFT
catapult .... ONAGER
cataract .... FALLS
catch .... NAB, HAUL, HOOK,
    SNAG, TRAP, DETENT
catchword ..... CUE, SLOGAN

c catechu-like resin ..... KINO
category .... GENRE, SPECIES
cater ...... PANDER, PURVEY
caterpillar .... LARVA
caterpillar hair .... SETA
caterpillar, N. Z. .... WERI
catfish, Egypt ...... DOCMAC
catfish, S. Am. .... DORAD
cathedral .... MINSTER
cathedral city, Eng. ..... ELY
cathedral, famous .. CHARTRES
cathedral passage ..... SLYPE
cathedral, Russian ..... SOBOR
Catholic, Greek UNIAT, UNIATA
Catholic tribunal ...... ROTA
catkin ..... AMENT, AMENTA
catnip .... NEP
catspaw DUPE, TOOL, STOOGE
cattail ...... TULE, MATREED
cattail india, narrow .. REREE
cattail, N. Z. .... RAUPO
cattle, breed of .... DEVON
cattle dealer .... DROVER
cattle genus .... BOS
cattle stealing, crime of
                    ABIGEAT
CAUCASIAN .... see
            CAUCASUS NATIVE
Caucasian bharal .... TUR
Caucasian goat .... TUR, TEHR
Caucasian ibex .... ZAC
d Caucasian language
                ANDI, AVAR
Caucasion Moslem
                LAZ, LAZZI
Caucasian race in China
                LOLO, NOSU
Caucasus native
        SVAN, SVANE, OSSET
caucho tree .... ULE
caudal appendage ..... TAIL
caulk lightly .... CHINSE
cause ...... CAUSA, REASON
caustic ... LYE, LIME, ACRID,
            ERODENT, MORDANT
caustic poison ...... PHENOL
cauterize .... SEAR
cautery plant .... MOXA
cautious WARE, WARY, CHARY
"Cavalleria Rusticana" heroine
                    LOLA
cavalryman .... ULAN, UHLAN
cavalryman, Turk., Alg.
                SPAHI, SPAHEE
cave: archaic .... ANTRE
cave explorer .... SPELUNKER
cave: poet. .... GROT
cavern .. CAVE, GROT, GROTTO
caviar .... ROE, IKRA
caviar fish .... SHAD, STERLET
cavil .... CARP, OBJECT

Cavity

a cavity .... ATRIA, ANTRA, SINUS, ANTRUM
cavity, ear, nose .... VUG, VOOG, VUGG, VUGH, GEODE
cavy .... APEREA
ceasel .... HALT, AVAST
Cecrops' daughter ...... HERSE
cedar, E. Ind. ...... DEODAR
Celebes ox .... ANOA
celebrated .... EMINENT
celery-like plant .... UDO
cella .... NAOS
cellulose acetate ...... ACETOSE
cellulose: comb. form .. CELLO
Celt .... ERSE, GAEL
Celt, legendary IR, ITH, MILED
Celtic ... ERSE, MANX, WELSH
Celtic church early center IONA
Celtic dart .... COLP
Celtic god ...... TARANIS
Celtic goddess
ANA, ANU, DANA, DANU
Celtic mother of gods
ANA, ANU, DANA, DANU
Celtic name meaning black
DHU
Celtic Neptune .... LER
b Celtic paradise ..... AVALON
Celtic sea god .... LER
Celtic sun god .... LUG, LUGH
cement ..LUTE, PUTTY, SOLDER
cement well lining .... STEEN
cenobite .... MONK
censure. BLAME, CHIDE, SLATE
center .... HUB, CORE, FOCI, FOCUS, HEART
center, away from .... DISTAL
center, toward ...... ENTAD
centerpiece .... EPERGNE
centesimal unit ..GRAD, GRADE
centesimi, 100 .... LIRA
centipede: Tahiti .... VERI
central .... MID, FOCAL
Cent. Am. gum tree
TUNO, TUNU
Cent. Am. tree .... EBO, EBOE
central line .... AXIS
central points .... FOCI
century plant .... AGAVE
century plant fiber..PITA, PITO
cere .... WAX
cereal .... FARINA
cereal grain .... OAT, RYE
cereal grass ...... OAT, RYE, WHEAT, MILLET
cereal grass, E. Ind. ... MAND, RAGI, RAGGI, RAGGEE

c cereal grass genus ... SECALE
cereal plant: obs. ...... RIE
cereal spike ...... COB, EAR
ceremonial chamber .... KIVA
Ceres' mother .... OPS
certificate, money ..... SCRIP
cerulean blue COELIN, COELINE
cervine animal .... DEER
cesspool .... SUMP
cetacean . ORC, WHALE, NAR-WAL, NARWHAL, PORPOISE
cetacean, dolphinlike, genus
INIA
Ceylon ape .... MAHA
Ceylon foot soldier ..... PEON
Ceylon governor .... DISAWA
Ceylon moss .... AGAR
Ceylon native
VEDDA, VEDDAH, WEDDAH
Ceylon sandstone ...... PAAR
Ceylon trading vessel .. DONI
chafe RUB, FRET, FROT, GALL
chaff .... BANTER
chaffinch ..... CHINK, SPINK
chain .... CATENA
chain, nautical .... TYE
chainlike .... CATENATE
chair .... SEDAN
chair part ...... RUNG, SPLAT
d chaise .... GIG
chalcedony .... ONYX, AGATE
chalcedony, red .... SARD
Chaldean astron. cycle .. SAROS
Chaldean city .... UR
chalice
AMA, AMULA, CALIX, GRAIL
chalice veil .... AER
chalky silicate .... TALC
challenge .. DARE, DEFY, CAGE
chamber .... ROOM, CAMERA
chamber, pert. to ... CAMERAL
champagne, Marne .... AY
chance .... HAP, LOT, LUCK
chances, excess of ..... ODDS
chanced upon .... MET
chancel part .... BEMA
chancel screen .... JUBE
chancel seat .. SEDILE, SEDILIA
change .... FLUX, VARY, ALTER, AMEND
change appearance .. OBVERT
change direction CANT, KANT, TACK, TURN, VEER
change: music .... MUTA
channel .... GAT, MEDIA, STRIA, MEDIUM, STRIAL
Channel Island .... SARK
channel marker .... BUOY
channels .... MEDIA

28

a chant .... INTONE
chanticleer .... COCK
chantry .... CHAPEL
chaos .... NU, NUN
chaos, Babyl. .... APSU
chaos, Egypt. ...... NU, NUN
chaos, Maori myth .... KORE
Chaos' son .... EREBUS
chap: S. Afr. .... KEREL
chapel, private .... ORATORY
chapel, sailor's ...... BETHEL
chaperon: Sp. DUENA, DUENNA
chaplain .... PADRE
chaplet .. ANADEM, WREATH
chapped .... KIBY
character .... NATURE
characteristic .... TRAIT
charcoal: Pharm. ...... CARBO
charge .... FEE, COST,
            DEBIT, INDICT
charge solemnly ..... ADJURE
charged particle .... ION
charger .... STEED
chariot, ancient Briton
        ESSED, ESSEDA, ESSEDE
chariot race site ...... CIRCUS
chariot, religious RATH, RATHA
charity .... ALMS
Charlemagne, race subdued by
                AVARS
b Charlemagne's father ... PEPIN
Charlotte —, dessert .. RUSSE
charm .... JUJU,
        SPELL, AMULET, GRIGRÍ
Charon, payment for .. OBOL
Charon, river of .... STYX
chart .... MAP
Charybdis, rock opp. .. SCYLLA
chasm GAP, ABYSS, CANYON
chaste .... PURE, VESTAL
chat, friendly .... COSE, COZE
Chateaubriand heroine, novel
                ATALA
chatelaine bag .... ETUI
chatter GAB, GAS, YAP, PRATE
chatterbox .... PIET
cheat .... RENIG, RENEGE
cheat .... BAM,
    CON, FOB, FUB, GIP, GYP,
    BILK, MUMP, COZEN, SHARP
cheaters: slang ..... GLASSES
check ...... NIP, TAB, REIN,
        STEM, BRAKE, STUNT
checking block .... SPRAG
cheek .... GENA, JOLE, JOWL
"cheek" . GALL, BRASS, NERVE
cheek, pert. to ...... MALAR
cheek-bone .... MALAR
cheer .... OLE, RAH,
        BRAVO, ELATE, ENCORE
cheer pine .... CHIR

c cheer up .... LIVEN
cheerless .... SAD, DRAB
cheese ..... EDAM, STILTON
cheese, Dutch .... EDAM
cheese, hard brown .. MYSOST
cheese, soft .... BRIE
cheesy .... CASEOUS
cheetah, Ind. . YOUSE, YOUZE
chela .... CLAW
Chemical compound ... IMID,
        AMIDE, AMINE, IMIDE,
        IMINE, ESTER
CHEMICAL ELEMENT .... see
            SPECIAL SECTION
chemical ending OL, INE, ENOL
chemical prefix ..... ACI, OXA,
            AMIDO, AMINO
chemical salt ...... SAL, ESTER,
            NITRE, BORATE
CHEMICAL SUFFIX .. see SUF-
    FIX, CHEMICAL
chemical unit .... TITER
chemist's pot .... ALUDEL
cherish ... FOSTER, TREASURE
cherry .... GEAN
cherry red .... CERISE
chess piece .... MAN
chess term,—passant ..... EN
chessman ..... KING, PAWN,
        ROOK, QUEEN, BISHOP,
d CASTLE, KNIGHT
chest, acacia wood ..... ARK
chest, antique .... CIST, KIST
chest, sacred ARK, ARCA, CIST
chest sound .... RALE
chestnut, Eur. ...... MARRON
chestnut, Polyn. ...... RATA
chevrotain . NAPU, MEMINNA
chew .... BITE, CHAM, GNAW
chew, leaf to .... COCA
chewink .... TOWHEE
Chibcha chief's title .... ZIPA
chick-pea .... GRAM
chicken snake .... BOBA
chide SCOLD, BERATE, REPROVE
chief ... ARCH, HEAD, MAIN
chief, Afr. tribe ...... KAID
chief, Am. Ind. ...... SACHEM
chief: Chinook .... TYEE
chief deity, Panopolis ... MIN
chief in Italy .... DUCE
chief, India .... SIRDAR
Chief Justice 1921-30 ... TAFT
Chief Justice 1941-46 .. STONE
chief, Moslem .... RAIS, REIS
chief officer, India .. DEWAN,
                DIWAN
chief Norse god ...... ODIN,
        WODAN, WODEN, WOTAN
chief, Pres. .... MIR
child .... TIKE, TYKE

29

a child of streets..ARAB, GAMIN
"Child of the Sun" .... INCA
child, pert. to :........ FILIAL
child: Scot. .... BAIRN
child: Tagalog, P. I. .... BATA
Chilean proletariat ..... ROTO
Chilean timber tree ..... PELU
Chilean volcano .... ANTUCO
chill .... ICE, AGUE
chills and fever
             AGUE, MALARIA
chimney: dialect .... LUM
chimney pipe .... FLUE
chin ...... MENTA, MENTUM
China .... CATHAY
China blue .... NIKKO
China grass .... BON
Chinese .. SERES, SERIC, SINIC
Chinese aborigine . YAO, MANS
Chin. aboriginal population
     division .... MIAO
Chin. are .... MU
Chin. boat .... JUNK
Chin. brick bed .... K'ANG
Chin. Causasian tribesman LOLO
Chin. characters in Jap. . MANA
Chin. club .... TONG
CHIN. COIN .. see also COINS
             Page 190

b Chin., coin, bronze LI
Chin., coin, early .... PU
Chin. Communist .. MAO, CHOU
Chin. cult .... JOSS
Chin. department .... FU
Chin. dialect .... WU
Chin. division .... MIAO
Chin. dynasty . HAN, KIN, SUI,
     WEI, YIN, CH'IN, CHOU,
     HSIA, T'ANG, MING, SUNG,
     TS'IN, YUAN
Chin. factory .... HONG
Chin. feudal state .... WEI
Chin. flute .... TCHE
Chin. god .... GHOS, JOSS
Chin. govt. section
             HIEN, HSIEN
Chin. guild .... HUI
Chin. idol .... GHOS, JOSS
Chin. instrument, stringed . KIN
Chin. kingdom, old
             WU, SHU, WEI
CHIN. MEASURE .see also pages
             188, 189
Chin. measure of length . TSUN
Chin. mile LI
Chin. monetary unit .... YUAN
CHIN. MONEY see also page 190
Chin. negative principle ... YIN
Chin. noodles .... MEIN
Chin. official .. KUAN, KWAN
Chin. philos. principle.LI, YANG

c Chin. plant .... UDO
Chin. pottery .... CHUN,
       KUAN, MING, TING
Chin. ruler .. YAO, YAU, YAOU
Chin. secret society ..... TONG
Chin. shop: Du. E. Ind. .. TOKO
Chin. silk .... PONGEE
Chin. wax, wax insect .. PELA
Chin. wormwood ...... MOXA
Chin. yellow .... SIL
chinin .... COYO
chink ..... RIFT, RIMA, RIME
chink-like .. RIMAL, RIMATE
chinky ...... RIMAL, RIMOSE,
             RIMOUS
chip .... NICK
chip of stone .. SPALL, GALLET
chipmunk .... HACKEE
chirp CHEEP, TWEET, TWITTER
chisel, primitive .... CELT
chisel, very broad .... TOOLER
chocolate powder ..... PINOLE
chocolate source ...... CACAO
choice .... CREAM, ELITE,
          PRIME, SELECT
choke up .... DAM, CLOG
choler ...... IRE, BILE, RAGE
choose .... OPT, ELECT
chop ..... AXE, CUT, HEW, LOP
chop fine .... MINCE
chopped .... HEWN
choral music
         MOTET, CANTATA

d chord, 3 tones .... TRINE
chore .... JOB, CHARE
Chosen .... COREA, KOREA
Christ's thorn .. NABK, NUBK
Christmas .... NOEL, YULE
Christmas crib ...... CRECHE
chromosome .... IDANT
chronicle .... ANNAL, ANNALS
chrysalis .... PUPA
chrysanthemum .. MUM, KIKU
chub, Furop. ...... CHEVIN
chunk .... GOBBET
church .... FANE
church bench .... PEW
church, body of ...... NAVE
church calendar .... ORDO
church contribution .... TITHE
church council .... SYNOD
church court .... ROTA
church dignitary. POPE, BISHOP,
     PRELATE, CARDINAL
church dish .... PATEN
church, India .... SAMAJ
church living .... BENEFICE
church maintenance, canon's
             PREBEND
church officer .... ELDER

a church official ..... SEXTON, VERGER
church part ..... APSE, BEMA, NAVE, ALTAR
church, Pope's ..... LATERAN
church porch .... PARVIS
church property .... GLEBE
church reader .... LECTOR
church recess .... APSE
church, Scot. .... KIRK, KURK
church vessel .. AMA, PIX, PYX
churchman .... PRELATE
churl. CEORL, VILLAIN, VILLEIN
churl: var. .... CARLE
churn plunger .... DASHER
cibol .... ONION
cicatrix .... SCAR
cigar .... CLARO, SMOKE, CORONA, CHEROOT
cigar, cheap ... STOGY, STOGIE
cigarette, medicinal ... CUBEB
cigarfish .... SCAD
cincture .... BELT
cinnamon, kind of .... CASSIA
cion .... GRAFT
cipher ...... ZERO, OUGHT
cipher system .... CODE
Circe's home .... AEAEA
circle .... CIRC, CIRQUE, RONDURE

b circle of light ... HALO, NIMB
circle, part of .... ARC
circle segment ...... SECTOR
circuit .... LAP, TOUR, AMBIT, ORBIT
circuit judge, court ..... EYRE
circular motion ...... GYRE
circular plate ..... DISC, DISK
circular turn .... LOOP
circular saw .... EDGER
cirque, geol. .... CWM
cistern .... BAC, VAT
citation .... CITAL
cite .... QUOTE, ADDUCE
citron ...... ETROG, CEDRAT, ETHROG
citrus fruit .... LIME, LEMON, ORANGE, SHADOCK, SHADDOCK
CITY .. see also TOWN and GAZETTEER
city, ancient, Asia Min. . MYRA, TYRE, SARDES, SARDIS
city, ancient Thessalian .... LARISSA
city: Gr. .... POLIS
City of a Hundred Towers PAVIA
City of Bridges ...... BRUGES
City of God .... HEAVEN
City of Kings .... LIMA
City of Lights .... PARIS

c City of Luxury ...... SYBARIS
City of Masts .... LONDON
City of Rams .... CANTON
City of Refuge ...... MEDINA
City of Saints .... MONTREAL
City of the Prophet .. MEDINA
City of the Seven Hills .. ROME
City of the Violet Crown .... ATHENS
City of Victory .... CAIRO
city, pert. to .. CIVIC, URBAN
city, Philistines' ...... EKRON
city political division ... WARD
civet, Chinese .... RASSE
civet, Indian .... ZIBET
civet, Java .... DEDES
civet, Madagascar .... FOSSA, FOUSSA
civetlike cat . GENET, GENETTE
civic goddess, Gr. ..... ALEA
Civil War commander ..... LEE, POPE, GRANT, EWELL, MEADE, SCOTT, SYKES, HOOKER, CUSTER, FORREST, JACKSON
civil wrong or injury .... TORT
claim .... ASSERT, DEMAND
clam genus .... MYA
clam, giant .... CHAMA
clam, razor .... SOLEN
clamor .... DIN, NOISE

d clamp .... VICE, VISE
clan .... GEN, SEPT, TRIBE
clan chieftain successor. TANIST
clan division: Gr. .... OBE
clan, Gr. .... GENOS
clan, head of .... ALDER
clarinet socket .... BIRN
clash .... JAR, COLLIDE
clasp . HASP, ENFOLD, INFOLD
clasp for a cope ..... MORSE
class ...... ILK, CASTE, GENUS, GENERA, SPECIES
class leader, Eng. .... DUX
class, lowest Jap. .... HEIMIN
class, scientific .... GENUS, GENERA
classic tongue .... LATIN
classification .... RATING
classification method . SYSTEM
classify .. RANK, RATE, SORT, TYPE, GRADE
claw .... NAIL, TALON, UNGUIS, UNGUES
claw, crustacean's .... CHELA, CHELAE
claw ornament .... GRIFF
claw: zool. .... UNCI, UNCUS
clay ..... BOLE, ARGIL, LOESS
clay, baked .... TILE

Clay

a clay bed .... **GAULT**
clay, building: Sp.
.... **ADOBE, TAPIA**
clay-covered .... **LUTOSE**
clay, friable .... **BOLE**
clay layer .... **SLOAM, SLOOM**
clay, melting pot ...... **TASCO**
clay mineral .... **NACRITE**
clay molding plate .... **DOD**
clay pigeon shooting ... **SKEET**
clay pipe .... **TD**
clay plug .... **BOTT**
clay, porcelain .... **KAOLIN**
clay, potter's .... **ARGIL**
clayey .... **BOLAR**
clayey soil **BOLE, MALM, MARL**
cleansing agent ...... **BORAX**
clear.**NET, RID, LUCID, LIMPID,**
AUDIBLE, TRANSPARENT
clear, as anchor .... **AWEIGH**
clear of charges ..... **ACQUIT**
clearing of land, Eng. ... **SART**
cleave ... **REND, RIVE, CLING**
cleaving tool .... **FROE**
cleft ...... **REFT, RIFT, RIMA**
Clemenceau's nickname . **TIGRE**
clement .... **MILD**
Cleopatra's attendant ... **IRAS**
Cleopatra's handmaid ... **IRAS**
b Cleopatra's needle ... **OBELISK**
Cleopatra's serpent .... **ASP**
clergyman ..... **ABBE, CANON,**
VICAR, CURATE, PRIEST,
RECTOR
cleric, Fr. .... **ABBE**
clerical cap .... **BIRETTA**
clerical, not .... **LAIC, LAICAL**
clever .... **APT, HABILE**
click beetle ...... **DOR, DORR,**
ELATER
climb .... **GRIMP, SCALE**
climbing plant ... **IVY, VINE,**
LIANA, LIANE
cling .... **STICK, ADHERE**
clingfish .... **TESTAR**
clinging, for .... **TENENT**
Clio, sister of .... **ERATO**
clip . **CUT, MOW, SNIP, SHEAR**
clique .... **SET**
CLOAK .... see also GARMENT
cloak ... **ABA, WRAP, CAPOT,**
CAPOTE, MANTLE
cloak, Ind. .... **CHOGA**
cloak, Rom. . **SAGUM, ABOLLA,**
ABOLLAE
cloak, woman's ...... **DOLMAN**
clock, ship-form .... **NEF**
clog-like shoe .... **PATTEN**
cloister .... **MONASTERY**
"Cloister-Hearth" author.**READE**

c close eyes of .... **SEEL**
close, keep .... **HUG**
close: musical .... **CODA**
close to . **AT, BY, NEAR, ANEAR**
close, to fit ..... **FAY, FADGE**
closed, as wings .... **PLIE**
closing measure, music .. **CODA**
CLOTH .... see also SILK,
COTTON, FABRIC
cloth, bark .... **TAPA**
cloth, figured old ..... **TAPET**
cloth measure .... **ELL**
cloth, old wool ..... **CHEYNEY**
cloth, stout .... **BRIN**
cloth strip, India .... **PATA**
cloth used in mourning . **CRAPE**
cloth, wrapping .... **TILLOT**
clothe .... **GIRD, VEST, ENDUE**
clothes moth .... **TINEA**
clothespress, old Dutch ... **KAS**
clothing .. **DUDS, GARB, GEAR,**
TOGS, RAIMENT
cloud .... **SMUR, CIRRI,**
NUBIA, CIRRUS
cloud dragon, Vedic ...... **AHI**
cloud, luminous ...... **NIMBUS**
clouds, broken .... **RACK**
clouds, wind-driven.**RACK, SCUD**
cloudberry .... **MOLKA**
cloudy .... **DULL, LOWERY**
d clout .... **HIT, SWAT**
cloven-footed ...... **FISSIPED**
clover .... **HUBAM,**
ALSIKE, MELILOT
clown .... **APER, GOFF, ZANY**
clown, Shakesperean . **LAVACHE**
cloy .... **PALL, SATE, ACCLOY**
club member, Gr. .... **ERANIST**
club, women's .... **ZONTA**
clubfoot ... **TALIPED, TALIPES**
clumsily, handle ... **PAW, BOTCH**
clumsy .... **INEPT, OAFISH**
cluster .... **NEP, TUFT**
cluster, grape .... **RACEME**
cluster pine .... **PINASTER**
coach dog ...... **DALMATIAN**
coach, Eastern .... **ARABA**
coagulate .... **GEL, CLOT**
coal dust ...... **COOM, SMUT**
coal, heat-treated ...... **COKE**
coal, live .... **EMBER**
coal, size of . **EGG, NUT, PEA**
coal refuse .... **CULM**
coal scuttle .... **HOD**
coalfish .... **CUDDY**
coalition .... **UNION, MERGER**
coarse .... **GROSS**
coarse sugar, E. Ind. .... **RAAB**
coast bird .... **GULL, TERN**
coast dweller ...... **ORARIAN**
coastal range, India .... **GHAT**

COAT ..... see also GARMENT
coat .... LAYER
coat, animal .... PELAGE
coat, Arab .... ABA
coat, soldier's ...... TUNIC
coat with alloy .... TERNE
cob .... SWAN
cobbler .... SUTOR
cobra ... HAJE, NAGA, MAMBA
cobra genus ..... NAIA, NAJA
cocaine source ... COCA, CUCA
cockatoo, Austral. ... GALAH
cockatoo, palm .. ARA, ARARA
cockboat .... COG
cockpit .... ARENA
coconut, dried ...... COPRA
coconut fiber ... COIR, KOIR,
              KYAR, COIRE
coconut, Ind. ...... NARGIL
coconut palm, P. I. ..... NIOG
cocoon insect .... PUPA
cocoon, silkworm ..... CLEW
cod genus .... GADUS
cod, pert. to .... GADOID
cod, young .... SCROD
code .... LAW, CIPHER
codfish, Eur. .... POOR
coffee ... RIO, JAVA, MOCHA
coffee-chocolate flavor .MOCHA
coffer-dam, Egypt ...... SADD
coffin stand .... BIER
cognizant .... AWARE
cognomen ... NAME, EPITHET
cohere .... BIND
coil .... WIND, TWINE
              TWIST, WREATHE
COIN ...... see also SPECIAL
              SECTION, Page 190
coin .... RIN, YEN, SPECIE
coin, cut edges of .... NIG
coin, edging .... REEDING
coin, gold .... LEV
coin, mill .... NURL
coin money .... MINT
coin, pewter .... TRA
coin, reverse side ...... VERSO
coin, silver .... SCEAT
coin tester, Orient
              SARAF, SHROFF
coin, tin .... TRA
coincide .... JIBE, AGREE
colander .... SIEVE
cold .... ALGID, GELID
cold, producing ..... ALGIFIC
cold tableland, Andes ... PUNA
collar .. ETON, FICHU, GORGET
collar, clerical ...... RABAT,
              RABATO, REBATO
collar, deep .... BERTHA
collar, wheel-shaped .... RUFF
collect ...... AMASS, GARNER

collection .... ANA, SET
collection .... SORTITE
collection, motley ..... RAFT
collection of facts .... ANA
collection of sayings .... ANA
COLLEGE DEGREE . see DEGREE
college, Iowa .... COE
college, N.J., East Orange
              UPSALA
college official ...... DEAN
college quadrangle ..... QUAD
colloquialism .... IDIOM
colonists greeting to Ind. NETOP
colonize .... SETTLE
colonizer .... OECIST
colonnade .... STOA
colony, Eng. ...... CAROLINA
colony, Fr. .... ALGERIA
color .... DYE, HUE, TINT
color .. ASH, BAY, RED, TAN,
    BLUE, FAON, FAWN, GRAY,
    GREY, HOPI, JADE, LIME,
    NAVY, NILE, PINK, PUCE,
    ROSE, SAXE, AMBER, BEIGE,
    CORAL, CREAM, EBONY,
    HENNA, IVORY, MAUVE,
    MOCHA, SEPIA, UMBER,
    CERISE, CITRON, COBALT,
    MAROON, RESEDA, SEVRES,
    SIENNA, SORREL, CAR-
    MINE, CELESTE, CITRINE,
    MAGENTA
color brown sugar ... CARAIBE
color changer, photo ... TONER
color, neutral .. GREGE, GREIGE
color, purplish-brown .. PUCE
color, slightly ... TINT, TINGE
color, stripe of .... PLAGA
color, terrapin ..... FEUILLE
Colorado park .... ESTES
coloring agent ...... RUDDLE
coloring matter in fustic .MORIN
colorless .... DRAB
colorless alkaloid ..... ESERIN
colorless oil .... CETANE
columbite, variety of .DIANITE
Columbus' birthplace .. GENOA
Columbus' city sailed from
              PALOS
Columbus' ship .. NINA, PINTA
column, Buddhist-Hindu, building
              LAT
column, Gr. .... DORIC, IONIC
column, memorial .... LAT
column, twisted . TORSE, TORSO
columns, arranged in TABULAR
coma .... TRANCE
comb horse .... CURRY
comb wool ..... CARD, TEASE
combat, field, place of . ARENA
combat, knight's ...... JOUST

33

Combat

a   combat, scene of ..... **ARENA**
combination .. **UNION, CARTEL**
combination, card .... **TENACE**

COMBINING FORMS:

above .... **SUR**
air ...... **AER, AERI, AERO**
all .... **PAN, OMNI**
ass .... **ONO**
bad .... **MAL**
bee .... **API**
beyond .... **SUR**
black .... **MELA**
blood .... **HEMO**
body ...... **SOMA, SOMATO**
bone .... **OSTEO**
both .... **AMBI**
boundary .... **ORI**
bread .... **ARTO**
bristle .... **SETI**
cetacean .... **CETO**
Chinese .... **SINO**
communications .... **TEL**
contemporary .... **NEO**
daybreak .... **EO**
dry .... **XER**
ear .... **OTO, AURI**
earth .... **GEO**
egg .... **OO, OVI**
eight .... **OCT, OCTO**
equal .... **ISO, PARI**

b   eye .... **OCULO**
far .... **TEL, TELE**
fat ... **SEBI, STEAT, STEATO**
fearful .... **DINO**
feast day .... **MAS**
female .... **GYNE**
firm .... **STEREO**
five .... **PENTA**
follower .... **IST**
food .... **SITO**
foot ..... **PED, PEDI, PEDO**
four-parted .... **TETRA**
fruit .... **CARPO**
gas .... **AER, AERO**
gate .... **PYLE**
glade .... **NEMO**
gland .... **ADEN**
gray .... **POLIO**
great .... **MEGA**
gums .... **ULO**
hair .... **PIL, PILI**
half .... **DEMI, SEMI**
heat ..... **THERM, THERMO**
hundred .... **CENTI, HECTO**
idea .... **IDEO**
ill .... **MAL**
individual .... **IDIO**
inner .... **ENTO**
in zoology .... **EAE**
late, latest .... **NEO**
line .... **STICH**

c   many .... **POLY**
medicine .... **IATRO**
middle .... **MEDI**
milk .... **LACT, LACTO**
monster .... **TERAT**
mountain .... **ORO**
mouth ...... **STOM, STOMO**
moving .... **KINO**
narrow .... **STENO**
neck types .... **DERA**
needle .... **ACU**
nerve .... **NEURO**
new .... **NEO**
nine .... **ENNE, ENNEA**
nose .... **NASI**
not .... **UN, NON**
numerical .... **UNI**
numerous .... **MULTI**
oil .... **OLEO**
one .... **UNI, MONO**
on this side .... **CIS**
other .... **HETER**
outside .... **ECTO**
peculiar .... **IDIO**
power .... **DYNA**
powerful .... **MEGA**
quality .... **ACY**
recent .... **NEO, CENE**
reversal .... **ALLO**
ribbon .... **TENE**

d   round .... **GYRO**
sad .... **TRAGI**
seeds .... **CARPO**
seizure of illness ..... **AGRA**
self .... **AUT, AUTO**
shoulder .... **OMO**
small .... **STENO**
solid .... **STEREO**
speak .... **LALO**
star .... **ASTRO**
stone .... **LITH**
strange .... **XENO**
sun .... **HELIO**
ten .... **DECA**
thin .... **SERO**
third .... **TRIT**
thread .... **NEMA**
threefold, thrice .... **TER**
tooth .... **ODONT**
touch .... **TAC**
thought .... **IDEO**
thousand .... **MILLE**
up .... **ANO**
vapor .... **ATMO**
various ...... **VARI, VARIO**
watery .... **SERO**
white .... **ALBO**
whole .... **TOTO**
wind .... **ANEMO**
within .... **ENT, ESO,
                ENDO, ENSO, ENTO**

34

a
without .... ECT
wood .... XYLO
worker .... ERGATE
come.ENSUE, ACCRUE, ARRIVE
come back .... RECUR
come forth .... ISSUE,
EMERGE, EMERSE
come forth from .. JET, GUSH,
SPEW, EMANATE
comedian's foil .... STOOGE
comedy .... FARCE
"Comedy of Errors" servant
LUCE
comfort .... EASE, SOLACE
comfortable .... COSH, SNUG
comforter .... SCARF
command .... BID, FIAT,
ORDER, DICTATE
command: archaic ..... HEST
command to horse
GEE, HAW, HUP
commander, Egypt .... SIRDAR
commander, Moslem
AGA, AGHA
commander, fortress CAID, QAID
commentary: Hebrew .... BIUR
commission, milit. ..... BREVET
commodity .... WARE, STAPLE
common ... VULGAR, GENERAL
common brant .... QUINK
b common: Hawaiian ..... NOA
common man .... PLEB
commonplace .. BANAL, TRITE
commotion . ADO, STIR, TO-DO
commune, Dutch, Holland EDE
COMMUNE see its country in
GAZETTEER
communion cup .... AMA
communion dish ...... PATEN
communion service ..... MASS
communion table ..... ALTAR
compact ...... DENSE, SOLID
companion .... PAL, MATE
comparative conjunction . THAN
comparative suffix ending . ER
compass point .... NE, SE, SW,
ENE, ESE, NNE, NNW, SSE,
SSW, WNW, WSW
compass point, mariner's RHUMB
compassion ...... PITY, RUTH
compel .... MAKE, FORCE,
COERCE
compendium .... SYLLABUS
compensate .... PAY
compensation, N. Z. ...... UTU
competent .... ABLE
complain .... FRET, FUSS,
GRIPE, REPINE
complainant .... RELATOR
complete ...... TOTAL, UTTER,
ENTIRE, PLENARY

c completely .... ALL, QUITE
completely occupy ... ENGROSS
complication ..... NODE, NODI
comply .... OBEY, YIELD
composer, Am. .. NEVIN, SOUSA,
FOSTER, COPLAND
composer, Eng. .... ARNE,
ELGAR, COATES
composer, Fr. .. LALO, AUBER
BIZET, IBERT, RAVEL
composer, Ger. ..... ABT, BACH,
WEBER
composer, Roum. ..... ENESCO
COMPOSITION.see also MUSIC
composition ... ESSAY, THEME
composition, mus. ...... OPUS,
ETUDE, MOTET, RONDO,
SUITE, SONATA, CON-
CERTO, FANTASIA
composition of selections.CENTO
composition, operatic .. SCENA
composition, sacred ... MOTET
compositor .... TYPO
compound, organic .... AMIDE
compound with oxygen . OXIDE
comrade-in-arms ...... ALLY
concave .... DISHED
conceal: law .... ELOIN
concealed ..... INNER, PERDU
concealed obstacle ...... SNAG
concede .... ADMIT,
d GRANT, YIELD
conceive .... IDEATE
concern .... CARE
concerning .... RE. INRE,
ABOUT, ANENT
conch .... SHELL
conciliate .... ATONE
conciliatory gift .... SOP
concise .. BRIEF, SHORT, TERSE
concluding passage music CODA
concoct .... BREW
concrete mixer .... PAVER
concur .. JIBE, AGREE, ASSENT
condescend ..... DEIGN, STOOP
condiment .... SALT,
CURRY, SPICE
condition .. IF, STATE, STATUS
condition in agreement PROVISO
conduct ...... LEAD, GUIDE
conductor .... MAESTRO
conductor's stick ...... BATON
conduit . MAIN, DRAIN, SEWER
cone ...... STROBIL, STROBILE
cone of silver .... PINA
confection .... COMFIT
confection, nut ...... PRALINE
confederate .... ALLY
Confederate soldier ...... REB
confederation .... LEAGUE
conference .... PALAVER

Confess

a confess .... AVOW, ADMIT
confession of faith .... CREDO
confidence .... FAITH, TRUST
confidences .... SECRETS
confident .... RELIANT
confidential .... ESOTERIC
confine ...... BOX, HEM, PEN,
CAGE, CRAMP
confined .... PENT
confront .... MEET
confused, make .... ADDLE
confusion .... BABEL
congealed dew .... RIME
conger .... EEL
congregate .. MEET, GATHER
conical mass of thread ... COP
coniferous tree ..... FIR, YEW,
PINE, CEDAR, SPRUCE
conjunction .... OR, AND,
BUT, NOR
connect ... JOIN, LINK, UNITE
connecting strip of land
ISTHMUS
connection
NEXUS, CORRELATION
connective .... AND, NOR
connective tissue ..... FASCIA
connubial .... MARITAL
conquer .... MASTER
conqueror, Mex.

b CORTES, CORTEZ
Conrad's "Victory" heroine
LENA
conscript .... DRAFT
consecrate .... BLESS
consecrated .... OBLATE
consequence .... OUTCOME
conservative .... TORY
consider .... DEEM, RATE,
TREAT, REGARD
consonant, hard ...... FORTIS
consonant, unaspirated .. LENE
conspire .... PLOT
Constantine VIII's daughter . ZOE
constellation ...... ARA, LEO,
APUS, ARGO, LYNX, LYRA,
PAVO, URSA, VELA, ARIES,
CANIS, CETUS, DRACO,
LIBRA, MENSA, ORION,
VIRGO, AQUILA, GEMINI,
PISCES, TAURUS
constellation, Altar ...... ARA
constellation, Aquila ... EAGLE
constellation, Ara ..... ALTAR
constellation, Aries ...... RAM
constellation, Balance .. LIBRA
constellation, Bear ...... URSA
constellation, Bull ... TAURUS
constellation, Crab ... CANCER
constellation, Crane ..... GRUS
constellation, Crow ... CORVUS

c constellation, Dog .... CANIS
constellation, Dragon .. DRACO
constellation, Hunter ... ORION
constellation, Lion .... LEO
constellation near South Pole
APUS
constellation, northern .... LEO
constellation, Peacock .... PAVO
constellation, Ram ..... ARIES
constellation, Southern ... ARA,
APUS, ARGO, GRUS, PAVO,
VELA, INDUS
constellation's main star .. COR
constitution supporter . CARTIST
constrictor ..... BOA, ABOMA
constructor .... ERECTOR
consume: obs. .... ETE
container .... BOX, CAN, TIN,
TUB, VAT, URN, CASE
containing ore .... ORY
contempt, exclamation of . PISH
contempt, look of ..... SNEER
contend .... VIE, COPE,
DEAL, COMPETE
contest .... AGON, BOUT
continent: abbr. ...... NA, SA,
AFR, EUR
continue .... LAST,
ENDURE, RESUME
contort . WARP, GNARL, TWIST

d contradict ..... DENY, REBUT,
NEGATE
contrition .... REMORSE
contrive ...... MAKE, DEVISE
control .... STEER
controversial .... ERISTIC
controversy .... DEBATE
conundrum .. ENIGMA, RIDDLE
convert to Judaism ...... GER
conveyance of estate .. DEMISE
convoy .... ESCORT
cony .. DAS, DAMAN, GANAM
cook in cream .... SHIR, SHIRR
cooking odor .... NIDOR
cooking pot .... OLLA
cooky .... SNAP
cool .... ICE
coolie woman ...... CHANGAR
Cooper novel .... PILOT
copal .... ANIME
copper .... CENT
Copperfield, Mrs. ...... DORA
copse .... HOLT, COPPICE
Coptic bishop .... ANBA
copy .... APE, MODEL, ECTYPE
copy, court record ... ESTREAT
coral .... POLYP
cord .... LINE, RAIP,
ROPE, WELT
cord, hat of Bedouin .... AGAL
cord, Hawaii .... AEA

a cordage fiber . **DA, COIR, ERUC,
FERU, HEMP, IMBE, JUTE,
RHEA, ABACA, SISAL**
cordage tree.............. **SIDA**
Cordelia's father .... **LEAR**
"Cordiale, —"......... **ENTENTE**
core ...... **AME, PITH, HEART**
core, casting mold ..... **NOWEL**
core material of earth ..... **NIFE**
core to fashion metal...... **AME**
core, wooden .... **AME**
cork .... **SPILE**
Cork County port......... **COBH**
cork, extract of .... **CERIN**
cork, flat .... **SHIVE**
cork helmet...... **TOPI, TOPEE**
corkwood............... **BALSA**
corm................... **BULB**
corn crake bird........... **RAIL**
corn crake genus........ **CREX**
corn, hulled........... **HOMINY**
corn, India .... **RAGEE, RAGGEE**
corn lily .... **IXIA**
corn meal .... **MASA**
cornbread .... **PONE**
corner... **NOOK, TREE, ANGLE**
cornerstone ..... **COIN, COYN,
COIGN, QUOIN, COIGNE**
cornice support .... **ANCON**
b Cornish prefix: town ...... **TRE**
Cornish prefix in names.... **LAN,
ROS**
cornu .... **HORN**
Cornwall mine .... **BAL**
corolla part .... **PETAL**
corona .. **AUREOLA, AUREOLE**
coronach, Scot.......... **DIRGE**
coronation stone .... **SCONE**
corpulent .... **OBESE**
corral: Sp............... **ATAJO**
correct. **OKEH, TRUE, AMEND,
EMEND, REVISE**
correct behaviour, Chin. ...... **LI**
correlative............. **OR, NOR**
correspond **JIBE, AGREE, TALLY**
corridor .... **HALL**
corrie .... **CWM**
corrode ... **EAT, RUST, ERODE**
corrupt .... **TAINT, VENAL,
VITIATE**
corrupt with money ..... **BRIBE**
corsair .... **PIRATE**
corset bone.............. **BUSK**
cortege .... **RETINUE**
corundum .... **EMERY**
cos lettuce .... **ROMAINE**
Cos, pert. to............ **COAN**
cosmic cycle............. **EON**
cosmic order: Vedic .... **RITA**
Cossack............... **TATAR**
Cossack chief........ **ATAMAN**

c Cossack headman.... **HETMAN**
Cossack regiment . **POLK, PULK**
cosset .... **PET**
costa .... **RIB**
coterie .... **SET**
cottage, Ind............. **BARI**
cotton batting........... **BATT**
cotton, Bengal .... **ADATI**
cotton, Egypt ...... **SAK, PIMA,
SAKEL**
cotton fabric..... **JEAN, LAWN,
LENO, DENIM,
SURAT, MADRAS**
cotton fabric, corded **CANTOON**
cotton machine .... **GIN**
cotton, matted........... **BATT**
cotton tree .... **SIMAL**
cottonwood, Texas ..... **ALAMO**
couch.................. **LAIR**
cougar .... **PUMA, PANTHER**
council .... **SOVIET**
council, ecclesiastical... **SYNOD**
council, king's .... **WITAN**
"Council of —" .... **TRENT**
counsel .... **REDE**
counselor............ **MENTOR**
count .... **ENUMERATE**
count, Ger. .... **GRAF**
counter .... **BAR**
counter, in cards .... **MILLE**
d countercurrent .... **EDDY**
countermand .... **REVOKE**
counterpart............... **LIKE**
countersink .... **REAM**
counting frame........ **ABACUS**
COUNTRY see also GAZETTEER,
SPECIAL SECTION
country, ancient......... **ELAM**
country, ancient, Asia Min., Gr.
EOLIS, AEOLIA, AEOLIS
country, ancient, Bib.... **SHEBA**
country, ancient Greek..... **ELIS**
country bumpkin ...... **RUBE,
YOKEL, RUSTIC**
country: law .... **PAIS**
COUNTY see also GAZETTEER,
SPECIAL SECTION
county: Dan.............. **AMT**
county: Eng............. **SHIRE**
county: Nor. ...... **AMT, FYLKE**
county: Swed.............. **LAN**
couple .... **TWO, PAIR**
courage .... **METTLE**
courier .... **ESTAFET,
ESTAFETTE**
course .... **WAY, ROAD,
TACK, ROUTE**
course, complete....... **CYCLE**
course, meal.. **SALAD, ENTREE**
course, part of ... **LAP, LEG**
court................... **AREA**

a
court action .... SUIT
court, A.-S. .. GEMOT, GEMOTE
court, church .... ROTA
court cry .... OYES, OYEZ
court hearing .... OYER
court, inner .... PATIO
court, Jap. ...... DARI, DAIRO
court, old English .... LEET
court order .... ARRET
court panel .... JURY
court, pert. to church .. ROTAL
court proceeding .... TRIAL
courtly .... AULIC
courtship strut, grouse's .. LAK
courtway .... AREA
courtyard .... PATIO
Covenant, — of the ...... ARK
cover inner surface ...... LINE
covering .. TEGMEN, TEGUMEN
covey .... BEVY, BROOD
cow .... BOSSY, BOVINE
cow house .... BYRE
cows .... KINE, BOSSIES
coward .... CRAVEN
cowboy garment .... CHAPS
cowboy, S. Am. ...... GAUCHO
cowfish .... RAY, TORO
cowl .... HOOD
cowlike .... COUS
coxcomb .... FOP

b
coy .... ARCH
coyotillo .... MARGARITA
coypu .... NUTRIA
cozy .... HOMY, SNUG
cozy place .... DEN, NEST
crab-eating mongoose .. URVA
crab, front of .... METOPE
crack . SNAP, CHINK, CREVICE
crackling .... CREPITANT
crackpot .... NUT
craft .... ART, TRADE
craftsman .... ARTISAN
crafty ...... SLY, FOXY, WILY
craggy hill .... TOR
cramp .... KINK
crane arm .... GIB, JIB
crane genus .... GRUS
crane, India .... SARUS
crane, pert. to .... GRUINE
crane, ship's .... DAVIT
cranelike bird .... CHUNGA

SERIEMA
cranial nerve ... VAGI, VAGUS
cravat .... TIE
crave . ASK, BEG, LONG, DESIRE
craw .... MAW, CROP
crayon ...... CHALK, PASTEL
craze .... FAD, MANIA
crazy .... LOCO, LUNY, WILD

c
cream .... ELITE
credit transfer system .. GIRO
creed .... CREDO, NICENE
creek .... RIA, KILL
creek: N.Y. .... VLEI
creeper .... IVY
creeping .. REPENT, REPTANT
Cremona .... AMATI
crescent moon's point ... CUSP
crescent-shaped ...... LUNATE
crescent-shaped figure .. LUNE
crescent-shaped mark . LUNULA
crest . TOP, COMB, PEAK, TUFT
crest, sharp rugged mountain

ARETE
crested as birds ..... PILEATE
Cretan princess ..... ARIADNE
Cretan spikenard .... PHU
CRETE . see SPECIAL SECTION
crevice ... CREVAS, CREVASSE
crew .... MEN, GANG,
TEAM, EIGHT
cribbage pin or score .... PEG
cribbage term .... NOB, NOBS
cricket .... GRIG
cricket, ball in .... EDGER
cricket, field parts ONS, OFFS
cricket, run in .... BYE
cricket term OVER, TICE, YORK

d
crime, Eccl. .... SIMONY
Crimean river .... ALMA
criminal .... FELON
crimp .... CURL, GOFFER
crimson ..... RED, CARMINE
crippled .... HALT, LAME
criticize .... SLATE
criticize in a small way

CARP, CAVIL
crocodile, India ...... GAVIAL
crocodile-head god, Egyp.

SOBK, SEBEK
crocus .... IRID
crocus bulb .... CORM
Croesus' land .... LYDIA
crony .. PAL, CHUM, BUDDY
crony: old Eng. .... EME
crooked ...... AGEE, AWRY
crooner, early ...... VALLEE
crop .... MAW, CRAW
crop, spring, India ...... RABI
cross ..... IRATE, TRAVERSE
cross, church .... ROOD
cross-examine .... GRILL
cross of life, Egypt .... ANKH
cross oneself .... SAIN
cross out .... DELETE
cross-stroke .... SERIF
cross timber, ship ...... SPALE
crossbeam .... TRAVE, TREVE
crossbill genus .... LOXIA
crossbow .... RODD

a
crossing, fence .... STILE
crosspiece . BAR, RUNG, CLEAT
crosspiece, vehicle ... EVENER
crossthreads ..... WEFT, WOOF
crosswise .... THWART
crossword champion, former
.... COOPER
crow .. ROOK, CRAKE, CORVUS
crow: Eng. .... BRAN
crow, Guam .... AGA
crow, kind of .... DAW
crowd, common ... MOB, RUCK
crowd together .. HERD, SERRY
crowded .... SERRIED
crown .... CAP, PATE,
.... TIARA, DIADEM
crown colony, Brit.
.... ADEN, BAHAMAS
crown of Osiris or Egypt .. ATEF
crown: poetic .... TIAR
crown, Pope's triple TIAR, TIARA
crucial point .... CRUX, PIVOT
crucible .... CRUSET
crucifix .... ROOD
crude . RAW, ROUGH, COARSE
crude metal .... ORE
crude sugar-molasses MELADA
cruel person .... SADIST
cruet .... AMA, CASTER
b
cruising .... ASEA
crumbled easily ..... FRIABLE
Crusader's foe ..... SARACEN
Crusader's headquarters . ACRE
crush .... MASH, SUBDUE
crustacean .... CRAB, ISOPOD,
.... SHRIMP, LOBSTER
crustacean order, one of
.... DECAPOD
cry .... HO, HOA, SOB, HOWL,
...... WAIL, WEEP, LAMENT
cry, Austral. ... COOEE, COOEY
cry for silence, court
.... OYES, OYEZ
crystal-clear .... PELLUCID
ctenophores, no tentacle .NUDA
Cuban dance .... CONGA
Cuban rodent .... PILORI
Cuban secret police ... PORRA
Cuban timber tree ..... CUYA
cubic decimeter .... LITER
cubic measure .. CORD, STERE
cubic meter .... STERE
cubicle .... CELL
cubitus .... ULNA
Cuchulain's wife . EMER, EIMER
cuckoo, black, keel-billed ANI
cuckoo, Oriental .. COEL, KOEL
cuckoopint .... ARUM
cucumber .... CUKE, PEPO
cud .... QUID, RUMEN

c
cudgel .... BAT, CLUB, DRUB,
.... BASTE, STAVE, STICK
cue .... HINT
cue, music .... PRESA
cuff fastener .... TAB
cuirass .... LORICA
cull .... SORT
culmination ..... ACME, APEX
cultivate land .... HOE, PLOW,
.... TILL, HARROW
cultivation method, Bengal
.... JUM, JOOM
cultivation, soil ...... TILTH
culture medium .... AGAR
cunning ... ART, CUTE, FOXY,
.... WILY, DEDAL, CALLID,
.... DAEDAL
cup .... CRUSE
cup, assaying .... CUPEL
cup, ceremonial .... AMA
cup, gem cutting .... DOP
cup stand of metal .... ZARF
cup to hold gem .... DOP
cupbearer .... SAKI
cupbearer of gods ...... HEBE
cupboard .... AMBRY, CLOSET
Cupid .... AMOR, EROS
Cupid's title .... DAN
cupola .... DOME
cur .... MUT, MUTT
d
curare ...... URALI, OORALI
curassow .... MITU
curassow genus .... CRAX
curdling powder ..... RENNET
cure-all .... ELIXIR, PANACEA
cure by salting .... CORN
cure with salt grass ..... DUN
curfew .... BELL
curios .... VIRTU
curl COIL, FRIZ, WIND, FRIZZ
curl of hair ...... FEAK, TRESS,
.... RINGLET
curling, mark aimed at ... TEE
currant genus .... RIBES
current .... AC, DC, EDDY,
...... RIFE, TIDE, STREAM
curt ...... BRUSK, BRUSQUE
curve .... ARC, BOW, ESS,
.... ARCH, BEND, SINUS
curve in a stream . HOEK, HOOK
curve, plane .... ELLIPSE,
.... PARABOLA
curve, sigmoid or double .. ESS
curved handle .... BOOL
curved in .. ADUNC, CONCAVE
curved out .... CONVEX
curved plank, vessel's .... SNY
Cush, son of .... SEBA
cushion ...... PAD, HASSOCK
custard .... FLAN
custard apple ...... ANNONA

a custard cake .... ECLAIR
custard dish .... FLAN
custody .... CHARGE
custom .... LAW, WONT,
  HABIT, USAGE
custom, India .... DASTUR
custom: Lat. .... RITUS
custom: obs. .... URE
customer .... PATRON
customs .... MORES
cut . HEW, LOP, MOW, DOCK,
  GASH, HACK, KERF, REAP,
  SLIT, SNEE, SNIP, TRIM,
  SEVER, SHEAR, SLIVE,
  CLEAVE, TREPAN
cut down .... FELL
cut edges of coins .... NIG
cut of meat .... LOIN
cut off ... DOCK, SNIP, ELIDE
cut off, as mane ..... ROACH
cut out .... EXCISE
cut: Shakespeare ...... SLISH
cut vertically
  SCARP, ESCARP, ESCARPE
cutter .... SLED
cutting .... SECANT, INCISAL

c cutting tool .. AX, ADZ, AXE,
  HOB, SAW, SAX, SYE, ADZE
cuttlefish ...... SEPIA, SQUID
cuttlefish fluid .... INK
Cyclades, one of, see GAZET-
  TEER
cycle, astronomical ..... SAROS
cyclorama .... CYKE
cylinder, moving ...... PISTON
cylindrical .... TERETE
cyma .... GOLA
cyma recta or reversa ... OGEE
cymbal, Orient .... ZEL
cymbals, India .... TAL
Cymbeline's daughter . IMOGEN
Cymric deity
  GWYN, LLEU, LLEW
Cymry .... WELSH
cypher system .... CODE
cyprinoid fish .... ID, IDE,
  CARP, CHUB
Cyrus' daughter ..... ATOSSA
cyst .... WEN
Czar .... IVAN, FEDOR
Czech .... SLAV
Czech, Eastern .... ZIPS

b Dadaist .... ERNST
dado, pedestal ...... SOLIDUM
Daedalus' son .... ICARUS
dagger . DIRK, SNEE, BODKIN
dagger, ancient . SKEAN, SKENE
dagger, Ir. DHU, SKENE, SKEAN
dagger, Malay ... CRIS, KRIS,
  CREES, KREES, CREESE,
  KREESE
dagger: obs. .... SNEE
dagger, thin .... STILETTO
Dahomey Negro .. FON, FONG
daily .... DIURNAL
dais .... ESTRADE
daisy . MOON, OXEYE, SHASTA
Dallas school .... SMU
dam .... WAER, WEIR
dam, Egypt ...... SADD, SUDD
dam site .... ASWAN
damage . MAR, HARM, IMPAIR
Damascus river ...... ABANA
damp .... DANK
domselfish .... PINTANO
dance .... HOP, JIG, REEL,
  GALOP, GAVOT, POLKA,
  TANGO, RUMBA, REDOWA,
  RHUMBA, GAVOTTA, GA-
  VOTTE
dance, country . REEL, ALTHEA
dance, Gr. .... HORMOS
dance, Israeli .... HORA

d dance, lively ..... JIG, REEL,
  GALOP, POLKA, BOLERO
dance, old Eng. .... MORRIS
dance, Sp. ... TANGO, BOLERO
dance, stately, old
  PAVAN, MINUET, PAVANE
dance step ..... PAS, CHASSE,
  GLISSADE
dancer ...... KELLY, SHAWN,
  BOLGER, ZORINA, ASTAIRE
dancing girl, Egypt .... ALMA,
  ALME, ALMEH
dancing girl, Jap. ..... GEISHA
dandy FOP, DUDE, JAKE, TOFF
DANISH ... see also DENMARK
  in SPECIAL SECTION
Danish astronomer .... BRAHE
Dan. borough (in Eng.) .. BORG
Dan. chieftain .... JARL, YARL
Don. division, territorial . AMT
Dan. fjord .... ISE
Dan. king ..... CNUT, KNUT,
  CANUTE
Dan. measure .... ALEN
Dan. money ..... ORA, ORAS
Dan. physicist .... BOHR
Dan. speech sound ...... STOD
dank .... WET
Dante's patron .... SCALA
Danube city ..... ULM, LINZ
Danube, old name of ... ISTER

a Danube tributary
    INN, OLT, ISAR, PRUT
daring .... BOLD, NERVE
dark .... MIRKY, MURKY
dark horse .... ZAIN
dark rock .... CHERT
dark wood ...... TEAK, EBONY
darkness .... MIRK, MURK
darling: Ir. . ROON, ACUSHLA,
    ASTHORE
darnel .... TARE
dart along .... FLIT
"Das Rheingold" role ... ERDA
dash .... ELAN
date, pert. to .... DATAL
date plum .... SAPOTE
date, Roman .... IDES, NONES
"David Copperfield" character
    DORA, HEEP, DARTLE
David's captain .... JOAB
David's commander ..... AMASA
David's daughter ..... TAMAR
David's father .... JESSE
David's nephew ...... AMASA
David's ruler, one of ...... IRA
David's son .... SOLOMON
David's wife .... MICHAL
dawn ...... DEW, EOS, AURORA
dawn, pert. to .... EOAN
day, Hebr. .... YOM

b day, Rom. ...... IDES, NONES
day-breeze, It. .... ORA
days: Lat. .... DIES
day's march .... ETAPE
daybreak .... DAWN
dazing larks, device for . DARE
deacon's stole ...... ORARION
dead .. FLAT, AMORT, INERT
dead, abode of . HADES, SHEOL
dead, region of: Egypt AMENTI
dead trees .... DRIKI
deadly .... FATAL, LETHAL
deadly carrot .... DRIAS
deadly sins, 7 ENVY, LUST, AN-
    GER, PRIDE, SLOTH, GLUT-
    TONY, COVETOUSNESS
dealer .... MONGER
dealer, cloth
    DRAPER, MERCER
dean ...... DOYEN, DOYENNE
dearth .... WANT
death ...... MORT, DEMISE
death deity: Rom. ...... MORS
death note on hunter's horn
    MORT
death notice .... OBIT
death rattle .... RALE
debate—debatable
    AGON, MOOT
debauchee ...... RAKE, ROUE
debris, rocky .... SCREE

c decade .... TEN
decamp ...... ELOPE, LEVANT
decay, dental .... CARIES
decay tree ...... CONK, KONK
deceit .... SHAM, WILE,
    FRAUD, GUILE
deceive .. BILK, DUPE, FOOL,
    GULL, TRICK, ILLUDE
decelerate .... RETARD
deception HOAX, STRATAGEM
decide: Rom. law .... CERN
decimal unit .... TEN
deck, ship's .... POOP
decks, cut away . RASEE, RAZEE
declaim .... RANT, RAVE,
    ORATE, RECITE
declaration in whist ... MISERE
declare .... AVER, AVOW,
    STATE, AVOUCH
declare, in cards .... MELD
decline .... EBB, SINK,
    WANE, REFUSE
declivity ...... SCARP, SLOPE
declivity in menage . CALADE
decorate ...... DECK, ADORN
decorated letter .... FAC
decorated wall part ..... DADO
decorous ..... STAID, DEMURE
decoy .... LURE, PLANT
decrease .... EBB, WANE,
    LESSEN, RECEDE

d decree .... ACT, FIAT,
    CANON, EDICT, ORDAIN
decree, Fr. law .... ARRET
decree, Moslem .... IRADE
decree, Rom. law ... DECRETE
decree, Russian .... UKASE
deduce .... INFER
deed .... GEST, GESTE
deeds .... ACTA
deer, Asia ...... AHU, KAKAR,
    SAMBAR, SAMBUR,
    SAMBHAR, SAMBHUR
deer, barking .... KAKAR
deer, Chile, Andes ..... PUDU
deer, female . DOE, ROE, HIND
deer genus, E. Ind. ..... RUSA
deer, India .... AXIS
deer, Jap. .... SIKA
deer, Kashmir ...... HANGUL
deer, red .... ROE, HART
deer, S. Am. .... GEMUL,
    GUEMAL, GUEMUL
deer, spotted .... CHITAL
deer, Tibet .... SHOU
deer track .... SLOT
deerlet .... NAPUS
deerlike .... CERVINE
defamation .... LIBEL
defeat, chess .... MATE
defeat utterly ... BEST, ROUT

Defect

a
- defect, weaving .... **SCOB**
- defendant's plea .... **NOLO**
- deference .... **RESPECT**
- defraud .... **GYP, BILK, GULL, CHEAT**
- defy .... **DARE**
- degrade ...... **ABASE, LOWER, DEBASE**
- degrading .... **MENIAL**
- degree .... **GRADE, STAGE**
- degree .. (dental) **DDS, DDSC;** (engineer) **CE, EE;** (divinity) **DD;** (science) **BSC;** (arts) **BA, MA, MFA;** (law) **LLB, LLD**
- degree, extreme .... **NTH**
- degree taken, Cambridge **INCEPTOR**
- degrees, angle of 57.30. **RADIAN**
- deified sky, Rom. ..... **CAELUS**
- **DEITY** . see also GOD, GODDESS and SPECIAL SECTION
- deity .... **GOD**
- deity, Buddhist ... **DEV, DEVA**
- deity, Hindu ...... **DEV, DEVA**
- deity, Jap. .. **AMIDA, AMITA**
- deity, primeval .... **TITAN**
- deity, Sumerian .... **ABU**
- deity, Syrian .... **EL**

b
- delay . **WAIT, DETAIN, LINGER**
- delay, law .... **MORA, MORAE**
- delicacy .... **FINESSE**
- delight .... **REVEL**
- delusion: Buddhism .... **MOHA**
- demand . **NEED, CLAIM, INSIST**
- demeanor .... **AIR**
- Demeter's daughter **CORA, KORE**
- demigod .... **HERO**
- demolish .... **RASE, RAZE**
- demon .. **IMP, DEVIL, FIEND**
- demon, Arab, Moslem, Oriental **JIN, JINN, GENIE, GENII, JINNI, JINNEE**
- demon, Hindu . **ASURA, DAITYA**
- demon, sun-swallowing, Hindu myth .... **RAHU**
- demon, Zoroastrian **DEV, DIV, DEVA**
- demonstrative pronoun **THAT, THIS, WHOM**
- den ...... **DIVE, LAIR, HAUNT**
- denary .... **TEN**
- denial .... **NO, NAY**
- **DENMARK** .. see also DANISH and SPECIAL SECTION
- denomination .... **SECT**
- denote .... **MEAN, SHOW, INDICATE**
- denoting unfit ships in Lloyd's registry .... **AE**

c
- dense . **CRASS, THICK, STUPID**
- density .... **DORD**
- dental tool .... **SCALER**
- deny .... **NEGATE**
- depart ..... **BEGONE, DECAMP**
- depart fast **VAMOSE, VAMOOSE**
- depart: Lat. .... **VADE**
- departed ... **GONE, LEFT, WENT**
- department, Chin. .. **FU, FOO**
- departure .... **EXODUS**
- dependent .... **MINION**
- depict .... **DRAW, PAINT, DESCRIBE**
- deplore .... **LAMENT**
- deposit, alluvial **DELTA, GEEST**
- deposit, clayey .... **MARL**
- deposit, geyser .... **SINTER**
- deposit, mineral .... **LODE**
- deposit, river **ALLUVIA, ALLUVIUM**
- deposit, wine cask ... **TARTAR**
- depressed .... **SAD**
- depression ...... **DENT, FOVEA**
- deprivation .... **LOSS**
- deprived .... **REFT**
- depute .... **SEND**
- deputy .... **AGENT, VICAR**
- derby .... **BOWLER**
- deride .... **GIBE, JIBE**
- derrick ...... **CRANE, STEEVE**

d
- dervish, "Arab. Nights" .. **AGIB**
- dervish, Moslem ...... **SADITE**
- descendant ...... **SON, CION**
- descendant, Fatima's **SAID, SEID, SAYID**
- descendants, male line .. **GENS**
- descent, deep .... **SCARP**
- descriptive term ..... **EPITHET**
- desert dweller ...... **EREMITE**
- desert, Mongolia .... **GOBI**
- desert plant .... **AGAVE**
- deserter .... **RAT**
- deserve .... **EARN, MERIT**
- design .... **AIM**
- desire .... **YEN, URGE, WANT, WISH**
- desire eagerly .... **ASPIRE**
- desirous .... **FAIN**
- desolate .... **LORN, BLEAK**
- despoil .... **RUIN**
- despot .. **CZAR, TSAR, TZAR, TYRANT, DICTATOR**
- dessert .. **ICE, PIE, MOUSSE, TRIFLE**
- destiny . **DOOM, FATE, KARMA**
- destroy .... **RASE, RAZE, DECIMATE**
- destruction .... **RUIN**
- detach .... **WEAN**
- detachable button ...... **STUD**
- detail .... **ITEM**

42

a detain **CHECK, DELAY, ARREST**
detecting device ..... **SONAR**
detective .... **TEC, DICK**
detent .... **PAWL**
determination ...... **WILL**
determine ...... **FIX, DECIDE, RESOLVE**
detest .... **HATE, LOATHE**
dethrone .... **DEPOSE**
detonator .... **CAP**
"— deum" .... **TE**
devaluate .... **DEBASE**
developed compound animal **ZOON**
Devil .... **UMA**
deviate ... **ERR, YAW, DIVERGE**
deviation .... **LAPSE**
deviation from course .... **YAW**
devil .. **DEMON, DEUCE, SATAN**
devil: Gypsy .... **BENG**
devil, Moslem **SHAITAN, SHEITAN**
devil, Russian folklore .. **CHORT**
devil worship ...... **SATANISM**
devilfish .... **MANTA**
Devon river .... **EXE**
devotee .... **FAN, IST**
devotion, nine-day .. **NOVENA**
devoutness .... **PIETY**
dewberry .... **MAYES**
b dewy .... **RORAL, RORIC**
dexterity .... **ART**
dexterous .... **CLEVER**
diadem .... **TIARA**
diagonal .... **BIAS**
DIALECT . see also LANGUAGE
dialect . **IDIOM, LINGO, PATOIS**
dialect, Chin. .... **CANTON**
dialect, Ethiopic .... **TIGRE**
dialect, Gr. .... **DORIC, IONIC**
diamond corner .... **BASE**
diamond fragments ..... **BORT**
diamond holder .... **DOP**
diamond, impure industrial **BORT**
diamond, perfect .... **PARAGON**
diamonds, low quality ... **BORT**
Diana .... **ARTEMIS**
Diana's grove .... **NEMUS**
Diana's mother ...... **LATONA**
diaphanous ..... **THIN, SHEER**
diaphragm, pert. to .. **PHRENIC**
diatonic note .... **MI**
diatribe .. **SCREED, HARANGUE**
dibble .... **DAP, DIB**
Dickens character .. **PIP, TIM, DORA, GAMP, HEEP, FAGIN, DORRIT**
Dickens' pseudonym ...... **BOZ**
"Die Fledermaus" girl .. **ADELE**
die for making drain pipe . **DOD**
die, gambling .. **TAT, TESSERA**

c "Dies —," "Day of Wrath" **IRAE**
diet .... **BANT, FARE**
differ ...... **VARY, DISAGREE**
difference between solar and lunar year ...... **EPACT**
different ...... **OTHER, DIVERS**
difficulty .... **RUB, KNOT**
dig ...... **GRUB, PION, DELVE**
digest .... **PANDECT**
digit, foot .... **TOE**
digraph **AE, EA, OA, OE, SH, TH**
dike .... **LEVEE**
dilation .... **ECTASIA**
dilatory ...... **SLOW, TARDY, REMISS**
dilemma .... **FIX**
dill herb .... **ANET**
dilute .... **THIN, WATER**
dim, become .. **BLEAR, DARKLE**
diminish ... **EBB, BATE, SINK, WANE, ABATE, TAPER**
diminish front: military .... **PLOY**
dingle ..... **DALE, DELL, GLEN**
dining room, ancient ... **OECUS**
diocese center .... **SEE**
Dioscuri .... **ANAX**
dip .... **DAP, DIB, DOPP, DUNK, LADE**
dip out .... **BAIL**
diplomacy .... **TACT**
d diplomat .... **ENVOY, CONSUL, ATTACHE**
diphthong ..... **AE, IA, OA, UO**
Dipper constellation ..... **URSA**
direct .... **AIM. LEAD**
direct attention .... **REFER**
direct steering of boat .. **CONN**
dirge .... **LINOS, LINUS**
dirigible .... **BLIMP**
dirk .... **SNY, SNEE**
dirty lock .... **FRIB**
disable ...... **LAME, MAIM**
disagreeable .... **ILL**
disappear gradually . **EVANESCE**
disavow ...... **DENY, RECANT**
disbeliever .... **ATHEIST**
disburse ...... **SPEND, EXPEND**
discard . **DROP, SCRAP, REJECT**
discernment .... **TACT**
discharge .... **EMIT, FIRE, SACK, SHOOT**
discharged .... **SHOT**
disciple .... **APOSTLE**
disciple: India .... **CHELA**
disciplinarian ...... **MARTINET**
disclaim .... **DENY**
disclose ...... **BARE, REVEAL**
discolored ...... **DOTY, LIVID**
disconcert ...... **FAZE, ABASH**
discourse .. **HOMILY, DESCANT**
discourse, art of ... **RHETORIC**

43

a
discover . SEE, SPY, ESPY, FIND
discriminate .... SECERN
discuss ...... TREAT, DEBATE
discussion group ...... FORUM
disease .... MAL, POX, HIVES
disease, Afr. .... NENTA
disease cause .... VIRUS
disease, diver's .... BENDS
disease, fowl ...... PIP, ROUP,
PEROSIS
disease, fungus .... ERGOT
disease, grape-vine
ESCA, ERINOSE
disease, plant ... SMUT, SCALD
disease, skin .... ECZEMA
disease spreader
VECTOR, CARRIER
disease, tropical .... SPRUE
disembark .... LAND
disembodied spirit: Chin.
KUEI, KWEI
disencumber .... RID
disengage .... FREE
disfigure .... MAR, DEFACE
disgrace .... SCANDAL
disguise .... MASK
disgust, word of .... AW
DISH .... also see VESSEL
dish .... PLATE

b
dish, Hawaiian .... POI
dish, highly seasoned
OLIO, OLLA
dish, hominy .... POSOLE
dish, Hungarian .... GOULASH
dish, It. .... RAVIOLI
dish, main .... ENTREE
dish, meat .... STEW, RAGOUT
dish, Mex. .. TAMAL, TAMALE,
TAMALI
dish, stemmed ..... COMPOTE
dishearten .... DAUNT, DETER
dishonor .... SHAME, VIOLATE
dishonorable .... BASE
disinclined .... AVERSE
disinfectant . CRESOL, PHENOL,
CRESSOL, CRESSYL
disk, ice hockey .... PUCK
disk, like a .. DISCAL, DISCOID
disk, metal .... PATEN
dislocate .... LUXATE
dismal .... DREAR
dismantle .... STRIP
dismay .... APPAL, DAUNT
dismiss .... DEMIT, FIRE
dismounted .... ALIT
disorder .... MESS, DERAY,
CLUTTER
disorderly flight .... ROUT
disparaging .... SNIDE
disparaging remark ...... SLUR
dispatch .... SEND, HASTE

c
dispatch boat .... AVISO
dispelled .... GONE
display .... AIR, SHEW, SHOW,
ARRAY, EVINCE
display proudly
VAUNT, OSTENT
displease .... VEX, MIFF,
ANGER, ANNOY
disposed .... PRONE
disposition .... MOOD, TEMPER
dispossess .... OUST, EVICT
disprove .... REFUTE
disputable .... MOOT
dissertation ... THESES, THESIS
dissolute person .. RAKE, ROUE
dissonant .... ATONAL
distance, at-from a . OFF, AFAR
distant ... FAR, YON, REMOTE
distilling vessel ..... MATRASS
distinctive air ... AURA, MIEN,
CACHET
distracted .... DISTRAIT
distraint: old Eng. law .. NAAM
distribute .. DEAL, DOLE, METE
DISTRICT .... see also REGION
district .... AREA, ZONE
district, old Eng. court
SOC, SOKE
disturb .... ROIL, MOLEST
disturbance ...... ROW, RIOT
ditch .... FOSS, RINE,
FOSSE, TRENCH
ditch, castle .... MOAT
ditch, fort. .... RELAIS
ditch millet .... HUREEK
ditto .... SAME
divan .... SOFA
dive .... DEN, HEADER
dive bomber .... STUKA
diverge .... DEVIATE
divers .... SEVERAL
divest .... STRIP, DEPRIVE
divide .... PART, SHARE
divide for study ..... DISSECT
divided .... REFT, SPLIT
divider .... MERIST
dividing wall, membrance, parti-
tion ..... SEPTA, SEPTUM
divination by lots: Lat.
SORS, SORTES
"Divine Comedy" author DANTE
divine favor .... GRACE
divine law: Rom. .... FAS
divine revelation TORA, TORAH
divine utterance ..... ORACLE
divinity .... DEITY
divorce bill, Jewish law
GET, GETT
divorce, Moslem ...... TALAK
"— dixit" .... IPSE
dizziness, pert. to ..... DINIC

a
docile .... TAME
dockyard barge .... LUMP
doctor ..... INTERN, INTERNE
Dr. Brown's dog hero .... RAB
Dr. Jekyll's other self .. HYDE
doctrinaire .... ISMY
doctrine .. ISM, DOGMA, TENET
documents, box for .. HANAPER
dodder .... AMIL
dodo genus .... DIDUS
doe .... HIND
doe, young .... TAG, TEG
dog, ... CANIS, CANINE
dog ...... POM, CHOW, PEKE,
    BASSET, POODLE, SPANIEL
dog, chops of .... FLEWS
dog-faced ape .... AANI
dog-fisher .... OTTER
DOG, GUN see DOG, HUNTING
dog, Hungarian PULI, KUVASZ
dog, hunting (bird) ... ALAN,
    ALAND, ALANT, BASSET,
    BEAGLE, SETTER, COURSER,
    HARRIER, POINTER
dog, John Brown's ...... RAB
dog, large .... ALAN
dog, "Odyssey" .... ARGOS
dog salmon .... KETA
dog, small-toy ..... POM, PUG,
                       PEKE

b
dog snapper, fish ...... JOCU
dog, Sputnik's .... LAIKA
dog star .... SEPT, SOPT,
            SEPTI, SIRIUS
dog, tropical .... ALCO
dog, Welsh .... CORGI
dog, wild, Austral. ..... DINGO
dog, wild, India ...... DHOLE
doge, office of ...... DOGATE
dogfish .... SHARK
dogma .... TENET
dogwood ..... OSIER, CORNEL
dole .... METE
dolphin fish .... DORADO
dolphin genus .... INIA
dolphin-like cetacean ... INIA
dolt .... ASS, OAF, CLOD,
            LOUT, DUNCE
domain .... BOURN, REALM,
    BOURNE, DEMENE, ESTATE,
    DEMESNE
dome .... CUPOLA
dome-shaped .... DOMOID
Domesday Book money ... ORA
domestic ...... MAID, LOCAL
domestic animal .. ASS, CAT,
        COW, DOG, HOG, PIG,
        RAM, SOW, MULE
domestic slave .... ESNE
domesticated .... TAME
dominion .... REALM, EMPERY

c
domino .... MASK
Don Juan's mother ...... INEZ
donkey .... ASS, MOKE,
            BURRO, NEDDY
doom ... CONDEMN, DESTINE
doom palm, Afr. .... DUM
door .... PORTAL
door: Lat. .... JANUA
door part ...... JAMB, SASH,
            SILL, LINTEL
door section .... PANEL
doorkeeper, Masonic ... TILER
dorado, color .... CUIR
Doric frieze slab ..... METOPE
dormant ..... ASLEEP, LATENT
dormouse .... LOIR
dormouse, garden ..... LEROT
dormouse genus .... GLIS
dorsal .... NOTAL
dote .... DRIVEL
dots, paint with ...... STIPPLE
dotted with figures ..... SEME
double . DUAL, TWIN, BINATE
double cocoon ...... DUPION
double dagger ...... DIESIS
double, Egypt .... KA
double salt .... ALUM
double tooth .... MOLAR
doubletree .... EVENER

d
dovkie ...... ROTCH, ROTGE,
                ROTCHE
Dovyalis .... ABERIA
dowel ..... PIN, COAG, COAK
dower, pert. to ...... DOTAL
dower property .... DOS
down ...... FUZZ, PILE, EIDER
down, facing. PRONE, PRONATE
down quilt .... DUVET
"downunder" native clan .. ATI
downward, curve ..... DEFLEX
dowry .... DOS, DOT
drag ... LUG, TUG, HAUL, SNIG
dragnet .... TRAWL
dragon, like a ... DRACONTINE
dragon of darkness, Bibl. RAHAB
drain . SAP, DEPLETE, VITIATE
drain .... SUMP, SEWER
dram, small .... NIP
DRAMA ..... see also PLAY
Dravidian KOTA, MALE, NAIR,
        TODA, TULU, TAMIL
draw ...... TIE, TOW, LIMN,
            PULL, DEPICT
draw forth .... EDUCE
draw from .... DERIVE
draw out . EDUCE, ATTENUATE
draw tight: naut. ...... FRAP
drawing curve .... SPLINE
drawing room .... SALON
dreadful .... DIRE
dream, day .... REVERIE

45

Dream

"Dream Girl" playwright . **RICE**
dregs . . . . **FAEX, LEES,**
DROSS, SEDIMENT
drench . . . . **SOUSE, TOUSE**
drenched . . . . **WET, DEWED**
DRESS . . . . see also GARMENT
dress . . . . **GARB, CLOTHE,**
ACCOUTER
dress, as stone . . . . . **DAB, NIG**
dress feathers . . . . **PREEN**
dress leather . . . . . . **DUB, TAN**
dress up . . . . . . **TOG, PREEN**
dressed . . . . **CLAD**
dressing wounds, material for
LINT, LINTS
dried berry: Sp. . . . . **PASA**
dried up . . . . **SERE**
drift . . . . **TREND**
drill . . . . **BORE, TRAIN**
drilling rod . . . . **BAR, BIT**
DRINK . . . . see also BEVERAGE
drink . . . . **GULP, SWIG,**
QUAFF, IMBIBE
drink, Christmas **NOG, WASSAIL**
drink, fermented . . . . . . **MEAD**
drink, honey . . . . **MEAD**
drink, hot . . . . **TODDY**
drink, hot milk . . . . . . **POSSET**
drink of gods . . . . **NECTAR**
drink of liquor . . **NIP, BRACER**
drink, old honey . . . . . **MORAT**
drink, palm . . . . **NIPA**
drink, rum-gin . . . . . **BUMBO**
drink slowly . . . . **SIP, SUP**
drink, small . . . . . . **NIP, PEG,**
DRAM, SLUG
drink to excess . . **TOPE, BOUSE**
drink, whiskey . . . . . **STINGER**
drinking bowl . . . . . . **MAZER**
drinking cup, Gr. . . . . **HOLMOS**
drinking vessel . . . . **CUP, MUG,**
TIG, TYG, JORUM,
STEIN, TANKARD
drive . . . . **RIDE, URGE, IMPEL**
drive away . . . . . **SHOO, DISPEL**
drive back
ROUT, REPEL, REPULSE
drive in . . . . **TAMP**
drivel . . . . **DROOL, SLAVER**
driver, fast reckless . . . . . **JEHU**
drizzle . . **MIST, SMUR, SMURR**
droll . . . . **ODD**
dromedary, female . . . . **DELUL**
dromedary, swift . . . . **MEHARI**
drone . . . . **BEE, DOR, HUM**
droop . . . . **LOP, SAG, WILT**
drooping . . . . **ALOP**
drop . . . . . . **DRIB, FALL, SINK,**
GUTTA, GLOBULE
drop a fish line or bait . . **DAP**
drop, one . . . . **MINIM**

drop: Prov. Eng. . . . . . **SIE, SYE**
dropsy . . . . **EDEMA**
dross . . **SLAG, SPRUE, SCORIA**
drought-tolerant plant . . **GUAR**
drove . . . . **HERD, RODE**
drove of horses . . . . **ATAJO**
drowse . . . . **NOD**
drudge . . . **MOIL, TOIL, LABOR**
drug . . . . . **DOPE, SINA, ALOES,**
OPIATE, DILANTIN
drug, Hippocrates' . . . . **MECON**
drugged bliss . . . . **KEF**
drum-call to arms . . . . **RAPPEL**
drum roll, reveille . . . . . . **DIAN**
drum, small . **TABOR, TABOUR,**
TABRET
drum, W. Ind. . . . . **GUMBY**
drumbeat . . . . **DUB, TATOO,**
TATTOO
drunkard . . . . **SOT, SOAK,**
SOUSE, TOPER
dry . . . . **SEC, ARID, SERE**
dry, as wine . . . . **SEC**
dry bed of river . . . . **WADI**
dry goods dealer . . . . . **DRAPER**
dub . . . . **NAME, KNIGHT**
duck . . . . **ANAS, SMEE,**
TEAL, PEKIN
duck, Arctic . . . . **EIDER**
duck, breed of . . . . **ROUEN**
duck, diving . . . . **SMEW**
duck eggs, Chin. . . . . . . **PIDAN**
duck, fresh water . . . . . . **TEAL**
duck genus . . **AEX, AIX, ANAS**
duck, like a . . . . **ANATINE**
duck lure . . . . **DECOY**
duck, male . . . . **DRAKE**
duck, Muscovy . . . . **PATO**
duck, pintail . . . . **SMEE**
duck, ring-necked . . . . . **DOGY**
duck, river . . . . . **TEAL, EIDER,**
SHOVELER
duck, sea . . . . . . **COOT, SCAUP**
duck, sea, northern . . . **SCOTER**
duck-shooting boat . . . . **SKAG**
duck to cook: Fr. . . . **CANETON**
duct: anat. . . . . **VAS, VASA**
dude . . . . **FOP, DANDY**
due, India . . . . **HAK, HAKH**
duet . . . . **DUI, DUO**
dugout canoe **BANCA, PIROGUE**
dugout, India . **DONGA, DUNGA**
duke's dominion . . . . . . **DUCHY**
dulcimer . . . . **CITOLE**
dulcimer, Oriental . . . . **SANTIR**
dull . **DRY, DUN, DRAB, LOGY,**
BLUNT, PROSY, BORING
dull color . . **DUN, MAT, DRAB,**
MATTE, TERNE
dull in finish . . . . **MAT, MATTE**

46

a dull silk fabric .... GROS
dullard .... BOOR
Dumas hero
    ATHOS, ARAMIS, PORTHOS
dummy whist .... MORT
dung beetle .... DOR
dunlin bird .... STIB
dupe .... USE, FOOL
duration measure .... TIME
dusk .... EVE
dusky .... DIM, DARK, SWART
dusty: Scot. .... MOTTY
DUTCH see also NETHERLANDS,
        SPECIAL SECTION
Dutch: bit ....DOIT
     cupboard .... KAS
     donkey .... EZEL
     "mister" .... HEER
     out .... UIT
     woman .... FROW
Dutch cheese .... EDAM
Dutch commune .... EDE
Dutch early geographer .. AA
Dutch fishing boat .. DOGGER
Dutch measure, old ..... AAM
Dutch meter .... EL
Dutch minor coin ...... DOIT
Dutch news agency, old ANETA
Dutch painter
    LIS, HALS, LELY, STEEN
Dutch two-masted vessel KOFF
duty .... CHORE, TARIFF
dwarf .. RUNT, STUNT, TROLL

c dwarf cattle, S. Am.
           NATA, NIATA
dwell ...... BIDE, LIVE, ABIDE
dwelling .... ABODE
dwindle .... PETER
Dyak knife .... PARANG
Dyak, sea .... IBAN
dye base .... ANILINE
dye, blue .... WOAD
dye, blue-red ...... ORSELLE
dye gum .... KINO
dye, indigo .... ANIL
dye, lichen
    ARCHIL, ORCHAL, ORCHIL
dye plant .... ANIL
dye, red .. AAL, ANATO, AURIN,
    EOSIN, ANATTA, ANATTO,
    AURINE, EOSINE, ANNAT-
    TA, ANNATTO, ANNOTTO,
    ARNATTO
dye, red, poisonous
        AURIN, AURINE
dye stuff .. EOSINE, MADDER
dye, yellow .... WELD,
        WOLD, WOALD
dyeing apparatus ...... AGER
dyeing reagent .... ALTERANT
dyestuff from lichens .. LITMUS
dyewood tree .... TUI
dynamite inventor .... NOBEL
DYNASTY see CHIN. DYNASTY
dynasty, first Chin. ..... HSIA
dynasty, It. .... SAVOY

E

b eager .. AGOG, AVID, ARDENT
eagle .... ERN, ERNE
eagle, Bible .... GIER
eagle, tried to mount to heaven
    on .... ETANA
eagle, sea .... ERN, ERNE
eagle's nest
  AERY, EYRY, AERIE, EYRIE
eaglestone ... ETITE, AETITES
ear .... LUG, HANDLE
ear canal .... SCALA
ear cavity .... UTRICLE
ear doctor .... AURIST
ear inflamation ...... OTITIS
ear of wheat: archeol.
      SPICA, SPICAE
ear, pert. to .... OTIC, AURAL
ear, prominence TRAGI, TRAGUS
ear shell .. ORMER, ABALONE
ear stone .. OTOLITE, OTOLITH
earache ... OTALGY, OTALGIA
eared seal .... OTARY

d early Britisher .... PICT
early Christian priest ... ARIUS
earnest
    ARDENT, INTENT, SINCERE
earnest money: law .... ARRA,
       ARLES, ARRHA
earth .... GEO
earth deposit in rocks .. GUHR
earth: dial. .... ERD
earth god, Egypt. GEB, KEB, SEB
earth goddess .... GE, ERDA,
       GAEA, GAIA
earth goddess, Khonds' .. TARI
earth goddess, Rom.
      CERES, TERRA
earth, kind of .... LOAM
earth, pert. to .... GEAL
earth's surface, made on
      EPIGENE
earthenware maker ... POTTER
earthly .... TERRENE
earthquake .. SEISM, TEMBLOR

47

a
earthquake, pert. to .. **SEISMIC**
earthquake, shock of. **TREMOR**
earthwork, Rom. .... **AGGER**
East .. **ASIA, LEVANT, ORIENT**
E. African native ... **SOMALI**
E. Afr. spiritual power .. **NGAI**
E. Indian animal .... **TARSIER**
E. Ind. dye tree .... **DHAK**
E. Ind. fruit **DURIAN, DURION**
E. Ind. grass .... **KASA**
E. Ind. herb ..... **PIA, SESAME**
E. Ind. herb root **CHAY, CHOY**
E. Ind. palm .... **NIPA**
E. Ind. plant .. **JUTE, SESAME**
E. Ind. shrubby herb .... **SOLA**
E. Ind. tanning tree .. **AMLA, AMLI**
E. Ind. term of address **SAHIB**
E. Ind. timber tree..**ACH, SAJ, SAL, SAIN, SAUL, TEAK**
E. Ind. tree, large .... **SIRIS**
E. Ind. vine ..... **AMIL, GILO, ODAL, ODEL, SOMA**
E. Ind. vine, milky .... **SOMA**
E. Ind. weight .... **TOLA**
E. Ind. wood, strong, heavy **ENG**
E. Ind. woody vine **ODAL, GILO**
East Indies .... **INDONESIA**
east wind .... **EURUS**
east wind's opposite .... **AFER**
Easter ...... **PASCH, PASCHA**

b
Eastern .... **ORTIVE**
Eastern Catholic ...... **UNIAT**
Eastern Church doxology **DOXA**
Eastern European ...... **SLAV**
Eastern garment .... **SARI**
Eastern name ..... **ALI, ABOU**
Eastern title ..... **AGA, RAS**
Eastern Turkey tribesman **KURD**
easy .... **SOFT**
easy gait .... **LOPE**
easy job **SNAP, CINCH, SINECURE**
eat away .... **ERODE**
eat voraciously **RAVEN, RAVIN, RAVINE**
eaten away .... **EROSE**
eating away **CAUSTIC, ERODENT**
eccentric person ...... **GINK**
eccentric piece, rotating .. **CAM**
ecclesiastic .... **PRELATE**
ECCLESIASTICAL see CHURCH
eclipse .... **DIM**
eclipse demon, Hindu **KETU, RAHU**
ecru .... **BEIGE**
Ecuadorian extinct Indians **CARA**
edentate genus .... **MANIS**
edge .... **HEM, LIP, RIM, ARRIS, BRINK, MARGE**
edged unevenly .... **EROSE**
edging .... **PICOT**

c
edging, make .... **TAT**
edible fungus .... **CEPE**
edible root .... **OCA, YAM, TARO, CASAVA, CASSAVA**
edible shoot, Jap. .... **UDO**
edict ... **LAW, FIAT, DECREE**
Edinburgh: poet ...... **EDINA**
edit ...... **REVISE, REDACT**
editorial "I" .... **WE**
Edom district .... **TEMAN**
Edomite .... **OMAR**
Edomite city .... **PAU**
Edomite duke **UZ, ARAN, IRAM**
Edomite king, ruler ..... **BELA**
educated .... **BRED, LETTERED**
educator, Am. .... **MANN**
educe .... **EVOKE, ELICIT**
Edward Bradley's pseudo. **BEDE**
eel, marine .... **CONGER**
eel: old Eng. .... **ELE**
eel-shaped amphibian .. **OLM**
eel, S. Am. .... **CARAPO**
eel, young .... **ELVER**
eelworm .... **NEMA**
Eghbal's land .... **IRAN**
effervescent, to make . **AERATE**
effigy .... **IDOL**
effluvium ... **MIASM, MIASMA**
effort .... **DINT, ASSAY, NISUS, TRIAL**

d
effusive .... **GUSHING**
eft .... **EVET, NEWT**
egg .... **OVUM**
egg dish .. **OMELET, OMELETTE**
egg drink .... **NOG, NOGG**
egg, insect .... **NIT**
egg-shaped **OOID, OVAL, OVATE, OVOID**
egg-shaped ornaments ... **OVA**
egg white, raw .... **GLAIR**
eggs .... **OVA, ROE**
ego .... **SELF**
Egypt, pert. to ..... **COPTIC**
Egyptian bird .... **IBIS**
Egyp. Christian .... **COPT**
Egyp. city, ancient **SAIS, THEBES**
Egyp. cobra .... **HAJE**
Egyp. crown .... **ATEF**
Egyp. dog-headed ape, deity **AANI**
Egyp. gateway .... **PYLON**
Egyp. god of creation ... **PTAH**
EGYPTIAN GODS — GODDESSES —DEITY see also GODS and SPECIAL SECTION
Egyp. guard .... **GHAFIR**
Egyp. heaven **AALU, AARU, IALU, YARU**
Egyp. immortal heart **AB, HATI**
Egyp. king .. **MENES, RAMESES**
Egyp. lute .... **NABLA**

a
Egyp. nationalist party . WAFD
Egyp. precious alloy .... ASEM
Egyp. primeval chaos ...... NU
Egyp. queen of gods .... SATI
Egyp. sacred bird .. BENU, IBIS
Egyp. sacred bull .... APIS
Egyp. season .... AHET
Egyp. tambourine ...... RIKK
Egyp. thorn .... KIKAR
Egyp. writing surfaces PAPYRI
eh?: obs. ....ANAN
eight days after feast .. UTAS
eight, group of
OCTAD, OCTET, OCTAVE
eight, set of .... OGDOAD
eighth day of feast .... UTAS
eighth day, on ...... OCTAN
eighth note .... UNCA
Eire legislature .... DAIL
ejaculation, mystic ...... OM
eject ...... EMIT, OUST, SPEW
elaborate .... ORNATE
Elam, capital of .... SUSA
eland .... IMPOFO
elanet .... KITE
elasmobranch fish RAY, SHARK
Elbe, river to ...... EGER, ISER
Elbe tributary .... EGER, ISER
elbow .... ANCON
elder .... SENIOR

b
elder son of Zeus ...... ARES
elder statesmen, Jap. .. GENRO
eldest: law ...... AINE, EIGNE
electric catfish .... RAAD
electric force .... ELOD
electric force unit ...... VOLT
electric reluctance unit .. REL
electric unit .. ES, AMP, MHO,
OHM, REL, PERM, FARAD,
HENRY, AMPERE
electrified particle ...... ION
electrode .. ANODE, CATHODE
electromagnet .... RELAY
electron tube
TRIODE, KLYSTRON
elegance .... GRACE
elegant .... FINE, POSH
elegist .... POET
elegy .... NENIA
ELEMENT, non-metallic and metallic, gaseous on page 195
elemi .... ANIME
element, radioactive of URANIC
elephant goad .... ANKUS
elephant: India .... HATHI
elephant's cry .... BARR
elephant's ear .... TARO
elevated ground MESA, RIDEAU
elevation of mind . ANAGOGE
elevator: Brit. .... LIFT

c
elf .... SPRITE
elf, Egypt. .... OUPHE
elfin .... FEY
Elia .... LAMB
elicit .... EDUCE
elide .... DELE, OMIT
Elija .... ELIAS
eliminate ... DELETE, REMOVE
Elizabeth I, name for ORIANA
elk, Am. .... WAPITI
elk, Europ. .... MOOSE
elk, Europ. genus ...... ALCES
elliptical ...... OVAL, OVOID
elm .... ULM, ULME
elm fruit seed ...... SAMARA
elongated .... PROLATE
else .... OTHER
elude .... DODGE, EVADE
elver .... EEL
emaciation .... TABES, MACIES
emanation .... AURA
emanation, star .... BLAS
embankment ... DAM, BUND,
DIKE, DYKE, DIGUE, LEVEE
embellish
GILD, ADORN, DECORATE
embellished .... ORNATE
ember .... ASH, COAL
emblem ... INSIGNE, INSIGNIA

d
emblem of authority .... MACE
emblem of U.S. .... EAGLE
embrace
HUG, CLASP, ENARM, INARM
embrocation ...... LINIMENT
embroidery frame
TABORET, TABOURET
emend .... EDIT
emerald .... BERYL, SMARAGD
emerge RISE, ISSUE, EMANATE
emetic .... IPECAC
eminent .... NOTED
emit .... REEK, EXUDE
emmer .... SPELT
emmet .... ANT
Emperor of Russia
CZAR, TSAR, TZAR
emphasis .... ACCENT, STRESS
empire .... REALM
employ .... USE, HIRE, PLACE
employed for wine, meas. AAM
employees .... PERSONNEL
employer .... BOSS, USER
employment .... PLACE
emporium ...... MART, STORE
Empress, Byzant. ...... IRENE
Empress, Russian ... CZARINA,
TSARINA, TZARINA
empty .... VOID, INANE,
DEPLETE
emulate .... RIVAL
enamel ware .... LIMOGES

49

a enchantress .... **CIRCE, MEDEA**
encircle .... **ORB, GIRD, GIRT, RING, EMBAY**
encircled
GIRT, RINGED, SURROUNDED
encircling band .... **ZONE**
enclose .... **MEW**
enclosure .... **MEW, PEN, REE, STY, CORRAL**
enclosure, cattle ..... **ATAJO**
enclosure: Sp. Am. ... **CANCHA**
encomium .... **ELOGE**
encompass .. **GIRD, GIRT, RING**
encompassed by .... **AMID**
encore .... **BIS**
encounter .... **MEET**
encourage .... **ABET**
end **TIP, FINIS, LIMIT, OMEGA**
end: music .... **FINE**
end result .... **PRODUCT**
end, tending to an ..... **TELIC**
endeavor .. **TRY, ESSAY, NISUS**
ENDING ... see also SUFFIX or type of ending
ending, comparative . **IER, IOR**
ENDING, NOUN see SUFFIX, NOUN ENDING
ending, plural .... **EN, ES**
ending, superlative ...... **EST**
endow ...... **DOWER, INVEST**
b endue .... **ENDOW**
endure .. **BEAR, LAST, WEAR**
endure: dial. .... **BIDE**
energy ...... **PEP, VIM, ZIP, POWER, VIGOR, VIGOUR**
energy, potential ...... **ERGAL**
energy unit **ERG, RAD, ERGON**
enfeeble **WEAKEN, DEBILITATE**
engage **HIRE, ENTER, CHARTER**
engender .... **BEGET, BREED, PROMOTE, GENERATE**
engine, donkey ...... **YARDER**
engine of war .... **RAM**
engine part .... **STATOR**
engine, rotary ...... **TURBINE**
engineer, Am. .... **EADS**
engineer, military .... **SAPPER**
English actor .... **EVANS**
Eng. actress .... (Nell) **GWYN, TERRY, NEAGLE**
Eng. architect .... **WREN**
Eng. author .... **MORE, WEST, ARLEN, BACON, CAINE, DEFOE, DORAN, ELIOT, HARDY, READE, SHUTE, WAUGH, WELLS, AMBLER, AUSTEN, BARRIE, BELLOC, BRONTE, ORWELL, STERNE**
Eng. car .... **ROVER**
Eng. cathedral city **ELY, YORK**
Eng. city, historic **COVENTRY**

c Eng. college ... **ETON, BALIOL**
ENG. COMPOSER
see COMPOSER, ENG.
Eng. country festival .... **ALE**
Eng. dramatist
SHAW, PEELE, DRYDEN
Eng. emblem .... **ROSE**
Eng. essayist .... **SALA, STEELE**
Eng. explorer ... **ROSS, CABOT**
Eng. historian .... **BEDE**
Eng. king
BRAN, CNUT, KNUT, CANUTE
Eng. monk ..... **BEDE, BAEDA**
Eng. murderer .... **ARAM**
Eng. musician .... **ARNE**
ENG. NOVELIST .... see ENG. AUTHOR
Eng. painter .... **OPIE, ORPEN**
Eng. philosopher ..... **HUME, JOAD, BACON, SPENCER**
Eng. playwright .... **SHAW**
Eng. poet ..... **GRAY, AUDEN, BLAKE, BYRON, CAREW, DONNE, ELIOT**
Eng. queen ...... **ANNE, MARY**
Eng. rebel leader, 1450 .. **CADE**
Eng. royal house **YORK, TUDOR**
Eng. scholar, schoolmaster
ARAM
Eng. school, boys' ...... **ETON**
Eng. sculptor .... **EPSTEIN**
d Eng. spa .... **BATH, MARGATE**
Eng. spy .... **ANDRE**
Eng. statesman ... **EDEN, PITT**
Eng. theologian ..... **ALCUIN**
Eng. woman politician ... **ASTOR**
ENG. WRITER ..... see ENG. AUTHOR and ENG. ESSAYIST
engraver ... **CHASER, ETCHER, GRAVER**
engraver, famous ... **PYE, DORE**
engraver's tool .... **BURIN**
engrossed .... **RAPT**
enigma .... **RIDDLE**
enlarge
DILATE, EXPAND, INCREASE
enlarge a hole .... **REAM**
enlarging, as chimneys .. **EVASE**
enmity .... **ANIMUS**
Enoch's father .... **CAIN**
enough .... **ENOW**
enrol .... **ENTER, ENLIST**
ensign .... **FLAG**
ensnare .... **NET, WEB**
entangle .... **MAT, MESH**
enter .... **ENROL**
entertain
AMUSE, DIVERT, REGALE
enthusiasm
ELAN, ARDOR, VERVE, SPIRIT
enthusiastic .... **RABID**

a entice .... BAIT, LURE,
     TOLE, TEMPT, ALLURE
enticement .... TICE
entire man .... EGO
entity .... ENS, ENTIA
entomb .... INURN
entrance
   ADIT, DOOR, GATE, PORTAL
entrance halls .... ATRIA
entreat .... PRAY, PLEAD
entreaty .... PLEA
entry, separate .... ITEM
entwine
   WEAVE, ENLACE, WREATHE
enumerate .... COUNT
envelop WRAP, ENFOLD, INFOLD
environment .... MILIEU
envoy .... LEGATE
envy .... COVET
enzyme .... ASE, LOTASE,
    RENNIN, MALTASE
eon .... OLAM
ephah, 1/10 .... OMER
epic poetry .... EPOS, EPOPEE
epoch .... ERA
epochal .... ERAL
epode .... POEM
eponymous ancestor ... EBER
equal IS, ARE, TIE, EVEN, PEER
equality .... PAR, PARITY

b equally .... AS
equilibrium .... POISE
equine .... HORSE
equip .... FIT, RIG
equitable ... JUST, IMPARTIAL
equivalence .... PAR
equivocate .... EVADE
era .... EPOCH
eradicate .... ERASE, UPROOT
eral .... EPOCHAL
erase .... DELE, DELETE
erect .... REAR, RAISE
ergo .... HENCE
Eris' brother .... ARES
ermine, summer .... STOAT
Eros .... CUPID
errand boy .... PAGE
error, publication ...... TYPO,
   ERRATA, ERRATE, ERRATUM
Esau .... EDOM
Esau's brother .... JACOB
Esau's father-in-law .... ELON
Esau's grandson .... OMAR
Esau's home .... SEIR
Esau's wife .... ADAH
escape .. LAM, ELUDE, EVADE
eschew .... SHUN
escutcheon band .... FESS
Esdra's angel .... URIEL
eskers .... OSAR
Eskimo .... ITA

c Eskimo boat
   KIAK, KYAK, KAYAK
Eskimo boot .... MUKLUK
Eskimo coat
  PARKA, NETCHA, TEMIAK
Eskimo curlew .... FUTE
Eskimo house
  IGLU, IGLOE, IGLOO, IGLOU
Eskimo settlement ..... ETAH
Eskimo summer hut .... TOPEK
Eskimos of Asia YUIT, INNUIT
esoteric .... INNER
espy .... SEE, SPY
esquire .... ARMIGER
essay ... TRY, TEST, ATTEMPT
essay, scholarly
   THESIS, TREATISE
essence: Hindu religion .. RASA
essence, rose .... ATTAR
essential oils fluid ..... NEROL
essential part .... CORE, PITH
"— est" (that is) .... ID
establish ...... BASE, FOUND
established value .... PAR
estate, landed, large .. MANOR
estate manager ..... STEWARD
estate, not held by feudal tenure ALOD, ALLOD, ALODIUM
esteem .... HONOR,
   PRIZE, ADMIRE, HONOUR

d ester, hydriodic acid ... IODIDE
ester, liquid .... ACETIN
ester, oleic acid ...... OLEATE
estimate .... RATE, APPRAISE
Estonian .... ESTH
estuary .... RIA
estuary, Brazil .... PARA
estuary, S. Am. .... PLATA
Eternal City .... ROME
eternity ..... AGE, EON, OLAM
ether compound .... ESTER
ethereal ...... AERY, AERIAL
ETHIOPIA see also ABYSSINIA
Ethiopia .... CUSH
Ethiopian title .... RAS
Ethiopic .... GEEZ
ethos, opposed to .... PATHOS
Etruscan god .... LAR
Etruscan Juno .... UNI
Etruscan Minerva .... MENFRA
Etruscan title, peer LAR, LARS
eucalyptus secretion
   LAAP, LARP, LERP
eucalyptus tree .... YATE
Eucharist case ...... PIX, PYX
Eucharist cloth
  FANO, FANON, FANUM
Eucharist spoon .... LABIS
Eucharist wafer .... HOST
eulogy .... ELOGE
euphorbia .... SPURGE

a

Eurasian dock plant .. **PARELLE**
eureka red .... **PUCE**
Euripides heroine ..... **MEDEA**
EUROPEAN see also specific
    word, as FISH, ANIMAL,
    etc.
European .... **POLE, SLAV**
Eur. colorful fish ...... **BOCE**
EUROP. FISH .. see FISH, EUR.
European, in Moslem East
              FRANGI
Europ. iris .... **ORRIS**
Europ. kite ..... **GLED, GLEDE**
Europ. porgy .... **PARGO**
Eurytus' daughter ...... **IOLE**
evade
  SHUN, DODGE, ELUDE, SHIRK
evaluate .... **RATE, ASSESS**
Evangelist ...... **LUKE, MARK**
Evans, Mary Ann ...... **ELIOT**
Eve's grandson .... **ENOS**
even ...... **EEN, LEVEL, PLANE**
even if .... **THO**
evening party .... **SOIREE**
evening prayer ...... **VESPER**
eventual lot .... **FATE**
ever .... **EER**
evergreen .... **FIR, YEW, PINE,**
    CAROB, CEDAR, OLIVE,
    SAVIN, LAUREL, SABINE,
    SAVINE, SPRUCE

b

evergreen, bean ...... **CAROB**
evergreen genus
    OLAX, ABIES, CATHA
evergreen, red-berry
        YEW, WHORT
evergreen, tropical .. **CALABA**
everlasting ... **ETERN, ETERNE**
evict .... **OUST**
evident **CLEAR, PLAIN, PATENT**
evil .... **MAL**
evil god, Egypt. ... **SET, SETH**
evil intent: law ...... **DOLUS**
evil spirit, Haiti **BAKA, BOKO**
evil spirit, Hindu ..... **ASURA**
evolve .... **EDUCE**
ewe, old .... **CRONE**
exact **BLEED, DEMAND, EXTORT**
exacerbate .... **IRE**
exact point .... **TEE**
examine ..... **PRY, SPY, SCAN**
excavate .. **DIG, PION, DREDGE**
excavation for extracting ore
           STOPE
excavation, mine .. **PIT, STOPE**
exceed .... **TOP**
exceedingly: music ..... **TRES**
excellence .... **VIRTU**
excellent .... **AONE**
except .... **BUT, SAVE**
excess ...... **LUXUS, NIMIETY**

c

excess, fill to ... **GLUT, SATE**
excess of solar year ... **EPACT**
exchange medium, Chin. **SYCEE**
exchange premium, discount
           AGIO
exchequer .... **FISC, FISK**
excite .... **ELATE, ROUSE**
excited .... **AGOG, MANIC**
excitement, public
      FUROR, FURORE
exclamation .. **AH, EH, HA, HI,**
    MY, OH, OW, UM, ACH,
    AHA, AUH, BAH, BAW, FIE,
    FOH, GRR, HAH, HAW,
    HAY, HEM, HEP, HEU, HEY,
    HIC, HIP, HOI, HOY, HUH,
    OHO, OUF, PAH, PEW, POH,
    PUE, SOH, TCH, TCK, TUT,
    UGH, WEE, WHY, WOW,
    YAH, YOI, YOW, ALAS,
    PHEW, ALACK
exclamation, Fr. .... **HEIN**
exclamation, Ger. ..... **HOCH**
exclamation, Ir. ...... **ADAD,**
    AHEY, ARAH, ARRA, ARRO,
    BOOH, EHEU, OCHONE
exclude ... **BAR, OMIT, DEBAR**
exclusive .... **SOLE**
exclusive set .... **ELECT, ELITE**
exclusively .... **ONLY**

d

excoriate .... **ABRADE**
excrete from skin ..... **EGEST**
excuse .. **PLEA, ALIBI, REMIT**
excuse, court **ESSOIN, ESSOINE**
execrated ..... **CURST, SWORE**
exemplar ... **MODEL, PATTERN**
exhaust
  SAP, TIRE, SPEND, DEPLETE
exhausted .... **EFFETE**
exhibits leaping ..... **SALTATE**
exigency .... **NEED**
exist .... **LIVE**
exist .. all forms of verb "BE"
exist, beginning to .. **NASCENT**
existence .... **ENS, ESSE**
existentialist leader ... **SARTRE**
existing **ALIVE, BEING, EXTANT**
exit .. **LEAVE, DEPART, EGRESS**
expand ..... **DILATE, DISTEND**
expanse .... **SEA**
expatriate .... **EXILE**
expectation .... **HOPE**
expedite .... **HURRY, HASTEN**
expedition .. **SAFARI, SUFFARI**
expert ... **ACE, ONER, ADEPT**
expiate .... **ATONE**
explain .... **DEFINE**
explode
  POP, DETONATE, FULMINATE
exploit
  DEED, FEAT, GEST, GESTE

Explosive

a explosive
CAP, TNT, GAINE, TONITE
explosive sound ... POP, CHUG
expose .... AIR, DISPLAY
expression, elegant . ATTICISM
expression, local .... IDIOM
expressionless ..... WOODEN
expunge DELE, ERASE, DELETE
extend
JUT, LIE, REACH, BEETLE
extend the front ..... DEPLOY
extensive .... AMPLE
extent .... AREA
external .... EXOTERIC
external covering. HIDE, HUSK,
PEEL, PELT, RIND, SKIN
extinct wild ox .... URUS
extirpate .. ROOT, ERADICATE
extort .... BLEED, EXACT
extra .... ODD, SPARE
extra leaf .... INSERT
extra, theatrical .... SUPE
extract DRAW, ELICIT, EVULSE
extraneous .... EXOTIC
extraordinary person, thing
ONER

c extravagance .... ELA
extreme .... ULTRA
extreme unction, give
ANELE, ENELE
exudate, plant
GUM, LAC, RESIN
exude ..... EMIT, OOZE, REEK
exult .... ELATE
eye .... ORB, SEE, OGLE
eye cosmetic ... KOHL, KUHL
eye inflammation STY, IRITIS
eye, inner coat ...... RETINA
eye, layer .... UVEA
eye of bean .... HILA, HILUM
eye of insect .... STEMMA
eye, part of the .... IRIS,
UVEA, CORNEA, RETINA
eye, pert. to .... OPTIC
eye socket .... ORBIT
eye, symbolic .... UTA
eye-worm, Afr. .... LOA
eyelash .... CILIA, CILIUM
eyes: old Eng. .... NIE
eyestalk .... STIPE
eyewink ...... LOOK, GLANCE
eyot .... ISLE, ISLET

F

b Fabian .... SHAW
fable .... APOLOG, APOLOGUE
fable writer .... ESOP, AESOP
fabled bird .... ROC, RUKH
"Fables in Slang" author ADE
fabric .... REP, ACCA, BAFT,
DRAB, DUCK, IKAT,
LAWN, LENO, MOFF, REPP,
SILK, SUSI, TAPA, TUKE,
CRAPE, CREPE, MOIRE,
NINON, ORLON, RAYON,
CANVAS, COVERT, MAN-
TUA, MOHAIR
fabric, Angora ..... CAMLET,
MOHAIR
fabric, coarse cotton .. SURAT
fabric, coarse wool
TAMIN, TAMINE
fabric, corded REP, REPP, PIQUE
fabric, cotton ... LENO, MULL,
DENIM, MANTA, SCRIM,
CALICO, CRETON, NAN-
KIN, PENANG, NANKEEN,
CRETONNE
fabric, curtain ... NET, SCRIM
fabric, felt-like .... BAIZE
fabric, fig'd DAMASK, PAISLEY
fabric from remnants MUNGO
fabric, Ind. .. SHELA, SHELAH

d fabric, knitted .... TRICOT
fabric, light wool .... ALPACA
fabric, lustrous POPLIN, SATEEN
fabric, mourning ALMA, CRAPE
fabric, net .. TULLE, MALINE
fabric, plaid .. MAUD, TARTAN
fabric, printed BATIK, BATTIK
FABRIC, RIBBED
see RIBBED FABRIC
fabric, satin .. PEKIN, ETOILE
fabric, satiny
SATINET, SATINETTE
fabric, sheer .... GAUZE,
BEMBERG, ORGANZA
fabric, short nap .... RAS
fabric, silk .... SURAH,
PONGEE, SAMITE, TOBINE
fabric, silk, gold, medieval ACCA
fabric, silk, thick ...... GROS
fabric, stiff .... WIGAN
fabric stretcher
TENTER, STENTER
fabric, striped .. SUSI, DOREA,
DORIA, DOOREA, MADRAS
fabric, thick .... DRAB
fabric, twilled .... REP
fabric, upholstery .. BROCATEL,
BROCATALL, BROCATELL
BROCATELLE

53

Fabric

a fabric, velvet-like .... PANNE
fabric, voile-like .. ETAMINE
fabric, wool .. SERGE, TAMIN,
    TAMIS, MERINO, TAMINE,
    TAMINY, TAMISE, TAM-
    MIN, ESTAMIN, ETAMINE,
    STAMMEL, ESTAMINE
fabric, worsted ...... ETAMINE
fabricate .... MAKE
fabulist .... ESOP, AESOP
fabulous bird ..... ROC, RUKH
face MAP, MUG, PHIZ, FACADE
face with stone .... REVET
facet of gem .. BEZEL, BEZIL,
    CULET, COLLET
facile .... EASY
facing glacier .... STOSS
fact .... DATUM
fact, by the: law ..... FACTO
facts .... DATA
faction .... SECT, SIDE, CABAL
factor .... GENE
factory .... PLANT
faculty .... SENSE
fade ...... DIE, DIM, WITHER
"Faerie Queene" iron man
    TALUS
"Faerie Queene" lady .... UNA
failure .... DUD, FLOP
fainting: med. .... SYNCOPE
b fair . BAZAR, FERIA, BAZAAR
    KERMIS, KIRMES
fair JUST, CLEAR, IMPARTIAL
fair-haired .. BLOND, BLONDE
fair-lead, naut. .... WAPP
fairy .. ELF, FAY, PERI, SPRITE
fairy fort .... LIS, LISS
fairy king .... OBERON
fairy queen ... MAB, TITANIA
fairy, Serbo-Croat VILA, VILY
fairylike creature .... PERI
faith, article of ...... TENET
faith, pert. to ...... PISTIC
faithful .... LEAL
    TRUE, STANCH, STAUNCH
falcon .... SACER, SAKER,
    LANNER, MERLIN, SAKERET
falcon, Asia LAGGAR, LUGGAR
falcon genus .... FALCO
falcon-headed god
    MENT, MENTU
falcon, Ind. SHAHIN, SHAHEEN
falcon of sea ...... ERN, ERNE
falconer's bait .... LURE
fall DROP, PLAP, PLOP, SPILL
fall back .... RETREAT
fallacy ...... IDOLA, IDOLUM
fallow-deer, female ...... TEG
false excuse .... SUBTERFUGE
false friend .. IAGO, TRAITOR
false fruit of rose .... HIP

c false god .... IDOL
Falstaff's follower ...... NYM
fame .... ECLAT, KUDOS,
    RENOWN, REPUTE
famed .... NOTED
familiar .... VERSANT
familiar saying ... SAW, TAG
family, Florentine .... MEDICI
family, Genoese ...... DORIA
family: Scot. .... ILK
famous .... NOTED
fan .... ROOTER
fan palm genus ...... INODES
fan's stick .... BRIN
fanatical .... RABID
fancy ... IDEA, WHIM, IDEATE
fanfare .... TANTARA,
    TANTARO, TANTARARA
fanning device
    PUNKA, PUNKAH
fare .... DIET
farewell ... AVE, VALE, ADIEU
farinaceous .... MEALY
farinaceous food SAGO, SALEP
farm group .... GRANGE
farm, small, Sp. Am. CHACRA
farm, Sw. small leased .. TORP
farm: Swedish .... TORP
farm, tenant .... CROFT
farmer .... KULAK, GRANGER
farmyard, S. Afr. ...... WERF
d Faroe Is. wind .... OE
Faroe judge .... FOUD
Farouk's father ...... FUAD
fashion .... FORM, MODE,
    MOLD, MODEL, STYLE
fasten ..... BOLT, LOCK, NAIL
    SEAL, SNIB, TACK, RIVET
fasten: naut BELAY, BATTEN
fastener .... NUT, PIN, BRAD,
    CLIP, HASP, NAIL, SNAP,
    STUD, CLASP, RIVET,
    CLEVIS, COTTER
fastener, wire .... STAPLE
fastener, naut. .... BITT
fastener, wood
    FID, NOG, PEG, PIN
fastening .... LATCH
fastidious .... NICE
fasting month .... RAMADAN
fasting period .... LENT
fat LARD, LIPA, SUET, OBESE
fat, animal .. ADEPS, TALLOW
fat: comb. form STEAT, STEATO
fat, liquid part .... ELAIN,
    OLEIN, ELAINE, OLEINE
fat, natural .... ESTER
fat, of .... SEBAIC
fat, solid part
    STEARIN, STEARINE
fatal ...... FUNEST, LETHAL

54

a fate .... **LOT, DOOM, KISMET**
Fates, Gr. & Rom. .... **MOIRA, MORTA, PARCA, CLOTHO, DECUMA, MOIRAI, PARCAE, ATROPOS, LACHESIS**
fateful .... **DIRE**
father .... **SIRE, BEGET**
father: Arab. .... **ABU, ABOU**
father: Hebr. .... **ABBA**
father of modern engraving **PYE**
father's side, kinship on **AGNAT, AGNATE**
fathom .... **PROBE, SOUND**
fatigue .. **FAG, TIRE, WEARY**
Fatima's huband .... **ALI**
fatty .... **ADIPOSE**
fatty gland secretion **SEBUM**
fatuous .... **INANE**
faucet ... **TAP, COCK, SPIGOT**
fault find ..... **CARP, CAVIL**
faultfinder .. **MOMUS, CAVILER**
faulty .... **BAD**
faux pas ...... **ERROR, GAFFE**
favor .... **BOON**
favorable vote .. **AY, AYE, YES**
favorite .... **PET, IDOL**
fawn color .... **FAON**
fawning favorite ...: **MINION**
fear .... **PHOBIA**
fearful .... **TREPID**
b feast .... **REGALE**
feast day: comb. form .... **MAS**
feather **PENNA, PINNA, PLUME**
feather grass .... **STIPA**
feather palms .... **EJOO, IROK**
feather: zool. .... **PLUMA**
feathers, cast .... **MEW**
feathers of o-o .... **HULU**
feathered scarf .... **BOA**
feeble .. **PUNY, WEAK, DEBILE**
feel .... **SENSE**
feel one's way .... **GROPE**
feeler **PALP, PALPI, ANTENNA**
feet, having .... **PEDATE**
feet, pert. to **PEDAL, PEDARY**
feign .... **ACT, SHAM**
feline .... **CAT, PUMA**
felis leo .... **LION**
fellow ..... **GUY, LAD, BOZO, CHAP, DICK, CHAPPY, CHAPPIE**
felt .... **GROPED, SENSATE**
female animal, parent **DAM, DOE**
female camel .... **NAGA**
female disciple at Joppa **DORCAS**
female insect .... **GYNE**
fence of shrubs .... **HEDGE**
fence of stakes .... **PALISADE**
fence step .... **STILE**

c fence, sunken, hidden **AHA, HAHA**
fence to restrain cattle .. **OXER**
fencer's cry .. **HAI, HAY, SASA**
fencing dummy .... **PEL**
fencing position **CARTE, SIXTE, QUARTE, QUINTE, TIERCE, SECONDE, SEPTIME**
fencing sword ...... **EPEE, FOIL**
fencing term .... **TOUCHE**
fencing thrust ...... **LUNGE, PUNTO, REMISE, RIPOST, RIPOSTE, REPRISE**
fend .... **WARD**
fennel: P. I. .... **ANIS**
"Ferdinand the Bull" author **LEAF**
feria, pert. to .... **FERIAL**
ferment .... **YEAST**
ferment: med. .... **ZYME**
fermented milk dessert **LACTO**
fern, climbing, P. I. .... **NITO**
fern, Polyn., edible .... **TARA**
fern root, N. Z. .... **ROI**
fern "seed" .... **SPORE**
fern species .... **WEKI**
fern spore ...... **SORI, SORUS**
Ferrara ducal family .... **ESTE**
ferrum .... **IRON**
ferryboat .... **BAC**
d ferryboat, Afr. .... **PONT**
fertilizer ..... **MARL, GUANO**
fervent .... **ARDENT**
fervor ... **ZEAL, ZEST, ARDOR**
fester .... **RANKLE**
festival .... **ALE, FAIR, FETE, GALA, FERIA, FIESTA, KERMIS, KIRMES**
festival, Creek Indian .. **BUSK**
festival, Gr. **AGON, DELIA, HALOA**
fetid .... **OLID, RANK**
fetish .... **OBI, JUJU, OBIA, ZEME, ZEMI, CHARM, OBEAH, GRIGRI**
fetish, P. I. .... **ANITO**
fetter .... **GYVE, IRON**
feud, opposed to ...... **ALOD, ALLOD, ALODIUM, ALLODIUM**
feudal benefice .... **FEU**
feudal estate **FEOD, FEUD, FIEF**
feudal land .... **BENEFICE**
feudal service, form of **AVERA**
feudal tax **TAILAGE, TALLAGE, TAILLAGE**
feudal tenant .... **VASSAL**
fever, intermittent **AGUE, TERTIAN**
feverish .... **FEBRILE**
fez .... **TARBUSH, TARBOOSH, TARBOUCHE**

a fiber .... JUTE, PITA, RAFFIA, STAPLE, THREAD
fiber, bark
TAPA, OLONA, TERAP
fiber, coarse .... ADAD
fiber, cordage .... DA, COIR, FERU, HEMP, IMBE, JUTE, RHEA, ABACA, SISAL
fiber from palm .... ERUC
fiber, hat or basket .... DATIL
fiber knot .... NEP
fiber plant
ISTLE, IXTLE, IXLE, RAMIE
fiber plant, Brazil .... CAROA
fiber plant, E. Ind. SANA, SUNN
fiber, textile .... SABA
fiber, tropical
IXLE, ISTLE, IXTLE
fiber, woody .... BAST, BASTE
fictional submarine character
NEMO
fiddle, medieval .... GIGA
fiddler crab genus ...... UCA
field LEA, ACRE, WONG, CROFT
field deity ...... PAN, FAUN
field, enclosed: law ..... AGER
field, stubble .... ROWEN
fifth segment crustacean
CARPOS
b fig marigold, Afr. ...... SAMH
figs, Smyrna .. ELEME, ELEMI
fight
CLEM, FRAY, MELEE, AFFRAY
figurative use of word .. TROPE
figure .... SOLID
figure, equal angles
ISAGON, ISOGON
figure, 4-sided .... TETRAGON
figure, geom. .... SECTOR
figure of speech
TROPE, SIMILE, METAPHOR
figure, oval .... ELLIPSE
figure, 10-sided .... DECAGON
figwort .... MULLEIN
Fiji chestnut .... RATA
Fiji tree .... BURI
filament .... FIBER, HAIR
filament, flax ... HARL, HARLE
filament, plant
ELATER, THREAD
filch .... STEAL
file .... ROW
file, coarse .... RASP
file, three-square single-cut
CARLET
filled to capacity
SATED, REPLETE
fillet, architectural ORLE, ORLO
fillet, narrow heraldic
ORLE, ORLO, LISTEL
fillet, shaft's ..... ORLE, ORLO

c fillip .... SNAP
film, old green ..... PATINA
filthy .... VILE
filthy lucre .... PELF
finale: music .... CODA
finally: Fr. .... ENFIN
finback whale .... GRASO
finch .. MORO, LINNET, SISKIN
finch, Europ.
TARIN, TERIN, SERIN
finch, S. Afr. .... FINK
find fault ...... CARP, CAVIL
fine, as a line .... LEGER
fine, punish by ...... AMERCE
fine, record of ...... ESTREAT
finesse .... ART, SKILL
Fingal's kingdom .... MORVEN
finger .... DIGIT
finger cymbals ... CASTANETS
finger, 5th PINKIE, MINIMUS
finger inflammation ... FELON
finger nail half-moon
LUNULA, LUNULE
fingerless glove .... MIT, MITT
fingerprint pattern .... WHORL
finial ornament, slender .. EPI
finisher .... EDGER, ENDER
finishing tool .... REAMER
FINLAND, FINNISH
see also SPECIAL SECTION
d Finland .... SUOMI
Finn in Ingria ..... VOT, VOTE
Finns .... SUOMI
Finnish god .... JUMALA
Finnish poetry ...... RUNES
Finnish steam bath ... SAUNA
fire basket .... CRESSET
fire bullet .... TRACER
fire god .... VULCAN
fire god, Hindu .. AGNI, AKAL, CIVA, DEVA, KAMA, SIVA
fire in heart: Buddhism RAGA
fire opal: Fr. ...... GIRASOL
fire, sacrificial, Hindu .. AGNI
fire worshipper PARSI, PARSEE
firearm . GUN, RIFLE, MAUSER, PISTOL, CARBINE, REVOLVER
firecracker .... PETARD
fired clay .... TILE
firedog .... ANDIRON
fireplace
GRATE, INGLE, HEARTH
fireplace side shelf .... HOB
firewood bundle BARIN, FAGOT
firewood, Tex. .... LENA
firework .... GERB
firm FAST, STANCH, STAUNCH
firm: Hawaii .... HUI
firmament .... SKY
firn .... NEVE
firs, true .... ABIES

a first **PRIME, INITIAL, ORIGINAL**
first American-born white
child .... **DARE**
first appearance ...... **DEBUT**
first born: law .... **EIGNE**
first fruits of a benefice
.... **ANNATES**
first miracle site ...... **CANA**
first mortal, Hindu ..... **YAMA**
first part in duet ..... **PRIMO**
first principles .... **ABCS**
first-rate .... **ACE**
firth: Scot. .... **KYLE**
fish .. **ANGLE, TRAWL, TROLL**
fish ..... **ID, EEL, IDE, CARP,
DACE, HAKE, HIKU, JOCU,
LIJA, LING, MADO, MASU,
OPAH, ORFE, PEGA, PETO,
PIKE, POGY, ROUD, RUDD,
SCAD, SCUP, SESI, SHAD,
SIER, SKIL, SOLE, SPET,
TOPE, TUNA, ULUA, PAR-
GO, POWAN, POWEN,
ROACH, SKATE, CONGER,
MULLET, SABALO, TOMCOD**
fish, ancient .. **ELOPS, ELLOPS**
fish, Atlant. **TAUTOG, ESCOLAR**
fish, boneless .. **FILET, FILLET**
fish, bony .... **CARP, TELEOST**
fish, butterfly .... **PARU**
b fish by trolling .... **DRAIL**
fish, Calif. surf .... **SPRAT**
fish, carplike
.... **RUD, DACE, ROUD, RUDD**
fish cleaner .... **SCALER**
fish, climbing .... **ANABAS**
fish, cod-like **CUSK, HAKE, LING**
fish, colorful
.... **BOCE, OPAH, WRASSE**
fish, Congo .... **LULU**
fish, Cuban .... **DIABLO**
fish, cyprinoid
.... **ID, IDE, ORF, ORFE**
fish, edible .... **SPRAT**
fish eggs .... **ROE**
fish, Egypt. .... **SAIDE**
fish, elongated **EEL, GAR, PIKE**
fish, Europ. .. **ID, BOCE, DACE,
BREAM, SPRAT, UMBER,
BARBEL, BRASSE, PLAICE,
SENNET, WRASSE**
fish, flat .. **DAB, RAY, SOLE,
BRILL, FLUKE, FLOUNDER**
fish, Florida .... **TARPON**
fish, food .. **COD, CERO, HAAK,
HAIK, HAKE, LING, SHAD,
TUNA, TUNNY, SARDINE**
fish, food: Ind. .... **HILSA**
fish, fresh water
.... **IDE, BASS, DACE, ESOX**
fish from boat .... **TROLL**

c fish, game .... **BASS,
MARLIN, TARPON, TARPUN**
fish, gobeylike .... **DRAGONET**
fish, Gr. Lakes .. **CISCO, PERCH**
fish, Hawaiian .... **AKU**
fish, herringlike .... **SHAD**
fish, hook for **GIG, GAFF, DRAIL**
fish, lancet .... **SERRA**
fish line ...... **SNELL, TRAWL**
fish line cork .... **BOB**
fish, linglike .... **COD**
fish, long-nosed .... **GAR**
fish, mackerellike
.... **CERO, TUNNY, TINKER**
fish, many .... **SHOAL**
fish, marine **BONITO, TARPON**
fish measure .... **MEASE**
fish, Medit. .... **NONNAT**
fish, nest-building .... **ACARA**
fish net
.... **SEINE, TRAWL, SPILLER**
fish, N. Z. .... **IHI**
fish, No. Pacif. .... **INCONNU**
fish, parasitic .... **REMORA**
fish, perch-like .... **DARTER**
fish, Pers. myth .... **MAH**
fish pickle .... **ALEC**
fish, piece of ... **FILET, FILLET**
fish, pikelike .... **GAR**
d fish-pitching prong . **PEW, GAFF**
fish-poison tree .... **BITO**
fish, predatory .... **GAR**
fish, river .... **BLAY**
fish, Russian .... **STERLET**
fish sauce .... **ALEC, GARUM**
fish sign .... **PISCES**
fish, silvery .... **MULLET**
fish, small .. **ID, IDE, DARTER**
fish, snouted .... **SAURY**
fish, S. Am. .... **ARAPAIMA**
fish, sparoid .... **SAR, SARGO**
fish, spiny ..... **GOBY, PERCH**
fish, sucking .... **REMORA**
fish, trap ...... **WEEL, WEIR**
fish, tropical
.... **SARGO, ROBALO, SALEMA**
fish, warm sea
.... **GUASA, GROUPER**
fish, W. Ind.
.... **BOGA, CERO, TESTAR**
fish whisker .... **BARBEL**
fish with moving line .. **TROLL**
fish with net .. **SEINE, TRAWL**
fish, young .... **FRY**
fisherman's hut, Orkney
.... **SKEO, SKIO**
fishhook line-leader ... **SNELL**
fishhook part .... **BARB**
fishing expedition: Scot. **DRAVE**
fishing grounds, Shetlands **HAAF**

a fissure. . . . . **RENT,**
RIFT, RIMA, RIME, CLEFT
fissures, full of **RIMOSE, RIMOUS**
fist . . . . **NEAF**
fit . . **APT, RIPE, SUIT, ADAPT**
fit for cultivation . . . . **ARABLE**
fit for human consumption
POTABLE
fit of sulks . . . . **HUFF**
five-dollar bill . . . . **VEE**
five-franc piece . . . . **ECU**
five, group of . . . . **PENTAD**
five in cards . . . . **PEDRO**
fix or fixed . . . . **SET**
fixed charge . . . . **FEE**
fixed income person . . **RENTIER**
fixed payment . . . . **KIST**
flaccid . . . . **LIMP**
flag. **JACK, ENSIGN, BANDEROLE**
flag, flower, blue . . . . **IRIS**
flag, military . . . . **GUIDON**
flag, pirate . . . . **ROGER**
flag, small
BANNERET, BANNERETTE
flagellants . . . . **ALBI**
flag's corner . . . . **CANTON**
flank . . . . **SIDE**
flank: dialect . . . . **LEER**
flannel . . . . **LANA**

b flap . . . . **TAB, LOMA**
flap, as sails . . . . **SLAT**
flare . . . . **FUSEE, FUZEE**
flaring edge . . . . **LIP, FLANGE**
flashed lightning . . . **LEVINED**
flask, drinking . . . . **CANTEEN**
flat . . . . **EVEN, LEVEL, PLANE**
flat-bottomed boat
ARK, DORY, PUNT, SCOW
flat, music . . . . . . **MOL, MOLLE**
flatfish . . . . **DAB, RAY, SOLE,**
BRILL, FLUKE, FLOUNDER
flatten out . . . . **CLAP**
flattened . . **OBLATE, PLANATE**
flatter . . . . **PALP**
flattery . . . . **PALAVER**
flavor . . . . **LACE, TANG,**
AROMA, SAPOR, SEASON
flavoring plant . . **HERB, LEEK,**
MINT, ANISE, BASIL
flavoring root . . . . . . **LICORICE**
flax fiber . . . . **TOW**
flax, like . . . . **TOWY**
flax, prepare . . . . **RET**
flee . . . . **LAM, BOLT**
fleece . . . . **FELL, WOOL**
fleece, poorest . . . . **ABB**
fleet . . . . **NAVY**
fleet, esp. Span.
ARMADA, ARMADO, ARMATA
fleet, merchant . . . . . **ARGOSY**
fleur-de-lis . . . . **LIS, LYS, LISS**

c fleur-de-lis, obs. . . . . . . **LUCE**
flexible . . . . **LITHE**
flexible wood: dial. . . . . . **EDDER**
flight . . . . **HEGIRA, HEJIRA**
flight of ducks . . . . **SKEIN**
flight organ . . . . **WING**
flight, pert. to . . . . **AERO**
flightless bird
EMU, KIWI, WEKA, PENGUIN
flip . . . . **SNAP**
flit . . . . **FLY, GAD**
float
BUOY, RAFT, SWIM, WAFT
floating . . . . **NATANT**
floating vegetation on Nile
SADD, SUDD
floating wreckage . . **FLOTSAM**
flock of quail . . . . **BEVY**
flock of swans . . . . **BANK**
flock, pert. to . . . . **GREGAL**
flock, small . . . . **COVEY**
flog
BEAT, LASH, WHIP, SWINGE
flood . . . . **SEA, EAGRE,**
SPATE, FRESHET, TORRENT
floodgate . . . . . . **CLOW, SLUICE**
flora and fauna . . . . **BIOTA**
floral leaf . . . . **BRACT, SEPAL**
Florentine family . . . . . **MEDICI**

d Florida tree . . . . **MABI**
flounder
DAB, SOLE, FLUKE, PLAICE
flour sieve . . . . **BOLTER**
flour, unsorted Ind. **ATA, ATTA**
flourish, music . . . . . **ROULADE**
flourishing: dialect . . . . . **FRIM**
flow . . . . **RUN, FLUX**
flow out . . . . . . **EMIT, SPILL**
flow, to stop
STANCH, STAUNCH
flower cluster
CYME, ANADEM, RACEME
flower extract
ATAR, OTTO, ATTAR, OTTAR
flower, fall
ASTER, COSMOS, SALVIA
flower, field . . . . **GOWAN**
flower, genus of . . . . **ROSA**
flower-goddess, Norse **NANNA**
flower-goddess, Rom. . . **FLORA**
flower leaf . . . **BRACT, SEPAL**
flower, Oriental . . . . **LOTUS**
flower part . . . . **PETAL,**
SEPAL, CARPEL, SPADIX
flower, showy . . . . **CALLA**
flower spike . . . . **AMENT**
flowering plant . . . . **ARUM**
fluctuate . . . . **WAVER**
fluent . . . . **GLIB**
fluff, yarn . . . . **LINT**

a
fluid, aeriform .... GAS
fluid, medical ... SERA, SERUM
fluid, serous .... SERA, SERUM
fluidity unit .... RHE
flume .... SHUTE, SLUICE
flushed .... RED
flute, ancient Gr. ... HEMIOPE
flute, India ... BIN, MATALAN
flute, small .... FIFE
flutter .. FLAP, WAVE, HOVER
fly GNAT, SOAR, WING, AVIATE
fly agaric .... AMANITA
fly aloft .... SOAR
fly, artificial
   HARL, HERL, CAHILL, CLARET
fly, kind of .... BOT
fly, small ...... GNAT, MIDGE
fly, S. Afr. .... TSETSE
flycatcher
   TODY, ALDER, PEWEE, PHOEBE
flying .... VOLANT, VOLITANT
"Flying Dutchman" saver SENTA
flying fox .... KALONG
flying lemur .... COLUGO
flying, of .... AERO
flying saucer .... UFO
foam .... SUD, SUDS
focus .... CONCENTRATE
fodder pit .... SILO
fodder storage place .... SILO

b
fodder, to store ...... ENSILE,
   ENSILO, ENSILAGE, ENSILATE
fog .... MIST
fog horn .... SIRENE
fog: old Eng. .... RAG
foist .... FOB, PALM
fold .... LAP, PLY, PLIE,
   RUGA, PLEAT, CREASE
fold of skin .... PLICA
folds, arrange in ..... DRAPE
folded .... PLICATE
folio .... PAGE
folk dance, Slavic ...... KOLO
folklore being .... TROLL
folkway .... MOS
folkways .... MORES
follow .... DOG, TAIL,
   ENSUE, TRACE, SHADOW
follow suit, not RENIG, RENEGE
follower .. IST, ITE, ADHERENT
foment .... ABET
fondle .... PET, CARESS
fondness: Ir. .... GRA
font .... LAVER, STOUP
food .... FARE, MEAT,
   MANNA, ALIMENT, PABULUM
food bit .... ORT
food, farinaceous ...... SAGO
food for animals .... FORAGE
food forbidden Israelites TEREFA

c
food, Hawaii .... POI
food: Maori, N. Z. ...... KAI
food of gods
   AMRITA, AMREETA, AMBROSIA
food: Polyn. .... KAI
food, provide .... CATER
food, soft invalid's ...... PAP
foods, choice .... CATES
fool..ASS, DOLT, GABY, RACA,
   SIMP, IDIOT, NINNY
fool's bauble .... MAROTTE
fool's gold .... PYRITE
foolish .. DAFT, ZANY, INANE,
   SILLY, HARISH, ASININE
foot, animal's ..... PAD, PAW
foot, Chin. .... CHEK
foot, Gr. poet. .... IONIC
foot, having .... PEDATE
foot part, horse's ... PASTERN
foot, poet. ..... IAMB, IAMBIC,
   IAMBUS, ANAPEST, ANAPAEST
foot soldier .... PEON
foot soldier, Ir. KERN, KERNE
foot, two-syllable
   SPONDEE, TROCHEE
foot, verse .... IAMB,
   DACTYL, ANAPEST, ANAPAEST
football position: abbr. ... FB,
   HB, LE, LT, QB, RE, RT

d
footless .... APOD, APODAL
footless animal APOD, APODE
footless animal genus .. APODA
footlike .... PEDATE
footlike part .... PES
footpad .... WHYO
footstalk, leaf .... STRIG
footstool HASSOCK, OTTOMAN
for .... PRO
for example .... EG
for fear that .... LEST
for shame .... FIE
forage plant .. GUAR, ALSIKE,
   LUCERN, ALFALFA, LUCERNE
foramen .... PORE
foray .... RAID
forbidden
   TABU, TABOO, BANNED
Forbidden City .... LASSA
forbidding .... STERN
force ...... VIS, DINT, DRIVE,
   IMPEL, POWER, ENERGY,
   VIOLENCE
force, alleged
   OD, BIOD, ELOD, ODYL
force, hypothetical .... OD
force, unit of .... DYNE
force, with .... AMAIN
foreboding .... OMEN
forefather .... SIRE
forefoot .... PUD
forefront .... VAN

a forehead, of the .... **METOPIC**
forehead strap .... **TUMP**
foreign in origin ...... **EXOTIC**
foreign trade discount .. **AGIO**
foreigner: Hawaii ..... **HAOLE**
foreigners' quarter, Constanti-
 nople .... **PERA**
foremost part
            BOW, VAN, FRONT
foremost segment, insect's
                ACRON
foreordain .... **DESTINE**
foreshadow .... **BODE**
forest: Brazil .... **MATTA**
forest clearing .... **GLADE**
forest: obsolete .... **WOLD**
forest ox .... **ANOA**
forest partly inundated **GAPO**
forest, pert. to
    SILVAN, SYLVAN, NEMORAL
forest, P. I. .... **GUBAT**
forest warden .... **RANGER**
forestall .... **AVERT, PREVENT**
foretell ...... **AUGUR, INSEE**
foreteller .... **SEER**
foretoken .... **OMEN**
forever .... **AY, AYE**
forever: Maori .... **AKE**
forever: poet. **ETERN, ETERNE**
forfeit .... **LOSE, LAPSE**

b forfeits, Jap. .... **KEN**
forgetfulness fruit .... **LOTUS**
forgetfulness water ... **LETHE**
forgive .... **REMIT**
forgiving .... **CLEMENT**
forgo .... **WAIVE**
form a network .... **PLEX**
form: Buddhism .... **RUPA**
form into line **ALIGN, ALINE**
form, pert. to .... **MODAL**
form, philos. .... **EIDOS**
formal choice .... **VOTE**
formation, military .. **ECHELON**
former .... **ERST**
former ruler **CZAR, TSAR, TZAR**
formerly .... **NEE, ERST, ONCE**
formerly: pref. .... **EX**
formic acid source ..... **ANT**
formicid .... **ANT**
formula .... **LAW**
forsaken .... **LORN**
fort .... **DIX, ORD, REDAN,**
   CITADEL, REDOUBT, RAVELIN
fort, N. Z. .... **PA, PAH**
forth .... **OUT**
forth, issuing .... **EMANANT**
forthwith .... **NOW**
fortification
    REDAN, RAVELIN, REDOUBT

c fortification, ditchside
    SCARP, ESCARP, ESCARPE
fortification, felled trees
                ABATIS
fortification, slope .... **TALUS**
fortified place ...... **LIS, LISS**
fortify .... **ARM, MAN**
fortunate (India) .... **SRI**
fortune: Gypsy .... **BAHI**
forty days fast ...... **CARENE**
forty: Gr. .... **MU**
forward .... **ON, AHEAD**
fossil, mollusk .... **DOLITE**
fossil resin .... **RETINITE**
fossil worm track ... **NEREITE**
foul smelling
        OLID, FETID, REEKY
found .... **BASE**
found, thing .... **TROVE**
foundation .. **BED, BASE, BASIS**
fountain .... **FONS**
four, group of .... **TETRAD**
four-inch measure .... **HAND**
fourth calif (caliph) .... **ALI**
fourth estate .... **PRESS**
fowl .... **HEN, CAPON, POULT**
fowl's gizzard, etc. .... **GIBLET**
fox .... **TOD**
fox, Afr. .... **FENNEC**
fox hunter's coat ...... **PINK**
d fox, S. Afr. .... **ASSE, CAAMA**
"Fra Diavolo" composer **AUBER**
fraction ...... **PART, DECIMAL**
fragment, pottery
    SHARD, SHERD, SHEARD
fragments .... **ANA, ORTS**
fragrant .... **OLENT**
frame, supporting
        TRESSEL, TRESTLE
framework .... **TRUSS**
France .... **GAUL**
franchise .... **CHARTER**
Franciscan .... **MINORITE**
frank .... **OPEN, HONEST**
Franks, pert. to ...... **SALIC**
frankincense ...... **OLIBANUM**
Frankish law .... **SALIC**
Frankish peasant .. **LITI, LITUS**
fraud .... **SHAM**
fraught .... **LADEN**
fray .... **MELEE**
free .... **RID, GRATIS**
free-for-all .... **FRAY, MELEE**
free from discount ...... **NET**
free from knots: obs. .. **ENODE**
freebooter .... **PIRATE**
freedman, Kentish law .. **LAET**
freehold land, Turkey .. **MULK**
freeman ...... **CEORL, THANE**
freight-boat .... **ARK**

a freight car .... **GONDOLA**
FRENCH WORDS: (accent marks
omitted throughout)
according to ..... **ALA, AUX**
after .... **APRES**
again .... **ENCORE**
airplane .... **AVION**
alas .... **HELAS**
all .... **TOUT**
among .... **ENTRE**
and .... **ET**
angel .... **ANGE**
annuity .... **RENTE**
arm .... **BRAS**
article ...... **LA, LE, DE,**
(plural) **DES, LAS, LES, UNE**
at the home of ..... **CHEZ**
aunt .... **TANTE**
baby .... **BEBE**
bacon .... **LARD**
back .... **DOS**
ball .... **BAL**
bang! .... **PAN**
bath .... **BAIN**
beach .... **PLAGE**
beast .... **BETE**
before .... **AVANT**
being .... **ETRE**
bench .... **BANC**
between .... **ENTRE**

b beware .... **GARE**
bitter .... **AMER**
black .... **NOIR, NOIRE**
blue .... **BLEU**
bread crumbs ..... **PANURE**
bridge .... **PONT**
business house .... **CIE**
but .... **MAIS**
cabbage .... **CHOU**
cake .... **GATEAU**
carefully groomed .. **SOIGNE**
carriage .... **FIACRE**
charmed .... **RAVI**
chicken .... **POULE**
child .... **ENFANT**
clear .... **NET**
climax, theatre ..... **CLOY**
cloth .... **DRAP**
cloud .... **NUAGE**
coarse cloth .... **BURE**
connective .... **ET**
cowardly .... **LACHE**
cup .... **TASSE**
dance, formal .... **BAL**
dare .... **OSER**
daughter .... **FILLE**
deal .... **DONNE**
dear .... **CHER, CHERI**
deed .... **FAIT**
defy .... **DEFI**

c department .... see SPECIAL
SECTION, GAZETTEER
depot .... **GARE**
detective force .... **SURETE**
devil .... **DIABLE**
dirty .... **SALE**
donkey .... **ANE**
down with .... **ABAS**
dream .... **REVE**
duck to cook .... **CANETON**
dugout .... **ABRI**
duke .... **DUC**
dungeon .... **CACHOT**
ear of grain .... **EPI**
east .... **EST**
egg .... **OEUF**
elegance .... **LUXE**
enamel .... **EMAIL**
equal .... **PAREIL**
evening .... **SOIR**
exaggerated .... **OUTRE**
exclamation .... **HEIN**
exist .... **ETRE**
fabric .... **RAS, DRAP**
father .... **PERE**
fear .... **PEUR**
finally .... **ENFIN**
fingering .... **DOIGTE**
fire .... **FEU**
five .... **CINQ**
for .... **CAR**
friend .... **AMI, AMIE**
froth .... **BAVE**
full .... **PLEIN**
game .... **JEU, JEUX**
gift .... **CADEAU**
god .... **DIEU**
golden .... **DORE**
good .... **BON**
good-bye **ADIEU, AU REVOIR**
grain ear .... **EPI**
gray .... **GRIS**
gravy .... **JUS**
grimace .... **MOUE**
ground .... **TERRE**

d half-mask .... **LOUP**
hall .... **SALLE**
handle .... **ANSE**
head .... **TETE**
health .... **SANTE**
here .... **ICI**
hill .... **PUY**
his .... **SES**
house .... **MAISON**
hunting match .... **TIR**
husband .... **MARI**
idea .... **IDEE**

(French words continued on
pages 62 and 63)

French

FRENCH:

impetuosity	ELAN
in	DANS
income, annual	RENTE
is	EST
island	ILE
kind	SORTE
king	ROI
lamb	AGNEAU
land	TERRE
laugh	RIRE
laughter	RISEE
law	LOI, DROIT
leather	CUIR
lift	LEVE
lily	LIS
little	PEU
lively	VIF
lodging place	GITE
low	BAS
maid	BONNE
mail	POSTE
mask, half	LOUP
material	DRAP
May	MAI
meat dish	SALMI
milk	LAIT
mine	AMOI
mother	MERE
mountain	MONT
museum	MUSEE
nail	CLOU
name	NOM
near	PRES
network	RESEAU
night	NUIT
no	NON
nose	NEZ
nothing	RIEN
number, one	UNE
nursemaid	BONNE
of	DE
one	UNE
our	NOS, NOUS
out	HORS
outbreak	EMEUTE
over	SUR
oyster farm	PARC
petticoat	JUPE, COTTE
picnic spot	BOIS
pinion	AILE
poem	DIT
pork	SALE
pout	MOUE
preposition	DES
pretty	JOLI, JOLIE
pronoun	CES, ILS, MES, TOI, UNE, ELLE
queen	REINE
quickly	VITE
rabbit	LAPIN
railway station	GARE
read	LIRE
rear	ARRIERE
reception	ACCUEIL
rent	LOUER
river	RIVIERE
roast	ROTI
royal edict	ARRET
saint: abbr.	STE
salt	SEL
salted	SALE
school	ECOLE, LYCEE
scow	ACON
sea	MER
security	RENTE
senior	AINE
servant	BONNE
she	ELLE
sheath	ETUI
sheep	MOUTON
shelter	ABRI
shine	LUSTRE
shooting match	TIR
sickness	MAL
silk	SOIE
situated	SISE
small	PETIT
smitten	EPRISE
soldier	POILU
some	DES
son	FILS
soul	AME
spirit	AME
star	ETOILE
state	ETAT
stocking	BAS
storm	ORAGE
summer	ETE
superior quality	LUXE
superfluous	DETROP
surnamed	DIT
sweetmeat	DRAGEE
that	CE, CET, QUE, QUI, CELA
thee	TE
there!	VOILA
they	ILS
thirty	TRENTE
this	CE
thou	TOI
to be	ETRE
to go	ALLER
to love	AIMER
too much	TROP
under	SOUS
upon	SUR
us	NOUS
verb	ETRE
verse	RONDEL

a **FRENCH:**

very	TRES
vineyard	CRU
wall	MUR
water	EAU
wave	ONDE
weapon	ARME
well	BIEN
wine	VIN
wine, delicacy of	SEVE
wine-plant	CEP
with	AVEC
with the	AU
without	SANS
wing	AILE
wood	BOIS
yesterday	HIER
you	TOI
your	VOTRE

Fr., annuity	RENTE
Fr. art group	FAUVES
Fr. artist	DORE, DUFY, GROS, COROT, DEGAS, MANET, MONET, BRAQUE, DERAIN, RENOIR, CHAGALL, CHIRICO, MATISSE, UTRILLO
Fr. artist cult	DADA

b

Fr. author	SUE, GIDE, HUGO, LOTI, ZOLA, CAMUS, DUMAS, RENAN, STAEL, VERNE, RACINE, SARTRE, COCTEAU
Fr. Calvinist	CALAS
Fr. chalk	TALC
Fr. coin, old	SOU
Fr. commercial company	CIE
FR. COMPOSER see COMPOSER, FR.	
Fr. dramatist	RACINE
Fr. ecclesiastic city	SENS
Fr. explorer	CARTIER
Fr. fort, battle of Verdun	VAUX
Fr. general	FOCH, HOCHE GAMELIN
Fr.-Ger. river basin	SAAR
Fr. guerillas	MAQUIS
Fr. Guiana tribesman	BONI
Fr. historical area	ANJOU
Fr. honeysuckle	SULLA
Fr. illustrator	DORE
Fr. island	ILE
Fr. lace-making town	CLUNY
Fr. marshal	NEY, MURAT
FR. NOVELIST see FR. AUTHOR	
FR. PAINTER see FR. ARTIST	
Fr. philosopher	COMTE
Fr. premier, former	LAVAL
Fr. priest	ABBE, PERE
Fr. protectorate	TUNIS
Fr. psychologist	BINET

c

Fr. Revolution month	NIVOSE, FLOREAL, PRAIRAL, VENTOSE, BRUMAIRE, FERVIDOR, FRIMAIRE, MESSIDOR, PLUVIOSE, THERMIDOR
Fr. revolutionist	MARAT
Fr. sculptor	RODIN
Fr. security	RENTE
Fr. singer	PIAF, SABLON
Fr. soprano	PONS, CALVE
Fr. statesman	COTY
FR. WRITER .. see FR. AUTHOR	
Frenchman	GAUL
frenzied	AMOK
frequently	OFT
fresh	NEW, SPICK
fresh supply	RELAY
freshet	FLOOD, SPATE
freshwater worm	NAID, NAIS
fretted	EROSE
Frey's wife	GERD
friar	FRA, MONK
friar, mendicant	SERVITE
friend: law	AMY
friends	KITH
Friendly Islands	TONGA
friendship	AMITY
frigate bird, Hawaiian	IWA
Frigg's brother-in-law	VE
Frigg's husband	ODIN

d

fright	FUNK, PANIC
frighten	FLEY, ALARM, SCARE
frill, neck	RUFF, JABOT
fringe of curls	FRISETTE
fringe: zool.	LOMA
frisk	PLAY, ROMP
frisky	PEART
FROCK see GARMENT	
frog	TOAD
frog genus	RANA
frogs, order of	ANURA
frogs, pert. to	RANINE
frolic	LARK, PLAY, ROMP, CAPER, SPORT, SPREE
from head to foot	CAP-A-PIE
from: Lat.	DE
from: prefix	AB
front	VAN, FORE, FACADE
front page weather box	EAR
front, to extend	DEPLOY
frontier post	FORT
frontiersman	BOONE, CARSON
frost	ICE, HOAR, RIME
frosty	RIMY
froth	FOAM, SPUME
frothlike	SPUMY, YEASTY
frown	LOUR, GLOOM, LOWER, SCOWL, GLOWER
frugal	CHARY
fruit	BERRY, OLIVE
fruit, Afr.	PECEGO

Fruit

a
fruit, aggregate ..... ETAERIO
fruit decay .... BLET
fruit dish
    COMPOTE, COMPOTIER
fruitdots, fern .... SORI, SORUS
fruit, dry .... ACHENE
fruit, fleshy ...... PEAR, PEPO
fruit, hard-shelled NUT, GOURD
fruit, India .... BEL
fruit-jelly .... RHOB
fruit, lemonlike ...... CITRON
fruit of maple ...... SAMARA
fruit pigeon, Polyn. ...... LUPE
fruit, plumlike .... SLOE
fruit, pulpy ..... UVA, DRUPE
fruit shrub, E. Ind. .... CUBEB
fruit, small, 1-seeded
  AKENE, ACHENE, ACHENIUM
fruit, southern ...... PAPAW
fruit squeezer ...... REAMER
fruit, tropical .. DATE, MANGO
fruit, vine .... MELON
fruit, yellow tropical
  PAPAW, PAPAYA, PAWPAW
fruiting spike .... EAR
frustrate ... SCOTCH, THWART
fry lightly .... SAUTE
Fuegan Indian .... ONA
fuel   LOG, COAL, COKE, PEAT
fuel ship .... OILER, TANKER
fuel, turf .... PEAT, PEET
fugue theme .... DUX
fulcrum, oar .... THOLE
full .... PLENARY
full and clear ..... OROTUND
fullness .... PLENUM
fulmar .... NELLY, MALDUCK
fume .... REEK, SMOKE

c
fun .... SPORT
function ...... GO, USE, WORK
function, trig. .... SINE, COSINE
fundamental
    BASIC, ELEMENTAL
funeral bell KNELL, MORTBELL
funeral music .... DIRGE
funeral notice .... OBIT
funeral oration .... ELOGE
funeral pile .... PYRE
funeral song .... NENIA
fungi, tissue in ...... TRAMA
fungus .... AGARIC
fungus, edible
  MOREL, MORIL, TRUFFLE
fungus, white-spored AMANITA
fur ...... SEAL, VAIR, GENET
  MARTEN, NUTRIA, MINIVER
fur cape .... PELERINE
fur: Her. PEAN, VAIR, VAIRE
furbelow ...... FRILL, RUFFLE
Furies, Gr. .... ERINYS
ERINNYS, ERINYES, ERINNYES
Furies, one of
  ALECTO, MEGAERA, TISIPHONE
Furies, Rom. .... DIRAE
furlongs, eight .... MILE
furnish crew .... MAN
furnish with .... ENDOW
furnishings, mode of .. DECOR
furrows, with RIVOSE, RUTTED
further .... AID, YET
furtive .... SLY, SNEAKY
fury .... IRE
furze .... WHIN, WHUN,
  GORSE, GORST, GORSTE
fuse partly .... FRIT
fuss .... ADO, TO-DO

G

b
gabi .... TARO
Gad, son of .... ARELI
gadget .... GISMO
Gael .... SCOT
Gaelic .. ERSE, CELTIC, KELTIC
Gaelic poem .... DUAN
Gaelic sea god .... LER
gaff .... SPAR
gain .... GET, WIN, EARN
gait .. LOPE, CANTER, GALLOP
gait, horse's ... PACE, RACK
Galahad's mother ..... ELAINE
Galatea's beloved ..... ACIS
Galilee town .... CANA
galla ox ...... SANGA, SANGU
gallery, art .... SALON
gallery: hist. .... ALURE

d
gallery, open .... LOGGIA
gallery protecting troops
    ECOUTE
galley, armed, old Northmen's
    AESC
galley, fast
    DROMON, DROMOND
galley, 1 oar bank   UNIREME
galley, 2 oar banks .. BIREME
galley, 3 oar banks TRIREME
gallop, rapid .... TANTIVY
gallop slowly .... LOPE
Galsworthy heroine .... IRENE
Galway Bay, isles in .... ARAN
gamble .... GAME
gambling place ...... CASINO

a gambol.......... **DIDO, CAPER**
game ... **LOTO, BINGO, LOTTO**
game, Basque .... **PELOTA**
game, board ... **CHESS, HALMA**
game, card ... **LU, LOO, NAP,
PAM, PUT, FARO, CINCH,
MACAO, MONTE, OMBER,
OMBRE, STUSS, TAROT,
WHIST, BASSET, CASINO,
ECARTE, ROUNCE,
CANASTA**
game, child's .... **TAG**
game, dice .... **LUDO**
game, follow .... **STALK**
game, gambling ... **FARO, PICO,
STUSS**
game, Hawaii .... **HEI**
game, Ind. guessing ... **CANUTE**
game, It. guessing ... **MORA**
game of skill..... **POOL, CHESS**
game piece..... **MAN, DOMINO**
gamecock .... **STAG**
gamekeeper .... **RANGER**
gaming cube........ **DIE, DICE**
Ganges boat........... **PUTELI**
gangplank .... **RAMP**
gangster ... **MUG, THUG, WHYO**
gannet, common .... **SOLAN**
gannet genus .... **SULA**
gap .... **HIATUS, LACUNA**
gap in hedge
b .... **MUSE, MEUSE, MUSET**
gar fish .... **SNOOK**
garland.......... **LEI, ANADEM**
GARMENT. see **COAT, BLOUSE**
garment................. **ROBE**
garment, Arab .... **ABA**
garment, bishop's .... **CHIMAR,
CHIMER, CHIMERE**
garment, church .... **COTTA**
**GARMENT, CLERICAL OR EC-
CLESIASTIC,.... see GARMENT,
PRIESTLY**
garment, fitted .... **REEFER**
garment, India, Hindu..... **SARI,
SAREE, BANIAN, BANYAN**
GARMENT, LITURGICAL ... see
GARMENT, PRIESTLY
garment, loose **CAMIS, CAMUS,
CYMAR, SIMAR, CAMISE**
garment, Malay .... **SARONG**
garment, Moslem .... **IZAR**
garment, N. Afr......... **HAIK**
garment, Old Ir........... **INAR**
garment, outer....... **CAPOTE,
PALETOT**
garment, Polyn........ **PAREU**
garment, priestly... **ALB, COPE,
AMICE, EPHOD, STOLE**
garment, rain .... **PONCHO**
garment, scarflike ...... **TIPPET**

c garment, Turk........ **DOLMAN**
garment, woman's..... **BODICE,
MANTUA**
garnishment .... **LIEN**
garret .... **ATTIC**
garter snake genus...... **ELAPS**
gas .... **FUEL, NEON**
gas apparatus .... **AERATOR**
gas, charge with ...... **AERATE**
gas, colorless.......... **OXAN**
gas, inert..... **ARGON, XENON**
gas, radioactive .... **RADON,
NITON**
GASEOUS ELEMENT...... see
**ELEMENTS, SPECIAL
SECTION, Page 195**
gaseous sky "cloud" .. **NEBULA**
GASTROPOD see also **MOLLUSK**
gastropod .... **WELK, WILK,
WHELK, LIMPET**
gastropod, Haliotis .. **ABALONE**
gate .... **PORTAL**
gate, water .... **SLUICE**
gateway............... **PYLON**
gateway, Buddhist temple
TORAN, TORANA
gateway, Pers........... **DAR**
gateway, Shinto shrine.... **TORII**
gather........ **AMASS, GLEAN,
GARNER, MUSTER**
gather, as grouse .... **LEK**
d gather in bundles .... **SHEAVE**
gathers, put in .... **SHER, SHIR,
SHIRR**
gaunt .... **SPARE**
Gawain's father .... **LOT**
gazelle .... **ARIEL**
gazelle, Afr....... **ADMI, DAMA,
MOHR, KORIN, MHORR**
gazelle, Asia .... **AHU**
gazelle, black-tailed........ **GOA**
gazelle, Pers......... **CORA**
gazelle, Sudan .... **DAMA**
gazelle, Tibetan .... **GOA**
gear .... **CAM**
gear tooth................. **COG**
gear wheel, smallest.... **PINION**
Geb's consort............. **NUT**
Gelderland city............. **EDE**
gelid .... **ICY, COLD**
GEM........... see also **STONE**
gem ..... **JADE, ONYX, OPAL,
RUBY, SARD, AGATE, PEARL,
STONE, GARNET, SPINEL,
EMERALD, PERIDOT**
gem-bearing earth, Burma **BYON**
gem, carved .... **CAMEO**
gem facet ...... **BEZEL, BEZIL,
CULET, COLLET**
gem weight............. **CARAT**
Gemini's mortal half ... **CASTOR**

65

Gender

a
gender, a .... NEUTER
genealogy .... TREE
GENERAL, CIVIL WAR
  see CIVIL WAR COMMANDER
general, Morocco .... KAID
general Sitting Bull defeated
                      CUSTER
generation .... AGE
Genesis matriarch ...... SARAI
genie, Egypt. .... HAPI
genip tree .... LANA
genipap wood .... LANA
gentle . MILD, TAME, TENDER
gentle breeze .... AURA
gentle heat .... TEPOR
genuflect .... KNEEL
GENUS . see PLANT or
             ANIMAL named
genus of plants .... ARUM
geode VUG, VOOG, VUGG, VUGH
geological division . LIAS, LYAS
geol. epoch BALA, ECCA, LIAS,
         MUAV, ERIAN, UINTA,
         PLIOCENE
geol. formation ..... TERRAIN,
         TERRANE, TERRENE
geol. period .... DYAS,
         EOCENE, MIOCENE
geol. stage ... RISS, ACHEN
geol. vein angle .... HADE

b
geometric ratio .... SINE
geometric solid
         CONE, CUBE, PRISM
geometrical lines ...... LOCI,
         LOCUS, SECANT
geometry rule .... THEOREM
geometry term .... VERSOR
geophagy .... PICA
George Sand novel ..... LELIA
Geraint's wife .... ENID
geranium lake color . NACARAT
germ . BUG, VIRUS, MICROBE
germ-free ASEPTIC, ANTISEPTIC
germs, produced by ... SEPTIC
GERMAN . see also TEUTONIC
GERMAN WORDS: (umlauts
omitted throughout)
  "A" .... EIN
  above .... UBER
  again .... UBER
  alas .... ACH
  article ...... DAS, DER, EIN
  ass .... ESEL
  beer .... BIER
  blood .... BLUT
  conjunction .... UND
  count .... GRAF
  donkey .... ESEL
  dumpling .... KNODEL
  eat .... ESSEN

c
  eight .... ACHT
  evening .... ABEND
  everything .... ALLES
  exclamation .... HOCH
  four .... VIER
  gentleman .. HERR, HERREN
  hall .... AULA, SAAL
  heaven .... HIMMEL
  hunter .... JAGER
  "I" .... ICH
  ice .... EIS
  iron .... EISEN
  is .... IST
  it .... ES
  league (s) .... BUND, BUNDE
  love .... LIEBE
  mister .... HERR
  nation .... VOLK
  never .... NIE
  new .... NEUE
  no .... NEIN
  noble .... EDEL
  old .... ALT
  one .... EIN, EINE
  out of .... AUS
  pronoun .... ICH
  people .... VOLK
  school hall .... AULA
  softly .... LEISE

d
  song .... LIED
  spirit .... GEIST
  state .... STAAT
  steel .... STAHL
  temperament .... GEMUT
  than .... ALS
  the .... DAS, DER
  three .... DREI
  thunder .... DONNER
  title .... VON, PRINZ
  town .... STADT
  us .... UNS
  very .... SEHR
  with .... MIT
  without .... OHNE
  yes .... JA
  you .... SIE
  your ...... IHR, DEIN, EUER

German .... BOCHE
Ger. admiral .... SPEE
Ger. bacteriologist ..... KOCH
Ger. camp, war ...... STALAG
GER. COMPOSER
         see COMPOSER, GER.
Ger.-Czech region ... SUDETEN
Ger. district, old ...... GAU
Ger. dive bomber ...... STUKA
Ger. emperor .... OTTO
Ger. highway ..... AUTOBAHN
Ger. John .... HANS

Ger. king .... **OTTO**
Ger. landscape painter .. **ROOS**
Ger. name prefix .... **VON**
Ger. philosopher . **KANT, HEGEL**
Ger. physicist .. **OHM, ERMAN**
Ger. president .... **EBERT**
Ger. princely family ..... **WELF**
Ger. theologian .... **ARND**
Ger. title .. **VON, GRAF, PRINZ**
Ger. tribal region
　　　　　　GAU, GAUE, GAUS
Germanic deity .... **DONAR**
Germanic letter .... **RUNE**
gesture dance, Samoa; Fiji **SIVA**
get out! . **SCAT, SHOO, SCRAM**
ghastly .... **LURID**
ghost .... **HANT, SPOOK,**
　　　　　SPECTER, SPECTRE
ghost, India .... **BHUT**
ghost-town state: abbrev.: **UT**
giant .... **TITAN**
giant, frightful .... **OGRE**
giant, Hindu myth ..... **BANA**
giant, killed by Apollo .. **OTUS**
giant, Norse, Scand. myth **YMER,**
　　　　YMIR, JOTUM, MIMIR
giant, Rom. .... **CACA**
giant, 1000-armed, Hindu **BANA**
giants, Bibl. .... **ANAK, EMIM**
gibbon, Malay .... **LAR**
gift, receiver of .... **DONEE**
gig .... **NAPPER**
gigantic person .... **TITAN**
"Gil —" LeSage novel .. **BLAS**
Gilead's descendant .... **ULAM**
Gilgit language, Kashmir **SHINA**
gills, four .... **PINT**
gilt .... **DORE**
gin .... **TRAP**
gingerbread tree .... **DUM**
ginkgo tree .... **ICHO**
GIPSY .... see **GYPSY**
giraffe-like animal .... **OKAPI**
girasol .... **OPAL**
girder .... **TRUSS**
girdle .... **OBI, CEST, SASH**
girl .... **SIS, CHIT,**
　　　　　　　DAME, SKIRT
GIRL'S NAME
　　　see **WOMAN'S NAME**
girth, saddle .... **CINCH**
gist .... **NUB, PITH**
give: law .... **REMISE**
give reluctantly ..... **GRUDGE**
give up ... **CEDE, WAIVE, YIELD**
give up wholly ...... **DEVOTE**
give way .... **YIELD**
glacial hill .... **PAHA**
glacial ice block, pinnacle **SERAC**
glacial ridge .... **AS, OS, ASAR,**
　　KAME, OSAR, ESCAR,
　　ESKAR, ESKER

glacial snow field **FIRN, NEVE**
glacial stage .... **WURM**
glacier chasm
　　　CREVAS, CREVASSE
glacier, facing a .... **STOSS**
gladiolus .... **IRID**
gladly .... **FAIN**
gland .... **PINEAL, THYROID**
gland, edible .... **NOIX**
glass .... **LENS**
glass, blue .... **SMALT**
glass bubble .... **BLEB**
glass defect .... **TEAR**
glass, flatten ...... **PLATTEN**
glass furnace mouth .. **BOCCA**
glass ingredient ...... **SILICON**
glass-like material .. . **PLASS**
glass maker .... **GLAZIER**
glass, molten .... **PARISON**
glass, partly fused **FRIT, FRITT**
glass, transparent ..... **UVIOL**
glass vial .. **AMPULE, AMPOULE**
glassmaker's oven . **LEER, LEHR**
glasswort .... **KALI**
glossy .... **HYALINE**
glazier's tack .... **BRAD**
gleam .... **GLINT**
glide .... **SKIM, SLIP,**
　　　　　SKATE, SLIDE
glittering piece ..... **SPANGLE**
globe .... **ORB, SPHERE**
global .... **ROUND, SPHERAL**
gloom .... **MIRK, MURK**
gloomy .... **DARK, DOUR,**
　　　　DREAR, DREARY
"Gloomy Dean" .... **INGE**
glossy-surfaced ...... **GLACE**
glottal stop: Dan. ...... **STOD**
glove leather ..... **KID, NAPA,**
　　　　MOCHA, SUEDE
glove shape, unstitched **TRANK**
glowing .... **CANDENT**
glucoside, root .... **GEIN**
glut ... **SATE, GORGE, SATIATE**
gnarl ..... **NUR, KNUR, NURR**
gnat, small .... **MIDGE**
gnome .... **NIS, GREMLIN**
go .... **WEND**
go astray .... **ABERRATE**
go astray slightly .... **ERR**
go back .... **REVERT**
go forth .... **FARE**
go hence: Lat. .... **VADE**
go on! .... **GARN, SCAT**
go shufflingly .. **MOSY, MOSEY**
goad .... **PROD, SPUR, INCITE**
goal .... **AIM, END**
goat, Alpine mountain .. **IBEX**
goat antelope .... **GORAL**
goat, Asian .... **JAGLA**

67

Goat

a
goat, genus .... **CAPRIA**
goat god .... **PAN**
goat, wild .. **TUR, IBEX, TAHR,**
TAIR, TEHR, THAR
goatsucker .... **POTOO**
gob .... **TAR**
Gobi Desert .... **SHAMO**
goblet .... **HANAP**
goblin .... **POOK, PUCA, PUCK**
goblin, Egypt .... **OUPHE**
goblin, Norse **NIS,NISSE,KOBOLD**
goby, small .... **MAPO**
GOD . see also DEITY, and see
also SPECIAL SECTION
god, Babyl. **EA, ABU, ANU, BEL**
GOD, CHIEF see CHIEF NORSE
GOD, also BABYLONIAN
CHIEF GOD
god: Chin. .... **SHEN**
god: Hebrew .... **EL**
god: Jap .... **KAMI**
god: Lat. .... **DEUS**
god of alcoholic drinks, **SIRIS**
god of Arcadia .... **PAN**
GOD OF CHAOS ... see CHAOS
god of darkness—evil, Egyp.
SET, SETH
god of dead, Hindu .... **YAMA**
god of dead, Rom. .... **ORCUS**
b
god of discord, Norse
LOK, LOKE, LOKI
god of earth, Babyl. .. **DAGAN**
GOD OF EARTH, Egyptian
see EARTH GOD
god of evil: Egyp... **SET, SETH**
god of evil, to ward off **BES,BESA**
god of fertility, Norse ... **FREY**
god of fields, flocks, forest
PAN, FAUN
god of fire ... **AGNI, VULCAN**
god of Hades ..... **DIS, PLUTO**
god of harvests ...... **CRONUS**
god of light, Norse
BALDR, BALDER, BALDUR
god of love, Gr. .... **EROS**
god of love, Rom. **AMOR, CUPID**
god of love, Vedic .... **BHAGA**
god of mirth .. **COMUS, KOMOS**
god (goddess) of mischief . **ATE**
god of michief, Norse
LOK, LOKE, LOKI
GOD OF MOON see MOON GOD
god of music .... **APOLLO**
god of north wind ... **BOREAS**
god of pleasure ..... **BES, BESA**
god of procreation, Egyp. **MIN**
god of prosperity, Teutonic **FREY**
god of revelry, Gr. ... **COMUS,**
KOMOS
god of ridicule .... **MOMUS**
GOD OF SEA .... see SEA GOD
GOD OF SKY .... see SKY GOD

c
God of Southeast Wind: Gr.
EURUS
GOD OF STORMS
see STORM GOD
GOD OF SUN .... see SUN GOD
god of thunder **THOR, DONAR**
god of Tuesday **TIU, TIW, TYR**
GOD OF UNDERWORLD
see UNDERWORLD GOD
god of war, Assyrian
ASUR, ASSUR
god of war, Babyl. . **IRA, IRRA**
god of war, Gr. .... **ARES**
god of war, Norse
TY, TYR, TYRR
god of war, Rom. .... **MARS**
god of war, Teut. .... **ER**
god of wind, Norse .. **VAYU**
god of wind, storm, Babylonian
ZU, ADAD, ADDA, ADDU
god of winds, Gr. ... **AEOLUS**
god of wisdom, Babyl.
NABU, NEBO
god of wisdom, Norse .. **ODIN**
god of youth .... **APOLLO**
god skilled with bow, Norse **ULL**
god, Sumerian .... **ABU**
god, unknown, Hindu ..... **KA**
gods, Chief Teut., Norse **AESIR**
gods: Lat. .... **DI**
d
gods, mother of .... **RHEA**
gods, mother of: Ir. **ANA, ANU**
GODS, QUEEN OF
see QUEEN OF GODS
gods, the .... **DEI, DII**
GODDESS see also SPECIAL SECT.
GODDESS, CHIEF see BABY-
LONIAN CHIEF GODDESS
goddess, cow-headed ..... **ISIS**
goddess: Latin .... **DEA**
GODDESS, MOTHER
see MOTHER GODDESS
goddess of agriculture
CERES, DEMETER
goddess of art or science . **MUSE**
goddess of astronomy **URANIA**
goddess of beauty: Norse **FREYA**
goddess of betrothal, Norse **VOR**
goddess of chase .**DIAN, DIANA**
goddess of crops, Rom. **ANNONA**
goddess of dawn, Gr. ..... **EOS**
goddess of dawn, Rom.
AURORA
goddess of dawn, Vedic .. **USAS**
goddess of dead ... **HEL, HELA**
goddess of deep, Babyl. . **NINA**
goddess of destiny, Norse
URD, URTH
goddess of destruction ... **ARA**
goddess of discord .. **ATE, ERIS**
goddess of earth, Teut. . **ERDA**

Goddess

a goddess of earth ... GE, ERDA,
GAEA, GAIA, TARI
goddess of earth: Rom.
CERES, TERRA
goddess of faith, Rom. . FIDES
goddess of fate, Rom.
NONA, PARCA
goddess of fate, Teutonic NORN
goddess of fertility ASTARTE
goddess of fertility, Anatolian
MA
goddess of field, Rom. . FAUNA
goddess of flowers, Gr. CHLORIS
goddess of flowers, Norse
NANNA
goddess of flowers, Rom. FLORA
goddess of grain
CERES, DEMETER
goddess of harvest ...... OPS
goddess of harvest, Attica
CARPO
goddess of healing ...... EIR
goddess of hearth ..... VESTA
goddess of heavens, Egyp. . NUT
goddess of hope .... SPES
goddess of hunt . DIAN, DIANA
goddess of infatuation .. ATE
goddess of justice . MA, MAAT
b goddess of love ...... VENUS,
ASTARTE, APHRODITE
goddess of love, Babylonian
ISTAR, ISHTAR
goddess of love, Norse
FREYA, FREYJA
goddess of magic .... HECATE
GODDESS OF MATERNITY
see MATERNITY GODDESS
goddess of mischief .... ATE
GODDESS OF MOON
see MOON GODDESS
goddess of nature
CYBELE, ARTEMIS
GODDESS OF NIGHT, NORSE
see NIGHT, NORSE
goddess of night: Rom.NOX,NYX
goddess of peace IRENE, EIRENE
goddess of plenty .... OPS
goddess of prosperity: Rom.
SALUS
goddess of retribution .... ATE
goddess of retribution, Gr. ARA
goddess of revenge .. NEMESIS
GODDESS OF SEA
see SEA GODDESS
goddess of seasons .... HORAE
goddess of splendor, Hindu
UMA
goddess of truth, Egypt
MA, MAAT
GODDESS OF UNDERWORLD
see UNDERWORLD GODDESS

c goddess of vegetation .. CORA,
KORE, CERES
goddess of vengeance .... ARA
goddess of victory ...... NIKE
goddess of volcanoes, Hawaii
PELE
goddess of war, Gr. .... ENYO
goddess of wisdom
ATHENA, PALLAS
goddess of woods ..... DIAN,
DIANA, ARTEMIS
goddess of youth .... HEBE
goddess, Queen .. HERA, JUNO
goddesses of destiny ... FATES
goddesses of fate, Gr. MOERAE
goddesses of fate, Norse NORNS
Goethe drama .... FAUST
Goethe heroine ...... MIGNON
golconda .... MINE
gold ...... AU, CYME, GILT
gold alloy, ancient ..... ASEM
Gold Coast Negro .... GA
Gold Coast tong. CHI, TWI, TSHI
gold-colored metal . ORMOLU
gold, cover with .... GILD
gold deposit .... PLACER
gold district-field, Afr. .. RAND
gold: Her. .... OR
gold, mosaic .... ORMOLU
gold, pert. to .... AURIC
golden .... AUREATE
d Golden Fleece keeper .. AEETES
Golden Fleece seeker .. JASON
golden in color .. DORE, DURRY
golden oriole .... PIROL
golden oriole, Eur. .... LORIOT
golden-touch king .... MIDAS
golf attendant .. CADY, CADDY
golf club ...... IRON, CLEEK,
MASHIE, PUTTER
golf club, part .... TOE
golf club socket .... HOSEL
golf hole .... CUP
golf pro .... SNEAD
golf score .... PAR
golf stroke-shot .. PUT, BAFF,
CHIP, LOFT, PUTT, DRIVE,
SCLAFF
golf term ..... LIE, PAR, TEE
golfer .... TEER
gomuti .... ARENGA
gondolier's song
BARCAROLE, BARCAROLLE
gone .... OUT, AWAY
gone by .... AGO, PAST, YORE
gonfalon .... BANNER
good-bye: Fr. ADIEU,AU REVOIR
good digestion ..... EUPEPSIA
good health, in .... PEART
"Good King" .... HAL
good news EVANGEL, EVANGILE

69

Good

a

"Good Queen Bess," name for ORIANA
good: Tagalog .... MABUTI
goods .... WARES
goods in sea .... JETSAM
goods sunk at sea
                LAGAN, LIGAN
goose barnacle genus .. LEPAS
goose cry ...... HONK, YANG
goose genus .... ANSER
goose, male .... GANDER
goose, sea .... SOLAN
goose, wild .... BRANT
gooseberry .... FABES
gopher tortoise ...... MUNGOFA
gorge .... GLUT, CHASM,
             FLUME, RAVINE
Gorgons, one of ...... MEDUSA
gorse ... WHIN, WHUN, FURZE
goshawk genus . ASTUR, BUTEO
gospel ... EVANGEL, EVANGILE
gossamer .... WEB
gossip .... EME
gossip: India .... GUP
Gottfried's sister ...... ELSA
gourd fruit .... PEPO
gourd rattle .... MARACA
gourmet .... EPICURE
gout of knee ...... GONAGRA
government .... STATE

b

government control .... REGIE
             STATISM
governor .... REGENT
governor, Mecca
        SHERIF, SHEREEF
governor, Persia ..... SATRAP
governor, Turkish .... BEY
GOWN .... see GARMENT
grace .... ADORN
Graces' mother .... AEGLE
Graces, The . AGLAIA, THALIA
graceful .... GAINLY
grackle .... DAW, MINA,
           MYNA, MYNAH
grade .... RANK, RATE,
          SORT, STEP
gradient .... SLOPE
Graf —, ship .... SPEE
graft .... CION, SCION
grafted: Her. .... ENTE
Grail, Holy, finder of .... BORS
grain .... OAT, RYE, SEED,
     WALE, SPELT, MILLET
grain beetle .... CADELLE
grain, chaff of .... BRAN
grain, coarse .... SAMP
grain given Romans . ANNONA
grain, sorghum, Ind. .. DARI,
  DORA, DURR, MILO, CHENA,
  DARRA, DARSO, DURRA,
  DHURRA, DOURAH, HEGARI

c

grain, sorghum, U. S. FETERITA
grain, stalks of ...... HAULM
grain to grind .... GRIST
gram molecule .... MOL
grammatically, describe . PARSE
grampus .... ORC
granary, India
    GOLA, GUNJ, GUNGE
grandparental .... AVAL
grandson, Adam's, Eve's . ENOS
grant .... CEDE, MISE, REMISE
grant, India, Hindu .... ENAM
grant of rights
    PATENT, CHARTER
granular snow .... FIRN, NEVE
grape .... UVA, MUSCAT,
    CATAWBA, CONCORD
grape conserve .... UVATE
grape disease .... ESCA
grape genus .... VITIS
grape jelly .... SAPA
grape juice DIBS, MUST, STUM
grape juice sirup .... SAPA
grape-like .. UVA, UVAL, UVIC
grape-like fruit .... UVA
grape refuse .... MARC
grape, white .... MALAGA
grapefruit .. POMELO, PUMELO
graphite .... KISH
grasp .... SEIZE

d

grass .... POA, REED, DARNEL
grass, Andes .... ICHU
grass, blue .... POA
grass, coarse .... REED, SEDGE
grass genus ...... AIRA, COIX,
    AVENA, STIPA
grass, kind of .... RIE
grass, marsh .... REED
    SEDGE, FESCUE
grass, N. Afr. .... ALFA
grass, pasture .... GRAMA
grass rope: Sp. .... SOGA
grass, rope-making
    MUNG, MUNJ
grass, sour .... SORREL
grass stem .... CULM
grass tuft .... HASSOCK
grass, yard, wire .... POA
grasshopper .... GRIG
grassland
    SAVANNA, SAVANNAH
grassland, S. Afr. ..... VELDT
grasslands, Western ... RANGE
grate ...... JAR, RASP, GRIDE
gratify . SATE, ARRIDE, PLEASE
grating . GRID, GRILL, GRILLE
gratuitous .... FREE
gratuity .... FEE, TIP
gratuity, customer ..... PILON
grave .... SOBER

70

a gravestone, Gr. & Rom. **STELA, STELE, STELAE, STELAI**
graving tool .... **STYLET**
Gray, botanist .... **ASA**
gray .... **OLD, HOAR, ASHEN, SLATE**
gray kingbird .... **PIPIRI**
gray, mole .... **TAUPE**
gray parrot .... **JAKO**
gray plaid, gray shawl .. **MAUD**
grayish-brown .. **DUN, TAUPE**
graze ..... **AGIST, BROWSE**
grease ... **OIL, LARD, AXUNGE**
great barracuda .... **PICUDA**
Great Barrier Island, N. Z. **OTEA**
"Great Emancipator" .... **ABE**
great: Gypsy .... **BARO**
greater ...... **MORE, MAJOR**
Greece, ancient name . **HELLAS**
Greece, modern .... **ELLAS**
greedy .... **AVID**

Greek Letters, Numbers:
Greek A, One .... **ALPHA**
Greek B, Two .... **BETA**
Greek D, Four ...... **DELTA**
Greek E, Eight .... **ETA**
Greek I, Ten .... **IOTA**
Greek M, Forty .... **MU**
b Greek N, Fifty .... **NU**
Greek O, 800 ...... **OMEGA**
Greek P, Eighty .... **PI**
Greek R, 100 .... **RHO**
Greek T, 300 .... **TAU**
Greek Z, Seven ...... **ZETA**
Greek 90 .... **KOPPA**
Greek 900 .... **SAMPI**
Gr. ancient .... **ATTIC**
Gr. assembly .... **AGORA**
Gr. athletic contest .... **AGON**
Gr. authors .... **ZENO, AESOP, HOMER, PLATO, TIMON, HESIOD, PINDAR, SAPPHO, STRABO, THALES, PLUTARCH**
Gr. city, ancient **ELIS, SPARTA**
Gr. city, word for ..... **POLIS**
Gr. colony, ancient ... **IONIA**
Gr. column ..... **DORIC, IONIC**
Gr. commonalty ...... **DEMOS**
Gr. community .... **DEME**
Gr. dialect ..... **EOLIC, AEOLIC**
Gr. district, ancient ... **ATTICA**
Gr. drama .... **MIME**
Gr. festival city ...... **NEMEA**
Gr. galley **TRIREME, UNIREME**
Gr. garment .... **CHITON**
Gr. ghost .... **KER**
GREEK GODS, GODDESSES . see SPECIAL SECTION and see GODS, GODDESSES
Gr. hero ...... **AJAX, JASON**

c Gr. historian .... **CTESIAS**
Gr. January .... **GAMELION**
Gr. legendary hero ..... **IDAS**
Gr. market place ..... **AGORA**
Gr. meeting place of voters **PNYX**
Gr. musical term .. **MESE, NETE**
Gr. myth flier .... **ICARUS**
Gr. native .... **CRETAN**
Gr. patriarch .... **ARIUS**
Gr. philosopher **PLATO, THALES**
Gr. poet ..... **ARION, HOMER, PINDAR**
Gr. poetess ... **SAPHO, SAPPHO**
Gr. poetry, simple ..... **DORIC**
Gr. priest .... **MYST**
Gr. princess .... **IRENE**
Gr. province .... **NOME**
Gr. resistance group ..... **EDES**
Gr. rose .... **CAMPION**
Gr. sculptor .... **PHIDIAS**
Gr. shield .... **PELTA**
Gr. slave .... **PENEST**
Gr. statesman ..... **ARISTIDES**
Gr. temple .... **MAOS**
Gr. theologian .... **ARIUS**
Gr. township-commune .. **DEME**
Gr. underground .... **ELAS**
Gr. vase .... **PELIKE**
d Gr. weight, old .. **MNA, MINA**
green ..... **NILE, VERD, VERT, OLIVE, RESEDA**
green chalcedony .... **JASPER**
green cheese .... **SAPSAGO**
green chrysolite ..... **PERIDOT**
green copper arsenate . **ERINITE**
green fly .... **APHID**
green: Her. .... **VERT**
Green Mountain hero ... **ALLEN**
green parrot: P. I. .... **CAGIT**
green stone ... **JADE, PERIDOT**
greenish yellow **OLIVE, RESEDA**
Greenland Eskimo ...... **ITA**
Greenland geol. div. .... **KOME**
Greenland settlement, town, base .... **ETAH**
Greenland's colonizer ... **ERIC**
greeting .. **AVE, HAIL, SALUTE**
gridiron .... **GRILL**
grief ..... **DOLOR, DOLOUR**
griffon genus .... **GYPS**
grimalkin .... **CAT**
grinding .... **MOLAR**
grindstone, Indian .... **MANO**
grit .... **SAND**
grivet .... **WAAG**
grivet monkey .... **TOTA**
grommet, naut. ..... **BECKET**
groom, India . **SAIS, SICE, SYCE**
groove .... **RUT, SCARF**

a

groove, pilaster **STRIA, STRIAE**
grooved ..... **LIRATE, STRIATE**
grope .... **FEEL**
gross .... **CRASS**
ground grain .... **MEAL**
ground wheat-husk ..... **BRAN**
groundhog .... **MARMOT**
group .... **BAND, BODY, CREW, TEAM**
group, animal ..... **NID, NYE, HERD, NIDE, COVEY, DROVE, CLUTCH**
grouper .... **MERO**
grouse .... **PTARMIGAN**
grouse, red: Scot. . **MUIRFOWL**
grove, small-tree ..... **COPSE**
grow .... **WAX, RAISE**
grow together ...... **ACCRETE**
growing out .... **ENATE**
growl .... **YAR, GNAR, YARR, SNARL**
growth, skin .... **WEN**
grub .... **LARVA**
grudge .... **SPITE**
gruel, maize .... **ATOLE**
gruesome .. **GRISLY, MACABRE**
guarantees .... **SURETIES**

b

guard .... **SENTRY**
guard, as door .... **TILE**
guardhouse .... **BRIG**
guardian, alert
ARGUS, CERBERUS
Guatemala fruit .... **ANAY**
guava .... **ARACA**
Gudrun's husband
ATLI, SIGURD
Guenon monkey .... **MONA**
guest house .... **INN**
Guiana tree .... **MORA**
guide .... **LEAD, PILOT, STEER**
guiding .... **POLAR**
guiding rule .... **MOTTO**
Guido's note .... **UT, ELA**
guild, merchants' .... **HANSE**
guillemot ...... **COOT, MURR, MURRE**
guilty .... **NOCENT**
guinea fowl's young ..... **KEET**
guinea pig .... **CAVY**
gulch: Sp. .... **ARROYO**
GULF, ... also see GAZETTEER
gulf, Ionia sea .... **ARTA**
gulf, Medit. .... **TUNIS**

c

gull ..... **MEW, SKUA, TERN, WAEG, XEMA**
gull, fork-tailed .... **XEMA**
gull genus ...... **LARI, XEMA**
gulls, of, like .... **LARINE**
gullet .... **MAW, CRAW**
gullible person .. **DUPE, GULL**
"Gulliver's Travels," men
YAHOOS
gully: Afr. .... **DONGA**
gulp .... **SWIG**
gum .... **RESIN, BALATA**
gum arabic
ACACIA, ACACIN, ACACINE
gum, astringent .... **KINO**
gum resin .... **ELEMI, LOBAN, MYRRH**
gum resin, aromatic .... **MYRRH**
gum, Somaliland ..... **MATTI**
gums .... **ULA**
gumbo .. **OCRA, OKRA, OKRO**
gumbo limbo tree ... **GOMART**
gun .... **GAT**
gun, British .... **STEN**
gun fire, burst of ..... **SALVO**
gun, Ger. .... **BERTHA**

d

gun, kind of .... **BREN**
gun lock catch .... **SEAR**
gun, P. I. .... **BARIL**
gun, slang ..... **ROD, HEATER, ROSCOE**
gun: S. Afr. ..... **ROER, ROHR**
gunny cloth .... **TAT**
gusto .... **ZEST**
gutta mixture .... **SOH**
gutta, Sumatra .... **SIAK**
guy-rope .. **STAT, STAY, VANG**
gym feat .... **KIP**
gymnast .... **TURNER**
gypsum, kind of . **YESO, GESSO, YESSO, SELENITE**
gypsy ..... **ROM, CALE, CALO, ROAMER, ROMANY**
gypsy boy .... **ROM**
gypsy gentleman .... **RYE**
gypsy girl .... **CHAI**
gypsy husband .... **ROM**
gypsy lady .... **RANI**
gypsy married woman .. **ROMI**
gypsy: Sp. .... **GITANO**
gypsy tent, camp .... **TAN**
gypsy village .... **GAV**
gypsy word .... **LAV**
gypsy word for paper, book .**LIL**

H

H .... AITCH
habit .... RUT, WONT, USAGE
habitat plant form ..... ECAD
habitation .... ABODE
habituate .... ENURE, INURE
habituated .... USED
hackney coach, Fr. ... FIACRE
hackneyed ..... STALE, TRITE
Hades ... DIS, ORCUS, PLUTO,
           SHEOL, TARTARUS
Hades: Old Eng. .... ADES
Hades, place before .. EREBUS
Hades river
     STYX, LETHE, ACHERON
hag .... CRONE
haggard .... DRAWN
Haggard, H. Rider, novel .. SHE
hail .... AVE, GREET
hail: naut. .... AVAST
hair, arrange .... COIF
hair, caterpillar .... SETA
hair coat .... MELOTE
hair-do, old .... TETE
hair dressing .... POMADE
hair, false . RAT, WIG, TOUPEE
hair, head of .... CRINE
hair, knot of .. BUN, CHIGNON
hair, lock of .... CURL, TRESS
hair net .... SNOOD
hair, remove .... EPILATE
hair, rigid .... SETA
hair, rough, matted ..... SHAG
hair shirt .... CILICE
hair, standing .... ROACH
hair unguent .... POMADE
hairless: Sp. Am. ..... PELON
hairlike process
             CILIA, CILIUM
hairy . PILAR, COMOSE, PILOSE
Haiti bandit .... CACO
Halcyone's husband .... CEYX
half .... MOIETY
half-boot .... PAC
half-breed ... MESTEE, MUSTEE
half-caste .... METIS
half-moon figure .... LUNE
half-way .... MID
halfway house .... INN
halfpenny: Brit. .... MAG
hall: Ger. .... AULA, SAAL
hallow .... BLESS
halo .... NIMB, CORONA,
     NIMBUS, AUREOLA, AUREOLE
halt .... LAME, STOP
halting place, troops' .. ETAPE
Hamilton's party .... FEDERAL

Hamite .... SOMAL, BERBER,
                      SOMALI
Hamitic language AGAO, AGAU
hamlet ... BURG, DORP, TOWN
Hamlet's castle .... ELSINORE
hammer .... KEVEL
hammer head part ...... PEEN
hammer, heavy .... MAUL
hammer, large .... SLEDGE
hammer, lead .... MADGE
hammer, tilt .... OLIVER
hamper ... CRAMP, FETTER,
                    TRAMMEL
Ham's son .... CUSH
hand .... PUD, NEAF, MANUS
hand, pert. to .... CHIRAL
hand, whist .... TENACE
handbill .... LEAF
handcuff .... MANACLE
handle .... EAR, LUG, PAW,
           ANSA, HILT, KNOB,
           HELVE, TREAT
handle, bench plane .... TOTE
handle, having ...... ANSATE
handle roughly ... PAW, MAUL
handle, scythe ...... SNATH,
           SNEAD, SNEED, SNATHE
handstone for grinding . MANO
handwriting .... SCRIPT
handwriting on the wall . MENE,
     MENE, TEKEL, UPHARSIN
hang ...... DRAPE, DROOP,
           HOVER, IMPEND
hank of twine .... RAN
Hannibal's defeat ..... ZAMA
Hannibal's victory ... CANNAE
happen ...... OCCUR, BEFALL,
           BETIDE, CHANCE
happening .... EVENT
happiness god, Jap.
           EBISU, HOTEI
harangue .... ORATE,
           TIRADE, DIATRIBE
Haran's son .... LOT
harass .... NAG, BESET
harbinger .... HERALD
harbor .... BAY, COVE,
           PORT, HAVEN
hard cash .... SPECIE
harden .... GEL, SET
     ENURE, INURE, INDURATE
hardship .... TRIAL
hardtack .... PANTILE
hardwood .... ASH, OAK
Hardy novel heroine ..... TESS
hare: dialect .... WAT

73

a hare, genus .... **LEPUS**
hare, young, 1 year .. **LEVERET**
harem ... **ZENANA, SERAGLIO**
harem room .... **ODA**
harlot of Jericho, Bibl. .. **RAHAB**
harm .**BANE, DAMAGE, INJURE**
harm: old Eng. .... **DERE**
harm: poetic .... **BALE**
harmful .... **NOCENT**
harmonize .... **ATTUNE**
harmony .. **UNISON, CONCORD**
harp, ancient .... **TRIGON**
Harp constellation ...... **LYRA**
harp guitar key .... **DITAL**
harp, kind of .... **EOLIC**
harp, Nubian .... **NANGA**
harpy, Gr. myth .... **AELLO**
harquebus projection .... **CROC**
harrow .... **DRAG**
harsh to taste .... **ACERB**
hartebeeste ..... **ASSE, TORA,
CAAMA, KAAMA**
harvest .... **REAP**
harvest festival, Rom. . **OPALIA**
harvest goddess .... **OPS**
harvest, India ... **RABI, RABBI**
has not: Old Eng. .... **NAS**
hashish .... **BHANG**
hasty pudding .... **SEPON**
HAT .... see HEADGEAR

b hat: Anglo-Ir. ...... **CAUBEEN**
hat plant .... **SOLA**
hat, straw .. **MILAN, PANAMA**
hatchet, archeol. ...... **HACHE**
hatchet, stone .... **MOGO**
hatred ... **ODIUM, AVERSION**
hatred: Buddhism ..... **DOSA**
hatter's mallet .... **BEATER**
haul tight, naut. .. **BOUSE, TRICE**
haunt, low .. **DEN, DIVE, NEST**
hautboy .... **OBOE**
haven .... **LEE**
having buttery account:
Oxford .... **BATTEL**
having holes, as cheese .. **EYEY**
having true luster when uncut
NAIF
haw!: P.I. .... **MANO**
haw, as cattle .... **HOI**
Hawaiian bird .. **IO, O-O, IIWI**
Hawaiian bird, extinct . **MAMO**
Hawaiian bird, red-tailed **KOAE**
Hawaiian blueberry ... **OHELO**
Hawaiian chant ...... **MELE**
Hawaiian cloth .. **TAPA, KAPA**
Hawaiian cudweed ... **ENAENA**
Hawaiian dance .... **HULA**
Hawaiian farewell, greeting
ALOHA
Hawaiian feather cloak . **MAMO**
Hawaiian fern .... **HEII**

c Hawaiian floral emblem **LEHUA**
Hawaiian food .... **POI**
Hawaiian food-game fish .**ULUA**
Hawaiian garland .... **LEI**
Hawaiian god .... **KANE**
Hawaiian goddess, fire .. **PELE**
Hawaiian goose .... **NENE**
Hawaiian gooseberry ... **POHA**
Hawaiian governor, 1st . **DOLE**
Hawaiian grass .... **HILO**
Hawaiian hawk .... **IO**
Hawaiian herb .... **HOLA**
Hawaiian loincloth .... **MALO**
Hawaiian musical instrument
PUA
Hawaiian porch ...... **LANAI**
Hawaiian president, 1st .. **DOLE**
Hawaiian royal chief ... **ALII**
Hawaiian shrub ...... **AKIA**
Hawaiian staple .... **POI**
Hawaiian starch ...... **APII**
Hawaiian timber tree ... **OHIA**
Hawaiian tree
KOA, AULU, ALANI, ILIAHI
Hawaiian tree, dark .... **AALII**
Hawaiian tree fern ..... **PULU**
Hawaiian vine .... **IE**
Hawaiian volcano goddess.**PELE**
Hawaiian windstorm .... **KONA**
hawk .... **KITE**

d hawk, falconry ...... **BATER**
hawk, fish .... **OSPREY**
hawk genus .... **BUTEO**
hawk-head god, Egypt . **HORUS**
hawk, India .... **SHIKRA**
hawk-like bird .... **KITE**
hawk, Scot. .... **ALLAN**
hawk, young ..... **BRANCHER**
hawks .... **IOS**
hawk's cage .... **MEW**
hawk's leash .... **LUNE**
hawthorn .... **MAY**
hawthorn berry .... **HAW**
hay, spread to dry .... **TED**
haystack .... **RICK**
hazard .. **DARE, RISK, PERIL**
hazardous .... **CHANCY**
haze: Old Eng. .... **HASE**
hazelnut .... **FILBERT**
hazy, make .. **DIM, BEDIM**
"he remains": Lat. .... **MANET**
head ..... **NOB, LEAD, PATE,
POLL, TETE, CAPUT, CHIEF,
CAPITA, LEADER, NODDLE,
NOODLE**
head covering .... **CAP, HAT,
TAM, HOOD, VEIL, BERET**
head covering, fleecy .. **NUBIA**
head, crown of .... **PATE**
head, having round ... **RETUSE**
head, membrane covering **CAUL**

a head, Moslem .... **RAIS, REIS**
head of Benjamin's clan .. **IRI**
head, shaved .... **TONSURE**
head: slang .... **NOGGIN**
head wrap .... **NUBIA, SHAWL**
headband, Gr. .... **TAENIA**
HEADDRESS
   see also HEADGEAR
headdress, bishop's
   MITER, MITRE
headgear, brimless .... **TOQUE**
headgear, clerical
   BERETTA, BIRETTA
headgear, dervish .... **TAJ**
headgear, kind of ... **PANAMA**
headgear, military ...... **SHAKO**
headgear, Moslem .. **TARBUSH, TARBOOCH, TARBOOSH, TARBOUCHE**
headgear, poetic .... **TIAR**
headgear, priest's
   BERETTA, BIRETTA
headgear, tropics
   TOPI, TERAI, TOPEE
headgear, Turk. .... **FEZ**
headland .. **RAS, CAPE, NASE, NESS, NOZE**
headless: Her. .... **ETETE**
headstrong .... **RASH**
healing goddess .... **EIR**
health, in good .... **FIT**
b health-drinking word
   SALUD, PROSIT
health resort .... **SPA**
heap .... **PILE, RAFF, RAFT**
hear ye! .... **OYES, OYEZ**
hearing: law .... **OYER**
hearken .. **HEAR, HEED, LIST, ATTEND, LISTEN**
heart .... **COR, CORE**
heart auricle . **ATRIA, ATRIUM**
heart contraction ..... **SYSTOLE**
heart, immortal, Egyp. .... **AB**
heart trouble .... **ANGINA**
heartleaf .... **MEDIC**
heartless ... **CRUEL, SARDONIC**
heat .... **WARM, CALOR**
heated to whiteness .**CANDENT**
heath .... **MOOR**
heath genus .... **ERICA**
heathen .... **PAGAN**
heathen god .... **IDOL**
heather .... **LING, ERICA**
heating apparatus, vessel.**ETNA**
heave upward .... **SCEND**
heaven .. **SION, ZION, URANO**
heaven, eagle-borne flier to
   ETANA
heaven personified: Babyl.. **ANU**
heavens, pert. to .... **URANIC**
heavenly .... **EDENIC**

c heavenly being .... **ANGEL, SERAPH, SERAPHIM**
heavenly Jerusalem **SION, ZION**
heavy blow .... **ONER**
HEBREW see also **JEWISH** and **BIBLICAL**
Hebr. Bible books .... **NEBIIM**
Hebr. Bible pronunciation aid
   GRI, KRI, KERE, KERI, QERE, QERI, QUERI
Hebr. drum .... **TOPH**
Hebr. dry measure .. **CAB, KAB**
Hebr. lyre .... **ASOR**
Hebr. measure .... **KOR, EPHA, OMER, EPHAH**
Hebr. precept .... **TORA**
HEBREW PROPHETS see
   SPECIAL SECTION, Page 196
Hebr. proselyte .... **GER**
Hebr. reclaimer .... **GOEL**
Hebr. teacher ...... **RAB, REB**
Hebr. universe .... **OLAM**
Hebrews' ancestor, legend
   EBER
Hector's mother ..... **HECUBA**
hedge plant .... **PRIVET**
hedgerow: Eng. .... **REW**
heed .... **HEAR, MIND, OBEY, RECK**
heel .... **CAD, CALX**
d height .... **STATURE**
heir .... **SON, SCION, HERITOR, LEGATEE**
held, able to be .... **TENABLE**
Helen: It. .... **ELENA**
Helen of Troy's mother . **LEDA**
Helen's lover .... **PARIS**
helical .... **SPIRAL**
Helios .... **SUN**
hell .... **HADES, SHEOL**
Hellespont swimmer . **LEANDER**
helm position .... **ALEE**
helmet, light .... **SALLET**
helmet, medieval
   ARMET, HEAUME
helmet, Rom. .... **GALEA**
helmet-shaped ...... **GALEATE**
helmet-shaped part ... **GALEA**
helmsman .... **PILOT**
Heloise's husband ... **ABELARD**
help .. **AID, ABET, BACK, TIDE, ASSIST, SUCCOR, SUCCOUR**
helper .... **AIDE**
Helvetic .... **SWISS**
hem in .... **BESET**
hemp .... **TOW, RINE, RAMIE**
hemp, Afr. .... **IFE**
hemp, India ...... **KEF, BANG, KEEF, KEIF, KIEF, BHANG, DAGGA, RAMIE**
hemp, Manila .... **ABACA**

a
hemp narcotic ...... **CHARAS**
hemp shrub, India
PUA, POOA, POOAH
hen .... **LAYER**
hen harrier, Europ. ..... **FALLER**
hence .... **SO, OFF, AWAY**
Hengist's brother ..... **HORSA**
Henry IV birthplace ...... **PAU**
"Henry IV" character ... **PETO**
"Henry V" knave ...... **NYM**
"Henry VI" character ... **IDEN**
hep .... **ONTO**
her: obs. .... **HIR**
Hera's son .... **ARES**
herald .... **USHER**
HERALDIC TERMS . see also
SPECIAL SECTION, Page 194
herald's coat .... **TABARD**
heraldic bearing **ORLE, FILLET**
heraldic cross .... **PATEE**
heraldic wreath .... **ORLE**
herb ...... **RUE, LEEK, MINT,**
MOLY, WORT, ANISE, TANSY,
YARROW, OREGANO
herb, aromatic **BASIL, DITTANY**
herb, bitter ..... **RUE, ALOE**
herb, carrot family .... **ANISE**
herb eve .... **IVA**
herb, fabulous **MOLY, PANACE**
herb, forage .... **SULLA**

b
herb genus .... **ABFA**
GEUM, RUTA, ALETRIS
herb, medicinal .. **ALOE, SENNA**
herb of grace .... **RUE**
herb, snake-charm .. **MUNGO**
herb with aromatic root **NONDO**
herb, wooly .... **POLY**
Hercules' captive .... **IOLE**
Hercules, monster slain by
HYDRA
Hercules' mother .. **ALCMENE**
herd .... **DROVE**
herd of horses ...... **CAVIYA**
herd of whales .. **GAM, POD**
herdsman, Swiss ...... **SENN**
hereditary right .... **UDAL**
hereditary factor .. **GEN, GENE**
heretic, 4th cent.
ARIAN, ARIUS
heretofore .... **ERENOW**
Hermes' mother .... **MAIA**
Hermes' son .... **PAN**
hermit . **EREMITE, ANCHORITE**
hero, legendary .... **PALADIN**
Hero's love .... **LEANDER**
heroic ...... **EPIC, EPICAL**
heroic poem **EPIC, EPOS, WORK**
heroic song .... **EDDA**
heron .... **EGRET**
heron brood, flock .... **SEDGE**
heron, kind of ...... **BITTERN**

c
herring .... **ALEC, BRIT, SILL**
herring, grayback ..... **CISCO**
herring keg .... **CADE**
herring small Eur. ...... **SPRAT**
hesitate
DEMUR, FALTER, TEETER
hesitation syllable .... **ER, UM**
Hesperides, one of .... **AEGLE**
Heyward, Du Bose, heroine. **BESS**
Hezekiah's mother ...... **ABI**
hiatus .... **GAP, LACUNA**
hickory tree ...... **SHELLBARK**
hidden ..... **INNER, ARCANE,**
COVERT, LATENT
hide .... **VEIL, CACHE**
hide of beast ..... **FELL, SKIN**
hide, thongs of .... **RIEM**
hide, undressed .... **KIP**
hides, Russian leather ... **JUFTI**
hiding in .... **PERDU**
high in pitch: mus. ...... **ALT**
high on scale .... **ELA**
high priest ...... **ELI, AARON,**
ANNAS
highest note .... **ELA**
highest point .. **APEX, ZENITH**
highway ...... **ITER, PIKE**
highway, Alaska-Canada **ALCAN**
highwayman .. **PAD, LADRONE**
hike .... **TRAMP**

d
hill .... **TOR**
hill, broad ... **LOMA, LOMITA**
hill dweller, Ceylon .... **TODA**
hill dweller, India ..... **DOGRA**
hill, flat-topped .... **MESA**
hill fort: Ir. .... **RATH**
hill, isolated .... **BUTTE**
hill, pointed .... **TOR**
hill, Rome
CAELIAN, PALATINE
hill, S. Afr. ...... **KOP, BULT**
hill: Turk. .... **DAGH**
hillock .... **TUMP**
hillside: Scot. .... **BRAE**
hilltop .... **KNAP**
hilt, sword .... **HAFT, HANDLE**
Himalayan animal .... **PANDA**
Himal. broadmouth ..... **RAYA**
Himal. ibex .... **KYL**
Himal. monkshood ..... **ATIS**
Himal. mountain .... **API**
Himal. wild goat . **KRAS, TAHR,**
TAIR, THAR
hind ...... **ROE, BACK, REAR**
hinder by fear .... **DETER**
hindrance .... **BAR, LET**
Hindu age, cycle ...... **YUGA**
Hindu ancestor .... **MANU**
Hindu ascetic .... **JOGI,**
YATI, YOGI, FAKIR,
SADHU, FAKEER

a Hindu bible .... **VEDA**
Hindu charitable gift ... **ENAM**
Hindu cymbal .... **TAL**
Hindu deity .... **DEVA, RAMA,
SIVA, SHIVA**
HINDU DEITY see also GOD
and see SPECIAL SECTION
Hindu divorce law ..... **TALAK**
Hindu female slave ..... **DASI**
Hindu festival .... **HOLI**
Hindu festival, religious . **PUJA**
Hindu gentlemen **BABU, BABOO**
HINDU GODS .... see SPECIAL
SECTION, Page 200, and
also GOD
Hindu guitar .... **BINA,
VINA, SITAR**
Hindu holy man .... **SADH**
Hindu laws, giver of ... **MANU**
Hindu legendary hero ... **NALA**
Hindu life energy .... **JIVA**
Hindu, low caste .... **KORI**
Hindu magic .... **MAYA**
Hindu mantra .... **OM**
Hindu mendicant .... **NAGA**
Hindu monastery ...... **MATH**
Hindu "Olympus" ...... **MERU**
Hindu philosophy ...... **YOGA**
Hindu poet .... **TAGORE**
Hindu prince
RAJA, RANA, RAJAH
b Hindu progenitor, myth **MANU**
Hindu queen .... **RANI, RANEE**
Hindu religious adherent
JAIN, JAINA
Hindu rites .... **ACHARA**
Hindu sacred literature .. **VEDA**
Hindu sacred word .... **OM**
Hindu scripture .... **AGAMA**
Hindu scriptures, pert. to **VEDIC**
Hindu sect, one of **SEIK, SIKH**
Hindu teacher .... **GURU**
Hindu temple .... **DEUL**
Hindu term of respect **SAHIB**
Hindu title .... **AYA, SRI**
Hindu trader
BANIAN, BANYAN
Hindu unknown god ..... **KA**
Hindu, unorthodox ... **JAINA**
Hindu widow, suicide .. **SUTTEE**
Hindu woman's garment
SARI, SAREE
Hindu word .... **OM**
Hindu writings .... **VEDA**
Hinduism, elixir
AMRITA, AMREETA
Hindustani .... **URDU**
hinge, kind of .... **BUTT**
hint .... **TIP, CLEW, POINTER**
hip ...... **COXA, ILIA, ILIAC**
hipbone, of the .... **ILIAC**

c Hippocrates' birthplace ... **KOS**
Hippodrome .... **ARENA**
hire
LET, RENT, ENGAGE, CHARTER
hired carriage .... **HACK**
hired labor: S. Afr. ..... **TOGT**
history .... **LORE**
hitherto .... **YET**
Hittites ancestor .... **HETH**
hive for bees .... **SKEP**
hives .... **UREDO**
hoard .... **AMASS, STORE**
hoarder .... **MISER**
hoarfrost .... **RIME**
hoarfrost: Eng. .... **RAG**
hoary .... **OLD, GRAY**
hoax .... **RUSE, CANARD**
hobgoblin ..... **PUCK, SPRITE**
hock, horse's ...... **GAMBREL**
hockey ball .... **ORR**
hodgepodge ... **MESS, OLIO**
hog cholera .... **ROUGET**
hog deer .... **AXIS**
hog, female .... **GILT**
hog plum, W. Ind. **AMRA, JOBO**
hog, wild .... **BOAR, PECCARY**
hog's heart, liver, etc. .. **HASLET**
Hogan, golfer .... **BEN**
hoist .... **HEAVE**
hold, as in war .... **INTERN**
d hold back .... **DETER**
hold fast: naut. ...... **BELAY**
holding .... **TENURE**
holding device .. **VISE, TONGS**
hole for molten metal .. **SPRUE**
hole in embankment .... **GIME**
hole in mold .... **GEAT**
hole-in-one .... **ACE**
holidays, Roman .... **FERIA**
HOLLAND see NETHERLANDS
SPECIAL SECTION
hollow .... **DENT, HOWE**
holly .... **HOLM, ILEX**
holly, U. S. .... **ASSI,
YAPON, YUPON, YAUPON**
holm oak .... **ILEX**
"Holy Hill," Gr. .... **ATHOS**
Holy Land city .... **DAN**
holy orders, give .... **ORDAIN**
holy water font .... **STOUP**
homage .... **HONOR**
home .... **ABODE**
home of gods, Norse .. **ASGARD**
"Home Sweet Home" author
PAYNE
homeopath school-founder
HERING
Homer's epic .... **ODYSSEY**
hominy, Indian coarse .. **SAMP**
honey .... **MEL**
honey-badger .... **RATEL**

a honey buzzard .... **PERN**
honey drink .. **MEAD, MORAT**
honey eater bird
    IAO, MOHO, MANUAO
honeybee .... **DESERET**
honeycomb, like a ... **FAVOSE**
honor .... **EXALT, REVERE**
honorarium .... **TIP**
honorary commission .. **BREVET**
Honshu bay .... **ISE**
Honshu port .... **KOBE**
hooded garment ...... **PARKA**
hoodoo .... **JINX, JYNX**
hoof .... **UNGUES, UNGUIS**
hook, bent into ..... **HAMATE**
hook, double curve .... **ESS**
hook, engine .... **GAB**
hook for pot .... **CLEEK**
hook money .... **LARI, LARIN**
hooks .... **HAMI**
hookah .... **NARGILE**
hooked .... **HAMUS,**
   HAMATE, HAMOSE, FALCATE
Hoover Dam lake ...... **MEAD**
hop-picker's basket ...... **BIN**
hope goddess, Rom. ..... **SPES**
hop plant .... **LUPULUS**
hopscotch stone ...... **PEEVER**
Horae, one of .... **DIKE,**
    EIRENE, EUNOMIA
Horeb .... **SINAI**
b horizontal stripe .... **BAR**
horizontal timber ..... **LINTEL**
horn .... **CORNU**
horn, crescent-moon ..... **CUSP**
horn, Hebr. **SHOFAR, SHOPHAR**
horn quicksilver .... **CALOMEL**
horn-shaped structure . **CORNU**
horn sounded for kill ... **MORT**
horn tissue, bit of ..... **SCUR**
horneblende .... **EDENITE**
hornless, Eng. dial. ...... **NOT**
hornless stag .... **POLLARD**
hors d'oeuvre ...... **CANAPE**
horse .. **BAY, COB, NAG, ARAB,**
   MARE, MERE, ROAN,
   MOUNT, STEED, EQUINE,
   JENNET
horse, Austral. .... **WALER**
horse, Barbary native ... **BARB**
horse blanket .... **MANTA**
horse breed .... **MORGAN**
horse, brown
   BAY, ROAN, SORREL
horse color **BAY, ROAN, SORREL**
horse dealer, Eng. .... **COPER**
horse, disease of .... **SPAVIN**
horse, draft .... **SHIRE**
horse genus .... **EQUUS**
horse: gypsy .. **GRI, GRY, GRAS**
horse-mackerel .... **SCAD**

c horse-man, myth ... **CENTAUR**
horse, piebald .... **PINTO**
horse, race .... **PACER**
horse-radish, fruit of ... **BEN**
horse, saddle .... **MOUNT**
horse, small .... **GENET,**
   GENNET, JENNET, GENETTE
horse, Sp. Am. ..... **CABALLO**
horse, swift .. **ARAB, COURSER**
horse, talking, Gr. ..... **ARION**
horse, war .... **CHARGER**
horse, white-flecked ... **ROAN**
horse, wild Asiatic ... **TARPAN**
horse, young ..... **COLT, FOAL**
horses, goddess of ..... **EPONA**
horse's sideways tread ... **VOLT**
horsehair .... **SETON**
horsemanship, art of **MANEGE**
horseshoe gripper ...... **CALK**
horseshoeing stall
   TRAVE, TREVE
Horus' mother .... **ISIS**
Hosea's wife .... **GOMER**
host .... **ARMY, HORDE**
hostelry .... **INN**
hot air chamber ...... **OVEN**
hot iron to sear ..... **CAUTER**
hot spring, eruptive .. **GEYSER**
Hottentot .... **NAMA**
hourly .... **HORAL**
d house **ROOF, VILLA, COTTAGE**
house, like a .... **DOMAL**
house, mud, Afr. ..... **TEMBE**
house urn: Rom. ... **CAPANNA**
housefly genus ...... **MUSCA**
housefly genus, lesser **FANNIA**
household **MENAGE, MAINPOST**
household god .... **LAR, LARES**
howl .... **ULULATE**
howling monkey **MONO, ARABA**
hub .. **NAVE, BOSTON, CENTER**
hubbub .. **ADO, STIR, TUMULT**
hue .... **COLOR, TINGE**
huge .... **VAST, ENORM**
Huguenot leader ..... **ADRETS**
hull .... **POD, HUSK**
humble .... **ABASE**
hummingbird
   AVA, TOPAZ, COLIBRI
humorist .... **WIT**
humpback salmon
   HADDO, HOLIA
Humphreys, Mrs. (pseudo.)
   RITA
hundred .... **CENTUM**
hundredweight ...... **CENTAL**
Hungarian dog .... **PULI**
Hungarian hero .... **NAGY**
Hungarian king .... **BELA**
Hungarian people ... **MAGYAR**
Hungarian pianist ... **SANDOR**

a Hungarian playwright **MOLNAR**
Hungarian violinist .... **AUER**
Huns, king of
      ATLI, ETZEL, ATTILA
hunt, Ind. .... **SHIKAR**
hunter ...... **ORION, NIMROD**
hunter, India .... **SHIKARI**
hunting cry . **HO, YOI, TOHO,**
    HALLOO, YOICKS, TALLY-
    HO
hunting hat .... **TERAI**
hunting hound .... **ALAN**
huntress .... **ATALANTA**
huntsman .... **JAGER**
HUNTSMAN'S CRY see **HUNT-**
    ING CRY
hup: army .... **ONE**
hurdy-gurdy ..... **LIRA, ROTA**
hurry .... **HIE, HASTEN**
hurt .... **MAR, ACHE, LESION**

c hurt: old Eng. .... **DERE**
hurtful .... **MALEFIC**
husband's brother .... **LEVIR**
hush .... **SH, HSH**
husk, cereal .... **BRAN**
hut, India .... **BARI**
hut, Mex. .... **JACAL**
hydrate, as lime ..... **SLAKE**
hydraulic pump .... **RAM**
hydrocarbon . **TOLAN, ETHANE,**
    OCTANE, RETENE, TERPENE
hydrogen compound ... **IMINE**
hydrogen isotope ... **PROTIUM**
hymn .... **ODE**
hymn of praise ..... **ANTHEM**
hypnotic state ...... **TRANCE**
hypothetical force
    OD, BIOD, ELOD, ODYL
hypothetical force of ... **ODIC**
hyson .... **TEA**

I .... **EGO**
"I have found it" .... **EUREKA**
"I love": Lat. .... **AMO**
Iago's wife .... **EMILIA**
Iberians .... **IBERI, IBERES**
b ibex .... **KYL, TUR, KAIL**
Ibsen character ... **ASE, NORA**
ice block, glacial ... **SERAC**
ice mass .... **BERG, FLOE**
ice, slushy ...... **SISH, LOLLY**
iced .... **GLACE**
Iceland epic, literature, tales
    EDDA
Icelandic narrative ..... **SAGA**
icy .... **GELID**
"id —" (that is) .... **EST**
idea, Plato .... **EIDOS**
ideal .... **UTOPIAN**
ideal republic, imaginary
    OCEANA
ideal state .... **UTOPIA**
identical .... **ONE, SAME**
ideology .... **ISM**
idiocy .... **ANOESIA**
idiot .... **AMENT, CRETIN**
idle .... **OTIANT, OTIOSE**
idle, to be ...... **LAZE, LOAF**
idol: archaic .... **PAGOD**
idol: philos. .... **EIDOLON**
idolatrous .... **PAGAN**
ids, pert. to .... **IDIC**
Idumaea .... **EDOM**
if ever .... **ONCE**
if not .... **ELSE**
ignoble .... **BASE**

ignominy .... **SHAME**
ignorance, Hindu philos. **TAMAS**
ignorant .. **STUPID, UNAWARE**
ignore .... **ELIDE**
Igorot's neighbor tribesman **ATA**
ill .... **EVIL**
d ill-will .... **SPITE, RANCOR**
illumination unit ...... **LUX**
illusion .... **CHIMERA**
illusory riches .... **MINE**
image .... **IDOL,**
    IDOLON, IDOLUM, EIDOLON
image, pert. to ...... **ICONIC**
image, religious .. **ICON, IKON**
imagine: arch. .... **WIS**
imbecile .... **AMENT,**
    ANILE, CRETIN
imbibe .... **SIP, GULP, DRINK**
imitate ... **APE, MIME, MIMIC**
imitation .... **MIMESIS**
imitation gems .... **PASTE**
immature seed .... **OVULE**
immature: zool. ..... **NEANIC**
immeasurable .... **BOUNDLESS**
immediately ..... **NOW, ANON**
immense .... **VAST**
immerse .. **DIP, DUNK, DOUSE**
immigrant, Greek ..... **METIC**
immunizing substance
    SERUM, HAPTEN, HAPTENE
imou pine .... **RIMU**
impair .. **MAR, DAMAGE, SPOIL**
impart .... **GIVE, LEND**
impartial .... **EVEN**
impede ...... **ESTOP, HAMPER**
impel .... **URGE**

Impertinent

a
impertinent ..... **PERT, SAUCY**
IMPLEMENT .... see also **TOOL**
implement, pounding .. **PESTLE**
implement to skid logs .. **TODE**
implied .... **TACIT**
import .... **SENSE**
important, critically ... **VITAL**
importune .... **URGE**
impose .... **LAY**
impost .... **TAX**
imposture .... **SHAM**
impoverish .... **IMPOOR**
impressionist painter .. **DEGAS**
      MANET, MONET, RENOIR
imprison .... **IMMURE**
improve .... **AMEND**
improvise music .... **VAMP**
impudence .... **LIP,**
      BRASS, CHEEK, NERVE
impure metal product .. **MATTE**
in addition .. **TOO, ALSO, YET**
in agreement .... **UNITED**
in disagreement .... **OUT**
in half, in — .... **TWO**
"in medias —" .... **RES**
in name only ...... **NOMINAL**
in same place .... **IBID**
in so far as .... **QUA**
in the know .... **AWARE**
in the matter of .... **INRE**
in the past .... **OVER**
b
in the very near future. **ANON**
in unison .... **ONE**
in very truth .... **AMEN**
inability to hear ..... **ASONIA**
inactive .... **INERT**
inadequate .... **SCANT**
inborn .... **NATIVE**
incarnation, Hindu .... **RAMA,**
      AVATAR
incense ingredient
      GUM, SPICE, STACTE
incense receptacle, Rom.**ACERRA**
incense, Somali ...... **MATTI**
incentive .... **GOAD, MOTIVE**
incessantly .... **EVER**
inch, .001 of .... **MIL**
incidentally .... **OBITER**
incinerate .... **CREMATE**
incite ..... **EGG, PROD, URGE,**
      IMPEL, SET ON, SUBORN
inciter .... **EGGER**
inclination .... **BENT**
incline .. **TEND, SLOPE, TREND**
inclined .... **APT, PRONE**
inclined way .... **RAMP**
income, annual, Fr. .... **RENTE**
incompletely .... **SEMI**
inconsiderable ..... **NOMINAL**
increase .... **WAX, RISE**
incrustation .... **SCAB**

c
incursion, predatory .... **RAID**
indeed: Ir. ...... **ARU, AROO**
indentation
      CRENA, CRENAE, CRENELET
index mark .... **FIST**
INDIA, INDIAN .... see also
      SPECIAL SECTION and see
      also HINDU
India farmer .... **MEO**
India minstrel .... **BHAT**
India native chief .... **SIRDAR**
India native servant ... **MATY**
India: poet. .... **IND**
India, swamp belt of .. **TERAI**
INDIAN .. see also page 192
Indian .... **SAC**
INDIAN, ALGONQUIN .... see
      page 192
Indian, Arawak ...... **ARAUA**
Indian, Arikara .... **REE**
Indian, Athapasca ..... **TAKU**
Indian buzzard .... **TESA**
Indian corn .... **MAIZE**
Indian corn: N. Z. ... **KANGA**
Indian elk .... **SAMBAR**
Indian farmer, Fla. .. **CALUSA**
Indian in Chaco ...... **TOBA**
Indian mahogany tree .. **TOON**
Indian mulberry **AL, AAL, ACH**
Indian of Jalisco ...... **CORA**
Indian of Keresan ...... **SIA**
Indian of Mex., scattered **CORA**
d
Indian ox .... **ZEBU**
Indian, Panamint ...... **KOSO**
INDIAN, PLAINS . see page 193
Indian race .... **JAT**
Indian shell currency
      ULO, UHLLO
INDIAN, SIOUAN see page 193
Indian, S. Peru ..... **CHANCA**
INDIAN TREE.see **TREE, INDIA**
Indian, warlike ...... **APACHE**
Indian weight ..... **SER, TOLA**
Indian, whaler .... **HOH**
Indian yellow .... **PURI,**
      PIURI, PURREE
indicating succession **ORDINAL**
indict .... **ARRAIGN**
indifferent to pain
      STOIC, STOICAL
indigo plant .... **ANIL**
indistinct, make ...... **BEDIM**
indite .... **PEN, WRITE**
individual .... **ONE, SELF**
Indo-Chin. native **LAO,MRU,TAI**
Indo-Chin. tribe **TAI,LAOS,SHAN**
Indo-Chin. tribes ...... **MOI**
Indo-European **ARYA, ARYAN**
Indo-Malayan animal .. **NAPU**
indolent ...... **OTIOSE, SUPINE**
Indonesian ..... **ATA, NESIOT**

a

induce .... LEAD
Indus tribesman .... GOR
ineffectual .... VAIN
inelastic .... LIMP
inert .... SUPINE
infatuation .... ATE
infertile moor .... LANDE
infinity .... OLAM
infirm .... ANILE, SENILE
inflamed, be .... RANKLE
inflammable liquid .. ACETONE
inflammation: med. .. ANGINA
inflexible ...... IRON, RIGID
inflict .... DEAL, IMPOSE
inflorescence RACEME, SPADIX
inflorescence, racemose AMENT
influence .... AFFECT
informer: slang .... NARK
infusion .... TEA
ingenuous .... NAIVE
inhabitant .... ITE
inhabitant of a town ..... CIT
inheritance .... ENTAIL
inheritor .... LEGATEE
initiate .. OPEN, BEGIN, START
initiate, Gr. ... EPOPT, EPOPTA
injure ... MAR, HARM, MAIM
injury ..... LESION, TRAUMA
inlaid .... MOSAIC
inlaid decoration ...... BUHL

b

inlet .. ARM, BAY, RIA, FIORD
inlet: Dutch .... ZEE
inlet, Orkneys .... VOE
inn, ... KHAN,
    HOSTEL, POSADA, HOSPICE
inn, "Canterbury Tales" TABARD
inn, Oriental .... SERAI
inn, Turkish .... IMARET
inner .... ENTAL
inner meaning .. CORE, HEART
inner parlor: Scot. ...... BEN
innkeeper PADRONE, BONIFACE
insect .. ANT, BEE, BUG, DOR,
    FLY, FLEA, GNAT, MITE,
    APHID, CADEW, EMESA,
    BEETLE, CADDIS, CICADA,
    CICALA, MANTIS
insect, adult .... IMAGO
insect body
    THORAX, THORACES
insect, immature ...... PUPA,
    LARVA, INSTAR
insect mature .... IMAGO
insect order .... DIPTERA
insect, plant sucking .. APHID
insect, ruinous APHID, BORER
insertion mark .... CARET
inset .... PANEL
insidious .... SLY
insincere talk .... CANT
insipid, become .... PALL

c

insist .... URGE, PRESS
inspire .... IMBUE
install .... INSTATE
instance .... CASE
instant .... MO, TRICE
instar .. PUPA, IMAGO, LARVA
instigate .. EGG, ABET, INCITE
instruct ..... BRIEF, EDUCATE
INSTRUMENT .. see also MUS-
    ICAL INSTRUMENT
instrument, Afr. reed
    GORA, GORAH, GOURA
instrument, Chin. ancient KIN
instrument, Hebr. ... TIMBREL
instrument, India ..... RUANA
instrument, Jap. ..... SAMISEN
instrument, lutelike BANDORE
instrument, lyrelike ... KISSAR
instrument, math. ... SECTOR
instrument, medieval .. ROCTA
instrument, naut.
    PELORUS, SEXTANT
instrument, Sp. ..... CASTANET
instrument, stringed ... LYRE,
    NABLA, REBAB, REBEC,
    SAROD, SITAR, VIOLA,
    CITHER, CITHARA, CITH-
    ERN, CITTERN, GITTERN
instrument, surveying TRANSIT
instrumentality MEDIA, MEDIUM

d

insulate .... ISLE
insult .... CAG
insurgent .... REBEL
intact .... WHOLE
intellect .... MIND,
    NOUS, MAHAT, REASON
inter .... BURY, INHUME
intercharged ..... PERMUTED
interdict .... BAN
interferometer ...... ETALON
interior, ancient temple CELLA
interjection for silence .... TST
interlace .... WEAVE
interlock .... LINK
international language RO, IDO
inter. money unit .... BANCOR
international pact ... ENTENTE
interpret .... REDE
intersect .... MEET
interstice, small
    AREOLA, AREOLE
interstices, with .... AREOLAR
intervening: law ..... MESNE
interweave .. TWINE, RADDLE
intimidate AWE, COW, DAUNT
intone .... CHANT
intoxicant: India ...... SOMA
intoxicated .... SOSH
intricate .... DEDAL, DAEDAL,
    GORDIAN

a intrigue .... CABAL
introduce
  BROACH, INSERT, PRESENT
Introducer of jetties for deepening .... EADS
Inundation .... SPATE
inveigle ...... LURE, ENTICE
inventor, claim of rights PATENT
inventor, elevator .... OTIS
inventor, sewing machine HOWE
inventor, steam engine WATT
invest ...... ENDOW, ENDUE,
  INDUE, CLOTHE, ORDAIN
Invested .... CLAD
investigate .... PROBE
investigator .... TRACER
invite .... ASK, BID
involve ENTAIL, ENTRAMMEL
Io butterfly .... KIHO
iodine source .... KELP
ion, negative .... ANION
ion, positive .... CATION
Ionian city .... TEOS
iota .... JOT, MITE
Iowa college town ..... AMES
ipecac source .... EVEA
IRAN .. see also PERSIAN
Iran, former part of ... ELAM
Iranian ...... TAT, KURD

b Iranian Turk .... SART
irascible .... TESTY
irate .... MAD
Ireland ...... EIRE, ERIN
Ireland, old name ..... IERNE
Ireland personified .... IRENA
iridescent gem .... OPAL
iris .... FLAG
iris, Florentine, European ORRIS
iris, layer of .... UVEA
iris, of a layer ...... UVEAL
iris root .... ORRIS
IRISH .. see also IRELAND
Irish .... ERSE
Ir. alphabet, early
  OGAM, OGUM
Ir. ancestor IR, MIL, ITH, MILED
Ir. assembly .... DAIL
Ir. church .... KIL
Ir. city, ancient ...... TARA
Ir. clan, ancient ...... SEPT
Ir. competitive meet .... FEIS
Ir. crowning stone, — Fail LIA
Ir. dramatist .... SYNGE
Ir. exclamation .... ARU,
  AROO, ARRA, WHIST, WURRA
Ir. fairies .... SHEE
Ir. family .... CINEL
Ir. Free State .... EIRE
Irish-Gaelic .... ERSE
Ir. goddess, battle BADB, BODB

c **IR. GODS' MOTHER** see page 200
Ir. kings' home .... TARA
Ir. law, tribe .... CINEL
Ir. lower house parliament DAIL
Ir. nobleman .... AIRE
Ir. poet
  AE, COLUM, MOORE, YEATS
Ir. rebel group .... IRA
Ir. tribe .... SIOL
Ir. writing .... OGAM, OGHAM
Irishman .. AIRE, CELT, MICK
iron disulfide .... PYRITE
iron, pert. to .... FERRIC
ironwood ...... ACLE, COLIMA
irony .... SATIRE
Iroquoian .... ERIE
Iroquois demon .... OTKON
irrational number ...... SURD
irregularity .... JOG
irrigation ditch FLUME, SLUICE
irritate .... VEX, GALL, RILE,
  NETTLE, RANKLE
Isaac's son EDOM, ESAU, JACOB
Ishmael .... PARIAH
Ishmael, son of ...... DUMAH
Ishmael's mother ..... HAGAR
isinglass .... MICA
Isis, husband of ...... OSIRIS
ISLAM .... see MOSLEM

d island .... OE, AIT, CAY, KAY,
  KEY, EYOT, HOLM, ILOT,
  ISLE, ATOLL, ISLET, ISLOT
ISLAND, AEGEAN .... see
  GAZETTEER
Island, Argyll .... IONA
island, coral .... ATOLL
island, Dodecanese . COO, KOS,
  CASO, LERO, SIMI
island, Great Barrier ... OTEA
island, Gr. (fine marble) PAROS
island, Gr., pert. to ... CRETAN
island, inhabiting an .. NESIOTE
ISLAND, INNER HEBRIDES
  see HEBRIDES GAZETTEER
island, Ionian .... ZANTE
island, Micronesia ... PONAPE
island near Ireland .... ARAN
island, near Italy .... CAPRI
island off Scotland .... IONA,
  ARRAN
island, Riga Gulf ...... OESEL
island, river AIT, EYOT, HOLM
island, South Seas .... ARU,
  TAITI, TAHITI, OTAHEITE
island, west of Sumatra .. NIAS
islands, Gulf of Bothnia ALAND
islands, Irish .... ARAN
islands, off Timor ..... LETI
Isle of Man, pert. to ... MANX
islet .... AIT, CAY, HOLM
isolate .... ENISLE

Israel .... **JACOB**
ISRAEL, KING OF ... see KING
             OF ISRAEL
ISRAELITE .. see also HEBREW
     and BIBLICAL
ISRAELITE JUDGE .... see
          BIBLICAL JUDGE
ISRAELITE KING .. see KING
            OF ISRAEL
Israelite tribe .... **DAN**
Israelites .... **SION, ZION**
issue EMIT, EMERGE, EMANATE
isthmus .... **NECK**
istle fiber ...... **PITA, PITO**
it proceeds: music ...... **VA**
ITALIAN WORDS: (accent marks
omitted throughout)
   arts .... **ARTES**
   article .... **LA**
   canal (s) **CANALE, CANALI**
   chest .... **CASSO**
   custom house ..... **DOGANA**
   day-breeze .... **ORA**
   dear .... **CARA, CARO**
   dough .... **PASTA**
   drink .... **BEVERE**
   enough .... **BASTA**
   evening .... **SERA**
   enthusiasm .... **ESTRO**
   feast .... **FESTINO**
   field .... **CAMPO**
   food .... **PASTO**
   from beginning .... **DACAPO**
   gentleman .... **SER**
   goodby .... **ADDIO**
   gondola cabin ...... **FELZE**
   hamlet .... **CASAL, CASALE**
   hair .... **PELO**
   hand .... **MANO**
   harbor .... **PORTO**
   harp .... **ARPA**
   hatred .... **ODIO**
   Helen .... **ELENA**
   holiday .... **FESTA, FESTE**
   host .... **OSTE**
   Italy .... **ITALIA**
   judge .... **PODESTA**
   lady .... **DONNA, SIGNORA**
   lake .... **LAGO**
   little .... **POCO**
   love .... **AMORE**
   lover .... **AMOROSO**
   mother .... **MADRE**
   mountain peak ...... **CIMA**
   nine .... **NOVE**
   ninth .... **NONO**

   one .... **UNO**
   paste .... **PASTA**
   peak .... **CIMA**
   pronoun .... **MIA**
   right .... **DESTRO**
   Rome .... **ROMA**
   sign .... **SEGNO**
   somebody .... **UNO**
   street .... **CALLE**
   three .... **TRE**
   time .... **TEMPO**
   tour .... **GIRO**
   town ...... **CASAL, CASALE**
   you .... **TU**
   voice .... **VOCE**
   well .... **BENE**
   with .... **CON**

Italian actress .... **DUSE**
It., ancient
     ITALI, OSCAN, SABINE
It. astronomer ...... **GALILEO**
It. author .... **SILONE**
It. car .... **FIAT**
It. cathedral city .... **MILAN**
It. commune .... **ESTE**
It. composer .... **BOITO,**
    GUIDO, VERDI, ROSSINI
It. day breeze .... **ORA**
It. family .... **ESTE,**
    CENCI, DORIA, MEDICI
It. family royal name .... **ESTE**
It. gambling game ..... **MORA**
It. gentleman .... **SER**
It. guessing game ..... **MORA**
It. lady ..... **DONA, SIGNORA**
It. millet ...... **BUDA, MOHA**
It. painter .... **RENI,**
    LIPPI, VINCI, ANDREA,
    CRESPI, GIOTTO
It. poet
   DANTE, TASSO, ARIOSTO
It. resort .... **LIDO**
It. rice dish .... **RISOTTO**
It.: Rome .... **ROMA**
It. sculptor .... **LEONI**
It. singer .... **AMATO**
It. title, early .... **SER**
It. university city **BARI, PADUA**
It. violin maker ..... **AMATI**
It. wine .... **ASTI**
Italy .... **ITALIA**
itch .... **PSORA**
itemize .... **LIST**
ivory nut ...... **ANTA, TAGUA**
ivy crowned ...... **HEDERATED**
ivy thicket .... **TOD**

J

jack in cribbage .... **NOB**
jack-in-the-pulpit **ARAD, AROID**
jack tree .... **JACA**
jackal, Afr. .... **THOS**
jackal, India .... **KOLA**
jackal, N. Afr. .... **DIEB**
jackdaw .... **DAW**
jackdaw: Scot. .... **KAE**
JACKET: see also **GARMENT**
jacket .. **ETON, JUPE, BOLERO**
jacket, armor .... **ACTON**
jacket, Malay .... **BAJU**
Jackson heroine .. **RAMONA**
Jacob's brother .. **EDOM, ESAU**
Jacob's son ..**DAN, GAD, ASER,**
LEVI, ASHER
Jacob's twin brother .... **ESAU**
Jacob's wife .. **LEAH, RACHEL**
jaeger gull ..... **SKUA, ALLAN**
jagged line .... **ZAG, ZIG**
jai alai .... **PELOTA**
Jamashid .... **YIMA**
James II daughter ..... **ANNE**
Janizaries, Chief of ..... **DEY**
JAPANESE: see also **SPECIAL**
SECTION
Jap. aborigine ... **AINO, AINU**
Jap. admiral .... **ITO**
Jap.-Am. .... **ISSEI,**
KIBEI, NISEI, SANSEI
Jap. army reserve ..... **HOJU**
Jap. army second line ... **KOBI**
Jap. art of self-defense **JUDO**
Jap. badge, family ..... **MON**
Jap. badge, imperial **KIRIMON**
Jap. beer, rice .... **SAKE, SAKI**
Jap. beverage .... **SAKE**
Jap. box, girdle .... **INRO**
Jap. bush clover .... **HAGI**
Jap. cedar .... **SUGI**
Jap. celery-like vegetable **UDO**
Jap. cherry .... **FUJI**
Jap. clogs .... **GETA**
Jap. deer .... **SIKA**
Jap. drama ...... **NO, KABUKI**
Jap. emperor's title ... **TENNO**
Jap. festival .... **BON**
Jap. fish .... **TAI, FUGU**
Jap. food, seaweed
KOBU, KOMBU
Jap. gods .... **KAMI**
Jap. happiness god
EBISU, HOTEI
Jap. harp .... **KOTO**
Jap. herb, stout .... **UDO**

Jap. Immigrant .... **ISSEI**
Jap. mile measure .... **RI**
Jap. monastery .... **TERA**
Jap. national park ..... **ASO**
Jap. naval station ..... **KURE**
Jap. news agency ... **DOMEI**
Jap. nobleman .... **KUGE**
Jap. outcast
ETA, YETA, RONIN
Jap. outer garment
MINO, HAORI, KIMONO
Jap. parliament .... **DIET**
Jap. perfecture .... **FU**
Jap. persimmon .... **KAKI**
Jap. plant .... **UDO**
Jap. plane .... **ZERO**
Jap. primitive .... **AINO, AINU**
Jap. province, old ... **ISE, KAI**
Jap. receptacle .... **INRO**
Jap. salad plant .... **UDO**
Jap. salmon .... **MASU**
Jap. sash, kimono .... **OBI**
Jap. school of painting **KANO**
Jap. ship name .... **MARU**
Jap. sock .... **TABI**
Jap. statesman .... **ITO**
Jap. straw cape .... **MINO**
Jap. sword .. **CATAN, CATTAN**
Jap. vegetable ... **UDO, GOBO**
Jap. verse .... **UTA**
Jap. village .... **MURA**
Jap. volcano .... **FUJI**
Jap. writing .... **KANA**
Japheth, son of .... **GOMER**
jar ...... **EWER, OLLA, CRUSE**
jar ring .... **LUTE**
jar, wide-mouthed ..... **OLLA**
jargon **CANT, ARGOT, PATOIS**
Jason's father .... **AESON**
Jason's 2d wife ...... **CREUSA**
Jason's ship .... **ARGO**
Jason's wife .... **MEDEA**
jaunty .... **PERK**
Java plum: P. I. ..... **DUHAT**
Javanese carriage ..... **SADO**
Javanese language **KAVI, KAWI**
Javanese poison tree ... **UPAS**
javelin, Afr. **ASSAGAI, ASSEGAI**
javelin game .. **JERID, JEREED**
javelin, Rom. .... **PILUM**
jeer .... **GIBE, SCOFF**
jeer at ...... **TAUNT, DERIDE**
Jehoshaphat, father of ... **ASA**
Jehovah .... **GOD**
Jehovah: Hebr. .... **JAH,**
JAVE, JAVEH, YAHWEH

84

a jejune .. **DRY, ARID, BARREN**
jelly base .... **PECTIN**
jelly fruit .... **GUAVA**
jelly, meat .... **ASPIC**
jeopardize .... **ENDANGER**
Jericho, land opposite .. **MOAB**
jersey, woollen ...... **SINGLET**
Jerusalem, ancient name **SALEM**
Jerusalem: poet. ...... **ARIEL**
jest .... **JAPE**
jester ...... **MIME, BUFFOON**
jet, U.S. ..... **SABRE, SCORPION**
Jether, son of .... **ARA**
jetty .... **MOLE**
Jew .... **SEMITE**
JEWEL .... see GEM, STONE
jewelry setting .... **PAVE**
jewels, adorn with ..... **BEGEM**
JEWISH .. see also HEBREW
Jewish ascetic ...... **ESSENE**
Jewish benediction ... **SHEMA**
Jewish bride .... **KALLAH**
Jewish ceremony **SEDAR, SEDER**
Jewish feast of tabernacles
SUCCOTH
Jewish festival **PURIM, SEDER**
Jewish law, body of .. **TALMUD**
Jewish marriage contract
KETUBA
Jewish offering ..... **CORBAN**
b Jewish prayer book . **MAHZOR**
Jewish scholar .... **RAB**
Jewish sect, ancient .. **ESSENES**
Jewish teacher ... **REB, RABBI**
Jewish title of honor
RAB, GAON
Jezebel's husband ..... **AHAB**
Joan of Arc's victory **ORLEANS**
Job's-tears .... **COIX**
jog .... **TROT, NUDGE**
John: Gaelic, Scot. **IAN, EOAN**
John: Ir. .... **EOIN, SEAN**
John: Russ. .... **IVAN**
johnny-cake .... **PONE**
Johnson, Dr., hero .. **RASSELAS**
join ..... **LINK, PAIR, SEAM,**
WELD, YOKE, MERGE,
UNITE, ATTACH
join corners ... **MITER, MITRE**
join wood .... **RABBET**
joining bar .... **YOKE**
joint **HIP, KNEE, NODE, HINGE**
joint part **TENON, MORTISE**
joke with **KID, RIB, JAPE, JOSH**
joker .... **WAG, WIT**
Jordan city, ancient region
PETRA
Joseph's father .... **JACOB**
Joseph's nephew .... **TOLA**

c Joshua tree .... **YUCCA**
Joshua's father .... **NUN**
jostle .... **JOG, ELBOW**
jot .... **IOTA, TITTLE**
journey .... **ITER, RIDE, TOUR,**
TREK, TRIP, TRAVEL
journey in circuit ...... **EYRE**
joy ..... **DELIGHT, RAPTURE**
joyous .... **GLAD**
Judah, city in ... **ADAR, ENAM**
Judah's son ..... **ER, ONAN**
Judaism scriptures
TORA, TORAH
Judge .. **DEEM, RATE, ARBITER**
JUDGE, BIB. ... see BIBLICAL
JUDGE
judge in Hades ...... **MINOS**
judge of dead, Egypt ... **OSIRIS**
judge's bench .... **BANC**
judge's chamber .... **CAMERA**
judges' rule, Israel **KRITARCHY**
judgment, Fr. law ...... **ARRET**
JUDICIAL see also LEGAL, LAW
judicial assembly ..... **COURT**
jug, large beer ...... **RANTER**
jug shaped like man ... **TOBY**
jug, wide-mouthed .... **EWER**
juice .... **SAP**
juice, thickened .... **RHOB**
jujitsu .... **JUDO**
jujube .... **BER, ELB**
Jules Verne character .. **NEMO**
d Juliet's betrothed ..... **PARIS**
Juliet's father, family **CAPULET**
jumble .... **PI, PIE, MESS**
jump: music .... **SALTO**
jumping disease, Malay .. **LATA**
jumping rodent ..... **JERBOA**
juncture, line of ...... **SEAM**
June bug .... **DOR**
Jungfrau's site .... **ALPS**
jungle clearing .... **MILPA**
juniper .... **GORSE,**
SAVIN, SABINE, SAVINE
juniper, Europ. .... **CADE**
juniper tree, Bibl. **EZEL, RETEM**
Jupiter .... **JOVE**
Jupiter's moon, inner .... **IO**
Jupiter's wife ... **HERA, JUNO**
jurisdiction .... **VENUE**
jurisdiction, old Eng. **SOC, SOKE**
jurisprudence .... **LAW**
jury list .... **PANEL**
jury, writ summoning **VENIRE**
just .... **MORAL**
justice, goddess of . **MA, MAAT**
jute .... **DESI**
Jutlander .... **DANE**
jutting rock .... **TOR**
juxtaposition, place in **APPOSE**
lynx .... **SPELL**

K

Kaffir language .... XOSA
Kaffir tribe .... ZULU
Kaffir war club .... KIRI
Kaffir warrior .... IMPI
Kalmuck ..... ELEUT, ELEUTH
Kandh language .... KUI
kangaroo, male ..... BOOMER
kangaroo, young ...... JOEY
Katmandu's country ... NEPAL
kava .... AVA
kava bowl .... TANOA
Kaw .... AKHA
Keats poem-1820 ... LAMIA
keel .... CAREEN
keel, at right angle to ABEAM
keel block wedge ... TEMPLET
keel, having no ...... RATITE
keel, kind of .... FIN
keel, part of .... SKEG
keel-shaped part
                  CARINA, CARINAE
keen ACUTE, SHARP, ASTUTE
keep account of .... TAB
keepsake .... TOKEN
keeve .... KIVER

b Kentucky coffee tree . CHICOT
Kentucky college ..... BEREA
kerchief .... MADRAS
kernel .... NUT
ketch, Levant .... SAIC
ketone, liquid ...... ACETONE
ketone, oily .... CARONE
kettledrum .. NAKER, ATABAL,
    ATTABAL, TIMPANI, TIM-
    PANO, TYMPANO
key .... ISLE
key fruit .... SAMARA
key notch .... WARD
key part .... BIT
key-shaped ...... URDE, URDY
keyed up .... AGOG
Khedive's estate ..... DAIRA
kid, undressed .... SUEDE
kidney .... NEER
kidney bean .... BON
kidneys, pert. to ..... RENAL
killer whale .... ORCA
kiln ...... OST, OAST, OVEN
kiloliter .... STERE
kind
    ILK, SORT, GENRE, SPECIES
kind: Gr. .... GENOS
kindle: dialect .... TIND
kindly .... BENIGN
kindness .... LENITY
kindred .... SIB

c king .... REX, REY, REGES
king —, cartoon character
                         AROO
King Alfred's city: abbr. .. LON
king, Amalekite .... AGAG
King Arthur's abode
  AVALON, AVALLON, CAMELOT
King Arthur's burial place
          AVALON, AVALLON
King Arthur's court CAMELOT
King Arthur's father .. UTHER
King Arthur's fool .. DAGONET
King Arthur's lance ..... RON
King Arthur's mother IGERNA,
    IGERNE, YGERNE, IGRAINE
King Arthur's queen
       GUINEVER, GUINEVERE
KING, BIBLICAL .... see
             BIBLICAL KING
King Ethelred "The —"
                     UNREADY
king, Gr. .... MINOS
King Gradlon's capital .... IS
king, Hebrew .... HEROD
king, Midianite .... REBA
king, mythical .... MIDAS
king of beasts .... LION

d King of Colchis' daughter
                        MEDEA
king of Crete .... MINOS
king of elves ...... ERLKING
king of gods, Egypt
        AMEN, AMON, AMUN
king of Greece, ancient MINOS
king of Israel ... AHAB, ELAH,
        OMRI, SAUL, NADAB
king of Jews .... HEROD
king of Judah ... ASA, AHAZ,
             AMON, UZZIAH
king of Judea .... HEROD
king of Naples ...... MURAT
king of Persia ...... CYRUS
king of Sodom .... BERA
king, pert. to ...... REGNAL
king, Phrygian ...... MIDAS
king, rich .... CROESUS
king, Spartan AGIS, LEONIDAS
king, Teut. Visigoth .. ALARIC
king's bodyguard ..... THANE
king's yellow .... ORPIMENT
KINGDOM ..see also COUNTRY
kingdom, ancient ...... MOAB
KINGDOM, BIB. .. see page 197
kingfish .... HAKU, OPAH
kinkajou .... POTTO
kinship, Moslem law ... NASAB
Kipling hero .... KIM

86

a kismet .... FATE
kiss .... BUSS, SMACK
kitchen, ship's ...... GALLEY
kitchen tool
   CORER, RICER, GRATER
kite, bird
   GLED, GLEDE, ELANET
kittiwake gull, Shetlands WAEG
kitty, feed the .... ANTE
kiwi .... ROA
knave .... ROGUE
knave, in cribbage ..... NOBS
knave of clubs .... PAM
knead .... ELT
knead, in massage .... PETRIE
knee: Lat. .... GENU
kneecap .. ROTULA, PATELLA
KNIFE .. see also DAGGER
knife .... CHIV, STAB,
   MACHETE, MACHETTE
knife, Burmese .... DAH, DOW
knife dealer .... CUTLER
knife, Eskimo .... ULU
knife, large ...... SNY, SNEE
knife, loop-cutting
   TREVAT, TRIVAT, TRIVET
knife, P. I. .... BOLO
knife, single-edge .... BOWIE
knife, surgical ...... SCALPEL
knight SIR, RITTER, TEMPLAR
knight, heroic ...... PALADIN
knight, make .... DUB
knight, medieval ...... BEVIS
knight's mantel ..... TABARD

c knight's wife .... DAME
knitting stitch .... PURL
knob: anat. .... CAPUT
knobbed .... TOROSE
knoblike .... NODAL
knobkerrie .... KIRI
knockout .... KO, KAYO
knot .... MILE, NODE, NODI,
   SNAG, GNARL, KNURL,
   NODUS
knot, fiber .... NOIL, NOYL
knot in wood .... BURL
knot KNAR, KNOR, KNUR, NURL
knot, insecure .... GRANNY
knot lace ...... TAT, TATT
knot, like a .... NODAL
knot of thread .... BURL
knots, fiber .... NEP
knots, having .... NODED
know .... KEN, WIST
knowledge .... KEN, LORE
knowledge, pert. to .. GNOSTIC
knowledge, pure .... NOESIS
known as milo maize, grain
   MILO
knucklebones, sheep ... DOLOS
kobold .... NIS, NISSE
Kol dialect .... HO
kopecks, 100 .... RUBLE
Koran chapter .... SURA
Koran interpreters .... ULEMA
Korea .... CHOSEN
Korean president ..... RHEE
Korean soldier .... ROK
Kronos' wife .... RHEA
kurrajong tree .... CALOOL

L

b "La Boheme" heroine ... MIMI
Laban, daughter of .... LEAH
label .... TAG, PASTER
LABOR GROUP ... see UNION
laborer, China . COOLY, COOLIE
laborer, India .... TOTY
Labrador tea .... LEDUM
labyrinth .... MAZE
lac .... RESIN
lace .... BEAT, LASH
lace, barred GRILLE, GRILLEE
lace, Fr. ... CLUNY, ALENCON
lace, gold, silver ..... ORRIS
lace, metal tip of
   AGLET, AIGLET
lace, square hole ...... FILET
lacerate .... RIP, TEAR
laceration .... RIP, TEAR
lack .... NEED, WANT
lack of power .... ATONY

d Laconian clan group ..... OBE
Laconian subdivision ..... OBE
ladder, scale fort wall with
   SCALADE, SCALADO, ES-
   CALADE, ESCALADO
ladderlike .... SCALAR
lady, India .... BIBI
"Lady of the Lake" outlaw DHU
ladylove, in poetry ..... DELIA
lagoon .... LIMAN
lake .... MERE
lake, Afr. salt .. SHAT, SHOTT
lake, Blue Nile source .. TANA
Lake Erie battle officer PERRY
Lake, Great (5) ERIE, HURON,
   ONTARIO, MICHIGAN, SU-
   PERIOR
lake, mountain .... TARN
lake near Galilee sea .. MEROM
lake, resort .... TAHOE

Lake

a lake: Scot. .... **LOCH**
Lake Tahoe trout ..... **POGY**
lake whitefish .... **POLLAN**
lama, head .... **DALAI**
lamb .... **EAN, EWE, YEAN**
lamb, holy .... **AGNUS**
lamb: Lat. .... **AGNI, AGNUS**
lamb, young .... **COSSET**
Lamb's pen name ...... **ELIA**
Lamech, ancestor of ... **CAIN**
Lamech's son
　　　　NOAH, JABAL, JUBAL
lament .... **KEEN, WAIL,**
　　WEEP, GRIEVE, PLAINT
lamentation .... **LINOS**
lamp black .... **SOOT**
lamprey .... **EEL**
lance head .... **MORNE**
lance, mythical .... **RON**
lance rest, breastplate **FAUCRE**
lance, short .... **DART**
Lancelot's beloved ... **ELAINE**
lancer, Ger. ... **ULAN, UHLAN**
lancewood .... **CIGUA**
land, absolute property **ALOD,**
　　ALLOD, ALODIUM, ALLODIUM
land amid water .. **ISLE, ISLET**
land breeze .... **TERRAL**
land, church's .... **GLEBE**
b land held in fee simple
　　　　　ODAL, UDAL
land: law .... **SOLUM**
LAND MEASURE .. see also
　　AREA in SPECIAL SECTION
land measure
　AR, ARE, ROD, ACRE, ROOD
land ownership, pert. to **ODAL**
land snail genus ...:. **CERION**
land spring .... **LAVANT**
land, tilled, plowed: Sp.
　　　　　ARADA, ARADO
land under tenure: Scot. .. **FEU**
landing place ..... **KEY, PIER,**
　　QUAI, QUAY, LEVEE
landing place, India
　　　　　GAUT, GHAT
landing ship .... **LST**
landmark .... **COPA**
landmark: Sp. ...... **SENAL**
lands .... **ACRES**
language, Aramaic ... **SYRIAC**
language, Assam .... **AO, AKA**
language, dead ...... **LATIN**
language, early It. .... **OSCAN**
language, Egypt. ..... **COPTIC**
language, Finnish .... **UGRIC**
language form, peculiarity
　　　　　　IDIOM
language, Gilgit ...... **SHINA**
language, Hittite ...... **PALA**
language, Indic .... **HINDI**

c language, Indo-Chin. .... **AO,**
　WA, AKA, ANU, LAI, LAO,
　MRO, MRU, PWO, SAK,
　AHOM, AKHA, AMOY,
　BODO, GARO, KAMI, NAGA,
　RONG, SGAU, SHAN
language, Ir. .. **CELTIC, KELTIC**
language, Kandh .... **KUI**
language, Kashmir .... **SHINA**
language, Mossi .... **MO, MOLE**
language, N. Afr. .... **BERBER**
language of Bible days
　　　　　　ARAMAIC
language, P. I.
　　　　TAGAL, TAGALOG
language, Scot. **CELTIC, KELTIC**
language, Semitic .... **ARABIC**
language, Siberian
　　　　ENISEI, YENISEI
language, S. Afr. ...... **TAAL**
language, Sudanic .. **MO, MOLE**
language, synthetic .. **RO, IDO**
language, Welsh **CELTIC, KELTIC**
languages, E. Europ. ... **UGRIC**
languish .... **FLAG, PINE**
languor, drug-induced
　　　　KEF, KAIF, KIFF
langur .... **MAHA**
lantern feast .... **BON**
d Laomedon's father ...... **ILUS**
Laomedon's son
　　　　PRIAM, TITHONUS
Laos aborigine ... **KHA, YUN**
lapel .... **REVER**
lapidate .... **STONE**
Lapp's sledge ... **PULK, PULKA**
larboard .... **APORT**
larch **TAMARAC, TAMARACK**
large amount .... **SCAD**
lariat .... **LAZO, ROPE,**
　　LASSO, REATA, RIATA
lariat, metal eye of
　HONDA, HONDO, HONDOO
larva .... **GRUB**
larva of fly ...... **BOT, BOTT**
lash .... **TIE, WHIP**
lasso
ROPE, REATA, RIATA, LARIAT
last .... **FINAL, OMEGA**
last but one .... **PENULT**
"Last Days of Pompeii" char-
　acter .... **IONE**
last Imam .... **MAHDI**
last section .... **FINALE**
Last Supper picture .... **CENA**
Last Supper room .. **CENACLE**
latching: naut. ...... **LASKET**
late ... **NEW, TARDY, RECENT**
late, one at school ..... **SERO**
lateen-rigged boat ..... **DOW,**
　DHOW, SETEE, MISTIC

a
latent .... DORMANT
lateral .... SIDE
lath .... SLAT
LATIN ...... see also ROMAN
LATIN:
abbot .... ABBAS
above ...... SUPER, SUPRA
about .... CIRCITER
across .... TRANS
act .... ACTU, ACTUS
after .... POST
aged .... AET (abbr.)
all .... TOTO
alone .... SOLO, SOLUS
and .... ET
and others .... ETAL (abbr.)
around .... CIRCUM
art .... ARS
backward .... RETRO
before .... ANTE
behold .... ECCE
being .... ESSE
believe, I .... CREDO
beneath .... INERA
bird .... AVIS
book .... LIBER
blessed .... BEATA
bronze .... AES
but .... SED
cattle .... PECORA

b
country .... RUS, RURIS
cup .... CALIX
custom .... RITUS
day .... DIEM
days .... DIES
depart! .... VADE
divination by lots ...... SORS,
                        SORTES
door .... JANUA
earth .... TERRA
egg .... OVUM
eight .... OCTO
error .... LAPSUS
event .... REI
evil .... MALA, MALUM
fate .... NONA
field .... AGER
fields .... AGRI
fire .... IGNIS
first .... PRIMUS
fish .... PISCES
force .... VIS
from .... DE
go! .... VADE
god .... DEUS
goddess .... DEA
gods .... DI
gold .... AURUM
good ...... BONUM, BONUS
grandfather .... AVUS
he .... ILLE

c
he remains .... MANET
he was .... ERAT
head .... CAPUT
high .... ALTA
himself .... IPSE
I love .... AMO
in so far as .... QUA
is .... EST
itself .... IPSO
ivory .... EBUR
journey .... ITER
knee .... GENU
lamb .... AGNI, AGNUS
land .... AGER
learned .... DOCTUS
life ...... VITA, ANIMA
lo .... ECCE
man .... VIR
mass .... MISSA
mine .... MEUM
more than .... SUPER
mountain .... MONS
name .... NOMEN
nose, of the .... NAS
not .... NON
observe .... NOTA
offense ..... MALA, MALUM

d
once .... SEMEL
or .... AUT
other .... ALIA
over .... SUPER
pardon .... VENIA
palm .... VOLA
part .... PARS
partly .... PARTIM
peace .... PAX
pin .... ACUS
pledge .... VAS
possessive .... SUA
power .... VIS
pronoun .... SUA
property .... BONA
quickly .... CITO
rate .... RATA
religious law .... FAS
right .... DEXTER
same .... IDEM
scarcely VIX
see .... VIDE
side .... LATUS
table .... MENSA
tail .... CAUDA
that is .... "ID EST"
that one .... ILLE
the same .... IDEM
thing .... RES

89

Latin

LATIN(continued from page 89)

this one .... HIC, HAEC
thus .... SIC
throat .... GULA
to be .... ESSE
to use .... UTOR
tooth .... DENS
toward .... AD
twice .... BIS
under .... SUB
unless .... NISI
vein .... VENA
voice .... VOX
water .... AQUA
we .... NOS
well .... BENE
where .... UBI
within .... INTRA
without .... SINE
wool .... LANA
wrong ...... MALA, MALUM

Latvia, native of .... LETT
laugh .... FLEER
laugh, able to .... RISIBLE
laughing .... RIANT
laughing, pert. to .. GELASTIC
laurel .... BAY, DAPHNE
laurel bark, medicinal .. COTO
lava .... AA, LATITE, SCORIA
lava, rough .... AA
lavender, Eur. .... ASPIC
lavish affection .... DOTE
law
JURE, RULE, CANON, EDICT
law, abstract .... JUS
law, D. E. Ind. .... ADAT
law excluding women from
reign .... SALIC
law of Moses .. TORA, TORAH
law, Rom. .... JUS, LEX
lawful .... LEGAL, LICIT
lawgiver, Gr.
DRACO, MINOS, SOLON
lawgiver, Hebr. ...... MOSES
lawmaker .... SOLON
lawyer .... LEGIST
lawyers' patron saint ... IVES
lay .... PUT, DITTY
layer .... PLY,
LAMINA, STRATA, STRATUM
layer of a plant ..... PROVINE
layer, wood .... VENEER
layman .... LAIC
lazar .... LEPER
lazy .... OTIOSE
lead-colored .... LIVID
lead: music PRESA, PRECENT
lead, ore .... GALENA

lead, pellets of .... SHOT
lead, pencil ...... GRAPHITE
lead sulphide, native GALENA
lead telluride ...... ALTAITE
lead, white .... CERUSE
leaden color, having ... LIVID
leader, fishing .... SNELL
leader of movement .... VAN
leader, Rom. .... DUX
leaf appendage ...... STIPEL
leaf-cutting ant ...... ATTA
leaf division .... LOBE
leaf, fern .... FROND
leaf, flower .... BRACT, SEPAL
leaf-miner beetle ...... HISPA
leaf of book .... FOLIO
leaf vein .... RIB
league, Ger. .... BUND
league, trading ...... HANSE
Leah's father .... LABAN
Leah's son .... LEVI
lean .. CANT, GAUNT, SPARE
lean-to .... SHED
Leander's love .... HERO
"Leaning Tower" city .... PISA
leap LUNGE, VAULT, CURVET
leap: music .... SALTO
leap: Scot. LOUP, LOWP, STEND
leaping .... SALTANT
learned .. ERUDITE, LETTERED
learning .... LORE
learning, man of
SAGE, PEDANT, SAVANT
Lear's daughter ...... REGAN
Lear's faithful follower KENT
least bit .... RAP
leather bottle .... MATARA
leather flask, Gr. ..... OLPE
leather, glove
KID, NAPA, MOCHA, SUEDE
leather, kind of ... ELK, BOCK
leather, prepare—make into
TAN, TAW
leather, soft
NAPA, ALUTA, SUEDE
leather thong, hawk's .. BRAIL
leatherfish .... LIJA
"leatherneck" .... MARINE
leave
GO, QUIT, EXEAT, DEPART
leave destitute ...... STRAND
leave of absence, school EXEAT
leave-taking .... CONGE
leaves, having: Her. .. POINTE
leaven .... YEAST
leaving .... ORT
leavings .... DREGS, RESIDUE
Lebanese port, old .... TYRE
ledge, fort .... BERM, BERME
ledger entry
ITEM, DEBIT, CREDIT

a lee, opposed to .... STOSS
leeangle .. LEAWILL, LEEWILL
leer .... OGLE
Leeward Island .... NEVIS
left: comb. form ...... LEVO
left-hand .... LEVO
left-hand page .... VO, VERSO
left, to turn .... HAW
leftover .... ORT
leg, covering, ancient PEDULE
leg, front of .... SHIN
leg joint, animal ..... HOCK
leg-like part .... CRUS
leg of mutton, lamb .. GIGOT
leg, part of .... SHIN, SHANK
leg, pert. to calf of .. SURAL
legal action suit .. RES, CASE
legal claim .... LIEN
legal delays .... MORAE
legal injury .... TORT
legal job .... CASE
legal matter .... RES
legal offense .. DELIT, DELICT
legal order .... WRIT
legal paper .... DEED
legal profession ... BAR, LAW
legal prosecution ..... SUIT
legend ... MYTH, SAGA, TALE
legion division, Rom. COHORT
legislate .... ENACT

b legislative assembly, Afr. RAAS
legislator ... SOLON, SENATOR
legislature .. DIET, SENATE
legislature: Sp. ...... CORTES
legume ..... PEA, POD, BEAN
leisure .... REST, OTIUM
lemur .... MAKI, INDRI,
    LORIS, AYE-AYE, SEMIAPE
lemur, Afr. .... GALAGO
lemur, Asia, Ceylon LORI, LORIS
lemur, Ceylonese ...... LORI
lemur, flying .... COLUGO
lemur, ruffed .... VARI
lemuroid .... POTTO
lengthily, address ... PERORATE
Leningrad's river ..... NEVA
lens, hand .... READER
lentil .... ERVUM
leopard .... PARD
Leporidae, one of the ... HARE
leprosy .... LEPRA
Lepus genus, one of .. HARE
lerp .... LAAP
Lesbos, poet of ...... ARION
"Les Etats —" .... UNIS
less .... MINUS
lessen BATE, ABATE, MITIGATE
let HIRE, RENT, LEASE, PERMIT
let bait drop .... DAP
let it stand! .... STA, STET

c let up .... ABATE
lethal .... FATAL
lethargy
    COMA, STUPOR, TORPOR
letter .. AR (18), EF (6), EM
    (13), EN (14), EX (24),
    WY (25), BEE (2), CEE
    (3), DEE (4), ESS (19),
    GEE (7), JAY (10), PEE
    (16), TEE (20), VEE (22),
    WYE (25), ZED (26), ZEE
    (26), AITCH (8)
letter, according to .. LITERAL
letter, Ang.-Sax. .. EDH, ETH
letter, early Gr. ...... SAN
LETTER, GR. and NUMBER . see
    also GREEK LETTER
letter, Gr. ... MU, NU, PI, XI,
    CHI, ETA, PHI, PSI, RHO,
    TAU, BETA, IOTA, ZETA,
    ALPHA, DELTA, GAMMA,
    KAPPA, OMEGA, SIGMA,
    THETA, LAMBDA, EPSILON,
    OMICRON, UPSILON
letter, Hebr. ... HE (5), PE (17),
    AIN (16), MEM (13),
    NUN (14), SIN (21), TAV
    (22), TAW (22), VAU
    (16), WAW (16), ALEF
    (11), AYIN (16), BETH
    (2), CAPH (11), ELEF (1),
    KAPH (11), KOPH (19),
    QOPH (19), RESH (20),
    SADE (18), SHIN (21),
    TETH (9), YODH (10),
    ALEPH (13), GIMEL (3),
    LAMED (12), DALETH (4),
    LAMEDH (12)
letter of resignation .. DEMIT
letters, sloping ...... ITALICS
lettuce, kind of COS, ROMAINE
Levantine ketch .... SAIC
levee .... DIKE, DYKE
level EVEN, RASE, RAZE, PLANE
leveling slip .... SHIM
lever ..... PRY, PEVY, PEAVY,
    PEEVY, PEAVEY, PEEVEY,
    TAPPET
levy ... TAX, CESS, IMPOST
Lew Wallace hero ...... HUR
Lhasa holy man .... LAMA
Lhasa's country .... TIBET
liability .... DEBT
liana .... CIPO
liang .... TAEL
liar .... ANANIAS
Liberian native .... VAI, VEI
Liberian tribes .. GI, KRA, KRU
license: slang .... READER
lichen .... MOSS
lichen genus USNEA, EVERNIA

a

lichen, kind **PARELLA, PARELLE**
lie in wait .... **LURK**
Liege, town near .... **ANS**
liegeman .... **VASSAL**
lieu .... **STEAD**
life .... **BIOS, BIOTA**
life: Lat. ...... **VITA, ANIMA**
life, of .... **VITAL**
life principle .... **PRANA**
life principle, Hindu .. **ATMAN**
life prolonger .... **ELIXIR**
life, relating to
         BIOTIC, BIOTICAL
life tenant .... **LIVIER**
lifeless **AMORT, AZOIC, INERT**
lifetime .... **AGE**
lifted with effort ...... **HOVE**
ligament .... **BOND**
light .... **LAMP, KLEIG,
         KLIEG, TAPER, ILLUME**
light and fine, as lines .. **LEGER**
light as a line .... **LEGER**
light bulb filler ...... **ARGON**
light, circle of
         HALO, NIMB, NIMBUS
light intensity unit ...... **PYR**
light, kind of .... **ARC**
light ring .... **CORONA**
light, science of ..... **OPTICS**
light, sun's **AUREOLA, AUREOLE**

b

light unit **PYR, LUMEN, HEFNER**
lighter, lamp .... **SPILL**
lighter, make .... **LEAVEN**
lighthouse .... **PHAROS**
lightning: poet. .... **LEVIN**
ligulate .... **LORATE**
like .... **AS, AKIN**
likely .... **APT**
likeness .... **ICON, IMAGE**
likewise not .... **NOR**
lily .... **LIS, LYS, ALOE,
         ARUM, SEGO, CALLA**
lily family plant .... **CAMAS
         CAMASS, CAMMAS**
lily genus .... **ALOE**
lily genus, plantain .... **HOSTA**
Lily Maid of Astolat
         ELAIN, ELAINE
lily, palm .... **TI**
limb ...... **ARM, LEG, MANUS**
limber .... **LITHE**
lime, to hydrate ..... **SLAKE**
lime tree .... **TEIL, TEYL**
limestone, grainy ..... **OOLITE**
limestone, Irish .... **CALP**
limestone, soft **MALM, CHALK**
limicoline bird **SNIPE, PLOVER**
limit .... **TERM, BOURN,
         STENT, STINT, BOURNE**
limn.......... **DRAW, PAINT**
Lindbergh's book .... **WE**

c

linden .... **LIN, TEIL, TEYL**
line .... **ROW, RANK**
line, cutting .... **SECANT**
line, fine, on type letter **CERIF,
         SERIF, CERIPH**
line, fishing .... **SNELL**
line, in a .... **AROW**
line, intersecting .... **SECANT**
line inside of .... **CEIL**
line, math. .... **VECTOR**
line, naut. . **EARING, MARLINE**
line not forming angle **AGONE**
line on a letter .... **SERIF**
line, pert. to .... **LINEAR**
line, thin ..... **STRIA, STRIAE**
line, waiting .... **CUE, QUEUE**
line with stone **STEAN, STEENE**
lines, marked with
         RULED, STRIATE, STRIATED
lines, telescope-lens .. **RETICLE**
linen .... **CREA**
linen, fine ..... **LAWN, TOILE**
linen, household, table **NAPERY**
linen, one caring for royal
         NAPERER
linen tape, braid ...... **INKLE**
linger .... **WAIT, TARRY**
lingo .... **ARGOT**
lingua .... **GLOSSA**
liniment .... **ARNICA**

d

link .... **YOKE, CATENATE**
links connected ..... **CATENATE**
linnet ...... **TWITE, LENARD**
lion .... **LEO, SIMBA**
lion group .... **PRIDE**
lion killed by Hercules **NEMEAN**
lion of God .... **ALI**
lionet .... **CUB**
lips, pert. to .... **LABIAL**
liqueur .... **CREME, NOYAU**
liqueur, sweet .... **GENEPI**
liquid element
         BROMIN, BROMINE
liquid, made ... **FUSIL, FUSILE**
liquid, without ..... **ANEROID**
liquor .. **GIN, RUM, RYE, GROG**
liquor, malt .... **ALE, PORTER**
liquor, oriental ..... **ARRACK**
liquor, P. I. .... **VINO**
liquor, Russian **VODKA, VODKI**
liquor, sugar-cane
         TAFIA, TAFFIA
Lisbon's river .... **TAGUS**
lissome .... **SVELTE**
list ....**ROTA, SLATE,
ROSTER, CATALOG, CATALOGUE**
list of persons
         ROTA, PANEL, ROSTER
list, one of a .... **ITEM**
listen .... **HARK, HEAR**
listless, be .... **MOPE**

a listlessness... **ENNUI, APATHY**
liter, Dutch .... **AAM, KAN**
literary collection........... **ANA**
literary extracts .... **ANALECTA, ANALECTS**
literary master .... **STYLIST**
literary scraps, bits....... **ANA, NOTES**
literate .. **LEARNED, LETTERED**
lithograph .... **CHROMO**
Lithuanian ...... **BALT, LETT**
litter, E. Ind. .... **DOOLI, DOOLY, DOOLEE, DOOLEY, DOOLIE**
"Little Boy Blue" poet .... **FIELD**
little casino .... **TWO**
little chief hare........... **PIKA**
little: music.............. **POCO**
liturgy................... **RITE**
live .... **all forms of verb "BE"**
live oak, Calif.......... **ENCINA**
lively.... **PERT, BRISK, PEART**
lively, make.............. **PERK**
lively: music ..... **VIVO, DESTO, ANIMATO**
lively person............. **GRIG**
lively song................ **LILT**
liver.................... **HEPAR**
liver, pert. to....... **HEPATIC**
liverwort genus .... **RICCIA**
b livid...................... **BLAE**
living in currents .... **LOTIC**
Livonian .... **LIV**
lixivium........... **LYE, LEACH**
lizard............ **GILA, GECKO, GUANA, SKINK, VARAN, IGUANA**
lizard, Am....... **ANOLE, ANOLI**
lizard, beaded.............. **GILA**
lizard, changeable **CHAMELEON**
lizard genus ..... **UTA, AGAMA**
lizard, large... **GILA, MONITOR**
lizard, old world .... **SEPS**
lizard, small...... **EFT, GECKO**
lizard, starred........... **AGAMA**
lizard, tropical.......... **AGAMA**
lizardlike............. **SAURIAN**
llamalike animal .... **ALPACA**
load............... **LADE, ONUS**
loadstone............ **MAGNET**
loaf, small: dial. .... **BAP**
loam .... **LOESS**
loam, India............. **REGUR**
loath .... **AVERSE**
loathe .... **ABHOR**
lobster box .... **CAR**
local .... **TOPICAL**
locale .... **SITE**
locality .... **AREA, LOCUS, VENEW, VENUE**
location ... **SITE, SPOT, PLACE**
lock............. **CURL, TRESS**

c locks, Panama Canal ... **GATUN**
lockjaw... **TETANUS, TRISMUS**
locust..... **ACACIA, CICADA, CICALA**
locust, N. Z............... **WETA**
lodge, soldier's......... **BILLET**
lofty dwelling .... **AERIE**
log birling contest ...... **ROLEO**
log drive, escape work on.. **SNIB**
log, spin floating .... **BIRL**
log splitter.............. **WEDGE**
logarithmic unit .... **BEL**
loge................... **STALL**
logger's implement..... **PEAVY, PEAVEY**
logic, omission of step in proof **SALTUS**
logician .... **DIALECTOR**
Lohengrin's wife .... **ELSA**
Loire, city on .... **BLOIS**
loiter..................... **LAG**
Loki's daughter ..... **HEL, HELA**
Loki's son .... **NARE**
Loki's wife .... **SIGYN**
London district............ **SOHO**
long...... **YEN, PINE, CRAVE, YEARN, ASPIRE**
long ago .... **ELD, YORE**
long journey .. **TREK, ODYSSEY**
d long line (fishing) with hooks **TROT**
long live! .... **VIVA, VIVE**
long-suffering .... **MEEK**
look.................... **LO, SEE**
look after........ **MIND, TEND**
look askance............. **LEER**
look at ...... **EYE, SCAN, VIEW**
look here! .... **HIST**
look narrowly**PEEK, PEEP, PEER**
look slyly......... **LEER, OGLE**
loom, heddles of .... **CAAM**
loom, lever in .... **LAM**
loon, genus............. **GAVIA**
loon, kind of .... **DIVER**
loop, edging .... **PICOT**
loophole........ **MUSE, MEUSE**
looplike structure, anat.... **ANSA**
loose...................... **LAX**
loose coat**PALETOT, MANTEVIL**
loose robe............... **SIMAR**
loosen .... **UNDO, UNTIE**
lop.... **SNED, PRUNE, SNATHE**
lopsided......... **ALOP, ALIST**
loquat tree .... **BIWA**
Lord High Executioner in "Mikado" **KOKO**
Lord: Jacobite Church ..... **MAR**
lord, Oriental............ **KHAN**
lord, Pers........ **KAAN, KAUN, KAWN, KHAN**
lord, privileged ...... **PALATINE**

a
lord, Scot.	LAIRD
lore, Norse	RUNE
lorica	CUIRASS
"Lorna Doone" character	RIDD
lose	AMIT
"Lost Chord" finale	AMEN
lot	FATE
Lotan's father	SEIR
Lot's birthplace	UR
Lot's father	HARAN
Lot's son	MOAB
lottery prize	TERN
lotus enzyme	LOTASE
Lotus: poet	LOTE
lotus tree	SADR
loud: music	FORTE
loud-voiced one	STENTOR
loudness, measurement unit	PHON
loudspeaker for high sound	TWEETER
loudspeaker for low sound	WOOFER
Louis XVI's nickname	VETO
Louisiana county	PARISH

b
Louisiana native	CREOLE
lounge	LOAF, LOLL
love	JO, GRA, ADORE, AMOUR
love: Anglo-Irish	GRA
love apple	TOMATO
love feast	AGAPE
love god	
LOVE GOD . see GOD OF LOVE	
LOVE GODDESS . see GODDESS OF LOVE	
love, inflame with	ENAMOR, ENAMOUR
love knot	AMORET
love to excess	DOAT, DOTE
lover	ROMEO
"Love's Labour's Lost" constable	DULL
loving	FOND, AMATIVE, AMATORY
low	MOO, BASE
low caste Hindu	PASI, TELI
low caste Indian	DOM, MAL, GADDI
Lowell, poetess	AMY
lower	ABASE, DEBASE, NETHER
lower: arch.	VAIL
lower jaw, bird's	MALA
lower world gods, Rom.	MANES
lowest deck	ORLOP
lowest part of base	PLINTH

c
lowest point	NADIR
loyal	LEAL, TRUE, STANCH, STAUNCH
loyalist	TORY
lozenge	PASTIL, ROTULA, TROCHE, PASTILE, PASTILLE
loyalty fulfilling religious obligations: Rom.	PIETAS
Lubeck, pert. to	LUBS
lucerne	MEDIC, ALFALFA
luck: Ir.	CESS
luck, pert. to	ALEATORY
lucky stroke	FLUKE
lugubrious	SAD
lukewarm	TEPID
lumber along	LOB, LOBB
Lumber State	see page 223
lumberman	SAWYER
lumberman's boot	PAC
lumberman's boots	PACS, OVERS
lumberman's hook	PEVY, PEAVY, PEEVY, PEAVEY, PEEVEY
luminaire	LAMP
luminary	STAR

d
lump	NUB, WAD, CLOT, NODE, SWAD
lunar crater	LINNE
lunar god, Phrygian	MEN
luncheon	TIFFIN
lurch	CAREEN
lure	BAIT, DECOY
luster	GLOSS, SHEEN
lusterless	DIM, MAT, MATTE
lustrous	NITID
lute, Oriental	TAR
luxuriant	LUSH, RANK
luxuriate	BASK
Luzon native	ATA, ITA, AETA, ATTA, TAGAL, TAGALA
Luzon negrito	ATA, AETA, ITA, ATTA
Luzon pagan	ITALON
Lynette's knight	GARETH
lynx, Afr.	SYAGUSH
lynx, Pers.	CARACAL
lyrebird genus	MENURA
lyric	ODE, MELIC
lyric Muse	ERATO
Lytton heroine	IONE

M

macaque Indian **BRUH, RHESUS**
macaw .... **ARA, ARARA**
macaw, Braz.
    ARA, ARARA, MARACAN
mace-bearer .... **BEADLE**
macerate .... **RET, STEEP**
machine, finishing .... **EDGER**
machine, grain cleaner **AWNER**
machine gun .... **BREN, STEN**
machine, hummeling .. **AWNER**
machine, ore-dressing **VANNER**
machine part
    CAM, PAWL, TAPPET
machine, rubber .. **EXTRUDER**
mackerel net .... **SPILLER**
mackerel, young .... **SPIKE**
Madagascar mammal .. **LEMUR**
Madagascar native .... **HOVA**
madam .... **MUM, MAAM**
madder ..... **RUBIA, MUNJEET**
madder, common Eu. **GARANCE**
madder shrub genus ... **EVEA**
madness .... **MANIA**
mafura tree .... **ROKA**
maggot .... **LARVA**
Magi, one of .... **GASPAR**
magic .... **RUNE**
magic: Hindustan **JADU, JADOO**
magic, pert. to .... **GOETIC**

b

magic stone .... **AGATE**
magic: W. Ind. .... **OBEAH**
magician .... **MAGE**
    MAGI, MAGUS, MERLIN
magistrate, Athens **ARCHON**
magistrate, It. .... **DOGE**
magistrate, Rom. .... **EDILE,**
    AEDILE, CONSUL, PRETOR
magnate ... **MOGUL, TYCOON**
magnifying glass .... **LENS**
Magog, ruler of .... **GOG**
magpie .. **MAG, PIE, MAGG,**
    PIET, PIOT, PYAT, PYET,
    NINUT, PIANET
magpie genus .... **PICA**
mah-jongg piece .... **TILE**
mahatma
    ARAHT, ARHAT, ARAHAT
mahogany pine ...... **TOTARA**
mahogany, Sp. .... **CAOBA**
mahogany streak .... **ROE**
mahogany tree, Ind. ... **TOON**
MAHOMET .. see **MOHAMMED**
MAHOMETAN ... see **MOSLEM**
maid .... **LASS, BONNE**
maid, lady's .... **ABIGAIL**
maid-of-all-work ..... **SLAVEY**
maid, Oriental
    AMA, IYA, AMAH, EYAH
maiden .... **DAMSEL**

c

maiden name, signifying..**NEE**
maiden of myth .... **IO**
mail .... **POST, SEND**
mail, coat of . **BRINIE, BYRNIE**
mail, India **DAK, DAUK, DAWK**
main point ... **NUB, GIST, PITH**
maintain.**AVER, HOLD, ASSERT**
maize .... **CORN**
maize bread .... **PIKI**
maize genus .... **ZEA**
major: music .... **DUR**
major third: Gr. mus. .. **DITONE**
make .... **RENDER**
make as one: obs. ...... **UNE**
make evident .... **EVINCE**
make fast: naut. ...... **BELAY**
make good by action . **REDEEM**
make happy .... **ELATE**
make public: Old Eng. **DELATE**
Makua .... **KUA**
malarial fever .... **AGUE**
malarial poison
    MIASM, MIASMA
Malay apple .... **KAWIKA**
Malay canoe
    PRAH, PRAO, PRAU, PROA
Malay chief or headman.**DATO,**
    DATU, DATTO

d

Malay dagger ... **CRIS, KRIS,**
  CREES, KREES, CREESE, KREESE
Malay lanseh tree ..... **DUKU**
Malay law .... **ADAT**
Malay lugger .... **TOUP**
malay negrito ..... **ATA, ITA**
Malay nerve ailment ... **LATA**
MALAY OUTRIGGER see **MALAY**
    CANOE
Malay title of respect .. **TUAN**
Malay ungulate .... **TAPIR**
Malay verse form ... **PANTUN**
Malay vessel
    PRAH, PRAO, PRAU, PROA
Malay, word meaning dark **AETA**
Malayan ape .... **LAR**
male cat .... **GIB, TOM**
male figure, used as support
    ATLAS, TELAMON
male swan .... **COB**
malefic .... **EVIL**
malic acid, fruit with
    ATTA, APPLE, GRAPE
malign .... **REVILE**
malignant .... **EVIL**
malignant spirit ... **KER, KERES**
malleable ..... **SOFT, DUCTILE**
mallet .... **MALL, GAVEL**
malt drink, pert. to ..... **ALY**
malt infusion .... **WORT**
maltreat .... **ABUSE**

Mammal

a
MAMMAL .. see also ANIMAL
mammal, sea aquatic .. SEAL, OTTER, WHALE, DUGONG, MANATEE
mammoth .... GIANT
man-eating monster ... LAMIA
man, handsome ...... ADONIS
man, rich .... CROESUS
man's name .. ELI, GUY, IAN, IRA, JOB, LEE, RAY, REX, ADAM, ALAN, AMOS, BRAM, CARL, DANA, DION, EBEN, EMIL, ENOS, ERIC, EVAN, EZRA, HANS, HUGH, HUGO, IVAN, JOEL, JOHN, JOSE, JUAN, JUDE, KARL, KNUT, LEON, LUKE, MARC, MARK, NEIL, NOEL, OTTO, OWEN, PAUL, SEAN, SETH, TEIG, BASIL, CALEB, CLARE, ENOCH, HIRAM, HOMER, SERGE, STEVE, TERRY, DEXTER, GASPAR, GEORGE, OLIVER, SAMSON, STEVEN, WARREN
man's nickname .AL, ABE, ALF, BEN, BOB, DON, GUS, JIM, JOE, KIT, LEW, LON, LOU, MAC, MAT, MAX, MOE, NED, PAT, ROB, SAM, SID, SIM, TED, TOM, ABIE, ALGY, ANDY, BART, BERT, BILL, BONY, DAVE, DAVY, DICK, DODE, FRED, GENE, JACK, JAKE, JOCK, JOEY, MART, MIKE, MOSE, NOLL, PETE, PHIL, RUBE, TOBY, TONY, WALT, ZACH, ZEKE

b
manageable .... YARE
manager .... GERENT
Manasseh, city of ...... ANER
Manasseh, son of ..... AMON
mandarin's home
                 YAMEN, YAMUN
manducate .... EAT
maned .... JUBATE
manger ...... CRIB, CRECHE
mangle .... MAUL
mango, P. I. ...... CARABAO
mania .... CRAZE
manifest .... SHOW, OVERT, ATTEST, EVINCE
manifestation .... AURA
manifestation of god of lower
    world .... SERAPIS
maniple FANO, FANON, FANUM
manner
    AIR, WAY, MIEN, MODE
manner of walking ..... GAIT
manners .... MORES
manor .... DEMENE, DEMESNE

c
mantis crab .... SQUILLA
mantle .... CAPE
manual training, Swed. . SLOID, SLOYD
manuao .... IAO
Manxman .... GAEL
many .... MAINT
many-colored
            PIED, PINTO, MOTLEY
many-colored stone ... AGATE
Maori tattooing .... MOKO
Maori village ... KAIK, KAIKA
Maori wages .... UTU
Maori war club MERE, MARREE
Maori war-club wood .... RATA
map .... PLAT
map in a map .... INSET
maple fruit, seed .... SAMARA
maple genus .... ACER
maple tree tap .... SPILE
mar .... DEFACE
marabou .... ARGALA
marble MIB, MIG, TAW, MIGG, AGATE, AGGIE, MARMOR, MEALIE, SHOOTER
marble, Belgian RANCE, RANSE
marble, choice ALAY, ALLEY
marble, It. .... CARRARA
marble, Rom. .... CIPOLIN
marble, white .... DOLOMITE

d
marbles, game at ...... TAW
March King .... SOUSA
mare: Gypsy .... GRASNI
margin .... RIM, EDGE, MARGE
marginal reading, Hebrew
    Bible .... KRI
margosa tree .... NIM, NEEM
Marie Wilson, character played
    by .... IRMA
MARINE .. see also SEA
marine annelid .... LURG
marine fish, E. Ind. ... DORAB
marine measure, Jap. ..... RI
marine snail
            WELK, WILK, WHELK
marine snail genus .. NERITA
marine turtle genus..CARETTA
marine worm .... SYLLID
marionette maker ..... SARG
mark .... STIGMA, STIGMATA
mark, diacritic TILDE, MACRON
mark of omission ..... CARET
mark, reference
        OBELI, OBELUS, OBELISK
mark, short vowel .... BREVE
marked with spots: bot. NOTATE
marker, Gr. & Rom. ... STELA, STELE, STELAE, STELAI

a market .... MART, SELL, VEND, RIALTO
market: India .... PASAR
market, Oriental SUQ, SOOK, SOUK
market place BAZAR, BAZAAR
market place, Gr. .... AGORA
marksman .... AIMER
marmalade tree MAMEY, SAPOTE
marmoset .... MICO
marmoset, S. Am. .. TAMARIN
"Marner, — " Eliot novel SILAS
marriage, absence of .. AGAMY
marriage notice BAN, BANNS
marriage portion, pert. to DOTAL
marriage portion: Scot. DOS, DOTE
marriage settlement DOS, DOT, DOWRY, DOWERY
marriage vows .... TROTH
marriageable .... NUBILE
marrow .... PITH
marry .... WED, WIVE
Mars .... ARES
Mars' outer satellite .. DEIMOS
Mars, pert. to .... AREAN
"Marseillaise" author .. LISLE
b marsh .... BOG, FEN, SLUE, LIMAN, SWALE
marsh elder .... IVA
marsh fever .... HELODES
marsh gas .... METHANE
marsh hen .... RAIL
marsh mallow .... ALTEA
marsh marigold ...... CAPER
marsh plant REED, SEDGE, FESCUE
marshal, Waterloo ...... NEY
marshy . PALUDAL, PALUDINE
marsupial, arboreal COALA, KOALA, POSSUM
marten .... SOBOL
martyr, 1st Christian . STEPHEN
marvel .... MIRACLE
Mascagni heroine ...... LOLA
MASCULINE see also MALE, MAN'S
mashy .... IRON
masjid ...... MOSK, MOSQUE
mask, half .... DOMINO
mask topknot, Gr. ..... ONKOS
masons' pickax ...... GURLET
masquerade cloak ... DOMINO
mass ...... GOB, WAD, BULK
mass book .... MISSAL
mass meeting .... RALLY
mass, pert. to .... MISSATICAL
mass, rounded .... BOLUS
mast .... SPAR

c mast: obs. .... SPIR
mast, support .... BIBB
mast, wood for .... POON
master: archaic .... DAN
master, India MIAN, SAHEB, SAHIB
master, pert. to ...... HERILE
master, S. Afr. .... BAAS
master-stroke .... COUP
mastic tree .... ACOMA
masticate ...... CHAW, CHEW
mat, ornamental ...... DOILY
match, friction . FUSEE, FUZEE
match, wax .... VESTA
matchmaker .... EROS
MATERIAL ... see also FABRIC
maternity goddess, Egypt . APET
matgrass .... NARD
math quantity .SINE, OPERAND
math ratio, quantity .. PI, SINE
math term, hyperbolic function COSH, SECH, SINH, TANH
matter: law .... RES
matter-of-fact ...... LITERAL
matter: philos. .... HYLE
mattress case .... TICK
mature ... AGE, RIPE, RIPEN
mature reproductive cell GAMETE
d maul .... MALLET
Mau Mau territory .... KENYA
Mauna — .... LOA
mausoleum, at Agra ..... TAJ
maw: dialect .... MAA
maxilla ...... JAW, MALA
maxim . SAW, ADAGE, AXIOM, GNOME, MOTTO, SAYING
maxwell per ampere turn . PERM
May 1, Celtic ...... BELTANE
May fly .... DUN
MAYAN . see MAYAN INDIAN, page 192
Mayan year .... HAAB
Mayan year-end days .. UAYEB
mayor, Sp. . ALCADE, ALCALDE
meadow .... LEA, MEAD
meadow barley .... RIE
meadow grass genus ..... POA
meadow mouse .... VOLE
meadow saxifrage ..... SESELI
meadowsweet SPIREA, SPIRAEA
meager .... SCANT, LENTEN, SCANTY
meal .... REPAST
meal, boiled .... MUSH
meal, fine .... FARINA
meal, grain . PINOLA, PINOLE
meal, Indian, Hindu ATA, ATTA
meal, light .... BEVER

Meaning

a meaning .... **SENSE, PURPORT**
meantime .... **INTERIM**
MEASURE ... Area, Liquid, Dry
Length, Distance
see SPECIAL SECTION
measure ...... **EM, EN, GAGE,
METE, PACE, GAUGE**
MEASURE, BIB. .. see **HEBREW
MEASURE**
measure, Chin. length .... **LI**
"Measure for Measure"
character .... **ANGELO**
MEASURE, DRY, BIB. .... see
HEBREW DRY MEASURE
measure, Jap. distance ... **RI**
measure of distance, Ang.-Ind.
COSS
measure of spirits .... **PEG**
measure, old Arab .... **SAA**
measure, old length ...... **ELL**
measure, poetry .... **SCAN**
measure, square .... **AR, ARE**
meat, cut of ...... **HAM, RIB,
CHOP, LOIN, FILET,
STEAK, FILLET**
meat on skewer .... **CABOB,
KABOB, KEBAB**
meat roll, fried .... **RISSOLE**
Mecca pilgrim garb .... **IHRAM**
Mecca shrine .... **CAABA,
KAABA, KAABEH**

b Mecca, trip to .... **HADJ**
mechanical man .... **ROBOT**
mechanical part .... **CAM**
mechanics, branch of . **STATICS**
mechanics of motion
DYNAMICS
meddle .... **PRY, TAMPER**
Medea's father .... **AEETES**
median line of valve ... **RAPHE**
medical .... **IATRIC**
medical fluid .... **SERUM**
medicinal capsule ..... **CACHET**
medicinal fruit shrub ... **ALEM**
medicinal gum .... **KINO**
medicinal herb .... **ALOE,
IPECAC, BONESET**
medicinal plant .... **ALOE**
medicinal plant, leaves **SENNA**
medicinal tablet ..... **TROCHE**
medicine man ...... **SHAMAN**
medicine man, S. Am.
PEAI, PIAY
medieval lyric .... **ALBA**
medieval society **GILD, GUILD**
medieval tale, poem . **LAI, LAY**
Medina Arab .... **AUS**
MEDITERRANEAN .... see also
GAZETTEER
Mediterranean, East of.**LEVANT**
Medit. grass .... **DISS**

c Medit. herb genus ...... **AMMI**
Medit. island: It. .... **RODI**
Medit. resort .... **NICE**
medlar .... **MESPIL**
medley .... **OLIO**
Medusa's slayer ..... **PERSEUS**
meet .... **SIT**
meeting .... **TRYST, SESSION**
meeting, political .... **CAUCUS**
megapode .... **MALEO**
melancholy . **SAD, BLUE, DREAR**
melancholy: poet. ..... **DOLOR**
mellow .... **AGE, RIPE**
melodic .... **ARIOSE**
melodious .... **ARIOSO**
melody .... **AIR, ARIA,
TUNE, MELOS**
melon ...... **PEPO, CASABA**
melt together ..... **FUSE, FUZE**
melted .... **MOLTEN**
membership .... **SEAT**
membrane ...... **WEB, TELA,
VELA, VELUM**
memento .... **RELIC**
memorabilia .... **ANA**
memorandum .... **CHIT, NOTE**
memorial post, Indian ... **TOTEM**
memory, pert. to
MNESIC, MNEMONIC
Memphis chief god .... **PTAH**

d Memphis street, famous.**BEALE**
men .... **SONS**
mendacious person ..... **LIAR**
mender, chief ...... **TINKER**
mendicant, Mos.
FAKIR, FAKEER
Menelaus' wife .... **HELEN**
menhaden fish .... **POGY**
menhaden, young ... **SARDINE**
Mennonite .... **AMISH**
Menotti heroine ...... **AMELIA**
men's party .... **STAG**
mental .... **PHRENIC**
mental deficiency ..... **AMENTIA**
mental deficient **IDIOT, MORON**
mention .... **CITE**
Mercator .... **MAP, CHART**
mercenary . **VENAL, HIRELING**
merchandise .... **WARES**
merchant .... **TRADER**
merchant: India .... **SETH**
"Merchant of Venice" heiress
PORTIA
merchant ship ...... **ARGOSY**
merchant vessel, Gr. . **HOLCAD**
Mercury, Gr. .... **HERMES**
Mercury's wand ... **CADUCEUS**
mercy, show .... **SPARE**
mere .... **SIMPLE**
merely .... **ONLY**

a merganser duck SMEW, GARBILL
merge .... MELD
merit .... EARN
merriment .... GLEE
merry-go-round ... CAROUSAL,
CAROUSEL, CARROUSAL
"Merry Widow" composer LEHAR
"Merry Wives" character
PISTOL
mesh .... NET, WEB
Mesopotamia .... IRAK, IRAQ
Mesopotamian boat GUFA, KUFA
Mesopotamian city .... URFA
mesquite bean flour ... PINOLE
mess, to make a ...... BOTCH
mestizo .... METIS
metal .... TIN, MONEL

metal alloy .... BRASS,
MONEL, BRONZE
metal, bar of .... INGOT
metal bar on house door . RISP
metal casting .... PIG, INGOT
metal, coat with .PLATE, TERNE
metal-decorating art .. NIELLO
metal disk .... MEDAL
metal dross .... SLAG
metal filings .... LEMEL
metal fissure .... LODE
b metal leaf .... FOIL
metal mixture .... ALLOY
metal refuse .... SCORIA
metal spacer: print. .... SLUG
metal suit .... MAIL
metal sulfide, impure . MATTE
metal, white .... TIN
metallic rock .... ORE
metalware, lacquered ... TOLE
metalwork, god of .. VULCAN
metarabic acid ..... CERASIN
meteor .... LEONID
meteor, exploding
BOLIS, BOLIDE
meter, Dutch .... EL
meter, one-millionth .. MICRON
meters, 100 sq. ...... AR, ARE
metheglin .... MEAD
method .... PLAN, ORDER
Methuselah's grandson .. NOAH
methyl-phenol
CRESOL, CRESSOL
metric measure ..... AR, ARE,
GRAM, KILO, LITER, METER,
STERE, DECARE, HECTARE
metric "quart" ...... LITER
metrical beat .... ICTUS
metrical unit .... MORA
metropolitan .... URBAN
mew .... GULL
mew, cat's .... MIAU, MIAW,
MIAOU, MIAUL

c Mexican dollar .... PESO
Mex. mush .... ATOLE
Mex. painter .... RIVERA
Mex. persimmon ..... CHAPOTE
Mex. plant .... JALAP
Mex. president ..... ALEMAN,
CALLES, MADERO
Mex. resin tree ...... DRAGO
Mex. rodent .... TUCAN
Mex. slave .... PEON
Mex. spiny tree ..... RETAMA
Mex. timber tree ..... ABETO
Mex. wind instrument . CLARIN
mezzanine .... ENTRESOL
miasma .... MALARIA
mica, kind of ...... BIOTITE
mica of muscovite ..... TALC
microbe .... GERM
microspores .... POLLEN
middle .... MESAL,
MESNE, MEDIAN
middle, in the ...... ATWEEN
middle, toward ...... MESAD
middling .... SOSO
Midgard Serpent slayer .. THOR
midge .... GNAT
midship, off .... ABEAM
d "Midsummer Night's Dream"
character .. PUCK, SNUG
midwife: India .... DHAI
MID-EAST land .. IRAK, IRAQ
mien .... AIR
might .... POWER
mignonette ... GREEN, RESEDA
migrate .... TREK
migratory worker
OKIE, ARKIE
Mikado's court . DAIRI, DAIRO
Milanion's wife ... ATALANTA
Milan's "Met" ..... LA SCALA
mild ...... SHY, MEEK, SOFT,
BLAND, GENTLE
mildness .... LENITY
mile: naut. .... KNOT
mile, part of, Burma ... DHA
Miled, son of .... IR, ITH, EBER
milestone .... STELE
milfoil .... YARROW
military award .... DSO
military cap .... KEPI
military command ... AT EASE
military group . CADRE, CORPS
military maneuvers ... TACTICS
milk, coagulated ..... CURD
milk coagulator ..... RENNIN
milk, curdled ...... CLABBER
milk, part of SERUM, LACTOSE
milk, pert. to .... LACTIC
milk: pharm. .... LAC
milk protein .... CASEINE

Milk

a milk, watery part of .... **WHEY**
milkfish .... **AWA, SABALO**
Milky Way .... **GALAXY**
mill .... **QUERN**
MILLET
     see also GRAIN SORGHUM
millet, India **JOAR,JUAR,CHENA**
millimeter, 1000th part **MICRON**
millstone support .... **RYND**
millwheel board .... **LADE**
millwheel bucket .... **AWE**
Milton, masque by .... **COMUS**
Milton rebel angel ..... **ARIEL**
mime .... **APER**
mimic ...... **APE, APER, MIME**
mimicking, practice of . **APISM**
mimosa .... **ACACIA**
minced oath .. **GAD, GED, GEE,
LUD, DRAT, EGAD, HECK,
OONS, SWOW, MAFEY,
MACKINS**
mind .... **CARE, TEND**
mind, opposite of: Hindu
     ATTA, ATMAN
mind: philos. .... **NOUS**
Mindanao native, Indonesian
     ATA, AETA, MORO
mine ceiling .... **ASTEL**
mine entrance .... **ADIT**
mine narrow veins ..... **RESUE**

b mine passage .... **STULM**
mine roof support .... **NOG**
mine shaft drain pit .... **SUMP**
mine step .... **LOB**
mineral, alkaline ..... **TRONA**
mineral, blue .... **IOLITE**
mineral group ..... **URANITE**
mineral group, pert. to . **SALIC**
mineral, hard **SPINEL, SPINELLE**
mineral, lustrous .... **SPAR**
mineral, raw, native .... **ORE**
mineral salt .... **ALUM**
mineral, soft .... **TALC**
mineral spring .... **SPA**
mineral tar .... **BREA**
mineral, transparent ... **MICA**
mineral used gun-powder **NITER**
Minerva .... **ATHENA**
minim .... **DROP**
mining refuse .... **ATTLE**
mining road .... **BORD**
mining tool ..... **GAD, BEELE**
minister, Moslem **VIZIR, VIZIER**
minister (to) .... **CATER**
mink, Amer. .... **VISON**
minority, legal ...... **NONAGE**
Minos' daughter .... **ARIADNE**
Minotaur's slayer .... **THESEUS**
minstrel .... **RIMER**
minstrel, medieval ... **GOLIARD**
minstrel, Norse . **SCALD, SKALD**

c mint .... **COIN**
mint, Europ. .... **CLARE, CLARY,
CLARRY, HYSSOP, DITTANY**
mint genus .... **MENTHA**
mint herb .... **SAGE**
mints, the .... **NEPETA**
minus .... **LESS**
minute ... **WEE, TINY, SMALL**
mira .... **STAR**
miracle, scene of first .. **CANA**
mirage .... **SERAB**
miscellany .... **ANA**
mischief .... **HOB**
mischievous spirit ...... **PUCK**
misconceive .... **ERR**
Mishnah section . **ABOT, ABOTH**
Mishnah section festivals .**MOED**
misinterpret .... **ERR**
mislay .... **LOSE**
misplay .... **ERROR**
misrepresent .... **BELIE**
Miss Dombey's suitor .. **TOOTS**
missile .... **DART, SNARK**
missile, guided .. **JUNO, NIKE,
THOR, ATLAS, TITAN,
BOMARC, JUPITER, PERSH-
ING, REGULUS, REDSTONE,
BOLD ORION,MINUTEMAN**
mist ... **HAZE, SMUR, MISLE**
mist: Eng. .... **RAG**

d mistake, stupid .... **BONER**
mistakes .... **ERRATA**
mistakes, make .... **ERR**
mite ...... **ACARI, ATOMY,
ACARID, ACARUS**
mite genus .. **ACARI, ACARUS**
mite, tick, order of
     ACARIDA, ACARINA
mitigate . **EASE, ABATE, ALLAY**
mix .... **STIR, ADDLE, KNEAD**
mixture .... **OLIO**
mixture, mineral ..... **MAGMA**
Moab city, chief .... **UR**
Moab king .... **MESHA**
Moabites, Bibl. .... **EMIM**
moat .... **FOSS, FOSSE**
"Moby Dick" pursuer .. **AHAB**
moccasin .... **PAC**
mock .... **GIBE, JIBE, FLEER,
TAUNT, DERIDE**
mock blow .... **FEINT**
mock orange ...... **SYRINGA**
mockingbird genus .... **MIMUS**
model, perfect ..... **PARAGON**
moderate .... **BATE,
ABATE, LESSEN**
modernist .... **NEO**
modest .... **SHY, DEMURE**
modify .... **VARY, ALTER,
EMEND, TEMPER**
Mogul emperor ...... **AKBAR**

100

a MOHAMMEDAN .. see MOSLEM
Mohammedanism ...... ISLAM
Mohammed's adopted son . ALI
Mohammed's birthplace . MECCA
Mohammed's daughter . FATIMA
Mohammed's descendant
SAID, SEID, SAYID
Mohammed's son-in-law . . ALI
Mohammed's supporters . ANSAR
Mohammed's title .... ALI
Mohammed's tomb city MEDINA
Mohammed's uncle .... ABBAS
Mohammed's wife ..... AISHA
Mohawk, city on .... UTICA
Mohicans, last of the .. UNCAS
moiety .... HALF
moist .... WET, DAMP, DANK,
DEWY, UVID, HUMID
moist spot, rock-ledge .... SIPE
moisten ... DAMPEN, IMBRUE
moisture, having medium MESIC
mojarra fish .... PATAO
molasses .. TREACLE, TRIACLE
molasses, rum made from
TAFIA
mold .... MUST
mold, hole in casting . GIT, GEAT
molded clay .... PUG
molding .. CYMA, GULA, OGEE,
b   TORUS, REGLET, REEDING
molding, concave
CONGE, SCOTIA
molding, convex
OVOLO, TORUS, ASTRAGAL
molding, curved . CYMA, OGEE
molding, edge of . ARIS, ARRIS
molding, flat .... FILLET
molding, rounded TORI, TORUS
molding, S-shaped ...... OGEE
molding, square ...... LISTEL
moldings, quarter-round . OVOLI
moldy .... MUSTY
mole ...... NEVUS, NAEVUS
mole cricket, S. Am. . CHANGA
mole genus .... TALPA
molecule part .... ION
molelike mammal ... DESMAN
MOLLUSK. see also GASTROPOD
mollusk ...... CLAM, CHITON,
MUSSEL, ABALONE
mollusk, bivalve ..... SCALLOP
mollusk, chamber-shelled
NAUTILUS
mollusk, gastropod
SNAIL, ABALONE
mollusk genus ARCA, MUREX,
OLIVA, ANOMIA
mollusk, largest ...... CHAMA
mollusk's rasp organ .. RADULA
molt .... MEW, SHED

c molten rock ... LAVA, MAGMA
moment ..... MO, JIFF, TRICE
Monaco, pert. to
MONACAN, MONEGASQUE
monad .... ATOM, UNIT
monastery .... MANDRA
monastery church .. MINSTER
MONEY . see also SPECIAL
SECTION COINS
money ... CASH, CUSH, GELT
money, Amer. Ind. .. WAMPUM
money, bronze .... AES
money certificate . BOND, SCRIP
money, copper .... AES
money: dialect .... SPENSE
money, early Eng. .... ORA
money drawer .... TILL
money exchange fee .... AGIO
money, fishhook . LARI, LARIN
money, medieval .... ORA
money of account .... ORA
money, piece of .... COIN
money premium .... AGIO
money, put in .... INVEST
money reserve .... FUND
money, shell . SEWAN, SEAWAN
money, trade unit .... UNITAS
moneylender .... USURER
moneylender, Ind. .. MAHAJAN
Mongol ... HU, ELEUT, TATAR,
d   ELEUTH, TARTAR
Mongol dynasty ...... YUAN
Mongol warrior .... TATAR
Mongolian tent .... YURT
Mongoloid .... TURK, DURBAN
Mongoloid in Indo-China . SHAN
mongrel .... CUR, MUTT
monitor lizard .... URAN
monk .. FRA, FRIAR, CENOBITE
monk, Buddhist ...... ARAHT,
ARHAT, ARAHAT
monk, Eng. ..... BEDA, BEDE
monk, Gr. Church ... CALOYER
monk, head .... ABBOT
monk settlement . SCETE, SKETE
monk's hood .... COWL
monk's title ..... FRA, ABBOT
monkey .... APE, LAR, SAI,
SIME, SIMIAN, MARMOSET
monkey, Afr. .... MONA,
WAAG, GRIVET
monkey, Asia .... LANGUR
monkey, capuchin .... SAI
monkey, Chin. .... DOUC
monkey genus .... CEBUS
monkey, guenon ..... NISNAS
monkey, howling ...... ARABA
monkey, P. I. .... MACHIN
monkey puzzle ...... PINON
monkey, red, Afr. ..... PATAS
monkey, small .... LEMUR

a monkey, S. Am. ... SAKI, TITI, ACARI, ARABA, SAJOU, TETEE, PINCHE, SAGUIN, SAMIRI, SAIMIRI, SAPAJOU
monkey, spider, genus .QUATA, ATELES, COAITA
monkshood .... ATIS, ATEES, ACONITE
monolith .... MENHIR
monopoly ..... TRUST, CARTEL
monosaccharide .... OSE
Mons, language of ...... PEGU
monster .. GOUL, GOWL, OGRE
monster, Gr. myth .. CHIMERA
monster, half-man-bull MINOTAUR
monster: med. ...... TERAS
monster, 100 eyes ..... ARGUS
monster slain by Hercules HYDRA
month, Egypt. .... AHET, APAP, TYBI
month, first day, Rom. CALENDS, KALENDS
month, Hindu .... ASIN, JETH, KUAR, MAGH
month, in last ...... ULTIMO
month, Jewish ancient ... AB (11th), BUL (8th), ZIF (8th), ABIB (7th), ADAR (6th), ELUL (12th), IYAR, (8th), NISAN (7th), SEBAT (5th), SIVAN (9th), TEBET (4th), TIZRI (1st), TEBETH (4th), TISHRI (1st)

b month, Moslem .... RABIA, RAJAB, SAFAR, SHABAN, RAMADAN
month, Nisan .... ABIB
monument, stone .LECH, CAIRN, DOLMEN, CROMLECH
moon . LUNA, DIANA, PHOEBE
moon, age at beginning of calendar year ..... EPACT
moon angel .... MAH
moon flower .... ACHETE
moon god, Babyl. ... SIN, ENZU
moon goddess .... ASTARTE
moon goddess, Gr. .... SELENA, SELENE, ARTEMIS
moon goddess, Rom. ... LUNA, DIAN, DIANA
moon nearest earth, point PERIGEE
moon valley ..... RILL, RILLE
moor grass .... NARD
moorhen .... GORHEN
Moorish .... MORISCAN
moose genus .... ALCES
mop .... SWAB, SWOB

c Moqul, one of .... HOPI
morals overseer ...... CENSOR
morass .... QUAG, MARSH
moray .... EEL
Mordecai, enemy of .. HAMAN
more .... PLUS
more! ..... BIS, PIU, ENCORE
more than enough ..... TOO, EXTRA, EXCESS
More's island .... UTOPIA
morepork, N. Z. .. PEHO, RURU
morindin dye .... AL
moringa seed .... BEN
morning glory .... IPOMEA
morning music ...... AUBADE
morning: P. I. .... UMAGA
morning prayer ...... MATINS
morning song .... MATIN
Moro .... SULU, LANAO
Moro chief DATO, DATU, DATTO
Moro mantle .... JABUL
Moroccan Berber .... RIFF
Moroccan land, public .. GISH
Moroccan native ...... MOOR
moron .... AMENT, IDIOT
morose ... BLUE, GLUM, GRUM
morsel .... ORT
mortar implement .... PESTLE
d mortar ingredient ...... LIME
mortar mixer .... RAB
mortar tray .... HOD
mortise insert .... TENON
Mosaic law .... TORA, TORAH
mosaic piece .... TESSERA
Moselle, river to .... SAAR
Moses, law given to here SINA, SINAI
Moses' brother .... AARON
Moses' death mountain .. NEBO
Moses' father-in-law .. JETHRO
Moses' spy in Canaan .. CALEB
MOSLEM ..... see also MECCA
Moslem .... TURK
Moslem ablution before prayer WIDU, WUDU, WUZU
Moslem, Afr. .... MOOR
Moslem beggar .FAKIR, FAKEER
Moslem bible .... KORAN
Moslem call to prayer ADAN, AZAN
Moslem chief .... AGA, IMAM, DATTO
Moslem chief gold coin .DINAR
Moslem converts ...... ANSAR
Moslem deity ... JANN, ALLAH
Moslem demon .. JANN, EBLIS
Moslem Easter .... EED
Moslem fast ...... RAMADAN
Moslem festival ...... BAIRAM

102

a Moslem fiat .... **IRADE**
Moslem fourth Caliph .... **ALI**
Moslem grant of property
  WAKF, WAQF, WUKF
Moslem guide .... **PIR**
Moslem holy city ..... **MECCA**
Moslem holy man
  IMAM, IMAUM
Moslem, hostile to Crusaders
  SARACEN
Moslem in Turkestan ... **SALAR**
Moslem judge ... **CADI, CAZI,**
  CAZY, KADI, KAZI, KAZY
Moslem leader . **IMAM, IMAUM**
Moslem marriage.**MOTA, MUTA**
Moslem marriage settlement
  MAHR
MOSLEM MORO ... see MORO
  CHIEF
Moslem mystic .... **SUFI**
Moslem name .... **ALI**
Moslem Negroids .... **MABA**
Moslem noble ... **AMIR, EMIR,**
  AMEER, EMEER
Moslem, N. W. India ... **SWAT**
Moslem official .... **AGA**
Moslem, orthodox ..... **HANIF**
Moslem, P.I. .... **MORO**
Moslem potentate .... **AGA**
Moslem prayer .... **SALAT**
Moslem prayer place ... **IDGAH**
Moslem priest . **IMAM, IMAUM**

b Moslem prince ... **AMIR, EMIR,**
  AMEER, EMEER
Moslem principle .... **IJMA**
Moslem pulpit ...... **MIMBAR**
Moslem reformer ..... **WAHABI**
Moslem religion .... **ISLAM**
Moslem religious college
  ULEMA
Moslem ruler .... **HAKIM**
Moslem saber ...... **SCIMITAR**
Moslem saint .... **PIR**
Moslem school .... **MADRASA**
Moslem spirit ... **JINN, JINNI**
Moslem spiritual guide ... **PIR**
Moslem teacher .. **ALIM, COJA**
Moslem temple .**MOSK, MOSQUE**
Moslem theologians ... **ULEMA**
Moslem title .... **AGA, RAIS,**
  REIS, SEID, SIDI, SYED,
  SYUD, CALIF, SAYID,
  SEYID, CALIPH
Moslem tunic ... **JAMA, JAMAH**
Moslem weight .... **ROTL**
Moslem woman's dress .. **IZAR**
Moslems, Sunnite .... **SART**
Moslemized Bulgarian . **POMAK**
mosque .... **MASJID**
mosque, central .... **JAMI**
mosque, Jerusalem .... **OMAR**
mosque student .... **SOFTA**

c mosquito, genus, yellow-fever
  AEDES
mossbunker fish .... **POGY**
moss of Ceylon .... **AGAR**
moth .... **IO, LUNA,**
  EGGER, TINEA
moth, clearwing, genus . **SESIA**
moth, clothes .... **TINEA**
moth, green .... **LUNA**
mother goddess; Baby. . **ERUA**
mother goddesses. Hindu **MATRIS**
mother of Arthur .... **IGRAINE**
mother of gods .... **RHEA**
MOTHER OF IRISH GODS .. see
  page 200
mother-of-pearl ...... **NACRE**
mother-of-pearl shell.**ABALONE**
mother turned to stone . **NIOBE**
mother's side, related on
  ENATE, ENATIC
mother's side, relation on
  ENATE, ENATION
motherless calf .. **DOGY, DOGIE**
motion, producing .... **MOTILE**
motionless ..... **INERT, STILL**
motive .... **CAUSE, REASON**
motmot, S. Am. ...... **HOUTOU**
motor part .... **ROTOR**
mottled .... **PIED, PINTO**

d mottled, as wood ...... **ROEY**
MOULDING .... see MOLDING
mound ...... **TUMP, BARROW**
mound, Polyn. .... **AHU**
Mount of Olives ...... **OLIVET**
mountain, Alps ...... **BLANC**
mountain ash ... **SORB, ROWAN**
mountain, Asia Minor ... **IDA**
mountain, Bibl. .. **HOR, NEBO,**
  SEIR, SINA, HOREB,
  SINAI, ARARAT
  (see others on page 197)
mountain chain .... **SIERRA**
mountain climbing staff .**PITON**
mountain crest .... **ARETE**
mountain, Crete .... **IDA**
mountain, Edom .... **HOR**
mountain, fabled Hindu . **MERU**
mountain, famous .... **IDA**
mountain, Gr. ...... **HELICON**
mountain in Thessaly ... **OSSA**
mountain lion .... **PUMA**
mountain mint .... **BASIL**
mountain, Moab .... **NEBO**
mountain pass .... **COL**
mountain pass, Alps **CENIS**
mountain pass, India
  GAUT, GHAT
mountain peak .... **ALP**
mountain pool .... **TARN**
mountain recess .... **CWM**
mountain ridge ...... **ARETE**

a mountain ridge, Port. ... SERRA
mountain, 2nd highest N.A. LOGAN
mountain sickness PUNA, VETA
mountain spinach ..... ORACH
mountain spur .... ARETE
mountains, Asia ..... ALTAI
mountains, myth ... KAF, QAF
mourn .... WEEP, GRIEVE, LAMENT
mournful .... SAD, DIRE
mourning band .... CRAPE
mouse .... VOLE
mouse, field .... VOLE
mouse genus .... MUS
mousebird ..... COLY, SHRIKE
mouth .... OS, ORA
mouth, away from .... ABORAL
mouth open .... AGAPE
mouth, river .... DELTA
mouth, tidal river ...... FRITH
mouth, toward .... ORAD
mouthful .... SIP, SUP
mouthlike orifice ...... STOMA
mouthpiece ..... REED, BOCAL
move .... STIR, AFFECT
move a camera .... PAN
move back ..... EBB, RECEDE
move to and fro WAG, FLAP, SWAY
b movement: biol. .... TAXIS
movement, capable of . MOTILE
movement: music ...... MOTO
movement,with:music CONMOTO
movie: Sp. .... CINE
moving part .... ROTOR
mow, barn's .... LOFT
mow of hay .... GOAF
mowed strip .... SWATH
Mowgli's bear friend ... BALU, BALOO
Mozambique native ...... YAO
muck .... MIRE
mud ...... MIRE, MURGEON
mud deposit .... SILT
mud, slimy .... OOZE
mud, stick in .... MIRE
mud, viscous .... SLIME
mud, volcano .... SALSE
muddle .... MESS, ADDLE
muddy .... ROIL
muffin .... GEM
mug .... STEIN, NOGGIN
mug, small .... TOBY
mugger .... GOA
mulatto .... METIS
mulberry bark cloth .... TAPA
mulberry genus ...... MORUS
mulberry, India ...... AL, AAL
mulct .... FINE, AMERCE
mullet, red .... SUR

c multiform .... DIVERSE
multiplicand: math. . FACIEND
multiplier: math. .... FACIENT
multitude ...... HOST, HORDE
mum .... ALE
munch .... CHAMP
mundane .... TERRENE
Munich's river .... ISAR
municipal officer, Sp. . ALCADE, ALCAID, ALCAIDE, ALCAYDE
muntjac deer . KAKAR, RATWA
murder by suffocation . BURKE
murder fine, Scot. .... CRO
murderer, first .... CAIN
murmuring sound CURR, PURL, PURR
Musci, plant of .... MOSS
muscle .... THEW, SINEW
muscle coordination, lack of ATAXIA
muscle, deep, pert. to SCALENE
muscle, kind of ERECTOR, LEVATOR
muscle, like .... MYOID
muscle, round, rolling .. TERES
muscle, stretching .... TENSOR
muscles .... BRAWN
muscular action, irregular
d ATAXIA
muscular spasm .... TIC
Muse, chief .... CALLIOPE
muse in reverie .... REVE
Muse of astronomy ... URANIA
Muse of comedy ..... THALIA
Muse of dancing .TERPSICHORE
Muse of history .... CLIO
Muse of lyric poetry CLIO, ERATO
Muse of music ...... EUTERPE
Muse of poetry ...... ERATO
Muse of sacred lyric POLYMNIA
Muse of tragedy . MELPOMENE
Muses, 9 .... PIERIDES
Muses' region ...... AONIA
Muses, The .... NINE
musette .... OBOE
museum head ...... CURATOR
mush .... ATOLE, SEPON
mushroom .... MOREL, MORIL
mushroom cap .... PILEUS
music: as written .... STA
music character .... DOT, CLEF, REST
music drama .... OPERA
music for nine .... NONET
music for three .... TRIO
music for two .... DUET
music from the sign: abbr. . DS

a music hall .... ODEA,
      ODEON, ODEUM
music interval .... TRITONE
music: it proceeds .... VA
music lines .... STAFF
music piece
   SERENATA, SERENATE
music, sacred
   CHORAL, CHORALE
music symbols, old ... NEUME
MUSICAL .... see also MUSIC
musical beat .... TAKT
musical composition, India
   RAGA
musical direction . STA, TACET
musical instrument ..... ASOR,
   DRUM, FIFE, GIGA, HARP,
   HORN, LUTE, LYRE, OBOE,
   PIPE, REED, TCHE, TUBA,
   TURR, VINA, VIOL, CELLO,
   RAPPEL, SPINET, CLAVIER,
   HELICON, OCARINA
musical sign .. DOT, CLEF, REST
musical study .... ETUDE
musical work .... OPUS
musician, 11th century . GUIDO

c musket ball, India ...... GOLI
Musketeer .... ATHOS,
   ARAMIS, PORTHOS
mussel, fresh-water ..... UNIO
must .... STUM
mustache monkey ... MOUSTOC
mustard family plant ... CRESS
musteline animal
   OTTER, RATEL
mustiness .... FUST
mutilate .... MAIM
muttonbird .... OII
muttonfish .... SAMA
"My Name is —" ..... ARAM
mysteries .... ARCANA
mysterious .... OCCULT
mystery .... RUNE
mystic word, Hindu ...... OM
mystic writing .... RUNE
mythical land ...... LEMURIA
mythical stream .... STYX
mythical submerged island
   ATLANTIS
mythical warrior .... ARES
MYTHOLOGY ..... see SPECIAL
   SECTION, Page 198

N

b nab .... GRAB, ARREST
Nabal's wife: Bibl. ... ABIGAIL
NaCl .... SALT
nahoor sheep .... SNA
nail .... CLAW, TALON,
   UNGUES, UNGUIS
nail, hooked .... TENTER
nail, mining, surveying .. SPAD
nail, thin .... BRAD
nail with aperture ...... SPAD
nails, 100 lbs. .... KEG
namaycush .... TOGUE
NAME .... see also MAN'S
   NAME, WOMAN'S NAME
name .... DUB, TERM, CLEPE,
   NOMEN, TITLE, ENTITLE
name: Dan. .... NAAM
name plate, shop's .... FACIA
named ... Y-CLEPT, Y-CLEPED
namely .... VIZ
Naomi, name claimed by MARA
Naomi's daughter-in-law . RUTH
naos .... CELLA
nap, coarse, long ...... SHAG
nap-raising device .... TEASEL,
   TEASLE, TEAZEL, TEAZLE
nap-raising machine ...... GIG
nap, to raise .... TEASE
napoleon, game like ..... PAM

d Napoleon's brother-in-law
   MURAT
Napoleon's isle .... ELBA
Napoleon's marshal general NEY
Napoleonic victory .JENA, LODI
Narcissus, nymph who loved
   ECHO
narcotic .... DOPE, DRUG,
   HEROIN, OPIATE
narcotic, India . BANG, BHANG
narcotic plant .... DUTRA
narcotic shrub
   KAT, KAAT, KHAT
narcotic shrub, S. Am.
   COCA, CUCA
narrate .... TELL
narrow ...... LINEAL, STRAIT
nasal .... RHINAL
Nata's wife: myth ..... NANA
nation: Ger. .... VOLK
nation, pert. to ...... STATAL
NATIVE .... see TRIBES in
   SPECIAL SECTION, Page 191
native .... ITE, RAW, NATAL,
   ENDEMIC, INDIGENE
natural luster, having ... NAIF
natural talent . DOWER, FLAIR
nature ...... OUSIA, ESSENCE
nature goddess ...... CYBELE

Nature

a
nature principal: Hindu... **GUNA**
nature spirit .... **NAT**
nature story writer ..... **SETON**
nautical .... **MARINE**
nautical cry...... **AHOY, OHOY,**
AVAST
Navaho hut............. **HOGAN**
naval hero............. **PERRY**
navy jail................. **BRIG**
near ...... **AT, NIGH, ABOUT,**
CLOSE
Near East native .. **ARAB, TURK**
Near East river valley..... **WADI**
near the ear .... **PAROTIC**
near to................. **BY, ON**
nearest.................. **NEXT**
nearsighted person..... **MYOPE**
nearsightedness ..... **MYOPIA**
neat ...... **TIDY, TOSH, TRIG,**
TRIM, SPRUCE
neat cattle.............. **NOWT**
neatly................. **FEATLY**
necessitate .... **ENTAIL**
neck, nape of .... **NUCHA**
necklace ..... **BEADS, RIVIERE**
neckline shape..... **VEE, BOAT,**
CREW
neckpiece ..... **ASCOT, STOLE**
neckpiece, feather........ **BOA**
neckpiece, woman's ..... **FICHU**
NECKTIE .... see **TIE**

b
need........ **WANT, REQUIRE**
needle .... **PROD, BODKIN**
needle bug .... **NEPA**
needle case.............. **ETUI**
needle-shaped .... **ACUATE,**
ACERATE
needlefish .... **GAR**
needlelike bristle ..... **ACICULA**
negative......... **NE, NO, NAY,**
NON, NOT
negative pole .... **CATHODE**
neglect.................. **OMIT**
neglected school subject: abbr.
LAT.
negligent .... **LAX**
negotiate............... **TREAT**
negrito .... **ATA, ATI, ITA,**
AETA, ATTA
Negro dance............. **JUBA**
Negro: India .... **HUBSHI**
NEGRO TRIBE .... see SPECIAL
SECTION, AFRICAN TRIBES
Nelson's victory site....... **NILE**
nematocyst.............. **CNIDA**
nemesis................. **BANE**
Nepal Mongoloid .... **RAIS**
Nepal native.............. **KHA**
Nepal people.............. **RAIS**
nephew .... **NEPOTE**

c
nephew, Fijian .... **VASU**
Neptune................... **LER**
Neptune's spear...... **TRIDENT**
nerve cell.............. **NEURON**
nerve-cell process....... **AXON**
nerve layers, brain ...... **ALVEI**
nervous .... **EDGY**
nervous disease....... **CHOREA**
nest .. **NID, NIDE, NIDI, NIDUS**
nest, eagle's ..... **AERY, AERIE,**
EYRY, EYRIE
nested boxes .... **INRO**
nestling .... **EYAS**
net .... **CLEAR**
net, fishing ..... **SEINE, STENT,**
TRAWL
net of hair-lines .... **RETICLE**
NETHERLANDS... see SPECIAL
SECTION
netlike .... **RETIARY**
nettle family ... **RAMIE, RAMEE**
network .... **WEB, MESH,**
RETE, RETIA
neuroglia .... **GLIA**
neve .... **FIRN**
— Nevis, Gt. Brit. peak .... **BEN**
new .... **NOVEL, RECENT**
New Caledonia bird....... **KAGU**
New England state: abbr. .... **RI**

d
New Guinea area........ **PAPUA**
New Guinea tribesman.. **KARON**
New Guinea victory...... **GONA**
New Guinea wild hog ..... **BENE**
New Jerusalem foundation
JASPER
new, lover of .... **NEO**
new star .... **NOVA**
new wine .... **MUST**
New York harbor isle ..... **ELLIS**
New Zealand aborigine...... **ATI**
N.Z. bird......... **HUIA, KAKI,**
PEHO, RURU
N.Z. clan .... **ATI**
N.Z. evergreen .... **TAWA**
N.Z. fruit pigeon......... **KUKU**
N.Z. laburnum............ **GOAI**
N.Z. mollusk .... **PIPI**
N.Z. native............. **MAORI**
N.Z. native fort........ **PA, PAH**
N.Z. parson bird........ **KOKO**
N.Z. plant................ **KARO**
N.Z. rail bird........... **WEKA**
N.Z. scabbard fish........ **HIKU**
N.Z. shrub .... **KARO**
N.Z. shrub, poisonous..... **TUTU**
N.Z. subtribe........... **HAPU**
N.Z. timber tree ... **GOAI, HINO,**
MIRO, PELU, RATA, RIMU,
HINAU, HINOU, KAURI,
KAURY, TOTARA

a N.Z. tree..... **AKE, KOPI, NAIO,**
PUKA, TORO, WHAU
N.Z. tribe .... **ATI**
N.Z. wages .... **UTU**
N.Z. wood hen .... **WEKA**
news agency, Eng. ... **REUTERS**
news agency, former Dutch
ANETA
news agency, Jap....... **DOMEI**
news agency, Rus. Soviet. **TASS**
news paragraph........... **ITEM**
newspaper service ..... **AP, UP,**
INS, UPI, REUTERS
newspapers.............. **PRESS**
newt...... **EFT, EVET, TRITON**
nibble .... **GNAW, KNAB, KNAP**
niche............... **RECESS**
Nichols' hero .... **ABIE**
Nick Charles' dog .... **ASTA**
Nick Charles' wife....... **NORA**
nickel steel alloy .... **INVAR**
nicotine acid........... **NIACIN**
nictitate .... **WINK**
Niger delta native .... **IJO**
NIGERIA.......... see SPECIAL
SECTION
Nigerian Negro....... **ARO, IBO**
Nigerian tribe............. **EDO**
NIGERIAN TRIBE OR PEOPLE
see also SPECIAL SECTION
page 191

b niggard................. **MISER**
nigh................... **NEAR**
night, Norse ...... **NATT, NOTT**
nightingale, Pers....... **BULBUL**
nightjar................. **POTOO**
nightmare demon, Teut. . **MARA**
nightmare, the....... **INCUBUS**
nightshade, black ..... **MOREL,**
MORIL
Nile, as god.............. **HAPI**
Nile island .... **RODA**
Nile native............. **NILOT**
Nile sailboat .... **CANGIA**
Nile valley depression ... **KORE**
Nile, waste matter on.... **SADD,**
SUDD
Nilotic Negro ...... **JUR, LUO,**
LWO, SUK
nimble .... **SPRY, AGILE**
nimbus........... **HALO, NIMB**
nimrod .... **HUNTER**
nine-angled polygon . **NONAGON**
nine, based on .... **NONARY**
nine, group of......... **ENNEAD**
nine inches .... **SPAN**
nine, music for........ **NONET**
Nineveh's founder....... **NINUS**
ninth day, every....... **NONAN**
ninth: mus............. **NONA**
niton................. **RADON**

c nitrogen.......... **AZO, AZOTE**
Noah, pert. to.......... **NOETIC**
Noah's landing .... **ARARAT**
Noah's 1st son .... **SEM, SHEM**
Noah's 2nd son .... **HAM**
Nobel prize, literature '04
MISTRAL
Nobel prize, science...... **UREY**
noble, nobleman . **DUKE, EARL,**
LORD, PEER, BARON, COUNT
noble: Ger...... **GRAF, RITTER**
NOBLEMAN .... see NOBLE
nobleman, Jap........... **KAMI**
nocturnal mammal **BAT, LEMUR**
nod................ **BOW, BECK**
Nod, west of............. **EDEN**
nodding .... **NUTANT**
noddy tern: Hawaii ...... **NOIO**
node........... **KNOB, KNOT,**
KNUR, NODUS
"— noire" .... **BETE**
nomad .... **ARAB, SCENITE**
Nome in Greece.......... **ELIS**
nomenclature .... **NAME**
nominal value............ **PAR**
nominate .... **NAME**
non-gypsy: Romany....... **GAJO**
non-Jew............. **GOI, GOY**
non-Moslem of Turkey or

d Ottoman Empire.... **RAIA, RAYA**
non-professional .... **LAY, LAIC**
non-union worker........ **SCAB**
nonchalant .... **COOL**
none: dialect............ **NIN**
nonsense. **PISH, POOH, HOOEY**
nonsense creature ...... **GOOP**
noodles: Yiddish ...... **FARFEL,**
FERFEL
nook, sheltered .... **COVE**
noose................. **LOOP**
Norn, one of **URD, URTH, WYRD**
Norse "Adam"........... **ASKR**
Norse bard .... **SCALD, SKALD**
Norse chieftain.... **JARL, YARL**
Norse epic.............. **EDDA**
Norse explorer...... **ERIC, LEIF**
NORSE GOD or GODDESSES
see also GODS and GODDESSES
and see also SPECIAL SECTION
Page 200
Norse gods **VANS, AESIR, VANIR**
Norse letter............. **RUNE**
Norse myth. hero .. **EGIL, EGILL**
Norse myth. king.......... **ATLI**
Norse myth. "Life" force.... **LIF**
Norse myth. woman ...... **IDUN**
Norse neighbor .... **FINN**
Norse poetry........... **RUNES**
Norse prose .... **EDDA**
Norse sea goddess .... **RAN**
Norseman ...... **DANE, SWEDE**

a
North African .... **BERBER**
N. Afr. outer garment .. **HAIK**
North Carolina college .. **ELON**
North Carolinian .... **TARHEEL**
North Caucasian language
　　　　UDI, AVAR, UDIC, UDISH
North, Mrs. of fiction .. **PAMELA**
North Sea fishing boat .. **COBLE**
North Sea, river into **ELBE, TEES**
North Star .... **POLARIS**
North Syrian deity .... **EL**
northern .... **BOREAL**
northern Scandinavian ... **LAPP**
northern tribe, China .... **HU**
northernmost land ..... **THULE**
Northumberland river ... **TYNE**
Norway coin .... **ORE**
Norway territorial division. **AMT**
Norwegian author ... **HAMSUN**
Norwegian composer ... **GRIEG**
Norwegian county **AMT, FYLKE**
Norwegian saint .... **OLAF**
nose .... **CONK, NASI,**
　　　　　　NASUS, SNOOP
nose, having large .... **NASUTE**
nose, having snub .... **SIMOUS**
nose openings .. **NARES, NARIS**
nose, snub .... **PUG**
nostrils .... **NARES, NARIS**

b
nostrils, of .... **NARIC,**
　　　　NARIAL, NARINE
"— Nostrum," Mediterranean
　　　　　　　　　MARE
not at home .... **OUT**
not ever: poet. .... **NEER**
not genuine .... **TIN**
not in style ...... **OUT, PASSE**
not long ago .... **LATELY**
not moving .... **INERT, STATIC**
not one .... **NARY, NONE**
not so great .... **LESS, FEWER,**
　　　　　　　　SMALLER
notch ... **KERF, NICK, NOCK,**
　　　　　　CRENA, CRENAE
notched .. **SERRATE, SERRATED**
note .... **CHIT, MEMO**
note, double, whole .... **BREVE**
note, Guido's .... **UT, ELA**
note, Guido's low ..... **GAMUT**
note, half .... **MINIM**
note, high, highest .... **ELA**
note, marginal
　　　　POSTIL, APOSTIL
note: music .. **DI, DO, FA, FI,**
　　LA, LE, LI, ME, MI, RA, RE,
　　RI, SE, SI, SO, TE, TI, SOL
note, old Gr. musical .... **NETE**
note, old musical .... **ELA**
NOTE, SCALE ..... see **NOTE:**
　　　　　　　　MUSIC
notes, furnish with . **ANNOTATE**

c
notes in Guido's scale .. **ELAMI**
nothing . **NIL, NIX, NUL, NULL,**
　　　　　　ZERO, NIHIL
notion .... **BEE, IDEA**
notion, capricious ..... **WHIM**
notional .... **IDEAL**
notorious .... **ARRANT**
Nott's son .... **DAG**
notwithstanding .... **YET**
nought .... **ZERO, NULL**
NOUN ENDING
　　　　　see **SUFFIX, noun**
noun form .... **CASE**
noun suffix of condition .. **ATE**
noun with only 2 cases. **DIPTOTE**
nourish .... **FEED, FOSTER**
nourishment .... **PABULUM**
Nova Scotia .... **ACADIA**
novel, advocate of ...... **NEO**
novel by A. France ..... **THAIS**
novelty .... **FAD**
novice .... **TIRO, TYRO**
now: dial. .... **NOO**
noxious .... **MIASMIC**
Nubian .... **NUBA**
nucha .... **NAPE**
nuclear element ...... **PROTON**
nudge .... **POKE**
nuisance .... **PEST**
nullify .... **NEGATE**

d
nullify, legally .... **VOID**
number, describable by .**SCALAR**
number under 10 ...... **DIGIT**
number, whole .... **INTEGER**
numbered: Bib. .... **MENE**
numerous .. **MANY, MULTIPLE**
nun, Franciscan .... **CLARE**
nun, head .... **ABBESS**
nun's dress .... **HABIT**
nunbird .... **MONASE**
nuque .... **NAPE**
nurse, Oriental, India .. **AMA,**
　　IYA, AMAH, AYAH, EYAH
nurse, Slavic .... **BABA**
nursemaid: Fr. .... **BONNE**
nut ...... **COLA, KOLA, LICHI,**
　　　　ALMOND, CASHEW,
　　　　LICHEE, LITCHI
nut, beverage .... **COLA, KOLA**
nut, hickory .... **PECAN**
nut, pert. to .... **NUCAL**
nut, P. I. .... **PILI**
nut, pine .... **PINON**
nut, stimulating .... **BETEL**
nut tree, Afr. .... **COLA, KOLA**
nuts for food .... **MAST**
nuthatch genus .... **SITTA**
nutlike drupe .... **TRYMA**
nutmeg husk .... **MACE**
nutria .... **COYPU**

a nutriment ... **FOOD, ALIMENT**
nutritive .... **ALIBLE**
nymph .... **MAIA, LARVA**
nymph, fountain ...... **EGERIA**
nymph, laurel .... **DAPHNE**
nymph, Moslem .... **HOURI**

c nymph, mountain ..... **OREAD**
nymph, ocean ...... **OCEANID**
nymph, water . **NAIAD, NEREID**
nymph, wood . **DRYAD, NAPEA,**
NAPAEA, HAMADRYAD
Nyx's daughter .... **ERIS**

O, plural .... **OES**
oaf .... **LOUT**
oak, Calif. .... **ENCINA**
oak, dried fruit of ... **CAMATA**
oak, evergreen .... **HOLM**
oak moss .... **EVERNIA**
oak, Turkey .... **CERRIS**
oakum, seal with ...... **CALK**
oar .... **ROW, BLADE, PROPEL**
oar at stern .... **SCULL**
oasis, N. Afr. ... **WADI, WADY**
oat genus .... **AVENA**
oats as rent .... **AVENAGE**
oath, knight's .... **EGAD**
oath, old-fashioned . **ODS, EGAD**
oath, say under ...... **DEPOSE**
obeisance, Oriental
BOW, SALAAM
b obey .... **HEED, MIND**
object ... **AIM, CAVIL, DEMUR**
object of art .... **CURIO**
objection, petty .... **CAVIL**
objective ...... **AIM, GOAL**
obligation .... **TIE, DEBT**
DUTY, ONUS
oblique ...... **CANT, BEVEL,**
SLANT, SLOPE
obliterate .... **ERASE, EFFACE**
obliteration .... **RASURE**
oblivion .... **LETHE, LIMBO**
oblivion stream .... **LETHE**
obscure .... **DIM, FOG, DARK**
BEDIM, CLOUD
obscure, render ...... **DARKLE**
observe .. **SEE, NOTE, BEHOLD,**
REMARK, CELEBRATE
obstinate .... **SET, HARD**
obstruction, petty .... **CAVIL,**
obtain .... **GET**
obvious ...... **OPEN, PATENT**
obvious, not . **SUBTLE, SUBTILE**
occasional .... **ODD**
Occident .... **WEST**
occipital protuberances .. **INIA**
occultism .... **CABALA**
occupant .... **TENANT**
occupation .... **TRADE**
occupy .... **USE, FILL**
occurrence .... **EVENT**

ocean's rise, fall ...... **TIDE**
oceanic .... **PELAGIC**
oceanic tunicate .... **SALP**
ocher, black .... **WAD, WADD**
octave, designating high .. **ALT**
octave of church feast ... **UTAS**
octopus .... **POULPE**
octoroon **METIS, MESTEE, MUSTEE**
odd-job man .... **JOEY**
Odin. **WODAN, WODEN, WOTAN**
Odin's brother ...... **VE, VILI**
Odin's granddaughter . **NANNA**
Odin's son ... **TY, TYR, THOR,**
TYRR, VALE, VALI
Odin's wife .... **RIND**
odor .... **AROMA, SCENT**
ODYSSEUS ... see also **ULYSSES**
d Odysseus' companion . **ELPENOR**
Odysseus' friend ..... **MENTOR**
Odyssey beggar .... **IRUS**
Odyssey singer .... **SIREN**
Oedipus' father ...... **LAIUS**
Oedipus' mother .... **JOCASTA**
of speed of sound .... **SONIC**
of the age: abbr. .... **AET**
off .... **AWAY**
offend .... **CAG**
offense .... **CRIME**
offense: law .. **MALA, MALUM**
offer .... **BID, TENDER**
offered up .... **OBLATE**
offhand .... **CASUAL**
office, ecclesiastic .. **MATINS**
office, priest's .... **MATINS**
office, R. C. curia
DATARY, DATARIA
officer, church ...... **BEADLE**
officer, court: Scot. ... **MACER**
officer, municipal: Scot. **BAILIE**
officer, Rom. .... **LICTOR**
officer, synagogue .... **PARNAS**
officer, university
DEAN, BEADLE, BURSAR
official, Moslem .... **HAJIB**
official, Rom.
EDILE, AEDILE, TRIBUNE
official, subordinate .. **SATRAP**
official, weights .... **SEALER**
offspring .... **SONS, HEIRS**

109

a ogygian .... AGED
Ohio college town ...... ADA
oil .... FAT, LARD, LUBE,
ATTAR, OLEUM
oil beetle .... MELOE
oil bottle ..... CRUCE, CRUET,
CRUSE, CRUIZÉ
oil, cruet .... AMPULLA
oil, edible .... ACEITE
oil, orange .... NEROLI
oil, pert. to .... OLEIC
oil, rub with .... ANOINT
oil-yielding Chinese tree .. TUNG
oil-yielding tree ... EBO, EBOE
oilfish .... ESCOLAR
oilstone .... HONE
oily ketone .... IRONE
ointment .... BALM, NARD,
SALVE, CERATE, POMADE
Ojibway secret order
MEDA, MIDE
O.K. .... ROGER
okra .... GOMBO, GUMBO
old .... AGED, ANILE, SENILE
"Old Curiosity Shop" girl . NELL
old English army .... FYRD
old Eng. gold piece ..... RYAL
old Eng. rune ... WEN, WYN
old Greek coin .... OBOL
old Irish coin .... RAP
old Persian money .... DARIC
OLD TESTAMENT see BIBLICAL
and SPECIAL SECTION
Old Testament objects ... URIM

b Old Test. people . PHUD, PHUT
old person .... DOTARD
old Sp. gold coin ...... DOBLA
old times .... ELD, YORE
old-womanish .... ANILE
oleaginous .... OILY
oleander genus .... NERIUM
oleic acid salt .... OLEATE
oleoresin .... ANIME,
ELEMI, BALSAM
olive fly genus .... DACUS
olive genus .... OLEA
olive, inferior .... MORON
olive, stuffed .... PIMOLA
Oliver's nickname ...... NOLL
Olympian deity-god-goddess
ARES, HERA, APOLLO,
ATHENA, HERMES, AR-
TEMIS, DEMETER
Olympus, mountain near . OSSA
Olympus queen .... HERA
Olympus, region by ... PIERIA
omen .... BODE, PRESAGE
omission, vowel ...... ELISION
omit ...... DELE, PASS, SKIP
omit in pronunciation .. ELIDE

c omitted, having part
ELLIPTIC, ELLIPTICAL
onager .... ASS
once: dial. .... ANES
one .... AIN, UNIT
one-base hit .... SINGLE
one behind other .... TANDEM
one-eighth Troy ounce .. DRAM
one-eyed giant ..... CYCLOPS
one-horse carriage ..... SHAY
one hundred sq. meters AR, ARE
one hundred thousand rupees
LAKH
one, music by .... SOLI, SOLO
one-spot .... ACE
one thousand .... MIL
one-year record ...... ANNAL
O'Neill heroine .... ANNA
onion .... CEPA
onion, Welsh .... CIBOL
onionlike plant .. CIVE, LEEK,
CHIVE, SHALLOT, ESCHALOT
only .... MERE, SAVE, SOLE
onward .... AHEAD, FORTH
onyx, Mex. .... TECALI
oorial .... SHA
ooze .... LEAK, SEEP, SEIP,
SIPE, SYPE, EXUDE
open .... AJAR, OVERT,
BROACH, PATENT, UNWRAP

d open court .... AREA
open plain .... VEGA
opening .... GAP, HOLE,
RIFT, SLOT, VENT, HIATUS
opening; long ..... RIMA, SLOT
opening, mouthlike
STOMA, STOMATA
opening, slit-like .... RIMA
opening, small .... PORE
opera ... AIDA, BORIS, ORFEO
opera, Beethoven .... FIDELIO
opera, Bizet .... CARMEN
opera composer, modern
BRITTEN, MENOTTI
opera, Gounod .... FAUST
opera hat .... GIBUS
opera heroine .. AIDA, ELSA,
MIMI, SENTA, ISOLDE
opera house, Milan ... SCALA
opera, Massenet
MANON, THAIS
opera, Puccini .... TOSCA
opera scene .... SCENA
opera singer .... MELBA
opera soprano, star . ALDA, PONS
BORI, RISE, RAISA, STEBER
opera star .... DIVA
opera, Verdi ... AIDA, ERNANI
opera, Wagner .... RIENZI
operate .... RUN, MANAGE
operetta composer ..... FRIML

a opium poppy seed ...... MAW
opossum, S. Am. ...... QUICA
opponent .. FOE, ANTI, RIVAL
opportune .... TIMELY
opportunity .... CHANCE
oppose .... IMPUGN
opposed, one .... ANTI
opposed to solo .... TUTTI
opposite extremities ... POLES
opposite .... REVERSE
Ops' daughter .... CERES
Ops' husband .... SATURN
optical glass .... LENS
optical illusion ...... MIRAGE
optical instrument lines RETICLE
optimistic .... ROSY, ROSEATE
oracle, Apollo's .... DELOS
oracle, Gr. .. DELPHI, DELPHOI
oral .... PAROL
orange-red stone ...... SARD
orange tincture, Her. ... TENNE
orangutan, Malay ...... MIAS
orarion .... STOLE
orator .... OTIS, RHETOR
orb of day .... SUN
orbit point .. APSIS, APOGEE
orchid genus .... DISA
orchid leaves for tea
                FAAM, FAHAM
orchid tuber .... SALEP
b ordain .... DECREE
order .... BID, FIAT,
                ARRAY, EDICT, DECREE
order, one of Catholic. MARIST
order, put in .... TIDY, SETTLE
orderliness .... SYSTEM
ordinance .... LAW
ordnance piece ...... MORTAR
ore deposit ...... LODE, MINE
ore of iron .... OCHER, OCHRE
ore receptacle ...... MORTAR
organ .... EAR, EYE
organ of algae .... PROCARP
organ part .... STOP
organ pipe .... REED
organ pipe, displayed MONTRE
organ prelude .... VERSET
organ, seed-bearing .. PISTIL
organ stop REED,SEXT,DOLCAN,
                CELESTE, MELODIA
organism, 1-cell
                AMEBA, AMOEBA
organism, simple
                MONAD, MONAS
organization .... SETUP
orgy .... REVEL
Orient .... EAST
Oriental ..... ASIAN, TATAR
Oriental dwelling .... DAR

c Oriental lute .... TAR
Oriental nursemaid .... AMA,
                IYA, AMAH, AYAH, EYAH
Oriental plane tree .. CHINAR
Oriental porgy .... TAI
Oriental potentate ...... AGA
Oriental sailing ship .. DHOW
Oriental servant ...... HAMAL
Oriental ship captain .... RAS
Oriental weight .... ROTL
orifice. PORE, STOMA, OSTIOLE
orifices, sponge ...... OSCULA
origin .... SEED
original .... NEW
original sin .... ADAM
originate ARISE, START, CREATE
Orinoco tributary .... ARO
oriole, golden .... LORIOT
ornament .... FRET
ornament, curly ...... SCROLL
ornament in relief ... EMBOSS
ornament, spire .... EPI
ornamental border .... DADO
ornamental grass .... EULALIA
ornamental nailhead .... STUD
Orpheus' destination ... HADES
Orpheus' instrument ..... LYRE
orris .... IRIS
orris-root ketone, oil ... IRONE
oscillate .... WAVE
osier .... WITHE
d Osiris' brother .... SET
Osiris' wife, sister ...... ISIS
ostentation .... POMP
ostracism .... TABU, TABOO
ostrich, Am. .... RHEA
ostrich-like bird
                EMU, EMEU, RATITE
Otaheite apple .... HEVI
Othello was one .... MOOR
Othello's lieutenant, foe IAGO
otherwise .... ELSE
otic .... AURAL
otologist .... AURIST
otter brown, color ... LOUTRE
otter genus .... LUTRA
Ottoman .... TURK
Ottoman court .... PORTE
Ottoman official ...... PASHA
"Our Mutual Friend," ballad-
                seller in .... WEGG
oust .... EJECT, EVICT
out .... AWAY, FORTH
out-and-out .... ARRANT
out: Dutch .... UIT
out of style .... PASSE
out of the way .... ASIDE
outbreak, unruly ...... RIOT
outburst, sudden ..... SPATE
outcast
                LEPER, PARIAH, ISHMAEL

Outcome

outcome, final .... **UPSHOT**
outcry .... **CLAMOR**
outer .... **ECTAL**
outer portion of earth ... **SIAL**
outfit .. **KIT, RIG, GEAR, SUIT**
outfit, queer .... **GETUP**
outlet .... **VENT**
outline .... **PERIMETER**
outlook .... **VISTA**
outmoded .... **PASSE**
OUTRIGGER see **MALAY CANOE**
outward .... **ECTAD**
ova .... **EGGS**
oval ... **ELLIPTIC, ELLIPTICAL**
oven .... **KILN, OAST**
oven, annealing ..... **LEER, LEHR**
oven, Polyn. native ...... **UMU**
over .... **ATOP, ABOVE,**
AGAIN, ENDED, ACROSS
over-nice .... **FINICAL**
overnice person .... **PRIG**
over: poet. .... **OER**
over there ..... **YON, YONDER**
overact .... **EMOTE**
overcoat ... **ULSTER, PALETOT**
overdue payment ..... **ARREAR**
overflow .... **DEBORD**
overfond, be ..... **DOAT, DOTE**
overjoy .... **ELATE**
overlay .... **CEIL**
overripe grain .... **BRITE**
overseer, ranch: Sp. Am.
.... **CAPORAL**
overshadow .... **DOMINATE**
overshoe
GOLOE, GALOSH, GALOSHE
overskirt .. **PANIER, PANNIER**
overspreading mass ..... **PALL**

overt .... **OPEN, FRANK**
overwhelm .... **DELUGE**
overwhelming amount .... **SEA**
Ovid's "— Amatoria" .... **ARS**
ovule .... **SEED**
ovum .... **EGG**
owala tree .... **BOBO**
owl, barn, Samoa ...... **LULU**
owl, eagle .. **BUBO, KATOGLE**
owl, horned .... **BUBO**
owl, S. Asia .... **UTUM**
owl's cry .... **HOOT**
own up to .... **AVOW**
ownership, of land, old law
.... **ODAL, UDAL**
ox, extinct wild .... **URUS**
ox, forest .... **ANOA**
ox, long-haired .... **YAK**
ox of Caesar's time .... **URUS**
ox, wild .... **ANOA**
ox, wild: India .... **GAUR**
GOUR, ZEBU, GAYAL
oxalis, S. Amer. .... **OCA**
oxen .... **KINE**
oxhide strap ..... **REIM, RIEM**
oxide .... **CALX**
oxidize .... **RUST**
oxygen compound **OXID, OXIDE**
oxygen, form of ...... **OZONE**
oxygen radical .... **OXYL**
oyster bed material
CULCH, CUTCH, CULTCH
oyster drill .... **BORER**
oyster farm: Fr. .... **PARC**
oyster, young .... **SPAT**
oysterfish .... **TAUTOG**
Ozarks, town west of in Okla.
.... **ADA**
Oz books author ...... **BAUM**

P

pace .... **RATE, STEP**
pachisi, kind of .... **LUDO**
pachyderm .... **ELEPHANT**
Pacific aroid food plant **TARO**
Pacific Island cloth ..... **TAPA**
Pacific pine .... **HALA**
Pacific shrub .... **SALAL**
pacify
CALM, SOOTHE, PLACATE
pack .... **WAD, STOW**
pack animal .... **ASS,**
BURRO, LLAMA, SUMPTER
pack horse .... **SUMPTER**
pack down .... **RAM, TAMP**
package .... **ROBBIN**
package of spun silk .. **MOCHE**
pad .... **TABLET**

padded jacket under armor
.... **ACTON**
padnag .... **TROT, AMBLE**
Padua, town near ...... **ESTE**
pagan god .... **IDOL**
page, "Love's Labor Lost" **MOTH**
page number .... **FOLIO**
pageantry .... **POMP**
"Pagliacci" character .. **CANIO**
"Pagliacci" heroine ... **NEDDA**
pagoda, Chinese ...... **TA, TAA**
pagoda ornament ... **EPI, TEE**
paid notice .... **AD**
pail .... **SKEEL**
pain, dull .... **ACHE**
pain reliever **OPIATE, ANODYNE**
paint, face .... **FARD, ROUGE**

pain-killer alkaloid source **COCA**
painted bunting: Creole .. **PAPE**
PAINTER .. see also ARTIST
    and country of each artist
painter, modernist
       KLEE, MIRO, ERNST
painting style .... **GENRE**
painting, wall .... **MURAL**
pair .... **DUO, DIAD,**
      DUAD, DYAD, MATE
pair of horses ... **SPAN, TEAM**
pairing .... **MATING**
palanquin .... **JAUN**
palanquin bearer ..... **HAMAL**
palanquin, Jap. .... **KAGO**
palatable, very .... **SAPID**
pale .... **WAN, ASHY,**
      ASHEN, PASTY
pale color .... **PASTEL**
pale-colored .... **MEALY**
Palestine in Jewish use **ERETS**
palisade: fort. .... **RIMER**
Pallas .... **ATHENA**
pallid .... **WAN, PALE**
palm ...... **TI, COCO, TALA,**
  TALIPAT, TALIPOT, TALI-
  PUT
palm, Afr. .... **DUM**
palm, Asia .... **ARENG, BETEL**
palm, betel .... **ARECA**
palm, book .... **TARA**
palm, Brazil .... **ASSAI**
palm, climbing ...... **RATTAN**
palm cockatoo .... **ARARA**
palm, dwarf genus .... **SABAL**
palm fiber **DOH, TAL, RAFFIA**
palm fiber, S. Amer. ... **DATIL**
palm genus .... **ARECA**
palm genus, Asia .... **ARENGA**
palm juice, fermented .. **SURA**
palm leaf
    OLA, OLE, OLAY, OLLA
palm-leaf mat .... **YAPA**
palm lily .... **TI**
palm, liquor ..... **BENO, BINO**
palm, N. Z. .... **NIKAU**
palm, nipa ..... **ATAP, ATTAP**
palm off .... **FOB, FOIST**
palm, palmyra leaf ..... **OLA,**
    OLE, OLLA, OLAY
palm sago, Malay ... **GOMUTI**
palm sap .... **TODDY**
palm starch .... **SAGO**
palm, W. Ind. **GRIGRI, GRUGRU**
palmetto .... **SABAL**
palmyra leaf ...... **OLA, OLE,**
    OLAY, OLLA
palmyra palm .... **BRAB**
palp .... **FEELER**
palpitation .... **PALMUS**

pamper .... **COSHER, COSSET**
pamphlet .... **TRACT**
panacea .... **ELIXIR**
Panama gum tree **COPA, YAYA**
Panama, old name .. **DARIEN**
Panama tree, large .. **CATIVO**
Panay negrito .... **ATI**
panda .... **WAH, BEAR**
panel .... **PANE**
panel of jurors ...... **VENIRE**
pang .... **THROE**
pangolin .... **MANIS**
panic .... **FEAR, FUNK**
pannier .... **DOSSER**
Panopolis, chief god of .. **MIN,**
    KHEM
pant .... **GASP**
pantry .... **AMBRY, LARDER,**
    SPENCE, BUTTERY
— Paulo, Brazil .... **SAO**
papal cape ... **FANO, FANON,**
  FANUM, ORALE, PHANO,
  FANNEL
papal church .... **LATERAN**
papal collar ... **FANO, FANON,**
  FANUM, ORALE, PHANO,
  FANNEL
papal court ...... **SEE, CURIA**
papal fanon .... **ORALE**
papal letter .... **BULL, BULLA**
papal scarf .... **ORALE**
papal veil .... **FANO, FANON,**
  FANUM, ORALE, PHANO,
  FANNEL
papal vestment .... **FANO,**
  FANON, FANUM, ORALE,
  PHANO, FANNEL
paper folded once ..... **FOLIO**
paper, imperfect, poor
    CASSE, CASSIE, RETREE
paper, lighting .... **SPILL**
paper measure .. **REAM, QUIRE**
paper mulberry .... **KOZO**
paper mulberry bark .... **TAPA**
paper size
    DEMY, POTT, OCTAVO
paper, thin crisp ...... **PELURE**
par, 2 under .... **EAGLE**
Para, Brazil, capital .. **BELEM**
parade .... **MARCH, STRUT**
paradise .... **EDEN**
paradise, Buddhist ..... **JODO**
paradise, like ...... **EDENIC**
"Paradise Lost" angel .. **ARIEL**
paragraph .... **ITEM**
parallelogram .... **RHOMB**
paralysis .... **PARESIS**
parapet, solid portion of **MERLON**
parasite .... **LEECH**

Parasite

a
parasite in blood .... TRYP
parasitic insect MITE, ACARID
parasitic plant MOSS, DODDER
paravane .... OTTER
Parcae .... FATES
Parcae, one of
    NONA, MORTA, DECUMA
parcel of land .... LOT, PLAT
parchment, book
    FOREL, FORREL
pardon .... REMIT, CONDONE
pardon, general .... AMNESTY
pare .... PEEL
Paris art exhibit ...... SALON
Paris, first bishop of
    DENIS, DENYS
Paris section .... PASSY
Paris subway .... METRO
Paris thug .... APACHE
Paris' father .... PRIAM
Paris' wife .... OENONE
parish head .... RECTOR
parley .... PALAVER
Parliament report .. HANSARD
parol .... ORAL
paroxysm .... FIT, SPASM
parrot
    KEA, LORY, VASA, VAZA
parrot, Brazil ... ARA, ARARA
parrot-fish

b
    LORO, LAUIA, SCARID
parrot, hawk .... HIA
parrot, monk .... LORO
parrot, N. Z. large KEA, KAKA
parrot, P. I., green ... CAGIT
parrot, sheep-killing ... KEA
parrot's bill, part of .... CERE
parrotlike .... ARINE
parry .... FEND, EVADE
Parsi priest .... MOBED
Parsi scripture ...... AVESTA
parsley camphor ...... APIOL
parsley, plant kin to
    ANISE, CELERY
parson bird
    POE, TUE, TUI, KOKO
parsonage .... MANSE
part .... ROLE, SOME, PIECE,
    BREAK, SEVER, SHARE,
    CLEAVE, ELEMENT
part, Greek play
    EXODE, EXODOS
part of church .... BEMA
    NAVE, AISLE, ALTAR
part of horse's foot .. PASTERN
part of speech .. NOUN, VERB
parted .... PARTITE
participle ending .... ING
parti-colored .... PIED, PINTO

c
parti-colored horse
    ROAN, CALICO
particle ...... ACE, BIT, ION,
    JOT, ATOM, IOTA, DROP,
    MITE, MOTE, GRAIN,
    SHRED, TITTLE
particle, electrically charged
    ION
particle in cosmic rays MESON
particle of chaff ...... PALEA
particle, small
    JOT, ATOM, IOTA, MOTE
particular .... ITEM
Partlet .... HEN, BIDDY
partnership: Hawaii HUI, HOEY
partridge call ... JUCK, JUKE
partridge, sand ...... SEESEE
partridge, snow ...... LERWA
party .... SECT
parvenu .... UPSTART
pasha .... DEY
pass .... HAND, ELAPSE
pass a rope through ... REEVE
pass between peaks .... COL
pass by .... BYGO
pass on .... RELAY
pass over ... OMIT, SKIP, ELIDE
pass through .... REEVE
pass through mountains .. COL,
    DEFILE

d
passable .... SOSO
passage .... GUT, ITER,
    CANAL, TRANSIT
passage, bastion .... POSTERN
passage, covered .... ARCADE
passage: hist. .... ALURE
passage: music TUTTI, STRETTA
passage out ...... EXIT, EGRESS
passageway ADIT, HALL, AISLE
Passover .... PASCH, PASCHA
Passover meal SEDAR, SEDER
passport endorsement VISA, VISE
past AGO, GONE, OVER, AGONE
paste .... STRASS
pasteboard .... CARD
pasted-up art work .. COLLAGE
pastel .... TINT
pastoral .... IDYLLIC
pastoral place ...... ARCADIA
pastoral poem .. IDYL, IDYLL
pastoral staff .. PEDA, PEDUM
pastry
    PIE, FLAN, TART, ECLAIR
pasture .... LEA
pasture: N. Eng. ...... ING
pasture, to .... AGIST
pasty .... DOUGHY
pat .... DAB, TAP
pat, very .... APT
Patagonian cavy ...... MARA
patchwork, literary .... CENTO

a
patella .... ROTULA
paten ...... ARCA, ARCAE
patent from monarch .. BERAT
path: Anglo-Ir. ..... CASAUN
path: math. .... LOCUS
path of planet .... ORBIT
pathos, false .... BATHOS
patriarch Jacob ...... ISRAEL
patriarch's title .... NASI
patron .... CLIENT
patron saint of France
　　　　　　　DENIS, DENYS
patronage ...... EGIS, AEGIS
pattern ...... NORM, TYPE,
　　IDEAL, MODEL, PARAGON
pattern, large square DAMIER
Paul, Apostle .... SAUL
Paul's birthplace ..... TARSUS
paulownia tree .... KIRI
pause: poet. .... REST
pause: poet. & music
　　SELAH, CESURA, CAESURA
paver .... TUP
paver's mallet .... TUP
pavilion .... TENT
paving stone .... FLAG, SETT
paw .... PUD, FOOT
pawl .... DETENT
b
pawn .... HOCK
Pawnee Indian rite .... HAKO
Pawnee tribes .... CHAUI
pay .... ANTE, WAGE, REMIT
pay dirt .... ORE
pay, fixed ...... STIPEND
pay for another ...... TREAT
pay homage: feudal law
　　　　　　　　　ATTORN
pay one's part .... ANTE
pay out .... SPEND
payable .... DUE
paymaster, India ...... BUXY
payment back .... REBATE
payment for a bride, S. Afr.
　　　　　　　　　LOBOLA
payment for death, feudal CRO
payment for homicide ... ERIC
payment, press for ...... DUN
payment to owner: Fr. law CENS
pea .... LEGUME
peace .... PAX
peace god, Anglo-Saxon .. ING
peace of mind .... REST
peaceful ... IRENE, IRENICAL
peach, clingstone ...... PAVY
peacock .... MAO, PAVO
peacock blue .... PAON
peacock butterfly .... IO
peacock fish .... WRASSE
peacock genus .... PAVO
peacock: Kipling .... MAO

c
peak ...... ALP, TOR, ACME,
　　　APEX, PITON, ZENITH
peak: Scot. .... BEN
peanut ...... MANI, GOOBER
pear, autumn .... BOSC
pear cider .... PERRY
pearl blue color ...... METAL
Pearl Buck heroine .... OLAN
pearl, imitation ...... OLIVET
pearl millet ... BAJRA, BAJRI
pearlweeds .... SAGINA
peasant.CARL, CEORL, CHURL
peasant, India .... RYOT
peasant, Scot.
　　　　　COTTAR, COTTER
peat .... TURF
peat spade .... SLADE
pecan tree .... NOGAL
peccary, collared ...... JAVALI
peck ...... DAB, NIP, KNIP
pedal .... TREADLE
peddle .... HAWK, SELL, VEND
peddle: Eng. .... TRANT
pedestal .... GAINE
pedestal part .. DADO, PLINTH
peduncle, plant ...... SCAPE
peel . BARK, PARE, RIND, SKIN
peep-show .... RAREE
PEER ...... see also NOBLE
peer .... PEEK, PEEP
d
Peer Gynt's mother ...... ASE
peevish .... PETULANT
peg .... KNAG
peg, golf .... TEE
peg, wooden
　　NOG, TRENAIL, TREENAIL
Pegu ironwood .... ACLE
Peleg's son .... REU
pellucid ...... CLEAR, LIMPID
pelma .... SOLE
pelota court .... FRONTON
pelt ...... FELL, SKIN, STONE
pelvic bone, pert. to .... ILIAC
pelvic bones .... ILIA
pen name, Dickens ...... BOZ
pen name, G. Russell ...... AE
pen name, Lamb .... ELIA
pen point .... NEB, NIB
pen-text .... RONDE
penman, Yutang .... LIN
penalty .... FINE
pendulum weight ...... BOB
Penelope's father .... ICARIUS
penetrate
　　GORE, ENTER, PERMEATE
penitential season ..... LENT
penmanship .... HAND
pennies .... PENCE
Pennsylvania sect ..... AMISH
Pentateuch .... TORA, TORAH

115

People

PEOPLE .. see also TRIBES in SPECIAL SECTION
people .... **MEN, FOLK, ONES, RACE, DEMOS**
people, ancient Asian ... **SERES**
people: Ger. .... **VOLK**
people: Ir. .... **DAOINE**
people, Nigerian . **BENI, BENIN**
people: Sp. .... **GENTE**
people, spirit of ...... **ETHOS**
people, the .... **DEMOS**
pepper, climbing ...... **BETEL**
pepper, garden .... **PIMIENTO**
pepper plant, Borneo .... **ARA**
pepper shrub
AVA, CAVA, KAVA, KAWA
pepper vine .... **BETEL**
Pequod's captain ...... **AHAB**
"per —" ..... **DIEM, ANNUM**
perceive .. **SEE, SENSE, DESCRY**
perception . **EAR, TACT, SENSE**
perch .... **SIT, ROOST**
perch genus .... **PERCA**
perchlike fish ...... **DARTER**
percolate .. **OOZE, SEEP, LEACH**
peregrine .... **ALIEN**
perenially shifting sands region
AREG
perfect ...... **IDEAL, MODEL**
perforate ...... **BORE, DRILL, PUNCH, RIDDLE**
perform .... **RENDER**
performer
DOER, ACTOR, ARTISTE
perfume
ATAR, OTTO, AROMA, ATTAR
perfume base .... **MUSK**
perfume with incense .... **CENSE**
perfumed pad ...... **SACHET**
Pericles' consort .... **ASPASIA**
periphery ... **RIM, PERIMETER**
period .... **DOT**
period, time
AGE, EON, ERA, STAGE
periodic as Med. winds **ETESIAN**
permit .. **LET, ALLOW, LICENSE**
permission .... **LEAVE**
pernicious, something .... **PEST**
perplex
BAFFLE, CONFUSE, BEWILDER
Persephone ..... **CORA, KORE**
Persephone's husband
HADES, PLUTO
Persia .... **IRAN**
Persian .... **IRANI**
Persian coin, ancient .. **DARIC**
Pers. demigod .... **YIMA**
Pers. elf .... **PERI**
Pers. enameled tile .... **KASI**
Pers. fairy .... **PERI**
Pers. governor, old ... **SATRAP**
Pers. headdress, ancient **TIARA**

Pers. lord ..... **KAAN, KHAN**
Pers. mystic .... **SUFI**
Pers. native .... **LUR**
Pers. poet .... **OMAR**
Pers. potentate .... **SHAH**
Pers. priestly caste .... **MAGI**
Pers. province, ancient .. **ELAM**
Pers. race, tribesman **LUR,KURD**
Pers. rug .. **SENNA, HAMADAN**
Pers. ruler .... **SHAH**
Pers. ruler of dead .... **YIMA**
Pers. sect .... **BABI**
Pers. sprite .... **PERI**
PERS. TITLE ...... see TITLE, PERSIAN
Pers. tribe member ..... **LUR**
Pers. weight .... **SER**
persimmon, E. Ind. **GAB, GAUB**
person of mixed blood
METIS, MESTIZO
person, overnice .... **PRIG**
personage .... **NIBS**
personification of folly ... **ATE**
personification of light: Polyn.
AO
personnel .... **STAFF**
perspiration .. **SUDOR, SWEAT**
perspire ...... **EGEST, SWEAT**
pert girl ...... **CHIT, MINX**
pertaining to the chin **MENTAL**
pertinent .... **APT, PAT**
perturb .... **DERANGE, DISTURB, AGITATE, TROUBLE**
PERU INDIAN .. see page 193
peruse ..... **CON, READ, SCAN**
peruser .... **CONNER**
Peruvian fertility goddess **MAMA**
Peruvian plant .... **OCA**
pervade .... **PERMEATE**
pester ...... **ANNOY, TEASE**
pestle .... **PILUM**
pestle vessel ...... **MORTAR**
pet .... **CADE**
pet lamb ..... **CADE, COSSET**
"Peter Pan" dog ...... **NANA**
"Peter Pan" pirate ...... **SMEE**
petiole .... **STIPE**
Petrarch's love ...... **LAURA**
petrol .... **GAS**
peyote .... **MESCAL**
phantoms .... **EIDOLA**
Pharaoh .... **RAMESES**
Pharaoh after Rameses I .. **SETI**
phase ...... **FACET, STAGE**
pheasant brood **NID, NYE, NIDE**
pheasant, Himal. . **CHIR, CHEER**
pheasant, India ...... **MONAL**
Phidias statue ...... **ATHENA**
philippic .... **TIRADE**
PHILIPPINE ISLANDS
see also SPECIAL SECTION

a Philippine Islands attendant **ALILA**
P.I. bast fiber ...... **CASTULI**
P.I. cedar .... **CALANTAS**
P.I. chief **DATO, DATU, DATTO**
P.I. DWARF see P. I. **NEGRITO**
P.I. dyewood tree
    TUI, IPIL, TUWI
P.I. food .... **POI, SABA**
P.I. fort .... **COTA, KOTA**
P.I. grass ...... **BOHO, BOJO**
P.I. lighter .... **CASCO**
P.I. lizard .... **IBID, IBIT**
P.I. Moslem .... **MORO**
P.I. negrito, native, dwarf
    ATA, ATI, ITA,
    AETA, ATTA
P.I. palm wine ... **BENO, BINO**
P.I. peasant .... **TAO**
P.I. poisonous tree .... **LIGAS**
P.I. rice ...... **PAGA, MACAN**
P.I. sash .... **TAPIS**
P.I. servant .... **ALILA**
P.I. shrub, rope **NABO, ANABO**
P.I. skirt .... **SAYA**
P.I. tree ..... **DAO, IBA, TUA,**
    TUI, BOGO, DITA, IFIL,
    IPIL, YPIL
P.I. warrior .... **MORO**
Philistine city .... **GATH,**
    GAZA, EKRON
b Philistine deity, principal **DAGON**
philosopher's stone .... **ELIXIR**
philosophical element ... **RECT**
philosophical theory **MONISM**
philosophy, pert. to Gr. **ELEATIC**
phloem .... **BAST**
phoebe .... **PEWEE, PEWIT**
Phoebus .... **SOL, SUN**
Phoenician city .... **TYRE**
Phoenician goddess .. **ASTARTE**
Phoenician port .... **SIDON**
Phoenician princess .. **EUROPA**
phonetic notation system
    ROMIC
phonetical sound .... **PALATAL**
phosphate of lime ... **APATITE**
photo-developing powder **METOL**
photography solution ... **HYPO**
Phrygian god .... **ATTIS**
Phrygian lunar god ..... **MEN**
physical ... **SOMAL, SOMATIC**
physician ..... **GALEN, MEDIC**
physician's group .... **AMA**
physician's symbol **CADUCEUS**
physicist, Am. .... **EINSTEIN**
physicist, Eng. .... **BOYLE**
physicist, Fr. .... **CURIE**
physicist, Nobel prize-winner
    1944 .... **RABI**
physiological individual .. **BION**

c piano, upright ...... **CLAVIAL**
pick, miner's: Eng.
    MANDREL, MANDRIL
pick out ...... **CULL, GLEAN**
picket .... **PALE**
pickled bamboo shoots **ACHAR**
pickled meat .... **SOUSE**
pickling fluid .... **BRINE**
pickling herb .... **DILL**
pickpocket .... **DIP**
"Picnic" author .... **INGE**
picture ... **DRAW, PORTRAIT**
picture border .... **MAT**
picture, composite .. **MONTAGE**
picturesque .... **SCENIC**
pie, meat, small .... **PASTY**
piebald .... **PINTO**
piebald pony ... **PIED, PINTO**
piece of eight .... **REALS**
piece out .... **EKE**
piece, thin .... **SLAT**
pier .... **KEY, DOCK,**
    MOLE, QUAI, QUAY
pier, architectural ..... **ANTA**
pier support ... **PILE, PILING**
pierce ... **GORE, STAB, SPEAR**
pig.**HOG, SOW, SHOAT, SHOTE**
pig, wild .... **BOAR**
pig, young .... **ELT, GRICE**
pigs .... **SUS**
pigs' feet .... **PETTITOES**
d pigs, litter of .... **FARROW**
pigs, red .... **DUROC**
pigeon ... **NUN, BARB, DOVE,**
    POUTER, ROLLER
pigeon hawk .... **MERLIN**
pigeon pea.**DAL, TUR, GANDUL**
piglike animal ..... **PECCARY**
pigment, blue-green .... **BICE**
pigment, brown .... **SEPIA**
pigment, brown, from soot
    BISTER, BISTRE
pigment, deep blue .... **SMALT**
pigment, red .... **LAKE**
pigment test crystalline **DOPA**
pigment, without .... **ALBINO**
pigmentation, lack of
    ACHROMA
pigtail .... **CUE, QUEUE**
pike, full grown . **LUCE, LUCET**
pike, walleyed .... **DORE**
pilaster .... **ANTA**
pilchard .. **FUMADO, SARDINE**
pilchard-like fish ..... **SPRAT**
pile ...... **NAP, HEAP, SPILE**
pile driver .... **OLIVER**
pile driver ram .... **TUP**
pile of hay .... **RICK, STACK**
pilfer .... **STEAL**
pilgrim .... **PALMER**

117

a   pilgrimage city .... MECCA
pilgrimage to Mecca .... HADJ
pill, large .... BOLUS
pillage .... LOOT, SACK, STEAL
pillage .... RAPINE
pillar, as of ore .... JAMB
pillar, Hindu .... LAT
pillar, resembling ..... STELAR
pillar, tapering .... OBELISK
pillow .... BOLSTER
pilot .... GUIDE, STEER
pimento or —spice ..... ALL
pin .... BROOCH
pin, firing .... TIGE
pin, gunwale .... THOLE
pin, machine .... COTTER
pin, metal .... RIVET
pin, pivot .... PINTLE
pin, rifle firing .... TIGE
pin, Roman .... ACUS
pin, small, very LILL
pin, splicing .... FID
pin, wooden .. FID, NOG, PEG,
     COAG, COAK, DOWEL
pin wrench .... SPANNER
pinafore .... TIER
pincer claw .... CHELA
pinch .... NIP
pinched with cold ..... URLED
Pindar work .... ODE
b   pine-cone, like a ..... PINEAL
pine, Mex. .... OCOTE, PINON
pine, Scot. .... RIGA
pine, textile screw
     ARA, PANDAN
pineapple NANA, PIÑA, ANANA
pineapple genus .... PUYA
pinfeather .... PEN
pinion .... WING
pink .... DAMASK
pinnacle .... TOP, APEX
pinnacle, ice .... SERAC
pinniped .... SEAL
pinochle score, term
     DIX, MELD
pint, half .... CUP
pintado fish .... SIER
pintail .... SMEE
pinworm .. ASCARID, ASCARIS
pious Biblical Jew ..... TOBIT
pipe .... TUBE, RISER
pipe, Irish .... DUDEEN
pipe joint, fitting .... TEE
pipe, pastoral .... REED
pipe, tobacco
     BRIAR, BRIER, DUDEEN
pipe, water .HOOKAH, NARGILE
pipe with socket ends
     HUB, HUBB
pipelike .... TUBATE
pique .... PEEVE

c   pirate ..... ROVER, CORSAIR
pirate in War of 1812 LAFITTE
pismire .... ANT, EMMET
pistil part .... CARPEL
pistol .... DAG, DAGG,
     MAUSER, SIDEARM
pistol: slang .... HEATER
pit ...... HOLE, ABYSS, STONE
pit for roots, Maori ..... RUA
pit: medical .... FOSSA
pit, small .. FOVEA, LACUNA
pitch .... KEY, TAR, TONE
pitcher .... JUG, EWER
pitcher's false move ..... BALK
pith .... NUB, GIST
pith helmet .... TOPI, TOPEE
pithy .... TERSE
pithy plant .... SOLA
pitiful quality .... PATHOS
pittance .... DOLE
pitted .... FOVEATE
pity .... RUTH
placard .... POSTER
place ...... SET, LIEU, LOCI,
     SPOT, LOCUS, STEAD, LO-
     CALE
place before .... APPOSE
place, camping .... ETAPE
place case is tried .... VENUE
place in office again .. RESEAT
d   place, in relation ...... POSIT
place, market .... FORUM
place of shelter .. GITE, HAVEN
placid .... CALM, SERENE
plagiarize .... STEAL
plague .... PEST, TEASE
plain, arctic .... TUNDRA
plain, Argentine ...... PAMPA
plain, Asia .... CHOL
plain, Palestine .... ONO
plain, Russia .... STEPPE
plain, S. Am. .... LLANO
plain, treeless ...... SAVANNA
plain, treeless Arctic .. TUNDRA
plain, upland .. WOLD, WEALD
Plains Indian .... see page 193
plainly woven .... UNI
plait .... PLY, BRAID
plan .... PLOT, INTEND
plane, Fr. .... SPAD
plane, Ger. .... STUKA
plane, Jap. .... ZERO
plane part .... FLAP,
     NOSE, TAIL, WING
plane, Russ. fighter ...... MIG
planets (in order of distance from
     sun) MERCURY (1), VE-
     NUS (2), EARTH (3),
     MARS (4), JUPITER (5),
     SATURN (6), URANUS (7),
     NEPTUNE (8), PLUTO (9)

a planets in distance from Earth
(closest first)

1—VENUS	5—SATURN
2—MARS	6—URANUS
3—MERCURY	7—NEPTUNE
4—JUPITER	8—PLUTO

planets in size
(largest first)

1—JUPITER	6—VENUS
2—SATURN	7—PLUTO
3—NEPTUNE	8—MARS
4—URANUS	9—MERCURY
5—EARTH	

planetarium .... **ORRERY**
planetary aspect **CUSP, TRINE**
plank's curve on ship ..... **SNY**
plant .... **SOW, SEED**
plant, bayonet .... **DATIL**
plant broom .... **SPART**
plant, bulb
   CAMAS, CAMASS, CAMMAS
plant cutter bird ...... **RARA**
plant cutting .. **SLIP, PHYTON**
plant disease .... **RUST, SMUT**
plant joined to another **GRAFT**
plant life .... **FLORA**
PLANT, LILY ...... see LILY
plant, lily-like
   CAMAS, CAMASS, CAMMAS
plant louse .... **APHID**
plant, male .... **MAS**
b plant, medicinal, S. Am.
   ALOE, SENNA, IPECAC
plant modified by environment
   to abnormal development
     ECAD
plant, mustard family
   KALE, CRESS
plant organ .... **LEAF**
plant pod .... **BOLL**
plant, poisonous .... **LOCO**
plant, sea-bottom .... **ENALID**
plant stem: bot. ..... **CAULIS**
plant stem tissue ...... **PITH**
plant used as soap ... **AMOLE**
plants of area .... **FLORA**
plantain lily genus .... **HOSTA**
plantation, osier ...... **HOLT**
planter .... **SEEDER**
plaster .... **SMEAR**
plaster, artist's painting.**GESSO**
plaster of Paris .... **GESSO**
plastic .... **LUCITE**
plate, battery .... **GRID**
plate, Eucharist ...... **PATEN**
plate, reptile's .... **SCUTE**
plate to hurl .... **DISCUS**
plateau .... **MESA**
plateau, Andes .... **PUNA**
platform ..... **DAIS, STAGE**
platform, ancient ...... **BEMA**

c platform, mine shaft
   SOLLAR, SOLLER
platinum, of .... **OSMIC**
platinum wire loop ..... **OESE**
Plato's "Idea" ... **EIDE, EIDOS**
play .... **DRAMA**
play on words .... **PUN**
play, part of ..... **ACT, SCENE**
play unskillfully ...... **STRUM**
player .... **ACTOR**
playing card, old It. ... **TAROT**
playwright .... **INGE**
plea, to end: law .... **ABATER**
plead ...... **SUE, ENTREAT**
pleading: law .... **OYER**
please .... **SUIT**
pleasing .... **NICE**
pleasure god, Egypt. . **BES, BESA**
pledge .... **VOW,**
   **GAGE, OATH, PAWN,
   TROTH, ENGAGE**
pledge, Rom. law .... **VAS**
plexus .... **RETE, RETIA**
pliable .... **WAXY**
pliant .... **LITHE**
plinth .... **ORLO, SOCLE**
plot .... **LOT,**
   PLAT, CABAL, CONSPIRE
plow, cutter **COLTER, COULTER**
d plow part .... **SHETH, SHEATH**
plow, sole of .... **SHARE**
plowed field ... **ERD, ARADA**
plug .... **BUNG,**
   CORK, SPILE, STOPPER
plum .... **GAGE, SLOE**
plume ..**EGRET, PREEN, AIGRET**
plummet .... **FATHOM**
plump child .... **FUB**
plunder .... **ROB, LOOT, PREY,
   SACK, BOOTY, RAVEN,
   RAVIN, REAVE, PILFER,
   RAPINE, RAVAGE, RAVINE**
plunder ruthlessly ... **MARAUD**
plunge .... **DIVE, DOUSE**
plural ending ..... **EN, ES**
plus .... **AND**
Pluto .... **DIS, HADES, ORCUS**
Pluto's mother-in-law **DEMETER**
pneumonia, kind of .... **LOBAR**
Po tributary .... **ADDA**
pochard .... **SMEE**
pocket billiards .... **POOL**
pocket gopher, Mex. .... **TUZA**
pod, cotton .... **BOLL**
pods for tanning .... **PIPI**
Poe poem .... **RAVEN**
poem .... **ODE, ELEGY, EPODE**
poem division, or part . **CANTO**
poem, 8 line .... **TRIOLET**

Poem

a
poem, long heroic .. EPIC, EPOS
poem, love .... SONNET
poem, lyric ...... ODE, EPODE
poem, mournful .... ELEGY
poem, of a .... ODIC
poem, old Fr. .... DIT
poem, sacred .... PSALM
poet .... BARD, ODIST
poet, A.-S. .... SCOP
poet, Bengal .... TAGORE
poet, blind, epic ..... HOMER
poet, lyric .... ODIST
poet, Norse ... SCALD, SKALD
poet, poor .... RIMER
poetry .... EPOS, POESY
poetry, early .... RUNE
poetry, Finnish .... RUNES
poetry, mournful, pert. to
.... ELEGIAC
poetry, Norse god of
.... BRAGE, BRAGI
poi, source of .... TARO
point END, TIP, BARB, PUNTO
point in moon's orbit nearest
earth .... PERIGEE
point of curve .... NODE
point of land .... SPIT
point of moon .... CUSP
point of view .... ANGLE

b
point on mariner's compass
.... RUMB
point on tooth's crown .. CUSP
point, tennis or golf .... ACE
point won .... GOAL
pointed ..... SHARP, ACUATE
pointed arch .... OGEE
pointed end .... CUSP
pointed missile DART, SPEAR
pointed remark .... BARB
pointed staff .... PIKE
pointer .... WAND
pointless .... INANE
poison .... BANE, TAINT
poison, arrow .. INEE, UPAS,
URALI, URARE, URARI,
CURARE, CURARI
poison, hemlock ..... CONINE
poison, India BISH, BISK, BIKH
poisonous protein RICIN, RICINE
poisonous weed .... LOCO
poke ..... JAB, PROD, NUDGE
poker stake ..... POT, ANTE
pokeweed ..... POCAN, SCOKE
Polar explorer .... BYRD
pole .... MAST
pole, Gaelic games
.... CABER, CABIR
Pole .... SLAV
pole, naut. ... MAST, SPRIT
pole to handle fish .... PEW
pole to pole, from AXAL, AXIAL

c
polecat, Cape ZORIL, ZORILLA
police line .... CORDON
policeman ..... COP, PEELER
policeman, state .... TROOPER
policeman, S. Afr. ..... ZARP
polish .... RUB, WAX,
SHINE, LEVIGATE
POLISH ... see also POLAND
SPECIAL SECTION
Polish assembly ... SEIM, SEJM
Polish cake .... BABA
Polish general .. BOR, ANDERS
Polish title of address
.... PAN, PANI
polished ...... SHINY, SLEEK,
URBANE, ELEGANT
polisher .... EMERY
polishing material
.... RABAT, ROUGE
polite CIVIL
political booty .... GRAFT
pollack fish .... SEY
pollen brush .. SCOPA, SCOPAE
Pollux or Castor .... ANAX
Pollux' mother .... LEDA
Pollux' twin .... CASTOR
polo stick .... MALLET
Polynesian .... MAORI
Polyn. "Adam" .... TIKI
Polyn. chestnut .... RATA

d
Polyn. cloth .... TAPA
Polyn. dance .... SIVA
Polyn. deity, demon
.... AKUA, ATUA
Polyn. drink .... AVA
Polyn. for nature's power MANA
Polyn. god .... ATEO
Polyn. god of forest ... TANE
Polyn. herb .... PIA
Polyn. hero .... MAUI
Polyn. island group ... SAMOA
Polyn. languages
.... MAORI, MAHORI
Polyn. lily .... TI
Polyn. stone heap ...... AHU
pome .... APPLE
"Pomp and Circumstance" Com-
poser .... ELGAR
pompous .... TURGID
pond .. MERE, POOL, LOCHAN
ponder .... MUSE, PORE
pontiff .... POPE
pony .... CAVY
pony, student's .... CRIB
pool ..... MERE, TARN,
LAGOON, PUDDLE
pool: Scot. .... DIB, CARR,
LINN, LLYN
poon tree DILO, DOMBA, KEENA
poor .... NEEDY
poor joe .... HERON

120

poor player .... DUB
poorly ILL
POPE .. see also PAPAL
Pope ... JOHN, PIUS, ADRIAN
Pope, English .... ADRIAN
Pope John XXIII first name
.... ANGELO
Pope John XXIII last name
.... RONCALLI
Pope Pius XI .... RATTI
Pope Pius XII ...... PACELLI
POPE'S CAPE, COLLAR ... see
PAPAL CAPE, COLLAR
Pope's triple crown TIAR, TIARA
poplar .... ALAMO, ASPEN
poplar, white ... ABELE, ASPEN
poppy red .... GRANATE
poppy seed .... MAW
populace, the .... DEMOS
popular girl .... BELLE
porcelain
.... CHINA, SEVRES, LIMOGES
porcelain, ancient .... MURRA
porcelain, Chin. ...... JU, KO
porcelain, Eng. .... SPODE
porch .... ANTA, STOOP,
VERANDA, VERANDAH
porch, Gr. .... STOA
porch, Hawaiian ...... LANAI
porch swing .... GLIDER
porcupine anteater .. ECHIDNA
porcupine, Canada .... URSON
pore .... PORUS, STOMA,
OSTIOLE, STOMATA
porgy .... SCUP
porgy, Europ. .... PARGO
porgy genus .... PAGRUS
porgy, Jap. (Oriental) .... TAI
porkfish .... SISI
porous rock ..... TUFA, TUFF
porpoise .... DOLPHIN
porridge .... POB, BROSE
porridge, corn meal .... SAMP
porridge: Sp. Am. ..... ATOLE
Porsena of Clusium ..... LARS
PORT .. see also SPECIAL SEC-
TION — GAZETTEER
port .... HAVEN
port, banana, Honduras .. TELA
port, Black Sea ...... ODESSA
Port Moresby land ... PAPUA
port of Rome .... OSTIA
port opp. Gibraltar .... CEUTA
port, South Seas ...... APIA
port, Suez .... SAID
port wine city .... OPORTO
portable chair .... SEDAN
portal .... DOOR, GATE
portend BODE, AUGUR, PRESAGE

portent .... OMEN, SIGN
porter, Orient
.... HAMAL, HAMMAL
Portia's waiting woman NERISSA
portico .... STOA
portion. PART, SOME, SEGMENT
portion out DOLE, METE, ALLOT
portray .... DRAW,
LIMN, DEPICT, DELINEATE
Portuguese coin .... REI
Port. colony, India ...... GOA
Port. folk tune .... FADO
Port. lady .... DONA
Port. man .... DOM
Port. navigator .... GAMA
Port. title ..... DOM, DONNA
pose .... SIT
Poseidon .... NEPTUNE
Poseidon's son .... TRITON
posited .... SET
position ...... SITUS, STATUS
position without work SINECURE
positive .... THETIC
positive pole, terminal ANODE
possession, landed .... ESTATE
possum .... COON
possum, comic-strip .... POGO
post .... MAIL, SEND
post-hole digger (slick) ...LOY
postpone .... DEFER
postulate .... POSIT
posture .... STANCE
pot .... OLLA
pot, chem. .... ALUDEL
pot, earthen .... CRUSE
pot herb .... WORT
pot, India LOTA, LOTO, LOTAH
pot liquor .... BREWIS
pot metal .... POTIN
potassium .... KALITE
potassium chloride .. MURIATE
potassium nitrate
.... NITER, GROUGH
potation, small .... DRAM
potato .... SPUD
potato, sweet .. YAM, BATATA
pother .... ADO
potpourri .... OLIO
potter's blade .... PALLET
pottery fragment .... SHARD
pottery, pert. to .... CERAMIC
pouch .... SAC
pouch-shaped ...... SACCATE
poultry .... HENS, BIRDS
poultry disease .... PIP, ROUP
pounce .... SWOOP
pound .... TUND
pound down ...... RAM, TAMP
pour .... RAIN, TEEM
pour off gently ...... DECANT

121

a

pour out .... LIBATE
poverty .... NEED, WANT
powder, astringent .... BORAL
powder, mineral ingredient
.... TALC
powder of aloes .... PICRA
powdered pumice .... TALC
power .. DINT, MANA, FORCE
practical joke .... HOAX
practice .... HABIT
practice exercise, musical ETUDE
praise LAUD, EXTOL, EXTOLL
prance .... CAPER
prank .... DIDO, CAPER
prate .... GAB, YAP
prate: India ..... BUKH, BUKK
pray: Yiddish .... DAVEN
prayer AVE, BEAD, BENE, PLEA,
CREDO, MATIN, ORISON
prayer form .... LITANY
prayer, 9-day .... NOVENA
prayer-rug, Hindu ..... ASANA
prayer stick, Am. Ind.
.... BAHO, PAHO, PAJO
prayers, deacon's
.... ECTENE, EKTENE
prayerbook
ORDO, PORTAS, PORTASS
praying figure .... ORANT
preacher, Gospel .... EVANGEL

b

precepts .... DICTA
precipice, Hawaii .... PALI
precipitous .... STEEP
preclude ..... AVERT, DEBAR
preconceive .... IDEATE
predicament .... SCRAPE
predicate
BASE, FOUND, AFFIRM
predict
AUGUR, FORECAST, FORETELL
predisposed .... PRONE
preen .... PLUME, PRINK
preface .... PROEM
prefecture, Jap. .... KEN
PREFIX:
about .... PERI
above .... HYPER
across .... DIA, TRANS
again .... RE
against .... ANTI
ahead .... PRE
an .... AE
apart .... DIS
away ...... DE, DI, APO
back .... ANA
backward .... RETRO
bad .... MAL
badly .... MIS
beauty .... CALLI
before ..... OB, PRE, ANTE
blood .... HAEM, HEMO

c

both .... AMBI
CHEMICALS .. see page 29
common .... PRE
distant .... TEL, TELE
double .... DI
down .... DE, CATA
eight ... OCT, OCTA, OCTO
equal .... ISO
far .... TEL, TELE
faulty .... MIS
fire .... PYR
former, formerly ...... EX
four .... TETRA
from .... EC
half ..... DEMI, HEMI, SEMI
ill .... MIS
mountain .... ORO
negative .... IR, NON
new .... NEO
not ... IL, IM, IR, UN, NON
not fully .... SEMI
numerical .... UNI
of atmospheric pressure BARO
of the stars .... ASTRO
on this side .... CIS
one .... UNI
out of .... EC, EX

d

outer .... ECT, EXO, ECTO
outer skin .... EPI
outside .... ECT, EXO
over .... EPI, SUPER,
SUPRA, SUPERB
partly .... SEMI
people .... DEMO
pray .... ORA
recent .... NEO
same .... ISO, EQUI, HOMO
separation .... DIS
single .... MONO
ten .... DEC, DECA
thousand .... KILO
three .... TER, TRI
thrice .... TER, TRIS
threefold .... TRI
through .... DIA, PER
to .... AP
together .... COM
town .... TRE
turning .... ROTO
twice .... BI
two .... DI, DUA
twofold .... DI
under .... SUB
upon .... EPI
upward .... ANA, ANO
with .... SYN
within .... ENDO
wrong .... MIS

a prehistoric implement ... CELT
prehistoric mound ...... TERP
prejudice .... BIAS
prelate, high .... PRIMATE
prelude .... PROEM
premium, exchange ..... AGIO
prepare .... FIT, GIRD,
    MAKE, ADAPT, EQUIP
prepare for publication .. EDIT
prepared opium
    CHANDU, CHANDOO
preposition ...... AT, IN, ON,
    UP, INTO
presage
   OMEN, HERALD, PORTEND
prescribed .... THETIC
prescribed quantity ..... DOSE
present .. GIFT, GIVE, DONATE
present, be .... ATTEND
present in brief .... SUM
presently .ANON, ENOW, SOON
preserve .... CAN, JAM, KEEP,
   SAVE, PROTECT, MAINTAIN
preserve in brine .. CORN, SALT
Presidential nickname .... ABE,
    CAL, IKE, TEDDY
press together .... SERRY
pressure .... DURESS
pressure unit .. BARAD, BARIE
pretend .. FAKE, SHAM, FEIGN
b pretense .... SHAM
pretensions .... AIRS
pretentious .... SIDY
prevail .... WIN
prevail on .... INDUCE
prevalent .... RIFE
prevent ... DETER, PRECLUDE
prevent by law .... ESTOP
prey .... RAVIN
prey upon
   RAVEN, RAVIN, RAVINE
Priam's son
   PARIS, HECTOR, HEKTOR
price .... RATE
price of transportation .. FARE
prickle .... SETA
prickles .... SETAE
prickly pear
   TUNA, NOPAL, CACTUS
prickly plant ... BRIAR, BRIER,
    NETTLE
prickly seed coat .. BUR, BURR
pride .... PLUME
PRIEST .. see also CLERGYMAN
priest
   FRA, ABBE, CURE, PADRE
priest, Celtic .... DRUID
priest, Gr. .... MYST

c PRIEST, HIGH, see HIGH PRIEST
priest in "Iliad" .... CALCHAS
priest, Mongol ...... SHAMAN
priest, Moro SARIP, PANDITA
priestess, Gr. .... AUGE
priestess, Rom. ...... VESTAL
priesthood, Rom. ...... SALII
priestly caste ... MAGI, MAGUS
prima donna .... DIVA
PRIMA DONNA ...... see also
   OPERA SOPRANO
prime minister: Brit. ... EDEN,
    PEEL
primeval .... OLD,
   EARLY, PRIMAL, PRISTINE
prince, Abyssin. .... RAS
prince, Arabian .. EMIR, SAYID,
   SAYYID, SHERIF, SHEREEF
prince, India
   RAJA, RANA, RAJAH
prince of Argos ...... DANAE
Prince of Darkness .... SATAN
prince, Oriental ...... KHAN
prince, Persian .. AMIR, AMEER
prince, petty .... SATRAP
prince, Slavic .... KNEZ
Prince Val's father ... AGUAR
princeling .... SATRAP
princely .... ROYAL
princess, Gr. myth ..... IOLE
princess, India .. RANI, RANEE
d principal .... TOP, ARCH
   MAIN, CHIEF
principal commodity .. STAPLE
principle, accepted
   AXIOM, PRANA, TENET
print .... STAMP
print measure .... EM, EN
printer, 1st colonial .... DAYE
printer's direction ..... STET
printer's mark .... DELE
printer's mistake
   TYPO, ERRATUM
printer's mistakes .... ERRATA
printing plate .... STEREO
printing roller .... PLATEN
prison .JUG, GAOL, JAIL, QUOD
prison sentence .... RAP
prison spy .... MOUTON
privation .... LOSS
privilege, commercial .. OCTROI
prize .... PRY, AWARD
pro .... FOR
"— pro nobis" .... ORA
probe, medical .... STYLET
problem .... POSER
proboscis .... SNOUT
proboscis monkey ..... KAHA
proceed ... WEND, ADVANCE
proceedings .... ACTA

123

a procession .... TRAIN, PARADE, MOTORCADE
proclaim .... CRY, VOICE, HERALD, DECLARE
prod .... URGE
produce .... BEGET, YIELD CREATE, INWORK, GENERATE
produce as an effect ... BEGET
produced, quantity ..... YIELD
producing cold .... ALGIFIC
production, artistic .. FACTURE
profane .... VIOLATE
profane, Hawaiian ...... NOA
profession ART, CAREER, METIER
professional, not LAIC, LAICAL
profit ... GAIN, VAIL, AVAIL
profit, to yield .... NET
profits, taker of: law . PERNOR
profitable ...... FAT, USEFUL
profound .... DEEP
"— profundis" .... DE
progenitor ...... SIRE, PARENT
progeny .... ISSUE
prohibit .... BAN, BAR, VETO, DEBAR, ESTOP
prohibition BAN, VETO, EMBARGO
Prohibition, against ...... WET
project ...... JUT, IDEA, PLAN

b projectile .... MISSILE
projecting edge RIM, FLANGE
projecting piece ARM, RIM, TENON, FLANGE
projecting rim .... FLANGE
projecting tooth .... SNAG
projection . EAR, BARB, PRONG
projection, fireplace.HOB, HOBB
projection, jagged SNAG, TOOTH
projection, studlike .... KNOP
promenade .... MALL
promise .... WORD
promise to pay .... IOU, NOTE
"Promised Land" fountain AIN
promontory ..... CAPE, NASE, NAZE, NESS
promontory, Orkneys .... NOUP
promontory, rocky ...... TOR
promote .... FOSTER
prompt .... CUE, YARE
prone .... APT, FLAT
prong .... TINE, TOOTH
pronghorn .... CABREE, CABRET, CABRIE, CABRIT
pronoun .. IT, ME, US, WE, YE, HER, HIM, ONE, SHE, THAT, THIS, THEE, THEM, THEY, THOU, THESE, THOSE

c pronoun, possessive . MY, HER, HIS, ITS, OUR, HERS, MINE, OURS, YOUR
pronounce indistinctly ... SLUR
pronounce strongly .... STRESS
pronouncement DICTA, DICTUM
proof, corrected .... REVISE
proof, printer's .... GALLEY
proofreader's mark DELE, STET, CARET
prop .... HOLD, STAY, BRACE, BOLSTER, SUSTAIN
propeller .... OAR
proper .... DUE, FIT
properly .... FEATLY
property, hold on .... LIEN
property, India .... DHAN
property, item of ASSET, CHATTEL
property, landed ...... ESTATE
property owned absolutely ALOD, ALLOD, ALODIUM, ALLODIUM
property, receiver of . . ALIENEE
prophesy .... FORETELL
prophet .... SEER, AUGUR, PREDICTOR, FORETELLER
PROPHETS, BIBLICAL ..... see SPECIAL SECTION
prophets .... VATES

d prophetic ... VATIC, VATICAL
proportion .... RATIO
proportionally assess PRORATE
proposition THESES, THESIS, PREMISE
proposition, logic .... LEMMA
proposition: math. .. THEOREM
prosecutor .... SUER
prosecutor: abbr. .... DA
proselyte to Judaism .... GER
"— prosequi," .... NOLLE
Proserpina ...... CORA, KORE
prospect .... VISTA
prosperity .... WEAL
prosperity god, Teut. .... FREY
Prospero's servant ...... ARIEL
prostrate .... PRONE, REPENT
protagonist .... HERO
protected .... HOUSED
protection .... EGIS, AEGIS
protection right, Old Eng. MUND
protective building ... REDAN
protective influence EGIS, AEGIS
Protestant denomination: abbr. ME, PE, BAP, PRESB
prototype .... IDEAL
protozoan order .... LOBOSA
protuberance ... JAG, NUB, HUMP, KNOB, KNOT, NODE, WART, KNURL, TORUS

124

protuberant .... TOROSE
prove: law .... DERAIGN
proverb ...... SAW, ADAGE,
AXIOM, MAXIM, SAYING
provide ...... ENDOW, ENDUE
provided .... IF
provided that .... SO
province, Rom. .... DACIA
provisional clause ... PROVISO
proviso .... CLAUSE
provoke............ IRE, RILE,
ANGER, ANNOY
prow .... BOW, STEM
prune: prov. Eng. ...... SNED
pruning knife .... DHAW
Prussian spa, town ...... EMS
pry .... NOSE, LEVER, SNOOP
Psalm, 51st .... MISERERE
Psalmist .... DAVID
Psalms, selection of .. HALLEL
Psalms, word in ...... SELAH
pseudonym ...... NOM, ALIAS
pseudonym of Louise Del La
Ramee .... OUIDA
psyche .... SOUL
psychiatrist
JUNG, ADLER, FREUD
Ptah, embodiment of ... APIS
ptarmigan .... RYPE
pteropod genus ...... CLIONE
pua hemp ...... POOA
public .... OPEN, OVERT
public: Chin. .... KUNG
public esteem .... REPUTE
public, make ... AIR, DELATE
public vehicle .... BUS, TAXI
publication, style of .. FORMAT
publish .... ISSUE, PRINT
publish illegally ...... PIRATE
Puccini heroine .... MIMI
puck, hockey .... RUBBER
pudding .... DUFF, SAGO
pueblo dweller .... HOPI
Pueblo Indian ... HOPI, ZUNI,
KERES, MOQUI, TANOA
Pueblo sacred chamber .. KIVA
Pueblo, Tanoan .... HANO
Puerto Rican plant ...... APIO
puff up .... ELATE
puffbird, Brazil .... DREAMER
puffbird genus ..... MONASA
puffer fish .... TAMBOR
Pulitzer poet .... FROST
pull .. TOW, TUG, DRAG, HALE
pull with nautical tackle BOUSE
pulley .... SHEAVE
pulp, fruit .... POMACE
pulpit .... AMBO, BEMA
pulpy mass left in cider POMACE
pulverize .... MICRONIZE

c pump handle .... SWIPE
pumpkin .... PEPO
punch .... JAB
"Punch and Judy" dog .. TOBY
punch, engraver's .. MATTOIR
punctuation mark DASH, COLON
pungent .. TEZ, SPICY, TANGY
punish by fine ...... AMERCE
punishment .... FERULE
punishment, of .... PENAL
punitive .... PENAL
Punjab native .... JAT
punk .... AMADOU
pupa .... INSTAR
pupil of eye .... GLENE
puppet .... DOLL
puppet, famous JUDY, PUNCH
puppeteer, famous ...... SARG
pure sirup .... CLAIRCE
pure thought .... NOESIS
purification, ancient Roman
LUSTRUM
purloin .... STEAL
purple
MAUVE, MODENA, TYRIAN
purple dye source .... MUREX
purple medic
LUCERN, ALFALFA, LUCERNE
purple ragwort ...... JACOBY
purple seaweed . SION, LAVER
d purport, general ...... TENOR
purpose .... AIM, END,
GOAL, SAKE, INTENT
purposive .... TELIC
purse net .... SEINE
pursy .... STOUT
push up .... BOOST
put aside .... DAFF
put away .... STORE
put back .... REPLACE
put forth .... EXERT
put in bank .... DEPOSIT
put off .... DEFER
put out .... OUST, EJECT
put up .... ANTE
puzzle .... POSER,
REBUS, BAFFLE, ACROSTIC
puzzles .... CRUCES
Pygmalion's statue .. GALATEA
pygmy .... ATOMY
pygmy people, Congo
AKKA, ACHUAS
pygmy people, Equatorial Africa
BATWA, ABONGO, OBONGO
Pylos, kin of .... NESTOR
Pyramus, lover of .... THISBE
pyromaniac .... FIREBUG
Pythias' friend .... DAMON
python .... BOA

Q

a
qua .... AS
"— qua non" .... SINE
quack IMPOSTOR, CHARLATAN
quack medicine .... NOSTRUM
quadrant .... ARC
quadrate .... SQUARE
"quae —" which see .... VIDE
quaff .... DRINK
quail .... COLIN, COWER
quake .... SHAKE,
    SHIVER, TREMOR, TREMBLE
Quaker .... FRIEND
Quaker Poet .... WHITTIER
quaking .... TREPID
qualify .... FIT, ADAPT,
            EQUIP, PREPARE
qualified .... FIT, ABLE
quality .... CALIBER, CALIBRE
quantity, indeterminate . SOME
quantity: math.
            SCALER, VECTOR

b
quarrel .... ROW, FEUD,
            SPAT, TIFF
quarter of a year: Scot. RAITH
quartz .... JASPER
quartz, green .... PRASE
quartz, translucent ... PRASE
quash: law .... CASSARE
quaternion .... TETRAD
quay .... LEVEE
Quebec, district, town .. LEVIS
Quebec's patron saint .. ANNE
Queen .... CLEO
queen: Moslem BEGUM, BEEGUM
queen of gods, Egypt. ... SATI
queen of gods, Rom. ... HERA,
                JUNO
Queen of Italy .... ELENA
Queen of Ithaca ... PENELOPE
Queen of Roumania ... MARIE
Queen of Scots .... MARY
Queen of Spain, last ..... ENA
queen, "Romeo and Juliet"
                MAB

c
queenly .... REGAL, REGINA[
Queensland hemp plant
                SIDA
Queensland tribe .... GO[
quell .... CALM, CRUSH
quench .... SLAK[
quench steel ..... AUSTEMPE[
quern .... MIL[
query .... AS[
queue .... LIN[
question .... ASK, GRIL[
question, hard .... POSE[
quetzal .... TROGON
quibble .... CAVIL, EVAD[
quick .... FAST, AGILE
            ALIVE, RAPI[
quick: music .... TOST[
quicken ... HASTEN, ENLIVE[
quickly .... CITO, APACE
            PRESTO, PRONTO
quickly, move
            SCAT, SCUD, SKIT[
quicksilver ...... HEAUTARI[
quid .... CU[

d
"quid — quo," equivalent . PR[
quiescent LATENT, DORMAN[
quiet .... CALM, LULL
            STILL, SMOOTH
quiet! .... SH, PST, TS[
quilkin .... FROG, TOAD
quill .... PEN, SPIN[
quill feathers REMEX, REMIGES
quill for winding silk ..... CO[
quilt .... EIDER, COVE[
quince, Bengal .... BEL, BHE[
quinine .... KINA
quintessence ... PITH, ELIXI[
quirt, cowboy's ...... ROMA[
quit .... CEASE, LEAVE
quite .... ALL
quivering ... ASPEN, TREMOR
"quod — demonstrandum"
                ERAT
"Quo Vadis" tyrant character
                NERO
quoits, mark of .... MO[
quote .... CITE

126

R

Ra, consort of .... **MUT**
Ra, son of .... **SU, SHU**
rabbi, law-teaching ... **AMORA**
rabbit cage .... **HUTCH**
rabbit, Europ. . **CONY, CONEY**
rabbit, female .... **DOE**
rabbit fur .... **LAPIN**
rabbit home .... **WARREN**
rabbit, small swamp .. **TAPETI**
rabbit, So. Am. .... **TAPETI**
rabble .... **MOB**
rabies .... **LYSSA**
raccoon-like mammal .. **COATI**
RACE .. see also TRIBES in
SPECIAL SECTION
race, boat .... **REGATTA**
race, kind of .... **RELAY**
race, short .... **SPRINT**
race-track .... **OVAL**
race-track circuit .... **LAP**
race-track tipster ...... **TOUT**
races, pert. to .... **ETHNIC**
Rachel's father ...... **LABAN**
racing boat .... **GIG**
racket, game .... **PELOTA**
radar screen .... **SCOPE**
radiate .... **EMANATE**
radical .... **RED**
radicle .... **STEMLET**
radio advertiser .... **SPONSOR**
radio bulletin ..... **NEWSCAST**
radio-guided bomb ...... **AZON**
radio wave ...... **MICROWAVE**
radio wire .... **LITZ**
radio-TV awards ..... **EMMIES**
radioactive counter .. **GEIGER**
radioactive element ... **NITON**
radioactive ray ...... **GAMMA**
radium discoverer ...... **CURIE**
radium emanation .... **NITON**
radius, pert. to ...... **RADIAL**
radon .... **NITON**
raft, kind of ... **CATAMARAN**
raft, Maori .... **MOKI**
rag doll .... **MOPPET**
rage .... **RAMP, RANT,
RESE, STORM**
ragged person: Sp. ...... **ROTO**
raging monster, Bibl. .. **RAHAB**
ragout, game .... **SALMI**
ragweed genus .... **IVA**
raid ...... **FORAY, INROAD**
raid, soldier's .... **COMMANDO**
rail at .... **REVILE**
rail bird **SORA, WEKA, CRAKE**
railing .... **PARAPET**

railroad bridge ..... **TRESSEL,
TRESTLE**
railroad light .... **FLARE**
railroad signal
TRIMMER, SEMAPHORE
railroad tie .... **SLEEPER**
railroad timber .... **TIE**
railway station: Fr. ..... **GARE**
rain after sunset ...... **SEREIN**
rain, fine .... **MISLE**
rain forest .... **SELVA**
rain gauge ...... **UDOMETER**
rain serpent, Hindu .... **NAGA**
rain spout: Scot. ...... **RONE**
rain tree .... **SAMAN**
rainbow .... **ARC, IRIS**
rainbow goddess .... **IRIS**
rainbow, pert. to ..... **IRIDAL**
raincoat .... **PONCHO**
rainy .... **WET**
raise . **REAR, BREED, ELEVATE**
raised .... **BRED**
raisin: Sp. .... **PASA**
raising device .... **JACK**
Rajah's lady .... **RANI, RANEE**
rake ...... **ROUE, LOTHARIO**
rake with gunfire .. **ENFILADE**
ram . **TUP, BUTT, TAMP, ARIES**
ram, male .... **TUP**
ram-headed god, Egypt
AMEN, AMON, AMUN
Ramachandra, wife of .. **SITA**
ramble .... **GAD, ROVE**
Ramee, de la, penname . **OUIDA**
rammed earth building material
PISE
rampart ..... **AGGER, VALLUM**
range ...... **AREA, GAMUT,
SCOPE, SIERRA**
Rangoon's state .... **PEGU**
rank .... **ROW, RATE, DEGREE**
ranks, press in ...... **SERRY**
rankle .... **FESTER**
ransom .... **REDEEM**
rapeseed ..... **COLSA, COLZA**
rapid, more: music .. **STRETTA,
STRETTE, STRETTI, STRETTO**
rapids, river .... **SOO**
rapidly .... **APACE**
rapier .... **BILBO**
rare earth element ... **ERBIUM**
rascal .... **IMP, ROGUE**
rase .... **INCISE**
rasorial .... **GNAWING**
rasp .... **FILE, GRATE**

127

a

raspberry, variety . **BLACKCAP**
rasse .... **CIVET**
rat .... **DESERTER**
rat, Ceylon, India . **BANDICOOT**
rat hare .... **PIKA**
rate .... **ESTIMATE**
rate, relative .... **AT**
ratify .... **SEAL**
ratio .... **RATE**
RATIO: MATH see MATH, RATIO
rational .... **SANE**
rational integer .... **NORM**
rational principle ...... **LOGOS**
rationalize .... **THOB**
ratite bird ...... **CASSOWARY**
rattan .... **CANE**
rattlesnake
    RATTLER, CROTALUS
rave .... **RANT**
"Raven" author .... **POE**
"Raven" character .... **LENORE**
ravine
    GAP, DALE, VALE, GORGE
ravine, Afr. .... **WADI, WADY**
ravine, Arabia .. **WADI, WADY**
rawboned .... **LEAN**
rawboned animal ...... **SCRAG**
ray fish .... **SKATE**
rays, like .... **RADIAL**
rayon ... **ACETATE, CELANESE**

b

raze .... **DEVASTATE**
razor-billed auk
    ALCA, MURR, MURRE
reach across .... **SPAN**
react .... **RESPOND**
read, inability to ..... **ALEXIA**
read metrically .... **SCAN**
read publically ...... **PRELECT**
reader, first .... **PRIMER**
reading desk .... **AMBO**
reading substituted: Bibl.
    KERE, KERI
ready: dialect .... **YARE**
ready-made tie .... **TECK**
real being, pert. to .... **ONTAL**
real thing .... **MCCOY**
reality .... **FACT**
realm .... **DOMAIN**
reamer .... **BROACH**
rear ... **ERECT, RAISE, ARRIERE**
rear, to the
    AFT, ABAFT, ASTERN
rearhorse .... **MANTIS**
rearing of horse ...... **PESADE**
reason .... **NOUS**
reason, deprive of ... **DEMENT**
reasoning .... **LOGIC**
reasoning, deductive .. **APRIORI**
reata
    LAZO, ROPE, LASSO, LARIAT

c

rebec of India .... **SAROD**
Rebecca's hairy son ..... **ESAU**
rebound .. **CAROM, RICOCHET**
rebuff .... **SLAP, SNUB**
rebuke
    CHIDE, SCOLD, REPROVE
recalcitrant ...... **RENITENT**
recant .... **RETRACT**
recede .... **EBB**
recent
    NEO, NEW, LATE, NEOTERIC
receptacle .... **BIN, BOX,**
    TRAY, VESSEL
reception, a.m. .... **LEVEE**
reception: Fr. .... **ACCUEIL**
reception, India ...... **DURBAR**
recess .... **APSE, ALCOVE**
recess, wall .... **NICHE**
recipient .... **DONEE**
recite metrically .... **SCAN**
reckon ...... **ARET, COUNT**
reckoning .... **TALLY**
reclaim .... **REDEEM**
recline .... **LOLL**
recluse ...... **ASCETIC, EREMITE**
    ANCHORET, ANCHORITE
recoil .... **SHY, RESILE**
recommit .... **REMAND**
recompense .. **PAY, FEES, MEED**
reconnaissance **RECCO, RECON**

d

reconnoiter .... **SCOUT**
reconstruct .... **REMODEL**
record .. **TAB, NOTE, ENROL**
    ENTER, ENTRY, REGISTER
record of investigation **REPORT**
record, ship's .... **LOG**
record, year's .... **ANNAL**
records .... **ANNALS**
recorded proceedings ... **ACTA**
recording device .... **TAPE**
records, one who ...... **NOTER**
recourse, have .... **REFER**
recover strength .... **RALLY**
recovery, legal .... **TROVER**
recruit .... **BOOT**
rectifier, current ...... **DIODE**
rectify ...... **AMEND, EMEND**
recurring pattern ...... **CYCLE**
red .... **CARMINE,**
    MAGENTA, NACARAT
red, Brazil .... **ROSET**
red cedar .... **SAVIN, SAVINE**
red circle: Her. .... **GUZE**
red currant .... **RISSEL**
red deer .... **ELAPHINE**
red dye root ... **CHAY, CHOY**
red garden flower .... **CANNA**
red: Her. .... **GULES**
red horse .... **BAY, ROAN**
red ocher .... **KEEL, KIEL,**
    TIVER, RADDLE, RUDDLE

a red pigment .... ROSET,
ASTACIN, ASTACENE
red pine .... RIMU
red planet .... MARS
red powder, India ...... ABIR
red, painter's .... ROSET
Red River Rebellion leader
RIEL
red: Sp. .... ROJO
red squirrel ...... CHICKAREE
red swine .... DUROC
red, Venetian .... SIENA
red-yellow color ...... ALOMA
redact .... EDIT
redbreast .... ROBIN
redcap .... PORTER
reddish yellow .... SUDAN
redeem .... RANSOM
redshank .... CLEE
reduce ...... PARE, DEMOTE
reduce sail .... REEF
reduce taxes .... DERATE
reebok .... PEELE
reedbuck .... NAGOR
reek .... FUG, FUME
reef .... SHOAL
reel, fishing-rod ...... PIRN
refer .... PERTAIN
refer to repeatedly ..... HARP
refined grace ...... ELEGANCE
b reflection .... GLARE
refracting device ...... LENS
refractor, light .... PRISM
refrain .... FORBEAR
refrain in songs .. FALA, LALA,
DERRY, LUDDEN
refrigerant .... FREON
refuge ...... HAVEN, SHELTER
refugee .... EMIGREE
refuse .... DENY
refuse .... ORT, DROSS,
SCUM, OFFAL, TRASH
refuse, bit of .... SCRAP
refuse, flax .... POB
refuse: law .... RECUSE
refuse, metal . DROSS, SCORIA
refuse, wool .... COT
refute .... REBUT, DISPROVE
regale .... FETE
regard ...... ESTEEM, RESPECT
regarding .... RE, ANENT
regenerate .... RENEW
regiment's framework .. CADRE
REGION .... see also DISTRICT
region ...... CLIME, SECTOR
region, Afr. .. CONGO, NUBIA
region, Boeotia ...... AONIA
region, Cent. Afr.
SUDAN, SOUDAN
region, Fr. .... ALSACE

c region, Gr. .... DORIC
region, Indo-China ..... LAOS
region, pert. to .... AREAL
register .... ENROL,
ENROLL, RECORD
reiterate .... REPEAT
regret .... RUE, DEPLORE
reign: India .... RAJ
reign, pert. to ...... REGNAL
reigning .... REGNANT
reigning beauty .... BELLE
reimbursed .... PAID
reindeer .... CARIBOU
reindeer, Santa's .... DASHER,
DONDER, BLITZEN,
PRANCER
reinstate .... REVEST
reject ...... SPURN, REPULSE
relate .... TELL,
RECITE, NARRATE
related .... AKIN, TOLD,
COGNATE, GERMANE
related by blood .... SIB
related on mother's side ENATE
relation .... SIB
relative.SIB, SIS, AUNT, NIECE
relative amount ...... RATION
relative pronoun ...... WHO,
THAT, WHAT
relative speed .... TEMPO
d relatives .... KIN
relatives, favoring .. NEPOTAL
relax .... EASE
relaxing of state tensions
DETENTE
relay of horses ..... REMUDA
release .... LOOSE
release: law .... REMISE
release, phonetic .... DETENTE
relevant .... GERMANE
reliable .... HONEST
relief, — .... BAS
relief .... DOLE
relieve .... EASE, ALLAY
relieve: Scot. .... LISS
religieuse .... NUN
religion .... FAITH
religion, Jap. .... SHINTO
religious art, work of .. PIETA
religious brother ...... FRA,
MONK, FRIAR
religious festival ..... EASTER
religious festival, India .. MELA
religious law, Rom. ...... FAS
religious laywoman .. BEGUINE
religious opinion .... DOXY
religious order, one in . OBLATE
religious sayings ...... LOGIA
relinquish .... CEDE,
WAIVE, YIELD

129

a reliquary .... APSE, ARCA, ARCAE, CHEST
relish .... GUSTO
reluctant ..... LOATH, AVERSE
rely .... TRUST
remain .... BIDE, STAY
remainder .... REST
remaining .... OVER
remark, witty .... MOT, SALLY
remiss .... LAX
remit .... SEND
remnant ...... END, SHRED
remora fish . PEGA, LOOTSMAN
remove .. DELE, DOFF, DELETE
remove interior .... GUT
remove: law .... ELOIN, ELOIGN, ELOIGNE
remunerate .... PAY
rend ...... RIP, TEAR, WREST
render fat .... TRY
rendezvous .... TRYST
renegade .... APOSTATE
renounce .... ABNEGATE
renovated hat .... MOLOKER
renown .... FAME, NOTE, EMINENCE, PRESTIGE
rent ...... LET, HIRE, TEAR, TORN, LEASE
rent, old Eng. law ...... TAC
renter .... LESSEE
b repair .... DARN, MEND
repartee .... RIPOST, RIPOSTE
repast .... MEAL
repay .... REQUITE
repay in kind .. RETALIATE
repeat ...... ECHO, ITERATE
repeat: music .... BIS
repeat performance .. ENCORE
repeat sign: music .... SEGNO
repeat tiresomely .. DIN, DING
repeated phrase .... REPRISE
repeatedly hit ...... POMMEL
repetition .... ROTE
replete .... FULL
report, small .... POP
repose .... EASE, REST
representation .... IDOL
representative .... AGENT
reproach ..... BLAME, TAUNT
reproach, old term ...... RACA
reproductive body .. GAMETE
reproductive cell ..... SPORE
reptile, pert. to ..... SAURIAN
repulse .... REPEL
reputation .... NAME, REPUTE
repute .... CHARACTER
request .... PLEA
rescind .... REPEAL
resentment .... IRE
reserve supply .... STORE

c residence ..... HOME, ABODE
residence, ecclesiastical . MANSE
resident of .... ITE
resign .... QUIT, DEMIT
resin ..... GUM, LAC, ANIME, COPAL, ELEMI, JALAP, MYRRH, BALSAM, MASTIC
resin, fossil . AMBER, GLESSITE
resin, fragrant .... ELEMI
resist .... OPPOSE
resist authority ...... REBEL
resisting pressure ... RENITENT
resistor, current ... RHEOSTAT
resort .... SPA
resort, Fr. .... PAU, NICE, CANNES
resources .... FUND, MEANS, ASSETS
respect .... ESTEEM
respond .... REACT
rest ...... SIT, EASE, REPOSE
rest, lay at .... REPOSE
restaurant, small ..... BISTRO
resthouse ...... CHAN, KHAN
resting .... ABED
restive .... BALKY
restore .... RENEW
restrain .. CURB, REIN, DETER, STINT, TETHER
d restrict .... LIMIT
retaliate .... REPAY
retain .... HOLD, KEEP
retaliation .... TALION
retinue .... SUITE, TRAIN
retort, quick . RIPOST, RIPOSTE
retract .... RECANT
retreat .... RECEDE
retreat, cosy . DEN, NEST, NOOK
retribution .... NEMESIS
retribution, get .... VENGE
retrograde .... RECEDE
return ...... RECUR, RESTORE
return a profit .... PAY
return blow .... TIT
return on investment .. YIELD
returning .... REDIENT
reunion, hold a .... REUNE
reveille, call to .... DIAN
revelry, cry of .... EVOE
revelry, drunken ...... ORGY
revenue, church: Scot. ANNAT
reverberate .... ECHO
reverberating ...... REBOANT
revere ...... HONOR, HONOUR
reverence .... AWE
reversed in order .. CONVERSE
reversion to type .... ATAVISM

a **revert to state (land)**
ESCHEAT
revise .... EDIT, AMEND
revive wine .... STUM
revoke legacy, grant .. ADEEM
Revolution hero . HALE, ALLEN
revolutions per minute .. REVS
revolve . SPIN, TURN, ROTATE
revolve: logging .... BIRL
revolver.GAT, GUN, ROD, COLT
reward .... MEED
rhebok .... PEELE
Rhine city .... MAINZ
Rhine tributary .... AAR
rhinoceros beetle ...... UANG
rhinoceros, black
BORELE, NASICORN
rhinoceros: obs.
ABADA, ABATH
Rhone tributary .... SAONE
rhythm .... TIME, METER,
METRE, CADENCE
rhythmical accent ...... BEAT
rhythmical swing .... LILT
rib .... COSTA
rib. pert. to .... COSTAL
rib, woman from .... EVE
ribs, with .... COSTATE
ribbed fabric ..... REP, CORD,
REPP, PIQUE

b ribbon, badge ...... CORDON
ribbon: comb. form ..... TENE
ribbonfish .... GUAPENA
rice .... PADI, PADDY
rice dish ...... PILAU, PILAW
rice field, Java .... PADI
rice grass, P.I. .... BARIT
rice in husk .... PALAY
rice paste, Jap. .... AME
rice polishings .... DARAC
rich man .... MIDAS,
NABOB, NAWAB
rich silk cloth .... CAFFA
riches .... PELF
rid .... FREE
riddle .... ENIGMA
ridge .... ARETE,
SPINE, MOUNTAIN
ridge, camp's .... RIDEAU
ridge, glacial, sandy ...... OS,
OSAR, ESKER, OESAR
ridge on cloth .... WALE
ridge on skin .... WELT
ridge, stony .... RAND
ridges, rounded .... GYRI
ridged area, Balkan ..... BILO
ridicule .... GUY, MOCK,
RAZZ, DERIDE
ridicule personified, Gr.
MOMUS

c riding academy ..... MANEGE
riding dress .... HABIT
rifle .... KRAG, MINIE,
GARAND, CARBINE
rifle ball .... MINIE
rifleman, Ger. .... JAGER
right conduct, Buddhist ... TAO
right conduct: Taoism ..... TE
right hand: music .... DM
right-hand page .. RO, RECTO
right: law .... DROIT
right, pert. to .... DEXTER
right to speak .... SAY
right, turn .... GEE
rights, of ..... JURAL, UDAL
Rigoletto's daughter ... GILDA
rigorous ...... HARSH, STERN,
STRICT, SEVERE, AUSTERE
rim ...... LIP, EDGE, FLANGE
rim of wheel .. FELLY, FELLOE
"Rime cold giant" . YMER, YMIR
ring ...... PEAL, TOLL, KNELL
ring, boxing .... ARENA
ring for reins . TERRET, TERRIT
ring, gun carriage ..... LUNET
ring, harness pad
TERRET, TERRIT
ring, lamp condensing ... CRIC
ring, little .... ANNULET
ring, naut. .... GROMMET

d ring of light ...... HALO, NIMB,
NIMBUS, AUREOLA,
AUREOLE
"Ring of the Nibelung" goddess
ERDA
"Ring of the Nibelung" smith
MIME
ring out .... PEAL
ring, part of .... CHATON
ring, rubber jar .... LUTE
ring, seal .... SIGNET
ring-shaped ...... CIRCINATE
ring-shaped piece ..... QUOIT
ring, stone of .... CHATON
ringlet .... CURL, TRESS
ringworm ..... TINEA, TETTER
ripening agent .... AGER
ripple ...... LAP, RIFF, WAVE
rise above .... TOWER
rise aloft .... TOWER
rise: old Eng. .... RIS
risible .... GELASTIC
rites, religious .... SACRA
ritual .... RITE
RIVER . see also GAZETTEER in
SPECIAL SECTION
river .... RIO
river, Balmoral Castle's ... DEE
river bank .... RIPA
river bank, growing by
RIPARIAN

a river-bank stair, Ind. **GAUT, GHAT**
river bed, dry, Afr. **WADI, WADY**
river between Europe and Asia **KARA**
river, Bremen's .... **WESER**
river Caesar crossed . **RUBICON**
river, Dutch Meuse ..... **MAAS**
river in Baltic .... **ODER**
river in Essex .... **CAM**
river in Orleans .... **LOIRE**
river in Petrograd ...... **NEVA**
river into Moselle ...... **SAAR**
river into Rhone ...... **SAONE**
river islet .... **AIT**
river, "Kubla Khan" .... **ALPH**
river, Munich's .... **ISAR**
river mouth ..... **LADE, DELTA**
river nymph .... **NAIS**
river to the Humber **OUSE, TRENT**
River of Woe ..... **ACHERON**
river, Southwest .... **PECOS**
river: Sp. .... **RIO**
river: Tagalog .... **ILOG**
river to Medit. .... **EBRO**
river valley .... **STRATH**
rivulet .... **RILL**
road .... **VIA, PATH, ITER, AGGER**

b road: Roman .... **ITER**
road: Gypsy .... **DRUN**
roadhouse .... **INN**
roam .... **GAD, ROVE**
roast .... **CALCINE**
roasted meat strip .... **CABOB**
roasting rod .... **SPIT**
rob .... **REAVE, DESPOIL**
Rob Roy .... **CANOE**
robber .... **THIEF**
ROBE ..... see also GARMENT
robe .... **MANTLE**
robe to ankles .... **TALAR**
"Roberta" composer .... **KERN**
robot drama .... **RUR**
rock aggregate .... **AUGE**
rock, basic igneous .... **SIMA**
rock cavity ..... **VOOG, VUGG, VUGH, GEODE**
rock, dangerous ...... **SCYLLA**
rock, dark .... **BASALT**
rock, fine grained ..... **TRAP**
rock, flintlike .... **CHERT**
rock, granitoid **DUNITE, GNEISS**
rock, hard .... **WHIN**
rock, jutting .... **TOR**
rock, laminated ...... **SHALE SLATE, GNEISS**
rock, melted .... **LAVA**
rock, mica-bearing ... **DOMITE**

c rock, projecting ... **TOR, CRAG**
rock, rugged .... **CRAG**
rock snake .... **PYTHON**
rock whiting genus ..... **ODAX**
rock-wren .... **TURCO**
ROCKET .. see under MISSILE, GUIDED
rocket's goal .... **MOON**
rockfish ... **RASHER, TAMBOR**
rockfish, Calif. .. **RENA, REINA**
rockweed ...... **FUCI, FUCUS**
Rocky Mt. peak ...... **ESTES**
Rocky Mt. range **TETON, UINTA**
rocky peak, eminence, pinnacle .... **TOR**
rod .... **POLE, WAND, BATON, PERCH, STAFF**
rod, barbecue .... **SPIT**
rod, basketry .... **OSIER**
rod, billiard .... **CUE**
rod, chastening ...... **FERULE**
rodent .... **RAT, HARE**
rodent genus .... **MUS**
rodent, rabbit-like ...... **PIKA**
rodent, S. Am. .. **CAVY, DEGU, PACA, COYPU, AGOUTI**
rodent, W. Ind. ...... **HUTIA**
Rhoderick Dhu .... **SCOT**
rogue .... **PICARO**
roguish .... **SLY, ARCH**

d roister .... **REVEL**
Roland's destroyer ..... **GAN, GANO, GANELON**
roll and heave .... **TOSS**
roll of bread: dialect. .... **BAP**
roll of cloth .... **BOLT**
roll of paper .... **SCROLL**
roll up .... **FURL**
romaine .... **COS**
ROMAN GODS see SPECIAL SECTION
Rom. assembly ...... **COMITIA**
Rom. authors .... **CATO, LIVY, OVID, LUCAN, NEPOS, PLINY, CICERO, HOR-ACE, SENECA, SILIUS, VERGIL, SALLUST**
Rom. barracks **CANABA, CANNABA**
Rom. box .... **CAPSA**
Rom. boxing glove ... **CESTUS**
Rom. bronze .... **AES**
Rom. brooch .... **FIBULA**
Rom. building .... **INSULA**
Rom. cap .... **PILEUS**
Rom. cavalry body **TURM, TURMA**
Rom. circus post .... **META**
Rom. clan ..... **GENS, GENTES**
Rom. cloak ... **TOGA, ABOLLA**

a Rom. coin, ancient **SEMIS, DINDER**
Rom. coins .... **AS, AES, ASSES, SOLIDUS**
Rom. Curia court ...... **ROTA**
Rom. date ...... **IDES, NONES**
Rom. dictator .... **SULLA**
Rom. dish .... **LANX**
Rom. emperor .... **NERO, OTHO, TITUS**
Rom. farce .... **EXODE**
Rom. galley **TRIREME, UNIREME**
Rom. gaming cube ..... **TALUS**
Rom. garment .. **TOGA, STOLA, TUNIC, PLANETA**
Rom. goal post in racing . **META**
Rom. highway ..... **VIA, ITER**
Rom. historian .. **LIVY, NEPOS**
Rom. judge .... **EDILE, AEDILE**
Rom. law control ..... **MANUS**
Rom. legendary king ... **NUMA**
Rom. liquid measure ... **URNA**
Rom. list ...... **ALBE, ALBUM**
Rom. magistrate or official **EDILE, AEDILE, ARCHON, CONSUL, PRETOR, TRIBUNE**
Rom. market ... **FORA, FORUM**
Rom. meal .... **CENA**
b Rom. money, copper ..... **AES**
Rom. numerals 1-**I**, 5-**V**, 10-**X**, 50-**L**, 100-**C**, 500-**D**, 1000-**M**
ROMAN OFFICIAL see ROMAN MAGISTRATE
Rom. patriot .... **CATO**
Rom. philosopher **CATO, SENECA**
Rom. platter .... **LANX**
Rom. pledge .... **VAS**
Rom. poet ..... **OVID, LUCAN, HORACE, VERGIL, VIRGIL**
Rom. pound .... **AS**
Rom. province .... **DACIA**
Rom. public games ...... **LUDI**
Rom. public lands ...... **AGER**
Rom. religious festivals . **VOTA**
Rom. road .... **VIA, ITER**
Rom. robe .... **TOGA**
Rom. room, principal **ATRIA, ATRIUM**
Rom. scroll .... **STEMMA**
Rom. statesman .... **CATO**
Rom. sword .... **FALX**
Rom. vessel .... **PATERA**
Rom. war garb .... **SAGUM**
Rom. weight .... **AS**

c Rom. well-curb ...... **PUTEAL**
Rom. writer .... **MACER**
romance, tale of . **GEST, GESTE**
ROMANIA .... see RUMANIA
Rome, a founder of ... **REMUS**
Rome's cathedral church **LATERAN**
Rome's conqueror ..... **ALARIC**
Rome's river .... **TIBER**
Romulus' twin .... **REMUS**
rood .... **CROSS**
roof .... **MANSARD**
roof edge .... **EAVE**
roof of mouth ...... **PALATE**
roof of mouth, pert. to **PALATAL**
roof ornament .... **EPI**
roof, rounded . **DOME, CUPOLA**
roof, rounded like a ... **DOMAL**
roof, truncated .... **HIP**
roofing piece ...... **RAG, TILE**
roofing slate .... **TILE**
roofing timber .... **PURLIN**
rook's cry .... **CAWK**
room, Eng. college supply **BUTTERY**
room, snug .... **DEN**
room, rooms .... **SPACE, SUITE**
room, architecture ..... **OECUS**
room for household goods, linen, etc. **EWRY, EWERY**
d room, main, Rom. **ATRIA, ATRIUM**
room, mineshaft . **PLAT, PLATT**
room, Rom. .... **ALA**
roomy .... **WIDE**
roost .... **PERCH**
rooster .... **COCK**
root .... **RADIX, RADICES**
root, drug-yielding ... **JALAP**
root, edible .... **OCA, TARO, CASSAVA**
root, tree used for sewing **WATAP**
root, word .... **ETYM**
rootlet .... **RADICEL, RADICLE**
rootstock, edible .... **TARO**
rootstock, fern (Maori) ... **ROI**
rootstock, fragrant .... **ORRIS**
rope ...... **JEFF, LAZO, LASSO, LONGE, REATA, RIATA, LARIAT, MARLINE**
rope, cringle **LEEFANG, LEEFANGE**
rope fiber .. **DA, COIR, FERU, HEMP, IMBE, JUTE, RHEA, ABACA, SISAL**
rope for animals ..... **TETHER**
rope guide: naut. ...... **WAPP**
rope loop .... **BIGHT**

133

a rope, naut. ... **FOX, TYE, STAY, VANG, HAWSER, RATLIN, LANIARD, LANYARD, RATLINE, SNOTTER**
rope to tie boat ..... **PAINTER**
rope, weave .... **REEVE**
rope, yardarm ..... **SNOTTER**
ropes, unite .... **SPLICE**
rosary bead .... **AVE**
rose: Byron .... **GUL**
rose fruit .... **HIP**
rose genus .... **ROSA, ACAENA**
rose-like plant .... **AVENS**
rose of Sharon
ALTHEA, ALTHAEA
rose oil derivative ..... **ATAR, OTTO, ATTAR, OTTAR**
rose ornament ...... **ROSETTE**
rose, Pers. .... **GUL**
rosewood .... **MOLOMPI**
rosolic acid ... **AURIN, AURINE**
rostellum .... **ROSTEL**
roster .... **LIST, ROTA**
rotate .... **ROLL, GYRATE**
rotating muscle ..... **EVERTOR**
rotating part .... **CAM, ROTOR**
rotation producer .... **TORQUE**
rotten .... **PUTRID**
rouge ...... **RADDLE, RUDDLE**
b rough ...... **RUDE, UNEVEN**
rough, as country ..... **HILLY**
rough copy .... **DRAFT**
rough in voice .... **GRUFF**
rough rock .... **KNAR**
roughness, sea .... **LIPPER**
roulette bet ...... **BAS, NOIR, MILIEU**
round, a ...... **ROTA, ROTULA**
round hand .... **RONDE**
round room .... **ROTUNDA**
Round Table Knight .... **KAY, BORS, BORT, BALAN, BALIN, BOHORT, GARETH, GAWAIN, GALAHAD, PELLEAS**
round-up .... **RODEO**
rounded projection ..... **LOBE**
rounder ...... **RAKE, ROUE**
roundworm .... **NEMA, ASCARID, ASCARIS**
rouse . **WAKE, AWAKE, WAKEN**
Rousseau novel, hero ... **EMILE**
route .... **WAY, PATH**
route, plane's fixed ..... **LANE**
routine, fixed .... **ROTE**
row .... **LINE, SPAT, TIER**
rowan tree .... **ASH, SORB**
rowdy: slang .... **B'HOY**
rower .... **OAR**
rower's bench .... **ZYGA, ZYGON, THWART**

c royal authority ..... **SCEPTRE**
royal court, relating to . **AULIC**
royal edict: Fr. .... **ARRET**
royal family, Fr. ..... **VALOIS**
royal rights, having . **PALATINE**
royal rod .. **SCEPTER, SCEPTRE**
royal treasury ..... **FISC, FISK**
royalty, Hawaii ...... **ALII**
rub harshly .... **GRATE**
rub off .... **ABRADE**
rub out .... **ERASE**
rub roughly .... **SCRAPE**
rub to polish ... **BUFF, SHINE**
rub to soreness ...... **CHAFE**
rubber .... **PARA, LATEX, CAUCHO, ELASTIC**
rubber, black ...... **EBONITE**
rubber source .... **KOKSAGYZ**
rubber, S. Am. . **PARA, CEARA**
rubber tree ...... **ULE, HULE, SERINGA**
rubber, wild .... **CEARA**
rubbery substance
GUTTA, NOREPOL
rubbish .... **ROT, JUNK, CULCH, RUBBLE**
rubble masonry ..... **MOELLON**
rubella .... **MEASLES**
ruby .... **RED**
ruby red quartz ..... **RUBASSE**
d ruby spinel ... **BALAS, BALASS**
rudder bushing ...... **PINTLE**
rudder fish .... **CHOPA**
ruddle ...... **KEEL, KIEL**
rudiment .... **GERM**
rudiments .... **ABC**
rue .... **REGRET**
rue herb genus .... **RUTA**
ruff, female ..... **REE, REEVE**
ruffed lemur .... **VARI**
ruffer .... **NAPPER**
ruffle .... **CRIMP**
ruffle, neck ... **JABOT, RUCHE**
RUG ...... see also CARPET
rug, long narrow
KANARA, RUNNER
ruin .... **DOOM**
rule ...... **LAW, DOMINEER**
"Rule Britannia" composer
ARNE
rules, dueling .... **DUELLO**
ruler .... **REGENT**
ruler, Afghanistan ..... **EMIR, AMEER, CALIF, EMEER, CALIPH, SULTAN**
ruler, Arabian .. **EMIR, AMEER, CALIF, EMEER, CALIPH, SULTAN**
RULER, BIBLICAL .... see
SPECIAL SECTION

134

a **RULER IN EAST** ... see RULER, ARABIAN
ruler, India............. **NAWAB**
ruler, Morocco .... **SHERIF, SHEREEF**
ruler, Moslem ... **EMIR, AMEER, CALIF, EMEER, CALIPH, SULTAN**
ruler of gods............. **ZEUS**
ruler, Oriental .... **CALIF**
ruler, Tunis .... **DEY**
RUMANIA .... see also SPECIAL SECTION
Rumanian composer... **ENESCO**
Rumanian folk song ..... **DOINA**
Rumanian king's title .... **DOMN**
rumen................... **CUD**
ruminant .... **DEER, GOAT, CAMEL, LLAMA, ANTELOPE**
ruminant genus .... **CAPRA**
ruminant, horned........ **DEER, GOAT**
ruminate ..... **MULL, PONDER**
Rumor personified....... **FAMA**
rumor, to..... **BRUIT, NORATE, REPORT**

b rumple .... **MUSS**
run at top speed .... **SPRINT**
run before wind .... **SCUD**
run of the mill .... **PAR**
run out.................. **PETER**
runner .... **SCARF, STOLO, STOLON**
runner, distance........ **MILER**
runner, plant.. **STOLO, STOLON**
rupees, 100,000.......... **LAC**
rural ..... **RUSTIC, PASTORAL**
rural deity ...... **PAN, FAUNUS**
rural poem............ **GEORGIC**
rush .... **HASTE, SPEED**
rush, marsh .... **SPART**
Russell's viper .... **DABOIA, DABOYA**
RUSSIA....... see also SOVIET and SPECIAL SECTION
Russia, most northern town **KOLA**
Russian .... **RED, RUSS, SLAV, KULAK, TATAR**
Russ. basso .... **KIPNIS**
Russ. author............ **BUNIN**

c Russ. beer....... **KVAS, QUAS, KVASS**
Russ. community........... **MIR**
Russ. convention........ **RADA**
Russ. cooperative society **ARTEL**
Russ. council .... **DUMA**
Russ. dress......... **SARAFAN**
Russ. edict ... **UKASE, DECREE**
Russ. emperor .... **CZAR, TSAR, TZAR**
Russ. fiddle........... **GUDOK**
Russ. folk dance .... **KOLO**
Russ. girl's name........ **OLGA**
Russ. hemp................ **RINE**
Russ. labor union........ **ARTEL**
Russ. lagoon........... **LIMAN**
Russ. Lapland capital ..... **KOLA**
Russ. leather............ **YUFT**
Russ. liquid measure ... **STOF, STOFF, STOOF**
Russ. log hut .... **ISBA**
Russ. marsh .... **LIMAN**
Russ. mile .... **VERST**
Russ. mountain range .... **ALAI, URAL**

d Russian mts., pert. to.... **ALTAIC**
Russ. name, given.. **AKIM, IGOR**
Russ. news agency .... **TASS**
Russ. official............ **BERIYA**
Russ. opera............ **BORIS**
Russ. peninsula .... **KOLA**
Russ. sea, inland .... **ARAL, AZOF, AZOV**
Russ. secret police .... **KGB, NKVD, OGPU**
Russ. tavern .... **CABACK**
Russ. tax, old .... **OBROK**
Russ. tea urn .... **SAMOVAR**
Russ. trade guild .... **ARTEL**
Russ. vehicle ... **ARBA, ARABA**
Russ. village .... **MIR**
Russ. whip............... **PLET**
Russ. writer.... **GORKI, GORKY**
Russ. "yes"................. **DA**
rust.............. **EAT, ERODE**
Rustam's father............ **ZAL**
rustic .... **BOOR, RUBE, CARL, CARLE, YOKEL, BUCOLIC, PEASANT**
Ruth's husband .... **BOAZ**
Ruth's son............... **OBED**
rye, disease of......... **ERGOT**

S

sable .... **SOBOL, MARTEN**
sac .... **BURSA**
saccharine source .... **TAR**
sack fiber .... **JUTE**
sack, to .... **LOOT**
saclike cavity .... **BURSA**
sacred asp, symbol .... **URAEUS**
sacred bull, Egypt . **APIS, HAPI**
sacred chalice .... **GRAIL**
sacred city, India ... **BENARES**
sacred enclosure, Gr. .. **SEKOS**
sacred fig .... **PIPAL**
sacred Hindu word .... **OM**
sacred image .... **ICON, IKON**
sacred lily .... **LOTUS**
sacred object: Oceania . **ZOGO**
sacred picture ... **ICON, IKON**
sacred place .... **SHRINE**
sacred place, Gr.
　　　　　ABATON, HIERON
sacred tree, Hindu .. **BO, PIPAL**
sacrifice, place of ..... **ALTAR**
sacrificial drink, Zoroaster's
　　　　　　　　　　SOMA
sacrificial offerings .... **HIERA**
sad: comb. form ...... **TRAGI**
sad cry .... **ALAS, ALACK**
sad: music .... **MESTO**
saddle horses, fresh . **REMUDA**
saddle knob .... **POMMEL**
saddle, rear of .... **CANTLE**
safe .... **SECURE**
safe place ..... **PORT, HAVEN**
safe: thief's slang ...... **PETE**
safety lamp .... **DAVY**
safflower .... **KUSUM**
saga .... **EDDA**
sage .... **WISE**
sagacious .... **WISE,**
　　　　　　ASTUTE, SAPIENT
sage genus .... **SALVIA**
soil fastener .... **CLEW**
sail-line .... **EARING**
sail nearer wind ...... **LUFF**
sail, square .... **LUG**
sail, square, edge of ... **LEECH**
sail, triangular .... **JIB**
sail yard: Scot. .... **RAE**
sail's corner .... **CLEW**
"Sails" of constellation Argo
　　　　　　　　　　VELA
sailboat .... **YAWL, KETCH**
sailing race .... **REGATTA**
SAILING VESSEL ...... see
　　　　　VESSEL, SAILING
sailmaker's awl ..... **STABBER**

sailor . **GOB, TAR, SALT, SEADOG**
sailor, India .... **LASCAR**
St. Anthony's cross ..... **TAU**
saint, British .... **ALBAN**
saint, Buddhist
　　　ARAHT, ARHAT, ARAHAT
St. Catherine's home ... **SIENA**
saint, female: abbr. ..... **STE**
saint, 14th century ..... **ROCH**
St. Francis' birthplace .. **ASSISI**
St. John's-bread ..... **CAROB**
"St. Louis Blues" composer
　　　　　　　　　HANDY
saint, Moslem .... **PIR**
St. Paul, deserter from . **DEMAS**
St. Vitus dance ...... **CHOREA**
sainte: abbr. .... **STE**
saint's relic box ...... **CHASSE**
salad green ...... **UDO, CRESS,**
　　　　KERSE, CRESSE, ENDIVE
salamander .. **EFT, EVET, NEWT**
salient angle .... **CANT**
Salientia, the .... **ANURA**
sally .... **START, SORTIE**
"Sally in Our Alley" composer
　　　　　　　　　CAREY
salmon, female .... **HEN**
salmon, male .... **COCK**
salmon net .... **MAUD**
salmon, silver .... **COHO**
salmon, third year ..... **MORT**
salmon, 2 yr. .. **SMOLT, SPROD**
salmon, young .. **PARR, GRILSE**
salt ..... **SAL, HALITE, SALINE**
salt factory .... **SALTERN**
salt lake, Turkestan .... **SHOR**
salt of tartaric acid .. **TARTAR**
salt pond or spring ... **SALINA**
salt, resembling ...... **HALOID**
salt, rock .... **HALITE**
salt, solution .. **BRINE, SALINE**
salt tax .... **GABELLE**
salt tree, Tamarisk ..... **ATLE**
salted .... **ALAT**
saltpeter .... **NITER, NITRE**
saltwort .... **KALI**
saltworks ,........ **SALINA**
salty water .... **BRINE**
salutation .... **AVE**
salutation: Ir. ...... **ACHARA**
Salvation Army leader . **BOOTH**
salver .... **TRAY**
salvia .... **CHIA**
Sambal language .... **TINO**
sambar deer .... **MAHA, RUSA**
same .... **ILK, DITTO**

136

same place: abbr. .... **IBID**
samlet .... **PARR**
Samoan maiden .... **TAUPO**
Samoan mollusk .... **ASI**
Samoan political council . **FONO**
Samuel, king killed by .. **AGAG**
Samuel, teacher of .... **ELI**
Samuel's son .... **ABIA**
samurai, straying ..... **RONIN**
sanction .... **AMEN, FIAT**
sanctuary ...... **BEMA, FANE,**
　　　　　　　　NAOS, CELLA,
　　　　　　　　GRIT
sand bar .... **REEF, SHOAL**
sand expanses .... **AREG**
sand hill .... **DENE, DUNE**
sand island .... **BAR**
sand, sea bottom .... **PAAR**
sand snake genus ...... **ERYX**
sandal, Egypt .... **TATBEB**
sandal, Mex.
　　　　HUARACHE, HUARACHO
sandalwood tree .... **MAIRE**
sandarac powder .... **POUNCE**
sandarac tree .... **ARAR**
sandbox tree genus .... **HURA**
sandpiper .. **REE, RUFF, STIB,**
　　　　　　REEVE, STINT
sandpiper, Europ. ...... **TEREK**
sandpiper, red .... **KNOT**
sandpiper, small ..... **KNOT,**
　　　　　　　　PUME, STINT
sandstone .... **GRIT**
sandstorm .... **HABOOB**
sandwich .... **HERO**
Sandwich Island discoverer
　　　　　　　　　COOK
sandy .... **ARENOSE**
Sankhya philos. term ... **GUNA**
Sanskrit dialect .... **PALI**
Sanskrit precept
　　　　　　　SUTRA, SUTTA
Sanskrit school .... **TOL**
Sao —, Brazil .... **PAULO**
Sao Salvador .... **BAHIA**
sap spout .... **SPILE**
sapodilla ... **SAPOTA, SAPOTE**
sapota tree .... **ACANA**
Saracen ..... **MOOR, MOSLEM**
Sarah's slave .... **HAGAR**
sarcasm .... **IRONY**
Sardinia gold coin ... **CARLINE**
sargeant fish .... **SNOOK**
Sargon's capital ...... **ACCAD**
Sarmatia cave-dwellers . **TAURI**
sartor .... **TAILOR**
sash, C. Amer. .... **TOBE**
sash, Jap. kimono .... **OBI**
sassafras tree .... **AGUE**
Satan .... **DEVIL**
Satan: Arab .... **EBLIS**

satellite .... **MOON, PLANET**
satellite .... **LUNIK, SPUTNIK,**
　　　　PIONEER, EXPLORER,
　　　　VANGUARD, ATLAS-
　　　　SCORE, DISCOVERER
satellite, navigation . **TRANSIT**
satellite, television .... **TIROS**
satellite's path .... **ORBIT**
satiate .. **CLOY, GLUT, SATE**
satirical .... **DRY**
satisfaction Maori .... **UTU**
satisfy ... **SATE, SUIT, PLEASE**
saturate . **SOAK, IMBUE, STEEP**
Saturn, satellite of ..... **DIONE**
Saturn's rings projection.**ANSA**
Saturn's wife .... **OPS**
Saturnalia .... **ORGY**
satyr .... **FAUN**
sauce .... **GRAVY**
sauce, Chinese, Oriental .. **SOY**
sauce, fish .... **ALEC**
sauce, peppery ...... **TABASCO**
sauce, tomato .... **CATSUP,**
　　　　CATCHUP, KETCHUP
saucy .... **PERT**
Saul's army leader ..... **ABNER**
Saul's chief herdsman .. **DOEG**
Saul's father .... **KISH**
Saul's grandfather . **NER, ABIEL**
Saul's successor ...... **DAVID**
Saul's uncle .... **NER**
Sault Ste. Marie .... **SOO**
saurel fish .... **SCAD**
sausage, spiced ..... **SALAME,**
　　　　　　　　　SALAMI
savage .... **FERAL**
Savage Island language .. **NIUE**
save ....../.. **HOARD, STINT,**
　　　　REDEEM, CONSERVE
saviour .... **REDEEMER**
savory .... **SAPID, TASTY**
saw .... **ADAGE, AXIOM,**
　　　　　　MAXIM, SAYING
saw-leaved centaury
　　　　　　BEHN, BEHEN
saw, notched like .... **SERRATE**
saw notching .... **REDAN**
saw, surgical **TREPAN,TREPHINE**
sawbill duck .... **SMEW**
sawlike organ, or part .. **SERRA**
sawlike parts . **SERRAS, SERRAE**
sawtooth ridge .... **SIERRA**
saxhorn .... **TUBA**
Saxon god .... **ER, EAR**
Saxon king ...... **INE, ALFRED**
Saxony natives .... **SORBS**
say .... **UTTER**
say again .... **ITERATE**
saying ... **MOT, SAW, ADAGE,**
　　　　AXIOM, MAXIM
sayings .... **LOGIA**

137

a
scabbard fish .... **HIKU**
scabbard, put into .. **SHEATHE**
scaffolding .... **STAGING**
scale .... **GAMUT**
scale, syllable of .. **DO, FA, LA, MI, RE, SO, TI, SOL**
scale under blossom
.... **PALEA, PALET**
scales, having large . **SCUTATE**
scallop ..... **CRENA, CRENAE**
scallops, cut in small ... **PINK**
scalloped .... **CRENATE**
scalp disease .... **FAVI, FAVUS**
scamp ...... **ROGUE, RASCAL**
SCANDINAVIAN
.... see also **NORSE**
SCANDINAVIAN . see also
SWEDEN, NORWAY, In
SPECIAL SECTION
Scandinavian ... **DANE, SWEDE**
Scand., ancient ...... **NORSE**
Scand. countryman ..... **GEAT**
Scand. explorer .... **ERIC**
Scand. fertility god .... **NJORD**
Scand. legend .... **SAGA**
Scand. measure .... **ALEN**
Scand. nation .... **GEATAS**
Scandinavians in Russia
.... **ROS, RUS**

b
scanty .... **SPARSE**
scar, resembling a .... **ULOID**
scarce .... **RARE**
scarcely: Lat. .... **VIX**
scare away .... **SHOO**
scarf .... **BOA, TIE, ASCOT, ORALE**
scarf, long .... **STOLE**
scarf, Sp. Am. .... **TAPALO**
scarlet flower .... **SALVIA**
Scarlett O'Hara's home .. **TARA**
scatter ... **SOW, TED, STREW**
scatter: dial. .... **SCOAD**
scatter on .... **LITTER**
scattered: Her. .... **SEME**
scenario .... **SCRIPT**
scene ..... **VIEW, TABLEAU**
scene of action .**ARENA, SPHERE**
scenic view .... **SCAPE**
scent .... **ODOR, AROMA**
scented .... **OLENT**
schedule .... **LIST**
scheme .... **PLAN, PLOT**
schism .... **RENT**
scholar .... **PEDANT**
scholars, Moslem .... **ULEMA**
scholarship .... **BURSE**
school, boy's .... **PREP**
school, Fr. ..... **ECOLE, LYCEE**
school grounds ...... **CAMPUS**

c
SCHOONER ... see also **BOAT, SHIP, VESSEL**
schooner, 3-masted ..... **TERN**
sciences .... **ARTS**
scientific farmer . **AGRONOMIST**
scientific study: abbr. .. **ANAT.**
scientist, Am. . **UREY, HOOTON, PARRAN, COMPTON, WAKSMAN, MILLIKAN**
scientist, Austr. .... **MEITNER**
scientist, Czech .... **CORI**
scientist, Dan. .... **BOHR**
scientist, Eng. ...... **HOGBEN, FLEMING, HALDANE**
scientist, Ger. .. **BAADE, HABER**
scientist, Ital. .... **FERMI**
scissors .... **SHEARS**
scoff .... **GIBE, JEER, JIBE, RAIL, SNEER**
scold ...... **JAW, NAG, RATE**
scold: dialect .... **FRAB**
scone: Scot. ..... **FARL, FARLE**
scoop .... **DIP**
scoot: Scot. ..... **SKYT, SKITE**
scope .. **AREA, AMBIT, RANGE**
scorch .... **CHAR, SEAR, SERE, SINGE**
score .... **TALLY**
scoria .... **SLAG, DROSS**

d
scorpion fish .... **LAPON**
Scotch cake .... **SCONE**
scoter .... **COOT**
Scotland .... **SCOTIA**
Scott character ...... **ELLEN**
Scott heroine .... **ELLEN**
Scott, poem by .. **MARMION**
SCOTTISH
see Pages of SCOTTISH WORDS
Scot. alderman .... **BAILIE**
Scot. author .... **BARRIE**
Scot. chemist ... **URE, DEWAR**
Scot. chief landholder
.... **THANE, THEGN**
Scot. cultural congress ... **MOD**
Scot. explorer .... **RAE**
Scot. highlander ...... **GAEL**
Scot. king .... **BRUCE**
Scot. lord ..... **THANE, THEGN**
Scot. pillory .... **JOUG**
Scot. playwright ...... **BARRIE**
Scot. poet .... **BURNS**
Scot. pottage .... **BROSE**
Scot. proprietor ...... **LAIRD**
Scot. scholar .... **NICOLL**
Scot. singer .... **LAUDER**
SCOTTISH WORDS:
accept .... **TAE**
advise .... **REDE**
afraid .... **RAD, RADE**
age .... **EILD**

138

a
against	GIN
alder tree	ARN, ELLER
an	AE
animal, lean	RIBE
any	ONY
article	TA
ashes	ASE
ask	AX
at all	AVA
away	AWA
awry	AJEE
babbler	HAVEREL
ball	BA
bank	BRAE
barter	TROKE
beg	SORN
bind	OOP
biscuit	BAKE
blockhead	CUIF, NOWT
bloodhound	LYAM
bone	BANE
bound	STEND
breeches	TREWS
broth	BREE, BROO
brow of hill	SNAB
built	BAG
burden	BIRN
bushel	FOU
calves	CAUR, CAURE

b
came	CAM
catch	KEP
chalk	CAUK
check	WERE
chest	KIST
child	BAIRN
church	KIRK, KURK
comb	KAME
contend	KEMP
court, bring to	SIST
cut	KNAP, SNEG
dairymaid	DEY
damage	TEEN
damaged	LESED
dare	DAUR
devil	DEIL
did not know	KENNA
die	DEE
dig	HOWK
dining room	SPENCE
do	DAE, DIV
do not know	KENNA
dread	DREE
drip	SIE, SYE
dusty	MOTTY
earth	EARD
elder	ELLER
else	ENSE
empty	TOOM
endeavor	ETTLE
endure	DREE

c
extra	ORRA
eye	EE
eyes	EEN, EES
family	ILK
fidget	FIKE
firth	KYLE
fishing expedition	DRAVE
fit of sulks	GEE
flax refuse	PAB, POB
fog	DAG, HAR, HAAR
foretell	SPAE
give	GIE
glimpse	STIME
grandchild	OY, OYE
grant as property	DISPONE
great-grandchild	IEROE
grief	TEEN
have	HAE
hawk	ALLAN
heavy	THARF
hill	BEN, DOD, BRAE, DODD
hillside	BRAE
howl	YOWT
hurt	LESED
injure	TEEN
injured	LESED
intent	ETTLE
keg	KNAG

d
kinsman	SIB
kiss	PREE
knead	ELT
knock	KNOIT
lake	LOCH
leap	LOUP, LOWP, STEND
learning	LEAR
list of candidates	LEET
loaf	SORN
lop	SNATHE
lout	CUIF
love	LOE
loyal	LEAL
marriage portion	DOTE
millrace	LADE
mire	GLAUR
mist	URE
mountain	BEN
mouth, river	BEAL
mouth	BEAL
mud	GLAIR
must	MAUN
name	IAN
near, nearest	NAR
no	NAE
none	NANE
not matched	ORRA
now	NOO
nowhere	NAEGATE
oak	AIK

(Scottish words continued 140)

Scottish

a
oatmeal dish . . . . **BROSE**
odd . . . . **ORRA**
old age . . . . **EILD**
once . . . . **ANES**
one . . . . **AIN, ANE, YIN**
otherwise . . . . **ELS**
out . . . . **OOT**
own . . . . **AIN, ANE, AWN**
pantry . . . . **SPENCE**
parlor . . . . **BEN**
payment . . . . **MENSE**
paw ground . . . . **PAUT**
peat cutter . . . . **PINER**
pig . . . . **GRICE**
pike . . . . **GED, GEDD**
pillory . . . . **TRONE**
pipe . . . . **CUTTY**
pluck wool . . . . **ROO**
pool . . . . **DIB, CARR,**
LINN, LLYN
present . . . . **GIE**
pretty . . . . **GEY**
prop . . . . **RANCE**
propriety . . . . **MENSE**
prune . . . . **SNED**
puddle . . . . **DUB**
pull . . . . **PU**
quagmire . . . . **HAG**
quarter of a year . . . . . . **RAITH**
relieve . . . . **LISS**

b
revenue, church . . . . . **ANNAT**
ridge of a hill . . . . **SHIN**
river . . . . **DOON**
rowboat . . . . **COBLE**
sailyard . . . . **RAE**
same . . . . **ILK**
scone . . . . **FARL, FARLE**
scoot . . . . **SKYT, SKITE**
scratch . . . . **RIT**
seep . . . . **SIPE**
seize . . . . **VANG**
self . . . . **SEL**
serve . . . . **KAE**
severe blow . . . . **DEVEL**
sheepfold . . . . **REE**
sheep tick . . . . **KED**
sheep walk . . . . **SLAIT**
shelter . . . . **BIELD, SHEAL**
sift . . . . **SIE**
since . . . . **SIN, SYNE**
slope . . . . **BRAE**
slouch . . . . **LOUCH**
sly . . . . **SLEE**
small . . . . **SMA**
snow . . . . **SNA**
so . . . . **SAE**
son of . . . . **MAC**
song . . . . **STROUD**
sore . . . . **SAIR**
sorrow . . . . **TEEN**
sow . . . . **SOO**

c
steward . . . . **MORMAOR**
stipend . . . . **ANNAT**
stone **STANE, STEAN, STEEN**
stretch . . . . **STENT**
stupid one . . . . **CUIF**
suffer . . . . **DREE**
summit . . . . **DOD, DODD**
sweetheart . . . . **JO**
than . . . . **NA**
to . . . . **TAE**
toe . . . . **TAE**
tone . . . . **TEAN**
trench . . . . **GAW**
truant, play . . . . **TRONE**
try . . . . **ETTLE**
tune . . . . **PORT**
turnip . . . . **NEEP**
uncanny . . . . **UNCO**
uncle . . . . **EME**
urge . . . . **ERT**
very . . . . **VERA**
vex . . . . **FASH**
village . . . . **REW**
void, to render . . . . **CASS**
waterfall . . . . . **LIN, LYN, LINN**
wealthy . . . . **BIEN**
weep . . . . **ORP**
week . . . . **OUK**

d
weighing machine . . . . . **TRON,**
TRONE
well . . . . **AWEEL**
wet . . . . **WAT**
whirlpool . . . . . . **WEEL, WIEL**
whiskey drink . . . . **ATHOL,**
ATHOLE
widow's third . . . . **TERCE**
workhouse . . . . **AVER**
year, ¼ of . . . . **RAITH**
yell . . . . **GOWL**
scoundrel . . . . **ROGUE, VARLET**
scout unit . **DEN, PACK, TROOP**
scow . . . . **BARGE, LIGHTER**
scow: Fr. . . . . **ACON**
scrap, table . . . . **ORT**
scraps of literature . . . . **ANA**
scrape . . . **RAKE, RASP, GRAZE**
scrape bottom . . . . **DREDGE**
scratch . . . . **MAR, RAKE**
scrawny animal . . . . **SCRAG**
screamer bird . . . . **CHAJA**
screed . . . . **TIRADE**
screen . . . . **SIFT, SHADE**
screen, altar . . . . **REREDOS**
screen, wind . . . . **PARAVENT**
script, modern Syriac . . . . **SERTA**
script, upright . . . . **RONDE**
scripture, early . . . . **ITALA**
scripture passage . . . . **TEXT**
scriptures, occult interpretation
CABALA
scrutinize . . . . **EYE, SCAN**

a scuffle .... MELEE
sculptor of "Thinker" . RODIN
scum, metal .... DROSS
scup .... BREAM, PORGY
scuppernong ..... MUSCADINE
scuttle .... HOD
scuttle, coal .... HOD
scythe .... SY, SYE
scythe handle . SNATH, SNEAD,
                SNEED, SNATHE
sea anemone .. POLYP, OPELET
sea bird ... ERN, ERNE, GULL,
     SKUA, SCAUP, TERN, FUL-
     MAR, GANNET, PETREL,
     SCOTER
sea bird, north .... PUFFIN
sea cow . DUGONG, MANATEE
sea cucumber .... TREPANG
sea demon, Teut. ...... WATE
sea duck ...... COOT, EIDER,
              SCAUP, SCOTER
sea eagle .... ERN, ERNE
sea-ear .... ABALONE
sea: Fr. .... MER
sea girdles .... CUVY
sea god .... LER, TRITON,
               NEPTUNE
sea god, Gr. . NEREUS, TRITON,
               POSEIDON
sea god, Rom. ...... NEPTUNE
sea god, Teut. .. HLER, AEGIR
sea goddess, Norse ..... RAN
b sea green .... CELADON
sea gull, Eur. .... MEW
sea, kept bow on . ATRY, ATRIE
sea lettuce ..... ALGA, LAVER
sea lettuce genus ULVA, ULUA
sea marker .... DAN
sea pheasant .... SMEE
sea robber .... PIRATE
sea mile, Austral. ...... NAUT
sea nymph .... NEREID
sea shell .... TRITON
   (see also SHELL)
sea skeleton .... CORAL
sea slug genus . DOTO, ELYSIA
sea snail . WELK, WILK, WHELK
sea snake, Asia ...... KERRIL
sea soldier .... MARINE
sea worm . SAO, LURG, NEREIS
seal .... SIGIL
seal, eared .... OTARY
seal, fur .... URSAL
seal, letter .... CACHET
seal, official .... SIGNET
seal, papal .... BULLA
seal, young .... PUP
seals, group of .... POD
seamark .... BEACON
seamen: Brit. .... RATINGS
seamlike ridge .... RAPHE

c seams of boat, fill ..... CALK
SEAPORT .... see PORT
search .... GROPE
search for ...... HUNT, SEEK
search for food ...... FORAGE
season ...... AGE, FALL, SALT,
              TIDE, SPRING
season, church . LENT, ADVENT
season, Fr. .... ETE
seasons, goddesses of .. HORAE
seasonal phenomenon .. EPACT
seasoning .... SAGE, SALT
seasoning herb .... SAGE,
              BASIL, THYME
seat, chancel .... SEDILE
seat, long ...... PEW, SETTEE
seat of oracle of Zeus. DODONA
seat, Rom. .... SELLA
seaweed ... ORE, AGAR, ALGA,
           KELP, ALGAE, LAVER,
           VAREC
seaweed ashes .... KELP
seaweed, brown .... KELP
seaweed, edible .... AGAR
seaweed, edible Hawaiian LIMU
seaweed, purple ...... LAVER
seaweed, purple, Jap. ... NORI
seaweed, red .... DULSE
Seb, consort of .... NUT
d secluded .... REMOTE
second . ABET, TRICE, MOMENT
second brightest star ... BETA
second-growth crop .... ROWEN
Second Punic War's end,
   site of .... ZAMA
second team .... SCRUB
secondary .... BYE, LESS
secret ...... RUNE, ARCANE,
           COVERT, MYSTERY,
           ESOTERIC
secret agent .... SPY
secret society, Afr..EGBO, PORO
secret society in Sierra Leone
                      PORO
secrets .... ARCANA
secrets, one learning .. EPOPT
secretion, sweet
           LAAP, LERP, LAARP
sect .... CULT
sect, Nepal . ACHAR, ACHARA
section of journey .... LEG
secular ... LAY, LAIC, LAICAL
secure .. FIX, GET, PIN, FAST,
          NAIL, SAFE, FASTEN
secure firmly . MOOR, ANCHOR
secure with rope ...... BELAY
security .... BOND
Sec'y of State, 1933-44 .. HULL
sedate .... STAID
sedative .... NEMBUTAL

141

a sediment .... LEES, SILT, DREGS, SILTAGE
see .... ESPY, LOOK
see: Lat. .... VIDE
seed .... PIP, PIT, GRAIN, SPORE, PYRENE
seed coat or covering .. ARIL, HULL, HUSK, TESTA, TEGMEN, TESTAE, TEGUMEN, TEGIMINA
seed, edible ...... PEA, BEAN, LENTIL, PINOLE
seed, edible, Asia .... SESAME
seed, immature .... OVULE
seed, lens-shaped ..... LENTIL
seed, nutlike .... PINON
seed, opium poppy ..... MAW
seed plant .... ENDOGEN
seeds, remove .... GIN
seedless plant .... FERN
seek to attain .... ASPIRE
seem .... LOOK
seesaw .... TEETER
segment, last .... TELSON
segment of body ..... SOMITE
segment of circle ...... ARC
segment, pert. to ...... TORIC
seine .... NET
seize .... NAB, GRAB, GRASP, USURP, ARREST, COLLAR

b seize: archaic .... REAVE
selections, literary
ANA, ANALECTA
self .... EGO
self-assurance ...... APLOMB
self-defense, art of ..... JUDO
self-denying .... ASCETIC
self-education doctrine
BIOSOPHY
self-locking nut ..... PALNUT
self-reproach .... REMORSE
sell .... VEND
seller .... COSTER, VENDER, VENDOR
semblance .... GUISE
semester .... TERM
semi-precious stone
ONYX, SARD
semicircular room ..... APSE
semidiameter .... RADIUS
semidiameters .... RADII
Seminole chief ..... OSCEOLA
Semitic deity .... BAAL
sen, tenth of .... RIN
senate house .... CURIA
senate houses .... CURIAE
Senator, former ...... BORAH
send back ... REMIT, REMAND
send money .... REMIT

c send out .... EMIT, ISSUE
sending forth .... EMISSIVE
Senegambia gazelle ... KORIN
senility .... DOTAGE
senior .... ELDER
senior: Fr. .... AINE
senna, source of ..... CASSIA
sennet .... SPET
sense .... FEEL
senseless .... INANE
sensitive .... SORE
sentence, analyze ..... PARSE
sentence part .... CLAUSE
"Sentimental Journey" author
STERNE
sentinel, mounted ... VEDETTE
separate . SIFT, APART, SECERN
separated .... APART
separation .... SCHISM
sequence, 3-card ..... TIERCE
sequester .... ISOLATE
Sequoia national park ... MUIR
seraglio .... HAREM, SERAI
serene .... SERENO
serf .... ESNE
serf, Rom. .... COLONA
serf, Spartan, ancient .. HELOT
sergeant fish .... COBIA
series .... SET, GAMUT
series, in a .... SERIATIM

d series of tones .... SCALE
serious ..... GRAVE, EARNEST
sermon .... HOMILY
serow .... JAGLA
SERPENT ..... see also SNAKE
serpent, Egypt. myth .... APEPI
serpent goddess, Egypt. . BUTO
serpent, Gr. .... SEPS
serpent, large .. BOA, PYTHON
serpent monster ...... ELLOPS
serpent, myth. ...... BASILISK
serpent worship ...... OPHISM
serpentine .... OPHITE
servant........... BOY, MAN, MAID, MENIAL
servant, India .... HAMAL, FERASH, HAMMAL
servant, man's .... VALET
servant, P. I. .... BATA
servants, for .... MENIAL
serve soup .... LADLE
server .... TRAY
service, religious ...... MASS
service tree .... SORB
servile .... MENIAL
serving boy .... PAGE
sesame .... TIL, TEEL
sesame oil ...... BENI, BENNE
sesame seed .... GINGILI
session, hold .... SIT, MEET

a
set aside	DEFER
set in type	PRINT
set limits to	STINT
set price	RATE
set system	ROTE
set thickly	STUD
setback	REVERSE
Seth's brother	CAIN
Seth's mother	EVE
Seth's son	ENOS
setting	SCENE, MILIEU
setting sun, Egyp. god of	TEM, TUM, ATMU, ATUM
settled	ALIT
settler	BOOMER
seven	SEPT
Seven Dwarfs	DOC, DOPEY, HAPPY, GRUMPY, SLEEPY, SNEEZY, BASHFUL
seven, group of	HEPTAD, PLEIAD, SEPTET, SEPTETTE
"Seventh Heaven" heroine	DIANE
seventh order, of	SEPTIC
seventh, pert. to	SEPTAN
sever	CUT, LOP, REND
severe	STERN
severely criticize	PAN, SLATE, ROAST

b
sew hawk's eyelids	SEEL
"Seward's —," Alaska	FOLLY
sexes, common to both	EPICENE
shabby	WORN
shabby woman	DOWD
shackle	BOND, GYVE, IRON, FETTER
shad	ALLIS, ALOSA, ALOSE, ALLICE
shaddock	POMELO, PUMELO
shade	HUE, SCREEN
shade of difference	NUANCE
shade of meaning	NUANCE
shaded walk	MALL
shadow	TAIL
shadow, eclipse	UMBRA
shaft	POLE, SPINDLE
shaft column, feather	SCAPE
shaft horse	THILLER
shaft of column	FUST
shaft, wooden	ARROW
shafter	HORSE
shake	JAR, JOLT, NIDGE
Shakespeare's elf	PUCK
Shakespeare's river	AVON
Shakespeare's theatre	GLOBE
Shakespeare's wife	ANNE
Shakesperian clown	BOTTOM
Shakesperian forest	ARDEN
Shakesperian king	LEAR

c
Shakesperian shrew	KATE
Shakesperian villain	IAGO
shallow receptacle	TRAY
sham	FAKE
Shamash, wife of	AI, AYA
"Shane," star of	LADD
Shang dynasty	YIN
shank	CRUS, SHIN
shanks	CRURA
shanty	HUT
shape	FORM, MOLD
shaped like a club	CLAVATE
shaped like a needle	ACUATE, ACERATE
shaping tool	LATHE, SWAGE
share	LOT, RATION
share	PARTAKE
shark	TOPE
shark, Eur. small	TOPE
shark, long-nosed	MAKO
shark, nurse	GATA
shark parasite fish	REMORA
sharp	ACERB, ACUTE, ACUATE
sharp	CHEAT
sharp ridge	ARETE
sharpen	EDGE, HONE, WHET
sharpshooter	JAGER, SNIPER
shavetail: abbr.	LT
shawl	MAUD, PAISLEY

d
shea tree	KARITE
sheaf of grain: Her.	GERB
shear	CLIP
sheath, petiole	OCREA
Sheba: Lat.	SABA
shed, as feathers	MOLT, MOULT
shed for sheep	COTE
sheen	GLOSS
sheep	EWE, RAM, MERINO
sheep, Afr. domestic	ZENU
sheep, Afr. wild	ARUI, UDAD, AOUDAD
sheep, Asia wild	ARGALI
sheep, Asia, wild, mountain	SHA, SNA, RASSE, URIAL, BHARAL, NAHOOR, OORIAL
sheep cry	BAA, MAA
sheep disease	COE, GID, ROT
sheep dog	COLLIE
sheep, Eng. black-faced	LONK
sheep, female	EWE
sheep genus	OVIS
sheep in 2nd year	TEG, TEGG, BIDENT
sheep, India, wild	SHA, SNA, URIAL, NAHOOR, OORIAL
sheep, large-horned	AOUDAD, ARGALI
sheep, Leicester	DISHLEY
sheep, male	RAM, TUP

Sheep

a
sheep, N. Afr. wild .... ARUI, UDAD, AOUDAD
sheep, of .... OVINE
sheep owner, Bibl. .... NABAL
sheep pasture, old Eng. .. HEAF
sheep, pert. to .... OVINE
sheep, Tibet .... SHA, SNA, URIAL, BHARAL, NAHOOR, OORIAL
sheep tick .... KED, KADE
sheep, unshorn .. HOGG, HEDER
sheep walk: Scot. .... SLAIT
sheep, wild .. SHA, SNA, ARUI, UDAD, RASSE, BHARAL, NAHOOR, AOUDAD, AR-GALI, OORIAL
sheep, young ...... TAG, TEG
sheepfold .... REE, COTE
sheeplike .... OVINE
sheepskin leather ...... BOCK, ROAN, SKIVER
sheerly .... SOLELY
shekel, ¼, Hebrew ...... REBA
shelf .... LEDGE
shelf above altar ... RETABLE
shell .... BOMB
shell .. TEST, LORICA, TUNICA
shell beads .... PEAG
shell, large .... CONCH
shell, marine .... TRITON
shell money .... ULLO, COWRY, UHLLO, COWRIE

b
shellfish, edible ...... CRAB, ABALONE, SCALLOP
shelter .... LEE, COTE, SHED, HAVEN, SCREEN
shelter, hillside .... ABRI
shelter: Scot. .. BIELD, SHEAL
shelter, to .... ALEE
sheltered .... ALEE
Shem descendant ..... SEMITE
Shem's brother .... HAM
Shem's son ...... LUD, ARAM, ELAM, ASSHUR
Sheol .... HADES
shepherd prophet ...... AMOS
shepherd's crook PEDA, PEDUM
shepherd's pipe .... OAT, REED
shepherd's song .. MADRIGAL
shepherdess, "Winter's Tale" MOPSA
sheriff substitute ..... ELISOR
sheriff's men .... POSSE
Sherwood .... FOREST
Shetland court president FOUD
Shetland hill pasture ... HOGA
shield .. ECU, EGIS, AEGIS, PAVIS, DEFEND, PROTECT
shield, Athena's .... AEGIS
shield, Austral. ...... MULGA
shield-bearing or border.ORLE

c
shield, medieval .... ECU
shield, Rom. ..... SCUTA, SCUTUM, CLIPEUS
shield-shaped PELTATE, SCUTATE
shield, small .... ECU
shield strap .... ENARME
shield's corner: Her. CANTON
shift .... VEER
shift position.GIBE, GYBE, JIBE
shin .... CNEMIS
shine GLOW, GLISTEN, ERADIATE
shingle, wedge-shaped .. SHIM
shingles .... ZONA
shining .... NITID
Shinto deity .... KAMI
Shinto temple .... SHA
Shinto temple gate .... TORII
ship .... KEEL, SEND, LINER, TANKER, TENDER, VESSEL, CARAVEL
ship, back part .... STERN
ship boat ...... GIG, DORY
ship body or frame ..... HULL
ship bow, curve of ...... LOOF
ship canvas .... SAIL
ship clock .... NEF

d
ship drainage hole .. SCUPPER
ship employee ...... STEWARD
ship, 1st Northwest Passage GJOA
ship, forward part BOW, PROW
ship, fur-hunting ..... SEALER
ship, ironclad ...... MONITOR
ship: Jap. ...... MARO, MARU
ship keel, rear part ..... SKEG
ship, large .... TONNER
ship, lowest part ...... BILGE
ship, Medit. ... SETEE, SETTEE
ship, middle part ...... WAIST
ship mooring place DOCK, BERTH
ship, oar-propelled ... GALLEY
ship, part of RIB, DECK, HULL, KEEL
ship plank .... STRAKE
ship platform .... DECK
ship pole .... MAST, SPAR
ship shaped clock .... NEF
ship side, opp. middle ABEAM
ship timber, bevel ..... SNAPE
ship timber curve ...... SNY
ship timber, extra ..... RIDER
ship wheel .... HELM
ship, wrecked .... HULK
ship, 1-masted .... SLOOP
ship, 2-masted ... BRIG, SNOW
ship's kitchen .... GALLEY
shipboard covering .... CAPOT

144

a shipbuilding curve ..... SNY
shipbuilding piece
SPALE, THWART
shipworm .... BORER, TEREDO
shipwreck, causing
NAUFRAGEOUS
shirk .... GOLDBRICK
SHIRT .... see also GARMENT
shirt .... KAMIS, CAMISE
shirt, Oriental .... CAMISE
shoal .... REEF
shoal water deposit .... CULM
shock .... STUN,
APPAL, APPALL, TRAUMA
shock absorber ..... SNUBBER
shod, as monks ...... CALCED
shoe .... GAITER, SANDAL
shoe form .... LAST
shoe front .... VAMP
shoe gripper .... CLEAT
shoe, heavy.BROGAN, BROGUE
shoe latchet .... TAB
shoe, mule .... PLANCH
shoe part
LAST, RAND, WELT, INSOLE

b shoe strip ...... RAND, WELT
shoe, wooden ... GETA, SABOT
shoe, wooden-soled .... CLOG
shoes .... SHOON
shoes, Mercury's winged
TALARIA
shoelace .... LACET
shoemakers' saint ... CRISPIN
shoemaker's tool .... AWL
shoot .... BAG, POT
shoot at from ambush ... SNIPE
shoot at, marble to ...... MIG
shoot, cotton .... RATOON
shoot, plant ...... BINE, CION,
GEMMA, SPRIT,
STOLO, STOLON
shoot, small .... SPRIG
shoot, sugar cane ... RATOON
shooter, hidden ...... SNIPER
shooter marble .... TAW,
AGATE, AGGIE
shooting match .... TIR
shooting match: Fr. ...... TIR
shooting star .... LEONID
shop .... STORE
shop, Rom. wine .. TABERNA
shops, Rom. wine .. TABERNAE
shop's name plate ...... FACIA
shore .... COAST, STRAND
SHORE BIRD . see BIRD, SHORE
short .... CURT,
BRIEF, TERSE, STUBBY

c short-breathed .... PURSY
short comedy sketch .... SKIT
short-spoken ... CURT, TERSE
short tail .... SCUT
shorten .... CUT, DELE, ELIDE
shortly
ANON, SOON, PRESENTLY
Shoshonean .... UTE
shoulder blade ..... SCAPULA
shoulder, of the
ALAR, SCAPULAR
shoulder ornament
EPAULET, EPAULETTE
shoulder, road .... BERM
shoulder wrap .... SHAWL
shout.CRY, CALL, ROAR, YELL
shove .... PUSH
shovel .... SPADE
show as false .... BELIE
show off .... FLAUNT
show place, Rom. .... CIRCUS
show, street .... RAREE
"Showboat" author .... FERBER
showy .... LOUD
shrew ...... ERD, TARTAR
shrewd.SAGE, CANNY, ASTUTE
shrike genus .... LANIUS
shrill .... PIPY
shrill, to .... STRIDULATE
shrimplike crustacean ... PRAWN
shrine .... ALTAR
shrink .... CONTRACT
shroud-stopper: naut. .... WAPP
SHRUB .... see also TREE
shrub and tree .... ALDER
shrub, Asia .... CHE
shrub, berry-bearing ... ELDER
shrub, berry, Pacific ... SALAL
shrub, Chin. .... TEA
shrub, Congo medical .. BOCCA
shrub, desert
RETEM, OCOTILLO
shrub, Eng. .... HEATH
shrub, evergreen .. BOX, YEW,
TITI, ERICA, HEATH, SAL-
AL, OLEANDER
shrub, flowering ITEA, AZALEA,
PRIVET, SPIREA, SPIRAEA,
SYRINGA
shrub genus BIXA, INGA, ITEA,
ROSA, ALDER, IXORA,
AZALEA
shrub, Hawaiian ..... OLONA
shrub, low spiny .... GORSE
shrub, Medit. .... CAPER
shrub, poisonous
SUMAC, SUMACH
shrub, prickly .... CAPER

a shrub, Rhus genus .... SUMAC, SUMACH
shrub, strong-scented .. BATIS
shrub with grapelike fruit SALAL
shrub, yellow flowers OLEASTER
shun .... AVOID, DODGE
shut up .... IMMURE
shy .... JIB, BALK
SIAM .. see also SPECIAL SECTION
Siamese .... THAI
Siam. coin .... ATT
Siam. garment ...... PANUNG
Siam. group ...... KUI, LAO
Siam. monetary unit ...... BAHT
Siamese twin ... ENG, CHANG
SIBERIAN .. see also RUSSIAN
Siberian .... TATAR
Siberian wild cat .... MANUL
Siberian squirrel ..... MINIVER
sibilant sound .... HISS
Sicilian resort .... ENNA
sickle, curved like ... FALCATE
sickle: variant .... SIVE
side, jewel's .... FACET
side arm .... GUN, SWORD, PISTOL, REVOLVER
b side: Lat. .... LATUS
side of head ... LORA, LORUM
side, pert. to COSTAL, LATERAL
side-post, door's ...... JAMB
sidetrack .... SHUNT
side street, Chin. ... HUTUNG
side timber: naut. ...... BIBB
side, toward the .... LATERAD
sidereal .... ASTRAL
sidewalk .... PAVEMENT
sidewalk edge ... CURB, KERB
sidewinder ...... CROTALUS
sidle .... EDGE
Siegfried's murderer ... HAGEN
siesta .... NAP
sieve ... SIFT, PUREE, BOLTER
sieve for clay .... LAUN
Sif, son of ...... ULL, ULLR
sift .... SCREEN
sift: dialect .... REE
sift: old Eng. .... LUE
sift: Scot. .... SIE
sifter .... SIEVE
sigh .... SOUF, SOUGH
sight, come into ...... LOOM
sight, dimness of ..... CALIGO
sight on gun .... BEAD
sight, pert. to .... OCULAR
sign ... MARK, OMEN, TOKEN

c sign, music .... PRESA, SEGNO
sign: old Eng. .... SEIN
sign, pert. to .... SEMIC
sign up ...... ENROL, ENROLL
signal for attention ...... PST
signal for parley ... CHAMADE
signal to act .... CUE
signal to begin .... CUE
signature, affix SIGN, ENDORSE
signet .... SIGIL
signify ...... MEAN, DENOTE
"Silas Marner" author .. ELIOT
silence .... GAG, HUSH
silence: music .... TACET
silent ... MUM, MUTE, TACIT
silica .... SAND, SILEX
silica, rich in .... ACIOLIC
silicate .... MICA
silk-cotton tree CEIBA, KAPOK
silk-cotton tree fiber KAPOK, KUMBI
silk fabric ..... GROS, MOFF, PEKIN, SATIN, TULLE
silk filament .... BRIN
silk, fine ...... CRIN, TULLE
silk, heavy .... GROS
silk in cocoon .... BAVE
silk, India ... ROMAL, RUMAL
silk, old heavy ..... CAMACA
d silk, raw .... GREGE
silk substitute ...... NYLON, RAYON, ORLON, DACRON
silk thread .... FLOSS
silk, twilled .... ALMA
silk, unravel .... SLEAVE
silken .... SERIC
silkworm, Assam ... ERI, ERIA
silkworm, China ...... TASAR
silkworm disease .... UJI
silly .... INANE
silver: Her. .... ARGENT
silver lactate .... ACTOL
silver ore .... PACO
silver, uncoined, in ingots SYCEE
silverfish .. TARPON, TARPUN
silverize .... PLATE
silvery .... ARGENT
silvery-white metal .. COBALT
simian .... APE
similar .... LIKE, SUCH
Simon .... PETER
simper .... SMIRK
simple .... EASY, MERE
simple sugar .... OSE
simpleton ... ASS, DAW, OAF, BOOB, COOT, FOOL, GABY, GAWK, GOWK, SIMP, GOOSE
simulate APE, SHAM, FEIGN, PRETEND

146

a sin .... ERR, EVIL
sin, grief for ..... ATTRITION
Sinai .... HOREB
Sinbad's bird .... ROC
since .... AGO
since: Scot. ...... SIN, SYNE
Sinclair Lewis character .. CASS
sine — non .... QUA
sine qua — .... NON
sinew .... TENDON
sinewy .... WIRY
sing, as a round ...... TROLL
sing, as a round ...... TROLL
sing softly .... CROON
sing, Swiss style
    JODEL, YODEL, YODLE
singer, synagogue ... CANTOR
singing bird .... OSCINE
singing girl, Egyptian .. ALMA,
    ALME, ALMAH, ALMAI,
    ALMEH
singing, suitable for .... MELIC
single .... ONE, BILL, MONO,
    ONLY, UNAL
single out .... CHOOSE
single: prefix .... MONO
single thing ...... ONE, UNIT
singleton .... ACE
sink, as putt .... HOLE
sink: geol. .... DOLINA

b sinuous .. WAVY, SERPENTINE
sinus cavities .... ANTRA
Sioux, Siouan .... OTO, OTOE
sir: India .... MIAN
sir: Malay .... TUAN
siren, Rhine .... LORELEI
Sisera's killer .... JAEL
sister .... NUN, SIB
"Sistine Madonna" painter
    RAPHAEL
sitatunga, Afr. ...... NAKONG
sitting
    POSING, SEANCE, SESSION
sitting on .... ASTRIDE
situation, difficult .... STRAIT
siva snake .... COBRA
Siva, wife of DEVI, KALI, SATI
six, group of
    SENARY, SESTET, SEXTET
six-line verse SESTET, SESTINA
six on a die .. CISE, SICE, SISE
six, series of .... HEXAD
six: Sp. .... SEIS
sixpence: slang .... SICE
sixteen annas .... RUPEE
sixth: music .... SEXT
sixth sense: abbr. ...... ESP
size of shot ..... BB, FF, TT
sizing .... SEALER
skate .... RAY
skate genus .... RAIA

c skating area .... RINK
skegger .... PARR
skein of yarn .... RAP, HANK
skeletal .... BONY
skeleton, sea animal
    CORAL, SPONGE
skeptic .... AGNOSTIC
sketch ...... DRAW, OUTLINE
ski, heel spring .... AMSTUTZ
ski race .... SLALOM
ski run ..... SCHUSS, SLALOM
ski wax .... KLISTER
skier, mark of ..... SITZMARK
skiing position ...... VORLAGE
skiing, zigzag .... SLALOM
skilled person .... ADEPT
skillful ...
    ABLE, DEFT, ADEPT, HABILE
skillfully .... ABLY
skim over .... SKIP
skin .... FLAY, DERMA
skin, deeper layer ..... CUTIS
skin, design on
    TATOO, TATTOO
skin disease ... ACNE, MANGE,
    PSORA, TETTER
skin disease, horse's .. CALORIS
skin disease, Peru ...... UTA
skin infection .... LEPRA
skin layer .... DERM, CUTIS,

d DERMA, CORIUM, ENDERON
skin of a beast .... FELL
skin, pert. to .. DERIC, DERMIC
skinflint .... MISER
skink, Egypt. .... ADDA
skip .... OMIT
skip a stone .... DAP
skip happily .... CAPER
skipjack .... ELATER
skirmish .... MELEE
skirt, ballet .... TUTU
skirt section .... PANEL
skittle .... PIN
skulk .... LURK
skull, pert. to .. INIAL, INION
skull protuberance .... INION
skullcap, Arab. ..... CHECHIA
skunk .. CHINCHA, CHINCHE
sky .... FIRMAMENT
sky god, Assyrian ...... ANAT
sky: Chin. .... TIEN
sky god, Babyl. .... ABU, ANU
sky god, Norse .... TIU,
    TIW, TYR, ZIO, ZIU
sky, highest part .... ZENITH
sky: Polyn. .... LANGI
sky serpent, Vedic ...... AHI
slab, engraved ...... TABLET
slab, flooring, decorative DALLE
slag .... DROSS, SCORIA

a
slam .... BANG
slam in cards .... VOLE
slander ...... LIBEL, ASPERSE
slang .... ARGOT
slant .... BEVEL, SLOPE
slanted edge .... BEVEL
slanted: naut. .... ARAKE
slanting .... SKEW, ASKEW
slanting type .... ITALIC
slantingly, drive .... TOE
slap .... CUFF, SPANK
slash .... JAG, SLISH
slater's tool, same as slate-
    trimming tool
slate-trimming tool
    SAX, ZAT, ZAX
Slav .... SERB
Slav, ancient
    VEND, WEND, VENED
Slav, E. Ger. .... WEND
Slav in Saxony .... SORB
slave .... ESNE, SERF, THRALL
slave, fugitive ...... MAROON
slave, Spartan .... HELOT
sled, Swiss .... LUGE
sled to haul logs ...... TODE
sleep .... NAP, NOD, DOZE
sleep, deep .... SOPOR
sleep lightly .... DOZE

b
sleeping .... DORMANT
sleeping place BED, COT, BERTH
sleeping sickness fly .. TSETSE
sleeve, large .... DOLMAN
sleigh .... PUNG
sleight-of-hand .... MAGIC
slender .... LANK, LEAN,
    SLIM, THIN, REEDY
slender woman .... SYLPH
slice, bacon .... RASHER
slice of meat .... COLP
slice, thick .... SLAB
slick .... LOY
slide .... SKID, SLUE
sliding door, Jap. ... FUSUMA
sliding piece .... CAM
sliding valve .... PISTON
slight .... MERE, SLIM, FAINT
slight intentionally SLUR, SNUB
slimy .... OOZY
sling around .... SLUE
slip. ERR, BONER, GLIDE, LAPSE
slip by .... ELAPSE
slip out of course ...... SLUE
slip, plant .... CION, CUTTING
slipknot .... NOOSE
slipper .... MULE, MOYLE
slipper, P. I. .... CHINELA
slope .... RAMP, GRADIENT
slope: fort. .... GLACIS

c
slope of vein or lode ... HADE
slope: Scot .... BRAE
slope of land ...... VERSANT
slope, steep ... SCARP, ESCARP
sloping edge
    BASIL, BEZEL, BEZIL
sloth, three-toed .... AI
sloth, two-toed .... UNAU
slouch: Scot. .... LOUCH
slow .... POKY
slow loris .... KOKAM
slow: music .. TARDO, LARGO
    LENTO, ADAGIO, ANDANTE
slower: music .... RIT
sluggish .... DOPEY
sluice .... CLOW
slump .... RECESSION
slur over .... ELIDE
slushy mass .... POSH
sly look .... LEER, OGLE
sly: old Eng. .... SLEE, SLOAN
sly: Scot: .... SLEE
smack .... BUSS, KISS, SLAP
small .... PETIT, WEE, TINY,
    PETIT, PETTY, PETITE
small amount .. DRAM, MINIM
small arachnid .... MITE
small bottle .... VIAL
small bunch .... WISP
small case .... ETUI

d
small cluster .... SPRIG
small coin .... MITE
small creature MITE, MINIMUS
small dog .... POM, PUG,
    PUP, PEKE, FEIST
small goby, Atlantic ... MAPO
small: law .... PETIT
small marine animal ... SALP
small monkey .... LEMUR
small pearl .... PEARLET
small poem .... ODELET
small: Scot. .... SMA
small stream RUN, RILL, RILLET
small: suffix .... ING
small weight ... GRAM, MITE
smallest .... LEAST
smallest integer .... ONE
smallpox .... VARIOLA
smaragd .... EMERALD
smart .... STING
smart CHIC, ASTUTE, CLEVER
smartly dressed ... CHIC, TRIG
smear on .... DAUB
smell, disagreeable
    OLID, REEK, FETOR
smelting mixture ...... MATTE
smelting waste .. SLAG, DROSS
smirch .... SULLY
smith, aided Siegfried .. MIME

a
smock .... CAMISE
smoke .... FUME, REEK
smoke-colored .... FUMOUS
smoke, wisp of .... FLOC
smoked beef ...... PASTRAMI
smokeless powder .... FILITE
smoking .... AREEK
smoking pipe .. BRIAR, BRIER
smoking pipe, Oriental
       HOOKAH, NARGILE
smoky .... FUMID
smooth
   EVEN, IRON, LEVEL, PREEN
smooth-breathing ..... LENE
smooth, make .... LEVIGATE
smooth: phonetics ...... LENE
smooth-spoken .... GLIB
smoothing tool .... PLANE
snail, large.WHELK, ABALONE
snail, marine .... TRITON
snake .... ASP, BOA, ADDER,
   VIPER, PYTHON, REPTILE
snake, Amer. .. ADDER, RACER
snake-bite antidote
       GUACO, CEDRON
snake, black .... RACER
snake charmer's clarinet BEEN
snake-haired woman GORGON,
   MEDUSA, STHENO, EURYALE
b
snake, India .... COBRA,
   KRAIT, DABOIA, DABOYA
snake-like .... SINUOUS
snake, S. Amer. ...... ABOMA
snake, tree .... LORA
snake, venomous, Ind..BONGAR
snakebird .... DARTER
snakeroot, white ...... STEVIA
snap up bargains ...... SNUP
snapper ...... SESI, PARGO
snapper fish: Maori .. TAMURE
snapper: N. Z. ...... TAMURE
snare .. GIN, NET, WEB, TRAP
snarl .... GNAR, GNARR
snatch .... GRAB, SEIZE
sneer.GIBE, JIBE, FLEER, SCOFF
sniff .... NOSE
snipe, Europ. ...... BLEATER
snipe's cry .... SCAPE
snoring .... STERTOR
snow field, Alpine.FIRN, NEVE
snow goose genus ...... CHEN
snow, ground down ... LOLLY
snow house
   IGLU, IGLOE, IGLOO, IGLOU
snow leopard .... OUNCE
snow lily .... VIOLET
snow, living in ...... NIVAL
snow mouse .... VOLE

c
snow panther .... OUNCE
snow runner ...... SKI, SKEE
snow: Scot. .... SNA
SNOW WHITE
       see SEVEN DWARFS
snuff .... RAPPEE
snuffbox bean
   CACOON, MACKAYBEAN
snug .... COSY, COZY
snuggery .... NEST
so .... THUS, TRUE, VERY
so be it! .... AMEN
so much: music ...... TANTO
so: Scot. .... SAE
soak .... RET, SOG, SOP, WET
soak flax .... RET
soap, fine .... CASTILE
soap-frame bar .... SESS
soap: pharm. .... SAPO
soap plant .... AMOLE
soap substitute ...... AMOLE
soap vine .... GOGO
soapstone .... TALC
soapy mineral .... TALC
sober .... GRAVE, STAID
social affair .... TEA
social division ...... CASTE
social unit or group .. SEPT
society, entrance into .. DEBUT
d
society swell .... NOB
sock, Jap. .... TABI
sock, Rom. .... UDO
sod .... TURF
sodium alum .... MENDOZITE
sodium carbonate .... TRONA
sodium chloride ...... SALT
sodium chloride: pharm. .. SAL
sodium compound ..... SODA
sodium nitrate .. NITER, NITRE
sofa .... DIVAN
soft
   LOW, EASY, WAXY, TENDER
soft area on bill .... CERE
soft drink
   ADE, POP, COLA, SODA
soft feathers ... DOWN, EIDER
soft ice from floes .... LOLLY
soft job ..... SNAP, SINECURE
soft mass .... WAD
soft palate .... VELUM
soft palate lobe ...... UVULA
soft palate, pert. to
       VELAR, UVULAR
soft palates .... VELA
soft-spoken .... MEALY
soften in temper ..... RELENT
softly: music .... SOAVE
soil: comb. form ..... AGRO
soil, organic part .... HUMUS

149

Soil

a soil, rich .... **LOAM**
soil, sticky .. **GOMBO, GUMBO**
soil, type of ...... **PEDOCAL**
solar disc ...... **ATEN, ATON**
solar over lunar year,
    excess of .... **EPACT**
soldier: Am. Rev. .. **BUCKSKIN**
soldier, Austral., N. Z. **ANZAC**
soldier, Brit. .... **ATKINS**
soldier, former ...... **LANCER**
soldier, Gr. .... **HOPLITE**
soldier, Indo-Brit. ..... **SEPOY**
soldier, native India ... **SEPOY**
soldier's shelter ..... **FOXHOLE**
sole .... **PELMA**
sole of foot .... **VOLA**
sole of plow .... **SLADE**
solemn declaration .**VOW, OATH**
solicit .... **BEG, URGE,**
      COURT, CANVASS
solicitor's chamber ...... **INN**
solicitude .... **CARE**
solid ... **CONE, CUBE, PRISM**
solid, become **GEL, SET, HARDEN**
solid: comb. form .... **STEREO**
solidify .. **GEL, SET, HARDEN**
solitary .... **LONE, ONLY, SOLE**
solo .... **ARIA**
Solomon's aid giver ... **HIRAM**

b Solomon's temple rebuilder
              HIRAM
solution .... **KEY**
solution, strength of
         TITER, TITRE
solvent .... **ACETONE**
solvent, treat with .. **SOLUTIZE**
some .... **ANY**
somite .... **MEROSOME**
son: Fr. .... **FILS**
son-in-law .... **GENER**
son: Ir. .... **MAC**
son of .... **MAC**
son of Agrippina .... **NERO**
son of Joktan .... **OPHIR**
son of Reuben .... **PALLU**
son of: Scot. .... **MAC**
song ..... **LAY, ODE, DITE,**
    DITTY, MELOS, TROLL
song, Christmas
   NOEL, CAROL, WASSAIL
song for solo voices ..... **GLEE**
song: Ger. .... **LIED**
song, Hawaiian .... **MELE**
song, Jap. .... **UTA**
song, morning: poet. .. **MATIN**
song, of a .... **MELIC**
song of praise, joy
   PEAN, PAEAN, ANTHEM
"Song of the South" Uncle
             REMUS

c song, operatic .... **ARIA**
song, religious
   HYMN, CHANT, ANTHEM
song, sacred
   HYMN, CHANT, ANTHEM
song, sad .... **DIRGE**
song: Scot. .... **STROUD**
song, simple .... **DITTY**
song, Sp. .... **CANCION**
song thrush ... **MAVIE, MAVIS**
sonship .... **FILIETY**
soon .... **ANON**
sooner .... **ERE, ERER**
soot .... **COOM, SMUT**
soot: old Eng. .... **SOTE**
soothe .... **EASE, LULL**
soothing **ANODYNE, LENITIVE**
soothsayer .... **SEER**
Sophocles, play by .. **OEDIPUS**
soprano, prima donna .. **ALDA,**
    BORI, PONS, RISE,
   RAISA, CALLAS, STEBER
sora bird .... **RAIL**
sorceress .... **CIRCE**
sorceress, Hindu .... **USHA**
sorceress, myth. ...... **LAMIA**
sorceress, "Odyssey," Greek
             CIRCE

d sorcery, W. Ind.
   OBE, OBI, OBEAH
sore, make .... **RANKLE**
sore: Scot. .... **SAIR**
sorghum variety .... **MILO**
sorrow .. **DOLOR, REMORSE**
sorrow, feel
   RUE, LAMENT, REPENT
sorrowful . **SAD, BLUE, DOLENT**
sort .... **KIND,**
   CLASS, GROUP, SPECIES
sortie .... **SALLY**
sortilege .... **LOT**
sorting machine ..... **GRADER**
soul .... **ANIMA**
soul, Egyp. .... **BA, KA**
soul, Hindu .. **ATMA, ATMAN**
sound .. **TONE, NOISE, VALID**
sound, kind of ...... **PALATAL**
sound loudly .. **BLARE, LARUM**
sound, monotonous
      HUM, DRONE
sound perception .... **EAR**
sound, pert. to ...... **SONANT**
sound reasoning ...... **LOGIC**
sound, resemblance of
       ASSONANT
sound, solid .... **KLOP**
sound the ocean
    PLUMB, FATHOM

a sound waves, of ...... **AUDIO**
sound, without ..... **ASONANT**
sounding .... **SONANT**
soundless .... **ASONANT**
soup, heavy .. **PUREE, POTAGE**
soup spoon .... **LADLE**
soup, thick .... **BISK,
HOOSH, PUREE, BISQUE**
soup vessel .... **TUREEN**
soupfin shark .... **TOPE**
sour ...... **ACID, ACERB,
ACIDIC, ACETOSE**
sour curdled milk: Nor. .. **SKYR**
sour-leaved plant ...... **SORREL**
sour milk drink.**LEBAN, LEBEN**
source, mineral .... **ORE**
source, obsidian's ...... **LAVA**
soursop .... **ANNONA**
south: Sp. .... **SUR**
South African ...... **BOER**
SOUTH AFRICA ..... see also
SPECIAL SECTION
S. Afr. assembly .... **RAAD**
S. Afr. dialect .... **TAAL**
S. Afr. Dutch .. **BOER, TAAL**
S. Afr. garter snake .... **ELAPS**
S. Afr. grass country .... **VELD**
S. Afr. greenhorn ..... **IKONA**
S. Afr. gully .... **DONGA**
S. Afr. "out" .... **UIT**
b S. Afr. town .... **STAD**
S. Afr. village .... **KRAAL**
SOUTH AMERICA ... see also
SPECIAL SECTION
South American animal . **TAPIR**
S. Amer. bird .. **GUAN, JACU,
SYLPH, TURCO, SERIEMA**
S. Amer. game bird **TINAMOU**
S. Amer. Indian group .... **GES**
S. Amer. lizard .... **TEJU**
S.Amer.tree **VERA,CEBIL,FOTUI**
S. Amer. ungulate .... **TAPIR**
"South Pacific" hero .. **EMILE**
Southern Cross constellation
CRUX
Southern France .... **MIDI**
Southern river .... **PEEDEE**
Southern state: abbr. .... **ALA**
Southwest river .... **RED**
sovereign (coin) .... **SKIV**
sovereignty .... **EMPERY**
SOVIET .... see also RUSSIAN
Soviet news agency .... **TASS**
Soviet newspaper .... **PRAVDA**
sow .... **PIG, GILT**
sow .... **SEED, PLANT**
sow: Prov. Eng. .... **YELT**
sow: Scot. .... **SOO**
sower .... **SEEDER**
sown: her. .... **SEME**
soybean .... **SOJA, SOYA**

c spa, Bohemian .... **BILIN**
spa, Eng. .... **BATH**
spa, Ger. .... **EMS, BADEN**
space between bird's eye
and bill ..... **LORA, LORE,
LORUM**
space between triglyphs
METOPE
space, small **AREOLA, AREOLE**
spaces on bird's face
LORAE, LORES
spade .... **LOY, SHOVEL**
spade, narrow .... **LOY, SPUD**
spade-shaped .... **PALACEOUS**
spade, turf .... **SLANE**
Spain, ancient ...... **IBERIA**
SPANISH see also SPAIN, SPE-
CIAL SECTION
SP. ARTIST
see SP. PAINTER
Sp. belle .... **MAJA**
Sp. cellist .... **CASALS**
Sp. coin, old .... **PISTOLE**
Sp. dance ..... **JOTA, BOLERO**
Sp. epic .... **CID**
Sp. explorer
CORTEZ, BALBOA, CORTES
d Sp. fabric .... **CREA**
Sp. fortress commander .. **CAID**
Sp. game of ball .... **PELOTA**
Sp. general, duke.**ALBA, ALVA**
Sp. hero .... **CID**
Sp. kettle .... **OLLA**
Sp. lady ..... **DONA, SENORA**
Sp. length unit .... **VARA**
Sp. man .... **DON, SENOR**
Sp. nun .... **AVILA**
Sp. painter
GOYA, MIRO, SERT, PICASSO
Sp. poet .... **ENCINA**
Sp. pot .... **OLLA**
Sp. title.**DON, SENOR, SENORA**

SPANISH WORDS:
(tilde omitted throughout)
abbey .... **ABADIA**
afternoon .... **TARDE**
annatto seeds ... **ACHIOTE**
another .... **OTRO**
article .... **EL, LA, LAS,
LOS, UNO**
ass .... **ASNO**
aunt .... **TIA**
bay .... **BAHIA**
bean .... **HABA**
before .... **ANTES**
being .... **ENTE**
black .... **NEGRA**
blue .... **AZUL**
box canyon .... **CAJON**

151

Spanish

a
boy .... NINO
bravo! .... OLE
bull .... TORO
but .... PERO
canal .... CANO
chaperon . DUENA, DUENNA
chest .... CAJETA
chief ...... JEFE, ADALID
child .... NINO
church .... IGLESIA
city .... CIUDAD
clay building . ADOBE, TAPIA
cloak .... CAPA
clothes .... ROPA
corral .... ATAJO
cut .... TAJO
day .... DIA
dining hall .... SALA
dove .... PALOMA
drawing room .... SALA
estuary .... RIA
evening .... TARDE
evil .... MALO
first .... PRIMUS
for .... POR
friend .... AMIGO
funds .... CAJA
girl .... NINA
God .... DIOS
gold .... ORO

b
good-bye .... ADIOS
grass fiber rope ..... SOGA
grille .... REJA
gulch .... ARROYO
gypsy .... GITANO
hall .... SALA
hamlet .... ALDA
harbor entrance ..... BOCA
health .... SANO
hello .... HOLLA
hill . ALTO, CERRO, MORRO
hillside .... FALDA
hotel .... POSADA
house .... CASA
Indian .... INDIO
inlet .... RIA, ESTERO
jail keeper .... CAID
judge .... JUEZ
king .... REY
lady .... DAMA
lake .... LAGO
landmark .... SENAL
latter .... ESTE
lawsuit .... ACTO
letter .... CARTA
lime .... LIMA
love .... AMOR
man .... HOMBRE
manservent .... MOZO
mayor .. ALCADE, ALCALDE

c
mouth .... BOCA
movie house .... CINE
meadow .... VEGA
my .... MIO
of .... DE
open space .... COSO
other .... OTRA
parish priest ...... CURA
peak .... PICO
people .... GENTE
pine .... PINO
pole .... PALO
pole, wooden ...... PALO
porridge .... ATOLE
post office ...... CORREO
pot .... OLLA
priest ...... CURA, PADRE
queen .... REINA
ragged person ..... ROTO
raisin .... PASA
red .... ROJO
river .... RIO
road .... CAMINO
room .... SALA
rum .... RON
saint, feminine .... SANTA
she .... ELLA
silver .... PLATA
six .... SEIS
snake .... CULEBRA

d
song .... CANCION
south .... SUR
street ...... CALLE, CALLI
sweet potato ..... CAMOTE
tall .... ALTA
this .... ESTA, ESTE
three .... TRES
to be .... SER, ESTE
tomorrow .... MANANA
trench .... TAJO
uncle .... TIO
very .... MUY
water .... AGUA
wax .... CERA
wit .... SAL
with .... DE
work .... OBRA
yes .... SI
you .... TE

spar ...... BOX, BOOM, GAFF,
           MAST, YARD, SPRIT
spar for colors .... GAFF
spar, heavy .... BARITE
spar, loading .... STEEVE
spar, small .... SPRIT
spare .... LEAN, EXTRA,
          GAUNT, LENTEN
sparkle .... GLITTER
sparkling, as wine . MOUSSEUX
sparrow, hedge .... DONEY

152

a
Sparta queen .... LEDA
Spartan army division .. MORA
Spartan magistrate ... EPHOR
spasm ...... FIT, TIC, JERK
spawning place .... REDD
speak
UTTER, ORATE, DECLAIM
speak: comb. form ..... LALO
speak, inability to .... ALALIA
speak theatrically ..... EMOTE
speaker .. ORATOR, LOCUTOR
speaking tube, pilot's.GOSPORT
spear .... DART, LANCE
spear, Afr. ASSAGAI, ASSEGAI
spear, fish .... GIG, GAFF
spear-like weapon PIKE, LANCE
spear-shaped .... HASTATE
spear, 3-prong ..... TRIDENT
spear thrower, Austral.
WOMERA
special: Moslem law
KHAS, KHASS
species .... KIND, SORT
specific date .... DAY
specified time .... DATE
specimen .... SAMPLE
speck .... DOT, MOTE, FLECK
speckle .... DOT, STIPPLE
spectacle .... PAGEANT
specter .... BOGY, BOGEY,
GHOST, SHADE

b
speech ... LECTURE, ORATION
speech, art of ..... RHETORIC
speech defect
LISP, ALOGIA, STAMMER
speech goddess, Hindu
VAC, DEVI, VACH
speech, local .... PATOIS
speech, long .... SPIEL
speech, loss of ...... APHASIA
speech peculiarity .... IDIOM
speech, violent ...... TIRADE
speechless ...... DUMB, MUTE
speed ..... HIE, RUN, PACE,
RACE, HASTE, HASTEN,
RAPIDITY
speed, at full .... AMAIN
spelt .... ADOR, EMMER
Spenser heroine .... UNA
Spenser's name for Ireland
IRENA
sphere .... ORB
sphere of action ..... ARENA
spice .... MACE
spice ball .... FAGOT, FAGGOT
spicknel .... MEU, MEW
spicy .... RACY
spider crab genus MAIA, MAJA
spider fluid: Pharm. ARANEIN

c
spider monkey
QUATA, ATELES, COAITA
spider nest .... NIDUS
spigot .... TAP
spike .... EAR, GAD, BROB
spikenard .... NARD
spin
BIRL, REEL, TWIRL, ROTATE
spinal column ... AXIS, AXON
spinal cord .... MYELON
spinal membrane ...... DURA
spindle .... COP, AXLE
spindle, yarn .... HASP
spine .... AXIS, AXON
spine bones .... SACRA
spine, slender .... SETA
spineless cactus ...... CHAUTE
spiniform .... SPINATE
spinning jenny .... MULE
spiny shrub genus ..... ULEX
spiral formation ..... VOLUTE
spire ornament .... EPI
spirit .... ELAN, SOUL, METAL
spirit: Egyp. myth ..... BA, KA
spirit: Ger. .... GEIST
spirit, Ir. . BANSHEE, BANSHIE
spirit lamp .... ETNA
spirit, Moslem ..... JIN, JINN,
GENIE, GENII, JINNI, JINNEE
spirit of air .... ARIEL
spirit of evil .. DEMON, DEVIL

d
spirit of man: Egypt ... AKH
spirit raiser .. ELATER, ELATOR
spirits and water ...... GROG
spirits of the dead .... MANES
spirited .... EAGER, CONMOTO
spirited horse .... STEED
spiritual body: Egypt. .. SAHU
spiritual struggle ..... PENIEL
spiritualist meeting ... SEANCE
splash .... LAP
spleen .... MILT
splendid .... GRAND
splendor .... ECLAT
splendor, goddess of: Hindu
UMA
split .... RIT, RENT, RIVE,
CLEFT, RIVEN, CLEAVE
split pulse .... DAL
spoil .... ROT, BOTCH
spoil, as eggs .... ADDLE
spoils of war .... LOOT
spoken .... ORAL
spoken word .... AGRAPH
spokes, having .... RADIAL
sponge, calcareous .... LEUCON
sponge gourd ... LOOF, LOOFA
sponge on ..... MUMP, LEACH
sponge spicule, bow-shaped
OXEA, TOXA, PINULUS
sponge, young .... ASCON

a

spongewood .... SOLA
sponsor .... PATRON
sponsorship ...... EGIS, AEGIS
spool .... REEL
spore .... SEED
spore cluster .... SORUS
spore fruit of rust fungi
    AECIA, TELIA, AECIUM,
    TELIUM
spore sac, fungus ASCI, ASCUS
sport .... RUX, GAME,
    GOLF, PLAY, POLO
sports arena STADIA, STADIUM
sports center ... RINK, ARENA
sports hall .... GYM
spot in mineral ..... MACLE
spot on card .... PIP
spotted ...... PIED, PINTO,
    DAPPLED, MACULOSE
spotted cavy .... PACA
spotted deer KAKAR, CHITAL
spotted moth ...... FORESTER
spotted sting-ray ..... OBISPO
spotted, to make
    DAPPLE, STIPPLE
spouse .... MATE, WIFE
spray .... ATOMIZE
spray, sea .... LIPPER

b

spread .... TED
spread by peening .... RIVET
spread by report
    BRUIT, NORATE
spread out .... FAN
spread rumor .... GOSSIP
spread the word .... TELL
spread to dry, as hay ... TED
sprightly .... PERT, PEART
spring .... SPA
spring back .... RESILE
spring: Bible .... AIN
spring-like .... VERNAL
spring: old Eng. .... KELD
spring, mineral .... SPA
spring rice, India ...... BORO
spring, small .... SEEP
springs, warm ...... THERMAE
springboard .... BATULE
sprinkle DEG, WATER, SPARGE
sprinkling: her. .... SEME
sprint .... RUN, RACE
sprite .. ELF, FAY, PIXY, PIXIE
sprite, tricksy .... ARIEL
sprout ... CION, GROW, SCION
spruce ... TRIG, TRIM, NATTY
spruce, Jap. .... YEDDO
spruce, white ...... EPINETTE
spume .... FOAM
spun wool .... YARN
spur .... GAD, GOAD, CALCAR
spur of mountain ..... ARETE

c

spur part .... ROWEL
spur wheel .... ROWEL
spurs, having .... CALCARATE
spurt .... JET, GUSH
spy, garment-trade slang KEEK
spy, British, Revolution ANDRE
squama .... ALULA
squander .... SPEND
square dance .... REEL
square-meshed net ..... LACIS
squash .... PEPO,
    CRUSH, GOURD, FLATTEN
squash bug .... ANASA
squaw .... MAHALA
squawfish .... CHUB
squid genus .... LOLIGO
squirrel fur, Siberian
    CALABAR, CALABER
squirrel, ground Europ. .. SISEL
squirrel-like animal DORMOUSE
squirrel skin .... VAIR
squirrel's nest ... DRAY, DREY
ST. .... see SAINT
stab .... GORE
stabilize .... STEADY
stable .... FIRM, SOLID
stable compartment ..... STALL
stable-keeper, royal .. AVENER
stables, royal .... MEWS
stableman .... OSTLER

d

stack of hay .... RICK
staff .... ROD, MACE
staff-bearer .... MACER
staff, bishop's ...... CROSIER
staff of office .... MACE
staff, royal SCEPTER, SCEPTRE
stag ... DEER, HART, MALE
stage direction
    MANET, SENET, EXEUNT
stage equipment ...... PROPS
stage extra ... SUPE, SUPER
stage horn signal ... SENNET
stage setting .... SCENE
stage whisper .... ASIDE
stagger .... REEL
stagger: Prov. Eng. ..... STOT
stagnation .... STASIS
stagnation, blood .... STASIS
stain, DYE, SOIL, SPOT, TASH
stair part ...... RISER, TREAD
stair post .... NEWEL
staircase spindle ...... SPEEL
stake .... ANTE, WAGER
stake, like a .... PALAR
stake, pointed ..... PALISADE
stake, poker .... ANTE
stakes .... POT
stakes, —, Epsom Downs Race
    OAKS
stale .... TRITE
stalk .... STEM

154

a
stalk, flower . **SCAPE, PEDICEL**
stalk, frond .... **STIPE**
stalk, plant .... **CAULIS**
stalk, short .... **STIPE**
stalk, sugarcane....... **RATOON**
stall in mud.............. **STOG**
stammer .... **HAW, HEM**
stammering sound .... **ER**
stamp............ **MARK, SIGIL**
stamp battery block .... **VOL**
stamp of approval.......... **OK**
stamp-sheet part .... **PANE**
stamping device .... **DIE**
stamping machine...... **DATER**
stanch .... **STEM**
stand .... **RISE**
stand . **BEAR, ABIDE, ENDURE**
stand, cuplike............ **ZARF**
stand in awe of .... **FEAR**
stand, small .... **TABORET,
TABOURET**
stand, 3-legged .... **TRIPOD,
TRIVET**
standard . **PAR, FLAG, ENSIGN**
standard **NORM, TYPE, NORMA**
standard of chemical strength
TITER
standard, Turk .... **ALEM**
standing.............. **STATUS**
stannum.................. **TIN**
stanza, last .... **ENVOY**

b
stanza, Nor .... **STEV**
stanza, part of .... **STAVE**
star.................... **ASTRO**
star, blue............... **VEGA**
star, brightest............ **COR**
star cluster, distant... **NEBULA,
NEBULAE**
star, day .... **SUN**
star, evening . **VENUS, HESPER,
VESPER, HESPERUS**
star facet................ **PANE**
star, fixed .... **SUN, ALYA**
star: Fr. .... **ETOILE**
star in Aquarius .... **SKAT**
star in Aquilla.......... **ALTAIR**
star in Argo............. **NAOS**
star in Big Dipper .... **PHAD**
star in Bootes............ **IZAR**
star in Cetus............ **MIRA**
star in Cygenus . **SADR, DENEB**
star in Draco....... **ADIB, JUZA**
star in Eridanus .... **AZHA, BEID**
star in Leo... **DUHR, REGULUS**
star in Lyra ...... **VEGA, WEGA**
star in Orion .... **RIGEL**
star in Pegasus . . **ENIF, MATAR**
star in Pleiades .... **MAIA**
star in Perseus.......... **ATIK**
star in Scorpio .... **ANTARES**

c
star in Serpens .... **ALYA**
star in Taurus... **NATH, PLEIAD**
star in Virgo............. **SPICA**
star near Mizar......... **ALCOR**
star, new .... **NOVA**
star-shaped.......... **STELLATE**
star-shaped spicule..... **ACTER,
ACTINE**
star, temporary .... **NOVA**
stars, dotted with .... **SEME**
stars, pert. to......... **ASTRAL**
starch........... **AMYL, ARUM,
SAGO, FARINA, CASSAVA**
starchy rootstock .... **TARO**
starfish.............. **ASTEROID**
starnose................. **MOLE**
— Starr, comic strip character
BRENDA
starred lizard **AGAMA, HARDIM**
start ... **BEGIN, SALLY, ROUSE**
starvation .... **INEDIA**
starwort................. **ASTER**
state.................... **AVER**
STATE.... see also GAZETTEER
STATE FLOWERS. see SPECIAL
SECTION
state, New England: abbr..... **RI**
state of affairs............ **PASS**
state, pert. to............. **CIVIL**

d
state of: suffix .... **ERY**
state of being: suffix ...... **URE**
state precisely .... **SPECIFY**
stately home... **DOME, ESTATE**
statements, confused
RIGMAROLE
statesman, Brit........... **PITT**
station . **POST, DEPOT, PLACE**
stationary ..... **FIXED, STATIC**
stationary motor part.. **STATOR**
statistician............. **STATIST**
statute .... **ACT, LAW**
stave, barrel.............. **LAG**
stay............. **WAIT, TARRY**
stay rope................. **GUY**
stays................. **CORSET**
stead .... **LIEU, PLACE**
steal .... **COP, ROB, GLOM,
SNITCH**
steal cattle .... **RUSTLE**
steal: Eng................ **GLOM**
steal, Eng. dialect .... **NIM**
steel beam .... **GIRDER**
steel: Ger.............. **STAHL**
steel splint, armor skirt .. **TACE,
TASSE, TASSET**
steep .... **RET, SOP**
steep .... **SHEER**
steep in lime............. **BOWK**
steer wildly.............. **YAW**
steer, young: Prov. Eng.... **STOT**

155

Steering

a steering, direct ship's .... **COND, CONN**
steersman .... **COX**
stellar ...... **ASTRAL, STARRY**
stem **CION, CORM, SCAPE, STALK**
stem, fungus .... **STIPE**
stem, hollow .... **CANE**
stem, jointed .... **CULM**
stem of hop .... **BINE**
stem, rudimentary .. **CAULICLE**
stem, ship's .... **PROW**
stench .... **ODOR, FETOR**
stentorian .... **LOUD**
step .... **GRADE, PHASE**
step ... **PACE, STAIR, TREAD**
step, dance ..... **PAS, CHASSE**
step up to mark .... **TOE**
step, upright part of .. **RISER**
steps, outdoor .... **PERRON**
steps over fence .... **STILE**
steppes, storm on ..... **BURAN**
stern **GRIM, HARSH, AUSTERE**
steward: Scot. ..... **MORMAOR**
stick .. **BAR, BAT, ROD, CANE,
WAND, BATON, MUNDLE**
stick .... **GLUE,
PASTE, ADHERE, CLEAVE**
stick, conductor's ..... **BATON**
stick together ...... **COHERE**
stick used in hurling .. **CAMAN**
b sticks, bundle of ...... **FAGOT**
stickler for formality .. **TAPIST**
sticky substance ... **GOO, GUM**
stiffly nice .... **PRIM**
stigma .... **BRAND**
stigmatic point of mango **NAK**
still .... **BUT, YET**
stimulant, coffee **CAFFEIN, CAFFEINE**
stimulant, tea **THEIN, THEINE**
stimulate .. **FAN, WHET, ELATE**
sting .... **BITE, SMART**
stinging ant .... **KELEP**
stinging herb .... **NETTLE**
stingy .... **MEAN**
stint .... **TASK**
stipend, church ..... **PREBEND**
stipend: Scot. .... **ANNAT**
stipulation .... **CLAUSE**
stir .. **ADO, MIX, TODO, ROUSE**
stir up .... **RILE, ROIL**
stitch .... **PUNTO**
stitchbird .... **IHI**
stitched fold .... **TUCK**
stithy .... **ANVIL**
stock .... **BREED**
stock .... **STORE**
stock exchange, membership in **SEAT**
stock exchange, Paris **BOURSE**

c stock market crash .... **PANIC**
stockade: Russ. .... **ETAPE**
stocking run .... **LADDER**
stockings .... **HOSE**
stocky .... **STUB**
stolen goods .... **SWAG**
stomach .... **MAW, CRAW**
stomach division, ruminant's **OMASUM**
stomach, first ..... **RUMEN**
stomach, ruminant's .... **TRIPE**
stone .. **AGATE, LAPIS, SLATE**
Stone Age tool .... **CELT,
EOLITH, NEOLITH**
stone, aquamarine .... **BERYL**
stone, breastplate .... **JASPER**
stone chest .... **CIST**
stone chip .... **SPALL**
stone: comb. form .... **LITH**
stone-cutter's chisel .... **DROVE**
stone fruit .... **DRUPE**
stone, green . **BERYL, OLIVINE**
stone hammer .... **MASH**
stone, hard .... **ADAMANT**
stone heap ... **CARN, KARN,
CAIRN, CARNE, CAIRNE**
stone, hollow .... **GEODE**
stone implement ...... **CELT,
EOLITH, NEOLITH**
stone, like a .... **LITHOID**
stone, monument ..... **MENHIR**
d stone paving block ..... **SETT**
stone pillar .... **STELE**
stone, red ..... **SARD, SPINEL**
stone roller fish ...... **TOTER**
stone, rough .... **RUBBLE**
stone: Scot. .... **STEAN, STEEN**
stone set .... **PAVER**
stone, squared ...... **ASHLAR**
stone to death .... **LAPIDATE**
stone, woman turned to **NIOBE**
stone worker .... **MASON**
stone, yellow **TOPAZ, CITRINE**
stonecrop **ORPIN, SEDUM, ORPINE**
stonecutter **MASON, LAPICIDE**
stonecutter's chisel ... **DROVE**
stoneware: Fr. .... **GRES**
stool pigeon .... **NARK**
stop .... **DAM, BALK, HALT,
STEM, WHOA, DESIST**
stop, as engine .. **CONK, STALL**
stop by accident ...... **STALL**
stop: naut. ... **AVAST, BELAY**
stop short .... **BALK**
stoppage .... **JAM**
stopper .... **BUNG, PLUG**
storage battery plate ... **GRID**
storage place **BIN, BARN, SILO**
store, army .... **CANTEEN**
store fodder .... **ENSILE**

156

a storehouse .... ETAPE
storehouse, army ..... DEPOT
storehouse, India .... GOLA
storehouse, public ..... ETAPE
stork .... MARABOU
storm FUME, FURY, RAGE, RAVE
storm, away from ..... ALEE
storm, dust .... SIMOON
storm: Fr. .... ORAGE
storm god, Babyl. ZU, ADAD,
　　　　　　ADDA, ADDU
story, Norse .... SAGA
story, short .... CONTE
stoss, opposite of .... LEE
stout .... BURLY
stout, kind of .... PORTER
stove .... ETNA, RANGE
"Stowe" character
　　　　EVA, TOM, TOPSY
straight .... DIRECT
straight-edge .... RULER
strain .... EXERT
strained .... TENSE
strainer .... SIEVE
strainer, wool cloth ... TAMIS
Straits Settlement region
　　　　　　　PENANG
strange .... ODD
strap on falcon's leg .... JESS
strap-shaped .... LORATE
b strass .... PASTE
stratagem .... RUSE, WILE
stratagem, sudden ..... COUP
stratum .... LAYER
straw hat ...... BAKU, MILAN
stray .... ERR
stray .... WAIF
stray animal .... CAVY
streak ...... ROE, LINE, VEIN,
　　STRIA, STRAKE, STRIAE
streaky .... LINY, ROWY
stream
　FLOW, RILL, BOURN, RIVER
streamlet ...... RILL, RUNNEL
street Arab .... GAMIN
street: It., Sp. .. CALLE, CALLI
street, narrow .... LANE
street roisterer .... MUN
street urchin .... ARAB
street, Venice water .. RIO, RII
strength .... POWER
strengthening .... ROBORANT
stress .... ICTUS
stressed beat, syllable .. ARSIS
stretch: Scot. .... STENT
stretched out ...... PROLATE
stretcher .... LITTER
stretching frame .... TENTER,
　　　　　　　STENTER
strewn with flowers: Her. SEME

c strife .... WAR
strife, civil .... STASIS
strike .. BAT, HIT, RAP, CONK,
　SLOG, SLUG, SOCK, SWAT,
　WHAM, SMITE
strikebreaker ..... FINK, SCAB
striking effect .... ECLAT
string of mules .... ATAJO
stringy .... ROPY
strip .. BARE, DIVEST, STRAKE
strip of land ... DOAB, DUAB
strip of wood .... LATH
strip off skin .... FLAY
strip, oxhide, S. Afr. ... RIEM
strip, wood, metal ... SPLINE
stripe .... BAR, BAND, WALE,
　　　　　WEAL, STREAK
stripe of color: zool. .. PLAGA
stripling .... BOY, LAD
strive .... AIM, VIE
strobile .... CONE
stroke .... FIT, ICTUS
stroke, brilliant .... COUP
stroll .... AMBLE
strong-arm man ...... GOON
strong, as cigars ... MADURO
strong desire .... HUNGER
strong man .... SAMSON
strong man, Gr. ...... ATLAS
strong point .... FORTE
d strong-scented ... OLID, RANK
strongbox .... SAFE
stronghold .. FORT, SION, ZION
struck with horror ... AGHAST
structure, tall .... TOWER
struggle .... COPE
struggle helplessly. FLOUNDER
struggled .... HOVE
stud .... BOSS
student in charge ... MONITOR
studio, art .... ATELIER
study ...... CON, PORE, READ
study group .... SEMINAR
stuff .... PAD, RAM, CRAM
stuffing .... KAPOK
stum .... MUST
stumble: prov. Eng. ..... STOT
stump of branch .... SKEG
stunted trees .... SCRUB
stupefied .... MAZED
stupefy .... DAZE, MAZE,
　　　　　　STUN, BESOT
stupid .... CRASS, DENSE
stupid person ...... ASS, OAF
　CLOD, COOT, DOLT, LOON,
　LOUT, LOWN, MOKE
stupor ...... COMA, SOPOR
sturgeon, small .... STERLET
style .... MODE, NAME
style of art .... DADA, GENRE

157

Stylet

a
stylet, surgical ...... TROCAR
stymie .... IMPEDE
Styx ferryman ...... CHARON
subbase .... PLINTH
subdued shade ...... PASTEL
subject ..... TOPIC, VASSAL
subject in grammar .... NOUN
subjoin .... ADD
sublime .... NOBLE
submarine PIGBOAT, SNORKEL
submit .... BOW, YIELD
subordinate
     MINOR, DEPENDENT
subside
  EBB, SINK, ABATE, RELAPSE
substance, lustrous ...... METAL
substances, class of .... LIPIN
substantiate .... VERIFY
substantive word ...... NOUN
substitute
    VICE, PROXY, ERSATZ
substitute for: suffix .... ETTE
subtle emanation ...... AURA
subtle variation ...... NUANCE
subtract .... DEDUCT
subway, Eng. .... TUBE
subway entrance ...... KIOSK
subway, Fr. .... METRO
success .... HIT, WOW

b
succession .... LINE
successively .... AROW
succinct .... TERSE
succor .... AID
succulent plant .. ALOE, HERB
such .... SO
sucking fish ... PEGA, REMORA
Sudan lake .... CHAD
Sudan native .... FUL
Sudan Negroid .... SERE
Sudan people .... HAUSA
sudden attack: Med. .. ICTUS
suet .... TALLOW
suffer .... LET, BIDE
suffer from hunger
    CLEM, STARVE
suffer: Scot. .... DREE
sufficient: poet. .... ENOW

SUFFIXES:
act of .... TION
action .... ANCE
adjective ... ENT, IAL, INE,
    ISH, IST, ITE, OUS
agent .... URE
alcohol .... OL
carbohydrate .... OSE
chemical or chemistry . ANE,
  ENE, IDE, INE, OLE, ONE,
  ENOL, ITOL, OLIC

c
common ending ENT, INE,
    ING, ION
common suffix ..... ES, ESE,
    ESS, INE, IVE, ETTE,
    YNONE
condition .... ATE, ILE, ISE,
    ANCE, SION, STER
comparative ...... IER, IOR
compound .... ICAL, ILITY
diminutive .... ET, IE, ULA,
    ULE, ETTE
feminine ... INA, INE, ELLA
feminine noun .... ESS
follower .... IST, ITE
forming nouns from verbs. ER
full of .... OSE
inflammation .... ITIS
inhabitant of .... ITE
into .... EN
like .... OID
little .... ET
made of .... EN
make .... ISE
medical .... IA, OMA
mineral .... ITE, LITE
native of .... ITE
noun .... IA, OR, ATE, ENT,
  ERY, ESS, IER, ISE, IST,
  ITE, ANCY, ENCE, ENSE,
  STER

d
noun ending .... STER
noun forming diminutive.CLE
number .... TEEN
or ordinal number .... ETH
oil .... OL, OLE
one who does ... IST, STER
one who does .... IST
order of animals ...... INI
ordinal .... ETH
origin, denoting ...... OTE
participle .... ING
person .... ER
plural .... (old EN), ES
quality ...... ANCE, ILITY
rocks, of .... ITE, LITE
science of .... ICS
skin .... DERM
small .... ING
state of ...... ERY, ANCE
state of being .... URE
substitute for .... ETTE
superlative .... EST
sympathizer .... ITE
town .... TON
tumor .... OMA
verb .... ISE, ESCE
with mineral names ... LITE
zoological .... ATA
Sufi disciple .... MURID
sugar .... OSE, SUCROSE
sugar cane disease ..... ILIAU

158

a sugar cane residue .. **BAGASSE**
sugar, crude .... **GUR**
sugar, fruit .... **KETOSE**
sugar, raw ...... **CASSONADE**
sugar, simple .... **OSE**
sugar source .... **CANE**
suggestion .... **CUE, HINT**
suit of mail .... **ARMOR**
suitable **.APT, FIT, PAT, PROPER**
suitcase ... **BAG, GRIP, VALISE**
suitor .... **SWAIN**
sullen .. **DOUR, GLUM, MOROSE**
sullen, act .... **MOPE**
sullen, be ...... **POUT, SULK**
sully .... **SOIL, DIRTY**
sultan, Turkish .... **SELIM**
sultan's order .... **IRADE**
sultan's residence ...... **SERAI**
sultanate .... **OMAN**
sultry .... **HUMID**
Sulu Moslem .... **MORO**
"sum," infinitive following **ESSE**
sum paid as punishment .. **FINE**
sumac genus .... **RHUS**
sumac, P. I. ... **ANAM, ANAN**
Sumatra squirrel shrew .. **TANA**
Sumatra wildcat ...... **BALU**
Sumatran silk .... **IKAT**
b "summa — laude" ...... **CUM**
summary
   DIGEST, PRECIS, EPITOME
summer: Fr. .... **ETE**
summer-house
         ARBOR, PERGOLA
summer, pert. to ..... **ESTIVAL**
summit
   APEX, KNAP, PEAK, SPIRE
summits .... **APICES**
summon .... **CALL, CITE,**
         PAGE, CLEPE, EVOKE
sun .... **SOL, HELIOS**
sun apartments ..... **SOLARIA**
sun bittern .... **CAURALE**
sun: comb. form ...... **HELIO**
sun disk ...... **ATEN, ATON**
sun-dried brick
   DOBE, DOBY, ADOBE, DOBIE
sun god, Babyl. ... **UTU, UTUG,**
         BABBAR, SHAMASH
sun god, Egypt. ..... **RA, TEM,**
         TUM, AMON, AMEN,
         AMUN, ATMU, ATUM
sun god, Gr., Rom. ..... **SOL,**
         APOLLO, HELIOS
sun god, Inca .... **INTI**
sun, halo around .... **CORONA**
sun, pert. to .... **SOLAR**
sun porches .... **SOLARIA**
sun tree, Jap. .... **HINOKI**

c sunbaked building
   DOBE, DOBY, ADOBE, DOBIE
Sunday of Lent, 4th .. **LAETARE**
sunder
   PART, REND, SPLIT, DIVIDE
sundial, style of ..... **GNOMON**
sunfish .... **BREAM**
sunfish genus .... **MOLA**
sunken fence .... **AHA, HAHA**
sunset, occurring at **ACRONICAL**
sunspot center
         UMBRA, UMBRAE
supercilious person ..... **SNOB**
superfluous: Fr. .... **DE TROP**
superintendent, office
               MANAGER
superior, most ... **BEST, TOPS**
superior quality: Fr. .... **LUXE**
superiority, belief in .. **RACISM**
superlative, absolute .. **ELATIVE**
superlative ending ...... **EST**
supernatural .... **OCCULT**
supernatural being, Melanesia
               ADARO
supernatural power, E. Afr. **NGAI**
supernatural power, Polyn.
               MANA
superscribe .... **DIRECT**
superstition, object of
         FETICH, FETISH
d supper .... **TEA**
supplication, make ..... **PRAY**
supply .... **STOCK, ENDUE**
supply, fresh .... **RELAY**
supply of horses ...... **REMUDA**
support ...... **LEG, RIB, ABET,**
         BACK, PROP, BRACE
support, one-legged .. **UNIPOD**
suppose ... **ASSUME, IMAGINE**
suppose: archaic ...... **TROW**
suppress ...... **ELIDE, QUASH**
Supreme Being, Hebrew . **IHVH,**
         JHVH, JHWH, YHVH, YHWH
surety agreement ...... **BOND**
surf, roar of .... **ROTE**
surface, attractive ... **VENEER**
surface of gem .... **FACET**
surface of a tool .... **FACE**
surfeit .... **CLOY, GLUT, SATE**
surfeited .... **BLASE**
surge .... **TIDE, BILLOW**
surgeon's instrument .. **TREPAN,**
         TROCAR, ABLATOR, LE-
         VATOR, SCALPEL
surgical thread .... **SETON**
Surinam toad .... **PIPA**
surly .... **GRUFF, SULLEN**
surmise .. **INFER, GUESS, OPINE**
surnamed: Fr. .... **DIT**

a surpass ...... **CAP, TOP, BEST**
surplice, chorister's .... **COTTA**
surplus .... **EXTRA, EXCESS**
surrender
    CEDE, YIELD, DEDITION
surrender: law .... **REMISE**
surround **GIRD, BESET, INARM**
surrounding area ...... **ZONE**
surtout .... **COAT**
survey .... **MAP, POLL**
surveyor's assistant .. **RODMAN**
surveyor's instrument
    ROD, ALIDADE
surveyor's rod, sight on **TARGET**
Susa inhabitant ..... **ELAMITE**
suspend .... **HANG**
suspenders .... **BRACES**
suture .... **SEAM**
svelte .... **SLIM, TRIM**
swab .... **MOP**
swain .... **LOVER**
swallow **BOLT, GULP, MARTIN**
swallow, sea .... **TERN**
swamp ..... **BOG, FEN, MARSH,**
  MORASS, SLEW, SLOO, SLUE
swamp gas .. **MIASM, MIASMA**
swamp, S. Afr. ... **VLEI, VLEY**
swampy belt, India ..... **TERAI**
swan, female .... **PEN**
swan genus .... **OLOR**

b swan, male .... **COB**
swan, whistling .... **OLOR**
swap .... **TRADE**
sward .... **SOD, TURF**
swarm .... **NEST, HORDE**
swarthy .... **DUN, DARK**
swastika .... **FYLFOT**
sway .... **ROCK, ROLL**
swear .... **AVER, CURSE**
sweat ...... **SUDOR, PERSPIRE**
SWEDISH .... see also SPECIAL
    SECTION—SWEDEN
Swedish:
    beer .... **OL**
    tea .... **TE**
    toe .... **TA**
    you .... **ER**
Swedish coin .... **ORE**
Swedish county, district .. **LAN**
Swedish explorer ...... **HEDIN**
Swedish order of merit .. **VASA**
Swedish royal guard **DRABANT**
Swedish sculptor ..... **MILLES**
sweep, scythe's ...... **SWATH**
sweet flag .. **SEDGE, CALAMUS**
sweet gale .... **GAGL**
sweet liquid .... **NECTAR**
sweet potato
  YAM, BATATA, OCARINA
sweet potato: Sp. .... **CAMOTE**

c sweet red wine .... **ALICANTE**
sweet-smelling
    OLENT, REDOLENT
sweet spire .... **ITEA**
sweetfish .... **AYU**
sweetheart: Ir. .... **GRA**
sweetheart: Scot. .... **JO**
sweetmeat: Fr. ...... **DRAGEE**
sweetsop .... **ATA,**
  ATES, ATTA, ANNONA
swell .... **DILATE**
swell of water .... **WAVE**
swelling **LUMP, NODE, EDEMA**
swelling on plants ..... **GALL**
swerve .... **SHY, SKEW**
swift .... **FAST, FLEET**
swift, common .... **CRAN**
swift horse .. **ARAB, PACOLET**
swiftly, run ..... **DART, SCUD**
swimming .... **NATANT**
swimming bell .. **NECTOPHORE**
swindle **GIP, GYP, DUPE, SWIZ**
swindler .... **COZENER**
swine .. **HOG, PIG, SOW, BOAR**
swine, feeding of ... **PANNAGE**
swine fever .... **ROUGET**
swine genus .... **SUS**
swing music .... **JIVE**
swing musician ...... **HEPCAT**

d swinish .... **PORCINE**
swipe .... **GLOM**
swirl .... **EDDY, GURGE**
SWISS .. see also SPECIAL SEC-
    TION—SWITZERLAND
Swiss capital ... **BERN, BERNE**
Swiss card game ...... **JASS**
Swiss critic .... **AMIEL**
Swiss patriot .... **TELL**
Swiss state .... **CANTON**
switch .... **TOGGLE**
swollen .... **TURGID**
swoon .... **FAINT**
swoon: old Eng. .... **SWEB**
sword ... **PATA, EPEE, BLADE,**
  SABER, SABRE, RAPIER
sword, Arthur's
  EXCALIBAR, EXCALIBUR
sword, curved .. **SABER, SABRE**
sword, fencing .... **EPEE**
sword, matador's ... **ESTOQUE**
sword, medieval ...... **ESTOC**
sword, Norse myth. ... **GRAM**
sword, put away .... **SHEATHE**
sword, St. George's
  ASCALON, ASKELON
sword-shaped .... **ENSATE**
sword, Siegfried's ..... **GRAM**
sword, slender .... **RAPIER**
swordsman's dummy stake **PEL**
syllable, last .... **ULTIMA**

a syllable, scale .... **DO, FA, LA,**
           MI, RE, SO, TI, SOL
syllable, short .. **MORA, MORAE**
sylvan deity **PAN, FAUN, SATYR**
SYMBOL, CHEMICAL .... see
      SPECIAL SECTION
symbol .... **TOKEN**
symbol of authority ... **MACE**
symbol of Crusaders ... **CROSS**
symbol of protection ... **EGIS**
sympathizer: suffix ...... **ITE**
synagogue ... **SHUL, TEMPLE**
syncopated music .... **RAG**
syncope ...... **FAINT, SWOON**
synod, Russian .... **SOBOR**
syntax, give the .... **PARSE**

c synthetic fabric or fiber **NYLON,**
    ORLON, RAYON, DACRON
synthetic rubber
      BUNA, ELASTOMER
Syria, ancient .... **ARAM**
Syrian, ancient port ... **SIDON**
Syrian bear .... **DUBB**
Syrian bishop's title .... **ABBA**
Syrian city, old ...... **ALEPPO**
system .... **ISM**
system of rule ...... **REGIME**
system of rules .... **CODE**
system of weights ..... **TROY**
system of worship ...... **CULT**
systematic regulation ... **CODE**

T

b
T-shaped .... **TAU**
tab .... **FLAP, LABEL**
tabard .... **CAPE**
table mountain, Abyssin. **AMBA**
tableland .... **MESA**
tablet .... **PAD, SLATE**
taboo, opposite of .... **NOA**
tabor, Moorish
    ATABAL, ATTABAL
Tacoma's Sound ...... **PUGET**
tack: naut. .... **BUSK**
tact .... **FINESSE**
tackle, anchor .... **CAT**
tael, part of .... **LI**
tag .... **LABEL**
tag, metal .... **AGLET, AIGLET**
Tagalog for river ...... **ILOG**
Tahitian national god ... **ORO**
Tai race branch .... **LAO**
tail, of .. **CAUDAL, CAUDATE**
tail of coin .... **VERSO**
tail, rabbit's .... **SCUT**
tail: zool. .... **CAUDA**
tailor .... **SARTOR**
Taino fetish .... **ZEME, ZEMI**
Taj Mahal site .... **AGRA**
take away by force ..... **REAVE**
take away: law ...... **ADEEM**
take back .... **RECANT**
take effect again ..... **REVEST**
take off .... **DOFF**
take one's ease .... **REST**
take on cargo ... **LADE, LOAD**
take out **DELE, ELIDE, EXPUNGE**
take part .... **SIDE**
take up again ...... **RESUME**
take up weapons .... **ARM**
tale .... **SAGA, YARN, STORY**
tale, medieval Fr. .... **LAI**

tale, Norse .... **SAGA**
"Tale of Two Cities" girl **LUCIE**
"Tales of a Wayside —" .. **INN**
talent .... **FLAIR**
talented .... **SMART**
talisman .... **CHARM**
talisman, Afr. .... **GRIGRI**
talk ...... **GAB, GAS, CHAT,**
    PRATE, PALAVER
d talk: slang .... **YAK**
talk freely .... **DESCANT**
talk pompously
    ORATE, HARANGUE
talk, rambling ... **RIGMAROLE**
talk wildly ..... **RANT, RAVE**
Tallinn .... **REVAL**
tallow tree .... **CERA**
tally .... **SCORE**
Talmud commentary .. **GEMARA**
talon .... **CLAW, NAIL**
tamarack .... **LARCH**
tamarisk .... **ATLE**
tame, as hawks .... **MAN**
tan .... **BUFF, BEIGE**
tan skins .... **TAW**
tanager .... **YENI, REDBIRD**
tanager, S. Am. **HABIA, LINDO**
tanbark .... **ROSS**
tangle ...... **SNARL, SLEAVE**
tangled mass ..... **MAT, SHAG**
tanning gum .... **KINO**
tanning, plant for ..... **ALDER**
tanning shrub **SUMAC, SUMACH**
tanning tree, India **AMLA, AMLI**
tantalize .... **TEASE**
Tantalus' daughter .... **NIOBE**
tantra .... **AGAMA**
tantrum .... **RAGE**
tap **PAT, COCK, SPIGOT, FAUCET**

Tapering

a tapering dagger .... **ANLACE**
tapering piece .... **SHIM**
tapestry .... **ARRAS, TAPIS, DOSSER**
tapestry center .... **ARRAS**
tapeworm .... **TAENIA**
tapeworm larva .... **MEASLE**
tapioca-like food .... **SALEP**
tapioca source .... **CASAVA, CASSAVA**
tapir, S. Amer. .... **DANTA**
Tapuyan .... **GE**
tarboosh .... **FEZ**
target .... **BUTT**
Tariff Act writer .... **SMOOT**
Tarkington character ...... **SAM**
tarnish .... **SPOT, SULLY**
taro .... **GABE, GABI, DASHEEN**
taro paste .... **POI**
taro root ... **EDO, EDDO, KALO**
tarpaulin .... **PAULIN**
tarpon .... **SABALO**
tarradiddle .... **FIB, LIE**
tarry .... **BIDE, WAIT, STAY, LINGER**
tarsus .... **ANKLE**
tarsus, insect .... **MANUS**
tart .... **ACID**
tartar, crude ... **ARGAL, ARGOL**
Tartini's B-flat .... **ZA**

b task .... **DUTY, CHORE, STENT, STINT**
task, punishing .... **PENSUM**
taste .... **SIP, SUP, SAPOR, SNACK, PALATE**
tasteful .... **ELEGANT**
tasty .... **SAPID**
Tatar .... **HU**
Tatar dynasty, China .... **WEI**
Tatar tribe, W. Siberia .... **SHOR**
tattle .... **BLAB**
tattler, idle .... **GOSSIP**
Tattler publisher .... **STEELE**
tau cross .... **ANKH**
taunt ...... **JEER, MOCK, TWIT**
taut .... **TENSE**
taut, pull .... **STRETCH**
tavern .... **INN**
tax .... **CESS, GELD, LEVY, SCOT, SESS, STENT, ASSESS, EXCISE, IMPOST**
tax, church .... **TITHE**
tea .... **CHA, CHAA**
tea, black .... **PECO, BOHEA, PEKOE**
tea bowl .... **CHAWAN**
tea box .... **CADDY, CALIN, CANISTER**
tea, China ... **BOHEA, CONGOU**
tea, Chin. green .... **HYSON**

c tea genus .... **THEA**
tea-growing region ..... **ASSAM**
tea, kind of . **OOPAK, OOLONG, OOPACK**
tea, Labrador .... **LEDUM**
tea, marsh .... **LEDUM**
tea, medicinal . **PTISAN, TISANE**
tea, Oriental .... **CHA**
tea, Paraguay ... **MATE, YERBA**
tea, rolled ... **CHA, TCHA, TSIA**
tea tree .... **TI**
teacake ...... **SCON, SCONE**
teacher.... **DOCENT, MENTOR**
teacher, Hebrew .... **RABBI**
teacher, Islam religious ... **ALIM, MOLLA, MULLA**
teacher, Jewish ... **RAB, REB**
teacher, Moslem .... **ALIM, MOLLA, MULLA**
teacher, Xenophon's **ISOCRATES**
teacher's association: abbr. **NEA**
team of horses .... **SPAN**
team, 3-horse .... **RANDEM**
teamster's command **GEE, HAW**
tear .... **RIP, REND, RENT**
tear apart ..... **REND, TATTER, DIVULSE**
tease .... **TWIT, BOTHER**
technical name: biol...... **ONYM**
technique .... **ART**
tedious writer .... **PROSER**

d teem .... **RAIN, POUR**
teeth, false .... **DENTURES**
teeth, incrustation ..... **TARTAR**
Telamon's son .... **AJAX**
telegraph inventor ...... **MORSE**
telegraph key .... **TAPPER**
telegraph signal .... **DOT, DASH**
telegraph, underwater ... **CABLE**
telegraphic speed unit .... **BAUD**
telephone exchange ... **CENTRAL**
telephone inventor .... **BELL**
telephone wire .... **LINE**
telescope part .... **LENS**
television .... **VIDEO**
television broadcast . **TELECAST**
television cable ...... **COAXIAL**
television recording **KINESCOPE**
television tube .. **MONOSCOPE, ICONSCOPE**
tell .... **IMPART, RELATE, NARRATE**
tell in detail .... **RECOUNT**
Tell, site of legend .... **URI**
telling blow .... **COUP, ONER**
temper .... **ANNEAL**
temper, fit of .... **PET**
temperament: Ger. ..... **GEMUT**
"Tempest" sprite .... **ARIEL**
"Tempest" slave ..... **CALIBAN**
temple ... **FANE, RATH, RATHA**
temple, Asian .... **PAGODA**

a temple chamber, Gr. ... NAOS
temple, inner part ..... CELLA
temple: Siam. .... VAT, WAT
temple tower, India .. SHIKARA
tempo: music .... TAKT
temporary decline ...... SLUMP
temporary fashion .... FAD
temporary relief ... REPRIEVE
tempt .... LURE, TOLE
temptation .... ALLURE
ten .... DECAD
ten ares .... DECARE
Ten Commandments
   DECALOG, DECALOGUE
"Ten Days that Shook the
   World" author ..... REED
ten million ergs ...... JOULE
tenant .... LESSEE
tenant, early Ir. .... SAER
tend .... SERVE
tender .... SOFT, OFFER
tending toward .... FOR
tendril: bot. ...... CAPREOL
tennis score .... LOVE, DEUCE
tennis shoe .... SNEAKER
tennis stroke ACE, LOB, LOBB
tennis term .... LET
Tennyson character .... ENID,
                     ARDEN

b Tennyson heroine
               ELAIN, ELAINE
Tennyson sailor ...... ENOCH
tenon .... COG
tenonlike piece .. COAG, COAK
tenor, famous ..... MELCHIOR
tense .... TAUT
tent dweller
            KEDAR, SCENITE
tent dwelling Arabs ... KEDAR
tent flap .... FLY
tentmaker, the .... OMAR
tents .... CAMP
tentacle .... FEELER
tenth part .... DECI, TITHE
tepid .... WARM
Tereus' son .... ITYS
term .... NAME
term .... SESSION
term: algebra .... NOME
TERM, GEOMETRY ...... see
   GEOMETRY, GEOMETRIC
term in office ...... TENURE
term, math. .... SINE, COSINE
term of address .... SIR, SIRE,
                    MADAM
termagant .... SHREW
terminable .... ENDABLE
termite, P. I. .... ANAI, ANAY
tern .... SKIRK

c tern, black .... DARR
tern genus .... STERNA
tern, Hawaii .... NOIO
terpene alcohol ...... NEROL
terpene compound . TEREBENE
terrapin .... EMYD,
               POTTER, SLIDER
terrapin, red-bellied
               POTTER, SLIDER
terrestrial .... GEAL
terrible .... DIRE
terrier, kind of .. SKYE, CAIRN
terrier, Scottish breed of . SKYE
terrified .... AFRAID
territorial division .... AMT
territory ...... LAND, SOIL
territory, additional
               LEBENSRAUM
territory, enclosed .. ENCLAVE
terror .... PANIC
terrorist .... GOON
tessellated .... MOSAIC
tessera .... TILE
test .... ASSAY, TEMPT,
            TRIAL, EXAMINE
test ground .... BOSE
testament .... WILL
testifier .... DEPONENT
testify ...... DEPONE, DEPOSE

d tetrachord, upper tone of. NETE
Teutonic, ancient ...... GOTH
Teutonic barbarian ..... GOTH
Teutonic deity .... ER
Teut. Fate ...... NORN, URTH
TEUTONIC GODS, GODDESSES,
   DEITY see NORSE SPECIAL
   SECTION
Teut. legendary hero ... OFFA
Teut. letter of alphabet . RUNE
Teut. people .... GEPIDAE
Teut. sea goddess ...... RAN
Teut. sky god .. TY, TIU, TIW,
            TYR, ZIO, ZIU, TYRR
Texas shrine .... ALAMO
textile screw pine
               ARA, PANDAN
texture .... WALE,
               WOOF, GRAIN
Thailand .... SIAM
Thames estuary .... NORE
than: Ger. .... ALS
than: Scot. .... NA
thankless person .... INGRATE
that is: abbr. ...... E.G., I.E.
that not .... LEST
that one: Lat. .... ILLE

a

that which follows .... **SEQUEL**
thatch, grass to .... **NETI**
thatching palm .... **NIPA**
the: Ger. .... **DAS, DER**
"The Ballad of Reading —"
                            GAOL
"The Jairite" .... **IRA**
"The Lion of God" .... **ALI**
"The Red" .... **ERIC**
the same: Lat. .... **IDEM**
the squint .... **SKEN**
theatre .... **ODEA, ODEON,**
                    ODEUM, STAGE
theatre box seat .... **LOGE**
theatre district .... **RIALTO**
theatre floor .... **PIT**
theatre, Grecian .... **ODEA,**
                    ODEON, ODEUM
theatre group .... **ANTA**
theatre, part of Greek . **SKENE,**
        SCENA, SCENAE, SKENAI
theatre sign .... **SRO**
"Theban Bard" ...... **PINDAR**
Thebes deity ... **AMEN, AMON,**
    AMUN, MENT, AMENT, MENTU
Thebes, king of
                    CREON, OEDIPUS
theme .... **MOTIF**
theme: music .... **TEMA**
then .... **ANON**

b

then: music .... **POI**
theoretical .... **PLATONIC**
there: Fr. .... **VOILA**
therefore .... **ERGO**
theseli veil .... **TEMPE**
Theseus' father ..... **AEGEUS**
thesis, opp. of .... **ARSIS**
thespian .... **ACTOR**
Thessaly, king of .... **AEOLUS**
Thessaly mountain ...... **OSSA**
Thessaly valley .... **TEMPE**
they: Fr. .... **ILS**
thick-lipped .... **LABROSE**
thicket .. **BOSK, SHAW, COPSE,**
        COPPICE, SPINNEY
thicket: dialect .... **RONE**
thicket, game .... **COVERT**
thickness .... **PLY**
thief, gypsy .... **CHOR**
thief: Yiddish ..... **GANEF, GONOF,**
        GANOF, GONOF
thigh bone .... **FEMUR**
thigh, of the ...... **FEMORAL**
thin ...... **LANK, LEAN, RARE,**
    SHEER, DILUTE, PAPERY,
        SPARSE, TENUOUS
thin cake .... **WAFER**
thin: comb. form ...... **SERO**
thin disk .... **WAFER**
thin layer .... **FILM**

c

"Thin Man" dog ...... **ASTA**
"Thin Man" wife ...... **NORA**
thin-toned .... **REEDY**
thin out .... **ATTENUATE**
thing: law (Latin) ...... **RES**
things added .... **ADDENDA**
things done .... **ACTA**
things to be done
                AGENDA, AGENDUM
think ... **DEEM, TROW, OPINE**
think: archaic .... **WIS**
think (over) .... **MULL, MUSE**
third: comb. form ...... **TRIT**
third day, every .... **TERTIAN**
third king of Judah ..... **ASA**
third: music .... **TIERCE**
Third Reich special police: abbr.
                            SS
thirst-tortured king: Gr. myth
                        TANTALUS
thirsty .... **DRY, ADRY**
thirty: Fr. .... **TRENTE**
thirty, series of .... **TRENTAL**
this: Fr. .... **CE**
this: Sp. .... **ESTA, ESTE**
this one: Lat. ..... **HIC, HAEC**
thither .... **THERE**
Thomas Hardy heroine ... **TESS**
thong .... **STRAP**
thong, braided .... **ROMAL**
thong-shaped .... **LORATE**
thong, S. Afr. .... **RIEM**

d

Thor's stepson ..... **ULL, ULLR**
Thor's wife .... **SIF**
thorax, crustacean's . **PEREION**
thorn ... **BRIAR, BRIER, SPINE**
thorn apple .... **METEL**
thorn, bearing a ..... **SPINATE**
thornback ray .. **DORN, ROKER**
Thorne Smith character. **TOPPER**
thorny plant ... **BRIAR, BRIER**
thorny shrub ... **NABK, NUBK**
thoroughfare .... **WAY, ROAD,**
        AVENUE, STREET
thoroughgoing ..... **ARRANT**
those .... **YON, YOND**
those in power or office ... **INS**
thou: Fr. .... **TU**
thought .... **IDEA**
thought: comb. form .... **IDEO**
thoughts, form .... **IDEATE**
thousand .... **MIL**
thousand: comb. form . **MILLE**
Thrace, ancient people of **EDONI**
thrall .... **ESNE, SLAVE**
thrash .... **LAM, BEAT**
thread: comb. form .... **NEMA**
thread, cotton ...... **LISLE**
thread, guiding ball of . **CLEW**
thread-like .... **NEMALINE**
thread-like process ..... **HAIR**

a	thread-like structure . . . . . **FILUM**	*c*	tibia. . . . . **CNEMIS**
	thread, of a. . . . . **FILAR**		Tichborne Claimant. . . . . **ORTON**
	threads, cross . . . . **RETICLE**		tick . . . . **ACARID**
	threads crossed by woof. **WARP**		tick genus . . . . **ARGAS**
	threads crossing warp . . . **WEFT,**		tick, S. Amer. . . . . . . **CARAPATO**
	WOOF		tickets, sell illegally. . . . . **SCALP**
	threads, lengthwise. . . . . . **WARP**		tickle. . . . . **TITILLATE**
	threaded fastener . . . . **NUT**		Ticonderoga's commander
	threaten. . . . **IMPEND, MENACE**		**GATES**
	three. . . . . **TER, TRIO, TRIAD**		tidal flood . . . . . . **BORE, EAGRE**
	three: Ger. . . . . **DREI**		tidal wave, flow or bore . **EAGRE**
	three: Ital. . . . . **TRE**		tidbit. . . . . **CATE**
	three-legged stand . . . . **TRIPOD,**		tide, lowest high . . . . **NEAP**
	TRIVET		tidings . . . . **NEWS, WORD**
	three-masted ship . . . . . . **XEBEC,**		tidings, glad . . . . **GOSPEL,**
	FRIGATE		**EVANGEL, EVANGILE**
	3 parts, divided into: Her.		tidy . . . . . . **NEAT, REDO, TRIM**
	TIERCE		tie . . . . **BIND, BOND, LASH,**
	3.1416 . . . . **PI**		**TRUSS, CRAVAT**
	three: Sp. . . . . **TRES**		tie, kind of. . . . . **ASCOT**
	three-spot . . . . **TREY**		tie-breaking game . . . . . **RUBBER**
	threefold . . . . . **TRINE, TREBLE,**		tie off . . . . **LIGATE**
	TERNARY, TERNATE		tie, railroad . . . . **SLEEPER**
	threefold: comb. form . . . . . **TER**		tier . . . . **ROW**
	threshold . . . . **SILL**		tiger cat, S. Amer. . . . . **CHATI**
	threshold, psychology . . . **LIMEN**		tiger, Persian . . . . . . **SHER, SHIR**
	thrice: music. . . . . **TER**		tight . . . . . . **SNUG, TAUT, TENSE**
	thrifty . . . . **FRUGAL, SAVING**		tight place. . . . **FIX, JAM, MESS**
	thrive . . . . . . **BATTEN, PROSPER**		tighten: naut. . . . . **FRAP**
b	throat. . . . . **GORGE, GULLET**		tightly stretched . . . . **TENSE**
	throat: Lat. . . . . **GULA**		til . . . . **SESAME**
	throat, pert. to . . . . **GULAR**	*d*	tile, hexagonal . . . . **FAVI**
	throb. . . . . **BEAT, PULSE,**		tile, roofing . . . . **PANTILE**
	PULSATE		tilelike. . . . . **TEGULAR**
	throe. . . . . **PANG**		till the earth . . . . . **FARM, PLOW**
	throng . . . . **MOB, HORDE,**		tilled land. . . . . **ARADA, ARADO**
	SWARM		tiller . . . . **HELM**
	through . . . . **PER**		tilt . . . . **TIP, CANT, LIST**
	through: prefix. . . . . **DIA**		tilt . . . . **JOUST**
	throw . . . . **CAST, PITCH**		tilting: naut. . . . . **ALIST**
	throw aside. . . . . **FLING**		timber bend . . . . **SNY**
	throw back . . . . **REPEL**		timber, flooring . . . . **BATTEN**
	thrush. . . . . **VEERY, MISSEL**		timber, nautical . . . . **KEVEL**
	thrush, Hawaiian . . . . **OMAO**		timber, pine: Asia . . . . . . **MATSU**
	thrush, India . . . . **SHAMA**		timber rot . . . . **DOAT, DOTE**
	thrush, missel. . . **MAVIE, MAVIS**		timber truck . . . . **WYNN**
	thrust . . . . **LUNGE**		timber wolf . . . . **LOBO**
	thrust back . . . . **REPEL**		timbrel . . . . . . **TABOR, TABOUR**
	thrust down . . . . **DETRUDE**		time . . . . . **ERA, TEMPI, TEMPO**
	thunderfish . . . . **RAAD**		time before. . . . . **EVE**
	thurible. . . . . **CENSER**		time being. . . . . **NONCE**
	Thuringian city . . . . **JENA**		time gone by . . . . **PAST**
	Thursday, source of name **THOR**		time out . . . . **RECESS**
	thus . . . . **SO, SIC**		time, space of . . . . **WHILE**
	thus far . . . . **YET**		time value, equalling in
	thwart. . . . . **FOIL**		**DIMORIC**
	Tiber tributary . . . . **NERA**		times, old . . . . **ELD, YORE**
	Tibetan chief . . . . **POMBO**		timid. . . . . **SHY, PAVID**
	Tibetan ox. . . . . **YAK**		timorous . . . . **TREPID**
	Tibetan priest. . . . . **LAMA**		timothy . . . . **HAY**
	Tibetan tribe . . . . **CHAMPA**		Timothy's grandmother: Bib.**LOIS**

165

a
tin .... CAN, STANNUM
tin, containing .... STANNOUS
tin foil .... TAIN
tin plate .... TAIN
tin roofing .... TERNE
tinamou .... YUTU
tincture: Her. .... OR, GULES,
    VERT, AZURE, SABLE,
    ARGENT, PURPURE
tinder .... PUNK, AMADOU
tine .... PRONG
tine of antler .... SNAG
tinge .... TAINT
tinge deeply .... IMBUE
tingle of feeling ..... THRILL
tinkle .... TING
tiny bird, W. Ind. ..... TODY
tip .... END, FEE, APEX, KNAP
tip .... CANT, LEAN,
    TILT, CAREEN
tipping .... ALIST, ATILT
tiptoe, on .... ATIP
tire .... FAG, JADE
tire casing .... SHOE
tire, face of .... TREAD
tire support .... RIM
tissue .... TELA
tissue, of a .... TELAR
tissue, pert. to ...... TELAR
TITAN . see SPECIAL SECTION,
    GREEK MYTH page 200

b
Titania's husband .... OBERON
titanic iron-ore sand . ISERENE
titlark .... PIPIT
title ..... EARL, NAME, TERM
title, baronet's .... SIR
title, Benedictine ...... DOM
title, church .... PRIMATE
title, East ...... COJA, HOJA
title, Ethiopian .... RAS
title Hindu gives Moslem
    MIAN
title, India .... AYA, NAWAB,
    SAHEB, SAHIB
title, Jewish . RAB, REB, RABBI
title, knight's .... SIR
title, king's .... SIRE
title, lady's ... DAME, MADAM
title, Moslem ...... AGA, ALI,
    MOLLA, MULLA,
    SHERIF, SHEREFF
title of address .... MME., MRS.,
    SIR, MAAM, MADAM
title of honor, Moslem . SAYID,
    SAIYID, SAYYID
title of kings of Edessa . ABGAR
title of respect ..... SIR, SIRE,
    MADAME
title of respect, Afr. ..... SIDI

c
title of respect, India .... SRI,
    SHRI, SAHIB, SHREE,
    HUZOOR
title of respect, Malay .. TUAN
title, Oriental .... BABA
title, Persian MIR, AZAM, KHAN
title, Spanish DOM, DON, SENOR
title to property or land . DEED
title, Turkish .. PACHA, PASHA
titleholder .... TITLIST
titmice, genus of ...... PARUS
titmouse ...... MAG, PARUS
tittle ..... JOT, IOTA, WHIT
Titus Andronicus' daughter
    LAVINIA
Tiwaz .... ER, TIU
to .... FOR, UNTO
to: prefix .... AP
to: Scot. .... TAE
to be: Fr. .... ETRE
to be: Lat. .... ESSE
"to be," part of ...... AM, IS,
    ARE, WAS
to go: Fr. .... ALLER
to love: Fr. .... AIMER
to the point that ..... UNTIL
to use: Lat. .... UTOR
toad genus .... BUFO
toad, huge .... AGUA
toad, order of .... ANURA

d
toad, tree genus ...... HYLA
toadfish .... SAPO
toast, bit of .... SIPPET
toasting word .... SALUD,
    SKOAL, PROSIT
tobacco ash . DOTTEL, DOTTLE
tobacco, chewing .... QUID
tobacco, coarse
    SHAG, CAPORAL
tobacco, Cuban .... CAPA
tobacco, low grade ..... SHAG
tobacco, Peru .... SANA
tobacco, roll .... CIGAR
toddy palm juice ...... SURA
toe .... DIGIT
toe, fifth .... MINIMUS
toe: Scot. .... TAE
togs .... DUDS
toilet case .... ETUI
Tokyo Bay city .... CHIBI
Tokyo, old name ... EDO, YEDO
tolerable .... SOSO
toll .... FEE, KNELL
Tolstoi heroine .... ANNA
tomb, Moslem TABUT, TABOOT
tomboy .... HOIDEN, HOYDEN
tomcat .... GIB
tone down .... SOFTEN
tone, lack of .... ATONY
tone, of .... TONAL
tone quality .... TIMBRE

a tone: Scot. .... **TEAN**
tones, series of ...... **OCTAVE**
tongue, gypsy .... **CHIB**
tongue of Agni .... **KALI**
tongue, pert. to ..... **GLOSSAL**
tongue, using the ..... **APICAL**
tongue, wagon .... **NEAP**
tonic .... **ROBORANT**
tonic, dried India
.... **CHIRATA, CHIRETTA**
tonic herb ...... **ALOE, TANSY**
Tonkin native .... **THO**
too early ...... **PREMATURE**
too much: Fr. .... **TROP**
tool, boring .... **AWL, BIT,
AUGER, GIMLET**
tool, cutting .. **AX, ADZ, AXE,
HOB, SAW, SAX, SYE, ADZE**
tool, engraver's
.... **BURIN, MATTOIR**
tool, enlarging ...... **REAMER**
tool, grass-cutting .... **SITHE,
SCYTHE, SICKLE**
tool, machine .... **LATHE**
tool, molding .... **DIE**
tool, pointed .... **BROACH**
tool, post hole digging .... **LOY**
tool shaper .... **SWAGER**
tool, splitting .... **FROE, FROW**
b tool, stone, prehistoric
.... **CELT, EQLITH**
tool, threading ...... **CHASER**
tool's biting edge .... **BIT**
tooth ..... **COG, TINE, MOLAR,
CANINE, CUSPID, FANG**
tooth-billed pigeon ... **DODLET**
tooth, canine .... **CUSPID**
tooth: comb. form .... **ODONT**
tooth, gear .... **COG**
tooth: Lat. .... **DENS**
tooth-like ornament .. **DENTIL**
tooth, long **FANG, TUSH, TUSK**
tooth pulp .... **NERVE**
toothed formation ..... **SERRA**
toothed margin, having
.... **DENTATE**
toothed wheel .... **GEAR**
toothless .... **EDENTATE**
toothless mammals . **EDENTATA**
top .... **APEX, CAP, LID**
top-notch .... **AONE**
top ornament ..... **EPI, FINIAL**
topaz humming bird ..... **AVA**
topee material .... **SOLA**
toper .... **SOT, SOUSE**
topic .... **THEME**
topmast crossbar support .. **FID**
topsail .... **RAFFE**
torment .... **BAIT, ANNOY,
DEVIL, HARRY, TEASE**
torn: archaic .... **REFT**

c torn place .... **RENT**
torrid region or zone .. **TROPIC**
tortoise .... **GALAPAGO**
tortoise, fresh water .... **EMYD**
tortoise, marsh genus ... **EMYS**
tortoise, order of ... **CHELONIA**
torturer .... **RACKER**
"Tosca" villain ...... **SCARPIA**
toss ...... **CAST, FLIP, HURL,
FLING, PITCH**
tosspot ... . **SOT**
total .... **ADD, SUM, UTTER**
total abstinence .. **NEPHALISM**
totalitarian ruler ... **DICTATOR**
totem pole .... **XAT**
toucan .... **TOCO**
toucan, S. Am. .... **ARACARI**
touch .... **ABUT**
touch lightly .... **PAT**
touch, organ of .... **PALP**
touch, pert. to **HAPTIC, TACTIC,
TACTILE, TACTUAL**
touch sense, pert. to .. **HAPTIC**
touchwood .... **PUNK**
tough .... **WIRY, HARDY,
ROWDY, CHEWY**
tour: It. .... **GIRO**
tourmaline, colorless
.... **ACHROITE**
d tow .... **PULL, DRAW**
towai .... **KAMAHI**
toward: Lat. .... **AD**
toward stern ..... **AFT, ABAFF,
ABAFT, ASTERN**
towel .... **WIPER**
towel fabric .... **HUCK, TERRY**
tower, Bibl. .... **BABEL**
tower, India .... **MINAR**
tower, little .... **TURRET**
tower, mosque, slender
.... **MINARET**
towering .... **STEEP**
towhead .... **BLOND, BLONDE**
town, Arcadia ancient ... **ALEA**
town: Cornish prefix .... **TRE**
town: Dutch .... **STAD**
town: Ger. .... **STADT**
town, India pilgrimage . **SORON**
town: It. .... **CASAL, CASALE**
town: Jap. .... **MACHI**
town: suffix .... **TON**
township, ancient Attica . **DEME**
townsman .... **CIT**
toxic protein .... **ABRIN**
toy with .... **TRIFLE**
trace .... **TINGE, VESTIGE**
track .... **TRACE**
track, animal ... **RUN, SLOT,
SPUR, SPOOR**
track circuit .... **LAP**

167

a

track of ship .... **WAKE**
track, deer's .... **SLOT**
track, otter's .... **SPUR, SPOOR**
track, put off .... **DERAIL**
track, put on another
           SHUNT, SWITCH
tracker, India .... **PUGGI**
tract .... **LOT, AREA**
tract of farm land .... **FIELD**
trade .... **SWAP, SWOP**
           BARTER, TRAFFIC
trade .... **METIER**
trade agreement ...... **CARTEL**
trader ..... **DEALER, MONGER**
trader selling to soldiers
           SUTLER
trading exchange .... **PIT**
trading vessel of Ceylon
           DONI, DHONI
traditional story .... **SAGA**
traduce .... **SLUR, DEFAME**
traffic .... **TRADE**
trail .... **SLOT, SPOOR, TRACK**
train of attendants
           SUITE, RETINUE
train, overhead .... **EL**
train, slow, many-stops . **LOCAL**
tramp .... **BO, HOBO**
trample .... **TREAD**
tranquil or tranquilize

b
           SERENE, SOOTHE
transaction ...... **DEAL, SALE**
transfer .... **CEDE**
transfer, property
           DEED, GRANT
transfer, sovereignty .. **DEMISE**
transferer, property .. **ALIENOR**
transform .... **CONVERT**
transgress .... **ERR, SIN**
transit coach .... **BUS**
"— transit gloria mundi" . **SIC**
translator of Freud, Amer.
           BRILL
transmit .... **SEND**
transom .... **TRAVE**
transpire .... **OCCUR, HAPPEN,**
           DEVELOP
transverse pin .... **TOGGLE**
trap .... **SNARE, ENSNARE**
trap door .... **DROP**
trap, mouse: dial. .... **TIPE**
trap, rabbit: dial. .... **TIPE**
trappings .... **REGALIA**
travel .... **TREK**
traveler .... **PASSENGER**
tray .... **SALVER, SERVER**
tread softly ...... **PAD, SNEAK**
treasure ...... **ROON, TROVE**
treasurer, college ..... **BURSAR**
treasury agents .... **TMEN**
treat .... **USE**

c

treat with acid ..... **ACIDIZE**
treat with malice .... **SPITE**
treatment .... **USE**
tree   (3 letters) **ASH, ELM,**
     FIR, LIN, OAK, YEW;
     (4 letters) **AKEE, AMLA,**
     AMLI, ANAM, ANDA,
     ARAR, ASAK, AULU, AUSU,
     AUZU, BARU, BIJA, BITO,
     BIWA, BOBO, BOGO, DALI,
     DILO, DOON, DOUM, DUKU,
     EBOE, EJOO, GOAI, GUAO,
     HINO, IFIL, IPIL, KINO,
     KIRI, KOPI, KOZO, LIME,
     LINN, MAKO, MYXA,
     NAIO, NEEM, NIOG, NIPA,
     ODUM, OHIA, PALM, PELU,
     PINE, PUKA, RATA, RIMU,
     ROKA, SAUL, SHEA, SUPA,
     TALA, TARA, TAWA, TEAK,
     TEIL, TEYL, TOON, TORO,
     TUNG, TUNO, TUWI, UPAS,
     WHAU, YATE, YAYA, YPIL;
     (5 letters) **ASPEN**; (6 let-
     ters) **LINDEN**
tree, African .... **AKEE, BAKU,**
     COLA, KOLA, ROKA,
     SHEA, AEGLE, ARTAR

d

tree, Afr. & Asia .... **SIRIS**
tree, Afr. gum .... **BUMBO**
tree, Afr. tallow .... **ROKA**
TREE, AMER. TROPICAL...see
     TREE, TROPICAL AMER.
tree, Argentine timber ... **TALA**
TREE, ASIATIC .. see ASIATIC
     TREE
tree, arrow poison ...... **UPAS**
TREE, AUSTRAL. .... see
     AUSTRAL. TREE
tree, Bengal quince ...... **BEL**
tree, black gum ...... **TUPELO**
tree, body of .... **TRUNK**
tree, boxwood yielding . **SERON**
tree, buckwheat .... **TITI**
tree, butter .... **SHEA**
tree, caucho-yielding ..... **ULE**
tree, chicle .... **SAPOTA**
tree, Chin. ... **GINKO, GINKGO**
tree clump, prairie ..... **MOTTE**
tree cobra .... **MAMBA**
tree, coniferous (cone) .. **FIR,**
     YEW, PINE, LARCH
TREE. E. IND. .... see E. IND.
     TREE and TREE, IND.
TREE, EVERGREEN ...... see
     EVERGREEN
tree, flowering ..... **CATALPA**
tree genus .... **MABA**
tree genus, Afr. .... **OCHNA**

a tree genus, elms
ULMUS, CELTIS
tree genus, small ... CATALPA
tree, gum .... ICICA
tree, hardwood ASH, OAK, IPIL
tree, India .... DAR, MEE, SAJ,
SAL, AMLA, AMLI, DHAK,
MYXA, NEEM, SHOQ, MA-
HUA, BANYAN
tree knot .... BURL
tree, locust .... ACACIA
tree, maidenhair ..... GINKGO
tree, Malay .... TERAP
tree, Medit. .... CAROB
tree, mimosaceous ...... SIRIS
tree moss .... USNEA
tree, N. Am.
TAMARAC, TAMARACK
TREE, N. Z.
see NEW ZEALAND TREE
tree, oak .... ENCINA
tree of olive family ..... ASH
tree, Pacific .... KOU
tree, palm .. GRIGRI, GRUGRU
tree, palm, Asiatic .... ARENG
TREE, P.I. ..... see P. I. TREE
tree, pod .... CAROB
tree, resinous .... FIR, PINE,
BALSAM
b tree, showy Asia .... ASAK
tree-snake .... LORA
tree, sun, Jap. .... HINOKI
tree, swamp .... ALDER
tree, tamarisk salt ...... ATLE
tree, tea .... TI
tree, thorny .... ACACIA
tree tiger .... LEOPARD
tree toad genus .... HYLA
tree, tropical .... EBOE, PALM,
BALSA, MANGO, COLIMA,
SAPOTA, LEBBEK
tree, tropical Amer. CEBA, DALI,
GUAO, CEIBA, COLIMA,
GUAMA, CEDRON
tree trunk .... BOLE
tree, W. Ind. .... GENIP,
SAPOTE, LIBIDIBI
trees of a region .... SILVA
treeless plain .... PAMPAS,
TUNDRA, STEPPES
tremble ...... QUAKE, DIDDER
trembling ..... ASPEN, TREPID
trench .... SAP
trench extension .... SAP
trench, rear wall of .. PARADOS
trend .... TENOR
trespass .. INFRINGE, INTRUDE

c trespass for game .... POACH
trespass to recover goods
TROVER
triad .... TRIO
trial .... TEST
triangle .... TRIGON, SCALENE
triangle, side of .... LEG
triangular insert .... GORE
tribal symbol .... TOTEM
TRIBE
see also SPECIAL SECTION
tribe ...... CLAN, FOLK, RACE
TRIBE, BIBLICAL .... see
SPECIAL SECTION
tribe: Bib. tent-dwellers. KEDAR
tribe division, Rom.
CURIA, CURIAE
TRIBE, ISRAELITE .... see
ISRAELITE TRIBE
TRIBESMAN .. see TRIBES in
SPECIAL SECTION
tribulation .... TRIAL
tribunal .... BAR, FORUM
tribute .... SCAT, SCATT
tribute: Gaelic .... CAIN
trick FLAM, GAWD, JEST, RUSE,
WILE, DODGE, FICELLE,
STRATAGEM
tricks, game for no .... NULLO
tricks, win all .... CAPOT
d Trieste measure ... ORNA, ORNE
trifle .... TOY, DOIT, FICO,
STRAW, NIGGLE, PALTER
trifling .... SMALL, SLIGHT
trig .... NEAT, TRIM
trigonometry function
SINE, COSINE
trigonometry line ..... SECANT
trill, bird's .... TIRALEE
trim .... NEAT, TRIG,
ADORN, DECORATE
trimmed .... SNOD
trimming, dress . GIMP, RUCHE
trimmings, overlapping . FLOTS
Trinidad tree .... CYP
trinket .... GAUD
triple .... TRI, TREBLE
triplet .... TRIN
tripletail, P. R. .... SAMA
tripod, 6-footed .... CAT
Tripoli: measure . see page 188
"Tristram Shandy" author
STERNE
Tristram's beloved ..... ISOLT,
YSEUT, ISAUDE, ISAULT,
ISEULT, ISOLDE, ISOLTA,
ISOUDE, ISULTE
trite .. BANAL, CORNY, STALE
triton ...... EFT, EVET, NEWT

169

a troche ...... **PASTIL, ROTULA, PASTILE, PASTILLE**
TROJAN .... see also TROY
Trojan hero .. **PARIS, ENEAS, AENEAS, AGENOR, DARDAN, HECTOR, HEKTOR, ACHILLES**
trolley .... **TRAM**
troop-carrying group: abbr. **ATS**
troop, division, Gr. .... **TAXIS**
troops .... **MEN**
troops, spread .... **DEPLOY**
trophy .... **CUP**
tropic .... **SOLAR**
tropical Am. bird genus **CACICUS**
tropical disease . **BUBA, BUBAS**
tropical fever .... **DENGUE**
TROPICAL FRUIT .... see **FRUIT, TROPICAL**
tropical plant .... **TARO**
tropical shrub genus **INGA, SIDA**
trot .... **JOG, AMBLE**
trouble ... **ADO, AIL, WORRY, EFFORT, MOLEST**
troubles .... **ILLS**
troublesome person **PEST, AGITATOR**
trough, inclined ...... **CHUTE**
trough, mining ...... **SLUICE**
b trout, British .. **SEWEN, SEWIN**
trout, brook .... **CHAR**
trowel, plasterers' ..... **DARBY**
Troy .... **ILION, ILIUM**
Troy, founder of .... **ILUS**
Troy, land of .... **TROAS**
Troy, last king of ...... **PARIS, PRIAM, PRIAMOS**
Troy, of ancient **ILIAC, ILIAN**
Troy: poetic .... **ILIUM**
truant, play: Scot. .... **TRONE**
truck .... **LORRY, CAMION**
trudge .... **PACE, PLOD, SLOG**
true copy: law .... **ESTREAT**
true olives .... **OLEA**
trumpet .... **HORN, CLARION**
trumpet call, reveille .... **DIAN**
trumpet, mouth of .... **CODON**
trumpet shell .... **TRITON**
trumpeter perch .... **MADO**
trumpeter, pigeon-like .. **AGAMI**
trundle, as ore .... **RULL**
trunk of body .... **TORSO**
trunkfish .... **CHAPIN**
truss up .... **TIE**
trust .... **RELY, TROW, RELIANCE**
trustee of a wakf. **MUTAWALLI**
trusting .... **RELIANT**
truth: Chin. .... **TAO**

c truth drug ...... **PENTOTHAL**
Truth personified .... **UNA**
try .... **TEST, ESSAY, ATTEMPT**
try to equal ... **VIE, EMULATE**
tsetse fly .... **MAU, KIVU**
tsetse fly genus .... **GLOSSINA**
tub ...... **VAT, KNAP, KNOP**
tub, brewer's .... **KEEVE**
tub, broad .... **KEELER**
tub, wooden: dialect ...... **SOE**
tube .... **DUCT**
tube, glass ... **PIPET, PIPETTE**
tube, plane's .... **PITOT**
tuber delicacy ...... **TRUFFLE**
tuber, edible **OCA, OKA, YAM, TARO, POTATO**
tuber, orchid .... **SALEP**
tuber, S. Amer. .... **OCA, OKA**
Tuesday, god who gave name to **TIU, TYR**
tuft .... **CREST**
tuft: bot. .... **COMA**
tufted plant .... **MOSS**
tulip tree .... **POPLAR**
TUMERIC ..... see TURMERIC
tumor .... **OMA, WEN**
tumor, skin .... **WEN**
tumult .... **RIOT**
tune .... **AIR, ARIA, SONG, MELODY**
tune, bagpipe .... **PORT**
d tune: Scot. .... **PORT**
tungstite ..... **OCHER, OCHRE**
tuning fork ...... **DIAPASON**
Tunis, ruler of ..... **BEY, DEY**
tunnel, train, Alps .... **CENIS**
tunny .... **AMIA, TUNA**
turban, Oriental .... **MANDIL**
turbid, make .... **ROIL**
turf .... **SOD**
turf, bit of: golf ...... **DIVOT**
Turkestan town dwellers . **SART**
turkey buzzard .... **AURA**
turkey red .... **MADDER**
turkeys, collection of .. **RAFTER**
Turkic person **TATAR, TARTAR**
Turkic person, 8th century **OGOR**
Turkish army corps ..... **ORDU**
Turkish army officer ..... **AGA**
Turkish caliph .... **ALI**
Turkish chamber .. **ODA, ODAH**
Turkish chieftain ...... **AMIR, ZAIM, AMEER**
Turkish commander . **AGA, ALI**
Turkish copper coin .... **PARA**
Turkish decree .... **IRADE**
Turkish flag .... **ALEM**
Turkish general .... **AGA**
Turkish gold coin ...... **LIRA, ALTUN, MAHBUB**

170

a Turkish government .... **PORTE**
Turkish govt. summer residence
          YALI
Turkish governor .. **VALI, WALI**
Turkish hostelry ..... **IMARET**
Turkish judge .... **CADI, KADI**
Turkish leader .... **AGA**
Turkish liquor ...... **MASTIC**
Turkish magistrate.**CADI, KADI**
Turkish military district . **ORDO**
Turkish money of account
          ASPER
Turkish officer .. **AGA, AGHA**
Turkish oxcart . **ARBA, ARABA**
Turkish palace .... **SERAI**
Turkish pavilion .... **KIOSK**
Turkish president, former
          INONU
Turkish regiment .... **ALAI**
Turkish standard . **ALEM, TOUG**
Turkish sultan .... **SELIM**
Turkish title .... **AGA, AGHA,**
    BABA, EMIR, EMEER,
    PASHA, BASHAW
Turkish tribesman ..... **TATAR**
Turkish tribesman, Persia
          GHUZ
Turkoman tribesman **SEID, SHIK**
turmeric .... **REA, ANGO**
b turmoil .... **WELTER**
turn ..... **BEND, GYRE, VEER,**
    ROTATE, SWERVE
turn aside.**SKEW, VEER, SHUNT**
turn back to .... **REVERT**
turn direction .... **VERT**
turn inside out .... **EVERT**
turn over: mus. .... **VERTE**
turning point ... **CRISES, CRISIS**
turning: prefix .... **ROTO**
turnover .... **PIE**
turnip ... **BAGA, NEEP, SWEDE**
turnip: Scot. .... **NEEP**
turpentine derivative
    ROSIN, PINENE
turpentine distillate .... **ROSIN**
turpentine resin
    ALK, GALLIPOT, GALIPOT
turtle, Amazon ...... **ARRAU**
turtle, edible
    TERAPIN, TERRAPIN
turtle, edible part of . **CALIPEE**
turtle enclosure ...... **CRAWL**
turtle genus .... **EMYS**
turtle, hawkbill ...... **CARET**
turtle, order of .... **CHELONIA**
Tuscany art city ...... **SIENA**
tusk, elephant .... **IVORY**
tutelary god ..... **LAR, LARES**
tutor .... **TUTE**

c TV advertiser ...... **SPONSOR**
"Twelfth Night" clown .. **FESTE**
"Twelfth Night" heroine
          VIOLA
twelve and one-half cents . **BIT**
twenty-fourth part
    CARAT, KARAT
twenty quires .... **REAM**
twice .... **BIS**
twice: prefix .... **BI**
twig, willow .. **WITHE, WITHY**
twilight .... **EVE, DUSK,**
    GLOAM, EVENTIDE
twilled coth .... **REP**
twilled wool fabric ..... **SERGE**
twin .... **GEMEL**
twin crystal .... **MACLE**
twin gods, Teut. ...... **ALCIS**
twine .... **COIL, WIND, TWIST**
twining stem .... **BINE**
twist .... **PLY, COIL, FEAK,**
    KINK, SKEW, GNARL,
    WREATHE, CONTORT
twist inwards .... **INTORT**
twist out of shape ...... **WARP**
twisted .... **AWRY, SKEW,**
    TORTILE
twisted roll of fibers .... **SLUB**
twisted spirally .... **TORSE**
twitch .... **TIC**
d twitching .... **TIC**
two ...... **DUO, DUAD, PAIR**
two ears, affecting the **DIOTIC**
two elements, having . **BINARY**
two feet, verse of .... **DIPODY**
two-footed ... **BIPED, BIPEDAL**
two-horse chariot ...... **BIGA**
two-hulled boat . **CATAMARAN**
two-masted ship . **YAWL, ZULU**
two-month period .. **BIMESTER**
two, music for .... **DUET**
two notes, group of .... **DUOLE**
two-pronged, as sponges
    DICELLATE
two-pronged weapon .. **BIDENT**
two-spot .... **DEUCE**
two tenacles, having.**DICEROUS**
two-toed sloth .... **UNAU**
two-wheeled vehicle **GIG, CART**
two-year-old sheep
    TEG, TEGG, BIDENT
"Two Years Before the Mast"
    author .... **DANA**
twofold .. **DUAL, TWIN, BINAL**
twofold: prefix .... **DI**
tycoon .... **NABOB**
tymp arch of furnace ... **FAULD**
Tyndareus, wife of ..... **LEDA**
type collection .... **FONT**

a type, conforming to . **TYPICAL**
type face .... **RUNIC, CASLON**
type, 5½ point .... **AGATE**
type, jumbled .... **PI, PIE**
type, kind of .... **ELITE**
type measure .... **EM, EN**
type metal piece ...... **QUAD**
type, mixed .... **PI, PIE**
type of script .... **RONDE**
type part .... **KERN**
type set .... **FONT**

c type size ..... **PICA, AGATE,**
BREVIER
type, skanting .... **ITALIC**
type square .... **EM**
type tray .... **GALLEY**
typewriter roller ..... **PLATEN**
Tyr, Norse war god ...... **ER**
tyrant .... **DESPOT**
tyrant of Rome .... **NERO**
Tyre, king of .... **HIRAM**
Tyre, princess of .... **DIDO**
tyro .... **NOVICE**

U

Uganda native .... **KOPI**
ukase .... **EDICT**
Ukraine legislature ..... **RADA**
"Ulalume" author .... **POE**
ulexite .... **TIZA**
ultra-conservative ..... **TORY**
ULYSSES ... see also ODYSSEUS
Ulysses' swineherd ... **EUMAEUS**
Ulysses' voyages .... **ODYSSEY**
umbrella .... **GAMP**
umbrella finial, Burma ... **TEE**
umbrella, India ...... **CHATTA**
umbrella part .... **RIB**
b umpire .... **REFEREE**
unaccented vowel sound **SCHWA**
unadulterated .... **PURE**
unaffected .. **SIMPLE, ARTLESS**
Unalaskan .... **ALEUT**
unaspirate .... **LENE**
unassuming
MODEST, NATURAL
unbeliever .... **HERETIC**
unbleached ..... **ECRU, BEIGE**
unburnt brick .. **DOBE, ADOBE**
Uncas' beloved .... **CORA**
uncanny ...... **EERY, EERIE,**
WEIRD
unceasing **ETERNAL, PERPETUAL**
uncinate .... **HAMATE**
uncivil .... **RUDE**
uncle, dial. .... **EME**
uncle: Scot. .... **EME**
"Uncle Remus" author
HARRIS
"Uncle Remus" rabbit ... **BRER**
unclean: Jewish law .... **TREF**
unclose .... **OPE, OPEN**
uncommon .... **RARE, SPECIAL**
unconcerned .... **CALM, OPEN,**
SERENE
unconscious state ...... **COMA**
unconstrained .... **EASY**

uncouth person ... **CAD, BOOR,**
YAHOO, GALOOT
unction .... **BALM**
unctuous ..... **OILY, SUAVE**
under .... **INFRA, NEATH,**
SOTTO, NETHER
under: Fr. .... **SOUS**
under: naut. .... **ALOW**
under: prefix .... **SUB**
under side, pert. to .. **VENTRAL**
undergo: obs. .... **DREE**
underground bud .... **BULB**
d underground reservoir, natural
water .... **CENOTE**
underground stream, S. Afr.
AAR
underhand, throw ...... **LOB**
undernsong .... **TIERCE**
undershirts .... **SKIVVIES**
undersized animal ...... **RUNT**
understand .... **GRASP**
understanding ... **KEN, SENSE,**
ENTENTE
underwater box ..... **CAISSON**
underworld .... **HADES, SHEOL**
underworld, Egypt.
DUAT, AMENTI
underworld god ... **DIS, PLUTO**
underworld god, Egypt. **OSIRIS,**
SERAPIS
underworld goddess ..... **HEL**
underwrite ... **ENSURE, INSURE**
undeveloped .... **LATENT**
undraped .... **NUDE**
undulant fever .. **BRUCELLOSIS**
undulating .... **WAVY**
undulation .... **WAVE**
unequal .... **UNIQUE**
unequal angled ..... **SCALENE**
unequal conditions ...... **ODDS**
uneven .... **ODD, EROSE**
unevenly shaped .... **EROSE**

a unfadable .... FAST
unfair move .... FOUL
unfair shove in marbles . FULK
unfasten ..... UNTIE, LOOSEN
unfavorable .... BAD, ILL
unfeeling ... HARSH, CALLOUS
unfermented grape juice
         STUM
unfit to eat, make . DENATURE
unfledged bird .... EYAS
unfold .... EVOLVE
unguent, Roman wrestlers'
         CEROMA
ungula .. CLAW, HOOF, NAIL
ungulate, S. Am. ...... TAPIR
unhappy .... SAD, BLUE,
     MOROSE, RUEFUL
unicorn fish ...... LIJA, UNIE
uniform .... EVEN
uniform in hue .. FLAT, FLOT
uninteresting .... DULL
union .... MERGER
union, labor ... AFL, CIO, ILA,
     ITA, ILGWU
union, political .... BLOC
union, Russ. workers' ... ARTEL
unique person .... ONER
unique thing: slang ..... ONER
unit .... ACE, ONE
b unit of capacity ...... FARAD
unit of conductance ..... MHO
unit of electrical intensity:
   abbr. .... AMP
unit of electrical resistance or
   reluctance .... REL
unit of electricity . OHM, WATT,
   FARAD, WEBER
unit of electromotive force
         VOLT
unit of energy .... ERG,
     RAD, ERGON
unit of fluidity .... RHE
unit of force .... DYNE
unit of heat .... CALORIE
unit of illumination ...... PHOT
unit of jet propulsion ... JATO
unit of light .... PYR, LUMEN,
     HEFNER
unit of power .... DYNE
unit of power, electric ... OHM,
   WATT, FARAD, WEBER
unit of pressure BARAD, BARIE
unit of reluctance .... REL
unit of resistance .... OHM
unit of weight .... WEY
unit of work ..... ERG, ERGON
unit, pert. to ...... MONADIC
unit, power ratio .... BEL

c unite .... WED, ALLY, JOIN,
    KNIT, WELD, YOKE,
    MERGE, INTEGRATE
unite edges .... RABBET
UNITED STATES
         see AMERICAN
unity .... ONE
univalent element .... MONAD
universal .. WORLD, GENERAL
universal language .. RO, IDO
universe .... WORLD, COSMOS
universe: Hindu .... LOKA
universe, pert. to ..... COSMIC
university degree-holder
         LICENTIATE
University in Conn. ..... YALE
unkeeled .... RATITE
unkind ILL
unknown Hindu god .... KA
unless .... BUT, SAVE
unless: Lat. .... NISI
unlock .... OPE, OPEN
unmarried .... CELIBATE
unmatched .... ODD
unmixed ...... PURE, SHEER
unmusical clang ...... TONK
unnecessary .... NEEDLESS
unplowed strip .... HADE
unpredictable .... ERRATIC
d unprincipled person .... CAD,
    SCAMP, BOUNDER,
    REPROBATE
unprofitable, as rents .... SECK
unrefined .... EARTHY
unrelenting . IRON, ADAMANT
unruffled .... CALM, SERENE
unruly outbreak .... RIOT
unruly person .... RANTIPOLE
unsophisticated .... NAIVE
unsorted flour .... ATA, ATTA
unspoken .... TACIT
unstable . ASTATIC, ERRATIC
unsuitable ..... INAPT, INEPT
untamed ...... WILD, FERAL
untidy person .... SLOB
untidiness .... MESS, MUSS
until .... TILL
untrained .... RAW
unusual .... RARE, EXOTIC
unusual person or thing . ONER
unwavering .... SURE, STEADY
unwholesome ILL
unwieldly thing .... HULK
unwilling .... LOTH, LOATH,
     AVERSE
unwilling, be: archaic ... NILL
unyielding .. FIRM, ADAMANT
unyielding: naut. .... FAST

a up: comb. form .... ANO
Upanishad .... ISHA
upland plain .... WOLD
upbraid ...... CHIDE, SCOLD,
REPROACH
upon ...... EPI, ATOP, ONTO
upon: law .... SUR
Upper Nile Negro ...... MADI
Upper Nile tribesman ... MADI
Upper Silurian .... ONTARIAN
uppermost part .... TOP
upright ...... ERECT, HONEST
upright column .... STELE
upright piece .... JAMB, STUD
uprising .... REVOLT
uproar .... DIN
upward, heave: naut. ... SCEND
uraeus .... ASP
Uranus' satellite .... ARIEL
urban office-holder ... MAYOR
urchin .... IMP, TAD, GAMIN
Urfa, modern .... EDESSA
urge .... EGG, PLY, YEN,
IMPEL, PRESS
urge: Scot. .... ERT

c urial .... SHA
urticaria .... HIVES
urus .... TUR
us: Ger. .... UNS
usage .... WONT
use a divining rod ..... DOWSE
use, be of .... AVAIL
use exertions .... STRIVE
use one's efforts ..... EXERT
used up ...... ATE, DEPLETED
useful ..... UTILE, PRACTICAL
useless .... IDLE, FUTILE,
OTIOSE, INUTILE
usual .... NORMAL
Utah State flower .... SEGO
utmost .... LAST, FINAL,
GREATEST
utmost hyperbole .... ELA
utter .... SAY, SHEER,
SPEAK, STARK
utter, as greeting .... BID
utter loudly ..... VOCIFERATE
uttered ... ORAL, SAID, SPOKE
utterly .... STARK
Uz, brother of .... ARAN

V

b V-shaped piece ...... WEDGE
vacant .... IDLE, EMPTY
vacuum .... VOID
vacuum, opposite of .. PLENUM
vacuum tube .... DIODE
vagabond . VAG, HOBO, TRAMP
vague .... HAZY, LOOSE
vainglory .... PRIDE
valance, short .... PELMET
vale ..... DALE, DELL, VALLEY
Vali, mother of .... RIND
valiant ... BRAVE, STALWART
Valkyrie .... DIS, NORN
valley ..... DALE, DELL, VAIL,
VALE, GLADE
valley, deep .... COULEE
valley, Jordan .... GHOR
value .... RATE, PRIZE,
WORTH, APPRAISE
value, thing of little ... TRIFLE
valve .... COCK
vampire .... LAMIA
van .... FORE
vandal .... HUN
vanish .... EVANESCE
vanity .... PRIDE
vanity case .... ETUI
vantage, place of ... COIGN
vapid .... INANE, STALE

d vapor .... STEAM
vapor: comb. form ..... ATMO
vapor: dialect........... ROKE
vapor in air ... HAZE, MIST
Varangians .... ROS
variable .... PROTEAN
variable, most ...... PROTEAN
variable star .... MIRA, NOVA
variation, small
SHADE, NUANCE
variegated .... SHOT
variegated in color
PIED, CALICO
variety .... KIND
variety of bean
SOY, LIMA, PINTO
various: comb. form
VARI, VARIO
varnish ingredient
LAC, COPAL, RESIN
varnish, kind of
SHELLAC, SHELLACK
varnish material .... ELEMI
vase .... URN
vat ...... BAC, TUB, CISTERN
vat, beer ... GAAL, GAIL, GYLE
vat, brewer's ... KIVE, KEEVE
vat, large .... KEIR, KIER
vault .... SAFE

a vault, church .... **CRYPT**
vaulted alcove .... **APSE**
vaunt .... **BRAG, BOAST**
vector, that which turns a
.... **VERSOR**
Vedic dialect .... **PALI**
VEDIC GODS
see SPECIAL SECTION
veer ..... **SHY, TURN, SHIFT**
veer off .... **SHEER**
vegetable ... **PEA, BEAN, BEET,
KALE, OCRA, OKRA, OKRO,
CHARD, ENDIVE, TOMATO,
WOBBIE, CELTUCE**
vegetable fuel .... **PEAT**
vegetables, pod .... **PEASE**
vehicle .... **CAR, CART,
CYCLE, HANSOM**
vehicle, Am. Ind.
.... **TRAVOIS, TRAVOISE**
vehicle 4-wheeled .... **LANDAU**
vehicle, light, India ... **TONGA**
vehicle, Near East ..... **ARABA**
vehicle, Russ. .... **TROIKA**
vehicle, war .... **TANK**
veil, chalice .... **AER**
vein: Lat. .... **VENA**
b vein of body .... **CAVA**
vein, ore .... **LODE, SCRIN**
vein, ore: prov. Eng. ... **ROKE**
vein, ore beside .... **RIDER**
vein, throat .... **JUGULAR**
vellum .... **PARCHMENT**
velocity per second ..... **VELO**
velum .... **PALATE**
velvet .... **PANNE**
velvet grass .... **HOLCUS**
vend .... **SELL**
vendetta .... **FEUD**
venerable .... **OLD, HOARY**
"Venerable" monk ...... **BEDE**
venerate ..... **ESTEEM, REVERE**
veneration .... **AWE**
Venetian nobleman ..... **DOGE**
Venetian painter ..... **TITIAN**
Venetian red .... **SIENA**
Venetian resort .... **LIDO**
Venetian rose .... **SIENA**
Venetian traveler ...... **POLO**
Venezuela copper center **AROA**
Venezuela Ind. language **PUME**
vengeance goddess ...... **ARA**
Venice marble bridge ..**RIALTO**
Venice canals .... **RII**
Venice district .... **RIALTO**
ventral .... **HEMAD, HAEMAD**
venture .... **DARE**

c Venus, island of ..... **MELOS**
Venus' son .... **CUPID**
Venus, youth loved by **ADONIS**
veranda, Dutch, S. Afr. **STOEP**
veranda, Hawaii ...... **LANAI**
veranda, India .... **PYAL**
verb form .... **IS, AM, ARE,
WAS, TENSE**
verbal .... **ORAL**
verbal ending .. **ED, ER, ES, ING**
verbal noun .... **GERUND**
verbal rhythm .... **METRE**
verbally .... **ALOUD**
Verdi heroine .... **AIDA**
verily .... **YEA, AMEN**
verity .... **TRUTH**
versatile .... **MOBILE**
verse .... **LINE, STICH**
verse, Fr. .... **RONDEL**
verse, Ir. .... **RANN**
verse, pert. to kind of **IAMBIC**
version, Bible .... **ITALA**
vertebral bones **SACRA, SACRUM**
verticle line, in a ..... **APEAK**
verticle timber: naut. ... **BITT**
vertigo .... **DINUS**
very .... **SO**
very abundant ... **LUXURIANT**
very: Fr. .... **TRES**
very: Scot. .... **VERA**
d very: Span. .... **MUY**
Ve's brother .... **ODIN**
vesicle, skin .... **BLISTER**
VESSEL .. see also BOAT, SHIP,
GALLEY
vessel .... **ARK**
vessel, anat. .... **VAS, VASA**
vessel, Arab .... **DOW, DHOW**
vessel, chemical ...... **ETNA**
vessel, coasting, E. Ind.
.... **PATAMAR**
vessel, cooking .... **PAN, POT**
vessel, drinking ...... **GOURD**
vessel for liquors .. **DECANTER**
vessel, glass .... **BOCAL**
vessel, Gr. **CADUS, AMPHORA**
vessel, heating .... **ETNA**
vessel, large .... **TANK**
vessel, liquor .... **FLAGON**
vessel, Medit. .. **SETEE, MISTIC**
vessel, Rom. .... **PATERA**
vessel, sacred ...... **PIX, PYX**
vessel, sailing .... **SAIC,
SETEE, XEBEC**
vessel, shallow .... **BASIN**
vessel, supply .... **COALER**
vessel, 3-masted
.... **XEBEC, FRIGATE**
vessel, 2-masted **YAWL, ZULU**

a vessel with two handles, Gr. .... DIOTA
vessel's curved planking .. SNY
vestal .... CHASTE
vestige .... IOTA, RELIC, TRACE
vestment .. ALB, COPE, AMICE, EPHOD, STOLE
vestment, white .. ALB, AMICE
vesuvianite, brown ... EGERAN
vetch .... TARE
vetch, bitter .... ERS
vetch, India .... AKRA
vetiver, grass .... BENA
vex GALL, RILE, ROIL, HARRY
vex persistently ...... NETTLE
vex: Scot. .... FASH
vexed .... RILY
via .... PER
viands .... DIET
viands, dainty .... CATES
Viaud's pseudonym ..... LOTI
vibrate .... THRILL
vibration: music .... TREMOLO
vice .... SIN
viceroy .... VALI
Vichy Premier .... LAVAL
vicious man .... YAHOO
victim .... PREY
victorfish .... AKU
victor's crown .... LAUREL
victory, Eng. .. CRECY, CRESSY
victory trophy .... SCALP

b victuals .... FOOD
"— victus," woe to the conquered .... VAE
"—vide," "which see" .. QUAE
vie with .... EMULATE
Viennese park .... PRATER
view .... SCENE, VISTA
vigilant ...... WARY, ALERT
vigor .... PEP, VIM, VIS, ZIP, FORCE
Viking ... ERIC, OLAF, ROLLO
Viking explorer .... ERIC
vilify .... REVILE
village .. DORP, VILL, HAMLET
village, Afr. .... KRAAL
village, Java .... DESSA
village, Russ. .... MIR
village, Scot. .... REW
village, S. Afr. native .. STAD
villain .... KNAVE
villein .... CEORL
vindicate .... AVENGE
vindication .... REVENGE
vine .... IVY, BINE
vine: comb. form ..... VITI
vine, N. Z. .... AKA
vine, P. I. .... IYO

c vine, woody .. ABUTA, LIANA
"vin du —," wine of the country .... CRU
vinegar of ale .... ALEGAR
vinegar, pert. to ..... ACETIC
vinegar worm .... EEL, NEMA
vinous .... WINY
viol, ancient type ..... REBEC
viol, bass .... GAMBA
viol, Shetlands .... GUE
viola .... ALTO
violent .... HOT
violet-odored ketone .. IRONE
violin, bass .... CELLO
violin, early .. REBAB, REBEC
violin, famous ...... STRAD
violin, It. .. AMATI, CREMONA
violin, small .... KIT
violin, tenor ..... ALTO, VIOLA
violinist ...... ELMAN, YSAYE
viper .... ASP, ADDER
viper genus .... ECHIS
viper, horned ...... CERASTES
Virgil's hero .. ENEAS, AENEAS
Virgin Mary pictured mourning .... PIETA
virus-fighting substance .... ANTIVIRAL
visage .... FACE
viscous

d .... LIMY, ROPY, SIZY, SLIMY
viscous substance .. TAR, SLIME
Vishnu, incarnation, 7th RAMA
Vishnu, soul of universe VASU
Vishnu's bow .... SARAN
Vishnu's serpent ...... NAGA
visible juncture ...... SEAM
Visigoth king ALARIC, ALARIK
vision, defective ...... ANOPIA
vision, pert. to .... OPTIC
visionary ...... AIRY, IDEAL, DREAMY, UNREAL, IDEALIST
visit ...... SEE, CALL, HAUNT
visit at sea .... GAM
visit between whalers ... GAM
vison .... MINK
vital energy .... HORME
vital fluid .... SAP
vital principle .... SOUL
vitalize .... ANIMATE
vitamin ... CITRIN, ADERMIN, ANEURIN, TORULIN
vitamin B NIACIN, THIAMINE
vitamin B2 .... FLAVIN
vitamin H .... BIOTIN
vitiate ...... SPOIL, TAINT, POLLUTE, INVALIDATE
vitriol-infused earth .... SORY
vituperate .... SCOLD

a
vivacious ..... AIRY, BRIGHT
vivacity .... ELAN, LIFE
vocal flourish ...... ROULADE
vocation .... CAREER
"— voce" .... SOTTO
voice .... SAY
voice
ALTO, BASS, VOCE, TENOR
voice: It. .... VOCE
voice: Lat. .... VOX
voice, loss of ...... APHONIA
voiced .... SONANT
voiced, not .... ASONANT
voiceless .... SPIRATE
voiceless consonant ..... SURD
void .... NUL, NULL,
ABYSS, SPACE, INVALID
void, to make.ANNUL, CANCEL
void, to render: Scot. ... CASS
voided escutcheon ...... ORLE
volcanic cinder ...... SCORIA
volcanic islands, Atlantic
FAROE
volcanic rock
TUFA, TUFF, LATITE
volcanic scoria-matter
LAVA, SLAG
volcano .. ETNA, AETNA, PELEE
volcano crater .... MAAR
volcano hole .... CRATER

c
volcano, Martinique Is. .. PELEE
volcano mouth ...... CRATER
volcano, P. I. .... APO
volcano pit .... CRATER
volcano, Sicily ETNA, AETNA
volcano, W. Indies .... PELEE
volition .... WILL
volt-ampere .... WATT
Voltaire .... AROUET
Voltaire play: Fr. ...... ZAIRE
voluble .... GLIB
volume .... MO, TOME
vomiting .... EMESIS
voodoo charm .... MOJO
voodoo snake deity .... ZOMBI
vote .... BALLOT
vote into office .... ELECT
vote, right to .... FRANCHISE
vote, take a .... POLL
votes ...... AYES, NOES, YEAS
vouch for .... SPONSOR
voucher .... CHIT, NOTE
"vous —": Fr., you are .. ETES
vowel, line over ..... MACRON
vowel suppression .... ELISION
voyaging .... ASEA
vulcanite .... EBONITE
Vulcan's wife .... MAIA
vulgar .... COARSE
vulture AURA, URUBU, CONDOR

W

b
"W", old English .... WEN
wade across .... FORD
wading bird IBIS, RAIL, CRANE,
EGRET, HERON, STILT,
AVOCET, AVOSET, JAC-
ANA, FLAMINGO
wag .... WIT
wages .... PAY
Wagner heroine . ELSA, SENTA,
ISOLDE
Wagnerian role .... ERDA
wagon .. CART, DRAY, WAIN
wagon pin .... CLEVIS
wagon, Russ. .... TELEGA
wagon shaft .... THILL
wagon tongue .... NEAP, POLE
wagtail .... LARK
wahoo, fish .... PETO
wail .... KEEN, LAMENT
waist ...... CAMISA, TAILLE
waistcoat VEST, GILET, JERKIN
wait .... BIDE
waken ...... ROUSE, AROUSE

d
wale .... WELT
Wales emblem .... LEEK
walk ..... PACE, STEP, TREAD
walk affectedly .... MINCE
walk heavily .... PLOD, SLOG
walk, inability to .... ABASIA
walk lamely .... LIMP
walk stiffly .... STALK
walk, tree-lined .... ALAMEDA
walking stick ... CANE, STILT
wall, arena .... SPINA
wall around fortified place
RAMPART
wall, divided by .... SEPTATE
wall: Fr. .... MUR
wall material .... COB
wall, of a .... MURAL
wall paneling .... WAINSCOT
wall piece TEMPLET, TEMPLATE
wall section .... DADO, PANEL
wall, squeeze against .. MURE
walls .... SEPTA
wallaba tree, Brazil ..... APA
walled city, Nigeria ..... KANO

a wallflower .... KEIRI
wallop .... LAM
wallow .... WELTER
walrus .... MORSE
wampum PEAG,SEWAN,SEAWAN
wan ... ASHY, PALE, ASHEN
wand .... BATON
wander .. ERR, HAAK, ROAM,
ROVE, RAMBLE, DIGRESS
wander idly .... GAD
wanderer .... VAG, NOMAD
"Wandering Jew" author .. SUE
wane .... EBB
want .... LACK, NEED, DESIRE
wapiti .... ELK
war-club, medieval ..... MACE
war correspondent
PYLE, BALDWIN
war cry, ancient Gr. .... ALALA
war god .... ARES, MARS
war god, Babyl. ... IRA, IRRA
war god, Norse TY, TYR, TYRR
war god, Teut. .... ER
war goddess, Gr. ...... ENYO
war horse .... CHARGER
war, religious ...... CRUSADE
war, Russ.-Eng. ...... CRIMEA
war vessel .... CRUISER
warble .. SING, TRILL, YODEL
b ward off .... FEND, AVERT,
PARRY, REPEL, STAVE
ward politician ...... HEELER
warden, fire .... RANGER
warehouse .... DEPOT
warehouse room .... LOFT
warm .... CALID, TEPID
warning of danger: biol.
SEMATIC
warning signal .... SIREN
warning system, attack
DEW, BMEWS
warp yarn .... ABB
warrant, from monarch BERAT
warrior, Samoa .... TOA
warship, sailing ..... FRIGATE
wary .... CAGY
was not: dialect .... NAS
wash .... LAVE
wash leather .... LOSH
wash out .... ELUTE
washings: chem. ..... ELUATE
Washington Irving character RIP
wasp .... HORNET
wasps, the .... VESPA
waste .... LOSS
waste allowance .... TRET
waste away GNAW, ATROPHY
waste fiber .... NOIL
waste land .... MOOR
waste matter .... DROSS
waste silk ..... KNUB, FRISON

c waste time .... IDLE
wastes, growing in .. RUDERAL
watch .... SEE, GLOM
watch chain .... FOB
watchdog, Hel's .... GARM
watchful .... ALERT
watchful guardian .... ARGUS
watchful, name meaning IRA
watchman, alert ...... ARGUS
watchman, night .... SERENO
watchtower .... MIRADOR
water ... SPRINKLE, IRRIGATE
water arum .... CALLA
water chestnut, Chin. ... LING
water cock .... KORA
water, covered by .... AWASH
water: Fr. .... EAU, EAUX
water: Lat. .... AQUA
water lily .... LOTUS
water passage SLUICE, STRAIT
water pipe
HOOKA, HOOKAH, NARGILE
water raising device
TABUT, TABOOT
water reservoir, natural
CENOTE
water scorpion genus ... NEPA
water, seek .... DOUSE
water, sound of ...... PLASH
water: Sp. .... AQUA
d water spirit
ARIEL, SPRITE, UNDINE
water sprite ..... NIX, NIXIE
water sprite: Gaelic .. KELPIE
water surface .... RYME
water vessel, India
LOTA, LOTO, LOTAH
water wheel
NORIA, DANAIDE, TURBINE
water wheel, Persian .. NORIA
water's surface: naut. ... RYME
watercourse ... LADE, BROOK,
CANAL, RIVER, STREAM
watered apearance .... MOIRE
watered silk .... MOIRE
waterfall, Scot. LIN, LYN, LINN
watering place .. SPA, BADEN
waterproof canvas ..... TARP
waterskin .... MATARA
watertight, make CALK, CAULK
waterway .... BAYOU, CANAL
waterway, narrow .... STRAIT
watery .... SEROUS
watery: comb. form .... SERO
wattle tree .... BOREE
wattled honeyeater
IAO, MANUAO
wave .... FLY, SEA
wave-crest comb. ...... COOM
wave: Fr. .... ONDE
wave, huge .... SEA

a
white acid, pert. to .. **TROPIC**
white alkaline .... **SODA**
white ant, P. I. ... **ANAI, ANAY**
white, bitter compound **LININ**
white: comb. form ..... **ALBO**
"White Elephant" land .. **SIAM**
white ermine **LASSET, MINIVER**
white-flecked .... **ROAN**
White Friar ..... **CARMELITE**
white: Ir. .... **BAWN**
white man: P. I. ... **CACHILA**
white matter, brain .... **ALBA**
white oak .... **ROBLE**
white poplar .... **ABELE**
white spruce ...... **EPINETTE**
white with age .... **HOAR**
whitefish .... **CISCO**
whiten .... **ETIOLATE**
whitish .... **HOARY**
whitlow grass .... **DRABA**
Whittier heroine ...... **MAUD**
whiz ..... **PIRR, WHIR, ZIZZ**
whoa .... **HOLLA**
whole amount .... **GROSS**
whole: comb. form ..... **TOTO**
wholesome .... **SALUTARY**
wholly .... **ALL**
wicked .... **EVIL**
wicker basket .... **CESTA,
KIPSY, PANNIER**

b
wicker basket, Guiana **PEGALL**
wickerwork .... **RATAN**
wickerwork hut .... **JACAL**
wicket, croquet .... **HOOP**
wide-mouthed vessel
EWER, OLLA
widgeon .... **SMEE**
widgeon genus ...... **MARECA**
widow .... **RELICT**
widow in cards .... **SKAT**
widow monkey .... **TITI**
widow's bit or coin .... **MITE**
widow's third: Scot. .... **TERCE**
wield .... **PLY, USE**
wife, Moroccan ruler's **SHERIFA**
wife ... **FEME, FRAU, FEMME**
wife's property .... **DOS**
wig .... **PERUKE**
wigwam .. **TIPI, TEPEE, TEEPEE**
wild .... **FERAL, SAVAGE**
wild animals, collection of
ZOO, MENAGERIE
wild animal's trail
SLOT, SPUR, SPOOR
wild apple ... **CRAB, DOUCIN**
wild ass, Afr. ...... **QUAGGA**
wild ass, Asia ...... **ONAGER**
wild boar genus .... **SUS**
wild buffalo, India
ARNA, ARNI, ARNEE

c
wild buffalo, Malay ... **GAUR,
SLADANG, SALADANG,
SELADANG**
wild cat, Siberia, Tibet, steppes
MANUL
wild cattle, India **GAUR, GOUR**
wild cry .... **EVOE**
wild dog .... **DHOLE**
wild dog genus .... **THOS**
wild dog, Japan ...... **TANATE**
"Wild Duck" author .... **IBSEN**
wild garlic .... **MOLY**
wild ginger .... **ASARUM**
wild hog .... **BOAR**
wild honeybee, E. Ind. **DINGAR**
wild horse of Tartary **TARPAN**
wild lime .... **COLIMA**
wild olive tree ..... **OLEASTER**
wild ox .... **ANOA**
wild ox, Malay. ..... **BANTENG**
wild plum .... **SLOE**
wild plum, Calif. ..... **ISLAY**
wild sheep, Asia
RASSE, ARGALI
wild sheep, horned . **MOUFLON**
wild sheep, India ... **SHA, SNA,
URIAL, NAHOOR, OORIAL**
wild sheep, N. Afr.
ARUI, UDAD, AOUDAD
wild sheep, Tibet .... **SHA**

d
SNA, BHARAL, NAHOOR
wild turnip .... **NAVEW**
wild vanilla .... **LIATRIS**
wildcat .... **BALU, LYNX**
wildcat, Afr. & India .. **CHAUS**
wildcat, S. Am. ...... **EYRA**
wildcat, Sumatra ...... **BALU**
wildebeest .... **GNU**
wile .... **ART**
will addition .... **CODICIL**
will, one inheriting from
DEVISEE
will, one making .... **DEVISOR**
will power, loss of .... **ABULIA**
William: Ir. .... **LIAM**
William I, half brother of **ODO**
William the Conqueror's
daughter .... **ADELA**
willingly .... **LIEF**
willow .... **ITEA, OSIER**
willow, Europ. .... **SALLOW**
willow genus, Virginia ... **ITEA**
Wilson's thrush .... **VEERY**
wilt .... **FADE, DROOP**
wily .... **FOXY**
wimple .... **GORGET**
win .... **GAIN**
winch .... **WHIN**
wind .... **GALE**
wind, Adriatic .... **BORA**

Wind

a wind, Andes ... **PUNA, PUNO**
wind, Austral. .... **BUSTER**
wind, away from .... **ALEE**
wind, cold Malta ... **GREGALE**
wind, cold Medit. .... **MISTRAL**
wind, cold Swiss Alps **BISE, BIZE**
wind: comb. form .... **ANEMO**
wind-deposited loam ... **LOESS**
wind, dry, from Sahara .. **LESTE**
wind, east .... **EURUS**
wind god, Babyl.
    ADAD, ADDA, ADDU
wind god, Hindu ...... **VAYU**
wind god, pert. to
    EOLIAN, AEOLIAN
wind, hot, dry ...... **KAMSIN,**
SIMOOM, SIMOON, SIROCCO
wind, hot, Medit. .... **SOLANO**
wind indicator .. **SOCK, VANE**
wind instrument
HORN, OBOE, PIPE, BUGLE
wind, Levant .... **ETESIAN**
wind, Madeira .... **LESTE**
wind, Medit. .... **ETESIAN**
wind, Medit., poet. ..... **SIROC**
wind, Mesop. .... **SHAMAL**
wind, north .... **BOREAS**
wind off Faroe Islands .... **OE**
wind, Peru Andes **PUNA, PUNO**
wind, sand-laden
SAMIEL, SIMOOM, SIMOON
b wind, Sahara .... **LESTE**
wind, South .. **NOTUS, AUSTER**
wind, southeast .... **EURUS**
wind, southwest .... **AFER**
wind, Trieste, cold ..... **BORA**
wind, warm dry **FOHN, FOEHN**
wind, west .... **AFER**
winds, south, Peru ..... **SURES**
windborne .... **AEOLIAN**
windflower .... **ANEMONE**
windlass .... **CAPSTAN**
windmill sail .... **AWE**
window lead .... **CAME**
window ledge .... **SILL**
window part .... **SASH**
window, semipolygonal .. **ORIEL**
window setter ...... **GLAZIER**
windrow .... **SWATH**
windstorm
OE, BURAN, TORNADO
windstorm, Asia **BURA, BURAN**
wine ...... **VIN, HOCK, PORT,**
SACK, VINO, MEDOC, TO-
KAY, CLARET, MALAGA,
MUSCAT, SHERRY, MO-
SELLE
wine, Am. .... **CATAWBA**
wine, ancient .... **MASSIC**
wine cask ...... **TUN, BUTT**
wine city, It. .... **ASTI**

c wine cup .... **AMA**
wine, delicacy of: Fr. ... **SEVE**
wine disorder .... **CASSE**
wine district, Calif. .... **NAPA**
wine drink .... **NEGUS**
wine, dry .... **SEC, BRUT**
wine, golden .... **BUAL**
wine, heavy .... **TOKAY**
wine, honey and ...... **MULSE**
wine, Madeira .... **BUAL**
wine measure, Trieste
    ORNA, ORNE
wine merchant .... **VINTNER**
wine, new .... **MUST**
wine pitcher, Gr. .... **OLPE**
wine, red **PORT, TINTA, CLARET**
wine, sweet .... **MUSCAT**
wine, sweet: Fr. ..... **MASDEU**
wine, to make .... **VINT**
wine vessel ...... **AMA, OLPE,**
AMULA, CHALICE
wine, white .... **HOCK,**
SHERRY, SAUTERNE
wineberry, N. Z. ..... **MAKO**
wing .... **ALA, PENNA,**
PINNA, PINION
wing, bastard .... **ALULA**
wing, beetle **TEGMAN,**
TEGMINA, TEGUMEN
wing: Fr. .... **AILE**
d wing-footed animal .. **ALIPED**
winglike .... **ALAR**
wing-like part ..... **ALA, ALAE**
wing movement .... **FLAP**
wing tip, pert. to ... **ALULAR**
wings .... **ALAE**
wings, divested of
DEALATA, DEALATED
wings, having .. **ALAR, ALATE**
wings: her. .... **VOL, AILE**
winged figure, Gr.
IDOLON, IDOLUM, EIDOLON
winged fruit, indehiscent
    SAMARA
winged god ..... **EROS, CUPID**
winged seed .... **SAMARA**
winged victory .... **NIKE**
wingless .... **APTERAL**
wingless invertebrates **APTERA**
wink rapidly .... **BAT**
winning at bridge ...... **SLAM**
winnow .... **FAN**
winter, pert. to .... **BRUMAL,**
HIEMAL, HYEMAL, HIBERNAL
winter squash ...... **CUSHAW**
wipe out .... **ERASE**
wire measure .... **MIL**
wire service .... **AP, UP,**
INS, UPI, REUTERS

182

a wires, cross .... **RETICLE**
Wisconsin college ...... **RIPON**
wisdom ...... **LORE, GNOSIS**
wisdom god of: Babyl.
NABU, NEBO
wisdom goddess of: Gr.
ATHENA, PALLAS
wisdom, goddess of: Rom.
MINERVA
wise .... **SAGE, SENSIBLE**
wise adviser .... **MENTOR**
wise man
SAGE, SOLON, NESTOR
Wise Men .... **MAGI, GASPAR,**
MELCHIOR, BALTHASAR
wise men, A-S .... **WITAN**
wisecrack .. **GAG, JOKE, QUIP**
wish for ..... **YEARN, DESIRE**
wish undone .... **RUE**
wisp of hair .... **TATE**
wit .... **WAG, HUMOR**
wit: Sp. .... **SAL**
witless chatter .... **GAB**
witch ... **HAG, HECAT, LAMIA,**
HECATE, HECCAT, HEKATE
witch city .... **SALEM**
witch doctor .... **GOOFER**
witch in "Faerie Queene"
DUESSA
witchcraft .... **OBEAH**
with: Fr. .... **AVEC**
b with: Ger. .... **MIT**
with joy .... **FAIN**
with: prefix .... **SYN**
withdraw .. **RECEDE, REMOVE,**
RETIRE, SECEDE, RETRACT
wither .... **FADE**
withered .... **SERE**
within ...... **INTO, INTERIOR**
within: comb. form
ESO, ENDO, ENSO, ENTO
within: prefix .... **ENDO**
without: comb. form ..... **ECT**
without energy .... **ATONY**
without: Fr. .... **SANS**
without: Ger. .... **OHNE**
without: Lat. .... **SINE**
without: poetic .... **SANS**
without teeth, claws, lion
MORNE
without veins ...... **AVENOUS**
witness .... **SEE**
witness, law . **TESTE, DEPONENT**
witness, to bear ...... **ATTEST**
witty remark ..... **MOT, QUIP**
witty reply .... **REPARTEE**
wobble .... **TEETER**
Woden .... **ODIN**
woe .... **MISERY**
woe is me .... **ALAS**

c wolf, gray .... **LOBO**
wolf, Odin's ...... **GERE, GERI**
wolf, timber .... **LOBO**
wolfhound .... **ALAN**
wolfish .... **LUPINE**
wolframite .... **CAL**
wolverine genus .... **GULO**
woman diplomat, first U.S.
OWEN
woman: Gr. .... **GYNE**
woman, ill-tempered
SHREW, VIRAGO
woman personified, Ir.
EMER, EIMER
woman's name (3 letters) **ADA,**
AMY, ANN, EVA, EVE, FAY,
IDA, INA, MAE, MAY, NAN,
RAE, UNA, ZOE, (4 let-
ters) AFRA, ALIX, ALMA,
ALYS, ANNA, ANNE, AVIS,
BONA, CARA, CLOE, CORA,
DORA, EDNA, ELLA, ELSA,
EMMA, ENID, ERMA, ETTA,
INEZ, JANE, JEAN, JOAN,
JUNE, LEAH, LIDA, LILA,
LOIS, LORA, LUCY, MARY,
MAUD, MYRA, NONA,
NORA, OLGA, RITA, ROSA,
ROSE, RUTH, SARA, VERA,
VIDA, (5 letters) ALICE,
ANITA, CLARE, DELIA,
d **DIANA, ELAIN, ELSIE,**
ERICA, FAITH, FLORA,
GRACE, IRENE, SARAH,
SELMA, (6 letters) AL-
THEA, BERTHA, DAPHNE,
EDWINA, ELAINE, EMILIA,
PHOEBE, (7 letters) ABI-
GAIL, CELESTE, LAVINIA
woman's nickname **CAT, DEB,**
HAT, KIT, LOU, MAB, MAG,
MEG, SAL, SUE, ABBY,
ADDY, BESS, BETH, CARO,
DORA, GAIL, JILL, JOSY,
JUDY, JULE, KATE, KATY,
LINA, LISA, LULU, MART,
MIMI, MINA, MOLL, NELL,
NINA, ROXY, SUSY, TAVE,
TAVY, TESS, TINA, XINA,
SALLY, SALLIE
Wonderland girl ...... **ALICE**
wont .... **HABIT**
wood .... **ALOE**
wood apple, Ind. .... **BEL**
wood, black .... **EBONY**
wood, flexible .... **EDDER**
wood, fragrant . **ALOES, CEDAR**
wood: comb. form ...... **XYLO**
wood: Fr. .... **BOIS**
wood gum .... **XYLAN**

183

Wood

a wood, light .... **BALSA**
wood, long piece .... **POLE**
wood: obsolete .... **WOLD**
wood, piece of ...... **SLAT, SPRAG, BILLET**
wood pussy .... **SKUNK**
wood robin, N. Z. ...... **MIRO**
wood sorrel .... **OCA, OKA**
wood, timber: P. I. ..... **CAHUY**
woodchuck .... **MARMOT**
woodchuck: dialect **MOONACK**
wooden .... **TREEN**
wooden brick .... **DOOK**
wooden collar, convict's **CANG**
wooden pail .... **SOE**
wooden peg .... **SKEG**
wooden shoe **SABOT, PATTEN**
woodland deity **FAUN, SATYR**
woodland god .... **PAN**
woodpecker genus **JYNX, YUNX**
woodpecker, green **HICKWALL**
woodpecker group ...... **PICI**
woodpecker, red-bellied . **CHAB**
woodpecker, small ... **PICULE**
woodpeckers, of ...... **PICINE**
woodwind
OBOE, BASSOON, CLARINET
woodworking tool ..... **SAPPER**
woodworm .... **TERMITE**
woody fiber .... **BAST**
b woody hill .... **HOLT**
woody plant .... **TREE**
woof .... **WEFT**
wool ...... **ANGORA, MERINO**
wool cluster .... **NEP**
wool, coarse .... **GARE**
wool fat . **LANOLIN, LANOLINE**
wool: Lat. .... **LANA**
wool measure .... **HEER**
wool package .... **FADGE**
wool, reclaimed .... **MUNGO**
woolen cloth .... **ETAMINE**
woolen cloth, coarse, twilled
KERSEY
woolen fabric .... **FRISCA**
woolen thread .... **YARN**
woolly ...... **LANATE, LANOSE**
woolly pyrol .... **URD**
word by word .... **LITERAL**
word expressing action .. **VERB**
word meanings, pert. to
SEMANTIC
word of affirmation .... **AMEN**
word of choice .... **OR**
word of God .... **LOGOS**
word of honor, promise
PAROL, PAROLE
word of mouth, by
PAROL, PAROLE
word of ratification .... **AMEN**
word, scrambled ... **ANAGRAM**

c work
MOIL, TOIL, CHARE, LABOR
WORK ..see also **COMPOSITION**
work aimlessly .... **POTTER**
work at steadily .... **PLY**
work hard
PEG, MOIL, TOIL, SLAVE
work, in terms of heat **ERGON**
work, musical
OPUS, OPERA, ORATORIO
work persistently .... **PEG**
work, piece of .... **JOB, STINT**
work: Sp. .... **OBRA**
work unit .... **ERG, ERGON**
workbasket .... **CABA, CABAS**
worker .... **HAND, OPERANT, OPERATOR**
worker ant .... **ERGATE**
worker: comb. form .. **ERGATE**
worker's group, worldwide .. **ILO**
worker's union, Soviet .. **ARTEL**
workhorse: Scot .... **AVER**
working boat, Chesapeake Bay
FLATTIE
workman, mine .... **CAGER**
workman, S. Afr. ...... **VOLK**
workshop .... **ATELIER**
world: Hindu myth .... **LOKA**
world, holder of .... **ATLAS**
World War I battle site
MONS, MARNE
d World War I group . **AEF, AMEX**
World War II area ...... **ETO**
worm ... **ESS, TINEA, ANNELID**
worm, African .... **LOA**
worm, bait .... **LURG**
worm, eye-infesting ...... **LOA**
worm, S-shaped .... **ESS**
worm track, fossil .. **NEREITE**
worn, as rope .... **MAGGED**
worn by friction .... **ATTRITE**
worn out .... **EFFETE**
worn-out horse
NAG, HACK, PLUG
worry .... **RUX, CARE, CARK, FRET, STEW**
worship .... **ADORE**
worship, form of ...... **RITUAL**
worship, house of .... **BETHEL**
worship, object of .... **IDOL**
worship of saints ...... **DULIA**
worship, place of
ALTAR, TEMPLE
worthless **BAD, RACA, TRASHY**
worthless bit from table ... **ORT**
worthless rock .... **GANGUE**
wound: Her. .... **VULN**
wound mark .... **SCAR**
wrangle .... **HAGGLE**
wrap .... **SWATHE, SWADDLE**

a

wrapping	PLIOFILM
wrath	IRE
wrathful	IRATE
wreath	CHAPLET
wreath: Her.	TORSE
wreathe	COIL, WIND
wrest	REND
wrestle	TUSSLE
wrestling throw	HIPE, HYPE
wriggling	EELY
wrinkle	RUCK, RUGA, SEAM, RUGAE, RIMPLE
wrinkled	RUGATE, RUGOSE
wrist	CARPUS
wrists	CARPI
wrist bone	CARPAL
wrist guard	BRACER
writ of execution	ELEGIT
writ, sheriff's	VENIRE
writ to arrest	CAPIAS

c

write	PEN, SCRIVE
write comments	POSTIL
write music	NOTATE
writer	DITER, SCRIBE
writer, Ger.	MANN
writing instrument	PEN
writing on the wall	MENE, TEKEL
writing paper size	CAP
writing table	ESCRITOIRE
writing well, art of	RHETORIC
wrong	OUT, EVIL, AMISS
wrong: Lat.	MALA, MALUM
wrong, legal	TORT
wrong: prefix	MIS
wrongdoing	EVIL
wrongdoing, serious	CRIME
wryneck	LOXIA
Wyoming peak, highest	GANNETT

Y

b

Y, In Middle Eng.	YOK, YOGH
Y's	WIES
yacht	SAIL
yacht pennant	BURGEE
Yale	ELI
yam, Hawaii	HOI
yam, white	UBE, UBI, UVE, UVI
Yang, opposite of	YIN
Yangtze tributary	HAN
Yap Island stone money	FEI
yarn	GARN, TALE, CREWEL
yarn count	TYPP
yarn for warp	ABB
yarn measure	LEA, HEER
yarn projection	KNAP, KNOP
yarn, quantity of	SKEIN
Yarura language	PUME
yataghan	BALAS
yaupon holly	CASSENA
yawn	GAPE
yawn: obs.	GANE
yearly	ETESIAN
yearly church payment	ANNAT
yearn	ACHE, LONG
year's crops	ANNONA
yeast	BEES
yeast, brewer's	BARM
yeast, Jap.	KOJI
yeast, wild	ANAMITE
yell: Scot.	GOWL
yellow	AMBER, OCHER, OCHRE, MELINE, CITRINE
yellow-brown	TOPAZ
yellow bugle	IVA

d

yellow dye plant	AMIL
yellow fish	ORF, ORFE
yellow ide	ORF, ORFE
yellow iris	SEDGE
yellow ocher	SIL
yellow pigment	SIL
yellow wood	AVODIRE
yellowhammer, Eur.	AMMER
yellowish	SALLOW
yelp	KIYI, YOUP
Yemenite	ARAB
Yemen's capital	SANA
yes: Sp.	SI
yesterday: Fr.	HIER
yesterday, pert. to	HESTERNAL
yet	E'EN, STILL
yew, pert. to	TAXINE
yield	CEDE, ACCEDE, CONCEDE
Yogi	SWAMI
yoke bar, S. Afr.	SKEY
yokel	OAF, HICK, RUBE
yolk of egg	VITELLUS
yolky	EGGY
yon	THERE
yorker: cricket	TICE
Yorkshire city	LEEDS
Yorkshire river	URE, OUSE
you: It.	TU
you: Sp.	TE
young animal	CUB, PUP, COLT, WHELP
young female hog	GILT
young girl of Burma	MIMA
young hog	SHOAT, SHOTE
young kangaroo	JOEY

Young

a
young man, handsome **ADONIS**
young ox: Eng. .... **STOT**
young plant .... **SET**
young rowdy ..... **HOODLUM**
youngest son .... **CADET**
youngster
  KID, TAD, TOT, SHAVER
youth .... **LAD**
youth .... **GOSSOON**
youth shelter .... **HOSTEL**

Z

b
zeal .... **ELAN, ARDOR**
zealot .... **BIGOT**
zealous .... **AVID**
Zebedee, son of **JOHN, JAMES**
zebra, young .... **COLT**
zebrawood .... **ARAROBA**
zebu-yak hybrid **ZO, ZOH, ZOBO**
zenith .... **TOP, ACME, PEAK**
zenith, opposite of .... **NADIR**
Zeno's follower .... **STOIC**
zeppelin .... **BLIMP**
Zeppelin .... **GRAF**
zero .... **CIPHER**
zest .... **TANG**
zetetic .... **SEEKER**
Zeus, epithet of ..... **AMMON**
Zeus, maiden loved by
  IO, LEDA, EUROPA
Zeus, mother of .... **RHEA**
Zeus, old Doric name for **ZAN**
Zeus' daughter
  ATE, HEBE, IRENE
Zeus' sister .... **HERA**

c
youthful: zool. .... **NEANIC**
Yucatan Indian .... **MAYA**
yucca-like plant .... **SOTOL**
Yugoslav .... **SERB, CROAT**
Yugoslav leader .... **TITO**
Yum-Yum's friend
  KOKO, NANKIPOO
Yutang .... **LIN**

d
Zeus' son ..... **ARES, ARCAS,
  MINOS, APOLLO**
Zeus' wife ..... **HERA, METIS**
Zilpah's son ..... **GAD, ASHER**
zinc in slabs .... **SPELTER**
zinc ingot .... **SPELTER**
Zionist group .... **ITO**
zipper .... **TALON**
zodiac sign ...... **LEO, ARIES,
  LIBRA, VIRGO, CANCER,
  PISCES, TAURUS, SCORPIO**
Zola novel .... **NANA**
zone .... **AREA**
zone: Lat. .... **ZONA**
zoophyte, marine ...... **CORAL**
Zophah, son of .... **BEERA**
Zoroastrian .. **PARSI, PARSEE**
Zoroastrian bible .... **AVESTA**
zounds .... **OONS**
Zulu headman ..... **INDUNA**
Zulu language .... **BANTU**

SPECIAL SECTION

READY REFERENCE WORD LISTS

In one compact section, here are lists of the most useful and widely used word categories. Some of these words, having certain customary definitions, are also listed in the DEFINITIONS section of this book, but these word lists will be of greatest help when you are confronted with GENERALIZED definitions such as "Roman goddess," "South American Indian," "Heraldic term," "African tribe," "U.S. author," or "Ice hockey great."

In most cases, the words in each separate listing are placed according to the number of letters in the words. This is a tremendous advantage to puzzle solvers, who are more concerned with the length of a word than with its alphabetical placement. However, in some lists of people's names (U.S. Authors, Award-Winning Ice Hockey Players, and the like) you may be looking for either the first name or the last name, but it was impossible to list both ways, so they are listed alphabetically by the last name.

This section is intended as a handy reference for crossword puzzle solvers, and contains words and names often found in crosswords. Therefore, some of the lists are complete (such as Chemical Elements), but many are not (Some Names from the Baseball Hall of Fame, for example).

The listings for this Special Section are shown on the Table of Contents.

MEASURES

AREA MEASURES

AR, ARE, ACRE, DECARE (10 ARES), CENTIAR, CENTIARE

Annam .... MAU, QUO, SAO
Bengal .... BEGA
Czechoslovakia ... LAN, MIRA
Dutch E. Ind. .... BOUW
England, Old .... HYDE
Japan .... BU, SE, TAN
Norway .... MAL, MAAL
Paraguay .... LINO
Poland .... MORG
Rome, Ancient ...... CLIMA, CLIMATA
Serbia .... RIF, RALO
Shetlands, Orkney .... URE
Siam .... RAI, NGAN
Sweden .... MORGEN

DRY MEASURES

PECK, PINT, STERE

Algeria .... TARRI
Austria .... MUTH
Borneo .... GANTANG
Brazil .... MOIO
Burma .... TENG
Calcutta ...... KUNK, RAIK
Channel Is. .... CABOT
China .... HO, HU
Dutch .... KOP, ZAK
Egypt ...... KADA, KILAH
Hebrew ..... CAB, KAB, KOR, EPHA, OMER, SEAH, EPHAH
Italy .... SALM, SALMA
Japan .... SHO
Morocco .... SAHH
Netherlands ...... KOP, ZAK
Portugal .... MEIO, PIPA
Russia .... LOF
Tangier .... MUDD
Tunis ..... SAA, SAAH, UEBA

LENGTH, DISTANCE MEASURES

ELL, ROD, FOOT, HAND, INCH, MILE, YARD, METER, METRE, PERCH, MICRON, FURLONG

Annam .... LY, GON, NGU
Brazil .... PE
Calcutta .... DHAN, JAOB
China ...... HU, LI, PU, TU, CH'IH, TCHI, TSUN
Czechoslovakia .. SAH, LATRO
Denmark FOD, MIL, MUL, ALEN
Domin. Repub. .... ONA
Dutch .... DUIM, VOET
D. E. Indies .... DEPA
Egypt .. PIC, PIK, KHET, THEB
Eritrea .... CUBI
Estonia .... LIIN, SULD
France .... AUNE
Greece .. PIC, PIK, BEMA, PIKI, POUS, ACAENA
Hebrew .... EZBA
Iceland .... FET, ALIN, LINA
India .. GAZ, GEZ, GUZ, JOW, KOS, JAOB, KOSS
Italy .... CANNA
Japan .. BU, JO, RI (marine), CHO, DJO, KEN, RIN, HIRO

Java .... PAAL
Libya .... DRA, PIK, DRAH
Malabar .... ADY
Malacca .... ASTA
Netherlands ... DUIM, VOET
Norway ...... FOT, ALEN
Persia ...... GAZ, GEZ, GUZ, ZAR, ZER
Poland .... MILA, PRET
Prussia .... RUTE
Rangoon . LAN, DAIN, TAUN
Rome, ancient .... ACTUS, .. GRADUS, STADIA, STADIUM
Russia .... FUT, VERST
Siam .... WA, KUP, NIU, SEN, SOK, WAH, NIOU, SAWK
Spain .... BARA, CODO, DEDO, VARA
Sweden ...... FOT, REF, FAMN
Switzerland .... TOISE
Tripoli .... DRA, DRAA
Turkey .... PIC, PIK, KHAT, ZIRA

(liquid measures on page 189)

WEIGHTS

KIP, TON, GRAM, KILO, CARAT, GRAIN, OUNCE, CENTRAL
Abyssinia .... KASM, NATR, OKET, ALADA, NETER
Annam .... BINH
Arabia .... KELA
Austria .... UNZE
Bavaria .... GRAN
Brazil .... ONCA
Bulgaria .... OKA, OKE
Burma ..... VIS, KYAT, VISS
Calcutta .. PANK, PAWA, RAIK
China ... LI, FEN, HAO, KIN, SSU, TAN, YIN, TAEL
Columbia .... SACO
Denmark ES, ORT, VOG, ESER, PUND
Dutch .... ONS, LOOD
Dutch E. Ind ...... TJI, HOEN, TALI, WANG
Egypt ... KAT, KET, OKA, OKE, HEML, KHAR, OHIA, OKIEH
England .... STONE
Estonia .... NAEL, PUUD
Ethiopia .... See Abyssinia
France .... GROS
Germany .... LOT, LOTE, LOTH, STEIN
Greece .... MNA, MINA, OBOLE, OBOLUS
Guinea .... AKEY, PISO, UZAN, SERON

Hebrew .... BEKA, REBA
India .... SER, BHAR, PALA, RATI, TOLA, VISS, RATTI
Italian .... SALM, SALMA
Japan ...... KIN, SHI, MORIN
Malay .... CHEE
Malta .... SALM, SALMA
Mexico ...... LIBRA, ONZA
Mongolia .... LAN
Morocco .... ARTEL
Moslem .... ROTL
Netherlands ...... ONS, LOOD
Norway .... PUND
ORIENT .... MANN, ROTL, TAEL, ARTAL
Palestine ...... ROTLA, ZUZA
Persia .... SER
Poland .... LUT
Portugal GRAO, ONCA, LIBRA
Rangoon .... RUAY
Rome, Ancient .... AS, BES, LIBRA, SOLIDUS
Russia .... LAN, PUD, DOLA, POOD, POUD
Siam .... PAI, KLAM, KLOM, TICAL
Shetland Island .. URE (ounce)
Spain .... ONZA
Sweden ASS, ORT, STEN, UNTZ
Turkey ..... OCK, OKA, OKE, KILE, OCHA, KERAT

LIQUID MEASURES

TUN, DRAM, GILL, PINT, MINIM
Abyssinia ...... CUBA, KUBA
Annam .... TAO
Arabia .... SAA
Austria .... FASS
Brazil .... PIPA
Burma .... BYEE, SEIT
China ...... KO, QUEI, SHIH
Cyprus .... CASS
Dutch .. (old) AAM, AUM, KAN
Egypt .... HIN
England .... PIN, CRAN
Ethiopia .... see ABYSSINIA
Germany ...... AAM, EIMER
Hebrew .... HIN

Hungary .... AKO
Japan .... KOKU, SHO
Malaya .... PAU
Netherlands . AAM, AUM, KAN
Portugal .... BOTA, PIPA
Rangoon .... BYEE, SEIT
Rome, Ancient .... URNA
Russia ... STOF, STOFF, STOOF
Somaliland .... CABA
Spain .... COPA
Sweden .... AM, AMAR, KAPP
Switzerland ..... IMMI, SAUM
Tangier .... KULA
Trieste .... ORNA, ORNE
Yugoslavia .... AKOV

189

COINS, MONEY

Abyssinia ..... BESA, GIRSH,
TALARI
Afghanistan .... AMANIA
Albania .... LEK
Anglo-Saxon .... ORA, SCEAT
Annam .... QUAN
Austria .... DUCAT
Biblical .. BEKA, MITE (small),
SHEKEL, TALENT
Brazil .... REI
Bulgaria ... LEV, LEW, DINAR
Chile .... COLON
China .. LI, CASH, TAEL, TIAO,
YUAN, PU (early)
Colombia .... REAL
Costa Rica .... COLON
Czechoslovakia .... DUCAT,
KRONE (plural, KRONEN)
Denmark .... ORA, ORE, ORAS,
KRONE (plural, KRONER)
Dutch OORD, DALER, GULDEN,
STIVER
D. E. Indies ..... BONK, DUIT
Egypt .... GIRSH
England .... ORA, RIAL (gold),
RYAL, RYEL, GROAT,
PENCE, FLORIN, GUINEA
Equador .... SUCRE
Ethiopia ...... see ABYSSINIA
Europe .... (old) GROS, DUCAT
France .. ECU (old), SOL, SOU,
AGNEL (old), FRANC,
LIARD (old), LOUIS, OBOLE,
BESANT or BEZANT (old).
Genoa .... JANE (old)
Germany ..... MARK, KRONE
(former), TALER, THALER
Ger. E. Africa .... PESA
Greece .. OBOL or OBOLI (old),
STATER (old)
Hungary ...... GARA, PENGO
Iceland .... AURAR,
EYRIR, KRONA
India.LAC, PIE, ANNA, DAWM,
FELS, HOON, LAKH, PICE
(small bronze), TARA,
MOHUR (old), RUPEE
Iran .... see PERSIA
Iraq .... DINAR
Ireland .... RAP (old)

Italy .... LIRA, LIRE, SOLDO,
TESTER, TESTON, TESTONE,
TESTOON
Japan .... BU, RIN,
SEN, YEN, OBAN
Latvia .... LAT, LATU
Lithuania .. LIT, LITAI, LITAS
Macao .... AVO
Malaya TRA (tin, pewter), TRAH
Mexico ..... PESO, CENTAVO
Montenegro .... PARA
Morocco .... OKIA, RIAL
Nepal .... MOHAR
Netherlands .... DAALDER
Norway .... ORE,
KRONE (KRONER)
Oman .... GAJ, GAZ,
GOZ, GHAZI
Persia.PUL, KRAN, POUL, RIAL
DARIC, DINAR, MOHUR
(old), TOMAN, STATER
Peru .... SOL, DINERO
Poland .... DUCAT
Portugal ..... JOE, REI, PECA,
DOBRA (former)
Rome, ancient . SEMIS, DINDER
Roman .... AS, AES, ASSES,
SOLIDUS
Rumania ..... LEU, LEY, BANI
Russia . COPEC, KOPEK, RUBLE
Siam .... AT, ATT, BAHT,
TICAL or TIKAL
Sicily .... TARI
Somaliland .... BESA
South Africa .... DAALDER
Spain ..... COB, DURO, PESO,
REAL, DOBLA (old), PESETA,
PISTOLE (old)
Sweden ORE, KRONA (KRONOR),
KRONE (KRONER)
Switzerland .... BATZ
Thailand .... see SIAM
Timor .... AVO
Turkey .. LIRA (gold), PARA,
ALTUN (gold), ASPER,
MAHBUB (gold), PIASTER
United States .. CENT, DIME,
EAGLE
Venice .... BETSO (old silver)
Yugoslavia .... DINAR

TRIBES (Including Peoples, Natives)

EUROPE:

Albania............. GEG, CHAM, GHEG, TOSK
Balto-Slav.................. LETT
Celtic on Danube........... BOII
Finnish near Volga........ VEPS, VEPSA
Finnish, Ingria....... VOT, VOTE, VOTH, WOTE
Lithuania.................. BALT
Syryenian.................. KOMI
Teuton, ancient............ UBII

MIDDLE EAST:

Arab.................. AUS, IBAD
Bedouin............. ABSI, HARB
Turkey..................... KURD
East Turkey................ KURD
Persia........... see under ASIA

ASIA:

Afghanistan................ SAFI
Assam........... AO, AKA; AHOM, GARO, NAGA
Borneo.... DYAK, IBAN; DAYAK
Burma....... WA, LAI, KAW, MON, WAS; AKHA, CHIN, KADU, KUKI, TSIN; KAREN
Caucasus .... IMER, KURI, LASI, LAZE, LAZI, SVAN; OSSET, SVANE
Celebes, Malayan.......... BUGI
China, Miao................ HEH
China, Nord....... USUN, UZUN; USSUN
China, Tatar............... TOBA
India.............. AWAN, BHIL, BHEEL, TURI
Kolarian (India)........... BHAR
Japan, aborigine..... AINO, AINU
Madagascar................ HOVA
Manchu.................... DAUR
Mongol.................... CHUD
Nepal.............. AOUL, KHAS
Persia............. LUR, KURD, FARSI, IRANIAN
Tibet.................. CHAMPA

AFRICA:

Abyssinian................ SHOA
Bantu........ KUA; BANE, BAYA, BIHE, BULE, FANG, FUNG, GOGO, GOLO, GOMA, GUHA, HAKU, HEHE, JAGA, LUBA, MAKA, NAMA, SOGA, SUKU,

VIRA, YAKA, ZULU (largest); KAFIR; KAFFIR
Bedouin.................... ABSI
Berber . DAZA, RIFF, TEDA, TIBU
Bushman..... SAN, SAAN, QUNG
Congo.............. FIOT, SUSU
Central Africa...... ABO; BULO, DOMA, KALI, KURI, LURI, YAKO; LUREM
Dahomey .... FON, FONG
East Africa...... JUR, LUR, YAO; AKKA, ALUR, ASHA, BARI, BONI, GOLO, MADI, NUER, VITI
Ethiopian................. SHOA
Gold Coast........ AKAN, AKIM, AKRA
Hamitic ..... AFAR, BEJA, BENI, BOGO, GALA, HIMA
Kaffir .... XOSA, ZULU
Kenya..................... BONI
Lake Albert......... ALUR, LURI
Liberia.............. GI; KRA, KRII, VAI, VEI; KROO, TOMA
Libya.......... FUL, FULA, MZAB
Mozambique .... YAO
Nigeria...... ARO, EDO, IBO, IJO; BENI, BINI, EBOE, EKOI, IDJO, IDYO, IDZO, NUPE; BENIN
Nilotic.............. SUK, BARI
Pygmy............. AKKA, DOKO
Slave Coast.............. EGBA
Sudan..... FUL, FUR, VEI; FULA, GOLO, MABA, MEGE, NUBA, SUSU, TAMA
West Africa...... GA; AJA, EWE, IBO, KRU, KWA; AGNI, AKIM, APPA, BAGA, BINI, EFIK, EGBA, EKOI, GENG, GOLA, HABE, IKWE, JEBU, JOAT, JOLA, KETU, NALU, ONDO, REMO, SAPE, TCHI, TSHI, VACA, WARI

ALASKA:
Aleutians.................. ATKA

GREENLAND .... ITA

AUSTRALIA .... KOKO
NEW GUINEA............ KARON

SOUTH AMERICA:
Fr. Guiana................. BONI

191

INDIANS, INDIAN TRIBES

Alaska .... ALEUT, SITKA

Algonquin or Algonkian
Indians ... FOX, SAC, WEA;
CREE, SAUK; MIAMI; LEN-
APE, OTTAWA, PIEGAN;
SHAWNEE

Amazon .... (lower) MURA,
(upper) ANDOA

Apache .... LIPAN

Araucanian .... AUCA

Arawak ..... ARAUA, CAMPA,
INERI

Arikara .... REE

Arizona .. HANO, HOPI, MOKI,
PIMA, TEWA, YUMA;
MOQUI; APACHE

Athapascan Indians ..... DENE,
HUPA, TAKU; LIPAN,
TINNE; APACHE, NAV-
AHO

Aymara .... COLLA

Bolivia ...... ITE, URO, URU;
ITEN, LECA, MOJO, MOXO,
URAN; CHOLO

Brazil .... GE; YAO; CAME,
DIAU, MAKU, MURA, PURI,
PURU, TUPI; ACROA,
ANDOA, ARAUA, CARIB,
GUANA, SIUSI; ZAPARO

Caddoan Indians .. REE; ADAI;
IONI, CADDO, BIDAI;
PAWNEE

California ...... HUPA, KOSO,
MONO, NOZI, POMO, SERI,
TATU, YANA; MAIDU,
YANAN; SALINA

Canada .... AHT, CREE, DENE,
TAKU; NISKA, TINNE;
SARCEE

Carib .... YAO, TRIO

Carolina .... CATAWBA

Chaco .... TOBA

Chile .... AUCA

Colorado .... UTE

Colombia ...... BORO, DUIT,
MUSO, MUZO, TAMA,
TAPA; CHOCO; COLIMA

Costa Rica ...... BOTO VOTO

Cowichan Indians .. NANAIMO

Dakotas .. REE, SIOUX, TETON;
MANDAN, SANTEE;
ARIKARA

Delaware .... LENAPE

Ecuador: ..... CARA (extinct);
ANDOA, ARDAN

Eskimo .... ATKA; ALEUT

Florida: .... CALUSA

Fuegan .... ONA

Great Lakes .... ERIE; HURON

Guatemala .... MAM; CHOL,
ITZA, IXIL, IXLI, MAYA,
ULVA, VOTO; KICHE, PIPIL

Honduras .... PAYA

Iowa .... FOX, SAC; SAUK

Indiana .... WEA; MIAMI

Iroquoian Indians,
Iroquois: ...... ERIE, HURON,
CAYUGA, MOHAWK,
ONEIDA, SENECA

Jalisco: .... CORA

Keresan Indians: . SIA; ACOMA

Kusan .... COOS

Lesser Antilles .... INERI

Mayan Indians: ... MAM, CHOL

Mexico ... MAM, CHOL, CORA,
MAYA, MIXE, PIMA, PIME,
SERI, TECA, TECO, WABI;
AZTEC, OTOMI, SERIA;
TOLTEC

Miami .... WEA

Mississippi ..... TIOU, BILOXI

Montana ...... CROW, HOHE

Muskohegan Indians: . CREEK,
YAMASI, CHOCTAW,
SEMINOLE

Nebraska .... KIOWA

Nevada .... PAIUTE

New Mexico . SIA, PIRO, TANO,
TAOS, TEWA, ZUNI;
ACOMA, KERES, PECOS

New York .... SENECA

Nicaragua . MIXE, RAMA, ULVA

Oklahoma .. KAW, OTO; LOUP,
OTOE; CADDO, CREEK,
KANSA, KIOWA, OSAGE,
PONCA; PAWNEE

Oregon .... COOS, KUSAN,
MODOC, CHINOOK

Panamint .... KOSO
Panama .... CUNA, CUEVA
Pawnee Indians .... LOUP
Payaguas .... AGAZ
Peru: ...., ANDE, ANTI, BORO,
    CANA, INCA, INKA, LAMA,
    PEBA, PIBA, PIRO, YNCA;
    CAMPA, CHIMU, CHOLO,
    COLAN, YUNCA; CHANCA;
    QUICHU
Peru South .... CANA, COLLA,
    CHANCA
Piman Indians .. CORA, JOVA,
    MAYO, PIMA, XOVA, YAKI,
    YAQUI
Plains Indians ... CREE, CROW;
    KIOWA, OSAGE; PONCA,
    TETON, PAWNEE
Pueblo Indians .. HOPI, MOKI,
    TANO, TAOS, ZUNI;
    KERES, MOQUI
Rio Grande .... TANO
Sacramento Valley ..... YANA
Salishan Indians ..... ATNAH,
    LUMMI
Sheshonean Indians .... UTE;
    HOPI, KOSO, MOKI,
    MONO; MOQUI, PIUTE;
    UINTA, PAIUTE
Siouan Indians ... KAW, OTO;
    CROW, IOWA, OTOE;
    KANSA, OMAHA, OSAGE,
    PONCA; BILOXI, DAKOTA,
    MANDAN; CATAWBA

Sonora .... JOVA, PIMI, SERI

South America (widely
    distributed) .... GES, ONA,
    YAO; LULE, MOXO, PANO,
    PIRO, TOBA; CARIB,
    INERI; ARAWAK

South Carolina ..... CATAWBA

Tacanan Indians ..... CAVINA

Tanoan .... TEWA

Tapuyan Indians .... GE, GES,
    GHES, ACROA

Texas .... LIPAN

Tierra del Fuego: .... ONA

Tlingit: .... AUK, SITKA

Tupian .... ANTA

Utah: .... UTE

Washington .... HOH, LUMMI,
    MAKAH

Yucatan .... MAYA

Yukian .... TATU

Yukon .... TAKU

Yuncan .... CHIMU

ARMOR

Head .... COIF, HELM; ARMET, VISOR; BEAVER, CAMAIL; BASINET, HAUBERK
Neck .... GORGET
Shoulder .... AILETTE, PAULDRON, EPAULIERE, PASSEGARDE
Body .... TACE; CULET, TASSE; CORIUM, GORGET, LORICA; TASSET; CUIRASS, HAUBERK, SURCOAT; BRAGUETTE
Arm .... BRASSARD, PALLETTE, VAMBRACE; CUBITIERE, REREBRACE
Hand .... GAUNTLET
Thigh .... CUISH, TASSE, TUILE; CUISSE, TASSET, TUILLE
Leg, foot .... JAMB, JAMBE; GREAVE; CHAUSSE, PEDIEUX; SOLLERET
Complete suit .... BARD, MAIL; BARDE

HERALDRY—HERALDIC TERMS

Heraldic bearings: BEND, ENTE, FESS, ORLE, FESSE, GIRON, GYRON, LAVER, PHEON; SALTIRE
Heraldic tinctures:
gold, OR; fur, PEAN, VAIR, VAIRE; green, VERT; blue, AZURE; red, GULES; black, SABLE; orange, TENNE; silver, ARGENT; blood-red, MURREY; purple, PURPURE
attitude of animal
SEJANT, GARDANT, PASSANT, RAMPANT
ball .... ROUNDEL
band ..... FESS, ORLE, FESSE
barnacle .... BREY
bend .... COTISE
bird .... MARTLET
circle .... BEZANT, ANNULET
colter .... LAVER
creature .. LION, PARD; BISSE, WYVER; CANNET, WYVERN; GRIFFON, MARTLET
cross .. CRUX, NOWY, PATY; FLORY, FORMY, PATEE, PATTE; CLECHE; SALTIRE
curved in middle ...... NOWY
curves, made of ..... NEBULE
division .... PALE, PALY
dog, short-eared ...... ALANT
drops, seme of .... GUTTE
duck ..... CANNET, CANETTE
fillet .... ORLE
fish trap .... WEEL
flower strewn .... SEME

flying in air .... FLOTANT
fountain .... SYKE
grafted .... ENTE
headless .... ETETE
horizontal band ......see band
leaves, having .... POINTE
lines .... UNDE, UNDY, URDY, NEBULY
lozenge ..... FUSIL, MASCLE
manacle .... TIRRET
pointed .... URDE
powdered .... SEME
scattered .... SEME
sheaf of grain .. GERB, GERBE
shield .... PAVIS
shield division .... ENTE
shield's corner ..... CANTON
silver .... ARGENT
sitting .... ASSIS
snake .... BISSE
sown .... SEME
spangled .... SEME
star-strewn .... SEME
strewn .... SEME
three parts, divided into
TIERCE
triangle ..... GIRON, GYRON
two-winged .... VOL
voided escutcheon ...... ORLE
walking .... PASSANT
wavy .... ONDE, UNDE, UNDY, UNDEE, NEBULE
winged .... VOL, AILE
wound .... VULN
wreath .... ORLE, TORSE

CHEMICAL ELEMENTS AND SYMBOLS

All elements are natural, metallic elements unless otherwise indicated. The chemical symbol of each element is indicated by the letter or letters in dark type that follow it. (Syn.) indicates synthetically produced.

3 letters
TIN **Sn**

4 letters
GOLD **Au**
IRON **Fe**
LEAD **Pb**
NEON **Ne** (gaseous)
ZINC **Zn**

5 letters
ARGON **Ar** (gaseous)
BORON **B** (nonmetallic)
RADON **Rn** (gaseous)
XENON **Xe** (gaseous)

6 letters
BARIUM **Ba**
CARBON **C**
 (nonmetallic)
CERIUM **Ce**
CESIUM **Cs**
COBALT **Co**
COPPER **Cu**
CURIUM **Cm** (syn.)
ERBIUM **Er**
HELIUM **He** (gaseous)
INDIUM **In**
IODINE **I**
 (nonmetallic)
NICKEL **Ni**
OSMIUM **Os**
OXYGEN **O** (gaseous)
RADIUM **Ra**
SILVER **Ag**
SODIUM **Na**
SULFUR **S**
 (nonmetallic)

7 letters
ARSENIC **As**
 (semimetallic)
BISMUTH **Bi**
BROMINE **Br**
 (nonmetallic)

CADMIUM **Cd**
CALCIUM **Ca**
FERMIUM **Fm** (syn.)
GALLIUM **Ga**
HAFNIUM **Hf**
HOLMIUM **Ho**
IRIDIUM **Ir**
KRYPTON **Kr** (gaseous)
LITHIUM **Li**
MERCURY **Hg**
NIOBIUM **Nb**
RHENIUM **Re**
RHODIUM **Rh**
SILICON **Si**
 (nonmetallic)
TERBIUM **Tb**
THORIUM **Th**
THULIUM **Tm**
URANIUM **U**
YTTRIUM **Y**

8 letters
ACTINIUM **Ac**
ALUMINUM **Al**
ANTIMONY **Sb**
ASTATINE **At**
 (semimetallic)
CHLORINE **Cl** (gaseous)
CHROMIUM **Cr**
EUROPIUM **Eu**
FLUORINE **F** (gaseous)
FRANCIUM **Fr**
HYDROGEN **H** (gaseous)
LUTETIUM **Lu**
NITROGEN **N** (gaseous)
NOBELIUM **No** (syn.)
PLATINUM **Pt**
POLONIUM **Po**
RUBIDIUM **Rb**
SAMARIUM **Sm**
SCANDIUM **Sc**
SELENIUM **Se**
 (nonmetallic)
TANTALUM **Ta**
THALLIUM **Tl**

TITANIUM **Ti**
TUNGSTEN **W**
VANADIUM **V**

9 letters
AMERICIUM **Am** (syn.)
BERKELIUM **Bk** (syn.)
BERYLLIUM **Be**
GERMANIUM **Ge**
LANTHANUM **La**
MAGNESIUM **Mg**
MANGANESE **Mn**
NEODYMIUM **Nd**
NEPTUNIUM **Np** (syn.)
PALLADIUM **Pd**
PLUTONIUM **Pu**
POTASSIUM **K**
RUTHENIUM **Ru**
STRONTIUM **Sr**
TELLURIUM **Te**
 (nonmetallic)
YTTERBIUM **Yb**
ZIRCONIUM **Zr**

10 letters
DYSPROSIUM **Dy**
GADOLINIUM **Gd**
LAWRENCIUM **Lr** (syn.)
MOLYBDENUM **Mo**
PHOSPHORUS **P**
 (nonmetallic)
PROMETHIUM **Pm**
TECHNETIUM **Tc**

11 letters
CALIFORNIUM **Cf**
 (syn.)
EINSTEINIUM **Es**
 (syn.)
MENDELEVIUM **Md**
 (syn.)

12 letters
PRASEODYMIUM **Pr**
PROTACTINIUM **Pa**

BIBLICAL REFERENCES

BOOKS OF THE BIBLE

Names and order of books of the:

OLD TESTAMENT

1 GENESIS	11 KINGS 1	21 ECCLESIASTES	30 AMOS
2 EXODUS	12 KINGS 2	22 SONG OF	31 OBADIAH
3 LEVITICUS	13 CHRONICLES 1	SOLOMON	32 JONAH
4 NUMBERS	14 CHRONICLES 2	23 ISAIAH	33 MICAH
5 DEUTERONOMY	15 EZRA	24 JEREMIAH	34 NAHUM
6 JOSHUA	16 NEHEMIAH	25 LAMENTATIONS	35 HABAKKUK
7 JUDGES	17 ESTHER	26 EZEKIEL	36 ZEPHANIAH
8 RUTH	18 JOB	27 DANIEL	37 HAGGAI
9 SAMUEL 1	19 PSALMS	28 HOSEA	38 ZECHARIAH
10 SAMUEL 2	20 PROVERBS	29 JOEL	39 MALACHI

Names and order of books of the:

NEW TESTAMENT

1 MATTHEW	9 GALATIANS	15 TIMOTHY 1	23 JOHN 1
2 MARK	10 EPHESIANS	16 TIMOTHY 2	24 JOHN 2
3 LUKE	11 PHILIPPIANS	17 TITUS	25 JOHN 3
4 JOHN	12 COLOSSIANS	18 PHILEMON	26 JUDE
5 THE ACTS	13 THESSALON-	19 HEBREWS	27 REVELATION
6 ROMANS	IANS 1	20 JAMES	
7 CORINTHIANS 1	14 THESSALON-	21 PETER 1	
8 CORINTHIANS 2	IANS 2	22 PETER 2	

BIBLICAL PROPHETS

AMOS (minor), ESAY, EZRA, JOEL (minor), HOSEA (minor), JONAH (minor), MICAH (minor), MOSES, DANIEL (major), NAHUM (minor), ELISHA, HAGGAI (minor), ISAIAH (major), EZEKIEL (major), JEREMIAH (major)

BIBLICAL PATRIARCHS

REU; ADAM, EBER, ENOS, NOAH, SETH, SHEM; ISAAC, JACOB, JARED, NAHOR, PELEG, SERUG, TERAH; LAMECH

BIBLICAL RULERS

OG; ASA (Judah), GOG, IRA; AGAG, AHAB, AHAZ, AMON, ELAH, JEHU, OMRI, SAUL; CYRUS, DAVID, DEBIR, HEROD, HIRAM, JORAM, NADAB, PEKAH, PIRAM, REZIN, SIHON, ZIMRI; ABIJAH, BAASHA. CAESAR, DARIUS, HEZION, HOSHEA, JAPHIA, JOSHUA, JOSIAH, JOTHAM, UZZIAH

BIBLICAL PEOPLES—TRIBES

DAN, GOG; ANAK, ARAD, CUSH, EMIM, MOAB, PHUD, PHUT (o.t.); ARKITE, HAMITE, HIVITE, KENITE, SEMITE, SHELAH, SINITE; EDOMITE, HITTITE, LEHABIM, MOABITE, REPHAIM

BIBLICAL PLACES

City . DAN, GATH, GAZA, ZOAR; BABEL, EKRON, SODOM; HEBRON	Mt. HOR, EBAL, NAIN, NEBO, PEOR; HOREB, SEIR, SINA, SINAI, TABOR; ARARAT, GILEAD, HERMON
Country .... EDOM, ENON, SEBA; SHEBA	Place .... ENON, AENON; JORDAN, SHILOH
Hill, Jerusalem's .... ZION	Pool .... SILOAM
Kingdom .... ELAM, MOAB; SAMARIA	Region .. ARAM, EDAR; BASHAN
Land .... NOD	Town ...... CANA (1st miracle), NAIN (miracle site); BETHEL
Land of plenty .... GOSHEN	River .... ARNON, JORDAN

BIBLICAL MEN

OG, UZ; ARA, DAN, ELI, GOG, HAM, IRA, LOT, NUN, URI; ABEL, AMOS, BOAZ, CAIN, CUSH, DOEG, EBAL, ENON, ENOS, ESAU, HETH, IRAD, JADA, JEHU, JOAB, KISH, LEVI, MASH, MOAB, OBAL, OBED, OMAR, OREB, OZEM, SETH, SODI, ULAM, UNNI, URIA; AARON (high priest), ABIAH, ABIEL, AHIRA, AMASA, ANNAS, CALEB, CHUZA, ENOCH, HAMAN, HARAN, HIRAM, HOHAM, IBZAN, ISAAC, JACOB, JAMES, JARED, MASSA, MOREH, NABAL, NAHBI, NAHOR, OPHIR, REZON, SACAR, TERAH, URIAH, ZAHAM; SAMSON; ANANIAS, ISHMAEL

BIBLICAL WOMEN

EVE; ADAH, JAEL, LEAH, MARY, RUTH; DINAH, EGLAH, HAGAR, JULIA, JUNIA, LYDIA, MERAB, NAOMI, PHEBE, RAHAB, SARAH, SARAI, SHUAH, TAMAR; ABITAL, BILHAH, DORCAS, ESTHER, HANNAH, HOGLAH, MAACAH, MAHLAH, MICHAL, MILCAH, MIRIAM, PERSIS, RACHEL, RIZPAH, SALOME, VASHTI, ZILLAH, ZILPAH; ABIGAIL, HAMUTAL

BIBLICAL NAMES

ED, ER; IRI, NER, ONO, REI, TOI; ABIA, ADER, ANER, ANIM, ASOM, DARA, ELON, ENOS, IRAD, IVAH, REBA; ABIAM, AHIRA, AMASA, ASEAS

GODS (DEITIES), GODDESSES AND MYTHOLOGY

ASSYRIAN GODS
ANAT (sky), ASUR or ASSUR (war)

BABYLONIAN GODS
Chief gods: EA, ABU or ANU, BEL
EA (chief), ZU (wind), ABU or ANU (chief, sky, sun), BEL (chief), HEA (see EA), IRA (war), SIN (moon), UTU (sun), ADAD or ADDA or ADDU (wind, storm), APSU (chaos), ENKI (see EA), ENZU (see SIN), IRRA (war), NABU or NEBO (wisdom), UTUG (sun), DAGAN (earth), ETANA (eagle rider), SIRIS (alcoholic drinks), BABBAR (sun), SHAMASH (sun)

BABYLONIAN GODDESSES
AI or AYA (consort of Shamash), ERUA (mother), NINA (watery deep), NANAI (daughter of Anu), ISTAR or ISHTAR (chief, love)

BRYTHONIC GODDESS
DON (ancestress of gods)

CELTIC GODS—GODDESS
ANA, ANU, DANA, DANU (mother, queen), LER (sea), LUG, LUGH (light, sun), DAGDA (chief)

CYMRIC GODS
GWYN, LLEU, LLEW (solar)

EGYPTIAN GODS
RA (sun), SU (solar deity), BES (evil, pleasure), GEB (earth), KEB (earth), MIN (procreation), SEB (earth), SET (evil), SHU (see SU), TEM or TUM (sun), AANI (dog-headed ape, sacred to Thoth), AMEN (king), AMON (sun and king), AMUN (king), ATMU or ATUM (sun), BESA (see BES), HAPI (the Nile as a god), KHEM (see MIN), MENT (falcon-headed), PTAH (Memphis god), SETH (evil), SOBK (crocodile-headed), AMMON (see AMEN), HORUS (hawk-headed), MENTU (see MENT), SEBEK (see SOBK), THOTH (wisdom, magic), OSIRIS (underworld), SERAPIS (see OSIRIS)

EGYPTIAN GODDESSES
MA (same as MAAT), MUT (Amen's wife), NUT (heavens), ANTA, APET (maternity), BAST (cat- or lion-headed), BUTO (serpent), ISIS (cow-headed, Horus' mother), MAAT (truth, justice), SATI (queen), ATHOR (see HATHOR), HATHOR (love, mirth, cow-headed)

EGYPTIAN MYTH

BA (soul of man), KA (body of man), NU (chaos), AKH (spirit of man), NUN (see NU), APIS (sacred bull), ATEN (solar disk), DUAT (see AMENTI), HAPI (Nile or Amenti's jinnee), AMENTI (underworld region)

GREEK GODS

DIS (underworld), PAN (field, flocks, forest), ZAN (old name for Zeus), ARES (war, Eris' brother), EROS (love), ZEUS (chief of Olympian gods), COMUS (mirth and revelry), EURUS (southeast wind), HADES (underworld), KOMOS (see COMUS), MOMUS (ridicule), PLUTO (underworld), AEOLUS (wind), APOLLO (sun, youth), AUSTER (south wind), BOREAS (north wind), CRONUS (a Titan, Rhea's spouse; harvest), HELIOS (sun), HERMES (herald), KRONOS (see CRONUS), NEREUS (sea), PLUTUS (wealth), TRITON (sea), BACCHUS (wine), POSEIDON (sea)

GREEK GODDESSES

GE (earth, mother of Titans), ARA (destruction, retribution, vengeance), ATE (discord, mischief, infatuation), EIR (healing), EOS (dawn), ALEA (ATHENA), CORA (see KORE), DICE or DIKE (one of Horae), ENYO (Ares' mother, war), ERIS (discord, sister of Ares), GAEA or GAIA (see GE), HEBE (youth), HERA (queen), HORA (one of Horae), KORE (vegetation), LEDA (Tyndareus' wife), NIKE (victory), RHEA (mother of gods, wife of Kronos), UPIS, ARTEMIS, HORAE (three goddesses of seasons), IRENE (peace), METIS (Zeus' first wife), MOIRA (fate or Fates), ATHENA (wisdom), CLOTHO (a Fate, thread spinner), CYBELE (nature), EIRENE (see IRENE), HECATE (moon, magic), MOERAE (see MOIRA), PALLAS (wisdom), SELENA and SELENE (moon), ARTEMIS (moon, woods, nature), ATROPOS (one of the Fates, thread cutter), DEMETER (grain, agriculture), CHLORIS (flowers), NEMESIS (revenge), LACHESIS (one of the Fates, thread length), APHRODITE (love)

GREEK MYTH

IO (Zeus' beloved changed to a heifer), INO (Cadmus' daughter), PAN (field, flocks, forest), ANAX (one of Dioscuri), AUGE (Arcadian princess), CEYX (Halcyone's husband turned into kingfisher), CLIO (Muse of History), FAUN (see PAN), IDAS (hero, killed Castor), IOLE (Hercules' captive), LETO (Apollo's mother), MAIA (Hermes' mother), OTUS (giant killed by Apollo), ALTIS (sacred grove, Olympic games), ATLAS (held up heavens), CREON (Oedipus' brother-in-law), DIONE (Aphrodite's mother), ENEAS (Troy's defender), ERATO (Clio's sister), HADES (underworld), HELLE (fell into Hellespont with golden fleece), HYDRA (9-headed monster), MINOS (king), NIOBE (weeping stone), SATYR (part-horse demigod), THEIA (Hyperion's sister, wife), ADONIS (beautiful youth), AENEAS (see ENEAS), AGENOR (Trojan warrior), ALECTO (a Fury), DAPHNE (Apollo's nymph turned into tree), EUROPA (carried off by Zeus in form of white bull), HECTOR (Trojan warrior), NEREID (sea nymph to Poseidon), NESTOR (wise king, fought Troy), THETIS (Achilles' mother), TITHON (see TITHONUS), TRITON (sea demigod,

Poseidon's son), URANIA (astronomy), ARIADNE (Theseus' love), ATHAMAS (Ino's husband), CENTAUR (half man, half horse), CYCLOPS (1-eyed giant), SILENUS (woodland deity, horse-goat-human), ATALANTA (picked up golden apples—lost the race), TARTARUS (infernal regions), TITHONUS (immortal king of Troy, Eos' favorite), TISIPHONE (one of Erinyes)
The Gorgons: MEDUSA, STHENO, EURYALE
The Graces: AGLAIA, THALIA
The Titans or Titanesses: primeval deities: GAEA or GE (mother of Titans). URANUS (father of Titans). Titans: RHEA, COEUS, CREUS, THEIA, CRONUS or KRONOS, PHOEBE, THEMIS

HINDU GODS

KA (unknown), AGNI (fire), AKAL (immortal), CIVA (see SIVA), DEVA or DEWA (divine being), KAMA (love), RAMA (incarnation of Vishnu), SIVA (supreme), VAYU (wind), YAMA (judge of dead), BHAGA (love), DYAUS (heaven, sky), VISHNU (supreme), KRISHNA (avatar of Vishnu)

HINDU GODDESSES

SRI (beauty, wealth, luck, Vishnu's wife), UMA (splendor), VAC (speech), DEVI (any divinity, Siva's consort), KALI (evil), SHRI (see SRI), USAS (dawn), VACH (see VAC), SHREE (see SRI), MATRIS (mothers), LAKSHMI (see SRI)

HINDU MYTH

BANA (1,000-arm giant), KALI (tongue of Agni), KETU (Rahu's tail), NAGA (Vishnu's serpent), RAHU (dragon, swallows sun), USHA (Bana's daughter)

INCA GOD

INTI (sun)

IRISH—see CELTIC

NORSE GODS

ER (war), TY (see TIU), VE (Odin's brother, slayed Ymir), EAR (see ER), LOK (see LOKI), TIU (sky, war, Tiwaz), TIW (see TIU), TYR (sky, war), ULL (bow skill), VAN (sea), ZIO (sky), ZIU (see ZIO), FREY (fertility), HLER (sea), HOTH (blind god), LOKE or LOKI (discord, mischief), ODIN chief god, war, wisdom, slayed Ymir), THOR (thunder), TYRR (war), ULLR (see ULL), VALE (see VALI), VALI (Odin's son), VANS (see VANIR), VILI (Odin's brother), AEGIR (sea), AESIR (chief), ALCIS (twin gods), BALDR (see BALDER), BRAGE or BRAGI (poetry), DONAR (see THOR), HODER or HOTHR (see HOTH), VANIR (early race of gods), WODAN or WODEN or WOTAN (see ODIN), BALDER or BALDUR (light)
The Aesir or chief gods: TIU, TYR, ULL, FREY, LOKI, ODIN, THOR, VALI, BRAGI, DONAR, WODEN, BALDER

NORSE GODDESSES

EIR (healing), HEL (Loki's daughter, underworld, dead), RAN (sea, death, wife of Aegir), SIF (Thor's wife), URD (destiny), VOR (betrothal), ERDA (earth), FREA or FRIA (see FRIGG), GERD (Frey's wife), HELA (see HEL), NORN (fate), RIND (Odin's wife, Vali's mother), SAGA (golden beaker), URTH (see URD), FREYA (love, beauty), FRIGG (Odin's wife), NANNA (flowers), NORNA or NORNS (see NORN), FREYJA (see FREYA)

NORSE MYTH

ASK (see ASKR), DIS (female spirit), ASKR (first man), ATLI (king), EGIL (story hero), GARM (Hel's watchdog, slays Tyr), GERI (Odin's wolf), IDUN (Bragi's wife), MARA (nightmare demon), NATT or NOTT (night), WATE (giant), YMIR or YMER ("rime-cold giant"), EGILL (see EGIL), MIMIR (giant), ASGARD (abode of gods)

PHOENICIAN GODDESS
ASTARTE (fertility, love)

ROMAN GODS

DIS (underworld), SOL (sun), AMOR (love), FAUN (field, herds, half goat), JOVE (chief god), MARS (war), MORS (death), COMUS (mirth, joy), CUPID (love), EURUS (southeast wind), KOMOS (see COMUS), MANES (spirits of dead, gods of underworld), ORCUS (dead), APOLLO (sun, music), AUSTER (south wind), BOREAS (north wind), FAUNUS (rural deity), VULCAN (fire), NEPTUNE (sea)

ROMAN GODDESSES

NOX or NYX (night), OPS (harvest, plenty), DIAN (moon, chase, woods), IRIS (rainbow, Zeus' messenger), JUNO (queen), LUNA (moon), MAIA (Vulcan's consort), NONA (Fate), SPES (hope), CERES (earth, grain, agriculture, vegetation), DIANA (see DIAN), EPONA (horses), FIDES (faith), FAUNA (field), FLORA (flowers), MORTA (a Fate), PARCA (a Fate), SALUS (prosperity), TERRA (earth), VENUS (love), VESTA (hearth), ANNONA (crops), AURORA (dawn), DECUMA (a Fate), PARCAE (the Fates), VACUNA (Sabine huntress)
The Fates or Parcae: NONA, MORTA, DECUMA

TEUTONIC GODS—see NORSE GODS

TEUTONIC GODDESSES—see NORSE GODDESSES

VEDIC GODS—see HINDU GODS

VEDIC GODDESSES—see HINDU GODDESSES

WELSH GOD
DYLAN

FIRST AND LAST NAMES
COMMON TO CROSSWORD PUZZLES

You often find in crossword puzzles definitions like "Writer Aldous ———"
or "——— Pavlova." The following list contains the most commonly used
names, first names and last names. The part of the name which is usually given
in the definition is here in light-face type, arranged alphabetically. The rest of
the person's name follows in bold-face type.

Aaron . **BURR, HANK**
Abbot . . . . **BUD**
Abzug . . . . **BELLA**
Acheson. . . . . . . **DEAN**
Adam . . . . **BEDE**
Adams . . . . **EDIE,
MAUDE**
Addams . . . . **JANE**
Adoree . . . . **RENEE**
Agar . . . . **JOHN**
Alain . . . . **DELON**
Alan. . . . **ALDA, KING,
LADD, ARKIN,
BATES, PATON**
Albert . . . . **CAMUS**
Albertus. . . **MAGNUS**
Albrecht. . . . . **DURER**
Aldo. . . . . **RAY**
Aldous . . . . . **HUXLEY**
Alejandro. . . . . . . **REY**
Alexander . . . **POPE,
SEROV, CALDER,
FLEMING**
Alexandre . . . **DUMAS**
Alfred **LUNT, DRAKE**
Alfred B. . . . . . **NOBEL**
Alighieri . . . . . **DANTE**
Allegra . . . . **KENT**
Allen . . . . **MEL, FRED,
ETHAN, STEVE,
WOODY**
Allison. . . . . **FRAN**
Allyson . . . . **JUNE**
Alpert . . . . **HERB**
Ambler . . . . **ERIC**
Ambrose . . . **BIERCE,
FLEMING**
Amelia . . . **BLOOMER**
Amundsen. . . **ROALD**
Anais. . . . . **NIN**
Anatole. . . . . **FRANCE**
Andersen. . . . . **HANS**
Anderson. . . . . . **LONI**
Andersson. . . . . **BIBI**
Andre . . . . **GIDE**
Andrea . . . . **DORIA**
Andrea del . . . **SARTO**
Andress . . . **URSULA**
Andrew. . . . . . **YOUNG**

Andrews. . . . . . **DANA,
JULIE**
Andy . . . . **HARDY,
DEVINE**
Aneurin Bevan. . **NYE**
Angelico. . . . . . . **FRA**
Angelo . . . . . **MOSSO,
PATRI, GIOTTO**
Anita . . . . **LOOS**
Anna . . . **CASE, HELD,
STEN, MOFFO,
NEAGLE**
Anouk . . . . **AIMEE**
Anthony . . . . . . **EDEN,
SUSAN, TUDOR**
Anton . . . . **DOLIN,
SUSAN**
Antony . . . . . . **MARK**
Anya . . . . **SETON**
Arden . . . . **EVE, TONI,
ENOCH**
Arlene. . . . . **DAHL**
Arnaz . . **DESI, LUCIE**
Arnold. . . . . **HAP**
Arsene . . . . **LUPIN**
Artemus. . . . . . **WARD**
Arthur. . . . . **BEA**
Arthur Conan **DOYLE**
Ataturk. . . . . . **KEMAL**
Attlee . . . . **CLEMENT**
Auguste. . . . **COMTE,
RODIN**
Autry. . . . . **GENE**
Ayres . . . . **LEW**
Baba . . . . **ALI**
Babe . . . . **RUTH**
Baer. . . . . **MAX**
Bagnold . . . . . . **ENID**
Bailey . . . . **PEARL**
Bainter . . . . **FAY**
Baird . . . . **BIL**
Ballard . . . . **KAYE**
Balzac . . . . . **HONORE**
Bambi . . . . **LINN**
Bara. . . . . **THEDA**
Barbara . . . . . . **EDEN,
HALE, RUSH**
Barkley. . . . . . **ALBEN**
Barry. . . **GENE, JACK**

Barrymore. . . . **DREW,
JOHN, ETHEL,
LIONEL**
Bartok. . . **EVA, BELA**
Barton. . . . . . . **CLARA**
Basie. . . . . . . **COUNT**
Bates . . . . **ALAN**
Bayes . . . . **NORA**
Bea, Beatrice . . **LILLIE**
Bean . . **ROY, ORSON**
Becky. . . . . . . **SHARP**
Bede . . . . **ADAM**
Beerbohm . . . . . **MAX**
Beery . . . . **NOAH**
Begley . . . . **ED**
Beiderbecke . . . . **BIX**
Ben **HOGAN, SHAHN**
Bennett . . . . . **CERF,
JOAN, TONY**
Bergen . . . . . . **EDGAR,
POLLY**
Bernhardt . . . **SARAH**
Berra. . . . . **YOGI**
Bert . . . . **LAHR**
Best. . . . . **EDNA**
Bette **DAVIS, MIDLER**
Beverly. . . . . . . **SILLS**
Bevin. . . . . . . **ERNEST**
Billings . . . . **JOSH**
Billy . . . . **MAY, ROSE,
SUNDAY**
Bing. . . . . **CROSBY**
Bjorn . . . . **BORG**
Blaise . . . . . . **PASCAL**
Blake. . . . . **EUBIE**
Blakeley . . . . . **RONEE,
SUSAN**
Blanc. . . . . **MEL**
Blas. . . . . **GIL**
Bloch. . . . . **RAY**
Bloomer . . . . **AMELIA**
Blue. . . . . **BEN**
Blum . . . . **LEON**
Blyth. . . . . **ANN**
Bobby . . . **ORR, HULL**
Bogarde . . . . . . **DIRK**
Bohan . . . . **MARC**
Bohr. . . . . **NIELS**
Boleyn . . . . **ANNE**

202

Bolger.......... RAY
Bolivar .... SIMON
Bonheur....... ROSA
Boone . PAT, DEBBY,
DANIEL,
RICHARD
Bovary .... EMMA
Bradley....... OMAR
Brendan..... BEHAN
Bret......... HARTE
Brice .... FANNY
Bridges....... BEAU,
JEFF, LLOYD
Brigham .... YOUNG
Brodie........ STEVE
Bronte .... EMILY
Brooke ..... SHIELDS
Brooks .... HERB
Brown.......... LES
Broz............ TITO
Bruce DERN, CABOT
Brynner .... YUL
Buck .... FRANK,
HENRY, OWENS,
PEARL, ROGERS
Buddy . RICH, HOLLY
Buffalo Bill ... CODY
Bull .... OLE
Bunche....... RALPH
Burbank.... LUTHER
Burl .... IVES
Burr........ AARON,
RAYMOND
Burrows........ ABE
Burstyn ...... ELLEN
Buttons .... RED
Byington .... SPRING
Cabeza de.... VACA
Caesar .... SID
Calloway ...... CAB
Campbell...... GLEN
Canada.......... LEE
Cannon....... DYAN
Cantrell ...... LANA
Capek........ KAREL
Carl .... CORI, JUNG,
FROST, SAGAN
Carl Marie von
WEBER
Carnegie ...... DALE
Carnera ...... PRIMO
Carney .... ART
Carpenter ... KAREN,
SCOTT
Carrie Chapman
CATT
Carrie Jacobs BOND
Carrillo........ LEO
Carroll LEO, BAKER,
LEWIS
Carson .... KIT

Carter... AMY, CHIP,
JACK, JUNE,
LYNDA
Caruso ..... ENRICO
Cass .... PEGGY
Casals....... PABLO
Castle........ IRENE,
VERNON
Cather .... WILLA
Catherine...... PARR
Cavalieri...... LINA
Celeste....... HOLM
Chagall....... MARC
Champion .... GOWER
Chaney......... LON
Channing.... CAROL
Chaplin. LETA, OONA
Chapman....... CEIL
Charisse...... CYD
Charles.. RAY, NICK,
NORA, DARWIN
Charlie . RICH, PRIDE
Charlotte .. BRONTE,
CORDAY
Chase. ILKA, CHEVY
Chekhov..... ANTON
Christian ..... DIOR
Christie..... AGATHA
Cid............... EL
Claire .... INA
Clapton......... ERIC
Clara BOW, BARTON
Clare Booth ... LUCE
Clarence ...... DAY,
DARROW
Clark... ROY, DANE,
DICK, KENT,
MARK, GABLE
Claude ..... MONET,
RAINS
Clay......... HENRY,
CASSIUS
Clemens...... MARK
TWAIN
Clement..... ATTLEE
Cleveland... AMORY,
GROVER
Cliburn........ VAN
Clifton........ WEBB
Cobb......... TY, LEE
Cole.. NAT, PORTER
Columbo ..... RUSS
Como .... PERRY
Conde......... NAST
Connelly...... MARC
Connery....... SEAN
Connie ...... MACK,
FRANCIS
Conway .. TIM, TOM,
SHIRL
Cooper .... GARY

Copland ..... AARON
Cordell .... HULL
Cornel....... WILDE
Costello .... LOU
Cotton .... MATHER
Coty .... RENE
Count .... BASIE
Coward....... NOEL
Cox .... WALLY
Crane .... HART
Cregar ...... LAIRD
Crockett...... DAVY
Cronyn....... HUME
Crosby . BING, GARY
Crystal ...... GAYLE
Curie ... EVE, MARIE,
PIERRE
Curtis .... TONY
Dailey .... DAN
Dale......... EVANS
Daniel ..... BOONE,
DEFOE
Daniels .... BEBE
Danny........ KAYE
Dantes .... EDMOND
David.. SOUL, BOWIE
Davis.... MAC, JEFF,
BETTE
Dawber........ PAM
Day DORIS, LARAINE
De l'Enclos ... NINON
De Leon...... PONCE
De Maupassant. GUY
De Valera... EAMON
Dean .. RUSK, DIZZY,
JAMES, MARTIN
Deborah....... KERR
Della REESE, STREET
Delmar .... VINA
Delon .... ALAIN
Dennis ... DAY, KING
Derek .... BO, JOHN
Descartes ..... RENE
Devine .... ANDY
Dewey .. TOM, JOHN
DeLuise .... DOM
Diamond Jim BRADY
Diana... DORS, ROSS
Dickinson..... EMILY
Dionne ...... MARIA,
OLIVA, CECILE,
EMELIE, YVONNE,
ANNETTE
Disney .... WALT
Dolin .... ANTON
Don .... HO, ADAMS,
KNOTTS
Donahue PHIL, TROY
Donlevy ...... BRIAN
Donna........ REED,
SUMMER

203

Doone....... **LORNA**
Dorfmann ..... **ANIA**
Doris ... **DAY, DUKE**
Dorothy ... **DIX, GISH**
Dors .... **DIANA**
Dostoevsky. **FEODOR**
Doubleday... **ABNER**
Downs .... **HUGH**
Drew .... **ELLEN**
Dreyfus .. **ALFRED**
Dufy .... **RAOUL**
Duke .... **DORIS**
Duke Astin .. **PATTY**
Dunaway .... **FAYE**
Duncan. **SARA, TODD**
Dunne....... **IRENE**
Durocher .. **LEO, LIP,**
            LIPPY
Dvorak ...... **ANTON**
Dwight ...... **MOODY**
Eamon de .. **VALERA**
Earhart ..... **AMELIA**
Eartha......... **KITT**
Eastwood..... **CLINT**
Eddie........... **FOY**
Edgar . **POE, DEGAS,**
           GUEST
Edith .... **PIAF**
Edmond .... **DANTES**
Edmund .... **BURKE**
Edna **BEST, FERBER,**
         MILLAY
Edouard ..... **MANET**
Eduard **LALO, BENES**
Edvard ...... **GRIEG**
Edward ...... **ELGAR**
Edward Everett **HALE**
Edwards **GUS, VINCE**
Edwin .... **BOOTH,**
         WEEKS
Eisaku......... **SATO**
Ekberg .... **ANITA**
Ekland .... **BRITT**
Elaine .... **MAY**
Eleanora...... **DUSE**
Elia... **LAMB, KAZAN**
Elias.......... **HOWE**
Elihu ... **ROOT, YALE**
Ellen . **DREW, TERRY**
Ellington..... **DUKE**
Elliott........ **GOULD**
Ellsworth ..... **VINES**
Elmer .. **RICE, CRAIG**
Elmo .... **ROPER**
Emerson .... **FAYE,**
   RALPH WALDO
Emile.......... **ZOLA**
Emily **POST, BRONTE**
En-lai......... **CHOU**
Enoch **ARDEN, LIGHT**
Enrico........ **FERMI**

Erica .... **JONG**
Erik .... **SATIE**
Erikson........ **LIEF**
Ernest....... **BEVIN,**
   BLOCK, SETON
Ernie ... **FORD, PYLE**
Errol .. **LEON, FLYNN**
Estrada......... **ERIK**
Ethan **ALLEN, FROME**
Ethel....... **WATERS**
Ethelbert .... **NEVIN**
Eugene. **DEBS, FIELD**
Eva .... **GABOR**
Eva Marie .... **SAINT**
Evans .... **DALE**
Everett...... **CHAD**
Evita .... **PERON**
Ewell.......... **TOM**
Eydie....... **GORME**
Eyre.......... **JANE**
Ezra. **POUND, STONE**
Fanny .... **BRICE**
Farrow .... **MIA**
Ferber........ **EDNA**
Ferde....... **GROFE**
Ferenc .... **MOLNAR**
Fermi ...... **ENRICO**
Fernand ..... **LEGER**
Fernando.... **LAMAS**
Ferrer.... **MEL, JOSE**
Field .... **SALLY**
Filippino .... **LIPPI**
Fisher .. **BUD, HAM,**
   CARRIE, EDDIE
Fitzgerald.... **ELLA,**
  BARRY, F. SCOTT
Flynn........ **ERROL**
Foch .... **NINA**
Fonda **JANE, HENRY,**
        PETER
Ford.. **EDSEL, ERNIE,**
        HENRY
Foscolo .... **UGO**
Fra Filippo..... **LIPPI**
Francesco.... **NITTI**
Franchot .... **TONE**
Francis ..... **BACON,**
        DRAKE
Francis Scott ... **KEY**
Franck ...... **CESAR**
Francoise.... **SAGAN**
Frank.... **FAY, BUCK,**
        CAPRA
Frank Lloyd. **WRIGHT**
Frankie...... **CARLE,**
        LAINE
Frans.......... **HALS**
Franz....... **KAFKA,**
   LEHAR, LISZT
Frederick.... **LOEWE**
Frobe .... **GERT**

Frome....... **ETHAN**
Gabor . **EVA, MAGDA,**
      ZSA ZSA
Gagarin ...... **YURI**
Gale......... **STORM**
Gam .... **RITA**
Garbo ...... **GRETA**
Gardner . **AVA, ERLE**
Garner .... **JAMES,**
      ERROLL
Garson .... **GREER**
Gavin......... **MUIR**
Gayle...... **CRYSTAL**
Gazzara .... **BEN**
Gehrig......... **LOU**
Geller .... **URI**
Genghis...... **KHAN**
George.. **ADE, OHM,**
   BUSH, RAFT,
  SAND, BROWN,
  CLARK, DEWEY,
  GOBEL, LUCAS,
  SCOTT, SEGAL,
  CUSTER, PATTON
George Bernard
        SHAW
George Frederick
      HANDEL
George Herman
       RUTH
Georges...... **BIZET,**
     SEURAT
Gerald........ **FORD**
Geraldine...... **PAGE**
Gershwin....... **IRA,**
     GEORGE
Gert.......... **FROBE**
Gertrude ..... **BERG,**
      STEIN
Getz............ **STAN**
Gibson ...... **HOOT**
Gil .... **BLAS**
Gillespie...... **DIZZY**
Giuseppe .... **BELLI,**
     VERDI
Gladys ..... **KNIGHT**
Glasgow...... **ELLEN**
Glenn . **FORD, JOHN,**
     MILLER
Gluck......... **ALMA**
Golda .... **MEIR**
Goldberg ..... **RUBE**
Goldie ...... **HAWN**
Gordon **RUTH, FLASH**
Gorky .... **MAXIM**
Gorme ...... **EYDIE**
Gould .... **JAY**
Grace ...... **KELLY**
Graham ..... **BILLY,**
  GREENE, MARTHA
Grandma .... **MOSES**

Grant... **LEE, WOOD, TINKER**
Gray .... **ASA**
Greco ..... **EL, JOSE**
Greeley..... **HORACE**
Greene ...... **LORNE, GRAHAM**
Gregor ..... **MENDEL**
Gregory .... **PECK**
Grey ... **JANE, ZANE**
Griffith .... **ANDY**
Grissom **GUS, VIRGIL**
Grofe......... **FERDE**
Gueden........ **HILDE**
Guevara........ **CHE**
Guido .... **RENI**
Guitry .... **SACHA**
Gulager .... **CLU**
Gustav ..... **MAHLER**
Guthrie....... **ARLO, WOODY**
Guy .... **MOLLET**
Gypsy Rose ..... **LEE**
Hackett....... **JOAN, BUDDY**
Hackman ..... **GENE**
Hagen.......... **UTA**
Hal .... **MARCH, LINDEN, PRINCE**
Hale............ **ALAN**
Haley.......... **ALEX**
Hallstrom...... **IVAR**
Hals .... **FRANS**
Halsey......... **BULL**
Hammarskjold .. **DAG**
Hamsun ...... **KNUT**
Hank **SNOW, AARON**
Hansson........ **OLA**
Harold. **ROME, TEEN, UREY**
Harriet Beecher **STOWE**
Harris ... **JOEL, PHIL, JULIE**
Harrison........ **REX, FORD, NOEL, GEORGE**
Hart......... **CRANE**
Harte......... **BRET**
Haver .... **JUNE**
Havoc .... **JUNE**
Hawn......... **GOLDIE**
Hayward..... **SUSAN**
Hayworth....... **RITA**
Hazel......... **SCOTT**
Hefner .... **HUGH**
Heifetz ..... **JASCHA**
Heinrich ...... **HEINE**
Held.......... **ANNA**
Hemingway.... **PAPA, ERNEST**

Hendrix........ **JIMI**
Henri ...... **MATISSE, ROUSSEAU**
Henrik........ **IBSEN**
Henry . **CLAY, FORD, LUCE, FONDA, HUDSON**
Henry Cabot. **LODGE**
Herbert.... **HOOVER, VICTOR**
Herbert George **WELLS**
Herbie........ **MANN**
Herman ..... **HESSE, WOODY**
Hernando... **CORTES, DE SOTO**
Hernando de... **SOTO**
Hess .... **MYRA**
Heywood..... **BROUN**
Hieronymus . **BOSCH**
Hildegarde..... **NEFF**
Hirt .... **AL**
Ho Chi .... **MINH**
Hobson...... **LAURA**
Hogan........ **BEN**
Hogg........... **IMA**
Holbein........ **HALS**
Holbrook........ **HAL**
Horace ...... **MANN**
Horatio .... **ALGER**
Horne .... **LENA**
Houdini...... **HARRY**
Houston .... **SAM**
Howard.. **RON, KEEL**
Howe........ **ELIAS**
Hubbell........ **CARL**
Hudson........ **ROCK**
Hugh........ **DOWNS**
Hume .... **DAVID**
Hunter .... **IAN, KIM, TAB, EVAN**
Hus .... **JAN**
Hyerdahl ...... **THOR**
Ian .... **HUNTER**
Ibn .... **SAUD**
Ilka.......... **CHASE**
Immanuel...... **KANT**
Imogene...... **COCA**
Imre.......... **NAGY**
Ina .... **CLAIRE**
Inonu........ **ISMET**
Irene . **RICH, DUNNE, CASTLE**
Irving........ **BERLIN**
Isaac......... **STERN**
Isadora.... **DUNCAN**
Ismet........ **INONU**
Italo......... **TAJO**
Iturbi .... **JOSE**
Ives .... **BURL**

J. Carrol...... **NAISH**
Jack..... **SOO, LORD, PAAR, WEBB, OAKIE, LONDON**
Jacob .... **RIIS**
Jagger . **DEAN, MICK**
James. **AGEE, CAAN, COCO, DEAN, WATT, HARRY, HENRY, JESSE, JOYCE, BARRIE, GARNER**
Jamie .... **FARR**
Jan.... **HUS, SMUTS, STEEN, PEERCE, VERMEER**
Jan Van ...... **EYCK**
Jane .. **EYRE, GREY, FONDA, AUSTEN**
Janet. **BLAIR, LEIGH, GAYNOR**
Janice......... **RULE**
Janis.... **IAN, PAIGE**
Jannings ...... **EMIL**
Janos .... **KADAR**
Jawaharlal... **NEHRU**
Jay.......... **GOULD**
Jean-Paul... **MARAT**
Jeanmaire.... **RENEE**
Jeanne ...... **CRAIN, EAGELS**
Jefferson..... **DAVIS**
Jenny .... **LIND**
Jerome .... **KERN**
Jesse ...... **JAMES**
Jessica....... **TANDY**
Jim... **RYUN, CROCE**
Jimmy........ **SAVO**
Joan ...... **RIVERS**
Joanne .... **DRU**
Joel Chandler **HARRIS**
Johan .... **SARS**
Johann Sebastian **BACH**
John ... **HAY, AGAR, DALY, DREW, ALDEN, KEATS, LOCKE, SAXON, CALVIN, LENNON**
John Foster **DULLES**
John Godfrey.. **SAXE**
John Jacob.. **ASTOR**
John Maynard **KEYNES**
John Philip .. **SOUSA**
John Singer **SARGENT**
John Stuart.... **MILL**
John Wilkes . **BOOTH**
Johnnie .... **RAY**

Johnny . . . . CASH, MERCER
Johnson . . OSA, VAN, ARTE
Jolson . . . . AL
Jonas . . . . SALK
Jonathan . . . . . SWIFT
Jones . . TOM, DEAN, JACK
Jong . . . . ERICA
Jonson . . . . BEN
Joplin JANIS, SCOTT
Jose GRECO, MARTI
Joseph . . . . . COTTEN
Josif . . . . STALIN
Josip Broz . . . . . TITO
Jubal . . . . EARLY
Jule . . . . STYNE
Jules . . . . VERNE
Julia Ward . . . . HOWE
Julie ADAMS, HARRIS
June HAVER, HAVOC
Kadar . . . . JANOS
Kafka . . . . FRANZ
Karel . . . . CAPEK
Karen . . . . BLACK
Karenina . . . . . ANNA
Karl . . . . MARX
Katherine . . . . . . ROSS
Kay . KYSER, STARR
Kazan . . . . ELIA
Keach . . . . STACY
Keller . . . . HELEN
Kelly . . GENE, WALT, GRACE, EMMET
Kenton . . . . STAN
Khachaturian . ARAM
Khan . AGA, ALI, ALY
Khayyam . . . . OMAR
Kibbee . . . . GUY
Kim DARBY, NOVAK, HUNTER
King. ALAN, CAROLE
Kingsley . . . . BEN
Kirkegaard . . SOREN
Klee . . . . PAUL
Knight. TED, GLADYS
Korbut . . . . OLGA
Koussevitzky . SERGE
Kovacs . . . . . . ERNIE
Kreisler . . . . FRITZ
Kristofferson . . . KRIS
Kruger . . . . . . HARDY
Krupa . . . . GENE
Kublai . . . . KHAN
Kurt . . . . ADLER
Kyser . . . . KAY
Ladd ALAN, CHERYL
Lagerlof . . . . . SELMA
Lahr . . . . BERT
Lancaster . . . . . BURT

Lanchester . . . . ELSA
Lange . . . . HOPE
Lanny . . . . ROSS
Lanza . . . . MARIO
Lardner . . . . RING
Laurel . . . . STAN
Laurence . . . OLIVIER
Laurie . . . . PIPER
Lazarus . . . . . EMMA
Learned . . . . . . HAND
Lee . . PEGGY, PINKY, GRANT, GYPSY, CANADA, HARPER, MAJORS
Lehar . . . . FRANZ
Lehmann . . . . . LOTTE
Lehr . . . . LEW
Leinsdorf . . . . . ERICH
Lena . . . . HORNE
Lennon . . . . JOHN
Lenya . . . . LOTTE
Levant . . . . . . OSCAR
Lew . . CODY, AYRES
Lewis . . . . ADA, TED, JOHN, LAWES, SHARI, STONE
LeGallienne . . . . . EVA
Light . . . . ENOCH
Light-horse Harry LEE
Lillian . . BLAIR, ROTH
Lillie . . . . . . BEA, PEEL
Linda . BLAIR, LAVIN
Linkletter . ART, JACK
Linn . . . . BAMBI
Liszt . . . . FRANZ
Little . . . . RICH
Lollobrigida . . . . GINA
Lombardo . . . . . GUY CARMEN
Long . . . . HUEY
Loos . . . . ANITA
Loren . . . . SOPHIA
Lorenz . . . . HART
Loretta SWIT, YOUNG
Lorna . . . . DOONE
Lorre . . . . PETER
Lotte . . . . LENYA
Louis . . . . JOE
Louise . . TINA, ANITA
Loy . . . . MYRNA
Lucretia . . . . . . MOTT
Lucrezia . . . . BORGIA
Lucy . . . . STONE
Ludwig . . . . EMIL
Lugosi . . . . BELA
Luise . . . . RAINER
Lupino . . . . IDA
Lynn . . . . BARI
Lyon . . . . SUE
Mack . . . . TED
MacGraw . . . . ALI

Madame de . . . STAEL
Magda . . . . . . GABOR
Maglie . . . . SAL
Magnani . . . . . ANNA
Mailer . . . . NORMAN
Major . . . . . . BOWES
Majors . . . . LEE
Malbin . . . . . ELAINE
Malden . . . . . . KARL
Malone . . . . . MOLLY
Mann . . . . . HERBIE, HORACE, THOMAS
Manuel de . . . . FALLA
Marceau . . . MARCEL
Marco . . . . . . POLO
Margaret . . . . MEAD
Margaret Chase SMITH
Maria . . . . CALLAS
Marie . . . . CURIE
Mario . . . . . . LANZA
Mark . . . . . . CLARK
Marner . . . . . . SILAS
Marquette . . . . PERE
Marquis . . . . . . DON
Marshall . . . . . PENNY
Martha . HYER, RAYE
Marti . . . . JOSE
Martin . DEAN, MARY, ROSS, BUBER, STEVE, LUTHER
Martin Luther . . KING
Marx . KARL, CHICO, HARPO, ZEPPO, GROUCHO
Mary . . . URE, ASTOR
Mary Baker . . . EDDY
Masaryk JAN, TOMAS
Mason . . . . . . JAMES, MARSHA, PERRY
Massey CURT, ILONA
Mata . . . . HARI
Mather . . . . COTTON
Matisse . . . . . HENRI
Maude . . . . . ADAMS
Maurice . . . . . EVANS, RAVEL, UTRILLO
Maurois . . . . ANDRE
Maxim . . . . . . GORKI, GORKY
Maxwell . . . . . ELSA
McDaniel . . . . HATTIE
McLeod . . . . . GAVIN
McPherson . . . AIMEE
Mel . . . . . OTT, ALLEN, BLANC, TORME, TILLIS
Meriwether . . . LEWIS
Merkel . . . . UNA
Merman . . . . . ETHEL
Merrill . . . . DINA

Meryl....... **STREEP**
Meyerson...... **BESS**
Mickey ..... **MANTLE**
Midler........ **BETTE**
Miles . **VERA, SARAH, STANDISH**
Miller.. **ANN, GLENN, ROGER**
Mineo .... **SAL**
Minnelli........ **LIZA**
Minnie....... **PEARL**
Minuit .... **PETER**
Mischa .... **AUER, ELMAN**
Mitchell . **GUY, JONI, BILLY**
Moffo .... **ANNA**
Mohandas .. **GANDHI**
Mollet .... **GUY**
Mondrian ...... **PIET**
Montand....... **YVES**
Montez **LOLA, MARIA**
Montgomery... **WES**
Monty .... **HALL**
Moorhead ... **AGNES**
Moreno....... **RITA**
Morgana **FATA, NINA**
Morley .... **SAFER**
Mostel .... **ZERO**
Mountbatten.. **EARL, LOUIS**
Mowbray ...... **ALAN**
Muhammad...... **ALI**
Munson .... **ONA**
Murray ... **DON, JAN, KEN, MAE, ANNE**
Musial........ **STAN**
Myra .... **HESS**
Myrna .... **LOY**
Nagy .... **IMRE**
Nahum .... **TATE**
Nancy ...... **HANKS**
Natalie .... **WOOD**
Nathan ...... **HALE**
Nazimova...... **ALLA**
Ned .... **SPARKS**
Negri .... **POLA**
Nelson **EDDY, GENE, MILES, RIDDLE**
Nero .... **PETER**
Newton....... **ISAAC**
Newton-John **OLIVIA**
Nicholas...... **AMATI**
Niels .... **BOHR**
Nikola .... **TESLA**
Noel....... **COWARD**
Nora . **KAYE, BAYES**
Norman ...... **LEAR, MAILER**
Normand .... **MABEL**
Novarro ..... **RAMON**

Novello........ **IVOR**
O'Casey .... **SEAN**
O'Neal....... **RYAN, TATUM**
O'Neill........ **OONA**
O. Henry ... **PORTER**
Ogden.. **NASH, REID**
Oley........ **SPEAKS**
Oliver **REED, HARDY, PERRY**
Oliver Wendell **HOLMES**
Olsen........... **OLE**
Omar....... **SHARIF, BRADLEY**
Onegin ...... **EUGEN**
Opie........... **READ**
Orson **BEAN, WELLES**
Orville...... **WRIGHT**
Oscar .... **WILDE, LEVANT**
Ott .... **MEL**
Pablo....... **CASALS**
Pacino............ **AL**
Paderewski.. **IGNACE**
Page .... **PATTI**
Paine........ **TOM**
Palmer **ARNIE, LILLI, ARNOLD**
Pancho...... **SANZA, VILLA**
Parker......... **FESS**
Parton........ **DOLLY**
Pasternak ... **BORIS**
Pasteur....... **LOUIS**
Pastor........ **TONY**
Paton........ **ALAN**
Patti.......... **PAGE**
Paul... **ANKA, KLEE, MUNI**
Pauling....... **LINUS**
Pavlova ...... **ANNA**
Pearl . **BUCK, WHITE, BAILEY, MINNIE**
Pearson ..... **LESTER**
Peerce .... **JAN**
Peewee ...... **REESE**
Peggy ... **LEE, CASS, WOOD**
Peron ... **EVA, JUAN, EVITA**
Perry **COMO, MASON**
Pete. **ROSE, SEEGER, FOUNTAIN**
Peter.. **ARNO, NERO, ROSE, LORRE**
Peter Paul .. **RUBENS**
Petula .... **CLARK**
Phileas .... **FOGG**
Philip.... **HALE, NERI**

Philo .... **VANCE**
Picasso...... **PABLO**
Pickens........ **SLIM**
Picon........ **MOLLY**
Pierre .. **LOTI, CURIE**
Pierre-Auguste **RENOIR**
Pinky .... **LEE**
Pinza........... **EZIO**
Pirandello...... **LUIGI**
Pola .... **NEGRI**
Polo......... **MARCO**
Ponce de...... **LEON**
Pons .... **LILY**
Ponselle....... **ROSA**
Porter .... **COLE**
Pound .... **EZRA**
Preminger..... **OTTO**
Priscilla...... **ALDEN, MULLEN**
Prokofiev..... **SERGE**
Proust...... **MARCEL**
Pyle.......... **ERNIE**
Radner .... **GILDA**
Rainer .... **LUISE**
Rainer Maria.. **RILKE**
Raines........ **ELLA**
Rains....... **CLAUDE**
Ralph..... **NADER, BUNCHE**
Rand..... **AYN, SALLY**
Rathbone..... **BASIL**
Ray .. **ALDO, BLOCH, NOBLE**
Rayburn........ **SAM**
Raymond..... **BURR, GENE**
Read.......... **OPIE**
Rebecca...... **WEST**
Red, the........ **ERIC**
Reed . **ALAN, DONNA**
Reese .... **DELLA, PEEWEE**
Rehan......... **ADA**
Reiner... **ROB, CARL**
Rene .... **COTY**
Rex .... **BELL, REED, STOUT**
Reynolds ...... **BURT**
Rhodes ...... **CECIL**
Richard.. **DIX, BYRD, LONG, ROWE, CONTE, STRAUSS**
Ringo........ **STARR**
Rip.. **TORN, TAYLOR**
Rita .... **GAM**
Ritter.... **TEX, JOHN, THELMA**
Rivera **CHITA, DIEGO**
Robb........... **INEZ**
Rockne....... **KNUTE**

207

Roger .... **BACON**
Rogers .. **ROY, CARL,**
    WILL, KENNY,
    GINGER
Romero ..... **CESAR**
Ronstadt ..... **LINDA**
Root .. **OREN, ELIHU**
Roper .... **ELMO**
Rose .... **PETE**
Rousseau..... **HENRI**
Rowlands...... **GENA**
Rubinstein.. **ANTON,**
    ARTUR, ARTURO
Ruby .... **DEE**
Rudolf. **BING, FRIML,**
    DIESEL
Runyon..... **DAMON**
Russell .... **SAGE**
Ruth **BABE, GORDON**
Saarinen....... **EERO**
Sagan.......... **CARL**
Saint,—Marie ... **EVA**
Sally .. **RAND, FIELD**
Salmon P.... **CHASE**
Salvador........ **DALI**
Sam......... **SNEAD,**
    HOUSTON
Samuel...... **MORSE**
Sand .... **GEORGE**
Sandra .... **DEE**
Sarah .... **MILES**
Saud .... **IBN**
Savalas....... **TELLY**
Schmeling....... **MAX**
Scholem........ **ASCH**
Schulberg ..... **BUDD**
Seegar .... **ALAN**
Seeger .... **PETE**
Seeley.... **BLOSSOM**
Segovia .... **ANDRES**
Selassie ...... **HAILE**
Serling .... **ROD**
Seton .... **ANYA**
Sevareid........ **ERIC**
Shahn .... **BEN**
Shankar .... **RAVI**
Sharif .... **OMAR**
Sharp .... **BECKY**
Shaw.......... **ARTIE**
Shawn .... **TED**
Shelley .... **PERCY**
    BYSSHE,
    WINTERS
Shields ..... **BROOKE**
Shire .... **TALIA**
Shirley .... **BOOTH**
Sidney ...... **LANIER**
Sigmund .... **FREUD**
Signe........ **HASSO**
Silvers .... **SID, PHIL**

Sinatra ...... **FRANK,**
    NANCY
Sinclair....... **LEWIS,**
    UPTON
Skelton........ **RED**
Skinner......... **OTIS**
Smith .... **AL, ADAM,**
    ALEXIS, ALFRED
Snead.......... **SAM**
Sommer....... **ELKE**
Sonja......... **HENIE**
Sonny **BONO, TUFTS**
Sophia ...... **LOREN**
Sothern .... **ANN**
Spacek....... **SISSY**
Sparks .... **NED**
Speaker .... **TRIS**
Speaks .... **OLEY**
Spencer.... **TRACY**
Spewack ..... **BELLA**
St. John **JILL, ADELA**
St. Vincent Millay
    EDNA
Stacy........ **KEACH**
Stalin........ **JOSIF**
Standish...... **MILES**
Stanford...... **WHITE**
Starr ... **KAY, RINGO**
Steen .... **JAN**
Steiger .... **ROD**
Stengel ...... **CASEY**
Stephen..... **CRANE**
Stephen V. ...**BENET**
Sterling .... **JAN**
Stern .... **ISAAC**
Steve .... **ALLEN**
Stevens **CAT, MARK,**
    RISE, STELLA
Stevenson.... **ADLAI**
Stevie ..... **WONDER**
Stewart **ROD, JIMMY**
Stoker....... **BRAM**
Stone .. **LUCY, EZRA**
Storm .. **GALE, FIELD**
Stravinsky..... **IGOR**
Streep........ **MERYL**
Stuart .... **JEB**
Styne .... **JULE**
Sullivan .... **ED**
Sumac .... **YMA**
Summer...... **DONNA**
Sunday...... **BILLY**
Susan .... **DEY**
Susan B.. **ANTHONY**
Syngman ...... **RHEE**
Tab .... **HUNTER**
Tajo........ **ITALO**
Talia .... **SHIRE**
Tamiroff....... **AKIM**
Tanguay....... **EVA**
Tarbell .... **IDA**

Tarkington... **BOOTH**
Taylor. **LIZ, RIP, ROD**
Teasdale ...... **SARA**
Tebaldi..... **RENATA**
Templar ...... **SIMON**
Templeton..... **ALEC**
Tennessee .. **ERNIE,**
    WILLIAMS
Terry........ **ELLEN**
Tex .... **RITTER**
Thatcher .... **BECKY**
Theda........ **BARA**
Thelma...... **RITTER**
Thelonious ... **MONK**
Thomas ...... **ARNE,**
    GRAY, HOOD,
    MANN, NAST,
    DYLAN, HARDY,
    HICKS, DANNY,
    MARLO, MOORE,
    WOLFE, HOBBES
Thompson..... **SADA**
Thornton .... **WILDER**
Tilden .... **BILL**
Tillis........... **MEL**
Tillstrom ...... **BURR**
Timothy .. **BOTTOMS**
Tito .... **BROZ**
Tolstoy.......... **LEO**
Tom.... **MIX, EWELL,**
    PAINE
Tomlin .... **LILY**
Tony **SARG, CURTIS,**
    PASTOR
Toren .... **MARTA**
Torme......... **MEL**
Torn .... **RIP**
Toscanini... **ARTURO**
Trotsky....... **LEON**
Truex .... **ERNIE**
Truman ...... **BESS,**
    HARRY, CAPOTE
Trygve .... **LIE**
Tse-tung .... **MAO**
Tuesday...... **WELD**
Tunney...... **GENE**
Turner.... **IKE, NAT,**
    LANA, TINA
Turpin......... **BEN**
Twain .... **MARK**
Ty............. **COBB**
Ulanova ..... **GALINA**
Ullmann .... **LIV**
Uriah .... **HEEP**
Vallee .... **RUDY**
Vance ..... **CYRUS,**
    ETHEL, PHILO
Vaughan..... **SARAH**
Velez......... **LUPE**
Venerable, the . **BEDE**
Vera.......... **MILES**

Verdon . . . . **GWEN**
Verdugo . . . . . . **ELENA**
Vereen . . . . **BEN**
Vermeer . . . . **JAN**
Verne . . . . **JULES**
Vernon . . . . . **CASTLE**
Victor **HUGO, BORGE,**
             BUONO
Vigoda . . . . **ABE**
Vincent . . . . **PRICE**
Virginia . . . . **DARE,**
    MAYO, WOOLF
Virna . . . . **LISI**
Vivien . . . . **LEIGH**
Vladimir . . . . . . **LENIN**
Voight . . . . **JON**
W.C. **HANDY, FIELDS**
Wallace . . . . **LEW,**
    HENRY, AGARD
Wallach . . . . **ELI**
Waller . . . . **FATS**
Wally . . . . . . **COX, PIP**
Walter . . **ABEL, REED,**
           BRUNO
Walton . . . . **IZAAK**
Warburg . . . . **OTTO**
Warhol . . . . **ANDY**
Warren . . . . **EARL**
Washington . . **DINAH,**
     BOOKER T.
Waters . . . . **ETHEL**
Waugh . . . . **ALEC**
Webb . . . **ALAN, JACK**

Webster . . . . . . **NOAH,**
          DANIEL
Weill . . . . **KURT**
Weld . . . . **TUESDAY**
Welles . . . . **ORSON,**
         SUMNER
Wendell . . . . . **COREY,**
        WILLKIE
Werner Von . **BRAUN**
Wharton . . . . . . **EDITH**
White . . . . . . **BYRON,**
         PEARL,
  WILLIAM ALLEN
Whiteman . . . . . **PAUL**
Whitman . . . . . **WALT**
Whitney . . . . **ELI**
Wilbur . . . . **CROSS,**
       WRIGHT
Wilde . . . . **OSCAR**
Wilder . . **GENE, BILLY**
Wiley . . . . **POST**
Wilhelm von . . . **OPEL**
Wilkins . . . . **ROY**
Willa . . . . **CATHER**
William **HART, HULL,**
    INGE, PENN,
    PITT, BOOTH,
  HANDY, HOLDEN
William Butler. **YEATS**
William Cullen
       BRYANT
William Randolph
      HEARST

William Rose . . **BENET**
William Sidney
      PORTER
Williams **TED, ROBIN,**
         ROGER
Wills . . . . **CHILL,**
        HELEN
Wilson . . . . **FLIP**
Winding . . . . **KAI**
Winslow . . . . . **HOMER**
Winterhalter . . **HUGO**
Wolfgang Amadeus
      MOZART
Wood . . . . **GRANT**
Wray . . . . **FAY**
Wynn . . . . **ED, EARLY**
Wynter . . . . **DANA**
Xavier . . . . **CUGAT**
Yale . . . . **ELIHU**
Yat-sen . . . . **SUN**
Yogi . . . . **BERRA**
Yoko . . . . **ONO**
Young . . . . . . **CY, GIG,**
    ALAN, CHIC
Youskevitch . . . **IGOR**
Yutang . . . . **LIN**
Zasu . . . . **PITTS**
Zebulon . . . . **PIKE**
Zeppo . . . . **MARX**
Zetterling . . . . **MAI**
Zola . . . . **EMILE**
Zorina . . . . **VERA**
Zubin . . . . **MEHTA**

CELEBRITIES' ORIGINAL NAMES

Abbot, Bud....... **William Abbot**
Adams, Edie..... **Elizabeth Edith Enke**
Adoree, Renee .... **Jeanne de la Fonte**
Aimee, Anouk .. **Francoise Sorya**
Albert, Eddie ..... **Edward Albert Heimberger**
Alda, Robert **Alphonso d'Abruzzo**
Alexander, Jane ... **Jane Quigley**
Allen, Fred ...... **John F. Sullivan**
Allen, Woody .. **Allen Konigsberg**
Allyson, June...... **Ella Geisman**
Anderson, Dame Judith. **Frances Margaret Anderson**
Andrews, Dana.... **Carver Daniel Andrews**
Andrews, Julie........ **Julia Wells**
Angeli, Pier....... **Anna Maria Pierangeli**
Ann-Margret **Ann-Margret Olsson**
Arden, Eve..... **Eunice Quedens**
Arlen, Harold..... **Hyman Arluck**
Arliss, George.. **George Andrews**
Arness, James .. **James Aurness**
Arthur, Jean...... **Gladys Greene**
Astaire, Fred ..... **Frederick Austerlitz**
Astor, Mary. **Lucille Langehanke**
Auer, Mischa........... **Mischa Ounskowsky**
Aumont, Jean-Pierre. **Jean-Pierre Salomons**
Avalon, Frankie. **Francis Avallone**
Bacall, Lauren **Betty Joan Perske**
Ballard, Kaye.. **Catherine Balotta**
Bancroft, Anne...... **Anna Maria Italiano**
Bara, Theda **Theodosia Goodman**
Bardot, Brigitte.... **Camille Javal**
Bari, Lynn....... **Marjorie Fisher**
Barry, Gene ...... **Eugene Klass**
Barrymore, John ... **John Blythe**
Barrymore, Lionel . **Lionel Blythe**
Bartholomew, Freddie . **Frederick Llewellyn**
Bayes, Nora...... **Dora Goldberg**
Bennett, Tony........ **Anthony Benedetto**
Benny, Jack. **Benjamin Kubelsky**
Berg, Gertrude .... **Gertrude Edelstein**
Bergen, Polly...... **Nellie Burgin**
Berkeley, Busby .... **William Berkeley Enos**
Berle, Milton .. **Mendel Berlinger**
Berlin, Irving .... **Israel Baline**
Bishop, Joey .... **Joseph Gottlieb**
Black, Karen ...... **Karen Ziegler**
Blaine, Vivian **Vivienne Stapleton**

Blair, Janet........ **Martha Janet Lafferty**
Blake, Amanda .... **Beverly Neill**
Blake, Robert... **Michael Gubitosi**
Blue, Ben ... **Benjamin Bernstein**
Bogarde, Dirk ... **Derek Van Den Bogaerde**
Boone, Pat ...... **Charles Eugene Boone**
Borgnine, Ernest **Ermes Borgnino**
Bowie, David **David Robert Jones**
Brice, Fanny...... **Fanny Borach**
Bridges, Beau ..... **Lloyd Vernet Bridges III**
Britt, May..... **Maybritt Wilkens**
Brodie, Steve........ **John Stevens**
Bronson, Charles........ **Charles Buchinsky**
Brooks, Mel ... **Melvin Kaminsky**
Burns, George. **Nathan Birnbaum**
Burstyn, Ellen ... **Edna Gilhooley**
Burton, Richard. **Richard Jenkins**
Buttons, Red..... **Aaron Chwatt**
Byrnes, Edd (Kookie) .... **Edward Breitenberger**
Caine, Michael......... **Maurice Micklewhite**
Calhoun, Rory.... **Francis Durgin**
Callas, Maria.............. **Maria Kalogeropoulos**
Cannon, Dyan..... **Samille Diane Friesen**
Cantor, Eddie... **Edward Iskowitz**
Capucine.... **Germaine Lefebvre**
Carroll, Diahann .. **Carol Diahann Johnson**
Castle, Irene........ **Irene Foote**
Castle, Vernon ... **Vernon Blythe**
Chandler, Jeff........ **Ira Grossel**
Charisse, Cyd **Tula Ellice Finklea**
Checker, Chubby.. **Ernest Evans**
Cher......... **Cherilyn Sarkisian**
Clark, Dane .... **Bernard Zanville**
Cobb, Lee J.......... **Leo Jacoby**
Colbert, Claudette **Lily Claudette Chauchoin**
Cole, Nat (King). **Nathaniel Coles**
Connery, Sean **Thomas Connery**
Connors, Michael......... **Kreker Ohanian**
Conrad, Robert... **Conrad Robert Falk**
Cooper, Alice.... **Vincent Furnier**
Cooper, Gary... **Frank J. Cooper**
Cord, Alex..... **Alexander Viespi**
Corday, Mara.... **Marilyn Watts**
Cosell, Howard ... **Howard Cohen**
Costello, Elvis. **Declan McManus**
Costello, Lou...... **Louis Cristillo**
Crawford, Joan. **Lucille Le Sueur**

Crosby, Bing **Harry Lillis Crosby**
Curtis, Tony.. **Bernard Schwartz**
Damone, Vic ...... **Vito Farinola**
Darby, Kim...... **Deborah Zerby**
Darren, James... **James Ercolani**
Davis, Bette...... **Ruth Elizabeth Davis**
Day, Dennis.... **Eugene McNulty**
Day, Doris. **Doris von Kappelhoff**
Day, Laraine.... **Laraine Johnson**
DaSilva, Howard.......... **Harold Silverblatt**
De Carlo, Yvonne. **Peggy Yvonne Middleton**
Dee, Ruby.... **Ruby Ann Wallace**
Dee, Sandra.... **Alexandra Zuck**
Deneuve, Catherine.... **Catherine Dorleac**
Denver, John........ **Henry John Deutschendorf Jr.**
Derek, John........ **Derek Harris**
Devine, Andy **Jeremiah Schwartz**
DeWolfe, Billy ..... **William Jones**
Dickinson, Angie **Angeline Brown**
Dietrich, Marlene .... **Maria von Losch**
Diller, Phyllis ...... **Phyllis Driver**
Donahue, Troy ... **Merle Johnson**
Dors, Diana .... **Diana Fluck**
Douglas, Kirk.. **Issur Danielovitch**
Douglas, Melvyn......... **Melvyn Hesselberg**
Drake, Alfred... **Alfredo Capurro**
Dressler, Marie.... **Leila Koerber**
Drew, Ellen........... **Terry Ray**
Dylan, Bob .. **Robert Zimmerman**
Ebsen, Buddy ... **Christian Ebsen**
Eden, Barbara . **Barbara Huffman**
Ely, Ron.......... **Ronald Pierce**
Evans, Dale .... **Frances Octavia Smith**
Everett, Chad **Raymond Cramton**
Ewell, Tom.. **S. Yewell Tompkins**
Fabian . **Fabian Forte Bonaparte**
Fairbanks, Douglas ..... **Douglas Ullman**
Farrow, Mia .... **Maria Farrow**
Faye, Alice .... **Ann Leppert**
Fernandel ... **Fernand Contandin**
Fetchit, Stepin..... **Lincoln Perry**
Fields, Gracie .. **Grace Stansfield**
Fields, W. C...... **William Claude Dukinfield**
Finch, Peter.... **William Mitchell**
Fitzgerald, Barry. **William Shields**
Fleming, Rhonda .. **Marilyn Louis**
Fontaine, Joan **Joan de Havilland**
Ford, Glenn .... **Gwyllyn Ford**
Ford, John ..... **Sean O'Fearna**
Forsythe, John ..... **John Freund**
Foxx, Redd.. **John Elroy Sanford**

Franciosa, Tony .... **Anthony Papaleo**
Francis, Arlene ... **Arlene Francis Kazanjian**
Francis, Connie....... **Constance Franconero**
Gabor, Zsa Zsa .... **Sari Gabor**
Garbo, Greta .. **Greta Gustafsson**
Gardenia, Vincent ...... **Vincente Scognamiglio**
Gardner, Ava...... **Lucy Johnson**
Garfield, John ... **Julius Garfinkle**
Garland, Beverly......... **Beverly Fessenden**
Garland, Judy ... **Frances Gumm**
Garner, James .... **James Baumgarner**
Gaynor, Janet ..... **Laura Gainer**
Gaynor, Mitzi... **Francesca Mitzi von Gerber**
Gentry, Bobbie **Roberta Streeter**
Gershwin, George .... **Jacob Gershowitz**
Gershwin, Ira.. **Israel Gershowitz**
Gilbert, John ..... **John Pringle**
Gilford, Jack ..... **Jacob Gellman**
Gish, Dorothy **Dorothy de Guiche**
Gish, Lillian..... **Lillian de Guiche**
Goddard, Paulette .. **Marion Levy**
Goldwyn, Samuel........ **Samuel Goldfish**
Gordon, Gale.... **Gaylord Aldrich**
Gould, Elliott ... **Elliott Goldstein**
Goulet, Robert........... **Stanley Applebaum**
Granger, Stewart......... **James Lablanche Stewart**
Grant, Cary ... **Archibald Leach**
Grant, Kathryn ... **Olive Kathryn Grandstaff**
Grant, Lee...... **Lyova Rosenthal**
Graves, Peter .... **Peter Aurness**
Grayson, Kathryn.......... **Zelma Kathryn Hedrick**
Grey, Joel.............. **Joel Katz**
Hackett, Buddy.. **Leonard Hacker**
Harlow, Jean **Harlean Carpentier**
Harris, Barbara .... **Sandra Markowitz**
Harvey, Laurence...... **Larushka Mischa Skikne**
Haver, June ..... **June Stovenour**
Hayden, Sterling.. **John Hamilton**
Hayes, Helen..... **Helen Hayes Brown**
Hayward, Louis... **Seafield Grant**
Hayward, Susan......... **Edythe Marrener**
Hayworth, Rita .... **Margarita Carmen Cansino**
Heflin, Van . **Emmett Evan Heflin**

211

Hepburn, Audrey .... **Audrey Hepburn-Ruston**
Heston, Charlton . **John Charlton Carter**
Holden, William.. **William Beedle**
Holliday, Judy ...... **Judith Tuvim**
Hope, Bob.. **Leslie Townes Hope**
Hopper, Hedda .... **Elda Furry**
Houdini, Harry ..... **Ehrich Weiss**
Houseman, John .... **Jacques Haussmann**
Howard, Leslie .... **Leslie Stainer**
Hudson, Rock .. **Roy Scherer, Jr.**
Humperdinck, Engelbert .. **Arnold Dorsey**
Hunter, Jeffrey .... **Henry H. McKinnies**
Hunter, Kim .... **Janet Cole**
Hunter, Ross .... **Martin Fuss**
Hussey, Ruth......... **Ruth Carol O'Rourke**
Hutton, Betty........ **Betty Jane Thornburg**
Hutton, Lauren ..... **Mary Hutton**
Ives, Burl..... **Burle Icle Ivanhoe**
Jagger, Dean...... **Dean Jeffries**
Janssen, David .... **David Meyer**
John, Elton..... **Reginald Dwight**
Johnson, Van....... **Charles Van Johnson**
Jolson, Al .... **Asa Yoelson**
Jones, Jennifer...... **Phyllis Isley**
Jones, Tom . **Thomas Woodward**
Jourdan, Louis..... **Louis Gendre**
Karloff, Boris..... **William Pratt**
Kaye, Danny .... **David Daniel Kaminsky**
Kazan, Elia .... **Elia Kazanjoglous**
Keel, Howard....... **Harold Leek**
Kerr, Deborah .... **Deborah Kerr-Trimmer**
King, Alan..... **Irwin Kinberg**
King, Carole........ **Carole Klein**
Knight, Ted .. **Tadeus Wladyslaw Konopka**
Ladd, Cheryl .... **Cheryl Stoppelmoor**
Lahr, Bert ...... **Irving Lahrheim**
Laine, Frankie .... **Frank Paul Lo Vecchio**
Lake, Veronica .... **Constance Ockleman**
Lamarr, Hedy.... **Hedwig Kiesler**
Lamour, Dorothy .... **Dorothy Kaumeyer**
Lanchester, Elsa....... **Elizabeth Sullivan**
Lanza, Mario ... **Alfredo Cocozza**
Laurel, Stan ..... **Arthur Stanley Jefferson**
Laurie, Piper .... **Rosetta Jacobs**

Lawrence, Gertrude... **Alexandra Dagmar Lawrence-Klasen**
Lawrence, Steve.......... **Sidney Leibowitz**
Lee, Canada..... **Lionel Canegata**
Lee, Gypsy Rose . **Louise Hovick**
Lee, Peggy..... **Norma Egstrom**
Leigh, Janet.. **Jeanette Morrison**
Leigh, Vivien ..... **Vivien Hartley**
Lenya, Lotte.. **Caroline Blamauer**
Lewis, Jerry..... **Joseph Levitch**
Liberace .... **Wladziu Valentino Liberace**
Lillie, Beatrice .... **Constance Sylvia Munston**
Linden, Hal ..... **Harold Lipshitz**
Lisi, Virna .... **Virna Pieralisi**
Lockwood, Gary ...... **John Gary Yusolfsky**
Lombard, Carole...... **Jane Alice Peters**
London, Julie......... **Julie Peck**
Lord, Jack.... **John Joseph Ryan**
Loren, Sophia ..... **Sophia Scicoloni**
Lorre, Peter . **Laszlo Loewenstein**
Louise, Tina ..... **Tina Blackmer**
Loy, Myrna ..... **Myrna Williams**
Lynley, Carol .... **Carolyn Lee**
Lynn, Diana ...... **Dolores Loehr**
Maclaine, Shirley .... **Shirley Maclean Beaty**
Madison, Guy ... **Robert Moseley**
Main, Marjorie.. **Mary Tomlinson**
Malden, Karl. **Malden Sekulovich**
Mansfield, Jayne ...... **Vera Jane Palmer**
March, Frederic .... **Ernest Frederick McIntyre Bickel**
Martin, Dean . **Dino Paul Crocetti**
Martin, Ross . **Martin Rosenblatt**
Martin, Tony .... **Alvin Morris**
May, Elaine........ **Elaine Berlin**
Mayo, Virginia.... **Virginia Jones**
McGee, Fibber.... **James Jordan**
McQueen, Butterfly...... **Thelma McQueen**
Meredith, Burgess ...... **George Burgess**
Merman, Ethel **Ethel Zimmerman**
Merrill, Dina ..... **Nedenia Hutton Rumbough**
Miles, Vera........ **Vera Ralston**
Milland, Ray.. **Reginald Truscott-Jones**
Miller, Ann ... **Lucille Ann Collier**
Miller, Marilyn .... **Mary Ellen Reynolds**
Monroe, Marilyn .... **Norma Jean Baker**
Montand, Yves .... **Ivo Levi**

Moore, Garry.. **Thomas Garrison Morfit**
Moreno, Rita ..... **Rosita Dolores Alverio**
Morgan, Dennis . **Stanley Morner**
Morgan, Harry.. **Harry Bratsburg**
Morgan, Helen..... **Helen Riggins**
Mostel, Zero. **Samuel Joel Mostel**
Muni, Paul... **Muni Weisenfreund**
Murray, Mae..... **Marie Adrienne Koenig**
Naldi, Nita.. **Anita Donna Dooley**
Neagle, Anna **Marjorie Robertson**
Nelson, Barry .... **Robert Neilson**
Newmar, Julie.. **Julia Newmeyer**
Nichols, Mike....... **Michael Igor Peschkowsky**
North, Sheree ..... **Dawn Bethel**
Novak, Kim ..... **Marilyn Novak**
Novarro, Ramon.......... **Ramon Samaniegos**
Nuyen, France... **France Nguyen Vannga**
O'Brian, Hugh ..... **Hugh Krampe**
O'Brien, Margaret .... **Angela Maxine O'Brien**
O'Hara, Maureen .... **Maureen Fitzsimmons**
O'Keefe, Dennis .... **Edward Flanagan**
Oakie, Jack..... **Lewis D. Offield**
Oberon, Merle..... **Estelle Merle O'Brien Thompson**
Page, Patti .... **Clara Ann Fowler**
Paige, Janis .. **Donna Mae Jaden**
Palmer, Betsy .. **Patricia Brumek**
Palmer, Lilli .... **Lilli Peiser**
Papas, Irene....... **Irene Lelekou**
Parks, Bert....... **Bert Jacobson**
Pearl, Minnie ..... **Sarah Ophelia Cannon**
Peters, Bernadette .. **Bernadette Lazzaro**
Pickens, Slim. **Louis Bert Lindley**
Pickford, Mary..... **Gladys Smith**
Pinza, Ezio ..... **Fortunato Pinza**
Powell, Jane..... **Suzanne Burce**
Powers, Stefanie .... **Stefania Federkiewicz**
Prentiss, Paula .... **Paula Ragusa**
Preston, Robert .... **Robert Preston Meservey**
Raft, George ...... **George Ranft**
Raines, Ella.......... **Ella Raubes**
Randall, Tony .... **Leonard Rosenberg**
Ray, Aldo .... **Aldo da Re**
Raye, Martha.. **Margaret O'Reed**
Reed, Donna .. **Donna Mullenger**
Reese, Della.......... **Dolloreese Patricia Early**

Reynolds, Debbie.. **Mary Frances Reynolds**
Rhue, Madlyn.. **Madeleine Roche**
Ritter, Tex .... **Woodward Ritter**
Rivera, Chita .. **Dolores Conchita Figueroa del Rivero**
Robinson, Edward G. . **Emmanuel Goldenberg**
Rogers, Ginger . **Virginia McMath**
Rogers, Roy....... **Leonard Slye**
Rooney, Mickey .... **Joe Yule, Jr.**
Roth, Lillian ..... **Lillian Rutstein**
Russell, Lillian ..... **Helen Louise Leonard**
Sales, Soupy .... **Milton Hines**
Savalas, Telly . **Aristotle Savalas**
Saxon, John...... **Carmen Orrico**
Scala, Gia..... **Giovanna Scoglio**
Schneider, Romy ..... **Rosemarie Albach-Retty**
Scott, Lizabeth .... **Emma Matzo**
Sharif, Omar ... **Michel Shalhoub**
Shearer, Moira ...... **Moira King**
Sheen, Martin ... **Ramon Estevez**
Shire, Talia .... **Talia Coppola**
Shore, Dinah ...... **Frances Rose Shore**
Signoret, Simone........ **Simone Kaminker**
Sills, Beverly .... **Belle Silverman**
Silverheels, Jay . **Harold J. Smith**
Singleton, Penny .... **Mariana McNulty**
Skelton, Red ... **Richard Skelton**
Smith, Alexis...... **Gladys Smith**
Somers, Suzanne....... **Suzanne Mahoney**
Sommer, Elke ..... **Elke Schletz**
Soo, Jack .... **Gogo Suzuki**
Sothern, Ann..... **Harriette Lake**
Sparks, Ned.. **Edward Sparkman**
St. James, Susan... **Susan Miller**
St. John, Jill..... **Jill Oppenheim**
Stack, Robert .... **Robert Modini**
Stanwyck, Barbara **Ruby Stevens**
Stapleton, Jean.. **Jeanne Murray**
Starr, Ringo .... **Richard Starkey**
Sterling, Jan ...... **Jane Sterling Adriance**
Sterling, Robert .... **William John Hart**
Stevens, Connie **Concetta Ingolia**
Stevens, Inger... **Inger Stensland**
Storm, Gale ... **Josephine Cottle**
Streep, Meryl....... **Mary Louise Streep**
Summers, Donna....... **LaDonna Gaines**
Sweet, Blanche.. **Daphne Wayne**
Tati, Jacques........... **Jacques Tatischeff**

Taylor, Robert.......... **Spangler Arlington Brugh**
Terry-Thomas .... **Thomas Terry Hoar-Stevens**
Thomas, Danny .. **Amos Muzyad Jacobs**
Thomas, Marlo .... **Margaret Thomas**
Tiffin, Pamela .... **Pamela Wonso**
Torn, Rip...... **Elmore Rual Torn**
Tucker, Sophie .... **Sophia Kalish**
Turner, Lana .. **Julia Jean Turner**
Twiggy........... **Lesley Hornby**
Twitty, Conway....**Harold Lloyd Jenkins**
Vague, Vera... **Barbara Jo Allen**
Vallee, Rudy........ **Hubert Prior Vallee**
Valli, Frankie . **Frank Castelluccio**
Van Devere, Trish .... **Patricia Dressel**
Van Doren, Mamie.. **Joan Lucille Olander**
Van, Bobby......... **Robert King**
Velez, Lupe... **Maria Guadeloupe Velez de Villalobos**
Vera-Ellen . **Vera-Ellen Westmeyr Rohe**

Walker, Nancy...... **Ann Swoyer Barto**
Wayne, John .... **Marion Michael Morrison**
Webb, Clifton.. **Webb Hollenbeck**
Welch, Raquel.... **Raquel Tejada**
Weld, Tuesday . **Susan Ker Weld**
Werner, Oskar...... **Oskar Josef Schliessmayer**
West, Adam... **William Anderson**
Wilder, Gene ... **Jerry Silberman**
Windsor, Marie . **Emily Marie Bertelson**
Winters, Shelley .. **Shirley Schrift**
Wonder, Stevie. **Stevland Morris**
Wong, Anna May ...... **Wong Liu Tsong**
Wood, Natalie .. **Natasha Gurdin**
Wynn, Ed.. **Isaiah Edwin Leopold**
Wynn, Keenan.... **Francis Xavier Aloysius Wynn**
Wynter, Dana . **Dagmar Spencer-Marcus**
York, Susannah .... **Susannah Yolande Fletcher**
Young, Gig . **Byron Elsworth Barr**
Young, Loretta .... **Gretchen Michaela Young**

SOME FAMOUS PEN NAMES

Boz............ **Charles Dickens**

Bell, Acton......... **Anne Bronte**
Bell, Carter.... **Charlotte Bronte**
Bell, Ellis.......... **Emily Bronte**
Boyd, Nancy ... **Edna St. Vincent Millay**
Elia .... **Charles Lamb**
Loti, Pierre.......... **Louis Viaud**
Saki .... **H. H. Munro**
Sand, George .. **Amandine Dupin Dudevant**
Ward, Artemus **Charles F. Browne**

Eliot, George ... **Mary Ann Evans**
Gorki, Maxim............ **Alexey Maximovich Peshkov**
Nasby, Petroleum ... **David Ross Locke**

Henry, O. **William Sydney Porter**
Ouida....... **Louise de la Ramee**
Twain, Mark.... **Samuel Clemens**

France, Anatole .... **Jacques Thibault**
Orwell, George . **Eric Arthur Blair**

Carroll, Lewis . **Charles Dodgson**
Colette........ **Sidonie Gabrielle Claudine Colette**
LeCarre, John....... **David John Cornwell**

Stendhal............ **Henri Beyle**
Voltaire .. **Francois Marie Arouet**

Westmacott, Mary....... **Agatha Christie**

SOME U.S. AUTHORS

Abbot, George
Ade, George
Albee, Edward
Alcott, Louisa May
Alger, Horatio
Asimov, Isaac
Austen, Jane
Baldwin, James
Barth, John
Baum, L. Frank
Behrman, S.N.
Bellow, Saul
Benchley, Peter
Benchley, Robert
Benet, Stephen
    Vincent
Bierce, Ambrose
Bishop, Jim
Blume, Judy
Bradbury, Ray
Brand, Max
Brown, Dee
Buck, Pearl
Burroughs, Edgar
    Rice
Burrows, Abe
Caldwell, Erskine
Caldwell, Taylor
Capote, Truman
Cather, Willa
Chase, Mary
Chayefsky, Paddy
Cheever, John
Clavell, James
Connelly, Marc
Cooper, James
    Fennimore
Crane, Hart
Crane, Stephen
Crews, Harry
Crichton, Michael
cummings, e.e.
Dickinson, Emily
Didion, Joan
Dos Passos, John
Drury, Allen
Emerson, Ralph
    Waldo
Farrel, James T.
Faulkner, William
Ferber, Edna
Fitzgerald, F. Scott
Frost, Robert
Gardner, Erle Stanley
Grey, Zane
Guest, Edgar A.

Hailey, Arthur
Haley, Alex
Hammett, Dashiell
Harris, Joel Chandler
Hart, Moss
Harte, Bret
Heller, Joseph
Hellman, Lillian
Hemingway, Ernest
Henry, O.
Hersey, John
Holmes, Oliver
    Wendell
Hughes, Langston
Inge, William
Irving, John
Irving, Washington
James, Henry
Kazan, Elia
Kerr, Jean
Kesey, Ken
Kilmer, Joyce
Knowles, John
Lardner, Ring
Lee, Harper
Levin, Ira
Lewis, Sinclair
London, Jack
Longfellow, Henry
    Wadsworth
Loos, Anita
Lowell, Amy
Lowell, James Russell
Lowell, Robert
Ludlum, Robert
MacInnes, Helen
Mailer, Norman
Malamud, Bernard
Masters, Edgar Lee
Matthison, Peter
McCarthy, Mary
McCullers, Carson
Melville, Herman
Mencken, H.L.
Michener, James
Millay, Edna St.
    Vincent
Miller, Arthur
Moore, Clement C.
Moore, Marianne
Nash, Ogden
Oates, Joyce Carol
Odets, Clifford
O'Hara, John
O'Neill, Eugene
Parker, Dorothy

Poe, Edgar Allan
Porter, Katherine Ann
Potok, Chaim
Pound, Ezra
Puzo, Mario
Rice, Elmer
Riley, James
    Whitcomb
Rinehart, Mary
    Roberts
Roth, Philip
Runyon, Damon
Salinger, J.D.
Sandburg, Carl
Saroyan, William
Schary, Dore
Schulberg, Budd
Segal, Erich
Shaw, Irwin
Simon, Neil
Sinclair, Upton
Singer, Isaac
    Bashevis
Slaughter, Frank
Stein, Gertrude
Steinbeck, John
Stone, Irving
Stout, Rex
Stowe, Harriet
    Beecher
Styron, William
Tarkington, Booth
Teasdale, Sara
Thurber, James
Tryon, Thomas
Twain, Mark
Updike, John
Uris, Leon
Vidal, Gore
Vonnegut, Kurt Jr.
Wallace, Irving
Warren, Robert Penn
Welty, Eudora
West, Nathaniel
Wharton, Edith
White, Theodore H.
Whitman, Walt
Whittier, John
    Greenleaf
Wilder, Thornton
Williams, Tennessee
Wolfe, Thomas
Wouk, Herman
Wylie, Elinor
Yerby, Frank

NAMES FROM SHAKESPEARE

Listed by Plays

(Plays are listed alphabetically by the titles that are commonly used. The actual title, if different, follows in parentheses.)

ALL'S WELL THAT ENDS WELL
DIANA, LAFEU; HELENA; BERTRAM, LAVACHE, MARIANA; PAROLLES, VIOLENTA

ANTONY AND CLEOPATRA
EROS, IRAS; MENAS, PHILO; ALEXAS, CAESAR (OCTAVIUS), GALLUS, SCARUS, SEXTUS (POMPEIUS), SILIUS, TAURUS; AGRIPPA, LEPIDUS, MARDIAN, OCTAVIA, THYREUS, VARRIUS; CANIDIUS, CHARMIAN, DERCETAS, DIOMEDES, MAECENAS, SELEUCUS; DEMETRIUS, DOLABELLA, VENTIDIUS; EUPHRONIUS, MENECRATES, PROCULEIUS

AS YOU LIKE IT
ADAM; CELIA, CORIN, PHEBE; AMIENS, AUDREY, DENNIS, JAQUES, LE BEAU, OLIVER; CHARLES, ORLANDO, SILVIUS, WILLIAM; ROSALIND; FREDERICK; TOUCHSTONE

COMEDY OF ERRORS, THE
LUCE; PINCH; AEGEON, ANGELO, DROMIO; ADRIANA, AEMILIA, LUCIANA, SOLINUS; BALTHAZAR; ANTIPHOLUS

CORIOLANUS (The Tragedy of Coriolanus)
CAIUS, TITUS; BRUTUS, JUNIUS, TULLUS; AGRIPPA, LARTIUS, MARCIUS, VALERIA, VELUTUS; AUFIDIUS, COMINIUS, MENENIUS, SICINIUS, VIRGILIA, VOLUMNIA

CYMBELINE
CAIUS (LUCIUS), HELEN; CLOTEN, IMOGEN; IACHIMO, PISANIO; BELARIUS, LEONATUS, PHILARIO; ARVIRAGUS, CORNELIUS, GUIDERIUS, POSTHUMUS

HAMLET (The Tragedy of Hamlet, Prince of Denmark)
OSRIC; HORATIO, LAERTES, OPHELIA; BERNARDO, CLAUDIUS, GERTRUDE, POLONIUS, REYNALDO; CORNELIUS, FRANCISCO, MARCELLUS, VOLTIMAND; FORTINBRAS; ROSENCRANTZ; GUILDENSTERN

JULIUS CAESAR (The Tragedy of Julius Caesar)
CATO, LENA; CASCA, CINNA, VARRO; BRUTUS, CICERO, CLITUS, DECIUS, LUCIUS, MARCUS, PORTIA, STRATO; CASSIUS, FLAVIUS, LEPIDUS, MESSALA, PUBLIUS; CLAUDIUS, LIGARIUS, LUCILIUS, MARULLUS, METELLUS, OCTAVIUS, PINDARUS, POPILIUS, TITINIUS; CALPURNIA, DARDANIUS, TREBONIUS, VOLUMNIUS; ARTEMIDORUS

KING HENRY IV, PART I (The First Part of King Henry IV)
JOHN, PETO; BLUNT, HENRY, PERCY, POINS; MICHAEL, QUICKLY; BARDOLPH, FALSTAFF, GADSHILL; ARCHIBALD, GLENDOWER

KING HENRY IV, PART II (The Second Part of King Henry IV)
DAVY, FANG, JOHN, PETO, WART; BLUNT, GOWER, HENRY, POINS, SNARE; FEEBLE, MORTON, MOULDY, PISTOL, RUMOUR, SCROOP, SHADOW, THOMAS; MOWBRAY, QUICKLY, SHALLOW, SILENCE, TRAVERS; BARDOLPH, BULLCALF, FALSTAFF, HARCOURT, HASTINGS, HUMPHREY; DOLL TEARSHEET

KING HENRY V (The Life of King Henry V)
NYM; GREY, JAMY; ALICE, BATES, COURT, GOWER, LEWIS; ISABEL, PISTOL; SCROOP; CHARLES, MONTJOY, QUICKLY; BARDOLPH, FLUELLEN, GRANDPRE, RAMBURES, WILLIAMS; ERPINGHAM, KATHARINE, MACMORRIS

KING HENRY VI, PART I (The First Part of King Henry VI)
LUCY; BASSET, TALBOT, VERNON; CHARLES, RICHARD; BEAUFORT, FASTOLFE, GARGRAVE, MARGARET, REIGNIER, WOODVILE; GLANSDALE, LA PUCELLE (Joan of Arc), PLANTAGENET

KING HENRY VI, PART II (The Second Part of King Henry VI)
SAY; CADE, DICK, HUME, IDEN, VAUX; BEVIS, GOFFE, PETER, SMITH; EDMUND, EDWARD, HORNER, SCALES, THOMAS; ELEANOR, HOLLAND, MICHAEL, RICHARD, SIMPCOX, STANLEY; BEAUFORT, CLIFFORD, HUMPHREY, JOURDAIN, MARGARET, MORTIMER, STAFFORD; ALEXANDER, SOUTHWELL; BOLINGBROKE, PLANTAGENET

KING HENRY VI, PART III (The Third Part of King Henry VI)
BONA, GREY; HENRY, LEWIS; EDMUND, EDWARD, GEORGE, RIVERS; RICHARD, STANLEY, CLIFFORD, HASTINGS, MARGARET, MORTIMER, STAFFORD; SOMERVILLE; MONTGOMERY; PLANTAGENET

KING HENRY VIII (The Famous History of the Life of King Henry VIII)
VAUX; BUTTS, DENNY, SANDS; LOVELL, WOLSEY; BRANDON, CRANMER; CAMPEIUS, CAPUCIUS, CROMWELL, GARDINER, GRIFFITH, PATIENCE; GUILDFORD, KATHARINE; ANNE BULLEN; ABERGAVENNY

KING JOHN (The Life and Death of King John)
BIGOT, HENRY, JAMES, LEWIS, MELUN, PETER; ARTHUR, BLANCHE, ELINOR, GURNEY, HUBERT, PHILIP, ROBERT; DE BURGH, LYMOGES; PANDULPH; CONSTANCE, CHATILLON

KING LEAR (The Tragedy of King Lear)
CURAN, EDGAR, REGAN; EDMUND, OSWALD; GONERIL; CORDELIA

KING RICHARD II (The Tragedy of King Richard II)
ROSS; BAGOT, BUSHY, GREEN, HENRY, PERCY; EDMUND, PIERCE, SCROOP, THOMAS; AUMERLE, HOTSPUR, MOWBRAY; FITZWATER; WILLOUGHBY; BOLINGBROKE, JOHN OF GAUNT

KING RICHARD III (The Tragedy of King Richard III)
 ANNE, GREY; HENRY, LOVEL; BLOUNT, EDWARD, GEORGE, MOR-
 TON, RIVERS, TYRREL; BRANDON, CATESBY, HERBERT, RICHARD,
 STANLEY, TRESSEL, URSWICK, VAUGHAN; BERKELEY, HASTINGS,
 MARGARET, RATCLIFF; BOURCHIER, ELIZABETH, ROTHERHAM;
 BRAKENBURY

MACBETH (The Tragedy of Macbeth)
 ROSS; ANGUS; BANQUO, DUNCAN, HECATE, LENNOX, SEYTON, SI-
 WARD; FLEANCE, MACDUFF, MALCOLM; MENTEITH; CAITHNESS,
 DONALBAIN

MEASURE FOR MEASURE
 ELBOW, FROTH, LUCIO, PETER; ANGELO, JULIET, POMPEY,
 THOMAS; CLAUDIO, ESCALUS, MARIANA, VARRIUS; ABHORSON,
 ISABELLA, OVERDONE; FRANCISCA, VINCENTIO; BARNARDINE

MERCHANT OF VENICE, THE
 GOBBO, TUBAL; PORTIA; ANTONIO, JESSICA, LORENZO, NERISSA,
 SALANIO, SALERIO, SHYLOCK; BASSANIO, GRATIANO, LEONARDO,
 SALARINO, STEPHANO; BALTHASAR

MERRY WIVES OF WINDSOR, THE
 NYM; ANNE, FORD, PAGE; CAIUS, EVANS, ROBIN, RUGBY; FENTON,
 PISTOL, SIMPLE; QUICKLY, SHALLOW, SLENDER, WILLIAM; BAR-
 DOLPH, FALSTAFF

MIDSUMMER-NIGHT'S DREAM, A
 MOTH, PUCK, SNUG; EGEUS, FLUTE, SNOUT; BOTTOM, COBWEB,
 HELENA, HERMIA, OBERON, QUINCE; THESEUS, TITANIA; LYSAN-
 DER; DEMETRIUS, HIPPOLYTA; STARVELING; PHILOSTRATE;
 PEASEBLOSSOM

MUCH ADO ABOUT NOTHING
 HERO; URSULA, VERGES; ANTONIO, CLAUDIO, CONRADE, DON
 JOHN, FRANCIS, LEONATO; BEATRICE, BENEDICK, BORACHIO,
 DOGBERRY, DON PEDRO, MARGARET; BALTHASAR

OTHELLO (The Tragedy of Othello, The Moor of Venice)
 IAGO; BIANCA, CASSIO, EMILIA; MONTANO; GRATIANO, LODOVICO,
 RODERIGO; BRABANTIO, DESDEMONA

PERICLES (Pericles, Prince of Tyre)
 BOULT, CLEON, DIANA, GOWER; MARINA, THAISA; CERIMON,
 DIONYZA, ESCANES, LEONINE; PHILEMON, THALIARD; ANTIO-
 CHUS, HELICANUS, LYCHORIDA, SIMONIDES; LYSIMACHUS

ROMEO AND JULIET (The Tragedy of Romeo and Juliet)
 PARIS, PETER; TYBALT; ABRAHAM, CAPULET, ESCALUS, GREG-
 ORY, SAMPSON; BENVOLIO, LAURENCE, MERCUTIO, MONTAGUE;
 BALTHASAR

TAMING OF THE SHREW, THE
SLY; BIANCA, CURTIS, GREMIO, GRUMIO, TRANIO; BAPTISTA, LU-CENTIO; BIONDELLO, HORTENSIO, KATHARINA, PETRUCHIO, VIN-CENTIO; CHRISTOPHER

TEMPEST, THE
IRIS, JUNO; ARIEL, CERES; ADRIAN, ALONSO; ANTONIO, CALIBAN; GONZALO, MIRANDA; PROSPERO, STEPHANO, TRINCULO; FERDI-NAND, FRANCISCO, SEBASTIAN

TIMON OF ATHENS (The Life of Timon of Athens)
CUPID, TITUS; CAPHIS, LUCIUS; FLAVIUS, PHRYNIA; LUCILIUS, LUCULLUS, PHILOTUS, TIMANDRA; APEMANTUS, FLAMINIUS, SER-VILIUS, VENTIDIUS; ALCIBIADES, HORTENSIUS, SEMPRONIUS

TITUS ANDRONICUS (The Tragedy of Titus Andronicus)
AARON; CHIRON, LUCIUS, MARCUS, MUTIUS, TAMORA; ALARBUS, LAVINIA, MARTIUS, PUBLIUS, QUINTUS; AEMILIUS; BASSIANUS, DEMETRIUS; SATURNINUS

TROILUS AND CRESSIDA
AJAX; HELEN, PARIS, PRIAM; AENEAS, HECTOR, NESTOR; AN-TENOR, CALCHAS, HELENUS, ULYSSES; ACHILLES, CRESSIDA, DI-OMEDES, MENELAUS, PANDARUS; AGAMEMNON, ALEXANDER, CASSANDRA, DEIPHOBUS, PATROCLUS, THERSITES; ANDROM-ACHE, MARGARELON

TWELFTH NIGHT (Twelfth Night; or, What You Will)
BELCH, CURIO, FESTE, MARIA, VIOLA; FABIAN, OLIVIA, ORSINO; AN-TONIO; MALVOLIO; AGUECHEEK, SEBASTIAN, VALENTINE

TWO GENTLEMEN OF VERONA, THE
JULIA, SPEED; LAUNCE, SILVIA, THURIO; ANTONIO, LUCETTA, PRO-TEUS; EGLAMOUR, PANTHINO; VALENTINE

WINTER'S TALE, THE
DION; MOPSA; DORCAS, EMILIA; CAMILLO, LEONTES, PAULINA, PERDITA; FLORIZEL, HERMIONE; ANTIGONUS, AUTOLYCUS, CLEO-MENES, MAMILLIUS, POLIXENES; ARCHIDAMUS

U.S. PRESIDENTS INFORMATION

Note: State indicates state of birth. First Ladies' maiden or original names are given directly under each president's name.

Name	Party	Vice-Pres.	State	Term
1. WASHINGTON, George Martha Dandridge Custis	Fed.	Adams	VA	1789–1797
2. ADAMS, John Abigal Smith	Fed.	Jefferson	MA	1797–1801
3. JEFFERSON, Thomas Martha Wayles Skelton	Dem.-Rep.	Burr, Clinton	VA	1801–1809
4. MADISON, James Dorothea Payne Todd "Dolley"	Dem.-Rep.	Clinton, Gerry	VA	1809–1817
5. MONROE, James Elizabeth Kortright	Dem.-Rep.	Tompkins	VA	1817–1825
6. ADAMS, John Quincy Louise Catherine Johnson	Dem.-Rep.	Calhoun	MA	1825–1829
7. JACKSON, Andrew Rachel Donelson Robards	Dem.	Calhoun, Van Buren	SC	1829–1837
8. VAN BUREN, Martin Hannah Hoes	Dem.	Johnson	NY	1837–1841
9. HARRISON, William Henry Anna Symmes	Whig	Tyler	VA	1841
10. TYLER, John Letitia Christian and Julia Gardiner	Dem.		VA	1841–1845
11. POLK, James Knox Sarah Childress	Dem.	Dallas	NC	1845–1849
12. TAYLOR, Zachary Margaret Smith	Whig	Fillmore	VA	1849–1850
13. FILLMORE, Millard Abigail Powers and Caroline Carmichael McIntosh	Whig		NY	1850–1853
14. PIERCE, Franklin Jane Mears Appleton	Dem.	King	NH	1853–1857
15. BUCHANAN, James	Dem.	Breckenridge	PA	1857–1861
16. LINCOLN, Abraham Mary Todd	Rep.	Hamlin, Johnson	KY	1861–1865
17. JOHNSON, Andrew Eliza McCardle	Dem.		NC	1865–1869
18. GRANT, Ulysses Simpson Julia Dent	Rep.	Colfax, Wilson	OH	1869–1877
19. HAYES, Rutherford Birchard Lucy Ware Webb	Rep.	Wheeler	OH	1877–1881
20. GARFIELD, James Abram Lucretia Rudolph	Rep.	Arthur	OH	1881
21. ARTHUR, Chester Alan Ellen Lewis Herndon	Rep.		VT	1881–1885
22. CLEVELAND, Stephen Grover Frances Folsom	Dem.	Hendricks	NJ	1885–1889
23. HARRISON, Benjamin Caroline Lavinia Scott and Mary Scott Lord Dimmick	Rep.	Morton	OH	1889–1893

Name	Party	Vice-Pres.	State	Term
24. CLEVELAND, Stephen Grover Frances Folsom	Dem.	Stevenson	NJ	1893–1897
25. MC KINLEY, William Ida Saxton	Rep.	Hobart, Roosevelt	OH	1897–1901
26. ROOSEVELT, Theodore Alice Hathaway Lee and Edith Kermit Carow	Rep.	Fairbanks	NY	1901–1909
27. TAFT, William Howard Helen Herron	Rep.	Sherman	OH	1909–1913
28. WILSON, Thomas Woodrow Ellen Louise Axson and Edith Bolling Galt	Dem.	Marshall	VA	1913–1921
29. HARDING, Warren Gamaliel Florence Kling De Wolfe	Rep.	Coolidge	OH	1921–1923
30. COOLIDGE, John Calvin Grace Anna Goodhue	Rep.	Dawes	VT	1923–1929
31. HOOVER, Herbert Clark Lou Henry	Rep.	Curtis	IA	1929–1933
32. ROOSEVELT, Franklin Delano Anna Eleanor Roosevelt	Dem.	Garner, Wallace Truman	NY	1933–1945
33. TRUMAN, Harry S Elizabeth (Bess) Wallace	Dem.	Barkley	MO	1945–1953
34. EISENHOWER, Dwight David Mamie Geneva Doud	Rep.	Nixon	TX	1953–1961
35. KENNEDY, John Fitzgerald Jacqueline Lee Bouvier	Dem.	Johnson	MA	1961–1963
36. JOHNSON, Lyndon Baines Claudia Alta Taylor "Lady Bird"	Dem.	Humphrey	TX	1963–1968
37. NIXON, Richard Milhous Thelma Catherine Patricia Ryan "Pat"	Rep.	Agnew, Ford	CA	1968–1974
38. FORD, Gerald Rudolph Elizabeth Bloomer Warren "Betty"	Rep.	Rockefeller	NE	1974–1977
39. CARTER, James Earl, Jr. Rosalynn Smith	Dem.	Mondale	GA	1977–1981
40. REAGAN, Ronald Wilson Anne Frances Robbins Davis "Nancy"	Rep.	Bush	IL	1981–

U.S. STATES INFORMATION

STATE	ABBREVIATIONS (official P.O. abbr. appears first)	RANK BY AREA	RANK BY POPULATION
ALABAMA	AL, Ala.	29	22
ALASKA	AK, Alas., Alsk.	1	50
ARIZONA	AZ, Ariz.	6	29
ARKANSAS	AR, Ark.	27	33
CALIFORNIA	CA, Calif., Cal.	3	1
COLORADO	CO, Colo.	8	27
*CONNECTICUT	CT, Conn.	48	25
*DELAWARE	DE, Del., Dela.	49	47
†DISTRICT OF COLUMBIA	DC, D.C.		
FLORIDA	FL, Fla.	22	7
*GEORGIA	GA, Ga.	21	12
HAWAII	HI, H., Haw.	47	40
IDAHO	ID, Id., Ida.	13	41
ILLINOIS	IL, Ill.	24	5
INDIANA	IN, Ind.	38	13
IOWA	IA, Ia.	25	28
KANSAS	KS, Kan., Kans.	14	32
KENTUCKY	KY, Ky.	37	24
LOUISIANA	LA, La.	31	18
MAINE	ME, Me.	39	39
*MARYLAND	MD, Md.	42	19
*MASSACHUSETTS	MA, Mass.	45	11
MICHIGAN	MI, Mich.	23	8
MINNESOTA	MN, Minn.	12	21
MISSISSIPPI	MS, Miss.	32	31
MISSOURI	MO, Mo.	19	15
MONTANA	MT, Mont.	4	45
NEBRASKA	NE, Nebr.	15	36
NEVADA	NV, Nev.	7	44
*NEW HAMPSHIRE	NH, N.H.	44	43
*NEW JERSEY	NJ, N.J.	46	9
NEW MEXICO	NM, N.M.	5	38
*NEW YORK	NY, N.Y.	30	2
*NORTH CAROLINA	NC, N.C.	28	10
NORTH DAKOTA	ND, N.D.	17	46
OHIO	OH, O.	35	6
OKLAHOMA	OK, Okla.	18	26
OREGON	OR, Ore.	10	30
*PENNSYLVANIA	PA, Penna., Penn.	33	4
*RHODE ISLAND	RI, R.I.	50	41
*SOUTH CAROLINA	SC, S.C.	40	24
SOUTH DAKOTA	SD, S.D.	16	45
TENNESSEE	TN, Tenn.	34	17
TEXAS	TX, Tex.	2	3
UTAH	UT, Ut.	11	36
VERMONT	VT, Vt.	43	48
*VIRGINIA	VA, Va.	36	14
WASHINGTON	WA, Wash.	20	20
WEST VIRGINIA	WV, W. Va.	41	34
WISCONSIN	WI, Wisc., Wis.	26	16
WYOMING	WY, Wyo.	9	49

†District   *One of the Thirteen Original States

STATE CAPITAL	STATE NICKNAME(S)	STATE FLOWER
Montgomery	Cotton, Heart of Dixie, Yellowhammer	Camellia
Juneau	The Last Frontier	Forget-Me-Not
Phoenix	Grand Canyon	Seguaro Cactus
Little Rock	Land of Opportunity	Apple Blossom
Sacramento	Golden, El Dorado	Golden Poppy
Denver	Centennial, Silver	Columbine
Hartford	Constitution, Nutmeg	Mountain Laurel
Dover	First, Diamond, Blue Hen	Peach Blossom
		American Beauty Rose
Tallahassee	Sunshine, Peninsular	Orange Blossom
Atlanta	Empire State of the South, Peach	Cherokee Rose
Honolulu	Aloha, Paradise of the Pacific	Hibiscus
Boise	Gem	Syringa
Springfield	Prairie, Sucker, The Inland Empire	Violet
Indianapolis	Hoosier	Peony
Des Moines	Hawkeye	Wild Rose
Topeka	Sunflower, Jayhawker	Sunflower
Frankfort	Bluegrass	Goldenrod
Baton Rouge	Pelican, Creole	Magnolia
Augusta	Pine Tree, Lumber	Pine Cone and Tassel
Annapolis	Old Line, Free, Cockade	Black-Eyed Susan
Boston	Bay, Old Colony	Mayflower
Lansing	Wolverine, Great Lake	Apple Blossom
St. Paul	North Star, Gopher	Lady's-Slipper
Jackson	Magnolia, Bayou	Magnolia
Jefferson City	Show Me, Bullion	Hawthorn
Helena	Treasure, Mountain	Bitterroot
Lincoln	Cornhusker, Blackwater	Goldenrod
Carson City	Sagebrush, Silver, Battle Born	Sagebrush
Concord	Granite	Purple Lilac
Trenton	Garden	Violet
Santa Fe	Sunshine, Land of Enchantment	Yucca
Albany	Empire, Excelsior	Rose
Raleigh	Tar Heel, Old North, Turpentine	Dogwood
Bismarck	Sioux, Flickertail	Wild Prairie Rose
Columbus	Buckeye	Scarlet Carnation
Oklahoma City	Sooner	Mistletoe
Salem	Beaver, Sunset, Valentine, Webfoot	Oregon Grape
Harrisburg	Keystone	Mountain Laurel
Providence	Little Rhody, Ocean	Violet
Columbia	Palmetto	Carolina Jessamine
Pierre	Coyote, Sunshine	Pasque Flower
Nashville	Volunteer	Iris
Austin	Lone Star	Bluebonnet
Salt Lake City	Beehive, Mormon	Sego Lily
Montpelier	Green Mountain	Red Clover
Richmond	Old Dominion, Mother of Presidents	Dogwood
Olympia	Evergreen, Chinook	Western Rhododendron
Charleston	Mountain	Big Rhododendron
Madison	Badger	Wood Violet
Cheyenne	Equality	Indian Paintbrush

GAZETTEER

OR

GEOGRAPHICAL DICTIONARY

Cities, States, Countries, Counties, Provinces, Towns, Rivers, Communes, Ports and Harbors, Regions, Lakes, Mountains, Islands, Volcanoes, Settlements, Kingdoms, Districts, Divisions, Peninsulas, Mountain Ranges, etc.

A

ABYSSINIA .... see ETHIOPIA

ADRIATIC ...... port and harbor, FIUME; peninsula, ISTRIA; resort, LIDO

AEGEAN..... gulf, SAROS; river, STRUMA; island, IOS, KOS, KEOS, CHIOS, DELOS, KASOS, LEROS, MELOS, NAXOS, PAROS, SAMOS, SYROS, TELOS, TENOS, THIRA, ANDROS, PATMOS, RHODES, SKYROS

AFGHANISTAN..... city, HERAT

AFRICA........ country, CHAD, MALI, TOGO, BENIN, CONGO, EGYPT, GABON, GHANA, KENYA, LIBYA, NIGER, SUDAN, ZAIRE, ANGOLA, (THE) GAMBIA, GUINEA, MALAWI, RWANDA, UGANDA, ZAMBIA, ALGERIA, BURUNDI, LESOTHO, LIBERIA, NIGERIA, SENEGAL, SOMALIA, TUNISIA; lake, CHAD, TANA, NYASA; mountains, ATLAS; river, NILE, CONGO, NIGER, ORANGE; canal, SUEZ

ALABAMA........ city, SELMA, ANNISTON

ALASKA.... city, NOME, SITKA; island, ADAK, ATKA, ATTU, UNGA; mountain, ADA; inlet, COOK; river, YUKON; highest peak in N. America, MCKINLEY; glacier, MUIR

ALBANIA ...... capital, TIRANA; river, DRIN

ALEUTIANS..... islands, ADAK, ATKA, ATTU

ALGERIA ... city, ORAN, SETIF, ALGIERS

ALPS... mountain, ROSA, VISO, BLANC, LEONE, MATTERHORN

ANGOLA .... city, LOBITO, LUANDA; mountain peak, MOCO

ANTARCTIC .... sea, ROSS

ARABIA ..... city, ADEN, SANA; district, TEMA (TAIMA); nation, OMAN, QATAR, YEMEN, KUWAIT; gulf, ADEN, OMAN; old kingdom, NEJD; cape, ASIR

ARCTIC .... gulf, OB; sea, KARA

ARGENTINA .... city, SALTA, CORDOBA, ROSARIO; province, CHACO; volcano, MAIPO

ARIZONA........... city, MESA, YUMA, TEMPE, TUCSON; county, GILA, PIMA, YUMA, PINAL, APACHE, MOHAVE, NAVAJO, COCHISE; lake, MEAD; river, SALT, GILA

ARKANSAS......... city, LITTLE ROCK; county, LEE, CLAY, DREW, PIKE, BOONE, CROSS, LOGAN, UNION; river, RED, WHITE

ARMENIA. river, **ARAS (ARAKS)**

ARU ISLANDS....... port, **DOBO**

ASIA... mountains, **ALTAI**; lake, **ARAL**; sea, **ARAL**; river, **OB, ILI, AMUR, LENA, ONON, TIGRIS**; kingdom, **NEPAL**; old kingdom, **SIAM**; country, **IRAN, IRAQ (IRAK), BURMA, CHINA, KOREA, TIBET**; desert, **GOBI**

ASIA MINOR..... district, **IONIA**; mountains, **IDA**

ASIATIC.............. see ASIA

AUSTRALIA.... peninsula, **EYRE**; river, **SWAN**; city, **PERTH**

AUSTRIA..... city, **GRAZ, LINZ, VIENNA (WIEN)**; river, **MUR, ENNS, RABA (RAAB)**; spa, **BADEN**

AZORES........ port and harbor, **HORTA**; island, **PICO, FAYAL (FAIAL), FLORES**; volcano, **PICO (ALTO)**

B

BAHAMAS..... capital, **NASSAU**

BAHRAIN.... capital, **MANAMA**

BALEARIC ISLANDS....... port, **PALMA**; island, **MAJORCA**

BALTIC...... capital, **RIGA**; gulf, **RIGA**; river, **ODER**

BANGLADESH . capital, **DACCA**; river, **GANGES**

BAVARIA ... river, **NAB (NAAB), ISAR**

BELGIUM . city, **GENT (GHENT), LIEGE**; commune or town, **ANS, ATH, HUY, SPA, MONS, NIEL, ROUX, NAMUR, MECHLIN (MALINES)**; river, **LYS, YSER, MEUSE, SENNE**; port and harbor, **OSTEND**; province, **LIEGE**

BENIN.......... city, **ABOMEY, COTONOU, PORTO-NOVO**; river, **VOLTA**

BOHEMIA.... river, **ELBE, ISER**;

BORNEO .. mountains, **KAPUAS, MULLER**; river, **BARITO, RAJANG**; state, **SABAH, SARAWAK**

BRAZIL...... city, **RIO, BELEM**; port and harbor, **PARA, NATAL, SANTOS, PELOTAS**; state, **PARA, BAHIA**; river, **APA, ICA, PARA**

BRITISH WEST INDIES.... island, **NEVIS**

BULGARIA....... capital, **SOFIA**

BURMA .. capital (former), **AVA**, (present), **RANGOON**; district, **PROME**

C

CALIFORNIA . city, **LODI, NAPA, POMONA, ALAMEDA, SALINAS**; town, **OJAI**; county, **NAPA, YOLO, MODOC, MADERA**; lake, **TAHOE**; mountain peak, **LASSEN, SHASTA**; valley, **NAPA**

CAMBODIA (KAMPUCHEA)...... capital, **PNOMPENH**; river, **MEKONG**

CAMEROON .... river, **SANAGA**

CANADA .... mountain, **LOGAN, ROBSON**; peninsula, **GASPE**; province, **ALBERTA (ALTA.), BRITISH COLUMBIA (B.C.), MANITOBA (MAN.), NEW BRUNSWICK (N.B.), NEWFOUNDLAND (NFLD.), NOVA SCOTIA (N.S.), ONTARIO (ONT.), PRINCE EDWARD ISLAND (P.E.I.), QUEBEC (QUE.), SASKATCHEWAN (SASK.)**; national park, **JASPER**

CAPE VERDE ..... island, **FOGO, MAIO (MAYO), BRAVA, SAL REI, BOA VISTA**

CARIBBEAN ...... island, **CUBA, ARUBA**

CAROLINES........ island, **YAP, TRUK, PALAU (PELEW), PONAPE**

CASPIAN .... seaport and harbor, **BAKU**

225

CENTRAL AMERICA . . . . river, **LEMPA**

CEYLON . . . . see SRI LANKA

CHAD . . . town, **SARH, ABECHE**

CHANNEL ISLANDS . . . . . . island, **SARK**

CHILE . . river, **LOA**; port, harbor, town, **ARICA**

CHINA (see also TAIWAN) . . . . . . city, **AMOY, IPIN, CANTON**; port and harbor, **AMOY**; old kingdom, **SHU**; river, **SI, WU, HAN, HSI, ILI, KAN, PEI, WEI, AMUR, HUAI (HWAI)**; province, **HONAN, HUNAN**; mountains, **OMEI (OMI)**

COLOMBIA river, **MAGDALENA**; city, **CALI**

COLORADO . . . . city, **LAMAR, OURAY, PUEBLO, DURANGO**; park, **ESTES**; range, **RATON**; mountain, **OSO, EOLUS**; peak, **OSO**; county, **OTERO, OURAY**; resort, **ASPEN**

CONNECTICUT . . town, **DARIEN, ANSONIA, MERIDEN**; city, **NEW HAVEN, HARTFORD, STAM-FORD**; river, **THAMES**

CORSICA . . . . port and harbor, **BASTIA**

CRETE . . . . port and harbor, **CANDIA**; capital, **CANEA**; mountain, **IDA**

CRIMEA . . . . port and harbor, **KERCH**; river, **ALMA**

CUBA . . . . . . town, **GUINES**; city, **HAVANA (HABANA)**

CYCLADES . . . island, **IOS (NIO), SYRA (SYROS), DELOS, MELOS (MILO), TENOS, THIRA**

CYPRUS . . . . capital, **NICOSIA**

CZECHOSLOVAKIA . . city, **BRNO (BRUNN)**; river, **GRAN, HRON, IPEL, ISER, ODER, OHRE (EGER), MOLDAU**; capital, **PRAGUE (PRAHA)**

D

DELAWARE . . . . . capital, **DOVER**; county, **KENT, SUSSEX**

DENMARK . . . . . . island off, **ALS, AERO**; islands, **FAROE**

DOMINICAN REPUBLIC . . . . . city, **MOCA**

DUTCH . . . . . . see NETHERLANDS

DUTCH EAST INDIES . . . . see INDONESIA

E

EAST ASIA . . . . former kingdom, **KOREA**

EAST EUROPEAN . . river, **DRAU (DRAVA, DRAVE), TISA (TISZA, THEISS)**

EAST INDIES . . . island, **BORNEO**

ECUADOR . . . . . . capital, **QUITO**; province, **EL ORO**

EGYPT . . . . . . city, **GIZA, CAIRO**; ancient city, **SAIS, THEBES**; province, **GIZA**; river, **NILE**

ENGLAND . . . . city, **ELY, BATH, YORK, LEEDS, COVENTRY**; port and harbor, **HULL, DOVER, POOLE**; town, **ETON**; river, **ALN (ALNE), CAM, DEE, EXE, NEN (NENE), URE, AVON, OUSE, TEES, TYNE, TRENT**; county, **KENT, YORK, BERKS, BUCKS, DERBY, DEVON, ESSEX, HANTS, WILTS, DORSET, SUR-REY, SUSSEX**

ESTONIA . . . . . capital, **TALLINN**; former capital, **REVAL (REVEL)**; town, **PARNU, TARTU**; river, **NARVA, PARNU, KASARI**

ETHIOPIA . . . . capital, **ADDIS ABABA**; lake, **TANA (TSANA), ABAYA**; province, **TIGRE**; river, **OMO, AWASH**; town, **HARER, GONDER**

EUROPE . . . . . . river, **ISAR, OISE, URAL, DANUBE**; lake, **BALA-TON**; peninsula, **IBERIA**; resort, **LIDO**

F

FAROE ISLANDS island, **STROMO**

FIJI . . . . capital, **SUVA**; island, **KORO**; island group, **LAU**

FINLAND . . . . capital, **HELSINKI**; city, **OULU, ESPOO (ESBO), LAHTI, TURKU**; lake, **ENARE (INARI)**; port and harbor, **ABO, PORI**; islands, **ALAND, KARLO**; town, northern, **ENARE (INARI)**; province, **HAME, OULU, LAPPI, VASSA**

FLANDERS . . . . city, **LISLE**

FLORIDA . . . . county, **DADE, DUVAL**; resort, **DE LAND**; city, **MIAMI, OCALA, TAMPA, ORLANDO**; cape, **SABLE**

FRANCE . . . . city, **AIX, AGEN, ALBI, CAEN, LYON (LYONS), METZ, NICE, OPPY, SENS, VAUX, ARLES, ARRAS, BLOIS, DINAN, LILLE, NANCY, NESLE, PARIS, REIMS, SEDAN, TOURS, TULLE, CANNES, NANTES, SEVRES**; commune, **AY, EU, AIX, AUX, DAX, PAU, AUBY, BRON, ISSY, LAON, LOOS, MERU, ORLY, VIMY**; port and harbor, **CAEN, MEZE, SETE, BREST**; resort, **PAU, NICE, CANNES**; department, **VAR, GARD, JURA, NORD, OISE, ORNE, MEUSE, VENDEE**; river, **AIN, LOT, LYS, AIRE, AUDE, CHER, EURE, LOIR, OISE, ORNE, RHIN (RHINE), SAAR, YSER, AISNE, ISERE, LOIRE (longest), MARNE, MEUSE, RHONE, SAONE, SARRE, SEINE, SELLE, VESLE, MOSELLE**; Mount, **BLANC**; mountains, **ALPS, JURA**; region, **ANJOU, ALSACE**

G

GABON . . . . capital, **LIBREVILLE**; city, **PORT-GENTIL**

GAMBIA (THE) . capital, **BANJUL**

GASCONY . . . . capital, **AUCH**

GEORGIA . . . . city, **MACON, SPARTA, AUGUSTA**; county, **BIBB, COBB, DE KALB**; river, **FLINT, OCONEE, SAVANNAH**

GERMANY . . . capital E. Germany, **E. BERLIN**; capital W. Germany, **BONN**; city, **AUE, EMS, ULM, GERA, JENA, LAHR, EMDEN, ESSEN, MAINZ, NEUSS**; spa, **AIX**; canal, **KIEL**; river, **EMS, ALLE, EDER, EGER, ELBE, ISAR, MAIN, ODER, REMS, RUHR, SAAR, LIPPE, MOSEL (MOSELLE), REGEN, RHINE (RHEIN), WESER**; mountain, **HARZ**; state, **HESSE**; district, **ALSACE**; former region, **SUDETEN**

GHANA . . . . capital, **ACCRA**; city, **KUMASI**; lake, **VOLTA**; region, **ASHANTI**; river, **VOLTA**

GREAT BARRIER ISLAND . . **OTEA**

GREECE . . . . . . ancient city, **ELIS**; ancient colony, **IONIA**; city, **SPARTA (SPARTI)**; island, **COS (KOS), IOS, NIO, MILO (MELOS), SCIO (CHIOS), CRETE, DELOS, PAROS, SAMOS, IONIAN**; mountain, **OETA, OSSA, HELICON**; river, **ARTA**; peninsula, **MOREA**; region, **DORIS**; ancient district, **ATTICA**

GREENLAND . . . . base, town, settlement, **ETAH**

GUAM . . . . . city, capital, **AGANA**; port and harbor, **APRA**

GUATEMALA . . . volcano, **AGUA**

GUINEA . . . . capital, **CONAKRY**; island, **TOMBO**; island group, **LOS**; town, **BOKE, LABE**

H

HAWAII. city, **HILO, HONOLULU**; island, **MAUI, OAHU, KAUAI, LANAI**; district, **HANA**; islet, **KURE**; volcanoes, **MAUNA KEA, MAUNA LOA**

HEBRIDES, INNER . island, **IONA, SKYE**

HOLLAND . . . see NETHERLANDS

HONDURAS . . . . port, **TELA**

HONSHU . . . . . bay, **ISE**; port and harbor, **KOBE**

HUNGARY . . . city, **EGER, PECS**;
river, **RAAB (RABA)**

I

IDAHO . . . . town, **ARCO**

ILLINOIS. . . city, **PANA, ALEDO,
CAIRO, ELGIN, PEKIN, CAN-
TON, MOLINE, PEORIA,
SPARTA**

INDIA . . . . . capital, **NEW DELHI**;
city, **AGRA, DELHI, POONA
(PUNE), SIMLA, BOMBAY,
KANPUR, MADRAS**; commune,
town, **DHAR, ARCOT, SORON,
SATARA**; mountains, **GHATS**;
region, **GOA, JIND, BERAR,
GWALIOR**; river, **SIND, INDUS,
GANGES**; state, **ASSAM, BIHAR,
MYSORE, PUNJAB**

INDIANA. . . . . city, **GARY, PERU,
MARION**

INDOCHINA. . . . . see BURMA,
CAMBODIA, LAOS, MALAYSIA,
THAILAND, and VIETNAM

INDONESIA island, **AROE (ARU),
BALI, JAVA, CELEBES, TER-
NATE**; island group, **ARU, KAI,
OBI, ALOR, LETI**; gulf, **BONE
(BONI)**; capital, **DJAKARTA**

IOWA . . . . . city, **AMES** (college);
county, **IDA**

IRAN . . . . capital, **TEHRAN**;
city, **AHVAZ, RASHT, ABADAN,
KERMAN, TABRIZ, MASHHAD**

IRAQ. . . . . capital, **BAGDAD
(BAGHDAD)**; port and harbor,
BASRA; ancient city, **KISH**

IRELAND (see also NORTHERN
IRELAND). . . . . old capital, **TARA**;
capital, **DUBLIN**; county, **CORK,
MAYO, CLARE**; islands, **ARAN**;
lake, **REE, ERNE**; port and harbor,
COBH, TRALEE; river, **LEE,
BANN, ERNE, NORE**; town,
TARA

ISLE OF WIGHT . . . port, **COWES**

ISRAEL. . . . . port and harbor,
ACRE, HAIFA; plain, **SHARON
(SARON)**; desert, **NEGEB
(NEGEV)**

ISTRIAN PENINSULA . . . . . . town,
PULA

ITALY. . capital, **ROMA (ROME)**;
city, **BARI, COMO, PISA, ROMA
(ROME), MILAN, PARMA,
SIENA, TRENT, NAPLES, VEN-
ICE, CASERTA**; commune, town,
**BRA, ALBA, ARCO, ASTI, ATRI,
DEGO, ESTE, LARI, NOLA,
ORIA, SAVA, TODI, ADRIA,
ASOLA, ASOLO, PADUA,
TURIN, EMPOLI**; resort, **LIDO**;
port and harbor, **OSTIA, TRANI**;
province, **ROMA, UDINE**; river,
**PO, ADDA, ARNO, NERA, RENO,
PIAVE, TIBER**; lake, **COMO,
ISEO, NEMI**; strait, **OTRANTO**;
gulf, **SALERNO**; isle, **CAPRI**;
mountain, **VISO**

IVORY COAST . . . . . . city, capital,
ABIDJAN; Mount, **NIMBA**; town,
MAN, DALOA

J

JAMAICA . . . capital, **KINGSTON**;
town, **MAY PEN**

JAPAN capital, **TOKYO (TOKIO,
old name, EDO)**; resort city, **HON-
SHU**; city, **KOBE, KOFU, NARA,
CHIBA, OSAKA, OTARU,
TOKYO (TOKIO)**; harbor, port, or
seaport, **OSAKA, OTARU**; island,
SADO, HONDO (HONSHU, larg-
est); volcano, **ASO, FUJI**; bay, **ISE**;
province, old, **ISE, YAMATO**;
mountain, **FUJI**; sea, **IYO**

JAVA . . stream, **SOLO**; mountain
peak, **SEMERU**

JORDAN. . capital, **AMMAN**; city,
ZARQA; gulf, **AQABA**

K

KAI ISLANDS . . . . . . sea, **BANDA**

KANSAS . . . . city, **ARMA, IOLA,
SALINA**; county, **OSAGE**; river,
SALINE

KENTUCKY. . . . . . county, **BATH,
BELL, ADAIR, BOONE, LARUE,
BUTLER**

KENYA. . . . . . . capital, **NAIROBI**;
river, **TANA, EWASO**

KIRIBATI ..... capital, **TARAWA**

KLONDIKE........ river, **YUKON**

KOREA, NORTH . city, **WONSAN;** river, **YALU**

KOREA, SOUTH........ capital, **SEOUL (KEIJO);** city, **PUSAN, SUWON, INCHON**

L

LAOS ..... capital, **VIENTIANE;** river, **MEKONG;** town, **PAKSE**

LATVIA...... capital, port, **RIGA;** river, **AA**

LEBANON .... port, **SIDON**

LESOTHO .... capital, **MASERU;** river, **ORANGE;** town, **HOEK**

LIBERIA ... capital, **MONROVIA,** cape, **PALMAS;** river, **MANO, CESTOS;** town, **HARPER**

LIBYA.......... port and harbor, **DERNA;** capital, **TRIPOLI;** gulf, **SIDRA;** town, **TOBRUK**

LITHUANIA .... capital, **VILNIUS**

LITTLE AMERICA..... sea, **ROSS**

LOUISIANA .. parish, **ORLEANS;** river, **RED, PEARL, SABINE**

LUZON........ province, **ABRA;** mountain, **LABO;** river, **ABRA, AGNO**

M

MAINE ...... bay, **CASCO;** town, **BATH,** (university) **ORONO;** city, river, **SACO**

MALAWI.... town, **ZOMBA;** lake, **NYASA;** river, **SHIRE**

MALAY ARCHIPELAGO.... island, **JAVA, LARAT, LUZON, BORNEO, CELEBES**

MALAYSIA.......... city, **IPOH, KANGAR, PENANG, MALACCA;** state, **KEDAH, PERAK, SABAH, JOHORE, PERLIS, SARAWAK**

MALDIVES....... capital, **MALE**

MALI.... capital, **BAMAKO;** city, **KAYES, SEGOU**

MALTA........... island, **GOZO, COMINO**

MARTINIQUE.... volcano, **PELEE**

MARYLAND... city, **BOWIE, BEL AIR;** Mount, **BACKBONE**

MASSACHUSETTS .... city, **SALEM, NEWTON;** cape, **ANN, COD;** mountain, **TOM;** town, **LENOX**

MAURITANIA ...... town, **ATAR**

MEDITERRANEAN ... island, **IOS, GOZO, RODI (RHODES), CAPRI, CRETE, MALTA;** gulf, **TUNIS;** resort, **LIDO, NICE**

MESOPOTAMIA ... river, **TIGRIS**

MEXICO .. city, **LEON, PUEBLA;** lake, **CHAPALA;** state, **COLIMA, SONORA, TABASCO;** town, **TULA, LERDO**

MICHIGAN......... city, **ALMA, CLARE, FLINT, SPARTA;** county, **LUCE, EATON**

MINDANAO .. volcano, **APO;** gulf, **DAVAO;** town, **MATI**

MINNESOTA..... city, **DULUTH;** Mount, **EAGLE;** river, **ST. CROIX**

MISSISSIPPI ...... city, **BILOXI;** county, **SCOTT;** river, **LEAF, YAZOO**

MISSOURI .... city, **AVA, LAMAR, LIBERTY, OSCEOLA, SEDALIA**

MONGOLIA .... desert, **GOBI**

MONTANA... city, **BUTTE;** peak, **KOCH;** river, **TETON**

MOROCCO .... capital, port, harbor, **RABAT;** city, **MEKNES, TANGIER;** mountains, **ATLAS;** region, **RIF (RIFF);** river, **TENSIFT;** town, **FES (FEZ), IFNI**

MOZAMBIQUE capital, **MAPUTO;** port and harbor, **BEIRA;** river, **SAVE (SABI), LIMPOPO, LUGENDA**

N

NEBRASKA . . . . capital, **LINCOLN;** city, **ORD;** river, **LOUP, PLATTE;** county, **LOUP, OTOE**

NEPAL . . . . mountain, **API;** river, **KOSI**

NETHERLANDS . . . . city, **UTRECHT;** commune or town, **EDE, EPE, BEEK, ECHT, EDAM, ELST, OLST, UDEN, GEMERT;** port and harbor, **EDAM;** river, **EEM, LEK, MAAS** (Dutch Meuse), **RIJN** (Dutch Rhine), **WAAL**

NEVADA . . . . city, **ELY, ELKO, RENO;** county, **NYE, ELKO, WASHOE;** lake, **TAHOE**

NEW GUINEA . . . . . city, port, and harbor, **LAE;** island, **PAPUA**

NEW HAMPSHIRE . . city, **KEENE, NASHUA, LACONIA;** county, **COOS;** lake, **OSSIPEE**

NEW HEBRIDES . . . . capital, port, harbor, **VILA;** island, **EPI (API), TANA (TANNA), EFATE**

NEW JERSEY . . . city, **NEWARK, TRENTON;** river, **RARITAN;** town, **LODI;** cape, **MAY**

NEW MEXICO . . . . . . town, **TAOS;** river, **GILA;** resort, **TAOS;** county, **LEA, LUNA, TAOS**

NEW YORK . . . . city, town, **ROME, TROY, OLEAN, UTICA, ELMIRA, OSWEGO;** island, **STATEN;** county, **TIOGA;** village, **ILION, MALONE**

NEWFOUNDLAND . . . . peninsula, **AVALON**

NEW ZEALAND . . . . bay, **HAWKE;** lake, **TAUPO;** peninsula, **MAHIA;** island, **OTEA**

NICARAGUA . . . . city, **LEON**

NIGER . . capital, **NIAMEY;** region, **AIR;** town, **MARADI, ZINDER**

NIGERIA . . . . capital, **LAGOS;** city, **IWO, KANO, BENIN;** river, **NIGER, BENUE;** town, **ABA, KUMO**

NORMANDY . . . . . . town, **ST.-LO**

NORTH CAROLINA . . river, **HAW, TAR, PEE DEE, YADKIN;** cape, **FEAR;** county, **ASHE**

NORTH DAKOTA . . city, **FARGO, MINOT;** river, **KNIFE**

NORTHERN IRELAND . . . . capital, **BELFAST;** city, **DERRY** (Londonderry), **NEWRY, ARMAGH;** county, **DOWN, TYRONE;** river, **BANN, FOYLE, LAGAN**

NORTHUMBERLAND . . . . river, **TYNE**

NORWAY . . . capital, **OSLO;** river, **KLAR, TANA, LAGEN;** city, **HAMAR**

O

OHIO . . county, **ROSS;** city, **ADA** (college town Ohio Northern), **KENT, LIMA, AKRON, BEREA, NILES, XENIA, CANTON, FOSTORIA;** river, **MAD, MIAMI**

OKINAWA . . . . . . port and harbor, **NAHA (NAFA, NAWA)**

OKLAHOMA . . . city, **ADA, ENID, TULSA, SHAWNEE;** county, **MAJOR, MAYES;** river, **RED**

OMAN . . . . capital, **MUSCAT (MASQAT);** port, **MATRAH**

OREGON . . . . city, **SALEM, ASTORIA;** peak, **HOOD**

ORKNEYS . . . . island, **HOY**

P

PACIFIC ISLANDS . . island, **YAP, GUAM, TRUK, WAKE, LEYTE, TAHITI;** island group, **FIJI, SULU, PALAU (PELEW), SAMOA**

PAHANG . . . . capital, **KUANTAN**

230

PAKISTAN....... city **LAHORE,**
KARACHI; province, **SIND, PUN-**
JAB; river, **SWAT, INDUS,**
KABUL, KUNDAR; mountain
pass, **BOLAN, GUMAL, KHYBER**

PANAMA......... city, **ANCON,**
COLON; lake, **GATUN**

PARAGUAY...... city, **ITA;** river,
APA

PENNSYLVANIA...... city, **ERIE,**
EASTON, CHESTER, TYRONE;
port, **ERIE**

PERSIA, Ancient..... city, **SUSA,**
NIRIZ

PERU .... capital, **LIMA;** city,
department, river, **ICA;** cold district, **PUNO;** port and harbor, **ILO,**
CALLAO; town, **LAMAS**

PHILIPPINE ISLANDS (see also
LUZON and MINDANAO).........
capital, (de facto) **MANILA;** city,
IBA, CEBU, LIPA, NAGA,
ILOILO; mountain or peak,
APO, IBA, LABO; volcano, **APO;**
port and harbor, **ILOILO, BATAN-**
GAS; province, **DAPA;** island,
CEBU, BATAN, SAMAR,
PANAY, LEYTE; island group,
SULU

POLAND... city, **LODZ, LUBAN,**
POSEN, SRODA; commune,
KOLO, KONIN; river, **SAN,**
BIALA, VISLA, STRYPA, VIS-
TULA; province, **KRAKOW (CRA-**
KOW)

PORTUGAL....... cape, **ROCA;**
capital, **LISBON;** city, **OPORTO;**
river, **LIS (LIZ), DOURO, MINHO,**
TAGUS

PUERTO RICO ..... capital, **SAN**
JUAN; city, **PONCE;** town,
LAJAS, LARES; highest point,
CERRO DE PUNTA

Q

QATAR.......... capital, **DOHA**

QUEBEC... city, **HULL, MAGOG,**
LAVAL, VERDUN; county,
LEVIS; lake, **MINTO;** peninsula,
GASPE

R

RHODE ISLAND .. city, **BRISTOL,**
NEWPORT, WARWICK

ROMANIA (RUMANIA) ...... city,
ARAD, CLUJ, IASI; county,
ALBA; river, **OLT**

RUSSIA .... city, **KEM, KIEV,**
LIDA, OMSK, OREL; port and har-
bor, **OREL, ODESSA;** river, **OB,**
OM, DON (DUNA), ILI, KEM,
OKA, UFA, LENA, NEVA, ONON,
SEIM, STYR, URAL, TEREK;
lake, **ONEGA;** sea, **ARAL, AZOF**
(AZOV); mountains, **ALAI, URAL,**
ALTAI; peninsula, **KOLA, KRYM**
(CRIMEA); lake in European
Russia, **SEG;** region, **OMSK**

RWANDA....... capital, **KIGALI**

S

SAMOA .... capital, port, and
harbor, **APIA**

SAUDI ARABIA.... city, **MECCA,**
MEDINA

SAVAGE ISLAND ... island, **NIUE**

SCOTLAND..... port and harbor,
OBAN; seaport, **AYR;** former
county, **AYR, BUTE, FIFE;** river,
DEE, TAY (longest), **DOON,**
SPEY, TYNE, AFTON; city, **AYR;**
lake, **AWE, LOCH (LOCHY), LAG-**
GAN; district, **KYLE, ATHOLE**
(ATHOLL); island off, **ARRAN**

SENEGAL. capital, port, **DAKAR;**
cape, **VERT**

SERBIA...... former capital, **NIS**
(NISH)

SEYCHELLES ..... island, **MAHE**

SIAM............ see THAILAND

SIBERIA (see also RUSSIA)......
river, **OB, YENISEI (ENISEI)**

SICILY volcano, **ETNA (AETNA);**
commune, town, **RAGUSA;** city,
province, resort, **ENNA**

SIERRA LEONE.......... capital,
FREETOWN; city, **BO**

SOCIETY ISLANDS . . . . island,
TAHITI

SOMALIA . . . . gulf, **ADEN**

SOUTH AFRICA . . city, **DURBAN**
region, **RAND**; river, **VAAL**

SOUTH AMERICA . . . river, **BENI,
PLATA, JAPURA (YAPURA)**;
district, **CHACO**; mountains,
ANDES

SOUTH CAROLINA . . . . river,
SANTEE; island, **PARRIS**

SOUTH DAKOTA . . . . capital,
PIERRE; city, **LEMMON**

SOUTH PACIFIC . . . . isle, **FIJI,
BALI, COOK, SAMOA**

SOUTHWEST . . . . . river, **PECOS**

SPAIN . . . . city, **JACA, JAEN,
LEON, AVILA**; province, **JAEN,
LEON, LUGO, AVILA, MALAGA**;
port and harbor, **ADRA, NOYA,
VIGO, MALAGA**; river, **EBRO,
MINHO, TAGUS**; old kingdom,
LEON, CASTILE; commune,
LALIN, LORCA

SRI LANKA . . . . city, **KANDY**;
province, **UVA**

SUDAN . . . . capital, **KHARTOUM**;
desert region, **NUBIA**; river, **NILE**;
town, **JUBA**

SUMATRA . . . . city, **MEDAN**;
stream, **DELI**

SWEDEN . . . . city, **LUND,
OREBRO**; river, **DAL, UME,
KLAR, LULE, LAGAN**; island off,
ALAND; port and harbor, **LULEA,
MALMO**; strait, **ORESUND**

SWITZERLAND . . . . city, **BALE
(BASEL, BASLE), BERN
(BERNE), GENF (GENEVA)**;
commune, town, **BEX, BIEL,
CHUR, SION, AARAU, MORAT**;
canton, **URI, ZUG (ZOUG), BERN
(BERNE), VAUD, BASEL
(BASLE)**; river, **AAR (AARE)**;
lake, **ZUG, JOUX, LUCERNE**;
mountain, **TODI, MATTERHORN**;
resort, **DAVOS**; capital, **BERN
(BERNE)**

SYRIA . . . . . capital, **DAMASCUS**;
city, **ALEP (ALEPPO), HAMA,
HOMS**; river, **EUPHRATES**

T

TAHITI . . . . . . capital, **PAPEETE**;
peak, **OROHENA**

TAIWAN (FORMOSA) . . . . capital,
TAIPEI; city, **TAI-NAN**

TALAUD ISLANDS . . . . town, **BEO**

TANIMBAR ISLANDS . . . . . island,
LARAT

TANZANIA . . . . capital, **DAR
ES SALAAM**; city, **TANGA,
MOSHI**; lake, **NYASA, RUKWA,
VICTORIA, TANGANYIKA**; is-
land, **MAFIA, PEMBA, ZANZI-
BAR**; region, **MARA**; town,
TABORA

TAPUL ISLANDS . . . . island,
LAPAC, LUGUS, SIASI

TASMANIA . . . . capital, **HOBART**

TENNESSEE . . . . city, **MEMPHIS**;
county, **KNOX, MAURY,
SHELBY**

TEXAS . . . . city, **WACO,
LAREDO, ABILENE**; county,
**CLAY, LAMB, CARSON, LOV-
ING**; river, **LEON**

THAILAND . . capital, **BANGKOK**;
gulf, **SIAM**; river, **PING, KLONG**;
town, **TAK**

TIBET . . . city, **LASSA (LHASA)**;
mountain pass, **DANGLA**; river,
INDUS

TOGO . . . . capital, **LOME**; Mount,
AGOU; town, **PALIME**

TRINIDAD . . . . . . port, **LA BREA**

TUNISIA . . . . capital, **TUNIS**

TURKEY . . . . . . capital, **ANKARA
(ANGORA)**; city, **ADANA, IZMIR**;
lake, **MANYAS**; river, **ARAS
(ARAKS), KURA**; town, city,
ORDU, URFA; island, **TENEDOS**

TUSCANY . . . . river, **ARNO**

232

U

UGANDA . . . capital, **KAMPALA;** lake, **KYOGA, ALBERT, EDWARD, GEORGE, VICTORIA;** Mount, **ELGON;** river, **NILE;** town, **LIRA, ENTEBBE**

UNITED ARAB EMIRATES . . . city, **ABU DHABI**

URUGUAY . . . . capital, **MONTEVIDEO;** city, **MELO, MINAS, SALTO, RIVERA;** river, **RIO NEGRO**

U.S.S.R. . . . . see RUSSIA

UTAH . . . . city, **LEHI, HEBER, LOGAN, OGDEN, PROVO;** county, **CACHE, DAVIS;** mountains, **UINTA;** peak, **KINGS;** river, **GREEN, SEVIER**

V

VENEZUELA . capital, **CARACAS;** town, **CORO, MERIDA;** island off coast, **ARUBA;** river, **META, APURE, ARAUCA, ORINOCO**

VERMONT . . . . city, **BARRE, RUTLAND;** creek, **OTTER;** county, **ESSEX, ORANGE, ORLEANS, WINDSOR;** mountains, **GREEN;** river, **WHITE**

VIETNAM . . . . capital, **HANOI;** city, **HUE, DA NANG, SAIGON** (now **HO CHI MINH CITY**); region, **ANNAM;** river, **RED (HONG), MEKONG**

VIRGINIA . . . . city, **SALEM, NORTON, BRISTOL, EMPORIA, FAIRFAX, HAMPTON, RADFORD, NORFOLK, ROANOKE;** Mount, **ROGERS;** river, **DAN, JAMES, POTOMAC, RAPIDAN, ROANOKE**

VIRGIN ISLANDS . . . . capital, **CHARLOTTE AMALIE**

W

WALES . . . . capital, **CARDIFF;** city, **RHONDDA, SWANSEA;** county, **GWENT;** lake, **BALA;** mountains, **BERWYN, SNOWDON;** river, **DEE, LUG (LUGG), USK, TAFF**

WASHINGTON . . . . city, **LACEY, TACOMA, SEATTLE, SPOKANE;** Mount, **RAINIER;** river, **SNAKE, NACHES, YAKIMA, COLUMBIA**

WESTERN AUSTRALIA . . . capital, **PERTH**

WEST INDIES . . . . isle, island, **CUBA, HAITI, NEVIS**

WEST VIRGINIA . . . . city, **ELKINS, WHEELING;** river, **OHIO, POTOMAC, BIG SANDY**

WISCONSIN . . . . city, **ALMA, RIPON, RACINE, KENOSHA, MADISON, GREEN BAY, EAU CLAIRE;** river, **BLACK;** lake, **MENDOTA**

WYOMING . . . . city, **CASPER, LARAMIE;** highest mountain peak, **GANNETT;** range, **TETON;** river, **GREEN, SNAKE, POWDER, BIGHORN**

Y

YEMEN, NORTH . . . . capital, **SAN'A (SANAA);** city, **MOCHA;** ancient ruins, **MARIB**

YEMEN, SOUTH . . capital, **ADEN**

YORKSHIRE . . . . river, **OUSE;** city, **LEEDS**

YUGOSLAVIA . . . . island, **RAB (ARBE), SOLTA;** city, **NIS (NISH);** port, **KOPER;** river, **LIM, KUPA, SAVA, DRINA, NERETVA (NARENTA);** former district and province, **BANAT**

YUKON . . . . city, **DAWSON;** district, **KLONDIKE;** peak, **KEELE;** lake, **TAGISH;** river, **PEEL, TANANA;** creek, **HESS**

Z

ZAIRE . . . . . . capital, **KINSHASA;** province, **KIVU, SHABA;** river, **UELE, CONGO, KASAI, LINDI, LULUA, UBANGI**

ZAMBIA . . . . . . capital, **LUSAKA;** waterfall, **VICTORIA;** river, **KAFUE, ZAMBEZI**

AEROSPACE

SATELLITES, CAPSULES, SPACECRAFT

NOTES: Where the country of origin is other than the U.S., that information is given. Many of these names are from a series of launches. For example, there were hundreds of Soyuz launches. The year given is that of the first launch.

3 letters

AMS.................... 1976
ANS .... Dutch, 1974
ATS 1966
BSE .... see YURI
CAT .... International, 1979
COS .... International, 1975
CTS .... Canadian, 1976
ETS .... see KIKU
FR-1............. French, 1965
GRS .... W. German, 1963
IMP 1973
IUE .... International, 1976
LEM 1967
LES................... 1965
OAO 1966
OFO 1970
OGO 1964
OSO 1962
OTS .... International, 1977
SMS 1974
TIP 1975
TTS 1967
UME.......... Japanese, 1976

4 letters

ANIK .... see TELESAT
ANNA 1962
AURA .... French, 1975
AZUR .... see GRS
BIOS 1966
DASH.................. 1963
DIALFrench & W. German, 1970
DMSP 1971
ECHO.................. 1960
EOLE............. French, 1971
ERTS 1972
ESRO....... International, 1968
ESSA 1966
EXOS............ see KYOKKO
GEOS....... International, 1976
GOES.................. 1975
HEAO.................. 1977
HEOS........ International, 1968
IQSY .... International, 1978
IRIS .... International, 1968
ISEE........ International, 1977
ISIS .... Canadian, 1965
ITOS................... 1970
KIKU .... Japanese, 1975
LUNA............ Soviet, 1959
MARS .... Soviet, 1962
NATO ...... International, 1970

NOAA 1970

NOSS.................. 1976
NOVA 1981
SAGE 1979
SERT 1964
SRET .... French, 1972
VELA 1963
YURI .... Japanese, 1978
ZOND............ Soviet, 1964

5 letters

AEROS ...... W. German, 1972
ARIEL .... British, 1962
ASTEX 1971
AYAME....... Japanese, 1979
CAMEO................. 1979
DENPA .... Japanese, 1972
DODGE 1967
DRIMS.......... see TELESAT
EKRAN .... Soviet, 1976
FAITH 1963
IDCSP 1966
INJUN 1961
LOFTI 1961
MAGIC ..... see INTERCOSMOS
MIDAS................. 1960
OSCAR 1961
PEOLE........... French, 1970
RELAY 1962
SAMOS................. 1961
SIGMA................. 1962
SIGNE .... French, 1977
SIRIO............ Italian, 1977
SOYUZ .... Soviet, 1967
TAIYO........ Japanese, 1975
TIROS 1960
TRAAC 1961
TRIAD 1972
UOSAT 1981
VENUS 1961

6 letters

APOLLO 1965
ARIANE .... International, 1979
AURORA 1962
BOREAS.... International, 1969
CASTOR .... French, 1975
COMSAT 1969
COSMOS .... Soviet, 1962
GEMINI................. 1964
HELIOS...... W. German, 1974
KYOKKO ..... Japanese, 1978

LAGEOS	1976	PIONEER		1958
MAGION	Czech, 1978	PROGNOZ	Soviet,	1972
MAGSAT	1979	SHINSEI	Japanese,	1971
NIMBUS	1964	SOLWIND		1979
OHSUMI	Japanese, 1970	SPUTNIK	Soviet,	1957
PAGEOS	1966	STAR-RAD		1962
PALAPA	Indonesian, 1976	TELESAT	Canadian,	1972
POLLUX	French, 1975	TELSTAR		1962
POLYOT	Soviet, 1963	TRANSAT		1977
PROTON	Soviet, 1965	TRANSIT		1960
RADOSE	1963	VOSKHOD	Soviet,	1964
RANGER	1961			

LAGEOS 1976
MAGION .... Czech, 1978
MAGSAT 1979
NIMBUS 1964
OHSUMI ...... Japanese, 1970
PAGEOS 1966
PALAPA ..... Indonesian, 1976
POLLUX .... French, 1975
POLYOT .... Soviet, 1963
PROTON .... Soviet, 1965
RADOSE 1963
RANGER 1961
ROHINI .... Indian, 1980
SAKURA ...... Japanese, 1977
SALYUT .... Soviet, 1971
SATCOM 1975
SCATHA 1979
SEASAT 1978
SKYLAB 1973
SKYNET .... British, 1969
SOLRAD 1976
SYNCOM 1963
TANSEI .... Japanese, 1971
VIKING 1975
VOSTOK .... Soviet, 1961
WESTAR 1974
WRESAT ..... Australian, 1967

7 letters
ASTERIX .... French, 1965
AUREOLE .... French, 1971
AURORAE .... see ESRO
BHASKAR .... Indian, 1979
COMSTAR 1976
COURIER 1960
DIADEME .... French, 1967
DIAPSON .... French, 1966
ESA-GEOS .. International, 1977
FREEDOM 1961
HAKUCHO .... Japanese, 1979
HAWKEYE 1974
INTASAT .... Spanish, 1974
JIKIKEN ...... Japanese, 1978
LANDSAT .... see ERTS
MARINER 1962
MARISAT 1976
MERCURY 1960
MIRANDA .... British, 1974
MOLNIYA .... Soviet, 1965
NAVSTAR 1978
ORBITER . see LUNAR ORBITER
PEGASUS 1965

PIONEER 1958
PROGNOZ .... Soviet, 1972
SHINSEI ...... Japanese, 1971
SOLWIND 1979
SPUTNIK .... Soviet, 1957
STAR-RAD 1962
TELESAT .... Canadian, 1972
TELSTAR 1962
TRANSAT 1977
TRANSIT 1960
VOSKHOD .... Soviet, 1964

8 letters
ALOUETTE .... Canadian, 1962
COLUMBIA 1981
ELEKTRON ...... Soviet, 1964
EXPLORER 1958
GORIZONT ...... Soviet, 1978
HIMAWARI .... Japanese, 1977
INTELSAT .. International, 1965
LANI BIRD .. International, 1966
METEOSAT . International, 1977
PROGRESS ...... Soviet, 1978
PROSPERO ...... British, 1971
SAN MARCO ..... Italian, 1964
SURVEYOR 1966
VANGUARD 1958

9 letters
ARYABHATA ..... Indian, 1975
EARLY BIRD International, 1965
FLTSATCOM 1978
STARLETTE ..... French, 1975
SYMPHONIE .... French & W. German, 1974
TOURNESOL ..... French, 1971
TRANSTAGE 1964

10 letters
CANNONBALL .... see LAGEOS
CHALLENGER 1983
COPERNICUS 1972
DISCOVERER 1959
DODECAPOLE 1965
FRIENDSHIP 1962

11 letters
INTERCOSMOS .. Soviet, 1969
LIBERTY BELL 1961

12 letters
LUNAR ORBITER 1966

ASTRONAUTS

NOTES: The first Russian Cosmonaut was Yuri Gagarin. The others are not listed because you are not apt to find their names in crosswords. This listing includes all U.S. missions up to June 1983.

Aldrin, Edwin (Buzz) .... Gemini-Titan 12, 1966; Apollo-Saturn 11, 1969
Allen, Joseph .... Columbia, November, 1982
Anders, William .... Apollo-Saturn 8, 1968
Armstrong, Neil .... Gemini-Titan 8, 1966; Apollo-Saturn 11, 1969
Bean, Alan.......................... Apollo-Saturn 12, 1969; Skylab 3, 1973
Bobko, Karol................................... Challenger, April, 1983
Borman, Frank .... Gemini-Titan 7, 1965; Apollo-Saturn 8, 1968
Brand, Vance .... Apollo 18, 1975; Columbia, November, 1982
Carpenter, M. Scott................................. Mercury-Atlas 7, 1962
Carr, Gerald.. Skylab 4, 1973–1974
Cernan, Eugene .... Apollo-Saturn 10, 1969; Apollo-Saturn 17, 1972
Collins, Michael .... Gemini-Titan 10, 1966; Apollo-Saturn 11, 1969
Conrad, Charles .... Gemini-Titan 5, 1965; Gemini-Titan 11, 1966;
                              Apollo-Saturn 12, 1969; Skylab 2, 1973
Cooper, L. Gordon .... Mercury-Atlas 9, 1963; Gemini-Titan 5, 1965
Crippen, Robert .... Columbia, April, 1981; Challenger, June, 1983
Cunningham, R. Walter.............................. Apollo-Saturn 7, 1968
Duke, Charles.................................... Apollo-Saturn 16, 1972
Eisele, Donn .... Apollo-Saturn 7, 1968
Engle, Joe .... Columbia, November, 1981
Evans, Ronald .... Apollo-Saturn 17, 1972
Fabian, John .... Challenger, June, 1983
Fullerton, C. Gordon .... Columbia, March, 1982
Garriott, Owen .... Skylab 3, 1973
Gibson, Edward .... Skylab 4, 1973–1974
Glenn, John.. Mercury-Atlas 6, 1962
Gordon, Richard .... Gemini-Titan 11, 1966; Apollo-Saturn 12, 1969
Grissom, Virgil (Gus)...... Mercury-Redstone 4, 1961; Gemini-Titan 3, 1965
Haise, Fred .... Apollo-Saturn 13, 1970
Hartsfield, Henry .... Columbia, June–July, 1982
Hauck, Frederick (Rick) .... Challenger, June, 1983
Irwin, James .... Apollo-Saturn 15, 1971
Kerwin, Joseph.................................... Skylab 2, 1973
Lenoir, William .... Columbia, November, 1982
Lousma, Jack .... Skylab 3, 1973; Columbia, March, 1982
Lovell, James .... Gemini-Titan 7, 1965; Gemini-Titan 12, 1966;
                          Apollo-Saturn 8, 1968; Apollo-Saturn 13, 1970
Mattingly, Thomas...... Apollo-Saturn 16, 1972; Columbia, June–July, 1982
McDivitt, James .... Gemini-Titan 4, 1965; Apollo-Saturn 9, 1969
Mitchell, Edgar .... Apollo-Saturn 14, 1971

```
Musgrave, Story.................................. Challenger, April, 1983
Overmeyer, Robert ........................... Columbia, November, 1982
Peterson, Donald ............................... Challenger, April, 1983
Pogue, William ................................ Skylab 4, 1973–1974
Ride, Sally ..................................... Challenger, June, 1983
Roosa, Stuart .................................. Apollo-Saturn 14, 1971
Schirra, Walter ............. Mercury-Atlas 8, 1962; Gemini-Titan 6-A, 1965;
                                                    Apollo-Saturn 7, 1968
Schmitt, Harrison.............................. Apollo-Saturn 17, 1972
Schweickart, Russell ........................... Apollo-Saturn 9, 1969
Scott, David ................. Gemini-Titan 8, 1966; Apollo-Saturn 9, 1969;
                                                    Apollo-Saturn 15, 1971
Shepard, Alan .......... Mercury-Redstone 3, 1961; Apollo-Saturn 14, 1971
Slayton, Donald (Deke)................................. Apollo 18, 1975
Stafford, Thomas................................ Gemini-Titan 6-A, 1965;
                                Apollo-Saturn 10, 1969; Apollo 18, 1975
Swigart, John ................................. Apollo-Saturn 13, 1970
Thagard, Norman................................. Challenger, June, 1983
Truly, Richard.............................. Columbia, November, 1981
Weitz, Paul ................. Skylab 2, 1973; Challenger, April, 1983
White, Edward..................................... Gemini-Titan 4, 1965
Worden, Alfred .................................. Apollo-Saturn 15, 1971
Young, John .............. Gemini-Titan 3, 1965; Gemini-Titan 10, 1966;
                          Apollo-Saturn 10, 1969; Apollo-Saturn 16, 1972;
                                                    Columbia, April, 1981
```

ROCKETS, LAUNCH VEHICLES

4 letters	5 letters	6 letters	8 letters
ABLE	AGENA	APACHE	ABLESTAR
ARGO	ARCAS	BIG JOE	ASTROBEE
HAWK	ARCON	SATURN	BLUE SCOUT
JUNO	ARIES	THORAD	MALEMUTE
NIKE	ATLAS		REDSTONE
TAID	CAJUN	7 letters	TOMAHAWK
THOR	DELTA	AEROBEE	VANGUARD
	JASON	CENTAUR	
	SCOUT	JAVELIN	9 letters
	TITAN	SHOTPUT	LITTLE JOE
		TERRIER	
			10 letters
			BLACKBRANT
			JOURNEYMAN

COMPUTER TERMINOLOGY

Note regarding computer languages: All computers actually work in machine language, which uses binary code. This is the "lowest" level of the languages. People don't think in binary codes, so "higher" level languages (symbolic languages), which are easier to understand, have been devised. The easier a language is to understand, the higher the level; hence the further it is from the computer's actual language.

3 letters

ADA......... High-level language
APL .... High-level language
BCD ..... Binary Coded Decimal
BIT........ Binary digit (1 or 0)
BOX......... Flow-chart symbol
BUG Error, defect, or malfunction
BUS . Conductor for transmitting signals
CAD.... Computer Aided Design
CAI Computer Assisted Instruction
CAL Computer Assisted Learning
CAM......... Computer Assisted Manufacturing
CAT Computer Assisted Training
COM Computer Output Microfilm
CPS .... Characters Per Second
CPU ... Central Processing Unit
CRT .... Cathode Ray Tube
DMA .... Direct Memory Access
DOS ..... Disk Operating System
EDP . Electronic Data Processing
HEX ..... (hexadecimal notation) Number system using 16 as a base
HIT ... The finding of a matching record
JCL ...... Job Control Language
JOB Unit of work for the computer
LOG .... Record events in chronological sequence
LPM .... Lines Per Minute
MAC ... Multi-Access Computing
MPU ... MicroProcessor Unit
PCM ..... Pulse Code Modulation
PL-1 ..... High-level language
RAM ... Random-Access Memory
ROM .... Read-Only Memory
RUN Begin execution of a program
ZAP .... Erase; wipe out

4 letters

ANSI .... American National Standards Institute
BAND Group of recording tracks on a magnetic disk or drum
BAUD Measurement unit of speed of data transmission
BEAD... Small unit of a program
BLIP.. Erratic signal on a screen

BOOT....... Protective housing
BYTE... Group of bits, usually 8 bits in length
CARD .... Circuit board
CHIP ...... Tiny piece of silicon embedded with many electronic circuits
CODE.... Representation of data or instructions in symbolic form
COPY .... Reproduce data from one storage device onto another
DATA.. Information of any type; computer "food"; computer input
DISK . Magnetic storage medium
DOWN......... Not in operation
DRUM . Magnetic storage device
DUMP . Clear memory and store data elsewhere
ECOM .... Electronic Computer-Oriented Mail
EDIT........... Prepare data for subsequent processing
FIFO.......... First In, First Out
FILE.... Organized collection of related data
FLOW ... Sequence of events in the solution of a problem
GATE......... Electronic switch
GIGO .. Garbage In, Garbage Out
HEAD...... Device used to read, record, or erase data on a magnetic storage medium
HOME ... Starting position for a cursor on a screen (top left-hand corner, usually)
KILO .... Prefix denoting one thousand
LIFO.......... Last In, First Out
LISP........ High-level language
LOAD. Transfer information from a storage device into the computer
LOGO...... High-level language, primarily for children
LOOP...... Closed sequence of instructions performed repeatedly

MEGA Prefix denoting one million
MENU . . List of program options
MODE . . . . . Method of operation
NODE . . . . . One component in a
   network
PACK Compress data in order to
   save space in storage
PASS . Single execution of a loop
PEEK BASIC language command
   that displays the value of a
   specific memory location
POKE BASIC language command
   that puts a one-byte value
   into a given memory
   location
PORT . . . . . . Computer outlet for
   plugging in a peripheral
PROM Programmable Read-Only
   Memory
READ . Retrieve information from
   memory
SCAN . . . . . . Read; examine each
   part in sequence
SORT Put data in order according
   to the desired rule
TAPE Magnetic medium for data
   storage
TASK . . . . . Single unit of work in
   multiprocessing
TEXT . . . . . Information part of a
   message
USER . . Computer network client
WORD . . . . . Group of characters
   representing a unit of data

5 letters
ALGOL . . . . . High-level language
ARRAY . Orderly arrangement of
   data in a list
ASCII . . . . Standard code that
   assigns values to numbers
   and letters; code which en-
   ables different computers
   to communicate
BASIC . . . . . . High-level language
BATCH . . Group of similar trans-
   actions collected for processing as a single unit
BLANK . . . . . . Character used to
   represent a space
BLOCK Group of records treated
   as a single unit of data
BOARD . . . . Sheet on which
   integrated circuits are
   mounted
BREAK . . . . Interrupt
CHART, FLOW . . . Diagrammatic
   representation of a data-
   processing problem
COBOL . . . . . High-level language
CORAL . . . . . High-level language

COUNT . . Total number of times
   an instruction is performed
CRASH . . . Hardware or software
   malfunction causing
   system breakdown
DEBUG . . . . Locate and eliminate
   errors
DRIVE . Device which causes the
   movement of a recording
   medium
ENTRY . . . . Item of data in a list
EPROM . . . . Electrically Program-
   mable Read-Only Memory
FAULT . . Failure of any part of a
   system
FIELD Part of a record containing a
   specific unit of information
FORTH . . . . . High-level language
FRAME Image in a display system
HERTZ . . . . Unit of frequency
INPUT Data that goes into a com-
   puter or its peripherals
LOG-ON . Sign onto a system or
   network
MERGE Combine two or more sets
   of records into a single file
MICRO . . . . Very small
MODEM . . . Device which allows
   computers to communicate
   over telephone lines
NEXUS Point in a system where
   interconnections occur
NOISE . . . . Spurious signals
OCTAL Number system using 8
   as a base
PILOT . High-level language used
   in classrooms
PIXEL Division of a display screen
QUEUE Waiting list of programs
   to be run
RADIX Base of a number system
RERUN . . . Repeat the execution
   of a program
SLAVE . . Unit which is under the
   control of a larger unit
SPACE Empty unit of data storage
STACK . . . . Area of memory
   reserved for storage of
   data; LIFO area
STORE . . . . . . Memory medium
TABLE . . Set of data arranged as
   an array
TRACK . . . . Channel on a
   magnetic medium
WRITE . . . . Record data on a
   storage medium

6 letters
ACCESS . . . . Retrieve data from
   a storage device or
   a peripheral

239

ANALOG Method of measurement that uses physical variables

ASSIGN Reserve part of a system for a specific purpose

BABBLE Cross-talk from several interfacing channels

BINARY . Notation system using only 1's and 0's to represent data

BUFFER .... Temporary storage space for data

CATENA.... Series of items in a chained list

CURSOR... Movable spot on the screen showing where the pointer is

DECADE.... Group of ten items

DUPLEX.. Communications line that allows simultaneous 2-way transmission

ENABLE.... Restore to ordinary operating conditions

ENCODE..... Represent data in digital form

FORMAT Specified arrangement of data; prepare (a diskette) for use

GLITCH.... Unwanted electronic pulse that causes errors

JITTER .... Signal instability

MASTER..... Unit that controls smaller (slave) units

MATRIX... Type of printer that forms letters by printing a pattern of dots

MEMORY The part of a computer that stores information

NIBBLE Four bit word; half a byte

ON-LINE . Under the control of a central processor

OUTPUT Information coming out of the computer; the end product of a program

PASCAL.... High-level language

PROMPT ..... Message from an operating system calling for action from the operator

RECORD. Set of information that contains all data about one item

SCREEN Surface of a CRT that is visible to the operator

SCROLL Move the contents of a screen up or down, one line at a time

SEARCH.... Look for a specific piece of data

SECTOR ...... Defined area of a track or band

SERIAL Pertaining to transmission of data one bit at a time

SNOBOL.... High-level language

STRING.... Set of consecutive characters

SUBSET .. Group of items which belongs to a larger group

SYNTAX. Grammatical rules that specify how an instruction can be written

THREAD. Group of beads which form a complete program

7 letters

ADDRESS.... Particular number associated with each memory location

CIRCUIT.... Closed-loop electric current path

COMMAND ..... Instruction to a computer

COMPILE... Translate symbolic language into machine language

COUNTER ...... Device used to accumulate totals and maintain a count

DECODER . Device used to alter data from one coded format to another

DIGITAL Describing a method of measurement using precise quantities to represent variables

DISABLE ... Inhibit or remove a hardware or software feature

DISPLAY . Output on the screen

EXECUTE....... Run a program

FLUTTER ...... Recurring speed variation

FORTRAN .. High-level language

GARBAGE .... Meaningless, unwanted data

MEGABIT...... One million bits

MONITOR . High-resolution CRT

NESTING Writing a program that has loops within loops

NETWORK..... System of inter-connecting components

OFF-LINE . Not under the control of a central processor

PLOTTER.... Special printer for graphics

PROGRAM... Set of instructions given a computer so it may perform a task

RAW DATA.. Information which has not been processed

READOUT Display of processed information on a screen

ROUTINE... Set of instructions; part of a program

SCANNER Device which samples the status of a file
SEGMENT . Division of a routine
STORAGE .. Place where data is held in the computer or its peripherals

8 letters
ALPHABET ...... Character set
ANNOTATE Add explanatory text to program instructions
ASSEMBLY .... Middle-level language
COMPILER . Program that translates symbolic language into machine language
COMPUTER .. Electronic device capable of accepting data, solving problems, and supplying results
CONSTANT . Item of data which does not vary in value
DATA BASE . Set of information available to the computer
DISCRETE ... Pertaining to data organized in distinct parts
DISKETTE .... Floppy disk
FUNCTION ...... The operation specified in an instruction
GRAPHICS . All non-alphanumeric displays generated by a computer
HARD COPY ... Output on paper
HARDWARE . The physical parts of a computer system
MEGABYTE ... One million bytes
OPERATOR ...... Person who is working the computer
PARALLEL .. Type of data transmission where all parts of an 8-bit word are sent simultaneously
REGISTER .. Specific location in memory
RESIDENT .... Any program permanently stored in the computer
RETRIEVE .. Search for, select, and extract data contained in a file
ROBOTICS ..... Area of artificial intelligence pertaining to industrial use of robots
SIMULATE .. Represent physical problems by mathematical formulas
SOFTWARE ... All programs that instruct the computer how to operate
TERMINAL ..... Peripheral of a computer system

VARIABLE . Symbol representing a quantity whose value can change

9 letters
ALGORITHM ...... Step-by-step procedure for giving instructions to a computer
ASSEMBLER Code that converts symbolic language into machine language
CHARACTER ..... Single letter, number, symbol, or space
CONNECTOR Flow-chart symbol
DECREMENT Decrease a variable by a specified amount
HANDSHAKE . Acknowledgment between two computers of ability to communicate
INCREMENT Increase a variable by a specified amount
INTERFACE ... Linkage between systems, programs, or between a person and a system
INTERRUPT Temporary break in the running of a program
MAIN FRAME .... Very large computer
PARAMETER Quantity which may be given variable values

10 letters
NANOSECOND .... Billionth of a second
PERIPHERAL ...... Any item of hardware that connects to a computer (printer, monitor, drive, etc.)
PHILOXENIC ... Friendly to uninformed users; user-friendly
REPERTOIRE Set of instructions a given computer can execute

11 letters
CYBERNETICS The study of the theory of control systems

12 letters
ALPHANUMERIC . Pertaining to characters that represent numbers, letters, and/or symbols
INTELLIGENCE ..... Processing capability

13 letters
CONFIGURATION ..... Specific makeup of the physical units of a computer system

MUSICAL TERMS

3 letters
AIR............. Tune or melody
BAR .... Vertical line dividing the
staff
CON..................... With
GAI................. Lively, brisk
PIU..................... More

4 letters
ALLA............. In the style of
BEAT..... Division of a measure
CHEF (D'ORCHESTRA) Conductor
CLEF.... Character on the staff
CODA .... Passage ending a
movement
ECCO.................... Echo
FINE..................... End
FINO.......... As far as; up to
FLAT.... Character on the staff
GLEE... English composition for
3 or more voices
HOLD.......... Sign indicating
prolongation of a note
IDYL ..... Romantic or pastoral
composition
LENO............. Faint; quiet
LIED............. German song
LOCO..................... Place
MANO.................... Hand
POCO..................... Little
POLO..... Syncopated Spanish
dance
REEL............. Lively dance
REST Pause between two tones;
character on the staff
SANS.................. Without
SINO...... As far as; up to
TEMA................. Theme
VAMP........... Improvise an
accompaniment
VIVO........... Lively; briskly
VOCE..................... Voice

5 letters
A DEUX .... For two hands
ANCOR....... Again; also; yet
BALLO................. Dance
BATON..... Conductor's wand
BOCCA................. Mouth
CANTO....... Melody or chant
CHANT...... Short sacred song
CHORD..... A harmony of 2 or
more tones
CLOSE....... Cadenza ending a
section or piece
DESTO .... Sprightly
DIRGE........... Funeral hymn

DOLCE .... Sweet; soft
ELEGY.. Melancholy composition
FLING............ Scottish dance
FOLIA.......... Spanish dance
GALOP .... Lively French dance
JALEO.......... Spanish dance
LARGO...... Slow and stately
LENTO .. Slow, but not dragging
MESTO......... Sad; melancholy
METER, METRE... Symmetrical
grouping of musical rhythms
MEZZO................... Half
MINIM............. Half-note
MOLTO.......... Very; much
PAUSA........ Rest; pause
PAVAN .. Stately Italian-Spanish
dance
PEZZO.................. Piece
PIANO........... Soft; softly
PIECE ..... Musical composition
PITCH..... Position of a tone in
the musical scale
POLKA .... Bohemian dance
SAMBA....... Brazilian dance
SCALE.... Series of tones which
form any major or minor key
SEGNO................. A sign
SENZA............... Without
SHARP .. Character on the staff
SOAVE ...... Suavely; flowingly
TANGO....... Argentine dance
TANTO..... As much; so much
TARDO...... Slow; lingering
TEMPO...... Rate of speed
VALSE.................. Waltz

6 letters
ADAGIO Slow; a slow movement
ANTHEM ...... Piece of sacred
vocal music
A TEMPO..... At the preceding
rate of speed
BOLERO........ Spanish dance
CHIARO .... Clear; pure
COMODO............ Leisurely
CON IRA .... Wrathfully
DA CAPO .. From the beginning
DECISO........... With decision
DI GALA.......... Gaily; merrily
EQUALE... Equal; even; smooth
FACILE............. Easy; fluent
FEBILE........... Feeble; weak
FEROCE................. Wildly
FINALE........ Last movement
FLORID.. Embellished with runs,
passages, etc.
GIUSTO................. Proper

242

INFINO . . . . As far as; up to
INTIMO . . . . Heartfelt; fervent
JARABE . . . . Mexican dance
LEGATO . . . Slurred; played with
    no break between notes
LITANY . . . . Song of supplication
MINUET . . . . Early French dance
    form
PAVANA Stately Italian-Spanish
    dance
REDOWA . . . . . Bohemian dance
SEMPRE . . . . Always; throughout
VELOCE . . . . Rapid
VIVACE . . . . Lively; animated

7 letters
AGILITA . . . . Vivacity
AGILITE . . . . Vivacity
AGITATO . . . . Agitated
ALLEGRO . . . . Lively or rapid
ALLONGE . . . . Prolonged
AMABILE . . . . Sweet and tender
ANDANDO . . . . Easy and flowing
ANDANTE . . . Moderately slowly
ANIMATO . . . . Vivaciously
ANIMOSO . . . . Spirited
BAROCCO . . . . Eccentric or
    whimsical
CADENCE . . . . Rhythm
CADENZA . . . . Elaborate ending
    passage
CALMATO . . . . Calmly
CAMPANA . . . . Bell
CANTATA . . . . . Vocal work with
    instrumental accompaniment
CANTATO . . . . Singingly
CANZONE . . . . Folk song or
    part-song in madrigal style
CHANSON . . . . Song
CLAVIER . . . . Keyboard
COMPASS . . . . Range of a voice
    or instrument
CON BRIO . . . . Spiritedly
CON MOTO . . With an energetic
    movement
DECIBEL . . . Unit of loudness or
    intensity of sound
DI COLTA . . . Suddenly; at once
DI MOLTO . . . . . Very; extremely
DOLENTE . . . . Sad
FERMATA . . . . A hold, pause, or
    interruption
FERVOSO . . . In an agitated style
GAVOTTE . . . Old French dance
GENTILE . . . . Gracefully; in a
    refined style
HANACCA . . . . . Moravian dance
HAUTBOY . . . . Oboe
INTRADA . . . . Short introduction
    or prelude
LEGGERO . . . . Light; airy

MAESTRO . . . Master; conductor
MARCATO . . . . With distinctness
    and emphasis
MAZURKA . . . . Polish dance
PARLATO . . . . Spoken
PASSAGE . . . . Portion or section
    of a composition
PENSOSO . . Pensive; thoughtful
PIETOSO . . . . Pitifully; movingly
PLACIDO . . . . Smooth; placid
REPLICA . . . A repeat or reprise
ROBUSTO . . . . Firmly and boldly
SCHERZO . . Vivacious movement
    in a symphony
SENTITO . . . . . . With expression
SERIOSO In a grave, impressive
    style

8 letters
A BALLATA . . . . In singing style
AFFABILE . . . . Sweetly and
    gracefully
BEL CANTO The art of beautiful
    song
BERCEUSE . . . . Lullaby
CALMANDO . . . . . Growing calm
CANTICLE . . . . Sacred chant
CAVATINA . . . . Short aria
CHACONNE . . . . Spanish dance
CON AMORE . . . . Lovingly
CON FURIA . . . . Furiously; wildly
CON GARBO . . . . Gracefully;
    elegantly
CON GIOCO . . . . Playfully
CON GIOIA . . . . Joyously
CON TINTO . . . . . . With shading;
    expressively
CON UMORE . . . . . . With humor
DAL SEGNO . . . . From the sign
DELICATO . . . In a delicate style
DIAPASON . . . . Octave
DISCRETO . . . . . . Comparatively
    subdued
DOLCIATO . . . . . . Softer; calmer
ELEGANTE . . . . Gracefully
ENFATICO . . . . . . With emphasis
FANDANGO . . . . Lively Spanish
    dance
FANTASIA . . . . Free-form
    composition
FERVENTE . . Ardently; fervently
HABANERA . . . . Cuban
    contradance
LARGANDO . . . Growing broader
LENTANDO . . . . Growing slower
LIBRETTO . . . . The words of an
    opera, oratorio, etc.
MACHUCHA . . . Dance similar to
    the bolero
MADRIGAL . . Vocal setting of a
    short lyric poem

MODULATE..... Pass from one key or mode into another
NOCTURNE.. Dreamily romantic composition
RHAPSODY....... Instrumental fantasia on folk songs
RIGAUDON Lively French dance
RIGOROSO .... In strict time
RISOLUTO... In a decided style
SARABAND.... Stately dance of Spanish or Oriental origin
SEMPLICE.... In a natural style
SERENADE ...... Love song for the evening
SOGGETTO ..... Subject; theme
VIGOROSO .... Vigorously

9 letters
A CAPPELLA .... Without instrumental accompaniment
ACOUSTICS Science of musical tones
AFTER NOTE ...... Unaccented note of a pair
ALL' OTTAVA An octave higher
ANTIPHONY Responsive singing
BAGATELLE.. Short, fairly easy piece of music
BARCAROLE .. Venetian boat-song
BELLICOSO... In a warlike style
BERGAMASK.. Clownish dance
CANTABILE .. In a singing style
CAPRICCIO.......... Free-form instrumental piece
CHROMATIC.. Relating to tones foreign to a given key
CON AFFETO...... With feeling
CON CALORE ..... Passionately
CON DOLORE.... Expressive of pain or grief
CON FRETTA........ Hurriedly
CON MAESTA ..... Majestically

CON RABBIA ...... With frenzy
CON RIPOSO ...... Calmly; in a tranquil manner
CON VIGORE .... Vigorously
FARANDOLA ..... Circle dance
GLISSANDO .... With a flowing, sliding move
IMPROMPTU ... Composition of extemporaneous form
MALAGUENA..... Spanish folk music
PIZZICATO ... Plucked with the fingers, as strings
POCO A POCO.... Little by little
POLONAISE ...... Polish dance

10 letters
ACCELERATO ... Livelier; faster
ACCIDENTAL... Chromatic sign not in the key-signature
ALLA MARCIA.. In march style
ALLARGANDO. Growing slower
ALLEGRETTO...... Quite lively
BERGERETTE.... Pastoral song
CAMPANELLO...... Small bell
CLAVICHORD..... Precursor of the pianoforte
CON ANIMATO ..... With spirit
CON AUDACIA .. With boldness
CON DELIRIO....... Deliriously
CON FERVORE ...... Ardently; fervently
CON GRAVITA Slowly; seriously
IMPRESARIO ... Manager of an opera or concert company
LARGAMENTE......... Broadly
LENTAMENTE.......... Slowly
NACHTMUSIK .... Serenade
RITARDANDO . Growing slower and slower
SEGUIDILLA .... Spanish dance
SEMIQUAVER 16th-note
TARANTELLA .... Italian dance

SOME NOTED COMPOSERS

3 letters
ABT .... Franz
BAX .... Arnold
CUI .... Cesar

4 letters
ADAM ..... Adolphe
ARNE....... Thomas
BACH....... Johann Sebastian
BACH.......... Karl
BERG........ Alban

BULL .... John
BYRD...... William
CAGE.......... John
FOSS .... Lukas
GADE......... Niels
IVES......... Charles
KERN....... Jerome
LALO ...... Edouard
PERI .... Jacopo
RAFF ...... Joachim
RIES...... Ferdinand

TOCH......... Ernst
WOLF......... Hugo

5 letters
AUBER ..... Daniel-Francois-Esprit
BALFE..... Michael
BIZET...... Georges
BLOCH ...... Ernest
BOITO...... Arrigo
BRUCH .... Max

244

CESTI.. Marc'Antonio
D'INDY..... Vincent
DUFAY... Guillaume
DUKAS......... Paul
ELGAR.... Edward
FALLA... Manuel de
FAURE...... Gabriel-
　　　　　　Urbain
FOOTE....... Arthur
FRIML...... Rudolf
GLUCK... Christoph
GRIEG..... Edvard
HAYDN....... Franz
　　　　　　Joseph
HOLST...... Gustav
IBERT.... Jacques
ISAAK..... Heinrich
LEHAR..... Franz
LISZT......... Franz
LOEWE........ Carl
LULLY Jean-Baptiste
MOORE.... Douglas
NEVIN... Ethelbert
PAINE John Knowles
RAVEL...... Maurice
REGER......... Max
SATIE......... Erik
SOUSA... John Philip
STILL. William Grant
SUPPE... Franz von
VERDI..... Giuseppe
WEBER.. Carl Maria
　　　　　　von
WEILL......... Kurt
WIDOR Charles-Marie

6 letters
BARBER.... Samuel
BARTOK........ Bela
BERLIN...... Irving
BOULEZ..... Pierre
BRAHMS.. Johannes
CADMAN... Charles
CARTER.... Elliott
CHAVEZ..... Carlos
CHOPIN... Frederic
COWELL.... Henry
DELIUS... Frederick
DUPARC.... Henri
DVORAK.... Antonin
ENESCO... Georges
FLOTOW... Friedrich
　　　　　　von
FOSTER... Stephen
FRANCK..... Cesar
GLIERE... Reinhold
GLINKA..... Mikhail
GOUNOD... Charles
GRETRY..... Andre
HALEVY... Jacques

HANDEL.... George
　　　　　Frederick
HANSON.... Howard
HARRIS........ Roy
HILLER... Ferdinand
JOPLIN....... Scott
KODALY.... Zoltan
KRENEK...... Ernst
KUHLAU... Friedrich
LASSUS. Roland de
LIADOV...... Anatol
MAHLER.... Gustav
MORLEY... Thomas
MOZART.. Wolfgang
　　　　　Amadeus
PIERNE Henri Gabriel
PISTON...... Walter
PLEYEL..... Ignaz
PORTER...... Cole,
　　　　　Quincy
RAMEAU..... Jean-
　　　　　Philippe
ROGERS.... James
SCHUTZ... Heinrich
STRAUS..... Oskar
TAYLOR.... Deems
THOMAS.. Ambroise
VECCHI...... Orazio
VITALI..... Giovanni
WAGNER... Richard
WALTON... William
WEBERN..... Anton

7 letters
ALBENIZ...... Isaac
ALLEGRI... Gregorio
ARENSKY... Anton
BABBITT... Milton
BELLINI... Vincenzo
BERLIOZ.... Hector
BORODIN Alexander
BRITTEN. Benjamin
CACCINI.... Giulio
CAVALLI. Francesco
COPLAND... Aaron
CORELLI. Arcangelo
CRESTON..... Paul
DEBUSSY... Claude
DELIBES........ Leo
DES PREZ... Josquin
DOWLAND... John
GIBBONS... Orlando
GRIFFES.... Charles
HASSLER..... Hans
HERBERT... Victor
JANACEK.... Leos
LE JEUNE... Claude
MARTINU. Bohuslav
MENOTTI Gian Carlo
MILHAUD.... Darius

NICOLAI....... Otto
OBRECHT.... Jakob
OKEGHEM Johannes
POULENC... Francis
PUCCINI... Giacomo
PURCELL.... Henry
RIEGGER Wallingford
RODGERS.... Richard
ROMBERG. Sigmund
ROSSINI Gioacchino
SCHUMAN.. William
SINDING... Christian
SMETANA... Bedrich
STRAUSS... Johann
STRAUSS... Richard
THOMSON... Virgil
VIVALDI... Antonio
WEELKES.. Thomas
YOUMANS.. Vincent

8 letters
ARCADELT.. Jacob
BRUCKNER.. Anton
CHAUSSON.. Ernest
CLEMENTI... Muzio
COUPERIN. Francois
DIABELLI.... Anton
GABRIELI... Andrea,
　　　　　　Giovanni
GERSHWIN. George
GIORDANO Umberto
GOLDMARK.... Karl
GRANADOS. Enrique
HONEGGER.. Arthur
JOMMELLI.. Niccolo
LOEFFLER... Charles
LORTZING.... Albert
MACHAUT.........
　　　　Guillaume de
MASCAGNI.. Pietro
MASSENET.. Jules
MESSIAEN.. Oliver
PAGANINI.. Nicola
PALMGREN.. Selim
PICCINNI.... Nicola
PIZZETTI Ildebrando
RESPIGHI.. Ottorino
SCHUBERT... Franz
SCHUMANN Robert
SCRIABIN Alexander
SESSIONS.... Roger
SIBELIUS.... Jean
SPONTINI.. Gasparo
SULLIVAN... Arthur
TELEMANN... Georg
　　　　　　Philipp
THOMPSON. Randall
VICTORIA... Tomas
　　　　　　Luis de

245

SPORTS

KENTUCKY DERBY WINNERS

YEAR	HORSE	JOCKEY	YEAR	HORSE	JOCKEY
1908	Stone Street	Pickens	1947	Jet Pilot	Guerin
1909	Wintergreen	Powers	1948	Citation	Arcaro
1910	Donau	Herbert	1949	Ponder	Brooks
1911	Meridian	Archibald	1950	Middleground	Boland
1912	Worth	Shilling	1951	Count Turf	McCreary
1913	Donerail	Goose	1952	Hill Gail	Arcaro
1914	Old Rosebud	McCabe	1953	Dark Star	Moreno
1915	Regret	Notter	1954	Determine	York
1916	George Smith	Loftus	1955	Swaps	Shoemaker
1917	Omar Khayyam	Borel	1956	Needles	Erb
1918	Exterminator	Knapp	1957	Iron Liege	Hartack
1919	Sir Barton	Loftus	1958	Tim Tam	Valenzuela
1920	Paul Jones	Rice	1959	Tomy Lee	Shoemaker
1921	Behave Yourself	Thompson	1960	Venetian Way	Hartack
1922	Morvich	Johnson	1961	Carry Back	Sellers
1923	Zev	Sande	1962	Decidedly	Hartack
1924	Black Gold	Mooney	1963	Chateaugay	Baeza
1925	Flying Ebony	Sande	1964	Northern Dancer	Hartack
1926	Bubbling Over	Johnson	1965	Lucky Debonair	Shoemaker
1927	Whiskery	McAtee	1966	Kauai King	Brumfield
1928	Reigh Count	Lang	1967	Proud Clarion	Ussery
1929	Clyde Van Dusen	McAtee	1968	Dancer's Image	Ussery
1930	Gallant Fox	Sande		(or Forward Pass)	
1931	Twenty Grand	Kurtsinger	1969	Majestic Prince	Hartack
1932	Burgoo King	James	1970	Dust Commander	Manganello
1933	Brokers Tip	Meade	1971	Canonero II	Avila
1934	Cavalcade	Garner	1972	Riva Ridge	Turcotte
1935	Omaha	Saunders	1973	Secretariat	Turcotte
1936	Bold Venture	Hanford	1974	Cannonade	Cordero
1937	War Admiral	Kurtsinger	1975	Foolish Pleasure	Vasquez
1938	Lawrin	Arcaro	1976	Bold Forbes	Cordero
1939	Johnstown	Stout	1977	Seattle Slew	Cruguet
1940	Gallahadion	Bierman	1978	Affirmed	Cauthen
1941	Whirlaway	Arcaro	1979	Spectacular Bid	Franklin
1942	Shut Out	Wright	1980	Genuine Risk	Vasquez
1943	Count Fleet	Longden	1981	Pleasant Colony	Velasquez
1944	Pensive	McCreary	1982	Gato del Sol	Delahoussaye
1945	Hoop, Jr.	Arcaro	1983	Sunny's Halo	Delahoussaye
1946	Assault	Mehrtens			

TRIPLE CROWN WINNERS

YEAR	HORSE	JOCKEY	YEAR	HORSE	JOCKEY
1919	Sir Barton	Loftus	1946	Assault	Mehrtens
1930	Gallant Fox	Sande	1948	Citation	Arcaro
1935	Omaha	Saunders	1973	Secretariat	Turcotte
1937	War Admiral	Kurtsinger	1977	Seattle Slew	Cruguet
1941	Whirlaway	Arcaro	1978	Affirmed	Cauthen
1943	Count Fleet	Longden			

SOME NAMES FROM THE BASEBALL
HALL OF FAME

Aaron, Hank
Alexander, Grover
    Cleveland
Anson, Cap
Appling, Luke
Baker, Home Run
Banks, Ernie
Bell, Cool Papa
Bender, Chief
Berra, Yogi
Boudreau, Lou
Brown, Mordecai
Campanella, Roy
Carey, Max
Chance, Frank
Chandler, Happy
Clarke, Fred
Clemente, Roberto
Cobb, Ty
Cochrane, Mickey
Combs, Earl
Conlan, Jocko
Connor, Roger
Cronin, Joe
Cummings, Candy
Cuyler, Kiki
Dean, Dizzy
Delahanty, Ed
Dickey, Bill
DiMaggio, Joe
Duffy, Hugh
Evers, John
Ewing, Buck
Faber, Urban
Feller, Bob
Flick, Elmer H.
Ford, Whitey
Foxx, Jimmy
Frick, Ford
Frisch, Frank
Gehrig, Lou
Giles, Warren
Gomez, Lefty

Goslin, Goose
Greenberg, Hank
Grove, Lefty
Hafey, Chick
Harridge, Will
Harris, Bucky
Hartnett, Gabby
Hooper, Harry
Hornsby, Rogers
Hoyt, Waite
Hubbard, Cal
Hubbell, Carl
Huggins, Miller
Irvin, Monte
Jackson, Travis
Johnson, Byron
Joss, Addie
Kaline, Al
Keefe, Timothy
Keeler, William
Kell, George
Kelley, Joe
Kelly, George
Kelly, King
Kiner, Ralph
Klein, Chuck
Klem, Bill
Koufax, Sandy
Lajoie, Napoleon
Landis, Kenesaw
    Mountain
Lemon, Bob
Lloyd, Pop
Lopez, Al
Mack, Connie
Mantle, Mickey
Manush, Henry
Marichal, Juan
Maranville, Rabbit
Marquard, Rube
Mays, Willie
McGinnity, Joe
McGraw, John

Medwick, Joe
Mize, Johnny
Musial, Stan
Nichols, Kid
Ott, Mel
Paige, Satchel
Plank, Ed
Rice, Sam
Rickey, Branch
Rixey, Eppa
Roberts, Robin
Robinson, Brooks
Robinson, Frank
Robinson, Jackie
Robinson, Wilbert
Roush, Edd
Ruffing, Red
Rusie, Amos
Ruth, Babe
Sisler, George
Snider, Duke
Spahn, Warren
Speaker, Tris
Stengel, Casey
Terry, Bill
Tinker, Joe
Traynor, Pie
Vance, Dazzy
Waddell, Rube
Wagner, Honus
Walsh, Ed
Waner, Lloyd
Waner, Paul
Ward, John
Weiss, George
Welch, Mickey
Wheat, Zach
Williams, Ted
Wilson, Hack
Wynn, Early
Yawkey, Tom
Young, Cy
Youngs, Ross

SOME NAMES FROM THE PRO FOOTBALL
HALL OF FAME

Adderley, Herb
Alworth, Lance
Atkins, Doug
Badgro, Morris (Red)
Battles, Cliff
Baugh, Sammy
Bednarik, Chuck
Bell, Bert
Bell, Bobby
Berry, Raymond
Blanda, George
Brown, Jim
Brown, Paul E.
Brown, Roosevelt
Butkus, Dick
Canadeo, Tony
Carr, Joe
Chamberlin, Guy
Christiansen, Jack
Clark, Earl (Dutch)
Connor, George
Conzelman, Jimmy
Davis, Willie
Donovan, Art
Driscoll, John (Paddy)
Dudley, Bill
Edwards, Albert (Turk)
Ewbank, Weeb
Fears, Tom
Flaherty, Ray
Ford, Leonard (Len)
Fortmann, Daniel J.
George, Bill
Gifford, Frank
Gillman, Sid
Graham, Otto
Grange, Harold (Red)
Gregg, Forrest
Groza, Lou

Guyon, Joe
Halas, George
Healey, Ed
Hein, Mel
Henry, Wilbur (Pete)
Herber, Arnie
Hewitt, Bill
Hinkle, Clarke
Hirsch, Elroy (Crazy-
  legs)
Hubbard, Robert (Cal)
Huff, Sam
Hunt, Lamar
Hutson, Don
Jones, David (Deacon)
Jurgensen, Sonny
Kinard, Frank (Bruiser)
Lambeau, Earl (Curly)
Lane, Richard (Night
  Train)
Lary, Yale
Lavelli, Dante
Layne, Bobby
Leemans, Alphonse
  (Tuffy)
Lilly, Bob
Lombardi, Vince
Luckman, Sid
Lyman, William Roy
  (Link)
Marchetti, Gino
Matson, Ollie
McAfee, George
McElhenny, Hugh
McNally, John (Blood)
Michalski, August
  (Mike)
Millner, Wayne
Mitchell, Bobby

Mix, Ron
Moore, Leonard
  (Lenny)
Motley, Marion
Musso, George
Nagurski, Bronko
Neale, Earle (Greasy)
Nevers, Ernie
Nitschke, Ray
Nomellini, Leo
Olsen, Merlin
Otto, Jim
Owen, Steven
Parker, Jim
Perry, Fletcher (Joe)
Pihos, Pete
Ringo, Jim
Robustelli, Andy
Sayers, Gale
Schmidt, Joe
Starr, Bart
Stautner, Ernie
Strong, Ken
Taylor, Jim
Thorpe, Jim
Tittle, Y.A.
Trafton, George
Trippi, Charley
Tunnell, Emlen
Turner, Clyde
  (Bulldog)
Unitas, Johnny
Van Brocklin, Norm
Van Buren, Steve
Warfield, Paul
Waterfield, Bob
Willis, Bill
Wilson, Larry

SOME NAMES FROM THE BASKETBALL
HALL OF FAME

Barlow, Thomas
Baylor, Elgin
Borgmann, Bennie
Bradley, Bill
Brennan, Joseph
Chamberlain, Wilt
Cooper, Charles
  (Tarzan)
Cousy, Robert
Davies, Robert
DeBernardi, Forrest
DeBusschere, Dave
Endacott, Paul
Foster, Harold (Bud)
Friedman, Max
Gale, Lauren (Laddie)
Gola, Thomas

Greer, Hal
Hagan, Clifford
Hanson, Victor
Holman, Nat
Krause, Edward
Kurland, Robert
Lapchick, Joe
Lucas, Jerry Ray
Luisetti, Angelo
McCracken, Branch
McCracken, Jack
Macauley, Edward
Martin, Slater
Mikan, George
Murphy, Charles
Pettit, Robert
Phillip, Andy

Pollard, James
Ramsey, Frank
Reed, Willis
Robertson, Oscar
Russell, John (Honey)
Russell, William
Schayes, Adolph
Schmidt, Ernest
Sedran, Barney
Sharman, William
Thompson, John
Twyman, Jack
Vandivier, Robert
  (Fuzzy)
West, Jerry Alan
Wooden, John

SOME AWARD-WINNING ICE HOCKEY PLAYERS

Beliveau, Jean
Bossy, Mike
Bourque, Ray
Bucyk, John
Clarke, Bobby
Cloutier, Real
Corlyle, Randy
Cournoyer, Yvan
Crozier, Roger
Devecchio, Alex
Dionne, Marcel
Dryden, Dave
Dryden, Ken
Esposito, Phil
Esposito, Tony
Ftorek, Robbie
Gainey, Bob
Giacomin, Ed
Goring, Butch

Goyette, Phil
Grant, Danny
Gretzky, Wayne
Hall, Glenn
Hawerchuk, Dale
Hodge, Charlie
Howe, Gordie
Howell, Harry
Hull, Bobby
Kasper, Steve
Kehoe, Rick
Keon, Dave
Lacroix, Andre
Lafleur, Guy
Laperriere, Jacques
Leach, Reg
Middleton, Rick
Mikita, Stan
Orr, Bobby

Parent, Bernie
Perreault, Gil
Pilote, Pierre
Plett, Willi
Potvin, Denis
Ratelle, Jean
Robinson, Larry
Sanderson, Derek
Savard, Serge
Selby, Brit
Smith, Billy
Stastny, Peter
Tardif, Marc
Trottier, Bryan
Vail, Eric
Vickers, Steve
Walton, Mike
Wharram, Ken
Wilson, Doug

ACRONYMS, INITIALS, ABBREVIATIONS

Acronyms (words or abbreviations formed by using key letters of the phrases they stand for) are seldom defined by those exact words. Hence, this special listing is arranged in sections to help you find the word you are looking for. For example, you may be given the definition "International pact" and you know it is a 4-letter word. Go to the INTERNATIONAL section and look at the 4-letter words (words are grouped by section, then word size, then alphabetically). Your answer will probably be NATO. You might also be given the definition "The 'A' in G.A.R."; you can then look for GAR in all the sections (it's in the MILITARY section) and find that A stands for ARMY. In each case, the letters from the acronym or initial-word have been capitalized, so you will know what the letters stand for. NOTE: Some of these organizations, acts, etc., no longer exist, but they have been included because they continue to appear in crossword puzzles.

Abbreviations Used in This Section

Admin.. Administration	Corp ...... Corporation	Inst .... Institute
Amer........ American	Dept ..... Department	Internat'l.. International
Assoc ..... Association	Fed .... Federal	Nat'l .... National
Conf ...... Conference	Govt...... Government	Org ...... Organization
	Inc....... Incorporated	

GOVERNMENTAL, POLITICAL

3 letters
AAA Agricultural Adjustment Act
AAA.... Agricultural Adjustment Admin.
AEC Atomic Energy Commission (now Nuclear Regulatory Commission)
ARA Area Redevelopment Admin.
BIA..... Bureau of Indian Affairs
BLM............. Bureau of Land Management
BLS .. Bureau of Labor Statistics
CAB.... Civil Aeronautics Board
CCA... Circuit Court of Appeals
CCC Civilian Conservation Corps
CIA.. Central Intelligence Agency
CRC... Civil Rights Commission
CSA Community Services Admin.
CSA..... Confederate States of America
CSC .. Civil Service Commission
CWA .... Civil Works Admin.
DEA .. Drug Enforcement Admin.
DOE............ Dept. of Energy
EDA .... Economic Development Admin.
EOP ..... Economic Opportunity Program
EPA ... Environmental Protection Agency
ERA ... Emergency Relief Admin.
ESA .... Employment Standards Admin.

FAA .... Fed. Aviation Admin.
FAC ...... Fed. Advisory Council
FBI . Fed. Bureau of Investigation
FCC ...... Fed. Communications Commission
FDA ..... Food and Drug Admin.
FEC .. Fed. Election Commission
FET .... Fed. Excise Tax
FHA ...... Fed. Housing Admin.
FRB .... Fed. Reserve Board
FRS ...... Fed. Reserve System
FTC .... Fed. Trade Commission
GAO. General Accounting Office
GPO... Gov't Printing Office
GSA ... General Services Admin.
HRA... Health Resources Admin.
HUD........ Housing and Urban Development
IRS .... Internal Revenue Service
NBS .. Nat'l Bureau of Standards
NFS ..... Nat'l Forest Service
NRA..... Nat'l Recovery Admin.
NRC....... Nuclear Regulatory Commission
NSA ...... Nat'l Security Agency
NSC ...... Nat'l Security Council
OEO .... Office of Economic Opportunity
OPA ..... Office of Price Admin.
OSS .... Office of Strategic Services
PHA ..... Public Housing Admin.
REA . Rural Electrification Admin.
RFC .... Reconstruction Finance Corp.

SBA	Small Business Admin.
SSA	Social Security Admin.
SSS	Selective Service System
TVA	Tennessee Valley Authority
WPA	Works Project Admin.

4 letters

ADAP	Airport Development Aid Program
ADEA	Age Discrimination Employment Act
AFDC	Aid to Families with Dependent Children
ALRB	Agriculture Labor Relations Board
BATF	Bureau of Alcohol, Tobacco, and Firearms
BEOG	Basic Education Opportunity Grant
CETA	Comprehensive Employment and Training Act
CHAP	Child Health Assessment Program
CWPS	Council on Wage and Price Stability
ECOA	Equal Credit Opportunity Act
EEOC	Equal Employment Opportunity Commission
FCRA	Fair Credit Reporting Act
FDIC	Fed. Deposit Insurance Corp.
FECA	Fed. Employees Compensation Act
FEPA	Fair Employment Practices Act
FERA	Fed. Emergency Relief Admin.
FERC	Fed. Energy Regulatory Commission
FHLA	Farmers Home Loan Admin.
FICA	Fed. Insurance Contributions Act
FLRB	Farm Labor Relations Board
FNMA	Fed. Nat'l Mortgage Assoc. (Fannie Mae)
FUTA	Fed. Unemployment Tax Act
GNMA	Gov't Nat'l Mortgage Assoc. (Ginnie Mae)
HHFA	Housing and Home Finance Agency
HOAP	Home Ownership Assistance Program
LMSA	Labor-Management Services Admin.
MDTA	Manpower Development and Training Act
MGIC	Mortgage Guaranty Insurance Corp. (Maggie Mae)

NASA	Nat'l Aeronautics and Space Admin.
NDSL	Nat'l Direct Student Loan
NEPA	Nat'l Environmental Policy Act
NLRA	Nat'l Labor Relations Act
NLRB	Nat'l Labor Relations Board
NOAA	Nat'l Oceanic and Atmospheric Admin.
NTSB	Nat'l Transportation Safety Board
OSHA	Occupation Safety and Health Admin.
SEOG	Supplemental Education Opportunity Grant
USBM	U.S. Bureau of Mines
USCC	U.S. Circuit Court
USDA	U.S. Dept. of Agriculture
USDC	U.S. Dept. of Commerce
USDE	U.S. Dept. of Energy
USDI	U.S. Dept. of the Interior
USDJ	U.S. Dept. of Justice
USDL	U.S. Dept. of Labor
USDT	U.S. Dept. of Transportation
USIA	U.S. Information Agency
USIS	U.S. Information Service

5 letters

FSLIC	Fed. Savings and Loan Insurance Corp.
MORGA	Municipal ORG. Act
NCPAC	Nat'l Conservative Political Action Committee
NIOSH	Nat'l Inst. for Occupational Safety and Health
VISTA	Volunteers In Service To America

6 letters

ADAMHA	Alcohol, Drug Abuse, and Mental Health Agency

MILITARY

3 letters

AAB	Army Air Base
AAM	Air-to-Air Missile
ABM	AntiBallistic Missile
ADC	Air Defense Command
AEF	Amer. Expeditionary Force
AGM	Air-to-Ground Missile
AMM	AntiMissile Missile
APO	Army Post Office
ARM	AntiRadar Missile
BAR	Browning Automatic Rifle
CEO	Chief Executive Officer
CIC	Commander-In-Chief
CNO	Chief of Naval Operations
DFC	Distinguished Flying Cross

DFM. Distinguished Flying Medal
DSC Distinguished Service Cross
DSM Distinguished Service Medal
DSO Distinguished Service Order
ETO .... European Theater of Operations
FPO .... Fleet Post Office
GAR Grand Army of the Republic
LCT .... Landing Craft Tank
LST.......... Landing Ship Tank
MAP Military Assistance Program
MIA .... Missing In Action
NCO. Non-Commissioned Officer
OCS ... Officer Candidate School
PFC ...... Private First Class
RAF .... Royal Air Force
SAC .... Strategic Air Command
SAM ..... Surface-to-Air Missile
SUM..... Surface-to-Underwater Missile
UAM .. Underwater-to-Air Missile
USN................. U.S. Navy
VAD............... Vice Admiral
WAC ..... Women's Army Corps
WAF .... Women in the Air Force

4 letters
AANS...... Advanced Automatic Navigation System
ADCC ..... Air Defense Control Center
ADIZ . Air Defense Identification Zone
AEAF... Allied Expeditionary Air Force
AWAC... Airborne Warning And Control
AWOL ... Absent WithOut Leave
ICBM .. InterContinental Ballistic Missile
ICCM .... InterContinental Cruise Missile
IRBM .... Intermediate Range Ballistic Missile
MASH .... Mobile Army Surgical Hospital
MATS .... Military Air Transport Service
RAAF. Royal Australian Air Force
RCAF. Royal Canadian Air Force
ROTC. Reserve Officers Training Corps
SLAM . Supersonic Low Altitude Missile
SLAR ..... Side-Looking Airborne Radar
SLBM...... Submarine-Launched Ballistic Missile
STOL Short TakeOff and Landing
TCBM TransContinental Ballistic Missile

USAR....... U.S. Army Reserve
USMA ... U.S. Military Academy
USMC .... U.S. Marine Corps
USMM ... U.S. Merchant Marine
USNA ...... U.S. Naval Academy
USNR....... U.S. Naval Reserve
WAAC. Women's Auxiliary Army Corps
WAAF ... Women's Auxiliary Air Force

5 letters
AICBM .... AntiInterContinental Ballistic Missile
CONAD CONtinental Air Defense
MIDAS... MIssile Defense Alarm System
NAVAR...... NAVigation radAR
NORAD....... NORth Amer. air Defense command
SHAPE . Supreme Headquarters, Allied Powers, Europe
USACE... U.S. Army Corps of Engineers
WAVES... Women Appointed for Volunteer Emergency Service (Naval Reserve)

6 letters
ACLANT....... Allied Command atLANTic
NAVAIR .... NAVal AIR
NAVCAD . NAVal aviation CADet

7 letters
CINCPAC. Commander-IN-Chief, PACific

INTERNATIONAL

3 letters
AID........ Agency for Internat'l Development
CMN .. Common Market Nations
EEC .... European Economic Community
FAO ...... Food and Agricultural Org. (U.N.)
IDA...... Internat'l Development Assoc.
ILA ... Internat'l Longshoreman's Assoc.
ILO .... Internat'l Labour Org.
ILU ..... Internat'l Laborers Union
IOC......... Internat'l Olympics Committee
IRO...... Internat'l Refugee Org.
ITO........ Internat'l Trade Org.
MFN..... Most Favored Nation
OAS ...... Org. of Amer. States
PAU .... Pan Amer. Union

UAE . . . . . . United Arab Emirates
UAR . . . . . . United Arab Republic
WEU . . . . . Western Europe Union
WHO . . . . World Health Org.

4 letters
CARE . . . . Cooperative for Amer.
Relief Everywhere
EFTA . . . . . European Free Trade
Assoc.
METO . . Middle East Treaty Org.
NATO North Atlantic Treaty Org.
OPEC . . . . Org. of Petroleum
Exporting Countries
SALT . Strategic Arms Limitation
Treaty

5 letters
ASEAN . . . Assoc. for SouthEast
Asia Nations
ASPAC . . . . . . ASian and PAcific
Council
CENTO . . . . CENtral Treaty Org.
LAFTA . . . . . . Latin America Free
Trade Assoc.
ODECA . . . . *Organizacion De
Estados CentroAmericanos* (Org.
of Central Amer. States)
SEATO . . SouthEast Asia Treaty
Org.
START . . . . STrategic Arms
Reduction Talks
SWAPO . . . . . . South West Africa
People's Org.
UNRRA . . . United Nations Relief
and Rehabilitation Admin.
UNRWA . . United Nations Relief
and Works Agency

6 letters
UNESCO . . . . United Nations
Educational, Scientific and
Cultural Org.
UNICEF . . . . United Nations
Internat'l Children's Emergency
Fund

7 letters
BENELUX BElgium, NEtherlands,
LUXembourg

8 letters
INTERPOL . . INTERnat'l criminal
POLice org.

ASSOCIATIONS

3 letters
AAA . . . Amateur Athletic Assoc.
AAO . . . . Amer. Assoc. of
Orthodontists
AAP . Assoc. of Amer. Publishers

AAU Assoc. of Amer. Universities
ABA . . . . Amer. Bar Assoc.
AEA . . . . . . Actors' Equity Assoc.
AFM . . . . Amer. Federation of
Musicians
AFT . . . . Amer. Federation of
Teachers
AMA . . . . . Amer. Medical Assoc.
APA . . . Amer. Psychiatric Assoc.
APA Amer. Psychological Assoc.
NEA . . . . . Nat'l Education Assoc.
SAG . . . . Screen Actors Guild

4 letters
AAMC . Amer. Assoc. of Medical
Colleges
AAPS . . . Amer. Assoc. of Plastic
Surgeons
AARP . . . Amer. Assoc. of Retired
Persons
AAUP . . . . Amer. Assoc. of
University Professors
AAUW . . . . Amer. Assoc. of
University Women
ABLA . . . . . . Amer. Business Law
Assoc.
AGVA . . . Amer. Guild of Variety
Artists
ALPA . . . . . Air Line Pilots Assoc.
ASTA . . . Amer. Society of Travel
Agents
ATLA . . . . . . Amer. Trial Lawyers
Assoc.
SACM . . . . . . Society of Authors
and Composers of Music

5 letters
AFTRA . . . . Amer. Federation of
Television and Radio Artists
ASCAP . . . . Amer. Society of
Composers, Authors, and
Publishers
PATCO . Professional Air Traffic
Controllers Org.

SPORTS

3 letters
AAA . . . Amateur Athletic Assoc.
AAU . . . . Amateur Athletic Union
ABA . . . Amer. Basketball Assoc.
ABC . . . Amer. Bowling Congress
AFC . . . . Amer. Football Conf.
AFL . . . . Amer. Football League
ASL . . . . . . Amer. Soccer League
ERA . . . . . . Earned Run Average
MVP . . . . . Most Valuable Player
NBA . . . . . Nat'l Basketball Assoc.
NFC . . . . Nat'l Football Conf.
NFL . . . . Nat'l Football League
NHL . . . . Nat'l Hockey League

NIT Nat'l Invitational Tournament
(basketball)
PBA Professional Bowlers Assoc.
PGA Professional Golfers' Assoc.
RBI .... Runs Batted In
WBA ...... World Boxing Assoc.

4 letters
LPGA .... Ladies Professional
Golfers Assoc.
NCAA .. Nat'l Collegiate Athletic
Assoc.
WPGA ... Women's Professional
Golfers' Assoc.

MISCELLANEOUS

3 letters
AAA ... Amer. Automobile Assoc.
ABS .... Amer. Bible Society
ACA .... Arts Council of America
ACT ..... Amer. College Testing
ADA .. Americans for Democratic
Action
ADF . Automatic Direction Finder
ADL .... Anti-Defamation League
AHA .... Amer. Heart Assoc.
AKA .... Also Known As
AKC .... Amer. Kennel Club
ALP .... Amer. Labor Party
APB .... All Points Bulletin
ARC .... Amer. Red Cross
BBB .... Better Business Bureau
BBC .. British Broadcasting Corp.
BMR ...... Basal Metabolic Rate
BTU ...... British Thermal Unit
CAP .... Civil Air Patrol
CDC . Center for Disease Control
CEA .... Council of Economic
Advisers
CED ... Committee for Economic
Development
CID . Criminal Investigation Dept.
(Scotland Yard)
CNS .. Central Nervous System
COD .... Cash On Delivery
CPI ...... Consumer Price Index
DAR .... Daughters of the Amer.
Revolution
DAV .. Disabled Amer. Veterans
DBA .... Doing Business As
DNA ..... DeoxyriboNucleic Acid
EAB ..... Ethics Advisory Board
EBS ..... Emergency Broadcast
System
EEG ..... ElectroEncephaloGram
EKG .... ElectroCardioGram
EMS Emergency Medical Service
EOE Equal Opportunity Employer
ERA .. Equal Rights Amendment
ESP ... ExtraSensory Perception
ETA .. Estimated Time of Arrival

ETV ..... Educational TeleVision
FAF .... Financial Aid Form
FCA .... Farm Credit Assoc.
FFA . Future Farmers of America
FOB .... Free On Board
FTA Future Teachers of America
GIM .... Gross Income Multiplier
GNI .... Gross Nat'l Income
GNP .... Gross Nat'l Product
GOP .... Grand Old Party
(Republican)
ICU .... Intensive Care Unit
IFO ..... Identified Flying Object
IFR ..... Instrument Flight Rules
IRA .... Individual Retirement
Account
JDL .... Jewish Defense League
KGB . *Komitet Gosudarstvennoye
Bezopastnosti* (Russian
Security Police)
LCD Least Common Denominator
LCD ..... Liquid Crystal Display
LED .... Light Emitting Diode
MDR Minimum Daily Requirement
NAM .... Nat'l Assoc. of
Manufacturers
NET Nat'l Educational Television
NHA . Nat'l Homebuilders Assoc.
NOW ..... Nat'l Org. for Women
NRA .... Nat'l Rifle Assoc.
OOB .... Off-Off Broadway
PAL ... Police Athletic League
PBS Public Broadcasting Service
PLO ... Palestine Liberation Org.
POC .... Port Of Call
POE .... Port Of Entry
PSE ... Pacific Stock Exchange
PTA ... Parent-Teacher's Assoc.
RCA .... Radio Corp. of America
RDF .... Radio Direction Finder
REM ...... Rapid Eye Movement
RFD .... Rural Free Delivery
RNA .... RiboNucleic Acid
ROI ...... Return On Investment
SAT ... Scholastic Aptitude Test
SEC .... Securities Exchange
Commission
SIG ...... Special Interest Group
SOP .... Standard Operating
Procedure
SRO .... Standing Room Only
SST ...... SuperSonic Transport
TLC ...... Tender Loving Care
TWU ... Transport Workers Union
UFO ... Unidentified Flying Object
UFW ...... United Farm Workers
UHF ...... Ultra High Frequency
UPI ... United Press International
USO .... United Service Org.
UWA ... United Way of America
VAT .... Value-Added Tax
VCR ... Video Cassette Recorder

VFR .... Visual Flight Rules
VFW .. Veterans of Foreign Wars
VHF ...... Very High Frequency
WPI ..... Wholesale Price Index
ZIP ..... Zone Improvement Plan
(post office)
ZPG .... Zero Population Growth

4 letters
AAAL... Amer. Academy of Arts
and Letters
ACLU...... Amer. Civil Liberties
Union
ALMA .... Adoptees Liberty
Movement Assoc.
AMEX ... AMer. stock EXchange
ANRC ... Amer. Nat'l Red Cross
ANSI Amer. Nat'l Standards Inst.
ANTA . Amer. Nat'l Theatre and
Academy
ASAP...... As Soon As Possible
BMOC ..... Big Man On Campus
BPOE.......... Benevolent and
Protective Order of Elks
CATV.... Community Antenna
TeleVision
CCTV.... Closed-Circuit TeleVision
CEEB......... College Entrance
Examination Board
CLEP . College Level Examination
Program
COLA. Cost Of Living Agreement
CORE....... Congress Of Racial
Equality
CWSP ...... College Work-Study
Program
FIFO.......... First In, First Out
GASP... Group Against Smoking
Pollution
HOLC. Home Owners Loan Corp.
IOOF ..... Independent Order of
Odd Fellows
KMPS ... KiloMeters Per Second
LEEP .... Law Enforcement
Education Program
LIFO.......... Last In, First Out
LOOM ... Loyal Order Of Moose
MDAR ..... Minimum Daily Adult
Requirement
MPAA . Motion Picture Assoc. of
America
NCOA ... Nat'l Council On Aging
NIFO .... Next In, First Out
NYSE New York Stock Exchange
OCTV... Open-Circuit TeleVision
PSAT.... Preliminary Scholastic
Aptitude Test
RADA .... Royal Academy of
Dramatic Arts
RCMP . Royal Canadian Mounted
Police

SASE .. Self-Addressed Stamped
Envelope
SBLI......... Savings Bank Life
Insurance
SCAN.. Senior Citizen Anticrime
Network
SNCC....... Student Nonviolent
Coordinating Committee
SPCA........... Society for the
Prevention of Cruelty
to Animals
SPCC........... Society for the
Prevention of Cruelty
to Children
SWAT .... Special Weapons And
Tactics force
TASS. *Telegraphnoye Agentstvo
Sovyetskovo Soyuza* (Soviet
News Agency)
USOC.. U.S. Olympic Committee
USSR.. Union of Soviet Socialist
Republics
WATS .... Wide Area Telephone
Service
WCTU ...... Woman's Christian
Temperance Union

5 letters
AMPAS..... Academy of Motion
Picture Arts and Sciences
ASPCA ... Amer. Society for the
Prevention of Cruelty to Animals
ATVAS .. Academy of TeleVision
Arts and Sciences
ENDEX .... ENvironmental Data
indEX
ILGWU..... Internat'l Ladies'
Garment Workers' Union
LASER.... Light Amplification by
Stimulated Emission of Radiation
LORAN . LOng-RAnge Navigation
MOPED... MOtor-assisted PEDal
cycle
NAACP..... Nat'l Assoc. for the
Advancement of Colored People
RADAR.... RAdio Detection And
Ranging
SCORE .... Service Corps Of
Retired Executives
SCUBA .... Self-Contained
Underwater Breathing Apparatus
SONAR ...... SOund NAvigation
Ranging

6 letters
AFL-CIO ... Amer. Federation of
Labor—Congress of Industrial
Organizations
AMVETS....... AMer. VETeranS
ENCONA .... ENvironmental
Coalition Of North America

THE WORD-FINDER
with cross-references

FOR THE SOLVER

You can complete any unfinished 2-, 3-, or 4-letter word in the crossword you are working by using this WORD-FINDER. Even though you are at first unable to locate it in the Definition section for some reason, if you have just two letters of your wanted word (just one if it's a 2-letter word) you can find it here.

The WORD-FINDER words are listed according to the following Letter-Combination system:

> XX - -   (for cases when the first two letters are known)
> - XX -   (when the second and third letters are known)
> - - XX   (when the last two letters are known)
> X - - X   (when the first and last letters are known)

Let us say that you need to complete a word that is four letters long.

STEP ONE: Find the Letter-Combination that is the same as the letters which you have written into the crossword puzzle. Have you, for example, found "ON" as the end of a 4-letter word? Then turn to the "- - ON" Letter-Combination. Of course, since the WORD-FINDER is thorough-going, a number of words, all containing the same letter combination, are listed under this Letter-Combination.

> - - ON   Acon, agon, Amon, anon,
> Avon, axon, azon, bion,
> boon, cion, coon, Dion,
> doon, ebon, Enon, Eton,
> faon, Gaon, hoon, icon,
> iron, Leon, lion, loon,
> moon, neon, etc.

STEP TWO: You may know, after looking through the words listed under your Letter-Combination, the word which is the only correct possibility. If not, you now begin to eliminate words in the list by working with the words in the crossword puzzle which CROSS your unfinished word. You do this by experimentally inserting words from the Letter-Combination list. When the experimental insert produces such impossible-looking combinations with the crossing word as "bv," "pv" etc. it can be discarded.

STEP THREE: After eliminating the words which make highly unlikely or "impossible" combinations with the crossing words, you still may not be sure how to complete your unfinished puzzle. Here you make use of the invaluable CROSS-REFERENCE listings following the words in the WORD-FINDER. Each number following a word is the number of the page of the Definitions Section on which the word and one of its definitions will be found. The alphabetical letters a, b, c, d indicate in exactly which section of the definition page you will be able to locate the word with its meaning.

Example: adat (90b,95d)

On page 90 of this Dictionary, in section b of the page, you will find the word ADAT in bold face type. The definition is "law, D. E. Ind". On page 95, section d, you will find another cross-reference to ADAT. The definition reads "Malay law."

STEP FOUR: Now re-examine the definition in your puzzle. Eliminate words in the WORD-FINDER by comparing definitions until you arrive at the "logical candidate" word for which you have been looking. Definitions in this dictionary and those in your puzzle will not always agree in exact wording. In that case, let the general meaning of the definitions be your guide. Everyday words are not always cross-referenced in this WORD-FINDER, nor are some words of exceptional terminology. Only some of the words listed in the Special Section are cross-referenced. If your definition calls for a word likely to be found in the Special Section, it is recommended that you look there first.

TWO-LETTER WORDS

A - Aa (47a), aa (90b), Ab (48d,75b,102a), ab (63d), AC (39d), ad (90a,112d,167d), ae (42b,43c,d,122b,139a), Ae (82c,115d), ah (52c), ai (143c,148c), al (8c,80c,102c,104b), am (166c,175c), an (11b, 13b), Ao (13d,88b,c,116c), AP (107a,182d), ap (122d,166c), ar (88b,91c,98a,99b,110c), as (51b,67b,92b,126a,133a,b,180d), at (25c,32c,106a,123a,128a), au (63a,69c), aw (44a), ax (40c,139a, 167a), ay (7c,8b,9b,28d,55a,60a)

- A Aa (47a), aa (90b), BA (42a), Ba (150a,153c), ba (139a), da (9b,37a, 56a,133d,135d), DA (124d), ea (43c), EA (15b,68a), fa (108b,138a, 161a), Ga (69c), ha (52c), ia (43d,158c), ja (66d), ka (45c), Ka (68c, 77b,150d,153c,173c), la (13b,61a,83a,108b,138a,151d,161a), ma, MA (42a), Ma (69a,b,85d), na (140c,163d), NA (36c), oa (43c,d), pa (60b,106d), ra (108b), Ra (159b), SA (36c), ta (112d,139a,160b), VA (83a), va (105a), wa (188), Wa (24c,d,88c), ya, za (162a)

B - BA (42a), ba (139a,150d,153c), bb (147b), be, bi (122d,171c), bo (23d,24c,136a,168a), bu (190), by (18b,32c,106a)

- B ab (63d,) Ab (48d,75b,102a), bb (147b), FB (59c), HB (59c), ob (122b), QB (59c)

C - ce (62d,164c), CE (42a)

- C DC (39d), ec (122c)

D - da (9b,37a,56a,133d,135d), DA (124d), DC (39d), DD (42a), de (63d,89b,122b,122c,124a,152c,d), di (68c,89b,108b,122b,122c, 122d,171d), dm (131c), do (108b,138a,161a)

- D ad, (90a,112d,167d), DD (42a), ed (175c), Ed (18d), id (26d, 40c,51c,57a,b,d), od (8d,59d,79c), td (32a)

E - ea (43c), EA (15b,68a), ec (122c), ed (175c), Ed (18d), ee (139c), EE (42a), ef (91c), eg (59d,163d), eh (52c), el (13b,42a,47a,99b, 151d,168a), El (68a,108a), em (91c,98a,123d,172a,c), en (15b, 29c,50a,91c,98a,119d,123d,158c,d,172a), eo (34a), er (35b,76c, 137d,155a,158c,d,160b,175c), Er (18d,68c,85c,163d,166c,172c, 178a), es (49b,50a,66c,119d,158c,d,175c), et (10b,61a,b,89a,158c), ex (60b,91c,122c)

- E ae (42b,43c,d,122b,139a), Ae (82c,115d), be, CE (42a), Ce (62d), ce (164c), de (63d,89b,122b,c,124a,152c,d), ee (139c), EE (42a), Ge (47d,69a), he (91c), ie (74c,158c,163d), LE (59c), le (13b,61a, 108b), me (108b,124d), Me. (124d), ne (35b,106b), oe (43c,54d, 82d,180d,182a,b), pe (91c), Pe. (124d), re (6b,10b,35d,108b,122b, 129b,138a,161a), RE (59c), se (35b,108b), te (43a,62d,108b,131c, 152d,160b,185d), Ve (63c,109c), we (48c,124b), We (92b), ye (124b)

F - fa (108b,138a,161a), FB (59c), ff (147b), Fi (108b), Fo (23d), fu (42c,84c), Fu (30b)

- F ef (91c), ff (147b), if (35d,125a), LF (16d), of (6b), RF 16d)

258

G - Ga (69c), Ge (47d,69a), Gi (91d), go (64c,90d)

- G eg (59d,163d), Og (16d,18c)

H - ha (52c), HB (59c), he (91c), hi (52c), ho (39b,79a), Ho (87c), Hu (101c,108a,162b)

- H ah (52c), eh (52c), oh (52c), Rh (20c), sh (17b,43c,79c,126d), th (43c)

I - Ia (43d,158c), id (26d,40c,51c,57a,b,d), Ie (74c,158c,163d), if (35d, 125a), iI (122c), im (122c), in (9d,123a), io (74b,74c,103c,115b), Io (25a,85d,95c,186b), ir ('9d,122c), Ir (10a,28a,82b), is (51a,166c, 175c), Is (15b,23c,86c), it (124b)

- I ai (143c,148c), bi (122d,171c), di (68c,89b,108b,122b,c,d,171d), fi (108b), Gi (91d), hi (52c) .i (30a,b,37b,98a,108b,161b), mi (43b, 108b,138a,161a), pi (71b,85d,91c,165a,172a), ri (84c,96d,98a, 108b), Ri (106c), si (108b,152d,185d), ti (92b,108b,113a,b,120d, 138a,161a,162c,169b), xi (91c)

J - ja (66d), jo (140c,160c), Jo (8c,94b), ju (121a)

K - ka (45c), Ka (68c,77b,150d,153c,173c), ko (22c,87c,121a)

- K OK (155a)

L - Ia (13b,61a,83a,108b,138a,151d,161a), Ie (13b,61a,108b), LE (59c), Lf (16d), II (30a,b,37b,98a,108b,161b), Lt (143c), LT (59c), Iu (65a), Io (17d,93d)

- L aI (8c,80c,102c,104b), AI (96b), eI (13b,42a,47a,99b,151d,168a), EI (68a,108a), iI (122c), oI (29c,158b,d,160b)

M - ma, Ma (69a,b,85d), MA (42a), me (108b,124b), Me. (124d), mi (43b,108b,138a,161a), mo (21d,81c,101c), Mo (88c,177c), mu (10a, 30a,60c,71a,91c), my (52c,124c)

- M am (166c,175c), em (91c,98a,123d,172a,c), dm (131c), im (122c), om (49a,77a,77b,105c,136a), um (52c,76c)

N - na (140c,163d), NA (36c), ne (35b,106b), no (42b,106b), No (84b), nu (71b,91c), Nu (29a,49a)

- N an (11b,13b), en (15b,29c,50a,91c,98a,119d,123d,158c,d,172a), in (9d,123a), on (8b,9a,60c106a,123a), un (34c,122c)

O - oa (43c,d), ob (122b), od (8d,59d,79c), oe (43c,54d,82d,180d, 182a,b), of (6b), Og (16d,18c), oh (52c), OK (155a), oI (29c, 158b, d,160b), om (49a,77a,b,105c,136a), on (8b,9a,60c,106a,123a), oo (34a,74b), or (9b,36a,37b,69c,158c,166a,184b), os (21d,67b,104a, 131b), ow (52c), ox (10c,22c), oy (139c)

- O Ao (13d,88b,c,116c), bo (23d,24c,136a,168a), do (108b,138a 161a), eo (34a), Fo (23d), go (64c,90d), ho (39b,79a), Ho (87c), Io (74b,c,103c,115b), Io (25a,85d,95c,186b), Jo (140c,160c), Jo (8c, 94b), ko (22c,87c,121a), Io (17d,93d), mo (21d,81c,101c), Mo (88c, 177c), no (42b,106b), No (84b), oo (34a,74b), Ro (13c,81d,88c,131c, 173c), so (76a,108b,125a,138a,158b,161a,165b,175c), to (10b, 13c), uo (43d), vo (91a), yo, zo (13d,186b)

P - pa (60b,106d), pe (91c), Pe. (124d), pi (71b,85d,91c,165a,172a), pu (30b,140a)

- P ap (122d,166c), AP (107a,182d), up (123a), UP (107a,182d)

Q - QB (59c), q.v. (180d)

R - ra (108b), Ra (159b), re (6b,10b,35d,108b,122b,129b,138a,161a), RE (59c), RF (16d), Rh (20c), ri (84c,96d,98a,108b), RI (106c), Ro (13c,81d,88c,131c,173c), RT (59c)

- R ar (88b,91c,98a,99b,110c), er (35b,76c,137d,155a,158c,d,160b, 175c), Er (18d,68c,85c,163d,166c,172c,178a), ir (99d,122c), Ir (10a, 28a,82b), or (9b,36a,37b,69c158c,166a,184b), Ur (6b,28d,94a, 100d)

S - SA (36c), se (35b,108b), Se, sh (17b,43c,79c,126d), si (108b,152d, 185d), so (76a,108b,125a,138a,158b,161a,165b,175c), SS (16d, 164c), Su (127a), Sw (35b), Sy (141a)

- S as (51b,67b,92b,126a,133a,b,180d), es (49b,50a,66c,119d,158c, d,175c), is (51a,166c,175c), Is (15b,23c,86c), os (21d,67b,104a, 131b), S.S. (16d,164c), us (124b)

T - ta (112d,139a,160b), td (32a), te (43a,62d,108b,131c,152d,160b, 185d), th (43c), ti (92b,108b,113a,b,120d,138a,161a,162c,169b), to (10b,13c), tt (147b), tu (83c,164d,185d), Ty (68c,109c,163d, 178a)

- T at (25c,32c,106a,123a,128a), et (10b,61a,b,89a,158c), it (124b), Lt (143c), LT (59c), RT (59c), tt (147b), ut (72b,108b), Ut (67a)

U - um (52c,76c), un (34c,122c), Uo (43d), up (123a), Ur (6b,28d, 94a,100d), UP (107a,182d), us (124b), ut (72b,108b), Ut (67a), Uz (48c)

- U au (63a,69c), bu (190), fu (42c,84c), Fu (30b), Hu (101c,108a, 162b), ju (121a), lu (65a), mu (10a,30a,60c,71a,91c), nu (71b, 91c), Nu (29a,49a), pu (30b,140a), Su (127a), tu (83c, 164d, 185d), Wu (30b), Zu (68c,157a)

V - va (105a), Va (83a), Ve (63c,109c), vo (91a)

- V q.v. (180d)

W - wa (188), Wa (24c,d,88c), we (48c,124b), We (92b), Wu (30b), wy (91c)

- W aw (44a), ow (52c), sw (35b)

X - xi (91c)

- X ax (40c,139a,167a), ex (60b,91c,122c), ox (10c,22c)

Y - ya, ye (12-tb), yo

- Y ay (7c,8b,9b,28d,55a,60a), by (18b,32c,106a), my (52c,124c), sy (141a), oy (139c), Ty (68c,109c,163d,178a), wy (91c)

Z - za (162a), zo (13d,186b), Zu (68c,157a)

- Z Uz (48c)

THREE-LETTER WORDS

AA - aal (47c,80c,104b), aam (47a,49d,93a), aar (172d), Aar (131a)

A - A aba (12a,25d,32b,33a,65b), Ada (110a,112c,183c), aea (26a,36d), aga (35a,39a,48b,102d,103a,b,111c,166b,170d,171a), aha (52c,55c, 159c), aka (88b,c,176b), Aka (13d), ala (6d,13a,15c,61a,133d,

260

182c,d), **Ala** (151b), **ama** (26a,28d,31a,35b,39c,95b,108d,111c, 117b,182c), **ana** (10b,33c,60d,93a,98c,122b,d,140d,142b), **Ana** (28a,68d,100c), **apa** (23a,177d), **ara** (33a,114a,116a,118b,163d), **Ara** (9b,18c,36b,c,68d,69b,c,85a,95a,175b), **Asa** (6a,18c,71a,84d, 86d,164c), **ata** (58d,97d,158d,160c,173d), **Ata** (79c,80d,94d, 95d,100a,106b,117a,), **ava** (78d,86a,116a,120d,139a,167b), **Ava** (24c), **awa** (100a,139a), **aya** (77b,166b)

- **AA**   baa (143d), maa (97d,143d), saa (98a), taa (112d)

AB -   aba (12a,25d,32b,33a,65b), abb (58b,178b,185b), ABC (134d), Abe (71a,96a,123a), Abi (76c), Abo (25d), Abt (34c), abu (17a), Abu (15b,42a,55a,68a,c,147d)

A - B   abb (58b,178b,185b), alb (65b,176a)

- **AB**   Bab (15a), cab (75c), dab (46a,57b,58b,d,114d,115c), gab (29b, 78a,116c,122a,161c,183a), jab (120b,125c), kab (75c), lab, Mab (54b,126b,183d), nab (13b,26c,27b,142a), pab (139c), rab (17c,75c, 85b,102d,162c,166b), Rab (45a), tab (29b,39c,58b,86a,128d,145a)

AC -   ace (7a,26c,52d,57a,77d,110c,114c,120b,147a,163a,173a), ach (8b, 48a,52c,66b,80c), aci (29c), act (41d,55b,119c,155c), acu (34c), acy (34c)

A - C   ABC (134d), are (31b,39d,92a,126a,127c,142a)

- **AC**   bac (31b,55c,174d), fac (41c), lac (53c,99d,130c,135b,174d), Mac (96a,140b,150b), pac (73b,94c,100d), sac (15d,121d), Sac (80c), tac (34d,130a), Vac (153b), zac (27c)

AD -   Ada (110a,112c,183c), add (10d,11d,14c,158a,167c), ade (18c, 149d), Ade (9c,53b), ado (22b,24d,35b,64c,78d,121d,156b,170a), ady (188), adz (40c,167a)

A - D   aid (14a,15b,64c,75d,158b), add (10d,11d,14c,158a,167c), and (36a,119d)

- **AD**   bad (55a,173a,184d), cad (22b,23b,75c,172c,173d), dad, fad (38b, 108c,163a), gad (58c,100a,b,127d,132b,153c,154b,178a), Gad (84a, 186d), had, lad (22c,25b,55b,157c,186a), mad (10c,82b), pad (39d, 59c,76c,157d,161a,168b), rad (50b,138d,173b), sad (29c,42c,94c, 98c,104a,150d,173a), tad (22c,174a,186a), wad (94d,97b,109c, 112b,149d)

AE -   aea (26a,36d), AEF (184d), aer (8b,28d,34a,b,175a), aes (23c, 89a,101c,132d,133a,b), aet (89a,109d), Aex (46d)

A - E   Abe (71a,96a,123a), ace (7a,26c,52d,57a,77d,110c,114c,120b, 147a,163a,173a), ade (18c,149d), Ade (9c,53b), age (51d,66a,92a, 97c,98c,116c,141c), ake (60a,107a), ale (17c,18c,50c,55d,92d, 104c), ame (37a,62d,131b), ane (61c,140a,158b), ape (36d,79d, 100a,101d,146d), are (51a,88b,98a,99b,110c,166c,175c), ase (51a, 139a), Ase (79b,115d), ate (81a,108c,158c,174c), Ate (20c,68b,d, 69a,b,116c,186b), ave (54c,71d,73a,122a,134a,136d), awe (81d, 100a,130d,175b,182b), axe (30c,40c,167a), aye (7c,9b,55a,60a)

- **AE**   dae (139b), eae (34b), hae (139c), kae (84a,140b), Mae (183c), nae (139d), rae (136b,138d,140b), Rae (183c), sae (140b,149c), tae (138d,140c,166c,d), vae (176b)

AF -   AFL (173a), Afr. (36c), aft (14a,15b,17d,128b,167d)

A - F   AEF (184d), Alf (96a)

- AF gaf (12b), kaf (12b), Kaf (104a), oaf (22a,45b,146d,157d,185d), Qaf (104a)

AG - aga (35a,39a,48b,102d,103a,b,111c,166b,170d,171a), age (51d, 66a,92a,97c,98c,116b,141c), ago (25a,69d,114d,147a)

- AG bag (26c,139a,145b,159a), cag (81d,109d), dag (11b,118c,139c), Dag (108c), fag (55a,166a), gag (146c,183a), hag (140a,183a), jag (124d,148a), lag (93c,155d), mag (73b,95b,166c), Mag (183d), nag (73d,78b,138c,184d), rag (59b,77c,100c,133c,161a), sag (46b), tag (45a,54c,65a,87b,144a), vag (174b,178a), wag (85b,104a,183a), zag (84a)

AH - aha (52c,55c,159c), Ahi (32c,147d), ahu (24c,41d,65d,103d,120d)

A - H ach (8b,48a,52c,66b,80c), akh (153d), ash (24d,33c,49c,73d,134b, 168c,169a), auh (52c)

- AH bah (52c), dah (24c,87a), hah (52c), Jah (84d), Mah (10b,57c, 102b), pah (52c,60b,106d), rah (29b), sah (188), wah (113c), yah (52c)

AI - aid (14a,15b,64c,75d,158b), aik (139d), ail (170a), aim (42d,43d, 67d,109b,125d,157c), ain (18d,91c,110c,124b,140a,154b,180a), air (11c,12c,42b,44c,53a,96b,98c,99d,125b,170c), ait (82d,132a), Aix (46d)

A - I Abi (76c), aci (29c), Ahi (32c,147d), Ali (7b,12a,25c,48b,55a,60c, 92d,101a,103a,164a,166b,170d), ami (61d), ani (19b,d,20b,39b), api (34a,76d), Ari (18d), asi (137a), ati (106d,107a), Ati (45d,106b, 113c,117a)

- AI hai (55c), kai (59c), Kai (14d,84c), lai (98b,161b), Lai (24c,d,88c), mai (62a), rai (188), sai (101d), tai (84b,111c,121b), Tai (80d), Vai (91d)

- AJ gaj (190), raj (129c), saj (48a,169a), taj (75a,97d)

AK - aka (176b), Aka (13d,88b,c), ake (60a,170a), akh (153d), ako (189), aku (57c,176a)

A - K aik (139d), aik (171b), ark (21a,29d,38a,58b,60d,175d), ask (38b, 82a,126c), auk (19b)

- AK dak (95c), hak (46d), lak (38a), nak (156b), oak (73d,168c,169a), sak (37c), Sak (88c), yak (112c,161d,165b), zak (188)

AL - ala (6d,13a,15c,61a,133d,182c,d), Ala. (151b), alb (65b,176a), ale (17c,18c,50c,55d,92d,104c), Alf (96a), Ali (7b,12a,25c,48b,55a,60c, 92d,101a,103a,164a,166b,170d), alk (171b), all (35c,118a,126d, 181a), alp (24b,103d,115c), als (66d,163d), alt (66c,76c,109c), aly (95d)

A - L aal (47c,80c,104b), AFL (173a), all (170a), ail (35c,118a,126d,181a), awl (145b,167a)

- AL aal (47c,80c,104b), bal (9d,37b,61a,61b), cal (183c), Cal (123a), dal (117d,153d), gal, Hal (69d), ial (158b), mal (34a,b,44a,52b,62c, 122b), Mal (94b), pal (35b,38d), sal (29c,48a,136d,149d,152d, 169a,183a), Sal (183d), tal (40c,77a,113b), Zal (135d)

AM - ama (26a,28d,31a,35b,39c,95b,108d,111c,117b,182c), ame (37a, 62d,131b), ami (61d), amo (79a,89c), amp (49b,173b), amt (37d, 40d,108a,163c), amy (63c), Amy (8c,94b,183c)

A - M aam (47a,49d,93a), aim (42d,43d,67d,109b,125d,157c), arm (22d, 60c,81b,92b,124b,161b), aum (189)

- AM aam (47a,49d,93a), bam (29b), cam (48b,65d,95a,98b,134a,139b, 148b,180c), dam (30c,49c,55b,156d,180a), gam (76b,176d,180c), ham (98a,144b), Ham (18d,107c), jam (123a,156d,165c), lam (51b, 58b,93d,164d,178a), Mam (192), pam (26c,65a,87a,105b), Ram (36b), ram (17a,45b,50b,79c,112b,121d,143d,157d), Sam (96a, 162a), tam (74d), yam (48c,121d,160b,170c)

AN - ana (10b,33c,60d,93a,98c,122b,d,140d,142b), Ana (28a,68d,100c), and (36a,119b), ane (61c,140a,158b), ani (19b,d,20b,39b), Ann (183c), ano (19d,20b,34d,122d,174a), Ans (92a), ant (49d,60b,81b, 118c), Anu (15b,28a,68a,d,75b,88c,147d), any (14b,150b)

A - N ain (18d,91c,110c,124b,140a,154b,180a), Ann (183c), arn (8c, 139a), awn (12c,17b,140a)

- AN ban (81d,97a,124a), can (24c,36c,123a,166c), dan (24c,97c), Dan (18c,39c,77d,83a,84a,141b), ean (17d,23b,88a), fan (43a,154b), 156b,182d), Gan (132d), Han (16c,30b,185b), Ian (85b,96a,139d), kan (93a), Ian (37b,37d,160b), man (29c,60c,64c,65a,142d,161d), Nan (183c), pan (34a,61a,104a,175d), Pan (56a,68a,68b,76b,120c, 135b,161a,184a), ran (73d), Ran (7c,107d,141a,163d), san (91c, San (24d), tan (23d,33c,46a,72d,90d), van (7b,59d,60a,63d,90c), wan (113a), Zan (186b)

A - O Abo (25d), ado (22b,24d,35b,64c,78d,121d,156d,170a), ago (25a, 69d,114d,147a), ako (189), amo (79a,89c), ano (19d,20b,34d, 122d,174a), Apo (122b,177c), Aro (107a,111c), Aso (84c), azo (107c)

- AO dao (117a), hao (189), iao (78a,96c,178d), Lao (80d,88c,146a, 161b), mao (115b), Mao (30b), sao (141b), Sao (113c), tao (10d, 131c,170b), Tao (117a), Yao (30a,c,104b)

AP - apa (23a,177d), ape (36d,79d,100a,101d,146d), api (34a,76d), apo (122b), Apo (177c), apt (11d,23b,32b,58a,80b,92b,114d,116d, 124b,159a)

A - P alp (24b,103d,115c), amp (49b,173b), asp (7b,32b,149a,174a, 176c)

- AP bap (93b,132d), Bap (124d), cap (19d,39a,43a,53a,74d,160a,167b, 185c), dap (43b,c,46b,91b,147d), gap (11b,23a,29b,76c,110d,128a), hap (17d,28d), Jap (31b,37d,59b,127a,131d,153d,167d), map (27a,29b,54a,98d,160a), nap (65a,117d,146d,148a), pap (59c), rap (90d,110a,147c,157c), sap (45d,52d,85c,169b,176d,179a), tap (55a,114d,153c), yap (16c,29b,122a)

AR - ara (33a,114a,116a,118b,163d), Ara (8c,9b,36b,c,68d,69b,c, 85a,95a,175b), arc (31b,39d,92a,126a,127c,142a), are (51a,88b, 98a,99b,110c,166c,175c), Ari (18d), ark (21a,29d,38a,58b,60d, 175d), arm (22d,60c,81b,92b,124b,161b), arn (8c,139a), Aro (107a, 111c), ars (13b,89a), Ars (112c), art (22d,38b,39c,43b,56c,124a, 162c,181d), aru (80c,82b), Aru (82d)

A - R aar (172d), Aar (131a), aer (8b,28d,34a,b,175a), Afr. (36c), air (11c,12c,42b,44c,53a,96b,98c,99d,125b,170c)

- AR aar (172d), Aar (131a), bar (37c,39a,46a,52c,76d,78b,91a,124a,

137a,156a,157c,169c), **car** (16a,61d,93b,175a) **dar,** (65c,111b,
169a), **ear** (14c,d,28c,63d,64a,73c,111b,116a,124b,137d,150d,
153c), **far** (44c), **gar** (57b,c,d,106b), **har** (139c), **jar** (31d,70d,143b),
lar (24c,51d,67a,78d,95d,101d,171b), **mar** (40b,44a,79a,d,81a,
140d), **Mar** (93d), **nar** (139d), **oar** (20b,124c,134b), **par** (15a,51a,
51b,c,69d,107c,135b,155a) **sar** (57d), **tar** (8c,68a,94d,111c,118c,
136a,c,176d), **war** (157c), **yar** (72a), **zar** (188)

AS -   **Asa** (6a,18c,71a,84d,86d,164c), **ase** (51a,139a), **Ase** (79b,115d),
ash (24d,33c,49c,73d,134b,168c,169a), **asi** (137a), **ask** (38b,82a,
126c) **Aso,** (84c), **asp** (7b,32b,149a,174a,176c), **ass** (17b,20c,45b,
c,59c,110c,112b,146d,157d)

A - S   **aes** (23c,89a,101c,132d,133a,b), **ais** (66d,163d), **Ans** (92a), **ars**
(13b,89a), **Ars** (112c), **ass** (17b,20c,45b,c,59c,110c,112b,146d,
157d), **aus** (66c), **Aus** (98b)

- AS   **bas** (62a,d,129d,134b), **das** (13b,15d,36d,66b,d,164a), **fas** (44d,89d,
129d), **gas** (10b,29b,59a,116d,161c), **has, kas** (32c,47a), **las** (13b,
(151d), **mas** (34b,55b,119a) **nas** (74a,89c,178b), **pas** (40d,
156a), **ras** (6c,26b,48b,51d,53d,61c,75a,111c,123c,166b), **vas** (46d,
89d,119c,133b,175d), **was** (166c,175c), **Was** (24d)

AT -   **ata** (58d,97d,158d,160c,173d), **Ata** (79c,80d,94d,95d,100a,
106b,117a), **ate** (81a,108c,158c,174c), **Ate** (20c,68b,d,69a,b,
116c,186b), **ati** (106d,107a), **Ati** (45d,106b,113c,117a), **att** (146a)

A - T   **Abt** (35c), **act** (41d,55b,119c,155d), **aet** (89a,109d), **aft** (14a,15b,
17d,128b,167d), **ait** (82d,132a), **alt** (66c,76c,109c), **amt** (37d,40d,
108a,163c), **ant** (49d,60b,81b,118c), **apt** (11d,23b,32b,58a,80b,92b,
114d,116d,124b,159a), **art** (22d,38b,39c,43b,56c,124a,162c,181d),
att (146a), **aut** (34d,89d)

- AT   **bat** (39c,107c,156a,157c,182d), **cat** (10a,45b,55b,71d,161b,169d,
180d,183d), **eat** (37b,96b,135d,179b), **fat** (110a,124a), **gat** (28d,
72c,131a), **hat** (74d), **Hat** (183d), **Jat** (80d,125c), **kat** (105d), **lat**
(24a,33d,106b,118a), **mat** (46d,50d,94d,117c,161d), **Mat** (96a),
nat (7a,24c,24d,106a), **oat** (15a,28b,70b,144b), **pat** (11d,116d,
159a,161d,167c), **Pat** (96a), **rat** 16a,42d,73b,132c), **sat** (13d), **tat**
(48c,72d,87c), **Tat** (82a), **vat** (31b,36c,163a,170c), **wat** (73d,140d,
163a,180b), **xat** (167c), **zat** (148a)

AU -   **auh** (52c), **auk** (19b), **aum** (189), **aus** (66c), **Aus** (98b), **aut** (34d,
89d), **aux** (6d,61a)

A - U   **abu** (17a), **Abu** (15b,42a,55a,68a,c,147d), **acu** (34c), **ahu** (24c,41d,
65d,103d,120d), **aku** (57c,176a), **Anu** (15b,28a,68a,d,75b,88c,
147d), **aru** (80c,82b), **Aru** (82d), **ayu** (160c)

- AU   **eau** (63a,178c), **gau** (66d,67a), **mau** (170c,188), **pau** (130c), **Pau**
(48c,76a), **tau** (71b,91c,136c,161a), **vau** (91c), **Yau** (30c)

AV -   **ava** (78d,86a,116a,120d,139a,167b), **Ava** (24c), **ave** (54c,71d,73a,
122a,134a,136d)

- AV   **gav** (72d), **lav** (72d), **tav** (91c)

AW -   **awa** (100a,139a), **awe** (81d,100a,130d,175b,182b), **awl** (145b,167a),
awn (12c,17b,140a)

- AW   **baw** (52c), **caw** (19b,d), **daw** (39a,70b,84a,146d), **gaw** (140c), **haw**
(35a,52c,74d,91a,155a,162c), **jaw** (97d,138c), **law** (26b,33a,40a,

264

48c,60b,85d,91a,111b,134d,155d), **maw** (38b,d,72c,111a,121a, 142a,156c), **paw** (32d,59c,73c), **raw** (20c,39a,105d,173d), **saw** (7a, 11b,40c,54c,97d,125a,137d,167a), **taw** (90d,91c,96c,d,145b,161d), **waw** (12b,91c), **yaw** (43a,155d)

AX - axe (30c,40c,167a)

A - X Aex (46d), Aix (46d), aux (6d,61a)

- AX lax (93d,130a), Max (96a), pax (89d,115b), sax (40c,148a,167a), tax (13a,14a,80a,91d), wax (28b,72c,80b,120c), zax (148a)

AY - aya (77b,143c,166b), aye (7c,9b,55a,60a), ayu (160c)

A - Y acy (34c), ady (188), aly (95d), amy (63c), Amy (8c,94b,183c), any (14b,150b)

- AY bay (12d,16c,33c,73d,78b,81b,90a,128d), cay (82d,180b), day (153a), fay (32c,54b,154b), Fay (183c), gay, Gay (17d), hay (52c, 55c,165d), jay (19b,91c), kay (82d), Kay (13b,134b), lay (16a,25c,80a,98b,107d,141d,150b), may (74d), May (183c), nay (42b,106b), pay (35b,128c,130a,d,177b), ray (38a,49a,57b, 58b,147b), Ray (96a), say (131c,174c,177a), way (37d,96b,134b, 164d)

AZ - azo (107c)

A - Z adz (40c,167a)

- AZ gaz (188,190), Laz (27d)

BA - baa (143d), Bab (15a), bac (31b,55c,174d), bad (55a,173a,184d), bag (26c,139a,145b,159a), bah (52c), bal (9d,37b,61a,b), bam (29b), ban (81d,97a,124a), bap (93b,132b), Bap. (124d), bar (37c, 39a,46a,52c,76d,78b,91a,124a,137a,156a,157c,169c), bas (62a,d, 129d,134b), bat (39c,107c,156a,157c,182d), baw (52c), bay (12d, 16c,33c,73d,78b,81b,90a,128d)

B - A baa (143d) boa (36c,55b,106a,125d,138b,142a,149a)

- BA aba (12a,25d,32b,33a,65b), iba (117a)

B - B Bab (15a), bib, bob (57c,115b), Bob (96a), bub (22c)

- BB abb (58b,178b,185b), ebb (6a,15b,41c,43c,104a,128c,158a,178a)

B - C bac (31b,55c,174d), BSC (42a)

- BC ABC (134d)

B - D bad (55a,173a,184d), bed (60c,148b), bid (35a,82a,109d,111b, 174c), bud (22c)

BE - bed (60c, 148b), bee (46b,81b,91c,108c), beg (38b,150a), bel (64a, 93c,168d,173b,183d), Bel (15b,68a,126b), ben (78c,81b,102c,115c), Ben (12d,77c,96a,106c,139d,140a), ber (85c), Bes (68b,119c), bet, bey (70b,170d)

B - E bee (46b,81b,91c), bye (38c,141d)

- BE Abe 71a,96a,123a), obe (31d,87d,150d), ube (185b)

B - G bag (26c,139a,145b,159a), beg (38b,150a), big, bog (97a,160a), bug (24b,66b,81b)

B - H bah (52c), boh (24c)

BI - bib, bid (35a,82a,109d,111b,174c), big, Bim (16c), bin (22c,59a, 78a,128c,156d), bis (50a,90a,102c,130b,171c), bit (46a,86b,114c, 167a,b,171c,180d), biz

265

- BI   **Abi** (76c), **obi** (55d,67b,84c,137b,150d), **ubi** (90a,180d,185b)

B - K   **Bok** (9c)

B - L   **bal** (9d,37b,61a,61b), **bel** (64a,93c,168d,173b,183d), **Bel** (15b,68a, 126d), **Bul** (25d,102a)

B - M   **bam** (29b), **Bim** (16c), **bum** (21b)

B - N   **ban** (81d,97a,124a), **ben** (78c,81b,102c,115c,139d,140a), **Ben** (12d, 77c,96a,106c), **bin** (22a,59a,78a,128c,156d), **bon** (30a,61d,86b,88c), **Bon** (84b), **bun** (25b,73b)

BO -   **boa** (36c,55b,106a,125d,138b,142d,149a), **bob** (57c,115d), **Bob** (96a), **bog** (97a,160a), **boh** (24c), **Bok** (9c), **bon** (30a,61d,86b,88c), **Bon** (84b), **boo**, **Bor** (120c), **Bos** (27c), **bot** (59a,88d), **bow** (11c,21b, 39d,60a,107c,109a,125a,144a,158a), **box** (36a,128c,145d,152d), **boy** (142d,157c), **Boz** (43b,115d)

B - O   **boo**

- BO   **Abo** (25d), **ebo** (28b,110a), **Ibo** (107a,180a)

B - P   **Bap.** (124d), **bap** (93b,132d)

B - R   **bar** (37c,39a,46a,52c,76d,78b,91a,124a,137a,156a,157c,169c), **ber** (85c), **Bor** (120c), **bur** (123b)

BS -   **BSC** (42a)

B - S   **bas** (62a,d,129d,134b), **Bes** (68b,119c), **bis** (50a,90a,102c,130b, 171c), **Bos** (27c), **bus** (125b,168b)

B - T   **bat** (39c,107c,156a,157c,182d), **bet**, **bit** (46a,86b,114c,167a,b, 171c,180d), **bot** (59a,88d), **but** (36a,52b,156b,173c)

- BT   **Abt** (35c)

BU -   **bub** (22c), **bud** (22c), **bug** (24b,66b,81b), **Bul** (25d,102a), **bum** (21b), **bun** (25b,73b), **bur** (123b), **bus** (125b,168b), **but** (36a,52b, 156b,173c), **buy**

- BU   **abu** (17a), **Abu** (15b,42a,55a,68a,c,147d)

B - W   **baw** (52c), **bow** (11c,21b,39d,60a,107c,109a,125a,144d,158a)

B - X   **box** (36a,c,128c,145d,152d)

BY -   **bye** (38c,141d)

B - Y   **bay** (12d,16c,33c,73d,78b,81b,90a,128d), **bey** (70b,170d), **boy** (142d,157c), **buy**

B - Z   **biz**, **Boz** (43b,115d)

CA -   **cab** (75c), **cad** (22b,23b,75c,172c,173d), **cag** (81d,109d), **cal** (183c), **Cal** (123a), **cam** (48b,65d,95a,98b,134a,139b,148b,180c), **can** (24c, 36c,123a,166a), **cap** (19d,39a,43a,53a,74d,160a,167b,185c), **car** (16a,61d,93b,175a), **cat** (10a,45b,55b,71d,161b,169d,180d), **Cat** (183d), **caw** (19b,d) **cay** (82d, 180b)

C - A   **cha** (162b,c)

- CA   **ECA** (8a), **oca** (48c,112c,116d,133d,170c,184a), **Uca** (56a)

C - B   **cab** (75c), **cob** (28c,78b,95d,160b,177d), **cub** (92d,185d)

C - D   **cad** (22b,23b,75c,172c,173d), **Cid** (151c,d), **cod** (57b,c), **cud** (126c, 135a)

CE -   **cee** (91c), **cep** (63a), **ces** (62b), **cet** (62d,180b)

C - E   **cee** (91c), **che** (145d), **cie** (61b,63b), **cle** (158d), **coe** (143d),

266

Coe (33c), **cue** (7a,27b,92c,117d,124b,132c,146c,159a)

- **CE** ace (7a,26c,52d,57a,77d,110c,114c,120b,147a,163a,173a), **ice** (30a, 36d,42d,63d)

C - G cag (81d,109d), cig, cog (33a,65d,163b,167b,180c)

CH - cha (162b,c), che (145d), chi (91c), Chi (69c), cho (188)

- **CH** ach (8b,48a,52c,66b,80c), ich (66c), och (8b), tch (52c)

CI - Cid (151c,d), cie (61b,63b), cig, CIO (173a), cis (34c,122c), **cit** (81a,167d)

C - I chi (91c), Chi (69c)

- **CI** aci (29c), ici (61d), lci (9b), LCI (21b)

- **CK** ock (189), tck (52c)

CL - cle (158d)

C - L cal (183c), Cal (123a), col (103d,114c)

C - M cam (48b,65d,95a,98b,134a,139d,148b,180c), com (122d), **cum** (159b), cwm (31b,37b,103d)

C - N can (24c,36c,123a,166a), con (7d,29b,83c,116d,157d)

CO - cob (28c,78b,95d,160b,177d), cod (57b,c), coe (143d), **Coe** (33c), cog (33a,65d,163b,167b,180c), col (103d,114c), com (122d), con (7d,29b,83c,116d,157d), coo (19b), Coo (82d), cop (36a,120c, 126d,153c,155d), cor (36c,75b,155b), cos (91d,132d), cot (129b, 148b), cow (22c,45b,81d), cox (156a), coy (16d), coz

C - O cho (188), CIO (173a), coo (19b), Coo (82d), cro (104c,115b,180a)

C - P cap (19d,39a,43a,53a,74d,160a,167a,185c), cep (63a), cop (36a, 120c,126d,153c,155d), cup (46b,69d,118b,170a), cyp (169d)

CR - cro (104c,115b,180a), cru (63a,176c), cry (25c,124a,145c,179d)

C - R car (16a,61d,93b,175a), cor (36c,75b,155b), cur (101d)

C - S ces (62b), cis (34c,122c), cos (91d,132d)

- **CS** ics (158d)

C - T cat (10a,45b,55b,71d,161b,169d,180d,183d), cet (62d,180b), **cit** (81a,167d), cot (148b), cut (30c,32b,145c)

- **CT** act (41d,55b,119c,155d), ect (35a,122d,183b), oct (34a,122c)

CU - cub (92d,185d), cud (126c,135a), cue (7a,27b,92c,117d,124b,132c, 146c,159a), cum (159b), cup (46b,69d,118b,170a), cur (101d), cut (30c,32b,145c)

C - U cru (63a,176c)

- **CU** acu (34c), ecu (58a,144b,c)

CW - cwm (31b,37b,103d)

C - W caw (19b,d), cow (22c,45b,81d)

C - X cox (156a)

CY - cyp (169d)

C - Y cay (82d,180b), coy (16d), cry (25c,124a,145c,179d)

- **CY** acy (34c), icy (65d)

C - Z coz

DA - dab (46a,57b,58b,d,114d,115c), dad, dae (139b), dag (11b,118c, 139c), Dag (108c), dah (24c,87a), dak (95c), dal (117d,153d), dam

267

(30c,49c,55b,156d,180a), **dan** (24c,97c), **Dan** (18c,39c,77d,83a, 84a,141b), **dao** (117a), **dap** (43b,c,46b,91b,147d), **dar** (65c,111b, 169a), **das** (13b,15d,36d,66b,d,164a), **daw** (39a,70b,84a,146d), **day** (153a)

D - A **dea** (68d,89b), **dha** (99d), **dia** (122b,d,152a,165b), **dra** (188), **dua** (122d)

- DA **Ada** (110a,112c,183c), **Ida** (103d,183c), **oda** (74a,170d)

D - B **dab** (46a,57b,58b,114d,115c), **deb**, **Deb** (183d), **dib** (21b,43b,c, 120d,140a), **dub** (25c,46a,c,87a,105b,121a,140a)

D - C **dec** (122d), **doc** (143a), **duc** (61c)

DD - **DDS** (42a)

D - D **dad**, **did**, **dod** (11a,32a,43b,140c), **dud** (21c,54a)

- DD **add** (10d,11d,14c,158a,167c), **odd** (46b,53a,109b,157a,172d,173c)

DE - **dea** (68d,89b), **deb**, **Deb** (183d), **dec** (122d), **dee** (91c), **Dee** (131d, 139b), **deg** (154b), **dei** (68d), **den** (38b,44d,74b,130d,133c,140d), **der** (13b,66b,d,164a), **des** (13b,61a,62b,d), **dev** (42a,b), **dew** (41a), **dey** (8d,84a,114c,135a,139b,170d)

D - E **dae** (139b), **dee** (91c), **Dee** (131d,139b), **die** (27b,54a,65a,155a, 167a), **doe** (41d,55b,127a), **due** (7b,115b,124c), **dye** (33c,154d)

- DE **ade** (18c,149d), **Ade** (9c,53b), **Ede** (35b,65d), **ide** (40c,57a,b,d, 158b), **ode** (26b,79c,94d,118a,119d,120a,150b)

D - G **dag** (11b,118c), **Dag** (108c,139c), **deg** (154b), **dig** (52b), **dog** (10b, 45b,59b), **dug**

DH - **dha** (99d), **dhu** (40b), **Dhu** (28a,87d)

D - H **dah** (24c,87a), **doh** (113b)

- DH **edh** (91c)

DI - **dia** (122b,d,152a,165b), **dib** (21b,43b,c,120d,140a), **did**, **die** (27b, 54a,65a,155a,167a), **dig** (52b), **dii** (68d), **dim** (47a,48b,54a,74d, 94d,109b), **din** (31c,130b,174a), **dip** (26a,79d,117c,138c), **dis** (122b,d), **Dis** (68b,73a,119d,172d,174b), **dit** (62b,d,120a,159d), **div** (42b,139b), **dix** (118b), **Dix** (60b)

D - I **dei** (68d) **dii** (68d), **dui** (46d)

- DI **Udi** (108a)

DJ - **djo** (188)

D - K **dak** (95c)

D - L **dal** (117d,153d)

D - M **dam** (30c,49c,55b,156d,180a), **dim** (47a,48b,54a,74d,94d,109b), **dom** (121c,166b,c), **Dom** (94b), **dum** (45c,67b,113a)

D - N **dan** (24c,97c), **Dan** (18c,39c,77d,83a,84a,141b), **den** (38b,44d,74b, 130d,133c,140d), **din** (130b,174a), **don** (151d,166c), **Don** (96a), **dun** (19a,39d,46d,71a,97d,115b,160b)

DO - **Doc** (143a), **dod** (11a,32a,43b,140c), **doe** (41d,55b,127a), **dog** (10b, 45b,59b), **doh** (113b), **dom** (121c,166b,c), **Dom** (94b), **don** (151d, 166c), **Don** (96a), **dop** (39c,43b), **dor** (17d,24b,32b,46b,47a,81b, 85d), **dos** (45d,61a,97a,181b), **dot** (45d,97a,104d,105a,116b,153a, 162d), **dow** (17d,87a,88d,175d)

D - O dao (117a) djo (188), DSO (99d), duo (46d,113a,171d)

- DO ado (22b,24d,35b,64c,121d,156b,170a), edo (162a), Edo (107a, 166d), Ido (13c,81d,88c,173c), Odo (181d), udo (28a,30c,48c,84b, c,d,136c,149d)

D - P dap (43b,c,46b,91b,147d), dip (26a,79d,117c,138c), dop (39c,43b)

DR - dra (188), dry (46d,85a,137c,164c)

D - R dar (111b,169a), der (13b,66b,d,164a), dor (17d,24b,32b,46b,47a, 81b,85d), dur (95c)

DS - DSO (99d)

D - S das (13b,15d,36d,66b,d,164a), DDS (42a), des (13b,61a,62b,d), dis (122b,d), Dis (68b,73a,119d,172d,174b), dos (45d,61a,97a,181b)

- DS DDS (42a), ods (109a)

D - T dit (62b,d,120a,159d), dot (45d,97a,104d,105a,116b,153a,162d)

DU - dua (122d), dub (25c,46a,c,87a,105b,121a,140a), duc (61c), dud (21c,54a), due (7b,115b,124c), dug, dul (46d), dum (45c,67b,113a), dun (19a,39d,46d,71a,97d,115b,160b), duo (46d,113a,171d), dur (95c), dux (31d,64a,90c)

D - U dhu (40b), Dhu (28a,87d)

D - V dev (42a,b), div (42b,139b)

D - W daw (39a,70b,84a), dew (41a), dow (17d,87a,88d,175d)

D - X dix (118b), Dix (60b), dux (31d,64a,90c)

DY - dye (33c,154d)

D - Y day (153a), dey (8d,84a,114c,135a,139b,170d), dry (46d,85a,137c, 164c)

- DY ady (188)

- DZ adz (40c,167a)

EA - eae (34b), ean (17d,23b,88a), ear (14c,d,28c,63d,64a,73c,111b, 116a,124b,137d,150d,153c), eat (37b,96b,135d,179b), eau (63a, 178c)

E - A ECA (8a), ela (21c,53c,72b,76c,108b,174c), Ena (8c,126b), era (8a, 51a,116b,165d), ESA (8a), eta (71a,84c,91c), Eva (157a,183c)

- EA aea (26a,36d), dea (68d,89b), Hea (15b), kea (114a,b), lea (56a, 97d,114d,185b), Lea (22d), N.E.A. (162c), pea (32d,91b,142a,175a), rea (9c,171a), sea (19a,52d,58c,112c,178d), tea (13d,18c,79c,81a, 145d,149c,159d), Wea (192), yea (7c,175c), zea (95c)

EB - ebb (6a,15b,41c,43c,104a,128c,158a,178a), ebo (28b,110a)

E - B ebb (6a,15b,41c,43c,104a,128c,158a,178a), eib (85c)

- EB deb, Deb (183d), Geb (47d), Keb (47d), neb (17b,19a,d,115d), reb (35d,75c,85b,162c,166b), Seb (47d), web (50d,70a,98c,99a,106c, 149b)

EC - ECA (8a), ect (35a,122d,183b), ecu (58a,144b,c)

E - C etc (10b)

- EC dec (122d), sec (46c,182c), tec (43a)

ED - Ede (35b,65d), edh (91c), edo (162a), Edo (107a,166d)

269

E - D   **Eed** (102d), **eid** (10b,93c,110b,165d), **end** (8b,67d,120a,125d,130a, 166a), **erd** (47d,119d,145c)

- ED   **bed** (60c,148b), **Eed** (102d), **fed, ged** (100a,140a), **ked** (140b,144a), **led, Ned** (96a), **ped** (16d,34b), **red** (33c,38d,59a,127b,134c,135b), **Red** (151b), **sed** (89a), **ted** (74d,138b,154b), **Ted** (96b), **wed** (97a, 173c), **zed** (91c)

EE -   **Eed** (102d), **eel** (36a,49c,57a,b,88a,102c,176c), **een** (52a,139c, 185d), **eer** (9b,52a), **ees** (139c)

E - E   **eae** (34b), **Ede** (35b,65d), **eke** (14c,117c), **ele** (48c), **eme** (38d,70a, 140c,172b), **ene** (35b,158b,c), **ere** (17d,150c), **ese** (35b,158c), **ete** (36c,62d,141c,159b), **eve** (47a,131a,143a,165d,171c), **Eve** (183c), **ewe** (88a,143d), **Exe** (43a), **eye** (93d,111b,140d)

- EE   **bee** (46b,81b,91c,108c), **cee** (91c), **dee** (91c), **Dee** (131d,139b), **fee** (29a,58a,70d,166a,d), **gee** (35a,91c,100a,131c,139c,162c), **lee** (74b, 144b), **Lee** (9c,31c,96a), **mee** (169a), **nee** (19d,22b,25c,60b,95c), **pee** (91c), **ree** (12c,50a,80c,134d,137a,140b,144b,146b), **Ree** (25a), **see** (20a,43c,44a,51c,53c,93d,109b,113c,116a,176d,178c,183b), **tee** (39d,52b,69d,91c,112d,115d,118b,172a), **vee** (58a,91c,106a), **wee** (52c,100c,148c), **zee** (81b,91c)

EF -   **eft** (93b,107a,136c,169d)

E - F   **elf** (54b,154b)

- EF   **AEF** (184d), **kef** (12a,46c,75d,88c), **nef** (32b,144c,d), **ref**

EG -   **egg** (32d,80b,81c,112c,174a), **ego** (51a,79a,142b)

E - G   **egg** (32d,80b,81c,112c,174a), **eng** (48a,146a), **erg** (50b,173b, 184c)

- EG   **beg** (38b,150a), **deg** (154b), **Geg** (8c), **keg** (27a,105b), **leg** (37d, 92b,141d,159d,169c), **Meg** (8c,183d), **peg** (38c,46b,54d,98a,118a, 184c), **teg** (45a,54b,171d)

E - H   **edh** (91c), **eth** (91c,158d)

- EH   **Heh** (191), **reh** (8d)

EI -   **ein** (66b,c), **Eir** (69a,75a), **eis** (66c)

E - I   **Eli** (18c,d,76c,96a,137a,185a), **epi** (56c,61c,d,111c,112d,122d, 133c,153c,167b,174a), **eri** (13d,21c,146d), **Eri** (18c)

- EI   **dei** (68d), **fei** (16a,185b), **lei** (65d,74c), **rei** (89b,121c), **Rei** (18d), **Vei** (91d), **Wei** (30b,162b)

EK -   **eke** (14c,117c)

E - K   **elk** (22c,90d,178a)

- EK   **lek** (65c)

EL -   **ela** (21c,53c,72b,76c,108b,174c), **elb** (85c), **eld** (10b,93c,110b, 165d), **ele** (48c), **elf** (54b,154b), **Eli** (18c,d,76c,96a,137a,185a), **elk** (22c,90d,178a), **ell** (10d,24b,32c,98a), **elm** (168c), **els** (140a), **elt** (87a,117c,139d), **Ely** (27c,50b)

E - L   **eel** (36a,49c,57a,b,88a,102c,176c), **ell** (10d,24b,32c,98a)

- EL   **bel** (64a,93c,168d,173b,183d), **Bei** (15b,68a,126b), **eel** (36a,49c, 57a,b,88a,102c,176c), **gel** (32d,73d,150a), **Hel** (68d,93c,172d), **mel** (77d), **pel** (55c,160d), **rel** (49b,173b), **sel** (62c,140b), **tel** (34a, b,122c), **zel** (40c)

EM -   **eme** (38d,70a,140c,172b), **Ems** (125a,151c), **emu** (19b,58c,111d)

270

E - M elm (168c)

- EM gem (104b), hem (22a,36a,48b,52c,155a), mem (91c), Sem (107c), Tem (143a,159b)

EN - Ena (8c,126b), end (8b,67d,120a,125d,130a,166a), ene (35b,158b, c), eng (48a,146a) ens (17d,18a,51a,52d), ent (34d,158b,c)

E - N ean (17d,23b,88a), een (52a,139c,185d), ein (66b,c), eon (8a,37b, 51d,116b), ern (19c,d,47b,54b,141a)

- EN ben (78c,81b,102c,115c), Ben (12d,77c,96a,106c,139d,140a), den (38b,44d,74b,130d,133c,140d), een (52a,139c,185d), fen (21c,97a, 160a), gen (31d,76b), hen (19a,60c,114c,136c), ken (60b,87c,122b, 172d), men (38c,116a,117b,170a), Men (94d), pen (36a,50a,80d, 118b,126d,160a,185c), sen (190), ten (19a,26c,41c,42b), wen (40c, 72a,110a,170c,177b), yen (33b,42d,93c,174a), Zen (24a)

EO - eon (8a,37b,51d,116b), Eos (14d,41a,68d)

E - O ebo (28b,110a), edo (162a), Edo (107a,166d), ego (51a,79a,142b), eso (34d,183b), ETO (184d), exo (122d)

- EO geo (34a,47d), Leo (36b,c,92d,186d), Meo (27b,80c), neo (34a,b, c,100d,106d,108c,122c,d,128c), Reo (26c)

EP - epi (56c,61c,d,111c,112d,122d,133c,153c,167b,174a)

E - P e.s.p. (147b)

- EP cep (63a), hep (52c), kep (139b), nep (27c,32d,56a,87c,184b), pep (50b,176b), rep (53b,d,131a,171c), yep, Zep

ER - era (8a,51a,116b,165d), erd (47d,119d,145c), ere (17d,150c), erg (50b,173b,184c), eri (13d,21c,146d), Eri (18c), ern (19c,d,47b,54b, 141a), err (21a,43a,67d,100c,d,147a,148b,157b,168b,178a), ers (20a,176a), ert (140c,174a), ery (155d,158c,d)

E - R ear (14c,d,28c,63d,64a,73c,111b,116a,124b,137d,150d,153c), eer (9b,52a), Eir (69a,75a), err (21a,43a,67d,100c,d,147a,148b,157b, 168b,178a), Eur. (36c)

- ER aer (8b,28d,34a,b,175a), ber (85c), der (13b,66b,d,164a), eer (9b, 52a), ger (8d,36d,75c,124d), her (124b,c), ier (50a,158c), Ker (71b, 95d), Ler (23d,28a,b,64b,106c,141a), mer (62c,141a), ner (137c), o'er (6b,112a), per (25c,122d,165b,176a), ser (80d,83b,d,116c, 152d,180a), ter (34d,122d,165a), xer (34a), zer (188)

ES - ESA (8a), ese (35b,158c), eso (34d,183b), esp (147b), ess (39d,78a, 91c,158c,184d), est (50a,61c,62a,79b,89c,158d,159c)

E - S ees (139c), eis (66c), els (140a), Ems (125a,151c), ens (17d,18a, 51a,52d), Eos (14d,41a,68d), ers (20a,176a), ess (39d,78a,91c,158c, 184d)

- ES aes (23c,89a,101c,132d,133a,b), Bes (68b,119c), ces (62b), des (13b,61a,62b,d), ees (139c), Ges (151b), ies (13b,61a), mes (62b), nes (26b), oes (109a), pes (59d), res (80a,89d,91a,97c,164c), ses (61d), yes (7c,55a)

ET - eta (71a,84c,91c), etc (10b), ete (36c,62d,141c,159b), eth (91c, 158d), ETO (184d)

E - T eat (37b,96b,135d,179h), ect (35a,122d,183b), eft (93b,107a,136c, 169d), elt (87a,117c,139d), ent (34d,158b,c), ert (140c,174a), est (50a,62a,79b,89c,158d,159c)

271

- ET aet (89a,109d), bet, cet (62d,180b), get (44d,64b,109b,141d), jet (20b,35a,154c), ket (189) let (9a,76d,77c,116b,130a,158b,163a), met (28d), net (26c,32a,50d,53b,60d,99a,124a,142a,149b), pet (26d,37c,55a,59b,162d), ret (58b,95a,149c,155d), set (7b,11d,13a, 23c,32b,33c,37c,58a,73d,109b,118c,121c,142c,150a,186a), Set (52b, 68a,b,111d), vet, wet (40d,46a,101a,124a,127c,149c), yet (18b, 24d,64c,77c,80a,108c,156b,165b)

EU - Eur. (136c)

E - U eau (63a,178c), ecu (58a,144b,c), emu (19b,58c,111d)

- EU feu (55d,61c,88b), heu (8b,30c,52c), jeu (61d), leu (190), meu (153b), peu (62a), Reu (115d)

EV - Eva (157a,183c), eve (47a,131a,143a,165d,171c), Eve (183c)

- EV dev (42a,b), lev (33b) rev

EW - ewe (88a,143d)

- EW dew (41a), few, hew (40a), Jew, lew (190), Lew (96a), mew (25b, 27b,50a,55b,72c,74d,101b,141b,153b), new (11a,63c,88d,111c, 128c), pew (30d,52c,57d,120b,141c), rew (75c,140c,176b), sew, yew (36a,52a,b,145d,168c,d)

EX - Exe (43a), exo (122d)

- EX Aex (46d), hex (18c), lex (90b), rex (86c,96a), sex, vex (7c,10d, 44c,82c)

EY - eye (93d,111b,140d)

E - Y Ely (27c,50b), ery (155d,158c,d)

- EY bey (70b,170d), dey (8d,84a,114c,135a,139b,170d), fey (49c), gey (140a), hey (25c,52c), key (14c,82d,88b,117c,118c,150b,180c), ley (190), Ney (63b,97b,105d), rey (86c,152b), sey (120c), wey (173b)

- EZ fez (75a,162a), gez (188), nez (62b), tez (125c), yez

FA - fac (41c), fad (38b,108c,163a), fag (55a,166a), fan (43a,154b, 156b,182d), far (44c), fas (44d,89d,129d), fat (110a,124a), fay (32c,54b,154b), Fay (183c)

F - A Fha (8a), fra (23c,63c,101d,123b,129d)

- FA MFA (42a)

F - B fib (162a), fob (29b,59b,113b,178c), fub (29b,119d)

F - C fac (41c)

F - D fad (38b,108c,163a), fed, fid (16b,54d,118a,167b), fod (188)

FE - fed, fee (29a,58a,70d,166a,d), fei (16a,185b), fen (21c,97a,160a), feu (55d,61c,88b), few, fey (49c), fez (75a,162a)

F - E fee (29a,58a,70d,166a,d), fie (52c,59d), foe (111a)

- FE ife (22c,75d)

- FF off (6b,15c,44c,76a)

F - G fag (55a,166a), fig, fog (109b), fug (129a)

FH - FHA (8a)

F - H foh (52c)

FI - fib (162a), fid (16b,54d,118a,167b), fie (52c,59d), fig, fin (86a), fir (16a,36a,52a,168c,d,169a), fit (7a,11d,51b,75a,114a,123a, 124c,126a,153a,157c,159a), fix (7b,10a,13a,14c,43a,c,141d,165c)

272

F – I	fei (16a,185b)
FL –	flo, flu, fly (58c,81b,163b,178d)
F – L	Ful (158b)
– FL	AFL (173a)
F – N	fan (43a,154b,156b,182d), fen (21c,97a,160a), fin (86a), Fon (40b), fun
FO –	fob (29b,59b,113b,178c), fod (188), foe (111a), fog (109b), foh (52c), Fon (40b), foo (42c), fop (38a,40d,46d), for (123d,163a,166c), fot (188), fou (139a), fox (134a)
F – O	Flo, foo (42c), fro (15b)
– FO	Ufo (59a)
F – P	fop (38a,40d,46d)
FR –	fra (23c,63c,101d,123b,129d), fro (15b), fry (57d)
F – R	far (44c), fir (16a,36a,52a,168c,d,169a), for (123d,163a,166c), fur
– FR	Afr. (36c)
F – S	fas (44d,89d,129d)
F – T	fat (110a,124a), fit (7a,11d,51b,75a,114a,123a,124c,126a, 153a,157c,159a), fot (188), fut (188)
– FT	aft (14a,15b,17d,128b,167d), oft (93b,107a,136c,169d), oft (63c)
FU –	fub (29b,119d), fug (129a), Ful (158b), fun, fur, fut (188)
F – U	feu (55d,61c,88b), flu, fou (139a)
F – W	few
F – X	fix (7b,10a,13a,14c,43a,c,141d,165c), fox (134a)
F – Y	fay (32c,54b,154c), Fay (183c), fey (49c), fly (58c,81b,163b,178d), fry (57d)
F – Z	fez (75a,162a)
GA –	gab (29b,78a,116c,122a,161c,183a), gad (58c,100a,127d,132b, 153c,154b,178a), Gad (84a,186d), gaf (12b), gag (146c,183a), gaj (190), gal, gam (76b,176d,180c), Gan (132d), gap (11b,23a,29b, 76c,110d,128a), gar (57b,c,d,106b), gas (10b,29b,59a,116d,161c), gat (28d,72c,131a), gau (66d,67a), gav (72d), gaw (140c), gay, Gay (17d), gaz (188,190)
G – A	goa (65d,104b,126c), Goa (121c), gra (59b,94b,160c)
– GA	aga (35a,39a,48b,102d,103a,b,111c,166b,170d,171a)
– GB	KGB (135d)
G – B	gab (29b,78a,116c,122a,161c,183a), Geb (47d), gib (17b,38b,95d, 166d,179d), gob (97b,136c)
G – D	gad (58c,100a,b,127d,132b,153c,154b,178a), Gad (84a,186d), ged (140a), Ged (100a), gid (143d), god (42a), God (84d)
GE –	Geb (47d), Ged (100a,140a), gee (35a,91c,100a,131c,139c,162c), Geg (8c), gel (32d,73d,150a), gem (104b), gen (31d,76b), geo (34a, 47d), ger (8d,36d,75c,124d), Ges (151b), get (44d,64b,109b,141d), gey (140a), gez (188)
G – E	gee (35a,91c,100a,131c,139c,162c), gie (139c,140a), gue (176c)
– GE	age (51d,66a,92a,97c,98c,116b,141c)
G – F	gaf (12b)

273

G - G   **gag** (146c,183a), **Geg** (8c), **gig** (26d,28d,57c,105b,127a,144c,153a, 171d), **gog** (95b)

- GG   **egg** (32d,80b,81c,112c,174a)

GH -   **ghi** (24d)

- GH   **ugh** (52c)

GI -   **gib** (17b,38b,95d,166d,179d), **gid** (143d), **gie** (139c,140a), **gig** (26d,28d,57c,105b,127a,144c,153a,171d), **gin** (37c,92d,139a,142a, 149b), **gip** (29b,160c), **git** (101a)

G - I   **ghi** (24d), **goi** (107c), **gri** (75c,78b)

G - J   **gaj** (190)

G - L   **gal, gel** (32d,73d,150a), **gul** (134a)

G - M   **gam** (76b,176d,180c), **gem** (104b), **gum** (7b,53c,80b,130c,156b), **gym** (154a)

GN -   **gnu** (11a,181d)

G - N   **gan** (132d), **gen** (31d,76b), **gin** (37c,92d,139a,142a,149b), **gon** (188), **gun** (56d,131a,146a)

GO -   **goa** (65d,104b,126c), **Goa** (121c), **gob** (97b,136c), **god** (42a), **God** (84d), **gog** (95b), **goi** (107c), **gon** (188), **goo** (156b), **Gor** (81a), **got, goy** (107c), **goz** (190)

G - O   **geo** (34a,47d), **goo** (156b)

- GO   **ago** (25a,69d,114d,147a), **ego** (51a,79a,142b)

G - P   **gap** (11b,23a,29b,76c,110d,128a), **gip** (29b,160c), **gup** (70a), **gyp** (29b,42a,160c)

GR -   **gra** (59b,94b,160c), **gri** (75c,78b), **grr** (52c), **gry** (78b)

G - R   **gar** (57b,c,d,106b), **ger** (8d,36d,75c,124d), **Gor** (81a), **grr** (52c), **gur** (159a)

G - S   **gas** (10b,29b,59a,116d,161c), **Ges** (151b), **Gus** (96a)

G - T   **gat** (28d,72c,131a), **get** (44d,64b,109b,141d), **git** (101a), **got, gut** (114d,130a)

GU -   **gue** (176c), **gul** (134a), **gum** (7b,53c,80b,130c,156b), **gun** (56d, 131a,146a), **gup** (70a), **gur** (159a), **Gus** (96a), **gut** (114d,130a), **guy** (55b,131b,155d), **Guy** (96a), **guz** (188)

G - U   **gau** (66d,67a), **gnu** (11a,181d)

- GU   **ngu** (188

G - V   **gav** (72d)

G - W   **gaw** (140c)

GY -   **gym** (154a), **gyp** (29b,42a,160c)

G - Y   **gay, Gay** (17d), **gey** (140a), **goy** (107c), **gry** (78b), **guy** (55b,131b, 155d), **Guy**\ (96a)

G - Z   **gaz** (188,190), **gez** (188), **goz** (190), **guz** (188)

HA -   **had, hae** (139c), **hag** (140a,183a), **hah** (52c), **hai** (55c), **hak** (46d), **Hal** (69d), **ham** (98a,144b), **Ham** (18d,107c), **Han** (16c,30b,185b), **hao** (189) **hap** (17d,28d), **har** (139c), **has, hat** (74d), **Hat** (183d), **haw** (35a,52c,74d,91a,155a,162c), **hay** (52c,55c,165d)

H - A   **Hea** (15b), **hia** (114b), **hoa** (39b)

274

- HA   aha (52c,55c,159c), cha (162b,c), dha (99c), FHA (8a), Kha (88d, 106b), sha (110c,143d,144a,c,174c,181c)

H - B   hob (40c,56d,100c,124b,167a,180c), hub (28b,118b,180c)

H - C   hic (52c,90a,164c)

H - D   had, hid, hod (23b,32d,102d,141a)

HE -   Hea (15b), Heh (191), hei (65a), Hel (68d,93c,172d), hem (22a,36a, 48b,52c,155a), hen (19a,60c,114c,136c), hep (52c), her (124b,c), heu (8b,30c,52c), hew (40a), hex (18c), hey (25c,52c)

H - E   hae (139c), hie (79a,153b), hoe (39c), hue (33c,143b)

- HE   che (145d), rhe (59a), she (124b), She (73a), the (13b)

H - G   hag (140a,183a), hog (45b,117c,160c), hug (32c,49d)

H - H   hah (52c), Heh (191), Hoh (80d), hsh (79c), huh (52c)

HI -   hia (114b), hic (52c,90a,164c), hid, hie (79a,153b), him (124b), hin (189), hip (52c,54b,85b,133c,134a), hir (76a), his (124c), hit (32d,157c,158a)

H - I   hai (55c), hei (65a), hoi (52c,74b,185b), hui (14a,30b,56d,114c)

- HI   Ahi (32c,147d), chi (91c), Chi (69c), ghi (24d), ihi (57c,156b), phi (91c)

H - K   hak (46d)

H - L   Hal (69d), Hel (68d,93c,172d)

H - M   ham (98a,144b), Ham (18d,107c), hem (22a,36a,48b,52c,155a), him (124b), hum (24d,46b,150d)

- HM   ohm (49b,67a,173b)

H - N   Han (16c,30b,185b), hen (19a,60c,114c,136c), hin (189), Hun (16c,21d,174b)

HO -   hoa (39b), hob (40c,56d,100c,124b,167a,180c), hod (23b,32d,102d, 141a), hoe (39c), hog (45b,117c,160c), Hoh (80d), hoi (52c,74b, 185b), hop (40b), Hor (103d), hot (10c,176c), how, hoy (16c,52c)

H - O   hao (189)

- HO   cho (188), mho (49b,173b), oho (52c), Rho (71b,91c), sho (188), tho (52a), Tho (167a), who (129c)

H - P   hap (17d,28d), hep (52c), hip (52c,54b,85b,133c,134a), hop (40b), hup (35a), hyp

H - R   har (139c), her (124b,c), hir (76a), Hor (103d), Hur (91d)

- HR   ihr (66d)

HS -   hsh (79c)

H - S   has, his (124c)

H - T   hat (74d), Hat (183d), hit (32d,157c,158a), hot (10c,176c), hut (143c)

HU -   hub (28b,118b,180c), hue (33c,143b,) hug (32c,49d), huh (52c), hui (14a,30b,56d,114c), hum (24d,46b,150d), Hun (16c,21d,174b), hup (35a), Hur (91d), hut (143c)

H - U   heu (8b,30c,52c)

- HU   ahu (24c,41d,65d,103d,120d), dhu (40b), Dhu (28a,87d), phu (38c), Shu (30b,127a)

H - W haw (35a,52c,74d,91a,155a,162c), hew (40a), how

H - X hex (18c)

HY - hyp

H - Y hay (52c,55c,165d), hey (25c,52c), hoy (16c,52c)

- HY shy (16d,99d,128c,160c,165d,175a), thy, why (52c)

IA - ial (158b), Ian (85b,96a,139d), iao (78a,96c,178d)

I - A iba (117a), Ida (103d,183c), Ila (16b), ILA (173a), ina (158c), Ina (183c), Ira (18c,d,41a,68c,82c,96a,164a,178a,c), Ita (51b,71d, 94d,95d,106b,117a), ITA (173a), Iva (76a,97b,127b,185b), iwa (63c), iya (95b,108d,111c)

- IA dia (122b,d,152a,165b), hia (114b), Lia (82b), mia (83c), pia (13b, 22d,48a,120d), ria (38c,51d,81b,152a,b), Sia (80c), tia (151d), via (132a,133a,b,179a)

IB - iba (117a), Ibo (107a,180b)

- IB bib, dib (21b,43b,c,120d,140a), fib (162a), gib (17b,38b,95d,166d, 179d), jib (38b,136b,146a), mib (8d,96c), nib (17b,19d,115d), rib (37c,85b,90c,98a,144d,159d,172a), sib (86b,129c,139d,147b)

IC - ice (30a,36d,42d,63d), ich (66c), ici (61d), Ici (9b), ics (158d), icy (65d)

- IC hic (52c,90a,164c), pic (188), sic (90a,165b,168b), tic (104d,153a, 171c,d)

ID - Ida (103d,183c), ide (40c,57a,b,d,158b), Ido (13c,81d,88c,173c)

I - D ind (80c)

- ID aid (14a,15b,64c,75d,158b), bid (35a,82a,109d,111b,174c), Cid (151c,d), did, fid (16b,54d,118a,167b), gid (143d), hid, kid (67d, 85b,90d,186a), lid (167b), mid (9d,28b,73b), nid (72a,106b,c,116d), old (158c), rid (32a,44a,60d), Sid (96a)

IE - ier (50a,158c)

I - E ice (30a,36d,42d,63d), Ide (40c,57a,b,d,158b), ife (22c,75d), Ike (123a), ile (62a,63b,158c), ine (29c,158b,c), Ine (10c,137d,180b), Ire (10c,30c,52b,64c,125a,130b,185a), ise (40d,158c,d), Ise (78a, 84c), ite (59b,81a,105d,130c,158b,c,d,161a), ive (158c)

- IE cie (61b,63b), die (27b,54a,65a,155a,167a), fie (52c,59d), gie (139c,140a), hie (79a,153b), lie (53a,69d,162a), nie (53c), pie (42d,85d,95b,114d,171b,172a), rie (28c,70d,97d), sie (46c,66d, 139b,140b,146b), tie (10a,14c,38b,45d,51a,88d,109b,127c,138b, 170b), vie (36c,157c,170c)

IF - ife (22c,75d)

- IF Lif (107d), rif (188), Sif (164d), vif (62a), Zif (102a)

I - G ing (114b,d,148d,158c,d,175c), Ing (10c,115b)

- IG big, cig, dig (52b), fig, gig (26d,28d,57c,105b,127a,144c, 153a,171d), jig (40b,d), mig (8d,96c,145b), Mig (118d), nig (33b, 40a,46a), pig (27a,45b,99a,151b,160c), rig (51b,112a), tig (46b), wig (73b), zig (84a)

IH - ihi (57c,156b), ihr (66d)

I - H ich (66c), ish (158b), Ith (10a,28a,82b,99d)

276

I - I lci (61d), lci (9b), ihi (57c,156b), ini (158d), iri (18a,d,75a)

- II dii (68d), oii (105c), rii (157b,175b)

IJ - ijo (107a)

IK - ike (123a)

I - K ilk (31d,54c,86b,136d,139c,140b), ink (20b,40c), irk (10d)

- IK aik (139d), pik (188)

IL - ila (16b), ILA (173a), ile (62a,63b,158c), ilk (31d,54c,86b,136d,
139c,140b), ill (43d,121a,173a,c,d), ILO (184c), ils (62b,d,164b)

I - L ial (158b), ill (43d,121a,173a,c,d)

- iL ail (170a), kil (82b), lil (72d), mil (80b,110c,164d,182d), Mil
(10a), nil (108c), oil (11a,71a), pil (34b), sil (30c,185c,d), til
(142d)

IM - imp (42b,127d,174a), imu (15d)

I - M ism (45a,79b,161c)

- IM aim (42d,43d,67d,109b,125d,157c), Bim (16c), dim (47a,48b,54a,
74d,94d,109b), him (124b), Jim (96a), Kim (86d), lim (21a), mim
(12b), nim (96d,155d), rim (22a,48b,96d,116b,124b,166a,180c),
Sim (96b), Tim (43b), vim (50b,176b)

IN - ina (158c), Ina (183c), Ind (80c), ine (29c,158b,c), Ine (10c,
137d,180b), ing (114b,d,158c,d,175c) Ing (10c,115b), ini (158d),
ink (20b,40c), inn (72b,73b,78c,132b,150a,161c,162b,179a), Inn
(41a), Ino (14b,25b), ins (164d), INS (107a,182d)

I - N Ian (85b,96a,139d), inn (72b,73b,78c,132b,150a,161c,162b,179a),
Inn (41a), ion (11c,29a,49b,101b,114c,158c)

- IN ain (18d,91c,110c,124b,140a,154b,180a), bin (22c,59a,78a,128c,
156d), din (31c,130b,174a), ein (66b,c), fin (86a), gin (37c,92d,
139a,142a,149b), hin (189), jin (42b,153c), kin (30b,81c,129d)
Kin (30b), lin (140c,168c,178d), Lin (115d,186c), Min (29d,68b,
113c), nin (107d), pin (45d,54d,141d,147d), rin (33b,142b), sin
(91c,140b,147a,168b,176a), Sin (102b), tin (36c,99a,b,108b,155a,
179c), vin (63a,182b), win (7a,17b,64b,123b), yin (140a), Yin (30b,
143c,185b)

IO - ion (11c,29a,101b,114c,158c), ior (50a,158c), ios (74d), IOU
(124b)

I - O iao (78a,96c,178d), ibo (107a,180b), Ido (13c,81d,88c,173c), ijo
(107a), ILO (184c), Ino (14b,25b), iso (34a,122c,d), ito (84a,c,
186d), iyo (7d,176b)

- IO CIO (173a), mio (152c), rio (33a,131d,132a,152c,157b), Rio (23a),
tio (152d), Zio (147d,163d)

I - P imp (42b,127d,174a)

- IP dip (26a,79d,117c,138c), gip (29b,160c), hip (52c,54b,85b,133c,
134a), kip (17c,72d,76c,189), lip (48b,58b,80a,131c), nip (20c,
29b,45d,46a,b,115c,118a), pip (11d,44a,121d,142a,154a), Pip
(43b), rip (87b,130a,162c), Rip (178b), sip (46b,79d,104a,162b),
tip (26b,d,50a,70d,77b,78a,120a,165d), yip (16c), zip (24b,50b,
176b)

IR - ira (18c,d,41a,68c,82c,96a,164a,178a,c), ire (10c,30c,52b,64c,

277

125a,130b,185a), **irl** (18a,d,75a), **irk** (10d)

I - R   **ier** (50a,158c), **ihr** (66d), **ior** (50a,158c)

 - IR   **air** (11c,12c,42b,44c,53a,96b,98c,99d,125b,170c), **Eir** (69a,75a), **fir** (16a,36a,52a,168c,d,169a), **hir** (76a), **mir** (29d,135c,d,166c,176b), **pir** (103a,b,136c), **sir** (163b,166b), **tir** (61d,62c,87a,145b), **vir** (89c)

IS -   **ise** (40d,158c,d), **Ise** (78a,84c), **-ish** (158b), **ism** (45a,79b,161c), **iso** (34a,122c,d), **ist** (7b,34b,43a,59b,66c,158c,d)

I - S   **ics** (158d), **ils** (62b,d,164b), **ins** (164d), **INS** (107a,182d), **ios** (74d), **its** (124c)

 - IS   **bis** (50a,90a,102c,130b,171c), **cis** (34c,122c), **dis** (122b,d), **Dis** (68b,73a,119d,172d,174b), **eis** (66c), **his** (124c), **lis** (54b, 58b,60c,62a,92b), **Lis** (47a), **mis** (122b,c,d,185c), **nis** (23d,67d, 68a,87c), **Nis** (19d), **ris** (131d), **sis** (67b,129c), **tis**, **vis** (59d,89b,d, 90b,176b), **wis** (79d,164c)

IT -   **ita** (51b,71d,94d,95d,106b,117a), **ITA** (173a), **ite** (59b,81a,105d, 130c,158b,c,d,161a), **Ite** (130c), **Ith** (10a,28a,82b,99d), **Ito** (84a, c,186d), **its** (124c)

I - T   **ist** (7b,34b,43a,59b,66c,158b,c,d)

 - IT   **ait** (82d,132a), **bit** (46a,86b,114c,167a,b,171c,180d), **cit** (81a, 167d), **dit** (62b,d,120a,159d), **fit** (7a,11d,51b,75a,114a,123a,124c, 126a,153a,157c,159a), **git** (101a), **hit** (32d,157c,158a), **kit** (112a, 176c), **Kit** (96a,183d), **lit**, **mit** (56c,66d,183b), **nit** (48d), **pit** (52b, 142a,164a,168a), **rit** (148c,140b,153d), **sit** (98c,116a,121c,130c, 142d), **tit** (19c,130d), **uit** (47a,111d,151a), **wit** (78d,85b,177b)

I - U   **imu** (15d), **I.O.U.** (124b)

 - IU   **piu** (102c), **Tiu** (7c,68c,147d,163d,166c,170c), **Ziu** (147d,163d)

IV -   **iva** (76a,97b,127b,185b), **ive** (158c), **ivy** (32b,38c,176b)

 - IV   **div** (42b,139b), **Liv** (93b)

IW -   **iwa** (63c)

 - IW   **Tiw** (68c,147d,163d)

 - IX   **Aix** (46b), **dix** (118d), **Dix** (60b), **fix** (7b,10a,13a,14c,43a,c,141d, 165c), **mix** (156b), **nix** (23d,108c,178d), **pix** (31a,51d,175d), **six** (26c), **vix** (89d,138c)

IY -   **iya** (95b,108d,111c), **iyo** (7d,176b)

I - Y   **icy** (65d), **ivy** (32b,38c,176b)

 - IZ   **biz**, **viz** (105b)

JA -   **jab** (120b,125c) **jag** (124d,148a) **Jah** (84d), **jam** (123a,156c,165c), **Jap**, **jar** (31d,70c,143b), **Jat** (80d,125c), **jaw** (97c,138c), **jay** (19b, 91c)

J - B   **jab** (120b,125c), **jib** (38b,136b,146a), **job** (30d,184d), **Job** (96a)

JE -   **jet** (20b,35a,154c), **jeu** (61d), **Jew**

J - E   **Joe** (96a)

J - G   **jag** (124d,148a), **jig** (40b,d), **jog** (82c,85c,170a), **jug** (118c,123d)

J - H   **Jah** (84d)

JI -   **jib** (38b,136b,146a), **jig** (40b,d), **Jim** (96a), **jin** (42b,153c)

 - JI   **tji** (189), **uji** (146d)

J – M   **jam** (123a,156d,165c), **Jim** (96a), **jum** (39c)

J – N   **jin** (42b,153c)

JO –   **job** (30d,184c), **Job** (96a), **Joe** (96a), **jog** (82c,85c,170a), **jot** (82a, 114c,166c,180d), **jow** (188), **joy**

– JO   **djo** (188), **ljo** (107a)

J – P   **Jap**

J – R   **jar** (31d,70d,143b), **Jur** (107b)

J – S   **jus** (61d,90b)

J – T   **Jat** (80d,125c), **jet** (20b,35a,154c), **jot** (82a,114c,166c,180d), **jut** (53a,124a)

JU –   **jug** (118c,123d), **jum** (39c), **Jur** (107b), **jus** (61d,90b), **jut** (53a,124a)

J – U   **jeu** (61d)

J – W   **jaw** (97d,138c), **Jew**, **jow** (188)

J – Y   **jay** (19b,91c), **joy**

KA –   **kab** (75c), **kae** (84a,140b), **kaf** (12b), **Kaf** (104a), **kai** (59c), **Kai** (14d,84c), **kan** (93a), **kas** (32c,47a), **kat** (105d), **kay** (82d), **Kay** (13b,134b)

K – A   **kea** (114a,b), **Kha** (88d,106b), **koa** (74c), **Kra** (11b,91d), **Kua** (95c)

– KA   **aka** (176b), **Aka** (13d,88b,c), **oka** (170c,184a,189)

K – B   **kab** (75c), **Keb** (47d), **KGB** (135d), **kob** (11a)

K – D   **ked** (140b,144a), **kid** (67d,85b,90d,186a)

KE –   **kea** (114a,b), **Keb** (47d), **ked** (140b,144a), **kef** (12a,46c,75d,88c), **keg** (27a,105b), **ken** (60b,87c,122b,172d), **kep** (139b), **Ker** (71b, 95d), **ket** (189) **key** (14c,82d,88b,117c,118c,150b,180c)

K – E   **kae** (84a,140b)

– KE   **ake** (60a,107a), **eke** (14c,117c), **Ike** (123a), **oke** (189)

K – F   **kaf** (12b), **Kaf** (104a), **kef** (12a,46c,75d,88c)

KG –   **KGB** (135d)

K – G   **keg** (27a,105b)

KH –   **Kha** (88d,106b)

– KH   **akh** (153d)

KI –   **kid** (67d,85b,90d,186a), **kil** (82b), **Kim** (86d), **kin** (30b,81c,129a), **Kin** (30b), **kip** (17c,72d,76c,189), **kit** (112a,176c), **Kit** (96a,183d)

K – I   **kai** (59c), **Kai** (14d,84c), **koi** (26d), **kri** (75c,96d), **Kri** (75c), **Kui** (86a,88c,146a)

– KI   **ski** (149c)

K – L   **kil** (82b), **Kol** (18b), **kyl** (76d,79b)

K – M   **Kim** (86d)

K – N   **kan** (93a), **ken** (60b,87c,122b), **kin** (30b,81c), **Kin** (30b)

KO –   **koa** (74c), **kob** (11a), **koi** (26d), **Kol** (18b), **kop** (76d), **kor** (75c), **Kos** (77c,82d), **kou** (169a)

– KO   **ako** (189), **TKO** (22c)

K – P   **kep** (139b), **kip** (17c,72d,76c,189), **kop** (76d), **kup** (188)

279

KR - **Kra** (11b,91d), **kri** (75c,96d), **Kru** (91d)

K - R **Ker** (71b,95d), **kor** (75c)

K - S **kas** (32c,47a), **Kos** (77c,82d)

K - T **kat** (105d), **ket** (189), **kit** (112a,176c), **Kit** (96a,183d)

KU - **Kua** (95c), **Kui** (86a,88c,146a), **kup** (188)

K - U **kou** (169a), **Kru** (91d)

- KU **aku** (57c,176a)

KY - **kyl** (76d,79b)

K - Y **kay** (82d), **Kay** (13b,134b), **key** (14c,82d,88b,117c,118c,150b, 180c)

- KY **sky** (56d)

LA - **lab, lac** (53c,99d,130c,135b,174d), **lad** (22c,25b,55b,157c,186a), **lag** (93c,155d), **Lai** (24c,d,88c), **lai** (98b,161b), **lak** (38a), **lam** (51b, 58b,93d,164d,178a), **lan** (37b,d,160b), **Lao** (80d,88c,146a,161b), **lap** (31b,37d,59b,127a,131d,153d,167d), **lar** (24c,51d,67a,78d,95d, 101d,171b), **las** (13b,151d), **lat** (24a,33d,106b,118a), **lav** (72d), **law** (26b,33a,40a,48c,60b,85d,91a,111b,134d,155d), **lax** (93d,130a), **lay** (16a,25c,80a,98b,107d,141d,150b), **Laz** (27d)

L - A **lea** (56a,97d,114c,185b), **Lea** (22d), **Lia** (82b), **loa** (7d,53c,97d,184d)

- LA **ala** (6d,13a,15c,61a,133d,182c,d), **Ala.** (151b), **ela** (21c,53c,72b, 76c,108b,174c), **lla** (16b), **ILA** (173a), **ola** (113b), **ula** (72c,158c)

L - B **lab, LLB** (42a), **lob** (15d,23b,94c,100b,163a,172d)

- LB **alb** (65b,176a), **elb** (85c), **LLB** (42a)

LC - **LCI** (21b)

L - C **lac** (53c,99d,130c,135b,174d)

L - D **lad** (22c,25b,55b,157c,186a), **led, lid** (167b), **LLD** (42a), **lud** (100a), **Lud** (23c,144b)

- LD **eld** (10b,93c,110b,165d), **LLD** (42a), **old** (8a,71a,77c,123c,175b)

LE - **lea** (56a,97d,114c,185b), **Lea** (22d), **led, lee** (74b,144b), **Lee** (9c, 31c,96a), **leg** (37d,92b,141d,159d,169c), **lei** (65b,74c), **lek** (65c), **Leo** (36b,c,92d,186d), **Ler** (23d,28a,b,64b,106c,141a), **les** (13b, 61a), **let** (9a,76d,77c,116b,130a,158b,163a), **leu** (190), **lev** (33b), **lew** (190), **Lew** (96a), **lex** (90b), **ley** (190)

L - E **lee** (74b,144b), **Lee** (9c,31c,96a), **lie** (53a,69d,162a), **loe** (139d), **lue** (146b), **lye** (8d,27d,93b)

- LE **ale** (17c,18c,50c,55d,92d,104c), **cle** (158d), **ele** (48c), **ile** (62a,63b, 158c), **ole** (24b,29b,113b,152a,158b,d), **ule** (23a,27d,134c,158c, 168d)

L - F **Lif** (107d), **lof** (188)

- LF **Alf** (96a), **elf** (54b,154b)

L - G **lag** (93c,155d), **leg** (37d,92b,141d,159d,169c), **log** (64a,128d), **lug** (27a,45d,47b,73c,136b), **Lug** (28b)

LI - **Lia** (82b), **lid** (167b),, **lie** (53a,69d,162a), **Lif** (107d), **lil** (72d), **lim** (21a), **lin** (92c,140c,168c,178d), **Lin** (115d,186c), **lip** (48b,58b,80a, 131c), **lis** (54c,58b,60c,62a,92b), **Lis** (47a), **lit, Liv** (93b)

280

L - I   **Iai** (98b,161b), **Lai** (24c,d,88c), **LCI** (21b), **Iei** (65b,74c), **Ioi** (62a)

- LI   **AII** (7b,12a,25c,48b,55a,60c,92d,101a,103a,164a,166b,170d),   **EII** (18c,d,76c,96a,137a,185a)

L - K   **Iak** (38a), **Iek** (65c), **Lok** (15d,68b)

- LK   **aIk** (171b), **eIk** (22c,90d,178a), **iIk** (31d,54c,86b,136d,139c,140b)

LL -   **LLB** (42a), **LLD** (42a)

L - L   **III** (72d)

- LL   **aII** (35c,118a,126d,181a), **eII** (10d,24b,32c,98a), **III** (43d,121a,173a, c,d), **UII** (7c,68c,146b,164d)

L - M   **Iam** (51b,58b,93d,164d,178a), **Iim** (21a), **Ium** (30a)

- LM   **eIm** (168c), **oIm** (48c), **uIm** (49c), **UIm** (40d)

L - N   **Ian** (37b,d,160b), **Iin** (140c,168c,178d), **Lin** (115d,186b), **Lon** (86c, 96a), **Iyn** (140c,178d)

LO-   **Ioa** (7d,53c,97d,184d), **Iob** (15d,23b,94c,100b,163a,172d), **Ioe** (139d), **Iof** (188), **Iog** (64a,128d), **Ioi** (62a), **Lok** (15d,68b), **Lon** (86c, 96a), **Ioo** (65a), **Iop** (30c,40a,46b,143a), **Ios** (13b,151d), **Iot** (24b, 28d,55a,65d,114a,119c,143c,150d,168a), **Lot** (6b,73d), **Lou** (96a, 183d), **Iow** (16c,149d), **Ioy** (121c,148b,151c,167a)

L - O   **Lao** (80d,88c,146a,161b), **Leo** (36b,c,92d,186d), **Ioo** (65a), **Luo** (107b), **Lwo** (107b)

- LO   **Fio, ILO** (184c), **uIo** (34b,80d)

L - P   **Iap** (31b,37d,59b,127a,131d,153d,167d), **Iip** (48b,58b,80a,131c), **Iop** (30c,40a,46b,143a)

- LP   **aIp** (24b,103d,115c)

L - R   **Iar** (24c,51d,67a,78d,95d,101d,171b), **Ler** (23d,28a,28b,64b,106c, 141a), **Lur** (116c)

LS -   **Lst** (21a,b,88b)

L - S   **Ias** (13b,151d), **Ies** (13b,61a), **Iis** (54b,58b,60c,62a,92b), **Lis** (47a), **Ios** (13b,151d), **Iys** (58b,92b)

- LS   **aIs** (66d,163d), **eIs** (140a), **IIs** (62b,d,164b)

L - T   **Iat** (24a,33d,106b,118a), **Iet** (9a,76d,77c,116b,130a,158b,163a), **Iit**, **Iot** (24b,28d,55a,65d,114a,119c,143c,150d,168a), **Lot** (6b,73d), **Lst** (21a,b,88b), **Iut** (189)

- LT   **aIt** (66c76c,109c), **eIt** (87a,117c,139d), **OIt** (41a)

LU-   **Iud** (100a), **Lud** (23c,144b), **Iue** (146b), **Iug** (27a,45d,47b,73c,136b), **Lug** (28b), **Ium** (30a), **Luo** (107b), **Lur** (116c), **Iut** (189), **Iux** (79d)

L - U   **Ieu** (190), **Lou** (96a,183d)

- LU   **fIu, uIu** (87a)

L - V   **Iav** (72d), **Iev** (33b), **Liv** (93b)

LW -   **Lwo** (107b)

L - W   **Iaw** (26b,33a,40a,48c,60b,85d,91a,111b,134d,155d), **Iew** (190), **Lew** (96a), **Iow** (16c,149d)

L - X   **Iax** (93d, 130a), **Iex** (90b), **Iux** (79d)

LY -   **Iye** (8d,27d,93b), **Iyn** (140c,178d), **Iys** (58b,92b)

L - Y   **Iay** (98b,107d,141d,150b), **Iey** (190), **Ioy** (121c,148b,151c,167a)

281

- LY   aly (95d), Ely (27c,50b), fly (58c,81b,163b,178d), ply (59b,90b, 118d,164b,171c,174a,181b,184c), sly (13b,38b,64c,81b,132c)

L - Z   Laz (27d)

MA -   maa (97d,143d), Mab (54b,126b,183d), Mac (96a,140b,150b), mad (10c,82b), Mae (183c), mag (73b,95b,166c), Mag (183d), Mah (10b, 57c,102b), mai (62a), mal (34a,b,44a,52b,62c,122b), Mal (94b), Mam (192), man (29c,60c,64c,65a,142d,161d), mao (115b), Mao (30b), map (27a,29b,54a,98d,160a), mar (40b,44a,79a,d,81a,140d), Mar (93d), mas (34b,55b,119a), mat (46d,50d,94d,117c,161d), Mat (96a), mau (170c,188), maw (38b,d,72c,111a,121a,142a,156c), Max (96a), may (74d), May (183c)

M - A   maa (97d,143d), MFA (42a), mia (83c), mna (71d,179d), moa (19b), Mya (31c)

- MA   ama (26a,28d,31a,35b,39c,95b,108d,111c,117b,182c), oma (158c,d, 170c), sma (140b,148d), Uma (43a,69b,153d)

M - B   Mab (54b,126b,183d), mib (8d,96c), mob (39a,127a,165b)

M - C   Mac (96a,140b,150b)

M - D   mad (10c,82b), mid (9d,28b,73b), Mod (138d), mud (6c)

ME -   mee (169a), Meg (8c,183d), mel (77d), mem (91c), men (38c,116a, 117b,170a), Men (94d), Meo (27b,80c), mer (62c,141a), mes (62b), met (28d), meu (153b), mew (25b,27b,50a,55b,72c,74d,101b,141b, 153b)

M - E   Mae (183c), mee (169a), Mme. (166b), Moe (96a)

- ME   ame (37a,62d,131b), eme (38d,70a,140c,172b), Mme. (166b), ume (11d)

MF -   MFA (42a)

M - G   mag (73b,95b,166c), Mag (183d), Meg (8c,183d), mig (8d,96c, 145b), Mig (118d), mug (46b,54a,65a)

MH -   mho (49b,173b)

M - H   Mah (10b,57c,102b)

MI -   mia (83c), mib (8d,96c), mid (9d,28b,73b), mig (8d,96c,145b), Mig (118d), mil (80b,110c,164d,182d), Mil (10a,82b), mim (12b), Min (29d,68b,113c), mio (152c), mir (29d,135c,d,166c,176b), mis (122b,c,d,185c), mit (56c,66d,183b), mix (156b)

M - I   mai (62a), Moi (80d)

- Mi   ami (61d)

M - L   mal (34a,b,44a,52b,62c,122b), Mal (94b), mel (77d), mil (80b,110c, 164d,182d), Mil (10a,82b), mol (58b,70c), mul (188)

MM -   Mme. (166b)

M - M   Mam (192), mem (91c), mim (12b), mom, mum (30d,95a,146c)

MN -   mna (71d,179d)

M - N   man (29c,60c,64c,65a,142d,161d), men (38c,116a,117b,170a), Men (94d), Min (29d,68b,113c), mon (15d,84b) Mon (24c), mun (157b)

MO -   moa (19b), mob (39a,127a,165b), Mod (138d), Moe (96a), Moi (80d), mol (58b,70c), mom, mon (15d,84b), Mon (24c), moo (94b), mop (160a), mos (59b), mot (126d,130a,137d,183b), mow (32b,40a)

282

M - O mao (115b), Mao (30b), Meo (27b,80c), mho (49b,173b), mio (152c), moo (94b), Mro (88c)

- MO amo (79a,89c), omo (34d)

M - P map (27a,29b,54a,98d,160a), mop (160a)

- MP amp (49b,173b), imp (42b,127d,174a)

MR - Mro (88c), Mrs. (166b), Mru (80d,88c)

M - R mar (40b,44a,79a,d,81a,140d), Mar (93d), mer (62c,141a), mir (29d, 135c,d,166c,176b), mur (63a,177d)

M - S mas (34b,55b,119a), mes (62b), mis (122b,c,d,185c), mos (59b), Mrs. (166b), Mus (104a,132c)

- MS Ems (125a,151c)

M - T mat (46d,50d,94d,117c,161d), Mat (96a), met (28d), mit (56c,66d, 183b), mot (126d,130a,137d,183d), mut (39c), Mut (9b,127a)

- MT amt (37d,40d,108a,163c)

MU - mud (6c), mug (46b,54a,65a), mul (188), mum (30d,95a,146c), mun (157b), mur (63a,177d), Mus (104a,132c), mut (39c), Mut (9b,127a), muy (152d,175d)

M - U mau (170c,188), meu (153b), Mru (80d,88c)

- MU emu (19b,58c,111d), imu (15d), SMU (40b), umu (112a)

M - W maw (38b,d,72c,111a,121a,142a,156c), mew (25b,27b,50a,55b,72c, 74d,101b,141b,153b), mow (32b,40a)

M - X Max (96a), mix (156b)

MY - Mya (31c)

M - Y may (74d), May (183c), muy (152d,175d)

- MY amy (63c), Amy (8c,94b,183c)

NA - nab (13b,26c,27b,142a), nae (139d), nag (73d,78b,138c,184d), nak (156b), Nan (183c), nap (65a,117d,146b,148a), nar (139d), nas (74a, 89c,178b), nat (7a,24c,d,106a), nay (42b,106b)

N - A NEA (162c), noa (35b,124a,161a), NRA (8a,20d)

- NA ana (10b,33c,60d,93a,98c,122b,d,140d,142b), Ana (28a,68d,100c), Ena (8c,126b), ina (158c), Ina (183c), mna (71d,179b), Ona (26b, 64a), sna (105b,140b,143d,144a,149c,181c,d), Una (54a,153b, 170c,183c)

N - B nab (13b,26c,27b,142a), neb (17b,19a,d,115d), nib (17b,19d,115d), nob (38c,74d,84a,149d) nub (67b,94d,95c,118c,124d)

N - D Ned (96a), nid (72a,106c,116d), nod (17c,46c), Nod (18d,25b)

- ND and (36a), end (8b,67d,120a,125d,130a,166a), ind (80c), und (66b)

NE - N.E.A. (162c), neb (17b,19a,d,115d), Ned (96a), nee (19d,22b,25c, 60b,95c), nef (32b,144c,d), neo (34a,b,c,100d,106d,108c,122c,d, 128c), nep (27c,32d,56a,87c,184b), ner (137c), nes (26b), net (26c, 32a,50d,53b,60d,99a,124a,142a,149b), new (11a,63c,88d,111c, 128c, Ney (63b,97b,105d), nex (62b)

N - E nae (139d), nee (19d,22b,25c,60b,95c), nie (53c,66c), NNE (35b), nye (72a,116b), Nye (9c,18b)

- NE ane (61c,140a,158b), ene (35b,158b,c), ine (29c,158b,c), Ine (10c, 137d,180b), NNE (35b), one (79a,b,80b,d,124b,147a,148d,173a,c),

283

une (13b,61a,62b,95c)

N - F nef (32b,144c,d)

NG - ngu (188)

N- G nag (73d,78b,138c,184d), nig (33b,40a,46a), nog (20c,46a,48d,54d, 100b,115d,118a)

- NG eng (48a,146a), ing (114b,d,148d,158c,d,175c), Ing (10c,115b)

N - H nth (42a)

NI nib (17b,19d,115d), nid (72a,106c,116d), nie (53c,66c), nig (33b, 40a,46a), nil (108c), nim (96c,155d), nin (107d), nip (20c,29b,45d,46a,b,115c,118a), nis (23d,67d,68a,87c), Nis (19d), nit (48d), nix (23d,108c,178d)

- NI ani (19b,d,20b,39b), ini (158d), oni (11b), uni · (34c,118d,122c), Uni (51d)

N - K nak (156b)

- NK ink (20b,40c)

N - L nil (108c), nul (108c,177a)

N - M nim (96c,155d), nom (62b,125a), Nym (54c,76a)

NN - NNE (35b), NNW (35b)

N - N Nan (183c), nin (107d), non (34c,62b,89c,106b,122c,147a), nun (24c,91c,117d,147b), Nun (29a,85c)

- NN Ann (183c), inn (72b,73b,78c,150a,161c,162b,179a), Inn (41a)

NO- noa (35b,124a,161a), nob (38c,74d,84a,149d), nod (17c,46c,148a), Nod (18d,25b), nog (20c,46a,48d,54d,100b,115d,118a), nom (62b, 125a), non (34c,62b,89c,106b,122c,147a), noo (108c,139d), nor (10b,36a,37b,92b), nos (62b,90a,179a), not (78b,106b), now (60b, 79d), Nox (69b)

N - O neo (34a,b,c,100d,106d,108c,122c,d,128c), noo (108c,139d)

- NO ano (19d,20b,34d,122d,174a), Ino (14b,25b), ono (34a), Ono (18d,118d), uno (83c,151d)

N - P nap (65a,117d,146b,148a), nep (27c,32d,56a,87c,184b), nip (20c, 29b,45d,46a,b,115c,118a)

NR - NRA (8a,20d)

N - R nar (139d), ner (137c), nor (10b,36a,37b,92b), nur (67d)

N - S nas (74a,89c,178b), nes (26b), nis (23d,67d,87c), Nis (19d), nos (62b,90a,179a)

- NS Ans (92a), ens (17d,18a,51a,52d), ins (164d), INS (107a,182d), ons (38c), uns (66d,174c)

NT - nth (42a)

N - T nat (7a,24c,d,106a), net (26c,32a,50b,53d,60d,99a,124a,142a, 149b), nit (48d), not (78b,106b), nut (24c,32d,38b,54d,64a,65d, 86b,141c,165a), Nut (69a)

- NT ant (49d,60b,81b,118c), ent (34d,158b,c), TNT (53a)

NU - nub (67b,94d,95c,118c,124d), nul (108c,177a), nun (24c,91c,117d, 147b), Nun (29a,85c,129d), nur (67d), nut (24c,32d,38b,54d,64a, 65d,86b,141c,165a), Nut (69a)

N - U ngu (188)

- NU   **Anu** (15b,28a,68a,d,75b,88c,147d), **gnu** (11a,181d), **Unu** (24d)

N - W   **new** (11a,63c,88d,111c,128c), **NNW** (35b), **now** (60b,79d)

- NW   **NNW** (35b), **WNW** (35b)

N - X   **nix** (23d,108c,178d), **Nox** (69b), **Nyx** (69b)

NY -   **nye** (72a,116d), **Nye** (9c,18b), **Nym** (54c,76a), **Nyx** (69b)

N - Y   **nay** (42b,106b), **Ney** (63b,97b,105d)

- NY   **any** (14b,150b), **ony** (139a), **sny** (18a,39d,43d,87a,119a,144d,145a, 165d,176a)

N - Z   **nez** (62b)

OA -   **oaf** (22a,45b,146d,157d,185d), **oak** (73d,168c,169a), **oar** (20b,124c, 134b), **oat** (15a,28b,70b,144b)

O - A   **oca** (48c,112c,116d,133d,170c,184a), **oda** (74a,170d), **oka** (170c, 184a,189), **ola** (113b) **oma** (158c,d,170c), **Ona** (26b,64a), **OPA** (8a), **ora** (10c,40d,41b,45b,83a,c,101c,104a,122d,123d), **ova** (48d), **oxa** (29c)

- OA   **boa** (36c,55b,106a,125d,138b,142d,149a), **goa** (65d,104b,126c), **Goa** (121c), **hoa** (39b), **koa** (74c), **loa** (7d,53c,184d), **Loa** (97d), **moa** (19b), **noa** (35b,124a,161a), **poa** (20d,70d,97d), **roa** (23d,87a), **toa** (17c,178b), **Zoa** (20b)

OB -   **obe** (31d,87d,150d), **obi** (55d,67b,84c,137b,150d)

O - B   **orb** (50a,53c,67d,153b)

- OB   **bob** (57c,115d), **Bob** (96a), **cob** (28c,78b,95d,160b,177d), **fob** (29b, 59b,113b,178c), **gob** (97b,136c), **hob** (40c,56d,100c,124b,167a, 180c), **job** (30d,184c), **Job** (96a), **kob** (11a), **lob** (15d,23b,94c,100b, 163a,172d), **mob** (39a,127a,165b), **nob** (38c,74d,84a,149d), **pob** (121b,129b,139c), **rob** (119d,155d), **Rob** (96a), **sob** (39b,179d)

OC -   **oca** (48c,112c,116d,133d,170c,184a), **och** (8b), **ock** (189), **oct** (34a, 122c)

O - C   **orc** (28c,70c,180b)

- OC   **Doc** (143a), **roc** (19c,53b,54a,147a), **soc** (44c,85d)

OD -   **oda** (74a,170d), **odd** (46b,53a,109b,157a,172d,173c), **ode** (26b,79c, 94d,118a,119d,120a,150b), **Odo** (181d), **ods** (109a)

O - D   **odd** (46b,53a,109b,157a,172d,173c), **oid** (158c), **old** (8a,71a,77c, 123c,175b), **Ord** (25b,60b)

- OD   **cod** (57b,c), **dod** (11a,32a,43b,140c), **fod** (188), **god** (42a), **God** (84d), **hod** (23b,32d,102d,141a), **Mod** (138d), **nod** (17c,46c), **Nod** (18d,25b), **pod** (76b,78d,91b,141b,180c), **rod** (6a,72d,88b,131a, 154d,156a,160a), **sod** (160b,170d), **tod** (24d,60c,83d), **Vod** (16a)

OE -   **o'er** (6b,112a), **oes** (109a)

O - E   **obe** (31d,87d,150d), **ode** (26b,79c,94d,118a,119d,120a,150b), **oke** (189), **ole** (24b,29b,113b,152a,158b,d), **one** (79a,b,80d,124b,147a, 148d,173a,c), **ope** (172c,173c), **ore** (39a,99b,108a,115b,141c,151a, 160b), **ose** (102a,146d,158b,c,d,159a), **owe**, **ote** (158d), **oye** (139c)

- OE   **coe** (143d), **Coe** (33c), **doe** (41d,55b,127a), **foe** (111a), **hoe** (39c), **Joe** (96a), **loe** (139d), **Moe** (96a), **poe** (114b), **Poe** (9c,d,128a, 172a), **roe** (27d,41d,48d,57b,76d,95b,157b), **soe** (170c,184a), **toe** (43c,69d,148a,156a), **voe** (17a,81b), **woe** (25b), **Zoe** (36b,183d)

285

OF - off (6b,15c,44c,76a), oft (63c)

O - F oaf (22a,45b,146d,157d,185d), off (6b,15c,44c,76a), orf (57b,185c), ouf (52c)

- OF lof (188)

- OG bog (97a,160a), cog (33a,65d,163b,167c,180c), dog (10b,45b,59b), fog (109b), gog (95b), hog (45b,117c,160c), jog (82c,85c,170a), log (64a,128d), nog (20c,46a,48d,54d,100b,115d,118a), sog (149c), tog (46a), vog (189)

OH - ohm (49b,67a,173b), oho (52c)

O - H och (8b)

- OH boh (24c), doh (113b), foh (52c), Hoh (80d), poh (52c), soh (52c, 72d,) zoh (13d,186b)

OI - oid (158c), oii (105c), oil (11a,71a)

O - I obi (55d,67b,84c,137b,150d), oii (105c), oni (11b), ori (34a), ovi (34a)

- OI goi (107c), hoi (52c,74b,185b), koi (26d), loi (62a), Moi (80d), poi (44a,59c,74c,117a,162a,164b), roi (55c,62a,133d), toi (62b,d,63a), Toi (18d), yoi (52c,79a)

OK - oka (170c,184a,189), oke (189)

O - K oak (73d,168c,169a), ock (189), ork (180b), ouk (140c)

- OK Bok (9c), Lok (15d,68b), Rok (87c), sok (188), yok (10c,185a)

OL - ola (113b), old (8a,71a,77c,123c,175b), ole (24b,29b,113b,152a, 158b,d), olm (48c), Olt (41a)

O - L oil (11a,71a), owl

- OL col (103d,114c), Kol (18b), mol (58b,70c), sol (108b), Sol (117b, 159b), tol (137b), vol (155a,182d)

OM - oma (158c,d,170c), omo (34d)

O - M ohm (49b,67a,173b), olm (48c)

- OM com (122d), dom (121c,166b,c), Dom (94b), mom, nom (62b,125a), pom (45a,148d), rom (72d), tom (95d), Tom (96b,157a), yom (41a)

ON - Ona (26b,64a), one (79a,b,80b,d,124b,147a,148d,173a,c), oni (11b), ono (34a), Ono (18d,118d), ons (38c) ony (139a)

O - N own (6d)

- ON bon (30a,61d,86b,88c), Bon (84b), con (7d,29b,83c,116d,157d), don (151d,166c), Don (96a), eon (8a,37b,51d,116b), Fon (40b), gon (188), ion (11c,29a,49b,101b,114c,158c), Lon (86c,96a), mon (15d,84b), Mon (24c), non (34c,62b,89c,106b,122c,147a), ron (152c), Ron (86c,88a), son (42d,75d), ton (158d,167d,179d), von (66d,67a), won, yon (44c,112a,164d)

OO - oop (139a), oot (140a)

O - O Odo (181d), oho (52c), omo (34d), ono (34a), Ono (18d,118d), oro (34c,122c,152a), Oro (161b), oto (34a) Oto (147b)

- OO boo, coo (19b), Coo (82d), foo (42c), goo (156b), loo (65a), moo (94b), noo (108c,139d), roo (140a), soo (127d,140b,151b), Soo (137c), too (18b,102c), woo, zoo (181b)

OP - OPA (8a), ope (172b,173c), Ops (28c,69a,b,74a,137c), opt (30c)

O - P oop (139a), orp (140c,179d)

- OP cop (36a,120c,126d,153c,155d), dop (39c,43b), fop (38a,40d,46b), hop (40b), kop (76d), lop (30c,40a,46b,143a), mop (160a), oop (139a), pop (52d,53a,130b,149d), sop (23b,35d,149c,155d), top (38c,52b,118b,123d,160a,174a,186b), wop

OR - ora (10c,40d,41b,45b,83a,c,101c,104a,122d,123d), orb (50a,53c, 67d,153b), orc (28c,70c,180b), Ord (25b,60b), ore (39a,99b,108a, 115b,141c,151a,160b), orf (57b,185c), orl (34a), ork (180b), oro (34c,122c,152a), Oro (161b), orp (140c,179d), orr (77c), ort (59b, 90d,91a,102c,129b,140d,180a,184d), ory (36c)

O - R oar (20b,124c,134b), oer (6b,112a), orr (77c), our (124c)

- OR Bor (120c), cor (36c,75b,155c), dor (17d,24b,32b,46b,47a,81b,85d), for (123d,163a,166c), Gor (81a), Hor (103d), ior (50a,158c), kor (75c), nor (10b,36a,37b,92b), por (152a), tor (38b,76d,85d,115c, 124b,132b,c), Vor (69a)

OS - ose (102a,146d,158b,c,d,159a), ost (15d,86b)

O - S ods (109a), oes (109a), ons (38c), Ops (28c,69a,b,74a,137c), ous (158b)

- OS Bos (27c), cos (91d,132d), dos (45d,61a,97a,181b), Eos (14d,41a, 68d), ios (74d), Kos (77c,82d), los (13b,151d), mos (59b), nos (62b, 90a,179a), ros (37b), Ros (138a,174d), SOS

OT - ote (158d), oto (34a), Oto (147b)

O - T oat (15a,28b,70b,144b), oct (34a,122c), oft (63c), Olt (41a), oot (140a), opt (30c), ort (59b,90d,91a,102c,129b,140d,180a,184d), ost (15d,86b), out (6b,14b,60b,69d,80a,108b,185c)

- OT bot (59a,88d), cot (129b,148b), dot (45d,97a,104d,105a,116b,153a, 162d), fot (188), got, hot (10c,176c), jot (82a,114c,166c,180d), lot (24b,28d,55a,65d,114a,119c,143c,150d,168a), Lot (6b,73d), mot (126d,130a,137d,183b), not (78b,106b), oot (140a), pot (120b, 145b,154d,175d), rot (22b,134c,143d,153d), sot (46c,167b,c), tot (186a), Vot (56d)

OU - ouf (52c), ouk (140c), our (124c), ous (158b), out (6b,14b,60b,69d, 80a,108b,185c)

- OU fou (139a), IOU (124b), kou (169a), Lou (96a,183d), sou (63b), you

OV - ova (48d), ovi (34a)

OW - owe, owl, own (6d)

- OW bow (11c,21b,39d,60a,107c,109a,125a,144d,158a), cow (22c,45b, 81d), dow (17d,87a,88d,175d), how, jow (188), low (16c,149d), mow (32b,40a), now (60b,79d), pow, row (44c,56b,92c,109a,126b, 127d,165c), sow (45b,117c,119a,138b,160c), tow (45d,58b,75d, 125b), vow (119c,150a), wow (52c,158a), yow (52c)

OX - oxa (29c)

- OX box (36a,c,128c,145d,152c), cox (156a), fox (134a), Nox (69b), pox (44a), vox (90a,177a)

OY - oye (139c)

O - Y ony (139a), ory (36c)

- OY boy (142d,157c), coy (16d), goy (107c), hoy (16c,52c), joy, loy (121c,148b,151c,167a), Roy, soy (17b,137c,74d), toy (169d)

287

- OZ   **Box** (43b,115d), **cox, goz** (190)

PA -   **pab** (139c), **pac** (73b,94c,100d), **pad** (39d,59c,76c,157d,161a,168b), **pah** (52c,60b,106d), **pal** (35b,38d), **pam** (26c,65a,87a,105b), **pan** (34a,61a,104a,175d), **Pan** (56a,68a,b,76b,120c,135b,161a,184a), **pap** (59c), **par** (15a,51a,b,c,69d,107c,135b,155a), **pas** (40d,156a), **pat** (11d,116d,159a,161d,167c), **Pat** (96a), **Pau** (48c,76a,130c), **paw** (32d,59c,73c), **pax** (89d,115b), **pay** (35b,128c,130a,d,177b)

P - A   **pea** (32d,91b,142a,175a), **pia** (13b,22d,48a,120d), **poa** (20d, 70d,97d), **pta** (6a), **pua** (74c,76a)

- PA   **apa** (23a,177d), **OPA** (8a), **spa** (75b,100b,130c,154b,178d)

P - B   **pab** (139c), **pob** (121b,129b,139c)

P - C   **pac** (73b,94c,100d), **pic** (188)

P - D   **pad** (39d,59c,76c,157d,161a,168b), **ped** (16d,34b), **pod** (76b,78d, 91b,141b,180c), **pud** (59d,73c,115a)

PE -   **pea** (32d,91b,142a,175a), **ped** (16d,34b), **pee** (91c), **peg** (38c,46b, 54d,98a,118a,184c), **pel** (55c,160d), **pen** (36a,50a,80d,118b,126d, 160a,185c), **pep** (50b,176b), **per** (25c,122d,165b,176a), **pes** (59d), **pet** (26d,37c,55a,59c,162d), **peu** (62a), **pew** (30d,52c,57d,120b, 141c)

P - E   **pee** (91c), **pie** (42d,85d,95b,114d,171b,172a), **poe** (114b), **Poe** (9c, d,128a,172a), **pre** (17d,122b,c), **pue** (52c), **Pye** (50d,55a)

- PE   **ape** (36d,79d,100a,101d,146d), **ope** (172b,173c)

P - G   **peg** (38c,46b,54d,98a,118a,184c), **pig** (27a,45b,99a,151b,160c), **pug** (45a,101a,108a,148d)

PH -   **phi** (91c), **phu** (38c)

P - H   **pah** (52c,60b,106d), **poh** (52c)

PI -   **pia** (13b,22d,48a,120d), **pic** (188), **pie** (42d,85d,95b,114d, 171b,172a), **pig** (27a,45b,99a,151b,160c), **pik** (188), **pil** (34b), **pin** (45d,54d,141d,147d), **pip** (11d,44a,121d,142a,154a), **Pip** (43b), **pir** (103a,b,136c), **pit** (52b,142a,164a,168a) **piu** (102c), **pix** (31a,51d, 175d)

P - I   **phi** (91c), **poi** (44a,59c,74c,117a,162a,164b), **psi** (91c)

- PI   **api** (34a,76d), **epi** (56c,61c,d,111c,112d,122d,133c,153c,167b, 174a), **UPI** (107a,182d)

P - K   **pik** (188)

PL -   **ply** (59b,90b,118d,164b,171c,174a,181b,184c)

P - L   **pal** (35b,38d), **pel** (55c,160d), **pil** (34b), **pul** (190), **Pul** (14a)

P - M   **pam** (26b,65a,87a,105b), **pom** (45a,148d)

P - N   **pan** (34a,61a,104a,175d), **Pan** (56a,68a,b,76b,120c,135b,161a, 184a), **pen** (36a,50a,80d,118b,126d,160a,185c), **pin** (45d,54d,141d, 147d), **pun** (119c)

PO -   **poa** (20d,70d,97d), **pob** (121b,129b,139c), **pod** (76b,78d,91b,141b, 180c), **poe** (114b), **Poe** (9c,d,128a,172a), **poh** (52c), **poi** (44a,59c, 74c,117a,162a,164b), **pom** (45a,148d), **pop** (52d,53a,130b,149d), **por** (152a), **pot** (120b,145b,154d,175d), **pow, pox** (44a)

P - O   **pro** (59d,126d), **Pwo** (88c)

288

- PO   apo (122b), Apo (177c)

P - P   pap (59c), pep (50b,176b), pip (11d,44a,121d,154a), Pip (43b), pop (52d,53a,130b,149d), pup (141b,148d,185d)

PR -   pre (17d,122b,c), pro (59d,126d), pry (52b,91d,98b,123d)

P - R   par (15a,51a,b,c,69d,107c,135b,155a), per (25c,122d,165b,176a), pir (103a,b,136c), por (152a), pur, pyr (92a,b,122c,173b)

PS -   psi (91c), pst (25c,126d,146c)

P - S   pas (40d,156a), pes (59d), pus

- PS   Ops (28c,69a,b,74a,137c)

PT -   Pta (6a)

P - T   pat (11d,116d,159a,161d,167c), Pat (96a), pet (26d,37c,55a,59b, 162d), pit (52b,142a,164a,168a), pot (120b,145d,154d,175d), pst (25c,126d,146c), put (65a,69d,90b)

- PT   apt (11d,23b,32b,58a,80b,92b,114d,116d,124b,159a), opt (30c)

PU -   pua (74c,76a), pud (59d,73c,115a), pue (52c), pug (45a,101a,108a, 148d), pul (190), pun (119c), pup (141b,148d,185d), pur, pus, put (65a,69d,90b), puy (61d)

P - U   Pau (48c,76a,130c), peu (62a), phu (38c), piu (102c)

PW -   Pwo (88c)

P - W   paw (32d,59c,73c), pew (30d,52c,57d,120b,141c), pow

P - X   pax (89d,115b), pix (31a,51d,175d), pox (44a), pyx (31a,51d,175d)

PY -   Pye (50d,55a), pyr (92a,b,122c,173b), pyx (31a,51d,175d)

P - Y   pay (35b,128c,130a,d,177b), ply (59b,90b,118d,164b,171c,174a, 181b,184c), pry (52b,91d,98b,123d), puy (61d)

- PY   spy (44a,51c,52b,141d)

QA -   Qaf (104a)

Q - A   qua (13c,80a,89c,147a)

Q - E   que (62d)

Q - F   Qaf (104a)

Q - I   qui (62d)

Q - O   quo (188)

QU -   qua (13c,80a,89c,147a), que (62d), qui (62d), quo (188)

RA -   rab (17c,75c,85b,102d,162c,166b), Rab (45a), rad (50b,138d,173b), rae (136b,138d,140b), Rae (183c), rag (59b,77c,100c,133c,161a), rah (29b), rai (188), raj (129c), ram (17a,45b,50b,79c,112b,121d, 143d,157d), Ram (36b), ran (73d), Ran (7c,107d,141a,163d), rap (90d,110a,147c,157c), ras (6c,26b,48b,51d,53d,61c,75a,111c,123c, 166b), rat (16a,42d,73b,132c), raw (20c,39a,105d,173d), ray (38a, 49a,57b,58b,147b), Ray (96a)

R - A   rea (9c,171a), ria (38c,51d,81b,152a,b), roa (23d,87a), rua (118c), Rua (16b)

- RA   ara (33a,114a,116a,118b,163d), Ara (9b,18c,36b,c,68d,69b,c,85a, 95a,175b), dra (188), era (8a,51a,116b,165d), fra (23c,63c,101d, 123b,129d), gra (59b,94b,160c), Ira (18c,d,41a,68c,82c,96a,164a, 178a,c), Kra (11b,91d), NRA (8a,20d), ora (10c,40d,41b,45b,83a,c,

289

101c,104a,122d,123d), **tra** (33b)

R - B   **rab** (17c,75c,85b,102d,162c,166b), **Rab** (45a), **reb** (35d,75c,85b,
     162c,166b), **rib** (37c,85b,90c,98a,144d,159d,172a), **rob** (119d,
     155d), **Rob** (96a), **rub** (6b,24d,28c,43c,120c,179b)

- RB   **orb** (50a,53c,67d,153b)

R - C   **roc** (19c,53b,54a,147a)

- RC   **arc** (31b,39d,92a,126a,127c,142a), **orc** (28c,70c,180b)

R - D   **rad** (50b,138d,173b), **red** (33c,38d,59a,127b,134c,135b), **Red**
     (151b), **rid** (32a,44a,60d), **rod** (6a,72d,88b,131a,154d,156a,160a),
     rud (26d,57b)

- RD   **erd** (47d,119d,145c), **Ord** (25b,60b), **urd** (17b,184b), **Urd** (68d,107d)

RE -   **rea** (9c,171a), **reb** (35d,75c,85b,162c,166b), **red** (33c,38d,59a,127b,
     134c,135b), **Red** (151b), **ree** (12c,50a,80c,134d,137a,140b,144a,
     146b), **Ree** (25a), **ref, reh** (8d), **rei** (89b,121c), **Rei** (18d), **rel** (49b,
     173b), **Reo** (26c), **rep** (53b,d,131a,171c), **res** (80a,89d,91a,97c), **ret**
     (58b,95a,149c,155d), **Reu** (115d), **rev, rew** (75c,140c,176b), **rex**
     (86c,96a), **rey** (86c,152b)

R - E   **rae** (136b,138d,140b), **Rae** (183c), **ree** (12c,50a,80c,134d,137a,
     140b,144a,146b), **Ree** (25a), **rhe** (59a,173b), **rie** (28c,70d,97d), **roe**
     (27d,41d,48d,57b,76d,95b,157b), **rue** (76a,b,129c,150d,183a), **rye**
     (28b,70b,72d,92d)

- RE   **are** (51a,88b,98a,99b,110c,166c,175c), **ere** (17d,150c), **ire** (10c,
     52b,30c,64c,125a,130b,185a), **ore** (39a,99b,108a,115b,141c,151a,
     160b), **pre** (17d,122b,c), **tre** (37b,83c,122d,165a,167d), **ure** (40a,
     139d,155d,158b,d), **Ure** (138d,185d)

R - F   **ref, rif** (188)

- RF   **orf** (57b,185c)

R - G   **rag** (59b,77c,100c,133c,161a), **rig** (51b,112a), **rug**

- RG   **erg** (50b,173b,184c)

RH -   **rhe** (59a,173b), **rho** (71b,91c)

R - H   **rah** (29b), **reh** (8d)

RI -   **ria** (38c, 51d, 81b, 152a, b), **rib** (37c, 85b, 90c, 98a, 144d,
     159d,172a), **rid** (32a,44a,60d), **rie** (28c,70d,97d), **rif** (188), **rig** (51b,
     112a), **rii** (157b,175b), **rim** (22a,48b,96d),116b,124d,166a,180c), **rin**
     (33b,142b), **rio** (33a,131d,132a,152c,157b), **Rio** (23a), **rip** (87b,
     130a,162c), **Rip** (178b), **ris** (131d), **rit** (140b,148c,153d)

R - I   **rai** (188), **rei** (89b,121c), **Rei** (18d), **rii** (157b,175b), **roi** (55c,62a,
     133d)

- RI   **Ari** (18d), **eri** (13d,21c,146d), **Eri** (18c), **gri** (75c,78b), **Iri** (18a,d,
     75a), **kri** (75c,96d), **ori** (34a), **sri** (60c,77b,166c), **Sri** (17c), **tri**
     (122d,169d), **Uri** (162d)

R - J   **raj** (129c)

R - K   **Rok** (87c)

- RK   **ark** (21a,29d,38a,58b,60d,175d), **irk** (10d), **ork** (180b)

R - L   **rel** (49b,173b)

R - M   **ram** (17a,45b,50b,79c,112b,121d,143d,157d), **Ram** (36b), **rim** (22a,

48b,96d,116b,124b,166a,180c), **rom** (72d), **rum** (8c,92d)

- RM   **arm** (22d,60c,81b,92b,124b,161b)

R - N   **ran** (73d), **Ran** (7c,107d,141a,163d), **rin** (33b),142b), **ron** (152c), **Ron** (86c,88a), **run** (10d,23c,58d,110d,148d,153b,154b,167d)

- RN   **arn** (8c,139a), **ern** (19c,d,47b,54b,141a), **urn** (36c,174d)

RO -   **roa** (23d,87a), **rob** (119d,155d), **Rob** (96a), **roc** (19c,53b,54a,147a), **rod** (6a,72d,88b,131a,154d,156a,160a), **roe** (27d,41d,48d,57b,76d, 95b,157b), **roi** (55c,62a,133d), **Rok** (87c), **rom** (72d), **ron** (152c), **Ron** (86c,88a), **roo** (140a), **ros** (37b), **Ros** (138a,174d), **rot** (22b, 134c,143d,153d), **row** (44··,56b,92c,109a,126b,127d,165c), **Roy**

R - O   **Reo** (26c), **rho** (71b,91c), **rio** (33a,131d,132a,152c,157b), **Rio** (23a), **roo** (140a)

- RO   **Aro** (107a,111c), **cro** (104c,115b,180a), **fro** (15b), **Mro** (88c), **oro** (34c,122c,152a), **Oro** (161b), **pro** (59d,126d), **S.R.O.** (6a,164a), **Uro** (192)

R - P   **rap** (90d,110a,147c,157c), **rep** (53b,d,131a,171c), **rip** (87b, 130a,162c), **Rip** (178b)

- RP   **orp** (140c,179d)

R - R   **rur** (132b)

- RR   **err** (21a,43a,67d,100c,d,147a,148b,157b,168b,178a), **grr** (52c), **orr** (77c)

R - S   **ras** (6c,26b,48b,51d,53d,61c,75a,111c,123c,166b), **res** (80a,89d, 91a,97c,164c), **ris** (131d), **ros** (37b), **Ros** (138a,174d), **rus** (89b), **Rus** (138a)

- RS   **ars** (13b,89a), **Ars** (112c), **ers** (20a,176a), **Mrs.** (166b)

R - T   **rat** (16a,42d,73b,132c), **ret** (58b,95a,149c,155d), **rit** (140b,148c, 153d), **rot** (22b,134c,143d,153d), **rut** (73a)

- RT   **art** (22d,38b,39c,43b,56c,124a,162c,181d), **ert** (140c,174a), **ort** (59b,90d,91a,102c,129b,140d,180a,184d)

RU -   **rua** (118c), **Rua** (16b), **rub** (6b,24d,28c,43c,120c,179b), **rud** (26d, 57b), **rue** (76a,b,129c,150d,183a), **rug**, **rum** (8c,92d), **run** (10d,23c, 58d,110d,148d,153b,154b,167d), **rur** (132b), **rus** (89b), **Rus** (138a), **rut** (73a), **rux** (154a,184d)

R - U   **Reu** (115d)

- RU   **aru** (80c,82b), **Aru** (82d), **cru** (63a,176c), **Kru** (91d), **Mru** (80d,88c), **Uru** (192)

R - V   **rev**

R - W   **raw** (20c,39a,105d,173d), **rew** (75c,140c,176b), **row** (44c,56b,92c, 109a,126b,127d,165c)

R - X   **rex** (86c,96a), **rux** (154a,184d)

RY -   **rye** (28b,70b,72d,92d)

R - Y   **ray** (38a,49a,57b,58b,147b), **Ray** (96a), **rey** (86c,152b), **Roy**

- RY   **cry** (25c,124a,145c,179d), **dry** (46d,85a,137c,164c), **ery** (155d,158c, d), **fry** (57d), **gry** (78b), **ory** (36c), **pry** (52b,91d,98b,123d), **try** (7c, 10d,14c,50a,51c,130a), **wry** (13d)

SA -   **saa** (98a), **sac** (15d,121d), **Sac** (80c), **sad** (29c,42c,94c,98c,104a,

291

150d,173a), sae (140b,149c), sag (46b), sah (188), sai (101d), saj (48a,169a), sak (37c), Sak (88c), sal (29c,48a,136d,149d,152d, 169a,183a), Sal (183d), Sam (96a,162a), san (91c), San (24d), sao (141b) , Sao (113c), sap (45d,52d,85c,169b,176d,179a), sar (57d), sat (13d), saw (7a,11b,40c,54c,97d,125a,137d,167a), sax (40c,148a,167a), say (131c,174c,177a)

S - A   saa (98a), sea (19a,52d,58c,112c,178d), sha (110c,143d,144a,c, 174c,181c), sia (80c), sma (140b,148b), sna (105b,140b,143d,144a, 149c,181c,d), spa (75b,100b,130c,154d,178d), sta (13c,91b,104d, 105a), sua (89d),

- SA   Asa (6a,18c,71a,84d,86d,164c), ESA (8a)

S - B   Seb (47d), sib (86b,129c,139d,147b), sob (39b,179d), sub (90a, 122d,172c)

S - C   sac (15d,121d), Sac (80c), sec (46c,182c), sic (90a,165b,168b), soc (44c,85d)

- SC   BSC (42a)

S - D   sad (29c,42d,94c,98c,104a,150d,173a), sed (89a), Sid (96a), sod (160b,170d), sud (59a)

SE -   sea (19a,52d,58c,112c,178d), Seb (47d), sec (46c,182c), sed (89a), see (20a,43c,44a,51c,53c,93d,109b,113c,116a,176d,178c,183b), sel (62c,140b), Sem (107c), sen (190) ser (80d,83b,d,116c, 152d,180a), ses (61d), set (7b,11d,13a,23c,32b,33c,37c,58a,73d, 109b,118c,121c,142d,150a,186a), Set (52b,68a,b,111d), sew, sex, sey (120c)

S - E   sae (140b,149c), see (20a,43c,44a,51c,53c,109b,113c,116a,176d, 178c,183b), she (124b), She (73a), sie (46c,66d,139b,140b,146b), soe (170c,184a), SSE (35b), ste (62c,136c), sue (119c), Sue (63a, 178a,183d), sye (40c,46c,139b,141a,167a)

- SE   ase (51a,139a), Ase (79b,115d), ese (35b,158c), ise (40d,158c,d), Ise (78a,84c), ose (102a,146d,158b,c,d,159a), SSE (35b), use (7b, 47a,49d,64c,109b,168b,c,181b)

S - F   Sif (164d)

S - G   sag (46b), sog (149c)

SH -   sha (110c,143d,144a,c,174c,181c), she (124b), She (73a), sho (188), Shu (30b,127a), shy (16d,99d,128c,160c,165d,175a)

S - H   sah (188), soh (52c,72d)

- SH   ash (24d,33c,49c,73d,134b,168c,169a), hsh (79c), ish (158b), ush

SI -   Sia (80c), sib (86b,129c,139d,147b), sic (90a,165b,168b), Sid (96a), sie (46c,66d,139b,140b,146b), Sif (164d), sil (30c,185c,d), Sim (96b), sin (91c,140b,147a,168b,176a), Sin (102b), sip (46b,79d, 104a,162b), sir (87a,163b,166b), sis (67b,129c), sit (98c,116a,121c, 130c,142d), six (26c)

S - I   sai (101d), Sia (80c), ski (149c), sri (60c,77b,166c), Sri (17c), sui (30b)

- SI   asi (137a), psi (91c)

S - J   saj (48a,169a)

SK -   ski (149c), sky (56d)

S - K sak (37c), Sak (88c), sok (188), Suk (107b)

- SK ask (38b,82a,126c)

SL - sly (13b,38b,64c,81b,132c)

S - L sal (29c,48a,136d,149d,152d,169a,183a), Sal (183d), sel (62c, 140b), sil (30c,185c,d), sol (108b), Sol (117b,159b)

SM - sma (140b,148d), SMU (40b)

S - M Sam (96a,162a), Sem (107c), Sim (96b), sum (8a,123a,167c)

- SM ism (45a,79b,161c)

SN - sna (105b,140b,143d,144a,149c,181c), sny (18a,39d,43d,87a,119a, 144d,145a,165d,176a)

S - N san (91c), San (24d), sen (190), sin (91c,140b,147a,168b,176a), Sin (102b), son (42d,75d), sun (75d,111a,117b,155b), syn (122d,183b)

SO - sob (39b,179d), soc (44c,85d), sod (160b,170d), soe (170c,184a), sog (149c), soh (52c,72d), sok (188), sol (108b) Sol (117b,159b), son (42d,75d), soo (127d,140b,151b), Soo (137c), sop (23b,35d, 149c,155d), SOS, sot (46c,167b,c), sou (63b), sow (45b,117c,119a, 138b,160c), soy (17b,137c,174d)

S - O sao (141b), Sao (113c), sho (188), soo (127d,140b,151b), Soo (137c), S.R.O. (6a,164a)

- SO Aso (84c), DSO (99d), eso (34d,183b), iso (34a,122c,d)

SP - spa (75b,100b,130c,154b,178d), spy (44a,51c,52b,141d)

S - P sap (45d,52d,85c,169b,176d,179a), sip (46b,79d,104a,162b), sop (23b,35d,149c,155d), sup (46b,104a,162b)

- SP asp (7b,32b,149a,174a,176c), e.s.p. (147b)

S - Q suq (22a,97a)

SR - sri (60c,77b,166c), Sri (17c), S.R.O. (6a,164a)

S - R sar (57d), ser (80d,83b,d,116c,152d,180a), sir (87a,163b,166b), sur (34a,62b,d,104b,151a,152d,174a)

SS - SSE (35b), ssu (189), SSW (35b)

S - S ses (61d), sis (67b,129c), SOS, sus (117c), Sus (160c,181b)

- SS ass (17b,20c,45b,c,59c,110c,112b,146d,157d), ess (39d,78a,91c, 158c,184d)

ST - sta (13c,91b,104d,105a), ste (62c,136c), sty (50a,53c)

S - T sat (13d), set (7b,11d,13a,23c,32b,33c,37c,58a,73d,109b,118c, 121c,142c,150a,186a), Set (52b,68a,b,111d), sit (98c,116a,121c, 130c,142d), sot (46c,167b,c)

- ST est (50a,61c,62a,79b,89c,158d,159c), ist (7b,34b,43a,59b,66c,158b, c,d), LST (21a,88b), ost (15d,86b), pst (25c,126d,146c), tst (81d, 126d)

SU - sua (89d), sub (90a,122d,172c), sud (59a), sue (119c), Sue (63a, 178a,183d), Sui (30b), Suk (107b), sum (8a,123a,167c), sun (75d, 111a,117b,155b), sup (46b,104a,162b), suq (22a,97a), sur (34a,62b, d,104b,151a,152d,174a), sus (117c), Sus (160c,181b)

S - U Shu (30b,127a), SMU (40b), sou (63b), ssu (189)

- SU ssu (189)

S - W saw (7a,11b,40c,54c,97d,125a,137d,167a), sew, sow (45b,117c, 119a,138b,160c), SSW (35b)

- SW SSW (35b), WSW (35b)

S - X sax (40c,148a,167a), sex, six (26c)

SY - sye (40c,46c,139b,141a,167a), syn (122d,183b)

S - Y say (131c,174c,177a), sey (120c), shy (16d,99d,128c,160c,165d, 175a), sky (56d), sly (13b,38b,64c,81b,132c), sny (18a,39d,43d,87a, 119a,144d,145a,165d,176a), soy (17b,137c,174d), spy (44a,51c, 52b,141d), sty (50a,53c)

TA - taa (112d), tab (29b,39c,58b,86a,128d,145a), tac (34d,130a), tad (22c,174a,186a), tae (138d,140c,166c,d), tag (45a,54c,65a,87b, 144a), tai (84b,111c,121b), Tai (80d), taj (75a,97d), tal (40c,77a, 113b), tam (74d), tan (23d,33c,46a,72c,90d), tao (10d,131c, 170b), Tao (117a), tap (55a,114d,153c), tar (8c,68a,94d,111c,118c, 136a,c,176d), tat (43b,48c,72d,87c), Tat (82a), tau (71b,91c,136c, 161a), tav (91c), taw (90d,91c,96c,d,145b,161d), tax (13a,14a,80a, 91d)

T - A taa (112d), tea (13d,18c,79c,81a,145d,149c,159d), tia (151d), toa (17c,178b), tra (33b), tua (117a)

- TA ata (58d,97d,158d,160c,173d), Ata (79c,80d,94d,95d,100a,106b, 117a), eta (71a,84c,91c), Ita (51b,71d,94d,95d,106b,117a), ITA (173a), Pta (6a), sta (13c,91b,104d,105a), uta (53c,84d,93b,147c, 150b)

T - B tab (29b,39c,58b,86a,128d,145a), tub (21a,27a,36c,174d)

TC - tch (52c), tck (52c)

T - C tac (34d,130a), tec (43a), tic (104d,153a,171c,d)

- TC etc (10b)

T - D tad (174a,186a), ted (74d,138b,154b), Ted (96b), tod (24d,60c,83d)

TE - tea (13d,18c,79c,81a,145d,149c,159d), tec (43a), ted (74d,138b, 154b), Ted (96b), tee (39d,52b,69d,91c,112d,115d,118b,172a), teg (45a,54b,143d,144a,171d), tel (34a,b,122c), Tem (143a,159b), ten (19a,26c,41c,42b), ter (34d,122c,165a), tez (125c)

T - E tae (138d,140c,166c,d), tee (39d,52b,69d,91c,112d,115d,118b, 172a), the (13b), tie (10a,14c,38b,45d,51a,88d,109b,127c,138b, 170b), toe (43c,69d,148a,156a), tre (37b,83c,122c,165a,167d), tue (114b), tye (28c,134a)

- TE ate (81a,108c,158c,174c), Ate (20c,68b,d,69a,b,116c,186b), ete (36c,62d,141c,159b), ite (59b,81a,105d,130c,158b,c,d,161a), ote (158d), ste (62c,136c), Ute (145c,180b)

T - G tag (45a,54c,65a,87b,144a), teg (45a,54b,143d,144a,171d), tig (46b), tog (46a), tug (45d,125b), tyg (46b)

TH - the (13b), tho (52a), Tho (167a), thy

T - H tch (52c)

- TH eth (91c,158d), lth (10a,28a,82b,99d), nth (42a)

TI - tia (151d), tic (104d,153a,171c,d), tie (10a,14c,38b,45d, 51a,88d,109b,127c,138b,170b), tig (46b), til (142d), Tim (43b), tin (36c,99a,b,108b,155a,179c), tio (152d), tip (26b,d,50a,70d,77b,78a,

294

120a,165d), **tir** (61d,62c,145b), **tis**, **tit** (19c,130d), **Tiu** (7c,68c, 147d,163d,166c,170c), **Tiw** (68c,147d,163d)

T - I **tai** (84b,111c,121b), **Tai** (80d), **tji** (189), **toi** (62b,d,63a), **Toi** (18d), **tri** (122d,169d), **tui** (47c,114b,117a), **Twi** (69c)

- TI **ati** (106d,107a), **Ati** (45d,106b,113c,117a)

TJ - **tji** (189)

T - J **taj** (75a,97d)

TK - **TKO** (22c)

T - K **tck** (52c)

T - L **tal** (40c,77a,113b), **tel** (34a,b,122c), **til** (142d), **tol** (137b)

T - M **tam** (74d), **Tem** (143a,159b), **Tim** (43b), **tom** (95d), **Tom** (96b, 157a), **tum** (26d), **Tum** (143a,159b)

TN - **TNT** (53a)

T - N **tan** (23d,33c,46a,72d,90d), **ten** (19a,26c,41c,42b), **tin** (36c,99a,b, 108b,155a,179c), **ton** (158d,167d,179d), **tun** (23b,27a,182b)

TO - **toa** (17c,178b), **tod** (24d,60c,83d), **toe** (43c,69d,148a,156a), **tog** (46a), **toi** (62b,d,63a), **Toi** (18d), **tol** (137b), **tom** (95d), **Tom** (96b, 157a), **ton** (158d,167d,179d), **too** (18b,102c), **top** (38c,52b,118b, 123d,160a,174a,186b), **tor** (38b,76d,85d,115c,124b,132b,c), **tot** (186a), **tow** (45d,58b,75d,125b), **toy** (169d)

T - O **tao** (10d,131c,170b), **Tao** (117a), **tho** (52a), **Tho** (167a), **tio** (152d), **TKO** (22c), **too** (18b,102c), **two** (26c,37d,80a,93a)

- TO **ETO** (184d), **Ito** (84a,c,186d), **oto** (34a), **Oto** (147b)

T - P **tap** (55a,114d,153c), **tip** (26b,d,50a,70d,77b,78a,120a,165b), **top** (38c,52b,118b,123d,160a,174a,186b), **tup** (115a,117d,127d,143d)

TR - **tra** (33b), **tre** (37b,83c,122d,165d,167d), **tri** (122d,169d), **try** (7c, 10d,14c,50a,51c,130a)

T - R **tar** (8c,68a,94d,111c,118c,136a,c,176d), **ter** (34d,122d,165a), **tir** (61d,62c,145b), **tor** (38b,76d,85d,115c,124b,132b,c), **tur** (14d,27c, 68a,79b,117d,174c), **tyr** (7c,68c,147d,163d,170c,178a)

TS - **tst** (81d,126d)

T - S **tis**

- TS **its** (124c)

T - T **tat** (43b,48c,72d,87c), **Tat** (82a), **tit** (19c,130d), **TNT** (53a), **tot** (186a), **tst** (81d,126d), **tut** (52c)

- TT **att** (146a)

TU - **tua** (117a), **tub** (21a,27a,36c,174d), **tue** (114b), **tug** (45d,125b), **tui** (47c,114b,117a), **tum** (26d), **Tum** (143a,159b), **tun** (23b,27a, 182b), **tup** (115a,117d,127d,143d), **tur** (14d,27c,68a,79b,117d, 174c), **tut** (52c)

T - U **tau** (71b,91c,136c,161a), **Tiu** (7c,68c,147d,163d,166c,170c)

- TU **utu** (35b,137c), **Utu** (96c,107a,159b)

T - V **tav** (91c)

TW - **Twi** (69c), **two** (26c,37d,80a,93a)

T - W **taw** (90d,91c,96c,d,145b,161d), **Tiw** (68c,147d,163d), **tow** (45d, 58b,75d,125b)

295

T - X   tax (13a,14a,80a,91d)

TY -   tye (28c,134a), tyg (46b), Tyr (7c,68c,109c,147d,163d,170c,178a)

T - Y   thy, toy (169d), try (7c,10d,14c,50a,51c,130a)

- TY   sty (50a,53c)

T - Z   tez (125c)

U - A   Uca (56a), ula (72c,158c), Uma (43a,69b,153d), Una (54a,153b, 170c,183c), uta (53c,84d,93b,147c,150b), uva (64a,70c)

- UA   dua (122d), Kua (95c), pua (74c,76a), qua (13c,80a,89c,147a), rua (118c), Rua (16b), sua (89d), tua (117a)

UB -   ube (185b), ubi (90a,180d,185b)

- UB   bub (22c), cub (92d,185d), dub (25c,46a,c,87a,105b,121a,140a), fub (29b,119d), hub (28b,118b,180c), nub (67b,94d,95c,118c 124d), rub (6b,24d,28c,43c,120c,179b), sub (90a,122d,172c), tub (21a,27a,36c,174d)

UC -   Uca (56a)

- UC   duc (61c)

UD -   Udi (108a), udo (28a,30c,48c,84b,c,d,136c,149d)

U - D   und (66b), urd (17b,184b), Urd (68d,107d)

- UD   bud (22c), cud (126c,135a), dud (21c,54a), lud (100a), Lud (23c, 144b), mud (6c), pud (59d,73c,115a), rud (26d,57b), sud (59a)

U - E   ube (185b), ule (23a,27d,134c,158c,168d), ume (11d), une (13b, 61a,62b,95c), ure (40a,139d,155d,158b,d), Ure (138d,185d), use (7b,47a,49d,64c,109b,168b,c,181b), Ute (145c,180b), uve (185b)

- UE   cue (7a,27b,92c,117d,124b,132c,146c,159a), due (7b,115b,124c), gue (176c), hue (33c,143b), lue (146b), pue (52c), que (62d), rue (76a,b,129c,150d,183a), sue (119c), Sue (63a,178a,183c), tue (114b)

UF -   ufo (59a)

- UF   ouf (52c)

UG -   ugh (52c)

- UG   bug (24b,66b,81b), dug, fug (129a), hug (32c,49b), jug (118c, 123d), lug (27a,45d,47b,73c,136b), Lug (28b), mug (46b,54a,65a), pug (45a,101a,108a,148d), rug, tug (45d,125b), vug (28a,66a)

U - H   ugh (52c), ush

- UH   auh (52c), huh (52c)

UI -   uit (47a,111d,151a)

U - I   ubi (90a,180d,185b), Udi (108a), uji (146d), uni (34c,118d,122c), Uni (51d), UPI (107a,182d), Uri (162d), uvi (185b)

- UI   dui (46d), hui (14a,30b,56d,114c), Kui (86a,88c,146a), qui (62d), Sui (30b), tui (47c,114b,117a)

UJ -   uji (146d)

- UK   auk (19b), ouk (140c), Suk (107b)

UL -   ula (72c,158c), ule (23a,27d,134c,158c,168d), Ull (7c,68c,146b, 164d), ulm (49c), Ulm (40d), ulo (34b,80d), ulu (87a)

U - L   Ull (7c,68c,146b,164d)

296

- UL **Bul** (25d,102a), **Ful** (158b), **gul** (134a), **mul** (188), **nul** (108c,177a), **pul** (190), **Pul** (14a)

UM - **Uma** (43a,69b,153d), **ume** (11d), **umu** (112a)

U - M **ulm** (49c), **Ulm** (40d)

- UM **aum** (189), **bum** (21b), **cum** (159b), **dum** (45c,67b,113a), **gum** (7b, 53c,80b,130c,156b), **hum** (24d,46b,150d), **Jum** (39c), **lum** (30a), **mum** (30d,95a,146c), **rum** (8c,92d), **sum** (8a,123a,167c), **tum** (26d), **Tum** (143a,159b)

UN - **Una** (54a,153b,170c,183c), **und** (66b), **une** (13b,61a,62b,95c), **uni** (34c,118d,122c), **Uni** (51d), **uno** (83c,151d), **uns** (66d,174c), **Unu** (24d)

U - N **urn** (36c,174d)

- UN **bun** (25b,73b), **dun** (19a,39d,46d,71a,97d,115b,160b), **fun, gun** (56d,131a,146a), **Hun** (16c,21d,174b), **mun** (157b), **nun** (24c,91c, 117d,129d,147b), **Nun** (29a,85c), **pun** (119c), **run** (10d,23c,58d, 110d,148d,153b,154b,167d), **sun** (75d,111a,117b,155b), **tun** (23b, 27a,182b), **wun** (24c), **Yun** (88d)

U - O **udo** (28a,30c,48c,84b,c,d,136c,149d), **ufo** (59a), **uio** (34b,80d), **une** (83c,151d), **Uro** (192)

- UO **duo** (46d,113a,171d), **Luo** (107b), **quo** (188)

UP - **UPI** (107a,182d)

- UP **cup** (46b,69d,118b,170a), **gup** (70a), **hup** (35a), **kup** (188), **pup** (141b,148d,185d), **sup** (46b,104a,162b), **tup** (115a,117d,127d, 143d)

- UQ **suq** (22a,97a)

UR - **urd** (17b,184b), **Urd** (68d,107d), **ure** (40a,139d,155d,158b,d), **Ure** (138d,185d), **Uri** (162d), **urn** (36c,174d), **Uro** (192), **Uru** (192)

- UR **bur** (123b), **cur** (101d), **dur** (95c), **Eur.** (36c), **fur, gur** (159a), **Hur** (91d), **Jur** (107b), **Lur** (116c), **mur** (63a,177d), **nur** (67d), **our** (124c), **pur, rur** (132b), **sur** (34a,62b,d,104b,151a,152d,174a), **tur** (14d,27c,68a,79b,117d,174c)

US - **use** (7b,47a,49d,64c,109b,168b,c,181b), **ush**

U - S **uns** (66d,174c)

-US **aus** (66c), **Aus** (98b), **bus** (125b,168b), **Gus** (96a), **Jus** (61d,90b), **Mus** (104a,132c), **ous** (158b), **pus, rus** (89b,138a), **sus** (117c), **Sus** (160c,181b)

UT - **uta** (53a,84d,93b,147c,150b), **Ute** (145c,180b), **utu** (35b, 137c), **Utu** (96c,107a,159b)

U - T **uit** (47a,111d,151a)

- UT **aut** (34d,89d), **but** (36a,52b,156b,173c), **cut** (30c,32b,145c), **fut** (188), **gut** (114d,130a), **hut** (143c), **jut** (53a,124a), **lut** (189), **mut** (39c), **Mut** (9b,127a), **nut** (24c,32d,38b,54d,64a,65d,86b,141c, 165a), **Nut** (69a), **out** (6b,14b,60b,69d,80a,108b,185c), **put** (65a, 69d,90b), **rut** (73a), **tut** (52c)

U - U **ulu** (87a), **umu** (112a), **Unu** (24d), **Uru** (192), **utu** (35b,137c), **Utu** (96c,107a,159b)

UV - **uva** (64a,70c), **uve** (185b), **uvi** (185b)

- UX aux (6d,61a), dux (31d,64a,90c), lux (79d), rux (154a,184d)
- UY buy, guy (55b,131b,155d), Guy (96a), muy (152d,175d), puy (61d)
- UZ guz (188)
VA - Vac (153b), vae (176b), vag (174b,178a), Val (91d), van (7b,59d, 60a,63d,90c), vas (46d,89d,119c,133b,175d), vat (31b,36c,163a, 170c), vau (91c)
V - A via (132a,133a,b,179a)
- VA ava (78d,86a,116a,120d,139a,167b), Ava (24c), Eva (157a,183c), iva (76a,97b,127b,185b), ova (48d), uva (64a,70c)
V - C Vac (153b)
V - D Vod (16a)
VE - vee (58a,91c,106a), Vei (91d), vet, vex (7c,10d,44c,82c)
V - E vae (176b), vee (58a,91c,106a), vie (36c,157c,170c), voe (17a,81b)
- VE ave (54c,71d,73a,122a,134a,136d), eve (47a,131a,143a,165d,171c), Eve (183c), ive (158c), uve (185b)
V - F vif (62a)
V - G vag (174b,178a), vog (189), vug (28a,66a)
VI - via (132a,133a,b,179a), vie (36c,157c,170c), vif (62a), vim (50b, 176b), vin (63a,182b), vir (89c), vis (59d,89b,d,90b,176b), vix, (89d,138b), viz (105b)
V - I Vai (91d), Vei (91d)
- VI ovi (34a), uvi (185b)
V - L vol (155a,182d)
V - M vim (50b,176b)
V - N van (7b,59d,60a,63d,90c), vin (63a,182b), von (66d,67a)
VO - Vod (16a), voe (17a,81b), vog (189), vol (155a,182d), von (66d, 67a), Vor (68d), Vot (56d), vow (119c,150a), vox (90a,177a)
V - R vir (89c), Vor (68d)
V - S vas (46d,89d,119c,133b,175d), vis (59d,89b,d,90b,176b)
V - T vat (31b,36c,163a,170c), vet, Vot (56d)
VU - vug (28a,66a)
V - U Vau (91c)
V - W vow (119c,150a)
V - X vex (7c,10d,44c,82c), vix (89d,138b), vox (90a,177a)
V - Z viz (105b)
- VY ivy (32b,38c,176b)
WA - wad (94d,97b,109c,112b,149d), wag (85b,104a,183a), wah (113c), wan (113a), war (157c), was (166c,175c), Was (24d), wat (73d, 140d,163a,180b), waw (12b,91c), wax (28b,72a,80c,120c), way (37d,96b,134b,164d)
W - A Wea (192)
- WA awa (100a,139a), iwa (63c)
W - B web (50d,70a,98c,99a,106c,149b)
W - D wad (94d,97b,109c,112b,149d), wed (97a,173c)

WE - Wea (192), web (50d,70a,98c,99a,106c,149b), wed (97a,173c), wee (52c,100c,148c), Wei (30b,162b), wen (40c,72a,110a,170c,177b), wet (40d,46a,101a,124a,127c,149c), wey (173b)

W - E wee (52c,100c,148c), woe (25b), wye (91c)

- WE awe (81d,100a,130d,175b,182b), ewe (88a,143d), owe

W - G wag (85b,104a,183a), wig (73b)

WH - who (129c), why (52c)

W - H wah (113c)

WI - wig (73b), win (7a,17b,64b,123b), wis (79d,164c), wit (78d,85b, 177b)

W - I Wei (30b,162b)

- WI Twi (69c)

- WL awl (145b,167a), owl

- WM cwm (31b,37b,103d)

WN - WNW (35b)

W - N wan (113a), wen (40c,72a,110a,170c,177b), win (7a,17b,64b,123b), won, wun (24c) wyn (110a)

- WN awn (12c,17b,140a), own (6d)

WO - woe (25b), won, woo, wop, wow (52c,158a)

W - O who (129c), woo

- WO Lwo (107b), Pwo (88c), two (26c,37d,80a,93a)

W - P wop

WR - wry (13d)

W - R war (157c)

WS - WSW (35b)

W - S was (166c,175c), Was (24d), wis (79d,164c)

W - T wat (73d,140d,163a,180b), wet (40d,46a,101a,124a,127c), wit (78d,85b,177b)

WU - wun (24c)

W - W waw (12b,91c), WNW (35b), wow (52c,158a), WSW (35b)

W - X wax (28b,72a,80b,120c)

WY - wye (91c), wyn (110a)

W - Y way (37d,96b,134b,164d), wey (173b), why (52c), wry (13d)

XA - xat (167c)

- XA oxa (29c)

XE - xer (34a)

- XE axe (30c,40c,167a), Exe (43a)

- XO exo (122d)

X - R xer (34a)

X - T xat (167c)

YA - yah (52c), yak (112c,161d,165b), yam (48c,121d,160b,170c), Yao (30a,c,104b), yap (16c,29b,122a), yar (72a), Yau (30c), yaw (43a, 155d)

Y - A yea (7c,175c)

- YA aya (77b,166b), Aya (143c), iya (95b,108d,111c), Mya (31c)

YE - yea (7c,175c), yen (33b,42d,93c,174a), yep, yes (7c,55a), yet (18b, 24d,64c,77c,80a,108c,156b,165b), yew (36a,52a,b,145d,168c,d) yez

- YE aye (7c,9b,55a,60a), bye (38c,141d), dye (33c,154d), eye (93d, 111b,140d), lye (8d,27d,93b), nye (72a,116d), Nye (9c,18b), oye (139c), Pye (50d,55a), rye (28b,70b,72d), sye (40c,46c,139b,141a, 167a), tye (28c,134a), wye (91c)

- YG tyg (46b)

Y - H yah (52c)

YI - yin (140a), Yin (30b,143c,185b), yip (16c)

Y - I yoi (52c,79a)

Y - K yak (112c,161d,165b), yok (10c,185a)

- YL kyl (76d,79b)

Y - M yam (48c,121d,160d,170c), yom (41a)

- YM gym (154a), Nym (54c,76a)

Y - N yen (33b,42d,93c,174a), yin (140a), Yin (30b,143c,185b), yon (44c,112a,164d), Yun (88d)

- YN lyn (140c,178d), syn (122d,183b), wyn (110a)

YO - yoi (52c,79a), yok (10c,185a), yom (41a), yon (44c,112a,164d), you, yow (52c)

Y - O Yao (30a,c,104b)

- YO iyo (7d,176b)

Y - P yap (16c,29b,122a), yep, yip (16c)

- YP cyp (169d), gyp (29b,42a,160c), hyp

Y - R yar (72a)

- YR pyr (92a,b,122c,173b), Tyr (7c,68c,109c,147d,163d,170c,178a)

Y - S yes (7c,55a)

- YS iys (58b,92b)

Y - T yet (18b,24d,64c,77c,80a,108c,156b,165b)

YU - Yun (88d)

Y - U Yau (30c), you

- YU ayu (160c)

Y - W yaw (43a,155d), yew (36a,52a,b,145d,168c,d), yow (52c)

- YX Nyx (69b), pyx (31a,51d,75d)

Y - Z yez

ZA zac (27c), zag (84a), zak (188), Zai (135d), Zan (186b), zar (188), zat (148a), zax (148a)

Z - A zea (95c), Zoa (20b)

Z - C zac (27c)

Z - D zed (91c)

ZE - zea (95c), zed (91c), zee (81b,91c), zel (40c), Zen (24a), Zep, zer (188)

Z - E zee (81b,91c), Zoe (36b,183c)

Z - F   **Zif** (102a)

Z - G   **zag** (84a), **zig** (84a)

Z - H   **zoh** (13d,186b)

ZI -   **Zif** (102a), **zig** (84a), **Zio** (147d,163d), **zip** (24b,50b,176b), **Ziu** (147d,163d)

Z - K   **zak** (188)

Z - L   **Zal** (135d), **zel** (40c)

Z - N   **Zan** (186b), **Zen** (24a)

ZO -   **zoa** (20b), **Zoe** (36b,183c), **zoh** (13d,186b), **zoo** (181b)

Z - O   **Zio** (147d,163d), **zoo** (181b)

- ZO   **azo** (107c)

Z - P   **Zep, zip** (24b,50b,176b)

Z - R   **zar** (188), **zer** (188)

Z - T   **zat** (148a)

Z - U   **Ziu** (147d,163d)

Z - X   **zax** (148a)

FOUR-LETTER WORDS

AA - -   **Aalu** (6b,48d), **Aani** (45a,48d), **Aare, Aaru** (6b,48d)

- AA -   **baal** (142b), **baas** (97c), **caam** (93d), **Faam** (111a), **gaal** (23b,174d), **Haab** (97d), **haaf** (57d), **haak** (57b,178a), **haar** (139c), **kaan** (93d, 116c), **kaat** (105d), **laap** (51d,91b,141d), **maal** (188), **ma'am** (95a, 166b), **maar** (177a), **Maas** (132a), **Maat** (69a,b,85d), **Naab, naam** (44c), **Naam** (105b), **paal** (188), **paar** (28c,137a), **raab** (32d), **raad** (14a,49b,151a,165b), **Raad** (151a), **raas** (91b), **Saad** (12b), **saah** (188), **saal** (66c,73b), **Saan** (24d), **Saar** (63b,102d,132a), **Taal** (7d, 88c,151a), **taar** (12b), **Waac, waag** (71d,101d)

- - AA   **blaa, chaa** (162b), **draa** (188)

A - - A   **Abba** (20a,55a,161c), **Abfa** (76b), **Abia** (18d,137a), **abra** (26b), **Abra, acca** (53b,d), **acta** (41d,123d,128d,164c), **adda** (147d), **Adda** (68c,119d,157a,182a), **aera** (8a), **Aeta** (94d,100a,106b,117a), **Afra** (183c), **agha** (35a,171a), **agla** (7a), **agra** (26d,34d), **Agra** (161b), **agua** (152d,166c,178c), **Aida** (110d,175c), **Aira** (70d), **Akha** (86a,c), **akia** (74c), **Akka** (125d), **akra** (176a), **Akra** (191), **akua** (120d), **alba** (98b,181a), **Alba** (151d), **Alca** (14c,128b), **alda** (152b), **Alda** (110d,150c), **Alea** (14b,31c,167d), **alfa** (70d), **alga** (141b,c), **alia** (89d), **alla** (6d), **alma** (40d,53d,146d,147a), **Alma** 38d, 183c), **alta** (89c,152d), **Alva** (151d), **Alya** (155b,c), **amba** (161a), **amia** (22c,170d), **amla** (48a,161d,168c,169a), **amma** (6a), **amra** (77c), **anba** (36d), **anda** (23a,168c), **anna** (190), **Anna** (110c,166d, 183c), **anoa** (28a,60a,112c,181c), **ansa** (73c,93d,137c), **anta** (83d, 117c,d,121a), **Anta** (164a), **apia** (121b), **aqua** (90a,178c), **arba** (135d,171a), **arca** (9a,22c,29d,115a,130a), **Arca** (101b), **area** (37d, 38a,44c,53a,93b,110d,127d,138c,168a,186d), **aria** (8b,98c,150a,c, 170c), **arna** (24a,181b), **Aroa** (175b), **arpa** (83b), **arra** (47d,52c,82b),

Arta (72b), **Arya** (80d), **asea** (39b,177c), **Asha** (191), **Asia** (48a), **asta** (188), **Asta** (107a,164c), **Atka** (11a), **atma** (150d), **atta** (58d, 90c,97d,160c,173d), **Atta** (94d,95d,100a,106b,117a), **atua** (120d), **Auca** (192), **aula** (66c,73b), **aura** (44c,49c,66a,96b,158a,170d, 177c), **Ausa, Azha** (155b)

AB - - **abas** (61c), **Abba** (20a,55a,161c), **abbe** (32b,63b,123b), **Abby** (183d), **ABC's** (57a), **abed** (130c), **Abel** (7a,25b), **abet** (8b,15b,50a, 59b,75d,81c,141d,159d), **Abfa** (76b), **Abia** (18d,137a), **Abib** (102 a,b), **Abie** (96b,107a), **abir** (129a), **able** (26b,35b,126a,147c), **ably** (147c), **aboo** (17a), **Abot** (100c), **Abou** (48b,55a), **abox** (22d), **abra** (26b), **Abra, abri** (61c,62c,144b), **Absi** (191), **abut** (22a, 167c)

- AB - **baba** (108d,120c,166c,171a), **babe, Babi** (116c), **babu** (77a), **baby, caba** (184c), **Faba, gabe** (162a), **gabi** (162a), **gaby** (59c,146d), **haba** (151d), **habe** (191), **Maba** (103a,168d), **mabi** (58d), **nabk** (30d, 164d), **nabo** (117a), **Nabu** (68c,183d), **Raba, rabi** (38d,74a), **Rabi** (14b,117b), **saba** (56a,117a), **Saba** (143d), **sabe, tabi** (84c, 149d), **tabu** (59d,111d), **Wabi** (192)

- - AB **Ahab** (18c,26c,85b,86d,100d,116a,180b), **Arab** (30a,78b,c,106a, 107c,157b,160c,185d), **blab** (162b), **brab** (113b), **chab** (184a), **crab** (39b,144b,181b), **doab** (157c), **drab** (23d,29c,33d,46d,53b,d), **duab** (157c), **frab** (138c), **grab** (105b,142a,149b), **Haab** (97d), **Joab** (41a), **knab** (107a), **Moab** (18d,85a,86d,94a), **Naab, raab** (32d), **scab** (80b, 107d,157c), **slab** (148b), **snab** (23c,139a), **stab** (14c,87a,117c), **swab** (102b)

A - - B **Abib** (102a,b), **Adib** (155b), **Agib** (12a,42d), **Akab** (18c,26c,85b, 86d,100d,116a,180b), **Arab** (30a,78b,c,106a,107c,157b,160c,185d)

AC - - **acca** (53b,d), **Acer** (96c), **ache** (79a,112d,185b), **acht** (66c), **achy, acid** (151a,162a), **Acis** (64b), **acle** (13d,82c,115d), **acme** (39c,115c, 186b), **acne** (147c), **acon** (62c,140d), **acor** (6d), **acre** (39b,56a,88b), **Acre, acta** (41d,123d,128d,164c), **acth** (13b), **acto** (152b), **Acts, actu** (7a,89a), **acus** (89d,118a), **acyl** (6d)

- A C - **Bach** (35c), **back** (75d,76d,159d), **Caca** (67a), **caco** (73b), **dace** (57a,b), **each, face** (159d,176c), **fact** (7a,128b), **hack** (40a,77c, 184d), **jaca** (84a), **jack** (26c,58a,127c), **Jack** (96b), **jacu** (19a,151b), **lace** (58b,179c), **lack** (178a), **lact** (34c), **lacy, mace** (49d,108d,153b, 154d,161a,178a), **mack, nach, paca** (132c,154a), **pace** (64b,98a, 153b,156a,170b,177d), **pack** (24b,140d), **paco** (9b,146d), **pacs** (94c), **pact** (8a), **raca** (19a,59c,130b,184d), **race** (116a,153b,154b, 169c), **rack** (32c,64b), **racy** (153b), **sack** (43d,118a,119d,182b), **saco** (189), **tace** (13a,155d), **tack** (28d,37d,54d), **tact** (43c,d,116a), **Vach** (153b), **Waco, Zach** (96b)

- - AC **utac** (22d), **Waac**

A - - C **aesc** (12d,64d), **alec** (10a,57c,d,76c,137c), **amic** (9d), **avec** (63a, 183a)

AD - - **adad** (52c,56a), **Adad** (68c,157a,182a), **Adah** (25b,51b), **Adam** (26b,96a,111c) **adan** (102d), **Adar** (85c,102a), **adat** (90b,95d), **adda** (147d), **Adda** (68c,119d,157a,182a), **Addu** (68c,157a,182a), **Addy** (183d), **aden** (34b), **Aden, Ader** (18d), **Ades** (73a), **Adib** (155b), **adit** (51a,100a,114d), **admi** (65d), **ador** (153b), **adry** (164c), **adze** (40c,167a)

302

- AD -   Badb (82b), bade, cade (25c,27a,76c,85d,116d), Cade (50c), cadi (12a,103a,171a), cady (69d), Dada (13b,63a,157d), dado (41c,111c, 115c,177d), Eads (23b,24b,50b,82a), fade (181d,183b), fado (121c), fady, gade, hade (66a,148c,173c), hadj (98b,118a), jade (33c,65d,71d,166a), jadu (95a), jady, kada (188), kade (144a), kadi (103a,171a), Kadu (191), lade (24c,26d,43c,93b,100a,132a,139d, 161b,178d), Ladd (143c), lady, made, Madi (174a), mado (14d,57a, 170b), padi (131b), rada (135c,172a), rade (138d), sadd (33a,40b, 58c,107b), sade (91d), sadh (77a), sado (26d,84d), sadr (94a), Sadr (155b), vade (42c,67d,89b), wadd (109c), wade, wadi (46c,106a, 109a,128a,132a), wady (109a,128a,132a)

- - AD   adad (52c,56a), Adad (68c,157a,182a), arad (13a,c,84a), bead (17a, 122a,146b), brad (54d,67c,105b), Chad (158b), clad (46a,82a), dead, diad (113a), duad (113a,171d), dyad (113a), ecad (73a, 119b), egad (100a,109a), Fuad (54d), glad (85c), goad (80b,154b), grad (28b), head (29d), ibad (191), irad (18d), Joad (50c), lead (35d,43d,72b,74d,81a), load (24c,26d,161b), mead (46a,78a,97d, 99b), Mead (78a), orad (104a), Phad (155b), quad (33c,172a), raad (14a,49b,151a,165b), read (116d,157d), road (37d,164d), Saad (12b), scad (31a,57a,78b,88d,137c), shad (27d,57a,b,c), spad (105b), Spad (118d), stad (151b,167d,176b), swad (94d), toad (10a, 17a,63d,126d), udad (143d,144a,181c), woad (20d,47c)

A - - D   abed (130c), acid (151a,162a), adad (52c,56a), Adad (68c,157a, 182a), aged (110a), alod (51c,55d,88a,124c), amid (9d,50a), apod (59d), arad (13a,c,84a), arid (46c,85a), Arnd (67a), Arod (86c), avid (47b,71a,186b)

AE - -   aera (8a), aeri (34a), aero (8b,34a,b,58c,59a), aery (47b,51d,106c), aesc (12d,64d), Aeta (94d,95d,100a,106b,117a)

- AE -   Caen, daer (22b), daez, faex (46a), Gaea (47d,69a), Gael (28a,96c, 138d), haec (90a,164c), haem (122b), Jael (147b), iaet (60d), nael (189), saer (163a), tael (91d,179d), waeg (19b,72c,87a), waer (40b)

- - AE   aiae (182d), biae (93b), brae (76d,139a,c,140b,148c), irae (43c), koae (74b), quae (176b), spae (139c)

A - - E   Aare, abbe (32b,63b,123b), Abie (96b,107a), able (26b,35b,126a, 147c), ache (79a,112d,185b), acle (13d,82c,115d), acme (39c,115c, 186b), acne (147c), acre (39b,56a,88b), Acre, adze (40c,167a), agee (13d,15c,38d), ague (30a,55d,95c,137b), aide (7b,14a,75d), aile (62b,63a,182c,d), aine (49b,62c,142c), aire (82c), Aire, ajee (15c,139a), akee (168c), alae (182d), albe (133a)
  alee (15c,75d,144b,157a,182a), Alle (14c), alme (40d,147a), aloe (7d,20a,76a,b,92b,98b,119b,158b,167a,183d), amie (61d), ance (158b,c,d), Ande (193), ange (61a), Anne (50c,84a,143b,183c), ante (87a,89a,115b,120b,122b,125d,154d), a-one (52b,167b), apse (9b, 20a,31a,128c,130a,142b,175a), arme (63a,179b), Arne (35c,50c, 134d), asse (25a,60d,74a), atle (136d,161d,169b), Aude, auge (123c,132b), aune (188), axle (153c,180c)

AF - -   afar (44c), Afar (6c), afer (48a,182b), affy (18b), Afra (183c)

- AF -   baff (69d), baft (14a,53b), cafe, daff (125d), daft (59c), gaff (57c, d,152d,153a), haft (76d), Kafa (6c), raff (75b), raft (27b,33c,58c, 75b), safe (141d,157d,174d), Safi (191), Taft (29d), Wafd (49a), waft (20d,58c)

303

- - AF   deaf, goaf (104b), Graf (37c,66b,67a,107c,186b), haaf (57d), heaf (144a), leaf (55c,73c,119b), loaf (79b,94b), neaf (58a,73c), Olaf (108a,176b), Piaf (63c), Wraf

A - - F   alef (91c), alif (12b), arif (127d), atef (39a,48d), Azof (20b,135d)

AG - -   Agag (18c,86c,137a), agal (17c,36d), Agao (6c,73c), agar (7d,28c, 39c,103c,141c), Agau (73c), Agaz (193), aged (110a), agee (13d, 15c,38d), ager (47c,56a,89b,c,131d,133b), agha (35a,171a), Agib (12a,42d), agio (52c,60a,101c,123a), Agis (86c), agla (7a), agni (88a,89c), Agni (56d,68b), agog (47b,52c,86b), agon (12c,36c,41b, 55d,71b), agra (26d,34d), Agra (161b), agri (89b), agro (149d), agua (152d,166c,178c), ague (30a,55d,95c,137b)

- AG -   baga (171b), bago (13d), cage (36a), cagy (178b), dagg (118c), dagh (76d), Dago, gage (28d,98a,119c,d), gagi (160b), hagg, hagi (84b), Iago (54b,111d,143c), Jaga (191), jagg, kago (113a), kagu (106c), lago (83b,152b), mage (95b), magg (95b), Magh (102a), magi (123c), Magi (95b,116c,183a), naga (13d,33a,55b,127c), Naga (24c,77a,88c,176d), Nagy (78d), Paga (117a), page (51b,59b, 142d,159b), raga (56d,105a), rage (10c,30c,157a,161d), ragi (28b), saga (79b,91a,138a,157a,161b,c,168a), Saga, sage (13a,90d,100c, 141c,145c,180b,183a), sago (54c,59b,113b,125b,155c), sagy, vagi (38b), wage (27a,115b), yage (23a)

- - AG   Agag (18c,86c,137a), brag (21a,175a), coag (45d,118a,163b), crag (132c), drag (74a,125b), flag (16b,50d,82b,88c,115a,155a), knag (115d,139c), krag (131c), peag (144a,178a), quag (21c,102c), shag (73b,105b,161d,166d), skag (7d,46d), slag (46c,99a,138c,148d, 177a), snag (11b,27b,35c,87c,124b,166a), stag (65a,98d), swag (22a,156c), waag (71d,101d)

A - - G   Agag (18c,86c,137a), agog (47b,52c,86b), ajog, areg (116a,137a)

AH - -   Ahab (18c,26c,85b,86d,100d,116a,180b), Ahaz (86d), ahem, Ahet (49a,102a), ahey (52c), Ahir (27b), Ahom (88c), ahoy (106a), ahum

- AH -   bahi (60c), baho (122a), baht (146a), haha (55c,159c), kaha (123d), kahu (14d), maha (28c,88c,136d), mahr (103a), Oahu, paha (67b), pahi (21b,26a), paho (122a), Rahu (42b,48b), saha, sahh (188), Saho (6c), sahu (153d), taha (179b), tahr (68a,76d)

- - AH   Adah (25b,51b), Amah (95b,108d,111c), arah (52c), ayah (108d), blah, drah (188), Elah (18c,86d), Etah (51c,71d), eyah (95b,108d, 111c), Ivah (18d), kyah (19a), Leah (19a,84a,87b,183c), Noah (88a, 99b), odah (170d), opah (23b,57a,b,86d), prah (21b,26a,95c,d), Ptah (48d,98c), saah (188), seah (188), shah (116c), Utah (180b), yeah

A - - H   acth (13b), Adah (25b,51b), aich (9a), Alph (132a), amah (95b, 108d,111c), ankh (38d,162b), arah (52c), arch (29d,38b,39d,123d, 132c), ayah (108d)

AI - -   aich (9a), Aida (110d, 175c), aide (7b,14a,75d), aile (62b,63a,182c, d), aine (49b,62c,142c), Aino (84a,c), aint, Ainu (84a,c), aipi (27a), Aira (70d), aire (82c), Aire, airs (123b), airy (177a,176d)

- AI -   bail (43c), bain (61a), bait (15d,51a,94d,167b), caid (35a,151d, 152b), cain (169c), Cain (6a,7a,50d,88a,104c,143a), Dail (49a, 82b, c), dain (188), dais (119b), fail, fain (42d,67c,183b), fair (17a,55d),

fait (6d,61b), **Gaia** (47d,69a), **gail** (23b,174d), **Gail** (183d), **gain** (7a,
b,124a,181d), **gait** (96b,179a), **haik** (57b,65b,108a), **hail** (6d,15a,
71d), **hair** (56b,164d), **jail** (123d), **Jain** (77b), **kaid** (29d,66a), **kaif**
(88c), **kaik** (96c), **kail** (18c,22a,25a,79b), **Kain, kair, laic** (32b,90b,
107d,124a,141d), **laid, lain, lair** (37c,42b), **Lais** (17c), **lait** (62a),
Maia (76b,109a,153b,155b,177c), **maid** (45b,142d), **mail** (12d,99b,
121c), **maim** (43d,81a,105c), **mair** (29d,35d,123d), **mais** (61b), **Naia**
(33a), **naid** (63c), **naif** (74b,105d), **naik, nail** (31d,54d,141d,161d,
173a), **naio** (107a,168c), **Nair** (45d), **nais** (63c,132a), **paid** (129c),
pail, pain (7c), **pair** (22d,37d,85b,171d), **pais** (37d), **qaid** (35a), **raia**
(107d), **Raia** (147b), **raid** (59d,80c), **raik** (188,189), **rail** (16b,19b,c,
37a,97b,138c,150c,177b), **rain** (121d,162d), **raip** (36d), **rais** (26c,
29d,75a,103b), **Rais** (106b), **saic** (86b,91d,175d), **said** (174c), **Said**
(42d,101a,121b), **sail** (144c,185a), **sain** (20c,38d,48a), **sair** (140b,
150d), **sais** (48d,71d), **tail** (11d,27d,59b,143b), **tain** (166a), **tair**
(68a,76d), **tait** (14d), **vail** (94b,124a,174d), **vain** (81a), **vair** (64c,
154c), **waif** (157b), **wail** (39b,88a), **wain** (177b), **Wain, wait** (26d,
42b,92c,155d,162a), **zaim** (170d), **zain** (41a)

- - **AI**   **alai** (171a), **Alai** (135c), **anai** (163b,181a), **chai** (72d), **goal** (106d,
168c), **ngai** (48a,159c), **peai** (98b), **quai** (88b,117c,180c), **Thai**
(146a)

A - - I   **Aani** (45a,48d), **abri** (61c,62c,144b), **Absi** (191), **admi** (65d), **aeri**
(34a), **agni** (88a,89c), **Agni** (56d,68b), **agri** (89b), **aipi** (27a), **aiai**
(171a), **Alai** (135c), **Albi** (58a), **alli** (74c,134c), **ambi** (34a,122c),
amli (48a,161d,168c,169a), **ammi** (98c), **amoi** (62a), **anai** (163b,
181a), **Andi** (27d), **anti** (7d,111a,122b), **Anti** (193), **apii** (74c), **arni**
(24a,181b), **arui** (11b,143d,144a,181c), **asci** (154a), **assi** (77d), **Asti**
83d,182b), **Atli** (14c,72b,79a,107d), **Atri, auri** (34a)

AJ - -   **ajar** (110c), **Ajax** (71b,162d), **ajee** (15c,139a), **ajog**

- **AJ -**   **baju** (84a), **caja** (152a), **caji** (180b), **gajo** (107c), **haje** (33a,48d),
maja (151c), **Maja** (153b), **majo, Naja** (33a), **pajo** (122a), **raja** (77a,
123c), **Raja, tajo** (152a,d), **yaje** (23a)

AK - -   **Akal** (56d), **Akan** (191), **akee** (168c), **akey** (189), **Akha** (86a,c), **akia**
(74c), **Akim** (135d,191), **akin** (8b,92b,129c), **Akka** (125d), **akov**
(189), **akra** (176a), **Akra** (191), **akua** (120d)

- **AK -**   **baka** (52b), **bake** (139a), **baku** (26d,157b,168c), **cake, caky, fake**
(123a,143c), **faky, hake** (57a,b), **hakh** (46d), **hako** (115b), **haku**
(86d), **jake** (40d), **Jake** (96b), **jako** (71a), **kaka** (114b), **kaki** (84c,
106d), **lake** (117d), **lakh** (110c), **laky, make** (35b,36d,54a,123a)
maki (91b), **mako** (18a,19a,20d,143c,168c,182c), **Maku** (192),
oaks (154d), **oaky, rake** (41b,44c,134b,140d), **Saka** (10a), **sake**
(84b,125d), **saki** (39c,84b,102a), **take, takt** (105a,163a), **Taku**
(80c), **taky, waka** (26a), **wake** (134b,168a), **wakf** (103a), **waky,
Yaka** (191), **Yaki** (193)

- - **AK**   **Anak** (67a), **asak** (13d,168c,169a), **beak** (19a), **coak** (45d,118a,
163b), **dhak** (48a,169a), **Dyak** (22b), **feak** (39d,171c), **flak** (11a),
haak (57b,178a), **Irak** (99a,d), **kiak** (51c), **kyak** (51c), **leak** (110c),
peak (9a,38c,159b,186b), **siak** (72d), **soak** (46c,137c), **teak** (41a,
48a,168c), **weak** (55b)

A - - K   **amok** (18b,63c), **Anak** (67a), **asak** (13d,168c,169a), **asok** (13d),
Atik (155b)

AL - - alae (182d), alai (171a), Alai (135c), alan (45a,79a,183), Alan, alar (15c,145c,182d), alas (52c,136b,183b), alat (136d), alay (96c), alba (98b,181a), Alba (151d), albe (133a), Albi (58a), albe (34d,181a), Alca (14c,128b), alco (45b), alda (152b), Alda (110d, 150c), Alea (14b,31c,167d), alec (10a,57c,d,76c,137c), alee (15c, 75d,144b,157a,182a), alef (91c), alem (98b,155a,170d,171a), alen (40d,138a), alfa (70d), alga (141b,c), Algy (96b), alia (89d), alif (12b), alii (74c,134c), alim (103b,162c), alin (188), alit (44b,143a), Alix (183c), alky, alla (6d), Alle (14c), allo (34c), ally (14a,35c,d, 173c), alma (40d,53d,146d,147a), Alma (38d,183c), alme (40d, 147a), alms (29a), alod (51c,55d,88a,124c), aloe (7d,20a,76a,b,92b, 98b,119b,158b,167a,183d) alop (13d,46b,93d), alow (18a,172c), Alph (132a), Alps (85d), also (10b,18b,80a), alta (89c,152d), alto (152b,176c,177a), alum (14a,45c), Alur (191), Alva (151d), Alya (155b,c), Alys (183c)

- AL - Aalu (6b,48d), Bala (26c,66a), bald (16c), bale (24b,74a), ball, Bali, balk (118c,146a,156b), ball, balm (110a,172c), Balt (93a), balu (104b,159a,181d), cale (72d), calf, calk (78c,109a,141c,178d), call (145c,159b,176d), calm (8d,11d,112b,118d,126c,d,172b,173d), calo (72d), calp (92b), calx (23c,75c,112c), dale (43c,128a,174b), dali (168c,169b), fala (129b), fall (46b,141c), falx (133b), gala (55d), Gala (191), gale (181d), gall (6c), gall (19a,28c,29b,82c,160c, 176a), galt, hala (112b), hale (125b), Hale (9d,131a), half (101a), hall (37b,114d), halm, halo (14d,31b,92a,107b,131d), Hals (47a), halt (13b,28a,38d,156d), lalu (48d), kala (19a), kale (22a,25a, 119b,175a), kali (26d,67c,136d,167a), Kali (147b), kalo (162a), lala (129b), lalo (16b,34d,153a), Lalo (35c), mala (89b,c,90a,94b, 97d,109d,185c), male (154d), Male (45d), mali (27b), mall (95d,124b,143b), malm (32a,92b), malo (23a,74c,152a), malt (17c), Nala (77a), pala (189), Pala (88b), pale (113a,117c,178a), pali (122b), Pali (23d,24a,137b,175a), pall (32d,81b,112a), palm (59b, 168c,169b), palo (152c), palp (11a,55b,58b,167c), paly (194), rale (7c,23a,29d,41b), ralo (188), sala (152a,b,c), Sala (50c), sale (14c,61c,62b,c,168b), salp (109c,148d), salt (35d,105b,123a,136c, 141c,149d), tala (16d,113a,168c,d), talc (28d,63b,99c,100b,122a, 149c), tale (91a,185b), tall (189), talk, tall (118d), vale (54c,128a, 174b), Vale (7c,109c), vali (171a,176a), Vali (7c,109c), wale (70b, 131b,157c,163d,179a,180a,c,d), wall (171a), walk, wall, Walt (96b), Yale (173c), yali (171a)

- - AL agal (17c,36d), Akal (56d), Aral (135d), aval (70c), axal (120b), Baal (142b), beal (139d), bual (182c), coal (49c,64a), cral, deal (11d,16c,36c,44c,81a,168b), dhal (12b), dial (25c), dual (45c,171d), eral (51a), etal (89a), foal (78c), gaal (23b,174d), geal (47d,163c), goal (8b,109b,120b,125d), heal, ical (158c), keal (25a), kral, leal (54b,94c,139d), maal (188), meal (72a,130b), Neal, odal (48a,88b, 112c), opal (20a,65d,67b,82b), oral (114a,153d,174c,175c), oval (48d,49c,127a), paal (188), peal (131c,d), pyal (175c), real (7a), rial (190), ryal (110a,190), saal (66c,73b), seal (10c,d,54d,64c,96a, 118b,128a), sial (112a), Taal (7d,88c,151a), teal (19b,20d,46c,d), udal (76b,88b,131c), unal (147a), ural, Ural (135c), uval (70c), veal, vial (148c), weal (124d,157c,180c,d), zeal (12c,55d)

A - - L Abel (7a,25b), acyl (6d), agal (17c,36d), Akal (56d), amil (45a,48a,

185c), amyl (155c), anil (47c,80d,180b), Aoul (191), Aral (135d), aril (142a), aval (70c), axal (120b), axil (10c), azul (151d)

AM - - amah (95b,108d,111c), amar (189), amba (161a), ambi (34a,122c), ambo (125b,128b), amen (14a,80b,94a,137a,149c,175c,184b), Amen (86d,127d,159b,164a), amer (61c), Ames (9c,82a), Amex (184d), amia (22c,170d), amic (9d), amid (9d,50a), amie (61d), amil (45a,48a,185c), amin (9d), amir (7c,12a,103a,b,123c,170d), amit (94a), amla (48a,161d,168c,169a), amli (48a,161d,168c,169a), amma (6a), ammi (98c), ammo (9d), ammu (9d), amol (62a), amok (18b,63c), Amon (86d,96d,127d,159b,164a), amor (152b), Amor (39c,68b), Amos (96a,144b), Amoy (88c), amra (77c), Amun (86d,127d,159b,164a), amyl (155c)

- AM - came (182b), Came (192), camp (163b), dama (65d,152b), dame (67b,87c,166b), damn, damp (101a), Fama (135a), fame (130a), famn (188), Gama (121c), game (64d,154a), gamp (172a), hami (78a), iamb (59c), jama (103b), jamb (12d,45c,118a,146b,174a), jami (103b), Kama (56d), kame (67b,139b), kami (68a,84b), Kami (88c,107c,144c), lama (23d,24a,91d,165b), Lamb (49c), lame (38d, 43d,73b), lamp (92a,94c), mama, Mama (116d), mamo (19a,d,74b), Nama (78c), name (8a,11b,d,25c,46c,107c,130b,157b,163b,166b), Rama (77a,80b,176d), rame (22d), rami (22d), ramp (65a,80b, 127b,148b), sama (105c,169d), same (44d,79b), samh (56b), samp (70b,77d,121b), Tama (192), tame (45a,b,66a), Tame, tamp (46b, 112b,121d,127d), vamp (80a,145a), Yama (57a,68a), Zama (73d, 141d)

- - AM Adam (26b,96a,111c), anam (159a,168c), Anam, Aram (18d,50c, 105c,144b,161c), Azam (166c), beam, Bram (96a), caam (93d), cham (20a,29d), Cham (8c), clam (20b,101b), cram (157d), dram (46b,110c,121d,148c), edam (29c), Elam (18d,37d,82a,116c,144b), enam (70c,77a), Enam (85c), exam, Faam (111a), flam (169c), foam (63d,154b), gram (29d,99b,148d,160d,180a), Gram, Guam, imam (25c,102d,103a), klam (189), Liam (181d), loam (47d,150a), lyam (139a), ma'am (95a,166b), miam (14d), naam (44c,105b), ogam (82b,c), olam (51a,d,75c,81a), pram (15a), ream (18c,37d, 50d,113d,171c), roam (178a), seam (85b,d,160a,176d,185a), sham (41c,55b,60d,80a,123a,b,146d), Siam (163d,181a), slam (180d, 182d), swam, team (38c,72a,113a), Tiam, tram (170a), Ulam (67b), wham (157c)

A - - M Adam (26b,96a,111c), ahem, Ahom (88c), ahum, Akim (135d,191), alem (98b,155a,170d,171a), alim (103b,162c), alum (14a,45c), anam (159a,168c), Anam, Anim (18d), Aram (18d,50c,105c,144b, 161c), arum (13a,39b,58d,92b,155c), Arum (66a), asem (9a,49a, 69c), Asom (18d), atom (101c,114c,180d), Atum (143a,159b), Azam (166c)

AN - - anai (163b,181a), Anak (67a), anam (159a,168c), anan (49a,159a, 180c), Anas (46c,d), Anat (138c,147d), Anax (43c,120c), anay (72b,163b,181a), anba (36d), ance (158b,c,d), ancy (158c), anda (23a,168c), Ande (193), Andi (27d), Andy (96b), Aner (18d,96b), anes (110c,140a), anet (43c), anew (7c), ange (61a), ango (171a), anil (47c,80d,180b), Anim (18d), anis (55c), ankh (38d,162b), anna (190), Anna (110c,166d,183c), Anne (50c,84a,143b,183c),

307

anoa (28a,60a,112c,181c), **anon** (7d,14d,79d,80b,123a,145c,150c, 164a), **ansa** (73c,93d,137c), **anse** (61d), **ansu** (11d), **anta** (83d, 117c,d,121a), **Anta** (164a), **ante** (87a,89a,115b,120b,122b,125d, 154d), **anti** (7d,111a,122b), **Anti** (193), **anzu** (11d)

- AN -   **Aani** (45a,48d), **Bana** (67a), **banc** (61a,85c), **band** (72a,157c), **bane** (74a,106b,120b,139a), **bang** (75d,105d,148a), **bani** (190), **bank** (18a,58c), **bans, bant** (43c), **Cana** (57a,64b,100c), **cane** (17b, 128a,156a,159a,177d), **Cane, cang** (184a), **cano** (152a), **cant** (28d, 81b,84d,90c,109b,136c,165d,166a), **Dana** (28a,96a,171d), **Dane** (85d,107d,138a), **dang, dank** (40b,101a), **dans** (62a), **Danu** (28a), **fana, fane** (30d,137a,162d), **fang** (167b), **Fano** (51d,96b,113c,d), **gane** (185b), **gang** (38c), **Gano** (132d), **hand** (60c,114c,115d,184c), **hang** (160a), **hank** (147c), **Hano** (125b), **Hans** (66d,96a), **hant** (67a), **Jane** (190), **Jane** (183c), **Jann** (102d), **kana** (84d), **Kane** (74c), **k'ang** (30a), **Kano** (84c,177d), **kant** (28d), **Kant** (67a), **lana** (58a,66a,90a,184b), **land** (44a,163c), **lane** (134b,157b), **lank** (148b,164b), **lanx** (133a,b), **mana** (30a,120d,122a,159c), **mand** (28b), **mane, mani** (115c), **mann** (189), **Mann** (9c,48c,185c), **mano** (71d,73d,74b,83b), **Mans** (30a), **Manu** (10a,76d,77a,b), **Manx** (27b, 28a,82d), **many** (108d), **nana** (118b), **Nana** (15c,105d,116d,186d), **nane** (139d), **Pana, pane** (113c,155a,b), **pang** (165b), **Pani** (120c), **pank** (189), **pant, rana** (77a,123c), **Rana** (63d), **rand** (16d,22a, 131b,145a,b), **Rand** (69c), **rang, rani** (72d,77b,123c,127c), **rank** (31c,55d,70b,92c,94d,157d), **rann** (175c), **rant** (41c,127b,128a, 161d), **sana** (56a,166d), **Sana** (185d), **sand** (71d,146c), **sane** (128a), **sang, sank, sano** (152b), **sans** (63a,183b), **tana** (159a), **Tana** (87d), **Tane** (120d), **tang** (30b,58b,186b), **tanh** (97c), **tank** (175a,d), **Tano** (192), **uang** (131a), **vane** (179b,182a), **vang** (72d,134a,140b), **Vans** (107d), **wand** (120b,132c,156a), **wane** (41c,43c), **wang** (189), **want** (41b,42d,87b,106b,122a), **wany, Yana** (192,193), **yang** (30b,70a), **yank, Yank, zany** (24a,32d,59c)

- - AN   **adan** (102d), **Akan** (191), **alan** (45a,79a,183c), **Alan** (96a), **anan** (49a,159a,180c), **Aran** (18c,48c,64d,82d,174c), **Awan** (191), **azan** (102d), **bean** (91b,142a,175a), **bran** (23c,39a,72a,79c,70b), **Bran** (23c,50c), **chan** (26c,130c), **clan** (169c), **Coan** (37b), **cran** (160c), **cyan, dean** (33c,109d), **dhan** (124c), **dian** (46c,130d,170b), **Dian** (68d,69a,c,102b), **duan** (64b), **elan** (12c,41a,50d,62a,153c,177a, 186b), **Eoan** (41a,85b), **Evan** (96a), **Ewan, flan** (39d,40a,114d), **gean** (29c), **Goan, gran, guan** (151b), **Iban** (47c), **Iran** (6a,48c, 116b), **Ivan** (40c,85b,96a), **Jean** (37c), **Jean** (183c), **Joan** (183c), **Juan** (113a), **Juan** (96a), **kaan** (93d,116c), **khan** (7c,26c,81b,93d, 116c,123c,130c,166c), **kran** (190), **kuan** (30b,c), **Kuan, kwan** (30b), **lean** (128a,148b,152d,164b,166a), **loan, mean** (15a,42b, 146c,156b), **mian** (97c,147b,166b), **moan, ngan, oban** (190), **Olan** (115c), **Oman** (159a), **Onan** (18c,85c), **Oran, oxan, pean** (65c), **plan** (99b,124a,138b), **quan** (190), **roan** (78b,c,114c,128d,144a, 181a), **Saan** (24d), **Sean** (85b,96a), **Shan** (13c,80d,88c,101d), **scan** (52b,93d,98a,116d,128b,c,140d), **span** (23b,107b,113a,128b,162c), **Svan** (27d), **swan** (19b,33a) **tean** (140c167a), **than** (35b), **tran** (7a), **tuan** (95d,147b,166c), **ulan** (27d,88a), **uran** (101d), **Uran, uzan** (189), **wean** (8d,42d), **yean** (88a), **yuan** (190), **Yuan** (30b,101d)

A - - N acon (62c,140d), adan (102d), aden (34b), Aden, agon (12c,36c, 41b,55d,71b), Akan (191), akin (8b,92b,129c), alan (45a,79a, 183c), Alan (96a), alen (40d,138a), alin (188), amen (14a, 80b,94a,137a,149c,175c,184b), Amen (86d,127d,159b,164a), amin (9d), Amon (86d,96b,127d,159b,164a), Amun (86d,127d, 159b,164a), anan (49a,159a,180c), anon (7d,14d,79d,80b,123a, 145c,150c,164a), Aran (18c,48c,64d,82d,174c), Asin (102a), aten (150a,159b), aton (150a,159b), Avon (143b), Awan (191) axon (106c,153c), ayin (91c), azan (102d), azon (127b)

AO - - aone (52b,167b), Aoul (191)

- AO - faon (33c,55a), gaol (123d), Gaol (164a), Gaon (85b), jaob, Laos (80d,129c), naos (28a,71c,137a,163a), Naos (155b), paon (115b), Taos (192), Yaou (30c)

- - AO Agao (6c,73c), dhao (24c), grao (189), guao (168c,169b), Miao (30a,b), omao (165b), prao (21b,26a,95c,d), tiao

A - - O aboo (17c), acto (152b), aero (8b,34a,b,58c,59a), Agao (6c,73c), agio (52c,60a,101c,123a), agro (149d), Aino (84a,c), albo (34d, 181a), alco (45b), allo (34c), also (10b,18b,80a), alto (152b,176c, 177a), ambo (125b,128b), ammo (9d), ango (171a), apio (125b), areo (34c), Argo (12c,36b,c), Arno (27a), aroo (80c,82b), arro (52c), arto (34a), asno (151d), Ateo (120d), atmo (34d,174d), auto (34d)

AP - - Apap (102a), apar (12d), aper (32d), Apet (97c), apex (39c,76c, 115c,118b,159b,166a,167b), apia (121b), apii (74c), apio (125b), Apis (17c,24b,49a,125a,136a), apod (59d), apse (9b,20a,31a,128c, 130a,142b,175a), Apsu (29a), Apus (36b,c)

- AP - capa (152a,166d), cape (75a,96c,124b,161a), caph (91c), capp (27a), gape (185b), gapo (60a), gapy, Hapi (66a,107b,136a), hapu (106d), jape (85a,b), kapa (74b), kaph (91d), kapp, Lapp (108a), mapo (68a,148d), napa (25c,67d,90d), Napa (182c), nape (15b, 108c,d), napu (29d,80d), papa, pape (19b,113a), rapt (6c,27a,50d), sapa (70c), sapo (149c,166d), tapa (16c,32c,53b,56a,74b,104b,112b, 113d,120d), tape (16a,19a,128d), tapu, wapp (54b,133d,145d), yapa (113b), Yapp (22a)

- - AP Apap (102a), atap (113b), chap (55b), clap (58b), drap (61b,c, 62a), flap (17b,59a,104a,118d,161a,182d), frap (45d,165c), heap (117d), knap (76d,107a,139b,159b,166a,170c,185b), laap (51d,91b, 141d), leap (26c), neap (165c,167a,177b), plap (54b), reap (7a,40a, 74a), shap, slap (24a,128c,148c), snap (23a,36d,38b,48b,54d,56c, 58c,149d), soap, swap (168a), trap (27b,67b,132b,149b), wrap (32b,51a)

A - - P alop (13d,46b,93d), Apap (102a), asop (180b), atap (113b), atip (14b,166a), atop (112a,174a)

AQ - - aqua (90a,178c)

- AQ - waqf (103a)

- - AQ Iraq (99a,d)

AR - - Arab (30a,78b,c,106a,107c,157b,160c,185d), arad (13a,c,84a), arah (52c), Aral (135d), Aram (18d,50c,105c,144b,161c), Aran (18c, 48c,64d,82d,174c), arar (137a,168c), Aras, arba (135d,171a), arca

309

(9a,22c,29d,115a,130a), **Arca** (101b), **arch** (29d,38b,39d,123d, 132c), **area** (37d,38a,44c,53a,93b,110d,127d,138c,168a,186d), **areg** (116a,137a), **areo** (34c), **Ares** (49b,51b,68c,76a,97a,105c,110b, 178a,186d), **aret** (128c), **Argo** (12c,36b,c), **aria** (8b,98c,150a,c, 170c), **arid** (46c,85a), **arif** (127d), **aril** (142a), **aris** (101b), **arme** (63a,179b), **arms, army** (78c), **arna** (24a,181b), **Arnd** (67a), **Arne** (35c,50c,134d), **arni** (24a,181b), **Arno** (27a), **arn't, Aroa** (175b), **Arod** (86c), **aroo** (80c,82b), **arow** (92c,158b), **arpa** (83b), **arra** (47d,52c,82b), **arro** (52c), **Arta** (72b), **arto** (34a), **arts** (138c), **arty, arui** (11b,143d,144a,181c), **arum** (13a,39b,58d,92b,155c), **Arum** (66a), **Arya** (80d)

- **AR** - **Aare, Aaru** (6b,48d), **bara** (188), **barb** (20b,57d,78b,117d,120a,b, 124b), **bard** (12d,120a), **bare** (43d,157c), **bari** (79c), **Bari** (37c,83d), **bark** (115c), **barm** (185b), **barn** (156d), **baro** (71a,122c), **barr** (49b), **Bart** (96b), **baru** (168c), **cara** (83a), **Cara** (48b,183c), **card** (33d, 114d), **care** (11b,14c,35d,150a,184d), **cark** (26d,184d), **carl** (115c, 135d), **Carl** (96a), **carn** (156c), **caro** (83a,183d), **carp** (27d,38d, 40c,55a,56c,57a), **carr** (120d,140a), **cart** (171d,175a,177b), **Dara** (18d), **Dard**, **dare** (28d,41b,42a,74d,175b), **Dare** (57a), **dari** (38a, 70b), **dark** (47a,67d,109b,160b), **darn** (130b), **darr** (163c), **dart** (13b,88a,100c,120b,153a,160c), **Dart** (100c), **earl** (107c), **earn** (42d,64b,99a), **fard** (112d), **fare** (43c,59b,67d,123b), **farl** (138c, 140b), **farm** (165d), **faro** (65a), **gara** (190), **garb** (32c,46a), **gare** (61b,c,62c,127c,184b), **Garm** (178c), **garn** (67d,185b), **Garo** (88c), **Harb** (191), **hard** (109b), **hare** (91b,132c), **hark** (92d), **harl** (16b,56b, 59a), **harm** (40b,81a), **harp** (105a,129a), **hart** (41d,154d), **jarl** (40d, 107d), **kara** (132a), **Kari** (14d), **Karl** (96a), **karn** (156c), **karo** (106d), **Lara** (25c), **lard** (54d,61a,71a,110a), **lari** (78a,101c), **Lari** (72c), **lark** (19a,63d,177b), **larp** (51d,121b), **mara** (114d), **Mara** (24a,d,105b,107b), **marc** (70c), **Marc** (96a), **mare** (78b,108b), **mari** (16a,61d), **mark, Mark** (52a,96a,146b,155a), **marl** (32a,42c, 55d), **maro** (144d), **Mars** (68c,118d,119a,178a), **mart** (49d,97a), **Mart** (96b,183d), **maru** (84c,144d), **Mary** (50c,126b,183c), **nard** (13a, 97c,102b,110a,153c), **Nare** (93c), **nark** (81a,156d), **nary** (108b), **oary, para** (134c,170d), **Para** (18a,51d), **parc** (62b,112c), **pard** (27b, 91b), **pare** (115c,129a), **pari** (34a,180a), **park, parr** (136d,147c), **pars** (89d), **part** (44d,60d,121c,159c), **paru** (57a), **rara** (119a), **rare** (138b,164b,172b,173d), **Sara** (24d,183c), **sard** (26d,28d,65d,111a, 142b,156d), **Sarg** (96d,125c), **sari** (48b,65b,77b), **Sark** (28d), **Sart** (82b, 103b, 170d), **tara** (22a, 55c, 113a, 168c), **Tara** (82b,c,138b), **tare** (9a,18d,41a,176a,179d), **tari** (47d,69a), **tarn** (87d,103d,120d), **taro** (13c,48c,49b,64b,112b,120a,133d,155c,170a, c), **tarp** (26b,178d), **tart** (114d), **vara** (151d), **vare** (179b), **vari** (34d,91b,134d,174d), **vary** (28d,43c), **ward** (31c,55c,86b), **ware** (27d,35a), **warf, warm** (7c,75b,163b), **warn** (7b), **warp** (36c,165a, 171c), **wart** (124d), **wary** (27d,176b), **yard** (152d), **yare** (96b,124b, 128b), **yark** (22c), **yarl** (40d,107d), **yarn** (154b,161b,184b), **yarr** (72a), **Yaru** (48d), **zarf** (39c,155a), **zarp** (120c)

- - **AR** **Adar** (85c,102a), **afar** (44c), **Afar** (6c), **agar** (7d,28c,39c,103c,141c), **ajar** (110c), **alar** (15c,145c,182d), **amar** (189), **apar** (12d), **arar** (137a,168c), **asar** (67b), **atar** (58d,116c,134a), **Avar** (27d,108a), **bear** (27a,50b,113c,155a), **Bhar** (191), **boar** (77c,117c,160c,181c), char (24d,138c,170b), czar (42d,49d,60b,135c), dear, Dhar, duar, Edar (18d), fear (113c,155a), gear (32c,112a,167b), gnar (72a), guar (46c,59d), haar (139c), hear (75b,c,92d), hoar (63d,71a, 181a), inar (65b), Isar (41a,104c,132a), Iyar (102b), izar (65b, 103b,155b), joar (100a), juar (100a), khar (189), knar (87c,134b), kuar (102a), kyar (33a), lear (139d), Lear (37a,143b, liar (98d), maar (177a), near (11d,32c,107b), omar (103b), Omar (48c,51b, 163b), osar (51b,67b,131b), paar (28c), pear (64a), rear (15b,23a, b,24a,51b,76d,127c), roar (145c) Saar (63b,102d,132a), scar (31a, 184d), sear (23d,27d,72d,138c), soar (59a), spar (22c,24c,64b, 97b,100b,144d), star (14a,21c,94c,100c), taar (12b), tear (67c, 87b,130a), thar (68a,76d), tiar (39a,75a,121a), tsar (42d,49d, 60b,135c), tzar (42d,49d,60b,135c), usar (8d,16c), wear (50b), year, Zoar

A - - R   **Abir** (129a), **Acer** (96c), **acor** (6d), **Adar** (85c,102a), **Ader** (18d), **ador** (153b), **afar** (44c), **Afar** (6c), **afer** (48a,182b), **agar** (7d,28c, 39c,103c,141c), **ager** (47c,56a,89b,c,131d,133b), **Ahir** (27b), **ajar** (110c), **alar** (15c,145c,182d), **Alur** (191), **amar** (189), **amer** (61b), **amir** (7c,12a,103a,b,123c,170d), **amor** (152b), **Amor** (39c,68b), **Aner** (18d,96b), **apar** (12d), **aper** (32d), **arar** (137a,168c), **asar** (67b), **Aser** (84a), **Askr** (107d), **asor** (75c,105a), **Asur** (68c), **atar** (58d,116b,134a), **Ater** (18c), **Auer** (79a), **Avar** (27d,108a), **aver** (7c,14a,15c,41c,95c,140d,155c,160b,184c)

AS - -   **asak** (13d,168c,169a), **asar** (67b), **asci** (154a), **asea** (39b,177c), **asem** (9a,49a,69c), **Aser** (84a), **Asha** (191), **ashy** (113a,178a), **Asia** (48a), **Asin** (102a), **Askr** (107d), **asno** (151d), **asok** (13d), **Asom** (18d), **asop** (180b), **asor** (75c,105a), **asse** (25a,60d,74a), **assi** (77d), **asta** (188), **Asta** (107a,164c), **Asti** (83d,182b), **Asur** (68c)

- AS   **base** (6a,43b,44b,51c,60c,79b,94b,122b), **bash**, **bask** (94d), **bass** (57b,c,177a), **bast** (16c,56a,117b,184a), **Bast** (27b), **casa** (152b), **case** (22c,36c,81c,91a,108c), **cash** (101c), **cask**, **Caso** (82d), **cass** (140c,177a), **Cass** (147a), **cast** (165b,167c), **dash** (125c,162d), **dasi** (77a), **ease** (7c,8d,35a,100d,129d,130b,c,150c), **East** (111b), **easy** (54a,146d,149d,172b), **fash** (140c,176a), **fass** (189), **fast** (56d, 126c,141d,160c,173a,d), **gash** (40a), **gasp** (113c), **hase** (74d), **hash**, **hasp** (31d,54d,153c), **hast** (17c,108d,120b,144d,152d), **jass** (160d), **kasa** (48a), **kasi** (116b), **kasm** (189), **lash** (58c,87b,165c,180d), **Lasi** (191), **lass** (95b), **last** (36c,50b,145a,174c), **masa** (37a), **mash** (39b,156c), **mask** (44a,45c), **mass** (8a,24b,35b,142d), **mast** (17c,108d,120b,144d,152d), **masu** (57a,84c), **nase** (26b,75a,124b), **Nash** (9c), **nasi** (34c,108a,115a), **Nast** (9c,27a), **oast** (15d,86b,112a), **pasa** (46a,127c,152c), **pasi** (94b), **pass** (110b,155c), **past** (25c,69d,165d), **rasa** (51c), **rase** (42b, d,91d), **rash** (75a), **rasp** (56b,70d,140d), **sasa** (55c), **sash** (18a,45c, 67b,182b), **sass** (154d), **tash** (156b), **Tass** (107a,135d,151b), **vasa** (46d,114a,160b,175d), **Vasa**, **vase** (78d,79d), **vast** (78d,79d), **vasu** (106c), **Vasu** (176d), **wash**, **wasp**, **wast**

- - AS   **abas** (61c), **alas** (52c,136b,183b), **Anas** (46c,d), **Aras**, **baas** (97c), **bias** (43b,123a), **blas** (6c,49c), **Blas** (67b), **bras** (61a), **Dyas** (66a), **ELAS** (71c), **eyas** (106c,173a), **gras** (78b), **Idas** (27b,71c), **iras** (11b,32a), **khas** (153a), **kras** (76d), **kvas** (135c), **Lias** (66a), **Lyas** (66a), **Maas** (132a), **mias** (111a), **Nias** (82d), **oras** (40d), **quas**

311

(135c), **upas** (84d,120b,168c,d), **Usas** (68d), **utas** (49a,109c), **Xmas,**
yeas (177c), **Zoas** (20b)

A - - S **abas** (61c), **ABC's** (57a), **Acis** (64b), **Acts, acus** (89d, 118a), **Ades**
(73a), **Agis** (86d), **Aias, Airs** (123b), **alas** (52c,136b,183b), **alms**
(29a), **Alps** (85d), **Alys** (183c), **Ames** (9c,82a), **Amos** (96a,144b),
Anas (46c,d), **Anes** (110c,140a), **anis** (55c), **Apis** (17c,24b,49a,
125a,136a), **Apus** (36b,c), **Aras, Ares** (49b,51b,68c,76a,97a,105c,
110b,178a,186d), **aris** (101b), **arms, arts** (138c), **ates** (160c), **atis**
(76d,102a), **Aves** (19d), **Avis** (89a,183c), **avus** (89b), **axis** (28b,
41d,77c,153c), **ayes** (177c)

AT - - **atap** (113b), **atar** (58d,116b,134a), **atef** (39a,48d), **aten** (150a,
159b), **Ateo** (120d), **Ater** (18c), **ates** (160c), **Atik** (155b), **atip**
(14b,166a), **atis** (76d,102a), **Atka** (11a), **atle** (136d,161d,169b),
Atli (14c,72b,79a,107d), **atma** (150d), **atmo** (34d,174d), **Atmu**
(143a,159b), **atom** (101c,114c,180d), **aton** (150a,159b), **atop** (112a,
174a), **Atri, atry** (141b), **atta** (58d,90c,97d,160c,173d), **Atta** (94d,
95d,100a,106b,117a), **Attu, atua** (120d), **Atum** (143a,159b)

- AT - **bata** (30a,142d), **bate** (43c,91b,100d), **bath, Bath** (50d,151c), **batt**
(37c), **batz** (190), **cata** (122c), **cate** (165c), **Cato** (132d,133b),
data (54a), **date** (64a,153a), **dato** (95c,102c,117a), **datu** (95c,102c,
117a), **eats, fate** (42d,52a,87a,94a), **gata** (143c), **gate** (51a,121b),
Gath (117a), **hate** (6a,43a), **hath, Hati** (48d), **jati** (27b), **jato** (173b),
Kate (143c,183d), **kath** (14a), **Katy** (183d), **lata** (85d,95d), **late**
(128c), **lath** (157c), **latu** (190), **mate** (18c,35b,41d,113a,154a,162c),
math (77a), **Matt, maty** (80c), **Nata** (15c,47c), **Nate** (22b), **Nath**
(155c), **Nato** (6a,8d), **natr** (189), **Natt** (107b), **oath** (119c,150a),
pata (32c,160d), **pate** (39a,74d), **path** (132a,134b), **pato** (46d), **patu**
(179b), **rata** (29d,56b,89d,96c,106d,120c,168c), **rate** (11d,14a,31d,
36b,51d,52a,70b,85c,112b,123b,127d,128a,138c,143a,174b), **rath**
(29a,76d,162d), **rati** (189), **rats, sate** (32d,52c,67d,70d,137c,159d),
sati, Sati (49a,126b,147b), **tate** (183a), **tatt** (87c), **tatu** (12d), **Tatu,**
Wate (141a), **watt, Watt** (82a,173b,177c), **yate** (51d,168c), **yati**
(76d), **zati** (21d)

- - AT **adat** (90b,95d), **alat** (136d), **Anat** (138c,147d), **beat** (58c,87b,131a,
164d,165b,180d), **bhat** (80c), **blat** (25b), **boat** (27b,106a), **brat,**
chat (9b,19c,161c), **coat** (160a), **doat** (17a,94b,112a,165d), **drat**
(100a), **Duat** (172d), **erat** (89c), **etat** (62d), **feat** (7a,52d), **fiat** (35a,
41d,48c,111b,137a), **Fiat** (83c), **flat** (41b,124b,173a), **frat, geat**
(77d,101a), **Geat** (138a), **ghat** (32d,88b,103d,132a), **gnat** (59a,
81b,99c), **goat** (135a), **heat, ikat** (53c,159a), **kaat** (105d), **khat**
(105d), **kyat** (189), **Maat** (69a,b,85d), **meat** (59b), **moat** (44d), **neat**
(165c,169d), **peat** (64a,175a), **piat** (11a), **plat** (22d,96c,114a,119c,
133d), **pyat** (95b), **scat** (26b,67a,d,126c,169c), **seat** (98c,156b),
shat (87d), **skat** (181b), **Skat** (155b), **slat** (58b,89a,117c,184a),
spat (112c,126b,134b), **stat** (72d), **swat** (15d,20d,32d,157c), **Swat**
(103a), **that** (42b,124b,129c), **what** (129c)

A - - T **abet** (8b,15b,50a,59b,75d,81c,141d,159d), **Abot** (100c), **abut** (22a,
167c), **acht** (66c), **adat** (90b,95d), **adit** (51a,100a,114d), **Ahet**
(49a,102a), **aint, alat** (136d), **alit** (44b,143a), **amit** (94a), **Anat**
(138c,147d), **anet** (43c), **Apet** (97c), **aret** (128c), **arn't, aunt** (129c)

AU - - **Auca** (192), **Aude, Auer** (79a), **auge** (123c,132b), **aula** (66c,73b),

312

auiu (74c,168c), **aune** (188), **aunt** (129c), **aura** (44c,49c,66a,96b, 158a,170d,177c), **auri** (34a), **Ausa, ausu** (168c,180b), **auto** (34d), **auza** (168c,180b)

- AU - baud (162d), baul (18b), Baum (9c,112c), cauk (139b), caul (16d, 74d), caur (139a), daub (148d), dauk (95c), Daur (139b), dauw (24c), eaux (178c), faun (56a,68b,137c,161a,184a), gaub (116c), gaud (169d), gaue (67a), Gaul (10a,60d,63c), gaup, gaur (112c, 181c), gaus (67d), gaut (88b,103d,132a), haul (27b,45d), jaun (113a), kaun (93d), laud (122a), laun (146b), maud (53d,136d, 143c), Maud (181a,183c), Maui (120d), maul (73c), maun (139d), naut (141b), Paul (96a), paun (18b), paut (140a), Sauk (192), saul (48a,168c), Saul (18c,86d,115a), saum (189), taun (188), taut (163b,165c), Vaux (63b), yaup

- - AU Agau (73c), beau, Diau (192), Drau, Esau (82c,84a,128c), frau (181b), miau (27b,99b), prau (21b,26a,95c,d), sgau (88c), unau (148c,171d), whau (107a,168c)

A - - U Aalu (6b,48d), Aaru (6b,48d), Abou (48b,55a), actu (7a,89a), Addu (68c,157a,182a), Agau (73c), Ainu (84a,84c), ammu (9d), ansu (11d), anzu (11d), Apsu (29a), Atmu (143a,159b), Attu, aulu (74c,168c), ausu (168c,180b), auzu (168c,180b)

AV - - aval (70c), Avar (27d,108a), avec (63a,183a), aver (7c,14a,15c,41c, 95c,140d,155c,160b,184c), Aves (19d), avid (47b,71a,186b), avis (89a), Avis (183c), Avon (143b), avow (6d,36a,41c,112c), avus (89b)

- AV - bave (61d,146c), cava (116a,175b), cave (27d), cavy (72b,120d, 132c,157b), Dave (96b), Davy (96b,136b), eave (133c), favi (138a, 165d), gave, have, Java (33a), Jave (84d), kava (18c,116a), Kavi (84d), lava (101c,132b,151a,177a), lave (16d,178b), nave (30d,31a, 78d,114b,180c), navy (33c,58b), pave (85a), pavo (115b), Pavo (36b,c), pavy (115b), rave (41c,157a,161d), ravi, Ravi (16b), save (52b,110c,123a,173c), Tave (183d), Tavy (183d), wave (19a, 59a,111c,131d,160c,172d), wavy (147b,172d), yava

- - AV Muav (66a), Slav (13c,40c,48b,52a,120b,135b)

A - - V akov (189), Azov (20b,135d)

AW - - Awan (191), away (6b,69d,76a,109d,111d), awry (13d,38d,171c)

- AW - bawl, bawn (181a), cawk (133c), dawk (95c), dawm (190), dawn (14d,41b), fawn (33c), gawd (169c), gawk (146d), gawp, hawk (19c, 115c), jawy, kawa (18c,116a), Kawi (84d), kawn (93d), lawn (20a, 37c,53b,92c), pawa (189), pawl (43a,95a), pawn (29c,119c), sawk (188), sawn, tawa (106d,168c), yawl (136b,171d,175d), yawn, yawp

- - AW chaw (97c), claw (29c,105b,161d,173a), craw (38d,72c,156c), dhaw (125a), draw (42c,53a,92b,117c,121c,167d), flaw, gnaw (20a,107a, 178b), miaw (27b,99b), shaw (164b), Shaw (50c,53b), slaw, thaw

A - - W alow (18a,172c), anew (7c), arow (92c,158b), avow (6d,36a,41c, 112c)

AX - - axal (120b), axil (10c), axis (28b,41d,77c,153c), axle (153c,180c), axon (106c,153c)

- AX - saxe (20d,33c), taxi (13a,125b), taxo (13a), waxy (119c,149d)

313

- - AX Ajax (71b,162d), Anax (43c,120c), coax (180c), Crax (19b,39d), flax, hoax (41c,122a), Odax (132c), Olax (52b)

A - - X abox (22d), Ajax (71b,162d), Alix (183c), Amex (184d), Anax (43d,120c), apex (39c,76c,115c,118b,159b,166a,167b),

AY - - ayah (108d), ayes (177c), ayin (91c)

- AY - baya (179b), Baya (191), cayo, Daye (123d), days, hayz, kayo (87c), maya (179b), Maya (23d,186c), Mayo (193), raya (19b,23c,76d, 107d), saya (117a), Vayu (68c,182a), ways, yaya (113c,168c)

- - AY alay (96c), anay (72b), away (6b,69d,76a,109d,111d), blay (57d), bray, chay (48a,128d), Clay (9d), dray (27a,154c,177b), esay, flay (147c,157c), fray (56b,60d), gray (33c,77c), Gray (50c), okay (8d), olay (113b), piay (98b), play (63d,154a), pray (18b,51a,159d), quay (88b,117c,180c), ruay (189), shay (110c), slay, stay (72d, 124c,130a,134a,162a), sway (104a)

A - - Y Abby (183d), ably (147c), achy, Addy (183d), adry, (164c), aery (47b,51d,106c), affy (18b), ahey (52c), ahoy (106a), airy (176d, 177a), akey (189), alay (96c), Algy (96b), alky, ally (14a,35c,d, 173c), Amoy (88c), anay (72b,163b,181a), ancy (158c), Andy (96b), army, arty, ashy (113a,178a), atry (141b), away (6b,69d,76a,109d, 111d), awry (13d,38d,171c)

AZ - - Azam (166c), azan (102d), Azha (155b), Azof (20b,135d), axon (127b), Azov (20b,135d), azul (151d)

- AZ - caza, cazi (103a), cazy (103a), Daza (191), daze (157d), dazy, faze (43d), Gaza (117a), gaze, gazi, gazy, haze (100c,174d), hazy (174b), jazz, Kazi (103a), kazy (103a), laze (79b), Laze (191), Lazi (191), lazo (88d,128b,133d), lazy, maze (87b,157d), naze (26b, 124b), Nazi, raze (42b,d,91d), razz (131b), vaza (114a)

- - AZ Agaz (193), Ahaz (86d), Boaz (135d)

A - - Z Agaz (193), Ahaz (86d)

BA - - Baal (142b), baas (97c), baba (108d,120c,166c,171a), babe, Babi (116c), babu (77a), baby, Bach (35c), back (75d,76d,159d), Badb (82b), bade, baff (69d), baft (14a,53b), baga (171b), bago (13d), bahi (60c), baho (122a), baht (146a), bail (43c), bain (61a), bait (15d,51a,94d,167b), baju (84a), baka (52b), bake (139a), baku (26d,157b,168c), Bala (26c,66a), bald (16c), bale (24b,74a), balk (118c,146a,156d), ball, balm (110a,172c), Balt (93a), balu (104b, 159a,181d), Bana (67a), banc (61a,85c), band (72a,157c), bane (74a,106b,120b,139a), bang (75d,105d,148a), bani (190), bank (18a,58c), bans, bant (43c), bara (188), barb (20b,57d,78b,117d, 120a,b,124b), bard (12d,120a), bare (43d,157c), bari (37c,79c), Bari (83d), bark (115c), barm (185b), barn (156d), baro (71a,122c), barr (49b), Bart (96b), baru (168c), base (6a,43b,44b,51c,60c,79b,94b, 122b), bash, bask (94d), bass (57b,c,177a), bast (16c,56a,117b, 184a), Bast (27b), bata (30a,142d), bate (43c,91b,100d), bath, Bath (50d,151c), batt (37c), batz (190), baud (162d), baul (18b), Baum (9c,112c), bave (61d,146c), bawl, bawn (181a), baya (179b), Baya (191)

- BA - abas (61c), ibad (191), iban (47c), oban (190)

- - BA Abba (20a,55a,161c), alba (98a,181a), Alba (151d), amba (161a), anba (36d), arba (135d,171a), baba (108d,120c,166c,171a), **boba** (29d), buba (170a), caba (184c), ceba (169b), cuba (189), **Cuba** (180b), Egba (191), Elba (105d), exba (188), Faba, haba (151d), isba (135c), juba (106b), koba (11a), kuba (26d,189), Luba (191), Maba (103a,168d), Nuba (108c), peba (12d), Peba (193), **Raba**, reba (144a), Reba (18d,86c), saba (56a,117a), Saba (143d), **Seba** (18c,39d), Toba (80c), tuba (105a,137d), ueba (188)

B - - A baba (108d,120c,166c,171a), baga (171b), baka (52b), Bala (26c, 66a), Bana (67a), bara (188), bata (30a,142d), baya (179b), **Baya** (191), Beda (101d), bega (188), Beja (6c,191), beka (189), **bela** (12a), Bela (18b,48c), bema (28d,31a,114b,119b,125b,137a), **bena**, (176a), Bera (86d), Besa (68b,119c), beta (71a,91c,141d), **biga** (171d), bija (168c), bina (77a), bisa (11a), biwa (93d,168c), **Bixa** (145d), blaa, boba (29d), boca (152b,c), boga (57d,180b), bola (16a, 179b), boma (7d), bona (89d,183c), Bona, bora (181d,182b), **bosa** (12a), bota (189), boza (12a), brea (100b), buba (170a), buda (83d), buna (161c), bura (182b)

- BB - Abba (20a,55a,161c), abbe (32b,63b,123b), Abby (183d)

- - BB bibb (97c,146b), Cobb (9c), dubb (161c), hobb (124b), **hubb** (118b), jibb, lobb (23b,94c,163a)

B - - B Badb (82b), barb (20b,57d,78b,117d,120a,b,124b), bibb (97c, 146b), blab (162b), bleb (20c,23d,67c), blob, blub, Bodb (82b), bomb (144a), boob (146d), brab (113b), brob (153c), bulb (37a, 172c)

- BC - ABC's (57a)

B - - C banc (61a,85c), bloc (173a), Bosc (115c)

B - - D bald (16c), band (72a,157c), bard (12d,120a), baud (162d), **bead** (17a,122a,146b), Beld (155b), bend (39d,171b), bind (33b,165c), blod (59d,79c), bird, bled, bold (41a), bond (92a,101c,141d,143b, 159d,165c), bord (100b), brad (54d,67c,105b), bred (23c,48c,127c), bund (49c,66c,90c), Byrd (9c,120b)

BE - - bead (17a,122a,146b), beak (19a), beal (139d), beam, bean (91b, 142a,175a), bear (27a,50b,113c,155a), beat (58c,87b,131a,164d, 165b,180d), beau, beck (107c), Beda (101d), Bede (48c,50c,101d, 175b), beef, been (149a), beer (18c), bees (185b), beet (175a), bega (188), behn (137d), Beid (155b), Beja (6c,191), beka (189), bela (12a), Bela (18b,48c,78d), Beli (23c), bell (24c,39d), **Bell** (162d), belt (16a,31a), bema (28d,31a,114b,119b,125b,137a), **bena** (176a), bend (39d,171b), bene (18a,83c,90a,106b,122a,180a), beng (43a), beni (116a,142d), Beni (191), beno (113b,117a), bent (80b), benu (49a), Bera (86d), berg (79b), berm (25d,90d,145c), **Bern** (160d), Bert (96b), Besa (68b,119c), Bess (76c,183d), best (41d, 159c,160a), beta (71a,91c,141d), bete (61a,107c), beth (91c), Beth (8c,183d), bevy (38a,58c)

- BE - abed (130c), Abel (7a,25b), abet (8b,15b,50a,59b,75d,81c,141d, 159d), Eben (96a), Eber (51a,75c,99d), ibex (67d,68a), obex (22d), obey (35c,75c), Obed (135d), uber (66b)

- - BE abbe (32b,63b,123b), albe (133a), babe, Bube (180b), cube (66b, 150a), dobe (159b,c,172b), Elbe (108a), gabe (162a), gibe (8a,42c, 84d,100d,138c,144c,149b), gybe (144c), Habe (191), **Hebe** (39c,

69c,186b), **imbe** (37a,56a,133d), **jibe** (8a,33b,35d,37b,42c,100d, 138c,144c,149b), **jube** (28d), **kibe, Kobe** (78a), **lobe** (90c,134b), **lube** (110a), **ribe** (139a), **robe** (65b), **rube** (37d,135d,185d), **Rube** (96b), **sabe, tobe** (7d,137b), **tube** (118b,158a)

B - - E   **babe, bade, bake** (139a), **bale** (24b,74a), **bane** (74a,106b,120b, 139a), **bare** (43d,157c), **base** (6a,43b,44b,51c,60c,79b,94b,122b), **bate** (43c,91b,100d), **bave** (61d,146c), **Bede** (48c,50c,101d,175b), **bene** (18a,83c,90a,106d,122a,180a), **bete** (61a,107c), **bice** (20d, 117d), **Bice** (27b), **bide** (47c,50b,130a,158b), **bike, bile** (30c), **bine** (145b,156a,171c,176b), **bise** (182a), **bite** (29d,156b), **bize** (182a), **blae** (93b), **blue** (33c,98c,102c,150d,173a), **boce** (23b,52a,57b), **bode** (14c,60a,110b,121b), **bole** (31d,32a,169b), **bone, bore** (14c, 25b,46a,116a,165c,179b), **bose** (163c), **brae** (76d,139a,c,140b, 148c), **bree** (139a), **Brie** (29c), **Bube** (180b), **bure** (61b), **byee** (189), **byre** (38a)

- BF -   **Abfa** (76b)

B - - F   **baff** (69d), **beef, biff, buff** (134c,161d)

B - - G   **bang** (75d,105d,148a), **beng** (43a), **berg** (79b), **bing, bong, borg** (40d), **brag** (21a,175a), **brig** (72b,106a,144d), **bung** (119d,156d), **burg** (22b,73c)

BH - -   **Bhar** (191), **bhat** (80c), **bhel** (126d), **Bhil** (191), **b'hoy** (134b), **bhut** (67a)

- - BH   **Cobh** (37a)

B - - H   **Bach** (35c), **bash, bath, Bath** (50d,151c), **beth** (91c), **Beth** (8c, 183d), **bikh** (120b), **binh** (189), **bish** (120b), **blah, booh** (52c), **bosh, both, bruh** (95a), **bukh** (122a), **bush**

BI - -   **bias** (43b,123a), **bibb** (97c,146b), **bibi** (87d), **bice** (20d,117d), **Bice** (27b), **bide** (47c,50b,130a,158b,162a,177d), **bien** (63a,140c,179a, 180a), **bier** (33b,66b), **biff, biga** (171d), **bija** (168c), **bike, bikh** (120b), **bile** (30c), **bilk** (29b,41c,42a), **bill** (17b,147a), **Bill** (96b), **bilo** (131b), **bina** (77a), **bind** (33b,165c), **bine** (145b,156a,171c, 176b), **bing, binh** (189), **Bini** (191), **binn** (22c), **bino** (113b,117a), **biod** (59d,79c), **bion** (117b), **bios** (92a), **bird, birl** (93c,131a,153c), **birn** (31d,139a), **birr** (180d), **bisa** (11a), **bise** (182a), **bish** (120b), **bisk** (120b,151a), **bite** (29d,156b), **biti** (20b), **bito** (7d,57d,168c), **bitt** (54d,175c), **biur** (35a), **biwa** (93d,168a), **Bixa** (145d), **bize** (182a), **bizz**

- BI -   **Abia** (18d,137a), **Abib** (102a,b), **Abie** (96b,107a), **abir** (129a), **ibid** (80a,117a,137a), **ibis** (48d,49a,177b), **ibit** (117a), **obia** (55d), **obit** (41b,64c), **Ubii** (191)

- - BI   **Albi** (58a), **ambi** (34a,122c), **Babi** (116c), **bibi** (87d), **Bubi** (180b), **cubi** (188), **gabi** (162a), **gobi, Gobi** (42d), **kobi** (84b), **mabi** (58d), **rabi** (38d,74a), **Rabi** (14b,117b), **sebi** (34b), **tabi** (84c,149d), **Tybi** (102a), **Wabi** (192), **Yobi**

B - - I   **Babi** (116c), **bahi** (60c), **Bali, bani** (190), **bari** (79c), **Bari** (37c, 83d), **Beli** (23c), **beni** (116a,142d), **Beni** (191), **bibi** (87d), **Bini** (191), **biti** (20b), **Boli** (191), **Boni** (63b), **Bori** (110d,150c), **Bubi** (180b), **Bugi** (191), **buri** (56b)

- - BK   **nabk** (30d,164d), **nubk** (30d,164d), **Sobk** (38d)

316

B - - K   back (75d,76d,159d), balk (118c,146a,156d), bank (18a,58c), bark (115c), bask (94d), beak (19a), beck (107c), bilk (29b,41c,42a), bisk (120b,151a), bock (17c,90d,144a), bonk (190), book, bosk (164b), bowk (155d), buck, bukk (122a), bulk (97b), bunk, busk (17b,37b,55d,161b)

BL - -   blaa, blab (162b), blae (93b), blah, blas (6c,49c), Blas (67b), blat (25b), blay (57d), bleb (20c,23d,67c), bled, blet (64a), bleu (61b), blew, blob, bloc (173a), blot, blow, blub, blue (33c,98c,102c,150d, 173a), blup, blur, blut (66b)

- BL -   able (26b,35b,126a,147c), ably (147c)

B - - L   baal (142b), bail (43c), ball, baul (18b), bawl, beal (139d), bell (24c,39d), Bell (162d), bhel (126d), Bhil (191), bill (17b,147a), Bill (96b), birl (93c,131a,153c), boil, boll (119b,d), bool (39d), bowl, bual (182c), buhl (81a), bull (113c), burl (87c,169a)

B - - M   balm (110a,172c), barm (185b), Baum (9c,112c), beam, berm (25d, 90d,145c), boom (152d), Bram (96a), brim

B - - N   bain (61a), barn (156d), bawn (181a), bean (91b,142a,175a), been (149a), behn (137d), Bern (160d), bien (63a,140c,179a,180a), binn (22c), bion (117b), birn (31d,139a), Bonn (17d), boon (18b,20c, 55a), born, bran (23c,39a,70b,72a,79c), Bran (23c,50c), bren (72d, 95a), brin (32c,54c,146c), bunn (25b), burn

BO - -   boar (77c,117c,160c,181c), boat (27b,106a), Boaz (135d), boba (29d,) bobo (112c,168c), boca (152b,c), boce (23b,52a,57b), bock (17c,90d,144a), Bodb (82b), bode (14c,60a,110b,121b), Bodo (88c), body (72a), Boer (151a), boga (57d,180b), bogo (117a,168c), Bogo (191), bogy (153a), boho (117a,179d), Bohr (14b,40d,138c), Boil (191), boil, bois (62b,63a,183d), bojo (117a), boko (52b), bola (16a, 179b), bold (41a), bole (31d,32a,169b), boll (119b,d), bolo (87a, 179b), bolt (13b,54d,58b,132d,160a), boma (7d), bomb (144a), bona (89d), Bona (183c), bond (92a,101c,141d,143b,159d,165c), bone, bong, Boni (63b), bonk (190), Bonn (17d), bony (147c), Bony (96b), boob (146d), booh (52c), book, bool (39d), boom (152d), boon (18b,20c,55a), boor (47a,135d,172c), boot (128d), bora (181d, 182b), bord (100b), bore (14c,25b,46a,116a,165c,179b), borg (40d), Bori (110d,150c), born, boro (154b), Boro (193), Bors (70b,134b), bort (43b), Bort (134b), bosa (12a), Bosc (115c), bose (163c), bosh, bosk (164b), boss (49d,157d), bota (189), both, Boto (192), bott (32a,88d), bout (36c), bouw (188), bowk (155d), bowl, boxy, boza (12a), boxo (55b)

- BO -   aboo (17a), Abot (100c), Abou (48b,55a), abox (22d), eboe (28b, 110a,168c,169b), Eboe, ebon (20b), oboe (74b,104d,105a,182a, 184a), obol (29b,110a)

- - BO   albo (34d,181a), ambo (125b,128b), bobo (112c,168c), bubo (112c), Egbo (141d), Gobo (84d), hobo (168a,174b), jobo (77c), lobo (165d,183c), nabo (117a), Nebo (68c,102d,103d,183a), umbo (22b), zobo (186b)

B - - O   bago (13d), baho (122a), baro (71a,122a), beno (113b,117a), bilo (131b), bino (113b,117a), bito (7d,52d,168c), bobo (112c,168c), Bodo (88c), bogo (117a,168c), Bogo (191), boho (117a,179d), bojo (117a), boko (52b), bolo (87a,179b), boro (154b), Boro (193), Boto

(192), boxo (55b), broo (139a), bubo (112c), Bufo (166c), Buto (142d), buyo (18b), bygo (114c)

B - - P blup, bump

BR - - brab (113b), brad (54d,67c,105b), brae (76d,139a,c,140b,148c), brag (21a,175a), Bram (96a), bran (23c,39a,70b,72a,79c), Bran (23c,50c), bras (61a), brat, bray, brea (100b), bred (23c,48c,127c), bree (139a), bren (72b,95a), Brer (172b), Bres, brew (35d), brey (194), Brie (29c), brig (72b,106a,144d), brim, brin (32c,54c,146c), brit (76c), brob (153c), broo (139a), brow, bruh (95a), brut (182c), Brut (23c)

- BR - abra (26b), Abra, abri (61c,62c,144b), Ebro (132a), obra (152d, 184c)

B - - R barr (49b), bear (27a,50b,113c,155a), beer (18c), Bhar (191), bier (33b,66b), birr (180d), blur (35a), blur, boar (77c,117c,160c,181c), Boer (151a), Bohr (14b,40d,138c), boor (47a,135d,172c), Brer (172b), buhr (180d), burr (123b)

- BS - Absi (191)

- - BS dibs (70c), Lubs (94b), nibs (116c), nobs (38c,87a)

B - - S baas (97c), bans, bass (57b,c,177a), bees (185b), Bess (76c,183d), bias (43b,123a), bios (92a), blas (6c,49c), Blas (67b), bois (62b, 63a,183d), Bors (70b,134b), boss (49d,157d), bras (61a), Bres, buss (87a,148c)

- - BT debt (91d,109b)

B - - T baft (14a,53b), baht (146a), bait (15d,51a,94d,167b), Bait (93a), bant (43c), Bart (96b), bast (16c,56a,117b,184a), Bast (27b), batt (37c), beat (58c,87b,131a,164d,165b,180d), beet (175a), belt (16a, 31a), bent (80b), Bert (96b), best (41d,159c,160a), bhat (80c), bhut (67a), bitt (54d,175c), blat (25b), blet (64a), blot, blut (66b), boat (27b,106a), bolt (13b,54d,58b,132d,160a), boot (128d), bort (43b), Bort (134b), bott (32a,88d), bout (36c), brat, brit (76c), brut (182c), Brut (23c), bult (76d), bunt (15d,180c), bust, butt (27a,77b,127d,162a,182b)

BU - - bual (182c), buba (170a), Bube (180b), Bubi (180b), bubo (112c), buck, buda (83d), buff (134c,161d), Bufo (166c), Bugi (191), buhl (81a), buhr (180d), bukh (122a), bukk (122a), bulb (37a,172c), bulk (97b), bull (113c), bult (76d), bump, buna (161c), bund (49c,66c,90c), bung (119d,156b), bunk (25b), bunt (15d, 180c), buoy (28d,58c), bura (182b), bure (61b), burg (22b,73c), buri (56b), burl (87c,169a), burn, burr (123b), bury (81d), bush, busk (17b,37b,55d,161b), buss (87a,148c), bust, busy, Buto (142d), butt (27a,77b,127d,162a,182b), buxy (115b), buyo (18b) buzz

- BU - abut (22a,167c), ebur (89c)

- - BU babu (77a), kobu (84b), Nabu (68c,183a), tabu (59d,111d), Tibu (191), zebu (22d,80d,112c)

B - - U babu (77a), baju (84a), baku (26d,157b,168c), balu (104b,159a, 181d), baru (168c), beau, benu (49a), bleu (61b)

B - - W blew, blow, bouw (188), brew (35d), brow

318

BY - -   byee, (189), bygo (114c), Byrd (9c,120b), byre (38a)

- - BY   Abby (183d), baby, doby (159b,c), gaby (59c,146d), goby (57d), kiby (29a), ruby (20a,65d,179c), toby (8c,85c,104b), Toby (96b, 125c)

B - - Y   baby, bevy (38a,58c), b'hoy (134b), blay (57d), body (72a), bogy (153a), bony (147c), Bony (96b), boxy, bray, brey (194), buoy (28d,58c), bury (81d), busy, buxy (115b)

B - - Z   batz (190), bizz, Boaz (135d), buzz

CA - -   caam (93d), caba (184c), Caca (67a), caco (73b), cade (25c,27a,76c, 85d,116d), Cade (50c), cadi (12a,103a,171a), cady (69d), Caen, cafe, cage (36a), cagy (178b), caid (35a,151d,152b), cain (169c), Cain (6a,7a,50d,88a,104c,143a), caji (180b), cake, caky, cale (72d), calf, calk (78c,109a,141c,178d), call (145c,159b, 176d), calm (8d,11d,112b,118d,126c,d,172b,173d), calo (72d), calp (92b), calx (23c,75c,112c), came (182b), Came (192), camp (163b), Cana (57a,64b,100c), cane (17b,128a,156a,159a,177d), Cane, cang (184a), cano (152a), cant (28d,81b,84d,90c,109b,136c,165d,166a), capa (152a,166d), cape (75a,96c,124b,161a), caph (91c), Capp (27a), cara (83a), Cara (48b,183c), card (33d,114d), care (11b, 14c,35d,150a,184d), cark (26d,184d), carl (115c,135d), Carl (96a), carn (156c), caro (83a), Caro (183d), carp (27d,38d,40c,55a,56c, 57a), carr (120d,140a), cart (171d,175a,177b), casa (152b), case (22c,36c,81c,91a,108c), cash (101c), cask, Caso (82d) cass (140c, 177a), Cass (147a), cast (165b,167c), cata (122c), cate (165c), Cato (132d,133b), Catt (9d), cauk (139b), caul (16d,74d), caup, caur (139a), cava (116a,175b), cave (27d), cavy (72b,120d,132c, 157b), cawk (133c), cayo, caza, cazi (103a), cazy (103a)

- CA -   ecad (73a,119b), ical (158c), scab (80b,107d,157c), scad (31a,57a, 78b,88d,137c), scan (52b,93d,98a,116d,128b,c,140d), scar (31a, 184d), scat (26b,67a,d,126c,169c)

- - CA   acca (53b,d), Alca (14c,128b), arca (9a,22c,29d,115a,130a), Arca (101b), Auca (192), boca (152b,c), Caca (67a), coca (29d,33a,105d, 113a), cuca (33a,105d), deca (34d,122d), Ecca (66a), esca (11c, 44a,70c), Inca (14b,30a), jaca (84a), juca (27a), mica (82c,100b, 146c), onca (189), orca (86b), paca (132c,154a), peca (190), pica (66b,95b,172c), puca (68a), raca (19a,59c,130b,184d), Teca (192), unca (49a), Ynca (193), yuca (27a)

C - - A   caba (184c), Caca (67a), caja (152a), Cana (57a,64b,100c), capa (152a,166d), cara (83a), Cara (48b,183c), casa (152b), cata (122c), cava (116a,175b), caza, ceba (169b), cela (62d), cena (88d,133a), cepa (110c), cera (152d,161d,179a), chaa (162b), chia (136d), cima (83b,c), Civa (56d), coca (29d,33a,105d,113a), coda (32c,35d,55d, 56c), coja (103b,166b), cola (25b,108d,149d,168c), coma (91c, 157d,170c,172b), copa (88b,113c), cora (65d), Cora (42b,69c,80c, 116b,124d,172b,183c), cota (117a), coxa (77b), crea (92c,151d), cuba (189), Cuba (180b), cuca (33a,105d), Cuna (193), cura (152c), cuya (39b), cyma (101a,b)

C - - B   chab (184a), chib (167a), chob (23c), chub (40c,154c), club (39c), Cobb (9c), comb (38c), crab (39b,144b,181b), crib (96b,120d), curb (130c,146b)

319

- CC -   acca (53b,d), Ecca (66a), ecce (17d,89a,c)

C - - C   chic (148d), circ (31a), cric (131c), croc (13a,74a)

C - - D   caid (35a,151d,152b), card (33d,114d), Chad (158b), chid, Chud
(191), clad (46a,82a), clod (22a,45b,157d), coed, cold (65d),
cond (156a), cord (39b,131a), curd (99d)

CE - -   ceba (169b), cede (67b,70c,129d,160a,168b,185d), ceil (92c,112a),
cela (62d), cell (39b), celt (30c,123a,156c,167b,179b), Celt (10a,
180a,b), cena (88d,133a), cene (34c), cens (115b), cent (36d), cepa
(110c), cepe (48c), cera (152d,161d,179a), cere (19a,114b,149d,
179a), cern (41c), cero (57b,c,d,180b), cess (91d,94c,162b), cest
(18a,67b), cete (180b,c), ceto (34a), Ceyx (73b)

- CE -   Acer (96c), icer

- - CE   ance (158b,c,d), bice (20d,117d), Bice (27b), boce (23b,52a,57b),
dace (57a,b), dice (65a), duce (29d), ecce (17d,89a,c), ence (158c),
esce (158d), face (159d,176c), lace (158b,179c), luce (58c,117d),
Luce (7b,35a), mace (49d,108d,153b,154b,161a,178a), mice (nice
(54d,119c,130c), Nice (98c), once (60b,79b), pace (64b,98a,153b,
156a,170b,177d), pice (190), puce (33c,d,52a), race (116a,153b,
154b), Rice (46a), sice (71d,147b), syce (71d), tace (13a,155d), tice
(9a,38c,51a,185d), vice (31d,158a), voce (83c,177a)

C - - E   cade (25c,27a,76c,85d,116d), Cade (50c), cafe, cage (36a), cake,
cale (72d), came (182b), Came (192), cane (17b,128a,156a,159a,
177d), Cane, cape (75a,96c,124b,161a), care (11b,14c,35d,150a,
184d), case (22c,36c,81c,91a,108c), cate (165c), cave (27d), cede
(67b,70c,129d,160a,168b,185d), cene (34c), cepe (48c), cere (19a,
114b,149d,179a), cete (180b,c), chee (189), cine (104b,152c), cise
(147b), cite (15a,98d,126d,159b), cive (110c), clee (19a,129a),
Cloe (183c), clue (161b), code (21c,31a,40c,161c), coke (32d,64a),
cole (25a), Cole, come, cone (66b,150a,157c), cope (12b,26b,36c,65b,
157d,176a), core (28b,51c,75b,81b), cose (29b), cote (19b,143d,
144a,b), cove (17a,73d,107d), coze (29b), Cree (192), cube (66b,
150a), cuke (39b), cure (123b,d), cute (39c), cyke (40c), cyme (58d,
69c)

C - - F   calf, chef, clef (104d,105a), coif (73a), cuff (148a), cuif (139a,d,
140c)

C - - G   cang (184a), chug (53a), clog (30c,145b), coag (45d,118a,163b),
crag (132c), crig (20d)

CH - -   chaa (162b), chab (184a), Chad (158b), chai (72d), cham (20a,29d),
Cham (8c), chan (26c,130c), chap (55b), char (24d,138c,170b),
chat (9b,19c,161c), chaw (97c), chay (48a,128d), chee (189), chef,
chek (59c), Chen (149b), cher (61b), chew (97c), chez (14b,61a),
chia (136d), chib (167a), chic (148d), chid, ch'ih (188), chil, chin,
Chin (30b), chip (69d), chir (29b,116d), chit (67b,98c,108b,116c,
177c), chiv (87a), chob (23c), chol (118d), Chol (192), chop (98a),
chor (164b), chou (61b), Chou (30b), chow (45a), choy (48a,128d),
chub (40c,154c), Chud (191), chug (53a), chum (38d), Chun (30c),
chut!

- CH -   ache (79a,112b,185b), acht (66c), achy, echo (130b,d), Echo (105d),
icho (67b), ichu (10b,70d), ocha (189), tcha (162c), tche (13d,30b,
105a), tchi, Tchi, tchu

- - CH   aich (9a), arch (29d,38b,39d,123d,132c), bach, Bach (35c), each, etch, Foch (63b), hoch (52c,66c), Hoch, inch, itch, Koch (66d), lech (102b), loch (88a,139d), much, nach, ouch, rich, Roch (136c), sech (97c), such (146d), Tech, Vach (153b), Zach (96b)

C - - H   caph (91c), Caph, cash (101c), ch'ih (188), Cobh (37a), cosh (35a, 97c), cush (101c), Cush (51d,73c)

CI - -   cima (83b,c), cine (104b,152c), cinq (61d), cion (42d,70b,145b, 148b,154b,156a), cipo (91d), circ (31a), ciri (24c), cise (147b), cist (22c,29d,156c), cite (15a,98d,126d,159b), cito (89d,126c), cits, city, Civa (56d), cive (110c)

- CI -   acid (151a,162a), Acis (64b), Scio

- - CI   asci (154a), deci (163b), foci (28b), fuci (132c), loci (66b,118c), Pici (19c,184a), unci (31d)

C - - I   cadi (12a,103a,171a), Cadi, caji (180b), cazi (103a), chai (72d), coli, Coni, Cori (138c), cubi (188)

- - CK   back (75d,76d,159d), beck (107c), bock (17c,90d,144a), buck, cock (19a,29a,55a,133d,136d,161d,174b), deck (13b,41c, 144d), dick (43a,55b), Dick (96b), dock (40a,117c,144d,179d), duck (26b,53b,179c), hack (40a,77c,184d), heck (100a), hick (185d), hoek (91a,115b,182b,c), huck (167d), jack (26c,58a,127c), Jack (96b), jock (96b), Jock, juck (114c), kick, lack (178a), lick, lock (54d), luck (28d), mack, mick (82c), mock (131b,162b), muck, neck (83a), nick (30c,108b), nock (13b,108b), pack (24b,140d), peck (24d), pick, puck (44b,68a,77c,100c), Puck (99d,143b), rack (32c,64b), reck (26d,75c), rick (74d,117c), rock (160b), ruck (39a, 185a), sack (43d,118a,119d,182b), seck (173d), sick, sock (157c, 182a), suck, tack (28d,37d,54d), teck (128b), tick (12b,20d,97c), tock (7d,19b), tuck (156b), wick

C - - K   calk (78c,109a,141c,178d), cark (26d,184d), cask, cauk (139b), cawk (133c), chek (59c), coak (45d,118a,163b), cock (19a,29a, 55a,133d,136d), conk (41c,108a,156d,157c), cook (137b), cork (119d), cusk (57b)

CL - -   clad (46a,82a), clam (20b,101b), clan (169c), clap (58b), claw (29c, 105b,161d,173a), clay, Clay (9d), clee (19a,129a), clef (104d,105a), clem (56b,158b), Cleo (126b), clew (16a,33a,77b,136b,164d), Clim (12b), Clio (104d), clip (54d,143d), clod (22a,45b,157d), Cloe (183c), clog (30c,145b), clop, clot (32d,94d), clou (62b), clow (58c,148c), cloy (61b,137c,159d), club (39c), clue, Clym (12b)

- CL -   acle (13d,82c,115d)

C - - L   call (145c,159b,176d), carl (115c,135d), Carl (96a), caul (16d,74d), ceil (92c,112a), cell (39b), chil, chol (118d), Chol (192), cirl (24c), coal (49c,64a), coel (39b), coil (39d,171c,185a), cool (25c,107d), cowl (101d), cral, cull (117c), curl (38d,73b,93b,131d)

- CM -   acme (39c,115c,186b)

C - - M   caam (93d), calm (8d,11d,112b,118d,126c,d,172b), cham (20a,29d), Cham (8c), chum (38d), clam (20b,101b), clem (56b,158b), Clim (12b), Clym (12b), coom (32d,150c,178d), corm (24b,38d,156a), cram (157d), Crom, culm (11a,32d,70d,145a,156a)

CN - -   Cnut (40d,50c)

321

- CN - acne (147c)

C - - N Caen, cain (169c), Cain (6a,7a,50d,88a,104c,143a), carn (156c), cern (41c), chan (26c,130c), Chen (149b), chin, Chin (30b), Chun (30c), cion (42d,70b,145b,148b,154b,156a), clan (169c), Coan (37b), coin (19b,37a,100c,101c,179d), conn (43d,156a), coon (121c), corn (39d,95c,123a), coyn (37a), cran (160c), crin (146c), cyan

CO - - coag (45d,118a,163b), coak (45d,118a,163b), coal (49c,64a), Coan (37b), coat (160a), coax (180c), Cobb (9c), Cobh (37a), coca (29d, 33a,105d,113a), cock (19a,29a,55a,133d,136d,161d,174b), coco, (113a), coda (32c,35d,56c), code (21c,31a,40c,161c), codo (188), coed, coel (39b), coho (136d), coif (73a), coil (39d,171c,185a), coin (19b,37a,100c,101c,179d), coir (33a,37a,56a,133d), Coix (70d,85b), coja (103b,166b), coke (32d,64a), coky, cola (25b,108d,149d,168c), cold (65d), cole (25a), Cole, coli, colp (28a,148b), colt (78c,131a, 185d,186b), Colt, coly (104a), coma (91c,157d,170c,172b), comb (38c), come, Como, cond (156a), cone (66b,150a,157c), Coni, conk (41c,108a,156d,157c), conn (43d,156a), cony (127a), cook (137b), cool (25c,107d), coom (32d,150c,178d), coon (121c), coop, Coos, (192), coot (19b,46d,72b,138d,141a,146d,157d), copa (88b,113a), cope (12b,26b,36c,65b,157d,176a), copt (48d), copy, cora (65d), Cora (42b,69c,80c,116b,124d,172b,183c), cord (39b,139a), core (28b,51c,75b,81b), Cori (138c), cork (119d), corm (24b,38c,156a), corn (39d,95c,123a), cose (29b), cosh (35a,97c), coso (152c), coss (98a), cost (29a), cosy (149c), cota (117a), cote (19b,143d,144a,b), coto (16c,90b), Coty (63c), coup (20d,97c,157b,c,162d), cous (38a), cove (17a,73d,107d), cowl (101d), coxa (77b) coyn (37a), coyo (15a,30c), coze (29b), cozy (149c)

- CO - acon (62c,140d), acor (6d), icon (79d,92b,136a), scob (42a), scon (162c), scop (120a), scot (14a,162b), Scot (64b,132c), scow (21a, 58b)

- - CO alco (45b), caco (73b), coco (113a), Duco, fico (169d), loco (38b, 119b,120b), mico (97a), paco (9b,146d), peco (162b), pico (65a, 152c), poco (83b,93a), saco (189), soco (22d), Teco (192), toco (19b,167c), unco (140c), Waco

C - - O caco (73b), calo (72d), cano (152a), caro (83a), Caro (183d), Caso (82d), Cato (132d,133b), cayo, cero (57b,c,d,180c), ceto (34a), cipo (91d), cito (89d,126c), Cleo (126b), Clio (104d), coco, (113a), codo (188), coho (136d), Como, coso (152d), coto (16c,90b), coyo (15a,30c)

C - - P calp (92b), camp (163b), Capp (27a), carp (27d,38d,40c,55a,56c, 57a), caup, chap (55b), chip (69d), chop (98a), clap (58b), clip (54d,143d), clop, colp (28a,148b), coop, coup (20d,97c,157b,c, 162d), crop (38b), cusp (38c,78b,119a,120a,b)

C - - Q cinq (61d)

CR - - crab (39b,144b,181b), crag (132c), cral, cram (157d), cran (160c), craw (38d,72c,156c), Crax (19b,39d), crea (92c,151d), Cree (192), crew (72a,106a), Crex (37a), crib (96b,120d), cric (131c), crig (20d), crin (146c), cris (40b,95d), croc (13a,74a), Crom, crop (38b), crow (19a), crus (91a,143c), crux (39a,151b)

322

- CR - acre (39b,56a,88b), Acre, ecru (17d,23d,172b), ocra (72c,175a)

C - - R carr (120d,140a), caur (139a), char (24d,138c,170b), cher (61b), chir (29b,116d), chor (164b), coir (33a,37a,56a,133d), cuir (45c,62a), curr (104c), Czar (42d,49d,60b,135c)

- - CS ABC's (57a), pacs (94c)

C - - S cass (140c,177a), Cass (147a), cens (115b), cess (91d,94c,162b), cits, Coos (192), coss (98a), cous (38a), cris (40b,95d), crus (91a, 143c), cuss

- CT - acta (41d,123d,128d,164c), acth (13b), acto (152b), Acts, actu (7a, 89a), ecto (34c,122d), octa (122c), octo (34a,89b,122c)

- - CT duct (170c), fact (7a,128b), lact (34c), pact (8a), Pict (23c,47d), rect (117b), sect (42b,54a,114c), tact (43c,d,116a)

C - - T cant (28d,81b,84d,90c,109b,136c,165d,166a), cart (171d,175a, 177b), cast (165b,167c), Catt (9d), celt (30c,82c,123a,156c,167b, 179b), Celt (10a,180a,b), cent (36d), cest (18a,67b), chat (9b,19c, 161c), chit (67b,98c,108b,116c,177c), chut!, cist (22c,29d,156c), clot (32d,94d), coat (160a), colt (78c,131a,185d,186b), Colt (131a), coot (19b,46d,72b,138d,141a,146d,157d), Copt (48d), cost (29a), cult (141d,161c), curt (145b,c), cyst

CU - - cuba (189), Cuba (180b), cube (66b,150a), cubi (188), cuca (33a, 105d), cuff (148a), cuif (139a,d,140c), cuir (45c,62a), cuke (39b), cull (117c), culm (11a,32d,70d,145a,156a), cult (141d,161c), Cuna (193), cura (152c), curb (130c,146b), curd (99d), cure (123b), curl (38d,73b,93b,131d), curr (104c), curt (145b,c), cush (101c), Cush (51d,73c), cusk (57b), cusp (38c,78b,119a,120a,b), cuss, cute (39c), cuvy (141a), cuya (39b)

- CU - acus (89d,118a), scud (32c,126c,135b,160c), scum (129b), scup (57a,121b), scur (78b), scut (145c,161b)

- - CU jacu (19a,151b), jocu (45b,57a)

C - - U chou (61b), Chou (30b), clou (62b)

C - - V chiv (87a)

C - - W chaw (97c), chew (97c), chow (45a), claw (29c,105b,161d,173a), clew (16a,33a,77b,136b,164d), clow (58c,148c), craw (38d,72c, 156c), crew (72a,106a), crow (19a)

C - - X calx (23c,75c,112c), Ceyx (73b), coax (180c), Coix (70d,85b), Crax (19b,39d), Crex (37a), crux (39a,151b)

CY - - cyan, cyke (40c), cyma (101a,b), cyme (58d,69c), cyst

- CY - acyl (6d)

- - CY ancy (158c), lacy, Lucy (183c), racy (153b)

C - - Y cady (69d), cagy (178b), caky, cavy (72b,120d,132c,157b), cazy (103a), chay (48a,128d), choy (48a,128d), city, clay, Clay (9d), cloy (61b,137c,159d), coky, coly (104a), cony (127a), copy, cosy (149c), Coty (63c), cozy (149c), cuvy (141a)

CZ - - czar (42d,49d,60b,135c)

C - - Z chez (14b,61b)

DA - - dace (57a,b), Dada (13b,63a,157d), dado (41c,111c,115c, 177d), daer (22b), daez, daff (125d), daft (59c), dagg (118c), dagh

323

(76d), **Dago**, **Dail** (49a,82b,c), **dain** (188), **dais** (119b), **dale** (43c, 128a,174b), **dali** (168c,169b), **dama** (65d,152b), **dame** (67b,87c, 166b), **damn**, **damp** (101a), **Dana** (28a,96a,171d), **Dane** (85d,107d, 138a), **dang**, **dank** (40b,101a), **dans** (62a), **Danu** (28a), **Dara** (18d), **Dard**, **dare** (28d,41b,42a,74d,175b), **Dare** (57a), **dari** (38a,70b), **dark** (47a,67d,109b,160b), **darn** (130b), **darr** (163c), **dart** (13b,88a, 100c,120b,153a,160c), **dash** (125c,162d), **dasi** (77a), **data** (54a), **date** (64a,153a), **dato** (95c,102c,117a), **datu** (95c,102c,117a), **daub** (148d), **dauk** (95c), **Daur** (139b), **dauw** (24c), **Dave** (96b), **Davy** (96b,136b), **dawk** (95c), **dawm** (190), **dawn** (14d,41b), **Daye** (123d), **days**, **Daza** (191), **daze** (157d), **dazy**

- **DA** - **adad** (52c,56a), **Adad** (68c,157a,182a), **Adah** (25b,51b), **Adam** (26b,96a,111c), **adan** (102d), **Adar** (85c,102a), **adat** (90b,95d), **Edam** (29c), **Edar** (18d), **Idas** (27b,71c), **odah** (170d), **odal** (48a,88b,112c), **Odax** (132c), **udad** (143d,144a,181c), **udal** (76b, 88b,131c)

- - **DA** **adda** (147d), **Adda** (68c,119d), **Aida** (110d,175c), **alda** (152b), **Alda** (110d,150c), **anda** (23a,168c), **Beda** (101a), **Buda** (83d), **coda** (32c,35d,56c), **Dada** (13b,63a,157d), **Edda** (76b,79b,107d), **Erda** (23d,41a,47d,68d,69a,131d,177b), **Juda** (188), **kada** (188), **Leda** (27b, 75d,120c,153a,171d,186b), **Lida** (183c), **meda** (110a), **nuda** (39b), **peda** (114d,144b), **rada** (135c,172a), **Roda** (107b), **sida** (37a, 126c,170a), **soda** (19a,149d,181a), **Teda** (191), **Toda** (45d,76d), **Veda** (77a,b), **Vida** (183c)

D - - **A** **Dada** (13b,63a,157d), **dama** (65d,152b), **Dana** (28a,96a,171d), **Dara** (18d), **data** (54a), **Daza** (191), **deca** (34d,122d), **depa** (188), **dera** (34c), **deva** (23d,42a,b,56d,77a), **dewa**, **dika** (23a), **Disa** (111a), **dita** (117a), **diva** (110d,123c), **dola** (189), **dona** (83d,121c,151d), **dopa** (117d), **dora** (70b), **Dora** (36d,41a,43b), **dosa** (74b), **doxa** (48b), **draa** (188), **Duma** (135c), **dura** (153c), **dyna** (34c)

- - **DB** **Badb** (82b), **Bodb** (82b), **Medb**

D - - **B** **daub** (148d), **dieb** (84a), **doab** (157c), **doob** (18b), **doub** (18b), **drab** (23d,29c,33d,46d,53b,d), **drib** (46b), **drub** (17b,39c), **duab** (157c), **dubb** (161c), **dumb** (153b)

D - **C** **disc** (31b), **douc** (101d)

DD - - **DDSC** (42a)

- **DD** - **adda** (147a), **Adda** (68c,119d,157a,182a), **Addu** (68c,157a,182a), **Addy** (183d), **Edda** (76b,79b), **eddo** (162a), **eddy** (37d, 39d,160d, 180d), **odds** (28d,172d)

- - **DD** **dodd** (139c,140c), **gedd** (140a), **Ladd** (143c), **ludd** (23c), **mudd** (188), **Nudd** (23c), **Redd** (153a), **Ridd** (94a), **rodd** (38d), **rudd** (26d, 57a,b), **sadd** (33a,40b,58c,107b), **sudd** (40b,58c,107b), **wadd** (109c)

D - - **D** **dard**, **dead**, **deed** (7a,52d,91a,166c,168b), **diad** (113a), **dord** (42c), **dowd** (143b), **duad** (13a,171d), **dyad** (113a)

DE - - **dead**, **deaf**, **deal** (11d,16c,36c,44c,81a,168b), **dean** (33c,109d), **dear**, **debt** (91d,109b), **deca** (34c,122d), **deci** (163b), **deck** (13b, 41c,144d), **dedo** (188), **deed** (7a,52d,91a,166c,168b), **deem** (36b, 85c,164c), **deep** (124a), **deer** (28c,135a,154d), **defi** (61b), **deft** (147c), **defy** (28d), **degu** (132c), **deil** (139b), **dein** (66d), **dele** (26a, 49c,51b,53a,110b,123d,124c,130a,145c,161b), **deli** (43c,174b),

deme (71b,c,167d), **demi** (34b,122c), **demo** (122d), **demy** (113d), **dene** (137a), **Dene** (192), **dens** (90a,167b), **dent** (42c,77d), **deny** (36d,43d,129b), **depa** (188), **dera** (34c), **dere** (74a,79c), **derm** (147c,158d), **desi** (85d), **desk**, **deul** (77b), **deus** (68a,89b), **Deva** (23d,42a,b,56d,77a), **Devi** (147b,153b), **dewa, dewy** (101a)

- DE - **aden** (34b), **Aden, Ader** (18d), **Ades** (73a), **edel** (66c), **Eden** (6b,50d, 107c,113d,123c), **Eder, EDES** (71c), **idea** (54c,108c,124a,164d), **idee** (61d), **idem** (89d,164a), **Iden** (76a), **ideo** (34b,d), **ides** (41a, b,133a), **odea** (105a,164a), **odel** (48a,112c), **Oder** (132a)

- - DE **aide** (7b,14a,75d), **Ande** (193), **Aude, bade, Bede** (48c,50c,101d, 175b), **bide** (47c,50b,130a,158b,162a), **bode** (14c,60a,110b,121b), **cade** (25c,27a,76c,85d,116d), **Cade** (50c), **cede** (67b,70c,129d, 160a,168b,185d), **code** (21c,31a,40c,161c), **Dode** (96b), **dude** (40d), **eide** (119c), **fade** (181d,183b), **fide, gade, Gide** (63a), **hade** (66a, 148c,173c), **hide** (53a), **hyde** (188), **Hyde** (45a), **inde, jade** (33c, 65d,71d,166a), **Jude** (11c,96a), **kade** (144a), **lade** (24c,26d,43c,93b, 100a,132a,139d,161b,178d), **lode** (42c,99a,111b,175b), **made**, **Mede** (10a,b,13c), **mide** (110a), **mode** (54d,96b,157d,179a), **nide** (23c,72a,106c,116d), **node** (35c,85b,87c,94d,120a,124d,160c), **nude** (16c), **onde** (63a,178d), **rede** (37c,81d,138d), **ride** (46b,85c), **rode** (46c), **rude** (134b,172b), **sade** (91d), **side** (13d,22a,b,54a,58a,89a, 161b), **tide** (39d,75d,109c,141c,159d), **Tide, tode** (80a,148a), **unde** (179a), **urde** (86b), **vade** (42c,67d,89b), **vide** (89d,126a,142a), **wade, wide** (133d)

D - - E **dace** (57a,b), **dale** (43c,128a,174b), **dame** (67b,87c,166b), **Dane** (85d,107d,138a), **dare** (28d,41b,42a,74d,175b), **Dare** (57a), **date** (64a,153a), **Dave** (96b), **Daye** (123d), **daze** (157d), **dele** (26a,49c, 51b,53a,110b,123d,124c,130a,145c,161b), **deme** (71b,c,167d), **dene** (137a), **Dene** (192), **dere** (74a,79c), **dice** (65a), **dike** (49c, 91d), **Dike** (78a), **dime, dine, dire** (45d,55a,104a,163c), **dite** (150b), **dive** (42b,74b,119d), **dobe** (159b,c,172b), **Dode** (96b), **doge** (95b), **dole** (44c,118c,121c,129d), **Dole** (74c), **dome** (39c,133c,155d), **done, dope** (46c,105d), **dore** (61d,67b,69d,117d), **Dore** (50d,63a,b), **dose** (123a), **dote** (17a,90b,94b,97a,112a,139d,165d), **dove** (19a, 117d), **doze** (148a), **dree** (139b,140c,158b,172c), **duce** (29d), **dude** (40d), **duff** (125b), **duke** (107c), **dune** (137a), **dupe** (27c,41c, 72c,160c), **duse** (83c), **dyke** (49c,91d), **dyne** (59d)

D - - F **daff** (125d), **deaf, doff** (130a,161b), **duff** (125b)

- DG - **edge** (22a,96d,131c,143c,146b), **edgy** (106c)

D - - G **dagg** (118c), **dang, ding** (130b), **Doeg** (137c), **dong, drag** (74a, 125b), **dreg, drug** (105d)

DH - - **dhak** (48a,169a), **dhal** (12b), **dhan** (124c), **dhao** (24c), **Dhar, dhaw** (125a), **dhow** (88d,111c,175d)

- - DH **sadh** (77a), **Sadh, yodh** (91d)

D - - H **dagh** (76d), **Dagh, dash** (125c,162d), **dish, doth, drah** (188)

DI - - **diad** (113a), **dial** (25c), **dian** (46c,130d,170b), **Dian** (68d,69a,c, 102b), **Diau** (192), **dibs** (70c), **dice** (65a), **dick** (43a,55b), **Dick** (96b), **dido** (11b,26c,65a,122a), **Dido** (27a,172c), **dieb** (84a), **diem** (89b,116a), **dier, dies** (41b,89b), **diet** (14a,54c,84c,91b,176a), **Dieu** (61d), **dika** (23a), **dike** (49c,91d), **Dike** (78a), **dill** (13a,117c), **dilo**

(120d,168c), **dime, dine, ding** (130b), **dino** (34b), **dint** (48c,59d, 122a), **Dion** (96a,152a), **dipt, dire** (45d,55a,104a,163c), **dirk** (40b), **dirt, Disa** (111a), **disc** (31b), **dish, disk** (31b), **diss** (98b), **dita** (117a), **dite** (150b), **diva** (110d,123c), **dive** (42b,74b,119d), **divi, dixi**

- DI - **Adib** (155b), **adit** (51a,100a,114d), **edit** (20d,49d,123a,129a,131a), **idic** (79b), **idio** (34b,c), **odic** (79c,120a), **Odin** (7c,29d,63c,68c,175d, 183b), **odio** (83b), **udic** (108a)

-- DI **Andi** (27d), **cadi** (12a,103a), **kadi** (103a,171a), **Lodi** (105d), **ludi** (133b), **Madi** (174a), **medi** (34c), **Midi** (151b), **nidi** (106c), **nodi** (35c,87c), **padi** (131b), **pedi** (34b), **rodi** (98c), **sidi** (103b), **wadi** (46c,106a,109a,128a,132a)

D -- I **dali** (168c,169b), **dari** (38a,70b), **dasi** (77a), **deci** (163b), **defi** (61b), **demi** (34b,122c), **desi** (85d), **Devi** (147b,153b), **divi, dixi, doni** (21a,28c,168a), **drei** (66d,165a)

- DJ - **Idjo** (191)

-- DJ **hadj** (98b,118a)

D -- K **dank** (40b,101a), **dark** (47a,67d,109b,160b), **dauk** (95c), **dawk** (95c), **deck** (13b,41c,144d), **desk, dhak** (48a,169a), **dick** (43a,55b), **Dick** (96b), **dirk** (40b), **disk** (31b), **dock** (40a,117c,144d,179d), **dook** (184a), **duck** (26b,53b,179c), **dunk** (43c,79d), **dusk** (171c), **Dyak** (22b)

- DL - **idle** (174b,c,178c), **idly**

D -- L **Dail** (49a,82b,c), **deal** (11d,16c,36c,44c,81a,168b), **deil** (139b), **dell** (43c,174b), **deul** (77b), **dhal** (12b), **dial** (25c), **dill** (13a,117c), **doll** (125c), **dowl, dual** (45c,171d), **duel, dull** (21a,32c,173a), **Dull** (94b)

- DM - **admi** (65d)

D -- M **dawm** (190), **deem** (36b,85c,164c), **derm** (147c,158d), **diem** (89b, 116a), **doom** (42d,55a,134d), **dorm, doum** (168c), **dram** (46b,110c, 121d,148c), **drum** (105a), **duim** (188)

- DN - **Edna** (183c)

D -- N **dain** (188), **darn, damn, dawn** (14d,41b), **dean** (33c,109d), **dein** (66d), **dhan** (124c), **dian** (46c,130d,170b), **Dian** (68d,69a,c,102b), **Dion** (96a,152a), **Domn** (135a), **doon** (140b,168c), **dorn** (164d), **down** (149d), **duan** (64b)

DO -- **doab** (157c), **doat** (17a,94b,112a,165d), **dobe** (159b,c,172b), **doby** (159b,c), **dock** (40a,117c,144d,179d), **dodd** (139c,140c), **Dode** (96b), **dodo** (19b), **Doeg** (137c), **doer** (8a,116b), **does, doff** (130a,161b), **doge** (95b,175b), **dogy** (46d,103c), **doit** (47a,169d,180d), **Doko** (191), **dola** (189), **dole** (44c,118c,121c,129d), **Dole** (74c), **doli, doll** (125c), **dolt** (20c,59c,157d), **dome** (39c,133c,155d), **Domn** (135a), **domy, dona** (83d,121c,151d), **done, dong, doni** (21a,28c, 168a), **don't, doob** (18b), **dook** (184a), **doom** (42d,55a,134d), **doon** (140b,168c), **door** (51a,121b), **dopa** (117d), **dope** (46c,105d), **dopp** (43c), **dora** (70b), **Dora** (36d,41a,43b,183c,d), **dord** (42c), **dore** (61d,67b,69d,117d), **Dore** (50d,63a,b), **dorm, dorn** (164d), **dorp** (73c,176b), **dorr** (32b), **dory** (21b,58b,144c), **dosa** (74b), **dose** (123a), **doss** (17c), **dost, dote** (17a,90b,94b,97a,112a,139d,165d), doth, Doto (141b), doty (43d), doub (18b), douc (101d), doum (168c), dour (67d,159a), dove (19a,117d), dowd (143b), dowl, down (149d), doxa (48b), doxy (129d), doze (148a), dozy

- DO - ador (153b), Edom (18c,51b,79b,82c,84a), idol (48c,54c,55a,75b, 79d,112d,130b,184d), odor (138b,156a)

- - DO Bodo (88c), codo (188), dado (41c,111c,115c,177d), dedo (188), dido (11b,26c,65a,122a), Dido (27a,172c), dodo (19b), eddo (162a), endo (34d,122d,183b), fado (121c), Jodo (113d), judo (84b,85c, 142b), Lido (83d,175b), ludo (65a,112b), mado (14d,57a,170b), ordo (22a,30d,122a,171a), pedo (34b), redo (165c), sado (26d, 84d), todo (22b,24d,35b,64c,156b), undo (11a,93d), Yedo (166d)

D - - O dado (41c,111c,115c,177d), Dago, dato (95c,102c,117a), dedo (188), demo (122d), dhao (24c), dido (11b,26c,65a,122a), Dido (27a,172c), dilo (120d,168c), dino (34b), dodo (19b), Doko (191), Doto (141b), Duco, duro (190)

D - - P damp (101a), deep (124a), dopp (43c), dorp (73c,176b), drap (61b, c,62a), drip, drop (43d,54b,100b,114c,168b), dump

DR - - draa (188), drab (23d,29c,33d,46d,53b,d), drag (74a,125b), drah (188), dram (46b,110c,121d,148c), drap (61b,c,62a), drat (100a), Drau, draw (42c,53a,92b,117c,121c,167d), dray (27a,154c,177b), dree (139b,140c,158b,172c), dreg, drei (66d,165a), drew, drey (154c), drib (46b), Drin, drip, drop (43d,54b,100b,114c,168b), drub (17b,39c), drug (105d), drum (105a), drun (132b)

- DR - adry (164c)

- - DR sadr (94a), Sadr (155b)

D - - R daer (22b), darr (163c), Daur (139b), dear, deer (28c,135a,154d), Dhar, dier, doer (8a,116b), door (51a,121b), dorr (32b), dour (67d, 159a), duar, Duhr (155b), durr (70b), dyer

- DS - DDSC (42a)

- - DS duds (32c,166d), Eads (23b,24b,50b,82a), odds (28d,172d), suds (59a)

D - - S dais (119b), dans (62a), days, dens (90a,167b), deus (68a,89b), dibs (70c), dies (41b,89b), diss (98b), does, doss (17c), duds (32c,166d), Duns, Dyas (66a)

D - - T daft (59c), dart (13b,88a,100c,120b,153a,160c), debt (91d,109b), deft (147c), dent (42c,77d), diet (14a,54c,84c,91b,176a), dint (48c,59d,122a), dipt, dirt, doat (17a,94b,112a,165d), doit (47a, 169d,180d), dolt (20c,59c,157d), don't, dost, drat (100a), Duat (172d), duct (170c), duet (104d,171d), duit (190), Duit (192), dunt, dust

DU - - duab (157c), duad (113a,171d), dual (45c,171d), duan (64b), duar, Duat (172d), dubb (161c), duce (29d), duck (26b,53b,179c), Duco, duct (170c), dude (40d), duds (32c,166d), duel, duet (104d,171d), duff (125b), Dufy (63a), Duhr (155b), duim (188), duit (190), Duit (192), duke (107c), duku (95d,168c), dull (21a,32c,173a), Dull (94b), Duma (135c), dumb (153b), dump, dune (137a), dunk (43c, 79d), Duns, dunt, dupe (27c,41c,72c,160c), dura (153c), duro (190), durr (70b), duse (83c), dusk (171c), dust, duty (109b,162b)

- DU - idun (107d), odum (168c,180a)

327

- - DU Addu (68c,157a,182a), Jadu (95a), Kadu (191), kudu (11a), ordu (170d), pudu (41d), Urdu (77b), widu (102d), wudu (102d)

D - - U Danu (28a), datu (95c,102c,117a), degu (132c), Diau (192), Dieu (61d), Drau, duku (95d,168c)

D - - W dauw (24c), dhaw (125a), dhow (88d,111c,175d), draw (42c,53a, 92b,117c,121c,167d), drew

DY - - dyad (113a), Dyak (22b), Dyas (66a), dyer, dyke (49c,91d), dyna (34c), dyne (59d,173b)

- DY - idyl (114d), Idyo (191), odyl (59d,79c)

- - DY Addy (183d), Andy (96b), body (72a), cady (69c), eddy (37d,39d, 160d,180d), fady, jady, Judy (125c,183d), lady, sidy (123b), tidy (106a,111b), tody (19b,d,59a,166a), undy (179a), urdy (86b), wady (109a,128a,132a)

D - - Y Davy (96b,136b), dazy, defy (28d), demy (113d), deny (36d,43d, 129b), dewy (101a), doby (159b,c), dogy (46d,103c), domy, dory (21b,58b,144c), doty (43d), doxy (129d), dozy, dray (27a,154c, 177b), drey (154c), Dufy (63a), duty (109b,162b)

- DZ - adze (40c,167a), Idzo (191)

- - DZ Lodz

D - - Z Daez

EA - - each, Eads (23b,24b,50b,82a), eard (139b), earl (107c,166b), earn (42d,64b,99a), ease (7c,8d,35a,100d,129d,130b,c,150c), east, East (111b), easy (54a,146d,149d,172b) eats, eaux (178c), eave (133c),

- EA - bead (17a,122a,146b), beak (19a), beal (139d), beam, bean (91b, 142a,175a), bear (27a,50b,113c,155a), beat (58c,87b,131a,164d, 165b,180d), beau, dead, deaf, deal (11d,16c,36c,44c,81a,168b), dean (33c,109d), dear, feak (39d,171c), fear (113c,155a), feat (7a, 52d), geal (47d,163c), gean (29c), gear (32c,112a,167b), geat (77d, 101a), Geat (138a), head (29d), heaf (144a), heal, heap (117d), hear (75b,c,92d), heat, jean (37c), Jean (183c), keal (25a), lead (35d,43d,72b,74d,81a), leaf (55c,73c,119b), Leah (19a,84a,87b, 183c), leak (110c), leal (54b,94c,139d), lean (128a,148b,152d, 164b,166a), leap (26c), lear (139d), Lear (37a,143b), mead (46a, 78a,97d,99b), Mead (78a), meal (72a,130b), mean (15a,42b,146c, 156b), meat (59b), neaf (58a,73c), Neal, neap (165c,167a,177b), near (11d,32c,107b), neat (165c,169d), peag (144a,178a), peal (98b), peak (9a,38c,159b,186b), peal (131c,d), pean (64c,150b), pear (64a), peat (64a,175a), read (116d,157d), real (7a), ream (18c,37d,50d,113d,171c), reap (7a,40a,74a), rear (15b,23a,b,24a, 51b,76d,127c), seah (188), seal (10c,d,54d,64c,96a,118b,128a), seam (85b,d,160a,176d,185a), Sean (85b,96a), sear (23d,27d,72a, 138c), seat (98c,156b), teak (41a,48a,168c), teal (19b,20d,46c,d), team (38c,72a,113a), tean (140c,167a), tear (67c,87b,130a), veal, weak (55b), weal (124d,157d,180c,d), wean (8d,42d), wear (50b), yeah, Yean (88a), year, yeas (177c), zeal (12c,55d)

- - EA Alea (14b,31c,167d), area (37d,38a,44c,53a,93b,110d,127d, 138c,168a,186d), asea (39b,177c), brea (100b), crea (92c,151d), evea (82a), Evea (95a), flea (81b), Frea, Gaea (47d,69a), idea (54c, 108c,124a,164d), Itea (145d,160c,181d), odea (105a,164a), olea

(170b), **Olea** (110b), **Otea** (71a,82d), **oxea** (153d), **plea** (51a,52d, 122a,130b), **rhea** (37a,56a,111d,133d), **Rhea** (19b,68d,87c,103c, 186b), **shea** (25a,168c,d), **Thea** (162c), **uvea** (53c,82b)

E - - A **Ecca** (66a), **Edda** (76b,79b,107d,136b), **Edna** (183c), **Egba** (191), **Ekka** (26d), **Elba** (105d), **Elia** (88a,115d), **ella** (152c, 158c), **Ella** (183c), **Elsa** (70a,93c,110d,177b,183c), **Emma** (183c), **Enna** (146a), **epha** (75c), **Erda** (23d,41a,47d,68d,69a,131d,177b), **eria** (13d,146d), **Erma** (183c), **Erua** (103c), **esca** (11c,44a,70c), **esta** (152d,164c), **etna** (75b,153c,157a,175d,177a,c), **Etta** (183c), **evea** (82a,95a), **eyra** (181d), **ezba** (188), **Ezra** (96a)

EB - - **Eben** (96a), **Eber** (51a,75c,99d), **Ebro** (132a), **eboe** (28b,110a,168c, 169b), **Eboe, ebon** (20b), **ebur** (89c)

- EB - **ceba** (169b), **debt** (91d,109b), **Hebe** (39c,69c,186b), **Nebo** (68c, 102d,103d,183a), **peba** (12d), **Peba** (193), **Reba** (18d,86c,144a), **Seba** (18c,39d), **sebi** (34b), **ueba** (188), **zebu** (22d,80d,112c)

- - EB **bleb** (20c,23d,67c), **dieb** (84a), **pleb** (10d,35b,180b), **Sieb** (12a), **sweb** (160d), **theb** (188)

EC - - **ecad** (73a,119b), **Ecca** (66a), **ecce** (17d,89a,c), **echo** (130b,d), **Echo** (105d), **ecru** (17d,23d,172b), **ecto** (34c,122d)

- EC - **beck** (107c), **deca** (34d,122d), **deci** (163b), **deck** (13b,41c,144d), **heck** (100a), **lech** (102b), **neck** (83a), **peca** (190), **peck** (24d), **peco** (162b), **reck** (26d,75c), **rect** (117b), **sech** (97c), **seck** (173d), **sect** (42b,54a,114c), **teca, Teca** (192), **Tech, teck** (128b), **Teco** (192)

- - EC **alec** (10a,57c,d,76c), **Alec** (137a), **avec** (63a,183a), **haec** (90a, 164c), **spec**

E - - C **epic** (76b,120a), **eric** (115b), **Eric** (71d,96a,107d,138a,164c,176b), **eruc** (37a,56a)

ED - - **Edam** (29c), **Edar** (18d), **Edda** (76b,79b,107d,136b), **eddo** (162a), **eddy** (37d,39d,160d,180d), **edel** (66c), **Eden** (6b,50d,107c,113d, 123c), **Eder, Edes** (71c), **edge** (22a,96d,131c,143c,146b), **edgy** (106c), **edit** (20d,49d,123a,129a,131a), **Edna** (183c), **Edom** (18c, 51b,79b,82c,84a)

- ED - **Beda** (101d), **Bede** (48c,50c,101d,175b), **cede** (67b,70c,129d,160a, 168b,185d), **dedo** (188), **gedd** (140a), **Leda** (27b,75d,120c,153a, 171d,186b), **meda** (110a), **Medb, Mede** (10a,b,13c), **medi** (34c), **peda** (114d,144b), **pedi** (34b), **pedo** (34b), **redd** (153a), **rede** (37c, 81d,138d), **redo** (165c), **Teda** (191), **Veda** (77a,b), **Yedo** (166d)

- - ED **abed** (130c), **aged** (110a), **bled, bred** (23c,48c,127c), **coed, deed** (7a,52d,91a,166c,168b), **feed** (108c), **fled, Fred** (96b), **gled** (19a, 52a,87a), **heed** (14c,75b,109b), **hued, lied** (66d,150b), **meed** (128c, 131a), **Moed** (100c), **need** (42b,52d,87b,122a,178a), **Obed** (135d), **pied** (96c,103c,114b,117c,154a,174d), **reed** (16a,70d,97b,105a, 111b,118b,144b), **Reed** (163a), **roed, seed** (70b,111c,112c,119a, 151b,154a), **shed** (27a,90c,101b,144b), **sled** (40a), **sned** (93d,125a, 140a), **sped, syed** (103b), **tied, toed, used** (6d,73a), **weed**

E - - D **eard** (139b), **ecad** (73a,119b), **egad** (100a,109a), **eild** (138d,140a), **elod** (49b,59d,79c), **emyd** (163c,167c), **Enid** (13b,25d,66b,163a, 183c)

EE - - **eely** (185a), **eery** (172b,180a)

329

- EE - beef, been (149a), beer (18c), bees (185b), beet (175a), deed (7a, 52d,166c,168b), deem (36b,85c,164c), deep (124a), deer (28c, 135a,154d), feed (108c), feel (72a,142c), fees (128c), Geez (6c, 51d), heed (14c,75b,109b), heel, Heep (41a,43b), heer (47a,184b, 185b), jeel, jeep, jeer (138c,162b), keef (75d), keek (154c), keel (128d,134d,144c,d), keen (15a,88a,177b), keep (123a,130d), keet (72b), leek (58b,76a,110c,177d), leer (9d,58a,67c,93d,112a,148c), lees (46a,142a), leet (26a,38a,139d), meed (128c,131a), meek (93d,99d), meer, meet (11d,13d,36a,50a,81d,142d), need (42b, 52d,87b,122a,178a), neem (96d,168c,169a), neep (140c,171b), neer (14b,86b,108b), peek (93d), peel (53a,114a), peen (73c), peep (93d,115c), peer (51a,107c), peet (64a), reed (16a,70d,97b,105a, 111b,118b,144b), Reed (163a), reef (129a,137a,145a), reek (49d, 53c,64a,148d,149a), reel (21b,40b,d,153c,154a,c,d,180d), reem (18d), seed (70b,111c,112c,119a,151b,154a), seek (141c), seel (20c,32c,143b), seem (11c), seen, seep (110c,116a,154b), seer (60a,124c,150c), teel (142d), teem (6b,121d), teen (139b,c,140b, 158d), teer (25b,69d), Tees (108a), veer (28d,144c,171b), weed week, weel (16d,57d,140d,180d), weep (39b,88a,104a), weet (19d)

- - EE agee (13d,15c,38d), ajee (15c,139a), akee (168c), alee (15c,75d, 144b,157a,182a), bree (139a), byee (189), chee (189), clee (19a, 129a), Cree (192), dree (139b,140c,158b,172c), epee (55c,160d), flee, free (44a,70d,131b), ghee (24d), glee (99a,150b), idee (61d), inee (120b), Klee (113a), knee (85b), ogee (40c,101a,b,120b), pree (139d), Rhee (87c), shee (82b), skee (149c), slee (140b,148c), smee (19b,46c,d,118b,119d,141b,181b), Smee (116d), snee (40a, b,43d,87a), Spee (66d,70b), thee (124b), tree (11d,37a,66a,184b), twee, tyee (29d), usee, whee

E - - E ease (7c,8d,35a,100d,129d,130b,c,150c), eave (133c), eboe (28b, 110a,168c,169b), Eboe, ecce (17d,89a,c), edge (22a,96d,131c, 143c,146b), elde (119c), eine (66c), Eire (82b), Elbe (108a), elle (62b,c), else (18b,79b,111d), ence (158c), enne (34c), ense (139b, 158c), ente (70b,151d), epee (55c,160d), Erie (82c,87d), erne (19c, d,47b,54b,141a) Erse (28a,64b,82b), esce (158d), esne (10c,45b, 142c,148a,164d), esse (7a,18a,52d,89a,90a,159a,166c), este (152b, d,164c), Este (55c,83c,112d), etre (61a,c,62d,166c), ette (158a,c,d), euge (180a), evoe (15b,130d,181c), eyre (23c,31b,85c), Eyre

EF - - Efik (191)

- EF - defi (61b), deft (147c), defy (28d), heft (179d), Heft, jefe (152a), jeff (133d), left (42c), reft (32a,42c,44d,167b), teff (6c), weft (39a,165a,184b)

- - EF alef (91c), atef (39a,48d), beef, chef, clef (104d,105a), elef (91c), fief (55d), keef (75d), klef (75d), lief (181d), reef (129a,137a, 145a), tref (172b)

E - - F elef (91c), Enif (155b)

EG - - egad (100a,109a), Egba (191), Egbo (141d), Eger (49a), eggs (112a), eggy (185d), Egil (107d), egis (14b,d,115a,124d,144b,154a,161a), egol (11b)

- EG - bega (188), degu (132c), hegh, mega (34b,c), pega (57a,130a, 158b), Pegu (24c,102a,127d), sego (24b,25a,92b,174c), tegg (143d,

171d), **vega** (110d,152c), **Vega** (155b), **Wega** (155b), **Wegg** (111d),
yegg (24c)

- - EG   **areg** (116a,137a), **Areg, Doeg** (137c), **dreg, Gheg** (8c), **skeg** (7d,
86a,144d,157d,184a), **sneg** (139b), **waeg** (19b,72c,87a)

EH - -   **eheu** (52c)

- EH -   **behn** (137d), **Hehe** (191), **jehu** (46b), **Jehu** (18c), **lehr** (67c,112a),
peho (19b,102c,106d), **sehr** (66d), **tehr** (27c,68a)

- - EH   **okeh** (8d,37b)

E - - H   **each, Elah** (18c,86d), **Esth** (16a,51d), **Etah** (51c,71d), **etch, eyah**
(95b,108d,111c)

EI - -   **eide** (119c), **eild** (138d,140a), **eine** (66c) **Eire** (82b)

- EI -   **Beid** (155b), **ceil** (92c,112a), **deil** (139d), **dein** (66d), **feis** (82b),
gein (67d), **heii** (74b), **hein** (52c,61c), **heir, keif** (75d), **keir** (20c,
174d), **Leif** (107d), **Leir, mein** (30b), **nein** (66c), **meio** (188), **Neil**
(96a), **reim** (112c), **rein** (29b,130c), **reis** (26c,29d,75a,103b), **seid**
(103b), **Seid** (42d,101a,171a), **Seik** (77b), **Seim** (120c), **sein** (146c),
seip (110c), **Seir** (51b,94a,103d), **seis** (147b,152c), **seit** (189), **Teig**
(96a), **teil** (92b,c,168c), **veil** (74d,76c), **vein** (20d,157b), **weir**
(40b,57d), **zein**

- - EI   **drei** (66d,165a), **kuei** (44a), **kwei** (44a), **Omei** (24a), **quei** (189),
vlei (38c,160a)

E - - I   **Ekoi** (191), **Enki** (15b), **equi** (122d), **etui** (27a,29b,62c,106b,148d,
166d,174b)

EJ - -   **ejoo** (55b,168c)

- EJ -   **Beja** (6c,191), **Nejd, reja** (152b), **Sejm** (120c), **teju** (151b)

EK - -   **Ekka** (26d), **Ekoi** (191)

- EK -   **beka** (189), **feke, Peke** (45a,148d), **Reki** (16a), **weka** (58c,106d,
107a,127b), **weki** (55c), **Zeke** (96b)

- - EK   **chek** (59c), **esek** (18d), **hoek** (39d), **keek** (154c), **leek** (58b,76a,
110c,177d), **meek** (93d,99d), **peek** (93d,115c), **reek** (49d,53c,
64a,148d,149a), **seek** (141c), **trek** (85c,93c,99d,168c)

E - - K   **Efik** (191), **esek** (18d)

EL - -   **Elah** (18c,86d), **Elam** (18d,37d,82a,116c,144b), **elan** (12c,41a,50d,
62a,153c,177a,186b), **ELAS** (71c), **Elba** (105d), **Elbe** (108a), **elef**
(91c), **Ella** (88a,115d), **Elis** (22c,37d,71b,107c), **ella** (152c,158c,
Ella (183c), **elle** (62b,c), **elmy, elod** (49b,59d,79c), **Elon** (18c,51b,
108a), **Elsa** (70a,93c,110d,177b,183c), **else** (18b,79b,111d), **Elui**
(102b)

- EL -   **bela** (12a), **Bela** (18b,48c,78d), **Beli** (23c), **bell** (24c,39d), **Bell**
(162d), **belt** (16a,31a), **cela** (62d), **cell** (39b), **celt** (30c,82c,123a,
156c,167b,179b), **Celt** (10a,180a,b), **dele** (26a,49c,51b,53a,110b,
123d,124c,130a,145c,161b), **dell** (43c,174b), **eely** (185a), **fell** (40a,
58b,76c,115d,147d), **fels** (190), **felt, geld** (162b), **gelt** (101c), **Hela**
(93c), **held, helm** (144d,165d), **help** (14a), **kela** (189), **keld** (154b),
kelp (82a,141c), **Kelt** (180b), **Lely** (47a), **mele** (74b,150b), **melt,
Nell** (110a,183d), **pela** (30c), **Pele** (69c,74c), **pelf** (131b), **pelo** (83b),
pelt (53a), **pelu** (30a,106d,168c), **rely** (16b,170b), **self** (48d,80d),
selt (97a,115c,175b), **tela** (22d,98c,121b,166a,179c), **tele** (34b,

331

122c), **teli** (94b), **tell** (105d,129c,154b), **Tell** (160d), **vela** (98c 136b,149d), **Vela** (36b,c), **veld** (151a), **velo** (175b), **weld** (47c,85b, 173c), **Welf** (67a), **welk** (65c,96d,141b), **well, welt** (36d,131b, 145a,b,177b,d), **yell** (145c), **yelp, yelt** (151b)

- - EL   **Abel** (7a,25b), **bhel** (126d), **coel** (39b), **duel, edel** (66c), **esel** (66b), **ezel** (47a,85d), **feel** (72a,142c), **fuel** (65c), **Gael** (28a,96c,138d), **goel** (15a,75c), **heel, Jael** (147b), **jeel, Joel** (96a), **keel** (128d,134d, 144c,d), **kiel** (128d,134d), **Kiel** (25d), **koel** (19a,b,39b), **nael** (189), **noel** (26d,150b), **Noel** (30d,96a), **odel** (48a,112c), **Orel, peel** (53a, 114a), **reel** (21b,40b,d,153c,154a,c,d,180d), **Riel** (129a), **ryel** (190), **seel** (20c,32c,143b), **tael** (91d,179d), **teel** (142d), **tuel, weel** (16d, 57d,140d,180d), **wiel** (140d,180d)

E - - L   **earl** (107c), **edel** (66c), **Egil** (107d), **egol** (11b), **Elul** (102b), **Emil** (96a), **enol** (29c,158b), **eral** (51a), **esel** (66b), **etal** (89a), **evil** (79c, 95d,147a,181a,185c), **ezel** (47a,85d)

EM - -   **Emer** (39b,183c), **emeu** (111d), **Emil** (96a), **Emim** (67a,100d), **emir** (12a,103a,b,123c,134d,135a,171a), **emit** (43d,49a,53c,58d,83a, 142c), **Emma** (183c), **emyd** (163c,167c), **Emys** (167c,171b)

- EM -   **bema** (28d,31a,114b,119b,125b,137a), **deme** (71b,c,167d), **demi** (34b,122c), **demo** (122d), **demy** (113d), **feme** (181b), **hemi** (122c), **hemo** (34a,122b), **hemp** (26a,37a,56a,133d), **kemp** (139b), **memo** (108b), **Nema** (34d,48c,134b,164d,176c), **nemo** (34b), **Nemo** (56a, 85c), **Remi** (10b), **Rems, seme** (45c,138b,151b,154b,155c,157b), **semi** (34b,80b,122c,d), **tema** (12a,164a), **Tema, xema** (72c), **Xema** (12c), **zeme** (55d,161b,180b), **zemi** (55d,161b,180b)

- - EM   **ahem, alem** (98b,155a,170d,171a), **asem** (9a,49a,69c), **clem** (56b, 158b), **deem** (36b,85c,164c), **diem** (89b,116a), **haem** (122b), **idem** (89d,164a), **item** (6d,13b,42d,51a,90d,92d,107a,113d,114c), **Khem** (113c), **neem** (96d,168c,169a), **poem** (51a), **reem** (18d), **riem** (76c, 112c,157c,164d), **seem** (11c), **Shem** (107c), **stem** (29b,125a,154d, 155a,156d), **teem** (6b,121d), **them** (124b)

E - - M   **edam** (29c), **Edom** (18c,51b,79b,82c,84a), **Elam** (18d,37d,82a,116c, 144b), **Emim** (67a,100d), **enam** (70c,77a), **Enam** (85c), **etym** (133d), **exam**

EN - -   **enam** (70c,77a,85c), **ence** (158c), **endo** (34d,122d,183b), **Enid** (13b,25d,66b,163a,183c), **Enif** (155b), **enin** (20d), **Enki** (15b), **Enna** (146a), **enne** (34c), **enol** (29c,158b), **Enon** (18c,d), **Enos** (7a,18d,52a, 70c,96a,143a), **enow** (50d,123a,158b), **ense** (139b,158c), **enso** (34d,183b), **ente** (70b,151d), **ento** (34b,d,183b), **envy** (41b), **Enyo** (12c,69c,178a), **Enzu** (102b)

- EN -   **bena** (176a), **bend** (39d,171b), **bene** (18a,83c,90a,106d,122a, 180a), **beng** (43a), **beni** (116a,142d), **Beni** (191), **beno** (113b,117a), **bent** (80b), **benu** (49a), **cena** (88d,133a), **cene** (34c), **cens** (115b), **cent** (36d), **dene** (137a), **Dene** (192), **dens** (90a,167b), **dent** (42c, 77d), **deny** (36d,43d,129b), **fend** (114b,178b), **gena** (29b), **gene** (54a,76b), **Gene** (96b), **gens** (42d,132d), **gent, genu** (6b,18a,87a, 89c), **hens** (121d), **Jena** (105d,165b), **keno, Kent** (90d), **lena** (56d), **Lena** (36b), **lend** (6d,79d), **lene** (36b,149a,172b), **leno** (37c, 53b), **lens** (67c,95b,111a,129b,162d), **lent** (54d), **Lent** (115d,141c), **mend** (130b), **mene** (19a,73d,108d,185c), **Ment** (54b,164a), **menu**

332

(19a,27a), **Menu, nene** (19b,74c), **pend, pene, pent** (36a), **rena** (25b,132c), **rend** (32a,159c,162c,185a), **Reni** (83d), **Reno, rent** (58a,91b,138b,153d,162c,167c), **send** (42c,44b,95c,121c,130a, 144c,168b), **senn** (76b), **Sens** (63b), **sent, tend** (26d,80b,93d,100a), **tene** (34d,131b), **teng** (188), **tent** (26b,115a), **vena** (90a,175a), **vend** (97a,115c,142b), **Vend** (10b,148a), **vent** (8b,11b,110d,112a), **wend** (67d,123d), **Wend** (10b,148a), **went** (42c), **xeno** (34d), **yeni** (19b,161d), **Zend, Zeno** (71b), **zenu** (143d)

- - **EN**   **aden** (34b), **Aden, alen** (40d,138a), **amen** (14a,80b,94a,137a,149c, 175c,184b), **Amen** (86d,127d,164a), **aten** (150a,159b), **been** (149a), **bien** (63a,140c,179a,180a), **bren** (72d,95a), **Caen, Chen** (149b), **Eben** (96a), **Eden** (6b,50d,107c,113d,123c), **even** (51a,58b,79d,91d, 149a,173a), **glen** (43c), **hien** (30b), **hoen** (189), **Iden** (76a), **Iren** (127c), **Iten** (192), **keen** (15a,88a,177b), **lien** (65c,91a,124c), **mien** (11c,17b,26d,44c,96b), **omen** (14c,59c,60a,121c,123a,146b), **open** (26a,60d,81a,109b,112c,125b,172b,173c), **oven** (15d,78c,86b), **Owen** (96a,183c), **oxen** (10c), **peen** (73c), **pien** (13b), **rien** (62b), **seen, Shen** (68a), **sken** (164a), **sten** (72c,95a), **teen** (139b,c,140b, 158d), **then, tien** (147d), **T-men** (168b), **when** (180d), **wren** (19b,c), **Wren** (50b)

E - - N   **earn** (42d,64b,99a), **Eben** (96a), **ebon** (20b), **Eden** (6b,50d,107c, 113d,123c), **elan** (12c,41a,50d,62a,153c,177a,186b), **Elon** (18c, 51b), **enin** (20d), **Enon** (18c,d), **Eoan** (41a,85b), **Eoin** (85b), **Erin** (82b), **Eton** (33b,50c,84a), **Evan** (96a), **even** (51a,58b,79d,91d, 149a,173a), **Ewan**

EO - -   **Eoan** (41a,85b), **Eoin** (85b)

- EO -   **feod** (55d), **Leon** (96a), **meou, meow, neon** (65c), **peon** (28c,59c, 99c), **Teos** (82a)

- - EO   **areo** (34c), **Ateo** (120d), **Cleo** (126b), **ideo** (34b,d,164d), **oleo** (34c), **skeo** (57d)

E - - O   **Ebro** (132a), **echo** (130b,d), **Echo** (105d), **ecto** (34c,122d), **eddo** (162a), **Egbo** (141d), **ejoo** (55b,168c), **endo** (34d,122d,183b), **enso** (34d,183b), **ento** (34b,d,183b), **Enyo** (12c,69c,178a), **ergo** (164b)

EP - -   **epee** (55c,160d), **epha** (75c), **epic** (76b,120a), **epos** (51a,76b,120a)

- EP -   **cepa** (110c), **cepe** (48c), **depa** (188), **kepi** (99d), **kept, Nepa** (106b, 178c), **pepo** (39b,64a,70a,98c,125c,154c), **repp** (53b,131a), **seps** (93b,142d), **sept** (31d,82b,143a,149c), **Sept** (45b), **Veps** (191), **wept**

- - EP   **deep** (124a), **Heep** (41a,43b), **jeep, keep** (123a,130d), **neep** (140c, 171b), **peep** (93d,115c), **prep** (138b), **seep** (110c,116a,154b), **skep** (16d,17c,77c), **step** (70b,112b,177b,d), **weep** (39b,88a,104a)

EQ - -   **equi** (122d)

ER - -   **eral** (51a), **erat** (89c), **Erda** (23d,41a,47d,68d,69a,131d,177b), **erer** (17d,150c), **ergo** (164b), **eria** (13d,146d), **eric** (115b), **Eric** (71d, 96a,107d,138a,164a,176b), **Erie** (82c,87d), **Erin** (82b), **Eris** (12c, 68d,109c), **Erma** (183c), **erne** (19c,d,47b,54b,141a), **Eros** (11c, 39c,68b,97c,182d), **Erse** (23a,64b,82b), **erst** (60b), **Erua** (103c), **eruc** (37a,56a), **eryx** (137a)

- ER -   **aera** (8a), **aeri** (34a), **aero** (8b,34a,b,58c,59a), **aery** (47b,51d,106c), **Bera** (86d), **berg** (79b), **berm** (25d,90d,145c), **Bern** (160d), **Bert**

(96b), **cera** (152d,161d,179a), **cere** (19a,114b,149d,179a), **cern** (41c), **cero** (57b,c,d, 180b), **dera** (34c), **dere** (74a,79c), **derm** 147c,158d), **eery** (172b,180a), **fern** (142a), **feru** (37a,56a,133d), **gerb** (56d,143d), **Gerd** (63c), **Gere** (183c), **Geri** (183c), **germ** (17d, 99c,134d), **Hera** (69c,85d,110b,126b,186b,d), **herb** (58b,158b), **herd** (39a,46c,72a), **here**, **herl** (16b,59a), **hero** (42b,124d,137b), **Hero** (90c), **Herr** (66c), **hers** (124c), **jerk** (153a), **kerb** (146b), **kere** (75c,128b), **kerf** (40a,108b), **keri** (75c,128b), **kern** (59c,172a), **Kern** (132b), **Kerr**, **Lero** (82d), **lerp** (51d,141d), **mere** (16c,22b, 62a,78b,87d,96c,110c,120d,146d,148b), **merl** (20b), **mero** (72a), **Meru** (77a,103d), **Nera** (165b), **Neri**, **Nero** (8a,126d,133a,172c), **Pera** (60a), **pere** (61c,63b), **peri** (54b,116b,c,122b), **perk** (84d, 93a), **perm** (49b,97d), **pern** (78a), **pero** (152a), **pert** (80a,93a,137c, 154b), **Peru**, **qere** (75c), **qeri** (75c), **sera** (11b,20d,59a,83a,180d), **Serb** (15d,148a,186c), **sere** (24d,46a,46c,138c,183b), **Sere** (158b), **serf** (21d,148a), **seri** (18b), **Seri** (192), **sero** (34d,88d,164b,178d), **Sert** (151d), **tera** (23d,84c), **term** (92b,105d,142b,166b), **tern** (19b, 32d,72c,94a,138c,141a,160a), **terp** (12b,123a), **vera** (140c,151b, 175c), **Vera** (183c), **verb** (7a,114b,184b), **verd** (71d), **veri** (28b), **vert** (71d,166a,171b), **very** (149c), **were** (139b), **werf** (54d), **werl** (15c,27c), **wert**, **zero** (31a,84c,108c), **Zero** (118d)

D - ER   **Acer** (96c) **Ader** (18d), **afer** (48a,182b), **ager** (47c,56a,89b,c,131d, 133b), **amer** (61b), **aner** (18d,96b), **aper** (32d), **Aser** (84a), **Ater** (18c), **Auer** (79a), **aver** (7c,14a,15c,41c,95c,140d,155c,160b, 184c), **beer** (18c), **bier** (33b,66b), **Boer** (151a), **Brer** (172b), **cher** (61b), **daer** (22b), **deer** (28c,135a,154d), **dier**, **doer** (8a,116b), **dyer**, **Eber** (51a,75c,99d), **Eder**, **Eger** (49a), **Emer** (39b,183c), **erer** (17d, 150c), **eser**, **euer** (66d), **ever** (9b,14b,80b), **ewer** (84c,85c,118c, 181b), **eyer**, **gier** (47b), **goer**, **heer** (47a, 184b, 185b), **hier** (63a, 185d), **Hier** (141a), **hoer**, **icer**, **Imer**, **Iser** (49a), **iter** (22d,76c,85c, 89c,114d,132a,b,133a,b), **jeer** (138c,162b), **kier** (20c,174d), **leer** (9d,58a,67c,93d,112a,148c), **meer**, **neer** (14b,86b,108b), **Oder** (132a), **omer** (51a,75c), **oner** (20d,53a,75c,162d,173a,d), **oser** (61b), **over** (6b,38c,80a,114d,130a), **oxer** (55c), **oyer** (38a,75b,119c), **peer** (51a,93d,107c), **pier** (23a,88b,180c), **rier** (180b), **roer** (72d), **ruer**, **saer** (163a), **seer** (60a,124c,150c), **sher** (65d,165c), **sier** (57a,118b), **ster** (158c,d), **suer** (124d), **teer** (25b,69d), **tier** (118a,134b), **tyer**, **uber** (66b), **user** (49d), **veer** (28d,144c,171b), **vier** (66c), **waer** (40b), **Ymer** (67a,131c), **Yser**

E - - R   **Eber** (51a,75c,99d), **ebur** (89c), **Edar** (18d), **Eder**, **Eger** (49a), **Emer** (39b,183c,), **emir** (12a,103a,b,123c,171a), **erer** (17d,150c), **eser**, **euer** (66d), **ever** (9b,14b,80b), **ewer** (84d,85c,118c,181b), **eyer**

ES - -   **Esau** (82c,84a,128c), **Esay**, **esca** (11c,44a,70c), **esca** (158d), **esek** (18d), **esel** (66b), **eser**, **esne** (10c,45b,142c,148a,164d), **Esop** (53b, 54a), **esox** (57b), **espy** (44a,142a), **esse** (7a,18a,52d,89a,90a,159a, 166c), **esta** (152d,164c), **este** (152b,d,164c), **Este** (55c,83c,d,112c), **Esth** (16a,51d), **Esus**

- ES -   **aesc** (12d,64d), **Besa** (68b,119c), **Bess** (76c,183d), **best** (41d,159c, 160a), **cess** (91d,94c,162b), **cest** (18a,67c), **desi** (85d), **desk**, **euer** (66d), **fess** (23c,51b), **fest**, **gest** (7c,41d,52d,133c), **hest** (35a), **jess** (157a), **jest** (169c), **Jesu**, **less** (100c,108b,141d), **lest** (59d,163d), mesa (49b,76d,119b,161a), mese (71c), mesh (50d,106c), mess (22b,44b,77c,85d,104b,165c,173d), ness (26b,75a,124b), nest (38b, 74b,130d,149c,160b), oese (15d,119c), pesa (190), peso (99c), pest (108c,116b,118d,170a), rese (127b), resh (91d), rest (15d,91b, 104d,105a,115a,b,130a,b,161b), sesi (20b,57a,149b), sess (149c, 162b), Tesa (80c), Tess (73d,164c,183d), test (26a,51c,144a,169c, 170c), vest (32c,177b), West (9c,50b,109b), Yeso (72d), zest (55d, 72d)

- - ES Ades (73a), Ames (9c,82a), anes (110c,140a), Ares (49b,51b,68c, 76a,97a,105c,110b,178a,186d), ates (160c), Aves (19d), bees (185b), Bres, dies (41b,89b), does, EDES (71c), fees (128c), Ghes (193), gres (156d), ides (41a,b,133a), Ives (9c,90b), lees (46a, 142a), ones (116a), oyes (38a,39b,75b), pres (62b), spes, Spes (69a,78a), Tees (108a), tres (19a,52b,63a,152d,165a,175c), uses (18a), wies (185a)

E - - S Eads (23b,24b,50b,82a), eats, EDES (71c), eggs (112a), egis (14b, d,115a,124d,144b,154a,161a), ELAS (71c), Elis (22c,37d,71b, 107c), Emys (167c,171b), Enns, Enos (7a,18d,52a,70c,96a,143a), epos (51a,76b,120a), Eris (12c,68d,109c), Eros (11c,39c,68b,97c, 182d), Esus, etes (177c), eyas (106c,173a)

ET - - Etah (51c,71d), etal (89a), etat (62d), etch, etes (177c), etna (75b, 153c,157a,175d,177a,c), Eton (33b,50c,84a), etre (61a,c,62d,166c), Etta (183c), ette (158a,c,d), etui (27a,29b,62c,106b,148d,166d, 174b), etym (133d)

- ET - Aeta (94d,95d,100a,106b,117a), beta (71a,91c,141d), beta (61a,107c), beth (91c), Beth (8c,183d), cete (180b,c), ceto (34a), fete (55d,129b), geta (84b,145a), gett (44d), Heth (77c), jete (16a), Jeth (102a), keta (45a), Keta, Ketu (48b), lete, Leti (82d), Leto (11c), Lett (16a,90a,93a), meta (132d,133a), Meta, mete (9a, 11d,22b,44c,45b,98a,121c), nete (71c,108b,163d), neti (164a), nett, pete (136b), Pete (96b), peto (57a,177b), Peto (76a), rete (106c,119c), seta (23b,27c,73a,b,123b,153c), seth (98d), Seth (7a, 52b,68a,b,96a,98d), seti (34a), Seti (116d), sett (115a,156d), tete (61d,73b,74d), teth (91d), veta (104a), veto (94a,124a), Veto, weta (93c), yeta (84c), zeta (71b,91c)

- - ET abet (8b,15b,50a,59b,75d,81c,141d,159d), Ahet (49a,102a), anet (43c), Apet (97c), aret (128c), beet (175a), biet (64a), diet (14a, 54c,84c,91b,176a), duet (104d,171d), evet (48d,107a,136c,169d), fret (28c,35b,111c,184d), keet (72b), khet (188), laet (60d), leet (26a,38a), meet (11d,13d,36a,50a,81d,142d), oket (189), peet (64a), piet (29b,95b), plet (135d), poet (49b), pret (188), pyet (95b), spet (16c,57a,142c), stet (91b,123b,124c), suet (54d), tret (9a,178b,179d), voet (188), weet (19d), whet (143c,156b)

E - - T east, East (111b), edit (20d,49d,123a,129a,131a), emit (43d,49a, 53c,58d,83a,142c), erat (89c), erst (60b), etat (62d), evet (48d, 107a,136c,169d), exit (114d), eyot (82d)

EU - - euer (66d), auge (180a)

- EU - deul (77b), deus (68a,89b), feud (55d,126b,175b), Geum (76b), jeux (61d), meum (27a,89c), Meum, neue (66c), peur (61c), Zeus (135a)

335

- - EU bleu (61b), Dieu (61d), eheu (52c), emeu (111d), lieu (118c,155d)

E - -U ecru (17d,23d,172b), eheu (52c), emeu (111d), Enzu (102b), Esau (82c,84a,128c)

EV - - Evan (96a), even (51a,58b,79d,91d,149a,173a), evea (82a,95a), ever (9b,14b,80b), evet (48d,107a,136c,169d), evil (79c,95d,147a, 181a,185c), evoe (15b,130d,181c)

- EV - bevy (38a,58c), Deva (23d,42a,b,56d,77a), Devi (147b,153b), hevi (111d), Leve (62a), Levi (84a,90c), levo (91a), levy (14a, 162b), Neva (91b,132a), neve (56d,67c,70c,149b), peva (12d), pevy (91d,94c), reve (61c,104d), revs (131a), seve (63a,182c)

- - EV Kiev, Stev (155b)

EW - - Ewan, ewer (84d,85c,118c,181b), ewry (133c)

- EW - dewa, dewy (101a), hewn, mewl (180d), mews (154c), news (165c), newt (48d,136c,169d), sewn, Tewa (193)

- - EW anew (7c), blew, brew (35d), chew (97c), clew (16a,33a,77b,136b, 164d), crew (72a,106a), drew, flew, grew, knew, Llew (40c), phew (52c), plew (17c), shew (44c), skew (148a,160c,171c), slew (160a), smew (19b,46d,99a,137d), spew (35a,49a), stew (21c,44b,184d), thew (104c), view (93d,138b), whew

E - - W enow (50d,123a,158b)

EX - - exam, exit (114d)

- EX - next (106a), sext (26b,111b,147b), text (21c,140d)

- - EX Amex (184d), apex (39c,76c,115c,118b,159b,166a,167b), Crex (37a), faex (46a), flex (18a), ibex (67d,68a), ilex (77d), obex (22d), plex (60b), spex, Ulex (153c)

E - - X eaux (178c), eryx (137a), esox (57b)

EY - - eyah (95b,108d,111c), eyas (106c,173a), eyer, eyey (74b), eyot (82d), eyra (181d), eyre (23c,31b,85c), Eyre, eyry (47b,106c)

- EY - Ceyx (73b), teyl (92b,c,168c)

- - EY ahey (52c), akey (189), brey (194), drey (154c), eyey (74b), fley (63d), Frey (7c,68b,124c), grey (33c), hoey (114c), joey (86a,185b), Joey (96b,109c), obey (35c,75c), prey (119d,176a), roey (103d), skey (185d), sley (179b), Spey, they (124b), trey (26c,165a), Urey (14b,107c,138c), whey (100a)

E - - Y easy (54a), eddy (37d,39d,160d,180d), edgy (106c), eely (185a), eery (172b,180a), eggy (185d), elmy, envy (41b), esay, espy (44a, 142a), ewry (133c), eyey (74b), eyry (47b,106c)

EZ - - ezba (188), ezel (47a,85d), Ezra (96a)

- - EZ chez (14b,61a), daez (189), Geez (6c,51d), Inez (45c,183c), juez (152b), knez (123c), oyez (38a,39b,75b)

FA - - Faam (111a), Faba, face (159d,176c), fact (7a,128b), fade (181d, 183b), fado (121c), fady, faex (46a), fail, fain (42d,67c,183b), fair (17a,55d), fait (6d,61b), fake (123a,143c), faky, fala (129b), fall (46b,141c), falx (133b), Fama (135a), fame (130a), famn (188), fana, fane (30d,137a,162d), fang (167b), fano (51d,96b,113c,d), faon (33c,55a), fard (112d), fare (43c,59b,67d,123c), farl (138c, 140b), farm (165d), faro (65a), fash (140c,176a), fass (189), fast (56d,126c,141d,160c,173a,d), fate (42d,52a,87a,94a), faun (56a,

68b,137c,161a,184a), **favi** (138a,165d), **fawn** (33c), **faze** (43d)

-FA - **afar** (44c), **Afar** (6c)

-- FA **Abfa** (76b), **alfa** (70d), **gufa** (21b,99a), **Kafa** (6c), **kufa** (21b,99a), **Offa** (163d), **sofa** (44d), **tufa** (121b,177a), **Urfa** (99a)

F -- A **Faba, fala** (129b), **Fama** (135a), **fana, flea** (81b), **fora** (133a), **Frea, Fria, fuga**

F -- B **flub** (22b), **frab** (138c), **frib** (43d)

F -- C **fisc** (52c,134c), **floc** (149a)

-- FD **Wafd** (49a)

F --D **fard** (112d), **feed** (108c), **fend** (114b,178b), **feod** (55d), **feud** (55d, 126b,175b), **find** (44a), **fled, fold, fond** (7c,94b), **food** (109a,176b), **ford** (177b), **foud** (54d,144b), **Fred** (96b), **Fuad** (54d), **fund** (6d, 101c,130c), **fyrd** (110a)

FE -- **feak** (39d,171c), **fear** (113c,155a), **feat** (7a,52d), **feed** (108c), **feel** (72a,142c), **fees** (128c), **feis** (82c), **feke, fell** (40a,58b,76c,115d, 147d), **fels** (190), **felt, feme** (181b), **fend** (114b,178b), **feod** (55d), **fern** (142a), **feru** (37a,56a,133d), **fess** (23c,51b), **fest, fete** (55d, 129b), **feud** (55d,126b,175b)

-FE - **afer** (48a,182b)

-- FE **cafe, fife** (59a,105a), **jefe** (152a), **life** (19a,177a), **nife** (37a), **orfe** (57a,b,185c), **rife** (6b,c,39d,123b), **safe** (141d,157d,174d), **wife** (154a)

F -- E **face** (159d,176c), **fade** (181d,183b), **fake** (123a,143c), **fame** (130a), **fane** (30d,137a,162d), **fare** (43c,59b,67d,123b), **fate** (42d,52a,87a, 94a), **faze** (43d), **feke, feme** (181b), **fete** (55d,129b), **fide, fife** (59a,105a), **fike** (139c), **file** (13a,127d), **fine** (49b,50a,104b,115d, 159a), **fire** (13a,43d,44b), **five, flee, floe** (79b), **flue** (8b,30a), **fore** (63d,174b), **free** (44a,70d,131b), **froe** (32a,167a,179d), **fume** (129a, 149a,157a), **fuse** (98c), **fute** (51c), **fuze** (98c), **fyke** (15d)

-FF - **affy** (18b), **offa, Offa** (163d), **offs** (38c)

-- FF **baff** (69d), **biff, buff** (134c,161d), **cuff** (148a), **daff** (125d), **doff** (130a,161b), **duff** (125b), **gaff** (57c,d,152d,153a), **goff** (32d), **guff, huff** (58a), **jeff** (133d), **Jeff, jiff** (101c), **kiff** (88c), **koff** (47a), **luff** (136b), **miff** (44c), **moff** (53b,146c), **muff, piff** (24b), **puff** (180d), **raff** (75b), **riff** (131d), **Riff** (18b,102c), **ruff** (19b,33b,63d, 137a), **teff** (6c), **tiff** (126b), **toff** (40d), **tuff** (121b,177a)

F -- F **fief** (55d)

F -- G **fang** (167b), **flag** (16b,50d,82b,88c,115a,155a), **flog** (180d), **Fong** (40b), **frog** (10a,17a,126d), **Fung** (191)

F -- H **fash** (140c,176a), **fish, Foch** (63b)

FI -- **fiat** (35a,41d,48c,111b,137a), **Fiat** (83c), **fico** (169d), **fide, fief** (55d), **fife** (59a,105a), **fike** (139c), **file** (13a,127d), **fill, fill** (109b), **film** (164b), **filo, fils** (62d,150b), **find** (44a), **fine** (49b,50a,104b, 115d,159a), **fink** (19a,56c,157c), **Finn** (107d), **Fiot** (191), **fire** (13a,43d,44b), **firm** (154c,173d), **firn** (67c,70c,106c,149b), **fisc** (52c,134c), **fish, fisk** (24d,52c,134c), **fist** (80c), **five**

-FI - **Efik** (191), **ifil** (117a,168c)

-- FI **defi** (61b), **Safi** (191), **sufi** (103a,116c)

337

F - - I favi (138a,165d), fili, foci (28b), fuci (132c), fuji (84b), Fuji (84d)

F - - J Funj

F - - K feak (39d,171c), fink (19a,56c,157c), fisk (24d,52c,134c), flak (11a), folk (116a,169c), fork, fulk (173a), funk (63d,113c)

FL - - flag (16b,50d,82b,88c,115a,155a), flak (11a), flam (169c), flan (39d,40a,114d), flap (17b,59a,104a,118d,161a,182d), flat (41b, 124b,173a), flaw, flax, flay (147c,157c), flea (81b), fled, flee, flew, flex (18a), fley (63d), flip (167c), flit (41a), flix, floc (149a), floe (79b), flog (180d), flop (54a), flot (173a), flow (157b), flub (22b), flue (8b,30a), flux (28d,58d)

F - - L fail, fall (46b,141c), farl (138c,140b), feel (72a,142c), fell (40a, 58b,76c,115d,147d), fill (109b), foal (78c), foil (15d,55c,165b), fool (24a,41c,47a,146d), foul (173a), fowl, fuel (65c), full (7b, 130b), furl (132c)

F - - M Faam (111a), farm (165d), film (164b), firm (154c,173d), flam (169c), foam (63d,154b), form (54d,143c), frim (58d), from

F - - N fain (42d,67c,183b), famn (188), faon (33c,55a), faun (56a,68b, 137c,161a,184a), fawn (33c), fern (142a), Finn (107d), firn (67c, 70c,106c,149b), flan (39d,40a,114d), fohn (182b)

FO - - foal (78c), foam (63d,154b), Foch (63b), foci (28b), fogy, fohn (182b), foil (15d,55c,165b), fold, folk (116a,169c), fond (7c,94b), Fong (40b), fono (137a), fons (60c), font (16b,171d,172a), food (109a,176b), fool (24a,41c,47a,146d), foot (115a), fora (133a), ford (177b), fore (63d,174b), fork, form (54d,143c), fort (63d, 157d), foss (44d,100d), foud (54d,144b), foul (173a), four (26c), fowl, foxy (38b,39c,181d)

- - FO Bufo (166c)

F - - O fado (121c), fano (51d,96b,113c,d), faro (65a), fico (169d), filo, fono (137a)

F - - P flap (17b,59a,104a,118d,161a,182d), flip (167c), flop (54a), frap (45d,165c)

FR - - frab (138c), frap (45d,165c), frat, frau (181b), fray (56b,60d), Frea, Fred (96b), free (44a,70d,131b), fret (28c,35b,111c,184d), Frey (7c,68b,124d), Fria, frib (43d), frim (58d), frit (64c,67c), frix (39d), froe (32a,167a,179d), frog (10a,17a,126d), from, frot (28c), frow (47a,167a)

- FR - Afra (183c)

F - - R fair (17a,55d), fear (113c,155a), four (26c)

- - FS offs (38c)

F - - S fass (189), fees (128c), feis (82b), fels (190), fess (23c,51b), fils (62d,150b), fons (60c), foss (44d,100d), fuss (22b,35b)

- - FT baft (14a,53b), daft (59c), deft (147c), gift (123a), haft (76d), heft (179d), Heft, left (42c), lift (49b), loft (14c,69d,104b,178b), raft (27b,33c,58c,75b), reft (32a,42c,44d,167b), rift (30c,32a,58a, 110d), sift (140d,142c,146b), soft (48b,95d,99d,163a), Taft (29d), tuft (24b,32d,38c), waft (20d,58c), weft (39a,165a,184b), yuft (135c)

F - - T   fact (7a,128b), fait (6d,61b), fast (56d,126c,141d,160c,173a,d), feat (7a,52d), felt, fest, Fiat (83c), fiat (35a,41d,48c,111b,137a), Fiot (191), fist (80c), flat (41b,124b,173a), flit (41a), flot (173a), font (16b,171d,172a), foot (115a), fort (63d,157d), frat, fret (28c, 35b,111c,184d), frit (64c,67c), frot (28c), fust (105c,143b)

FU - -   Fuad (54d), fuci (132c), fuel (65c), fuga, fugu (84b), fuji (84b), Fuji (84d), fulk (173a), full (7b,130b), fume (129a,149a,157a), fumy, fund (6d,101c,130c), Fung (191), funk (63d,113c), furl (132c), fury (157a), fuse (98c), fuss (22b,35b), fust (105c,143b), fute (51c), fuze (98c), fuzz (45d)

F - - U   feru (37a,56a,133d), frau (181b), fugu (84b)

F - - W   flaw, flew, flow (157b), frow (47a,167a)

F - - X   faex (46a), falx (133b), flax, flex (18a), flix, flux (28d,58d)

FY - -   fyke (15d), fyrd (110a)

- - FY   affy (18b), defy (28d), Dufy (63a)

F - - Y   fady, faky, flay (147c,157c), fley (63d), fogy, foxy (38b,39c,181d), fray (56b,60d), Frey (7c,68b,124d), fumy, fury (157a)

F - - Z   friz (39d), fuzz (45d)

GA - -   gaal (23b,174d), gabe (162a), gabi (162a), gaby (59c,146d), gade Gaea (47d,69a), Gael (28a,96c,138d), gaff (57c,d,152d,153a), gage (28d,98a,119c,d), gagl (160b), Gaia (47d,69a), gail (23b, 174d), Gail (183d), gain (7a,b,124a,181d), gait (96b,179a), gajo (107c), gala (55d), Gala (191), gale (181d), gali (6c), gall (19a, 28c,29b,82c,160c,176a), galt, Gama (121c), game (64d,154a), gamp (172a), gane (185b), gang (38c), Gano (132d), gaol (123d), Gaol (164a), Gaon (85b), gape (185b), gapo (60a), gapy, gara (190), garb (32c,46a), gare (61b,c,62c,127c,184b), Garm (178c), garn (67d,185b), Garo (88c), Gary, gash (40a), gasp (113c), gata (143c), gate (51a,121b), Gath (117a), gaub (116c), gaud (169d), gaue (67a), Gaul (10a,60d,63c), gaup, gaur (112c,181c), gaus (67a), gaut (88b,103d,132a), gave, gawd (169c), gawk (146d), gawp, Gaza (117a), gaze, gazi, gazy

- GA -   Agag (18c,86c,137a), agal (17c,36d), Agao (6c,73c), agar (7d,28c, 39c,103c,141c), Agau (73c), Agaz (193), egad (100a,109a), ngai (48a,159c), ngan (82b,c), Sgau (88c)

- - GA   alga (141b,c), baga (171b), bega (188), biga (171d), boga (57d, 180b), fuga, giga (56a,105a), goga (24a), hoga (144b), inga (145d, 170a), Jaga (191), juga (27a), mega (34b,c), muga (naga (13d, 33a,55b,127c), Naga (24c,77a,88c,176d), Olga (135c,183c), paga (117a), pega (57a,130a,158b), raga (56d,105a), riga (118b), ruga (59b,185a), saga (79b,91a,138a,157a,161b,c,168a), Saga, soga (70d,152b), Soga (191), toga (132d,133a,b), vega (152c), Vega (155b), Wega (155b), yoga (10b,13c,77a), Yuga (76d), zyga (134b)

G - - A   Gaea (47d,69a), Gaia (47d,69a), gala (55d), Gala (191), Gama (121c), gara (190), gata (143c), Gaza (117a), gena (29b), geta (84b, 145a), giga (56a, 105a), gila (93b), Gita, Gjoa (144d), glia (106c), goga (24a), gola (27b,40c,70c,157a), Goma (191), Gona (106d), gora (81c), Goya (151d), gufa (21b,99a),

Guha (191), guia (90a,101a,165b), guna (106a,137b)

- GB - Egba (191), Egbo (141d)

G - - B garb (32c,46a), gaub (116c), gerb (56d,143d), glib (58d,149a,177c), glub, grab (105b,142a,149b), grub (88d), guib (11a)

G - - D gaud (169d), gawd (169c), gedd (140a), geld (162b), Gerd (63c), gild (14a,49c,69c,98b), gird (32c,50a,123a,160a), glad (85c), gled (19a,52a,87a), goad (80b,154b), gold, Gond, good, grad (28b), grid (17a,70d,119b,156d)

GE - - geal (47d,163c), gean (29c), gear (32c,112a,167b), geat (77d,101a), Geat (138a), gedd (140a), Geex (6c,51d), gein (67d), geld (162b), gelt (101c), gena (29b), gene (54a,76b), Gene (96b), gens (42d, 132d), gent, genu (6b,18a,87a,89c), gerb (56d,143d), Gerd (63c), Gere (183c), Geri (183c), germ (17d,99c,134d), gest (7c,41d,52d, 133c), geta (84b,145a), gett (44d), Geum (76b)

- GE - aged (110a), agee (13d,15c,38d), ager (47c,56a,89b,c,131d,133b), Eger (49a), ogee (101a,b,120b)

- - GE ange (61a), auge (123c,132b), cage (36a), doge (95b,175b), edge (22a,96d,131c,143d,146b), euge (180a), gage (28d,98a,119c,d), huge, inge (24d,67d,117c,119c), kuge (84c), loge (164a), luge (148a), mage (95b), page (51b,59b,142d,159b), rage (10c,30c,157a, 161d), sage (13a,90d,100c,141c,145c,180b,183a), tige (118a), urge (42d,46b,79d,80a,b,81c,124a,150a), wage (27a,115b), yage (23a)

G - - E gabe (162a), gade, gage (28d,98a,119c,d), gale (181d), game (64d, 154a), gane (185b), gape (185b), gare (61b,c,62c,127c, 184b), gate (51a,121b), gaue (67a), gave, gaze, gene (54a,76b), Gene (96b), ghee (24d), gibe (8a,42c,84d,100d,138c,144c,149b), Gide (63a), gime (77d), gite (62a,118d), give (79d,123a), glee (99a, 150b), glue (7b,156a), gone (6b,15c,42c,44c,114d), gore (115d, 117c,154c,169c), guze (128d), gybe (144c), gyle (23b,174d), gyne (34b,55b,183c), gyre (31b,171b), gyve (55d,143b)

G - - F gaff (57c,d,152d,153a), goaf (104b), goff (32d), golf (154a), goof, Graf (37c,66b,67a,107c,186b), guff (6c), gulf (6c)

- GG - eggs (112a), eggy (185d)

- - GG dagg (118c), hagg, hogg (144a), jagg, magg (95b), migg (96c), nogg (48d), tegg (143d,171d), vugg (28a,66a,132b), Wegg (111d), wigg, yegg (24c)

G - - G gang (38c), Gheg (8c), glug, gong, grig (38c,70d,93a), grog (92d, 153d)

GH - - ghat (32d,88b,103d,132a), ghee (24d), Gheg (8c), Ghes (193), ghor (174b), ghos (30b), Ghuz (171a)

- GH - agha (35a,171a)

- - GH dagh (76d), hegh, high, Hugh (96a), Lugh (28b), Magh (102a), nigh (106a), ough, pugh, sigh, vugh (28a,66a,136b), yogh (10c, 185a)

G - - H gash (40a), Gath (117a), gish (102c), gosh, Goth (16c), gush (35a, 154c)

GI - - gibe (8a,42c,84d,100d,138c,144c,149b), Gide (63a), gier (47b),

340

gift (123a), **giga** (56a,105a), **gila** (93b), **gild** (14a,49c,69c,98b), **gill** (22d), **gilo** (48a), **gilt** (69c,77c,151b,185d), **gime** (77d), **gimp** (169d), **gink** (48b), **gird** (32c,50a,123a,160a), **girl**, **giro** (38c,83c, 167c), **girt** (50a), **gish** (102c), **gist** (95c,118c), **Gita**, **gite** (62a, 118d), **give** (79d,123a)

- GI - **Agib** (12a,42d), **agio** (52c,60a,101c,123a), **Agis** (86d), **Egil** (107d), **egis** (14b,d,115a,124d,144b,154a,161a)

- - GI **Bugi** (191), **hagi** (84b), **jogi** (76b), **magi** (123c), **Magi** (95b,116c, 183a), **ragi** (28b), **sugi** (84b), **vagi** (38c), **yogi** (76b)

G - - I **gabi** (162a), **gali** (6c), **gazi**, **Geri** (183c), **goai** (106d,168c), **gobi**, **Gobi** (42d), **goli** (105c), **Guti**, **gyri** (22d,131b)

GJ - - **Gjoa** (144d)

G - - J **gunj** (70c)

G - - K **gawk** (146d), **gink** (48b), **gowk** (146d)

GL - - **glad** (85c), **gled** (19a,52a,87a), **glee** (99a,150b), **glen** (43c), **glia** (106c), **glib** (58d,149a,177c), **glim**, **glis** (45c), **glom** (155d,160d, 178c), **glow** (144c), **glub**, **glue** (7b,156a), **glug**, **glum** (102c,159a), **glut** (52c,70a,137c,159d)

- GL - **agla** (7a), **iglu** (51c,149b), **ogle** (9d,53c,91a,93d,148c)

- - GL **gagl** (160b)

G - - L **gaal** (23b,174d), **Gael** (28a,96c,138d), **gagl** (160b), **gail** (23b,174d), **Gail** (183d), **gall** (19a,28c,29b,82c,160c,176a), **gaol** (123d), **Gaol** (164a), **Gaul** (10a,60d,63c), **geal** (47d,163c), **gill** (22d), **girl**, **goal** (8b,109b,120b,125d), **goel** (15a,75c), **Goll**, **goul** (102a), **gowl** (102a, 140d,185b), **gull** (32d,41c,42a,72c,99b,141a)

G - - M **Garm** (178c), **germ** (99c,134d), **Geum** (76b), **glim**, **glom** (155d, 160d,178c), **glum** (102c,159a), **gram** (29d,99b,148d,160d,180a), **Gram**, **grim** (156a), **grum** (102c), **Guam**

GN - - **gnar** (72a), **gnat** (59a,81b,99c), **gnaw** (20a,107a,178b)

- GN - **agni** (88a,89c), **Agni** (56d,68b)

- - GN **sign** (121c,146c)

G - - N **gain** (7a,b,124a,181d), **Gaon** (85b), **garn** (67d,185b), **gean** (29c), **gein** (67d), **glen** (43c), **Goan**, **goon** (157c,163c), **gown**, **gran**, **grin**, **guan** (151b), **Gwyn** (40c,50b)

GO - - **goad** (80b,154b), **goaf** (104b), **goal** (106d,168c), **goal** (8b,109b, 120b,125d), **Goan**, **goat** (135a), **gobi**, **Gobi** (42d), **gobo** (84d), **goby** (57d), **goel** (15a,75c), **goer**, **goff** (32c), **goga** (24a), **gogo** (16b,24a, 149c), **Gogo** (191), **gola** (27b,40c,70c,157a), **gold**, **golf** (154a) **goli** (105c), **Goll**, **Golo** (191), **Goma** (191), **Gona** (106d), **Gond**, **gone** (6b,15c,42c,44c,114d), **gong**, **good**, **goof**, **goon** (157c,163c), **Goop** (107d), **goor**, **gora** (81c), **gore** (115d,117c,154c,169c), **gory**, **gosh**, **Goth** (16c,163d), **goul** (102a), **gour** (112c,181c), **gout**, **gowk** (146d), **gowl** (102a,140d,185b), **gown**, **Goya** (151d)

- GO - **agog** (47b,52c,86b), **agon** (12c,36c,41b,55d),71b), **egol** (11b), **Igor** (135d), **Ogor** (170d)

- - GO **ango** (171a), **Argo** (12c,36b,c), **bago** (13d), **bogo** (117a, 168c), **Bogo** (191), **bygo** (114c), **Dago**, **ergo** (164b), **gogo** (16b,24a,

341

149c), Gogo (191), Hugo (63a,96a), Iago (54b,111d,143c), kago (113a), lago (83b,152b), mogo (74b), Pogo (121c), sago (54c, 59b,113b,125b,155c), sego (24b,25a,92b,174c), upgo (13c), zogo (136a)

G - - O gajo (107c), Gajo, Gano (132d), gapo (60a), Garo (88c), gilo (48a), giro (38c,83c,167c), gobo (84d), gogo (16b,24a,149c), Gogo (191), Golo (191), grao (189), guao (168c,169b), Gulo (183c), gyro (34d)

- GP - Ogpu (135d)

G - - P gamp (172a), gasp (113c), gaup, gawp, gimp (169d), Goop (107d), gulp (46a,79d,160a), Gump (43b), grip (159a)

GR - - grab (105b,142a,149b), grad (28b), Graf (37c,66b,67a,107c,186b), gram (29d,99b,148d,160d,180a), grao (189), gras (78b), gray (33c, 77c), Gray (50c), gres (156c), grew, grey (33c), grid (17a,70d, 119b,156d), grig (38c,70d,93a), grim (156a), grin, grip (159a), gris (61d), grit (137a,b), grog (92d,153d), gros (47a,53d,146c), Gros (63a), grot (27d), grow (154b), grub (43c,88d), grum (102c), Grus (36b,c,38b)

- GR - agra (26d,34d), Agra (161b), agri (89b), agro (149d), ogre (67a, 102a)

G - - R gaur (112c,181c), gear (32c,167b), Ghor (174b), gier (47b), gnar (72a), goer, goor, gour (112c,181c) guar (46c,59d), guhr (47d)

- - GS eggs (112a), togs (32c)

G - - S gaus (67a), gens (42d,132d), Gens, Ghes (193), ghos (30b), glis (45c), Glis, gras (78b), gres (156d), gris (61d), gros (47a,53d,146c), Gros (63a), Grus (36b,c,38b), gyps, Gyps (71d)

- - GT togt (77c), Vogt

G - - T gait (96b,179a), galt, gaut (88b,103d,132a), geat (77d,101a), Geat (138a), gelt (101c), gent, gest (7c,41d,52d,133c), gett (44d), ghat (32d,88b,103d,132a), gift (123a), gilt (69c,77c,151b), girt (50a), gist (95c,118c), glut (52c,70a,137c,159d), gnat (59a,81b,99c), goat (135a), grit (137a,b), grot (27d), gust

GU - - Guam, guan (151b), guao (168c,169b), guar (46c,59d), gufa (21b, 99a), guff, gugu, Guha (191), guhr (47d), guib (11a), gula (90a, 101a,165b), gulf (6c), gull (32d,41c,42a,72c,99b,141a), Gulo (183c), gulp (46a,79d,160a), Gump (43b), guna (106a,137b), gunj (70c), guru (77b), gush (35a,154c), gust, Guti, guze (128d)

- GU - agua (152d,166c,178c), ague (30a,55d,95c), ogum (82b)

- - GU degu (132c), fugu (84b), gugu, kagu (106c), Pegu (24c,102a,127d)

G - - U genu (6b,18a,87a,89c), gugu, guru (77b)

GW - - Gwyn (40c,50b)

G - - W glow (144c), gnaw (20a,107a,178b), grew, grow (154b)

GY - - gybe (144c), gyle (23b,174d), gyne (34b,55b,183c), gyps, Gyps (71d), gyre (31b,171b), gyri (22d,131b), gyro (34d), gyve (55d, 143b)

- - GY algy, Algy (96b), bogy (153a), cagy (178b), dogy (46d,103c), edgy (106c), eggy (185d), fogy, logy (46d), Nagy (78d), orgy (26d,130d, 137c), pogy (57a,88a,98d,103c), sagy

342

G - - Y gaby (59c,146d), Gaby, gapy, Gary, gazy, goby (57d), gory, gray (33c,77c), Gray (50c), grey (33c)

G - - Z Geez (6c,51d), Ghuz (171a)

HA - - Haab (97d), haaf (57d), haak (57b,178a), haar (139c), haba (151d), Habe (191), hack (40a,77c,184d) hade (66a,148c,173c), hadj (98b,118a), haec (90a,164c), haem (122b), haft (76d), hagg, hagi (84b), haha (55c,159c), haik (57b,65b,108a), hail (6d,15a,71d), hair (56b,164d), haje (33a,48d), hake (57a,b), hakh (46d), hako (115b), haku (86d), hala (112b), hale (125b), Hale (9d,131a), half (101a), hall (37b,114d), halm, halo (14d,31b,92a,107b,131d), Hals (47a), halt (13b,28a,38d,156d), hami (78a), hand (60c,114c,115d,184c), hang (160a), hank (147c), Hano (125b), Hans (66d,96a), hant (67a), Hapi (66a,107b,136a), hapu (106d), Harb (191), hard (109b), hare (91b,132c), hark (92d), harl (16b,56b,59a), harm (40b,81a), harp (105a,129a), hart (41d,154d), hase (74d), hash, hasp (31d, 54d,153c), hast, hate (6a,43a), hath, Hati (48d), haul (27b,45d), have, hawk (19c,115c), hayz, haze (100c,174d), hazy (174b)

- HA - Ahab (18c,26c,85b,86d,100d,116a,180b), Ahaz (86d), Bhar (191), bhat (80c), chaa (162b), chab (184a), Chad (158b), chai (72b), cham (20a,29d), Cham (8c), chan (26c,130c), chap (55b), char (24d,26c, 170b), chat (9b,19c,161c), chaw (97c), chay (48a,128d), dhak (48a, 169a), dhal (12b), dhan (124c), dhao (24c), Dhar, dhaw (125a), ghat (32d,88b,103d,132a), khan (7c,26c,81b,93d,116c,123c,130c, 166c), khar (189), khas (153a), khat (105d), Phad (155b), shad (27d,57a,b,c), shag (73b,105b,161d,166d), shah (116c), sham (41c, 55b,60d,80a,123a,b,146d), Shan (13c,80d,88c,101d), shap, shat (87d), shaw (164b), Shaw (50c,53b), shay (110c), Thai (146a), than (35b), thar (68a,76d), that (42b,124b,129c), thaw, wham (157c), what (129c), whau (107a,168c)

- - HA agha (35a,171a), Akha (86a,c), Asha (191), Azha (155b), epha (75c), Guha (191), haha (55c,159c), Isha (174a), kaha (123d), maha (28c,88c,136d), moha (42b,83d), ocha (189), paha (67b), poha (74c), saha, taha (179b), tcha (162c), Usha (16a,150c),

H - - A haba (151d), Haba, haha (55c,159c), hala (112b), Hela (93c), Hera (69c,85d,110b,126b,186b,d), hila (53c), Hima (191), hoga (144b), hoja (166b), hola (74c,152b), hora (22a,40b), Hova (95a), Hoya (14d), Hsia (30b,47c), huia (19a,106d), hula (74b), Hupa (192), hura (20a,137a), Hura, Hyla (10a,166d,169b)

H - - B Haab (97d), Harb (191), herb (58b,158b), hobb (124b), hubb (118b)

H - - C haec (90a,164c)

H - - D hand (60c,114c,115d,184c), hard (109b), head (29d), heed (14c, 75b,109b), held, herd (39a,46c,72a), Hild, hind (15b,41d,45a), hold (95c,124c,130d), hood (38a,74d), hued

HE - - head (29d), heaf (144a), heal, heap (117d), hear (75b,c,92d), heat, Hebe (39c,69c,186b), heck (100a), heed (14c,75b,109b), heel, Heep (41a,43b), heer (47a,184b,185b), heft (179d), Heft, hegh, Hehe (191), heil (74b), hein (52c,61c), heir, Hela (93c), held, helm (144d,165d), help (14a), hemi (122c), hemo (34a,122b), hemp (26a, 37a,56a,133d), hens (121d), Hera (69c,85d,110b),126b,186b,d), herb (58b,158b), herd (39a,46c,72a), here, herl (16b,59a), hero

(42b,124d,137b), **Hero** (90c), **Herr** (66c), **hers** (124c), **hest** (35a), **Heth** (77c), **hevi** (111d), **hewn**

- HE - **ahem**, **Ahet** (49a,102a), **ahey** (52c), **bhel** (126d), **chee** (189), **chef**, **chek** (59c), **Chen** (149b), **cher** (61b), **chew** (97c), **chez** (14b,61a), **eheu** (52c), **ghee** (24d), **Gheg** (8c), **Ghes** (193), **Hehe** (191), **Khem** (113c), **khet** (188), **phew** (52c), **rhea** (37a,56a,111d), **Rhea** (19b,68d, 87c,103c,186b), **Rhee** (87c), **shea** (25a,168c,d), **shed** (27a,90c,101b, 144b), **shee** (82b), **Shem** (107c), **Shen** (68a), **sher** (65d,165c), **shew** (44c), **Thea** (162c), **theb** (188), **thee** (124b), **them** (124b), **then**, **thew** (104c), **they** (124b), **whee**, **when** (180d), **whet** (143c,156b), **whew**, **whey** (100a)

- - HE **ache** (79a,112d,185b), **Hehe** (191), **Hohe** (192), **tche** (13d,30b,105a)

H - - E **Habe** (191), **hade** (66a,148c,173c), **haje** (33a,48d), **hake** (57a,b), **hale** (125b), **Hale** (9d,131a), **hare** (91b,132c), **hase** (74d), **hate** (6a, 43a), **have**, **haze** (100c,174d), **Hebe** (39c,69c,186b), **Hehe** (191), **here**, **hide** (53a), **hike**, **hipe** (185a), **hire** (49d,50b,91b,130a), **hive** (17c), **Hohe** (192), **hole** (6c,11b,110d,118c,147a), **home**, **hone** (110a,143c,180d), **hope** (13d,52d), **hose** (156c), **hove** (92a,157d), **howe** (77d), **Howe** (17a,82a), **huge**, **hule** (23a,134c), **Hume** (50c), **huse** (180c), **hyde** (188), **Hyde** (45a), **hyke**, **hyle** (97c), **hype** (185a)

H - - F **haaf** (57d), **half** (101a), **heaf** (144a), **hoof** (173a), **huff** (58a)

H - - G **hagg**, **hang** (160a), **hing** (13c), **hogg** (144a), **hong** (30b), **hung**

- - HH **sahh** (188)

H - - H **hakh** (46d), **hash**, **hath**, **hegh**, **Heth** (77c), **high**, **hish**, **hoch**, (52c, 66c), **Hoch**, **hoth**, **Hoth** (20c), **Hugh** (96a), **hunh?**, **hush** (17b,146c)

HI - - **hick** (185d), **hide** (53a), **hien** (30b), **hier** (63a,185d), **high**, **hike**, **hiku** (57a,106d,138a), **hila** (53c), **Hild**, **hill**, **hilo** (74c), **hilt** (73c), **Hima** (191), **hind** (15b,41d,45a), **hing** (13c), **hino** (106d,168c), **hint** (9a,39c,159a), **hipe** (185a), **hire** (49d,50b,91b,130a), **hiro**, **hish**, **hiss** (146a), **hist** (25c,93d), **hive** (17c)

- HI - **Ahir** (27b), **Bhil** (191), **chia** (136d), **chib** (167a), **chic** (148d), **chid**, **ch'ih** (188), **chil**, **chin**, **Chin** (30b), **chip** (69d), **chir** (29b,116d), **chit** (67b,98c,108b,116c,177c), **chiv** (87a), **jhil**, **ohia** (74c,168c), **Ohio**, **Phil** (96b), **phit** (24b), **phiz** (54a), **Rhin**, **shih** (189), **Shik** (171a), **shim** (91d,144c,162a,179d), **shin** (91a,d,140b,143c), **ship**, **shir** (36d, 65d,165c), **thin** (43b,c,148b), **this** (42b,124b), **Whig**, **whim** (26c, 54c,108c), **whin** (64c,70a,132b,181d), **whip** (58c,88d), **whir** (25c, 181a), **whit** (166c), **whiz** (25c)

- - HI **bahi** (60c), **Bahi**, **pahi** (21b,26a), **tchi**, **Tchi**, **tshi**, **Tshi** (69c)

H - - I **hagi** (84b), **hami** (78a), **Hapi** (66a,107b,136a), **Hati** (48d), **heii** (74b), **hemi** (122c), **hevi** (111d), **Holi** (77a), **hopi** (33c), **Hopi** (12c, 102c,125b), **hoti**

H - - J **hadj** (98b,118a)

H - - K **haak** (57b,178a), **hack** (40a,77c,184d), **haik** (57b,65b,108a), **hank** (147c), **hark** (92c), **hawk** (19c,115c), **heck** (100a), **hick** (185d), **hock** (91a,115b,182b,c), **hoek** (39d), **honk** (70a), **hook** (27b,39d), **howk** (139b), **huck** (167d), **hulk** (144d,173d), **hunk**, **husk** (53a,78d, 142a)

HL - - **Hier** (141a)

- - HL buhl (81a), kohl (53c), kuhl (53c)

H - - L hail (6d,15a,71d), hall (37b,114d), harl (16b 56b,59a), haul (27c, 45d), heal, heel, herl (16b,59a), hill, howl (39b), hull (141d,142a, 144c,d), hurl (167c)

H - - M haem (122b), haim, harm (40b,81a), helm (144d,165d), holm (77d, 82d,109a)

- HN - ohne (66d,183b)

- - HN behn (137d), fohn (182b), John (11c,96a,121a,186b)

H - - N hein (52c,61c), hewn, hien (30b), hoen (189), hoon (190), horn (11a, 105a,170b,182a), hymn (150c)

HO - - hoar (63d,71a,181a), hoax (41c,122a), hobb (124b), hobo (168a, 174b), hock (52c,66c), hock (91a,115b,182b,c), hoek (39d), hoen (189), hoer, hoey (114c), hoga (144b), hogg (144a), Hohe (192), hoja (166b), hoju (84b), hola (74c,152b), hold (95c,124c,130d), hole (6c,11b,110d,118c,147a), Holi (77a), holm (77d,82d,109a), holt (36d,119b,184b), holy, home, homo (122d), homy (38b), hone (110a,143c,180d), hong (30b), honk (70a), hood (38a,74d), hoof (173a), hook (27b,39d), hoon (190), hoop (181b), hoot (112c), hope (13d,52d), hopi (33c), Hopi (12c,102c,125b), hops (17c), hora (22a, 40h), horn (11a,105a,170b,187a), hors (62b), hose (156c), host (13a,51d,104c), Moth (20c), hoti, hour, Hova (95a), hove (92a, 157d), howe (77d), Howe (17a,82a), howk (139b), howl (39b), Hoya (14d)

- HO - Ahom (88c), ahoy (106a), b'hoy (134b), chob (23c), chol (118d), Chol (192), chop (98a), chor (164b), chou (61b), Chou (30b), chow (45a), choy (48a,128d), dhow (88d,111c,175d), Ghor (174b), ghos (30b), khof', mhor (180h), ohoy (106a), phon (94a), phoo, phos, phot (173b), rhob (64a,85c), Shoa (6c), shod, shoe (166a), shoo (46b,67a,138b), shop (169a), shoq (169a), shor (136d), Shor (162b), shot (9d,43d,90c,174d), shou (41d), show (42b,44c,96b), thob (128a), Thor (7c,68c,99c,100c,109c,165b), Thos (84a,181c), thou (124b), whoa (156d), whom (42b), whoo

- - HO baho (122a), boho (117a,179d), coho (136d), echo (130b,d), Echo (105d), icho (67b), kiho (82a), moho (19a,78a), otho (133a), paho (122a), peho (19b,102c,106d), Saho (6c), soho!, Soho (93c), toho (79a)

H - - O hako (115b), halo (14d,31b,92a,107b,131d), Hano (125b), hemo (34a,122b), hero (42b,124d,137b), Hero (90c), hilo (74c), hino (106d,168c), hiro, hobo (168a,174b), homo (168a,174b), Hugo (63a,96a), huso (180c), hypo (117b)

H - - P harp (105a,129a), hasp (31d,54d,153c), heap (117d), Heep (41a, 43b), help (14a), hemp (26a,37a,56a,133d), hoop (181b), hump (124d)

- HR - Shri (17c,166c)

- - HR Bohr (14b,40d,138c), buhr (180d), Duhr (155b), guhr (47d), lehr (67c,112a), mahr (103a), mohr (65d), rohr (72d), Ruhr, sehr (66d), tahr (68a,76d), tehr (27c,68a)

H - - R haar (139c), hair (56b,164d), hear (75b,c,92d), heer (47a,184b, 185b), heir, Herr (66c), hier (63a,185d), Hier (141a), hoar (63d,

71a,181a), hoer, hour
HS - - Hsia (30b,47c)
H - - S Hals (47a), Hans (66d,96a), hens (121d), hers (124c), hiss (146a), hops (17c), hors (62b), hyps
- - HT acht (66c), baht (146a)
H - - T haft (76d), halt (13b,28a,38d,156d), hant (67a), hart (41d,154d), hast, heat, heft (179d), Heft (35a), hest (35a), hilt (73c), hint (9a,39c, 159a), hist (25c,93d), holt (36d,119b,184b), hoot (112c), host (13a, 51d,104c), hunt (141c), hurt
HU - - hubb (118b), huck (167d), hued, huff (58a), huge, Hugh (96a), Hugo (63a,96a), huia (19a,106d), hula (74b), hule (23a,134c), hulk (144d,173d), hull (141d,142a,144c,d), hulu (55b), Hume (50c), hump (124d), hung, hunh?, hunk, hunt (141c), Hupa (192), hura (20a,137a), Hura, hurl (167c), hurt, huse (180c), hush (17b,146c), husk (53a,78d,142a), huso (180c), huzz
- HU - ahum, bhut (67a), chub (40c,154c), Chud (191), chug (53a), chum, (38d), Chun (30c), chut!, Ghuz (171a), jhum, Phud (110b), phut (24b), Phut (110b), rhum (8c), Rhus (159a), shul (161a), shun (15a, 51b,52a), shut, thud, thug (65a), thus (149c), whun (64c,70a)
- - HU ichu (10b,70d), jehu (46b), Jehu (18c), kahu (14d), Oahu, Rahu (42b,48b), sahu (153d), tchu
H - - U haku (86d), hapu (106d), hiku (57a,106d,138a), hoju (84b), hulu (55b)
- HV - IHVH (159d), JHVH (159d), YHVH (159d)
- HW - JHWH (159d), YHWH (159d)
H - - X hoax (41c,122c)
HY - - hyde (188), Hyde (45a), hyke, Hyla (10a,166d,169b), hyle (97c), hymn (150c), hype (185a), hypo (117b), hyps
- HY - whyo (59d,65a)
- - HY achy, ashy (113a,178a)
H - - Y hazy (174b), hoey (114c), holy, homy (38b)
H - - Z Hayz, huzz
IA - - Iago (54b,111d,143c), Ialu (48d), Iamb (59c)
- IA - bias (43b,123a), diad (113a), dial (25c), dian (46c,130d,170b), Dian (68d,69a,c,102b), Diau (192), fiat (35a,41d,48c,111b,137a), Fiat (83c), kiak (51c), Liam (181d), liar (98d), Lias (66a), miam (14d), mian (97c,147b,166b), Miao (30a,b), mias (111a), Mias, miau (27b,99b), miaw (27b,99b), Nias (82d), Piaf (63c), piat (11a), piay (98b), rial (190), siak (72d), sial (112a), Siam (163d,181a), Tiam, tiao, tiar (39a,75a,121a), vial (148c)
- - IA Abia (18d,137a), akia (74c), amia (22c,170d), apia (121b), aria (8b,98c,150a,c), Asia (48a), chia (136d), Elia (88a,115d), eria (13d, 146d), Fria, Gaia (47d,69a), glia (106d), Hsia (30b,47c), huia (19a, 106d), ilia (21d,77b,115d), inia (9b,109b), Inia (28c,45b), ixia (37a), Maia (76b,109a,153b,155b,177c), Naia (33a), obia (55d), ohia (74c, 168c), okia (190), raia (107d), Raia (147b), Soia, tsia (162c), Uria (14c,16d)

346

I - - A idea (54c,108c,124a,164d), ijma (103b), ikra (27d), ilia (21d,77b, 115d), Inca (14b,30a), inga (145d), inia (9b,109b), Inia (28c,45b), inka (193), Iola, Iona (28a,82d), iota (71a,85c,91c,114c,166c,176a, 180d), Iowa (193), irra (68c,178a), isba (135c), isha (174a), Itea (145d,160c,181d), Itza (192), ixia (37a)

IB - - Ibad (191), Iban (47c), ibex (67d,68a), ibid (80a,117a,137a), ibis (48d,49a,177b), ibit (117a)

- IB - bibb (97c,146b), bibi (87d), dibs (70c), gibe (8a,42c,84d,100d,138c, 144c,149b), jibb, jibe (8a,33b,35d,37b,42c,100d,138c,144c,149b), kibe, kiby (29a), nibs (116c), ribe (139a), Tibu (191)

- - IB Abib (102a,b), Adib (155b), Agib (12a,42d), chib (167a), crib (96b, 120d), drib (46b), frib (43d), glib (58d,149a,177c), guib (11a), snib (54d,93c), stib (19b,47a,137a)

I - - B iamb (59c)

IC - - ical (158c), icer, icho (67b), ichu (10b,70d), icon (79d,92b,136a)

- IC - aich (9a), bice (20d,117d), Bice (27b), dice (65a), dick (43a,55b), Dick (96b), fico (169d), hick (185d), kick, lick, mica (82c,100b, 146c), mice (82c), mico (97a), nice (54d,119c,130c), Nice (98c), nick (30c,108b), pica (66b,95b,172c), pice (190), Pici (19c, 184a), pick, pico (65a,152c), Pict (23c,47d), rice, Rice (46a), rich, rick (74d,117d,154d), sice (71d,147b), sick, tice (9a,38c,51a,185d), tick (12b,20d,97c), vice (31d,158a), wick

- - IC amic (9d), chic (148d) eric (131c), epic (76b,120a), eric (115b), Eric (71d,96a,107d,138a,164a,176b), idic (79b), laic (32b,90b,107d, 124a,141d), odic (79c,120a), olic (158b), otic (14c,d,47b), saic (86b, 91d,175d), Udic (108a), Uvic (70c)

I - - C idic (79b)

ID - - Idas (27b,71c), idea (54c,108c,124a,164d), idee (61d), idem (89d, 164a), Iden (76a), ideo (34b,d,164d), ides (41a,b,133a), idic (79b), idio (34b,c), Idjo (191), idle (174b,c,178c), idly, idol (48c,54c,55a 75b,79d,112d,130b,184d), idun (107d), idyl (114d), Idyo (191), Idzo (191)

- ID - Aida (110d,175c), aide (7b,14a,75d), bide (47c,50b,130a,158b, 162a,177b), dido (11b,26c,65a,122a), Dido (27a,172c), eide (119c), fide, Gide (63a) hide (53a), Lida (183c), Lido (83d,175b), mide (110a), Midi (151b), nide (23c,72a,106c,116b), nidi (106c), Ridd (94a), ride (46b,85c), sida (37a,126c,170a), side (13d,22a,b,54a, 58a,89a,161b), sidi (103b,166b), sidy (123b), tide (39d,75d,109c, 141c,159d), tidy (106a,111b), Vida (183c), vide (89d,126a,142a), wide (133d), widu (102d)

- - ID acid (151a,162a), amid (9d,50a), arid (46c,85a), avid (47b,71a, 186b), Beid (155b), caid (35a,151d,152b), chid, Enid (13b,25d,66b, 163a,183c), grid (17a,70d,119b,156d), ibid (80a,117a,137a), imid (29c), irid (38d,67c), kaid (29d,66a), laid (45b,142d), naid (63c), olid (55d,60c,148d,157d), ooid (48d), Ovid (132d,133b), oxid (112c), paid (129c), qaid (35a), quid (39b,166d), raid (59d,80c), said (174c), Said (42d,101a,121b), seid (103b), Seid (42d,101a, 171a), skid (148b), slid, uvid (101a), void (11a,49d,108d), zoid

I - - D Ibad (191), ibid (80a,117a,137a), imid (29c), Irad (18d), irid (38d, 67c)

347

- IE - bien (63a,140c,179a,180a), bier (33b,66b), dieb (84a), diem (89b, 116a), dier, dies (41b,89b), diet (14a,54c,84c,91b,176a), Dieu (61d), fief (55d), gier (47b), hien (30b), hier (63a,185d), kief (75d), kiel (128d,134d), Kiel (25d), kier (20c,174d), Kiev, lied (66d,150b), lief (181d), lien (65c,91a,124c), lieu (118c,155d), mien (11c,17b, 26d,44c,96b), pied (96c,103c,114b,117c,154a,174d), pien (13b), pier (23a,88b,180c), piet (29b,95b), Riel (129a), riem (76c,112c, 157c,164d), rien (62b), rier (180b), sier (57a,118b), tied, tien (147d), tier (118a,134b), vier (66c), view (93d,138b), wiel (140d, 180d), wies (185a)

- - IE Abie (96b,107a), Amie (61d), Brie (29c), Erie (82c,87d), Okie (99d), Opie (50c), plie (32c,59b), soie (62c), unie (173a)

I - - E idee (61d), idle (174b,c,178c), ille (89b,d,163d), imbe (37a,56a, 133d), inde, inee (120b), Inge (24d,67d,117c,119c), inre (35d,80a), lole (52a,76b,123c), lone (24b,88d,94d), ipse (44d,89c), Irae (43c), isle (8b,53c,81d,82d,86b,88a), ixle (56a)

IF - - ifil (117a,168c)

- IF - biff, fife (59a,105a), gift (123a), jiff (101c), kiff (88c), life (19a,177a), lift (49b), miff (44c), nife (37a), piff (24b), rife (6b,c, 39d,123b), riff (131d), Riff (18b,102c), rift (30c,32a,58a,110d), sift (140d,142c,146b), tiff (126b), wife (154a)

- - IF alif (12b), arif (127d), coif (73a), cuif (139a,d,140c), Enif (155b), kaif (88c), keif (75d), Leif (107d), luif, naif (74b,105d), waif (157b)

IG - - iglu (51c,149b), Igor (135d)

- IG - biga (171d), giga (56a,105a), high, migg (96c), nigh (106a), riga (118b), Riga, sigh, sign (121c,146c), tige (118a), wigg

- - IG brig (72b,106a,144d), crig (20d), grig (38c,70d,93a), prig (112a, 116c), snig (45d), swig (46a,72c), Teig (96a), trig (106a,148d,154a, 169d), twig, Whig

I - - G ilog (132a,161b)

IH - - IHVH (159d)

- IH - kiho (82a)

- - IH ch'ih (188), shih (189)

I - - H IHVH (159d), inch, itch, Ivah (18d)

II - - Iiwi (19a,74b)

- II - Iiin (188), Riis (9d)

- - II alii (74c,134c), apii (74c), Boii (191), heli (74b), Ubii (191)

I - - I Iiwi (19a,74b), immi (189), impi (86a), Inti (159b), Ioni (192)

IJ - - ijma (103b)

- IJ - bija (168c), Ilja (57a,90d,173a)

IK - - ikat (53b,159a), ikmo (18b), ikon (79d,136a), ikra (27d)

- IK - bike, bikh (120b), dika (23a), dike (49c,91d), Dike (78a), fike (139c), hike, hiku (57a,106d,138a), kiki (27b), kiku (30d), like (13c,37d,146d), mike, Mike (96b), Nike (69c,100c,182d), pika (93a,128a,132c), pike (57a,b,76c,120b,153a), piki (95c), piky,

rikk (49a), **sika** (41d,84b), **Sikh** (77b), **tike** (29d), **Tiki** (120c)

- - IK   **Atik** (155b), **Efik** (191), **haik** (57b,65b,108a), **kaik** (96c), **naik, raik** (188,189), **Seik** (77b), **Shik** (171a)

I - - K   **Irak** (99a,d), **irok** (55b)

IL - -   **ilex** (77d), **Illa** (21d,77b,115d), **ille** (89b,d,163d), **ills** (170a), **Ilog** (132a,161b), **ilot** (82d), **Ilus** (88d,170b)

- IL -   **aile** (62b,63a,182c,d), **bile** (30c), **bilk** (29b,41c,42a), **bill** (17b,147a), **Bill, bilo** (131b), **dill** (13a,117c), **dilo** (120d,168c), **eild** (138d,140a), **file** (13a,127d), **fili, fill** (109b), **film** (164b), **filo, fils** (62d,150b), **gila** (93b), **gild** (14a,49c,69c,98b), **gill** (22d), **gilo** (48a), **gilt** (69c,77c,151b,185d), **hila** (53c), **Hild, hill, hilo** (74c), **hilt** (73c), **Jill** (183d), **jilt, kile** (189), **kill** (38c), **kiln** (15d,112a), **kilo** (99b, 122d), **kilt, Lila** (183c), **lill** (15d,118a), **lilt** (93a,131a,147a), **lily, mila** (188), **mild** (32a,66a), **mile** (64c), **milk, mill** (126c), **milo** (70b, 87c,150d), **Milo, milt** (153d), **nile** (33c,71d), **Nile** (106b), **nili** (173d), **oily** (110b,172c), **pile** (45d,75b,117c), **pili** (34b,108d), **pill, pily, rile** (10c,d,82c,125a,156b,176a), **rill**   (23c,102b,132a,148d,157b), **rily** (176a), **silk** (53b,179c), **sill** (45c,76c,165a,182b), **silo** (59a, 156d), **silt** (104b), **tile** (31d,56d,72b,95b,133c,163c), **till** (39c,101c, 173d), **tilt** (26b,d,166a), **vila** (54b), **vile** (16c,56c), **vili** (54b), **Vili** (109c), **vill** (176b), **vily** (54b), **wild** (38b,173d), **wile** (13b,41c,157b, 169c), **wilk** (65c,96d,141b), **will** (18b,43a,163c,177c), **wilt** (46b), **wily** (13b,38b,39c)

- - IL   **amil** (45a,48a,185c), **anil** (47c,80d,180b), **aril** (142a), **axil** (10c), **bail** (43c), **Bhil** (191), **boil, ceil** (92c,112a), **chil, coil** (39d,171c, 185a), **Dail** (49a,82b,c), **deil** (139b), **Egil** (107d), **Emil** (96a), **evil** (79c,95d,147a,181a,185c), **fail, foil** (15d,55c,165b), **gail** (23c, 174d), **Gail** (183d), **hail** (6d,15a,71d), **ifil** (117a,168c), **ipil** (117a, 168c,169a), **Ixil** (192), **jail** (123d), **jhil, kail** (8c,22a,25a,79b), **mail** (12d,99b,121c), **moil** (46c,184c), **nail** (31d,54d,141d,161d,173a), **Neil** (96a), **noil** (87c,178b), **pail Phil** (96b), **rail** (16b,19b,c,37a,97b, 138c,150c,177b), **roil** (44c,104b,156b,170d,176a), **sail** (144c,185a), **skil** (57a), **soil** (154d,159a,163c), **tail** (11d,27d,59,143b), **teil** (92b, c,168c), **toil** (46c,184c), **vail** (94b,124a,174b), **veil** (74d,76c), **wail** (39b,88a), **ypil** (117a,168c)

I - - L   **ical** (158c), **idol**   (48c,54c,55a,75b,79d,112d,130b,184d), **idyl** (114d), **ifil** (117a,168c), **ipil** (117a,168c,169a), **itol** (158b), **Ixil** (192)

IM - -   **imam** (25c,102d,103a), **imbe** (37a,56a,133d), **imer, imid** (29c), **immi** (189), **impi** (86a)

- IM -   **cima** (83b,c), **dime, gime** (77d), **gimp** (169d), **Hima** (191), **lima** (17b,152b,174d), **Lima** (31b), **limb** (12d,22d), **lime** (25b,27d,31b, 33c,102d,168c), **limn** (45d,121c), **limp** (58a,81a,177d), **limu** (141c), **limy** (176d), **mima** (185d), **mime** (24a,71b,85a,100a), **Mime** (131d, 148d), **mimi** (14d), **Mimi** (87b,110d,125b,183d), **nimb** (31b, 73b,92a,107b,131d), **oime** (8b), **pima** (37c), **Pima** (192), **rima** (23a,30c,32a,58a,110d), **rime** (30c,36a,58a,63d,77c), **rimu** (79d,106d,129a,168c), **rimy** (63d), **sima** (132b) **sime** (101d), **Simi** (82d), **simp** (59c,146d), **time** (47a,131a), **Yima** (84a,116b,c), **Zimb** (6c)

349

--IM Anim (18d), Akim (135d,191), alim (103b,162c), brim, Clim (12b), duim (188), Emim (67a,100d), frim (58d), glim, grim (156a), maim (43d,81a,105c), prim (156b), Seim (120c), shim (91d,144c,162a, 179d), skim (67c), slim (148b,160a), swim (58c), trim (40a,106a, 154b,160a,165c,169d), urim (18d,23a,110a), wl:im (26c,54c,108c), zaim (170d)

I--M Idem (89d,164a), imam (25c,102d,103a), item (6d,13b,42d,51a, 90d,92d,107a,113d,114c)

IN-- inar (65b), Inca (14b,30a), inch, inde, inee (120b), Inez (45c,183c), inga (145d,170a), Inge (24d,67d,117c,119c), inia (9b,109b), Inia (28c,45b), Inka (193), inky (20b), inly (35d,80a), inro (84b,c, 106c), Inti (159b), into (123a,183b)

-IN- aine (49b,62c), Aine (142c), Aino (84a,c), aint, Ainu (84a,c), bina (77a), bind (33b,165c), bine (145b,156a,171c,176b), bing, binh (189), Bini (191), binn (22c), bino (113b,117a), cine (104b, 152c), cinq (61d), dine, ding (130b), dino (34b), dint (48c,59d, 122a), fine (49b,50a,104b,115d,159a), fink (19a,56c,157c), Finn (107d), gink (48b), hind (15b,41d,45a), hing (13c), hino (106d, 168c), hint (9a,39c,159a), jink, jinn (42b,103b,153c), jinx (78a), kina (126d), kind (150d,153a,174d), kine (38a,112c), king (26c, 29c), kink (38b,171c), kino (37c,34c,47c,72c,98b,161d,168c), lina (188), Lina (183d), line (12b,22b,36d,38a,126c,134b,157b,158b, 162d,175c), ling (24c,57a,b,75b,178c), link (36a,81d,85b), Linn (120d,140a,c,168c,178d), lino, lint (46a,58d), liny (157b), Linz (40d), mina (10b,70b,71d), Mina (23a,183d), mind (75c,81d,93d, 109b), mine (69c,79d,111b,124c), Ming (30b,c), mink (176d), mino (84c), mint (13a,33b,58b,76a), minx (116c), miny, nina (152a), Nina (26c,33d,68d,183d), nine (26c,104d), nino (152a), pina (35d,118b), pine (36a,52a,88c,93c,168c,d,169a), ping, pink (26d,33c,60c,138a), pino (152c), pint (67b), piny (rind (53a, 115c), Rind (109c,174b), rine (44d,75d,135c), ring (50a), rink (147c,154a), sina (46c), Sina (102d,103d), Sind, sine (64c,66b,90a, 97c,126a,163b,169d,183b), sing (26d,178a), sinh (97c), sink (41c, 43c,46b,158a), sino (34a), Tina (183d), tind (86b), tine (11b,124b, 167b), ting (166a), Ting (30c), Tino (136d), tint (33c,d,114d), tiny (100c,148c), vina (77a,105a), vine (32b), vino (92d,182b), vint (26c,182c), viny, wind (33b,39d,171c,185a), wine, wing (10d,58c, 59a,118b,d), wink (107a), winy (176c), Xina (183d), zinc (21a), zing

--IN akin (8b,92b,129c), alin (188), amin (9d), Asin (102a), ayin (91c), bain (61a), brin (32c,54c,146c), cain (169c), Cain (6a,7a,50d,88a, 104c,143c), chin, Chin (30b), coin (19b,37a,100c,101c,179d), crin (146c), dain (188), dein (66d), Drin, enin (20d), Eoin (85b), Erin (82b), fain (42d,67c,183b), gain (7a,b,124a), gein (67d), grin, hein (52c,61c), Jain (77b), join (36a,173c), Kain, Iain, Ilin (188), loin (98a), main (29d,35d,123d), mein (30b), nein (66d), Odin (7c, 29d,63c,68c,175d,183b), pain (7c), rain (121d,162d), rein (130c), Rhin, ruin (42d), sain (20c,38d,48a), sein (146c), shin (91a,d,140b, 143c), skin (53a,76c,115c), spin (131a,180d), tain (166a), thin (43b,c,148b), trin (169d), Tsin (30b), twin (45c,171d), vain (81a), vein (20d,157b), wain (177b), Wain, whin (64c,70a,132b,181d),

zain (41a), **zein**

I - - N **Iban** (47c), **icon** (79d,92b,136a), **Iden** (76a), **Idun** (107d), **ikon** (79d,136a), **Iran** (6a,48c,116b), **Iren** (127c), **iron** (55c,d,69d,81a, 97b,143b,149a,173d,179c), **Iten** (192), **Ivan** (40c,85b,96a)

IO - - **Iola**, **Iole** (52a,76b,123c), **Iona** (28a,82d), **Ione** (24b,88d,94d), **Ioni** (192), **iota** (71a,85c,91c,114c,166c,176a,180d), **Iowa** (193)

- IO - **biod** (79c,59d), **bion** (117b), **bios** (92a), **cion** (42d,70b,145b,148b, 154b,156a), **Dion** (96a,152a), **Fiot** (191), **lion** (55b,86c), **niog** (33a,168c), **niou** (188), **pion** (43c,52b), **piot** (95b), **riot** (44c, 111d,170c,173d), **siol** (82c), **sion** (125c,158c), **Sion** (75b,c,83a,157d), **tion** (158b), **Tiou** (192), **viol** (105a), **Zion** (75b,c,83a,157d)

- - IO **agio** (52c,60a,101c,123a), **apio** (125b), **Clio** (104d), **idio** (34b,c), **meio** (188), **moio** (188), **naio** (107a,168c), **noio** (107c,163c), **odio** (83b), **Ohio**, **olio** (44b,77c,98c,100d,121d), **Scio**, **skio** (57d), **trio** (104d,165a,169c), **Unio** (105c)

I - - O **Iago** (54b,111d,143c), **icho** (67b), **ideo** (34b,d,164d), **idio** (34b,c), **Idjo** (191), **Idyo** (191), **Idzo** (191) **ikmo** (18b) **inro** (84b,c,106c), **into** (123a), **ipso** (89c), **itmo** (18b)

IP - - **ipil** (117a,168c,169a), **Ipse** (44d,89c), **ipso** (89c)

- IP - **aipi** (27a), **cipo** (91d), **dipt**, **hipe** (185a), **kipp**, **lipa** (54d), **nipa** (14b, 46b,48a,164a,168c), **pipa** (159d) **pipe** (105a,180d,182a), **pipi** (106d, 119d), **pipy** (145d), **ripa** (16b,131d), **ripe** (58a,97c,98c), **Sipe** (101a, 110c,140b), **tipe** (168b), **tipi** (181b), **wipe**, **Xipe** (15c), **Zipa** (29d), **zipp**, **Zips** (40c)

- - IP **atip** (14b,166a), **chip** (69d), **clip** (54d,143d), **drip**, **flip** (167c), **grip** (159a), **knip** (115c), **quip** (183a,b), **raip** (36d), **seip** (110c), **ship**, **skip** (110b,114c,147c), **slip** (67c,119a), **snip** (32b,40a), **trip** (85c), **whip** (58c,88d)

I - - Q **Iraq** (99a,d)

IR - - **Irad** (18d), **Irae** (43c), **Irak** (99a,d), **Iran** (6a,48c,116b), **Iraq** (99a,d), **Iras** (11b,32a), **Iren** (127c), **irid** (38d,67c), **iris** (53c,58a,111c), **Iris** (127c), **Irma** (96d), **irok** (55b), **iron** (55c,d,69d,81a,97b,143b,149a, 173d,179c), **Irra** (68c,178a), **irus** (109d)

- IR - **Aira** (70d), **aire** (82c), **Aire**, **airs** (123b), **airy** (176d,177a), **bird**, **birl** (93c,131a,153c), **birn** (31d,139a), **birr** (180d), **ciri** (24c), **circ** (31a), **dire** (45d,55a,104a,163c), **dirk** (40b), **dirt**, **Eire** (82b), **fire** (13a,43d,44b), **firm** (154c,173d), **firn** (67c,70c,106c,149b), **gird** (32c,50a,123a,160a), **girl**, **giro** (38c,83c,167c), **girt** (50a), **hire** (49d,50b,91b,130a), **hiro**, **kiri** (86a,87c,115a,168c), **kirk** (31a,139b), **lira** (28b,79a,170d), **lire** (62c), **Mira** (155b,174d), **mire** (21c,104b), **mirk** (41a,67d), **miro** (19a,106d,184a), **Miro** (113a, 151d), **miry**, **pirn** (21b,129a,179b), **Piro** (192), **pirr** (181a), **rire** (62a), **sire** (17d,55a,59d,124a,163b,166b), **siri** (18b), **tire** (15a,22a, 52d,55a,179b,180d), **tiro** (9b,17d,108c), **Vira** (191), **vire** (11a,13b), **wire**, **wiry** (147a,167c), **zira** (188)

- - IR **Abir** (129a), **Ahir** (27b), **amir** (7c,12a,103a,b,123c,170d), **chir** (29b,116d), **coir** (33a,37a,56a,133d), **cuir** (45c,62a), **emir** (12a, 103a,b,123c,134d,135a,171a), **fair** (17a,55d), **hair** (56b,164d), **heir**, **kair**, **keir** (20c,174d), **koir** (33a), **lair** (37c,42b), **Leir**, **loir** (45c),

Loir, Muir (8b,142c), Nair (45d), noir (61b,134b), pair (22d,37d, 85b,171d), sair (140b,150a), Seir (51b,94a,103d), shir (36d,65d, 165c), skir, soir (61c), spir (97c), stir (8a,13a,35b,78d,100d), tair (68a,76d), vair (64c,154c), weir (40b,57d), whir (25c,181a), Ymir (67a,131c)

I - - R icer, Igor (135d), Imer, inar (65b), Isar (41a,104c,132a), Iser (49a), iter (22d,76c,85c,89c,114d,132a,b,133a,b), Iyar (102b), izar (65b,103b), Izar (155b)

IS - - Isar (41a,104c,132a), isba (135d), Iser (49a), Isha (174a), Isis (68d, 78c,111d), isle (8b,53c,81d,82d,86b,88a), ismy (45a)

- IS - bisa (11a), bise (182a), bish (120b), bisk (120b,151a), cise (147b), cist (22c,29d,156c), Disa (111a), disc (31b), dish, disk (31b), diss (98b), fisc (52c,134c), fish, fisk (24d,52c,134c), fist (80c), gish (102c), gist (95c,118c), hish, hiss (146a), hist (25c,93d), kish (16d,70c), Kish (137c), kiss (148c), kist (29d,58a,139b), Lisa (183d), lisp (153b), liss (54b,58b,60c,129d,140a), list (26d,27b, 75b,83d,134a,138b,165d), mise (8a,10a,70c), miss, mist (46b,59b, 59b,174d), Nish (19d), nisi (90a,173c), Oise, Pisa (90c), pise (127d), pish (36c,107d), pisk (9c,19b), piso (189), pist (25c), rise (49d,80b,155a), Rise (110d,150c), risk (74d), risp (99a), Riss (66a), sise (62c,147b), sish (79b), sisi (121b), sist (139b), visa (114d), vise (31d,77d,114d), viss (189), wise (136b), wish (42d), wisp (148c), wist (87c)

- - IS acis (64b), Agis (86d), anis (55c), Apis (17c,24b,49a,125a,136a), aris (101b), atis (76d,102a), avis (89a), Avis (183c), axis (28b, 41d,77c,153c), bois (62b,63a,183d), Bois, cris (40b,95d), dais (119b), egis (14b,d,115a,124d,144b,154a,161a), Elis (22c,37d, 71b,107c), Eris (12c,68d,109c), feis (82b), glis (45c), gris (61d), ibis (48d,49a,177b), iris (53c,58a,111c), Iris (127c), kris (40b,95d), Isis (68d,78c,111d), itis (158c), Lais (17c), Lois (165d,183c), mais (61b), nais (63c,132a), Otis (9c,d,24d,82a,111a), Ovis (143d), pais (37d), rais (26c,29d,75a,103b), Rais (106b), reis (26c,29d,75a, 103b), Riis (9d), sais (48d,71d), sels (147b,152c), this (42b,124b), tris (122d), unis (91b), Upis (13b)

I - - S ibis (48d,49a,177b), Ibis, Idas (27b,71c), ides (41a,b,133a), ills (170a), Ilus (88d,170b), Iras (11b,32a), iris (53c,58a,111c), Iris (127c), Irus (109d), Isis (68d,78c,111d), Itys (163b), Ives (9c,90b)

IT - - itch, Itea (145d,160c,181d), item (6d,13b,42d,51a,90d,92d,107a, 113d,114c), Iten (192), iter (22d,76c,85c,89c,114d,132a,b,133a,b), itis (158c), itmo (18b), itol (158b), itys (163b), Itza (192)

- IT - bite (29d,156b), biti (20b), bito (7d,57d,168c), bitt (54d,175c), cite (15a,98d,126d,159b), cito (89d,126c), cits, city, dita (117a), dite (150b), Gita, gite (62a,118d), jiti, kite (19c,49a,74c,d), kith (63c), lite (158c,d), lith (34d,156c), liti (60d) litz (127b), mite (12b,81b,82a,114a,c,148c,d,181b), mitt (56c), mitu (39d), mity, nito (55c), pita (9c,28b,56a,83a), pith (37a,51c,67b,95c,97a, 119b,126d), pitt (50d), Pitt (155d), pito (9c,28b,83a), pity (35b), rita, Rita (37b,78d,183c), rite (93a,131d), Sita (127d), site (93b), sito (34b), titi (20d,102a,145d,168d,181b), Tito (186c), vita (89c, 92a), vite (62b), viti (17ob), with (10b)

352

- - IT adit (51a,100a,114d), ait (44b,143a), amit (94a), bait (15d,51a, 94d,167b), brit (76c), chit (67b,98c,108b,116c,177c), doit (47a, 169d,180d), duit (190), Duit (192), edit (20d,49d,123a,129a,131a), emit (43d,49a,53c,58d,83a,142c), exit (114d), fait (6d,61b), flit (41a), frit (64c,67c), gait (96b,179a), grit (137a,b), ibit (117a), knit (173c,179b), lait (62a), nuit (62b), obit (41b,64c), omit (49c, 52c,106b,114c,147d), phit (24b), quit (90d,130c), seit (189), skit (145c), slit (40a), spit (120a,132b,c), suit (38a,58a,91a,112a,119c, 137c), tait (14d), trit (34d,164c), twit (162b,c), unit (101c,110c, 147a), wait (26d,42b,92c,155d,162a), whit (166c), writ (91a), Yuit (51c)

I - - T ibit (117a), ikat (53b,159a), ilot (82d)

- IU - biur (35a), Niue (137d), Pius (121a)

I - - U lalu (48d), ichu (10b,70d), iglu (51c,149b)

IV - - ivah (18d), Ivan (40c,85b,96a), Ives (9c,90b)

- IV - Civa (56d), cive (110c), diva (110d,123c), dive (42b,74b,119d), divi, five, give (79d,123a), hive (17c), jiva (77a), jive (160c), kiva (28c,125b), kive (174d), kivu (170c), live (47c), Livy (132d,133a), rive (32a,153d), siva (67a,120d), Siva (56d,77a), sive (146a), viva (93d), vive (93d), vivo (93a), wive (97a)

- - IV chiv (87a), skiv (151b)

- IW - Biwa (93d,168c), iiwi (19a,74b), kiwi (11d,19a,58c)

IX - - ixia (37a), Ixil (192), ixle (56a)

- IX - Bixa (145d), dixi, Mixe (192), mixy, pixy (154b)

- - IX Alix (183c), Coix (70d,85b), flix, noix (67c)

IY - - iyar (102b)

- IY - kiyi (185d)

I - - Y idly, inky (20b), inly, ismy (45a)

IZ - - izar (65b,103b), Izar (155b)

- IZ - bize (182a), bizz, size, sizy (176d), sizz, tiza (172a), zizz (181a)

- - IZ friz (39d), phiz (54a), swiz (160c), whiz (25c)

I - - Z Inez (45c,183c)

JA - - jaca (84a), jack (26c,58a,127c), Jack (96b), jacu (19a,151b), jade (33c,65d,71d,166a), jadu (95a), jady, Jael (147b), Jaga (191), jagg, jail (123d), Jain (77b), jake (40d), Jake (96b), jako (71a), jama (103b), jamb (12d,45c,118a,146b,174a), jami (103b), jane (190), Jane (183c), jann (102d), jaob, jape (85a,b), jari (40d,107d), jass (160d), jati (27b), jato (173b), jaun (113a), Java (33a), Jave (84d), jawy, jazz

- JA - ajar (110c), Ajax (71b,162d)

- - JA Beja (6c,191), bija (168c), caja (152a), coja (103b,166b), hoja (166b), iija (57a,90d,173a), maja (151c), Maja (153b), Naja (33a), puja (77a), raja (77a,123c), reja (152b), sɔja (151b)

J - - A jaca (84a), Jaca, Jaga (191), jama (103b), Java (33a), Jena (105d, 165b), jiva (77a), jota (151c), Jova (193), juba (106b), juca (27b), Juda, juga (27a), jula, jura, Juza (155b)

J - - B jamb (12d,45c,118a,146b,174a), jaob, jibb, Joab (41a)

353

- - JD   Nejd

J - - D   Joad (50c)

JE - -   jean (37c), Jean (183c), jeel, jeep, jeer (138c,162b), jefe (152a), jeff (133d), Jeff, jehu (46b), Jehu (18c), Jena (105d,165b), jerk (153a), jess (157a), jest (169c), Jesu, jete (16a), Jeth (102a), jeux (61d)

- JE -   ajee (15c,139a)

- - JE   haje (33a,48d), yaje (23a)

J - - E   jade (33c,65d,71d,166a), Jake (40d), Jake (96b), jane (190), Jane (183c), jape (85a,b), Jave (84d), jefe (152a), jete (16a), jibe (8a, 33b,35d,37b,42c,100d,138c,144c,149b), jive (160c), joke (183a), jole (29b), Jose (96a), Jove (85d), jube (28d), Jude (11c,96a), juke (114c), Jule (183d), June (183c), jupe (62b,84a), jure (90b), jute (37a,48a,56a,133d,136a), Jute

J - - F   jeff (133d), Jeff, jiff (101c)

J - - G   jagg, joug (138d), Jung (125a)

JH - -   Jhil, jhum, JHVH (159d), JHWH (159d)

J - - H   Jeth (102a), josh (85b), JHVH (159d), JHWH (159d)

JI - -   jibb, jibe (8a,33b,35d,37b,42c,100d,138c,144c,149b), jiff (101c), Jill (183d), jilt, jink, jinn (42b,103b,153c), jinx (78a), jiti, jiva (77a), jive (160c)

- - JI   caji (180b), Caji, fuji (84b), Fuji (84d), koji (185b), suji (180c)

J - - I   jami (103b), jati (27b), Jati, jiti, jogi (76d), joli (62b), joti

J - - K   jack (26c,58a,127c), Jack (96b), jerk (153a), jink, jock, Jock (96b), jonk, juck (114c), junk (30a,134c)

J - - L   Jael (147b), jail (123d), jarl (40d,107d), jeel, jhil, Jill (183d), Joel (96a), jowl (29b)

- JM -   ijma (103b)

- - JM   Sejm (120c)

J - - M   jhum, joom (39c)

J - - N   Jain (77b), jann, Jann (102d), jaun (113a), jean (37c), Jean (183c), jinn (42b,103b,153c), Joan (183c), John (11c,96a,121a,186b), join (36a,173c), juan (113a), Juan (96a)

JO - -   Joab (41a), Joad (50c), Joan (183c), joar (100a), jobo (77c), jock, Jock (96b), jocu (45b,57a), Jodo (113d), Joel (96a), joey (86a, 185d), Joey (96b,109c), jogi (76d), John (11c,96a,121a,186b), join (36a,173c), joke (183a), joky, jole (29b), joli (62b), jolt (143b), jonk, joom (39c), Jose (96a), josh (85b), joss (30b), Josy (183d), jota (151c), joti, joug (138d), Jova (193), Jove (85d), jowl 29b), Joxy

- JO -   ajog, ejoo (55b,168c), Gjoa (144d)

- - JO   bojo (117a), gajo (107c), Idjo (191), majo, mojo (177c), pajo (122a, rojo (129a,152c), tajo (152a,d)

J - - O   jako (71a), Jako, jato (173b), jobo (77c), Jodo (113d), judo (84b, 85c,142b), Juno (69c,85d,100c,126b)

J - - P   jeep, jump

354

J - - R   **jeer** (162b), **joar** (100a), **juar** (100a)

J - - S   **jass** (160d), **jess** (157a), **joss** (30b)

J - - T   **jest** (169c), **jilt, jolt** (143b), **just** (51b,54b)

JU - -   **juan** (113a), **Juan** (96a), **juar** (100a), **juba** (106b), **jube** (28d), **juca** (27a), **juck** (114c), **Juda, Jude** (11c,96a), **judo** (84b,85c,142b), **Judy** (125c,183d), **juez** (152b), **juga** (27a), **juju** (29b,55d), **juke** (114c), **jula, Jule** (183d), **jump, June** (183c), **Jung** (125a), **junk** (30a,134c), **Juno** (69c,85d,100c,126b), **jupe** (62b,84a), **jura, Jura, jure** (90b), **jury** (38a), **just** (51b,54b), **jute** (37a,48a,56a,133d, 136a), **Jute, Juza** (155b)

- - JU   **baju** (84a), **hoju** (84b), **juju** (29b,55d), **teju** (151b)

J - - U   **jacu** (19a,151b), **jadu** (95), **jehu** (46b), **Jehu** (18c), **Jesu, jocu** (45b,57a), **juju** (29b,55d)

J - - X   **jeux** (61d), **jinx** (78a), **jynx** (78a), **Jynx** (184a)

JY - -   **jynx** (78a), **Jynx** (184a)

J - - Y   **jady, jawy, joey** (86a,185d), **Joey** (96b,109c), **joky, Josy** (183d), **Jozy, Judy** (125c,183d), **July, jury** (38a)

J - - Z   **jazz, juez** (152b)

KA - -   **kaan** (93d,116c), **kaat** (105d), **kada** (188), **kade** (144a), **kadi** (103a, 171a), **Kadu** (191), **Kafa** (6c), **kago** (113a), **kagu** (106c), **kaha** (123d), **kahu** (14d), **kaid** (29d,66a), **kaif** (88c), **kaik** (96c), **kail** (18c, 22a,25a,79b), **Kain, kair, kaka** (114b), **kaki** (84c,106d), **kala** (19a), **kale** (22a,25a,119b,175a), **kali** (26d,67c,136d,167a), **Kali** (147b), **kalo** (162a), **Kama** (56d), **kame** (67b,139b), **Kami** (68a,84b,88c, 107c,144c), **kana** (84d), **Kane** (74c), **k'ang** (30a), **Kano** (84c,177d), **kant** (28d), **Kant** (67a), **kapa** (74b), **kaph** (91d), **Kapp, Kara** (132a), **Kari** (14d), **Karl** (96a), **karn** (156c), **karo** (106d), **kasa** (48a), **kasi** 116b), **kasm** (189), **Kate** (143c,183d), **kath** (14a), **Katy** (183d), **kaun** (93d), **kava** (18c,116a), **Kavi** (84d), **kawa** (18c,116a), **Kawi** (84d), **kawn** (93d), **kayo** (87c), **kazi** (103a), **kazy** (103a)

- KA -   **Akal** (56d), **Akan** (191), **ikat** (53b,159a), **okay** (8d), **skag** (7d, 46d), **skat** (181b), **Skat** (155b)

- - KA   **Akka** (125d), **Atka** (11a), **baka** (52b), **beka** (189), **dika** (23a), **Ekka** (26d), **Inka** (193), **kaka** (114b), **loka** (173c,184c), **pika** (93a, 128a,132c), **puka** (107a,168c), **roka** (95a,168c,d), **Saka** (10a), **sika** (41d,84b), **soka** (20c), **waka** (26a), **weka** (58c,106d,107a,127b), **Yaka** (191)

K - - A   **kada** (188), **Kafa** (6c), **kaha** (123d), **kaka** (114b), **kala** (19a), **Kama** (56d), **kana** (84d), **kapa** (74b), **kara** (132a), **kasa** (48a), **kava** (18c 116a), **kawa** (18c,116a), **keia** (189), **keta** (45a), **kina** (126d), **kiva** (28c,125b), **koba** (11a), **kola** (25b,84a,108d), **Kola** (135b,c,d), **kona** (74c), **kora** (19a,178c), **kota** (117a), **Kota** (45d), **kuba** (26d,189), **kufa** (21b,99a), **kula** (189), **kusa**

K - - B   **kerb** (146b), **knab** (107a), **knob** (73c,107c,124d), **knub** (178b)

K - - D   **kaid** (29d,66a), **keld** (154b), **kind** (150d,153a,174d), **Kurd** (48b, 82a)

KE - -   **keal** (25a), **keef** (75d), **keek** (154c), **keel** (128d,134d,144c,d), **keen** (15a,88a,177b), **keep** (123a,130d), **keet** (72b), **keif** (75d), **keir**

(20c,174d), **kela** (189), **keld** (154b), **kelp** (82a,141c), **Kelt** (180b), **kemp** (139b), **keno**, **Kent** (90d), **kepi** (99d), **kept**, **kerb** (146b), **kere** (75c,128b), **kerf** (40a,108b), **keri** (75c,128b), **kern** (59c,172a), **Kern** (132b), **Kerr**, **keta** (45a), **Ketu** (48b)

- KE - **akee** (168c), **akey** (189), **okeh** (8d,37b), **oket** (189), **skee** (149c), **skeg** (7d,86a,144d,157d,184a), **sken** (164a), **skeo** (57d), **skep** (16d,17c,77c), **skew** (148a,160c,171b,c), **skey** (185d)

- - KE **bake** (139a), **bike**, **cake**, **coke** (32d,64a), **cuke** (39b), **cyke** (40c), **dike** (49c,91d), **Dike** (78a), **duke** (107c), **dyke** (49c,91d), **fake** (123a,143c), **feke**, **fike** (139c), **fyke** (15d), **hake** (57a,b), **hike**, **hyke!**, **jake** (40d), **Jake** (96b), **joke** (183a), **juke** (114c), **lake** (117d), **like** (13c,37d,146d), **Loke** (15d,68b), **luke**, **Luke** (52a, 96a), **make** (35b,36d,54a,123a), **mike**, **Mike** (96b), **moke** (45c, 157d), **Nike** (69c,100c,182d), **Peke** (45a,148d), **pike** (57a,b,76c, 120b,153a), **poke** (108c), **rake** (41b,44c,134b,140d), **roke** (174d, 175b), **sake** (84b,125d), **soke** (44c,85d), **syke** (194), **take**, **tike** (29d), **tuke** (26b,53b), **tyke** (29d), **wake** (134b,168a), **woke**, **yoke** (85b,92d,173c), **Zeke** (96b)

K - - E **kade** (144a), **kale** (22a,25a,119b,175a), **kame** (67b,139b), **Kane** (74c), **Kate** (143c,183d), **kere** (75c,128b), **kibe kile** (189), **kine** (38a,112c), **kite** (19c,49a,74c,d), **kive** (174d), **Klee** (113a), **knee** (85b), **koae** (74b), **Kobe** (78a), **Kome** (71d), **kore** (107b) **Kore** (29a, 42b,116b,124d), **kuge** (84c), **Kure** (84c), **kyle** (57a,139c)

- - KF **wakf** (103a), **wukf** (103a)

K - - F **kaif** (88c), **keef** (75d), **keif** (75d), **kerf** (40a,108b), **kief** (75d), **kiff** (88c), **koff** (47a)

K - - G **k'ang** (30a), **king** (26c,29c), **knag** (115d,139c), **krag** (131c), **kung** (125b)

KH - - **khan** (7c,26c,81b,93d,116c,123c,130c,166c), **khar** (189), **khas** (153a), **khat** (105d), **Khem** (113c), **khet** (188), **khot**

- KH - **Akha** (86a,c)

- - KH **ankh** (38d,162b), **blkh** (120b), **bukh** (122a), **hakh** (46d), **lakh** (110c), **rukh** (53b,54a), **Sikh** (77b)

K - - H **kaph** (91d), **kath** (14a), **kish** (16d,70c), **Kish** (137c), **kith** (63c), **Koch** (66d), **koph** (91d), **Kush**, **kyah** (19a)

KI - - **kiak** (51c), **kibe**, **kiby** (29a), **kick**, **kief** (75d), **kiel** (128d,134c), **Kiel** (25d), **kier** (20c,174d), **Kiev** (20c,174d), **kiff** (88c), **kiho** (82a), **kiki** (27b), **kiku** (30d), **kile** (189), **kill** (38c), **kiln** (15d,112a), **kilo** (99b,122d), **kilt**, **kina** (126d), **kind** (150d,153a,174d), **kine** (38a,112c), **king** (26c,29c), **kink** (38b,171c), **kino** (27c,34c,47c,72c,98b,161d,168c), **kipp**, **kiri** (86a,87c,115a,168c), **kirk** (31a,139b), **kish** (16d,70c), **Kish** (137c), **kiss** (148c), **kist** (29d,58a,139b), **kite** (19c,49a,74c,d), **kith** (63c), **kiva** (28c,125b), **kive** (174d), **kivu** (170c), **kiwi** (11d, 19a,58c), **kiyi** (185d)

- KI - **akia** (74c), **Akim** (135d,191), **akin** (8b,92b,129c), **okia** (190), **Okie** (99d), **skid** (148b), **skil** (57a), **skim** (67c), **skin** (53a,76c,115c, d), **skio** (57d), **skip** (110b,114c,147c), **skir**, **skit** (145c), **skiv** (151b)

- - KI **Enki** (15b), **kaki** (84c,106d), **kiki** (27b), **Kuki** (191), **Loki** (7c,15d, 68b), **maki** (91b), **moki** (127b), **piki** (95c), **Reki** (16a), **saki** (39c,

356

84b,102a), **Tiki** (120c), **weki** (55c), **yaki** (193)

K - - I **kadi** (103a,171a), **kaki** (84c,106d), **kali** (26d,67c,136d,167a), **Kali** (147b), **Kami** (68a,84b,88c,107c,144c), **Kari** (14d), **kasi** (116b), **Kavi** (84d), **Kawi** (84d), **kazi** (103a), **kepi** (99d), **keri** (75c,128b), **kiki** (27b), **kiri** (86a,87c,115a,168c), **kiwi** (11d,19a,58c), **kiyi** (185d), **kobi** (84b), **koji** (185b), **Koli** (27b), **Komi** (191), **kopi** (107a, 168c), **Kopi** (172a), **kori** (7d,77a), **kuei** (44a), **Kuki** (191), **Kuli** (27b), **Kuri** (191), **kwei** (44a)

- KK - **Akka** (125d), **Ekka** (26d)

- - KK **bukk** (122a), **rikk** (49a)

K - - K **kalk** (96c), **kiak** (51c), **keek** (154c), **kick**, **kink** (38b,171c), **kirk** (31a,139b), **konk** (41c), **kunk** (188), **kurk** (31a,139b), **kyak** (51c)

KL - - **klam** (189), **Klee** (113a), **klom** (189), **klop** (150d)

K - - L **kail** (18c,22a,25a,79b), **Karl** (96a), **keal** (25a), **keel** (128d,134d, 144c,d), **kiel** (128d,134d), **Kiel** (25d), **kill** (38c), **koel** (19a,b,39b), **kohl** (53c), **kral**, **kuhl** (53c)

- KM - **ikmo** (18b)

K - - M **kasm** (189), **Khem** (113c), **klam** (189), **klom** (189)

KN - - **Knab** (107a), **knag** (115d,139c), **knap** (76d,107a,139b,159b,166a, 170c,185b), **knar** (87c,134b), **knee** (85b), **knew**, **knez** (123c), **knip** (115c), **knit** (173c,179b), **knob** (73c,107c,124d), **knop** (124b,170c, 185b), **knor** (87c), **knot** (43c,99d,107c,124d,137b), **knub** (178b), **knur** (67d,87c,107c), **knut**, **Knut** (40d,50c,96a)

K - - N **kaan** (93d,116c), **Kain**, **karn** (156c), **kaun** (93d), **kawn** (93d), **keen** (15a,88a,177b), **kern** (172a), **Kern** (132b), **khan** (7c,26c,81b,93d, 116c,123c,130c,166c), **kiln** (15d,112a), **kran** (190), **kuan** (30b), **Kuan** (30c), **kwan** (30b)

KO - - **koae** (74b), **koba** (11a), **Kobe** (78a), **kobi** (84b), **kobu** (84b), **Koch** (66d), **koel** (19a,b,39b), **koff** (47a), **kohl** (53c), **koir** (33a), **koji** (185b), **koko** (106d,114b), **Koko** (93d,186c), **koku** (189), **kola** (25b,84a,108d,168c), **Kola** (135b,c,d), **Koli** (27b), **kolo** (59b,135c), **Kome** (71d), **Komi** (191), **kona** (74c), **konk** (41c), **koop** (16c), **koph** (91d), **kopi** (107a,168c), **Kopi** (172a), **kora** (19a,178c), **Kora, kore** (107b), **Kore** (29a,42b,116b,124d), **kori** (7d,77a), **koso** (6c,80d), **Koso** (192,193), **koss** (188), **kota** (117a), **Kota** (45d), **koto** (84b), **kozo** (113d,168c)

- KO - **akov** (189), **Ekoi** (191), **ikon** (79d,136a)

- - KO **boko** (52b), **Doko** (191), **hako** (115b), **jako** (71a), **koko** (106d,114b), **Koko** (93d,186c), **mako** (18a,19a,20d,143c,168c,182c), **moko** (96c), **toko** (30c)

K - - O **kago** (113a), **kalo** (162a), **Kano** (84c,177d), **karo** (106d), **kayo** (87c), **keno**, **kiho** (82a), **kilo** (99b,122d), **kino** (27c,34c,47c,72c, 98b,161d,168c), **koko** (106d,114b), **Koko** (93d,186c), **kolo** (59b, 135c), **koso** (6c,80d), **Koso** (192,193), **koto** (84b), **kozo** (113d,168c), **Kroo** (191)

K - - P **Kapp**, **keep** (123a,130d), **kelp** ʼ82a,141c), **kemp** (139b), **kipp, klop** (150d), **knap** (76d,107a,139b,159b,166a,170c,185b), **knip** (115c), **knop** (124b,170c,185b), **koop** (16c)

357

KR - - krag (131c), kral, kran (190), kras (76d), kris (40b,95d), Kroe (191)

- KR - akra (176a), Akra (191), ikra (27d), okra (72c,175a), okro (72c, 175a)

- - KR Askr (107d)

K - - R kair, keir (20c,174d), Kerr, khar (189), kier (20c,174d), knar (87c,134b), knor (87c), knur (67d,87c,107c), koir (33a), Kuar (102a), kyar (33a)

- - KS oaks (154d)

K - - S khas (153a), kiss (148c), koss (188), kras (76d), kris (40b,95d), kvas (135c)

- - KT takt (105a,163a)

K - - T kaat (105d), kant (28d), Kant (67a), keet (72b), Kelt (180b), Kent (90d), kept, khat (105d), khet (188), khot, kilt, kist (29d,58a, 139b), knit (173c,179b), knot (43c,99d,107c,124d,137b), knut, Knut (40d,50c,96a), kyat (189)

KU - - Kuan (30c), kuan (30b), Kuar (102a), kuba (26d,189), kudu (11a), kuei (44a), kufa (21b,99a), kuge (84c), kuhl (53c), Kuki (191), kuku (19a,106d), kula (189), Kuli (27b), kung (125b), kunk (188), Kurd (48b,82a), Kure (84c), Kuri (191), kurk (31a,139b), kusa, Kush

- KU - akua (120d), skua (19b,72c,84a,141a)

- - KU baku (26d,157b,168c), duku (95d,168c), haku (86d), hiku (57a, 106d,138a), kiku (30d), koku (189), kuku (19a,106d), Maku (192), poku (11a), puku (11a), Suku (191), Taku (80c)

K - - U Kadu (191), kagu (106c), kahu (14d), Ketu (48b), kiku (30d), kivu (170c), kobu (84b), koku (189), kudu (11a), kuku (19a,106d)

KV - - kvas (135c)

- KV - NKVD (135d)

K - - V Kiev

KW - - kwan (30b), kwei (44a)

K - - W knew, know

KY - - kyah (19a), kyak (51c), kyar (33a), kyat (189), kyle (57a,139c)

- KY - Skye (163c), skyr (21d,151a), skyt (138c,140b)

- - KY alky, caky, coky, faky, inky (20b), joky, laky, oaky, piky, poky (148c), taky, waky

K - - Y Katy (183d), kazy (103a), kiby (29a)

K - - Z knez (123c)

LA - - laap (51d,91b,141d), lace (58b,179c), lack (178a), lact (34c), lacy, Ladd (143c), lade (24c,26d,43c,93b,100a,132a,139d,161b,178d), lady, laet (60d), lago (83b,152b), laic (32b,90b,107d,124a,141d), laid, lain, lair (37c,42b), Lais (17c), lait (62a), lake (117d), lakh (110c), laky, lala (129b), lalo (16b,34d,153a), Lalo (35c), lama (23d,24a,91d,165b), lamb, Lamb (49c), lame (38d,43d,73b), lamp (92a,94c), lana (58a,66a,90a,184b), land (44a,163c), lane (134b, 157b), lank (148b,164b), lant, lanx (133a,b), Laos (80d,129c), Lapp (108a), Lara (25c), lard (54d,61a,71a,110a), lari (78a,101c),

Lari (72c), **lark** (19a,63d,177b), **larp** (51d), **Lars** (51d,121b), **lash** (58c,87b,165c,180d), **Lasi** (191), **lass** (95b), **last** (36c,50b,145a, 174c), **lata** (85d,95d), **late** (128c), **lath** (157c), **latu** (190), **laud** (122a), **laun** (146b), **lava** (101c,132b,151a,177a), **lave** (16d,178b), **lawn** (20a,37c,53b,92c), **laze** (79b), **Laze** (191), **Laxi** (191), **lazo** (88d,128b,133d), **lazy**

- LA - **alae** (182d), **alai** (171a), **Alai** (135c), **alan** (45a,79a,183c), **Alan, alar** (15c,145c,182d), **alas** (52c,136b,183b), **alat** (136d), **alay** 5c), **blaa, blab** (162b), **blae** (93b), **blah, blas** (6c,49c), **Blas** (« 7b), **blat** (25b), **blay** (57d), **clad** (46a,82a), **clam** (20b,101b), **clan** (169c), **clap** (58b), **claw** (29c,105b,161d,173a), **Clay** (9d), **Elah** (18c,86d), **elan** (12c,41a,50d,62a,153c,177a,186b), **Elam** (18d,37d, 82a,116c,144b), **ELAS** (71c), **flag** (16b,50d,82b,88c,115a,155a), **flak** (11a), **flam** (169c), **flan** (39d,40a,114d), **flap** (17b,59a,104a, 118d,161a,182d), **flat** (41b,124b,173a), **flaw, flax, flay** (147c,157c), **glad** (85c), **klam** (189), **Olaf** (108a,176b), **olam** (51a,d,75c,81a), **Olan** (115c), **Olax** (52b), **olay** (113b), **plan** (99b,124a,138b), **plap** (54b), **plat** (22b,96c,114a,119c,133d), **play** (63d,154a), **slab** (148b), **slag** (46c,99a,138c,148d,177a), **slam** (180d,182d), **slap** (24a,128c, 148c), **slat** (58b,89a,117c,184a), **Slav** (13c,40c,48b,52a,120b,135b), **slaw, slay, Ulam** (67b), **ulan** (27d,88a)

- - LA **agla** (7a), **alla** (6d), **amla** (48a,161d,168c,169a), **aula** (66c,73b), **Bala** (26c,66a), **bela** (12a), **Bela** (18b,48c,78d), **bola** (16a,179b), **cela** (62d), **cola** (25b,108d,149d,168c), **dola** (189), **ella** (152c, 158c), **Ella** (183c), **fala** (129b), **gala** (55d), **Gala** (191), **gila** (93b), **gola** (27b,40c,70c,157a), **gula** (90a,101a,165b), **hala** (112b), **Hela** (93c), **hila** (53c), **hola** (74c,152b), **hula** (74b), **Hyla** (10a,166d, 169b), **lola, jula, kala** (19a), **kela** (189), **kola** (25b,84a,108d,168c), **Kola** (135b,c,d), **kula** (189), **lala** (129b), **Lila** (183c), **Loia** (27d,97b), **mala** (89c,90a,94b,97d,109d,185c), **mela** (34a,129d), **mila** (188), **Mola** (159c), **Nala** (77a), **Nola, olla** (36d,44b,84d,113b,121d, 151d,152c,181b), **pala** (189), **Pala** (88b), **pela** (30c), **Pola, pyla** (22d), **sala** (50c,152a,b,c), **Sala** (50c), **sola** (9a,48a,74b,118c, 154a,167b), **Sula** (65a), **tala** (16d,113a,168c,d), **tela** (22d,98c, 121b,166a,179c), **tola** (48a,80d,180a), **Tola** (85b), **tula** (9a), **Tula, upla, vela** (98c,136b,149d), **Vela** (36b,c), **vila** (54b), **vola** (89d), **Zola** (63a)

L - - A **lala** (129b), **lama** (23d,24a,91d,165d), **lana** (58a,66a,90a,184b), **Lara** (25c), **lata** (85d,95d), **lava** (101c,132b,151a,177a), **Leda** (27b, 75d,120c,153a,171d,186b), **lena** (56d), **Lena** (36b), **Lida** (183c), **lija** (57a,90d,173a), **Lila** (183c), **lima** (17b,152b,174d), **Lima** (31b), **lina** (188), **Lina** (183d), **lipa** (54d), **lira** (28b,79a,170d), **Lisa** (183d), **loka** (173c,184c), **Lola** (27d,97b), **loma** (58b,63d), **lora** (146b,149b, 151c,169b), **Lora** (183c), **lota** (24c,121d,178d), **Lota, lowa** (19a), **Luba** (191), **luna** (103c), **Luna** (102b), **lura** (22d,82a), **lyra, Lyra** (36b,74a)

- LB - **alba** (98b,181a), **Alba** (151d), **albe** (133a), **Albi** (58a), **albo** (34d, 181a), **Elba** (105d), **Elbe** (108a)

- - LB **bulb** (37a,172c)

L - - B **lamb, Lamb** (49c), **limb** (12d,22d), **lobb** (23b,94c,163a)

- LC - **Alca** (14c,128b), **alco** (45b)

- - LC **talc** (28d,63b,99c,100b,122a,149c)

L - - C **laic** (32b,90b,107d,124a,141d)

- LD - **Alda** (110d,150c), **alda** (152b)

- - LD **bald** (16c), **bold** (41a), **cold** (65d), **eild** (138d,140a), **fold, geld** (162b), **gild** (14a,49c,69c,98b), **gold, held, Hild, hold** (95c,124c, 130d), **Keld** (154b), **meld** (26a,41c,99a,118b), **mild** (32a,66a), **mold** (54d,143c), **sold, suld** (188), **told** (129c), **veld** (151a), **weld** (47c, 85b,173c), **wild** (38b,173d), **wold** (47c,60a,118d,174a,184a)

L - - D **Ladd** (143c), **laid, land** (44a,163c), **lard** (54d,61a,71a,110a), **laud** (122a), **lead** (35d,43d,72b,74d,81a), **lend** (6d,79d), **lied** (66d,150b), **load** (24c,26d,161b), **lood** (189) **lord** (107c), **loud** (156a), **Ludd** (23c)

LE - - **lead** (35d,43d,72b,74d,81a), **leaf** (55c,73c,119b), **Leah** (19a,84a, 87b,183c), **leak** (110c), **leal** (54b,94c,139d), **lean** (128a,148b,152d, 164b,166a), **leap** (26c), **lear** (139d), **Lear** (37a,143b), **lech** 102b), **Leda** (27b,75d,120c,153a,171d,186b), **leek** (58b,76a,110c,177d), **leer** (9d,58a,67c,93d,112a,148c), **lees** (46a,142a), **leet** (26a, 38a,139d), **left** (42c), **lehr** (67c,112a) **Leif** (107d), **Leir, Lely** (47a), **lena** (56d), **Lena** (36b), **lend** (6d,79d), **lene** (36b,149a, 172b), **leno** (37c,53b), **lens** (67c,95b,111a,129b,162d), **lent** (54d), **Lent** (115d,141c), **Leon** (96a), **Lero** (82d), **lerp** (51d,141d), **less** (100c,108b,141d), **lest** (59d,163d), **lete, Leti** (82d), **Leto** (11c), **Lett** (16a,90a,93a), **leve** (62a), **Levi** (84a,90c), **levo** (91a), **levy** (14a, 162b)

- LE - **Alea** (14b,31c,167d), **alec** (10a,57c,d,76c,137c), **alee** (15c,75d, 144b,157a,182a), **alef** (91c), **alem** (98b,155a,170d,171a), **alen** (40d, 138a), **bleb** (20c,23d,67c), **bled, blet** (64a), **bleu** (61b), **blew, clee** (19a,129a), **clef** (104d,105a), **clem** (56b,158b), **clew** (16a,33a,77b, 136b,164d), **elef** (91c), **flea** (81b), **fled, flee, flew, flex** (18a), **fley** (63d), **gled** (19a,52a,87a), **glee** (99a,150b), **glen** (43c), **Hler** (141a), **Ilex** (77d), **Klee** (113a), **Lleu** (40c), **Llew** (40c), **olea** (170b), **Olea** (110b), **oleo** (34c), **plea** (51a,52d,122a,130b), **pleb** (10d,35b,180b), **plet** (135d), **plew** (17c), **plex** (60b), **Sleb** (12a), **sled** (40a), **slee** (140b,148c), **slew** (160a), **sley** (179b), **Ulex** (153c), **vlei** (38c, 160a), **vley** (160a)

- - LE **able** (26b,35b,126a,147c), **acle** (13d,82c,115d), **aile** (62b,63a,182c, d), **Alle** (14c), **atle** (136d,161d,169b), **axle** (153c,180c), **bale** (24b, 74a), **bile** (30c), **bole** (31d,32a,169b), **cale** (72c), **cole** (25a), **Cole, dale** (43c,128a,174b), **dele** (26a,49c,51b,53a,110b,123b,124c,130a, 145c,161b), **dole** (44c,118c,121c,129d), **Dole** (74c), **elle** (62b,c), **file** (13a,127d), **gale** (181d), **gyle** (23b,174d), **hale** (125b), **Hale** (9d,131a), **hole** (6c,11b,110d,118c,147a), **hule** (23a,134c), **hyle** (97c), **idle** (174b,c,178c), **ille** (89b,d,163d), **iole** (52a,76b,123c), **isle** (8b,53c,81d,82d,86b,88a), **ixle** (56a), **jole** (29b), **Jule** (183d), **kale** (22a,25a,119b,175a), **kile** (189), **kyle** (57a,139c), **male** (154d), **Male** (45d), **mele** (74b,150b), **mile** (64c), **mole** (19d,23a,24d,85a, 117c,155c), **Mole** (88c), **mule** (45b,148b,153c,180b), **nile** (33c, 71d), **Nile** (106b), **ogle** (9d,53c,91a,93d,148c), **orle** (17b,56b,76a, 144b,177a), **pale** (113a,117c,178a), **Pele** (69c,74c), **pile** (45d,75b, 117c), **pole** (132c,143b,177b,184a), **Pole** (52a), **pule** (180d), **pyle** (34b), **Pyle** (9c,178a), **rale** (7c,23a,29d,41b), **rile** (10c,d,82c,125a,

156b,176a), **role** (114b), **rule** (11b,26b,90b), **sale** (14c,61c,62b,c, 168b), **sole** (52c,57a,b,58b,d,110c,115d,150a), **tale** (91a,185b), **tele** (34b,122c), **tile** (31d,56d,72b,95b,133c,163c), **tole** (9a,51a,99b, 163a), **tule** (24b,27c), **vale** (54c,128a,174b), **Vale** (7c,109c), **vile** (16c,56c), **vole** (97d,104a), **wale** (70b,131b,157c,163d,179a,180a, c,d), **wile** (13b,41c,157b,169c), **Yale** (173c), **Yule** (30d)

L - - E **lace** (58b,179c), **lade** (24c,26d,43c,93b,100a,132a,139d,161b), 178d), **lake** (117d), **lame** (38d,43d,73b), **lane** (134b,157b), **late** (128c), **lave** (16d,178b), **laze** (79b), **Laze** (191), **lene**(36b,149a, 172b), **lete, leve** (62a), **life** (19a,177a), **like** (13c,37d,146d), **lime** (25b,27d,31b,33c,102d,168c), **line** (12b,22b,36d,38a,126c,134b, 157b,158b,162d,175c), **lire** (62c), **lite** (158c,d), **live** (47c), **lobe** (90c,134b), **lode** (42c,99a,111b,175b), **loge** (164a), **Loke** (15d,68b), **Lome, lone** (150a), **lope** (48b,64b,d), **lore** (77c,87c,90d,151c,183a), **lose** (60a,100c), **lote** (24c,94a), **love** (163a), **lube** (110a), **luce** (58c,117d), **Luce** (7b,35a), **luge** (148a), **luke, Luke** (52a,96a), **luno** (38c,73b,74d), **lupe** (19a,64a), **lure** (41c,51a,54b,163a), **lute** (11c, 28b,84d,105a,131d), **luxe** (61c,62d,159c), **lyre** (11c,81c,105a,111c), **lyse**

- LF - **alfa** (70d)

- - LF **calf, golf** (154a), **gulf** (6c), **half** (101a), **pelf** (22a,56c,131b), **self** (48d,80d), **Welf** (67a), **wolf**

L - - F **leaf** (55c,73c,119b), **Leif** (107d), **lief** (181d), **loaf** (49b,94b), **loof** (144c,153d), **luff** (136b), **luif**

- LG - **alga** (141b,c), **Algy** (96b), **Olga** (135c,183c)

L - - G **ling** (24c,57a,b,75b,178c), **long** (38b,185b), **lung, lurg** (96d,141b, 184d)

L - - H **lakh** (110c), **lash** (58c,87b,165c,180d), **lath** (157c), **Leah** (19a,84a, 87b,183c), **lech** (102b), **lith** (34d,156c), **loch** (88a,139d), **losh** (178b), **loth** (15a,173d), **Lugh** (28b), **lush** (94d)

LI - - **Liam** (181d), **liar** (98d), **Lias** (66a), **lick, Lida** (183c), **Lido** (83d, 175b), **lied** (66d,150b), **lief** (181d), **lien** (65c,91a,124c), **lieu** (118c, 155d), **life** (19a,177a), **lift** (49b), **liin** (188), **lija** (57a,90d,173a), **like** (13c,37d,146d), **Lila** (183c), **lill** (15d,118a), **lilt** (93a,131a, 147a), **lily, lima** (17b,152b,174d), **Lima** (31b), **limb** (12d,22b), **lime** (25b,27d,31b,33c,102d,168c), **limn** (45d,121c), **limp** (58a,81a,177d), **limu** (141c), **limy** (176d), **lina** (188), **Lina** (183d), **line** (12b,22b,36d,38a,126c,134b,157b,158b,162d,175c), **ling** (24c,57a,b,75b,178c), **link** (36a,81d,85b), **linn** (120d,140a,c, 168c,178d), **lino, lint** (46a,58d), **liny** (157b), **Linz** (40d), **lion** (55b, 86c), **lipa** (54d), **lira** (28b,79a,170d), **lire** (62c), **Lisa** (183d), **lisp** 153b), **liss** (54b,58b,60c,129d,140a), **list** (26d,27b,75b,83d,134a, 138b,165d), **lite** (158c,d), **lith** (34d,156c), **liti** (60d), **litz** (127b), **live** (47c), **Livy** (132d,133a)

- LI - **alia** (89d), **alif** (12b), **alii** (74c,134c), **alim** (103b,162c) **alin** (188), **alit** (44b,143a), **Alix** (183c), **Clim** (12b), **Clio** (104d), **clip** (54d, 143d), **Elia** (88a,115d), **Elis** (22c,37d,71b,107c), **flip** (167c), **flit** (41a), **flix, glia** (106c), **glib** (58d,149a,177c), **glim, glis** (45c), **ilia** (21d,77b,115d), **ille** (89b,d), **olic** (158b), **olid** (55d,60c,148d,157d), **olio** (44b,77c,98c,100d,121d), **plie** (32c,59b), **slid, slim** (148b,

160a), **slip** (67c,119a), **slit** (40a)

- - LI   amli (48a,161d,168c,169a), **Atli** (14c,72b,79a,107d), **Bali, Beli** (23c), **coli, dali** (168c,169b), **doli, fili, gali** (6c), **goli** (105c), **Holi** (77a), **joli** (62b), **kali** (26d,67c,136d,167a), **Kali** (147b), **Koli** (27b, **Kuli** (27b), **mali** (27b), **pali** (122b), **Pali** (23d,24a,137b,175a), **pili** (34b,108d), **puli** (45a,78d), **soli** (12c,110c), **tali** (189), **teli** (94b), **vali** (171a,176a), **Vali** (7c,109c), **vili** (54b), **Vili** (109c), **wali** (171a), **yali** (171a)

L - - I   Lari (72c), **Iari** (78a,101c), **Lasi** (191), **Lazi** (191), **Leti** (82d), **Levi** (84a,90c), **liti** (60d), **loci** (66b,118c), **Lodi** (105d), **Loki** (7c,15d, 68b), **lori** (91b), **Loti** (63a,176a), **ludi** (133b), **Luri** (191)

- LK -   alky

- - LK   balk (118c,146a,156d), **bilk** (29b,41c,42a), **bulk** (97b), **calk** (78c, 109a,141c,178d), **folk** (116a,169c), **fulk** (173a), **hulk** (144d,173d), **milk** (60d), **mulk** (60d), **polk** (37c), **pulk** (37c,88d), **silk** (53b,179c), **sulk** (159a), **talk**, **volk** (66c,105d,116a), **Volk**, **walk**, **welk** (65c,96d, 141b), **yolk**

L - - K   lack (178a), **lank** (148b,164b), **lark** (19a,63d,177b), **leak** (110c), **leek** (58b,76a,110c,177d), **lick**, **link** (36a,81d,85b), **lock** (54d), **lonk** (143d), **look** (11c,53c,142a), **luck** (28d), **lurk** (92a, 147d)

LL - -   llyn (120d,140a), **Lleu** (40c), **Llew** (40c)

- LL -   alla (6d), **Alle** (14c), **allo** (34c), **ally** (14a,35c,d,173c), **ella** (152c, 158c), **Ella** (183c), **elle** (62b,c), **ille** (89b,d,163d), **ills** (170a), **olla** (36d,44b,84d,113b,121d,151d,152c,181b), **ullo** (6a,144a), **Ullr** (146b,164d)

- - LL   ball, bell (24c,39d), **Bell** (162d), **bill** (17b,147a), **Bill** (96b), **boll** (119b,d), **bull** (113c), **call** (145c,159b,176d), **cell** (39b), **cull** (117c), **dell** (43c,174b), **dill** (13a,117c), **doll** (125c), **dull** (21a,32c,173a), **Dull** (94b), **fall** (46b,141c), **fell** (40a,58b,76c,115d,147d), **fill** (109b), **full** (7b,130b), **gall** (19a,28c,29b,82c,160c,176a), **gill** (22d), **Goll, gull** (32d,41c,42a,72c,99b,141a), **hall** (37b,114d), **hill**, **hull** (141d,142a,144c,d), **Jill** (183d), **kill** (38c), **lill** (15d,118a), **loll** (94b,128c), **lull** (126d,150c), **mall** (95d,124b,143b), **mill** (126c), **moll, Moll** (183d), **mull** (53b,135a,164c), **Nell** (110a,183d), **nill** (173d), **Noll** (96b,110b), **null** (108c,177a), **pall** (32d,81b,112a), **pill, poll** (74d,160a,177c), **pull** (45d,167d), **rill** (23c,102b,132a,148d, 157b), **roll** (134a,160b), **rull** (170b), **sell** (97a,115c,175b), **sill** (45c, 76c,165a,182b), **tall** (118d), **tell** (105d,129c,154b), **Tell** (160d), **till** (39c,101c,173d), **toll** (131c), **vill** (176b), **wall, well, will** (18b,43a, 163c,177c), **yell** (145c)

L - - L   leal (54b,94c,139d), **lill** (15d,118a), **loll** (94b,128c), **lull** (25c,126d,150c)

- LM -   alma (40d,53d,146d,147a), **Alma** (38d,183c), **alme** (40d,147a), **alms** (29a), **elmy, ulme** (49c)

- - LM   balm (110a,172c), **calm** (8d,11d,112b,118d,126c,d,172b,173d), **culm** (11a,32d,70d,145a,156a), **film** (164b), **halm, helm** (144d, 165d), **holm** (77d,82d,109a), **malm** (32a,92b), **palm** (59b,168a,169b)

L - - M   Liam (181d), **loam** (47d), **loom** (11c,146b,179b), **lyam** (139a)

362

- LN - ulna (21d,39b)

- - LN kiln (15d,112a), vuln (184d)

L - - N Lain, laun (146b), lawn (20a,37c,53b,92c), lean (128a,148b,152d, 164b,166a), Leon (96a), lien (65c,91a,124c), liin (188), limn (45d, 121c), linn (120d,140a,c,168c,178d), lion (55b,86c), llyn (120d, 140a), loan, loin (40a,98a), loon (19a,b,c,157d,179c), lorn (42d, 60b), loun (19a,b), lown (157d)

LO - - load (24c,26d,161b), loaf (79b,94b), loam (47d,150a), loan, lobb (23b,94c,163a), lobe (90c,134b), lobo (165d,183c), loch (88a,139d), loci (66b,118c), lock (54d), loco (38b,119b,120b), lode (42c,99a, 111b,175b), Lodi (105d), Lodz, loft (14c,69d,104b,178b), loge (164a), logy (46d), loin (40a,98a), loir (45c), Loir, Lois (165d,183c), loka (173c,184c), Loke (7c,15d,68b), Loki (7c,15d,68b), Lola (27d, 97b), loll (94b,128c), Lolo (27d,30a), Lome (58b,63d), Lome, lone (150a), long (38b,185b), Lonk (143d), lood (189), loof (144c,153d), look (11c,53c,142a), loom (11c,146b,179b), loon (19a,b,c,157d, 179c), loop (31b,107d), Loos, loot (22a,118a,119d,136a,153d), lope (48b,64b,d), lora (146b,149b,151c,169b), Lora (183c), lord (107c), lore (77c,87c,90d,151c,183a), lori (91b), lorn (42d,60b), loro (19a,114b), lory (19a,114a), lose (60a,100c), losh (178b), loss (42c,123d,178b), lost, lota (24c,121d,178d), lote (24c,94a), loth (15a,173d), Loti (63a,176a), loto (65a,121d,178d), lots, loud (156a), loun (19a,b), loup (61d,62a,90c,139d), Loup (193), lour (13d,63d), lout (15c,22a,24b,45b,109a,157d), love (163a), Iowa (19a), lown (157d), lowp (90c,139d)

- LO - alod (51c,55d,88a,124c), aloe (7d,20a,76a,b,92b,98b,119b,158b, 167a,183d), alop (13d,46b,93d), alow (18a,172c), blob, bloc (173a), blot, blow, clod (22a,45b,157d), Cloe (183c), clog (30c,145b), clop, clot (32d,94d)ʼ, clou (62b), clow (58c,148c), cloy (61b,137c, 159d), elod (49b,59d,79c), Elon (18c,51b,108a), floc (149a), floe (79b), flog (180d), flop (54a), flot (173a), flow (157b), glom (155d, 160d,178c), glow (144c), ilog (132a,161b), ilot (82d), klom (189), klop (150d), Olor (160a,b), plod (170b), plop (54b), plot (25a,36b, 118d,138b), plow (39c,165d), ploy (43c), slob (173d), sloe (14a,20b, 64a,119d,181c), slog (157c,170b,177d), sloo (160a), slop, slot (10d, 11b,41d,110d,167d,168a,181b), slow (43c)

- - LO allo (34c), bilo (131b), bolo (87a), calo (72d), dilo (120d,168c), filo, gilo (48a), Golo (191), Gulo (183c), halo (14d,31b,92a), hilo (74c), kalo (162a), kilo (99b,122d), kolo (59b,135c), lalo (16b,34d), Lalo (35c), Lolo (27d,30a), malo (23a,74c,152a), milo (70b,87c), Milo, nolo (42a), orlo (56b,119c), Oslo (152c), palo (152c), pelo (83b), polo (154a), Polo (175b), ralo (188), silo (59a), solo (12c,89a,110c), ullo (6a,144a), velo (175b)

L - - O Iago (83b,152b), Ialo (16b,34d), Lalo (35c), lazo (88d,128b,133d), leno (37c,53b), Lero (82d), Leto (11c), levo (91a), Lido (83d,175b), lino, lobo (165d,183c), loco (38b,119b,120b), Lolo (27d,30a), loro (19a,114b), loto (65a,121d), ludo (65a,112b)

- LP - Alph (132a), Alps (85d), olpe (90d,182c)

- - LP calp (92b), colp (28a,148b), gulp (46a,79d,160a), help (14a), kelp (82a,141c), palp (11a,55b,58b,167c), pulp, salp (148d), yelp

L - - P laap (51d,91b,141d), lamp (92a,94c), Lapp (108a), larp (51d), leap (26c), lerp (51d,141d), limp (58a,81a,177d), lisp (153b), loop (31b,107d), loup (61d,62a,90c,139d), Loup (193), lowp (90c,139d), lump (45a,160c)

- - LR Ullr (146b,164d)

L - - R lair (37c,42b), lear (139d), Lear (37a,143b), leer (9d,58a,67c,93d, 112a,148c), lehr (67c,112a), Leir, liar (98d), loir (45c), Loir, lour (13d,63d)

- LS - also (10b,18b,80a), Elsa (70a,93c,110d,177b,183c), else (18b,79b, 111d)

- - LS fels (190), fils (62d,150b), Hals (47a), ills (170a)

L - - S Lais (17c), Laos (80d,129c), Lars (51d,121b), lass (95b), lees (46a, 142a), lens (95b,111a,129b,162d), less (100c,108b,141d), Lias (66a), liss (54b,58b,60c,129d,140a) Lois (165d,183c), Loos, loss (42c,123d,178b), lots, Lubs (94c), Lyas (66a)

- LT - alta (89c,152d), alto (152b,176c,177a)

- - LT Balt (93a), belt (13b,54d,58b,132d,160a), bult (76d), celt (30c,82c,123a,156c,167b,179b), Celt (10a,180a,b), colt (78c,131a,185d,186b), Colt, cult (141d,161c), dolt (20c,59c,157d), felt, galt, gelt (101c), gilt (69c,77c,151d,185d), halt (13b,28a,38d, 156d), hilt (73c), holt (36d,119b,184b), jilt, jolt (143b), Kelt (180b), kilt, lilt (93a,131a,147a), malt (17c), melt, milt (153d), molt (27a, 143d) pelt (53a), salt (35d,105b,123a,136c,141c,149d), silt (104b, 142a), tilt (26b,d,166a), tolt, volt (49b,78c), Walt (96b), welt (36d,131b,145a,b,177b,d), wilt (46b), yelt (151b)

L - - T lact (34c), laet (60d), lait (62a), lant, last (36c,50b,145a,174c), leet (26a,38a,139d), left (42c), lent (54d), Lent (115d,141c), lest (59d, 163d), Lett (16a,90a,93a), lift (49b), lilt (93a,131a,147a), lint (46a, 58d), list (26d,27b,75b,83d,134a,138b,165d), loft (14c,69d,104b, 178b), loot (22a,118a,119d,136a,153d), lost, lout (15c,22a,24b,45b, 109a,157d), lust (41b)

LU - - Luba (191), lube (110a), Lubs (94c), luce (58c,117d), Luce (7b,35a), luck (28d), lucy, Lucy (183c), Ludd (23c), ludi (133b), ludo (65a, 112b), luff (136b), luge (148a), Lugh (28b), luif, luke, Luke (52a, 96a), lull (25c,126d,150c), lulu (19a,57b,112c), Lulu (183d), lump (45a,160c), luna (103c), Luna (102b), lune (38c,73b,74d), lung, luny (38b), lupe (19a,64a), lura (22d,82a), lure (41c,51a,54b,163a), lurg (96d,141b,184d), Luri (191), lurk (92a,147d), lush (94d), lust (41b), lute (11c,28b,84d,105a,131d), luxe (61c,62d,159c)

- LU - alum (14a,45c), Alur (191), blub, blue (33c,98c,102c,150d,173a), blup, blur, blut (66b), club (39c), clue, Elul (102b), flub (22b), flue (8b,30a), flux (28d,58d), glub, glue (7b,156a), glug, glum (102c, 159a), glut (52c,70a,137c,159d), Ilus (88d,170b), plug (156b,184d), plum, plup, plus (10b,102c) slub (171c), slue (97b,148b,160a), slug (46b,99b,157c), slum, slur (44b,124c,148b,168a), ulua (57a,74c), Ulua (141b)

- - LU Aalu (6b,48d), aulu (74c,168c), balu (104b,159a,181d), hulu (55b), lalu (48d), iglu (51c,149b), lulu (19a,57b,112c), Lulu (183d), pelu (30a,106d,168c), pulu (74c), Sulu (102c), tolu (16a), Tulu (45d), zulu (171d,175d), Zulu (86a)

364

L - - U **latu** (190), **lieu** (118c,155d), **limu** (141c), **Lieu** (40c), **lulu** (19a,57b, 112c), **Lulu** (183d)

- LV - **Alva** (151d), **Ulva** (141b)

LW - - **Lwow**

L - - W **Llew** (40c), **Lwow**

- - LX **calx** (23c,75c,112c), **falx** (133b)

L - - X **lanx** (133a,b), **lynx** (26c,181d), **Lynx** (36b)

LY - - **lyam** (139a), **Lyas** (66a), **lynx** (26c,181d), **Lynx** (36b), **Lyra** (36b, 74a), **lyre** (11c,81c,105a,111c), **lyse**

- LY - **Alya** (155b,c), **Alys** (183c), **Clym** (12b), **llyn** (120d,140a)

- - LY **ably** (147c), **ally** (14a,35c,d,173c), **coly** (104a), **eely** (185a), **holy, idly, inly, July, Lely** (47a), **lily, moly** (76a,181c), **oily** (110b, 172c), **only** (24d,52c,98d,147a,150a), **Orly** (8b), **paly** (194), **pily, poly** (34c,76b), **puly, rely** (16b,170b), **rily** (176a), **ugly, vily** (54b), **wily** (13b,38b,39c)

L - - Y **Lacy, lady, laky, lazy, Lely** (47a), **levy** (14a,162b), **lily, limy** (176d), **liny** (157b), **livy** (132d,133a), **logy** (46d), **lory** (19a,114a), **lucy, Lucy** (183c), **luny** (38b)

L - - Z **Linz** (40d), **litz** (127b), **Lodz**

MA - - **maal** (188), **ma'am** (95a,166b), **maar** (177a), **Maas** (132a), **Maat** (69a,b,85d), **Maba** (103a,168d), **mabi** (58d), **mace** (49d,108d,153b, 154d,161a,178a), **mack, made, Madi** (174a), **mado** (14d,57a,170b), **mage** (95b), **magg** (95b), **Magh** (102a), **magi** (123c), **Magi** (95b, 116c,183a), **maha** (28c,88c,136d), **mahr** (103a), **Maia** (76b,109a, 153b,155b,177c), **maid** (45b,142d), **mail** (12d,99b,121c), **maim** (43d,81a,105c), **main** (29d,35d,123d), **mais** (61b), **maja** (151c), **Maja** (153b), **majo, make** (35b,36d,54a,123a), **maki** (91b), **mako** (18a,19a,20d,143c,168c,182c), **Maku** (192), **mala** (89b,c,90a,94b, 97d,109d,185c), **male** (154d), **Male** (45d), **mali** (27b), **mall** (95d, 124b,143b), **malm** (32a,92b), **malo** (23a,74c,152a), **malt** (17c), **mama, Mama** (116d), **mamo** (19a,74b), **mana** (30a,120d,122a, 159c), **mand** (28b), **mane, mani** (115c), **mann** (189), **Mann** (9c, 48c,185c), **mano** (71d,73d,74b,83b), **Mans** (30a), **Manu** (10a,76d, 77a,b), **Manx** (27b,28a,82d), **many** (108d), **mapo** (68a,148d), **mara** (114d), **Mara** (24a,d,105b,107b), **marc** (70c), **Marc** (96a) **mare** (78b), **Mare** (108b), **mari** (61d), **Mari** (16a), **mark** (146b,155a), **Mark** (52a, 96a), **marl** (32a,42c,55d), **maro** (144d), **Mars** (68c,118d,119a,129a, 178a), **mart** (49d,97a), **Mart** (96b,183d), **maru** (84c,144d), **Mary** (50c,126b,183c), **masa** (37a), **mash** (39b,156c), **mask** (44a,45c), **mass** (8a,24b,35b,142d), **mast** (17c,108d,120b,144d,152d), **masu** (57a,84c), **mate** (18c,35b,41d,113a,154a,162c), **math** (77a), **Matt, maty** (80c), **maud** (53d,71a,136d,143c), **Maud** (181a,183c), **Maui** (120d), **maul** (73c,96b), **maun** (139d), **maya** (77a,179b), **Maya** (23d, 186c), **Mayo** (193), **maze** (87b,157d)

- MA - **amah** (95b,108d,111c), **amar** (189), **imam** (25c,102d,103a), **Oman** (159a), **omao** (165b), **omar** (103b), **Omar** (48c,51b,116c,163b), **Xmas**

- - MA **alma** (40d,53d,146d,147a), **Alma** (38d,183c), **amma** (6a), **atma** (150d), **bema** (28d,31a,114b,119c,125b,137a), **boma** (7d),

eima (83b,c), **coma** (91c,157d,170c,172b), **cyma** (101a,b), **dama** (65d,152b), **Duma** (135c), **Emma** (183c), **Erma** (183c), **Fama** (135a), **Gama** (121c), **Goma** (191), **Hima** (191), **ijma** (103b), **Irma** (96d), **jama** (103b), **Kama** (56d), **lama** (23d,24a,91d,165b), **lima** (17b,152b,174d), **Lima** (31b), **loma** (58b,63d), **mama, Mama** (116d), **mima** (185d), **Nama** (78c), **Nema** (34d,48c,134b,164d,176c), **Numa** (133a), **pima** (37c), **Pima** (192), **puma** (27b,37c,55b,103d), **Rama** (77a,80b,176d), **rima** (23a,30c,32a,58a,110d), **Roma** (83c,d), **sama** (105c,169d), **sima** (132b), **soma** (10c,21c,34a,48a,81d,136b), **Tama** (192), **tema** (12a,164a), **Toma** (191), **xema** (72c), **Xema** (12c), **Yama** (57a,68a), **Yima** (84a,116b,c), **Yuma, Zama** (73d, 141d)

M - - A **Maba** (103a,168d), **maha** (28c,88c,136d), **Maia** (76b,109a,153b, 155b,177c), **maja** (151c), **Maja** (153b), **mala** (89b,c,90a,94b,97d, 109d,185c), **mama, Mama** (116d), **mana** (30a,120d,122a,159c), **mara** (114d), **Mara** (24a,d,105b,107b), **masa** (37a), **maya** (77a, 179b), **Maya** (23d,186c), **meda** (110a), **mega** (34b,c), **mela** (34a, 129d), **mesa** (49b,76d,119b,161a), **meta** (132d,133a), **Meta, mica** (82c,100b,146c), **mila** (188), **mima** (185d), **mina** (10b,70b,71d, 179d), **Mina** (23a,183d), **mira** (174d), **Mira** (155b), **moha** (42b, 83d), **Mola** (159c), **mona** (72b,101d), **mora** (42b,65a,72b,83d,99b, 153a,161a), **mota** (103a), **moxa** (27d,30c), **muga, mura** (84d), **Mura** (192), **Musa** (16a), **muta** (28d,103a), **myna** (19a,c,70b), **Myra** (10a, 31b,183c), **myxa** (168c,169a)

- MB - **amba** (161a), **ambi** (34a,122c), **ambo** (125b,128b), **imbe** (37a,56a, 133d), **umbo** (22b)

- - MB **bomb** (144a), **comb** (38c), **dumb** (153b), **lamb** (59c), **jamb** (12d, 45c,118a,146b,174a), **iamb, Lamb** (49c), **limb** (12d,22d), **nimb** (31b,73b,92a,107b,131d), **numb, rumb** (120b), **tomb, Zimb** (6c)

M - - B **medb, Moab** (18d,85a,86d,94a)

M - - C **marc** (70c), **Marc** (96a)

M - - D **maid** (45b,142d), **mand** (28b), **maud** (53d,71a,136d,143c), **Maud** (181a,183c), **mead** (46a,78a,97d,99b), **Mead** (78a), **meed** (128c, 131a), **meld** (26a,41c,99a,118b), **mend** (130b), **mild** (32a,66a), **mind** (75c,81d,93d,109b), **Moed** (100c), **mold** (54d,143c), **mood** (44c), **mudd** (188), **mund** (124d)

ME - - **mead** (46a,78a,97d,99b), **Mead** (78a), **meal** (72a,130b), **mean** (15a, 42b,146c,156b), **meat** (59b), **meda** (110a), **Medb, Mede** (10a,b,13c), **medi** (34c), **meed** (128c,131a), **meek** (93d,99d), **meer, meet** (11d, 13d,36a,50a,81d,142d), **mega** (34b,c), **mein** (30b), **meio** (188), **mela** (34a,129d), **meld** (26a,41c,99a,118b), **mele** (74b,150b), **melt, memo** (108b), **mend** (130b), **mene** (19a,73d,108d,185c), **Ment** (54b,164a), **menu** (19a,27a), **Menu, meou, meow, mere** (16c,22b, 62a,78b,87d,96c,110c,120d,146c,148b), **meri** (20b), **mero** (72a), **Meru** (77a,103d), **mesa** (49b,76d,119b,161a), **mese** (71c), **mesh** (50d,106c), **mess** (22b,44b,77c,85d,104b,165c,173d), **meta** (132d, 133a), **Meta, mete** (9a,11d,22b,44c,45b,98a,121c), **meum** (27a, 89c), **Meum, mewl** (180d), **mews** (154c)

- ME - **amen** (14a,80b,94a,137a,149c,175c,184b), **Amen** (86d,127d,159b, 164a), **amer** (61b), **Ames** (9c,82a), **Amex** (184d), **Emer** (39b,183c),

366

emeu (111d), **Imer, Omei** (24a), **omen** (14c,59d,60a,121c,123a, 146b), **omer** (51a,75c), **smee** (19b,46c,d,118b,119d,141b,181b), **Smee** (116d), **smew** (19b,46d,99a,137d), **T-men** (168b), **Ymer** (67a, 131c)

- - M E **acme** (39c,115c,186b), **alme** (40d), **arme** (63a,179b), **came** (182b), **Came** (192), **come, cyme** (58d,69c), **dame** (67b,87c,166b), **deme** (71b,c,167d), **dime, dome** (39c,133c,155d), **fame** (130a) **feme** (181b), **fume** (129a,149a,157a), **game** (64d,154a), **gime** (77d), **home, Hume** (50c), **kame** (67b,139b), **Kome** (71d), **lame** (38d,43d, 73b), **lime** (25b,27d,31b,102d,168c), **Lome, mime** (24a,71b,85a, 100a), **Mime** (131d,148d), **name** (8a,11b,d,25c,46c,107c,130b,157d, 163b,166b), **nome** (71c,163b), **Nome, olme** (8b), **pome** (11d), **Pume** (137b,175b,185b), **rame** (22d), **rime** (30c,36a,58a,63d,77c), **Rome** (31c,51d), **ryme** (178d), **same** (44d,79b), **seme** (45c,138b,151b, 154b,155c,157b), **sime** (101d), **some** (114b,121c,126a), **tame** (45a, 66a), **Tame, time** (47a,131a), **tome** (21d,177c), **ulme** (49c), **zeme** (55d,161b,180b), **zyme** (55c)

M - - E **mace** (49d,108d,153b,154d,161a,178a), **made, mage** (95b), **make** (35b,36d,54a,123a), **male** (154d), **Male** (45d), **mane, mare** (78b), **Mare** (108b), **mate** (18c,35b,41d,113a,154a,162c), **maze** (87b, 157d), **Mede** (10a,b,13c), **mele** (74b,150b), **mene** (19a,73d,108d, 185c), **mere** (16c,22b,62a,78b,87d,96c,110c,120d,146d,148b), **mese** (71c), **mete** (9a,11d,22b,44c,45b,98a,121c), **mice, mide** (110a), **mike, Mike** (96b), **mile** (64c), **mime** (24a,71b,85a,100a), **Mime** (131d,148d), **mine** (69c,79d,111b,124c), **mire** (21c,104b), **mise** (8a, 10a,70c), **mite** (12b,81b,82a,114a,c,148c,d,181b), **Mixe** (192), **mode** (54d,96b,157d,179a), **moke** (45c,157d), **mole** (19d,23a,24d,85a, 117c,155c), **Mole** (88c), **mope** (92d,159a), **more** (71a), **More** (50b), **Mose** (96b), **mote** (114c,153a), **moue** (61d,62b), **move, mule** (45b, 148b,153c,180b), **mure** (177d), **muse** (65b,93d,120d,164c), **Muse** (68d), **mute** (146c,153b)

M - - F **miff** (44c), **moff** (53b,146c), **muff**

M - - G **magg** (95b), **migg** (96c), **Ming** (30b,c), **morg** (188), **mung** (70d)

M H - - **mhor** (180b)

- - M H **samh** (56b)

M - - H **Magh** (102a), **mash** (39b,156c), **math** (77a), **mesh** (50d,106c), **moth, Moth** (112d), **much, mush** (97d), **muth** (188), **myth** (8b,91a)

M I - - **miam** (14d), **mian** (97c,147b,166b), **Miao** (30a,b), **mias** (111a), **miau** (27b,99b), **miaw** (27b,99b), **mica** (82c,100b,146c), **mice, mick** (82c), **mico** (97a), **mide** (110a), **Midi** (151b), **mien** (11c, 17b,26d,44c,96b), **miff** (44c), **migg** (96c), **mike, Mike** (96b), **mila** (188), **mild** (32a,66a), **mile** (64c), **milk, mill** (126c), **milo** (70b,87c, 150d), **Milo, milt** (153d), **mima** (185d), **mime** (24a,71b,85a,100a), **Mime** (131d,148d), **mimi** (14d), **Mimi** (87b,110d,125b,183d), **mina** (10b,70b,71d,179d), **Mina** (23a,183d), **mind** (75c,81d,93d,109b), **mine** (69c,79d,111b,124c), **ming** (30b,c), **mink** (176d), **mino** (84c), **mint** (13a,33b,58b,76a), **minx** (116c), **miny, Mira** (155b,174d), **mire** (21c,104b), **mirk** (41a,67d), **miro** (19a,106d,184a), **Miro** (113a, 151d), **miry, misu** (8a,10a,70c), **miss, mist** (46b,59b,174d), **mite** (12b,81b,82a,114a,c,148c,d,181b), **mitt** (56c), **mitu** (39d), **mity, Mixe** (192), **mixy**

- MI - amia (22c,170d), amic (9d), amid (9d,50a), amie (61d), amil (45a, 48a,185c), amin (9d), amir (7c,12a,103a,b,123c,170d), amit (94a), Emil (96a), Emim (67a,100d), emir (12a,103a,b,123c,134d,135a, 171a), emit (43d,49a,53c,58d,83a,142c), imid (29c), omit (49c, 52c,106b,114c,147d)

- - MI - admi (65d), ammi (98c), demi (34b,122c), hami (78a), hemi (122c), immi (189), jami (103b), kami (68a,84b), Kami (88c,107c,144c), Komi (191), mimi (14d), Mimi (87b,110d,125b,183d), rami (22d), Remi (10b), romi (72d), semi (34b,80b,122c,d), Simi (82d), zemi (55d,161b,180b)

M - - I Mabi (58d), Madi (174a), magi (123c), Magi (95b,116c,183a), maki (91b), mali (27b), mani (115c), mari (61d), Mari (16a), Maui (120d), medi (34c), Midi (151b), mimi (14d), Mimi (87b,110d,125b,183d), moki (127b), Moki

M - - J munj (70d)

M - - K Mack, mark (146b,155a), Mark (52a,96a), mask (44a,45c), meek (93d,99d), mick (82c), milk, mink (176d), mirk (41a,67d), mock (131b,162b), monk (28b,63c,129d), mosk (97b,103b), muck, mulk (60d), murk (41a,67d), musk (116b)

- ML - amla (48a,161d,168c,169a), amll (48a,161d,168c,169a)

M - - L maal (188), mail (12d,99b,121c), mall (95d,124b,143b), marl (32a, 42c,55d), maul (73c,96b), meal (72a,130b), merl (20b), mewl (180d), mill (126c), moil (46c,184c), moll, Moll (183d), mull (53b, 135a,164c)

- MM - amma (6a), ammi (98c), ammo (9d), ammu (9d), Emma (183c), immi (189)

M - - M ma'am (95a,166b), malm (43d,81a,105c), malm (32a,92b), meum (27a,89c), Meum, miam (14d)

- MN - omni (34a)

- - MN damn, Domn (135a), famn (188), hymn (150c), limn (45d,121c)

M - - N main (29d,35d,123c), mann (189), Mann (9c,48c,185c), maun (139d), mean (15a,42b,146c,156b), mein (30b), mian (97c,147b, 166b), mien (11c,17b,26d,44c,96b), moan, moon (40b,132c,137c), morn, mown

MO - - Moab (18d,85a,86d,94a), moan, moat (44d), mock (131b,162b), mode (54d,96b,157d,179a), Moed (100c), moff (53b,146c), mogo (74b), moha (42b,83d), moho (19a,78a), mohr (65d), moil (46c, 184c), moio (188), mojo (177c), moke (45c,157d), moki (127b), moko (96c), Mola (159c), mold (54d,143c), mole (19d,23a,24d,85a, 117c,155c), Mole (88c), moll, Moll (183d), molt (27a,143d), moly (76a,181c), mona (72b,101d), monk (28b,63c,129d), mono (34c, 78d,122d,147a), Mono (193), mons (89c), Mons (184d), mont (62b), mood (44c), moon (40b,132c,137c), moor (10a,75b,137b,141d, 178b), Moor (102c,d,111d), moot (41b,44c), mope (92d,159a), mora (42b,65a,72b,83d,99b,153a,161a), more (71a), More (50b), morg (188), morn, moro (19a,56c), Moro (100a,103a,117a,159a), Mors (41b), mort (41b,47a,78b,136d), Mose (96b), mosk (97b,103b), moss (91d,104c,114a,170c), most, mosy (67d), mota (103a), mote (114c,153a), moth, Moth (112d), moto (104b), moue (61d,62b), move, mown, moxa (27d,30c), Moxe (192), mozo (152b)

- MO - amoi (62a), amok (18b,63c), Amon (86d,96b,127d,159b,164a), amor (152b), Amor (39c,68b), Amos (96a,144b), Amoy (88c)

- - MO ammo (9d), atmo (34d,174d), Como, demo (122d), hemo (34a, 122b), homo (122d), ikmo (18b), itmo (18b), mamo (19a,b,74b), memo (108b), nemo (34b), Nemo (56a,85c), Pomo (192), Sumo

M - - O mado (14d,57a,170b), majo (18a,19a,20d,143c,168c,182c), malo (23a,74c,152a), mamo (19a,74b), mano (71d,73d,74b,83b), mapo (68a,148d), maro (144d), Mayo (193), meio (188), memo (108b), mero (72a), Miao (30a,b), mico (97a), milo (70b,87c, 150d), Milo, mino (84c), miro (19a,106d,184a), Miro (113a,151d), mogo, (74b), moho (19a,78a), moio (188), mojo (177c), moko (96c), mono (34c,78d,122d,147a), Mono (193), moro (19a,56c), Moro (100a,103a,117a,159a), moto (104b), Moxo (192), mozo (152b), Muso (192), Muzo (192), myxo

- MP - impi (86a), umph

- - MP bump, camp (163b), damp (101a), dump, gamp (172a), gimp (169d), Gump (43b), hemp (26a,37a,56a,133d), hump (124d), jump, kemp (139b), lamp (92a,94c), limp (58a,81a,177d), lump (45a, 160c), mump (29b,153d), pomp (111d,112d), pump, ramp (65a, 80b,127b,148b), romp (63d), rump, samp (70b,77d,121b), simp (59c,146d), sump (28c,45d,100b), tamp (46b,112b,121d), tymp (60a,76d,103d), tymp (20c), vamp (80a,145a)

M - - P mump (29b,153d)

- MR - amra (77c), Omri (18c,86d)

M - - R maar (177a), mahr (103a), meer, mhor (180b), mohr (65d), moor (10a,75b,137b,141d,178b), Moor (102c,d,111d), Muir (8b, 142c), murr (72b,128b)

- MS - Omsk

- - MS aims (29a), arms, Rems

M - - S Maas (132a), Mais (61b), Mans (30a), Mars (68c,118d,119a,129a, 178a), mass (8a,24b,35b,142d), mess (22b,44b,77c,85d,104b,165c, 173d), mews (154c), mias (111a), miss, mons (89c), Mons (184d), Mors (41b), moss (91d,104c,114a,170c), muss (135b,173d)

M - - T Maat (69a,b,85d), malt (17c), mart (49d,97a), Mart (96b,183d), mast (17c,108d,120d,144d,152d), Matt, meat (59b), meet (11d,13d,36a,50a,81d,142d), melt, Ment (54b,164a), milt (153d), mint (13a,33b,58b,76a), mist (46b,59b,174d), mitt (56c), moat (44d), moit (27a,143d), mont (62b), moot (41b,44c), mort (41b,47a, 78b,136d), most, must (70c,101a,106d,157d,182c), mutt (39c, 101d), myst (71c,123b)

MU - - Muav (66a), much, muck, mudd (188), muff, muga, Muir (8b, 142c), mule (45b,148b,153c,180b), mulk (60d), mull (53b,135a, 164c), mump (29b,153d), mund (124d), mung (70d), munj (70d), mura (84d), Mura (192), mure (177d), murk (41a,67d), murr (72b, 128b), Musa (16a), muse (65b,93d,120d,164c), Muse (68d), mush (97d), musk (116b), Muso (192), muss (135b,173d), must (70c,101a, 106d,157d,182c), muta (28d,103a), mute (146c,153b), muth (188), mutt (39c,101d), Muzo (192)

369

- MU - Amun (86d,127d,159b,164a), smug, smur (32c,46b,100c), smut (32d,44a,119a,150c)

- - MU ammu (9d), Atmu (143a,159b), limu (141c), rimu (79d, 106d,129a, 168c)

M - - U Maku (192), Manu (10a,76d,77a,b), maru (84c,144d), masu (57a, 84c), menu (19a,27a), Menu, meou, Meru (77a,103d), miau (99b), mitu (39d), Mitu

M - - V Muav (66a)

M - - W meow, miaw (27b,99b)

M - - X Manx (27b,28a,82d), minx (116c)

MY - - myna (19a,c,70b), Myra (10a,31b,183c), myst (71c,123b), myth (8b,91a), myxa (168c,169a), myxo

- MY - amyl (155c), emyd (163c,167c), Emys (167c,171b)

- - MY army (78c), demy (113d), domy, elmy, fumy, homy (38b), ismy (45a), limy (176d), rimy (63d)

M - - Y many (108d), Mary (50c,126b,183c), maty (80c), miny, miry, mity, mixy, moly (76a,181c), mosy (67d)

NA - - Naab, naam (44c,150b), nabk (30d,164d), nabo (117a), Nabu (68c, 183a), nach, nael (189), naga (13d,33a,55b,127c), Naga (24c,77a, 88c,176d), Nagy (78d), Naia (33a), naid (63c), naif (74b,105d), naik, nail (31d,54d,141d,161d,173a), naio (107a,168c), Nair (45d), nais (63c,132a), Naja (33a), Nala (77a), Nama (78c), name (8a, 11b,25c,46c,107c,130b,157d,163b,166b), nana (118b), Nana (15c, 105d,116d,186d), nane (139d), naos (28a,71c,137a,163a), Naos (155b), napa (25c,67d,90d), nape (15b,108c,d), napu (29d,80d), nard (13a,97c,102b,110a,153c), Nare (93c), nark (81a, 156d), nary (108b), nase (26b,75a,124b), Nash (9c), nasi (34c,108a, 115a), Nast (9c,27a), nata (47c), Nata (15c), Nate (22b), Nath (155c), Nato (6a,8d), natr (189), Natt (107b), naut (141b), nave (30d,31a,78d,114b,180c), navy (33c,58b), naze (26b,124b), Nazi

- NA - anai (163b,181a), Anak (67a), anam (159a,168c), Anam, anan (49a,159a,180c), Anas (46c,d), Anat (138c,147d), Anax (43c, 120c) anay (72b,163b,181a), enam (70c,77a), Enam (85c), gnar (72a), gnat (59a,81b,99c), gnaw (20a,107a,178b), inar (65b), knab (107a), knag (139c), knap (76d,107a,139b,159b,166a,170c,185b), knar (87c,134b), Onan (18c,85c), snab (23c,139a), snag (11b, 27b,35c,87c,124b,166a), snap (23a,36d,38b,48b,54d,56c,58c,149d), unai (147a), unau (148c,171d)

- - NA anna (190), Anna (110c,166d), arna (24a,181b), Bana (67a), bena (176a), bina (77a), bona (89d), Bona (183c), buna (161c), Cana (57a,64b,100c), cena (88d,133a), Cuna (193), Dana (28a,96a, 171d), dona (83d,121c,151d), dyna (34c), Edna (183c), Enna (146a), etna (75b,153c,157a,175d,177a,c), fana, gena (29b), Gona (106d), guna (106a,137b), Iona (28a,82d), Jena (105d,165b), kana (84d), kina (126d), kona (74c), lana (58a,66a,90a,184b), lena (56d), Lena (36b), lina (188), Lina (183d), luna (103c), Luna (102b), mana (30a,120d,122a,159c), mina (10b,70b,71d,179d), Mina (23a, 183d), mona (72b,101d), myna (19a,c,70b), nana (118b), Nana (15c,105d,116d,186d), nina (152a), Nina (26c,33d,68d,183d),

nona (89b,107b), **Nona** (69a,114a,183c), **orna** (169d,182c), **Pana,**
pina (35d,118b), **puna** (10b,33b,104a,119b,182a), **rana** (77a,123c),
Rana (63d), **rena** (132c), **sana** (56a,166d), **Sana** (185d), **sina** (46c),
Sina (102d,103d), **tana** (159a), **Tana** (87d), **Tina** (183d), **tuna** (57a,
b,123b,170d), **ulna** (21d,39b), **urna** (133a), **vena** (90a,175a), **vina**
(77a,105a), **Xina** (183d), **Yana** (192,193), **zona** (144c,186d)

N - - A naga (13d,33a,55b,127c), **Naga** (24c,77a,88c,176d), **Naia** (33a),
Naja (33a), **Nala** (77a), **Nama** (78c), nana (118b), **Nana** (15c,105d,
116d,186d), **napa** (25c,67d,90d), **Napa** (182c), **nata** (47c), **Nata**
(15c), **nema** (34d,48c,134b,164d,176c), **Nepa** (106b,178c), **Nera**
(165b), **Neva** (91b,132a), **Nina** (26c,33d,68d,183d), **nipa** (14b,
46b,48a,164a,168c), **Nola**, nona (89b,107b), **Nona** (69a,114a,183c),
Nora (79b,107a,164c,183c), **nota** (15c,89c), **nova** (20c,106d,155c,
174d), **noxa**, **Nuba** (108c), **Nuda** (39b), **Numa** (133a)

- NB - anba (36d)

N - - B **Naab, nimb** (31b,73b,92a,107b,131d), **numb**

- NC - ance (158b,c,d), **ancy** (158c), **ence** (158c), **Inca** (14b,30a), **inch,**
onca (189), once (60b,79b), **unca** (49a), **unci** (31d), **unco** (140c),
Ynca (193)

- - NC banc (61a,85c), **zinc** (21a)

- ND - anda (23a,168c), **Ande** (193), **Andi** (27d), **Andy** (96b), endo (34d,
122d,183b), **inde**, onde (63a,178d), **unde** (179a), **undo** (11a,93d),
undy (179a)

- - ND **Arnd** (67a), band (72a,157c), bend (39d,171b), **bind** (33b,165c),
bond (92a,101c,141d,143b,159d,165c), bund (49c,66c,90c), **cond**
(156a), fend (114b,178b), find (44a), fond (7c,94b), fund (6d,101c,
130c), **Gond**, hand (60c,114c,115d,184c), hind (15b,41d,45a),
kind (150d,153a,174d), land (44a,163c), lend (6d,79d), mand (28b),
mend (130b), mind (75c,81d,93d,109b), mund (124d), pend, pond,
pund (189), rand (16d,22a,131b,145a,b), **Rand** (69c), rend (32a,
159c,162c,185a), rind (53a,115c), **Rind** (109c,174b), rynd (100a),
sand (71d,146c), send (42c,44b,95c,121c,130a,144c,168b), **Sind,**
tend (26d,80b,93a,100a), tind (86b), tund (121d), vend (97a,115c,
142b), **Vend** (10b,148a), wand (120b,132c,156a), wend (67d,123d),
Wend (10b,148a), wind (33b,39d,171c,185a), yond (164d), **Zend**

N - - D naid (63c), nard (13a,97c,102b,110a,153c), need (42b,52d,87b,
122a,178a), **Nejd, NKVD** (135d), **Nudd** (23c)

NE - - neaf (58a,73c), **Neal, neap** (165c,167a,177b), near (11d,32c,107b),
neat (165c,169d), **Nebo** (68c,102d,103d,183a), neck (83a), need
(42b,52d,87b,122a,178a), **neem** (96d,168c,169a), **neep** (140c,
171b), neer (14b,86b,108b), **Neil** (96a), nein (66c), **Nejd, Nell**
(110a, 183d), **nema** (34d,48c,134b,164d,176c), nemo (34b), **Nemo**
(56a,85c), nene (19b,74c), neon (65c), **Nepa** (106b,178c), **Nera**
(165b), **Neri, Nero** (8a,126d,133a,150b,172c), ness (26b,75a,124b),
nest (38b,74b,130d,149c,160b), nete (71c,108b,163d), neti (164a),
nett, neue (66c), **Neva** (91b,132a), neve (56d,67c,70c,149b), news
(165c), newt (48d,136c,169d), next (106a)

- NE - Aner (18d,96b), anes (110c,140a), anet (43c), anew (7c), inee
(120b), **Inez** (45c,183c), knee (85b), knew, knex (123c), oner (20d,
53a,75c,162d,173a,d), ones (116a), sned (93d,125a,140a), snee

(40a,43d,87a), sneg (139b)

- - NE acne (147c), aine (49b,62c,142c), Anne (50c,84a,143b,183c), a-one
(52b,167b), Arne (35c,50c,134d), aune (188), bane (74a,106b,120b,
139a), bene (18a,83c,90a,106d,122a,180a), bine (145b,156a,171c,
176b), bone, cane (17b,128a,156a,159a,177d), Cane, cene (34c),
cine (104b,152c), cone (66b,150a,157c), Dane (85d,107d,138a),
dene (137a), Dene (192), dine, done, dune (137a), dyne (59d,173b),
eine (66c), enne (34c), erne (19c,d,47b,54b,141a), esne (10c,
45b,142c,148a,164d), fane (30d,137a,162c), fine (49b,50a,104b,
115d,159a), gane (185b), gene (54a), Gene (96b), gone (6b,15c,42c,
44c,114d), gyne (34b,55b,183c), hone (110a,143c,180d), Ione
(24b,88d,94d), jane (190), Jane (183c), June (183c), kane (74c),
kine (38a,112c), lane (134b,157b), lene (36b,149a,172b), line (12b,
22b,36d,38a,126c,134b,157b,158b,162d,175c), lone (150a), lune
(38c,73b,74d), mane, mine (69c,79d,111b,124c), mene (19a,73d,
108d,185c), nene (19b,74c), nine (26c,104d), none (108b), ohne
(66d,183b), orne (169d,182c), Orne (25b), pane (113c,155a,b), pene,
pine (36a,52a,88c,93c,168c,d,169a), pone (37a,85b), rine (44d,75d,
135c), rone (127c,164b), rune (9b,67a,94a,95a,105c,107d,120a,
141d,163d), sane (128a), sine (64c,66b,90a,97c,126a,163b,169d,
183b), syne (140b,147a), Tane (120d), tene (34d,131b), tine (11b,
124b,167b), tone (6c,118c,150d), tune (8b,12c,98c), tyne, Tyne
(108a), vane (179b,182a), vine (32b), wane (41c,43c), wine, zone
(44c,50a,160a)

N - - E name (8a,11b,d,25c,46c,107c,130b,157d,163b), nane (139d), nape
(15b,108c,d), Nare (93c), nase (26b,75a,124b), Nate (22b), nave
(30d,31a,78d,114b,180c), naze (26b,124b), nene (19b,74c), nete
(71c,108b,163d), neue (66c), neve (56d,67c,70c,149b), nice (54d,
119c,130c), Nice (98c), nide (23c,72a,106c,116d), nife (37a), Nike
(69c,100c,182c), nile (33c,71d), Nile (106b), nine (26c,104d), Niue
(137d), node (35c,85b,87c,94d,120a,124d,160c), nome (71c,163b),
Nome, none (108b), Nore (163d), nose (118d,125a,149b), note
(98c,109b,124b,128d,130a,177c), nove (83b), noze (75a), nude
(16c,172d), Nupe (191)

N - - F naif (74b,105d), neaf (58a,73c)

NG - - ngai (48a,159c), ngan

- NG - ange (61a), ango (171a), inga (145d,170a), Inge (24d,67d,117c
119c)

- - NG bang (75d,105d,148a), beng (43a), bing, bong, bung (119d,156d),
cang (184a), dang, ding (130b), dong, fang (167b), Fong (40b),
Fung (191), gang (38c), gong, hang (160a), hing (13c), hong (30b),
hung, Jung (125a), k'ang (30a), king (26c,29c), kung (125b), ling
(24c,57a,b,75b,178c), long (38b), lung, Ming (30b,c), mung (70d),
pang (165b), ping, pong, pung (22c,148b), Qung (191), rang, ring
(50a), Rong (88c), rung (28c,39a), sang, sing (26d,178a), song
(12c,170c), sung, Sung (30b), tang (30b,58b,186b), teng (188),
ting (166a), Ting (30c), tong (30a,c), tung (110a,168c), uang
(131a), vang (72d,134a,140b), wang (189), wing (10d,58c,59a,
118b,d), wong (56a), yang (30b,70a), zing

N - - G niog (33a,168c), nogg (48d)

372

- - NH   binh (189), hunh?, sinh (97c), tanh (97c)

N - - H   Nach, Nash (9c), Nath (155c), nigh (106a), Nish (19d), Noah (88a, 99b)

NI - -   Nias (82d), nibs (116c), nice (54d,119c,130c), Nice (98c), nick (30c,108b), nide (23c,72a,106c,116d), nidi (106c), nife (37a), nigh (106a), Nike (69c,100c,182d), nile (33c,71d), Nile (106b), nill (173d), nimb (31b,73b,92a,107b,131d), nina (152a), Nina (26c, 33d,68d,183d), nine (26c,104d), nino (152a), niog (33a,168c), niou (188), nipa (14b,46b,48a,164a,168c), Nish (19d), nisi (90a, 173c), nito (55c), Niue (137d)

- NI -   anil (47c,80d,180b), Anim (18d), anis (55c), Enid (13b,25d,66b, 163a,183c), Enif (155b), enin (20d), inia (9b,109b), Inia (28c,45b), knip (115c), knit (173c,179b), snib (54d,93c), snig (45d), snip (32b,40a), unie (173a), Unio (105c), unis (91b), unit (101c,110c, 147a)

- - NI   Aani (45a,48d), agni (88a,89c), Agni (56d,68d), arni (24a,181b), bani (190), beni (116a,142d), Beni (191), Bini (191), Boni (63b), Coni, doni (21a,28c,168a), Ioni (192), mani (115c), omni (34a), Pani (120c), rani (72d,77b,123c,127c), Reni (83d), yeni (19b,161d), Zuni (125b)

N - - I   nasi (34c,108a,115a), Nazi, Neri, neti (164a), ngai (48c,159c), nidi (106c), nisi (90a,173c), nodi (35c,87d), nori (8c,141c)

- - NJ   Funj, gunj (70c), munj (70d)

NK - -   NKVD (135d)

- NK -   ankh (38d,162b), Enki (15b), inka (193), inky (20b)

- - NK   bank (18a,58c), bonk (190), bunk, conk (41c,108a,156d,157c), dank (40b,101a), dunk (43c,79d), fink (19a,56c,157c), funk (63d, 113c), gink (48b), hank (147c), honk (70a), hunk, jink, jonk, junk (30a,134c), kink (38b,171c), konk (41c), kunk (188), lank (148b, 164b), link (36a,81d,85b), lonk (143d), mink (176d), monk (28b, 63c,129d), pank (189), pink (26d,33c,60c,138a), punk (9b,166a, 167c), rank (31d,55d,70b,92d,94d,157d), rink (147c,154a), sank, sink (41c,43c,46b,158a), sunk, tank (175a,d), tonk (173c), wink (107a), yank, Yank

N - - K   nabk (30d,164d), naik, nark (81a,156d), neck (83a), nick (30c, 108b), nock (13b,108b), nook (37a,130d), nubk (30d,164d)

- NL -   inly, only (24d,52c,98d,147a,150a)

N - - L   nael (189), nail (31d,54d,141d,161d,173a), Neal, Neil (96a), Nell (110a,183d), nill (173d), noel (26d,150b) Noel (30d,96a), noil (87c, 178b), Noll (96b,110b), noyl (87c), null (108c,177a), nurl (33b,87c)

N - - M   naam (44c,105b), Naam, neem (96d,168c,169a), norm (15a,115a, 128a,155a)

- NN -   Anna (110c,166d,183c), anna (190), Anne (50c,84a,143b,183c), Enna (146a), enne (34c), Enns

- - NN   binn (22c), Bonn (17d), bunn (25b), conn (43d,156a), Finn (107d), Jann (102d), jinn (42b,103b,153c), linn (120d,140a,c,168c,178d), mann (189), Mann (9c,48c,185c), rann (175c), senn (76b), sunn (56a), wynn (165d)

N - - N   nein (66c), neon (65c), ngan, noon, Norn (69a,163d,174b), noun (114b,158a)

NO - -   Noah (88a,99b), nobs (38c,87a), nock (13b,108b), node (35c,85b, 87c,94d,120a,124d,160c), nodi (35c,87c), noel (26d,150b), Noel (30d,96a), noes (177c), nogg (48d), noil (87c,178b), noio (107c, 163c), noir (61b,134b), noix (67c), Nola, Noll (96b,110b), nolo (42a), nome (71c,163b), Nome, nona (89b,107b), Nona (69a,114a, 183c), none (108b), nono (83b), nook (37a,130d), noon, Nora (79b, 107a,164c,183c), Nore (163d), nori (8c,141c), norm (15a,115a, 128a,155a), Norn (69a,163d,174b), nose (118d,125a,149b), Nosu (27d), nosy, nota (15c,89c), note (98c,109b,124b,128d,130a,177c), Nott (107b), noun (114b,158a), noup (124b), nous (81d,100a, 128b), nova (20c,106d,155c,174d), nowt (106a,139a), nowy (194), noxa, noyl (87c), noze (75a)

- NO -   anoa (28a,60a,112c,181c), anon (7d,14d,79d,80b,123a,145c,150c, 164a), enol (29c,158b), Enon (18c,d), Enos (7a,18d,52a,70c,96a, 143a), enow (50d,123a,158b), knob (73c), knop (124b,170c,185b), knor (87c), knot (43c,99d,107c,124b,137b), know, snob (159c), snod (169d), snow

- - NO   Aino (84a,c), Arno (27a), asno (151d), beno (113b,117a), cano (152a), dino (34b), fano (51d,96b,113c,d), fono (137a), Gano (132d), Hano (125b), hino (106d,168c), Juno (69c,85d,100c,126b), Kano (84c,177d), keno (161d,168c), kino (27c,34c,47c,72c,98b), leno (37c,53b), lino, mano (71d,73d,74b,83b), mino (84c), mono 34c,78d,122d,147a), Mono (193), nino (152a), nono (83b), pino (152c), puno (182a), Reno (152b), sino (34a), Tano (192), Tino (136d), tuno (28b,168c), vino (92d,182b), xeno (34d), Zeno (71b)

N - - O   nabo (117a), naio (107a,168c), Nato (6a,8d), Nebo (68c,102d,103d, 183a), nemo (34b), Nemo (56a,85c), Nero (8a,126d,133a,150b, 172c), nino (152a), nito (55c), noio (107c,163c), nolo (42a), nono (83b)

N - - P   neap (165c,167a,177b), neep (140c,171b), noup (124b)

- - NQ   cinq (61d)

- NR -   inre (35d,80a), inro (84b,c,106c)

N - - R   Nair (45d), natr (189), near (11d,32c,107b), neer (14b,86b,108b), noir (61b,134b), nurr (67d)

- NS -   ansa (73c,93d,137c), anse (61d), ansu (11d), ense (139b,158c), enso 34d,183b)

- - NS   bans, cens (115b), dans (62a), dens (90a,167b), Duns, Enns, fons (60c), gens (42d,132d), Hans (66d,96a), hens (121d), lens (67c, 95b,111a,129b,162d), Mans (30a), mons (89c), Mons (184d), oons (100a,186d), Pons (13d,63c,110d,150c), sans (63a,183b), Sens (63b), sons (98d,109d), Vans (107d)

N - - S   nais (63c,132a), naos (28a,71c,137a,163a), Naos (155b), ness (26b, 75a,124b), news (165c), Nias (82d), nibs (116c), nobs (38c,87a), noes (177c), nous (81d,100a,128b)

- NT -   anta (83d,117c,d,121a), Anta (164a), ante (87a,89a,115b,120b, 122b,125d,154d), anti (7d,111a,122b), Anti (193), ente (70b,151d),

ento (34b,d,183b), **inti** (159b), **into** (123a,183b), **onto** (76a,174a), **unto** (166c), **untz** (189)

- - NT **aint**, **arn't**, **aunt** (129c), **bant** (43c), **bent** (80b), **bunt** (15d,180c), **cant** (28d,81b,84d,90c,109b,136c,165d,166a), **cent** (36d), **dent** (42c,77d), **dint** (48c,59d,122a), **dont**, **dunt**, **font** (16b,171d,172a), **gent**, **hant** (67a), **hint** (9a,39c,159a), **hunt** (141c), **kant** (28d), **Kant** (67a), **Kent** (90d), **lant**, **lent** (54d), **Lent** (115d,141c), **lint** (46a,58d), **Ment** (54b,164a), **mint** (13a,33b,58b,76a), **mont** (62b), **oont** (25d), **pant, pent** (36a), **pint** (67b), **pont** (55d,61b), **punt** (21a,58b), **rant** (41c,127b,128a,161d), **rent** (58a,77c,91b,138b, 153d,162c,167c), **runt** (47a,172d), **sent, tent** (26b,115a), **tint** (33c, d,114d), **vent** (8b,11b,110d,112a), **vint** (26c,182c), **want** (41b, (38b,74b,106b,122a), **went** (42c), **wont** (6d,40a,73a,174c)

N - - T **Nast** (9c,27a), **Natt** (107b), **naut** (141b), **neat** (165c,169d), **nest** (38b,74b,130d,149c,160b), **nett, newt** (48d,136c,169d), **next** (106a), **Nott** (107b), **nowt** (106a,139a), **nuit** (62b)

NU - - **Nuba** (108c), **nubk** (30d,164d), **nuda** (39b), **Nudd** (23c), **nude** (16c, 172d), **nuit** (62b), **null** (108c,177a), **Numa** (133a), **numb, Nupe** (191), **nurl** (33b,87c), **nurr** (67d)

- NU - **Cnut** (40d,50c), **knub** (178b), **knur** (67d,87c,107c), **knut, Knut** (40d,50c,96a), **onus** (24c,93b,109b), **snub** (128c,148b), **snug** (35a, 38b,165c), **Snug** (99d), **snup** (149b)

- - NU **Ainu** (84a,c), **benu** (49a), **Danu** (28a), **genu** (6b,18a,87a,89c), **Manu** (10a,76d,77a,b), **menu** (19a,27a), **Menu, tunu** (28b), **zenu** (143d)

N - - U **Nabu** (68c,183a), **napu** (29d,80d), **niou** (188), **Nosu** (27d)

- NV - **envy** (41b)

- - NX **jinx** (78a), **jynx** (78a), **Jynx** (184a), **lanx** (133a,b), **lynx** (26c,181d), **Lynx** (36b), **Manx** (27b,28a,82d), **minx** (116c), **Yunx** (184a)

N - - X **noix** (67c)

- NY - **Enyo** (12c,69c,178a), **onym** (162c), **onyx** (25d,28d,65d,142b), **Pnyx** (71c)

- - NY **bony** (147c), **Bony** (96b), **cony** (127a), **deny** (36d,43d,129b), **liny** (157b), **luny** (38b), **many** (108d), **miny, piny, pony, puny** (55b, 179a), **tiny** (100c,148c), **tony, Tony** (96b), **tuny, viny, wany, winy** (176c), **zany** (24a,32d,59c)

N - - Y **Nagy** (78d), **nary** (108b), **navy** (33c,58b), **nosy, nowy** (194)

- NZ - **anzu** (11d), **Enzu** (102b), **onza** (189), **unze** (189)

- - NZ **Linz** (40d)

OA - - **Oahu, oaks** (154d), **oaky, oary, oast** (15d,86b,112a), **oath** (119c, 150a)

- OA - **boar** (77c,117c,160d,181c), **boat** (27b,106a), **Boaz** (135d), **coag** (45d,118a,163b), **coak** (45d,118a,163b), **coal** (49c,64a), **Coan** (37b), **coat** (160a), **coax** (180c), **doab** (157c), **doat** (17a,94b,112a,165d), **Eoan** (41a,85b), **foal** (78c), **foam** (63d,154b), **goad** (80b,154b), **goaf** (104b), **goai** (106a,168c), **goal** (8b,109b,120b,125d), **Goan, goat** (135a), **hoar** (63d,71a,181a), **hoax** (41c,122a), **Joab** (41a), **Joad** (50c), **Joan** (183c), **joar** (100a), **koae** (74b), **load** (24c,26d,161b), **loaf** (79b,94b), **loam** (47d,150a), **loan, Moab** (18d,85a,86d,94a), moan, moat (44d), Noah (88a,99b), road (37d,164d), roam (178a), roan (78b,c,114c,128d,144a,181a), roar (145c), soak (46c,137c), soap, soar (59a), toad (10a,17a,63d,126d), woad (20d,47c), Zoar, Zoas (20b)

- - OA anoa (28a,60a,112c,181c), Aroa (175b), Gjoa (144d), pooa (76a, 125b), proa (21b,26a,95c,d), Shoa (6c) stoa (33c,121a,c), tooa (17c), whoa (156d)

O - - A obia (55d), obra (152d,184c), ocha (189), ocra (72c,175a), octa (122c), odea (105d,164a), Offa (163d), ohia (74c,168c), okia (190), okra (72c,175a), olea (170b), Olea (110b), Olga (135c,183c), olla (36d,44b,84d,113b,121d,151d,152c,181b), onca (189), onza (189), orca (86b), orna (169d,182c), orra (139c,d,140a), ossa (21d), Ossa (103d,110b,164b), Otea (71a,82d), otra (152c), oxea (153d)

OB - - oban (190), Obed (135d), obex (22d), obey (35c,75c), obia (55d), obit (41b,64c), oboe (74b,104d,105a,182d,184a), obol (29b,110a), obra (152d,184c)

- OB - boba (29d), bobo (112c,168c), Cobb (9c), Cobh (37a), dobe (159b, c,172b), doby (159b,c), gobi, Gobi (42d), gobo (84d), goby (57d), hobb (124b), hobo (168a,174b), jobo (77c), Koba (11a), Kobe (78a), kobi (84b), kobu (84b), lobb (23b,94c,163a), lobe (90c, 134b), lobo (165d,183c), nobs (23b,87a), robe (65b), Sobk (38d), Toba (80c), tobe (7d,137b), toby (8c,85c,104b), Toby (96b,125c), Yobi, zobo (186b)

- - OB blob, boob (146d), brob (153c), chob (23c), doob (18b), jaob, knob (73c,107c,124d), rhob (64a,85c), scob (42a), slob (173d), snob (159c), swob (102b), thob (128a)

OC - - ocha (189), ocra (72c,175a), octa (122c), octo (34a,89b,122c)

- OC - boca (152b,c), boce (23b,52a,57b), bock (17c,90d,144a), coca (29d, 33a,105d,113a), cock (19a,29a,55a,133d,136d,161d,174b), coco, dock (40a,117c,144d,179d), Foch (63b), foci (28b), hoch (52c, 66c), hock (91a,115b,182b,c), jock, Jock (96b), jocu (45b,57a), Koch (66d), loch (88a,139d), loci (66b,118c), lock (54d), loco (38b, 119b,120b), mock (131b,162b), nock (13b,108b), poco (83b,93a), Roch (136c), rock (160b), sock (157c,182a), soco (22d), tock (7d, 19b), toco (19b,167c), voce (83c,177a)

- - OC bloc (173a), croc (13a,74a), floc (149a)

O - - C odic (79c,120a), olic (158b), otic (14c,d,47b)

OD - - odah (170d), odal (48a,88b,112c), Odax (132c), odds (28d,172d), Odea (105a,164a), odel (48a,112c), Oder (132a), odic (79c,120a), Odin (7c,29d,63c,68c,175d,183b), odio (83b), odor (138b,156a), odum (168c,180a), odyl (59d,79c)

- OD - Bodb (82b), bode (14c,60a,110b,121b), Bodo (88c), body (72a), coda (32c,35d,56c), code (21c,31a,40c,161c), codo (188), dodd (139c,140c), Dode (96b), dodo (19b), Jodo (113d), lode (42c,99a,111b,175b), Lodi (105d), Lodz, mode (54d,96b,157d, 179a), node (35c,85b,87c,94d,120a,124d,160c), nodi (35c,87c), Roda (107b), rodd (38d), rode (46c), rodi (98c), soda (19a,149d, 181a), Toda (45d,76d), tode (80a,148a), todo (22b,24d,35b,64c, 156b), tody (19b,d,59a,166a), yodh (91d)

- - OD alod (51c,55d,88a,124c), apod (59d), Arod (86c), biod (59d,79c),

376

clod (22a,45b,157d), **elod** (49b,59d,79c), **feod** (55d), **food** (109a, 176b), **good, hood** (38a,74d), **iood** (189), **mood** (44c), **plod** (170b, 177d), **pood** (189), **prod** (67d,80b,106b,120b), **quod** (123d), **rood** (38d,39a,88b), **shod, snod** (169d), **stod** (40d,67d), **trod, wood**

O - - D   **obed** (135d), **olid** (55d,60c,148d,157d), **ooid** (48d), **oord** (190), **orad** (104a), **Ovid** (132d,133b), **oxid** (112c)

OE - -   **oese** (15d,119c)

- OE -   **Boer** (151a), **coed, coel** (39b), **Doeg** (137c), **doer** (8a,116b), **does, goel** (15a,75c), **goer, hoek** (39d), **hoen** (189), **hoer, hoey** (114c), **Joel** (96a), **joey** (86a,185d), **Joey** (96b,109c), **koel** (19a,b,39b), **Moed** (100c), **noel** (26d,150b), **Noel** (30d,96a), **noes** (177c), **poem** (51a), **poet** (49b), **roed, roer** (72d), **roey** (103d), **toed, voet** (188)

- - OE   **aloe** (7d,20a,76a,b,92b,98b,119b,158b,167a,183d), **Cloe** (183c), **eboe** (28b,110a,168c,169b), **evoe** (15b,130d,181c), **floe** (79b), **froe** (32a,167a,179d), **oboe** (74b,104d,105a,182a,184a), **Otoe** (147b), **shoe** (166a), **sloe** (14a,20b,64a,119d,181c)

O - - E   **oboe** (74b,104d,105a,182a,184a), **oese** (15d,119c), **ogee** (40c,101a, b,120b), **ogle** (9d,53c,91a,93d,148c), **ogre** (67a,102a), **ohne** (66d, 183b), **Oime** (8b), **Oise, Okie** (99d), **olpe** (90d,182c), **once** (60b, 79b), **onde** (63a,178d), **ooze** (53c,104b,116a), **orfe** (57a,b,185c), **orle** (17b,56b,76a,144b,177a), **orne** (169d,182c), **Orne** (25b), **oste** (21d,83b), **Otoe** (147b), **Ouse** (132a,185d), **owse**

OF - -   **Offa** (163d), **offs** (38c)

- OF -   **doff** (130a,161b), **goff** (32d), **koff** (47a), **loft** (14c,69d,104b, 178b), **moff** (53b,146c), **sofa** (44d), **soft** (48b,95d,99d,163a), **toff** (40d)

- - OF   **Azof** (20b,135d), **goof, hoof** (173a), **loof** (144c,153d), **poof, roof** (78d), **stof** (135c), **woof** (39a,163d,165a,179d)

O - -F   **Olaf** (108a,176b)

OG - -   **ogam** (82b,c), **ogee** (40c,101a,b,120b), **ogle** (9d,53c,91a,93d,148c), **Ogor** (170d), **Ogpu** (135d), **ogre** (67a,102a), **ogum** (82b)

- OG -   **boga** (57d,180b), **bogo** (117a,168c), **Bogo** (191), **bogy** (153a), **doge** (95b,175b), **dogy** (46d,103c), **fogy, goga** (24a), **gogo** (16b,24a, 149c), **Gogo** (191), **hoga** (144b), **hogg** (144a), **jogi** (76d), **loge** (164a), **logy** (46d), **mogo** (74b), **nogg** (48d), **Pogo** (121c), **pogy** (57a,88a,98d,103c), **soga** (70d,152b), **Soga** (191), **toga** (132d,133a, b), **togs** (32c), **togt** (77c), **Vogt, yoga** (10b,13c,77a), **yogh** (10c, 185a), **yogi** (76d), **zogo** (136a)

- - OG   **agog** (47b,52c,86b), **ajog, clog** (30c,145b), **flog** (180d), **frog** (10a, 17a,126d), **grog** (92d,153d), **ilog** (132a, 161b), **niog** (33a,168c), **slog** (157c,170b,177d), **stog** (155a), **voog** (28a,66a,132b)

OH - -   **ohia** (74c,168c), **Ohio, ohne** (66d,183b), **ohoy** (106a)

- OH -   **boho** (117a,179d), **Bohr** (14b,40d,138c), **coho** (136c), **fohn** (182b), **Hohe** (192), **John** (11c,96a,121a,186b), **kohi** (53c), **moha** (42b,83d), **moho** (19a,78a), **mohr** (65d), **poha** (74c), **rohr** (72d), **soho!, Soho** (93c), **toho** (79a)

- - OH   **booh** (52c), **pooh** (22b,107d)

O - - H   **oath** (119c,150a), **odah** (170d), **okeh** (8d,37b), **opah** (23b,57a,b, 86d), **ouch!, ough**

OI - -   **oily** (110b,172c), **okme** (8b), **Oise**

- OI -   **Boii** (191), **boil, bois** (62b,63a,183d), **coif** (73a), **coil** (39d,171c, 185a), **coin** (19b,37a,100c,101c,179d), **coir** (33a,37a,56a,133d), **Coix** (70d,85b), **doit** (47a,169d,180d), **Eoin** (85b), **foil** (15d,55c, 165b), **join** (36a,173c), **koir** (33a), **loin** (40a,98a), **loir** (45c), **Loir, Lois** (165d,183c), **moil** (46c,184c), **moio** (188), **noil** (87c,178b), **noio** (107c,163c), **noir** (61b,134b), **noix** (67c), **ooid** (48d), **roil** (44c, 104b,156b,170d,176a), **Soia, sole** (62c), **soil** (154d,159a,163c), **soir** (61c), **toil** (46c,184c), **void** (11a,49d,108d,174b), **zoid**

- - OI   **amoi** (62a), **Ekoi** (191)

O - - I   **Omei** (24a), **omni** (34a), **Omri** (18c,86d)

- OJ -   **bojo** (117a), **coja** (103b,166b), **hoja** (166b), **hoju** (84b), **koji** (185b), **mojo** (177c), **rojo** (129a,152c), **soja** (151b)

OK - -   **okay** (8d), **okeh** (8d,37b), **oket** (189), **okia** (190), **Okie** (99d), **okra** (72c,175a), **okro** (72c,175a)

- OK -   **boko** (52b), **coke** (32d,64a), **coky, Doko** (191), **joke** (183a), **joky, koko** (106d,114b), **Koko** (93d,186c), **koku** (189), **loka** (173c,184c), **Loke** (15d,68b), **Loki** (7c,15d,68b), **moke** (45c,157d), **moki** (127b), **Moki, moko** (96c), **poke** (108c), **poku** (11a), **poky** (148c), **roka** (95a,168c,d), **roke** (174d,175b), **soka** (20c), **soke** (44c,85d), **toko** (30c), **woke, yoke** (85b,92d,173c)

- - OK   **amok** (18b,63c), **asok** (13d), **book, cook** (137b), **dook** (184a), **hook** (27b,39d), **irok** (55b), **look** (11c,53c,142a), **nook** (37a,130d), **pook** (68a), **rook** (19b,29c,39a), **sook** (22a,25c,97a), **took**

O - - K   **Omsk**

OL - -   **Olaf** (108a,176b), **olam** (51a,d,75c,81a), **Olan** (115c), **Olax** (52b), **olay** (113b), **Olea** (110b,170b), **oleo** (34c), **Olga** (135c,183c), **olic** (158b), **olid** (55d,60c,148d,157d), **olio** (44b,77c,98c,100d,121d), **olla** (36d,44b,84d,113b,121d,151d,152c,181b), **Olor** (160a,b), **olpe** (90d,182c)

- OL -   **bola** (16a), **bold** (41a), **bole** (31d,32a,169b), **boll** (119b,d), **bolo** (87a,179b), **bolt** (13b,54d,58b,132d,160a), **cola** (25b,108d,149d, 168c), **cold** (65d), **cole** (25a), **Cole, coli, colp** (28a,148b), **colt** (78c, 131a,185d,186b), **Colt, coly** (104a), **dola** (189), **dole** (44c,118c, 121c,129d), **Dole** (74c), **doli, doll** (125c), **dolt** (20c,59c,157d), **fold folk** (116a,169c), **gola** (27b,40c,70c,157a), **gold, golf** (154a), **goli** (105c), **Goil, Goio** (191), **hola** (74c,152b), **hold** (95c,124c,130d), **hole** (6c,11b,110d,118c,147a), **Holi** (77a), **holm** (77d,82d,109a), **holt** (36d,119b,184b), **holy, iola, iole** (52a,76b,123c), **jole** (29b), **joli** (62b), **jolt** (143b), **kola** (25b,84a,108d,168c), **Kola** (135b,c,d), **Koli** (27b), **kolo** (59b,135c), **Lola** (27d,97b), **loll** (94b,128c), **Lolo** (27d,30a), **Mola** (159c), **mold** (54d,143c), **mole** (19d,23a,24d,85a, 117c,155c), **Mole** (88c), **moll, Moli** (183d), **molt** (27a,143d), **moly** (76a,181c), **Nola, Noll** (96b,110b), **nolo** (42a), **Pola, pole** (132c,143b,177b,184a), **Pole** (52a), **polk** (37c), **poll** (74d,160a, 177c), **polo** (154a), **Polo** (175d), **poly** (34c,76b), **role** (114b), **roll** (134a,160b), **sola** (9a,48a,74b,118c,154a,167b), **sold, sole** (52c, 57a,b,58b,d,110c,115d,150a), **soli** (12c,110c), **solo** (12c,89a,110c), **tola** (48a,80d), **Tola** (85b,180a), **told** (129c), **tole** (9a,51a,99b,163a), **toll** (131c), **tolt, tolu** (16a), **vola** (89d,150a), **vole** (97d,104a,148a,

149b), **volk** (66c,105d,116a,184c), **Volk, volt** (49b,78c,173b), **wold** (47c,60a,118d,174a,184a), **wolf, yolk, Zola** (63a)

- - OL **bool** (39d), **chol** (118d), **Chol** (192), **cool** (25c,107d), **egol** (11b), **enol** (29c,158b), **fool** (24a,41c,47a,146d), **gaol** (123d), **Gaol** (164a), **idol** (48c,54c,55a,75b,79d,112d,130b,184d), **itol** (158b), **obol** (29b, 110a), **pool** (65a,119d,120d), **siol** (82c), **tool** (27c), **viol** (105a), **wool** (58b,179c)

O - - L **obol** (29b,110a), **odal** (48a,88b,112c), **odel** (48a,112c), **odyl** (59d, 79c), **opal** (20a,65d,67b,82b), **oral** (114a,153d,174c,175c), **Orel, oval** (48d,49c), **oxyl** (112c)

OM - - **Oman** (159a), **omao** (165b), **omar** (103b), **Omar** (48c,51b,116c, 163b), **Omei** (24a), **omen** (14c,59d,60a,121c,123a,146b), **omer** (51a,75c), **omit** (49c,52c,106b,114c,147d), **omni** (34a), **Omri** (18c, 86d), **Omsk**

- OM **boma** (7d), **bomb** (144a), **coma** (91c,157d,170c,172b), **comb** (38c), **come, Como, dome** (39c,133c,155d), **Domn** (135a), **domy, Goma** (191), **home, homo** (122d), **homy** (38b), **Kome** (71d), **Komi** (191), **loma** (58b,63d), **Lome, nome** (71c,163b), **Nome, pome** (11d), **Pomo** (192), **pomp** (111d,112d), **Roma** (83c,d), **Rome** (31c,51d), **romi** (72d), **romp** (63d), **soma** (10c,21c,34a,48a,81d,136b), **some** (114b, 121c,126a), **Toma** (191), **tomb, tome** (21d,177c)

- - OM **Ahom** (88c), **asom** (18d), **atom** (101c,114c,180d), **boom** (152d), **coom** (32d,150c,178d), **Crom, doom** (42d,55a,134d), **Edom** (18c, 51b,79b,82c,84a), **from, glom** (155d,160d,178c), **joom** (39c), **klom** (189), **loom** (11c,146b,179b), **room** (28d), **stom** (34c), **toom** (139b), **whom** (42b), **zoom**

O - - M **odum** (168c,180a), **ogam** (82b,c), **ogum** (82b), **olam** (51a,d,75c, 81a), **onym** (162c), **ovum** (48d)

ON - - **Onan** (18c,85c), **onca** (189), **once** (60b,79b), **onde** (63a,178d), **oner** (20d,53a,75c,162d,173a,d), **ones** (116a), **only** (24d,52c,98d, 147a,150a), **onto** (76a,174a), **onus** (24c,93b,109b), **onym** (162c), **onyx** (25d,28d,65d,142b), **onza** (189)

- ON - **a-one** (52b,167b), **bona** (89d), **Bona** (183c), **bond** (92a,101c,141d, 143b,159d,165c), **bone, bong, Boni** (63b), **bonk** (190), **Bonn** (17d), **bony** (147c), **Bony** (96b), **cond** (156a), **cone** (66b,150a,157c), **Coni, conk** (41c,108a,156d,157c), **conn** (43d,156a), **cony** (127a), **dona** (83d,121c,151d), **done, dong, doni** (21a,28c,168a), **don't, fond** (7c,94b), **Fong** (40b), **fono** (137a), **fons** (60c), **font** (16b,171d,172a), **Gona** (106d), **Gond, gone** (6b,15c,42c,44c,114d), **gong, hone** (110a, 143c,180d), **hong** (30b), **honk** (70a), **Iona** (28a,82d), **Ione** (24b, 88d,94d), **Ioni** (192), **jonk, kona** (74c), **konk** (41c), **lone** (150a), **long** (38b,185b), **lonk** (143d), **mona** (72b,101d), **monk** (28b,63c, 129d), **mono** (34c,78d,122d,147a), **Mono** (193), **mons** (89c), **Mons** (184d), **mont** (62b), **nona** (89b,107b), **Nona** (69a,183c), **none** (108b), **nono** (83b), **oons** (100a,186d), **oont** (25d), **pond, pone** (37a,85b), **pong, Pons** (13d,63c,110d,150c), **pont** (55d,61b), **pony, rone** (127c,164b), **Rong** (88c), **song** (12c,170c), **sons** (98d,109d), **tone** (6c,118c), **tong** (30a,c), **tonk** (173c), **tony, Tony** (96b), **wong** (56a), **wont** (6d,40a,73a), **yond** (164d), **zona** (144c,186d), **zone** (44c,50a,160d)

379

⊫-ON acon (62c,140d), agon (12c,36c,41b,55d,71b), Amon (86d,96b, 127d,159b,164a), anon (7d,14d,79d,80b,123a,145c,150c,164a), aton (150a,159b), Avon (143b), axon (106c,153c), azon (127b), bion (117b), boon (18b,20c,55a), cion (42d,70b,145b,148b,154b, 156a), coon (121c), Dion (96a,152a), doon (140b,168c), ebon (20b), Elon (18c,51b,108a), Enon (18c,d), Eton (33b,50c,84a), faon (33c, 55a), Gaon (85b), goon (157c,163c), hoon (190), icon (79d,92b, 136a), ikon (79d,136a), iron (55c,d,69d,81a,97b,143b,149a,173d, 179c), Leon (96a), lion (55b,86c), loon (19a,b,c,157d,179c), moon (40b,132c,137c), neon (65c), paon (115b), peon (28c,59c,99c), phon (94a), pion (43c,52b), poon (97c), roon (41a,168b), scon (162c), sion (125c,158c), Sion (75b,c,83a,157d), soon (123a), tion (158b), toon (80c,95b,168c), tron (180a), upon (6b), woon (24c), Zion (75b,c,83a,157d) zoon (43a)

O--N oban (190), Odin (7c,29d,63c,68c,175d,183b), Olan (115c), Oman (159a), omen (14c,59d,60a,121c,123a,146b), onan (18c), Onan (85c), open (26a,60d,81a,109b,112c,125b,172b,173c), Oran, oven (15d,78c,86b), Owen (96a,183c), oxan (65c), oxen (10c)

OO-- ooid (48d), oons (100a,186d), oont (25d), oord (190), ooze (53c, 104b,116a), oozy (148b)

-OO- boob (146d), booh (52c), book, bool (39d), boom (152d), boon (18b,20c,55a), boor (47a,135d,172c), boot (128d), cook (137b), cool (25c,107d), coom (32d,150c,178d), coon (121c), coop, Coos (192), coot (19b,46d,72b,138d,141a,146d,157d), doob (18b), dook (184a), doom (42d,55a,134d), doon (140b,168c), door (51a,121b), food (109a,176b), fool (24a,41c,47a,146d), foot (115a), good, goof, goon (157c,163c), Goop (107d), goor, hood (38a,74d), hoof (173a), hook (27b,39d), hoon (190), hoop (181b), hoot (112c), joom (39c), koop (16c), lood (189), loof (144c,153d), look (11c,53c,142a), loom (11c,146b,179b), loon (19a,b,c,157d,179c), loop (31b,107d), Loos, loot (22a,118a,119d,153d), mood (44c), moon (40b,132c, 137c), moor (10a,75b,137b,141d,178b), Moor (102c,d,111d), moot (41b,44c), nook (37a,130d), noon, pooa (76a,125b), pood (189), poof, pooh (22b,107d), pook (68a), pool (65a,119d,120d), poon (97c), poop (41c), poor (33a), poot!, rood (38d,39a,88b), roof (78d), rook (19b,29c,39a), room (28d), roon (41a,168b), roof (53a), Roos (67a), sook (22a,25c,97a), soon (123a,145c), soot (20b, 26c,88a), tooa (17c), took, tool (27c), toom (139b), toon (80c, 95b,168c), toot (28a,66a,132b), voog (28a,66a,132b), wood (39a,163d, 165a,179d), wool (58b,179c), woon (24c), yoop, zoon (43a)

--OO aboo (17a), aroo (80c,82b), broo (139a), ejoo (55b,168c), Kroo (191), phoo, shoo (46b,67a,138b), sloo (160a), whoo

O--O octo (34a,89b,122c), odio (83b), Ohio, okro (72c,175a), oleo (34c), olio (44b,77c,98c,100d,121d), omao (165b), onto (76a,174a), ordo (22a,30d,122a,171a), orlo (56b,119c), Oslo, otho (133a), otro (151d), otto (58d,116b,134a), Otto (14c,66d,67a,96a)

OP-- opah (23b,57a,b,86d), opal (20a,65d,67b,82b), open (26a,60d, 81a,109b,112c,125b,172b,173c), Opie (50c), opus (35c,105a,184c)

-OP- copa (88b,113c), cope (12b,26b,36c,65b,157d,176a), Copt (48d),

380

copy, dopa (117d), dope (46c,105d), dopp (43c), hope (13d,52d), hopi (33c), Hopi (12c,102c,125b), hops (17c), koph (91d), kopi (107a,168c), Kopi (172a), lope (48b,64b,d), mope (92d,159a), pope (20a,30d,31c,120d), qoph (91d), rope (36d,88d,128b), ropy (157c, 176d), soph, Sopt (45b), tope (24a,46b,57a,143c,151a), toph (75c), topi (37a,75a,118c), tops (159c)

- - OP alop (13d,46b,93d), asop (180b), atop (112a,174a), chop (98a), clop, coop, crop (38b), drop (43d,54b,100b,114c,168b), Esop (53b,54a), flop (54a), Goop (107d), hoop (181b), klop (150d), knop (124b,170c,185b), koop (16c), loop (31b,107d), plop (54b), poop (41c), prop (159d), scop (120a), shop, slop, stop (73b,111b), swop (168a), trop (62d,167a), yoop

- - OQ shoq (169a)

OR - - orad (104a), oral (114a,153c,174c,175c), Oran, oras (40d), orca (86b), ordo (22a,30d,122a,171a), ordu (170d), Orel, orfe (57a,b, 185c), orgy (26d,130d,137c), orle (17b,56b,76a,144b,177a), orlo (56b,119c), Orly (8b), orna (169d,182c), orne (169d,182c), Orne (25b), orra (139c,d,140a), orts (60d), oryx (11a)

- OR - bora (181d,182b), bord (100b), bore (14c,25b,46a,116a,165c, 179b), borg (10d), Bori (110d,150c), born, bore (154b), Boro (193), Bors (70b,134b), bort (43b), Bort (134b), cora (65d), Cora (42b, 69c,80c,116b,124d,172b,183c), cord (39b,131a), core (28b,51c, 75b,81b), cork (119d), Cori (138c), corm (24b,38d,156a), corn (39d,95c,123a), dora (70b), Dora (36d,41a,43b,183c,d), dord (42c), dore (61d,67b,69d,117d), Dore (50d,63a,b), dorm, dorn (164d), dorp (73c,176b), dorr (32b), dory (21b,58b,144c), fora (133a), ford (177b), fore (63d,174b), fork, form (54d,143c), fort (63d,157d), gora (81c), gore (115d,117c,154c,169c), gory, hora (22a,40b), horn (11a,105a,170b,182a), hors (62b), kora (178c), Kora, kore (107b), Kore (29a,42b,116b,124d), kori (7d,77a), lora (146b,149b,151c,169b), Lora (183c), lord (107c), lore (77c,87c, 90d,151c,183a), lori (91b), lorn (42d,60b), loro (19a,114b), lory (19a,114a), mora (42b,65a,72b,83d,99b,153a,161a), more (71a), More (50b), morg (188), morn, moro (19a,56c), Moro (100a,103a, 117a,159a), Mors (41b), mort (41b,47a,78b,136d), Nora (79b, 107a,164c,183c), Nore (163d), nori (8c,141c), norm (15a,115a, 128a,155a), Norn (69a,163d,174b), oord (190), pore (59d,110d, 111c,120d,157d), pork, Poro (141d), port (73d,136b,140c,170c,d, 182b,c), Rori (16b), sora (19b,c,127b), sorb (11d,103d,134b,142d), Sorb (148a,180a), sore (23d,142c), sori (55c,64a), sorn (139a,d), sors (44d,89b), sort (31d,39c,70b,86b,153a), sory (176d), tora (11a,44d,74a,75c,85c,90b,102d,115d), tore, tori (101b), torn (130a), toro (38a,107a,152a,168c), torp (54c), tort (31c,91a,185c), Tory (23c,36b,94c,172a), word (124b,165c), wore, work (64c,76b), worm, worn (143b), wort (76a,95d,121d), yore (10b,69d,93c,110b, 165d), york (38c), York (50b,c)

- - OR acor (6d), ador (153b), amor (152b), Amor (39c,68b), asor (75c, 105a), boor (47a,135d,172c), chor (164b), door (51a,121b), Ghor (174b), goor, Igor (135d), knor (87c), mhor (180b), moor (10a, 75b,137b,141d,178b), Moor (102c,d,111d), odor (138b,156a), Ogor (170b), Olor (160a,b), poor (33a), shor (136d), Shor (162b), Thor

381

(7c,68c,99c,100c,109c,165b), **utor** (90a,166c)

O - - R **Oder** (132a), **odor** (138b,156a), **Ogor** (170d), **Olor** (160a,b), **omar** (103b), **Omar** (48c,51b,116c), **omer** (51a,75c), **oner** (20d,53a,75c, 162d,173a,d), **osar** (51b,67b,131b), **oser** (61b), **over** (6b,38c,80a, 114d), **oxer** (55c), **oyer** (38a,75b,119c)

OS - - **osar** (51b,67b,131b), **oser** (61b), **Oslo**, **ossa** (21d) **Ossa** (103d,110b, 164b), **oste** (21d,83b)

- OS - **bosa** (12a), **Bosa**, **Bosc** (115c), **bose** (163c), **bosh**, **bosk** (164b), **boss** (49d,157d), **cosh** (35a,97c), **cose** (29b), **coso** (152c), **coss** (98a), **cost** (29a), **cosy** (149c), **dosa** (74b), **dose** (123a), **doss** (17c), **dost**, **foss** (44d,100d), **gosh**, **hose** (156c), **host** (13a,51d,104c), **Jose** (96a), **josh** (85b), **joss** (30b), **Josy** (183d), **koso** (6c,80d), **Koso** (192,193), **koss** (188), **lose** (60a,100c), **losh** (178b), **loss** (42c,123d, 178b), **lost**, **Mose** (96b), **mosk** (97b,103b), **moss** (91d,104c,114a, 170c), **most** (67d), **mosy** (67d), **nose** (118d,125a,149b), **Nosu** (27d), **nosy**, **pose** (14c,15d), **posh** (49b,148c), **post** (89a,95c,155d), **Rosa** (58d, 134a,145d,183c), **rose** (33c), **Rose** (6a,50c,183c), **ross** (16c,161d), **Ross** (50c), **rosy** (21a,111a), **sosh** (81d), **soso** (99c,114c,166c), **tosh** (106a), **Tosk** (8c), **toss** (24a,132d), **Xosa** (86a)

- - OS **Amos** (96a,144b), **bios** (92a), **Coos** (192), **Enos** (7a,18d,52a,70c, 96a,143a), **epos** (51a,76b,120a), **Eros** (11c,39c,68b,97c,182d), **ghos** (30b), **gros** (47a,53d,146c), **Gros** (63a), **Laos** (80d,129c), **Loos**, **naos** (28a,71c,137a,163a), **Naos** (155b), **phos**, **Taos** (192), **Teos** (82a), **Thos** (84a,181c)

O - - S **oaks** (154d), **odds** (28d,172c), **offs** (38c), **ones** (116a), **onus** (24c, 93b,109b), **oons** (100a,186d), **opus** (35c,105a,184c), **oras** (40d), **orts** (60d), **Otis** (9c,24d,82a,111a), **Otus** (67a), **ours** (124c), **Ovis** (143d), **oyes** (38a,39b,75b)

OT - - **Otea** (71a,82d), **Otho** (133a), **otic** (14c,d,47b), **Otis** (9c,d,24d,82a, 111a), **Otoe** (147b), **otra** (152c), **otro** (151d), **otto** (58d,116b,134a), **Otto** (14c,66d,67a,96a), **Otus** (67a)

- OT - **bota** (189), **both**, **Boto** (192), **bott** (32a,88d), **cota** (117a), **cote** (19b,143d,144a,b), **coto** (16c,90b), **Coty** (63c), **dote** (17a,90b,94b, 97a,112a,139d,165d), **doth**, **Doto** (141b), **doty** (43d), **Goth** (16c, 163d), **Hoth** (20c), **hoti** (71a,85c,91c,114c,166c,176a,180d), **jota** (151c), **joti**, **kota** (117a), **Kota** (45d), **koto** (84b), **lota** (24c, 121d,178d), **loth** (15a,173d), **lote** (24c,94a), **Loti** (63a,176a), **loto** (65a,121d,178d), **lots**, **mota** (103a), **mote** (114c,153a), **moth**, **Moth** (112d), **moto** (104b), **nota** (15c,89c), **note** (98c,109b,124b, 128d,130a,177c), **Nott** (107b), **pott** (113d), **rota** (27c,30d,38a,79a, 92d,133a,134a,b,180c), **rote** (130b,134b,143a,159d), **roti** (62c), **roti** (103b,111c), **roto** (30a,122d,127b,152c,171b), **sote** (150c), **tota** (71d), **tote** (27a,73c), **toto** (8d,15a,34d,89a,181a), **toty** (87b), **vota** (133b), **vote** (60b), **Vote** (56d), **Voth** (191), **Voto** (192), **Wote** (191)

- - OT **Abot** (100c), **blot**, **boot** (128d), **clot** (32d,94d), **coot** (19b,46d,72b, 138d,141a,146d,157d), **eyot** (82d), **Fiot** (191), **flot** (173a), **foot** (115a), **frot** (28c), **grot** (27d), **hoot** (112c), **liot** (82d), **khot**, **knot** (43c,99d,107c,124d,137b), **loot** (22a,118a,119d,136a,153d), **moot** (41b,44c), **phot** (173b), **piot** (95b), **plot** (25a,36b,118d,138b), **poot!**, **riot** (44c,111d,170c,173d), **root** (53a), **ryot** (115c), **scot** (14a,

382

162b), Scot (64b,132c), shot (9d,43d,90c,174d), slot (10d,11b,41d, 110d,167d,168a,181b), soot (20b,26c,88a), spot (93b,118c,154d, 162a), stot (154d,155d,157d,179b,186a), swot, toot, trot (85b, 93d,112d)

O - - T   oast (15d,86b,112a), obit (41b,64c), oket (189), omit (49c,52c, 106b,114c,147d), oont (25d), oust (44c,49a,52b,125d)

OU - -   ouch!, ough!, ours (124c), Ouse (132a,185d), oust (44c,49a,52b, 125d)

- OU -   Aoul (191), bout (36c), bouw (188), coup (20d,97c,157b,c,162d), cous (38a), doub (18b), douc (101d), doum (168c), dour (67d, 159a), foud (54d,144b), foul (173a), four (26c), goul (102a), gour (112c,181c), gout, hour, joug (138d), loud (156a), loun (19a,b), loup (61d,62a,90c,139d), Loup (193), lour (13d,63d), lout (15c, 22a,24b,45b,109a,157d), moue (61d,62b), noun (114b,158a), noup (124b), nous (81d,100a,128b), pouf, poul (190), pour (162d), pous (188), pout (159a), roud (57a,b), roue (41b,44c,127c,134b), roup (44a,121d), rout (41d,44b,46b), souf (146b), souk (22a,97a), soul (10d,125a,153c,176d), soup, sour, sous (62d,172c), toug (171a), toup (95d), tour (31b,85c), tout (61a,127a), youp (185d), your (124c)

 - OU   Abou (48b,55a), chou (61b), Chou (30b), clou (62b), meou, niou (188), shou (41d), thou (124b), Tiou (192), Yaou (30c)

O - - U   Oahu, Ogpu (135d), ordu (170d)

OV - -   oval (48d,49c,127a), oven (15d,78c,86b), over (6b,38c,80a,114d, 130a), Ovid (132d,133b), Ovis (143d), ovum (48d)

- OV -   cove (17a,73d,107d), dove (19a,117b), Hova (95a), hove (92a, 157d), Jova (193), Jove (85d), love (163a), move, nova (20c,106d, 155c,174d), nove (83b), rove (127d,132b,178a), wove, Xova (193)

- - OV   akov (189), Azov (20b)

OW - -   Owen (96a,183c), owse

- OW -   bowk (155d), bowl, cowl (101d), dowd (143b), dowl, down (149d), fowl, gowk (146d), gowl (102a,140d,185b), gown, howe (77d), Howe (17a,82a), howl (39b), howk (139b), Iowa (193), jowl (29b), lowa (19a), lown (157d), lowp (90c,139d), mown, nowt (106a,139a), nowy (194), powe, rowy (157b), town (73c), towy (58b), yowl, yowt (139c)

- - OW   alow (18a,172c), arow (92c,158b), avow (6d,36a,41c,112c), blow, brow, chow (45a), clow (58c,148c), crow (19a), dhow (88d,111c, 175d), enow (50d,123a,158b), flow (157b), frow (47a,167a), glow (144c), grow (154b), know, Lwow, meow, plow (39c,165d), prow (21b,22c,144d,156a), scow (21a,58b), show (42b,44c,96b), slow (43c), snow, stow (112b), swow (100a), trow (18a,21a,159d,164c, 170b)

OX - -   oxan (65c), oxes (153d), oxen (10c), oxer (55c), oxid (112c), oxyl (112c)

- OX -   boxy, coxa (77b), doxa (48b), doxy (129d), foxy (38b,39c,181d), moxa (27d,30c), Moxo (192), noxa, Roxy (183d), toxa (153d)

- - OX   abox (22d), esox (57b)

O - - X   obex (22d), Odax (132c), Olax (52b), onyx (25d,28d,65d,142b),

383

oryx (11a)

OY - -   oyer (38a,75b,119c), oyes (38a,39b,75b), oyez (38a,39b,75b)

- OY -   coyn (37a), coyo (15a,30c), Goya (151d), Hoya (14d), noyl (87c), soya (151b)

- - OY   ahoy (106a), Amoy (88c), b'hoy (134b), buoy (28d,58c), choy (48a,128d), cloy (61b,137c,159d), ohoy (106a), ploy (43c), troy (161c,180a), Troy

O - - Y   oaky, oary, obey (35c,75c), ohoy (106a), oily (110b,172c), okay (8d), olay (113b), only (24d,52c,98d,147a,150a), oozy (148b), orgy (26d,130d,137c), Orly (8b)

- OZ -   boza (12a), bozo (55b), coze (29b), cozy (149c), doze (148a), dozy, Jozy, kozo (113d,168c), mozo (152b), noze (75a), ooze (53c, 104b,116a), oozy (148b)

O - - Z   oyez (38a,39b,75b)

PA - -   paal (188), paar (28c), paca (132c,154a), pace (64b,98a,153b,156a, 170b,177d), pack (24b,140d), paco (9b,146d), pacs (94c), pact (8a), padi (131b), paga (117a), page (51b,59b,142d,159b), paha (67b), pahi (21b,26a), paho (122a), paid (129c), pail, pain (7c), pair (22d,37d,85b,171d), pais (37d), pajo (122a), pala (189), Pala (88b), pale (113a,117c,178a), pali (122b), Pali (23d,24a,137b,175a), pall (32d,81b,112a), palm (59b,168c,169b), palo (152c), palp (11a,55b, 58b,167c), paly (194), Pana, pane (113c,155a,b), pang (165b), Pani (120c), pank (189), pant, paon (115b), papa, pape (19b,113a), para (134c,170d), Para (18a,51d), parc (62b,112c), pard (27b, 91b), pare (115c,129a), pari (34a,180a), park, parr (136d,137a, 147c), pars (89d), part (44d,60d,121c,159c), paru (57a), pasa (46a,127c,152c), pasi (94b), pass (110b,155c), past (25c,69d,165d), pata (32c,160d), pate (39a,74d), path (132a,134b), pato (46d), patu (179b), paul, Paul (96a), paun (18b), paut (140a), pave (85a), pavo (115b), Pavo (36b,c), pavy (115b), pawa (189), pawi (43a, 95a), pawn (29c,119c)

- PA -   Apap (102a), apar (12d), opah (23b,57a,b,86d), opal (20a,65d,67b, 82b), spad (105b), Spad (118d), spae (139c), span (23b,107b,113a, 128b,162c), spar (22c,24c,64b,97h,100b,144d), spat (112c,126b, 134b), upas (84d,120b,168c,d)

- - PA   arpa (83b), capa (152a,166d), cepa (110c), copa (88b,113c), depa (188), dopa (117d), Hupa (192), kapa (74b), lipa (54d), napa (25c, 67d,90d), Napa (182c), Nepa, 106b,178c), nipa (14b,46b,48a,164a, 168c), papa, pipa (159d), pupa (30d,81b,c), ripa (16b,131d), ropa (152a), rupa (60b), sapa (70c), supa (168c), tapa (16c,32c,53b, 56a,74b,104b,112b,113d,120d), yapa (113b), Zipa (29d)

P - - A   paca (132c,154a), paga (117a), paha (67b), pala (189), Pala (88b), Pana, papa, para (134c,170d), Para (18a,51d), pasa (46a, 127c,152c), pata (32c,160d), pawa (189), peba (12d), Peba (193), peca (190), peda (114d,144b), pega (57a,130a), pela (30c), Pera (60a), pesa (190), peva (12d), pica (66b,95b,172c), pika (93a,128a, 132c), pima (37c), Pima (192), pina (35d,118b), pipa (159d), Pisa (90c), pita (9c,28b,56a,83a), plea (51a,52d,122a,130b), poha (74c), pola, pooa (76a,125b), proa (21b,26a,95c,d), puca (68a),

384

puja (77a), **puka** (107a,168c), **puma** (27b,37c,55b,103d), **puna** (10b,33b,104a,119b,182a), **pupa** (30d,81b,c), **Puya** (118b), **pyla** (22d)

P - - B   **pleb** (10d,35b,180b)

P - - C   **parc** (62b,112c)

P - - D   **paid** (129c), **pard** (27b,91b), **pend, Phad, Phud** (110b), **pied** (96c,103c,114b,117c,154a,174d), **plod** (170b,177d), **pond, pood** (189), **prod** (67d,80b,106b,120b), **pund** (189), **puud** (189)

PE - -   **peag** (144a,178a), **peal** (98b), **peak** (9a,38c,159b,186b), **peal** (131c,d), **pean** (64c,150b), **pear** (64a), **peat** (64a,175a), **peba** (12d), **Peba** (193), **peca** (190), **peck** (24d), **peco** (162b), **peda** (114d,144b), **pedi** (34b), **pedo** (34b), **peek** (93d,115c), **peel** (53a,114a), **peen** (73c), **peep** (93d,115c), **peer** (51a,93d,107c), **peet** (64a), **pega** (57a,130a,158b), **Pegu** (24c,102a,127d), **peho** (19b,102c,106d), **Peke** (45a,148d), **pela** (30c), **Pele** (69c,74c), **pelf** (22a,56c,131b), **pelo** (83b), **pelt** (53a), **pelu** (30a,106d,168c), **pend, pene, pent** (36a), **peon** (28c,59c,99c), **pepo** (39b,64a,70a,98c,125c,154c), **Pera** (60a), **pere** (61c,63b), **peri** (54b,116b,c,122b), **perk** (84d,93a), **perm** (49b,97d), **pern** (78a), **pero** (152a), **pert** (80a,93a,137c,154b), **Peru, pesa** (190), **peso** (99c), **pest** (108c,116b,118d,170a), **pete** (136b), **Pete** (96b), **peto** (57a,177b), **Peto** (76a), **peur** (61c), **peva** (12d), **pevy** (91d,94c)

- PE -   **aper** (32d), **Apet** (97c), **apex** (39c,76c,115c,118b,159b,166a,167b), **epee** (55c,160d), **open** (26a,60d,81a,109b,112c,125b,172b,173c), **spec, sped, Spee** (66d,70b), **spes, Spes** (69a,78a), **spet** (16c,57a,142c), **spew** (35a,49a), **spex, Spey**

- - PE   **cape** (75a,96c,124b,161a), **cepe** (48c), **cope** (12b,26b,36c,65b,157d,176a), **dope** (46c,105d), **dupe** (27c,41c,72c,160c), **gape** (185b), **hipe** (185a), **hope** (13d), **hype** (185a), **jape** (85a,b), **jupe** (62b, 84a), **lope** (48b,64b,d), **lupe** (19a,64a), **mope** (92d), **nape** (15b,108c,d), **Nupe** (191), **olpe** (90d), **pape** (19b,113a), **pipe** (105a,180d,182a), **pope** (20a,30d,31c,120d), **ripe** (58a,97c,98c), **rope** (36d,88d,128b), **rype** (19b,125a), **sipe** (101a,110c,140b), **supe** (53a,154d), **sype** (110c), **tape** (16a,19a,128d), **tipe** (168b), **tope** (24a,46b,57a,143c, 151a), **type** (31d,115a,155a), **wipe, Xipe** (15c)

P - - E   **pace** (64b,98a,153b,156a,170b,177d), **page** (51b,59b,142d,159b), **pale** (113a,117c,178a), **pane** (113c,155a,b), **pape** (19b,113a), **pare** (115c,129a), **pate** (39a,74d), **pave** (85a), **Peke** (45a,148d), **Pele** (69c,74c), **pene, pere** (61c,63b), **pete** (136b), **Pete** (96b), **pice** (190), **pike** (57a,76c,120b,153a), **pile** (45d,75b,117c), **pine** (36a, 52a,88c,93c,168c,d,169a), **pipe** (105a,180d,182a), **pise** (127d), **plie** (32c,59b), **poke** (108c), **pole** (132c,143b,177b,184a), **Pole** (52a), **pome** (11d), **pone** (37a,85b), **pope** (20a,30d,31c, 120d), **pore** (59d,110d,111c,120d,157d), **pose** (14c,15d), **powe, pree** (139d), **puce** (33c,d,52a), **pule** (180d), **pume** (137b), **Pume** (175b,185b), **pure** (29b,172b,173c), **pyle** (34b), **Pyle** (9c,178a), **pyre** (64c)

P - - F   **pelf** (22a,56c,131b), **Piaf** (63c), **piff** (24b), **poor, pouf, puff** (180d)

- PG -   **upgo** (13c)

P - - G   **pang** (165b), **peag** (144a,178a), **ping, plug** (156d,184d), **pong,**

prig (112a,116c), pung (22c,148b)

PH - - Phad (155b), phew (52c), Phil (96b), phit (24b), phiz (54a), phon (94a), phoo, phos, phot (173b), Phud (110b), phut (24b), Phut (110b)

- PH - epha (75c)

- - PH Alph (132a), caph (91c), kaph (91d), koph (91d), qoph (91d), soph, toph (75c), umph

P - - H path (132a,134b), pish (36c,107d), pith (37a,51c,67b,95c,97a, 119b,126d), pooh (22b,107d), posh (49b,148c), prah (21b, 26a,95c,d), Ptah (48d,98c), pugh!, push (145c)

PI - - Piaf t63c), piat (11a), piay (98b), pica (66b,95b,172c), pice (190), Pici (19c,184a), pick, pico (65a,152c), Pict (23c,47d), pied (96c, 103c,114b,117c,154a,174d), pien (13b), pier (23a,88b,180c), piet (29b,95b), piff (24b), pika (93a,128a,132c), pike (57a,b,76c,120b, 153a), piki (95c), piky, pile (45d,75b,117c), pili (34b,108d), pill, pily, pima (37c), Pima (192), pina (35d,118b), pine (36a,52a,88c, 93c,168c,d,169a), ping, pink (26d,33c,60c,138a), pino (152c), pint (67b), piny, pion (43c,52b), piot (95b), pipa (159d), pipe (105a, 180d,182a), pipi (106d,119b), pipy (145d), pirn (21b,129a,179b), Piro (192), pirr (181a), Pisa (90c), pise (127d), pish (36c,107d), pisk (9c, 19b), piso (189), pist (25c), pita (9c,28b,56a,83a), pith (37a, 51c,67b,95c,97a,119b,126d), pito (9c,28b,83a), Pitt (50d,155d), pity (35b), Pius (121a), pixy (154b)

- PI - apia (121b), apii (74c), apio (125b), Apis (17c,24b,49a,125a,136a), epic (76b,120a), ipil (117a,168c,169a), Opie (50c), spin (131a, 180d), spir (97c), spit (120a,132b,c), Upis (13b), ypil (117a,168c)

- - PI aipi (27a), Hapi (66a,107b,136a), Hopi (12c,102c,125b), hopi (33c), impi (86a), kepi (99d), kopi (107a,168c), Kopi (172a), pipi (106d,119d), tipi (181b), topi (37a,75a,118c), Tupi (192)

P - - I padi (131b), pahi (21b,26a), pali (122b), Pali, (23d,24a,137b,175a), Pani (120c), pari (34a,180a), pasi (94b), peal (98b), pedi (34b), peri (54b,116b,c,122b), Pici (19c,184a), piki (95c), pili (34b, 108d), pipi (106d,119d), puli (45a,78d), puri (80d)

P - - K pack (24b,140d), pank (189), park, peak (9a,38c,159b,186b), peck (24d), peek (93d,115c), perk (84d,93a), pick, pink (26d,33c,60c, 138a), pisk (9c,19b), polk (37c), pook (68a), pork, puck (44b,68a, 77c,100c), Puck (99d,143b), pulk (37c,88d), punk (9b,166a,167c)

PL - - plan (99b,124a,138b), plap (54b), plat (22d,96c,114a,119c,133d), play (63d,154a), plea (51a,52d,122a,130b), pleb (10d,35b,180b), plet (135d), plew (17c), plex (60b), plie (32c,59b), plod (170b, 177d), plop (54b), plot (25a,36b,118d,138b), plow (39c,165d), ploy (43c), plug (156d,184d), plum, plup, plus (10b,102c)

- PL - upia

P - - L paal (188), pail, pall (32d,81b,112a), paul, Paul (96a), pawl (43a, 95a), peal (131c,d), peel (53a,114a), Phil (96b), pili, poll (74d, 160a,177c), pool (65a,119b,120d), poul (190), pull (45d,167d), purl (87c,104c), pyal (175c)

P - - M palm (59b,168c,169b), perm (49b,97d), plum, poem (51a), pram (15a), prim (156b)

386

PN - -   **Pnyx** (71c)

P - - N   **pain** (7c), **paon** (115b), **paun** (18b), **pawn** (29c,119c), **pean** (64c, 150b), **peen** (73c), **peon** (28c,59c.99c), **pern** (78a), **phon** (94a), **pien** (13b), **pion** (43c,52b), **pirn** (21b,129a,179b), **plan** (99b,124a, 138b), **poon** (97c)

PO - -   **poco** (83b,93a), **poem** (51a), **poet** (49b), **Pogo** (121c), **pogy** (57a, 88a,98d,103c), **poha** (74c), **poke** (108c), **poku** (11a), **poky** (148c), **pola**, **pole** (132c,143b,177b,184a), **Pole** (52a), **polk** (37c), **poll** (74d,160a,177c), **polo** (154a), **Polo** (175b), **poly** (34c,76b), **pome** (11d), **Pomo** (192), **pomp** (111d,112d), **pond**, **pone** (37a,85b), **pong**, **Pons** (13d,63c,110d,150c), **pont** (55d,61b), **pony**, **pooa** (76a,125b), **pood** (189), **poof**, **pooh** (22b,107d), **pook** (68a), **pool** (65a,119d, 120d), **poon** (97c), **poop** (41c), **poor** (33a), **poot!**, **pope** (20a,30d, 31c,120d), **pore** (59d,110d,111c,120d,157d), **pork**, **Poro** (141d), **port** (73d,136b,140c,170c,d,182b,c), **pose** (14c,15d), **posh** (49b, 148c), **post** (89a,95c,155d), **pott** (113d), **pouf**, **poul** (190), **pour** (162d), **pous** (188), **pout** (159a), **powe**

- PO -   **apod** (59d), **epos** (51a,76b,120a), **spot** (93b,118c,154d,162a), **upon** (6b)

- - PO   **cipo** (91d), **gapo** (60a), **hypo** (117b), **mapo** (68a,148d), **pepo** (39b, 64a,70a,98c,125c,154c), **sapo** (149c,166d), **typo** (35c,51b)

P - - O   **paco** (9b,146d), **paho** (122a), **pajo** (122a), **palo** (152c), **pato** (46d), **pavo** (115b), **Pavo** (36b,c), **peco** (162b), **pedo** (34b), **peho** (19b, 102c,106d), **pelo** (83b), **pepo** (39b,64a,70a,98c,125c,154c), **pero** (152a), **peso** (99c), **peto** (57a,177b), **Peto** (76a), **phoo**, **pico** (65a, 152c), **pino** (152c), **Piro** (192), **piso** (189), **pito** (9c,28b,83a), **poco** (83b,93a), **Pogo** (121c), **polo** (154a), **Polo** (175b), **Pomo** (192), **Poro** (141d), **prao** (21b,26a,95c,d), **puno** (182a), **pyro**

- - PP   **Capp** (27a), **dopp** (43c), **kapp**, **kipp**, **Lapp** (108a), **repp** (53b,131a), **typp** (185b), **wapp** (54b,133d,145d), **Yapp** (22a), **zipp**

P - - P   **palp** (11a,55b,58b), **peep** (93d,115c), **plap** (54b), **p'op** (54b), **plup**, **pomp** (111d,112d), **poop** (41c), **prep** (138b), **prop** (159d), **pulp**, **pump**

PR - -   **prah** (21b,26a,95c,d), **pram** (15a), **prao** (21b,26a,95c,d), **prau** (21b, 26a,95c,d), **pray** (18b,51a,159d), **pree** (139d), **prep** (138b), **pres** (62b), **pret** (188), **prey** (119d,176a), **prig** (112a,116c), **prim** (156b), **proa** (21b,26a,95c,d), **prod** (67d,80b,106b,120b), **prop** (159d), **prow** (21b,22c,144d,156a), **prut!**, **Prut** (41a)

- PR -   **spry** (7a,107b)

P - - R   **paar** (28c), **pair** (22d,37d,85b,171d), **parr** (136d,137a,147c), **pear** (64a), **peer** (51a,93d,107c), **peur** (61c), **pier** (23a,88b,180c), **pirr** (181a), **poor** (33a), **pour** (162d), **purr** (104c)

- PS -   **apse** (9b,20a,31a,128c,130a,142b,175a), **Apsu** (29a), **ipse** (44d, 89c), **ipso** (89c)

- - PS   **Alps** (85d), **gyps**, **Gyps** (71d), **hops** (17c), **hyps**, **seps** (93b,142d), **tops** (159c), **Veps** (191), **Zips** (40c)

P - - S   **pacs** (94c), **pais** (37d), **pars** (89d), **pass** (110b,155c), **phos**, **Pius** (121a), **plus** (10b,102c), **Pons** (13d,63c,110d,150c), **pous** (188), **pres** (62b), **puss**

PT - - Ptah (48d,98c)

- - PT Copt (48d), dipt, kept, rapt (6c,27a,50d), sept (31d,82b,143a,149c), Sept (45b), Sopt (45b), wept

P - - T pact (8a), pant, part (44d,60d,121c,159c), past (25c,69d,165d), paut (140a), peat (64a,175a), peet (64a), pelt (53a), pent (36a), pert (80a,93a,137c,154b), pest (108c,116b,118d,170a), phit (24b), phot (173b), phut (24b), Phut (110b), piat (11a), Pict (23c, 47d), piet (29b,95b), pint (67b), plot (95b), pist (25c), Pitt (50d, 155d), plat (22d,96c,114a,119c,133d), plet (135d), plot (25a,36b, 118d,138b), poet (49b), pont (55d,61b), poot!, port (73d,136b, 140c,170c,d,182b,c), post (89a,95c,155d), pott (113d), pout (159a), pret (188), prut!, Prut (41a), punt (21a,58b), putt (69d), pyat (95b), pyet (95b)

PU - - puca (68a), puce (33c,d,52a), puck (44b,68a,77c,100c), Puck (99d,143b), pudu (41d), puff (180d), pugh!, puja (77a), puka (107a,168c), puku (11a), pule (180d), puli (45a,78d), pulk (37c, 88d), pull (45d,167d), pulp, pulu (74c), puly, puma (27b,37c,55b, 103d), pume (137b), Pume (175b,185b), pump, puna (10b,33b, 104a,119b,182a), pund (189), pung (22c,148b), punk (9b,166a, 167c), puno (182a), punt (21a,58b), puny (55b,179a), pupa (30d, 81b,c), pure (29b,172b,173c), puri (80d), purl (87c,104c), purr (104c), Puru (192), push (145c), puss, putt (69d), puud (189), puxy, Puya (118b)

- PU - Apus (36b,c), opus (35c,105a,184c), spud (121d,151c), spun, spur (10d,67d,167d,168a,181b), sput (21c)

- - PU hapu (106d), napu (29d,80d), Ogpu (135d), tapu

P - - U paru (57a), patu (179b), Pegu (24c,102a,127d), pelu (30a,106d, 168c), Peru, poku (11a), prau (21b,26a,95c,d), pudu (41d), puku (11a), pulu (74c), Puru (192)

P - - W phew (52c), plew (17c), plow (39c,165d), prow (21b,22c,144d, 156a)

P - - X plex (60b), Pnyx (71c)

PY - - pyal (175c), pyat (95b), pyet (95b), pyla (22d), pyle (34b), Pyle (9c,178a), pyre (64c), pyro

- - PY copy, espy (44a,142a), gapy, pipy (145d), ropy (157c,176d), typy

P - - Y paly (194), pavy (115b), pevy (91d,94c), piay (98b), piky, pily, piny, pipy (145d), pity (35a), pixy (154b), play (63d,154a), ploy (43c), pogy (57a,88a,98d,103c), poky (148c), poly (34c,76b), pony, pray (18b,51a,159a), prey (119d,176a), puly, puny (55b,179a), puxy

P - - Z phiz (54a)

QA - - Qaid (35a)

Q - - D Qaid (35a), quad (33c,172a), quid (39b,166d), quod (123d)

QE - - qere (75c), qeri (75c)

Q - - E qere (75c), quae (176b)

- - QF waqf (103a)

Q - - G quag (21c,102c), Qung (191)

Q - - H qoph (91d)

Q - - I   qeri (75c), quai (88b,117c,180c), quei (189)

Q - - N   quan (190)

QO - -   qoph (91d)

Q - - P   quip (183a,b)

Q - - S   quas (135c)

Q - - T   quit (90d,130c)

QU - -   quad (33c,172a), quae (176b), quag (21c,102c), quai (88b,117c, 180c), quan (190), quas (135c), quay (88b,117c,180c), quei (189), quid (39b,166d), quip (183a,b), quit (90d,130c), quiz, Qung (191), quod (123d)

- QU -   aqua (90a,178c), equi (122d)

Q - - Y   quay (88b,117c,180c)

Q - - Z   quiz

RA - -   raab (32d), raad (14a,49b,151a,165b), raas (91b), Raba, rabi (38d, 74a), Rabi (14b,117b), raca (19a,59c,130b,184d), race (116a,153b, 154b,169c), rack (32c,64b), racy (153b), rada (135c,172a), rade (138d), raff (75b), raft (27b,33c,58c,75b), raga (56d,105a), rage (10c,30c,157a,161d), ragi (28b), Rahu (42b,48b), Raia (107d,147b), raid (59d,80c), raik (188,189), rail (16b,19b,c,37a,97b,138c,150c, 177b), rain (121d,162d), raip (36d), rais (26c,29d,75a,103b), Rais (106b), raja (77a,123c), rake (41b,44c,134b,140d), rale (7c,23a, 29d,41b), ralo (188), Rama (77a,80b,176d), rame (22d), rami (22d), ramp (65a,80b,127b,148b), rana (77a,123c), Rana (63d), rand (16d,22a,131b,145a,b), Rand (69c), rang, rani (72d,77b,123c,127c), rank (31d,55d,70b,92c,94d,157d), rann (175c), rant (41c,127b, 128a,161d), rapt (6c,27a,50d), rara (119a), rare (138b,164b,172b, 173d), rasa (51c), rase (42b,91d), rash (75a), rasp (56b,70d,140d), rata (29d,56b,89d,96c,106d,120c,168c), rate (11d,14a,31d,36b,51d, 52a,70b,85c,112b,123b,127d,128a,138c,143a,174b), rath (29a, 76d,162d), rati (189), rats, rave,(41c,157a,161d), ravi (61b), Ravi (16b), raya (19b,23c,76d,107d), raze (42b,91d), razz (131b)

- RA -   Arab (30a,78b,c,106a,107c,157b,160c,185d), arad (13a,c,84a), arah (52c), Aral (135d), Aram (18d,50c,105c,144b,161c), Aran (18c,48c,64d,82d,174c), arar (137a,168c), Aras, brab (113b), brad (54d,67c,105b), brae (76d,139a,c,140b,148c), brag (21a,175a), Bram (96a), bran (23c,39a,70b,72a,79c), Bran (23c,50c), bras (61a), brat, bray, crab (39b,144b,181b), crag (132c), cral, cram (157d), cran (160c), craw (38d,72c,156c), Crax (19b,39d), draa, drab (23d,29c,33d,46d,53d), drag (74a,125b), drah (188), dram (46b,110c,121d,148c), drap (61b,c,62a), drat (100a), Drau, draw (42c,53a,92b,117c,121c,167d), dray (27a,154c), eral (51a), erat (89c), frab (138c), frap (45d,165c), frat, frau (181b), fray (56b,60d), grab (105b,142a,149b), grad (28b), Graf (37c,66b,67a, 107c,186b), gram (29d,99b,148d,160d,180a), grao (189), gras (78b), gray (33c,77c), Gray (50c), Irad (18d), Irae (43c), Irak (99a,d), Iran (6a,48c,116b), Iraq (99a,d), Iras (11b,32a), krag (131c), kral, kran (190), kras (76d), orad (104a), oral (114a,153d, 174c,175c), Oran, oras (40d), prah (21b,26a,95c,d), pram (15a), prao (21b,26a,95c,d), prau (21b,26a,95c,d), pray (18b,51a,159d), tram (170a), tran (7a), trap (27b,67b,132b,149b), tray (128c,136d,

142d,143c), **ural, Ural** (135c), **uran** (101d), **Wraf, wrap** (32b,51a)

- - RA **abra** (26b), **Abra, aera** (8a), **Afra** (183c), **agra** (26d,34d), **Agra** (161b), **Aira** (70d), **akra** (176a), **Akra** (191), **amra** (77c), **arra** (47d, 52c,82b), **aura** (44c,49c,66a,96b,158a,170d,177c), **bara** (188), **Bera** (86d), **bora** (181d,182b), **bura** (182b), **cara** (83a), **Cara** (48b, 183c), **cora** (65d), **Cora** (42b,69c,80c,116b,124d,172b,183c), **cura** (152c), **Dara** (18d), **dera** (34c), **dora** (70b), **Dora** (36d,41a,43b, 183c,d), **dura** (153c), **eyra** (181d), **Ezra** (96a), **fora** (133a), **gara** (190), **gora** (81c), **Hera** (69c,85d,110b,126b,186b,d), **hora** (22a,40b), **hura** (20a,137a), **Hura, ikra** (27d), **Irra** (68c, 178a), **jura, Jura, Kara** (132a), **kora** (19a,178c), **Kora, Lara** (25c), **lira** (28b,79a,170d), **lora** (146b,149b,151c,169b), **Lora** (183c), **lura** (22d,82a), **Lyra** (36b,74a), **mara** (114d), **Mara** (24a,d,105b,107b), **mira** (174d), **Mira** (155b), **mora** (42b,65a,72b,83d,99b,153a,161a), **mura** (84d), **Mura** (192), **Myra** (10a,31b,183c), **Nera** (165b), **Nora** (79b,107a,164c,183c), **ocra** (72c,175a), **okra** (72c,175a), **orra** (139c,d,140a), **otra** (152c), **para** (134c,170d), **Para** (18a,51d), **Pera** (60a), **Sara** (24d,183c), **sera** (11b,20d,59a,83a,180d), **sora** (19b,c, 127b), **sura** (87c,113b,166d), **Syra, tara** (22a,55c,113a,168c), **Tara** (82b,c,138b), **tera** (23d,84c), **tora** (11a,44d,74a,75c,85c,90b,102d, 115d), **vara** (151d), **vera** (140c,151b,175c), **Vera** (183c) **Vira** (191), **zira** (188)

R - - A **Raba, raca** (19a,59c,130b,184d), **rada** (135c,172a), **raga** (56d,105a), **Raia** (107d,147b), **raja** (77a,123c), **Rama** (77a,176d), **rana** (77a,123c), **Rana** (63d), **rara** (119a), **rasa** (51c), **rata** (29d,56b,89d), 96c,106d,120c,168c), **raya** (19b,23c,76d,107d), **reba** (144a), **Reba** (18d,86c), **rede** (37c,81d), **reja** (152b), **rena** (25b,132c), **rhea** (37a, 56a,111d,133d), **Rhea** (19b,68d,87c,103c,186b), **riga** (118b), **Riga**, **rima** (23a,30c,32a,58a,110d), **ripa** (16b,131d), **rita, Rita** (37b, 78d,183c,), **Roda** (107b), **roka** (95a,168c,d), **Roma** (83c,d), **ropa** (152a), **Rosa** (58d,134a,145d,183c), **rota** (27c,30d,38a,79a,92d, 133a,134a,b,180c), **ruga** (59b,185a), **rupa** (60b), **rusa, Rusa** (41d, 136d), **Ruta** (76b,134d)

- RB - **arba** (135d,171a)

- - RB **barb** (20b,57d,78b,117d,120a,b,124b), **curb** (130c,146b), **garb** (32c,46a), **gerb** (56d,143d), **Harb** (191), **herb** (58b,158b), **kerb** (146b), **Serb** (15d,148a,186c), **sorb** (11d,103d,134b,142d), **Sorb** (148a,180a), **verb** (7a,114b,184b)

R - - B **raab** (32d), **rhob** (64a,85c), **rumb** (120b)

- RC - **arca** (9a,22c,29d,115a,130a), **Arca** (101b), **arch** (29d,38b,39d,123d, 132c), **orca** (86b)

- - RC **circ** (31a), **marc** (70c), **Marc** (96a), **parc** (62b,112c)

- RD - **Erda** (23d,41a,47d,68d,69a,131d,177b), **ordo** (22a,30d,122a,171a), **ordu** (170d), **urde** (86b), **Urdu** (77b), **urdy** (86b)

- - RD **bard** (12d,120a), **bird, bord** (100b), **Byrd** (9c,120b), **card** (33d,114d), **cord** (39b,131a), **curd** (99d), **Dard, dord** (42c), **eard** (139b), **fard** (112d), **ford** (177b), **fyrd** (110a), **Gerd** (63c), **gird** (32c,50a,123a,160a), **hard** (109b), **herd** (39a,46c,72a), **Kurd** (48b, 82a), **lard** (54d,61a,71a,110a), **lord** (107c), **nard** (13a,97c,102b, 110a,153c), **oord** (190), **pard** (27b,91b), **sard** (26d,28d,65d,111a),

390

142b,156d), **Sard**, **surd** (82c,177a), **verd** (71d), **ward** (31c,55c,86b), **word** (124b,165c), **Wurd**, **Wyrd** (107d), **yard** (152d)

R - - D **raad** (14a,49b,151a,165b), **Raad** (151a), **raid** (59d,80c), **rand** (16d, 22a,131b,145a,b), **Rand** (69c), **read** (116d,157d), **redd** (153a), **reed** (16a,70d,97b,105a,111b,118b,144b), **Reed** (163a), **rend** (32a,159c, 162c,185a), **Ridd** (94a), **rind** (53a,115c), **Rind** (109c,174b), **road** (37d,164d), **rodd** (38d), **roed**, **rood** (38d,39a,88b), **roud** (57a,b), **rudd** (26d,57a,b), **rynd** (100a)

RE - - **read** (116d,157d), **real** (7a), **ream** (18c,37d,50d,113d,171c), **reap** (7a,40a,74a), **rear** (15b,23a,b,24a,51b,76d,127c), **reba** (144a), **Reba** (18d,86c), **reck** (26d,75c), **rect** (117b), **redd** (153a), **rede** (37c, 81d,138d), **redo** (165c), **reed** (16a,70d,97b,105a,111b,118b,144b), **Reed** (163a), **reef** (129a,137a,145a), **reek** (49d,53c,64a,148d,149a), **reel** (21b,40b,d,153c,154a,c,d,180d), **reem** (18d), **reft** (32a,42c, 44d,167b), **reim** (112c), **rein** (29b,130c), **reis** (26c,29d,75a,103b), **reja** (152b), **Reki** (16a), **rely** (16b,170b), **Remi** (10b), **Rems**, **rena** (25b,132c), **rend** (32a,159c,162c,185a), **Reni** (83d), **Reno**, **rent** (58a,77c,91b,138b,153d,162c,167c), **repp** (53b,131a), **rese** (127b), **resh** (91d), **rest** (15d,91b,104d,105a,115a,b,130a,b,161b), **rete** (106c,119c), **reve** (61c,104d), **revs** (131a)

- RE - **area** (37d,38a,44c,53a,93b,110d,127d,138c,168a,186d), **areg** (116a, 137a), **areo** (34c), **Ares** (49b,51b,68c,76a,97a,105c,110b), **aret** (128c), **brea** (100b), **bred** (23c,48c,127c), **bree** (139a), **bren** (72d, 95a), **Brer** (172b), **Bres**, **brew** (35d), **brey** (194), **crea** (92c), **Cree** (192), **crew** (72a,106a), **Crex** (37a), **dree** (139b,140c,158b,172c), **drei** (66d,165a), **dreg**, **drew**, **drey** (154c), **erer**, (17d,150c), **Frea**, **Fred** (96b), **free** (44a,70d,131b), **fret** (28c,35b,111c,184d), **Frey** (7c, 68b,124d), **gres** (156d), **grew**, **grey** (33c), **Iren** (127c), **Orei**, **pree** (139d), **prep** (138b), **pres** (62b), **pret** (188), **prey** (119d), **tree** (11d, 37a,66a,184b), **tref** (172b), **trek** (85c,93c,99d,168b), **tres** (19a,52b, 63a,152a,165a,175c), **tret** (9a,178b,179d), **trey** (26c,165a), **Urey** (107c,138c), **wren** (19b,c), **Wren** (50b)

- - RE **Aare**, **acre** (39b,56a,88b), **Acre**, **aire** (82c), **Aire**, **bare** (43d,157c), **bore** (14c,25b,46a,116a,165c,179b), **bure** (61b), **byre** (38a), **care** (11b,14c,35d,150a,184d), **cere** (19a,149d,179a), **core** (28b,51c, 75b,81b), **cure** (123b), **dare** (28d,41b,42a,74d,175b), **Dare** (57a), **dere** (74a,79c), **dire** (45d,55a,104a,163c), **dore** (61d,67b,69d, 117d), **Dore** (50d,63a,b), **Eire** (82b), **etre** (61a,c,62d,166c), **eyre** (23c,31b,85c), **Eyre**, **fare** (43c,59b,67d,123b), **fire** (13a,43d, 44b), **fore** (63d,174b), **gare** (61b,c,62c,127c), **Gere** (183c), **gore** (115d,117c,154c,169c), **gyre** (31b,171b), **hare** (91b,132c), **here**, **hire** (49d,50b,91b,130a), **inre** (35d,80a), **jure** (90b), **kere** (75c, 128b), **kore** (107b), **Kore** (29a,42b,116b,124d), **Kure** (84c), **lire** (62c), **lore** (77c,87c,90d,151c,183a), **lure** (41c,51a,54b,163a), **lyre** (11c,81c,105a,111c), **mare** (78b), **Mare** (108b), **mere** (16c,22b,62a, 78b,87d,96c,110c,120d,146d,148b), **mire** (21c,104b), **more** (71a), **More** (50b), **mure** (177d), **Nare** (93c), **Nore** (163d), **ogre** (67a,102a), **pare** (115c,129a), **pere** (61c,63b), **pore** (59d,110d,111c,120d,157d), **pure** (29b,172b,173c), **pyre** (64c), **qere** (75c), **rare** (138b,164b, 172b,173d), **rire** (62a), **sare** (24d,46a,c,138c,183b), **Sere** (158b), **sire** (17d,55a,59d,124a,163b,166b), **sore** (23d,142c), **sure** (173d), **tare** (9a,18d,41a,176a,179d), **tire** (15a,22a,52d,55a,179b,180d),

391

tore, tyre (15a), **Tyre** (31b,90d,117b), **vare** (179b), **vire** (11a,13b), **ware** (27d,35a), **were** (139b), **wire, wore, yare** (96b,124b,128b), **yore** (10b,69d,93c,110b,165d)

R - - E **race** (116a,153b,154b,169c), **rade** (138d), **rage** (10c,30c,157a, 161d), **rake** (41b,44c,134b,140d), **rale** (7c,23a,29d,41b), **rame** (22d), **rare** (138b,164b,172b,173d), **rase** (42b,d,91d), **rate** 11d,14a,31d,36b,51d,52a,70b,85c,112b,123b,127d,128a,138c,143a, 174b), **rave** (41c,157a,161d), **raze** (42b,d,91d), **rede** (37c,81d,138d), **rese** (127b), **rete** (106c,119c), **reve** (61c,104d), **ribe** (139a), **Rice** (46a), **ride** (46b,85c), **rife** (6b,c,39d,123b), **rile** (10c,d,82c,125a, 156b,176a), **rime** (30c,36a,58a,63d,77c), **rine** (44d,75d,135c), **ripe** (58a,97c,98c), **rire** (62a), **rise** (49d,80b,155a), **Rise** (110d,150c), **rite** (93a,131d), **rive** (32a,153d), **robe** (65b), **rode** (46c), **role** (114b), **Rome** (31c,51d), **rone** (127c,164b), **rope** (36d,88d,128b), **rose** (33c), **Rose** (6a,50c,183c), **rote** (130b,134b,143a,159d), **roue** (41b,44c,127c,134b), **rove** (127d,132b,178a), **rube** (37d,135d, 185d), **Rube** (96b), **rude** (134b,172b), **rule** (11b,26b,90b), **rune** (9b,67a,94a,95a,105c,107d,120a,141d,163d), **ruse** (13b,77c,157b, 169c), **rute** (188), **ryme** (178d), **rype** (19b,125a)

- RF - **orfe** (57a,b,185c), **Urfa** (99a)

- - RF **kerf** (40a,108b), **serf** (21d,148a), **surf** (23a), **turf** (115c,149d, 160b), **warf, werf** (54d), **zarf** (39c,155a)

R - - F **raff** (75b), **reef** (129a,137a,145a), **riff** (131d), **Riff** (18b,102c), **roof** (78d), **ruff** (19b,33b,63d,137a)

- RG - **Argo** (12c,36b,c), **ergo** (164b), **orgy** (26d,130d,137c), **urge** (42d, 46b,79d,80a,b,81c,124a,150a)

- - RG **berg** (79b), **borg** (40d), **burg** (22b,73c), **lurg** (96d,141b,184d), **morg** (188), **Sarg** (96d,125c)

R - - G **rang, ring** (50a), **Rong** (88c), **rung** (28c,39a)

RH - - **rhea** (37a,56a,111d,133d), **Rhea** (19b,68d,87c,105c,186d), **Rhee** (87c), **Rhin, rhob** (64a,85c), **rhum** (8c), **Rhus** (159a)

R - - H **rash** (75a), **rath** (29a,76d,162d), **resh** (91d), **rich, Roch** (136c), **rukh** (53b,54a), **rush, ruth** (35b,118c), **Ruth** (105b,183c)

RI - - **rial** (190), **ribe** (139a), **rice, Rice** (46a), **rich, rick** (74d,117c,154d), **Ridd** (94a), **ride** (46b,85c), **Riel** (129a), **riem** (76c,112c,157c,164d), **rien** (62b), **rier** (180b), **rife** (6b,c,39d,123b), **riff** (131d), **Riff** (18b, 102c), **rift** (30c,32a,58a,110d), **riga** (118b), **Riga, Riis** (9d), **rikk** (49a), **rile** (10c,d,82c,125a,156b,176a), **rill** (23c102b,132a,148d, 157b), **rily** (176a), **rima** (23a,30c,32a,58a,110d), **rime** (30c,36a,58a, 63d,77c), **rimu** (79d,106d,129a,168c), **rimy** (63d), **rind** (53a,115c), **Rind** (109c,174b), **rine** (44d,75d,135c), **ring** (50a), **rink** (147c, 154a), **riot** (44c,111d,170c,173d), **ripa** (16b,131d), **ripe** (58a,97c, 98c), **rire** (62a), **rise** (49d,80b,155a), **Rise** (110d,150c), **risk** (74d), **risp** (99a), **Riss** (66a), **rita, Rita** (37b,78d,183c), **rite** (93a,131d), **rive** (32a,153d)

- RI - **aria** (8b,98c,150a,c,170c), **arid** (46c,85a), **arif** (127d), **aril** (142a), **aris** (101b), **Brie** (29c), **brig** (72b,106a,144d), **brim, brin** (32c,54c,146c), **brit** (76c), **crib** (96b,120d), **cric** (131c), **crig** (20d), **crin** (146c), **cris** (40b,95d), **drib** (46b), **Drin, drip, eria** (13d,146d), **eric** (115b), **Eric** (71d,96a,107d,138a,164a,176b), **Erie** (82c,87d),

Erin (82b), **Eris** (12c,68d,109c), **Fria, frib** (43d), **frim** (58d), **frit** (64c,67c), **friz** (39d), **grid** (17a,70d,119b,156d), **grig** (38c,70d, 93a), **grim** (156a), **grin, grip** (159a), **gris** (61d), **grit** (137a,b), **irid** (38d,67c), **iris** (53c,58a,111c) **iris** (127c), **kris** (40b,95d), **prig** (112a, 116c), **prim** (156b), **trig** (106a,148d,154b,169d), **trim** (40a,106a, 154b,160a,165c,169d), **trin** (169d), **trio** (104d,165a,169c), **trip** (85c), **tris** (122d), **trit** (34d,164c), **Uria** (14c,16d), **urim** (18d,23a, 110a), **writ** (91a)

- - RI **abri** (61c,62c,144b), **aeri** (34a), **agri** (89b), **Atri, auri** (34a), **bari** (37c,79c), **Bari** (83d), **Bori** (110d,150c), **buri** (56b), **Cori** (138c), **dari** (38a,70b), **Geri** (183c), **gyri** (22d,131b), **kari** (14d), **keri** (75c,128b), **kiri** (86a,87c,115a,168c), **kori** (7d,77a), **Kuri** (191), **lari** (78a,101c), **Lari** (72c), **iori** (91b), **Luri** (191), **mari** (61d), **Mari** (16a), **Neri, nori** (8c,141c), **Omri** (18c,86d), **pari** (34a, 180a), **peri** (54b,116b,c,122c), **puri** (80d), **qeri** (75c), **Rori** (16b), **sari** (48b,65b,77b), **seri** (18b), **Seri** (192), **Shri** (17c,166c), **siri** (18b), **sori** (55c,64a), **Tari** (47d,69a), **tori** (101b), **Turi** (191), **vari** (34d,91b,134d,174d), **veri** (28b), **weri** (15c,27c)

R - - I **rabi** (38d,74a), **Rabi** (14b,117b), **ragi** (28b), **rami** (22d), **rani** (72d, 77b,123c,127c), **rati** (189), **ravi** (61b), **Ravi** (16b), **Reki** (16a), **Remi** (10b), **Reni** (83d), **rodi** (98c), **romi** (72d), **Rori** (16b), **roti** (62c)

- - RK **bark** (115c), **cark** (26d,184d), **cork** (119d), **dark** (47a,67d,109b, 160b), **dirk** (40b), **fork, hark** (92d), **jerk** (153a), **kirk** (31a,139b), **kurk** (31a,139b), **lark** (19a,63d), **lurk** (92a,147d), **mark** (146b, 155a), **Mark** (52a,96a), **mirk** (41a,67d), **murk** (41a,67d), **nark** (81a, 156d), **park, perk** (84d,93a), **pork, Sark** (28d), **Turk** (101d,102d, 106a,111d), **work** (64c,76b), **yark** (22c), **york** (38c), **York** (50b,c)

R - - K **rack** (32c,64b), **raik** (188,189), **rank** (31d,55d,70b.92c,94d,157d), **reck** (26d,75c), **reek** (49d,53c,64a,148d,149a), **rick** (74d,117d, 154d), **rikk** (49a), **rink** (147c,154a), **risk** (74d), **rock** (160b), **rook** (19b,29c,39a), **ruck** (39a,185a), **rusk** (23a)

- RL - **orle** (17b,56b,76a,144b,177a), **orlo** (56b,119c), **Orly** (8b)

- - RL **biri** (93c,131a,153c), **burl** (87c,169a), **carl** (115c,135d), **Carl** (96a), **cirl** (24c), **curl** (38d,73b,93b,131d), **earl** (107c), **farl** (138c,140b), **furl** (132d), **girl, harl** (16b,56b,59a), **herl** (16b,59a), **hurl** (167c), **jarl** (40d,107d), **Karl** (96a), **marl** (32a,42c,55d), **merl** (20b), **nurl** (33b,87c), **purl** (87c,104c), **yarl** (40d,107d)

R - - L **rail** (16b,19b,c,37a,97b,138c,150c,177b), **real** (7a), **reel** (21b,40b,d, 153c,154a,c,d,180d), **rial** (190), **Riel** (129a), **rill** (23c,102b,132a, 148d,157b), **roil** (44c,104b,156b,170d,176a), **roll** (134a,160b), **roti** (103b,111c), **rull** (170b), **ryal** (110a,190), **ryel** (190)

- RM - **arme** (63a,179b), **arms, army** (78c), **Erma** (183c), **Irma** (96d)

- - RM **barm** (185b), **berm** (25d,90d,145c), **corm** (24b,38d,156a), **derm** (147c,158d), **dorm, farm** (165d), **firm** (154c,173d), **form** (54d, 143c), **Garm** (178c), **germ** (17d,99c,134d), **harm** (40b,81a), **norm** (15a,115a,128a,155a), **perm** (49b,97d), **term** (92b,105b,142b,166b), **turm** (132d), **warm** (7c,75b,163b), **worm, wurm** (67c)

R - -M **ream** (18c,37d,50d,113d,171c), **reem** (18d), **reim** (112c), **rhum** (8c), **riem** (76c,112c,157c,164d), **roam** (178a), **room** (28d)

- RN - **arna** (24a,181b), **Arnd** (67a), **Arne** (35c,50c,134d), **arni** (24a,181b),

Arno (27a), **arn't, erne** (19c,d,47b,54b,141a), **orna** (169d,182c), **orne** (169d,182c), **Orne** (25b), **urna** (133a)

- - RN **barn** (156d), **Bern,** 160d), **birn** (31d), **born, burn, carn** (156c), **cern** (41c), **corn** (39d,95c,123a), **darn** (130b), **dorn** (164d), **earn** (42d, 64b,99a), **fern** (142a), **firn** (67c,70c,106c,149b), **garn** (67d,185b), **horn** (11a,105a,170b,182a), **karn** (156c), **kern** (59c,172a), **Kern** (132b), **lorn** (42d,60b), **morn, Norn** (69a,163d,174b), **pern** (78a), **pirn** (21b,129a,179b), **sorn** (139a,d), **tarn** (87d,103d,120d), **tern** (19b,32d,72c,94a,138c,141b,160a), **torn** (130a), **turn** (28d,131a, 175a), **warn** (7b), **worn** (143b), **yarn** (154b,161b,184b)

R - - N **rain** (121d,162d), **rann** (175c), **rein** (29b,130c), **Rhin, rien** (62b), **roan** (78b,c,114c,128d,144a,181a), **roon** (41a,168d), **ruin** (42d)

RO - - **road** (37d,164d), **roam** (178a), **roan** (78b,c,114c,128d,144a, 181a), **roar** (145c), **robe** (65b), **Roch** (136c), **rock** (160b), **Roda** (107b), **rodd** (38d), **rode** (46c), **rodi** (98c), **roed, roer** (72c), **roey** (103d), **rohr** (72d), **roil** (44c,104b,156d,170d,176a), **rojo** (129a, 152c), **roka** (95a,168c,d), **roke** (174d,175b), **role** (114b), **roll** (134a, 160b), **Roma** (83c), **Rome** (31c,51d), **romi** (72d), **romp** (63d), **rone** (127c, 164b), **Rong** (88c), **rood** (38d,39a,88b), **roof** (78d), **rook** (19b,29c,39a), **room** (28d), **roon** (41a,168b), **Roos** (67a), **root** (53a), **ropa** (152a), **rope** (36d,88d,128b), **ropy** (157c,176d), **Rori** (16b), **Rosa** (58d,134a,145d,183c), **rose** (33c), **Rose** (6a,50c,183c), **ross** (16c,161d), **Ross** (50c), **rosy** (21a,111a), **rota** (27c,30d,38a,79a,92d, 133a,134a,b,180c), **rote** (130b,134b,143a,159d), **roti** (62c), **roti** (103b,111c), **roto** (30a,122d,127b,152c,171b), **roud** (57a,b), **roue** (41b,44c,127c,134b), **roup** (44a,121d), **rout** (41d,44b,46b), **rove** (127d,132b,178a), **rowy** (157b), **Roxy** (183d)

- RO - **Aroa** (175b), **Arod** (86c), **aroo** (80c,82b), **arow** (92c,158b), **brob** (153c), **broo** (139a), **brow, croc** (13a,74a), **Crom, crop** (38b), **crow** (19a), **drop** (43d,54b,100b,114c,168b), **Eros** (11c,39c,68b,97c,182d), **froe** (32a,167a,179d), **frog** (10a,17a,126d), **from, frot** (28c), **frow** (47a,167a), **grog** (92d,153d), **gros** (47a,53d), **Gros** (63a), **grot** (27d), **grow** (154b), **irok** (55b), **iron** (55c,d,69d,81a,97b,143b, 149a,173d,179c), **Kroo** (191), **proa** (21b,26a,95c,d), **prod** (67d,80b, 106b,120b), **prop** (159d), **prow** (21b,22c,144b,156a), **trod, tron** (140d,180a), **trop** (62d,167a), **trot** (85b,93d,112d), **trow** (18a,21a, 159d,164c,170b), **trey** (161c,180a)

- - RO **aero** (8b,34a,b,58c,59a), **agro** (149d), **arro** (52c), **baro** (71a,122c), **boro** (154b), **Boro** (193), **caro** (83a), **Caro** (183c), **cero** (57b,c,d, 180b), **duro** (190), **Ebro** (132a), **faro** (65a), **Garo** (88c), **giro** (38c, 167c), **gyro** (34d), **hero** (42b,124d,137b), **Hero** (90c), **hiro, inro** (84b,c,106c), **karo** (106d), **Lero** (82d), **loro** (19a,114c), **maro** (144d), **mero** (72a), **miro** (19a,106d,184a), **Miro** (113a,151d), **moro** (19a,56c), **Moro** (100a,103a,117a,159a), **Nero** (8a,126d,133a,150b, 172c), **okro** (72c,175a), **otro** (151d), **pero** (152a), **Piro** (192), **Poro** (141d), **pyro, sero** (34d,88d,164b,178d), **taro** (13c,48c,49b,64b, 112b,120a,133d,155c,170a,c), **tiro** (9b,17d,108c), **toro** (38a,107a, 152a,168c), **tyro** (9b,17d,108c), **xero** (31a,84c,108c), **Zero** (118d)

R - - O **raio** (188), **redo** (165c), **Reno, rojo** (129a), **roto** (30a,122d,127b)

- RP - **arpa** (83b)

- - RP **carp** (27d,38d,40c,55a,56c,57a), **dorp** (73c,176b), **harp** (105a,129a),

larp (51d), **lerp** (51d,141d), **tarp** (26b,178d), **terp** (12b,123a), **torp** (54c), **turp, warp** (36c,165a,171c), **zarp** (120c)

R - - P   **raip** (36d), **ramp** (65a,80b,127b,148b), **rasp** (56b,70d,140d), **reap** (7a,40a,74a), **repp** (53b,131a), **risp** (99a), **romp** (63d), **roup** (44a, 121d), **rump**

- RR -   **arra** (47d,52c,82b), **arro** (52c), **Irra** (178a), **orra** (139c,d,140a)

- - RR   **barr** (49b), **birr** (180d), **burr** (123b), **carr** (120d,140a), **curr** (104c), **darr** (163c), **dorr** (32b), **durr** (70b), **Herr** (66c), **Kerr, murr** (72b,128b), **nurr** (67d), **parr** (136d,137a,147c), **pirr** (181a), **purr** (104c), **turr** (24d,105a), **Tyrr** (68c,109c,163d,178a), **yarr** (72a)

R - - R   **rear** (15b,23a,b,24a,51b,76d,127c), **rier** (180b), **roar** (145c), **roer** (72d), **rohr** (72d), **ruer, Ruhr**

- RS -   **Erse** (28a,64b,82c), **erst** (60b), **Ursa** (17b,36b,43d)

- - RS   **airs** (123b), **Bors** (70b,134b), **hers** (124c), **hors** (62b), **Lars** (51d, 121b), **Mars** (68c,118d,119a,129a,178a), **Mors** (41b), **ours** (124c), **pars** (89d), **sors** (44d,89b)

R - - S   **raas** (91b), **rais** (26c,29d,75a,103b), **Rais** (106b), **rats, reis** (26c, 29d,75a,103b), **Rems, revs** (131a), **Rhus** (159a), **Riis** (9d), **Riss** (66a), **Roos** (67a), **ross** (16c,161d), **Ross** (50c), **Russ** (135b)

- RT -   **Arta** (72b), **arto** (34a), **arts** (138c), **arty, orts** (60d), **Urth** (68d, 107d,163d)

- - RT   **Bart** (96b), **Bert** (96b), **bort** (43b), **Bort** (134b), **cart** (171d,175a, 177b), **curt** (145b,c), **dart** (13b,88a,100c,120b,153a,160c), **dirt, fort** (63d,157d), **girt** (50a), **hart** (41d,154d), **hurt, mart** (49d,97a), **Mart** (96b,183d), **mort** (41b,47a,78b,136d), **part** (44d,60d,121c, 159c), **pert** (80a,93a,137c,154b), **port** (73d,136b,140c,170c,d,182b, c), **Sart** (82b,103b,170d), **Sert** (151d), **sort** (31d,39c,70b,86b,153a), **tart** (114d), **tort** (31c,91a,185c), **vert** (71d,166a,171b), **wart** (124d), **wert, wort** (76a,95d,121d), **yurt** (101d)

R - - T   **raft** (27b,33c,58c,75b), **rant** (41c,127b,128a,161d), **rapt** (6c,27a, 50d), **rect** (117b), **reft** (32a,42c,44d,167b), **rent** (58a,77c,91b,138b, 153d,162c,167c), **rest** (15d,91b,104d,105a,115a,b,130a,b,161b), **rift** (30c,32a,58a,110d), **riot** (44c,111d,170c,173d), **root** (53a), **rout** (41d,44b,46b), **runt** (47a,172d), **rust** (37b,112c,119a), **ryot** (115c)

RU - -   **ruay** (189), **rube** (37d,135d,185d), **Rube** (96b), **ruby** (20a,65d, 179c), **ruck** (39a,185a), **rudd** (26d,57a,b), **rude** (134b,172b), **ruer ruff** (19b,33b,63d,137a), **ruga** (59b,185a), **Ruhr, ruin** (42d), **rukh** (53b,54a), **rule** (11b,26b,90b), **rull** (170b), **rumb** (120b), **rump, rune** (9b,67a,94a,95a,105c,107d,120a,141d,163d), **rung** (28c,39a), **runt** (47a,172d), **rupa** (60b), **ruru** (19b,102c,106d), **rusa, Rusa** (41d, 136d), **ruse** (13b,77c,157b,169c), **rush, rusk** (23a), **Russ** (135b), **rust** (37b,112c,119a), **Ruta** (76b,134b), **rute** (188), **ruth** (35b,118c), **Ruth** (105b,183c)

- RU -   **arul** (11b,143d,144a,181c), **arum** (13a,39b,58d,92b,155c), **Arum** (66a), **bruh** (95a), **brut** (182c), **Brut** (23c), **crus** (91a,143c), **crux** (39a,151b), **drub** (17b,39c) **drug** (105d), **drum** (105a), **drun** (132b), **erua** (103c), **eruc** (37a,56a), **grub** (43c,88d), **grum** (102c), **Grus** (36b,c,38b), **irus** (109d), **prutl, Prut** (41a), **true** (7a,8d,37b,54b, 94c,149c), **urus** (14d,53a,112c)

395

- - RU   **Aaru** (6b,48d), **baru** (168c), **ecru** (17d,23d,172b), **feru** (37a,56a, 133d), **guru** (77b), **maru** (84c,144d), **Meru** (77a,103d), **paru** (57a), **Peru, Puru** (192), **ruru** (19b,102c,106d), **Yaru** (48d)

R - - U   **Rahu** (42b,48b), **rimu** (79d,106d,129a,168c), **ruru** (19b,102c,106d)

- RV -   **urva** (38b)

RY - -   **ryal** (110a,190), **ryel** (190), **ryme** (178d), **rynd** (100a), **ryot** (115c), **rype** (19b,125a)

- RY -   **Arya** (80d), **eryx** (137a), **oryx** (11a), **tryp** (114a)

- - RY   **adry** (164c), **aery** (47b,51d,106c), **airy** (177a,176b), **atry** (141b), **awry** (13d,38d,171c), **bury** (81d), **dory** (21b,58b,144c), **eery** (172b, 180a), **ewry** (133c), **eyry** (47b,106c), **fury** (157a), **Gary, gory, jury** (38a), **lory** (19a,114a), **Mary** (50c,126b,183c), **miry, nary** (108b), **oary, sory** (176d), **spry** (7a,107b), **Tory** (23c,36b,94c,172a), **vary** (28d,43c), **very** (149c), **wary** (27d,176b), **wiry** (147a,167c)

R - - Y   **racy** (153b), **rely** (16b,170b), **rily** (176a), **rimy** (63d), **roey** (103d), **ropy** (157c,176d), **rosy** (21a,111a), **rowy** (157b), **Roxy** (183d), **ruay** (189), **ruby** (20a,65d,179c)

R - - Z   **razz** (131b)

SA - -   **Saad** (12b), **saah** (188), **saal** (66c,73b), **Saan** (24d), **Saar** (63b,102d, 132a), **saba** (56a,117a), **Saba** (143d), **sabe, sack** (43d,118a,119d, 182b), **saco** (189), **sadd** (33a,40b,58c,107b), **sade** (91d), **sadh** (77a), **sado** (26d,84d), **sadr** (94a), **Sadr** (155b), **saer** (163a), **safe** (141d,157d,174d), **Safi** (191), **saga** (79b,91a,138a,157a,161b,c, 168a), **Saga, sage** (13a,90d,100c,141c,145c,180b,183a), **sago** (54c, 59b,113b,125b,155c), **sagy, saha, sahh** (188), **Saho** (6c), **sahu** (153d), **saic** (86b,91d,175d), **said** (174c), **Said** (42d,101a,121b), **sail** (144c,185a), **sain** (20c,38d,48a), **sair** (140b,150d), **sais** (48d, 71d), **Saka** (10a), **sake** (84b,125d), **saki** (39c,84b,102a), **sala** (152a, b,c), **Sala** (50c), **sale** (14c,61c,62b,c,168b), **salp** (109c,148d), **salt** (35d,105b,123a,136c,141c,149d), **sama** (105c,169d), **same** (44d, 79b), **samh** (56b), **samp** (70b,77d,121b), **sana** (56a,166d), **Sana** (185d), **sand** (71d,146c), **sane** (128a), **sang, sank, sano** (152b), **sans** (63a,183b), **sapa** (70c), **sapo** (149c,166d), **Sara** (24d,183c), **sard** (26d,28d,65d,111a,142b,156d), **Sard, Sarg** (96d,125c), **sari** (48b,65b,77b), **Sark** (28d), **Sart** (82b,103b,170d), **sasa** (55c), **sash** (18a,45c,67b,182b), **sass, sate** (32d,52c,67d,70d,137c,159d), **sati, Sati** (49a,126b,147b), **Sauk** (192), **saul** (48a,168c), **Saul** (18c,86d, 115a), **saum** (189), **save** (52b,110c,123a,173c), **sawk** (188), **sawn saxe** (20d,33c), **saya** (117a)

- SA -   **asak** (13d,168c,169a), **asar** (67b), **Esau** (82c,84a,128c), **Esay, Isar** (41a,104c,132a), **osar** (51b,67b,131b), **tsar** (42d,49d,60b,135c), **usar** (8d,16c), **Usas** (68d)

- - SA   **ansa** (73c,93d,137c), **Ausa, Besa** (68b,119c), **bisa** (11a), **bosa** (12a), **casa** (152b), **Disa** (111a), **dosa** (74b), **Elsa** (70a,93c,110d, 177b,183c), **kasa** (48a), **kusa, Lisa** (183d), **masa** (37a), **mesa** (49b, 76d,119b,161a), **Musa** (16a), **ossa** (21d), **Ossa** (103d,110b,164b), **pasa** (46a,127c,152c), **pesa** (190), **Pisa** (90c), **rasa** (51c), **Rosa** (58d,134a,145d,183c), **rusa, Rusa** (41d,136d), **sasa** (55c), **Susa** (49a), **Tesa** (80c), **Ursa** (17b,36b,43d), **vasa** (46d,114a,160b,175d), **Vasa, visa** (114d), **Xosa** (86a)

S - - A saba (56a,117a), Saba (143d), saga (79b,91a,138a,157a,161b,c, 168a), saha, Saka (10a), sala (152a,b,c), Saia (50c), sama (105c, 169d), sana (56a,166d), Sana (185d), sapa (70c), Sara (24d,183c), sasa (55c), saya (117a), Seba (18c,39d), sera (11b,20d,59a,83a, 180d), seta (23b,27c,73a,b,123b,153c), shea (25a,168c,d), Shoa (6c), sida (37a,126c,170a), sika (41d,84b), sima (132b), sina (46c), Sina (102d,103d), Sita (127d), siva (67a,120d), Siva (56d,77a), skua (19b,72c,84a,141a), soda (19a,149d,181a), sofa (44d), soga (70d,152b), Soga (191), Soia, soja (151b), soka (20c), sola (9a,48a, 74b,118c,154a,167b), soma (10c,21c,34a,48a,81d,136b), sora (19b, c,127b), soya (151b), stoa (33c,121a,c), Sula (65a), supa (168c), sura (87c,113b,166d), Susa (49a), Syra

- SB - isba (135c)

S - - B scab (80b,107d,157c), scob (42a), Serb (15d,148a,186c), slab (148b), Sieb (12a), slob (173d), slub (171c), snab (23c,139a), snib (54d,93c), snob (159c), snub (128c,148b), sorb (11d,103d,134b, 142d), Sorb (148a,180a), stab (14c,87a,117c), stib (19b,47a,137a), stub (156c), swab (102b), sweb (160d), swob (102b)

SC - - scab (80b,107d,157c), scad (31a,57a,78b,88d,137c), scan (52b,93d, 98a,116d,128b,c,140d), scar (31a,184d), scat (26b,67a,d,126c, 169c), Scio, scob (42a), scon (162c), scop (120a), scot (14a,162b), Scot (64b,132c), scow (21a,58b), scud (32c,126c,135b,160c), scum (129b), scup (57a,121b), scur (78b), scut (145c,161b)

- SC - asci (154a), esca (11c,44a,70c), esce (158d)

- - SC aesc (12d,64d), Bosc (115c), DDSC (42a), disc (31b), fisc (52c,134c)

S - - C saic (86b,91d,175d), spec

S - - D Saad (12b), sadd (33a,40b,58c,107b), said (174c), Said (42d,101a, 121b), sand (71d,146c), sard (26d,28d,65d,111a,142b,156d), Sard, scad (31a,57a,78b,137c), scud (32c,126c,135b,160c), seed (70b, 111c,112c,119a,151b,154a), seid (103b), Seid 42d,101a, 171a), send (42c,44b,95c,121c,130a,144c,168b), shad (27d,57a, b,c), shed (27a,90c,101b,144b), shod, Sind, skid (148b), sled (40a), slid, sned (93d,125a), snod (169d), sold, spad (105b), Spad (118d), sped, spud (121d,151c), stad (151b,167d,176b), stod (40d,67d), stud (22b,25a,42d,54d,111c,143a,174a), sudd (40b,58c,107b), suld (188), surd (82c,177a), swad (94d), syed (103b), syud (103b)

SE - - seah (188), seal (10c,d,54d,64c,96a,118b,128a), seam (85b,d,160a, 176d,185a), Sean (85b,96a), sear (23d,27d,72c,138c), seat (98c, 156b), Seba (18c,39d), sebi (34b), sech (97c), seck (173d), sect (42b,54a,114c), seed (70b,111c,112c,119a,151b,154a), seek (141c), seel (20c,32c,143b), seem (11c), seen (105a,116a, 154b), seer (60a,124c,150c), sego (24b,25a,92b,174c), sehr (66d), seid (103b), Seid (42d,101a,171a), Seik (77b), Seim (120c), sein (146c), seip (110c), Seir (51b,94a,103d), seis (147b,152c), seit (189), Sejm (120c), self (48d,80d), sell (97a,115c,175b), seme (45c, 138b,151b,154b,155c,157b), semi (34b,80b,122c,d), send (42c, 44b,95c,121c,130a,144c,168b), senn (76b), Sens (63b), sent (42c, seps, (93b,142d), sept (31d,82b,143a,149c), Sept (45b), sera (11b,20d, 59a,83a,180d), Serb (15d,148a,186c), sere (24d,46a,c,138c,183b), Sere (158b), serf (21d,148a), seri (18b), Seri (192), sero (34d,88d,

397

164b,178d), **Sert** (151d), **sesi** (20b,57a,149b), **sess** (149c,162b), **seta** (23b,27c,73a,b,123b,153c), **seth** (98d), **Seth** (7a,52b,68a,b,96a, 98d), **seti** (34a), **Seti** (116d), **sett** (115a,156d), **seve** (63a,182c), **sewn, sext** (26b,111b,147b)

- SE - **asea** (39b,177c), **asem** (9a,49a,69c), **Aser** (84a), **esek** (18d), **esel** (66b), **eser, Iser** (49a), **oser** (61b), **used** (6d,73a), **usee, user** (49d), **uses** (18a), **yser**

- - SE **anse** (61d), **apse** (9b,20a,31a,128c,130a,142b,175a), **asse** (25a, 60d,74a), **base** (6a,43b,44b,51c,60c,79b,94b,122b), **bise** (182a), **bose** (163c), **case** (22c,36c,81c,91a,108c), **cise** (147b), **cose** (29b), **dose** (123a), **duse** (83c), **ease** (7c,8d,35a,100d,129d,130b,c,150c), **else** (18b,79b,111d), **ense** (139b,158c), **Erse** (28a,64b,82b), **esse** (7a,18a,52d,89a,90a,159a,166c), **fuse** (98c), **hase** (74d), **hose** (156c), **huse** (180c), **ipse** (44d,89c), **Jose** (96a), **lose** (60a,100c), **lyse, mese** (71c), **mise** (8a,10a,70c), **Mose** (96b), **muse** (65b,93d, 120d,164c), **Muse** (68d), **nase** (26b,75a,124b), **nose** (118d,125a, 149b), **oese** (15d,119c), **Oise, Ouse** (132a,185d), **owse, pise** (127d), **pose** (14c,15d), **rase** (42b,d,91d), **rese** (127b), **rise** (49d,80b,155a), **Rise** (110d,150c), **rose** (33c), **Rose** (6a,50c,183c), **ruse** (13b,77c, 157b,169c), **sise** (62c,147b), **vase, vise** (31d,77d,114d), **wise** (136b)

S - - E **sabe, sade** (91d), **safe** (141d,157d,174d), **sage** (13a,90d,100c,141c, 145c,180b,183a), **sake** (84b,125d), **sale** (14c,61c,62b,c,168b), **same** (44d,79b), **sane** (128a), **sate** (32d,52c,67d,70d,137c,159d), **save** (52b,110c,123a,173c), **saxe** (20d,33c), **seme** (45c,138b,151b,154b, 155c,157b), **sere** (24d,46a,c,138c,183b), **Sere** (158b), **sere** (63a, 182c), **shee** (82b), **shoe** (166a), **sice** (71d,147b), **side** (13d,22a,b, 54a,58a,89a,161b), **sime** (101d), **sine** (64c,66b,90a,97c,126a,163b, 169d,183b), **sipe** (101a,110c,140b), **sire** (17d,55a,59d,124a,163b, 166b), **sise** (62c,147b), **site** (93b), **sive** (146a), **size, skee** (149c), **Skye** (163c), **slee** (140b,148c), **sloe** (14a,20b,64a,119d,181c), **slue** (97b,148b,160a), **smee** (19b,46c,d,118b,119d,141b,181b), **Smee** (116d), **snee** (40a,b,43d,87a), **soie** (62c), **soke** (44c,85d), **sole** (52c, 57a,b,58b,d,110c,115d,150a), **some** (114b,121c,126a), **sore** (23d, 142c), **sote** (150c), **spae** (139c), **Spee** (66d,70b), **supe** (53a,154d), **sure** (173d), **syce** (71d), **syke** (194), **syne** (140b,147a), **sype** (110c)

S - - F **self** (48d,80d), **serf** (21d,148a), **souf** (146b), **stof** (135c), **surf** (23a)

SG - - **Sgau** (88c)

S - - G **sang, Sarg** (96d,125c), **shag** (73b,105b,161d,166d), **sing** (26d,178a), **skag** (7d,46d), **skeg** (7d,86a,144d,157d,184a), **slag** (46c,99a,138c, 148d,177a), **slog** (157c,170b,177d), **slug** (46b,99b,157c), **smug**, **snag** (11b,27b,35c,87c,124b,166a), **sneg** (139b), **snig** (45d), **snug** (35a,38b,165c), **Snug** (99d), **song** (12c,170c), **stag** (65a,98d), **stog** (155a), **sung, Sung** (30b), **swag** (22a,156c), **swig** (46a,72c)

SH - - **shad** (27d,57a,b,c), **shag** (73b,105b,161d,166d), **shah** (116c), **sham** (41c,55b,60d,80a,123a,b,146d), **Shan** (13c,80d,88c,101d), **shap**, **shat** (87d), **shaw** (164b), **Shaw** (50c,53b), **shay** (110c), **shea** (25a, 168c,d), **shed** (27a,90c,101b,144b), **shee** (82b), **Shem** (107c), **Shen** (68a), **sher** (65d,165c), **shet, shew** (44c), **shih** (189), **Shik** (171a), **shim** (91d,144c,162a,179d), **shin** (91a,d,140b,143c), **ship, shir** (36d, 65d,165c), **Shoa** (6c), **shod, shoe** (166a), **shoo** (46b,67a,138b), **shop**, **shoq** (169a), **shor** (136d), **Shor** (162b), **shot** (9d,43d,90c,174d), **shou**

(41d), **show** (42b,44c,96b), **Shri** (17c,166c), **shul** (161a), **shun** (15a, 51b,52a), **shut**

- **SH -** **Asha** (191), **ashy** (113a,178a), **Isha** (174a), **Tshi** (69c), **Usha** (16a, 150c)

- - **SH** **bash**, **bish** (120b), **bosh**, **bush**, **cash** (101c), **cosh** (35a,97c), **cush** (101c), **Cush** (51d,73c), **dash** (125c,162d), **dish**, **fash** (140c,176a), **fish**, **gash** (40a), **gish** (102c), **gosh**, **gush** (35a,154c), **hash**, **hish**, **hush** (17b,146c), **josh** (85b), **kish** (16d,70c), **Kish** (137c), **Kush** **lash** (58c,87b,165c,180d), **losh** (178b), **lush** (94d), **mash** (39b, 156c), **mesh** (50d,106c), **mush** (97d), **Nash** (9c), **Nish** (19d), **pish** (36c,107d), **posh** (49b,148c), **push** (145c), **rash** (75a), **resh** (91d), **rush**, **sash** (18a,45c,67b,182b), **sish** (79b), **sosh** (81d), **tash** (154d), **tosh** (106a), **tush** (167b), **wash**, **wish** (42d)

- S - - H **saah** (188), **sadh** (77a), **sahh** (188), **samh** (56b), **sash** (18a,45c,67b, 182b), **seah** (188), **sech** (97c), **seth** (98d), **Seth** (7a,52b,68a,b,96a, 98d), **shah** (116c), **shih** (189), **sigh**, **Sikh** (77b), **sinh** (97c), **sish** (79b), **soph**, **sosh** (81d), **such** (146d)

- SI - - **siak** (72d), **sial** (112a), **Siam** (163d,181a), **sice** (71d,147b), **sick**, **sida** (37a,126c,170a), **side** (13d,22a,b,54a,58a,89a,161b), **sidi** (103b, 166b), **sidy** (123b), **sier** (57a,118b), **sift** (140d,142c,146b), **sigh**, **sign** (121c,146c), **sika** (41d,84b), **Sikh** (77b), **silk** (53b,179c), **sill** (45c,76c,165a,182b), **silo** (59a,156b), **silt** (104b,142a), **sima** (132b), **sime** (101d), **Simi** (82d), **simp** (59c,146d), **sina** (46c), **Sina** (102d, 103d), **Sind**, **sine** (64c,66b,90a,97a,126a,163b,169d,183b), **sing** (26d,178a), **sinh** (97c), **sink** (41c,43c,46b,158a), **sino** (34a), **siol** (82c), **sion** (125c,158c), **Sion** (75b,c,83a,157d), **sipe** (101a,110c, 140b), **sire** (17d,55a,59d,124a,163b,166b), **siri** (18b), **sise** (62c, 147b), **sish** (79b), **sisi** (121b), **siss**, **sist** (139b), **Sita** (127d), **site** (93b), **sito** (34b), **siva** (67a,120d), **Siva** (56d,77a), **Sive** (146a), **size**, **sizy** (176d), **sixz**

- SI - **Asia** (48a), **Asin** (102a), **Hsia** (30b,47c), **Isis** (68d,78c,111d), **tsia** (162c), **Tsin** (30b)

- - SI **Absi** (191), **assi** (77d), **dasi** (77a), **desi** (85d), **kasi** (116b), **Lasi** (191), **nasi** (34c,108a,115a), **nisi** (90a,173c), **pasi** (94b), **sesi** (20b,57a), **sisi** (121b), **susi** (53b,d)

- S - - I **Safi** (191), **saki** (39c,84b,102a), **sari** (48b,65b,77b), **sati**, **Sati** (49a, 126b,147b), **sebi** (34b), **semi** (34b,80b,122c,d), **seri** (18b), **Seri** (192), **sesi** (20b,57a,149b), **seti** (34a), **Seti** (116d), **Shri** (17c,166c), **sidi** (103b,166b), **Simi** (82d), **siri** (18b), **sisi** (121b), **soli** (12c,110c), **sori** (55c,64a), **sufi** (103a,116c), **sugi** (84b), **suji** (180c), **susi** (53b,d)

- SK - - **skag** (7d,46d), **skat** (181b), **Skat** (155b), **skee** (149c), **skeg** (7d,86a, 144d,157d,184a), **sken** (164a), **skeo** (57d), **skep** (16d,17c,77c), **skew** (148a,160c,171b,c), **skey** (185d), **skid** (148b), **skil** (57a), **skim** (67c), **skin** (53a,76c,115c,d), **skio** (57d), **skip** (110b,114c,147c), **skir**, **skit** (145c), **skiv** (151b), **skua** (19b,72c,84a,141a), **Skye** (163c), **skyr** (21d,151a), **skyt** (138c,140b)

- SK - **Askr** (107d)

- - SK **bask** (94d), **bisk** (120b,151a), **bosk** (164b), **busk** (17b,37b,55d, 161b), **cask**, **cusk** (57b), **desk**, **disk** (31b), **dusk** (171c), **fisk** (24d,52c,134c), **husk** (53a,78d,142a), **mask** (44a,45c), **mosk** (97b,

399

103b), musk (116b), Omsk; pisk (9c,19b), risk (74d), rusk (23a), task (156b), Tosk (8c), tusk (167b)

S - - K sack (43d,118a,119d,182b), sank, Sark (28d), Sauk (192), sawk (188), seck (173d), seek (141c), Selk (77b), Shik (171a), siak (72d), sick, silk (53b,179c), sink (41c,43c,46b,158a), soak (46c,137c), Sobk (38d), sock (157c,182a), sook (22a,25c,97a), souk (22a,97a), suck, sulk (159a), sunk

SL - - slab (148b), slag (46c,99a,138c,148d,177a), slam (180d,182d), slap (24a,128c,148c), slat (58b,89a,117c,184a), Slav (13c,40c,48b,52a, 120b,135b), slaw, slay, Sleb (12a), sled (40a), slee (140b,148c), slew (160a), sley (179b), slid, slim (148b,160a), slip (67c,119a), slit (40a), slob (173d), sloe (14a,20b,64a,119d,181c), slog (157c,170b, 177d), sloo (160a), slop, slot (10d,11b,41d,110d,167d,168a,181b), slow (43c), slub (171c), slue (97b,148b,160a), slug (46b,99b,157c), slum, slur (44b,124c,148b,168a)

- SL - isle (8b,53c,81d,82d,86b,88a), Oslo

S - - L saal (66c,73b), sail (144c,185a), saul (48a,168c), Saul (18c,86d, 115a), seal (10c,d,54d,64c,96a,118b,128a), seel (20c,32c,143b), sell (97a,115c,175b), shul (161a), sial (112a), sill (45c,76c,165a, 182b) siol (82c), skil (57a), soil (154d,159a,163c), soul (10d,125a, 153c,176d)

SM - - smee (19b,46c,d,118b,119b,141b,181b), Smee (116d), smew (19b, 46d,99a,137d), smug, smur (32c,46b,100c), smut (32d,44a,119a, 150c)

- SM - ismy (45a)

- - SM kasm (189)

S - - M saum (189), scum (129b), seam (85b,d,160a,176b,185a), seem (11c), Seim (120c), Sejm (120c), sham (41c,55b,60d,80a,123a,b, 146d), Shem (107c), shim (91d,144c,162a,179d), Siam (163d,181a), skim (67c), slam (180d,182d), slim (148b,160a), slum, stem (29b, 125a,154d,155a,156d), stom (34c), stum (70c,105c,131a,173a), swam, swim (58c), swum

SN - - snab (23c,139a), snag (11b,27b,35c,87c,124b,166a), snap (23a, 36d,38b,48b,54d,56c,58c,149d), sned (93d,125a,140a), snee (40a, b,43d,87a), sneg (139b), snib (54d,93c), snig (45d), snip (32b, 40a), snob (159c), snod (169d), snow, snub (128c,148b), snug (35a,38b,165c), Snug (99d), snup (149b)

- SN - asno (151d), esne (10c,45b,142c,148a,164d)

S - - N Saan (24d), sain (20c,38d,48a), sawn, scan (52b,93d,98a,116d, 128b,c,140d), scon (162c), Sean (85b,96a), seen, sein (146c), senn (76b), sewn, Shan (13c,80d,88c,101d), Shen (91a,d,140b, 143c), shun (15a,51b,52a), sign (121c,146c), sion (125c,158c), Sion (75b,c,83a,157d), sken (164a), skin (53a,76c,115c,d), soon (123a, 145c), sorn (139a,d), span (23b,107b,113a,128b,162c), spin (131a, 180d), spun (72c,95a), stun (145a,157d), sunn (56a), Svan (27d), swan (19b,33a)

SO - - soak (46c,137c), soap, soar (59a), Sobk (38d), sock (157c,182a), soco (22d), soda (19a,149d,181a), sofa (44d), soft (48b,95d,99d, 163a), soga (70d,152b), Soga (191), soho!, Soho (93c), Soia, soie

400

(62c), **soil** (154d,159a,163c), **soir** (61c), **sojs** (151b), **soka** (20c), **soke** (44c,85d), **sola** (9a,48a,74b,118c,154a,167b), **sold**, **sole** (52c,57a,b, 58b,d,110c,115d,150a), **soli** (12c,110c), **solo** (12c,89a,110c), **soma** (10c,21c,34a,48a,81d,136b), **some** (114b,121c,126a), **song** (12c, 170c), **sons** (98d,109d), **sook** (22a,25c,97a), **soon** (123a,145c), **soot** (20b,26c,88a), **soph, Sopt** (45b), **sora** (19b,c,127b), **sorb** (11d,103d, 134b,142d), **Sorb** (148a,180a), **sore** (23d,142c), **sori** (55c,64a), **sorn** (139a,d), **sors** (44d,89b), **sort** (31d,39c,70b,86b,153a), **sory** (176d), **sosh** (81d), **soso** (99c,114c,166d), **sote** (150c), **souf** (146b), **souk** (22a,97a), **soul** (10d,125a,153c,176d), **soup, sour, sous** (62d,172c), **soya** (151b)

- SO - **asok** (13d), **asom** (18d), **asop** (180b), **asor** (75c,105a), **Esop** (53b, 54a), **esox** (57b)

- - SO **also** (10b,18b,80a), **Caso** (82d), **coso** (152c), **enso** (34d,183b), **huso** (180c), **ipso** (89c), **koso** (6c,80d), **Koso** (192,193), **Muso** (192), **peso** (99c), **piso** (189), **soso** (99c,114c,166d), **yeso** (72d)

S - - O **saco** (189), **sado** (26d,84d), **sago** (54c,59b,113b,125b,155c), **Saho** (6c), **sano** (152b), **sapo** (149c,166b), **Scio, sego** (24b,25a,92b,174c), **sero** (34d,88d,164b,178d), **shoo** (46b,67a,138b), **silo** (59a,156d), **sino** (34a), **sito** (34b), **skeo** (57d), **skio** (57d), **sloo** (160a), **soco** (22d), **sohol, Soho** (93c), **solo** (12c,89a,110c), **soso** (99c,114c,166d), **Sumo**

SP - - **spad** (105b), **Spad** (118d), **spae** (139c), **span** (23b,107b,113a,128b, 162c), **spar** (22c,24c,64b,97b,100b,144d), **spat** (112c,126b,134b), **spec, sped, Spee** (66d,70b), **spes, Spes** (69a,78a), **spet** (16c,57a, 142c), **spew** (35a,49a), **spex, spey, spin** (131a,180d), **spir** (97c), **spit** (120a,132b,c), **spot** (93b,118c,154d,162a), **spry** (7a,107b), **spud** (121d,151c), **spun, spur** (10d,67d,167d,168a,181b), **sput** (21c)

- SP - **espy** (44a,142a)

- - SP **cusp** (38c,78b,119a,120a,b), **gasp** (113c), **hasp** (31d,54d,153c), **lisp** (153b), **rasp** (56b,70d,140d), **risp** (99a), **wasp, wisp** (24b,148c)

S - - P **salp** (109c,148d), **samp** (70b,77d,121b), **scop** (120a), **scup** (57a, 121b), **seep** (110c,116a,154b), **seip** (110c), **shap, ship, shop, simp** (59c,146b), **skep** (16d,17c,77c), **skip** (110b,114c,147c), **slap** (24a, 128c,148c), **slip** (67c,119a), **slop, snap** (23a,36d,38b,48b,54d,56c, 58c,149d), **snip** (32b,40a), **snup** (149b), **soap, soup, step** (70b,112b, 177b,d), **stop** (73b,111b), **sump** (28c,45d,100b), **swap** (168a), **swop** (168a)

S - - Q **shoq** (169a)

S - - R **Saar** (63b,102d,132a), **sadr** (94a), **Sadr** (155b), **saer** (163a), **sair** (140b,150d), **scar** (31a,184d), **scur** (78b), **sear** (23d,27d,72c,138c), **seer** (60a,124c,150c), **sehr** (66d), **Seir** (51b,94a,103d), **sher** (65d, 165c), **shir** (36d,65d,165c), **shor** (136d), **Shor** (162b), **sier** (57a, 118b), **skir, skyr** (21d,151d), **slur** (44b,124c,148b,168a), **smur** (32c,46b,100c), **soar** (59a), **soir** (61c), **sour, spar** (22c,24c,64b,97b, 100b,144d), **spir** (97c), **spur** (10d,67d,167d,168a,181b), **star** (14a, 21c,94c,100c), **ster** (158c,d), **stir** (8a,13a,35b,78d,100d,104a), **suer** (124d)

- SS - **asse** (25a,60d,74a), **assi** (77d), **esse** (7a,18a,52d,89a,90a,159a, 166c), **ossa** (21d), **Ossa** (103d,110b,164b)

- - SS bass (57b,c,177a), Bess (76c,183d), boss (49d,157d), buss (87a, 148c), cass (140c,177a), Cass (147a), cess (91d,94c,162b), coss (98a), cuss, diss (98b), doss (17c), fass (189), fess (23c,51b), foss (44d,100d), fuss (22b,35b), hiss (146a), jass (160d), jess (157a), joss (30b), kiss (148c), koss (188), lass (95b), less (100c,108b,141d), liss (54b,58b,60c,129d,140a), loss (42c,123d,178b), mass (8a,24b, 35b,142d), mess (22b,44b,77c,85d,104b,165c,173d), miss, moss (91d,104c,114a,170c), muss (135b,173d), ness (26b,75a,124b), pass (110b,155c), puss, Riss (66a), ross (16c,161d), Ross (50c), Russ (135b), sass, sess (149c,162b), siss, Tass (107a,135d,151b), Tess (73d,164c,183d), toss (24a,132d), viss (189)

S - - S sais (48d,71d), sans (63a,183b), sass, seis (147b,152c), sens (63b), seps (93b,142d), sess (149c,162b), siss, sons (98d,109b), sors (44d, 89b), sous (62d,172c), spes, Spes (69a,78a), suds (59a)

ST - - stab (14c,87a,117c), stad (151b,167d,176b), stag (65a,98d), star (14a,21c,94c,100c), stat (72d), stay (72d,124c,130a,134a,162a), stem (29b,125a,154d,155a,156d), sten (72c,95a), step (70b,112b, 177b,d), ster (158c,d), stet (91b,123d,124c), stev (155b), stew (21c,44b,184d), stib (19b,47a,137a), stir (8a,13a,35b,78d,100d, 104a), stoa (33c,121a,c), stod (40d,67d), stof (135c), stog (155a), stom (34c), stop (73b,111b), stot (154d,155d,157d,179b,186a), stow (112b), stub (156c), stud (22b,25a,42d,54d,111c,143a,174a), stum (70c,105c,131a,173a), stun (145a,157d), Styx (29b,73a,105c)

- ST - asta (188), Asta (107a,164c), Asti (83d,182b), esta (152d,164c), este (152b,d,164c), Este (55c,83c,d,112d), Esth (16a,51d), oste (21d,83b)

- - ST bast (16c,56a,117b,184a), Bast (27b), best (41d,159c,160a), bust, cast (165b,167c), cest (18a,67b), dost, dust, east, East (111b), erst (60b), fast (56d,126c,141d,160c,173a,d), fest, fist (80c), fust (105c,143b), gest (7c,41d,52d,133c), gist (95c,118c), gust, hast, hest (35a), hist (25c,93d), host (13a,51d,104c), jest (169c), just (51b,54b), kist (29d,58a,139b), last (36c,50b,145a,174c), lest (59d, 163d), list (26d,27b,75b,83d,134a,138b,165d), lost, lust (41b), mast (17c,108d,120b,144d,152d), mist (46b,59b,174d), most, must (70c,101a,106d,157d,182c), Nast (9c,27a), nest (38b,74b,130d,149c,160b), oast (15d,86b,112a), oust (44c, 49a,52b,125d), past (25c,69d,165d), pest (108c,116b,118d,170a), pist (25c), post (89a,95c,155d), rest (15d,91b,104d,105a,115a,b, 130a,b,161b), rust (37b,112c,119a), sist (139b), test (26a,51c,144a, 169c,170c), vast (78d,79d), vest (32c,177d), wast, west, West (9c, 50b,109b), wist (87c), zest (55d,72d)

S - - T sait (35d,105b,123a,136c,141c,149d), Sart (82b,103b,170d), scat (26b,67a,d,126c,169c), scot (14a,162b), Scot (64b,132c), scut (145c,161b), seat (98c,156b), sect (42b,54a,114c), seit (189), sent, sept (31d,82b,143a,149c), Sept (45b), Sert (151d), sett (115a,156d), sext (26b,111b,147b), shat (87d), shot (9d,43d,90c, 174d), shut (89d), sift (140d,142c,146b), silt (104b,142a), skat (181b), Skat (155b), skit (145c), skyt (138c,140b), slat (58b,89a,117c, 184a), slit (40a), slot (10d,11b,41d,110d,167d,168a,181b), smut (32d,44a,119a,150c), soft (48b,95d,99d,163a), soot (20b,26c,88a), Sopt (45b), sort (31d,39c,70b,86b,153a), spat (112c,126b,134b),

spet (16c,57a,142c), **spit** (120a,132b,c), **spot** (93b,118c,154d,162a), **sput** (21c), **stat** (72d), **stet** (91b,123d,124c), **stot** (154d,155d,157d, 179b,186a), **suet** (54d), **suit** (38a,58a,91a,112a,119c,137c), **swat** (15d,20d,32d,157c), **Swat** (103a), **swot**

SU - -   **such** (146d), **suck**, **sudd** (40b,58c,107b), **suds** (59a), **suer** (124d), **suet** (54d), **sufi** (103a,116c), **sugi** (84b), **suit** (38a,58a,91a,112a, 119c,137c), **suji** (180c), **Suku** (191), **Sula** (65a), **suld** (188), **sulk** (159a), **Sulu** (102c), **Sumo**, **sump** (28c,45d,100b), **sung**, **Sung** (30b), **sunk**, **sunn** (56a), **supa** (168c), **supe** (53a,154d), **sura** (87c,113b, 166d), **surd** (82c,177a), **sure** (173d), **surf** (23a), **Susa** (49a), **susi** (53b,d), **susu** (20c), **Susu** (191), **Susy** (183d)

- SU -   **Asur** (68c), **Esus**, **tsun** (30b), **Usun** (191)

- - SU   **ansu** (11d), **Apsu** (29a), **ausu** (168c,180b), **Jesu**, **masu** (57a,84c), **Nosu** (27d), **susu** (20c), **Susu** (191), **vasu** (106c), **Vasu** (176d)

S - - U   **sahu** (153d), **Sgau** (88c), **shou** (41d), **Suku** (191), **Sulu** (102c), **susu** 20c), **Susu** (191)

SV - -   **Svan** (27d)

S - - V   **skiv** (151b), **Slav** (13c,40c,48b,52a,120b,135b), **stev** (155b)

SW - -   **swab** (102b), **swad** (94d), **swag** (22a,156c), **swam**, **swan** (19b,33a), **swap** (168a), **swat** (15d,20d,32d,157c), **Swat** (103a), **sway** (104a), **sweb** (160d), **swig** (46a,72c), **swim** (58c), **swiz** (160c), **swob** (102b), **swop** (168a), **swot**, **swow** (100a), **swum**

S - - W   **scow** (21a,58b), **shaw** (164b), **Shaw** (50c,53b), **shew** (44c), **show** (42b,44c,96b), **skew** (148a,160c,171b,c), **slaw**, **slew** (160a), **slow** (43c), **smew** (19b,46d,99a,137d), **snow**, **spew** (35a,49a), **stew** (21c, 44b,184d), **stow** (112b), **swow** (100a)

S - - X   **spex**, **Styx** (29b,73a,105c)

SY - -   **syce** (71d), **syed** (103b), **syke** (194), **syne** (140b,147a), **sype** (110c), **Syra**, **syud** (103b)

- - SY   **busy**, **cosy** (149c), **easy** (54a,146d,149d,172b), **Josy** (183d), **mosy** (67d), **nosy**, **rosy** (21a,111a), **Susy** (183d)

S - - Y   **sagy**, **shay** (110c), **sidy** (123b), **sizy** (176d), **skey** (185d), **slay**, **sley** (179b), **sory** (176d), **Spey** (7a,107b), **spry** (7a,107b), **stay** (72d,124c,130a, 134a), **Susy** (183d), **sway** (104a)

S - - Z   **sizz**, **swiz** (160c)

TA - -   **Taal** (7d,88c,151a), **taar** (12b), **tabi** (84c,149d), **tabu** (59d,111d), **tace** (13a,155d), **tack** (28d,37d,54d), **tact** (43c,d,116a), **tael** (91d, 179d), **Taft** (29d), **taha** (179b), **tahr** (68a,76d), **tail** (11d,27d,59b, 143b), **tain** (166a), **tair** (68a,76d), **tait** (14d), **tajo** (152a,d), **take**, **takt** (105a,163a), **Taku** (80c), **taky**, **tala** (16d,113a,168c,d), **talc** (28d,63b,99c,100b,122a,149c), **tale** (91a,185b), **tali** (189), **talk**, **tall** (118d), **Tama** (192), **tame** (45a,b,66a), **Tame**, **tamp** (46b,112b, 121d,127d), **tana** (159a), **Tana** (87d), **Tane** (120d), **tang** (30b,58b, 186b), **tanh** (97c), **tank** (175a,d), **Tano** (192), **Taos** (192), **tapa** (16c, 32c,53b,56a,74b,104b,112b,113d,120d), **tape** (16a,19a,128d), **tapu**, **tara** (22a,55c,113a,168c), **Tara** (82b,c,138b), **tare** (9a,18d,41a, 176a,179d), **Tari** (47d,69a), **tarn** (87d,103d,120d), **taro** (13c,48c, 49b,64b,112b,120a,133d,155c,170a,c), **tarp** (26b,178d), **tart** (114d), **tash** (154d), **task** (156b), **Tass** (107a,135d,151b), **tate** (183a), **tatt**

(87c), **tatu** (12d), **Tatu, taun** (188), **taut** (163b,165c), **Tave** (183d), **Tavy** (183d), **tawa** (106d,168c), **taxi** (13a,125b), **taxo** (13a)

- TA - **atap** (113b), **atar** (58d,116b,134a), **Etah** (71d,51c), **etal** (89a), **etat** (62d), **Ptah** (48d,98c), **stab** (14c,87a,117c), **stad** (151b,167d,176b), **stag** (65a,98d), **star** (14a,21c,94c,100c), **stat** (72d), **stay** (72d,124c, 130a,134a,162a), **utac** (22d), **Utah** (180b), **utas** (49a,109c)

-- TA **acta** (41d,123d,128d,164c), **Aeta** (94d,95d,100a,106b,117a), **alta** (89c,152d), **anta** (83d,117c,d,121a), **Anta** (164a), **Arta** (72b), **asta** (188), **Asta** (107a,164c), **atta** (58d,90c,97d,160c,173d), **Atta** (94d,95d,100a,106b,117a), **bata** (30a,142d), **beta** (71a, 91c,141d), **bota** (189), **cata** (122c), **cota** (117a), **data** (54a), **dita** (117a), **esta** (152d,164c), **Etta** (183c), **gata** (143c), **geta** (84b,145a), **Gita, iota** (71a,85c,91c,114c,166c,176a,180d), **jota** (151c), **keta** (45a), **kota** (117a), **Kota** (45d), **lata** (85d, 95d), **iota** (24c,121d,178d), **Lota meta** (132d,133a), **Meta, mota** (103a), **muta** (28d,103a), **nata** (47c), **Nata** (15c), **nota** (15c, 89c), **octa** (122c), **pata** (32c,160d), **pita** (9c,28b,56a,83a), **rata** (29d,56b,89d,96c,106d,120c,168c), **rita, Rita** (37b,78d,183c), **rota** (27c,30d,38a,79a,92d,133a,134a,b,180c), **Ruta** (76b,134d), **seta** (23b,27c,73a,b,123b,153c), **Sita** (127d), **tota** (71d), **veta** (104a), **vita** (89c,92a), **vota** (133b), **weta** (93c), **yeta** (84c), **zeta** (71b,91c)

T -- A **taha** (179b), **tala** (16d,113a,168c,d), **Tama** (192), **tana** (159a), **Tana** (87d), **tapa** (16c,32c,53b,56a,74b,104b,112b,113d,120d), **tara** (22a, 55c,113a,168c), **Tara** (82b,c,138b), **tawa** (106d,168c), **tcha** (162c), **teca, Teca** (192), **Teda** (191), **tela** (22d,98c,121b,166a,179c), **tema** (12a,164a), **Tema, tera** (23d,84c), **tesa** (80c), **Tewa** (193), **Thea** (162c), **Tina** (183d), **tiza** (172a), **Toba** (80c), **Toda** (45d,76d), **toga** (132d,133a,b), **tola** (48a,80d,180a), **Tola** (85b), **Toma** (191), **tooa** (17c), **tora** (11a,44d,74a,75c,85c,90b,102d,115d), **tota** (71d), **toxa** (153d), **tsia** (162c), **tuba** (105a,137d), **tufa** (121b,177a), **tula** (9a), **Tula, tuna** (57a,b,123b), **tuza** (119d)

T -- B **theb** (188), **thob** (128a), **tomb**

TC -- **tcha** (162c), **tche** (13d,30b,105a), **tchi, Tchi, tchu**

- TC - **etch, itch**

T -- C **talc** (28d,63b,99c,100b,122a,149c)

T -- D **tend** (26d,80b,93d,100a), **thud, tied, tind** (86b), **toad** (10a,17a, 63d,126d), **toed, told** (129c), **trod, tund** (121d)

TE -- **teak** (41a,48a,168c), **teal** (19b,20d,46c,d), **team** (38c,72a,113a), **tean** (140c,167a), **tear** (67c,87b,130a), **teca, Teca** (192), **Tech, teck** (128b), **Teco** (192), **Teda** (191), **teel** (142d), **teem** (6b,121d), **teen** (139b,c,140b,158d), **teer** (25b,69d), **Tees** (108a), **teff** (6c), **tegg** (143d,171d), **tehr** (27c,68a), **Teig** (96a), **teil** (92b,c,168c), **teju** (151b), **tela** (22d,98c,121b,166a,179c), **teli** (94b), **tell** (105d,129c,154b), **Tell** (160d), **tema** (12a,164a), **Tema, tend** (26d,80b,93d,100a), **tene** (34d,131b), **teng** (188), **tent** (26b), **Teos** (82a), **tera** (23d,84c), **term** (92b,105b,142b,166b), **tern** (19b,32d,72c,94a,138c,141a,160a), **terp** (12b,123a), **tesa** (80c), **Tess** (73d,164c,183d), **test** (26a,51c,144a,169c,170c), **tete** (61d,73b,74d), **teth** (91d), **Tewa** (193), **text** (21c,140d), **teyl** (92b, c,168c)

404

- TE - atef (39a,48d), aten (150a,159b), Ateo (120d), Ater (18c), ates (160c), Itea (145d,160c,181d), item (6d,13b,42d,51a,90d,92d,107a, 113d,114c), Iten (192), iter (22d,76c,85c,89c,114d,132a,b,133a,b), Otea (71a,82d), stem (29b,125a,154d,155a,156d), sten (72c,95a), step (70b,112b,177b,d), ster (158c,d), stet (91b,123d,124c), stev (155b), stew (21c,44b,184d)

- - TE ante (87a,89a,115b,120b,122b,125d,154d), bate (43c,91b,100d), bete (61a,107c), bite (29d,156b), cate (165c), cete (180b,c), cite (15a,98d,126d,159b), cote (19b,143d,144a,b), cute (39c), date (64a,153a), dite (150b), dote (17a,90b,94b,97a,112a,139d,165d), ente (70b,151d), este (152b,d,164c), Este (55c,83c,d,112d), ette (158a,c,d), fate (42d,52a,87a,94a), fete (55d,129b), fute (51c), gate (51a,121b), gite (62a,118d), hate (6a,43a), jete (16a), jute (37a,48a,56a,133d,136a), Jute, Kate (143c,183d), kite (19c,49a, 74c,d), late (128c), lete, lite (158c,d), lote (24c,94a), lute (11c,28b, 84d,105a,131d), mate (18c,35b,41d,113a,154a,162c), mete (9a, 11d,22b,44c,45b,98a,121c), mite (12b,81b,82a,114a,c,148c,d,181b), mote (114c,153a), mute (146c,153b), Nate (22b), nete (71c,108b, 163d), note (98c,109b,124b,128d,130a,177c), oste (21d,83b), pate (39a,74d), pete (136b), Pete, rate (11d,14a,31d,36b,51d,52a,70b, 85c,112b,123b,127d,128a,138c,143a,174b), rete (106c,119c), rite (93a,131d), rote (130b,134b,143a,159d), rute (188), sate (32d,52c, 67d,70d,137c,159d), site (93b), sote (150c), tate (183a), tete (61d, 73b,74d), tote (27a,73c), tute (171b), vite (62b), vote (60b), Vote (56d), Wate (141a), Wote (191), yate (51d,168c)

T - - E taco (13a,155d), take, tale (91a,185b), tame (45a,b,66a), Tame, Tane (120d), tape (16a,19a,128d), tare (9a,18d,41a,176a,179d), tate (183a), Tave (183d), tche (13d,30b,105a), tele (34b,122c), tene (34d,131b), tete (61d,73b,74d), thee (124b), tice (9a,38c,51a, 185d), tide (39d,75d,109c,141c,159d), tige (118a), tike (29d), tile (31d,56d,72b,95b,133c,163c), time (11b,124b), tine (47a,131a), tipe (168b), tire (15a,22a,52d,55a,179b,180d), tobe (7d, 137b), tode (80a,148a), toie (9a,51a,99b,163a), tome (21d,177c), tone (6c,118c,150d), tope (24a,46b,57a,143c,151a), tore, tote (27a, 73c), tree (11d,37a,66a,184b), true (7a,8d,37b,54b,94c,149c), tube (118b,158a), tuke (26b,53b), tule (24b,27c), tune (8b,12c, 98c), tute (171b), twee, tyee (29d), tyke (29d), tyne, Tyne (108a), type (31d,115a,155a), tyre (15a), Tyre (31b,90d,117b)

T - - F teff (6c), tiff (126b), toff (40d), tref (172b), tuff (121b,177a), turf (115c,149d,160b)

T - - G tang (30b,58b,186b), tegg (143d,171d), Teig (96a), teng- (188), thug (65a), ting (166a), Ting (30c), tong (30a,c,), toug (171a), trig (106a,148d,154b,169d), tung (110a,168c), twig

TH - - Thai (146a), than (35b), thar (68a,76d), that (42b,124b,129c), thaw, Thea (162c), theb (188), thee (124b), them (124b), then, thew (104c), they (124b), thin (43b,c,148b), this (42b,124b), thob (128a), Thor (7c,68c,99c,100c,109c,165b), Thos (84a,181c), thou (124b), thud, thug (65a), thus (149c)

- T H - Otho (133a)

- - TH acth (13b), bath, Bath (50d,151c), beth (91c), Beth (8c,183d), both, doth, Esth (16a,51d), Gath (117a), Goth (16c,163d), hath,

Heth (77c), Hoth (20c), Jeth (102a), kath (14a), klth (63c), lath (157c), lith (34d,156c), loth (15a,173d), math (77a), moth, Moth (112d), muth (188), myth (8b,91a), Nath (155c), oath (119c,150a), path (132a,134b), pith (37a,51c,67b,95c,97a,119b,126d), rath (76d,162d), ruth (35b,118c), Ruth (105b,183c), seth (98d), Seth (7a,52b,68a,b,96a,98d), teth (91d), Urth (68d,107d,163d), Voth (191), with (10b)

T - - H   tanh (97c), tash (154d), Tech, teth (91d), toph (75c), tosh (106a), tush (167b)

Tl - -   Tiam, tiao, tiar (39a,75a,121a), Tibu (191), tice (9a,38c,51a,185d), tick (12b,20d,97c), tide (39d,75d,109c,141c,159d), tidy (106a, 111b), tied, tien (147d), tier (118a,134b), tiff (126b), tige (118a), tike (29d), Tiki (120c), tile (31d,56d,72b,95b,133c,163c), till (39c, 101c,173d), tilt (26b,d,166a), time (47a,131a), Tina (183d), tind (86b), tine (11b,124b,167b), ting (166a), Ting (30c), Tino (136d), tint (33c,d,114d), tiny (100c,148c), tion (158b), Tiou (192), tipe (168b), tipi (181b), tire (15a,22a,52d,55a,179b,180d), tiro (9b,17d, 108c), titi (20d,102a,145d,168d,181b), Tito (186c), tiza (172a)

- Tl -   Atik (155b), atip (14b,166a), atis (76d,102a), itis (158c), otic (14c, d,47b), Otis (9c,d,24d,82a,111a), stib (19b,47a,137a), stir (8a, 13a,35b,78d,100d,104a)

- - Tl   anti (7d,111a,122b), Anti (193), Asti (83d,182b), blti (20b), Guti, Hati (48d), hoti, Inti (159b), jati (27b), jiti, joti, Leti (82d), liti (60d), Loti (63a,176a), neti (164a), rati (189), roti (62c), sati, Sati (49a,126b,147b), seti (34a), Seti (116d), titi (20d,102a,145d,168d, 181b), viti (176b), yati (76d), zati (21d)

T - - I   tabi (84c,149d), tali (189), Tari (47a,69a), taxi (13a,125b), tchi, Tchi, teli (94b), Thai (146a), Tiki (120c), tipi (181b), titi (20d,102a, 145d,168d,181b), topi (37a,75a,118c), tori (101b), tshi, Tshi (69c), Tupi (192), Turi (191), tuwi (117a,168c), Tybi (102a)

- TK -   Atka (11a)

T - - K   tack (28d,37d,54d), talk, tank (175a,d), task (156b), teak (41a, 48a,168c), teck (128b), tick (12b,20d,97c), tock (7d,19b),tonk (173c), took, Tosk (8c), trek (85c,93c,99d,168b), tuck (156b), Turk (101d,102d,106a,111d), tusk (167b)

- TL -   atle (136d,161d,169b), Atli (14c,72b,79a,107d)

- - TL   roti (103b,111c)

T - - L   Taal (7d,88c,151a), tael (91d,179d), tail (11d,27d,59b,143b), tall (118d), teal (19b,20d,46c,d), teel (142d), teil (92b,c,168c), tell (105d,129c,154b), Tell (160d), teyl (92b,c,168c), till (39c,101c, 173d), toil (46c,184c), toll (131c), tool (27c), tuel

TM - -   T-men (168b)

- TM -   atma (150d), atmo (34d,174d), Atmu (143a,159b), itmo (18b)

T - - M   team (38c,72a,113a), teem (6b), term (92b,105b,142b,166b), them (124b), tiam, toom (139b), tram (170a), trim (40a,106a,154b, 160a,165c,169d), turm (132d)

- TN -   etna (75b,153c,157a,175d,177a,c)

T - - N   tain (166a), tarn (87d,103d,120d), taun (188), tean (140c,167a), teen (139b,c;140b,158d), tern (19b,32d,72c,94a,138c,141a,160a),

406

than (35b), then, thin (43b,c,148b), tien (147d), tion (158b), T-men (168b), toon (80c,95b,168c), torn (130a), town (73c), tran (7a), trin (169d), tron (140d,180a), Tsin (30b), tsun (30b), tuan (95d,147b,166c), turn (28d,131a,175a), twin (45c,171d)

TO - - toad (10a,17a,63d,126d), Toba (80c), tobe (7d,137b), toby (8c, 85c,104b), Toby (96b,125c), tock (7d,19b), toco (19b,167c), Toda (45d,76d), tode (80a,148a), todo (22b,24d,35b,64c,156b), tody (19b,d,59a,166a), toed, toff (40d), toga (132d,133a,b), togs (32c), togt (77c), toho (79a), toil (46c,184c), toko (30c), tola (48a,80d,180a), Tola (85b), told (129c), tole (9a,51a,99b,163a), toll (131c), tolt, tolu (16a), Toma (191), tomb, tome (21d,177c), tone (6c,118c,150d), tong (30a,c), tonk (173c), tony, Tony (96b), tooa (17c), took, tool (27c), toom (139b), toon (80c,95b,168c), toot, tope (24a,46b,57a,143c,151a), toph (75c), topi (37a,75a, 118c), tops (159c), tora (11a,44d,74a,75c,85c,90b,102d,115d), tore, tori (101b), torn (130a), toro (38a,107a,152a,168c), torp (54c), tort (31c,91a,185c), Tory (23c,36b,94c,172a), tosh (106a), Tosk (8c), toss (24a,132d), tota (71d), tote (27a,73c), toto (8d,15a,34d, 89a,181a), toty (87b), toug (171a), toup (95d), tour (31b,85c), tout (61a,127a), town (73c), towy (58b), toxa (153d)

- TO - atom (101c,114c,180d), aton (150a,159b), atop (112a,174a), Eton (33b,50c,84a), itol (158b), Otoe (147b), stoa (33c,121a,c), stod (40d,67d), stof (135c), stog (155a), stom (34c), stop (73b,111b), stot (154d,155d,157d,179b,186a), stow (112b), utor (90a,166c)

- - TO acto (152b), alto (152b,176c), auto (34d), bito (7d,57d,168c), Boto (192), Buto (142d), Cato (132d,133b), ceto (34a), cito (89d,126c), coto (16c,90b), dato (95c,102c,117a), Doto (141b), ecto (34c,122d), ento (34b,d), into (123a,183b) jato (173b), koto (84b), Leto (11c), loto (65a,121d,178d), moto (104b), Nato (6a,8d), nito (55c), octo (34a,89b,122c), onto (76a,174a), otto (58d,116b,134a), Otto (14c,66d,67a,96a), pato (46d), peto (57a,177b), Peto (76a), pito (9c,28b,83a), roto (30a,122d,127b,152c,171b), sito (34b), Tito (186c), toto (8d,15a,34d,89a,181a), Tyto (16c), unto (166c), veto (94a,124a), Veto, Voto (192)

T - - O tajo (152a,d), Tano (192), taro (13c,48c,49b,64b,112b,120a,133d, 155c,170a,c), taxo (13a), Teco (192), tiao, Tino (136d), tiro (9b, 17d,108c), Tito (186c), toco (19b,167c), todo (22b,24d,35b,64c, 156b), toho (79a), toko (30c), toro (38a,107a,152a,168c), toto (8d,15a,34d,89a,181a), trio (104d,165a,169c), tuno (28b,168c), typo (35c,51b,123d), tyro (9b,17d,108c), Tyto (16c)

T - - P tamp (46b,112b,121d,127d), tarp (26b,178d), terp (12b,123a), torp (54c), toup (95d), trap (27b,67b,132b,149b), trip (85c), trop (62d,167a), tryp (114a), tump (60a,76d,103d), turp, tymp (20c), typp (185b)

TR - - tram (170a), tran (7a), trap (27b,67b,132b149b), tray (128c, 136d,142d,143c), tree (11d,37a,66a,184b), tref (172b), trek (85c, 93c,99d,168b), tres (19a,52b,63a,152d,165a,175c), tret (9a,178b, 179d), trey (26c,165a), trig (106a,148d,154b,169d), trim (40a,106a,154b,160a,165c,169d), trin (169d), trio (104d,165a, 169c), trip (85c), tris (122d), trit (34d,164c), trod, tron (140d, 180a), trop (62d,167a), trot (85b,93d,112d), trow (18a,21a,159d,

407

164c,170b), **troy** (161c,180a), **Troy, true** (7a,8d,37b,54b,94c,149c), **tryp** (114a)

- TR -   **Atri, atry** (141b), **etre** (61a,c,62d,166c)

- - TR   **natr** (189)

T - - R   **faar** (12b), **tahr** (68a,76d), **tair** (68a,76d), **tear** (67c,87b,130a), **teer** (25b,69d), **tehr** (27c,68a), **thar** (68a,76d), **Thor** (7c,68c,99c, 100c,109c,165b), **tiar** (39a,75a,121a), **tier** (118a,134b), **tour** (31b, 85c), **tsar** (42d,49d,60b,135c), **turr** (24d,105a), **tyer, Tyrr** (68c, 109c,163d,178a), **tzar** (42d,49d,60b,135c)

TS - -   **tsar** (42d,49d,60b,135c), **tshi, Tshi** (69c), **tsia** (162c), **Tsin** (30b), **tsun** (30b)

- - TS   **Acts, arts** (138c), **cits, eats, lots, orts** (60d), **rats**

T - - S   **Taos** (192), **Tass** (107a,135d,151b), **Tees** (108a), **Teos** (82a), **Tess** (73d,164c,183d), **this** (42b,124b), **Thos** (84a,181c), **thus** (149c), **tngs** (32c), **tops** (159c), **toss** (24a,132d), **tres** (19a,52b,63a,152d,165a, 175c), **tris** (122d)

- TT -   **atta** (58d,90c,97d,160c,173d), **Atta** (94d,95d,100a,106b,117a), **Attu, Etta** (183c), **ette** (158a,c,d), **otto** (58d,116b,134a), **Otto** (14c,66d,67a,96a)

- - TT   **batt** (37c), **bitt** (54d,175c), **bott** (32a,88d), **butt** (27a,77b,127c, 162a,182b), **Catt** (9d), **gett** (44d), **Lett** (16a,90a,93a), **Matt, mitt** (56c), **mutt** (39c,101d), **Natt** (107b), **nett, Nott** (107b), **Pitt** (50d,155d), **pott** (113d), **putt** (69d), **sett** (115a,156d), **tatt** (87c), **watt** (173b,177c), **Watt** (82a)

T - - T   **tact** (43c,d,116a), **Taft** (29d), **tait** (14d), **takt** (105a,163a), **tart** (114d), **tatt** (87c), **taut** (163b,165c), **tent** (26b,115a), **test** (26a, 51c,144a,169c,170c), **text** (21c,140d), **that** (42b,124b,129c), **tilt** (26b,d,166a), **tint** (33c,d,114d), **todt** (66b), **tolt, toot, tort** (31c,91a,185c), **tout** (61a,127a), **tret** (9a,178b,179d), **trit** (34d,164c), **trot** (85b,93d,112d), **tuft** (24b,32d,38c), **twit** (162b,c)

TU - -   **tuan** (95d,147b,166c), **tuba** (105a,137d), **tube** (118b,158a), **tuck** (156b), **tuel** (121b,177a), **tufa** (121b,177a), **tuff** (121b,177a), **tuft** (24b,32d, 38c), **tuke** (26b,53b), **tula** (9a), **Tula, tule** (24b,27c), **Tulu** (45d), **tump** (60a,76d,103d), **tuna** (57a,b,123b,170d), **tund** (121d), **tune** (8b,12c,98c), **tung** (110a,168c), **tuno** (28b,168c), **tunu** (28b), **tuny, Tupi** (192), **turf** (115c,149d,160b), **Turi** (191), **Turk** (101d,102d, 106a,111d), **turm** (132d), **turn** (28d,131a,175a), **turp, turr** (24d, 105a), **tush** (167b), **tusk** (167b), **tute** (171b), **tutu** (16a,106d,147d), **tuwi** (117a,168c), **tuza** (119d)

- TU -   **atua** (120d), **Atum** (143a,159b), **etui** (27a,29b,62c,106b,148d, 166d,174b), **Otus** (67a), **stub** (156c), **stud** (22b,25a,42d,54d,111c, 143a,174a), **stum** (70c,105c,131a,173a), **stun** (145a,157d), **Utug** (159b), **utum** (19b,112c)

- - TU   **actu** (7a,89a), **Attu, datu** (95c,102c,117a), **Ketu** (48b), **latu** (190), **mitu** (39d), **patu** (179b), **tatu** (12d), **Tatu, tutu** (16a,106d,147d), **yutu** (19b,166a)

T - - U   **tabu** (59d,111d), **Taku** (80c), **tapu, tatu** (12d), **Tatu, tchu, teju** (151b), **thou** (124b), **Tibu** (191), **Tiou** (192), **tolu** (16a), **Tulu** (45d), **tunu** (28b), **tutu** (16a,106d,147d)

TW - - **twee, twig, twin** (45c,171d), **twit** (162b,c)

T - - W **thaw, thew** (104c), **trow** (18a,21a,159d,164c,170b)

TY - - **Tybi** (102a), **tyee** (29d), **tyer, tyke** (29d), **tymp** (20c), **tyne, Tyne** (108a), **type** (31d,115a,155a), **typo** (35c,51b,123d), **typp** (185b), **typy, tyre** (15a), **Tyre** (31b,90d,117b), **tyro** (9b,17d,108c), **Tyrr** (68c,109c,163d,178a), **Tyto** (16c)

- TY - **etym** (133d), **Itys** (163b), **Styx** (29b,73a,105c)

- - TY **arty, city, Coty** (63c), **doty** (43d), **duty** (109b,162b), **Katy** (183d), **maty** (80c), **mity, pity** (35b), **toty** (87b)

T - - Y **taky, Tavy** (183d), **they** (124b), **tidy** (106a,111b), **tiny** (100c,148c), **toby** (8c,85c,104b), **Toby** (96b,125c), **tody** (19b,d,59a,166a), **tony, Tony** (96b), **tory, Tory** (23c,36b,94c,172a), **toty** (87b), **towy** (58b), **tray** (128c,136d,142d,143c), **trey** (26c,165a), **troy** (161c,180a), **Troy, tuny, typy**

TZ - - **tzar** (42d,49d,60b,135c)

- TZ - **Itza** (192)

- - TZ **batz** (190), **litz** (127b), **untz** (189)

UA - - **uang** (131a)

- UA - **bual** (182c), **duab** (157c), **duad** (171d), **dual** (45c,171d), **duan** (64b), **duar, Duat** (172d), **Fuad** (54d), **Guam, guan** (151b), **guao** (168c,169b), **guar** (46c,59d), **juan** (113a), **Juan** (96a), **juar** (100a), **kuan** (30b), **Kuan** (30c), **Kuar** (102a), **Muav** (66a), **quad** (33c,172a), **quae** (176b), **quag** (21c,102c), **quai** (88b,117c,180c), **quan** (190), **quas** (135c), **quay** (88b,117c,180c), **ruay** (189), **tuan** (95d,147b, 166c), **yuan** (190), **Yuan** (30b,101d)

- - UA **agua** (152d,166c,178c), **akua** (120d), **aqua** (90a,178c), **atua** (120d), **Erua** (103c), **skua** (19b,72c,84a,141a), **ulua** (57a,74c), **Ulua** (141b)

U - - A **ueba** (188), **ulna** (21d,39b), **ulua** (57a,74c), **Ulua** (141b), **Ulva** (141b), **unca** (49a), **upla, Urfa** (99a), **Uria** (14c,16d), **urna** (133a), **Ursa** (17b,36b,43d), **urva** (38b), **Usha** (16a,150c), **uvea** (53c,82b)

UB - - **uber** (66b), **Ubii** (191)

- UB - **buba** (170a), **Bube** (180b), **Bubi** (180b), **Bubo** (112c), **cuba** (189), **Cuba** (180b), **cube** (66b,150a), **cubi** (188), **dubb** (161c), **hubb** (118b), **juba** (106b), **jube** (28d), **kuba** (26d,189), **Luba** (191), **lube** (110a), **Lubs** (94c), **Nuba** (108c), **nubk** (30d,164d), **rube** (37d, 135d,185d), **Rube** (96b), **ruby** (20a,65d,179c), **tuba** (105a,137d), **tube** (118b,158a)

- - UB **blub, chub** (40c,154c), **club** (39c), **daub** (148d), **doub** (189), **drub** (17b,39c), **flub** (22b), **gaub** (116c), **glub, grub** (43c,88d), **knub** (178b), **slub** (171c), **snub** (128c,148b), **stub** (156c)

- UC - **Auca** (192), **buck, cuca** (33a,105d), **duce** (29d), **duck** (26b,53b, 179c), **Duco, duct** (170c), **fuci** (132c), **huck** (167d), **juca** (27a), **juck** (114c), **luce** (58c,117d), **Luce** (7b,35a), **luck** (28d), **lucy, Lucy** (183c), **much, muck, ouch!, puca** (68a), **puce** (33c,d,52a), **puck** (44b,68a,77c,100c), **Puck** (99d,143b), **ruck** (39a,185a), **such** (146d), **suck, tuck** (156b), **yuca** (27a)

- - UC **douc** (101d), **eruc** (37a,56a)

U - - C **Udic** (108a), **Utac** (22d)

UD - -   udad (143d,144a,181c), udal (76b,88b,131c), Udie (108a)

- UD -   Aude, buda (83d), Buda, dude (40d), duds (32c,166d), Juda, Jude (11c,96a), judo (84b,85c,142b), Judy (125c,183d), kudu (11a), Ludd (23c), ludi (133b), ludo (65a,112b), mudd (188), nuda (39b), Nudd (23c), nude (16c,172d), pudu (41d), rudd (26d,57a,b), rude (134b,172b), sudd (40b,58c,107b), suds (59a), wudu (102d)

- - UD   baud (162d), Chud (191), feud (55d,126b,175b), foud (54d,144b), gaud (169d), laud (122a), loud (156a), maud (53d,71a,136d,143c), Maud (181a,183c), Phud (110b), puud (189), roud (57a,b), scud (32c,126c,135b,160c), spud (121d,151c), stud (22b,25a,42d,54d, 111c,143a,174a), syud (103b), thud

U - - D   udad (143d,144a,181c), used (6d,73a), uvid (101a)

UE - -   ueba (188)

- UE -   Auer (79a), duel, duet (104d,171d), euer (66c), fuel (65c), hued, juez (152b), kuei (44a), quei (189), ruer, suer (124d), suet (54d), tuei

- - UE   ague (30a,55d,95c), blue (33c,98c,102c,150d,173a), clue, flue (8b,30a), gaue (67a), glue (7b,156a), moue (61d,62b), neue (66c), Niue (137d), roue (41b,44c,127c,134b), slue (97b,148b,160a), true (7a,8d,37b,54b,94c,149c)

U - - E   ulme (49c), unde (179a), unie (173a), unze (189), urde (86b), urge (42d,46b,79d,80a,b,81c,150a), usee

- UF -   buff (134c,161d), Bufo (166c), cuff (148a), duff (125b), Dufy (63a), gufa (21b,99a), guff (58a), huff (58a), kufa (21b,99a), luff (136b), muff, puff, (180d), ruff (19b,33b,63d,137a), sufi (103a, 116c), tufa (121b,177a), tuff (121b,177a), tuft (24b,32d,38c), yuft (135c)

- - UF   pouf, souf (146b)

UG - -   ugly

- UG -   auge (123c,132b), Bugi (191), euge (180a), fuga, fugu (84b), gugu, huge, Hugh (96a), Hugo (63a,96a), juga (27a), kuge (84c), luge (148a), Lugh (28b), muga (84b), ough, pugh (84b), ruga (59b,185a), sugi (84b), vugg (28a,66a,132b), vugh (28a,66a,132b), Yuga (76d)

- - UG   chug (53a), drug (105d), glug, joug (138d), plug (156b,184d), slug (46b,99b,157c), smug, snug (35a,38b,165c), Snug (99d), thug (65a), toug (171a), Utug (159b)

U - - G   uang (131a), Utug (159b)

- UH -   buhl (81a), buhr (180d), Duhr (155b), Guha (191), guhr (47d), kuhl (53c), Ruhr

- - UH   bruh (95a)

U - - H   umph, Urth (68d,107d,163d), Utah (180b)

- UI -   cuif (139a,d,140c), cuir (45c,62a), duim (188), duit (190), Duit (192), guib (11a), huia (19a,106d), luif, Muir (8b,142c), nuit (62b), quid (39b,166d), quip (183a,b), quit (90d,130c), quiz, ruin (42d), suit (38a,58a,91a,112a,119c,137c), Yuit (51c)

- - UI   arui (11b,143d,144a,181c), equi (122d), etui (27a,29b,62c,106b, 148d,166d,174b), Maui (120d)

410

U - - I   Ubii (191), unci (31d)

- UJ -   fuji (84b), Fuji (84d), juju (29b,55d), puja (77a), suji (180c)

- UK -   bukh (122a), bukk (122a), cuke (39b), duke (107c), duku (95d, 168c), juke (114c), Kuki (191), kuku (19a,106d), luke, Luke (52a,96a), puka (107a,168c), puku (11a), rukh (53b,54a), Suku (191), tuke (26b,53b), wukf (103a)

- - UK   cauk (139b), dauk (95c), Sauk (192), souk (22a,97a)

UL - -   Ulam (67b), ulan (27d,88a), Ulex (153c), ullo (6a,144a), Ullr (146b,164d), ulme (49c), ulna (21d,39b), ulua (57a,74c), Ulua (141b), Ulva (141b)

- UL -   aula (66c,73b), aulu (74c,168c), bulb 37a,172c), bulk (97b), bull (113c), bult (76d), cull (117c), culm (11a,32d,70d,145a,156a), cult (141d,161c), dull (21a,32c,173a), Dull (94b), fulk (173a), full (7b, 130b), gula (90a,101a,165b), gulf (6c), gull (32d,41c,42a,72c,99b, 141a), Gulo (183c), gulp (46a,79d,160a), hula (74b) hule, (23a, 134c), hulk (144d,173d), hull (141d,142a,144c,d), hulu (55b), jula, Jule (183d), July, kula (189), Kuli (27b), lull (25c,126d,150c), lulu (19a,57b,112c), Lulu (183d), mule (45b,148b,153c,180b), mulk (60d), mull (53b,135a,164c), null (108c,177a), pule (180d), pulk (37c,88d), pull (45d,167d), pulp, pulu (74c), puly, rule (11b,26b,90b), rull (170b), Sula (65a), suld (188), sulk (159a), Sulu (102c), tula (9a), Tula, tule (24b,27c), Tulu (45d), vuln (184d), Yule (30d), zulu (171d,175d), Zulu (86a)

- - UL   Aoul (191), azul (151d), baul (18b), caul (16d,74d), deul (77b), Elul (102b), foul (173a), Gaul (10a,60d,63c), goul (102a), haul (27b,45d), maul (73c,96b), paul, Paul (96a), poul (190), saul (48a, 168c), Saul (18c,86d,115a), shul (161a), soul (10d,125a,153c, 176d)

U - - L   udal (76b,88b,131c), unal (147a), Ural (135c), uval (70c)

UM - -   umbo (22b), umph

- UM -   bump, Duma (135c), dumb (153b), dump, fume (129a,149a,157a), fumy, Gump (43b), Hume (50c), hump (124d), jump, lump (45a, 160c), mump (29b,153d), Numa (133a), numb, puma (27b,37c,55b, 103d), Pume (137b,175b,185b), pump, rumb (120b), rump, Sumo, sump (28c,45d), tump (60a,76d,103d), Yuma

- - UM   ahum, alum (14a,45c), arum (13a,39b,58d,92b,155c), Arum (66a), Atum (143a,159b), Baum (9c,112c), chum (38d), doum (168c), drum (105a), Geum (76b), glum (102c,159a), grum (102c), jhum, meum (27a,89c), Meum, odum (168c,180a), ogum (82b), ovum (48d), plum, rhum (8c), saum (189), scum (129b), slum, stum (70c,105c,131a,173a), swum, Ulam (67b), utum (19b,112c)

U - - M   urim (18d,23a,110a), utum (19b,112c)

UN - -   unal (147a), unau (148c,171d), unca (49a), unci (31d), unco (140c), unde (179a), undo (11a,93d), undy (179a), unie (173a), Unio (105c), unis (91b), unit (101c,110c,147a), unto (166c), untz (189), unze (189)

- UN -   aune (188), aunt (129c), buna (161c), bund (49c,66c,90c), bung (119d,156d), bunk (25b), bunt (15d,180c), Cuna (193), dune (137a), dunk (43c,79d), Duns, dunt, fund (6d,101c,130c), Fung

411

(191), Funj, funk (63d,113c), guna (106a,137b), gunj (70c), hung, hunh?, hunk, hunt (141c), June (183c), Jung (125a), junk (30a, 134c), Juno (69c,85d,100c,126b), kung (125b), kunk (188), luna 103c), Luna (102b), lune (38c,73b,74d), lung, luny (38b), mund (124d), mung (70d), munj (70d), paun (18b), puna (10b,33b,104a, 119b,182a), pund (189), pung (22c,148b), punk (9b,166a,167c), puno (182a), punt (21a,58b), puny (55b,179a), Qung (191), rune (9b,67a,94a,105c,107d,120a,141d,163d), rung (28c,39a), runt (47a172d), sung, Sung (30b), sunk, sunn (56a), tuna (57a,b,123b, 170d), tund (121d), tune (8b,12c,98c), tung (110a,168c), tuno (28b,168c), tunu (28b), tuny, Yunx (184a), Zuni (125b)

-- UN Amun (86d,127d,159b,164a), Chun (30c), drun (132b), faun (56a, 68b,137c,161a,184a), Idun (107d), jaun (113a), kaun (93d), laun (146b), loun (19a,b), maun (139d), noun (114b,158a), paun (18b), shun (15a,51b,52a), spun, stun (145a,157d), taun (188), tsun (30b), Usun (191), whun (64c,70a)

U -- N ulan (27d,88a), upon (6b), uran (101d), Usun (191), uzan (189)

- UO - buoy (28d,58c), quod (123d)

U -- O ullo (6a,144a), umbo (22b), unco (140c), undo (11a,93d), Unio (105c), unto (166c), upgo (13c)

UP -- upas (84d,120b,168c,d), upgo (13c), Upis (13b), upla, upon (6b)

- UP - dupe (27c,41c,72c,160c), Hupa (192), jupe (62b,84a), lupe (19a, 64a), Nupe (191), pupa (30d,81b,c), rupa (60b), supa (168c), supe (53a,154d), Tupi (192)

-- UP blup, caup, coup (20d,97c,157b,c,162d), gaup, loup (61d,62a,90c, 139d), Loup (193), noup (124b), plup, roup (44a,121d), scup (57a, 121b), snup (149b), soup, toup (95d), yaup, youp (185d)

UR -- Ural (135c), uran (101d), urde (86b), Urdu (77b), urdy (86b), Urey (17b,36b,43d), Urth (68d,107d,163d), urus (14d,53a,112c), urva 150a), Uria (14c,16d), urim (18d,23a,110a), urna (133a), Ursa (17b,36b,43d), Urth (68d,107d,163d), urus (14d,53a,112c), urva (38b)

- UR - aura (44c,49c,66a,96b,158a,170d,177c), auri (34a), bura (182b), bure (61b), burg (22b,73c), buri (56b), burl (87c,169a), burn, burr (123b), bury (81d), cura (152c), curb (130c,146b), curd (99d), cure (123b), curl (38d,73b,131d), curr (104c), curt (145b,c), dura (153c), duro (190), durr (70b), furl (132d), fury (157a), guru (77b), hura (20a,137a), Hura, hurl (167c), hurt, jura, Jura, jure (90b), jury (38a), Kurd (48b,82a), Kure (84c), Kuri (191), kurk (31a,139b), lura (22d,82a), lure (41c,51a,54b,163a), lurg (96d,141b,184d), Luri (191), lurk (92a,147d), mura (84d), Mura (192), mure (177d), murk (41a,67d), murr (72b,128c), nurl (33b,87c), nurr (67d), ours (124c), pure (29b,172b,173c), puri (80d), puri (87c,104c), purr (104c), Puru (192), ruru (19b,102c,106b), sura (87c,113b,166d), surd (82c,177a), sure (173d), surf (23a), turf (115c,149d,160b), Turi (191), Turk (101d,102d,106a,111d), turm (132d), turn (28d, 131a,175a), turp, turr (24d,105a), Wurd, wurm (67c), yurt (101d)

-- UR Alur (191), Asur (68c), biur (35a), blur, caur (139a), Daur (139b), dour (67d,159a), ebur (89c), four (26c), gaur (112c,181c), gour (112c,181c), hour, knur (67d,87c,107c), lour (13d,63d), peur (61c),

412

pour (162d), scur (78b), slur (44b,124c,148b,168a), smur (32c,46b, 100c), sour, spur (10d,67d,167d,168a,181b), tour (31b,85c), your (124c)

U - - R uber (66b), Ulir (146b,164d), usar (8d,16c), user (49d), utor (90a, 166c)

US - - usar (8d,16c), Usas (68d), used (6d,73a), usee, user (49d), uses (18a), Usha (16a,150c), Usun (191)

- US - Ausa, ausu (168c,180b), bush, busk (17b,37b,55d,161b), buss (87a,148c), bust, busy, cush (101c), Cush (51d,73c), cusk (57b), cusp (38c,78b,119a,120a,b), cuss, duse (83c), dusk (171c), dust, fuse (98c), fuss (22b,35b), fust (105c,143b), gush (35a,154c), gust, huse (180c), hush (17b,146c), husk (53a,78d,142a), huso (180c), Just (51b,54b), kusa, Kush, lush (94d), lust (41b), Musa (16a), muse (65b,93d,120d,164c), Muse (68d), mush (97d), musk (116b), Muso (192), muss (135b,173d), must (70c,101a,106d,157d,182c), Ouse (132a,185d), oust (44c,49a,52b,125d), push, (145c) puss, rusa, Rusa (41d,136d), ruse (13b,77c,157b,169c), rush, rusk (23a), Russ (135b), rust (37b,112c,119a), Susa (49a), susi (53b,d), susu (20c), Susu (191), Susy (183d), tush (167b), tusk (167b),

- - US acus (89d,118a), Apus (36b,c), avus (89b), cous (38a), crus (91a, 143c), deus (68a,89b), Esus, gaus (67a), Grus (36b,c,38b), ilus (88d,170b), irus (109d), nous (81d,100a,128b), onus (24c,93b,109b), opus (35c,105a,184c), Otus (67a), Pius (121a), plus (10b, 102c), pous (188), Rhus (159a), sous (62d,172c), thus (149c), urus (14d,53a,112c), Zeus (135a)

U - - S unis (91b), upas (84d,120b,168c,d), Upis (13b), urus (14d,53a, 112c), uses (18a), Usas (68d), utas (49a,109c)

UT - - utac (22d), Utah (180b), utas (49a,109c), utor (90a,166c), Utug (159b), utum (19b,112c)

- UT - auto (34d), Buto (142d), butt (27a,77b,127d,162a,182b), cute (39c), duty (109b,162b), fute (51c), Guti, jute (37a,48a,56a,133d, 136a), Jute, lute (11c,28b,84d,105a,131d), muta (28d,103a), mute (146c,153b), muth (188), mutt (39c,101d), putt (69d), Ruta (76b, 134d), rute (188), ruth (35b,118c), Ruth (105b,183c), tute (171b), tutu (16a,106d,147d), yutu (19b,166a)

- - UT abut (22a,167c), bhut (67a), blut (66b), bout (36c), brut (182c), Brut (23c), chut!, Cnut (40d,50c), gaut (88b,103d,132a), glut (52c,70a,137c,159d), gout, knut, Knut (40d,50c,96a), lout (15c, 22a,24b,45b,109a,157d), naut (141b), paut (140a), phut (24b), Phut (110b), pout (159a), prut!, Prut (41a), rout (41d,44b,46b), scut (145c,161b), shut, smut (32d,44a,119a,150c), sput (21c), taut (163b,165c), tout (61a,127a)

U - - T unit (101c,110c,147a)

- UU - puud (189)

U - - U unau (148c,171d), Urdu (77b)

UV - - uval (70c), uvea (53c,82b), uvic (70c), uvid (101a)

- UV - cuvy (141a)

- UW - tuwi (117a,168c)

- - UW bouw (188), dauw (24c)

413

- UX - **buxy** (115b), **luxe** (61c,62d,159c), **puxy**

- - UX **crux** (39a,151b), **eaux** (178c), **flux** (28d,58d), **jeux** (61d), **Vaux** (63b)

U - - X **Ulex** (153c)

- UY - **buyo** (18b), **cuya** (39b), **Puya** (118b)

U - - Y **ugly**, **undy** (179a), **urdy** (86b), **Urey** (14b,107c,138c)

UZ - - **uzan** (189)

- UZ - **auzu** (168c,180b), **buzz**, **fuse** (98c), **fuzz** (45d), **guze** (128d), **huzz**, **Juza** (155b), **Muzo** (192), **tuza** (119d), **wuzu** (102d), **zuza** (189)

- - UZ **Ghuz** (171a)

U - - Z **untz** (189)

VA - - **Vach** (153b), **vade** (42c,67d,89b), **vagi** (38b), **vail** (94b,124a,174b), **vain** (81a), **vair** (64c,154c), **vale** (54c,128a,174b), **Vale** (7c,109c), **vali** (171a,176a), **Vali** (7c,109c), **vamp** (80a,145a), **vane** (179b, 182a), **vang** (72d,134a,140b), **Vans** (107d), **vara** (151d), **vare** 179b), **vari** (34d,91b,134d,174d), **vary** (28d,43c), **vasa** (46d,114a, 160b,175d), **Vasa**, **vase**, **vast** (78d,79d), **vasu** (106c), **Vasu** (176d), **Vaux** (63b), **Vayu** (68c,182a), **vaza** (114a)

- VA - **aval** (70c), **Avar** (27d,108a), **Evan** (96a), **ivah** (18d), **Ivan** (40c, 85b,96a), **kvas** (135c), **oval** (48d,49c,127a), **Svan** (27d), **uval** (70c)

- - VA **Alva** (151d), **cava** (116a,175b), **Civa** (56d), **deva** (23d,42a,42b, 56d,77a), **diva** (100d,123c), **Hova** (95a), **Java** (33a), **jiva** (77a), **Jova** (193), **kava** (18c,116a), **kiva** (28c,125b), **lava** (101c,151a, 177a), **Neva** (91b,132a), **nova** (20c,106d,155c,174d), **peva** (12d), **siva** (67a), **Siva** (56d,77a), **Ulva** (141b), **urva** (38b), **viva** (93d), **Xova** (193), **yava**

V - - A **vara** (151d), **vasa** (46d,114a,160b,175d), **Vasa**, **vaza** (114a), **Veda** (77a,b), **vega** (110d,152c), **Vega** (155b), **vela** (98c,136b,149d), **Vela** (36b,c), **vena** (90a,175a), **vera** (140c,151b,175c), **Vera** (183c), **veta** (104a), **Vida** (183c), **vila** (54b), **vina** (77a,105a), **Vira** (191), **visa** (114d), **vita** (89c,92a), **viva** (93d), **vola** (89d,150a), **vota** (133b)

V - - B **verb** (7a,114b,184b)

- - VD **NKVD** (135d)

V - - D **veld** (151a), **vend** (97a,115c,142b), **Vend** (10b,148a), **verd** (71d), **void** (11a,49d,108d,174b)

VE - - **veal**, **Veda** (77a,b), **veer** (28d,144c,171b), **vega** (110d,152c), **Vega** (155b), **veil** (74d,76c), **vein** (20d,157b), **vela** (98c,136b,149d), **Vela** (36b,c), **veld** (151a), **velo** (175b), **vena** (90a,175a), **vend** (97a, 115c,142b), **Vend** (10b,148a), **vent** (8b,11b,110d,112a), **Veps** (191), **vera** (140c,151b,175c), **Vera** (183c), **verb** (7a,114b,184b), **verd** (71d), **veri** (28b), **vert** (71d,166a,171b), **very** (149c), **vest** (32c, 177b), **veta** (104a), **veto** (94a,124a), **Veto**

- VE - **avec** (63a,183a), **aver** (7c,14a,15c,41c,95c,140d,155c,160b,184c), **Aves** (19d), **evea** (82a,95a), **even** (51a,58b,79d,91d,149a,173a), **ever** (9b,14b,80b), **evet** (48d,107a,136c,169d), **Ives** (9c,90b), **oven** (15d,78c,86b), **over** (6b,38c,80a,114d,130a), **uvea** (53c,82b)

- - VE **bave** (61d,146c), **cave** (27d), **cive** (110c), **cove** (17a,73d,107d),

414

Dave (96b), **dive** (42b,74b,119d), **dove** (19a,117d), **eave** (133c), **five, gave, give** (79d,123a), **gyve** (55d,143b), **have** (92a), **hive** (17c), **hove** (92a), **Jave** (84d), **jive** (160c), **jove** (85d), **kive** (174d), **lave** (16d,178b), **leve** (47c), **love** (163a), **move, nave** (30d,31a,78d,114b,180c), **neve** (56d,67c,70c,149b), **nove** (83b), **pave** (85a), **rave** (41c,157a,161d), **reve** (61c,104d), **rive** (32a,153d), **rove** (127d,132b,178a), **save** (52b,110c,123a,173c), **seve** (63a, 182c), **sive** (146a), **Tave** (183d), **vive** (93d), **wave** (19a,59a,111c, 131d,160c,172d), **wive** (97a), **wove**

V - - E   **vade** (42c,67d,89b), **vale** (54c,128a,174b), **Vale** (7c,109c), **vane** (179b,182a), **vare** (179b), **vase**, **vice** (31d,158a), **vide** (89d,126a, 142a), **vile** (16c,56c), **vine** (32b), **vire** (11a,13b), **vise** (31d,77d, 114d), **vite** (62b), **vive** (93d), **voce** (83c,177a), **vole** (97d,104a, 148a,149b), **vote** (60b), **Vote** (56d)

V - - G   **vang** (72d,134a,140b), **voog** (28a,66a,132b), **vugg** (28a,66a,132b)

- - VH   **IHVH** (159d), **JHVH** (159d), **YHVH** (159d)

V - - H   **Vach** (153b), **Voth** (191), **vugh** (28a,66a,132b)

VI - -   **vial** (148c), **vice** (31d,158a), **Vida** (183c), **vide** (89d,126a,142a), **vier** (66c), **view** (93d,138b), **vila** (54b), **vile** (16c,56c), **vili** (54b), **Vili** (109c), **vill** (176b), **vily** (54b), **vina** (77a,105a), **vine** (32b), **vino** (92d,182b), **vint** (26c,182c), **viny**, **viol** (105a), **Vira** (191), **vire** (11a,13b), **visa** (114d), **vise** (31d,77d,114d), **viss** (189), **vita** (89c, 92a), **vite** (62b), **viti** (176b), **viva** (93d), **vive** (93d), **vivo** (93a)

- VI -   **avid** (47b,71a,186b), **avis** (89a), **Avis** (183c), **evil** (79c,95d,147a, 181a,185c), **Ovid** (132d,133b), **Ovis** (143d), **uvic** (70c), **uvid** (101a)

- - VI   **Devi** (147b,153b), **divi, favi** (138a,165d), **hevi** (111d), **Kavi** (84d), **Levi** (84a,90c), **ravi** (61b), **Ravi** (16b)

V - - I   **vagi** (38b), **vali** (171a,176a), **Vali** (7c,109c), **vari** (34d,91b,134d, 174d), **veri** (28b), **vili** (54b), **Vili** (109c), **viti** (176b), **vlei** (38c,160a)

V - - K   **volk** (66c,105d,116a,184c)

VL - -   **vlei** (38c,160a), **vley** (160a)

V - - L   **vail** (94b,124a,174b), **veal, veil,** (74d,76c), **vial** (148c), **vill** (176b), **viol** (105a)

V - - N   **vain** (81a), **vein** (20d,157b), **vuln** (184d)

- VO - -   **voce** (83c,177a), **voet** (188), **Vogt, void** (11a,49d,108d,174b), **vola** (89d,150a), **vole** (97d,104a,148a,149b), **volk** (66c,105d,116a,184c), **volt** (49b,78c,173b), **voog** (28a,66a,132b), **vota** (133b), **vote** (60b), **Vote** (56d), **Voth** (191), **Voto** (192)

- VO -   **Avon** (143b), **Avow** (6d,36a,41c,112c), **evoe** (15b,130d,181c)

- - VO   **levo** (91a), **pavo** (115b), **Pavo** (36b,c), **vivo** (93a)

V - - O   **velo** (175b), **veto** (94a,124a), **Veto, vino** (92d,182b), **vivo** (93a), **Voto** (192)

V - - P   **vamp** (80a,145a)

V - - R   **vair** (64c,154c), **veer** (28d,144c,171b), **vier** (66c)

- - VS   **revs** (131a)

V - - S   **Vans** (107d), **Veps** (191), **viss** (189)

V - - T   **vast** (78d,79d), **vent** (8b,11b,110d,112a), **vert** (71d,166a,171b), vest (32c,177b), vint (26c,182c), voet (188), Vogt, volt (49b,78c, 173b)

VU - - vugg (28a,66a,132b), vugh (28a,66a,132b), vuln (184d)

- VU - avus (89b), ovum (48d)

- - VU kivu (170c)

V - - U vasu (106c), Vasu (176d), Vayu (68c,182a)

V - - W view (93d,138b)

V - - X Vaux (63b)

- - VY bevy (38a,58c), cavy (72b,120d,132c,157b), cuvy (141a), Davy (96b,136b), envy (41b), levy (14a,162b), Livy (132d,133a), navy (33c,58b), pavy (115b), pevy (91d,94c), Tavy (183d), wavy (147b, 172d)

V - - Y vary (28d,43c), very (149c), vily (54b), viny, vley (160a)

WA - - Waac, waag (71d,101d), Wabi (192), Waco, wadd (109c), wade, wadi (46c,106a,109a,128a,132a), wady (109a,128a,132a), waeg (19b,72c,87a), waer (40b), Wafd (49a), waft (20d,58c), wage (27a, 115b), waif (157b), wail (39b,88a), wain (177b), Wain, wait (26d, 42b,92c,155d,162a), waka (26a), wake (134b,168a), wakf (103a), waky (26a), wale (70b,131b,157c,163d,179a,180a,c,d), wali (171a), walk, wall, Walt (96b), wand (120b,132c,156a), wane (41c,43c), wang (189), want (41b,42d,87b,106b,122a), wany, wapp (54b,133d, 145d), waqf (103a), ward (31c,55c,86b), ware (27d,35a), warf, warm (7c,75b,163b), warn (7b), warp (36c,165a,171c), wart (124d), wary (27d,176b), wash, wasp, wast, Wate (141a), watt (173b, 177c), Watt (82a), wave (19a,59a,111c,131d,160c,172d), wavy (147b,172d), waxy (119c,149d), ways

- WA - Awan (191), away (6b,69d,76a,109d,111d), Ewan, kwan (30b), swab (102b), swad (94d), swag (22a,156c), swam, swan (19b,33a), swap (168a), swat (15d,20d,32d,157c), Swat (103a), sway (104a)

- - WA biwa (93d,168c), dewa, Iowa (193), kawa (18c,116a), Iowa (19a), pawa (189), tawa (160d,168c), Tewa (193)

W - - A waka (26a), Wega (155b), weka (58c,106d,107a,127b), weta (93c), whoa (156d)

W - - C Waac

- - WD dowd (143b), gawd (169c)

W - - D wadd (109c), Wafd (49a), wand (120b,132c,156a), ward (31c,55c, 86b), week, weld (47c,85b,173c), wend (67d,123d), Wend (10b, 148a), wild (38b,173d), wind (33b,39d,171c,185a), woad (20d,47c), wold (47c,60a,118d,174a,184a), wood, word (124b,165c), Wurd, Wyrd (107d)

WE - - weak (55b), weal (124d,157c,180c,d), wean (8d,42d), wear (50b), weed, week, weel (16d,57d,140d,180d), weep (39b,88a,104a), weet (19d), weft (39a,165a,184b), Wega (155b), Wegg (111d), weir (40b,57d), weka (58c,106d,107a,127b), weki (55c), weld (47c,85b, 173c), Welf (67a), welk (65c,96d,141b), well (36d,131b,145a, b,177b,d), wend (67d,123d), Wend (10b,148a), went (42c), wept, were (139b), werf (54d), weri (15c,27c), wert, west, West (9c,50b, 109b), weta (93c)

416

- WE -   **ewer** (84d,85c,118c,181b), **kwel** (44a), **Owen** (96a,183c), **sweb** (160d), **twee**

- - WE   **howe** (77d), **Howe** (17a,82a), **powe**

W - - E   **wade, wage** (27a,115b), **wake** (134b,168a), **wale** (70b,131c,157c, 163d,179a,180a,c,d), **wane** (41c,43c), **ware** (27d,35a), **Wate** (141a), **wave** (19a,59a,111c,131d,160c,172d), **were** (139b), **whee, wide** (133d), **wife** (154a), **wile** (13b,41c,157b,169c), **wine, wipe, wire, wise** (136b), **wive** (97a), **woke, wore, Wote** (191), **wove**

W - - F   **waif** (157b), **wakf** (103a), **waqf** (103a), **warf, Welf** (67a), **werf** (54d), **wolf, woof** (39a,163d,165a,179d), **Wraf, wukf** (103a)

W - - G   **waag** (71d,101d), **waeg** (19b,72c,87a), **wang** (189), **Wegg** (111d), **Whig wigg, wing** (10d,58c,59a,118b,d), **wong** (56a)

WH - -   **wham** (157c), **what** (129c), **whau** (107a,168c), **whee!, when** (180d), **whet** (143c,156b), **whew, whey** (100a), **Whig, whim** (26c, 54c,108c), **whin** (64c,70a,132b,181d), **whip** (58c,88d), **whir** (25c, 181a), **whit** (166c), **whiz** (25c), **whoa** (156d), **whom** (42b), **whoo!, whun** (64c,70a), **whyo** (59d,65a)

- - WH   **JHWH** (159d), **YHWH** (159c)

W - - H   **wash, wish** (42d), **with** (10b)

WI - -   **wick, wide** (133d), **widu** (102d), **wiel** (140d,180d), **wies** (185a), **wife** (154a), **wigg, wild** (38b,173d), **wile** (13b,41c,157b,169c), **wilk** (65c,96d,141b), **will** (18b,43a,163c,177c), **wilt** (46b), **wily** (13b,38b,39c), **wind** (33b,39d,171c,185a), **wine, wing** (10d,58c, 59a,118b,d), **wink** (107a), **winy** (176c), **wipe, wire, wiry** (147a, 167c), **wise** (136b), **wish** (42d), **wisp** (24b,148c), **wist** (87c), **with** (10b), **wive** (97a)

- WI -   **swig** (46a,72c), **swim** (58c), **swiz** (160c), **twig, twin** (45c,171d), **twit** (162b,c)

- - WI   **Iiwi** (19a,74b), **Kawi** (84d), **kiwi** (11d,19a,58c), **tuwi** (117a,168c)

W - - I   **Wabi** (192), **wadi** (46c,106a,109a,128a,132a), **wali** (171a), **weki** (55c), **weri** (15c,27c)

- - WK   **bowk** (155d), **cawk** (133c), **dawk** (95c), **gawk** (146d), **gowk** (146d), **hawk** (19c,115c), **sawk** (188)

W - - K   **walk, weak** (55b), **week, welk** (65c,96d,141b), **wick, wilk** (65c, 96d,141b), **wink** (107a), **work** (64c,76b)

- - WL   **bawl, bowl, cowl** (101d), **dowl, fowl, gowl** (102a,140d,185b), **howl** (39b), **jowl** (29b), **mewl** (180d), **pawl** (43a,95a), **yawl** (136b,171d, 175d), **yowl**

W - - L   **wail** (39b,88a), **wall, weal** (124d,157c,180c,d), **weel** (16d,57d,140d, 180d), **well, wiel** (140d,180d), **will** (18b,43a,163c,177c), **wool** (58b, 179c)

- - WM   **dawm** (190)

W - - M   **warm** (7c,75b,163b), **wham** (157c), **whim** (26c,54c,108c), **whom** (42b), **worm, wurm** (67c),

- - WN   **bawn** (181a), **dawn** (14d,41b), **down** (149d), **fawn** (33c), **gown, hewn, kawn** (93d), **lawn** (20a,37c,53b,92c), **lown** (157d), **mown, pawn** (29c,119c), **sawn, sewn, town** (73c), **yawn**

W - - N   **wain** (177b), **Wain, warn** (7b), **wean** (8d,42d), **when** (180d), **whin**

417

(64c,70a,132b,181d), **whun** (64c,70a), **woon** (24c), **worn** (143b), **wren** (19b,c), **Wren** (50b), **wynn** (165d)

WO - -   **woad** (20d,47c), **woke**, **wold** (47c,60a,118d,174a,184a), **wolf**, **wong** (56a), **wont** (6d,40a,73a,174c), **wood woof** (39a,163d,165a, 179d), **wool** (58b,179d), **woon** (24c), **word** (124b,165c), **wore**, **work** (64c,76b), **worm**, **worn** (143b), **wort** (76a,95d,121d), **Wote** (191), **wove**

- WO -   Lwow, swob (102b), swop (168a), swot, swow (100a)

W - - O   Waco, whoo, whyo (59d,65a)

- - WP   gawp, lowp (90c,139d), yawp

W - - P   **wapp** (54b,133d,145d), **warp** (36c,165a,171c), **wasp**, **weep** (39b, 88a,104a), **whip** (58c,88d), **wisp** (24b,148c), **wrap** (32b,51a)

WR - -   Wraf, wrap (32b,51a), wren (19b,c), Wren (50b), writ (91a)

- WR -   awry (13d,38d,171c), ewry (133c)

W - - R   waer (40b), wear (50b), weir (40b,57d), whir (25c,181a)

- WS -   owse

- - WS   mews (154c), news (165c)

W - - S   ways, wies (185a)

- - WT   newt (48d,136c,169d), nowt (106a,139a), yowt (139c)

W - - T   **waft** (20d,58c), **wait** (26d,42b,92c,155d,162a), **Walt** (96b), **want** (41b,42d,87b,106b,122a), **wart** (124d), **wast**, **watt** (173b,177c), **Watt** (82a), **weet** (19d), **weft** (39a,165a,184b), **welt** (36d,131b, 145a,b,177b,d), **went** (42c), **wept**, **wert**, **west**, **West** (9c,50b,109b), **what** (129c), **whet** (143c,156b), **wilt** (46b), **wist** (87c), **wont** (6d,40a,73a,174c), **wort** (76a,95d,121d), **writ** (91a)

WU - -   **wudu** (102d), **wukf** (103a), **Wurd**, **wurm** (67c), **wuzu** (102d)

- WU -   swum

W - - U   whau (107a,168c), widu (102d), wudu (102d), wuzu (102d)

W - - W   whew!

WY - -   wynn (165d), Wyrd (107d)

- WY -   Gwyn (40c,50b)

- - WY   dewy (101a), jawy, nowy (194), rowy (157b), towy (58b)

W - - Y   **wady** (109a,128a,132a), **waky**, **wany**, **wary** (27d,176b), **wavy** (147b,172d), **waxy** (119c,149d), **whey** (100a), **wily** (13b,38b,39c), **winy** (176c), **wiry** (147a,167c)

W - - Z   whiz (25c)

- XA -   axal (120b), exam, oxan (65c)

- - XA   Bixa (145d), coxa (77b), doxa (48b), moxa (27d,30c), myxa (168c, 169a), noxa, toxa (153d)

X - - A   xema (72c), Xema (12c), Xina (183d), Xosa (86a), Xova (193)

XE - -   xema (72c), Xema (12c), xeno (34d)

- XE -   oxea (153d), oxen (10c), oxer (55c)

- - XE   luxe (61c,62d,159c), Mixe (192), saxe (20d,33c)

X - - E   Xipe (15c)

XI - -   Xina (183d), Xipe (15c)

418

- XI - axil (10c), axis (28b,41d,77c,153c), exit (114d), ixia (37a), Ixil (192), oxid (112c)

- - XI dixi, taxi (13a,125b)

- XL - axle (153c,180c), ixle (56a)

XM - - Xmas

XO - - Xosa (86a), Xova (193)

- XO - axon (106c,153c)

- - XO Moxo (192), myxo, taxo (13a)

X - - O xeno (34d), xylo (35a,183d)

X - - S Xmas

- - XT next (106a), sext (26b,111b,147b), text (21c,140d)

XY - - xylo (35a,183d)

- XY - oxyl (112c)

- - XY boxy, buxy (115b), doxy (129d), foxy (38b,39c,181d), mixy, pixy (154b), puxy, Roxy (183d), waxy (119c,149d)

YA - - yage (23a), yaje (23a), Yaka (191), Yaki (193), Yale (173c), yali (171a), Yama (57a,68a), Yana (192,193), yang (30b,70a), yank, Yank, Yaou (30c), yapa (113b), Yapp (22a), yard (152d), yare (96b,124b,128b), yark (22c), yarl (40d,107d), yarn (154b,161b, 184b), yarr (72a), Yaru (48d), yate (51d,168c), yati (76d), yaup, yava, yawl (136b,171d,175d), yawn, yawp, yaya (113c,168c)

- YA - ayah (108d), cyan, dyad (113a), Dyak (22b), Dyas (66a), eyah (95b, 108d,111c), eyas (106c,173a), iyar (102b), kyah (19a), kyak (51c), kyar (33a), kyat (189), lyam (139a), Lyas (66a), pyal (175c), pyat (95b), ryal (110a,190)

- - YA Alya (155b,c), Arya (80d), baya (179b), Baya (191), cuya (39b), Goya (151d), Hoya (14d), maya (77a,179b), Maya (23d,186c), Puya (118b), raya (19b,23c,76d,107d), saya (117a), soya (151b), yaya (113c,168c)

Y - - A Yaka (191), Yama (57a,68a), Yana (192,193), yapa (113b), yava, yaya (113c,168c), yeta (84c), Yima (84a,116b,c), Ynca (193), yoga (10b,13c,77a), yuca (27a), Yuga (76d), Yuma

- YB - gybe (144c), Tybi (102a)

- YC - syce (71d)

- YD - hyde (188), Hyde (45a)

- - YD emyd (163c,167c)

Y - - D yard (152d), yond (164d)

YE - - yeah, yean (88a), year, yeas (177c), Yedo (166d), yegg (24c), yeli (145c), yelp, yelt (151b), yeni (19b,161d), yeso (72d), yeta (84c)

- YE - ayes (177c), byee (189), dyer, eyer, eyey (74b), oyer (38a,75b, 119c), oyes (38a,39b,75b), oyex (38a,39b,75b), pyet (95b), ryel (190), syed (103b), tyee (29d), tyer

- - YE Daye (123d), Skye (163c)

Y - - E yage (23a), yaje (23a), Yale (173c), yare (96b,124b,128b), yate (51d,168c), yoke (85b,92d,173c), yore (10b,69d,93c,110b,165d), Yule (30d)

419

- YG -   bygo (114c), zyga (134b)

Y - - G   yang (30b,70a), yegg (24c)

YH - -   YHVH (159d), YHWH (159d)

Y - - H   yeah, YHVH (159d), YHWH (159d), yodh (91d), yogh (10c,185a)

YI - -   Yima (84a,116b,c)

- YI -   ayin (91c)

- - YI   kiyi (185d)

Y - - I   Yaki (193), yali (171a), yati (76d), yeni (19b,161d), Yobi, yogi (76d)

- YK -   cyke (40c), dyke (49c,91d), fyke (15d), hyke!, syke (194), tyke (29d)

Y - - K   yank, Yank, yark (22c), yolk, york (38c), York (50b,c)

- YL -   gyle (23b,174d), Hyla (10a,166d,169b), hyle (97c), kyle (57a, 139c), pyla (22d), pyle (34b), Pyle (9c,178a), Xylo (35a,183d)

- - YL   acyl (6d), amyl (155c), idyl (114d), noyl (87c), odyl (59d,79c), oxyl (112c), teyl (92b,c,168c)

Y - - L   yarl (40d,107d), yawl (136b,171d,175d), yell (145c), yowl, ypil (117a,168c)

YM - -   Ymer (67a,131c), Ymir (67a,131c)

- YM -   cyma (101a,b), cyme (58d,69c), hymn (150c), ryme (178d), tymp (20c), zyme (55c)

- - YM   clym (12b), etym (133d), onym (162c)

YN - -   Ynca (193)

- YN -   dyna (34c), dyne (59d,173b), gyne (34b,55b,183c), jynx (78a), Jynx (184a), lynx (26c,181d), Lynx (36b), myna (19a,c,70b), rynd (100a), syne (140b,147a), tyne, Tyne (108a), wynn (165d)

- - YN   coyn (37a), Gwyn (40c,50b), llyn (120d,140a)

Y - - N   yarn (154b,161b,184b), yawn, yean (88a), yuan (190), Yuan (30b, 101d)

YO - -   Yobi, yodh (91d), yoga (10b,13c,77a), yogh (10c,185a), yogi (76d), yoke (85b,92d,173c), yolk, yond (164d), yoop, yore (10b,69d,93c, 110b,165d), york (38c), York (50b,c), youp (185d), your (124c), yowl, yowt (139c)

- YO -   eyot (82d), ryot (115c)

- - YO   buyo (18b), cayo, coyo (15a,30c), Enyo (12c,69c,178a), idyo (191), kayo (87c), Mayo (193), whyo (59d,65a)

Y - - O   Yedo (166d), yeso (72d)

YP - -   ypil (117a,168c)

- YP -   gyps, Gyps (71d), hype (185a), hypo (117b), hyps, rype (19b,125a), sype (110c), type (31d,115a,155a), typo (35c,51b), typp (185b), typy

- - YP   tryp (114a)

Y - - P   Yapp (22a), yaup, yawp, yelp, yoop, youp (185d)

- YR -   Byrd (9c,120b), byre (38a), eyra (181d), eyre (23c,31b,85c), Eyre, eyry (47b,106c), fyrd (110a), gyre (31b,171b), gyri (22d,

131b), **gyro** (34d), **Lyra** (36b,74a), **lyre** (11c,81c,105a,111c), **Myra** (10a,31b,183c), **pyre** (64c), **pyro**, **Syra**, **tyre** (15a), **Tyre** (31b,90d, 117b), **tyro** (9b,17d,108c), **Tyrr** (68c,109c,163d,178a), **Wyrd** (107d)

- - YR   **skyr** (21d,151a)
Y - - R   **yarr** (72a), **year**, **Ymer** (67a,131c), **Ymir** (67a,131c), **your** (124c), **Yser**
YS - -   **Yser**
- YS -   **cyst**, **lyse**, **myst** (71c,123b)
- - YS   **Alys** (183c), **Emys** (167c,171b), **days**, **Itys** (163b), **ways**
Y - - S   **yeas** (177c)
- YT -   **myth** (8b,91a), **Tyto** (16c)
- - YT   **skyt** (138c,140b)
Y - - T   **yelt** (151b), **yowt** (139c), **yuft** (135c), **Yuit** (51c), **yurt** (101d)
YU - -   **yuan** (190), **Yuan** (30b,101d), **yuca** (27a), **yuft** (135c), **Yuga** (76d), **Yuit** (51c), **Yule** (30d), **Yuma**, **Yunx** (184a), **yurt** (101d), **yutu** (19b,166a)
- YU -   **syud** (103b)
- - YU   **Vayu** (68c,182a)
Y - - U   **Yaou** (30c), **Yaru** (48d), **yutu** (19b,166a)
- YV -   **gyve** (55d,143b)
- YX -   **myxa** (168c,169a), **myxo**
- - YX   **Ceyx** (73b), **eryx** (137a), **onyx** (25d,28d,65d,142b), **oryx** (11a), **Pnyx** (71c), **Styx** (29b,73a,105c)
Y - - X   **Yunx** (184a)
- - YZ   **hayz**
ZA - -   **Zach** (96b), **zaim** (170d), **zain** (41a), **Zama** (73d,141d), **zany** (24a, 32d,59c), **zarf** (39c,155a), **zarp** (120c), **zati** (21d)
- ZA -   **Azam** (166c), **azan** (102d), **czar** (42d,49d,60b,135c), **izar** (65b, 103b), **Izar** (155b), **tzar** (42d,49d,60b,135c), **Uzan** (189)
- - ZA   **boza** (12a), **caza**, **Daza** (191), **Gaza** (117a), **Itza** (192), **Juza** (155b), **onza** (189), **tiza** (172a), **tuza** (119d), **vaza** (114a), **zuza** (189)
Z - - A   **Zama** (73d,141d), **zeta** (71b,91c), **Zipa** (29d), **zira** (188), **Zola** (63a), **zona** (144c,186d), **zuza** (189), **zyga** (134b)
- ZB -   **ezba** (188)
Z - - B   **Zimb** (6c)
Z - - C   **zinc** (21a)
Z - - D   **Zend**, **zoid**
ZE - -   **zeal** (12c,55d), **zebu** (22d,80d,112c), **zein**, **Zeke** (96b), **zeme** (55d,161b,180b), **zemi** (55d,161b,180b), **Zend**, **Zeno** (71b), **zenu** (143d), **zero** (31a,84c,108c), **Zero** (118d), **zest** (55d,72d), **zeta** (71b,91c), **Zeus** (135a)
- ZE -   **ezel** (47a,85d)
- - ZE   **adze** (40c,167a), **bize** (182a), **coze** (29b), **daze** (157d), **doze** (148a), **faze** (43d), **fuze** (98c), **gaze**, **guze** (128d), **haze** (100c,174d), **laze** (79b), **Laze** (191), **maze** (87b,157d), **naze** (26b,124b), **noze** (75a),

             ooze (53c,104b,116a), raze (42b,d,91d), size, unze (189)

Z - - E   Zeke (96b), zeme (55d,161b,180b), zone (44c,50a,160a), zyme
           (55c)

Z - - F   zarf (39c,155a)

Z - - G   zing

- ZH -   Azha (155b)

Z - - H   Zach (96b)

ZI - -   Zimb (6c), zinc (21a), zing, Zion (75b,c,83a,157d), Zipa (29d),
           zipp, Zips (40c), zira (188), zizz (181a)

- - ZI   cazi (103a), gazi, kazi (103a), Lazi (191), Nazi

Z - - I   zati (21d), zemi (55d,161b,180b), Zuni (125b)

Z - - L   zeal (12c,55d)

Z - - M   zaim (170d), zoom

Z - - N   zain (41a), zein, Zion (75b,c,83a,157d), zoon (43a)

ZO - -   Zoar, Zoas (20b), zobo (186b), zodi, zogo (136a), zoid, Zola (63a),
           zona (144c,186d), zone (44c,50a,160a), zoom, zoon (43a)

- ZO -   Azof (20b,135d), azon (127b), Azov (20b,135d), mozo (152b),
           Muzo (192)

- - ZO   bozo (55b), Idzo (191), kozo (113d,168c), lazo (88d,128b,133d)

Z - - O   Zeno (71b), zero (31a,84c,108c), Zero (118d), zobo (186b), zogo
           (136a)

Z - - P   zarp (120c), zipp

- ZR -   Ezra (96a)

Z - - R   Zoar

Z - - S   Zeus (135a), Zips (40c), Zoas (20b)

Z - - T   zest (55d,72c)

ZU - -   zulu (171d,175d), Zulu (86a), Zuni (125b), zuza (189)

- ZU -   azul (151d)

- - ZU   anzu (11d), auzu (168c,180b), Enzu (102b), wuzu (102d)

Z - - U   zebu (22d,80d,112c), zenu (143d), zulu (171d,175d), Zulu (86a)

ZY - -   zyga (134b), zyme (55c)

- - ZY   cazy (103a), cozy (149c), dazy, dozy, gazy, hazy (174b), Jozy,
           kazy (103a), lazy, oozy (148b), sizy (176d)

Z - - Y   zany (24a,32d,59c)

- - ZZ   bizz, buzz, fuzz (45d), huzz, jazz, razz (131b), sizz, zizz (181a)

Z - - Z   zizz (181a)